THE NATURE OF CONSCIOUSNESS

THE NATURE OF CONSCIOUSNESS
Philosophical Debates

edited by Ned Block, Owen Flanagan, and Güven Güzeldere

A Bradford Book
The MIT Press
Cambridge, Massachusetts
London, England

Third printing, 1998

© 1997 Massachusetts Institute of Technology

This book was set in Times Roman by Asco Trade
Typesetting Ltd, Hong Kong.
Printed and bound in the United States of America.

Library of Congress Cataloging-in-Publication Data

The nature of consciousness : philosophical debates /
  edited by Ned Block, Owen Flanagan, and Güven
  Güzeldere.
      p.   cm.
  "A Bradford book."
  Includes bibliographical references (p.   ) and index.
  ISBN 0-262-02399-7 (hb : alk. paper). —
  ISBN 0-262-52210-1 (pb : alk. paper)
  1. Consciousness. 2. Philosophy of mind. I. Block,
Ned Joel, 1942–   . II. Flanagan, Owen J.
III. Güzeldere, Güven.
B808.9N37   1997
126—dc20   96-17500
                                  CIP

In memory of Harry Bradford Stanton

Contents

Preface and Acknowledgments   ix

Sources   xvii

INTRODUCTION   **The Many Faces of Consciousness: A Field Guide**   1
Güven Güzeldere

I   **STREAM OF CONSCIOUSNESS**   69

1   **The Stream of Consciousness**   71
William James

2   **The Cartesian Theater and "Filling In" the Stream of Consciousness**   83
Daniel C. Dennett

3   **The Robust Phenomenology of the Stream of Consciousness**   89
Owen Flanagan

II   **CONSCIOUSNESS, SCIENCE, AND METHODOLOGY**   95

4   **Prospects for a Unified Theory of Consciousness or, What Dreams Are Made Of**   97
Owen Flanagan

5   **Consciousness, Folk Psychology, and Cognitive Science**   111
Alvin I. Goldman

6   **Can Neurobiology Teach Us Anything about Consciousness?**   127
Patricia Smith Churchland

7   **Time and the Observer: The Where and When of Consciousness in the Brain**   141
Daniel C. Dennett and Marcel Kinsbourne

8   **Begging the Question against Phenomenal Consciousness**   175
Ned Block

9   **Time for More Alternatives**   181
Robert Van Gulick

III   **THE PSYCHOLOGY AND NEUROPSYCHOLOGY OF CONSCIOUSNESS**   185

10   **Contrastive Phenomenology: A Thoroughly Empirical Approach to Consciousness**   187
Bernard J. Baars

11   **Visual Perception and Visual Awareness after Brain Damage: A Tutorial Overview**   203
Martha J. Farah

12   **Understanding Consciousness: Clues from Unilateral Neglect and Related Disorders**   237
Edoardo Bisiach

13   **Modularity and Consciousness**   255
Tim Shallice

14   **Towards a Neurobiological Theory of Consciousness**   277
Francis Crick and Christof Koch

IV   **CONSCIOUSNESS AND CONTENT**   293

15   **Consciousness and Content**   295
Colin McGinn

16   **Externalism and Experience**   309
Martin Davies

17   **A Representational Theory of Pains and Their Phenomenal Character**   329
Michael Tye

18   **Sensation and the Content of Experience: A Distinction**   341
Christopher Peacocke

V   FUNCTION OF
      CONSCIOUSNESS   355

19   Conscious Inessentialism and the
      Epiphenomenalist Suspicion   357
      Owen Flanagan

20   On a Confusion about a Function
      of Consciousness   375
      Ned Block

21   The Path Not Taken   417
      Daniel C. Dennett

22   Availability: The Cognitive Basis
      of Experience?   421
      David J. Chalmers

23   Fallacies or Analyses?   425
      Jennifer Church

24   Two Kinds of Consciousness   427
      Tyler Burge

25   Understanding the Phenomenal
      Mind: Are We All Just Armadillos?
      Part II: The Absent Qualia
      Argument   435
      Robert Van Gulick

VI   METAPHYSICS OF
      CONSCIOUSNESS   443

26   The Identity Thesis   445
      Saul A. Kripke

27   Reductionism and the Irreducibility
      of Consciousness   451
      John R. Searle

28   A Question about Consciousness 461
      Georges Rey

29   Finding the Mind in the Natural
      World   483
      Frank Jackson

30   Breaking the Hold: Silicon Brains,
      Conscious Robots, and Other Minds   493
      John R. Searle

31   The First-Person Perspective   503
      Sydney Shoemaker

VII   SUBJECTIVITY AND
      EXPLANATORY GAP   517

32   What Is It Like to Be a Bat?   519
      Thomas Nagel

33   Can We Solve the Mind-Body
      Problem?   529
      Colin McGinn

34   On Leaving Out What It's Like 543
      Joseph Levine

VIII THE KNOWLEDGE
      ARGUMENT   557

35   Understanding the Phenomenal
      Mind: Are We All Just Armadillos?
      Part I: Phenomenal Knowledge and
      Explanatory Gaps   559
      Robert Van Gulick

36   What Mary Didn't Know   567
      Frank Jackson

37   Knowing Qualia: A Reply to
      Jackson   571
      Paul M. Churchland

38   What Experience Teaches   579
      David Lewis

Contents

39 **Phenomenal States**   597
    Brian Loar

IX **QUALIA**   617

40 **Quining Qualia**   619
    Daniel C. Dennett

41 **The Inverted Spectrum**   643
    Sydney Shoemaker

42 **The Intrinsic Quality of Experience**   663
    Gilbert Harman

43 **Inverted Earth**   677
    Ned Block

44 **Curse of the Qualia**   695
    Stephen L. White

X   **HIGHER-ORDER
    MONITORING CONCEPTIONS
    OF CONSCIOUSNESS**   719

45 **What Is Consciousness?**   721
    David Armstrong

46 **A Theory of Consciousness**   729
    David M. Rosenthal

47 **Consciousness as Internal
    Monitoring**   755
    William G. Lycan

48 **Conscious Experience**   773
    Fred Dretske

49 **Is Consciousness the Perception of
    What Passes in One's Own Mind?**   789
    Güven Güzeldere

References to Introduction   807

Suggested Readings   817
compiled by Güven Güzeldere

Index   825

Preface and Acknowledgments

These are exciting times for thinking about consciousness, and this book contains a collection of essays that represents the cornerstones of contemporary philosophical thinking on the subject. Also included is a small corpus of articles representative of current psychology and neuropsychology research on consciousness that has given rise to fruitful discussions in the philosophy of mind. We hope that this book will be useful for philosophers in presenting a structured overview of the relevant literature on consciousness, bring philosophical problems of consciousness to bear on empirical issues being pursued in other fields, and be of interest to psychologists, neuroscientists, and other mind-scientists.

With the exception of chapter 1 on the stream of consciousness, a tribute to the remarkable body of William James's foundational work on consciousness and psychology in general, all the essays in this book belong to philosophers, psychologists, and neuropsychologists of our own day. Many of these essays revolve around ongoing debates concerning the nature of consciousness, often cross-cutting disciplinary boundaries. Hence the title, "The Nature of Consciousness: Philosophical Debates."

Consciousness, as a subject matter of research in philosophy and in science, has a fascinating history. Perhaps there is no other phenomenon for which the pendulum of intellectual credibility swung to such extremes as it did for consciousness within roughly a matter of a single century, steering it through times of both exaltation and of taboo treatment.

Consciousness was taken to be the "starting point of all psychology," only a few decades before it was condemned as being part and parcel of "superstition and magic."

It was characterized as "the only true reality" as well as "a nonentity with no right place among first principles."

It was regarded as "inert, uninfluential, a simple passenger in the voyage of life," as well as "an organ added for the sake of steering a nervous system grown too complex to regulate itself."

It was considered "something the meaning of which is known to everyone beyond doubt" as well as "something impossible to specify what it is, what it does, or why it evolved." (The quotations belong to William James, John Watson, George Miller, Thomas Huxley,—as paraphrased by James—Sigmond Freud, and Stuart Sutherland, respectively.)

Perhaps it is now time to ask, borrowing Julian Jaynes's words: "This consciousness that is myself of selves, that is everything, and yet nothing at all—what is it?"

The answer to this question, or attempts to formulate parts of such an answer, lie among the fifty essays in this book. But it is also important to ask: Where do we currently stand in the study of consciousness?

We are witnessing an upsurge of interest in consciousness concurrently in several disciplines —most notably, philosophy, psychology, and neuroscience. We try to give an explanation of this trend within its historical context in the introduction to this book. Today, it is not difficult to see the signs of the new "consciousness wave." In philosophy in the 1990s, several influential books have taken on the issue of consciousness: Daniel Dennett's *Consciousness Explained* (1991), Colin McGinn's *The Problem of Consciousness* (1991), Owen Flanagan's *Consciousness Reconsidered* (1992), John Searle's *The Rediscovery of the Mind* (1992), Paul Churchland's *The Engine of Reason, The Seat of the Soul* (1995), Fred Dretske's *Naturalizing the Mind* (1995), Michael Tye's *Ten Problems of Consciousness* (1995), David Chalmers's *The Conscious Mind* (1996), and William G. Lycan's *Consciousness and Experience* (1996). At present, an overwhelming number of new books exclusively on consciousness are waiting in the pipelines of respected publishers. In contrast, there were fewer such books published between the 1960s and 1980s. Consciousness seems to have become the topic of the decade for philosophy of mind.

In neuroscience and psychology, perhaps the biggest positive impact in favor of consciousness research was due to Francis Crick and Christoph Koch. Their 1990 article, "Towards a Neurobiological Theory of Consciousness," carrying the secure stamp of approval by a Nobel laureate, helped shatter the current psychological and professional barrier against the credibility of studying consciousness in science. Around the same time, many studies on neuropsychology, especially those on blindsight, generated interesting and approximately concurrent results, which relied on consciousness as an essential theoretial construct. Larry Weiskrantz's *Blindsight* (1986) and Bernard Baars's *A Cognitive Theory of Consciousness* (1988), although they were published in the 1980s, have gained more popularity in the 1990s.

There has also started a new industry of popular and semipopular books on consciousness. Dennett's *Consciousness Explained*, pitched at a level between laypeople and professional philosophers, became a best-seller. In 1994, Crick put together his ideas on consciousness in the form of a popular book, *The Astonishing Hypothesis: The Scientific Search for the Soul*. Later in the same year, Roger Penrose followed up on his ideas from his earlier book on artificial intelligence, this time on consciousness: *Shadows of the Mind: Search for the Missing Science of Consciousness*. Others are on their way. It is also worth mentioning the increased interest in consciousness in the scientific and semiscientific journals. See, for instance, the special "Mind and Brain" issue of *Scientific American*, which included consciousness as one of the eight topics covered (September 1992); the "10 Great Unanswered Questions of Science" of *Discover* magazine, which promoted the question, "What is consciousness?" (November 1992); and the special issue of *Omni*, "Science and the Soul" (October 1993). (What is dubbed "soul" in the titles turn out to be "consciousness" between the covers.)

Finally, a number of new edited volumes and journals on consciousness are appearing. In addition, the recent frequency of major conferences specifically on consciousness (for example, the success and popularity of the 1994 and 1996 Tucson conferences) is yet another indication of the new positive academic attitude toward consciousness. Among the anthologies, Davies and Humphreys's *Consciousness* (1993), Metzinger's *Conscious Experience* (1995), and Velman's *The Science of Consciousness* (1996) stand out. Among the volumes that are worthy outcomes of major conferences are Marcel and Bisiach's *Consciousness in Contemporary Science* (1988), Villanueva's *Philosophical Issues: Consciousness* (1991), Milner and Rugg's *The Neuropsychology of Consciousness* (1992), Bock and Marsh's *Experimental and Theoretical Studies of Consciousness*, Revonsuo and Kamppinen's *Consciousness in Philosophy and Cognitive Neuroscience* (1994), Cohen and Schooler's *Carnegie Symposium Proceedings on Consciousness* (in press), and Hameroff, Kaszhiak, and Scott's *Towards a Scientific Basis for Consciousness* (1996). Among the journals, *Consciousness and Cognition* (since 1992), *Psyche* (since 1993, first electronic journal on consciousness), and most recently *Journal of Consciousness Studies* (since 1994) are of special interest. All this booming activity belongs to the recent time frame of less than a decade, and it marks a novel period for the study of consciousness.

Now you may ask, among all the cited journals, conference proceedings, books, and anthologies, why should one acquire *this* book? Who would need it, and for what purposes can it be used? These are fair questions, and they have straightforward answers.

Despite the rapid growing interest in consciousness, no book has brought together all or most of the principal texts on the subject. This volume fills the gap, at least for philosophy, with a supplementary component for psychology and neuropsychology. *The Nature of Consciousness* contains fifty essays, including the Introduction, categorized under ten headings. Typically, each of these essays deals with a multitude of problems that are raised and debated in the literature about consciousness, and as such, would fall under more than a single heading. This is because almost any single problem addressed in this volume is theoretically interrelated to a number of others, and proposals for resolution do not carry much weight unless their scope simultaneously spans over a whole set of connected issues.

On the other hand, the intricacy of these interrelations sometimes results in theoretical tangles. For instance, as Güzeldere notes in the Introduction, different issues about qualia, subjectivity, the explanatory gap, and the knowledge argument recurrently get conflated and run together, at times making the controversies in the literature appear greater than they really are. Thus it is also important to try to "divide and conquer" the consciousness corpus.

In the face of these opposing factors, the categorization of the articles in this volume into the present sections aims at both distinguishing discrete areas of the relevant literature on the basis of distinct issues, as well as acknowledging the theoretical interconnections between them. Our goal is not only to bring together important essays on consciousness, but to present them within a superimposed structure so that this volume can be a road map for students of consciousness with which to explore and find major trails in the vast literature. To that end, we have also prepared a structured bibliography of additional readings on consciousness to serve as pointers for further study, and appended it to the end of the volume.

In putting this collection together, we have tried to strike a balance between composing it as a classic reference book, and making sure that it presents the leading edge of philosophical research on consciousness. Consequently, the present volume contains seminal works of the past few decades, as well as new essays. Naturally, given the enormous size of the relevant literature, we had to restrict our choices. Thus, this book is mostly a philosophy anthology. Nonetheless, many of the entries in it do explain, rely on, or argue about current scientific thinking on consciousness (touching on, e.g., works of neuroscientists, cognitive neuropsychologists, AI re-

searchers, psychologists). Finally, this volume had to leave out entirely the works of continental philosophers (e.g., Husserl, Merleau-Ponty, Sartre); each of these intellectual lineages we chose not to trace here could easily form main themes for separate books.

We hope that our anthology will serve many as a reference on debates on consciousness, a useful pedagogical tool in teaching medium- to advanced-level undergraduate courses and graduate seminars, and a guidebook for anyone trying to find his or her way through the large and confusingly interwoven literature on consciousness, for years to come.

The Essays

The volume opens with an Introduction by Güven Güzeldere in which he attempts to lay out conceptual foundations for the study of consciousness in a broader intellectual context. Güzeldere traces many of the contemporary problems and controversies about consciousness back to their historical antecedents, demonstrating the recurrent nature of these issues in a wide variety of schools of thought in philosophy and psychology. Among them are the scope and reliability of the introspectionist method, the nature of the (Freudian versus cognitive) unconscious, the distinction between first-person versus third-person perspectives, the explanatory gap, the knowledge argument, the controversy of "consciousness mysterianism," the question of "zombies" and epiphenomenalism, and the "hard problem." Güzeldere then distinguishes among four "W-questions" (What are the media and mechanisms of consciousness? Where, if anywhere, is the locus of consciousness? Who can be said to be a conscious being? Why is there consciousness at all?) and the "further-how" question (How does consciousness arise in, or emerge from, its underlying substance, structure, and mechanism, in the way it does?) in an attempt to probe into the inner structure of a body of interrelated problems about phenomenal consciousness. To that end, he further outlines a schema to tease out tangled issues about qualia, subjectivity, the knowledge argument, and "what it is like to be a certain organism." Finally, he presents an analysis of the current debates on consciousness in terms of a fundamental opposition between "essentialist" and "causal" intuitions, which he characterizes, respectively, by the mottos "consciousness is as consciousness feels" and "consciousness is as consciousness does."

Güzeldere's overarching diagnosis is that what lies at the bottom of some of the most persistent problems about consciousness has to do with the explanatory gap between the characterization of conscious experiences *as they are experienced* by their subjects versus *as they are investigated* from a third-person perspective, but the epistemological nature of this gap, to the extent that epistemology and ontology are separable, does not necessarily warrant ontological conclusions. Therefore, Güzeldere concludes, what seems the most promising direction in re-approaching consciousness and pursuing its deep-rooted problems in the present era involves rethinking epistemology and conceptual schemes (as opposed to a priori postulation of new ontology) to yield a cross-fertilization of the first-person and third-person perspectives, which would allow theorizing about the causal efficacy of how consciousness feels and the phenomenal quality of what consciousness does.

Section I of this volume, Stream of Consciousness, explores the nature and phenomenology of the inner goings-on of consciousness. In "The Stream of Consciousness," an all-time psychology classic, **William James** (chap. 1) starts out with the assertion that "the first and foremost concrete fact which everyone will affirm to belong to his inner experience is the fact that *consciousness of some sort goes on.*" He then explores the appearance and characteristics of the stream of consciousness: that it is continuous but in constant change, that every object of consciousness has a "fringe," and that consciousness always functions as a selective agency.

Daniel Dennett (chap. 2) and **Owen Flanagan** (chap. 3), in the two subsequent chapters, provide contemporary perspectives on James's idea. According to Dennett, the continuity of consciousness is, contrary to James and the received view at present, only apparent. Furthermore, Dennett claims, this appearance of continuity stems from the ability of the brain to not "notice" gaps, rather than "fill them in" in some suitable fashion. Flanagan stresses the singularity and definitiveness of the stream of consciousness as it is phenomenally experienced, while acknowledging the discontinuities at the level of underlying neural processes. So long as we don't think of consciousness as diaphanous, and expect to see through its causal structure, Flanagan concludes, the discontinuous nature of these underlying processes should neither undermine nor compete with its description as a continuous stream.

Section II, Consciousness, Science, and Methodology, brings together a number of essays on the nature of consciousness, its place within philosophy and science, and methodologies involved in its study. **Owen Flanagan** (chap. 4) gives a profile of prospects for a unified theory of consciousness, with a positive outlook. He argues that the best strategy to study consciousness is what he calls the "natural method," a triangulation of perspectives and data from phenomenology, psychology/cognitive science, and neuroscience. As a demonstration of the natural method in action, Flanagan presents a multifaceted account of the phenomenon of dreaming, drawing on a wide array of philosophical, psychological, and neuroscientific resources and combining them into a coherent explanatory framework. **Alvin Goldman** (chap. 5) explores the role of (phenomenal) consciousness in cognitive science, and argues that the folk-theoretic notion of qualia should not be hastily dismissed. Goldman suggests that qualia are the properties that uniquely allow us to recognize and classify our mental states, and, as such, they should be distinguished and credited for their significant role in scientific psychology and cognitive science.

Patricia Churchland (chap. 6) outlines a full-scale, multilayered, reductionist research strategy for consciousness, locating it in the general context of a reductionist scientific program. She argues that research on consciousness should allow for and welcome simultaneous generation and co-evolution of hypotheses at several levels of description, from neurobiological to psychological, for an integrated understanding of the phenomenon.

Daniel Dennett and **Marcel Kinsbourne** (chap. 7) present their "Multiple Drafts" model of consciousness as an alternative to what they call the "Cartesian Theater" model, a model based on the idea that there is single place, a "finish line" in the brain where different components of experiences all come together for subjective judgment. According to the Multiple Drafts model, all there is instead is a parallel stream of conflicting and continuously revised contents that can be probed at different times to elicit different narrative accounts from the subject. However, there is no single, canonical narrative that, independently of probing, represents the actual stream of consciousness.

On the basis of this model, Dennett and Kinsbourne diagnose errors that result from an equivocation between representational properties of time and temporal properties of representations in the brain in such previously puzzling phenomena. In particular, they criticize Benjamin Libet's work on "backward referral in time," and provide explanations for a number of previously puzzling temporal anomalies of conscious experience, such as the "color phi" and the "cutaneous rabbit" phenomena. **Ned Block** (chap. 8) and **Robert Van Gulick** (chap. 9) present critical commentaries on Dennett and Kinsbourne's work. Block accuses Dennett and Kinsbourne of begging the question against phenomenal consciousness by starting with the assumption that there is no such thing as phenomenal consciousness, and dismissing the question of how to distinguish between those revisions of contents that are phenomenally conscious, and those that are not. Van Gulick points out that the Multiple

Drafts model does not deal adequately with the Kantian view that consciousness involves continuous sensuous manifolds of space and time, and concludes, in accord with Block, that it remains inadequate as long as it eschews the distinction between phenomenal and non-phenomenal representations in the brain that can play different roles in the subject's mental life.

Section III, The Psychology and Neuropsychology of Consciousness, consists exclusively of essays by psychologists and neuroscientists, who examine and explicate various lines of empirical research that bear on philosophical problems about consciousness. **Bernard Baars** (chap. 10) suggests "treating consciousness as a variable" in empirical research, and delineates the differences between conscious and unconscious mental states and processes as constraints on any theory of consciousness. **Martha Farah** (chap. 11) gives a tutorial overview of various neuropsychological disorders of consciousness that result from brain damage, such as blindsight, prosopagnosia, and neglect, and attempts to locate them in a general theoretical framework.

Edoardo Bisiach (chap. 12) focuses on the phenomenon of unilateral neglect as it reveals clues about the spatiotemporal structure of the content of conscious visual experience, and he lends support to Dennett and Kinsbourne's critique of the "Cartesian Theater" model. **Tim Shallice** (chap. 13) gives an assessment of the modularity hypothesis of mental function, especially with regard to conscious mental states, and provides motivation for studying consciousness as part of a modular information-processing system. **Francis Crick** and **Christof Koch** (chap. 14) argue that the unity of conscious visual experience (underwritten by the "binding phenomenon") crucially depends on the semisynchronous firing of cortical neurons in the 40–70 Hz. frequency range, and they present reasons and further pointers for the pursuit of consciousness research at the neural level.

In Section IV, Consciousness and Content, the relation between intentional (contentful) and phenomenal (qualitative) properties of mental states is taken up. **Colin McGinn** (chap. 15) explores aspects of the problem of intentionality and the problem of consciousness that overlap with each other, observing that "phenomenology seems configured by content." Nonetheless, he argues, the pessimism surrounding the problem of consciousness does not have to spread to the problem of intentionality, insofar as the individuation of content, unlike the mind-body problem, is not inherently mysterious. **Martin Davies** (chap. 16) argues that perceptual experiences, like beliefs, have representational properties, but perceptual content is non-conceptual and different in kind from belief content. He notes that, as such, arguments for externalism for belief content do not readily apply to externalism for perceptual content, and proceeds to give a separate line of argumentation for the latter.

Michael Tye (chap. 17) also adopts the view that experiences are representational but non-conceptual. He argues, in particular, that the phenomenon of pain is a proper object of study for cognitive psychology because pains have representational content, and that their phenomenal character is utilized in the operation of the cognitive (belief/desire) systems. **Christopher Peacocke** (chap. 18) draws a distinction between representational and sensational properties of experiences. In accordance with the historical distinction between perception and sensation, he then argues that the latter, while indispensable for experiential content, are non-representational, and demonstrates his claim via examples from visual perception.

Section V deals with the question of the Function of Consciousness. **Owen Flanagan** (chap. 19) defends the view that phenomenal consciousness (he also calls it "subjective awareness") plays an important role in our mental lives. He argues in favor of teleological functionalism, a view that conceives of most mental capacities, consciousness in particular, as typically having an adaptive role for their subjects. Flanagan then presents reasons, based on current research in neuro-

science and evolutionary biology, why epiphenomenalism (the view that consciousness is inconsequential to mental life in general) should be rejected. In conclusion, Flanagan gives a critique of a distinction that **Ned Block** (chap. 20) draws between "phenomenal" and "access" consciousness in the following chapter, arguing in favor of an alternative distinction between "informational sensitivity" (access to information without phenomenal awareness) and "experiential sensitivity" (access to information as well as phenomenal awareness).

In contrast, Block's distinction is based on the thesis that phenomenal (experiential) properties of consciousness are different in kind from cognitive, intentional, or functional properties, and as such they constitute two distinct types of consciousness. According to Block, while the functional role of access consciousness in the guidance of rational thought and action is obvious, the function of phenomenal consciousness, when properly conceptualized and not confused with its cognitive counterpart (as it often is in the literature), is far from clear. Block points out instances of this kind of confusion, which he claims is prevalent among philosophers and neuropsychologists who write on consciousness, in the works of John Searle and Daniel Dennett, among others. He also presents a number of thought experiments, as well as examples from the current neuropsychology literature, to support his distinction.

The four successive chapters, by **Daniel Dennett** (chap. 21), **David Chalmers** (chap. 22), **Jennifer Church** (chap. 23), and **Tyler Burge** (chap. 24), provide different perspectives on Block's essay. Dennett and Church refuse to accept Block's distinction, arguing that it is untenable. In contrast, Chalmers and Burge promote some version of the distinction, even though they criticize Block in either not drawing it in the right way, or stopping short of drawing its full consequences. Dennett argues that Block's phenomenal versus access consciousness distinction points to, in effect, a difference in degree among conscious states of a single kind, with respect to two dimensions: "richness of content" and "degree of influence." According to Dennett, Block inflates this difference in degree into an imaginary difference in kind, and mislocates the question of the function of consciousness. Similarly, Church criticizes Block for not providing sufficiently good reasons to support the most fundamental elements of his thesis, that the concept of phenomenal consciousness is coherent, and furthermore, that the concepts of phenomenal and access consciousness are actually distinct. Chalmers, on the other hand, not only is sympathetic to Block's distinction, but also claims that Block stops short of carrying his own line of reasoning to a further conclusion— that, on the basis of this distinction, there simply is no function or explanatory role that can be attributed to phenomenal consciousness within our mental lives. Burge suggests that although there is a conceptual distinction between phenomenal and access consciousness, it must be acknowledged that any notion of consciousness in an individual, including access consciousness, has to presuppose phenomenal consciousness. He also draws a further distinction between phenomenal consciousness and phenomenal qualities, where the latter can be instantiated as being either "felt" or "unfelt," and argues that for a subject to be phenomenally conscious, the subject has to not only possess phenomenal qualities, but feel (or sense) them as well.

Finally, **Van Gulick** (chap. 25) approaches the question of the function of consciousness by way of discussing the well-known "absent qualia" objection to functionalism (see also Section IX). He argues that the reasoning that qualia have no functional role, since for any system that possesses qualia it is always possible to imagine functional isomorphs of that system that lack qualia, is question begging. Van Gulick maintains that it is an open empirical question whether it really makes no difference for a system to have phenomenal, as opposed to nonphenomenal, mental representations, and he suggests in accord with Baars (chap. 10) that phenomenal con-

sciousness may have the unique functional role of "broadcasting information within the nervous system."

In Section VI, Metaphysics of Consciousness, various metaphysical questions about the nature and ontological status of consciousness are explored. The well-known attack on identity theory presented by **Saul Kripke** (chap. 26) contends that the identification of certain types of physical and mental states involves unique difficulties that do not plague other theoretical reductions in science, such as the identification of temperature and mean kinetic energy of gas molecules. Kripke's argument is given in the broader framework of rigid designation and necessity: both the term "pain" and its counterpart "C-fiber firing" are rigid designators, and thus, if their referents are identical, they are necessarily identical. But they are not necessarily identical, Kripke maintains, given the possibility (based on the conceivability) of either one existing in the absence of the other. Therefore the thesis of identity between the mental and the physical fails. **John Searle** (chap. 27) draws distinctions among ontological, theoretical, logical, and causal kinds of reduction, and argues in favor of causal reduction of consciousness to its neurobiological underpinnings, while at the same time rejecting ontological reduction. Even though Searle agrees with Kripke on the failure of ontologically identifying the mental and the physical, unlike Kripke he claims that this fact stems from the pragmatics of our definitional practices vis-à-vis consciousness and has no deep metaphysical consequences for the unity of the overall "scientific worldview" he independently defends. **Frank Jackson** (chap. 29) examines the role of conceptual analysis in philosophy of mind, and argues that any credible materialist theory has to engage in some a priori reasoning in order to ontologically locate mental properties in the natural world, even in dealing with identifications that involve a posteriori necessity. According to Jackson, materialism cannot make a case for itself unless it provides an account of a priori relations between the physical and the mental.

Georges Rey (chap. 28) adopts an eliminativist perspective on phenomenal consciousness and claims that there is no place or need for our folk-theoretic notion of consciousness in the most plausible accounts of mental life. He argues that this notion, which likens consciousness to an "inner light," is underwritten by the "Cartesian Intuition" about the infallibility of first-person beliefs about consciousness. Once the Cartesian Intuition is dispelled, Rey concludes, we will see good reasons for "doubting there really is such a thing as consciousness at all." In contrast, **John Searle** (chap. 30) argues for the vindication of the common-sense notion of consciousness, and the ontological thesis that "behavior, functional role, and causal relations are irrelevant to the existence of conscious mental phenomena." Searle grounds his argument on an epistemic distinction between first-person and third-person points of view, and various thought experiments in which this distinction plays a central role, all the while recommending that regarding "possibility scenarios" involving consciousness, one should always ask oneself: "What would it be like for me?" In accord with Searle's suggestion, **Sydney Shoemaker** (chap. 31) turns to epistemology of modality, and explores the role and scope of the first-person perspective in assessing metaphysical claims about the mind. In particular, he examines Kripke's possibility argument against the identity of the mental and the physical, and Searle's thought experiments designed to establish the ontological independence of consciousness from behavioral, functional, and causal elements. Shoemaker's general approach is sympathetic to the first-person perspective, but he presents reasons that undermine the kind of absolute authority Searle seems to be suggesting. The moral Shoemaker ultimately draws is also very different from Searle's: whenever the first-person perspective seems to present a metaphysical possibility, "one should always ask whether the seeming discovery could be confirmed from the third-person point of view."

Section VII, Subjectivity and Explanatory Gap, begins with an essay that has become a phi-losophy of mind classic, "What is it like to be a bat?" **Thomas Nagel** (chap. 32) argues, in agreement with Kripke (chap. 26), that the mind-body relation is unique in nature and doesn't yield to reduction as other phenomena, e.g., lightning and electrical discharge, typically do. He characterizes an organism's possession of conscious states as there being "something it is like to be" that organism, and claims that this "subjective character" of experience is not capturable by any functional or causal analysis. For Nagel, physicalist accounts of any sort have to be objective, and as such they necessarily remain incomplete, leaving out the ineliminable subjectivity of the mental. However, the conclusion Nagel ultimately arrives at is agnostic: he maintains not that physicalism is false, but that "physicalism is a position we cannot understand because we do not at present have any conception of how it might be true."

Both **Colin McGinn** (chap. 33) and **Joseph Levine** (chap. 34) take up the issues Nagel raises, but carry them in different directions to different conclusions. McGinn argues not only that we have no conception of how the mind-body problem can be solved (e.g., how physicalism can explain consciousness), but that we should never expect to acquire such a conception. According to McGinn, an adequate explanation of the mind-body problem will forever elude human understanding, not because it is miraculous or involves divine intervention, but because it transcends our cognitive abilities, just as the understanding of quantum mechanics forever transcends the intellectual abilities of monkeys. This thesis makes McGinn a nonconstructive naturalist. Levine also thinks, drawing on Kripke's work, that there is an "explanatory gap" between theories that employ solely physical properties, on one hand, and phenomena that involve qualitative character on the other. However, unlike McGinn, he doesn't go on to make the further claim that this gap will remain forever for us human beings. Moreover, unlike Kripke, Levine argues that the explanatory gap points not to an ontological, but to a merely epistemological problem for physicalism. He concludes that as we improve our concept of qualitative character so as to include causal elements in it, the explanatory gap is likely to close.

Section VIII comprises five articles that focus on yet another form of argument designed to show that physicalism fails to account for consciousness. The Knowledge Argument is based on a thought experiment that involves a vision-scientist, Mary, who learns "everything physical there is to know" about color experiences but never experiences colors herself due to her special circumstances (being raised in a monochrome environment). The point of the argument is that Mary would learn something new upon her first experience of colors, and since she was supposed to already know, *ex hypothesi*, everything she could know in a physicalist framework, physicalism is false, or at best incomplete. This argument has generated a number of different but interrelated responses, and **Robert Van Gulick** (chap. 35) gives a schematic summary of various objections raised against it in the literature, including his own. (See Loar [chap. 39] below for a line similar to Van Gulick's response to the knowledge argument.) Van Gulick also examines the issue of the explanatory gap in the second half of his essay, and concludes that physicalism is not refuted by either family of arguments.

Frank Jackson (chap. 36) and **Paul Churchland** (chap. 37) present a continuation of an exchange between the authors that started with Jackson's "Epiphenomenal Qualia" (*Philosophical Quarterly*, 1982, 32:127–36), where the present form of the knowledge argument first appeared. Churchland's "Reduction, Qualia and the Direct Introspection of Brain States" (*Journal of Philosophy*, 1985, 82:8–28) presented a critique of the argument and charged Jackson with committing an intensional fallacy on the basis of an equivocation in his use of "knowing about" (brain states versus experiences); Churchland also argued there that Mary could very well be able to *imagine* what it would be like to have color experiences. In that case, Mary would not learn anything new upon actually having a color experience, and therefore physicalism would remain unrefuted.

In the present part of the exchange, Jackson restates the argument, and emphasizes that it doesn't rest on the claim that Mary cannot imagine what having color experiences is like unless she actually has them. Jackson's claim is that Mary, as a matter of fact, would not know the experiential facts, and this in itself is sufficient to show that physicalism is false. Jackson further adds that the intensionality of "knowing about," just like the powers of Mary's imagination, is orthogonal to the validity of his argument. Finally, he argues that the kind of knowledge that is to the point is Mary's knowledge about the experiences of others, not about her own. Churchland, in his rejoinder, insists that the equivocation of "knowing about" indeed invalidates Jackson's argument, and he presents an entirely physicalist alternative model of visual experience in which the premises of Jackson's argument come out true but the conclusion false. Hence, Churchland concludes, Jackson's argument is invalid, and physicalism survives his attack unscathed.

Churchland, while discussing possible responses to Jackson's argument, considers another approach but states that it is, although well-motivated, scientifically unsatisfactory. This approach is based on a distinction between "knowing how" and "knowing that," due to Laurence Nemirow and David Lewis, and is commonly known as the "ability analysis" of the knowledge argument. It maintains that what Mary gains upon actually having a color experience is not knowledge of new facts or propositions, which would undermine physicalism, but a new recognitional ability that involves color sensations. **David Lewis** (chap. 38) advances a detailed defense against Jackson on the basis of this line of reasoning: Learning what a particular experience is like amounts to gaining certain new abilities to remember, imagine, and recognize, and if gaining new abilities means gaining new information, there is good reason to think that this new information is neither a special kind of irreducibly non-physical, "phenomenal information," nor propositional information represented in the form of knowledge or belief. Therefore, Lewis concludes, the fact that one cannot learn what a new experience is like unless one actually has it, is not to be taken as a measure of the limits of science or the metaphysics of mind.

In the last article of this section, **Brian Loar** (chap. 39) defends physicalism against a number of objections, among them subjectivity, the explanatory gap, and the knowledge argument. His overarching solution is based on a distinction between properties and concepts, as they figure in discussions about the mental versus the physical. Loar argues that our phenomenal and functional (physical) concepts are distinct, and that while this accounts for the presence of the explanatory gap and the *prima facie* intuitive appeal of the knowledge argument, it doesn't imply that the phenomenal and functional properties are not identical. In accord with the general line of the ability analysis, Loar characterizes phenomenal concepts as recognitional concepts, grounded in discriminatory and recognitional dispositions of the subject, but he differs from Lewis in accepting that Mary comes to know new facts or propositions in having color experiences for the first time. Loar does not have to accept Jackson's verdict that physicalism is false, however, for the mode of individuation on which Loar takes Mary to acquire new propositions is laden with conceptual constituent structure. Thus what Mary learns makes reference not to new properties, but to properties she has already referred to in the past, albeit by means of different concepts. The conclusion Loar arrives at at the end of his essay expresses the gist of the physicalist approaches represented in this section: "Nothing in philosophy should make one doubt either that [phenomenal] qualities are real or that they are physical."

Section IX is a continuation of the debates on the nature and ontological status of phenomenal (qualitative) properties of experience, Qualia, with a particular focus on the "absent qualia" and "inverted spectrum" arguments. In the first piece of the section, **Daniel Dennett** (chap. 40) starts out with a common-sense description of qualia as "the ways things seem to us," but quickly moves on to a more specific set of definitional criteria that he thinks *essentially* characterizes the philosophically problematic notion of qualia. According to Dennett, what makes qualia lie at the bottom of notoriously vexing problems in philosophy of mind and metaphysics is the way qualia are traditionally taken to be "ineffable, intrinsic, private, and directly or immediately apprehensible in consciousness," supported by a belief in the infallibility and incorrigibility of first-person epistemic authority. Dennett's aim is not only to show that, under these criteria, there are no properties that fit the bill, but also to "make it just as uncomfortable for anyone to talk of qualia [...] with the standard presumption that they, and everyone else, knows what on earth they are talking about." To this end, he presents fifteen "intuition pumps" designed to demonstrate the conceptual confusions involving the notion of qualia. Ultimately, Dennett turns his strategical choice that it is "far better, tactically, to declare that there simply are no qualia at all" into an ontological resolution, and he concludes that "contrary to what seems obvious at first blush, there simply are no qualia at all."

The next three articles center around the possibility of a systematic difference between color experiences of subjects (or, the same subject at different times) that yields a complete inversion in their experienced "hue circle" which, nonetheless, does not manifest itself in language, or, more generally, in behavior. This possibility of an inverted spectrum (together with the different possibility of absent qualia, the complete absence of qualitative aspects of experience) is regarded as one of the most tenacious obstacles to functionalism, as well as to physicalism in general. The difficulty lies in the implication that qualia can neither be defined in terms of their functional role or physical make-up, nor be captured in a functionalist or physicalist explanatory framework.

The disagreements in the qualia debates are often underwritten by fundamental differences regarding the ontology of qualitative properties of experience, for instance differences over whether qualia form a class of properties metaphysically autonomous from intentional/representational, functional, or causal properties. This issue also figures as a substratal element in the debate in the present section. Drawing a distinction between "intentional" versus "qualitative" senses in which experiences may resemble or differ from one another, **Sydney Shoemaker** (chap. 41) opts for characterizing qualia as distinct from intentional properties. He maintains, however, that neither the absent qualia nor the inverted spectrum argument constitutes a refutation of functionalism, even though the latter presents a more veritable difficulty, since it involves, for Shoemaker, a genuine possibility, whereas the former does not. Shoemaker bases the plausibility of the full-scale intersubjective inverted spectrum scenario on the epistemically less problematic possibility of intrasubjective spectrum inversion, and he argues that while the functional/behavioral evidence may establish intentional similarities and differences between the (mental states of) subjects, it cannot capture qualitative similarities and differences. Shoemaker concludes his essay with a discussion of varieties of functionalist approaches to qualia.

Gilbert Harman (chap. 42) presents a defense of functionalism against three objections commonly raised in the literature: the claim that functionalism cannot account for the "intrinsic qualities" of experience, the knowledge argument, and the inverted spectrum. Against the first objection, Harman argues that the claim that we are ordinarily aware of the intrinsic properties of our experiences, as defended by sense-data theorists, involves a fallacy that stems from a confusion between "the properties of a represented object and the properties of a representation of that object." According to Harman, in perceiving an object we are aware of not the intrinsic properties of our experience (the representation, or the representing-vehicle of the object), but the properties of what we experience (the represented object). Thus, Harman concludes, the claim that functionalism fails to capture a psychologically relevant aspect of experiences because it takes into account solely non-intrinsic properties has no theoretical force. Harman's defense against the knowledge argument differs from those of Van Gulick (chap. 35), Churchland (chap. 37), Lewis (chap. 38), and Loar (chap. 39) in that he accepts that Mary comes to learn a new fact upon having color experiences, at the same time rejecting Jackson's premise that "Mary could know everything physical there is to know" while confined to her monolithic environment. Harman claims that Mary could not have a proper concept of redness (or any other color) since having concepts, being functionally determined, is dependent on the presence of perceptual inputs from red objects — something Mary, *ex hypothesi*, lacks. But then Mary could not possibly acquire all the facts about color experiences prior to having those experiences, Harman concludes, because "mental representations are constructed from concepts," and "to know what it is like to see something red is to be capable of representing [to oneself] something's being red."

Finally, Harman maintains that functionalism can plausibly reject the possibility of the inverted spectrum, unless the sense-data theorist's thesis that perception involves the awareness of intrinsic features of experience is held as a prior assumption. Having already argued against this thesis in the first objection, he states that in normal perception "there can be no distinction between how things look and how they are believed to be," thereby rejecting the distinction Shoemaker offers between intentional and qualitative properties of mental states. Consequently, Harman concludes, spectrum inversion is a possibility only when it comes simultaneously with inversion of belief and meaning. Since the latter can be captured in a functionalist framework, the inverted spectrum argument presents no genuine difficulty for functionalism.

Ned Block (chap. 43), in response to Harman, presents the "inverted earth" argument, while also challenging Harman's critique of the knowledge argument. Regarding the latter, Block maintains that Harman's rejection of the first premise of the knowledge argument, that Mary can learn "everything physical there is to know" without having color experiences herself, at best establishes that "the knowledge argument does not serve very well as a locus of controversy" between those who take qualia to be identical to intentional (broadly construed) properties and those who do not. Block chooses to bring out this controversy in his inverted earth thought experiment, a variation of the inverted spectrum scenario that, he maintains, avoids the complications of the original formulation. He argues both in favor of the existence of intrinsic mental features of experience, and against the thesis that functionalism can unproblematically reject the possibility of the inverted spectrum, and he grounds these two arguments on the kind of distinction Shoemaker defends and Harman rejects: a distinction between intentional and qualitative properties (or content) of experience. According to Block, intentional content is functionally characterizable but qualitative content is not, and Harman's identification of the two involves a fallacy, "the fallacy of intentionalizing qualia." Block asserts that the inverted spectrum scenario is designed precisely to drive a wedge between these two types of content, for it demonstrates the possibility of the invariance of intentional content (belief and meaning) in the case of inversion of qualitative content (qualia).

Block's inverted earth scenario is constructed to yield the same theoretical result, though it is the converse of the inverted spectrum case, as its aim is to demonstrate the invariance of qualitative content in the case of inversion of intentional content. In this scenario, we are asked to imagine ourselves being fitted with color-inverting lenses, without our knowledge, and transported to "inverted earth," a duplicate of our earth except for the fact that the colors of all

objects, as well as the color vocabulary of its inhabitants, are inverted. In other words, the experiences of the natives of inverted earth have inverted qualitative as well as intentional content with respect to ours. Block's contention is that on inverted earth, while the qualitative contents of our visual experiences would remain the same (the two inversions cancelling each other out), after a period of adaptation into our new physical and linguistic environment (but still without the knowledge of the fate that has befallen us), the "intentional contents would shift so as to be the same as those of the natives." The result is an exemplification of a case where intentional content is inverted while qualitative content remains invariant. This, Block concludes, is a vindication of the inversion objection against functionalism, without recourse to the original inverted spectrum argument.

In summary, while in this debate Harman takes the thesis that in perception we become aware of intrinsic properties of experience as a prior assumption that is required by the possibility of spectrum inversion, Block claims that it is the possibility of spectrum inversion that will, once convincingly established (as he tries to do with the inverted earth argument), "settle the issue of whether we are aware of intrinsic features of experience" (by showing that there indeed are intrinsic *mental* features of our experience). As such, Harman and Block seem to agree, in effect, on the following conditional as a premise in their respective arguments: *if* spectrum inversion is a genuine possibility, *then* perception involves the awareness of intrinsic properties of experience. Harman then goes on to argue that the idea that perception involves the awareness of intrinsic properties of our experience must be rejected, for it involves a fallacy based on "confusing intrinsic features of the intentional object of experience with intrinsic features of the experiences," and he concludes that the inverted spectrum argument as an objection against functionalism is untenable. In contrast, Block argues that inversion arguments against functionalism are tenable on the basis of his improved version of the inversion argument, and he concludes that this establishes what Harman rejects on the basis of his analysis of intentionality of experiences, namely that experiences have intrinsic mental properties of which we become aware in perception. (Harman also attempts to support his analysis of intentionality by introspective evidence but Block dismisses this effort as "an error in philosophical method.")

If this characterization of the controversy is correct, then an interesting feature in the dialectic of the disagreement between Harman and Block is worth pointing out: while Harman rejects the consequent of the conditional premise they both accept, which leads him to reject the antecedent, Block argues in favor of the antecedent, which leads him to accept the consequent. It seems, in other words, that in this debate Harman's *modus tollens* becomes Block's *modus ponens*.

In the last article of this section, **Stephen White** (chap. 44) presents a detailed analysis of qualia arguments and their consequences for physicalism and (orthodox) functionalism, as well as what he calls "physicalist-functionalism" and "transcendentalism." Physicalist-functionalism is the view that certain aspects of a subject's material constitution, even if they can vary without varying functional constitution, are relevant to the nature of the subject's qualia; as such it is a compromise between physicalism and functionalism. Transcendentalism differs from all varieties of physicalism and functionalism in maintaining that the qualitative character of mental states cannot be captured in either physical or functional terms, and that experiential facts are essentially irreducible "first-person" facts. White distinguishes two versions of physicalist-functionalism and attributes them to Ned Block and Sydney Shoemaker, respectively, while reserving transcendentalism for Thomas Nagel. The view he ultimately defends against the alternatives is one he attributes to Gilbert Harman, orthodox functionalism (akin to what is elsewhere called "analytic functionalism"), according to which

there is an a priori conceptual connection between qualitative and functional properties in virtue of the meaning of terms such as "pain" and expressions that describe the typical corresponding causal/functional dispositions.

For White, the criteria that distinguish the two versions of physicalist-functionalism are the positions each takes with respect to absent qualia and the inverted spectrum. Block differs from Shoemaker in that he believes in the possibility of both (and so holds that functionalism cannot distinguish among creatures with normal, absent, or inverted qualia) whereas Shoemaker rejects the former while accepting the latter (thereby upholding that functionalism can characterize what it is like to have experiences with qualitative content in general, but not what it is like to have experiences with particular qualitative content). White argues that while Shoemaker's position ultimately collapses into either orthodox functionalism or Block's position, Block's brand of physicalist-functionalism ends up with the unhappy consequence of "saddling itself with all the problems of pre-functionalist physicalist theories," while being deprived of "the only plausible solution those theories had generated," namely topic-neutral translation of mental terms. White's conclusion is that inversion arguments fail to provide any theoretical support for physicalist-functionalism over orthodox functionalism, and although orthodox functionalism "fails to capture *all* of our intuitions regarding qualia," leaving transcendentalism aside, it is the best theory of the mental at hand.

Section X, the last section of the volume, brings together five articles on the Higher-Order Monitoring Conceptions of Consciousness. The debate in this section centers around the idea of construing consciousness in terms of the awareness (or, more generally, some form of higher-order representation) of first-order mental states. **David Armstrong** (chap. 45), **David Rosenthal** (chap. 46), and **William Lycan** (chap. 47) all defend this view, but while Armstrong and Lycan characterize the higher-order representation as "perception-like," Rosenthal espouses the "higher-order-thought" characterization of consciousness. According to these "higher-order monitoring conceptions of consciousness" (so-called because they sometimes liken consciousness, in Armstrong's words, to "a self-scanning mechanism in the central nervous system"), what makes a belief, a perceptual state, or a particular pain conscious is the subject's having an accompanying higher-order awareness, in the form of perception or thought, of that first-order mental state.

David Armstrong, in an attempt to develop an "anti-Cartesian" account that regards consciousness as not the essence but a special and sophisticated development of mentality, distinguishes three kinds of consciousness and identifies consciousness "in the most interesting sense of the word" with a "perception-like awareness of current states and activities in our own mind." This is what Armstrong calls "introspective consciousness" (unlike Lycan and Rosenthal, who call it simply "consciousness"), and he regards it a late evolutionary development and a faculty highly specific to human beings, in contrast with "minimal consciousness" (the state of a creature who is normally conscious but at the time sound asleep or knocked out) and "perceptual consciousness" (first-order awareness one has of one's environment and bodily states). For Armstrong, introspective consciousness (which he essentially identifies with Kantian "inner-sense") is theoretically on a par with ordinary sense perception ("outer-sense"), in that they involve partial awareness of current states and activities of one's mind, and one's body and environment, respectively. Furthermore, both are selective, fallible, and causally characterizable. Armstrong concludes that the significance of introspective consciousness lies in the fact that it provides us with the awareness of the past history and present status of ourselves: "Without introspective consciousness, we would not be aware that we existed."

William Lycan also advocates a characterization of consciousness, which he calls the "Inner Sense" view, as a "perception-like second-order representation of our own psychological states and events." He defends this view against a number of questions and objections raised by various philosophers, including Daniel Dennett (who argues that this model allows the metaphysically dubious possibility of consciousness of a stimulus in the absence of the subject's belief in that consciousness), Fred Dretske (who questions why consciousness *of* certain physical states is enough to make those states *themselves* conscious), David Rosenthal (who argues the possibility of a regress threatens if second-order perception involves, as perceiving always does, some sensory quality), Christopher Hill (who charges that second-order attention to a mental state may transform that state into another), and Georges Rey (who objects that if all it takes to make a first-order state a conscious state is that it be monitored by a scanner that makes integrative use of the relevant information, then any notebook computer can be said to have conscious states). Having also noted similarities and differences between his, Armstrong's, and Rosenthal's views, Lycan concludes that the Inner Sense view of consciousness survives all criticisms unscathed.

David Rosenthal differs from Armstrong and Lycan in relying on thinking, rather than perceiving, as the form of higher-order awareness in his model of consciousness. For Rosenthal, "a mental state is a conscious state when, and only when, it is accompanied by a suitable higher-order thought." As such, the question of what it is for a mental state to be conscious can be separated and pursued independently from the question of what it is for mental states to have intentional or sensory properties. This is so, Rosenthal argues, because a state's being conscious is not intrinsic to its having intentional or sensory character, and further that if it *were* so intrinsic, "no theoretical understanding of what it is to be a conscious state would be possible at all." Drawing on a distinction between transitive and intransitive consciousness (in the sense of our being conscious *of* something versus our mental states' being of the conscious or unconscious kind), Rosenthal goes on to develop the details of his "higher-order thought" theory of consciousness and argues that the explanatory scope and power of the theory are enhanced, as it successfully predicts certain important aspects of our mental lives (e.g., that reporting one's mental states is distinct from verbally expressing them, and that we become aware of more fine-grained differences among sensory qualities as we acquire more fine-grained relevant conceptual distinctions). After criticizing the "higher-order perception" theories of consciousness, Rosenthal concludes that the higher-order thought theory constitutes our best hope of providing a credible account of consciousness while doing justice to our pretheoretic intuitions about the subject matter.

Fred Dretske (chap. 48), in contrast to Armstrong, Lycan, and Rosenthal, argues that a subject can have conscious experiences without necessarily being aware of those experiences, or aware of having them, and he thereby attempts to sever the conceptual link between consciousness of mental states and our higher-order awareness of those states. Dretske demonstrates his point by a number of examples, after having drawn a distinction between "consciousness of things" (experiences that do not necessarily involve any concepts about what is being experienced) and "consciousness of facts" (beliefs that necessarily deploy such concepts). Dretske's examples rely on two theses which he tries to motivate independently: that consciousness of a particular object does not necessarily entail consciousness of any facts about that object, and that a subject's being conscious of an object or a fact implies that that subject is in (or has) a conscious state of some sort. Having introduced this conceptual apparatus, he goes on to show that we can sometimes have experiences that are conscious in the absence of our consciousness of them, or our consciousness of the fact that we are having them.

Dretske's objection is not that we never form a higher-order awareness of our own mental states, or that such awareness is necessarily unlike perceiving or thinking; he in fact speculates that introspection is probably akin to coming to have thoughts that one has mental states such as beliefs, desires, and experiences of a certain kind. Rather, the thesis he argues against is that what makes mental states conscious consists in the subject's awareness of those states. According to Dretske, what makes our internal states conscious is, instead, "the way *they* make us conscious of something else—the world we live in and (in proprioception) the condition of our own bodies."

Finally, **Güven Güzeldere** (chap. 49) distinguishes between the higher-order perception and higher-order thought theories of consciousness by specifying their underlying assumptions in the writings of Armstrong, Lycan, Churchland, and Rosenthal, and argues that these two varieties of higher-order representation theories, upon close examination, do not survive as distinct competing models. In particular, he demonstrates that the higher-order perception accounts face a trilemma, if they are literally taken to be modeled after perception: they either must abandon their characteristic two-tiered structure, or commit themselves to what he calls "the fallacy of the representational divide," or turn into a species of their competitor, higher-order thought theories. Taking the first horn of this trilemma means simply giving up the essential introspective element in the theory, Güzeldere maintains, while taking the second horn involves a confusion between properties of what is represented in consciousness and properties of that which represents what is represented. Güzeldere concludes that if Locke's dictum that "consciousness is the perception of what passes in a man's own mind" cannot therefore be taken literally, to the extent that higher-order thought theories prove unsatisfactory, we should look in the direction of developing unilevel, nonintrospective accounts of consciousness.

Acknowledgments

We thank the three anonymous reviewers who provided several useful suggestions on the content and form of this collection. We express our thanks to Teri Mendelsohn, formerly of Bradford Books/MIT Press, who patiently and professionally accommodated our endless requests, alterations, and disagreements over the elongated period of the preparation of this book. Thanks also to Larry Russell, Murat Aydede, Altuğ Güzeldere, and Tomiko Yoda for editorial help, and to Judith Feldmann, Pam Quick, Sandra Minkkinen, and Betty Stanton of The MIT Press for overseeing the final editing and production of this book and bringing our efforts to completion.

Güven Güzeldere

Sources

Güven Güzeldere
Introduction
Adapted from "Consciousness: What it Is, How to Study it, What to Learn from its History" and "Problems of Consciousness: A Perspective on Contemporary Issues, Current Debates" in *Journal of Consciousness Studies*, 2:1, 30–51, and 2:2, 112–143, (1995), by permission of the author and publisher.

William James
"The Stream of Consciousness"
From *Psychology*, Chap XI (New York: Henry Holt and Co., 1910), 151–175.

Daniel C. Dennett
"The Cartesian Theater and 'Filling In' the Stream of Consciousness"
Adapted from *Consciousness Explained* (Boston: Little, Brown, and Co., 1991), by permission of the author and publisher.

Owen Flanagan
"The Robust Phenomenology of the Stream of Consciousness"
From *Consciousness Reconsidered* (Cambridge: MIT Press, 1992), 169–175, by permission of the author and publisher.

Owen Flanagan
"Prospects for a Unified Theory of Consciousness"
From *Scientific Approaches to the Study of Consciousness: 25th Carnegie Symposium*, eds. J. Cohen and J. Schooler (Hillsdale: J. Erlbaum Associates, 1996), by permission of the author and publisher.

Alvin Goldman
"Consciousness, Folk Psychology, and Cognitive Science"
From *Consciousness and Cognition*, 2 (1993), 364–382, by permission of the author and publisher.

Patricia Churchland
"Can Neurobiology Teach Us Anything About Consciousness?"
From the APA Proceedings, 67(4): 23–40, by permission of the author and publisher.

Daniel C. Dennett and Marcel Kinsbourne
"Time and the Observer: The Where and When of Consciousness in the Brain"
From *Behavioral and Brain Sciences*, 15 (1992), 183–247, by permission of the author and publisher.

Ned Block
"Begging the Question Against Phenomenal Consciousness"
From *Behavioral and Brain Sciences*, 15 (1992), 205–206, by permission of the author and publisher.

Robert Van Gulick
"Time for More Alternatives"
From *Behavioral and Brain Sciences*, 15 (1992), 228–229, by permission of the author and publisher.

Bernard J. Baars
"Contrastive Phenomenology: A Thoroughly Empirical Approach to Consciousness"
Adapted from a previous version that appeared in *Psyche*, 1:2 (1994), 32–55, by permission of the author and publisher.

Martha Farah
"Visual Perception and Visual Awareness after Brain Damage: A Tutorial Overview"
From *Attention and Performance XV: Conscious and Nonconscious Information Processing*, eds. Carlo Umiltà and Moris Moscovitch (Cambridge: MIT Press, 1995), 37–75, by permission of the author and publisher.

Edoardo Bisiach
"Understanding Consciousness: Clues from Unilateral Neglect and Related Disorders"
From *The Neuropsychology of Consciousness*, eds. A. D. Milner and M. D. Rugg (London: Academic Press, 1992), 113–137, by permission of the author and publisher.

Tim Shallice
"Modularity and Consciousness"
From *From Neuropsychology to Mental Structure* (Cambridge: Cambridge University Press, 1988), 381–404, by permission of the author and publisher.

Francis Crick and Christof Koch
"Towards a Neurobiological Theory of Consciousness"
From *Seminars in the Neurosciences*, 2 (1990), 263–275, by permission of the author and publisher.

Colin McGinn
"Consciousness and Content"
From *The Problem of Consciousness* (Oxford: Blackwell, 1991), 23–43, by permission of the author and publisher.

Martin Davies
"Externalism and Experience"
From *Philosophy And Cognitive Science: Categories, Consciousness, and Reasoning*, eds. A. Clark, J. Ezquerro, and J. M. Larrazabal (Dordrecht: Kluwer Academic Publishers, 1996), 1–33, by permission of the author and publisher.

Michael Tye
"A Representational Theory of Pains and Their Phenomenal Character"
From: *Philosophical Perspectives*, Vol. 9, ed. J. Tomberlin (Atascadero: Ridgeview Publishing Co., 1990), 223–239, by permission of the author and publisher.

Christopher Peacocke
"Sensation and Content of Experience: A Distinction"
From *Sense and Content* (Oxford: Clarendon Press, 1983), 4–26, by permission of the author and publisher.

Owen Flanagan
"Conscious Inessentialism and the Epiphenomenalist Suspicion"
From: *Consciousness Reconsidered* (Cambridge: MIT Press, 1992), 129–152, by permission of the author and publisher.

Ned Block
"On a Confusion About a Function of Consciousness"
From *Behavioral and Brain Sciences*, 18 (1995), 227–247, by permission of the author and publisher.

Daniel C. Dennett
"The Path Not Taken"
From Behavioral and Brain Sciences, 18 (1995), 252–253, by permission of the author and publisher.

Jennifer Church
"Fallacies or Analyses?"
From *Behavioral and Brain Sciences*, 18 (1995), 251–252, by permission of the author and publisher.

Robert van Gulick
"Understanding the Phenomenal Mind: Are We All Just Armadillos?", Part II
Adapted from a version in *Consciousness*, eds. M. Davies and G. Humphreys (Oxford: Blackwell, 1993), 149–154, by permission of the author and publisher.

Saul Kripke
"The Identity Thesis"
From *Naming and Necessity*, Lecture III (Cambridge: Harvard University Press, 1980), 144–155, by permission of the author and publisher.

John R. Searle
"Reductionism and the Irreducibility of Consciousness"
From *The Rediscovery of the Mind*, Chap. 5 (Cambridge: MIT Press, 1992), 111–126, by permission of the author and publisher.

Georges Rey
"A Question about Consciousness"
From *Perspectives on Mind*, eds. H. Otto and J. Tueidio (Norwell: Kluwer Academic Publishers, 1988), 5–24, by permission of the author and publisher.

Frank Jackson
"Finding the Mind in the Natural World"
From *Philosophy and the Cognitive Sciences: Proceedings of the 16th International Wittgenstein Symposium*, eds. R. Casati, B. Smith, and G. White (Vienna: Verlag Holder-Pichler-Tempsky, 1994), 101–112, by permission of the author and publisher.

John R. Searle
"Breaking the Hold: Silicon Brains, Conscious Robots, and Other Minds"
From *The Rediscovery of the Mind*, Chap. 3 (Cambridge: MIT Press, 1992), 65–82, by permission of the author and publisher.

Sydney Shoemaker
"The First-Person Perspective"
From the APA Proceedings, 68(2): 7–22, by permission of the author and publisher.

Thomas Nagel
"What Is it Like to Be a Bat?"
From *Philosophical Review*, 83:4 (1974), 435–450, by permission of the author and publisher.

Colin McGinn
"Can We Solve the Mind-Body Problem?"
From *Mind*, 98:891 (1989), 349–366, by permission of the author and publisher.

Joseph Levine
"On Leaving Out What It's Like"
From *Consciousness*, eds. M. Davies and G. Humphreys (Oxford: Blackwell, 1993), 121–136, by permission of the author and publisher.

Robert van Gulick
"Understanding the Phenomenal Mind: Are We All Just Armadillos?", Part I
Adapted from a version in *Consciousness*, eds. M. Davies and G. Humphreys (Oxford: Blackwell, 1993), pp. 137–149, by permission of the author and publisher.

Frank Jackson
"What Mary Didn't Know"
From *Journal of Philosophy*, 83:5 (1986), pp. 291–295, by permission of the author and publisher.

Paul M. Churchland
"Knowing Qualia: A Reply to Jackson"
From *A Neurocomputational Perspective* (Cambridge: MIT Press, 1989), 67–76, by permission of the author and publisher.

David Lewis
"What Experience Teaches"
From *Mind and Cognition*, ed. W. Lycan (Oxford: Blackwell, 1990), 499–519, by permission of the author and publisher.

Brian Loar
"Phenomenal States"
Adapted from a version in Philosophical Perspectives, ed. J. Tomberlin, Vol. 4 (Atascadero: Ridgeview Publishing Co., 1990), 81–108, by permission of the author and publisher.

Daniel C. Dennett
"Quining Qualia"
From *Consciousness in Contemporary Science*, eds. A. Marcel and E. Bisiach (Oxford: Oxford University Press, 1988), 43–77, by permission of the author and publisher.

Sydney Shoemaker
"The Inverted Spectrum"
From *Journal of Philosophy*, 74:7 (1981), 357–381, by permission of the author and publisher.

Gilbert Harman
"The Intrinsic Quality of Experience"
From *Philosophical Perspectives*, ed. J. Tomberlin, Vol. 4 (Atascadero: Ridgeview Publishing Co., 1990), 31–52, by permission of the author and publisher.

Ned Block
"Inverted Earth"
From *Philosophical Perspectives*, ed. J. Tomberlin, Vol. 4 (Atascadero: Ridgeview Publishing Co., 1990), 52–79, by permission of the author and publisher.

Stephen L. White
"The Curse of the Qualia"
From *Synthese*, 68 (1986), 333–368, by permission of the author and publisher.

David Armstrong
"What is Consciousness"
From *The Nature of Mind* (Ithaca: Cornell University Press, 1981), 55–67, by permission of the author and publisher.

David Rosenthal
"A Theory of Consciousness"
Adapted from ZiF Technical Report, Bielefeld, Germany, 1990, by permission of the author and publisher.

William G. Lycan
"Consciousness as Internal Monitoring"
Adapted from *Philosophical Perspectives*, Vol. 9, ed. J. Tomberlin (Atascadero: Ridgeview Publishing Co., 1990), 1–14, by permission of the author and publisher.

Fred Dretske
"Conscious Experience"
From *Mind*, 102:406 (1993), 263–283, by permission of the author and publisher.

Güven Güzeldere
"Is Consciousness the Perception of What Passes in One's Own Mind?"
From *Conscious Experience*, ed. T. Metzinger (Paderborn: Schoeningh-Verlag, 1995), 335–357, by permission of the author and publisher.

INTRODUCTION
The Many Faces of Consciousness: A Field Guide

Güven Güzeldere

There is perhaps no other phenomenon besides consciousness that is so familiar to each of us and yet has been so elusive to any systematic study, philosophical or scientific. In thinking about consciousness, the puzzlement one often finds oneself in is rather like St. Augustine's riddle in his contemplations about the nature of time: When no one asked him, he knew what it was; being asked, however, he no longer did. (Augustine of Hippo 1961: Book 11.)

What is at the heart of this puzzlement? Is there a genuine difficulty that underlies it? What are the specific issues that comprise *the* problem of consciousness? (Is there really a *"the* problem of consciousness"?) And are we facing a phenomenon the understanding of which lies forever beyond our intellectual capacities? These are the questions that I will pursue below.

The overarching goal of this introduction is to provide a *field guide* (with a particular perspective) for anyone interested in the history and present status of philosophical issues in the study of consciousness. Part One is a preliminary overview of the current philosophical positions in the literature, as well as a discussion of the unique difficulties inherent in the concept and nature of consciousness. Part Two is an account of the study of consciousness in the history of modern psychology. Finally, Part Three is an exposition of the mosaic of philosophical puzzles of consciousness, as well as an exploration of their interrelations.[1]

PART ONE
CONCEPTUAL FOUNDATIONS

The feeling of helplessness was terrifying. I tried to let the staff know I was conscious but I couldn't move even a finger or eyelid. It was like being held in a vice and gradually I realized that I was in a situation from which there was no way out. I began to feel that breathing was impossible, and I just resigned myself to dying.
—Patient: Male, aged fifty-four, bronchoscopy, 1978.

This testimonial was one of the many unsettling personal accounts of "becoming conscious" under general anesthesia, gathered in response to the following advertisement, which appeared in four national newspapers in Great Britain in 1984:

SURGERY: Have you ever been conscious during a surgical operation when you were supposed to be anaesthesized? A medical research team would like an account of your experiences. Write in confidence.

The goal of this advertisement was to gather firsthand accounts of gaining consciousness under general anesthesia, in order to investigate the truth of a number of patients' discomforting postsurgery reports and to provide legal guidance for the accumulating court cases.[2]

Whatever philosophical problems may be associated with the term *consciousness*, it might be thought that it would be a straightforward matter to specify an operational definition of being conscious for anesthesiologists to work with. Can consciousness simply not be detected on the basis of the patient's being alert and responsive? What is in question, after all, is neither the notoriously elusive problem of phenomenal experience nor the concept of the evanescent Humean self.

A brief look at the anesthesiology literature, brimming with terms like *real awareness* and *incipient consciousness*, quickly proves otherwise. (Cf. Rosen and Lunn 1987.) If anything, the consensus is that "with the spectral edge of the EEG [electroencephalogram] or median frequency, or any other processed EEG signal, there does not seem to be a clear cut-off, without overlap, between consciousness and unconsciousness" (Vickers 1987, p. 182). The phenomenon of consciousness does not have clear-cut boundaries, and its complex structure does not admit any easy formulations. (See, for instance, the *Roche Handbook of Differential Diagnosis* on "Coma" [1979] and on "Transient Loss of Consciousness" [1989].) Even if it is in principle possible to invent a "consciousness monitor," a device that would detect the physical signs of the presence of consciousness in a patient, no such technology is anywhere in sight, because it is not even known what exactly is to be measured.

The root of the problem lies deeper than the inadequacy of the technology or the lack of sufficient data, however. What seems to be critically lacking is a solid theoretical framework to ground and facilitate the experimental research. For example, there is no established consensus, even in the medical field, as to what should count as the criteria of consciousness, so as to demarcate the domain of the conscious from that of the unconscious or the nonconscious. The problem with building a consciousness monitor is not confined to a lack of sufficiently fine-grained measuring instruments; it ultimately has to do with not knowing where to begin measuring and where to end up with the measured quantities.[3]

Worse, it is not clear whether everyone means the same thing by the term *consciousness*, even within the bounds of a single discipline. There is considerable variation in people's pretheoretic intuitions, for instance, regarding the kinds of creatures to which consciousness can be attributed.[4]

And in the absence of well-grounded theories, the lack of robust pretheoretical intuitions becomes even more importunate. Consider again the case of anesthesia. A person who is totally unresponsive to stimuli can, in one very important sense, be said to have lost consciousness. Nonetheless, can she still be said to be conscious in another sense—in the sense of passively experiencing the sensations caused by the stimuli, for instance? Similarly, are we to grant consciousness to a patient in a vegetative state, even when she lacks a well-functioning brain stem? Or what would justify granting consciousness to the patient if she did have a functioning brain stem that maintained the autonomic functions of her body?[5] How many senses of consciousness are there anyway, and how are we to taxonomize them?

I The Puzzle of Consciousness

These questions do not have any easy, obvious answers. Nor is there at present anything that could be regarded as a received view on problems of consciousness in the scientific and philosophical community. Furthermore, it is common to find serious doubts expressed in the literature about whether there can ever be a complete understanding of the phenomenon of consciousness. The gloomy opening lines of Thomas Nagel's famous essay, "What Is It Like to Be a Bat?" have become formative for many in thinking about consciousness: "Consciousness is what makes the mind-body problem really intractable.... Without consciousness the mind-body problem would be much less interesting. With consciousness, it seems hopeless" (Nagel 1974, pp. 165–166).

The puzzle of consciousness can be regarded in various ways, all the way from a supernatural mystery that will forever elude naturalist explanations, to a natural but extremely complicated phenomenon about which we know very little. And some of the time, the blue line that lies in between becomes very thin. There are also those who express skepticism about the existence of consciousness as a real phenomenon or about the coherence of its conceptual grounding, as well as others with a much more positive outlook, busily constructing their own accounts of consciousness to solve the puzzle. A brief look at some of the representatives of these different positions is in order.

The Mystery of Consciousness and the Explanatory Gap

In the opening pages of *Consciousness Explained*, Daniel Dennett (1991) remarks:

Human consciousness is just about the last surviving mystery.... There have been other great mysteries: the mystery of the origin of the universe, the mystery of life and reproduction, the mystery of the design to be found in nature, the mysteries of time, space, and gravity.... We do not yet have the final answers to any of the questions of cosmology and particle physics, molecular genetics, and evolutionary theory, but we do know how to think about them. The mysteries haven't vanished, but they have been tamed.... With consciousness, however, we are still in a terrible muddle. Consciousness stands alone today as a topic that often leaves even the most sophisticated thinkers tongue-tied and confused. (pp. 21–22)

Dennett should not be taken as promoting the sense of mystery, however. After all, his book is entitled *Consciousness Explained*. Of course, it is hard to say that everyone (or even many) agrees with Dennett's conviction. In fact, the general sentiment among those who work on consciousness (including philosophers, psychologists, and neuroscientists) seems to be on the "puzzled" side.

Moreover, in the wake of a recent rise in interest in the study of consciousness, almost each appearance of consciousness as a subject matter in the popular press has been tagged with some element of mystery. For instance, Francis Crick and Christof Koch called consciousness the "most mysterious aspect of the mind-body problem" in their article that appeared in a special issue of *Scientific American* titled *Mind and Brain* (September 1992). *Discover* magazine enlisted consciousness as one of the "ten great unanswered questions of science" (November 1992), and *Omni* published a special issue on consciousness but titled it "Science and the Soul" (October 1993). (Perhaps the rather unusual title Francis Crick chose for his book that appeared shortly afterward was a response to *Omni*'s inquiry: *The Scientific Hypothesis: The Scientific Search for the Soul*.) Finally, *Time* magazine, in an issue that featured consciousness research, put the words "that evanescent thing called consciousness" on its cover (July 17, 1995).

Now, no one refers to other biological or psychological phenomena in such terms. There is never a special magazine issue that pronounces the problem of cell mutation with the question of the soul in the same breath, nor does anyone refer to language as "that evanescent thing." So it seems obvious that consciousness is perceived as special, possibly unique, and not readily amenable to ordinary scientific or philosophical explanation.

Some take this sense of mystery even further, and this attitude is not at all restricted to the popular press. It is in fact possible to find the same sentiments expressed in philosophical and scientific circles, by those whom Owen Flanagan (1991) calls the "New Mysterians." For instance, Colin McGinn (1989) finds it humanly impossible ever to understand "how technicolor phenomenology can arise from grey soggy matter," and approvingly quotes the English biologist Huxley who famously stated: "How it is that anything so remarkable as a state of consciousness comes about as a result of irritating nervous tissue is just as unaccountable as the appearance of Djin when Aladdin rubbed his lamp" (p. 349).[6]

The expression of this sort of puzzlement is hardly new. Similar perplexity has been expressed by a number of people over the years, especially since the mid-nineteenth century, with the advancement of neurology and neuropsychology and the consequently well-grounded conviction that facts about consciousness *must* have some explanatory basis in the facts about the brain. For instance, in 1874, physicist John Tyndall made the following remark: "We can trace the development of a nervous system, and correlate with it the parallel phenomena of sensation and thought. We see with undoubting certainty that they go hand in hand. But we try to soar in a vacuum the moment we seek to comprehend the connection between them. An Archimedean fulcrum is here required which the human mind cannot command; and the effort to solve the problem ... is like that of a man trying to lift himself by his own waistband" (p. 195).[7] In contemporary literature, Karl Popper, in a similar vein, finds "the emergence of full consciousness ... which seems to be linked to the human brain ... one of the greatest miracles" (Popper and Eccles 1993, p. 129). And most recently, McGinn (1989) delivers what he considers to be the final verdict on the mind-body problem: "We have been trying for a long time to solve the mind-body problem. It has stubbornly resisted our best efforts. The mystery persists. I think the time has come to admit candidly that we cannot solve the mystery" (p. 349).

There is, however, more than one way to read assertions about the mystery of consciousness. Accordingly, it is important not to lump together everyone who expresses puzzlement about consciousness into the same category. In particular, it is important to pay attention to the following two questions: Is the mystery essentially a result of a commitment to a materialist framework? Is the mystery essentially inherent in our (lack of) cognitive capacities?

As such, these questions constitute an ontological and an epistemic axis, respectively, that cross-cut each other. Not every combination in the matrix receives equal philosophical attention. A negative answer to both questions essentially leaves one out of the circle of those who find something mysterious in consciousness, and not many defend a view that find consciousness mysterious in both aspects. Rather, the focus is on views based on an exclusively positive answer to one or the other question.

Those who think that consciousness will remain a mystery in a materialist ontology suggest that the proper place to pursue investigation is instead an immaterial realm—such as the realm of the *res cogitans* for Descartes, or *World 2* of mental entities for Karl Popper. This move brings with it a problem perhaps larger than that it was presumed to solve: how to account for the link between consciousness in the immaterial realm and brains (and bodies) in the material realm. Descartes's notorious solution was to postulate the pineal gland as the gatekeeper of interaction between the two essentially different kinds of substances. Alternatively, Leibniz chose to rely on divine intervention to secure a "pre-established harmony" between the events of the two realms.

More than three centuries after Descartes, John Eccles (1991, pp. 190–191) makes a repeat attempt, although in neurologically sophisticated dress, by postulating *psychons* (mental units) as counterparts of dendrites in brains, to connect Popper's mental *World 2* to physical *World 1*. Another contemporary expression of the view that defends an antimaterialist framework for consciousness is given by Robert Adams (1987), who finds theism theoretically advantageous to materialism in explaining the relation of consciousness to bodily physical states.[8]

On the other hand are those who do not cut the bill of the mystery of consciousness to the presumed immaterial ontology of consciousness but rather to our lack of cognitive capacities that would enable us to understand the nature of the "psychophysical link" between brains and minds. Tyndall seems to be in this group, and so is McGinn, who states that although "we know that brains are the *de facto* causal basis of consciousness," we have no idea about how "the water of the physical brain is turned into the wine of consciousness" (McGinn 1989, p. 349). This is an epistemic rather than ontological problem. For McGinn, "there is, in reality, nothing mysterious about how the brain generates consciousness," but we human beings are forever "cognitively closed" to understanding the nature of this process, much the same way the understanding of quantum mechanics lies beyond the cognitive capacities of monkeys.[9]

The general difficulty involving consciousness forms a basis for what Joseph Levine (1983, 1993) called the "problem of the explanatory gap." Almost everyone agrees that there is indeed some explanatory gap in this area; what is controversial is, as I will note later, whether there is just an epistemic or also an ontological lesson that needs to be drawn from it.

In any case, these positions constitute only a fraction of the whole dialectical space. There are also the skeptics and the naturalists, and to them I now turn.

Skepticism About Consciousness

The skeptics among philosophers fundamentally doubt the coherence of the very concept of consciousness, and the merits of consciousness itself as a phenomenon fit for scientific or philosophical investigation. Patricia Churchland, in one of her early papers, compares the concept of consciousness (under a certain reading that she explicates) to such now-defunct concepts as ether, phlogiston, and demonic possession—concepts that "under the suasion of a variety of empirical-cum-theoretical forces ... lose their integrity and fall apart" (Churchland 1983, p. 80).

In a similar vein, Kathleen Wilkes claims not only that "science can dispense with the concept of consciousness and lose thereby none of its comprehensiveness and explanatory power," but "so too could ordinary language." She then suggests that "perhaps 'conscious' is best seen as a sort of dummy-term like 'thing', useful [only] for the flexibility that is assured by its lack of specific content" (Wilkes 1984, pp. 241–242). Along the same lines Georges Rey goes a step further and suggests that there are "reasons for doubting that oneself is conscious and ... thinking that nothing is conscious." Consciousness, Rey suggests, "may be no more real than the simple soul exorcised by Hume" (Rey 1988, p. 6).

Notice that this sort of skepticism about consciousness is a very different attitude from any form of "mysterianism." In particular, those who think that consciousness is mysterious are committed to the existence of some significant phenomenon, however elusive it may be in relation to scientific investigation or philosophical analysis. Consciousness skepticism, on the other hand, embraces an eliminativist stance: the concept of consciousness is defunct, and the phenomenon itself may actually be inexistent, at least so far as it is construed in the literature that the skeptics are attacking.

The Consciousness Naturalists

Finally, there are those who believe that consciousness is a real and perfectly natural phenomenon and that there will remain no mysterious unexplained residue about consciousness in a completely naturalist, but surely more advanced and mature, theoretical framework. Among the naturalists, however, there is a wide spectrum of positions representing different levels of confidence in the success of a naturalist program. For instance, one can straightforwardly distinguish between full-blown naturalists and naturalists-at-heart.[10]

Into the first group fall a number of philosophers who have explicitly defended a naturalist framework to explain consciousness, without theoretical reservations. However, some of the full naturalists, most significant among them Paul Churchland (1988) and Daniel Dennett (1991), have been charged with trying to do away with consciousness for the sake of explaining it. Some others have been more careful not to fall under this decree. For instance Owen Flanagan (1992), who proposes what he calls the *natural method*— a triangulated approach for studying consciousness that combines phenomenology, psychology, and neuroscience—states: "Consciousness exists, and it would be a mistake to eliminate talk of it because it names such a multiplicity of things. The right attitude is to deliver the concept from its ghostly past and provide it with a credible naturalistic analysis.... It will be our proudest achievement if we can demystify consciousness" (Flanagan 1995, p. 20).

Among the naturalists who give accounts of consciousness in terms of causal and functional roles (broadly construed) are Armstrong (1980b, 1993), Lewis (1966, 1972, 1980, 1995), Shoemaker (1975, 1991, 1994), Lycan (1987, 1997b), Van Gulick (1988, 1989, 1993), and Rosenthal (1986, 1997).

Most recently, Fred Dretske (1995) and Michael Tye (1995) came up with naturalist accounts that explain consciousness in entirely representational terms. Finally, one can add John Searle to this group, who dubs his view "biological naturalism":

The "mystery" of consciousness today is in roughly the same shape that the mystery of life was before the development of molecular biology or the mystery of electromagnetism was before Clerk-Maxwell equations. It seems mysterious because we do not know how the system of neurophysiology/consciousness works, and an adequate knowledge of how it works would remove the mystery.... [T]here has been no question of "naturalizing consciousness"; it is already completely natural. (Searle 1992, p. 102, 93, respectively)

Despite Searle's fully naturalist convictions, his views have, as I will point out later, significant disagreements with those of the above on many other (relevant) points. Nonetheless, his position also differs from a position that I call naturalism-at-heart.

Naturalists-at-heart are those who openly feel the pull of naturalism, while not quite being able to find a satisfactory place for consciousness in a naturalist framework. For example, Levine (1983, 1993), who thinks that the problem of explanatory gap poses ultimately no ontological problems for materialism, nonetheless expresses the following troubled sentiments: "The absent and inverted qualia hypotheses are thought experiments which give concrete expression to what I will call, following the Churchlands, the 'pro-qualia' intuition. This is the intuition that there is something special about conscious mental life that makes it inexplicable within the theoretical framework of functionalism, and, more generally, materialism" (Levine 1988, p. 272). Short of disbelieving materialism, Levine finds it difficult to place consciousness in a naturalist framework.

Perhaps the most eloquent proponent of this position is Thomas Nagel, possibly more so in his earlier writings than his later work. In one of his earlier works, Nagel examines and rejects "the reasons for believing that physicalism cannot possibly be true" and concludes: "My attitude toward physicalism [is that it] repels me although

I am persuaded of its truth" (Nagel 1965, p. 110). Later he moves to a position he calls "dual aspect theory"—a position that lies between asserting falsity of physicalism but remaining short of postulating nonphysical substances for accounting for the ontology of the mind—while admitting that "to talk about a dual aspect theory is largely hand waving" (Nagel 1986, pp. 29–30). So perhaps the early Nagel was a naturalist-at-heart, and now it is more accurate to characterize him as a half-hearted-naturalist. In either case, Nagel's position seems, at least fundamentally, somewhere in the naturalist camp, despite the skeptical and pessimistic undertones that make him sometimes look closer to the mysterians or skeptics.

To recapitulate: It is noteworthy that the spectrum of disagreements ranges over not only particular accounts of consciousness but, more fundamentally, whether any satisfactory naturalistic explanation of consciousness can *in principle* be given. Part of this disagreement owes, no doubt, to the difficulty in the *nature* of the phenomenon of consciousness. But there is also a part that stems from a conceptual disarray surrounding the *notion* of consciousness. It is thus instructive to examine these two dimensions that contribute to the puzzle of consciousness separately.

II Approaching Consciousness: A Multitude of Difficulties

What we are when we are awake, as contrasted with what we are when we sink into a profound and perfectly dreamless sleep or receive an overpowering blow upon the head—*that* it is to be conscious. What we are less and less, as we sink gradually down into dreamless sleep, or as we swoon slowly away: and what we are more and more, as the noise of the crowd outside tardily arouses us from our after-dinner nap, or as we come out of the midnight darkness of the typhoid fever crisis—*that* it is to become conscious.

This is how George Trumbull Ladd (1909), noted American psychologist (whose definition of psychology as the "description and explanation of states of consciousness *as such*" was adopted and promoted by William James), characterized the phenomenon of consciousness (p. 30). This characterization seems straightforward, commonsensical, and familiar to everyone. So familiar that perhaps, as George Stout (1899), another psychologist of the same era, declares in the opening pages of his *Manual of Psychology*, no precise definition is necessary, or even possible: "What is consciousness? Properly speaking, definition is impossible. Everybody knows what consciousness is because everybody is conscious" (p. 7). Similarly, William James never attempts to give a definition of consciousness anywhere in his two-volume work, *Principles of Psychology* (1950a, 1950b). This is not because James had no interest in, or nothing to say on, consciousness; on the contrary, many of the chapters in his two volumes are *about* consciousness—its underpinnings in the nervous system, its function in evolution, its streamlike phenomenology, and so on. Rather, according to James, consciousness was a phenomenon *too familiar* to be given a definition. James (1950a) was convinced that everyone took themselves to be possessors of conscious states that were accessible by introspection, and he regarded this belief as "the most fundamental of all the postulates of Psychology." In his refusal to discuss this postulate any further, James adds that he would "discard all curious inquiries about its certainty as too metaphysical" for the scope of his book (p. 185).

This somewhat peculiar "all-too-familiar a phenomenon" attitude toward consciousness has indeed been quite common among many other prominent investigators of consciousness. Sigmund Freud (1964), for instance, supports Stout's and James's convictions in his introductory lectures on psychoanalysis: "What is meant by consciousness we need not discuss; it is beyond all doubt" (p. 70). Closer to our times, neuroscientist Francis Crick and Christof Koch (1990) endorse the same line in the opening paragraphs of their article, "Towards a Neurobiological Theory of Consciousness," even though they are attempting

to lay out the foundations of a new theory of consciousness: they need not provide a precise definition of consciousness since "everyone has a rough idea of what is meant by consciousness" (p. 263).

On the other hand, it is not uncommon to come across statements about consciousness that convey a conviction opposite to those mentioned above: that not only is there no clear and generally accepted definition, but we are not even in possession of a stable *pretheoretical* conception of consciousness. And this view, too, has been around for quite a while, as expressed by Edward Titchener (1915) who cites two British psychologists, Alexander Bain and James Ward, of the late nineteenth century: "'Consciousness,' says Professor Ward, 'is the vaguest, most protean, and most treacherous of psychological terms'; and Bain, writing in 1880; distinguished no less than thirteen meanings of the word; he could find more today" (pp. 323–324).

Unfortunately, there is no hope of receiving help from antonyms, either. Here is the entry for "unconscious" in a psychology dictionary: "It is said that there are no less than 39 distinct meanings of 'unconscious'; it is certain that no author limits himself consistently to one. And nearly all meanings are closely linked to debatable theories. Any user of the term therefore risks suggesting agreement with theories he may deplore" (English and English 1958). Finally, Julian Jaynes (1976) rhetorically asks: "This consciousness that is myself of selves, that is everything, and yet nothing at all—what is it?" (p. 1).

Moreover, not only is there no consensus on what the term *consciousness* denotes, but neither is it immediately clear if there actually is a single, well-defined "*the* problem of consciousness" within disciplinary (let alone across disciplinary) boundaries. Perhaps the trouble lies not so much in the ill definition of the question, but in the fact that what passes under the term *consciousness* as an all too familiar, single, unified notion may be a tangled amalgam of several different concepts, each inflicted with its own separate problems.

What exactly, for example, is the problem of consciousness in philosophy, in psychology, and in the neurosciences? Are philosophers concerned with the same problem, or set of problems, as psychologists and neuroscientists who work on consciousness? Whereas Thomas Natsoulas (1992), a psychologist, questions: "Is consciousness what psychologists actually examine?" (p. 363), Kathleen Wilkes (1988), a philosopher, gives the following advice: "Just as psychologists do not study 'mind' *per se*, so they need not bother with consciousness [because] in all the contexts in which it tends to be deployed, the term 'conscious' and its cognates are, for *scientific* purposes, both unhelpful and unnecessary" (pp. 38–9).

An even more pessimistic view is enunciated by Stuart Sutherland (1995) under the entry "consciousness" in his *International Dictionary of Psychology*:

CONSCIOUSNESS: The having of perceptions, thoughts, and feelings; awareness. The term is impossible to define except in terms that are unintelligible without a grasp of what consciousness means.... Consciousness is a fascinating but elusive phenomenon: it is impossible to specify what it is, what it does, or why it evolved. Nothing worth reading has been written about it. (p. 95)

Why are there such glaring polarities? Why is consciousness characterized both as a phenomenon too familiar to require further explanation, *as well as* a source of obscurity that remains typically recalcitrant to systematic investigation by those who work largely within the same paradigm? There is something uniquely peculiar here. Is it the phenomenon of consciousness that is more puzzling, one sometimes wonders, or the magnitude of the puzzlement itself and the theoretical dissonance surrounding consciousness? Could it perhaps be as R. J. Joynt (1981) predicted: "Consciousness is like the Trinity; if it is explained so that you understand it, it hasn't been explained correctly" (p. 108)?

George Miller (1962), faced with these difficulties, tentatively entertains the interesting proposition that "maybe we should ban the word for a decade or two until we can develop more precise terms for the several uses which 'consciousness' now obscures." Nonetheless, he ultimately decides against it: "Despite all its faults, however, the term would be sorely missed; it refers to something immediately obvious and familiar to anyone capable of understanding a ban against it" (p. 25).[11]

In the end, I find myself in agreement with Miller's positive conclusion. It is historically accurate to note that consciousness as a phenomenon in need of not only explanation, but also definition, has persistently kept resurfacing. It also seems reasonable to think that further attempts to provide carefully constructed conceptual tools could only help the situation, providing a common platform of interaction among all who choose consciousness as their object of study. This is not to say that it is not crucial to proceed cautiously to steer clear of conceptual dead ends, as well as to make sure that one does not fall into the trap of reinventing the wheel of consciousness over and over. After all, if we hope that anything toward a better understanding of consciousness will come out of the joint efforts of different disciplines, it is of utmost importance to minimize crosstalk and make sure that common terms actually point to the same referents. As a result, it seems even more imperative to look for and try to delineate the specific *conceptions* and *aspects* of consciousness under which the different problems arise. The next section is a brief attempt to address conceptual issues along these lines, before turning to the epistemological and ontological difficulties that arise from the nature of consciousness.

Difficulties with the Concept of Consciousness

Because *consciousness* is a word whose semantics has shifted over time, a brief lexical and etymological exposition may be of some service as a preliminary step. Let us start with present definitions. The *Oxford English Dictionary* (*OED*:

unabridged second edition), for example, gives eight definitions of "consciousness," and twelve definitions of "conscious." For the purposes of this chapter, the eight *OED* entries for "consciousness" can be divided roughly into two groups. On the one hand, there is a largely social aspect of the term *consciousness*: joint or mutual knowledge shared by a community of people. This was indeed the earliest sense of consciousness, derived from the Latin term *conscius*.[12] It is this sense of consciousness that is used in talking about "class consciousness" in Marxist thought, or that appears in titles like Gerda Lerner's recent book, *The Creation of Feminist Consciousness* (1993).

On the other hand, *consciousness* has a largely psychological (mental) sense which relates to individuals, rather than groups, with no particularly ethical or political overtones.[13] This sense of consciousness, too, can be subdivided into two meanings—it means either "the state or faculty of being conscious, as a condition and concomitant of all thought, feeling, and volition" or "the state of being conscious, regarded as the normal condition of healthy waking life" (*OED*). The former sense is in accord with Descartes's usage of "consciousness," but it is more closely associated with, if it does not originate from, Locke's *An Essay Concerning Human Understanding*. It is also this sense of consciousness that bears an intentional component, inherent in the intentional states it subserves, leading to the *transitive* usage: "consciousness of." The latter is the *intransitive* usage of "consciousness," something more basic than, or perhaps a necessary constituent of the former, unless one wants to insist that all consciousness is consciousness of. The distinction between the transitive and the intransitive senses of the psychological concept of consciousness is alluded to numerous times in contemporary philosophy and psychology, and I will accept it here as such.[14]

Among the contemporary analytic philosophers, David Rosenthal (1997) has written substantially about the distinction between the transitive and intransitive senses of consciousness. He calls these two senses "creature consciousness" and "state consciousness," respectively. In taking consciousness as a property of organisms one can talk about a person's being conscious in the sense of being awake and alert, as opposed to being in a transient state of no consciousness, in a deep coma, or in non-REM sleep. In another vein, one can ask of a bat, or a spider, or a stickleback, or perhaps a robot if it is conscious. All of this has to do with *creature consciousness*. In addition, it makes sense to talk about whether a particular mental state is conscious. This is not quite the same as someone's being conscious. The creature sense of consciousness denotes an overall state one is in; the other classifies one's (mental) states as of one type or another. Further, a state that is not conscious can be among those that in principle cannot become conscious (e.g., certain computational states postulated by cognitive psychology), or those that can be made conscious only by such specific methods as Freudian psychoanalysis. In any case, this sense of consciousness which functions as a type-identifier for mental states is what I have in mind by *state consciousness*.[15] (Another important distinction is that of characterizing creature or state consciousness in causal versus phenomenal terms. This distinction will be introduced in the next section, and used recurrently throughout the chapter.)

In the rest of this discussion, I will largely put aside the social conception of consciousness and proceed with the psychological conception. This move approximately halves the size of the literature to be examined; yet there is still plenty that needs teasing apart and sorting out.[16]

Difficulties with the Nature of Consciousness

It is often remarked that conscious experiences are "immediately familiar" to any subject of such experiences. It is also argued that they are "so immediately close" that it is at times difficult, if not impossible, to separate their *appearance* from their *reality*. This ambiguity between the appearance versus the reality of consciousness is also regarded as unexampled; presumably nothing else in the world suffers from it. As such, it tends to uniquely blur the line between the epistemology and ontology of consciousness: if all there is to (the reality of) conscious states is their appearing in a certain way to subjects, and if they have no existential status independent of their so appearing, the ontology of consciousness seems to collapse into its epistemology.[17]

Ironically, on the other hand, the problem appears to be just the opposite from a different angle: the appearance of consciousness seems so different from its "physical reality" that a comprehensive theory that bridges this gap is regarded as a near impossibility. In Sellarsian terms, the scientific and manifest images of consciousness are considered to embody a theoretical gap perhaps greater than in any other subject matter. (Cf. Sellars 1991.)

The view that consciousness (or, in general, the mind) and its physical basis (or, in general, the body) seem essentially so different from one another that they must have distinct existences is based on a deep-rooted idea in the history of philosophy. This idea and its variants were constitutive of arguments for the metaphysical independence of mind and body throughout early modern philosophy of the seventeenth and eighteenth centuries, perhaps most notably exemplified in the work of Descartes. The essential and complete nature of mind, generally speaking, seems to consist solely in thinking, and, as such, it must be unextended, simple (with no parts), and essentially different from the body, and therefore immaterial. This was Descartes's argument in a nutshell, ultimately drawing a strong ontological conclusion (regarding the distinctness of mind and body) from a starting point constituted by epistemic considerations (regarding the distinctness of their appearances). As Ben Mijuskovic (1974) observes, in this type of argumentation, "the sword that severs the Gordian knot is the principle that what is conceptually distinct is on-

tologically separable and therefore independent" (p. 123).

Mijuskovic, in locating this form of reasoning in its historical context, also notes the presence of the converse of its inference: "If one begins with the notion, explicit or implicit, that thoughts or minds are simple, unextended, indivisible, then it seems to be an inevitable step before thinkers connect the principle of an unextended, immaterial soul with the impossibility of any knowledge of an extended, material, external world" and consequently, of the nature of the relation between them (p. 121). That is, this time an epistemological conclusion (regarding an epistemic gap between mind and body) is reached from a starting point constituted by ontological considerations (regarding the distinctness of their natures).

The difficulties inherent in the nature of consciousness constitute many of the philosophical problems that will be discussed in depth in the rest of this chapter. In particular, the nature and validity of inferences between matters epistemological and matters ontological, especially those that go from the former to the latter, will continually appear as a leitmotif. Of course, some of these difficulties may be overcome quite rapidly as the study of consciousness advances; others may prove more obstinate. But it may also turn out that certain problems that seemed unsolvable had appeared that way because of the specific ways in which they were formulated, or the implicit assumptions they rested on. This possibility, too, will emerge as a relevant concern later in the discussion.

The best way to gain insight into this sort of a difficulty may very well be through locating the analysis in a broad historical perspective. The long history of consciousness research no doubt contains hints that can be parlayed not only to draw methodological lessons for further study, but also to reveal the constituent fibers of the past paradigms which couched persistent core problems under different guises over and over. It is in fact the most striking feature of the consciousness literature, as I try to exemplify numerous times in this exposition, that the very same problems, analyses, and suggested solutions repeatedly appear, and the very same theoretical moves repeatedly get introduced at different times in the history of philosophy and psychology with little (if any) acknowledgement of past attempts and failures. In this regard, a historical approach that exposes the misleading implicit assumptions common to the past failures should prove useful in illustrating, at minimum, which steps *not* to take in approaching consciousness at present.

III Looking Ahead: The Two Faces of Consciousness

Before proceeding further, I will offer a brief first pass at a diagnosis that will be made at the end of this chapter: a principal reason underlying the confusion and seeming mystery surrounding the concept and phenomenon of consciousness lies in the presence of two influential, equally attractive, pretheoretic characterizations. These two characterizations not only shape the methods with which consciousness is studied, but more fundamentally, shape the way the problems to be studied are defined and delineated. They can be summarized in the following mottos: "Consciousness is as consciousness *does*" versus "Consciousness is as consciousness *seems*." The former is the *causal characterization*: it takes the causal role consciousness plays in the general economy of our mental lives as basic. The latter, in contrast, is the *phenomenal characterization*: it takes as fundamental the way our mental lives seem (or "feel," for lack of a better term) to us— that is, the phenomenal qualities that we typically associate with our perceptions, pains, tickles, and other mental states.

Most of the time, these two characterizations are taken to be mutually exclusive for explanatory purposes, to the extent that accounts of consciousness built around one characterization are typically accused of failing to capture the other. I believe that this undesirable consequence, which often seems to deadlock debates on consciousness, stems from a fundamental and ultimately misleading intuition that I will call the *segregationist intuition*: if the characterization of consciousness is causal, then it has to be *essentially* nonphenomenal, and if it is phenomenal, then it is *essentially* noncausal. (I call this formulation an "intuition" rather than a "thesis" due to its widely diffused, often implicit and unarticulated, but highly influential nature.)

In contrast with the segregationist intuition is what I call the *integrationist intuition*: what consciousness does, *qua* consciousness, cannot be characterized in the absence of how consciousness seems, but more importantly, that how consciousness seems cannot be conceptualized in the absence of what consciousness does. This counter intuition underwrites the project of trying to dissolve the stalemate between accounts of consciousness respectively based on the causal and the phenomenal characterizations, and marry them into a single unified account.

This introduction is not an attempt towards accomplishing such a project. Nevertheless, while presenting a conceptual mapping of the territory and locating in it contemporary problems and debates that center around consciousness, I hope to provide support for the integrationist intuition that motivates it. In doing so, I also aim to substantiate an *antiskeptical* position with respect to consciousness: there is a a deep-rooted and continuous theoretical thread connecting a set of recurrent problems in the history of philosophy and psychology typically associated with consciousness, indicating the presence of a persistent, significant, and challenging object of study.

PART TWO
A BRIEF HISTORY OF CONSCIOUSNESS: PHILOSOPHY AND PSYCHOLOGY

There is possibly no other subject matter in the history of philosophy and science with as fascinating a historical record as consciousness. Even within the past one hundred years, consciousness has more than once been crowned as the most significant aspect of human mentality, to be followed by periods of scapegoat treatment for the failures of philosophy and science (in particular, psychology) to give a satisfactory account of the mind. In either case, consciousness was hardly ever ignored. Explicitly or implicitly, it was an ever-present concern for everyone thinking about the human mind.

Following is a brief journey through the historical path that consciousness research has traversed in approximately the last hundred years, in particular via the schools of introspectionism, behaviorism, and cognitivism in psychology, with early modern philosophy taken as a starting point.

IV   Consciousness in Early Modern Philosophy

In accord with the fact that the origins of the word *consciousness* go back to early modern philosophy, it is generally agreed that Descartes gave the mind-body problem its modern formulation. Descartes's own account respectively characterized mind and body as thinking versus extended substances, and postulated that the nature of their relation was that of interaction between the *res cogitans* and the *res extensa*. But how did his notion of consciousness compare with his notion of mind? And to what extent does his notion of consciousness capture the notion that presently figures in contemporary debates?[18]

Descartes claimed that consciousness was an essential component of everything that was mental, and by "consciousness" he meant something akin to one's awareness of one's own mental states: "As to the fact that there can be nothing in the mind, in so far as it is a thinking thing, of which it is not aware, this seems to me to be self-evident. For there is nothing that we can understand to be in the mind, regarded in this way, that is not a thought or dependent on a thought" (Descartes 1993b, p. 171, fourth set of replies to

Arnauld). By "thought" Descartes must have had in mind something very similar to one of the contemporary usages of "consciousness," or "awareness," especially given his definition in the *Principles of Philosophy*: "By the term 'thought' I understand everything which we are aware of as happening within us, in so far as we have awareness of it" (Descartes 1992, p. 174).

Locke, coming after Descartes's rationalism from a distinctively empiricist tradition, was nonetheless largely in agreement with his predecessor with respect to the nature of the relation between what was mental and what was conscious: they were conceptually tied. In Locke's words, "thinking consists in being conscious that one thinks," and "the idea of thinking in the absence of consciousness is as unintelligible as the idea of a body which is extended without having parts" (Locke 1959, bk. 2, chap. 1, p. 138).

There is also another sense in which Descartes and Locke seem to be in agreement: the idea of construing consciousness in roughly something like higher-order awareness. For Descartes, proper sensations in adults exist only insofar as they are accompanied by a second-order reflective awareness: "When an adult feels something, and simultaneously perceives that he has not felt it before, I call this second perception *reflection*, and attribute it to the intellect alone, in spite of its being so linked to sensation that the two occur together and appear to be indistinguishable from each other" (Descartes 1991, p. 357: letter to Arnauld, 29 July 1648, AT V, 221). Along this theoretical line, Descartes concludes, for instance, that "pain exists only in the understanding" (Descartes 1991, p. 148: letter to Mersenne, 11 June 1640, AT III, 85).

In a somewhat similar vein, Locke famously stated that "consciousness is the perception of what passes in a man's own mind" (Locke 1959, bk. 2, chap. 1, §19, p. 138). However, it may be unfair to read too much into the "higher-order awareness" construal and make Descartes's and Locke's views seem more similar than they actually are. For instance, it is not altogether obvious that Locke's second-order "perception" is as cognitively loaded as Descartes's "reflective perception," although they seem to serve the same purpose in being responsible for consciousness of "first-order" mental goings on.[19] There are also contemporaries of Descartes and Locke, who located the epistemic locus of mind in qualitative conscious states rather than thoughts or reflective perceptions. Most notably, Malebranche holds this view.[20]

This brief characterization of the early modern philosophical thought on consciousness no doubt fails to do justice to the subtleties involved. But for the sake of finding a starting point common to both philosophy and "scientific psychology" in the study of consciousness, and tracing the issues in double-track to the contemporary debates, I will leap ahead to the late nineteenth century and, skipping over the problem of unity of consciousness and Kant's treatment of "unity of apperception," continue with the work of William James.

V The Last Hundred Years: William James's Puzzle

William James may be the philosopher and psychologist who thought and wrote more about consciousness than anyone else in history. Interestingly enough, the record of his stance(s) toward consciousness is also the most curious one. James allots a great deal of space to discussing the neural underpinnings, the evolutionary function, and the phenomenal nature of consciousness in his monumental work, *Principles of Psychology*. According to James of this book, consciousness is the starting place of all psychology, the most crucial aspect of human mentality. In a chapter on the methodology of psychology, he states: "*Introspective Observation is what we have to rely on first and foremost and always. The word introspection need hardly be defined—it means, of course, the looking into our own minds and reporting what we there discover. Every one agrees that we there discover states of consciousness*"

(James 1950a, p. 185; originally published in 1890). But only fourteen years later, James would bitterly denounce consciousness in an article titled, "Does Consciousness Exist?" with the following verdict:

For twenty years past I have mistrusted "consciousness" as an entity; for seven or eight years past I have suggested its non-existence to my students, and tried to give them its pragmatic equivalent in realities of experience. It seems to me that the hour is ripe for it to be openly and universally discarded....

[Consciousness] is the name of a non-entity, and has no right place among first principles. Those who still cling to it are clinging to a mere echo, the faint rumor left behind by the disappearing "soul," upon the air of philosophy. (James 1971, p. 4; originally published in 1904)

The reasons for this remarkable change of mind may partly lie deep in James's personal history, but they also have to do with the unique place of consciousness as a subject matter in philosophy and psychology.[21] A somewhat similar, almost neurotic shift of attitude, though in a much larger scale, spanning the whole discipline of psychology and, to some extent, philosophy, occurred in a relatively short period of transition, early in this century. This transition involved the collapse of the then very established school of introspectionism and the subsequent rise of behaviorism.[22]

VI Introspectionism

Introspectionism can be regarded as the first offspring of the effort of pulling psychology apart from philosophy and establishing it as an independent, "scientific" discipline on its own. Ironically, behaviorism would later denounce introspectionism as having tangled with metaphysics and present itself as the true, alternative scientific school of psychology. In actuality, in their struggle for identity, both schools borrowed a great deal from the scientific methodology of their times, and neither one's approach was intrinsically more "scientific" than the other.

Introspectionism's fundamental assumption was that psychology was the study of the "phenomenology" of the human mind; it attempted to give a full description of the mental landscape *as it appeared to the subject*. The data points consisted of discriminations in subjects' sensations of colors, sounds, smells, and the like. In doing so, introspectionism largely modeled its methodology after the modern chemistry of the day, which was enjoying a high reputation due to its successes in having put together the atomic table. The fundamental belief underlying most of introspectionist research was that a full understanding of the mind was possible only after completing an exhaustive inventory of its "atomic units," most elemental sensory impressions one can discriminate. Introspectionism, in other words, was in the business of constructing an atomic table of the human mind.[23] (Cf. Külpe 1901; Titchener 1915.)

Giving a full inventory of anything is no easy feat, and attempting this for the totality of the human "sensory space" was a daunting task, even in the hands of scrupulous researchers and meticulously trained subjects.[24] However, the fall of introspectionism did not result from depleted patience or the lack of a sufficient number of experiments. The failure had deeper reasons, both external and internal.

The external reason for failure was the overall changing intellectual climate in Europe and the United States, especially the rising influence of positivism in all sectors of science, as well as the humanities. The general positivist attitude constituted a significant motivation for psychologists, who had been trying hard to sever their professional ties with philosophers and to move away from anything "mental" in an attempt to relocate psychology among natural sciences. Consciousness was the subject matter of no natural science, so it could not be the subject matter of psychology either.[25]

The positivist atmosphere further provided a context in which it was easier for behaviorists to make introspectionism appear as a scientifically baseless enterprise, further burdened with the metaphysically dubious cargo of consciousness— so much so that John Watson, in the opening pages of his book that served as the behaviorist manifesto, belittled introspectionists' concern with consciousness by likening it to witchcraft: "Behaviorism claims that consciousness is neither a definite nor a usable concept. The behaviorist, who has been trained always as an experimentalist, holds, further, that belief in the existence of consciousness goes back to the ancient days of superstition and magic" (Watson 1970, p. 2).

In reality, introspectionism was as much an attempt to bring psychology up to par with natural sciences—to make it a "science of the mental," with ideas and methods inspired largely by chemistry. Although the founding adherents of behaviorism wholeheartedly denied any intellectual debt to their predecessors and did a good job of making themselves appear completely detached from their past, they were very similar to the introspectionists in aspiration and professional policy with regard to methodology.[26]

In any case, it would not be fair to place on solely external causes all responsibility for introspectionism's formidable downfall, which brought with it the downfall and disgrace of both consciousness (as a subject matter for research) and introspection (as a method for studying the mind) for several decades. There were serious reasons internal to the paradigm as well. Most important was the apparently irreconcilable conflict between results coming out of different laboratories. The most significant polarity was constituted by two main streams of research pursued in two different continents: the Würzburg school, represented by Külpe and his students in Leipzig, versus the Cornell school, lead by Titchener and his associates in Ithaca, New York. For instance, Titchener's laboratory reported that they discovered a total of "more than 44,435" discriminably different sensations, largely consisting of visual and auditory elements. In contrast, Külpe's published results pointed to a total of fewer than 12,000 (Boring 1942, p. 10). Who was telling the truth?

Conflicting results are no surprise in any experimental discipline. What led introspectionism to a dead end was an additional methodological shortcoming: the lack of a generally agreed-upon method of falsifying any of the results. The nature of introspective reports constituting the core of the data in the introspectionist paradigm was colored by the subjects' previous training. Titchenerian introspectionists were very careful not to work with "naive subjects," enforcing strict procedures to avoid "stimulus errors," but this policy worked against them in the end. Although a rigorous and careful training program and meticulous repetition of the experiments provided an acceptable degree of statistical consistency within individual laboratories, the results across different laboratories were sometimes highly contradictory. Unfortunately, when individual "seemings" (of colors, sounds, tactile sensations) were what counted as the sole data, each "phenomenal" report had to be taken at face value. And within such a framework, the degree and nature of previous training, which apparently was not standardized, made all the difference.

Edwin Boring recounts an anecdote in which Titchener and Edwin Holt debated, in front of an audience of other psychologists, whether green was an "atomic color" or a combination of blue and yellow. Each side insisted on his own judgment, and there was no means to settle the issue. One of the most serious conflicts, somewhat similar to this but larger in scope, involved a staunch disagreement between the followers of Titchener and those of Külpe on the existence of "imageless thought." Titchener was convinced that all conscious thought involved some form of imagery, at least some sensory elements. However, subjects from Külpe's laboratory came up with reports of having experienced thoughts with no associated imagery whatsoever. The debate came to a stalemate of, "You cannot experience X," of Titchenerians versus "Yes, we can!" of Külpeians, and

remained the theoretical knot that it was until introspectionism, as a whole, eventually disappeared against the rising tide of behaviorism.[27]

In sum, the fact that introspectionism ultimately located the locus of authority with regard to the data in the word of the subject, while training procedures for subjects were not standardized across laboratories to immunize against "stimulus-error," brought the death sentence to the movement. When the subjects' reports showed statistical inconsistencies, the whole introspectionist community found itself up against a theoretical wall. This impasse, which surfaced as a result of several years of careful laboratory work, brought with it a sad ending to a research paradigm of hundreds of experiments and thousands of subjects.[28]

VII Behaviorism

In contrast to introspectionism, behaviorism arrived with an extremely straightforward methodology (that would ultimately cut, rather than try to untangle, the knot of consciousness), and it appeared as a fresh alternative in the troubling times of introspectionism. There was one and only one element in its research agenda: publicly observable behavior. In the natural sciences, behaviorists argued, all phenomena under scrutiny were open to third-party observation. Behavior was a perfect candidate as a subject matter of this sort. Moreover, behaviorism was able to avoid introspectionism's fatal problem of irreconcilably conflicting subjective reports by, in Boring's words, shifting "the locus of scientific responsibility from an observing subject to the experimenter who becomes the observer *of* the subject" (Boring 1953, p. 184).

Watson championed this shift of locus and the change in the subject matter of the new psychology from "facts of the internal" to "facts of the external" in a rather rallying manner in the following advice to his colleagues:

Psychology as the behaviorist views it is a purely objective experimental branch of natural science. Its theoretical goal is the prediction and control of behavior. Introspection forms no essential part of its method nor is the scientific value of its data dependent upon the readiness with which they lend themselves to interpretation in terms of consciousness. (Watson 1913, p. 158)

You, as a psychologist, if you are to remain scientific, must describe the behavior of man in no other terms than those you would use in describing the behavior of the ox you slaughter. (Watson 1970, p. ix)

The term *consciousness* had never figured in the vocabulary of any natural science, and it had to leave the vocabulary of the scientific psychology as well. Watson was confident that behaviorism marked the beginning of an era that was also the point of no return for consciousness:

The time seems to have come when psychology must discard all reference to consciousness; when it need no longer delude itself into thinking that it is making mental states the object of observation.... This suggested elimination of states of consciousness as proper objects of investigation in themselves will remove the barrier from psychology which exists between it and the other sciences. (Watson 1913, p. 163, 177)

Behaviorism remained a very influential paradigm for psychology for over half a century and managed to have the words *consciousness* and *introspection* disappear from the face of the Anglo-American world.[29] There were obvious reasons for the enthusiastic acceptance of behaviorism by psychologists, motivated by its promising, "trouble-free" methodology. However, behaviorism became influential as a doctrine not only of methodology but also one of ontology. The behaviorist line turned into a fundamental belief not only that whatever psychology—*the discipline*—could study could be studied by observing behavior, but also that all there was to psychology—*the phenomenon*—was observable behavior.

This was what made (ontological) behaviorism both very strong and very weak: strong as a doctrine in its metaphysical claims and weak in grounding the strong claims it was making on what it took the world's constituents to be. The ultimate expression of the extreme view behaviorism came to hold about the ontology of consciousness is reflected in the formula Karl Lashley used to characterize "strict Behaviorism": "Consciousness is the particular laryngeal gesture we have come to use to stand for the rest" (Lashley 1923, p. 240). However, the metaphysical foundations of behaviorism, what it so passionately tried to detach itself from, turned out to be its own Achilles' heel, the cracked brick in the edifice. Even during the heyday of behaviorism, when all talk about consciousness was strictly taboo, consciousness was always present as a hidden variable in the minds and research agendas of psychologists. Boring was cognizant of this fact as early as the 1930s, when he declared: "Behaviorism owes its *ism* to consciousness. And what would it be without its *ism*? Well, it would be physiology" (Boring 1963, p. 275). Much later, Julian Jaynes would retrospectively note that "off the printed page, behaviorism was only a refusal to talk about consciousness" (Jaynes 1976, p. 15).

This make-believe attitude about the absence of *anything*, let alone consciousness, occurring somewhere between the input impinging on the subject and the subject's subsequent behavior was also precisely what provided cognitive psychology the fulcrum it needed to topple behaviorism. In Neisser's words, "the basic reason for studying cognitive processes has become clear as the reason for studying anything else: because they are there. Our knowledge of the world *must* be somehow developed from the stimulus input" (Neisser 1967, p. 5).[30]

VIII Cognitivism (and Beyond)

Ulric Neisser's *Cognitive Psychology* became a mark of a new era in psychology and proclaimed the name of the new game in its title. Neisser, in the introduction to his book, mentions the change in the intellectual atmosphere among psychologists in a wry tone: "A generation ago, a book like this one would have needed at least a chapter of self-defense against the behaviorist position. Today, happily, the climate of opinion has changed, and little or no defense is necessary. Indeed, stimulus-response theorists themselves are inventing hypothetical mechanisms with vigor and enthusiasm and only faint twinges of conscience" (Neisser 1967, p. 5).

For consciousness research, the era of cognitive psychology was marked with a few timid overtures. With the advent of cognitive psychology, whose fundamental ideas were largely inspired by computational models, consciousness found a new niche, though in terms completely foreign to its past: it became a kind of component or aspect of information-processing models. Although only a small percentage of the models developed at the time secured a role for consciousness, cognitivism brought about the first signs of the dissolution of a taboo. Nonetheless, even these cautious beginnings were not easy; consciousness would have to wait until the current ongoing ascent of neuropsychology research to come back under the spotlight. In cognitivism, cognition needed defense over behavior no more, but consciousness over cognition still did.

In this context, George Mandler's manifesto "Consciousness: Respectable, Useful, and Probably Necessary," even though it was not the first article that came out of the cognitivist literature on consciousness, and despite being written in a somewhat gingerly manner, stands out as a cornerstone.[31] Mandler opens his article with the following historical remarks: "I welcome this opportunity to act as *amicus curiae* on behalf of one of the central concepts of cognitive theory—consciousness. Another statement, however imperfect, may be useful to undo the harm that consciousness suffered during fifty years (approximately 1910 to 1960) in the oubliettes of behaviorism. It is additionally needed because so many of us have a history of collaboration with

the keepers of the jail and to speak freely of the need for a concept of consciousness still ties the tongues of not a few cognitive psychologists" (Mandler 1975, p. 229). Of course, Mandler was not alone in pointing to the importance of consciousness in cognitive psychology. Tim Shallice, for instance, had observed a few years earlier that "theoretical developments in cognitive psychology and the increasing use of introspective reports require a rationale, and that this should involve consideration of consciousness" (Shallice 1972, p. 383).

Interestingly, it was the success, not the failure, of information-processing models in explaining learning, memory, problem solving, and the like—actually almost everything except consciousness—that brought some attention to consciousness itself. The fact that consciousness seemed to be the last remaining unexplained phenomenon in an otherwise successful new research paradigm helped highlight old questions about consciousness buried during the behaviorist era. Furthermore, similar developments were taking place in philosophy. Functionalist accounts, largely inspired by computational ideas, were being met with noticeable success in explaining propositional attitudes, whereas consciousness (in the sense of the subjective character of experience, or qualia) was largely being regarded as the only aspect of mind escaping the net of functionalist explanation. (See, for instance, Ned Block's influential article, "Troubles with Functionalism" 1978, as well as Block and Fodor 1980.)

Shallice was one of the first to point out the special place consciousness occupied in the problem space of cognitive psychology: "The problem of consciousness occupies an analogous position for cognitive psychology as the problem of language behavior does for behaviorism, namely, an unsolved anomaly within the domain of the approach" (Shallice 1972, p. 383). Attempts to find some role for consciousness in a cognitive economy turned up results that at times exceeded expectations. Mandler, for instance, pointed to the possibility that consciousness might be the missing central element in a cognitivist frame-work, able to tie together several separate lines of cognitive research: "I hope to show that con-sciousness is ... probably necessary because it serves to tie together many disparate but ob-viously related mental concepts, including atten-tion, perceptual elaboration, and limited capacity notions" (Mandler 1975, p. 229).[32]

Of course, there were others on whose work Mandler was basing his claim. Most notably, Norman (1968) and Atkinson and Shiffrin (1968) had used consciousness as a property demarcat-ing processes of different kinds (conscious versus unconscious processes) in their respective unistore and multistore models of memory. Treisman (1969) and Posner and Boies (1971), among others, talked about consciousness as a limited capacity processing mechanism. Shallice's idea was to equate consciousness as selector input in his cognitive model of the dominant action sys-tem. Johnson-Laird characterized the "contents of consciousness" as the "current values of pa-rameters governing the high-level computations of the operating system" (1983a, p. 465; 1983b). All in all, the common presupposition driving the cognitivist research on consciousness was that "the basic phenomenological concept—con-sciousness—can be mapped onto an information-processing concept" (Shallice 1972, p. 383).[33]

Most of these models came complete with their flowcharts, with each functionally defined ele-ment confined to its own black box and arrows indicating the direction of information flow among them. Consciousness, then, became a box among boxes—a module connected to various other modules of processing in which input was registered, intermediate results were transmitted, and output was delivered. This approach to con-sciousness has, according to Neisser, a special strategical advantage: "It represents a theoretical coup: not only are the facts of attention appar-ently explained, but psychology's most elusive target is finally nailed down to a box in a flow chart" (Neisser 1976, p. 103).

A prominent account of consciousness in re-cent cognitive psychology, Bernard Baars's (1988) *A Cognitive Theory of Consciousness*, is similarly given in information-theoretic terms with substantial use of functional diagrams. This trend of diagramming in cognitive psychology, inspired largely by flowcharts of computational models in computer science, also got imported into philosophy of mind by empirically minded philosophers. A primary example is Daniel Den-nett's model in his "Toward a Cognitive Theory of Consciousness" (1986). Similar functional flowchart models are also being used in some of the present day neuropsychological accounts. (Cf. Schacter 1988 and Shallice 1988, especially chap. 16.)

IX The Study of the Unconscious

One important line of thought in the study of consciousness that has not yet been addressed in this chapter is the foundation of the crucial dis-tinction between the conscious and unconscious aspects of mentality. According to Johnson-Laird, "The division between conscious and un-conscious processes is the best available clue to the structure of the mind" (Johnson-Laird 1983a, p. 466). Freud would probably agree. None-theless, conceptions of the unconscious have changed from their Freudian origins to their cog-nitivist incarnations. Following is a brief histor-ical account of the unconscious.

The Freudian Unconscious

Until the time of Freud, there was no proper the-oretical framework in which to reject the Carte-sian idea of equating the mind with whatever lay within the scope of one's consciousness. In other words, consciousness was generally taken to be "the point of division between mind and not mind" (Baldwin 1901, p. 216)—the mark of the mental.

The received conception of the transparency of the mind to one's consciousness, found in Descartes and Locke, was not without exceptions, however.[34] Most notably, Leibniz, in his visionary reply to Locke in *New Essays*, can be said to have anticipated some very important developments to come in psychology two centuries ahead of their time, especially those with regard to the nature and role of the unconscious: "There are a thousand indications which lead us to think that there are at every moment numberless *perceptions* in us, but without apperception and without reflection.... In a word, *insensible* [unconscious] *perceptions* are of as great use in psychology as insensible corpuscles are in physics, and it is equally as unreasonable to reject the one as the other under the pretext that they are beyond the reach of our senses" (Leibniz 1951, pp. 374–378).

Nonetheless, taking consciousness as marking the boundaries of mind by and large remained an influential maxim until the time of Freud. For instance, the entry for "consciousness" in the 1901 edition of the *Encyclopedia of Philosophy and Psychology* reads as follows: "[Consciousness] is the distinctive character of whatever may be called mental life" (Baldwin 1901, p. 216). Within this context, the introspectionist conviction of the time—that psychology is the "science of the mental"— provided an especially strong basis for rejecting the unconscious as part of the mental, and hence as a subject matter for psychology. Titchener, for example, was resistant to the idea of the unconscious, to the extent of declaring it a theoretically dangerous construct for psychology: "The subconscious may be defined as *an extension of the conscious beyond the limits of observation.* ... [T]he subconscious is not a part of the subject-matter of psychology.... In the first place, *the construction of a subconscious is unnecessary....* Secondly, *the introduction of a subconscious is dangerous*" (Titchener 1915, pp. 326–327, emphases in the original text).[35]

None of this should be taken as claiming that the concept of the unconscious as a part or aspect of the mental was completely unheard of or unacknowledged, however. In other words, Freud was not really the inventor (or discoverer) of the concept of the unconscious in any way. On the contrary, the general intellectual atmosphere of the times preceding Freud's appearance allowed talk about mental activity of various sorts that occurred without the subject's awareness, at least in any direct way. For instance, the well-known metaphor of the mind as an iceberg, consisting of consciousness as the tip above the surface and of a subsurface unconscious component, constituted by hidden currents but nonetheless effective on one's conscious mental life, was generally recognized and used.

In particular, toward the end of the nineteenth century, the idea of the unconscious mind had become operative among many scientists, philosophers, and literary scholars, in a lineage traceable back from Rousseau to Goethe, to Fichte, and to Nietzsche (Whyte 1960). Freud apparently acknowledged this, as reported by Ernest Jones, one of the most prominent Freud scholars, in the following statement he made at his seventeenth birthday celebrations: "The poets and philosophers before me discovered the unconscious. What I discovered was the scientific method by which the unconscious can be studied" (quoted in MacIntyre 1958, p. 6). There were also attempts to study the unconscious empirically. For instance, Henri Ellenberger credits Gustav Fechner, a pioneer of psychophysics research, as the first person who tried to reveal the nature of the unconscious by experimental methods, though his work did not prove fruitful (Ellenberger 1970, chap. 5).

However, none of these ideas about mental processes going on in one's mind without being conscious were well formulated: there was no coherent account to explain the structure, functional role, or operation of the unconscious, or the modality of its relation to consciousness in the general scheme of an individual's mental life. There was consensus regarding neither the nature of the unconscious, nor its place in regard to consciousness, in the intellectual community. To this situation Freud brought a steadily evolving theoretical framework in which, for the first time, construction of hypotheses to answer each of these questions became possible. This is the sense in which Freud can be said to be the pioneer of the unconscious.[36]

In Freudian theory, the *unconscious proper* consists of repressed processes, exerting stress on the conscious component of the subject's mind and shaping his or her daily life in substantial ways. This is in contrast to the *preconscious*, which includes those processes that only contingently happen to lie outside awareness. What is preconscious can easily become conscious without special techniques or effort; what is unconscious has to be "brought to the surface" through the psychoanalytic technique with the help of an analyst.

The Freudian unconscious, although related, is not the same sense of unconsciousness employed in the current cognitive psychology research regarding unconscious processes—the "cognitive unconscious." Unconscious processes of both kinds are opaque to introspection, but there is a difference between them. The Freudian unconscious exists because of past events, explainable by repression mechanisms and the like, and is not *in principle* inaccessible. The cognitive unconscious, on the other hand, exists due to the way our perceptual-cognitive system is constituted and lies *in principle* outside our access. The mechanisms that subserve depth perception, for instance, are taken to be hard-wired: they are not there because of repression, and they can never become conscious through any method, psychoanalytic or otherwise.

The recognition and study of the cognitive unconscious goes even further back than Freud, at least to von Helmholtz's work on perceptual constancy, and spans a substantial period, all the way up to the thesis of "unconscious perceptual inference" by Rock (1983). Despite these differences, however, Freud's approach to the unconscious was very modern and in anticipation of the "cognitive revolution."

An encompassing account of the Freudian unconscious, including its structure and dynamics, is given in Erdelyi (1985). Erdelyi also makes a strong case that Freudian psychology was indeed very close, in essence, to the cognitive psychology of our day—especially in terms of its approach to understanding mental phenomena, and research methodology. He even goes on to reconstruct Freudian schemas of the structure of consciousness, quite plausibly, in modern flowchart style. Neisser (1976) also refers to Freud's diagrams depicting the structure of the tripartite division of consciousness, preconsciousness, and unconsciousness as "flowcharts" (See Freud 1950, p. 394).[37] It is true not only that Freud anticipated some of the developments in cognitive psychology but also that the Freudian unconscious, even if under different names, has played a significant role as an influential construct in cognitive psychology.

The Cognitive Unconscious

There has also been a whole research industry in contemporary cognitive psychology involved in investigating the nature of the unconscious: mental processes that underlie cognition but are themselves not conscious.[38] Over the past few decades, there has been an enormous wealth of data accumulated, operative in current psychological theory, in this area—from rules of Chomskian universal grammar, to computational mechanisms underlying vision and the $2\frac{1}{2}D$ *sketch* inspired by the work of the late David Marr (1982), and to Newell and Simon's work on cognitive constraints in planning, problem solving, and game playing (1972). Consequently, the classification of mental processes as conscious versus nonconscious is useful and not unusual (though controversial) in psychological practice, especially in research on psycholinguistics, attention, and perception.[39] Furthermore, as evidenced from contemporary psychology literature, research on type identifying mental states as conscious versus nonconscious, and research on the nature of consciousness of the subjects who have such states is being pursued on independent conceptual grounds. In fact, the dichotomy of conscious versus nonconscious processes is not the only such ground on which current research in cognitive psychology rests. There are several other such distinctions, all overlapping in various ways in their function to distinguish mental processes that are directly available to the subject ("introspectable," reportable, etc.) and those that are opaque and unavailable, as reflected in a recent note by cognitive psychologists Holyoak and Spellman:

Theorists of diverse persuasions have been led to propose cognitive dichotomies, which have been given a rather bewildering array of labels: unconscious vs. conscious, procedural vs. declarative, automatic vs. controlled, reflexive vs. reflective, and many others.

These distinctions do not always divide cognition along the same lines ... [but] there are tantalizing similarities among the proposed dichotomies. In particular, the first member of each pair is generally viewed as involving unconscious mental processes, a topic that has seen a recent resurgence of interest among experimental psychologists. (Holyoak and Spellman 1993, p. 265)

In sum, whether or not Johnson-Laird is right in his claim about the distinction between the conscious and the unconscious being the most important theoretical tool to study the mind, one can easily say that the investigation of the unconscious in cognitive psychology has proved to be at least as fruitful as the investigation of the conscious.[40]

X   Status Report: From Information Processing to Qualia

What is the current status of cognitive psychology? Information-processing models in psychology are still popular, but they do not constitute the sole dominant paradigm any more. This is also reflected in models of consciousness. But there are other reasons, too, for the shift in the research paradigm with respect to consciousness. One of them is the recognition that the functional diagrammatic depictions of consciousness seem to leave out something important: the subjective, experiential aspect of consciousness. Perhaps there is something about consciousness that makes its identification with specific modules of isolated functions fundamentally inadequate.

Interestingly, it was Neisser who registered such a concern about the information-processing models of consciousness during the heyday of cognitivism:

The treatment of consciousness as a processing stage is unsatisfactory in a still more fundamental way. It does justice neither to the usages of the word "consciousness" in ordinary discourse nor to the subtleties of experience. A better conception of consciousness, which has been suggested many times in the history of psychology, would recognize it as an aspect of activity rather than as an independently definable mechanism.... Consciousness is an aspect of mental activity, not a switching center on the intrapsychic railway. (Neisser 1976, pp. 104–105)

Many people, including philosophers, proceeded with Neisser's intuitions in the past few decades. Something essential to (at least our commonsense conception of) consciousness, it was largely believed, was necessarily left out in characterizing consciousness only by specifying its functional role in the cognitive economy of human mentation and behavior. This something—the phenomenal face of consciousness—brings us back full circle to the problem of the two faces of consciousness.

In the last part of this chapter, I will examine the dialectic of the opposition between the segregationist and the integrationist intuitions, in the context of the causal and phenomenal characterizations of consciousness.

PART THREE
PROBLEMS OF CONSCIOUSNESS: A PERSPECTIVE ON CONTEMPORARY ISSUES AND CURRENT DEBATES

"Consciousness is a word worn smooth by a million tongues," George Miller once said. "Depending upon the figure of speech chosen it is a state of being, a substance, a process, a place, an epiphenomenon, an emergent aspect of matter, or the only true reality" (Miller 1962, p. 25).

The conceptual and historical analyses I have presented are in agreement with Miller: it is probably best to regard and treat consciousness as a cluster concept. There are simply too many connotations that go under the term, and it seems futile to try to specify a single concept that would cover all aspects of consciousness or a single "*the* problem of consciousness." Nonetheless, I have tried to illustrate, there is a coherent theoretical thread constituted by certain problems and not others, that one can trace from texts in early modern (if not ancient Greek) philosophy to the emergence of scientific psychology in the nineteenth century, to the present.

The most troublesome feature of this thread is what has been most difficult to explain, and it is the topic I arrived at by the end of the historical analysis: the qualitative, or phenomenal aspects of consciousness, or qualia. Of course, the notion of consciousness theoretically outstrips the notion of qualia, and there are many fascinating aspects to consciousness that do not necessarily have a qualitative component (e.g., its representational aspect, its attentive and control components, and mechanisms of the unconscious). But it is also questionable whether qualitative and nonqualitative aspects of consciousness can really be understood or explained independent of one another. These are the questions I will focus on and pursue below.

XI Consciousness and Intentionality: Two Dimensions of Mind

Jerry Fodor once remarked: "There are, I think, three great metaphysical puzzles about the mind. How could anything material have conscious states? How could anything material have semantical properties? How could anything material be rational?" (Fodor 1991a, reply to Devitt, p. 285). Having enumerated these three questions,

Fodor chooses to stay away from the first, despite his career-long devotion to the latter two (which he takes to be closely related). This attitude is not at all uncommon. It is generally accepted as a received view that the two fundamental aspects of mind, consciousness and intentionality, can be studied in the absence of one another—at least that intentionality can be so studied with no reference to consciousness. Here, "consciousness" typically refers to the qualitative aspects of consciousness, and "intentionality" is taken sufficiently broadly to embrace questions about semantics, as well as rationality. Fodor's justification is the following:

It used to be universally taken for granted that the problem about consciousness and the problem about intentionality are intrinsically linked: that thought is ipso facto conscious, and that consciousness is ipso facto consciousness of some or other intentional object.... Freud changed all that. He made it seem plausible that explaining behavior might require the postulation of intentional but unconscious states. Over the last century, and most especially in Chomskian linguistics and in cognitive psychology, Freud's idea appears to have been amply vindicated.... Dividing and conquering—concentrating on intentionality and ignoring consciousness—has proved a remarkably successful research strategy so far. (Fodor 1991b, p. 12)

Not everyone agrees, however. In particular, John Searle recently argued for what he called the "connection principle": the thesis that consciousness and intentionality are immanently linked, and, contra Fodor's thesis, any research strategy that tries to explain the latter without recourse to the former is doomed to failure. Searle states the connection principle as follows: "Only a being that could have conscious intentional states could have intentional states at all, and every unconscious intentional state is at least potentially conscious.... [T]here is a conceptual connection between consciousness and intentionality that has the consequence that a complete theory of intentionality requires an account of consciousness" (Searle 1992, p. 132).[41] More recently,

Strawson (1994) takes the similar position that consciousness is the only distinctive characteristic of the mind.

The beginnings of this line of thought can be traced back to Brentano's discussion of the relation between mental and physical phenomena in *Psychology from an Empirical Standpoint*. Brentano is acknowledged as being first to postulate intentionality as the mark of the mental in modern terms. For instance, he says: "Every mental phenomenon is characterized by ... the intentional inexistence of an object, and what we might call, though not wholly unambiguously, reference to a content, direction toward an object (which is not to be understood here as meaning a thing). ... This intentional inexistence is characteristic exclusively of mental phenomena. No physical phenomenon exhibits anything like it" (Brentano 1874, pp. 88–89). And regarding consciousness, Brentano states, for instance, that "no mental phenomenon is possible without a correlative consciousness" (p. 121). Although the connotations of the terms *consciousness* and *intentionality* have somewhat shifted from Brentano's time to the present, I think it is fair to note that there is a great deal of theorizing in his work that lay the foundations of an account of the mental that attempts to incorporate these two dimensions of the mind in a principled way.

Another attempt to characterize (phenomenal) consciousness and intentionality as the two hallmarks of the mind, though for the purposes of a critique, is given by Richard Rorty (1979, p. 24) in terms of the diagram in figure I.1. There are in fact various ways to fill in such a diagram, and which elements of the mental are to occupy which cells is a matter of controversy. For instance, not everyone thinks that beliefs and desires are without a phenomenal component (Searle 1992), or that pains have no representational or intentional aspects (Dretske 1995, Tye 1995). And the adherents of panpsychism would probably maintain that the cell that holds what Rorty labels "the merely physical" is bound to remain nil.[42] Nonetheless, this way of depicting the dimensions of the mental is useful in terms of illustrating what has been the most problematic aspect of the study of consciousness. In this diagram, it is what Rorty calls "raw feels."[43]

Most of the current debates involving consciousness revolve around the (possible) inhabitants of this particular cell and their nature. Are there really such things as nonrepresentational but phenomenal properties? If there are, what is their ontological nature, what kinds of special epistemological problems do they present, and how can their semantics be given? Can they ever be captured in naturalistic explanatory scheme,

	With phenomenal properties	Without phenomenal properties
Intentional, representational	Occurrent thoughts, mental images	Beliefs, desires, intentions
Nonintentional, nonrepresentational	Raw feels (e.g., pains and what babies have when they see colored objects)	"The merely physical"

Figure I.1
Two dimensions of mind

or are they inherently bound to remain mysterious? These are the questions that constitute the consciousness debates today.

XII Perspectivity and Epistemic Asymmetry

Naturally, there can be several different entry points to the kind of exposition I aim to present here. The investigation of consciousness is as fascinating as it is difficult, and it presents unique epistemological and ontological difficulties. Although my overarching goal is to provide an overview of the contemporary problems of consciousness rather than try to present my own solutions to them, I will start by presenting a brief profile of what I take to be the primarily responsible component in the consciousness puzzle: the epistemic element of perspectivity. Perspectivity, or the fact that consciousness is a phenomenon that admits a distinction between "perspectives," or "points of view" in its explication, lies deep at the roots of the common understanding of consciousness, as well as the attitude of puzzlement. Furthermore, epistemically based theses about consciousness seem much less controversial than ontologically based theses. I start by sketching a commonsense conception of consciousness and try to reveal just how perspectivity figures in it. Then I will proceed to examine its possible ontological ramifications.

Why does consciousness keep appearing as an unsolved puzzle for philosophy, psychology, and neuroscience? There do not seem to be similar puzzles associated with the study of, say, memory or learning, or biological development and growth. What is so special about consciousness?

George Miller thinks that perhaps the unique difficulty involved in the understanding of consciousness stems from the fact that consciousness is both the phenomenon we try to investigate and the very tool we need to use to pursue this investigation. "Turning a tool on itself," he says, "may be as futile as trying to soar off the ground by a tug at one's bootstraps." He continues: "Perhaps we become confused because whenever we are thinking about consciousness, we are surrounded by it, and can only imagine what consciousness is *not*. The fish, someone has said, will be the last to discover water" (Miller 1962, p. 25).

Miller's observation is intriguing. One cannot, in principle, study the minute details of a microscope's outer surface, for instance, by using the very same microscope. This would be impossible simply because of the way the microscope, as a tool, is designed and used. Neither can one directly take the picture of a camera by using the camera itself. But why should these considerations apply to the study of consciousness using consciousness itself? One can certainly lay the body of a microscope under another microscope for examination or take pictures of one camera with another. It may be that the sort of recursive impossibility involved in the self-study of tools applies to the phenomenon of self-consciousness—for example, one's study of one's own consciousness by introspection. But Miller is concerned with the study of consciousness in general here, not only self-consciousness, and it is not clear why the analogy should hold.[44]

Nonetheless, Miller's point is related to what I see as the source of what makes consciousness puzzling. The difficulty lies in the curious duality inherent in the (epistemic) *study* of the phenomenon. This duality does not need to be inherent in the (ontological) *nature* of the phenomenon of consciousness itself or its properties. In fact, as I have mentioned, the ontology of consciousness is an issue open to current debates. But as far as the epistemology of the matter goes, there appears to be a genuine asymmetry between the *mode of access* to facts of one's own consciousness and the mode of access to facts about others' conscious states. This asymmetry is what grounds the important distinction between systematic approaches to consciousness from the *first-person perspective* versus the *third-person perspective*.

On the one hand, nothing is more intimately known by conscious human beings than the way the world (including themselves) appears to them.

We are all subjects of a variety of perceptual experiences, thoughts and ideas, pains and tickles, joys and sorrows. Under normal circumstances, there is nothing more familiar with the way the face of one's spouse looks, the way a favorite drink tastes, the way the chronic heartburn starts to make itself felt. We all have, it seems, firsthand, immediate, direct knowledge of the rich phenomenology of colors, sounds, tastes, aromas, and tactile sensations that embellish our experiences—the *qualia.* All these are constituents of a specific mode of being for every individual; they determine, in Thomas Nagel's famous phrase, *what it is like to be* that individual (Nagel 1974).

Moreover, we all seem to have a "privileged" way of knowing about our own thoughts, feelings, and sensations. Epistemological problems about knowledge notwithstanding, and even the question of the incorrigibility of the mental put aside, it seems that there is at least a special mode in which one's own experiences are present to one, in an immediate, direct way, not available for anyone else.[45]

Further, the common wisdom goes, we cannot genuinely entertain the possibility that we may be lacking consciousness; the very fact that we are questioning our own consciousness renders the possibility of our not being the entertainer of some occurrent thoughts logically contradictory. If in nothing else, Descartes was perhaps right in this regard: The mere fact of being the bearer of (these) thoughts is, in the Cartesian sense, unmistakable evidence, *for oneself,* that one is conscious. This is the characteristic of the first-person perspective; from the inside, consciousness seems all-pervasive, self-evident, and undeniable.

On the other hand, contemporary science tells us that the world is made up of nothing over and above "physical" elements, whatever their nature (waves, particles, etc.) may be. Where does this leave us with respect to the place of consciousness in an entirely physical world? "How can technicolor phenomenology arise from the soggy grey matter of brains?" as Colin McGinn asks (McGinn 1989, p. 349). Can one accommodate a respectable account of consciousness that does justice to the richness of our conscious experiences of sights and sounds within a framework based on a monistic materialist ontology? Consciousness just does not seem to be the kind of phenomenon that is amenable to the sort of scientific explanation that works so well with all other biological phenomena, such as digestion or reproduction. The facts that would settle the question of whether some organism—an animal or a fellow human being—is digesting do not seem to be available in the same way when it comes to the question of consciousness in others, especially in the case of organisms phylogenetically distant from ourselves. There seems to be no ordinary way to peek into the inner lives of others—to feel their pains, go through their sensations, or directly observe their consciousness.[46] That is, there seems to be an epistemic impossibility for anyone to have direct access to the qualia of others—literally share their first-person perspective, in short, to partake in the mode of what it is like to be them. These are the limitations of the third-person perspective: *from the outside,* firsthand exploration of the consciousness of others just seems to be out of the reach of ordinary scientific methods, others' experiences being neither directly observable nor noninferentially verifiable. And therein this asymmetry between the first- and the third-person perspectives lies the epistemic duality in the study consciousness.

But what exactly follows from this asymmetry? What do the limitations of the third-person approach entail, for example? Are there any insurmountable problems for a systematic study of consciousness—its nature, underlying mechanism, evolutionary function, ontological status? After all, the third-person perspective is what is and has successfully been operant in the scientific practice of the past several centuries, and no one doubts that it can provide valuable advances in the understanding of consciousness. But the issue is whether such an approach is always doomed to leave something essential to consciousness out of its explanatory scope. In short, is there an unbridgeable "explanatory gap" inherent in the third-person approaches to consciousness, and if so, can it be remedied by the deployment of a crossbred conceptual scheme that embodies a first-person approach in the investigation of consciousness?

XIII   First-Person versus Third-Person Approaches to Consciousness

The epistemic asymmetry inherent in the study of consciousness can be found as manifested under different names, roughly as variations of one another and as occupying critical roles in theoretical junctions. The notion of the first-person versus third-person perspectives is one such contrastive pair. Yet another similar distinction is that of the subjective versus the objective, or the "phenomenal" versus "physical."

One way of describing a particular experience, say, of tasting a particular vintage of a certain kind of wine, would be to try to state how the wine *tastes to me*—that is, what it is like for me to have that particular gustatory experience. This is indeed the ordinary, even if not so easy, way. It involves the usage of qualitative terms such as "fruity," "with a hint of tobacco," or "full-bodied," and the hope of conveying some sense of what the tasting of that wine would be like had it been experienced by the listener.

The other way would be to proceed by way of giving a description of the specific ways in which my tastebuds are excited, my olfactory nerves are activated, my blood chemistry has changed, and so forth. This would not be the most ordinary way of describing one's gustatory experiences, but perhaps one can overhear two devoted neurologists talking this way to one another at a conference reception. In any case, in the right context, it is clear that this alternative method would also be informative in conveying *something* about the nature of one's experience.

There is clearly an important difference between the two methods.[47] The first one attempts to describe an experience by stating its qualitative aspects as they seem to the experiencer. The fruity character is directly experienced *only* by the person whose gustatory and olfactory nerves are excited by the wine. As such, the experiencer has a privileged status; she gets to have the experience, whereas the listener only gets to hear the description. As far as the second method is concerned, however, the experiencer and the listener are epistemically on a par. The description of the perturbations in the experiencer's nervous system is open to public observation and verification, and ordinarily, no qualitative terms about the experience (how it feels) need to be involved. In other words, whereas the instantiation of the phenomenal properties of an experience is directly accessible only to the experiencer, the instantiation of its intrinsic neurophysiological properties can be equally observed by many.[48] In the latter case, what is at issue are the publicly observable aspects of the experience—not how it feels but what it does.

The important question is to determine whether these two methods have distinct scopes of explanation and whether they are necessarily committed to distinct ontologies. I have outlined two general approaches to consciousness, each of which respectively takes one of the two above methods as primary. The first of these approaches takes consciousness "as consciousness seems" and, in accord with the phenomenal characterization, regards its qualitative aspects as the primary components of any explanatory scheme. The second one takes consciousness "as consciousness does," and, in accord with the causal characterization, tries to account for consciousness in terms of what it does and the role it plays in one's cognitive economy. Put in different terms, one can call these the "first-person-perspectival" versus the "third-person-perspectival" approaches to consciousness.[49] The dichotomy of the "two faces of consciousness" manifests itself in yet other distinctions and under other names, to which I now turn.

XIV   The Two Faces of Consciousness Revisited

The phenomenal and the causal characterizations are merely expressions of what seems most important, or primary, in the understanding of the nature of consciousness. They are not, in themselves, in opposition with one another. It is only under the dictum of the *segregationist intuition* that they are considered essentially antipodal and mutually exclusive. The issue of how to locate the phenomenal and the causal characterizations with regard to each other is central to the dialectic of certain ongoing debates surrounding the "phenomenal" versus "access" senses and the "easy" versus "hard" problems of consciousness.

By "phenomenal characterization of consciousness" I mean a characterization given fundamentally in first-person terms, describing episodes of inner life in terms of how they feel or seem to the subject who experiences them. William James was interested in both the temporal and the spatial structure of consciousness, and his chapter "Stream of Thought" (James 1950a, pp. 224–290) provides an excellent example of such a characterization.[50] Apart from James and the continental phenomenologist philosophers, introspectionist psychologists were paradigmatically interested in the phenomenal aspects of experience, and they relentlessly pursued the project of "mapping the boundaries of the inner space of consciousness." Along those lines, Titchener defined consciousness as the occurrent parts of one's mind, accessible by introspection, at any given moment: "My 'consciousness' is the sum of mental processes which make up my experience *now*; it is the mind of any given 'present' time. We might, perhaps, consider it as a cross-section of mind" (Titchener 1902, p. 13).

But there is more to the phenomenal characterization in the way "problem of phenomenal consciousness" is understood today. In particular, the problem has now transformed into the exploration of explanatory laws that would account for how particular phenomenal aspects of

consciousness could arise from their physiological underpinnings.[51] Deep down, this problem is a manifestation of the gap that separates our direct understanding of consciousness in first-person terms, versus the objective, physicalist accounts of consciousness given in third-person terms. The roots of this problem are indeed unique; no other phenomenon presents us with two distinct epistemic perspectives from which it can be investigated. Given this duality, how does the "causal characterization" of consciousness fare against its phenomenal counterpart?

A causal characterization of consciousness can be given in many dimensions. One can try to account for consciousness in terms of behavioral manifestations, or of its role and place in the general mental economy. The former approach was behaviorists' failed solution to account for (or, rather, do away with) consciousness. The former became a canonical characterization in behaviorism's successor, cognitive psychology and in functionalist schools of philosophy.

Behaviorism, in its explicit form, is no longer around. But it is worth mentioning again how the most obvious difficulty in relying entirely on external criteria gave way to information-processing accounts of consciousness in particular, and of mental phenomena in general. Behaviorism left no room for the possibility of the presence of consciousness in the absence of external behavior. Put differently, the absence of evidence from the third-person perspective implied the theoretical rejection of all experience that is generally characterized in first-person terms. Given that the most familiar aspects of consciousness have to do with its phenomenology (think of James' stream), this result stood out as the most difficult one to accept. Even many behaviorists balked at biting the bullet and claiming that a person who is sitting perfectly still with no vocal cord activity whatsoever (behaviorists' characterization of "thinking") would ipso facto be unconscious.[52] This claim, it seemed, was readily refutable in one's own everyday phenomenology. There was, after all, an epistemic component to the phenomenon of consciousness that cried for a characterization in first-person terms. However, behaviorism, in its attempt to associate consciousness and behavior conceptually, and thereby fully externalize consciousness, left no room for talking about consciousness as it is experienced by the subject. Everyone smiled at the joke about one behaviorist's asking another, after having made love, "It was great for you; how was it for me?" but (fortunately) not many took the scenario as a serious possibility.[53]

A logical next step in trying to account for consciousness in causal terms was to reverse the behaviorist direction and, to some extent, re-internalize the causal criteria of consciousness. This provided a groundwork for functionalist philosophy of mind, and cognitive psychology. Under such a more relaxed framework, consciousness was allowed to be individualized by the role it played, as an integral component of the larger network of mental states and processes. With the promising application of computational ideas and information-processing models in psychology, it was canonically characterized as a process accomplishing a specific task, a module with a specific function in a cognitive diagram, or an abstract property of the overall system. Here is a paradigmatic characterization in the cognitivist framework:

Consciousness is a process in which information about multiple individual modalities of sensation and perception is combined into a unified multidimensional representation of the state of the system and its environment, and integrated with information about memories and the needs of the organism, generating emotional reactions and programs of behavior to adjust the organism to its environment.... The *content* of consciousness is the momentary constellation of these different types of information. (Thatcher and John 1977, p. 294)

What is important to note here is that this characterization is given largely in a third-person perspective. Consciousness is identified with *what it does* but not necessarily *how it feels* to the experiencing subject.

Once again, it is essential to ask at this stage whether these two perspectives are mutually exclusive regarding their explanatory roles—that is, whether an account of causal consciousness provides us with no understanding of how consciousness seems to the first-person subject, and whether an account of phenomenal consciousness has no elements that figure in the understanding of what consciousness does. As I will suggest below, my answer is "not necessarily." A further question along this line would be what ontological consequences the perspectival asymmetry in the epistemology of consciousness entails. There, my answer will be "not very much." But first let me bring into the picture another distinction, proposed by Ned Block, which aligns well with the distinction between the causal and phenomenal conceptions of consciousness.

Access Versus Phenomenal Consciousness

Block (1995) distinguishes between "access consciousness" and "phenomenal consciousness" as follows:

Access (A) consciousness: A state is access-conscious if, in virtue of one's having the state, a representation of its content is (1) inferentially promiscuous, that is, poised for use as a premise in reasoning, (2) poised for rational control of action, and (3) poised for rational control of speech.... These three conditions are together sufficient, but not all necessary.

Phenomenal (P) consciousness: P-consciousness is experience. P-conscious properties are experiential ones. P-conscious states are experiential, that is, a state is P-conscious if it has experiential properties. The totality of the experiential properties of a state are "what it is like" to have it. (pp. 230–231)

Defining A-consciousness is a straightforward matter. In the case of human beings, A-consciousness is a cognitively interwoven aspect of mental life, underlain by three crucial capacities centered around rationality: rational cogitation, speech, and action. (For the general case, not all three conditions are necessary for A-consciousness because, Block maintains, animals without speech can have mental states of the A-conscious type.) Construed as such, A-consciousness fits well in the domain of propositional attitudes in philosophy of mind, and it is just the perfect sort of subject matter for cognitive psychology.[54]

P-consciousness is more problematic. Block starts out his analysis of P-consciousness by stating the difficulty particular to it: "Let me acknowledge at the outset that I cannot define P-consciousness in any remotely noncircular way.... The best one can do for P-consciousness is ... *point* to the phenomenon" (Block 1995, p. 230). The way Block himself goes about characterizing P-consciousness is either "via rough synonyms" or by examples. P-consciousness, as expected, is what I have been referring to as the phenomenal aspect of consciousness. Among the P-conscious properties that endow a mental state with P-consciousness in virtue of its having them are, for instance, the way it feels to "see, hear, smell, taste, and have pains" and more generally, "the experiential properties of sensations, feelings, and perceptions". Furthermore, Block maintains, P-conscious properties are "distinct from any cognitive, intentional, or functional property" (p. 230).

Block thinks that it is not an embarrassment that he cannot provide a noncircular definition of P-consciousness. But why is it difficult to provide a straightforward definition of P-consciousness, and why should this not be considered a cause of disconcertment? According to Block, that there is no way to give a reductive definition of P-consciousness is not embarrassing given the "history of reductive definitions in philosophy," presumably full of failures.

It is still not clear, however, whether the inability to define P-consciousness reductively is sufficient reason to think that the only other alternative must be an ostensive definition. Even if it is, it may be useful to ask why the definition of P-consciousness is, unlike other definitions, thus obliged to ostention. In the case of A-consciousness, there seems to be no such problem. Block's

definition of A-consciousness is not, strictly speaking, reductive, and it serves its purpose well with no need for ostension. Could there be something inherent in the pretheoretical construal of P-consciousness such that it does not allow a nonreductive but also nonostensive definition? More importantly, could it be that the particular way Block's distinction carves out phenomenal consciousness, separating it completely from its causal and functional aspects in accord with the "segregationist intuition," renders its investigation by means of scientific methods theoretically impossible? Put differently, could we be painting ourselves into a corner by a conceptual commitment to Block's distinction such that we end up with a number of straightforward problems about A-consciousness and a conjured-up "hard problem" of P-consciousness that in principle admits no solution?[55] This last question leads directly into a related debate that has its roots in the "explanatory gap" problem, recently dubbed by David Chalmers the "easy and hard problems of consciousness."

The "Easy Problems of Consciousness" and the "Hard Problem"

Chalmers (1995) characterizes the "easy problems" as those concerning the explanation of various cognitive functions: discriminatory abilities, reportability of mental states, the focus of attention, the control of behavior. Of course these are not trivial problems at all, and labeling them "easy problems" should not be taken as downplaying their complicated nature. Rather, Chalmers's point is that "there is no real issue about whether these phenomena can be explained scientifically." They can be. "All of them are straightforwardly vulnerable to explanation in terms of computational or neural mechanisms" (p. 201). What makes "the hard problem" of consciousness a different *kind* of problem is, Chalmers maintains, its resistance to all the methods that explain, or have the potential to explain, the rest of the problems. Put differently, there is a different kind of problem about consciousness that may evade the successes of all standard scientific advances. Such a problem would be a hard problem indeed. What is it?

According to Chalmers, "The really hard problem is the problem of experience." More specifically, it is the "subjective" aspect of every experience that resists explanation. The notion of "subjective aspect" is given, as Block does, in Nagelian terms: There is something it is like to be a conscious organism and have experiences. In other words, "what it is like to be" constitutes the subjective character of the experiences of the organism in question. This much is also in line with Block's characterization of phenomenal consciousness.

I will give a sorted-out schema of the theoretically interwoven notions of "phenomenal aspect," "subjective character," and "what it is like to be" in section XVI below. For now, it is useful to observe that the line that separates Chalmers's "easy" and "hard" problems is the counterpart of the line that separates "access" and "phenomenal" consciousness in Block, which also mirrors the distinction between the causal versus phenomenal characterizations of consciousness outlined earlier. Given these distinctions Chalmers states the "hard problem" as the problem of bridging the explanatory gap between accounts of the causal-functional (physical) kind and the occurrence of specific phenomenal aspects. He asks:

Even when we have explained the performance of all the cognitive and behavioral functions in the vicinity of experience—perceptual discrimination, categorization, internal access, verbal report—there may still remain a further unanswered question: *Why is the performance of these functions accompanied by experience?* ... This further question is the key question in the problem of consciousness. Why doesn't all this information-processing go on "in the dark", free of any inner feel? (Chalmers 1995, p. 203).

There are two related questions Chalmers raises, and the roots of both go back at least a hundred years in the history of psychology and philosophy. The first has to do with how to bridge the explanatory gap between physical mechanism and phenomenal appearance, or brain and mind, as discussed in the "Mystery of Consciousness" section in section I. The second asks whether all the activity on the "physical" side could go on as usual in the total absence of any counterpart phenomenology. The former question is based on Levine's (1983, 1993) original formulation of the problem of the "explanatory gap," which has antecedents in considerations raised by Saul Kripke (1980) and Thomas Nagel (1974, 1986) (though reaching different conclusions). The latter question is a version of the so-called absent qualia problem.[56] Similar considerations also underlie what William Seager (1991) calls the *ultimate problem of consciousness*. He asks: "Why is it so hard to think about consciousness, to formulate reasonable models of the relation of particular modes of consciousness to their physical bases?" The answer Seager offers, in agreement with Nagel, has to do with the uniqueness of consciousness as a phenomenon: "There is no model by which we can satisfactorily understand the relation between conscious experience and subvening physical state since this relation is absolutely unique in nature" (pp. 223–234).

Before discussing the status of the hard problem further, let me first sketch a larger framework in which a number of relevant questions can be located and pursued. This framework will also be useful in revealing just how much explanation along one question-path can be useful in explaining issues in neighboring problems.

XV The Four W Questions and the Further-How Question

It is true that the enterprise of approaching consciousness within a scientific discipline has traditionally been very problematic, largely due to the inadequacy of the scientific third-person perspective *all by itself* as a penetrating tool for the study of the phenomenal character of consciousness.

The most influential assumption about consciousness, as evidenced by the diversity of the literature, is that what makes it a tough nut to crack is in some crucial way related to those properties of consciousness that have to do with its phenomenal aspect. Problems such as the irreducibility of consciousness, its imminent subjectivity, the status of its relation to its physical underpinnings, and so on all relate to the phenomenal side of consciousness.

In order to get into some of the inner structure of this difficulty, consider the following five questions, which I will call the four *W questions* and the *further-How question* of consciousness:

1. *What* are the media and mechanisms of consciousness? Can consciousness occur in any type of material substance, or does it have to have a specific kind of underpinning (e.g., a carbon-based molecular structure)? And what are the underlying mechanisms that facilitate consciousness?

2. *Where* is, if anywhere, the locus of consciousness? Can consciousness be localized in a specific organ, the brain (or a module in the brain), or is it endemic to the whole of the nervous system? Where is the seat of consciousness?

3. *Who* can be said to be a conscious being? Using consciousness as a type-identifying predicate, one can ask: Is a chimp, a spider, a protozoan, or a robot conscious or *non*conscious? (In a slightly different sense of consciousness, one can also ask of a person in a coma, or in sleep, or in a petit mal seizure whether she is conscious or *un*conscious.)

4. *Why* is there consciousness at all, and what is the role it plays in the general scheme of mental life and behavior of an organism? To put it in evolutionary terms, *which* function does consciousness serve such that it was selected as a trait in the phylogeny of certain classes of living things?

5. *How* does consciousness arise in, or emerge from, its underlying substance, structure, and mechanism, in the way it does?

Notice that the How question seems to be a further question, the answer to which may not be completely revealed even if all the previous four W questions are already adequately answered. The answer to the How question may involve the postulation of, in Chalmers's terms, an *extra ingredient*, which makes the question difficult in a unique way. Even when all the underpinnings of consciousness, including its medium, locus, and mechanism, are revealed, and conscious and nonconscious things are, at least according to some operational definition, properly categorized and explained, a further question may remain: Just *how* is it that one experiences the particular sort of phenomenal quality that one does, rather than a different quality, or even none at all? Or, more generally, how does any physical mechanism give rise to any kind of phenomenal experience? Because of this extra ingredient seemingly inherent in the How question, I call it the *further-How* question.

As must be clear from the formulation of the further-How question, the difficulty surrounding the extra ingredient, the gap that remains not bridged, owes its difficulty to the phenomenal aspect of consciousness. The further-How question is generally considered to be categorically more difficult compared to the other four—hence the dubbing: "the hard problem of consciousness" versus the rest, the "easy problems."

It is important to notice that the term *extra ingredient* can carry greatly different theoretical weights. For instance, the missing extra ingredient may be merely explanatory, due to an undeveloped concept, or some other theoretical tool. That would raise only an epistemological problem. But it may also mean a missing ingredient in the part and parcel of the world, in its ontology. It has been suggested that the missing ingredient is indeed ontological, and consciousness should be added to the list of fundamental physical elements of the universe. For instance, Chalmers (1995) claims that "a theory of consciousness requires the addition of *something* fundamental to our ontology" and suggests we take experience as fundamental "along-side mass, charge, and space-time" (p. 210; see also Chalmers 1996). Nagel and Searle have respectively made the same point in terms of the subjective properties of consciousness, in, for instance, the following passages:

The subjectivity of consciousness is an irreducible feature of reality—without which we couldn't do physics or anything else—and it must occupy as fundamental a place in any credible world view as matter, energy, space, time, and numbers. (Nagel 1986, pp. 7–8)

Conscious mental states and processes have a special feature not possessed by other natural phenomena, namely subjectivity. It is this feature of consciousness that makes its study so recalcitrant to the conventional methods of biological and psychological research, and most puzzling to philosophical analysis.... The world ... contains subjectivity as a rock-bottom element.... In the sense in which I am here using the tem, "subjective" refers to an ontological category, not to an epistemic mode. (Searle 1992, pp. 93, 95)[57]

The same idea has also been favored among those who try to find fundamental theoretical connections between consciousness and quantum physics, as well as those who popularize on this theme. For instance, an interview with Nick Herbert, the author of *Elemental Mind: Human Consciousness and the New Physics*, outlines his position as arguing that "consciousness itself must be considered a 'fundamental force' of the universe, 'elemental', on a par with such irreducible phenomena as gravity, light, mass, and electrical charge" (quoted in "The Consciousness Wars," *Omni*, October 1993, p. 56; see also Herbert 1993). In a somewhat similar spirit, theoretical physicist Henry Stapp claims that "an analysis of the measurement problem of quantum theory points to the need to introduce consciousness, per se, to physics," stressing as well that a complete account of consciousness can be given not in an "ontologically and dynamically monistic conceptualization of the world provided by classical-mechanics" but only "within a dualistic

quantum-mechanical conceptualization of nature" (Stapp 1996, p. i).

The study of consciousness can take any one of the above five questions as its entry point to investigation. Indeed, various people have made attempts to approach the phenomenon of consciousness by respectively addressing each of these issues. But the further-How question has typically generated less success than others. As a matter of fact, it led to grim diagnoses about the "explanatory gap," thought by some, such as Colin McGinn (1989), to lie possibly forever beyond the grasp of human understanding.

The seeming uniqueness of the further-How question, given the lack of apparent promising directions to pursue it in any existing methodology, led McGinn (1989) to take its conclusions perhaps too seriously. The very same considerations, on the other hand, can lead one to think that there is perhaps something fishy about the whole setup. The way the problem is presented relies obviously on a set of presumptions about the metaphysics of phenomenal consciousness, as well as the nature of scientific explanation. Could it be that the reason we seem to have no clue about how to explain the further-How question is that there is really nothing there to explain?[58] This brings up a metalevel issue: whether a complete explanation of the four W questions will in fact leave some further aspect of consciousness unexplained, such that the further-How question will remain untouched, unscathed, and in need of explanation as ever? To take up a favorite example of the Churchlands from the history of scientific explanation, what can assure us that the further-How question will not evaporate in time just as did questions about élan vital and phlogiston?

Note that this sort of skepticism against the further-How question need not entail a deflationary attitude toward consciousness in general. One can remain convinced that consciousness presents fascinating and real problems for philosophy and science and that this is already justified in the history of its study, while not believing that there is a further-How question in the way it is formulated, isolable from the four W questions such that no degree of understanding there will shed any light on it.

I do not know if there is a decisive way to settle the metaissue at this stage of our understanding of consciousness, and thereby decide the fate of the further-How question. I do not know if it is useful, or even yet possible, to settle it at present. It seems that the opposing attitudes toward consciousness stem largely from pretheoretical, though (or perhaps, hence) deep-rooted and very strongly held, intuitions. Of course, it is crucial to try to systematically examine and uncover the often implicit presumptions that these intuitions embody, but doing that also requires understanding what is currently known and accepted about consciousness at the present theoretical level—that is, understanding what is known about the four W questions. Each of these W questions is interesting in its own way, and each has generated some fruitful thinking independently in different fields. Thus, I now turn to a brief exposition of their current status, primarily the What and the Where questions.

The What Question

With regard to functionally characterized varieties of access consciousness, there is hardly any suspicion that consciousness is medium independent. But regarding phenomenal consciousness, this question is open to speculation. The functionalist intuitions suggest that if the existence of all mental phenomena, including P-consciousness, is a matter of the functional organization of the elements in the nervous system, then the possibility that consciousness is a trait that is not restricted to carbon-based animal brains of this planet should be allowed. Denying this possibility would be "neural chauvinism."

Perhaps Searle comes closest to claiming that consciousness, and actually the mind in general, can occur only in human and animal brains, or their causal (but not necessarily functional) equivalents, because of the "special powers of the brain," which cannot be matched by, for example, digital computers.[59] Notice that the question here is different from those in the various absent qualia arguments. The possibility being questioned is not one of non-emergence (i.e., absence) of consciousness in functional equivalents of human brains or in human brains themselves. Rather, somewhat symmetrically, it is the possibility of the emergence of consciousness in *non*-brains.

What about mechanism? Regarding the underlying mechanism of a very important component of consciousness, the binding of the various sensory features into a coherent whole in experience, the most promising recent results come from the work of Christof Koch and Francis Crick. In "Towards a Neurobiological Theory of Consciousness" (1990), they hypothesize that what underlies the phenomenon of binding is the pattern of synchronous oscillations in the brain within the 40 to 70 Hz range during visual experience.[60] (See also Llinás and Ribary 1994, in support of the 40 Hz hypothesis in the context of dream experiences. Metzinger 1995a explores how the binding problem relates to the integration of phenomenal content.)

Now, let's examine this hypothesis in light of the distinctions introduced so far. Does it, for instance, explain the access or the phenomenal senses of consciousness (or both)? Since Crick and Koch do not have such a distinction, it is hard to know what they think. According to Block, the hypothesis is designed to explain P-consciousness; failing that, it can explain, if anything, only A-consciousness. A true explanation of P-consciousness, Block maintains, has to explain further questions about why, for instance, it is the 40 to 70 Hz range and not some other. The discovery of an empirical correlation does not suffice to bridge the explanatory gap between the phenomenon as it appears to the subject and what its underlying mechanism does.

This formulation is just another expression of the "hard problem" and, as such, falls in the purview of the further-How question. Thus, while the Crick-Koch hypothesis (so far as it is correct) can be considered to explain successfully the What question of consciousness for some, it remains essentially incomplete for the defenders of a Blockean conception of phenomenal consciousness.

The Where Question

Is there a seat of consciousness? This question in its various incarnations has been discussed from the time of the ancient Greeks. What was once the question of the organ of reason in humans (e.g., the brain versus the heart) has now transformed into the question of the whole brain or a module in it, and if the latter, which?

As early as the late nineteenth century, James had discussed the question of the seat of consciousness and declared that the cortex, and not the rest of the brain, is what is responsible for consciousness:

For practical purposes, nevertheless, and limiting the meaning of the word consciousness to the personal self of the individual, we can pretty confidently answer the question prefixed to this paragraph by saying that *the cortex is the sole organ of consciousness in man*. If there be any consciousness pertaining to the lower centres, it is a consciousness of which the self knows nothing. (James 1950, pp. 66–67)

James's view was based on the experimental results of his day, which showed a significant correlation between cerebral processes and subjective reports of conscious experience. Note that James does not attempt to give an explanation of how the brain can possibly subserve conscious experience any further than outlining the relevant mechanism. In other words, James does not seem to be after anything beyond the ordinary W questions. Clearly this sort of explanation does not satisfy those who are after the further-How question.

But regardless of whether the further-How question is a well-formed formulation of inquiry, there is a lot of work to be done in explaining the mechanism of how and where consciousness emerges in a given organism. James was perhaps one of the first "consciousness modularists" by proposing that it was only a certain component of the brain that subserved consciousness.[61] Although it has always been in the scientific agenda, the belief in modularity in brain function has gained particular popularity over the last decade, especially due to the results coming from neuropsychology. Recent discoveries involving certain types of brain damage, such that the subjects become deprived of only very specific, encapsulated perceptual or cognitive abilities (e.g., prosopagnosia—the deficit of recognizing faces while almost all other visual capabilities remain intact), have provided support for theses of modular architecture.[62]

Extending this idea, one can transform the question of the modularity of mental function in general into the question of whether phenomenal consciousness in particular may be subserved by a module of some sort. Tim Shallice (1988) puts forth such a view, and a modularity hypothesis seems to lie behind Daniel Schacter's DICE model, where consciousness is depicted as a separate, functionally individuated box in the wiring diagram sketch (roughly speaking) of a nervous system (Schacter 1988). Block is also sympathetic to these models and calls the view "that treats consciousness as something that could be accomplished by a distinct system in the brain" *Cartesian modularism*, in contrast to Dennett and Kinsbourne's *Cartesian materialism*.

Cartesian materialism is the name Daniel Dennett and Marcel Kinsbourne (1992) give to the general belief that there is literally a place in the brain "where it all comes together"—something like a spatial or at least a temporal finish line that determines the outcome of various brain processes as a coherent, unitary, single experience. Dennett (1991) calls this the "Cartesian Theater" model of consciousness.[63] The idea of such a logical line in the brain makes it possible to ask questions about the temporality of certain events that take place inside the brain against the milepost of the phenomenology of experience. Denying that such a line exists makes it logically impossible to impose a fine-grained order on brain processes as having occurred prior to or following a particular experience. Dennett and Kinsbourne present a forceful argument against Cartesian materialism; for them it is the whole brain, if anything, that is in some sense the seat of consciousness. Today, the Where question, just like the What question, remains a hotly debated issue.[64]

The Who and the Why/Which Questions

The question of who can be classified as a conscious being is largely subordinate to the question of what the underlying medium and mechanism of consciousness are, at least in a materialist framework. Roughly speaking, those beings whose physical constitution (medium) allows the instantiation of those properties that indicate the working mechanism of consciousness can be safely allowed into the "charmed circle" of consciousness (barring difficulties inherent in the What question itself). It is also common practice in medicine to have a more or less circumscribed set of behavioral and psychological criteria to determine the occurrent presence or absence of consciousness in patients (e.g., see the *Roche Handbook of Differential Diagnosis* on "Transient Loss of Consciousness," 1989).

Of course, the issue is not *so* straightforward, especially when it comes to phenomenal consciousness. Is there anything it is like to be a bat catching prey with its sonar system, or a dogfish detecting electromagnetic fields in the ocean, or a robot clumsily walking about in an artificial intelligence laboratory? The answers and, more important, the advice on how to obtain these answers greatly vary. This question also leads to the discussion on "zombies"—whether there

could be, in nomological or just logical possibility, human replicas who nonetheless lack phenomenal consciousness. I come back to this issue in the discussion of epiphenomenalism.

Regarding the *Why/Which* question, the literature is somewhat barren. Perhaps this is partly as a result of the fact that it is nearly impossible to find any evolutionary role for *phenomenal* consciousness to play under the decree of the segregationist intuition, whereas the evolutionary contribution of consciousness, when it is taken as causally efficacious in accord with the causal characterization, is just too obvious. In other words, so long as consciousness is characterized as essentially noncausal and nonfunctional, rendered an *epiphenomenon* that makes no difference in the world, it drops out of the pool of factors that have survival value, and thus becomes explanatorily irrelevant to evolutionary theory. This is the conclusion Frank Jackson (1982) defends (using the term "qualia" for phenomenal consciousness): "[Qualia] are an excrescence. They *do* nothing, they *explain* nothing, they serve merely to soothe the intuitions of dualists, and it is left a total mystery how they fit into the world view of science.... Epiphenomenal qualia are totally irrelevant to survival" (p. 135)[65] On the other hand, if consciousness is taken as a *genus* for different modalities of perceptual awareness under a causal-representational characterization, pace Dretske (forthcoming), there remains no philosophically puzzling question about its evolutionary role. It would clearly be somewhat difficult for any creature to survive without sight, hearing, touch, smell, and so forth. (See also Dretske 1996 for a discussion of what kind of differences qualia make vis-à-vis judgments and beliefs.) Similarly, Armstrong (1980) attributes to introspective consciousness the biological function of making us aware of current mental states and activities of our own mind, such that it becomes "much easier to achieve *integration* of the states and activities, to get them working together in the complex and sophisticated ways necessary to achieve complex and sophisticated ends" (p. 65). See also Van Gulick (1988, 1989) for attempts to locate a functional role for phenomenal consciousness, and Dennett (1991), Flanagan (1992), Dretske (1995), and Flanagan and Polger (1995) for further evolutionary considerations.[66] Finally, Jaynes (1976) and Crook (1980) take entirely different approaches to the idea of the evolution of consciousness (characterized in terms closer to what I called the social sense of consciousness). Searle (1992) tries to strike a balance between defending a version of the essentialist intuition while assigning an evolutionary role to consciousness. Finally, a number of neuropsychological accounts identify consciousness with a specific information-processing module, in terms of a specific function it serves in the whole system. Although the concern is almost never evolutionary in such accounts, they can be mentioned here for their effort to find a specific function for consciousness (see, for example, Schacter 1988 and Shallice 1988). But on the whole, there is much about the Why/Which question that remains to be written than what is already there.

Having considered the various characterizations of consciousness and the various questions one can ask about them, I now turn to the examination of questions about phenomenal consciousness in the landscape of current philosophical debates.

XVI A Road Map for Phenomenal Consciousness and the Unbearable Lightness of *Whatitisliketobe*

As we have seen, the concept of consciousness is a hybrid that lends itself to several different characterizations. Part of my goal in this chapter was to tease them apart and treat them separately. Having done so, however, one sees that the problem of consciousness is like a Chinese box puzzle; for every distinction made, one discovers that further embedded distinctions are required.

In any case, given that the philosophical problems all revolve around the phenomenal characterization of consciousness, it is reasonable to focus discussion there. Doing so actually reveals that what is commonly referred to as "phenomenal consciousness" is also itself a hybrid. Consequently, it becomes imperative to bring the analytical microscope over there and to dissect the different elements in the tangle of phenomenal consciousness. Here I present a conceptual road map for locating various different philosophical problems, each associated with phenomenal consciousness in one way or another.

The term *phenomenal consciousness* is often used interchangeably with a variety of others, such as *qualitative character, qualia, phenomenal properties, subjective awareness, experience,* and *what it is like to be a certain organism.* (See, for instance, Block 1994, pp. 210–211.) This is a bunch. And to make matters worse, each of these concepts is known for its notorious elusiveness. Traditionally, the properties that go under the various names of "raw feels," "qualia," "qualitative character of experience," "phenomenal aspect of consciousness," and so on have all proved to be recalcitrant to systematic explanations. Dennett points out that attempts to give a straightforward account of phenomenal properties have typically been frustrating; "no sooner does [the concept of qualia] retreat in the face of one argument that 'it' reappears, apparently innocent of all charges, in a new guise" (Dennett 1988, p. 42).[67]

This elusiveness actually goes to the heart of the particular and long-standing problem of phenomenal consciousness, which is often labeled a mystery. Elusiveness by itself is not what makes the problem persistent, however. Otherwise, eliminativism could appear as a more appealing option. Rather, it is our unique epistemic relation to consciousness: phenomenal consciousness is perhaps the most difficult aspect of the mind to give up. An eliminativist stance toward the phenomenal aspect of mental life seems the most counter-intuitive of all eliminativist attitudes. That is why the question of phenomenal consciousness does not just disappear out of the philosophical and, in other guises, psychological and scientific landscapes. I thus find it important to lay out properly each conceptual component that contributes to the puzzle.

It is worth noting, however, that among all notions that are associated with phenomenal consciousness, one has particularly captured philosophical intuitions more than any other—so much so that it has become the central notion underlying almost any discussion about consciousness during the two decades since its publication. Unfortunately, it is also the most difficult to pin down or muster theoretical agreement upon. I have in mind Nagel's (1974) notion of "what it is like to be" a certain creature, or subject of experience.[68]

Nagel's notion of "what it is like to be" has been so influential that it seems to have an omnipresence in several distinct (even if related) problems with regard to consciousness. In particular, it gets pronounced in an intertwined way with the problem clusters that can be grouped under the headings of qualia, subjectivity, and the knowledge argument.

Nagel himself presents the issue of what it is like to be a certain creature as a theoretical basis for establishing the claim about that creature's having a certain ontologically irreducible point of view, which furnishes certain facts about the creature with subjectivity. For others, however, the notion of "what it is like to be" is taken to lay the ground for arguing for the reality of qualia, and for others, for the persuasiveness of the knowledge argument which claims that physicalism, as an ontological doctrine, is false. But the nature of the relations among each one of these problems is hardly ever spelled out in any detail. In fact, it seems that the notion of "what it is like to be" has become the *wild card* of consciousness problems. I will henceforth refer to it simply as the notion of *whatitisliketobe*.

Given this tangle, let me present the following schema as a conceptual road map to distinguish problems typically associated with phenomenal consciousness:

1. Qualia: Experiences have phenomenal and thus noncausal, nonrepresentational, nonfunctional, and perhaps nonphysical properties.

2. Subjectivity: Certain facts about experiences are subjective, that is, they cannot be completely understood except from a single kind of point of view.

3. Knowledge Argument: Certain facts about experiences are nonphysical.

To this, one can add the "base element" in the formula:

* Whatitisliketobe: There is something it is like to have experiences for a certain organism (or, simply, something it is like to be that organism).

I call *whatitisliketobe* a wild card, because it gets alluded to in discussions concerning any of the three problems mentioned above. To have certain qualia, it is generally presumed, is *whatitisliketobe* an organism undergoing a certain experience; certain facts about an experience are subjective because there is *somethingitisliketobe* having that experience; and finally, *whatitisliketobe* having a certain experience constitutes nonphysical facts about that experience. I think, however, that it can be questioned whether this common denominator is not in fact theoretically vacuous. Perhaps *whatitisliketobe* has turned into nothing but a wild card—a convenient way of talking about any one of the three problems of phenomenal consciousness, without, due to its intuitive charm, having to specify anything further. Then there would be no reason to look for a shared ingredient in need of explanation, above and beyond the explanation of these three problems.[69]

Nagel's original intention in introducing the notion of *whatitisliketobe* was, I think, to use it as an "intuition pump" for instating subjectivity rather than as a tool to talk about qualia. Further, for Nagel, the scope of applicability of the notion of subjectivity greatly transcends the problem of qualia, or consciousness in general; it also underlies problems about free will, personal identity, and the self, as well as the ontological doctrine of physicalism.[70]

The knowledge argument, formulated in contemporary literature by Frank Jackson, is also much closer in nature to issues surrounding subjectivity than to the problem of qualia. In fact, it can be seen as a logical conclusion of the difficulties Nagel raises about accommodating subjectivity in a physicalist ontology. In a nutshell, the knowledge argument is based on the claim that certain facts about experiences evade all physicalist accounts, and no matter how much one learns about the physical (causal, functional, representational, and so on) aspects of an experience, some facts about how the experience feels (to oneself, but more important, to others) will remain in the dark until one actually *has* that experience.

Jackson attempts to establish this claim by means of a thought experiment that involves an imaginary vision scientist, Mary, who learns "everything physical there is to know" about color experiences without ever having color experiences herself. Jackson's contention is that upon seeing a colored object for the first time in her life, Mary will learn something new, belying physicalism. The pivotal issue here is whether the having of an experience constitutes a special class of irreducible "first-person facts" or whether what is lacking in Mary has to do with her experiential "mode of access" to facts that she is already acquainted with (in the form of propositional knowledge); on this point of contention the knowledge argument has generated a fair amount of literature.[71] The interrelations between these problems need to be pursued further, but I will stop and opt for focusing on the most central player of the phenomenal consciousness debate: qualia. (I will henceforth use "phenomenal consciousness" and "qualia" interchangeably.)

XVII The Qualia Battles

The problem of qualia is one that surfaced under different guises in the philosophy literature during different periods. It is probably fair to state that qualia was the single most recalcitrant notion that resisted the rising wave of materialists in their program of giving an account of the mental by means of identity theory. For example, J. J. C. Smart mentions in his now-classic "Sensations and Brain Processes" (1959) that among the eight objections he considers, he feels the least confident in his answer to the one about phenomenal properties. (This is Objection 3, attributed to Max Black.) Both U. T. Place (1956) and B. A. Farrell (1950), philosophers of the same era, note that the identification of the so-called raw feels with the straightforwardly physical properties of the nervous system has been the most elusive component of the overall program of identity theory in "Is Consciousness a Brain Process?" and "Experience," respectively. Herbert Feigl also wrestles with the same problem in his lengthy manuscript, *The "Mental" and the "Physical"* (1967).[72]

A second wave in philosophy of mind came about, this time that of functionalism, in the 1970s. The problem of qualia was again on stage; the phenomenal feels were considered the "Achilles' heel of functionalism" (Shoemaker 1981a)—the only aspect of mentality that escaped the net of functional explanations.[73] It is during this period that the problems of *absent qualia* and a reincarnation of Locke's puzzle of *inverted spectrum* reached celebrity status. Critics of functionalism argued that a functionalist framework can provide an account of all components of mental life but cannot capture its qualia, lacking the theoretical tools to settle decisively questions about whether any two functionally equivalent systems differ (e.g., can be inverted) in their phenomenal aspects, or even whether a given system has any qualia at all. Thomas Nagel gives a concise characterization of the problem of absent qualia as follows: "The subjective character of experience ... is not captured by any of the familiar, recently devised reductive analyses of the mental, for all of them are logically compatible with its absence. [E.g.,] It is not analyzable in terms of any explanatory system of functional states, or intentional states, since these could be ascribed to robots or automata that behaved like people though *they experienced nothing*" (Nagel 1974, pp. 166–167; my emphasis).[74]

In a footnote to this passage, Nagel also entertains the possibility of the *impossibility* of absent qualia, but rejects it: "Perhaps there *could not* actually be such robots. Perhaps anything complex enough to behave like a person *would have* experiences. But that, if true, is a fact which cannot be discovered merely by *analyzing the concept of experience*" (fn. 2, p. 167; my emphasis). But what Nagel merely asserts as true has no argumentative force against certain causal-state identity theorists and some functionalists. For they take exactly the opposite of Nagel's assertion (broadly construed to include not only behavior, but also causal, functional, and intentional characterization) as a fundamental assumption.

For instance, David Lewis (1966) states: "The definitive characteristic of any (sort of) experience as such is [by analytic necessity] its causal role, its syndrome of most typical causes and effects" (p. 17). Similarly, the *concept* of a mental state for David Armstrong (1993) is that of a "state of the person apt for bringing about certain sorts of physical behavior," where he regards the mind as "an inner arena identified by its causal relations to outward act" (p. 129). As such, the relation between experiences and causal (and/or functional, intentional, etc.) characteristics *is* taken to be, contra Nagel's assumption, inherent in the concept of experience. This kind of fundamental disagreement where each side is vulnerable to the charge of question-begging against the other is a typical syndrome of the "qualia battles."

The possibility of absent qualia is closely related to the doctrine of epiphenomenalism (that phenomenal consciousness has no causal powers) and thus to the possibility of "zombies" (human replicas with all mental and behavioral attributes present save for phenomenal consciousness), as I argue below. The possibility of inverted spectrum, on the other hand, simply requires an inversion of a particular set of phenomenal qualities in some sensory domain, such as the hues in one's color space.[75]

But let us pause and ask the same question already posed about consciousness: When friends and foes of qualia disagree about whether qualia exist, are they really talking about the same thing? The ontologically rather ordinary fact that phenomenal properties of an experience exist only insofar as they belong to someone's experience (compare: geometric properties of a shadow exist only insofar as they belong to someone's shadow), when combined with the epistemologically rather extraordinary fact that experiences cannot epistemically be shared, and hence everyone can have "direct access" to only his or her qualia, seem to make it uniquely, even surprisingly difficult to investigate the ontological nature of qualia. As such, it gives rise to a wide variety of positions regarding what qualia *are*.

In "Quining Qualia," Dennett, one of the staunchest critics of the notion of qualia, tries to establish that "conscious experience has *no* properties that are special in *any* of the ways qualia have been supposed to be special." He attempts to show this by laying out what exactly it is that he wants to deny in denying the existence of qualia and sets up his target by identifying qualia with the "properties of a subject's mental states that are: 1. ineffable, 2. intrinsic, 3. private, and 4. directly or immediately apprehensible in consciousness" (Dennett 1988, pp. 43, 47). The final verdict Dennett arrives at, after an elaborate chain of "intuition pumps" designed to show that the very concept of qualia is inherently confused, is an eliminativist one: "There simply are no qualia at all" (p. 74).

In contrast to Dennett's eliminativist stance, the spectrum of other positions with respect to qualia extends from taking qualia to be non-physical properties that require a new ontology to reductively identifying qualia with neurophysiological properties. There are also midway, conciliatory positions. Paul and Patricia Churchland, for example, agree that when qualia are construed in the way Dennett does, the situation is indeed hopeless: "So long as introspectible qualia were thought to be ineffable, or epiphenomenal ... one can understand the functionalist's reluctance to have anything to do with them" (Churchland and Churchland 1982, p. 34). While promoting a realist attitude toward qualia, they claim that qualia will turn out to be properties intrinsic to the nervous system, such as spiking frequencies in the brain. Construed as such, qualia cease to be elusive, but their investigation also falls into the scope of disciplines other than philosophy or psychology. In the Churchlands' words: "The functionalist need not, and perhaps should not, attempt to deny the existence of qualia. Rather, he should be a realist about qualia.... [But, at the end], the nature of specific qualia will be revealed by neurophysiology, neurochemistry, and neurophysics" (Churchland and Churchland 1982, p. 31).

Owen Flanagan, who believes that an effort of triangulation involving phenomenology, psychology, and neuroscience, which he calls the "natural method," can penetrate the mystery of qualia and help dispel it, follows suit in promoting a more positive characterization of qualia: "Those who would quine qualia are bothered by the fact that they seem mysterious—essentially private, ineffable, and not subject to third-person evaluation. Qualia are none of these things." Although Flanagan does not necessarily share the Churchlands' conviction that qualia will turn out to be properties in the domain of neuroscience, he too concludes that "there are no qualia in Dennett's contentious sense, but there are qualia" (Flanagan 1992, p. 85).

A recent proposal in accounting for qualia comes from Fred Dretske's representational naturalism (Dretske 1995). According to this view, "all mental facts are representational facts" and hence, a fortiori, all facts about qualia are also representational. Dretske identifies qualia as properties that one's experience represents objects (or whatever the experience is about) as having. As such, qualia do not have to be given a functional characterization or identified with neurophysiological properties. Rather, Dretske locates qualia outside the mind, in accordance with his externalist theory of the mind. This view has the advantage of maintaining a realist stance toward qualia while remaining in a perfectly naturalistic framework.[76]

Finally, Ned Block brings the qualia issue back to the problem of "explanatory gap" and raises suspicions about the conceptual machinery of cognitive psychology to deal with qualia: "On the basis of the kind of conceptual apparatus now available in psychology, I do not know how psychology in anything like its present incarnation *could* explain qualia" (Block, 1978, p. 289). Block is neither as sure as the Churchlands about whether the answer to the nature of qualia will turn out to be in the domain of neuroscience, nor is he as optimistic as Flanagan in the promise of interdisciplinary methods to deliver a successful account of phenomenal properties. Nor is he convinced that qualia can be accounted for in a Dretskean representational framework. On the contrary, Block actually wants to raise more general doubts about the explanatory power of *any* mechanistic, functionalist, or in general physicalistic schemes to account for the presence or emergence of qualia. His worry, in other words, is about how qualia *can* be accounted for as part and parcel of any physical system, including (or rather, especially) a brain, even if one thinks that it *must* be so accounted. Block states: "*No* physical mechanism seems very intuitively plausible as a seat of qualia, least of all a *brain*.... Since we know that *we are brain-headed systems*, and that *we* have qualia, we know that brain-headed systems can have qualia. So even though we have no theory of qualia which explains how this is *possible*, we have overwhelming reason to disregard whatever *prima facie* doubt there is about the qualia of brain-headed systems" (Block 1978, p. 281).

As a consequence of this kind of general doubt about physicalism, the scenario involving beings physiologically and behaviorally similar to us, perhaps even identical down to the last molecular structure and behavioral trait, who nonetheless lack qualia altogether, is considered a genuine theoretical possibility. This step brings us to the debate on the notion of zombies and the doctrine of epiphenomenalism.

XVIII Epiphenomenalism and the Possibility of Zombies

Consciousness epiphenomenalism is the view that (phenomenal) consciousness has no causal powers and hence exhibits no effects in the world, though it may be the effect of some other cause itself. This doctrine and the possibility of zombies are closely related. If consciousness is an epiphenomenon, that is, not *essentially* linked to causal processes, or is only a recipient of but not a contributor to effects in a causal network, then there exists the possibility that the same organism that is taken to possess consciousness could be going through the very same mentations and behavior even if it had no phenomenal consciousness at all. Subtract away the consciousness, and you still get the same beliefs, desires, motives, preferences, reasoning capacities, and behavior in the organism. But what you get is a *zombie*. Its pains, tickles, and itches are all "ersatz." The zombie does not feel anything, even if it thinks and acts as if it does. Its experiences lack the qualitative feels altogether. There is nothing it is like to be *it*.[77]

Put differently, zombiehood becomes a possibility only under a view that accords with epiphenomenalism. If we maintain that consciousness has causal powers, then the absence of consciousness in my zombie twin, which is identical to me in every other respect, would make *some* difference. But by stipulation, there is no difference whatsoever between persons and their zombie twins except the fact that the latter lack consciousness. Hence, denying epiphenomenalism would also block the possibility of zombiehood. That is, if we accept that consciousness has causal powers, then my zombie twin cannot exist, even as a genuine theoretical creature.

The doctrine of epiphenomenalism has a deep-rooted history. The philosophers and the psychologists of the nineteenth century hotly debated whether consciousness was part and parcel of the causal network that was responsible for the decisions we make, actions we take, and so forth or whether it was just an idle spectator, riding along the causal processes, perhaps being caused by them, but without exerting any causal effect on those processes itself. Perhaps, the idea was, we are all automata, since all of our mental life and behavior seem to be determined by our nervous systems, in a purely mechanical framework, with no respectable place in it for consciousness.[78]

Thomas Huxley was one of the most influential advocates of such a thesis, known as the *automaton theory of consciousness*. The thesis was first formulated to apply to animals, in perfect agreement with Cartesian intuitions. Huxley put the matter as follows: "The consciousness of brutes would appear to be related to the mechanism of their body simply as a collateral product of its working, and to be as completely without any power of modifying that working as the steam whistle which accompanies the work of a locomotive engine is without influence upon its machinery" (Huxley 1901, p. 240). But, of course, the real target was human beings and the nature of human consciousness. This is where Huxley's automaton theory differed with Descartes's interactionist dualism. Huxley's account of the "brutes" was just a lead to make the same point for humans: "The argumentation which applies to brutes holds equally good of men.... It seems to me that in men, as in brutes, there is no proof that any state of consciousness is the cause of change in the motion of the matter of the organism" (pp. 243–244).[79]

In Huxley, consciousness plays no contributory role in the causal chains that take place in the nervous systems that totally determine the behavior of an organism; it only gets affected by the neural interactions. In contrast, Descartes's idea of consciousness was one of an equally causally efficacious parameter in the formula of mind-body interaction. As much as Descartes is thought to be the founder of interactionism, Huxley can be thought of as having laid out a clear foundation for epiphenomenalism with respect to the mind. The fundamental idea about epiphenomenalism remained intact until the present day, but what was then dubbed the "Automaton Theory" has been transformed into the "Problem of Zombies" in contemporary literature. Of course, it is important to note that even if we establish that it is the truth of some version of epiphenomenalism that makes zombiehood a possibility, there remain important issues about what the nature of this possibility is, for example, whether it is empirical, metaphysical, or conceptual. These are subtle issues that I cannot do justice to in the limited space here. Hence, rather than pursuing this line further, I will step back once again and examine how the background conditions for bringing the metaphysical disagreement on the possibility of zombiehood (just like the disagreement on the status of phenomenal consciousness) can be brought to a settlement.[80]

XIX Stalemate: How to Settle the Phenomenal Consciousness Dispute?

There are a variety of positions on the ontological status of phenomenal consciousness in the literature, all the way from substance dualism to property dualism, to reductionism (via some form of identity thesis), to eliminativism (usually coupled with some kind of antirealist stance), to representationalism (maintaining a naturalized realism). However, the literature does not contain any knock-down argument that would convince

a "friend of phenomenal consciousness" to a reconciliatory middle ground with a "qualia skeptic." Most often, the disagreement between the two parties comes down, for each side, to the charge of begging the question against the other. The eliminativists charge the defenders of phenomenal consciousness with believing in a fiction and creating a philosophical problem out of it. In return, the eliminativists get charged with holding the most preposterous philosophical fancy for denying their opponents' characterization of qualia.

As an example, consider Daniel Dennett, who is convinced that the notion of qualia "fosters nothing but confusion, and refers in the end to no properties or features at all" (Dennett 1988, p. 49). Ned Block, as a representative of the other side of the spectrum, accuses Dennett of begging the question against (the existence of) phenomenal consciousness (Block 1993, 1995). Interestingly, the dialectic of the debate seems to be at an impossible impasse: the contention is at the fundamental level of taking for granted versus denying the existence of a feature of mentality that can at best be defined *ostensively*. Friends of qualia, as exemplified by Block, claim that there is obviously *something* in their mental life that can be theorized about under the name "phenomenal consciousness," while the qualia skeptics, as exemplified by Dennett, state that there is *no* such thing to point at in their own experience.[81]

This is unfortunately the kind of philosophical junction at which most worthy disagreements hit rock bottom. Neither side is willing to concede their own point, and moreover neither side seems to have any way of demonstrating the validity of their claim. In another statement on the side of the friends of phenomenal consciousness, John Searle satirically asks: "How, for example, would one go about refuting the view that consciousness does not exist? Should I pinch its adherents to remind them that they are conscious? Should I pinch myself and report the results in the *Journal of Philosophy*?" (Searle 1992, p. 8). In contrast,

Dennett declares: "I cannot prove that no such sort of consciousness exists. I also cannot prove that gremlins don't exist. The best I can do is to show that there is no respectable motivation for believing in it" (Dennett 1991, p. 406).

Of course, the situation on the whole (and the particular state-of-the-art philosophical understanding of the mind-body problem we have arrived at after twenty-five hundred years of pondering) is more nuanced than I have just sketched. For instance, the eliminativist position has more resourceful ways of undermining belief in qualia, and the "friends of qualia" have intuitively appealing conceptual tools on their side, such as the absent and inverted qualia puzzles and the knowledge argument. Nonetheless, neither side can help finding the other's theoretical maneuvers equally unconvincing.

The eliminativist strategy largely depends on the deconstruction of the concept of phenomenal consciousness, thus revealing theoretical tensions internal to it. In different ways, both Daniel Dennett and Richard Rorty take this approach (Dennett 1988; Rorty 1979). Dennett does this by providing a number of "intuition pumps," designed to show that our pretheoretical intuitions about phenomenal consciousness are far from being reliable and sound. On the contrary, as Dennett attempts to show, our commonsense grasp of the facts about phenomenal consciousness can result in such conceptual dilemmas that it might be a better strategy to abandon any talk about phenomenal properties altogether. Dennett is quite straightforward in this approach; he says: "I want to make it just as uncomfortable for anyone to talk of qualia—or 'raw feels' or 'phenomenal properties' or 'subjective and intrinsic properties' or 'the qualitative character' or experience—with the standard presumption that they, and everyone else, knows what on earth they are talking about" (Dennett 1988, p. 43).

If there indeed is a conceptual disarray surrounding the notion of phenomenal consciousness, it seems only fair to demand from those who take the idea of phenomenal consciousness seriously and use it as a fundamental theoretical tenet to come up with a clarified conceptual network of terms that all go along with the umbrella term of *phenomenal consciousness*. On the other hand, there may be good reasons to respect the words of the supporters of phenomenal consciousness that the only definitional way open to them is by ostension. Being unable to provide a nonostensive definition is not, by itself, sufficient reason to pronounce the notion of phenomenal consciousness as theoretically illegitimate, and thereby promote its complete abandonment. The merits or shortcomings of an ostensive definition in revealing the essence of a phenomenon have to be judged on its own ground, in virtue of its success in providing conceptual clarity and theoretical agreement in the relevant discussions.

It should be acknowledged, however, that the strategy of revealing essences by means of "pointing" has not delivered any kind of agreement with respect to phenomenal consciousness thus far.[82] The same problem appears even more acutely in thinking about the possibility of zombies. How can you tell a zombie from a nonzombie, someone who has absent qualia from someone whose qualia are intact? If zombiehood is a possibility, not only could your closest friend turn out to be a zombie, without anyone's knowledge or awareness, so could you, and not know it yourself. Zombiehood brings with it not only the problem of other minds, and thus third-person skepticism, but first-person skepticism as well. If you, the reader of these lines, suddenly turned into a zombie, no one would notice any difference, and in a significant sense of "noticing," neither would you. Remember that knowing, judging, thinking, and being aware of—in a nonphenomenal sense—are all capabilities granted to a zombie, and furthermore, "there is no need to invoke qualia in the explanation of how we ascribe mental states to ourselves [because a zombie] after all, ascribes himself the same qualia; it's just that he's wrong about it"

(Chalmers 1993; Chalmers 1996 embraces the consequences of this result under the title "the paradox of phenomenal judgement").

Thus, to the extent that "seemings" of your own phenomenal states are constituted by self-ascriptive judgments, beliefs, thoughts, memories, expectations, and so forth about those states (and no doubt there is a significant extent to which such seemings are so constituted), it would be warranted to say that your inner life would continue to *seem* the same to you, despite the fact that you would cease to have any genuine phenomenal states once you turned into a zombie. Put differently, according to the zombie hypothesis, you could now be "hallucinating" your own phenomenology. You would, *ex hypothesi*, be confidently judging that nothing changed in your inner life, and be mistaken about it, but you would never be able to find this out. Indeed, for all you know, your present existence on earth could be continuing in alternating phases of humanhood versus zombiehood, switching every other minute. Hmm....

Coming back to a distinction I introduced at the beginning of this chapter, it is also important to note that the segregationist intuition plays into the hands of epiphenomenalism and the possibility of zombiehood. Characterizing consciousness in essentially noncausal (nonfunctional, nonrepresentational) terms leaves no epistemic hook for making it possible to detect the presence or absence of phenomenal consciousness, even from a first-person perspective.

But if we are to accept the possibility that any one of us can be a zombie and not know it, that is, if any one of us can be totally lacking phenomenal consciousness while not being able to find out about it, how can we possibly expect a stalemate over the ontology of phenomenon consciousness to be resolved, while fundamentally relying on ostention for its presence?

The stalemate seems unresolvable under the proposed terms. Perhaps, then, there is something fundamentally misleading here, and it is time to start looking for ways of building an alternative

conception of phenomenal consciousness based on the integrationist intuition—not one that eliminates phenomenal consciousness but not one that renders it completely inefficacious, or opaque even from the first-person perspective either. Rather, the conception should take the first-person characterization of experience seriously and support the commonsense understanding of phenomenal consciousness.

The bottom line of what seems most unacceptable here is the fact that under a framework that allows for the possibility of zombies, phenomenal consciousness is to be regarded as making no difference, in an epistemically significant sense, even in the first person. That is, a well-intended effort to promote phenomenal consciousness by conceptually separating it from all causal and representational properties actually yields a position with the opposite theoretical consequence: the demotion of phenomenal consciousness to a ghostly existence. If it is *this* sort of a property that we talk about when we consider phenomenal consciousness, would we really lose much (anything) by doing away with it?[83] And if we are committed to (internal) "pointing" as the only reliable way to verify the existence of phenomenal consciousness, the knowledge of the absence or presence of which is hidden even from the first-person perspective, that is, to the person who has it, should we perhaps not reconsider our very concept of phenomenal consciousness?

XX   In Place of a Conclusion

I would like to leave the reader with the two questions I just posed above. But let me also give a brief recapitulation and try to tie some of the loose ends.

I started by noting an epistemological asymmetry in the way one has access to (the facts about) one's own experiences versus those of others. This asymmetry leads us to the notion of perspectivity, something quite unique to (the study of) consciousness, and to the distinction between first-person and third-person points of view. This duality between points of view with respect to accessing facts about experiences also manifests itself in a duality in characterizing consciousness, in causal versus phenomenal terms.

Taking these characterizations as mutually exclusive, based on the presumption that phenomenal consciousness is essentially phenomenal *and* essentially noncausal, yields what I called the *segregationist intuition*. Opposing it is the *integrationist intuition*, which maintains that phenomenal consciousness can only be characterized by means of all causal, functional, or representational elements. Given these two intuitions, I briefly argued that the former plays into the hands of the doctrine of epiphenomenalism, which, when combined with considerations from the possibility of absent qualia and zombiehood, leads us into untenable and noncommonsensical conceptions of phenomenal consciousness. This is good evidence, on the other hand, to take the latter seriously and use it as the pretheoretical basis in reexamining our notion of phenomenal consciousness.[84]

Another domain where the epistemic element of perspectivity figures in is the problem of the explanatory gap and the question of the "hard problem" of consciousness. There seems to be an unbridged gap in the explanation of how physical embodiment and conscious experience are linked. The former is in general given a causal characterization from a third-person perspective, the latter a phenomenal characterization in first-person terms. It seems that under our existing conceptual scheme, bolstered by the segregationist intuition, the "hard problem" just does not, and cannot, lend itself to a solution.

What is important to note here is that the explanatory gap, in the way it is set up, stems from an epistemological issue. The further question that remains is whether its persistence is good enough evidence to yield ontological conclusions. Some think yes; introducing an "extra ingredient" into the picture and thus augmenting one's on-

tology to include consciousness as a fundamental element could indeed relieve one of the nagging problem of having to bridge mechanism and experience (by emergence, reduction, elimination, and so forth) or vice versa. Others think that the epistemological nature of the explanatory gap does not warrant ontological conclusions. Although I cannot go into this debate in any further detail here, I too would like to lend my support to this latter position. True, in the presence of the explanatory gap, the link between experience and its physical underpinnings may seem arbitrary, but I think that the decision to introduce a new fundamental element into the ontology, based on the explanatory gap, seems equally arbitrary as well. At least I fail to see how the most steadfast belief in a thus-expanded new ontology would leave one *less puzzled* about just how consciousness relates to its physical underpinnings, hence diminishing the explanatory gap and explaining away the further-How question. What seems the most promising direction in reapproaching consciousness and pursuing its deep-rooted problems in the present era involves rethinking epistemology and conceptual schemes (as opposed to a priori postulation of new ontology) to yield a cross-fertilization of the first-person and third-person perspectives, which would allow theorizing about how causal efficacy figures in *how consciousness feels*, and how phenomenal quality relates to *what consciousness does*.

In any case, at present it just does not seem as if there is a way to settle the dispute decisively about the "hard problem" or the consequences of the explanatory gap. And given the troublesome stalemate over the ontological nature of phenomenal consciousness, we seem to be not quite near a satisfactory understanding of the phenomenon. If anything, the survey of the contemporary issues and current debates surrounding consciousness points to a need for a careful reexamination of our pretheoretical intuitions and conceptual foundations on which to build better accounts of consciousness. It also seems probable that an entirely satisfactory understanding of consciousness will be possible, if at all, only when the constitutive elements of a more comprehensive framework, in which consciousness needs to be theoretically situated, are themselves better understood. And these elements include nothing less than causality, representation, indexicality, and personhood, and especially the deep-rooted dichotomies between mental and physical, and subjective and objective. As such, it is probably reasonable to assume, as Jerry Fodor likes to prognosticate regarding a complete account of rationality, that "no such theory will be available by this time next week."[85]

This being said, I conclude on a more positive note. Presently, there is an impressive rising tide of interest in the study of consciousness, and thanks to recent advances in interdisciplinary research, we are now in a better position to penetrate the mysteries of this great intellectual frontier. By integrating methodologies and perspectives from psychology, philosophy, neuroscience, cognitive science, and other disciplines and by keeping a mindful eye on the successes and failures of the past, we should be able to reach a higher vantage point and to see more broadly and more deeply than has ever before been possible. These are very exciting times for thinking about consciousness.

Acknowledgments

I would like to thank my coeditors, Ned Block and Owen Flanagan, for many helpful suggestions. Special thanks to Fred Dretske, John Perry, Roger Shepard, Brian C. Smith, and again to Owen Flanagan, for teaching me what I needed to know to write this chapter, and for their support throughout the preparation of this book.

Notes

1. The scope of my work has been limited to the philosophical and scientific paradigms rooted in Western intellectual history and, more specifically, in the analytic tradition. Obviously, there is a wealth of fascinating issues, questions, and approaches concerning consciousness that lie outside this limited scope. This chapter should not be taken as an attempt to give an exhaustive survey of all aspects of consciousness even within its own scope, and certainly not as embodying the grander ambition of covering all paradigms of the study of consciousness.

2. The results of this effort were discussed as part of a workshop attended by anesthesiologists, neurophysiologists, psychologists, and medicolegal experts in Cardiff, United Kingdom, in 1986. Rosen and Lunn (1987) is an outcome of this workshop.

3. Michenfelder makes the same point in another way, in concluding, "Thus there are a variety of end points one might choose to answer the question 'When is the brain anesthetized?' and there is no obvious basis for selecting one over another" (Michenfelder 1988, p. 36). However, cf. Nikolinakos (1994) for an optimistic outlook on the role of consciousness in anesthesia research. See, also, Flohr (1995) for an information-theoretic model of anesthesia where the "threshold of consciousness" is determined in terms of the brain's representational activity.

4. If we go down the phylogenetic ladder—for instance, from humans all the way to amoebae—where are we to cut the line and determine the bounds of the *charmed circle* to which only those who possess consciousness can belong? (The metaphor of the "charmed circle" is from Dennett 1987, p. 161.) Chimps, dogs, spiders? What about infants, fetuses, or comatose patients? On the other hand, if we insist on experience of sensations, itches, and tingles as necessary components of consciousness, is there any principled reason for stoping short of requiring something further, such as a conceptual overlay that makes possible one's situated awareness of one's own place and relations with others (not to talk of the Cartesian *res cogitans*), as essential to the nature of consciousness? The answers to these questions are all up for theoretical grabs.

It is also sociologically interesting to look at patterns in the common sense attributions of various mental abilities to various organisms. In contrast to widely dissenting opinions on the attribution of consciousness to others, there does not seem to be such a significant variation in pretheoretic intuitions with regard to attributions of intelligence, or perceptual capabilities. A preliminary survey study conducted on approximately one hundred Stanford students and faculty, based on a two-dimensional matrix of mental attributes (e.g., the ability to perceive, the ability to learn, intelligence, consciousness) versus kinds of organisms (e.g., protozoa, spiders, chimpanzees, humans) seemed to indicate a bias in our attributions toward reserving consciousness most exclusively for ourselves, while being more generous with the attributions of other mental abilities. (Güzeldere 1993).

5. This is, it turns out, a very tricky question. On the one hand, patients with only cortical brain damage make a striking contrast with those who further lack a functional brainstem. For instance, a report on the diagnosis of death, prepared by the President's Commission, makes the following statement:

> The startling contrast between bodies lacking *all* brain functions and patients with intact brain stems (despite severe neocortical damage) manifests [a tremendous difference with respect to responsiveness, and hence the attribute of life]. The former lie with fixed pupils, motionless except for the chest movements produced by their respirators. The latter can not only breathe, metabolize, maintain temperature and blood pressure, and so forth, *on their own*, but also sigh, yawn, track light with their eyes, and react to pain or reflex stimulation.

On the other hand, the commission shies away from reaching any conclusion with respect to the absence or presence of consciousness in patients of either kind: "It is not known which portions of the brain are responsible for cognition and consciousness; what little is known points to substantial interconnection among the brain stem, subcortical structures, and the neocortex" (President's Commission 1981, quoted in Capron 1988, pp. 161, 160, respectively).

Perhaps it is altogether misleading to think of the presence of consciousness in a binary fashion. It might be necessary to talk about degrees of consciousness, which could allow one to say that normal human beings are "more conscious" than those with brain damage, the brain-damaged patients more than those without a brainstem, and so forth.

6. Even though McGinn (1989) cites Julian Huxley as the author of this by now very popular, colorful quote (with no source), the credit belongs to T. H. Huxley (Julian Huxley's grandfather). In full, it reads: "But what consciousness is, we know not; and how it is that anything so remarkable as a state of consciousness comes about as the result of irritating nervous tissue, is just as unaccountable as the appearance of the Djin when Aladdin rubbed his lamp in the story, or as any other ultimate fact of nature" (Huxley 1866, 193). Interestingly, Huxley seems to have removed the reference to the Djin (as well as Aladdin's lamp) in the later editions of this book. For instance, in the 1876 edition, the same passage appears as: "But what consciousness is, we know not; and how it is that anything so remarkable as a state of consciousness comes about as the result of irritating nervous tissue, is just as unaccountable as any other ultimate fact of nature" (p. 188). Too bad the Djin is no longer around, for we could perhaps have wished from it to tell us if we would ever be able to solve the mind-body problem.

7. There is a longer passage in Tyndall's "Scientific Realism" where he addresses the mind-body problem in length, and concludes, in agreement with McGinn (though in 1868) that it is "as insoluble, in its modern form, as it was in the prescientific ages." Because the points Tyndall touches upon are so remarkably close to the contemporary formulations of the issues debated in the literature under the labels "explanatory gap" and the "hard problem" (e.g., the nature of the explanation between mind and body as opposed to other physical phenomena; the prospects for the mind-body problem upon reaching a fully advanced neuroscientific understanding of the brain; and the status of possible correlation-based accounts of consciousness), I quote this passage here in its entirety. (A more detailed discussion follows in section XIV.)

> The relation of physics to consciousness being thus invariable, it follows that, given the state of the brain, the corresponding thought or feeling might be inferred: or, given the thought or feeling, the corresponding state of the brain might be inferred. But how inferred? It would be at bottom not a case of logical inference at all, but of empirical association. You may reply, that many of the inferences of science are of this character—the inference, for example, that an electric current, of a given direction, will deflect a magnetic needle in a definite way. But the cases differ in this, that the passage from the current to the needle, if not demonstrable, is conceivable, and that we entertain no doubt as to the final mechanical solution of the problem. But the passage from the physics of the brain to the corresponding facts of consciousness is inconceivable as a result of mechanics.

Granted that a definite thought, and a definite molecular action in the brain, occur simultaneously; we do not possess the intellectual organ, nor apparently any rudiment of the organ, which would enable us to pass, by a process of reasoning, from the one to the other. They appear together, but we do not know why. Were our minds and senses so expanded, strengthened, and illuminated, as to enable us to see and feel the very molecules of the brain; were we capable of following all their motions, all their groupings, all their electrical discharges, if such there be; and were we intimately acquainted with the corresponding states of thought and feeling, we should be as far as ever from the solution of the problem, 'How are these physical processes connected with the facts of consciousness?'. The chasm between the two classes of phenomena would still remain intellectually impassable.

Let the consciousness of love, for example, be associated with a right-handed spiral motion of the molecules of the brain, and the consciousness of hate with a left-handed spiral motion. We should then know, when we love, that the motion is in one direction, and, when we hate, that the motion is in the other; but the 'WHY?' would remain as unanswerable as before. (Tyndall 1868, pp. 86–87)

It is worth noting that equally dissenting opinions were also available at the time. For instance, Huxley (1901) states: "I hold, with the Materialist, that the human body, like all living bodies, is a machine, all operations of which, sooner or later, be explained on physical principles. I believe that we shall, sooner or later, arrive at a mechanical equivalent of consciousness, just as we have arrived at a mechanical equivalent of heat" (p. 191).

8. For a materialist response to Adams, see Lewis (1995).

9. Antecedents of McGinn's view can be found in Nagel's work in several places, although Nagel only points out the possibility of McGinn's position without committing himself to it. For instance, he says:

We cannot directly see a necessary connection, if there is one, between phenomenological pain and a physiologically described brain state any more than we can directly see the necessary connection between increase in temperature and pressure of a gas at a constant volume. In the latter case the necessity of the connection becomes clear only when we descend to the level of molecular description: till then it appears as a contingent correlation. In the psychophysical case we have no idea whether there is such a deeper level or what it could be; but even if there is, the possibility that pain might be necessarily connected with a brain state at this deeper level does not permit us to conclude that pain might be directly analyzable in physical or even topic-neutral terms.... *Even if such a deeper level existed, we might be permanently blocked from a general understanding of it.* (Nagel 1986, pp. 48–49; my emphasis).

The possibility of a permanent cognitive closure in humans with regard to the understanding of the mind-body relation is an intriguing idea. But when it comes to taking this possibility as a statement of certainty, as McGinn does, it seems fair to question what warrants this conviction, especially in the absence of empirically grounded reasons. In particular, there is a curious tension between McGinn's confidence, on one hand, of his own cognitive ability to *assert* such a sweeping verdict on behalf of all human beings (at present as well as in the foreseeable future), and the aim of his argument, on the other hand, which ultimately strives to *attenuate* confidence in the powers of human cognitive abilities to solve the mind-body problem.

Put differently, McGinn wants his readers to simultaneously believe, as a result of his largely a priori reasoning, both that our cognitive abilities are limited to forever fall short of bringing a solution to the mind-body problem, *and* that they are nonetheless sufficiently powerful to foresee the exploratory limits of the human mind vis-à-vis the very same issue. By the same kind of reasoning, isn't there equally good reason to think, one wonders, that the opposite claim might rather be true— that it is more likely (or, at least not less likely) that we will someday come to a satisfactory understanding of the nature of the mind-body relation than it is that we will ever be able to determine how far the human understanding will extend? (For a thorough critique of McGinn's position, see Flanagan (1992), chap. 6.)

10. It is actually not a straightforward matter to give a precise definition of naturalism, and I will not attempt one here. Roughly speaking, I take "naturalism" to denote the view that everything is composed of fundamental entities recognized by the natural sciences (ontological dimension), and possibly that the accept-

able methods of theorizing about these entities are those commensurable with methods employed in the natural sciences (methodological dimension). For a comprehensive overview of naturalistic approaches in epistemology and philosophy of science in the twentieth century, see Kitcher (1992); for a recent analysis of the present status of naturalism, see Stroud (1996).

In philosophy mind, naturalism is often regarded as a close ally of two related but not identical views, materialism and physicalism, but there are exceptions. See, for instance, Post (1987) for a detailed attempt to lay out a fully naturalist but nonreductive metaphysics that is committed to a monism of entities with a pluralism of irreducible "emergent" properties. See also Chalmers (1996) for a somewhat similar view he calls "naturalistic dualism." For a thorough examination of the physicalist program, compare Poland (1994); for contemporary objections to physicalism, see Robinson (1993).

11. As it happens, Miller is not the first one to think about placing a ban on "consciousness" in order to help sort out the tangles in related terminologies. Here is a quote from the turn of the century, by philosopher and William James scholar Ralph Barton Perry (1904): "Were the use of the term 'consciousness' to be forbidden for a season, contemporary thought would be set for the wholesome task of discovering more definite terms with which to replace it, and a very considerable amount of convenient mystery would be dissipated. There is no philosophical term at once so popular and so devoid of standard meaning.... Consciousness comprises everything that is, and indefinitely much more. It is small wonder that the definition of it is little attempted" (p. 282). Hence, according to Perry, it is not (only) the ubiquitous familiarity with consciousness that renders attempts to give it a precise characterization or definition unnecessary; the reason is rather the difficulty of the analytic task involved in doing so.

12. A related term in Latin was *conscientia*, which can literally be translated as "knowledge with," which appeared in English and in French as "conscience." "Conscience" also had, and still has, a significant ethical aspect, which is reflected in another *OED* entry: "Internal knowledge, especially of one's own innocence, guilt, deficiencies, etc." (Cf. Baldwin 1901). Nonetheless, *consciousness* and *conscience* have been separate words with quite distinct meanings in English, at least since the time of Locke. In contrast, there is only one word in Romance languages like French (*conscience*)

and Italian (*coscienza*) that carries both meanings. Outside the boundaries of Indo-European languages, the term corresponding to consciousness in, say, Turkish—an Altaic language—carries a political, but not really ethical, connotation, in addition to the common psychological usage (*bilinç* or *şuur*, as opposed to *vicdan*). In any case, this little linguistic excursion gives no evidence of a semantic taxonomy that systematically relates to one based on language families.

13. The following quotation, taken from the circles where the concern with consciousness has to do primarily with the social rather than the psychological sense highlights this distinction quite eloquently:

> When you speak of "consciousness," you do not refer to the moral conscious: the very rigor of your methods ensures that you do not leave the strictly scientific domain which belong to you. What you have in mind exclusively is the faculty of perceiving and of reacting to perception, that is to say, the psychological concept which constitutes one of the accepted meanings of the word "consciousness." (Pope Paul VI, addressing a gathering of scientists for the conference *Brain and Conscious Experience* in Rome in 1964; quoted in Kanellakos and Lukas 1974, p. i)

14. This distinction is not uncontested, however. Some, especially in continental philosophy, think that there is no intransitive sense of consciousness: all consciousness is consciousness of. Jean-Paul Sartre, for example, is a typical representative of this view: "We establish the necessity for consciousness to be consciousness *of* something. In fact it is by means of that of which it is conscious that consciousness distinguishes itself in its own eyes and that it can be self-consciousness; a consciousness which would not be consciousness (of) something would be consciousness (of) nothing. (Sartre 1956, p. 173). The origins of this kind of an essentially intentional construal of consciousness goes back to Edmund Husserl's work from which Sartre adopted his view, most likely *Ideas* (Husserl 1913). (I thank Ron Brady for this pointer.)

15. See Güzeldere (1996) for an analysis of how the creature and state senses of consciousness can be connected by means of the "Introspective Link Principle," yielding various "higher-order monitoring" conceptions of consciousness. For other recent attempts to distinguish different senses of consciousness and sort

out some definitional issues, see Lycan (1987, preface; 1997b, chap. 1), Goldman (1993), and Natsoulas (1983, 1986).

16. My decision to address problems that bear only on the psychological sense of consciousness should not be taken to imply that the two subcategories are not related in interesting ways. In fact, it seems a philosophically significant task to investigate the nature of the relation between the social and the psychological senses of consciousness—is it something more like a genus-species relation, or one of family resemblance, or something completely unique? It can also be questioned whether one can fruitfully give an analysis of one of these halves while eschewing the other. Nonetheless, for the purposes of this chapter, I opt for focusing solely on the psychological sense of consciousness. Even if it may be impossible to fully understand the social sense of consciousness without referring to the psychological sense, or vice versa, due to the conceptual disarray surrounding the term "consciousness" such an analytic strategy seems essential as a first step.

17. For an exploration of the distinction between epistemological and ontological considerations, as well as the question of whether a set of criteria to distinguish the *mental* in general from the *physical* can be coherently formulated, see among others Rorty (1970a, 1970b) and Kim (1972).

18. The status of the mind-body problem in ancient Greek philosophy is also worth a visit. It is generally argued that there is no single term in ancient Greek that reflects the counterpart of the Cartesian/Lockean conception of consciousness, and that nothing like the contemporary debates on the mind-body problem or the problem of consciousness was ever in their horizon. For instance, Matson (1966) claims that "the Greeks had no mind-body problem" (p. 101), and Wilkes (1995) argues that "[Aristotle] paid absolutely no attention to consciousness per se" (p. 122). Similarly, Hamlyn (1968a) states: "There is an almost total neglect of any problem arising from psycho-physical dualism and the facts of consciousness. Such problems do not seem to arise for him. The reason appears to be that concepts like that of consciousness do not figure in his conceptual scheme at all; they play no part in his analysis of perception, thought, etc. (Nor do they play any significant role in Greek thought in general.) It is this perhaps that gives his definition of the soul itself a certain inadequacy for the modern reader" (p. xiii). See also Kahn (1966), Hamlyn (1968b), and Wilkes (1988) for similar views.

However, this view is not uncontested. For instance, Alastair Hannay (1990) suggests that in Greek philosophy one can find, contrary to the skepticism expressed above, something like a distinction between the social and psychological senses of consciousness. According to Hannay, Greeks distinguished between *syneidesis* (primarily ethical individual or shared knowledge) and *synaesthesia* (Aristotle's variation of the "unity of apperception"), in much the same way as modern philosophy proceeded in the seventeenth and eighteenth centuries. In alliance, Hardie (1976) argues against Matson, Kahn, and Hamlyn, and states that "it is . . . paradoxical to suggest that Aristotle was unaware of the mind-body problem" (p. 410). According to Hardie, Aristotle was "the first psychologist, and for him psychology without the conscious *psuchē* would have been Hamlet without the Prince" (p. 405). Ostenfeld (1987) goes a step further, and claims that both Plato and Aristotle were dealing with the mind-body problem in much the same sense Descartes did and we are. This debate, so far as I can see, is far from resolved at present.

19. The debate about whether consciousness consists in the higher-order awareness of first order mental states is very much alive in the contemporary literature. Among those who defend this view, some take the higher-order representation to be some form of perception (for example, Armstrong 1980, Churchland 1988, Lycan 1997), and others as some form of thought (for example, Rosenthal 1986, 1997; Carruthers 1989, 1996). For critiques, see Dretske (1993, 1995) and Shoemaker (1994). Despite the fact that such higher-order awareness accounts of consciousness have many promising aspects, I have to stop short of giving a proper exposition here. (A more detailed treatment of this approach can be found in Güzeldere 1995b.) I will also leave the discussion of "self-consciousness" (which is sometimes underwritten by such higher-order accounts) out of the scope of this chapter.

20. For Malebranche, although we can have a "clear idea" of our bodies, we cannot, unlike what Descartes believed, have a clear idea of our souls or minds. Put differently, we cannot know our minds through a clear idea; rather we know them "only through consciousness or inner sensation" such as "pain, heat, color, and all other sensible qualities" (Malebranche 1923, Elucidation 11: Knowledge of the Soul, pp. 86–87). As such, Malebranche gives qualitative aspects of the mind a much more central place in his theory, in contrast to the

Cartesian view. See Schmaltz (1996) for a thorough account of Malebranche's philosophy of mind. (I thank Tad Schmaltz for the relevant material and helpful discussion on this issue.)

21. Labeling the seemingly opposing views of James of 1890 and James of 1904 simply a "change of mind" is probably too superficial a conclusion in terms of historical scholarship, and not quite fair to James either. It is important to note that James's denouncement in the latter work is of "consciousness as an entity" rather than the reality of "conscious states." Regarding consciousness as an "entity" has close connotations to Cartesian substance dualism. Even though there is no straightforward advancement of such a metaphysical position in the *Principles of Psychology*, James's position with respect to the ontology of consciousness is not entirely clear there. Hence it might be better to characterize his 1904 article as marking merely the abandonment of consciousness as a nonmaterial entity, not consciousness per se as a subject matter. This interpretation is supported by James's own remark that he means to "deny that the word [*consciousness*] stands for an entity, but to insist most emphatically that it does stand for a function" (James 1971, p. 4).

Even though this much seems quite straightforward, we are by no means faced with an unproblematic account of consciousness. In fact, James never quite works out the metaphysical presuppositions and consequences of his view of characterizing consciousness as a function, as opposed to an entity. Moreover, the ontological turn he takes toward "radical empiricism" at around the same period as the publication of his "Does Consciousness Exist?" complicates matters. It is probably well warranted to remark that William James never held a long-standing metaphysical position with respect to consciousness void of internal tensions. At a certain stage in his life, roughly midway between the publication of the two above mentioned works, he went so far as to defend the plausibility of the immortality of consciousness in an article titled "Human Immortality," in the following words: "And when finally a brain stops acting altogether, or decays, that special stream of consciousness which it subserved will vanish entirely from the natural world. But the sphere of being that supplied the consciousness would still be intact; and in that more real world with which, even whilst here, it was continuous, the consciousness might, in ways unknown to us, continue still" (James 1956, pp. 17–18). Perhaps the historical fact of the matter regarding

James's attitude toward the metaphysics of consciousness is reflected most accurately in Gerald Myers's following remark, from his extensive study of James's life and thought: "James wanted to hold that in one way consciousness does not exist, but that in another way it does; yet he was never able, even to his own satisfaction, to define the two ways clearly enough to show that they are consistent rather than contradictory" (Myers 1986, p. 64). For related work, see among others Dewey (1940), Lovejoy (1963), and Reck (1972). (I thank Denis Phillips, Imants Baruss, and Eugene Taylor for helpful pointers and discussion on William James's views on consciousness.)

22. The claim of introspectionism's being well established here refers not as much to the soundness of its methodology and theoretical grounding as to its pervasiveness and preeminence in the field of psychology as a whole. To see this, one only needs to survey the monolithic psychology literature of the few decades roughly between the end of nineteenth and the beginning of the twentieth centuries: all major psychology journals are edited by the protagonists of the introspectionist school, all articles report studies involving introspection as their primary method, and so on. Ironically, the same observation holds of the period that immediately follows (roughly from late 1910s to early 1960s), except with behaviorism substituted for introspectionism.

It would be interesting to pursue the question of whether the fluctuation in James's life with respect to consciousness occurred as a result of, or was influenced by, the general air of dissatisfaction with the internal conflicts of the introspectionist school toward the end of its tenure, which led to behaviorism's rapid rise and takeover of the intellectual landscape. Or was the influence in the opposite direction? These are all intriguing questions, but unfortunately they lie outside the scope of this chapter.

23. This is only one (as it happens, also historically the most significant) use of the word *introspection*. A number of different phenomena have passed under the same name. For instance, toward the end of the last century, Brentano and Comte argued that introspection, as a second-order mental act that gathers information about first-order sensations, was misconstrued. Mill and James agreed and proposed a model of introspection as retrospection: the examination of one's own mental happenings retrospectively, through the medium of memory of the immediate past. (For details, see Lyons 1986, chap 1.) A second, separate phenomenon that

made its way to the cognitive psychology literature in the 1970s under the name *introspection* was the phenomenon of reasoning about the causes of one's own behavior, in terms of one's beliefs, desires, motivations, and so forth. (For a seminal article that piqued most of the initial interest in this literature, see Nisbett and Wilson 1977.) In any case, my analysis deals with introspection only in the former sense.

24. Edwin Boring notes that no subject left Wilhelm Wundt's laboratory without having provided 10,000 data points (Boring 1953, p. 172). William James humorously observes that if it had not been for the sustained patience and the inability to get bored of the leaders of introspectionism who came from the Germanic part of the continental Europe, the enterprise of introspectionism could have never endured. "They mean business," James remarks, "not chivalry" (James 1950, pp. 192–193).

25. The nature of the relation and the degree of influence between positivism and behaviorism are not uncontroversial. Even though it is generally taken for granted that the two movements enjoyed a genuine ally status, the details of this received view have recently been contested by Laurence Smith. Smith claims, "With their common intellectual background and orientation, behaviorism and logical positivism were naturally disposed to form some sort of alliance. But only after both movements were well under way was there any significant interaction between them" (Smith 1986, p. 5; cf. the rest of his book for further details).

26. In all fairness I should add that behaviorism did manage to bring in fresh air to psychology of the late nineteenth and early twentieth centuries at a time when an uncomfortable sense of containment within the rigid introspectionist paradigm was rapidly growing. The realization that psychology could employ nonhuman subjects and pursue research without being solely dependent on the linguistic data to be provided by trained introspectionists seemed, rightly, to open up new horizons. This should also explain, in part, the rather immediate success and popularity of behaviorism and the symmetrically rapid fall of introspectionism. Unfortunately, as I will detail below, behaviorism turned out to constrict psychology into an even more rigid cast in comparison to its predecessor.

27. John Watson would not miss the chance to put a nail in introspectionism's coffin by alluding to this controversy: "Psychology, as it is generally thought of, has something esoteric in its methods. If you fail to re-produce my findings, it is not due to some fault in your apparatus or in the control of your stimulus, but it is due to the fact that your introspection is untrained. The attack is made upon the observer and not upon the experimental setting" (Watson 1913, p. 163).

Interestingly, approximately two hundred years earlier, a similar debate had taken place between two empiricist philosophers, Locke and Berkeley, on almost exactly the same issue. The question was whether there were any "abstract ideas": ideas that are not of particular things but of universals—"types" of particular things. In the following quotation, notice that Berkeley rests his challenge of Locke's position on this question on exactly the same grounds that Titchener challenged Külpe: personal experience based on introspection.

> If any man has the faculty of framing in his mind such an idea of a triangle as is here described, it is in vain to pretend to dispute him out of it, nor would I go about it. All I desire is that the reader would fully and certainly inform himself whether he has such an idea or no. And this, methinks, can be no hard task for anyone to perform. What more easy than for anyone to look a little into his own thoughts, and there try whether he has, or can attain to have, an idea that shall correspond with the description that is here given of the general idea of a triangle, which is "neither oblique nor rectangle, equilateral, equicrural or scalenon, but all and none of these at once"? (Berkeley 1977, pp. 13–14)

28. There is of course a third, unmentioned but important school of psychology that emerged during the period of transition from introspectionism to behaviorism: Gestalt psychology. The fact that a separate account of Gestalt psychology is not being provided here is certainly not because it is intellectually unworthy of consideration. Quite the opposite, Gestaltists were very keen about the reasons for introspectionism's failure, and they brought a fresh new perspective on the basis of which a large number of facts in the psychophysics of perception could be fruitfully reinterpreted. Nonetheless, Gestalt psychology shared many of the same ontological assumptions with respect to consciousness and the role of phenomenology in studying the mind with introspectionism. As a result, as far as the history of consciousness in psychology research is concerned, it does not constitute the sort of sharp contrast that behaviorism provides. Hence, the brief treatment.

Finally, the emerging clinical wing of psychology, the psychoanalytic school, also had its disagreements with introspectionism, and it constituted the third distinct angle of attack alongside with behaviorism and Gestalt psychology. Unfortunately, I cannot go into a detailed analysis concerning these three movements here. For a well-documented historical account of introspectionism and the debates and movements that surrounded it, cf. the section on "Modern Experimental Psychology" in Boring (1929), as well as chapters 1 and 2 of Lyons (1986).

29. So much so that it is very rare, even today, to come across "consciousness" or "introspection" in any psychology or cognitive science textbook, or even psychology dictionaries. See, for example, Corsini (1984) or Stillings et al. (1987), which contain no entries for "consciousness," "awareness," or "introspection."

30. Naturally, there were internal disagreements, and thus different schools, within Behaviorism, and not each brand of the doctrine was as hardheaded. Most notably, the *analytical* (logical) behaviorists (who were mostly philosophers, e.g., Hempel 1949) were interested in analyzing meanings of mental terms in a purely behavioral vocabulary, whereas the *methodological* behaviorists (who were mostly psychologists) wanted merely to restrict their research to the study of publicly observable behavior without having to attempt any conceptual analysis or even deny the reality of the publicly unobservable mental phenomena.

For example, according to Edwin Holt (1914), "the true criterion of consciousness is not introspection, but specific responsiveness" (p. 206). Since making behavior the *criterion* of consciousness is not quite the same as *identifying* the two, consciousness thus becomes "externalized" by means of a publicly observable measure, but the metaphysical question of identity is left open. As such, the two phenomena could be said to be coexistent, as Holt (1915) acknowledges in a later work: "When one is conscious of a thing, one's movements are readjusted to it, and to precisely those features of it of which one is conscious. The two domains are coterminous" (p. 172). Edward Tolman's position in his "A Behaviorist's Definition of Consciousness" (1927) is also similar to Holt's in stopping short of advancing a metaphysical claim: "Whenever an organism at a given moment of stimulation shifts and there from being ready to respond in some relatively differentiated way to being ready to respond in some relatively more differentiated way, there is consciousness" (p. 435). (See also Tolman 1967 and note 43 for his position with respect to the study of "raw feels" in psychology.)

In contrast, the *ontological* behaviorists were in favor of doing away with consciousness, or any aspect of the mind, by *identifying* it with some piece of behavior. For example, Lashley (1923) maintained the following thesis: "The conception of consciousness here advanced is, then, that of a complex integration and succession of bodily activities which are closely related to or involve the verbal and gestural mechanisms and hence most frequently come to social expression" (p. 341).

Although the assumptions of these three schools are, by and large, logically independent of one another, Watson (1913, 1970), an indoctrinated behaviorist, seems to have believed in all of them, arguing that the time was ripe for psychology to discard all reference to consciousness. It is no doubt that a Watsonian universe would make life much easier for philosophers and psychologists. It would, for instance, remove the epistemic duality in the study of consciousness by collapsing the distinction between the first-person and third-person perspectives. Furthermore, by making consciousness ultimately an operationalized parameter in the domain of behavior, it would allow a set of behavioral criteria to settle questions about who or what possesses creature consciousness. But, as is evident from the history of psychology, life is never easy in the domain of mind. Questions about consciousness remained a nagging issue during behaviorism's tenure, and they eventually led its prominent figures like B. F. Skinner to not only acknowledge the existence of the phenomenon, but also adopt a conciliatory position in his later works. For example, Skinner (1974), after stating that the common conception of behaviorism as a school of thought that "ignored consciousness, feelings, and states of mind" was all wrong, concedes that the "early behaviorists wasted a good deal of time, and confused an important central issue, by attacking the introspective study of mental life" (pp. 3–5).

Undoubtedly, consciousness was not the only factor that brought the demise of behaviorism. A different line of attack, for example, came from the quarters of new-born modern linguistics on the issue of explanation of verbal behavior. In particular, Noam Chomsky's famous review (1959) of Skinner (1957) is a milestone that shook behaviorism (in psychology) in its foundations. For an influential critique of logical behaviorism (in philosophy), see Putnam (1963).

31. Of course, there were a few exceptions who spoke up while the reign of behaviorism was still tight and proved to be visionaries. Worth mentioning here is a

lengthy discussion Miller gave on consciousness in his excellent survey of psychology as early as 1962. It is possible to recount even earlier attempts to break the silence, and directly or indirectly talk about consciousness, especially in the fields of attention, learning, and cybernetics. Cf. Hebb (1949), Abramson (1951–55), Hilgard (1956), and Broadbent (1958). See also Hilgard's remarks on this issue in his lucid survey, "Consciousness in Contemporary Psychology" (1980). For an account of the "cognitive revolution" in psychology, see Baars (1985) and Hilgard (1987), chap. 7.

32. Years later, Alan Baddeley (1993), a prominent psychologist who has devoted his career to the investigation of memory, validates Mandler's insight in the following words: "I am rather surprised to find myself writing about consciousness.... There are very good reasons why the study of consciousness has been discretely ignored by cognitive psychology during its early years of development.... Why, then, have I changed my mind? In my own case, the strongest reason has come from the pressure of empirical evidence; I am an experimental psychologist who uses empirical data to drive theory, and it has become increasingly difficult to have a model of memory that is at all complete, without directly or indirectly including assumptions about consciousness" (pp. 11–13). (Note, by the way, that Baddeley 1990—in many respects a very thorough book on memory—contains no references to consciousness.)

33. The information-processing models of consciousness, although not the only game in town, are still very much alive today, in psychology as well as in philosophy. For instance, Dennett's central claim in his most recent *Consciousness Explained* is that "conscious human minds are more-or-less serial virtual machines implemented—inefficiently—on the parallel hardware that evolution has provided for us" (Dennett 1991, p. 218). See also Hofstadfer (1979), Harnad (1982), and Sommerhof (1990, 1996) for theorizing about consciousness in computational and systems-analysis terms. However, information-processing models of the mind (and, a fortiori, of consciousness in particular) have not always been everyone's favorite. For example Hubert Dreyfus, in his well-known critique of the research program and methodology of artificial intelligence, brought the whole information-processing approach under severe criticism (Dreyfus 1979, 1992, esp. chap. 4, "The Psychological Assumption"). Another line of attack was developed from neighboring quarters by philosopher John Searle. In an essay that later became known as the "Chinese room argument," Searle argued that no amount of information processing could alone provide a system with original (as opposed to derivative, assigned, etc.) semantics (Searle 1980). Dreyfus's critique never focused on consciousness per se, but Searle, in a newer work, deals exclusively with the problem of consciousness in cognitive science, and in general computational paradigms (Searle 1992). In contrast, a rival account of consciousness built entirely on computational ideas can be found in Jackendoff's *Consciousness and the Computational Mind* (1987). For a predecessor of the information-processing accounts of consciousness, see Donald Hebb's *The Organization of Behavior* (1949), a work that came out of the behaviorist era but anticipated what was ahead with foresight: Hebb argues to identify consciousness "theoretically with a certain degree of complexity of phase sequence in which both central and sensory facilitations merge, the central acting to reinforce now one class of sensory stimulations, now another" (p. 145).

34. Note, however, that a curious passage in Descartes's *Principles of Philosophy* suggests a theoretical commitment to something very much like Freud's unconscious, which does not sit squarely with his explicit commitment to the transparency of the mind:

> The strange aversions of certain people that make them unable to bear the smell of roses, the presence of a cat, or the like, can readily be recognized as resulting simply from their having been greatly upset by some such object in the early years of their life.... And the smell of roses may have caused severe headache in a child when he was still in the cradle, or a cat may have terrified him without anyone noticing and without any memory of it remaining afterwards; and yet the idea of an aversion he then felt for the roses or for the cat will remain imprinted on his brain till the end of his life (Descartes 1992), p. 195: *Principles of Philosophy*, pt. I, §9, AT, 429)

Unfortunately, I have not been able to find any further elaboration of this idea in Descartes's writings, which would surely be relevant in better understanding the nature of what seems to be an apparent theoretical tension.

35. The controversy over the status of unconscious mental states is multifaceted. Another staunch critic of the unconscious, though for reasons different from Titcheners' (that have to do with his stance against panpsychic views of consciousness), was William

James (1950a). He fretfully remarks: "The distinction ... *between the unconscious and the conscious being of the mental state* ... is the sovereign means for believing what one likes in psychology, and of turning what might become a science into a tumbling-ground for whimsies" (p. 163). As discussed in section XI, a different line of objection is also raised, this time in a Cartesian spirit, by Searle (1992) and Strawson (1994).

Note also that in Titchener, talk about the *unconscious* has switched to talk about the *subconscious*, but there is enough reason to think that nothing theoretically significant hangs on this implicit substitution. This terminological variation stems from the fact that Freud and his contemporary, Pierre Janet, had an initial disagreement that left them with two different terms (*unconscious* and *subconscious*), and each one adopted and perpetually owned his own term with a vengeance. But this was more a result of personal quarrels between the two personalities than a genuine theoretical dissonance on the nature and structure of *that which is not conscious*. And so far as I can tell, there is no evidence that Titchener's use of Janet's term, *subconscious*, rather than Freud's *unconscious* is the result of a "conscious decision" and a theoretical commitment. For an illuminating account of the relation between Freud and Janet, see Perry and Laurence (1984).

36. For an interesting discussion of the question of whether the Freudian unconscious is a "theoretical construct" on a par with scientific theoretical entities, see Dilman (1972).

37. Note that over time, Freud grew dissatisfied with his tripartite structure and eventually introduced the new elements of the id, the ego, and the superego into the picture:

> In the further course of psycho-analytic work, however, these distinctions (i.e., conscious, preconscious, and unconscious) have proved to be inadequate, and for practical purposes, insufficient. This has been clear in more ways than one; but the decisive instance is as follows. We have formed the idea that in each individual there is a coherent organization of mental processes; and we call this *ego*. (Freud 1962, p. 7)

Later Freud (1964) gives a schematic depiction of the structure of consciousness, with the id, the ego, and the superego being "superimposed" on the classical tri-partite division of the conscious, the preconscious, and the unconscious.

38. Cf. John Kihlstrom's work for a cognitivist overview of the various forms of the unconscious (e.g., Kihlstrom 1984, 1987).

39. For a thoughtful discussion of the theoretical issues involved, see Reingold and Merikle (1990).

40. Another paradigm in contemporary psychology that makes use of the conscious-unconscious distinction is that of implicit learning and implicit memory, as well as implicit perception. The focus of interest in this paradigm is on measuring the amount of learning and memory possible in the absence of subjects' awareness of the stimuli presented to them. A certain branch of this work became sensationalized in the media under the title "subliminal perception" in the 1970s. For a thorough and sympathetic account of the nature of this phenomenon, as well as the history of related research, see Dixon's *Subliminal Perception: The Nature of a Controversy* (1971) and his later *Preconscious Processing* (1981). For possibly the most influential recent work in this area (especially in masking studies), see Marcel (1983a, 1983b).

Naturally, there are also skeptics. For instance, Eriksen stated quite early on, "At present there is no convincing evidence that the human organism can discriminate or differentially respond to external stimuli that are at an intensity level too low to elicit discriminated verbal report. In other words, a verbal report is as sensitive an indicator of perception as any other response that has been studied" (Eriksen 1960, p. 298).

More recently, Holender (1986) presented a negative and rather controversial statement on subliminal perception, which also included a comprehensive survey of the field. For a collection of contemporary position papers in this paradigm, see the special issue of *Mind and Language* on "Approaches to Consciousness and Intention" (Spring 1990).

41. Searle also has an explanation to offer regarding the motivations underlying the sort of separationist view that Fodor promotes with respect to consciousness and intentionality:

> There has been in recent decades a fairly systematic effort to separate consciousness from intentionality. The connection between the two is being gradually lost, not only in cognitive science, but in linguistics and philosophy as well. I think the underlying—and perhaps unconscious—motivation for this urge to

separate intentionality from consciousness is that we
do not know how to explain consciousness, and we
would like to get a theory of the mind that will not
be discredited by the fact that it lacks a theory of
consciousness. (Searle 1992, p. 153)

Perhaps a piece of careful Freudian psychoanalysis
would resolve this issue for good. Lacking such expertise, I choose to leave the question open.

42. Panpsychism is a deep-rooted idea that can probably be traced, in one form or another, back to Thales
and other ancient Greek philosophers. Nagel (1988)
presents a contemporary discussion of panpsychism,
characterizing it as the view that "the basic physical
constituents of the universe have mental properties,
whether or not they are parts of living organisms"
(p. 181). Panpsychism was quite popular as a metaphysical doctrine among the psychologists (in particular,
the psychophysicists) of the nineteenth century, including such prominent figures as Gustav Fechner and Hermann Lotze. William James, in contrast, was never
sympathetic to this view; chapter VI of James (1950a)
contains a cogent critique of panpsychism (under the
title "Mind-Stuff Theory"). For recent discussions of
panpsychism in the context of ongoing consciousness
debates, see Seager (1995) and Hut and Shepard (1996).

43. The origins of the term *raw feels* goes back, so far
as I can trace, to the work of behaviorist psychologist
Edward Tolman. In outlining what falls outside the
scope of "scientific psychology," Tolman (1967) characterizes raw feels (from his opponents' perspective)
as follows: "Sensations, says the orthodox mentalist,
are more than discriminanda-expectations, whether
indicated by verbal introspection or by discrimination-
box experiments. They are in addition immediate
mental givens, 'raw feels'. They are unique subjective
suffusions in the mind" (Tolman 1967, pp. 250–251).
But it is probably Herbert Feigl (1967) who is responsible for the introduction and wide acceptance of *raw feels*
in the philosophical terminology.

44. In a short passage in the *Tractatus*, Wittgenstein
makes a similar point regarding the self (or subject-
hood):

> *5.633*   Where in the world is a metaphysical subject
> to be found?
> You will say that this is exactly like the case of the
> eye and the visual field. But really you do *not* see the
> eye.

And nothing *in the visual field* allows you to infer
that it is seen by an eye.
5.6331   For the form of the visual field is surely not
like this:

(Wittgenstein 1974, p. 57)

Keith Gunderson (1970) also discusses this issue under
the title, "The Investigational Asymmetries Problem"
and makes the similar point that "just as the eye does
not, cannot, see itself in its own visual field, so too, the
self will never, in its inventory-taking of the world, find
itself in the world in the manner in which it finds other
people and things" (p. 127).

Again, the point raised is well taken for consciousness
so far as one's own selfhood is involved in it, but it is not
obvious just how it generalizes into a difficulty (much
less an impossibility) with the study of consciousness in
general by (other) conscious beings.

45. This observation is intended to be ontologically
neutral. The emphasis here is on the "mode of access"
part and not on the "facts" themselves. In particular, it
does not entail the existence of a special class of facts,
"first-person facts," on the basis of an assumption of
ontological difference between facts of one's own consciousness and those of others.

46. Of course, technically speaking, it is not possible
to digest food in someone else's stomach either, but
"digestive epistemology" just does not seem to be a
fashionable topic these days.

47. Perhaps the most succinct expression of this difference is given in Sydney Shoemaker's question: "If
what I want when I drink fine wine is information about
its chemical properties, why don't I just read the label?"
(quoted in Dennett 1991, p. 383). There is a ready-
made answer to this question: It indeed *is* information
about the chemical properties of the wine that a con-
noisseur is interested in, but only if that information can
be accessed in a certain sensory modality—gustatorily,
not visually. Put in Fregean (1892) terms, reading the
label and sipping the wine would provide access to the

same referent via different "modes of presentation." Note, however, that Shoemaker's question remains not fully addressed until this answer is supplemented by a satisfactory account of something akin to modes of presentation regarding qualia.

48. Of course, not all publicly observable properties of an experience are intrinsic. There are often a great many extrinsic properties that determine what the experience is about that are equally accessible to the experiencer and the observer. Some think that all important properties of experiences, including those that determine an experience's phenomenal character, are extrinsic. See Dretske (1995).

49. There is a spectrum of positions with respect to these dichotomies that yield deep differences in the metaphysics of consciousness. Let me mention a few exemplary positions. Nagel (1979, 1986) takes the distinction between subjective and objective points of view as fundamental to important philosophical problems, such as personal identity, free will, and the mind-body problem. Velmans (1991) posits that first-person and third-person accounts of consciousness are complementary, but not reducible, to one another. In contrast, Dretske (1995) argues that as a "result of thinking about the mind in naturalistic terms, subjectivity becomes part of the objective order. For materialists, this is as it should be" (p. 65). This is in accord with an earlier statement by Lashley (1923), who claims that "the subjective and objective descriptions are not descriptions from two essentially different points of view, or descriptions of two different aspects, but simply descriptions of the same thing with different degrees of accuracy and detail" (p. 338). Papineau (1993) argues that it is a mistake to think that first-person and third-person thoughts refer to different entities on the basis of an epistemic difference, and calls it the "antipathetic fallacy." Finally, Perry (1979, 1993) examines the status of the first-person in relation to the role of indexicality in mind and language. Also, for two alternative approaches, see Hut and Shepard (1996) for a prioritization of the first-person over the third-person, and Smith (forthcoming) on how to get to the third-person from the first-person. For a scrutiny of the metaphysical foundations of such dichotomies as objectivity versus subjectivity, see among others Goodman (1978), Rorty (1979), Putnam (1981), and Smith (1996).

50. For a lucid analysis of James's account of the structure of "fringe consciousness," see Mangan (1993). Regarding works on the structure of phenomenal con-

sciousness, continental Europe was certainly more of a center than James's Cambridge. See, for instance, Brentano's chapter, "On the Unity of Consciousness," in his *Psychology from an Empirical Standpoint* (Brentano 1874), a work that slightly precedes James's *Principles of Psychology* (1890). A more detailed analysis of this sort was later given by Husserl. See, among others, his *Ideas: General Introduction to Pure Phenomenology* (1913) and *The Phenomenology of Internal Time-Consciousness* (1928). A more recent attempt along these lines, which comes from the analytic tradition, can be found in Searle (1992, chap. 6).

51. The idea of finding systematical bridging relations between the "mental" and the "physical" in order to establish explanatory hooks on consciousness was also the driving factor behind the emergence of psychophysics as a research program in the nineteenth century. This is exemplified in, for instance, Gustav Fechner's work where he sought ways of formalizing a logarithmic relation between the intensity of physical stimuli (measured in "physical units"), and the magnitude of felt sensory experience (measured in "psychological units") as reported by the subject. (Cf. Fechner 1966, see also Boring 1942 and Hilgard 1987, chap. 4.) The same idea was also operative in Gestalt psychology in the hypothesizing of a relation of isomorphism between "the structural characteristics of brain processes and of related phenomenal events" (Köhler 1971, p. 81; see also Köhler 1980 and Boring 1929, chap. 22).

52. John Searle presents a major attack on behaviorist theories of consciousness in his *Rediscovery of the Mind*, arguing for what he dubs "the principle of the independence of consciousness and behavior." His thesis is that "the capacity of the brain to cause consciousness is conceptually distinct from its capacity to cause motor behavior." One consequence he draws from this thesis is that "a system could have consciousness without behavior." Under certain qualifications, I find this view plausible. However, Searle goes further to claim that "*ontologically speaking, behavior, functional role, and causal relations are irrelevant to the existence of conscious mental phenomena*" (Searle 1992, p. 69; emphasis in original). This further and more encompassing claim does not directly follow from the weaker one. Moreover, it opens up a path the logical conclusion of which may turn into "epiphenomenalism": the view that consciousness plays no causal role itself, though it may be the causal effect of other phenomena. I find Searle's second thesis untenable and its consequence very

undesirable. I will come back to this issue in my discussion of epiphenomenalism and the possibility of zombies.

53. There are also scientifically documented cases where the relation between consciousness and externally observable behavior breaks down. I briefly discussed the phenomenon of "gaining consciousness' while under general anesthesia as one example. There are also several diseases of the nervous system that fall in the category of demyelinating neuropathies (diseases that result from loss of conduction of nerve impulses due to the lack of formation of myelin, a fatty substance essential to the insulation of axons in neurons), which result in the patient's gradual loss of reflexes and muscular strength, and hence behavior, while not resulting in substantial sensory changes (e.g., the Guillain-Barré syndrome). The ultimate state of such a patient involves very little outward behavior with no loss of consciousness, defying the behaviorist dogma. (Cf. Reeves 1981.) A moving account of a somewhat related nervous system disorder, encephalitis lethargica (commonly known as the sleeping sickness) was given in Oliver Sacks's popular book, *Awakenings*. Sacks's description of the victims of encephalitis lethargica is worth quoting at least for its literary value:

> Patients who suffered but survived an extremely severe somnolent/insomniac attack of [encephalitis lethargica] often failed to recover their original aliveness. They would be conscious and aware—yet not fully awake; they would sit motionless and speechless all day in their chairs, totally lacking energy, impetus, initiative, motive, appetite, affect or desire; they registered what went on about them with profound indifference. They neither conveyed nor felt the feeling of life; they were as insubstantial as ghosts, and as passive as zombies: von Economo compared them to extinct volcanoes. [However, . . .] one thing, and one alone, was (usually) spared amid the ravages of this otherwise engulfing disease: the "higher faculties"—intelligence, imagination, judgement, and humour. These were exempted—for better or worse. Thus these patients, some of whom had been thrust into the remotest or strangest extremities of human possibility, experienced their states with unsparing perspicacity, and retained the power to remember, to compare, to dissect, and to testify. Their fate, so to speak, was to become unique witnesses to a unique catastrophe. (Sacks 1974, pp. 9, 12)

54. Let me also mention that some philosophers think that the only legitimate sense of consciousness is phenomenal consciousness (e.g., Searle 1992, Flanagan 1992), while others believe only in access consciousness (e.g., Dennett 1991), and still others believe in phenomenal consciousness but try to account for it in causal, functional, or representational (i.e. "access-related") terms (e.g., Van Gulick 1988, Tye 1992, Dretske 1995).

55. Some of these ideas are briefly explored in Güzeldere and Aydede (forthcoming).

56. I will discuss absent qualia, an offspring of philosophical imagination that was conceived as a result of taking the "hard problem" (perhaps too) seriously, in discussing zombies below. Regarding the explanatory gap, here is a surprisingly contemporary expression of the problem from the nineteenth-century philosopher-psychologist Charles Mercier: "The change of consciousness never takes place without the change in the brain; the change in the brain never ... without the change in consciousness. But *why* the two occur together, or what the link is which connects them, we do not know, and most authorities believe that we never shall and can never know" (Mercier 1888, p. 11).

Note that the point Mercier is raising is very similar to the one expressed by John Tyndall in section I. A similar but more recent statement, though in a more determinedly pessimist tone, can be found in a rather unlikely source. Here is Freud on the "hard problem":

> We know two things concerning what we call our psyche or mental life: firstly, its bodily organ and scene of action, the brain (or nervous system), and secondly, our acts of consciousness, which are immediate data and cannot be more fully explained by any kind of description. Everything that lies between these two terminal points is unknown to us and, so far as we are aware, there is no direct relation between them. If it existed, it would at the most afford an exact localization of the processes of consciousness and would give us no help toward understanding them. (Freud 1949, pp. 13–14)

In contemporary philosophy of mind, Nagel's formulation of this problem has been most influential. The difficulties Nagel raises with respect to "bridging the explanatory gap" between things physiological and things phenomenal are also reflected in Kripke's attack against identity theory. Even though the latter follows a different path, using tools from philosophy of language, they arrive at very similar conclusions. (Cf.

Nagel 1974, 1979, 1986, and Kripke 1980.) The following quotation eloquently summarizes Nagel's (and presumably, Kripke's) position:

> We cannot directly see a necessary connection, if there is one, between phenomenological pain and a physiologically described brain state any more than we can directly see the necessary connection between increase in temperature and pressure of a gas at a constant volume. In the latter case the necessity of the connection becomes clear only when we descend to the level of molecular description: till then it appears as a contingent correlation. In the psychophysical case we have no idea whether there is such a deeper level or what it could be; but even if there is, the possibility that pain might be necessarily connected with a brain state at this deeper level does not permit us to conclude that pain might be directly analyzable in physical or even topic-neutral terms. (Nagel 1986, pp. 48–49)

57. Searle's position is not as straightforward as Nagel's, however. Although Searle talks about subjectivity as an irreducible ontological property unique to consciousness, he also maintains the following position, in a somewhat puzzling way, in the same book: "Consciousness is, thus, a biological feature of certain organisms, in *exactly the same sense* of 'biological' in which photosynthesis, mitosis, digestion, and reproduction are biological features of organisms.... One of the main aims of this book is to try to remove that obstacle, to bring consciousness back into the subject matter of science as a biological phenomenon *like any other*" (Searle 1992, pp. 93, 95; emphasis added).

58. As Wittgenstein somewhat sarcastically remarks:

> The feeling of an unbridgeable gulf between consciousness and brain-process: how does it come about that this does not come into the considerations of our ordinary life? This idea of a difference in kind is accompanied by slight giddiness.... When does this feeling occur in the present case? It is when I, for example, turn my attention in a particular way on to my own consciousness, and, astonished, say to myself: THIS is supposed to be produced by a process in the brain!—as it were clutching my forehead. But what can it mean to speak of "turning my attention on to my own consciousness"? This is surely the queerest thing there could be! (Wittgenstein 1958, §412, p. 124e)

59. Searle says: "For any artefact that we might build which had mental states equivalent to human mental states, the implementation of a computer program would not by itself be sufficient. Rather, the artefact would have to have powers equivalent to the powers of the human brain" (Searle 1984, p. 41).

Searle's argument is against functionalist accounts of consciousness. Even though he should not be taken to commit himself to a single specific underlying substance (i.e., neuronal structures), he nonetheless seems to think that consciousness is not medium-independent, at least so far as the causal powers of the medium go. This view seems to be based on the implicit assumption that there are causal powers that cannot be captured by functional organization, but it unfortunately leaves the central notion of causal power unexplicated.

60. Here is a noteworthy historical fact: Over a hundred years before Crick and Koch presented their findings on the 40–70 Hz phenomena, in 1879, Payton Spence published an essay in which he argued, on purely metaphysical grounds, that the basic form of consciousness consists of a constant alteration of conscious and unconscious states. But the alteration is so rapid that the subject never becomes aware of the discrete nature of her consciousness; she is under the illusion of having a continuous stream. Spence then speculated that there must be an underlying mechanism in the brain that is responsible for this alteration—something like a very rapid oscillation of neural tissue. In his own words:

> The simplest form of consciousness, or mental life, must consist in an alteration of a state of consciousness with a state of unconsciousness—a regular rhythmical revelation of the Affirmation, consciousness, by its Negation, unconsciousness, and *vice versa....* Perhaps it would be safer, for the present, to call it a pulsation, or an undulation in the brain, or a vibration of the molecules of the brain, paralleled in consciousness. This pulsation or vibration is, of course, very rapid; otherwise, we would not have to infer its existence, but would know it by perceiving the alterations of one state with another. (Spence 1879, p. 345)

The interesting part comes when M. M. Garver, a neurophysiologist of the same era, finds the idea plausible and follows up on it on experimental grounds. In particular, he investigates the neural basis of voluntary action (often associated with or regarded as an aspect of consciousness in those times, by psychologists including William James) and publishes his results in the *American Journal of Science* in 1880. According to Garver, mental activity is subserved by a cerebral oscillatory mechanism with a frequency range of 36–60 Hz. Garver hypothesizes that the change in the frequency of the neural oscillations correlates with minimum and maximum levels of mentation, which results in voluntary action. Garver formulates his hypothesis as follows: "The cerebral portion of the nervous system is continually varying in its activity, waxing and waning between certain limits, periods of maximum activity following periods of minimum activity at the rate of 36 to 60 times per second" (Garver 1880, p. 190).

At the end of his article, Garver claims that this pattern can be extended to accommodate Spence's hypothesis of alternating states of consciousness and suggests that the lower and upper limits of the oscillation frequency can be taken as the correlates of consciousness and unconsciousness, respectively.

While Spence and Garver cannot perhaps be said to be in pursuit of a solution to the binding problem, and thus have anticipated the Crick and Koch hypothesis over a hundred years ahead of its time, I find the similarity in the basic idea of seeking a neural oscillatory basis for consciousness fascinating. Except a passing remark by William James in his discussion of the continuity of consciousness (James 1950, p. 220, footnote), Spence and Garver's work seems to have gone, so far as I could trace, unnoticed to date.

61. The idea of localized functions in the brain precedes James's work, and goes back at least to the once-too-popular phrenology of Franz Gall in early 1800s (see, for instance, Ackerknecht and Vallois 1956). Jean Baptiste Bouillaud, in 1825, proposed a hemispheric asymmetry in brain function, but it was Carl Wernicke and Paul Broca who made the greatest contribution to the idea of modularity in the brain. Wernicke hypothesized that two particular areas in the left hemisphere of the brain (roughly, the left frontal lobe and the posterior cortex), which later became known as Broca's and Wernicke's areas, were responsible for language production and language understanding, respectively. For an elemental neuropsychological account of aphasias that result from damage to these areas and other related matters, see Kolb and Whishaw (1990).

62. For a comprehensive survey of similar neuropsychological disorders, see Farah (1995). I discuss some philosophical issues involved in the phenomenon of blindsight against the background of Block's access versus phenomenal consciousness distinction in Güzeldere (1995e).

63. The precursors to Dennett's *Cartesian Theater* metaphor can be found in the writings of Gilbert Ryle and U. T. Place. Ryle (1949) characterized and criticized the Cartesian notion of the mind as "a secondary theater in which the episodes enacted enjoy the supposed status of 'the mental'" (p. 158). Similarly, Place (1956) called it a mistake to suppose that "when the subject describes his experience, when he describes how things look, sound, smell, taste, or feel to him, he is describing the literal properties of objects and events on a peculiar sort of internal cinema or television screen, usually referred to in the modern psychological literature as the 'phenomenal field'" (p. 107). (The view that Ryle and Place criticize also constitutes a particular family of *sense-data* theories of perception that were quite popular at the time.)

Interestingly, while the metaphor of mind as an inner theater never occurs explicitly in the writings of Descartes (so far as I could tell), it can be found in a vivid passage in Hume (in his discussion of personal identity): "The mind is a kind of theatre, where several perceptions successively make their appearance; pass, re-pass, glide away, and mingle in an infinite variety of postures and situations." But Hume is also careful not to endorse, in virtue of using this metaphor, the kind of ontological conclusion Descartes is criticized as holding: "The comparison of the theatre must not mislead us. They are the successive perceptions only, that constitute the mind; nor have we the most distant notion of the place, where these scenes are represented, or of the materials, of which it is compos'd." (Hume 1955, Book I, IV:V, 85).

64. Another issue related to the Where question has to do with lateralization of brain function in light of the "split-brain" research of the last few decades. The performance of commissurotomy on humans (proposed and initiated by surgeon Joseph Bogen in 1960) to control interhemispheric spread of epilepsy produced a number of patients in whom individual investigation of specialized hemispheric capabilities became possible. The research on such patients (initially pursued by psychobiologist Roger Sperry and his collaborators) revealed a number of interesting facts about hemispheric specialization and resulted in a sizeable scientific literature, as well as a huge corpus of popular psychology writing on the so-called left-brain versus right-brain

distinction with regard to personality types, social behavior, and so on. One of the major results that came out of the commissurotomy research is the hypothesis proposed and defended by (among others) Michael Gazzaniga (1993), that human cognition as well as consciousness (in the sense of awareness of experience) are subserved by special brain circuitry normally located in the left hemisphere. For an account of the early work on commissurotomy, see Gazzaniga (1970). Galin (1974) explores the implications of hemispheric specialization for psychiatry. For a comprehensive collection of current research results in human neuropsychology, including articles on modularity of mental function and hemispheric specialization, see Gazzaniga et al. (1995).

65. It is interesting to note that this is a junction at which some upholders of the "pro-qualia intuition" meet on common ground with the most indoctrinated qualia skeptics, such as the behaviorist psychologists for whom exorcising qualia out of the scope of psychology was a primary goal. Notice, for instance, the similarity between Jackson's (1982) position (who characterizes himself as a "qualia freak," p. 127), and the position defended by Edward Tolman: "[Regarding visual perception in others] we never learn whether it 'feels' like our 'red' or our 'green' or our 'gray', or whether, indeed, its 'feel' is perhaps sui generis and unlike any of our own.... Whether your 'raw feels' are or are not like mine, you and I shall never discover. Your color 'feels' may be the exact complementaries of mine, but, if so, neither of us will ever find it out, provided only that your discriminations and my discriminations agree.... If there be 'raw feels' correlated with such discriminanda-expectations, these 'raw feels' are by very definition 'private' and not capable of scientific treatment. And we may leave the question as to whether they exist, and what to do about them, if they do exist, to other disciplines than psychology—for example, to logic, epistemology, and metaphysics. And whatever the answers of these other disciplines, we, as mere psychologists, need not be concerned" (Tolman 1967, pp. 252–253).

Whether this surprising "meeting of minds" between such arch-opponents as behaviorist psychologists and a certain brand of qualia defenders on presumably the very point of contention between them speaks in favor of the former or the latter party (if either), I leave open to the judgment of the reader.

66. William James (1950a), who characterizes consciousness as a "fighter for ends," makes the following statement (largely in agreement with Herbert Spencer 1891, 1898) in support of the causal construal and the evolutionary relevance of consciousness:

It is a well-known fact that pleasures are generally associated with beneficial, pains with detrimental experiences.... These coincidences are due, not to any pre-established harmony, but to the mere action of natural selection which would certainly kill off in the long-run any breed of creatures to whom the fundamentally noxious experience seemed enjoyable. An animal that should take pleasure in a feeling of suffocation would, if that pleasure were efficacious enough to make him immerse his head in water, enjoy a longevity of four or five minutes. But if the pleasures and pains have no efficacy, one does not see why the most noxious acts, such as burning, might not give thrills of delight, and the most necessary ones, such as breathing, cause agony.... The conclusion that [consciousness] is useful is ... quite justifiable. But, if it is useful, it must be so through its causal efficaciousness.

James's conclusion is that "the study *a posteriori* of the *distribution* of consciousness shows it to be exactly such as we might expect in an organ added for the sake of steering a nervous system grown too complex to regulate itself" (pp. 141, 143–144).

67. See also Kitcher (1979) and Revonsuo (1994) for related points.

68. Precursors to Nagel's thinking on this issue can be found in the writings of B. A. Farrell and Timothy Sprigge. Even though it was made famous by Nagel, the original formulation of the question "what is it like to be a bat?" goes back to Farrell's somewhat neglected essay, "Experience" (1950). In discussing the issue of experiential knowledge, Farrell imagines a Martian visitor about whose sensory capacities we obtain all the information there is. According to Farrell, "We would probably *still* want to say: 'I wonder what it would be like to be a Martian.'" He continues: "There *is* something more to be learned about the Martian, and that is what his experience is like." Farrell then extends the question to babies and mice, as well as an opium smoker, and finally a bat: "I wonder what it would be like to be, and hear like, a bat" (pp. 34–35).

The lessons Farrell draws out of his ruminations are quite the opposite of Nagel's conclusions, however. It is rather Sprigge (1971) who makes the connection between the "what it is like" aspect of experience and physicalism's difficulty with accommodating it in the particular way Nagel problematizes the issue: "When one imagines another's conscious state, there is no conclusive way of checking up whether one has done so correctly or not.... Presuming that the object (that is, at least normally, the organism) with which one is concerned, is indeed conscious, then *being that organism* will have a certain definite complex quality at every waking moment.... Physical science makes no reference to qualities of this kind. Thus consciousness is that which one characterises when one tries to answer the question what it is or might be like to *be* a certain object in a certain situation" (p. 168).

69. Lycan (1997b) also makes a similar point: "The phrase 'what it's like' is more sinning than sinned against; nothing whatever is clarified or explained by reference to it, and it itself is not only badly in need of explanation, in general, but at least three-ways ambiguous in particular" (p. 176).

70. See Nagel (1974, 1979, 1986) for a full range of problems that involve subjectivity. See Lycan (1990), Biro (1991), Akins (1993), and Dretske (1995), among others, for deflationary responses. See also Nagel (1983) for a discussion of how subjectivity figures in the problem of self, without ever touching on qualia, and Perry (forthcoming) for a penetrating analysis and critique of Nagel's account.

71. For Jackson's formulation, see Jackson (1982, 1986). For various critiques, see Nemirow (1980), Churchland (1989), Lewis (1990), Dennett (1991, chap. 10), Van Gulick (1993), Loar (1990), Harman (1993b), Dretske (1995, chap. 3), and Perry (1995). For a related empirical study on the conceptual representation of colors in the blind and the color-blind, see Shepard and Cooper (1992).

One of the earlier formulations of the knowledge argument can be found in C. D. Broad's thought experiment about the archangel who knows all about chemistry but lacks the sense of smell. Broad sets up the problem as follows:

> Would there be any theoretical limit to the deduction of the properties of chemical elements and compounds if a mechanistic theory of chemistry were true? Yes. Take any ordinary statement, such as we find in chemistry books; e.g., "Nitrogen and Hydrogen combine when an electric discharge is passed through a mixture of the two. The resulting compound contains three atoms of Hydrogen to one

of Nitrogen; it is a gas readily soluble in water, and possessed of a pungent and characteristic smell." If the mechanistic theory be true the archangel could deduce from his knowledge of the microscopic structure of atoms all these facts but the last. He would know exactly what the microscopic structure of ammonia must be; but he would be totally unable to predict that a substance with this structure must smell as ammonia does when it gets into the human nose. The utmost that he could predict on this subject would be that certain changes would take place in the mucous membrane, the olfactory nerves and so on. But he could not possibly know that these changes would be accompanied by the appearance of a smell in general or of the peculiar smell of ammonia in particular, unless someone told him so or he had smelled it for himself. (Broad 1962, p. 71)

Similarly, an early formulation of the knowledge argument, as well as an antecedent of the Nemirow-Lewis critique, appears in Feigl's discussion of "cognitive roles of acquaintance." Feigl asks: "What is it that the blind man cannot know concerning color qualities?" and proposes the following answer:

> If we assume complete physical predictability of human behavior, i.e., as much predictability as the best developed physical science of the future could conceivably provide, then it is clear that the blind man or the Martian would lack only *acquaintance* and *knowledge by acquaintance* in certain areas of the realm of qualia. Lacking acquaintance means not having those experiential qualia; and the consequent lack of knowledge by acquaintance simply amounts to being unable to label the qualia with terms used previously by the subject (or by some other subject) when confronted with their occurrence in direct experience. Now, mere *having* or *living through* is not *knowledge* in any sense. "Knowledge by acquaintance," however, as we understand it here, is propositional, it does make truth claims.

Feigl then goes on to suggest, anticipating many of the present-day critiques of the knowledge argument, that the blind person (or Jackson's fictional color scientist, Mary) does not lack any knowledge per se; all he or she lacks is a particular mode of knowing the same facts as do normally sighted people: "What one person *has* and *knows by acquaintance* may be identical with what someone else knows by description. The color experiences of the man who can see are known to him by acquaintance, but the blind man can have inferential knowledge, or knowledge by description *about* those same experiences" (Feigl 1967, p. 68). A related puzzle, based again on a thought-experiment, was posed as a "jocose problem" to John Locke by William Molyneux, an amateur philosopher, in a letter dated 1693: "Suppose a man *born* blind, and now adult, and taught by his *touch* to distinguish between a cube and a sphere of the same metal, and nighly of the same bigness, so as to tell, when he felt one and the other, which is the cube, which the sphere. Suppose then the cube and sphere placed on a table, and the blind man be made to see: *quaere*, whether *by his sight, before he touched them*, he could now distinguish and tell which is the globe, which the cube?" (Quoted in Locke (1959), Book II, Chapter IX, pp. 186–187.) As such, Molyneux's question transforms the inquiry of whether non-experiential facts can yield knowledge of experiential facts (in the knowledge argument) into a puzzle about *intersensory* translation— whether tactile facts can yield knowledge of visual facts ("facts" taken broadly). Locke's negative answer to this question was in agreement with Molyneux's opinion. But others disagreed, and Molyneux's question became one of the central topics of contention among such philosophers as Berkeley, Leibniz, Reid, Diderot, and Voltaire, in the greater context of the controversies over innateness and abstract ideas. See Morgan (1977) and Sanford (1983) for further exposition and discussion of the related issues.

72. For a classical treatment of the identity theory, see Sellars (1964). For recent arguments in its defense, see Enç (1983) and Hill (1991). A thus far unmentioned but related concept that has played a significant role in the philosophy of mind over the past few decades is *supervenience* (presumably imported from Rom Hare's work in ethics [1952] by Donald Davidson 1970). The thesis that the mental supervenes on the physical is put forth as a better materialist solution to the mind-body problem than the identity thesis. The supervenience thesis is roughly that the mental character of a state or event is wholly determined by its physical profile, such that there cannot be a change in the former without a change in the latter. Put differently, sameness in the (subvening) physical properties is hypothesized to guarantee sameness in the (supervening) mental properties.

But the status of the supervenience thesis vis-à-vis the mind-body problem, especially with regard to phenomenal consciousness, remains controversial. Are

supervenient properties ontologically distinct (autonomously emergent) from physical properties, for instance? Or (otherwise) does supervenience boil down to old-fashioned identity? How are we to explain the *nature* of the supervenience relation itself? Given the wide variety of possible supervenience relations (for example, weak versus strong, local versus global), there is a vast and technically complicated literature in this area, but there exist no clear-cut received views that are taken to unanimously answer all these questions. For a systematic and thorough exploration of the supervenience thesis in all its different characterizations, see Jaegwon Kim's essays collected in Kim (1993). Two other useful collections that contain representatives of contemporary theorizing on supervenience are Beckermann, Flohr, and Kim (1992), and Savellos and Yalçın (1995). See also McLaughlin (1989) for a discussion that relates supervenience to the question of epiphenomenalism, and McLaughlin (1992) for a thorough exposition of the thought of British emergentists in which one can find numerous clues for the present supervenience debates. In addition to philosophy of mind, notions of supervenience, emergence, and different kinds of reduction have been central to discussions in philosophy of biology, particularly during the first half of this century. See Brandon (1996) for an exposition of these issues that also ties them to debates in contemporary biology, and Harris (1993) for an exploration of the relations between the natures and the study of mind and life in philosophy, psychology, and biology.

73. It is interesting to note, by the way, that the word *consciousness* was hardly ever present in the philosophical literature around the time of functionalism, which was instead brewing with the term *qualia* and, to a lesser extent, terms like *raw feels* and *phenomenal aspect of consciousness*. In the 1990s, in contrast, many of the same old problems have gained new interest and impetus (perhaps from slightly but essentially similar perspectives) within a terminology populated with the magic word *consciousness* and its derivatives. The reasons for this terminological change probably lie partly outside philosophy, for example in the wide acceptance of the term *consciousness* into other fields with which philosophy interacts.

74. There is a sizeable literature regarding the absent qualia argument. Some of the most influential thought experiments that support the possibility of absent qualia are due to Block (1978, 1980b) and Block and Fodor (1980). See Shepard (1993) for a recent discussion in the

context of color vision and evolutionary theory. Shoe-maker (1975, 1981a) presents an eloquent defense of functionalism against the absent qualia arguments. See also Dretske (1995) who raises the possibility of absent qualia in an externalist context in relation to Donald Davidson's (1987) "swampman" argument, and Tye (1995) for a representationalist critique of absent qualia. For further discussion, see Lycan (1981), Levin (1985), Graham and Stephens (1985), White (1986), Fox (1989), Levine (1989), Horgan (1987), and Hardcastle (1996).

One of the most commonly cited absent qualia arguments is based on Block's (1978) "Chinese Nation" scenario, designed to "embarrass all versions of functionalism" by showing that functionalism is guilty of "classifying systems that lack mentality as having mentality" (p. 275). Block asks us to imagine the functional simulation of a human brain by the Chinese nation by connecting each of the billion inhabitants of China in appropriate ways through radio links, and having them communicate from a distance like neurons in a brain and thereby animate an artificial body for a certain period of time. According to Block, while this China-body system is "nomologically possible" and "it could be functionally equivalent to [a human being] for a short time," it is doubtful "whether it has any mental states at all—especially whether it has ... 'qualitative states', 'raw feels', or 'immediate phenomenological qualities'" (pp. 276–278). Block's point is to establish the short-comings of functional characterizations of qualia, by appealing to intuitions that he takes as common sensical, such as the intuition that such "distributed minds" are absurd.

A similar intuition was commonly employed in discussions regarding the unity of mind versus the divisibility of matter with the aim of embarrassing all forms of materialism in early modern philosophy. For example, the eighteenth century English theologian Samuel Clarke appeals to the absurdity of the distributed-minds intuition in a piece of hypothetical reasoning, similar to Block's, to make a case for the "immateriality and natural immortality of the soul" as follows: "That the soul cannot possibly be material is moreover demonstrable from the single consideration even of bare sense and consciousness itself. For suppose three, or three hundred, particles of matter, at a mile, or at any given distance, one from another; is it possible that all those separate parts should in that state be one individual conscious being?" But Clarke then takes his argument a step further to apply it to human beings: "Suppose then

all these particles brought together into one system, so as to touch one another; will they thereby, or by any motion or composition whatsoever, become any whit less truly distinct Beings, than they were at the greatest distance? How then can their being disposed in any possible system, make them one individual conscious being?" (Clarke 1707, p. 82)

75. The origins of this problem go back indeed to a puzzle about visual experience, described by John Locke a few centuries ago:

> Neither would it carry any imputation of falsehood to our simple ideas, if by the different structure of our organs it were so ordered, that the *same object should produce in several men's minds different ideas* at the same time; e.g. if the idea that a violet produced in one man's mind by his eyes were the same that a marigold produced in another man's, and *vice versa*. For, since this could never be known, because one man's mind could not pass into another man's body, to perceive what appearances were produced by those organs: neither the ideas hereby, nor the names, would be at all confounded, or any falsehood be in either. For all things that had the texture of a violet, producing constantly the idea that he called blue, and those which had the texture of a marigold, producing constantly the idea which he constantly called yellow, whatever those appearances were in his mind; he would be able as regularly to distinguish things for his use by those appearances, and understand and signify those distinctions marked by the name blue and yellow, as if the appearances or ideas in his mind received from those two flowers were exactly the same with the ideas in other men's minds (Locke 1959, bk. II, chap. 32, §15, p. 520).

There are also several positions with respect to the inverted spectrum argument. Here is a simple set: Block (1978) and Block and Fodor (1980) raise the possibility of inverted spectrum against functionalism, and Block (1990) presents an original twist on the same problem as a reply to Harman (1990), who argues against inverted spectrum on externalist grounds. Shoemaker (1975, 1981b, 1991) is more lenient toward accepting the possibility of inverted spectrum compared to his rejection of the possibility of absent qualia, but he presents an argument on how to accommodate qualia inversion within a broadly functionalist framework. However, see also Levine (1988), who argues that absent qualia and inverted spectrum stand or fall together as logical possibilities against functionalism. Dretske (1995) regards inverted spectrum as a problem for functionalism but not for representationalism (and hence, not for materialism in general). Tye (1995) argues for the conclusion that is somewhat similar to Shoemaker's: spectrum inversion is possible in narrow functional duplicates, but this does not constitute a problem for wide functionalism (that Tye defends).

76. A similarly externalist theory is put forth by Gilbert Harman (1990) where qualia are identified with intentional properties, as well as by Michael Tye (1995). David Armstrong had earlier suggested identifying qualia (what he called "secondary qualities") with properties of physical objects in his discussion of "Realist Reductionism" (Armstrong 1993, chap. 12, 270–290). Clues for these positions can be found in Elizabeth Anscombe's discussion of the intentional nature of sensations (Anscombe 1965).

77. Perhaps a caveat about the particular brand of epiphenomenalism and zombiehood I am referring to is in order here. Epiphenomenalism about phenomenal consciousness is, of course, different from epiphenomenalism about the mind in general. Discussions about epiphenomenalism earlier this century generally assumed the latter kind (see, for instance, Broad 1962). In the contemporary literature, however, the focus has somewhat shifted. Probably largely due to the advent of functionalist and computational-representational theories of mind in a materialist framework, many today take intentional states, such as beliefs and judgments, as contentful internal structures in the brain (see, for example, Fodor 1987). As such, no one thinks that beliefs, *qua* such physical structures, lack causal properties. The controversy is rather on whether their content (semantics) has a causal role in the explanation of behavior (cf. Dretske 1988).

But the real hot spot of the epiphenomenalism debate has to do with phenomenal consciousness—whether qualia play any role in the otherwise causally characterizable economy of our mental lives. Note, after all, that while there is a vast literature on the possibility of absent qualia, no one seems to be worrying about the possibility of "absent beliefs" or "absent judgments." There seems to be a crucial difference between beliefs and pains: while it is considered legitimate to *attribute* beliefs to someone who behaves in ways that can be explained by belief-attributions of the relevant sort, it is considered very problematic to so attribute pains, be-

cause the essence of pains, the reasoning goes, is not attributable (by a third party) but rather *accessible* in a privileged way (through the first-person perspective). There is something it is like to have pains, but there is nothing it is like to believe that there is no greatest prime number (or even that one is in pain). It is this difference that warrants epiphenomenalism, in the present literature, as a possibility with respect to pains, but not beliefs (about prime numbers, one's pains, or anything else).

Accordingly, under the stipulation of appropriate environmental and historical conditions, it is generally regarded as a possibility that a physical replica of a human being can lack all qualia, while not lacking beliefs or judgments (or other such intentional states). This is the possibility of the modern zombie that has center stage in debates about phenomenal consciousness. Ned Block (1995) calls such replicas *phenomenal zombies*: "the familiar ... robots that think but don't feel" (p. 234). Or, as David Chalmers (1996) describes: "My zombie twin ... will be psychologically identical to me. He will be perceiving the trees outside, in the functional sense, and tasting the chocolate, in the psychological sense [similar to its ordinary twin *modulo* qualia]. ... He will be awake, able to report the contents of his internal states, able to focus attention in various places, and so on. It is just that none of this functioning will be accompanied by any real conscious experience. There will be no phenomenal feel. There is nothing it is like to be a zombie" (p. 95).

It is important to notice that zombies, construed as such, are taken to be in possession of all sorts of beliefs, thoughts, and judgments that their human twins typically have, including the self-ascribed ones. As Chalmers (1993) states: "Zombie Dave's beliefs may not be colored by the usual phenomenological tinges, but it seems reasonable to say that they are nevertheless beliefs. Beliefs, unlike qualia, seem to be characterized primarily by the role that they play in the mind's causal economy." Accordingly, the zombie twin, too, takes aspirin because he *thinks* he has a headache, wants anesthetics at the dentist chair because he *believes* the root canal will hurt, and so on. It is just that all his beliefs and judgments about his own qualia are systematically false. Nothing hurts in him, even if he sincerely believes he has a splitting headache. Accordingly, we should not be motivated to put him under anaesthesia when his tooth is being drilled, despite all his screams, if it is the pain quale that matters.

Put differently, what distinguishes this kind of a zombie from its human twin is the *stipulated* ever-presence of a gap between the "appearance" and "reality" of the zombie's qualitative states—what qualia he judges himself to have versus what qualia he really has—and nothing much else. (Note that something like an "appearance-reality" distinction is required in order to coherently conceptualize the possibility of a zombie.) As such, there is a psychologically significant and explanatorily important sense in which things *seem* (i.e., are judged, thought, believed, expected, noticed, ... to be) a certain way to the zombie twin.

Consequently, to the extent that nonqualitative intentional states, (including self-ascribed beliefs about one's own qualitative states) are constitutive of a first-person perspective (cf. Chisholm 1981), the zombie can be said to have such a perspective (albeit a systematically misguided one). A zombie's life is not, after all, completely devoid of all mental elements. He only lacks an important component of an otherwise intact epistemic perspective. After all, it is in virtue of having such a perspective that receiving anaesthetics at the dentist chair *seems* to matter to the zombie twin, even if his preferences are entirely on the basis of false self-ascribed beliefs (about his own non-existent pain qualia). It is this characterization of zombiehood that is typically invoked in contemporary debates, and I will confine my discussion accordingly throughout the rest of this chapter.

78. Notice that this view, as such, does not deny that we are conscious. It comes close, however, in positing that our being conscious, in itself, makes no difference—hence the path to zombiehood.

79. James (1879) is a vigorous response to Huxley. See also Capek (1954) for a commentary on this exchange.

80. As far as I could trace, the term *zombie* enters the philosophical vocabulary with Kirk (1974) in an argument against materialism. For other arguments that defend the intuition in favor of the possibility of zombiehood, see Block (1978), Block and Fodor (1980), Searle (1992), and Chalmers (1996). For counterarguments, see Lewis (1972) and Shoemaker (1975), as well as Kirk (1994). For an expression of philosophical intolerance for epiphenomenalism and the possibility of zombies, see Dennett (1991, chp. 10). Güzeldere (1995d) distinguishes among physiological, functional, and merely behavioral zombies, and briefly examines their respective underlying metaphysical assumptions. (See

Journal of Consciousness Studies (2:4, 1995) for a symposium on zombies based on Moody 1994).

81. Here is Dennett (1979) on describing the phenomenology of one's own experience: "We are all, I take it, unshakably sure that we are each in a special position to report, or to know, or to witness or experience a set of something-or-others we may call, as neutrally as possible, *elements of our own conscious experience....* Propositional episodes ... comprise our streams of consciousness by embodying our semantic intentions of the moment, by being the standards against which we correct, or would correct, any failures of execution were we to utter anything at the time.... These are ... thinkings that p. ... I call them judgments.... Such judgments *exhaust* our immediate consciousness, that our individual streams of consciousness consist of nothing but such propositional episodes. My view, put bluntly, is that there is no phenomenological manifold in any such relation to our reports. There are the public reports we issue, and then there are the episodes of our propositional awareness, our judgments, and then there is—so far as *introspection* is concerned—darkness" (pp. 93–95).

This quotation probably represents a position at a far end of the spectrum of views on the nature of inner experience. There are, of course, many midway views between the positions that occupy the two endpoints. For instance, one can agree with "friends of qualia" that there *is* something crucial to theorize about under the term "phenomenal consciousness" distinct from "episodes of propositional awareness and judgments," but maintain that the way they choose to theorize about it is misguided.

82. The disagreement is not only between those who believe in phenomenal consciousness and those who deny it; it pervades the community of the supporters of this very notion. For instance, Block claims that Searle, in an attempt to point to consciousness, confounds too many senses of the term. As Block says, "It is important to point properly." But who has *the* omniscient pointer?

83. Jaegwon Kim (1996) makes a similar point with respect to mind in general: "Saving mentality while losing causality doesn't seem to amount to saving anything worth saving. For what good is the mind if it has no causal powers?" (p. 237). Or, to transform a point Fred Dretske (1988) makes with respect to the explanatory role of content into one about phenomenal consciousness (with apologies), "if having a mind is having *this*

kind of qualia (which don't *do* anything), one may as well not have a mind" (p. 80).

However, this position should be distinguished from eliminativism about consciousness, defended, for instance, by Rey (1988). Rey's suggestion is to do away with the largely folk-theoretic notion of consciousness because it contains Cartesian elements and plays no useful causal-explanatory role. I am suggesting (and probably Kim and Dretske would agree), in contrast, that because we do *not* want to do away with our common sense notion of consciousness (or, at least, a significant part of it), we need to seek to secure a genuine role for it in the causal web of the world.

84. Put differently, I am essentially in agreement with David Lewis (1980) on a point he makes regarding the status of pain that I take as an objection to the *segregationist intuition*: "Only if you believe on independent grounds that considerations of causal role and physical realization have no bearing on whether a state is pain should you say that they have no bearing on how a state feels" (p. 222). Along these lines, see Humphrey (1992); see also Hardin (1987, 1988) for an important attempt to deflate the explanatory gap between the causal and phenomenal aspects of consciousness in the case of visual perception and color qualia.

85. The Fodor quote is from Fodor 1987, p. 156. Fodor holds a much more pessimistic opinion regarding the prospects for a theory of consciousness in comparison to a theory of rationality, however. Regarding rationality, he thinks that "certain residual technical difficulties" notwithstanding, "we are (maybe) on the verge of solving a great mystery about the mind: *How is rationality mechanically possible?*" (Fodor 1987, pp. 156, 21). Regarding consciousness, here is what he says: "Nobody has the slightest idea how anything material could be conscious. Nobody even knows what it would be like to have the slightest idea about how anything material could be conscious. So much for the philosophy of consciousness" (Fodor 1992, p. 5).

Perhaps then, one thinks, Fodor should consider starting to think about consciousness and give those working in the field a helping hand. But similarly gloomy sentiments are expressed by Block (1994), a prominent figure in the consciousness literature, as well: "The notable fact is that in the case of thought, we actually have more than one substantive research programme, and their proponents are busy fighting it out, comparing which research program handles which phenomena best. But in the case of consciousness, we have nothing—zilch—worthy of being called a research program, nor are there any substantive proposals about how to go about starting one.... Researchers are *stumped*.... No one has yet come up with a theoretical perspective that uses these data to narrow the explanatory gap, even a little bit" (p. 211).

My ultimate conclusion, expressed in the last paragraph of this chapter and hopefully substantiated by the exposition presented thus far, differs from both.

References to the Introduction appear on pages 807–816.

I STREAM OF CONSCIOUSNESS

1 The Stream of Consciousness

William James

The order of our study must be analytic. We are now prepared to begin the introspective study of the adult consciousness itself. Most books adopt the so-called synthetic method. Starting with "simple ideas of sensation," and regarding these as so many atoms, they proceed to build up the higher states of mind out of their "association," "integration," or "fusion," as houses are built by the agglutination of bricks. This has the didactic advantages which the synthetic method usually has. But it commits one beforehand to the very questionable theory that our higher states of consciousness are compounds of units; and instead of starting with what the reader directly knows, namely his total concrete states of mind, it starts with a set of supposed "simple ideas" with which he has no immediate acquaintance at all, and concerning whose alleged interactions he is much at the mercy of any plausible phrase. On every ground, then, the method of advancing from the simple to the compound exposes us to illusion. All pedants and abstractionists will naturally hate to abandon it. But a student who loves the fullness of human nature will prefer to follow the "analytic" method, and to begin with the most concrete facts, those with which he has a daily acquaintance in his own inner life. The analytic method will discover in due time the elementary parts, if such exist, without danger of precipitate assumption. The reader will bear in mind that our own chapters on sensation have dealt mainly with the physiological conditions thereof. They were put first as a mere matter of convenience, because incoming currents come first. *Psychologically* they might better have come last. Pure sensations were described ... as processes which in adult life are well-nigh unknown, and nothing was said which could for a moment lead the reader to suppose that they were the *elements of composition* of the higher states of mind.

The Fundamental Fact

The first and foremost concrete fact which every one will affirm to belong to his inner experience is the fact that *consciousness of some sort goes on.* *"States of mind" succeed each other in him.* If we could say in English "it thinks," as we say "it rains" or "it blows," we should be stating the fact most simply and with the minimum of assumption. As we cannot, we must simply say that *thought goes on.*

Four Characters in Consciousness

How does it go on? We notice immediately four important characters in the process, of which it shall be the duty of the present chapter to treat in a general way:

1. Every "state" tends to be part of a personal consciousness.

2. Within each personal consciousness states are always changing.

3. Each personal consciousness is sensibly continuous.

4. It is interested in some parts of its object to the exclusion of others, and welcomes or rejects—*chooses* from among them, in a word—all the while.

In considering these four points successively, we shall have to plunge *in medias res* as regards our nomenclature and use psychological terms which can only be adequately defined in later chapters of the book. But everyone knows what the terms mean in a rough way; and it is only in a rough way that we are now to take them. This chapter is like a painter's first charcoal sketch upon his canvas, in which no niceties appear.

When I say *every "state" or "thought" is part of a personal consciousness,* "personal consciousness" is one of the terms in question. Its meaning we know so long as no one asks us to define it, but to give an accurate account of it is the most difficult of philosophic tasks....

In this room—this lecture-room, say—there are a multitude of thoughts, yours and mine, some of which cohere mutually, and some not. They are as little each-for-itself and reciprocally independent as they are all-belonging-together. They are neither: no one of them is separate, but each belongs with certain others and with none beside. My thought belongs with *my* other thoughts, and your thought with *your* other thoughts. Whether anywhere in the room there be a *mere* thought, which is nobody's thought, we have no means of ascertaining, for we have no experience of its like. The only states of consciousness that we naturally deal with are found in personal consciousnesses, minds, selves, concrete particular I's and you's.

Each of these minds keeps its own thoughts to itself. There is no giving or bartering between them. No thought even comes into direct *sight* of a thought in another personal consciousness than its own. Absolute insulation, irreducible pluralism, is the law. It seems as if the elementary psychic fact were not *thought* or *this thought* or *that thought*, but *my thought*, every thought being *owned*. Neither contemporaneity, nor proximity in space, nor similarity of quality and content are able to fuse thoughts together which are sundered by this barrier of belonging to different personal minds. The breaches between such thoughts are the most absolute breaches in nature. Every one will recognize this to be true, so long as the existence of *something* corresponding to the term "personal mind" is all that is insisted on, without any particular view of its nature being implied. On these terms the personal self rather than the thought might be treated as the immediate datum in psychology. The universal conscious fact is not "feelings and thoughts exist," but "I think" and "I feel." No psychology, at any rate, can question

the *existence* of personal selves. Thoughts connected as we feel them to be connected are *what we mean* by personal selves. The worst a psychology can do is so to interpret the nature of these selves as to rob them of their *worth*.

Consciousness is in constant change. I do not mean by this to say that no one state of mind has any duration—even if true, that would be hard to establish. What I wish to lay stress on is this, that *no state once gone can recur and be identical with what it was before.* Now we are seeing, now hearing; now reasoning, now willing; now recollecting, now expecting; now loving, now hating; and in a hundred other ways we know our minds to be alternately engaged. But all these are complex states, it may be said, produced by combination of simpler ones;—do not the simpler ones follow a different law? Are not the *sensations* which we get from the same object, for example, always the same? Does not the same piano-key, struck with the same force, make us hear in the same way? Does not the same grass give us the same feeling of green, the same sky the same feeling of blue, and do we not get the same olfactory sensation no matter how many times we put our nose to the same flask of cologne? It seems a piece of metaphysical sophistry to suggest that we do not; and yet a close attention to the matter shows that *there is no proof that an incoming current ever gives us just the same bodily sensation twice.*

What is got twice *is the same* OBJECT. We hear the same *note* over and over again; we see the same *quality* of green, or smell the same objective perfume, or experience the same *species* of pain. The realities, concrete and abstract, physical and ideal, whose permanent existence we believe in, seem to be constantly coming up again before our thought, and lead us, in our carelessness, to suppose that our "ideas" of them are the same ideas.... inveterate is our habit of simply using our sensible impressions as stepping-stones to pass over to the recognition of the realities whose presence they reveal. The grass out of the window now looks to me of the same green in the sun as in the shade, and yet a painter would have to paint one part of it dark brown, another part bright yellow, to give its real sensational effect. We take no heed, as a rule, of the different way in which the same things look and sound and smell at different distances and under different circumstances. The sameness of the *things* is what we are concerned to ascertain; and any sensations that assure us of that will probably be considered in a rough way to be the same with each other. This is what makes off-hand testimony about the subjective identity of different sensations well-nigh worthless as a proof of the fact. The entire history of what is called Sensation is a commentary on our inability to tell whether two sensible qualities received apart are exactly alike. What appeals to our attention far more than the absolute quality of an impression is its *ratio* to whatever other impressions we may have at the same time. When everything is dark a somewhat less dark sensation makes us see an object white. Helmholtz calculates that the white marble painted in a picture representing an architectural view by moonlight is, when seen by daylight, from ten to twenty thousand times brighter than the real moonlit marble would be.

Such a difference as this could never have been *sensibly* learned; it had to be inferred from a series of indirect considerations. These make us believe that our sensibility is altering all the time, so that the same object cannot easily give us the same sensation over again. We feel things differently accordingly as we are sleepy or awake, hungry or full, fresh or tired; differently at night and in the morning, differently in summer and in winter; and above all, differently in childhood, manhood, and old age. And yet we never doubt that our feelings reveal the same world, with the same sensible qualities and the same sensible things occupying it. The difference of the sensibility is shown best by the difference of our emotion about the things from one age to another, or when we are in different organic moods. What was bright and exciting becomes weary, flat, and unprofitable. The bird's song is tedious, the breeze is mournful, the sky is sad.

To these indirect presumptions that our sensations, following the mutations of our capacity for feeling, are always undergoing an essential change, must be added another presumption, based on what must happen in the brain. Every sensation corresponds to some cerebral action. For an identical sensation to recur it would have to occur the second time *in an unmodified brain.* But as this, strictly speaking, is a physiological impossibility, so is an unmodified feeling an impossibility; for to every brain-modification, however small, we suppose that there must correspond a change of equal amount in the consciousness which the brain subserves.

But if the assumption of "simple sensations" recurring in immutable shape is so easily shown to be baseless, how much more baseless is the assumption of immutability in the larger masses of our thought!

For there it is obvious and palpable that our state of mind is never precisely the same. Every thought we have of a given fact is, strictly speaking, unique, and only bears a resemblance of kind with our other thoughts of the same fact. When the identical fact recurs, we *must* think of it in a fresh manner, see it under a somewhat different angle, apprehend it in different relations from those in which it last appeared. And the thought by which we cognize it is the thought of it-in-those-relations, a thought suffused with the consciousness of all that dim context. Often we are ourselves struck at the strange differences in our successive views of the same thing. We wonder how we ever could have opined as we did last month about a certain matter. We have outgrown the possibility of that state of mind, we know not how. From one year to another we see things in new lights. What was unreal has grown real, and what was exciting is insipid. The friends we used to care the world for are shrunken to shadows; the women once so divine, the stars, the woods, and the waters, how now so dull and common!—the young girls that brought an aura of infinity, at present hardly distinguishable existences; the pictures so empty; and as for the books, what *was* there to find so mysteriously significant in Goethe, or in John Mill so full of weight? Instead of all this, more zestful than ever is the work, the work; and fuller and deeper the import of common duties and of common goods.

I am sure that this concrete and total manner of regarding the mind's changes is the only true manner, difficult as it may be to carry it out in detail. If anything seems obscure about it, it will grow clearer as we advance. Meanwhile, if it be true, it is certainly also true that no two "ideas" are ever exactly the same, which is the proposition we started to prove. The proposition is more important theoretically than it at first sight seems. For it makes it already impossible for us to follow obediently in the footprints of either the Lockian or the Herbartian school, schools which have had almost unlimited influence in Germany and among ourselves. No doubt it is often *convenient* to formulate the mental facts in an atomistic sort of way, and to treat the higher states of consciousness as if they were all built out of unchanging simple ideas which "pass and turn again." It is convenient often to treat curves as if they were composed of small straight lines, and electricity and nerve-force as if they were fluids. But in the one case as in the other we must never forget that we are talking symbolically, and that there is nothing in nature to answer to our words. *A permanently existing "Idea" which makes its appearance before the footlights of consciousness at periodical intervals is as mythological an entity as the Jack of Spades.*

Within each personal consciousness, thought is sensibly continuous. I can only define "continuous" as that which is without breach, crack, or division. The only breaches that can well be conceived to occur within the limits of a single mind would either be *interruptions, time*-gaps during which the consciousness went out; or they would be breaks in the content of the thought, so abrupt that what followed had no connection whatever with what went before. The proposition that consciousness feels continuous, means two things:

a. That even where there is a time-gap the consciousness after it feels as if it belonged together with the consciousness before it, as another part of the same self;

b. That the changes from one moment to another in the quality of the consciousness are never absolutely abrupt.

The case of the time-gaps, as the simplest, shall be taken first.

a. When Paul and Peter wake up in the same bed, and recognize that they have been asleep, each one of them mentally reaches back and makes connection with but *one* of the two streams of thought which were broken by the sleeping hours. As the current of an electrode buried in the ground unerringly finds its way to its own similarly buried mate, across no matter how much intervening earth; so Peter's present instantly finds out Peter's past, and never by mistake knits itself on to that of Paul. Paul's thought in turn is as little liable to go astray. The past thought of Peter is appropriated by the present Peter alone. He may have a *knowledge*, and a correct one too, of what Paul's last drowsy states of mind were as he sank into sleep, but it is an entirely different sort of knowledge from that which he has of his own last states. He *remembers* his own states, whilst he only *conceives* Paul's. Remembrance is like direct feeling; its object is suffused with a warmth and intimacy to which no object of mere conception ever attains. This quality of warmth and intimacy and immediacy is what Peter's *present* thought also possesses for itself. So sure as this present is me, is mine, it says, so sure is anything else that comes with the same warmth and intimacy and immediacy, me and mine. What the qualities called warmth and intimacy may in themselves be will have to be matter for future consideration. But whatever past states appear with those qualities must be admitted to receive the greeting of the present mental state, to be owned by it, and accepted as belonging together with it in a common self. This community of self is what the time-gap cannot break in twain, and is why a present thought, although not ignorant of the time-gap, can still regard itself as continuous with certain chosen portions of the past.

Consciousness, then, does not appear to itself chopped up in bits. Such words as "chain" or "train" do not describe it fitly as it presents itself in the first instance. It is nothing jointed; it flows. A "river" or "stream" is the metaphor by which it is most naturally described. *In talking of it hereafter, let us call it the stream of thought, of consciousness, or of subjective life.*

b. But now there appears, even within the limits of the same self, and between thoughts all of which alike have this same sense of belonging together, a kind of jointing and separateness among the parts, of which this statement seems to take no account. I refer to the breaks that are produced by sudden *contrasts in the quality* of the successive segments of the stream of thought. If the words "chain" and "train" had no natural fitness in them, how came such words to be used at all? Does not a loud explosion rend the consciousness upon which it abruptly breaks, in twain? No; for even into our awareness of the thunder the awareness of the previous silence creeps and continues; for what we hear when the thunder crashes is not thunder *pure*, but thunder-breaking-upon-silence-and-contrasting-with-it. Our feeling of the same objective thunder, coming in this way, is quite different from what it would be were the thunder a continuation of previous thunder. The thunder itself we believe to abolish and exclude the silence; but the *feeling* of the thunder is also a feeling of the silence as just gone; and it would be difficult to find in the actual concrete consciousness of man a feeling so limited to the present as not to have an inkling of anything that went before.

"Substantive" and "Transitive" States of Mind

When we take a general view of the wonderful stream of our consciousness, what strikes us first is the different pace of its parts. Like a bird's life, it seems to be an alternation of flights and perchings. The rhythm of language expresses this, where every thought is expressed in a sentence, and every sentence closed by a period. The resting-places are usually occupied by sensorial imaginations of some sort, whose peculiarity is that they can be held before the mind for an indefinite time, and contemplated without changing; the places of flight are filled with thoughts of relations, static or dynamic, that for the most part obtain between the matters contemplated in the periods of comparative rest.

Let us call the resting-places the "substantive parts," and the places of flight the "transitive parts," of the stream of thought. It then appears that our thinking tends at all times toward some other substantive part than the one from which it has just been dislodged. And we may say that the main use of the transitive parts is to lead us from one substantive conclusion to another.

Now it is very difficult, introspectively, to see the transitive parts for what they really are. If they are but flights to a conclusion, stopping them to look at them before the conclusion is reached is really annihilating them. Whilst if we wait till the conclusion *be* reached, it so exceeds them in vigor and stability that it quite eclipses and swallows them up in its glare. Let anyone try to cut a thought across in the middle and get a look at its section, and he will see how difficult the introspective observation of the transitive tracts is. The rush of the thought is so headlong that it almost always brings us up at the conclusion before we can arrest it. Or if our purpose is nimble enough and we do arrest it, it ceases forthwith to be itself. As a snowflake crystal caught in the warm hand is no longer a crystal but a drop, so, instead of catching the feeling of relation moving to its term, we find we have caught some substantive thing, usually the last word we were pronouncing, statically taken, and with its function, tendency, and particular meaning in the sentence quite evaporated. The attempt at introspective analysis in these cases is in fact like seizing a spinning top to catch its motion, or trying to turn up the gas quickly enough to see how the darkness looks. And the challenge to *produce* these transitive states of consciousness, which is sure to be thrown by doubting psychologists at anyone who contends for their existence, is as unfair as Zeno's treatment of the advocates of motion, when, asking them to point out in what place an arrow *is* when it moves, he argues the falsity of their thesis from their inability to make to so preposterous a question an immediate reply.

The results of this introspective difficulty are baleful. If to hold fast and observe the transitive parts of thought's stream be so hard, then the great blunder to which all schools are liable must be the failure to register them, and the undue emphasizing of the more substantive parts of the stream. Now the blunder has historically worked in two ways. One set of thinkers have been led by it to *Sensationalism*. Unable to lay their hands on any substantive feelings corresponding to the innumerable relations and forms of connection between the sensible things of the world, finding no *named* mental states mirroring such relations, they have for the most part denied that any such states exist; and many of them, like Hume, have gone on to deny the reality of most relations *out* of the mind as well as in it. Simple substantive "ideas," sensations, and their copies, juxtaposed like dominoes in a game, but really separate, everything else verbal illusion,—such is the upshot of this view. The *Intellectualists*, on the other hand, unable to give up the reality of relations *extra mentem*, but equally unable to point to any distinct substantive feelings in which they were known, have made the same admission that such feelings do not exist. But they have drawn an opposite conclusion. The relations must be known, they say, in something that is no feeling, no mental "state," continuous and consubstantial with the subjective tissue out of which sensations and other substantive conditions of consciousness are made. They must be known by something that lies on an entirely different plane, by an *actus purus* of Thought, Intellect, or Reason, all written with capitals and considered to mean something

unutterably superior to any passing perishing fact of sensibility whatever.

But from our point of view both Intellectualists and Sensationalists are wrong. If there be such things as feelings at all, *then so surely as relations between objects exist* in rerum natura, *so surely, and more surely, do feelings exist to which these relations are known*. There is not a conjunction or a preposition, and hardly an adverbial phrase, syntactic form, or inflection of voice, in human speech, that does not express some shading or other of relation which we at some moment actually feel to exist between the larger objects of our thought. If we speak objectively, it is the real relations that appear revealed; if we speak subjectively, it is the stream of consciousness that matches each of them by an inward coloring of its own. In either case the relations are numberless, and no existing language is capable of doing justice to all their shades.

We ought to say a feeling of *and*, a feeling of *if*, a feeling of *but*, and a feeling of *by*, quite as readily as we say a feeling of *blue* or a feeling of *cold*. Yet we do not: so inveterate has our habit become of recognizing the existence of the substantive parts alone, that language almost refuses to lend itself to any other use. Consider once again the analogy of the brain. We believe the brain to be an organ whose internal equilibrium is always in a state of change—the change affecting every part. The pulses of change are doubtless more violent in one place than in another, their rhythm more rapid at this time than at that. As in a kaleidoscope revolving at a uniform rate, although the figures are always rearranging themselves, there are instants during which the transformation seems minute and interstitial and almost absent, followed by others when it shoots with magical rapidity, relatively stable forms thus alternating with forms we should not distinguish if seen again; so in the brain the perpetual rearrangement must result in some forms of tension lingering relatively long, whilst others simply come and pass. But if consciousness corresponds to the fact of rearrangement itself, why, if the rearrangement stop not, should the consciousness ever cease? And if a lingering rearrangement brings with it one kind of consciousness, why should not a swift rearrangement bring another kind of consciousness as peculiar as the rearrangement itself?

The object before the mind always has a "Fringe." There are other unnamed modifications of consciousness just as important as the transitive states, and just as cognitive as they. Examples will show what I mean.

Suppose three successive persons say to us: "Wait!" "Hark!" "Look!" Our consciousness is thrown into three quite different attitudes of expectancy, although no definite object is before it in any one of the three cases. Probably no one will deny here the existence of a real conscious affection, a sense of the direction from which an impression is about to come, although no positive impression is yet there. Meanwhile we have no names for the psychoses in question but the names hark, look, and wait.

Suppose we try to recall a forgotten name. The state of our consciousness is peculiar. There is a gap therein; but no mere gap. It is a gap that is intensely active. A sort of wraith of the name is in it, beckoning us in a given direction, making us at moments tingle with the sense of our closeness, and then letting us sink back without the longed-for term. If wrong names are proposed to us, this singularly definite gap acts immediately so as to negate them. They do not fit into its mold. And the gap of one word does not feel like the gap of another, all empty of content as both might seem necessarily to be when described as gaps. When I vainly try to recall the name of Spalding, my consciousness is far removed from what it is when I vainly try to recall the name of Bowles. There are innumerable consciousnesses of *want*, no one of which taken in itself has a name, but all different from each other. Such a feeling of want is *toto coelo* other than a want of feeling: it is an intense feeling. The rhythm of a lost word may be there without a sound to clothe it; or the evanescent sense of something which is the initial vowel or consonant may mock us fitfully, without growing more distinct. Every one must know the tantalizing effect of the blank rhythm of some forgotten verse, restlessly dancing in one's mind, striving to be filled out with words.

What is that first instantaneous glimpse of someone's meaning which we have, when in vulgar phrase we say we "twig" it? Surely an altogether specific affection of our mind. And has the reader never asked himself what kind of a mental fact is his *intention of saying a thing* before he has said it? It is an entirely definite intention, distinct from all other intentions, an absolutely distinct state of consciousness, therefore; and yet how much of it consists of definite sensorial images, either of words or of things? Hardly anything! Linger, and the words and things come into the mind; the anticipatory intention, the divination is there no more. But as the words that replace it arrive, it welcomes them successively and calls them right if they agree with it, it rejects them and calls them wrong if they do not. The intention *to-say-so-and-so* is the only name it can receive. One may admit that a good third of our psychic life consists in these rapid premonitory perspective views of schemes of thought not yet articulate. How comes it about that a man reading something aloud for the first time is able immediately to emphasize all his words aright, unless from the very first he have a sense of at least the form of the sentence yet to come, which sense is fused with his consciousness of the present word, and modifies its emphasis in his mind so as to make him give it the proper accent as he utters it? Emphasis of this kind almost altogether depends on grammatical construction. If we read "no more," we expect presently a "than"; if we read "however," it is a "yet," a "still," or a "nevertheless," that we expect. And this foreboding of the coming verbal and grammatical scheme is so practically accurate that a reader incapable of understanding four ideas of the book he is reading aloud can nevertheless read it with the most delicately modulated expression of intelligence.

It is, the reader will see, the reinstatement of the vague and inarticulate to its proper place in our mental life which I am so anxious to press on the

attention. Mr. Galton and Prof. Huxley have ...
made one step in advance in exploding the ridiculous theory of Hume and Berkeley that we can
have no images but of perfectly definite things.
Another is made if we overthrow the equally ridiculous notion that, whilst simple objective
qualities are revealed to our knowledge in "states
of consciousness," relations are not. But these re-
forms are not half sweeping and radical enough.
What must be admitted is that the definite images
of traditional psychology form but the very
smallest part of our minds as they actually live.
The traditional psychology talks like one who
should say a river consists of nothing but pailsful,
spoonsful, quartpotsful, barrelsful, and other
molded forms of water. Even were the pails and
the pots all actually standing in the stream, still
between them the free water would continue to
flow. It is just this free water of consciousness that
psychologists resolutely overlook. Every definite
image in the mind is steeped and dyed in the free
water that flows round it. With it goes the sense of
its relations, near and remote, the dying echo
of whence it came to us, the dawning sense of
whither it is to lead. The significance, the value, of
the image is all in this halo or penumbra that
surrounds and escorts it,—or rather that is fused
into one with it and has become bone of its bone
and flesh of its flesh; leaving it, it is true, an image
of the same *thing* it was before, but making it
an image of that thing newly taken and freshly
understood.

*Let us call the consciousness of this halo of rela-
tions around the image by the name of "psychic
overtone" or "fringe."*

Cerebral Conditions of the "Fringe"

Nothing is easier than to symbolize these facts
in terms of brain-action. Just as the echo of the
whence, the sense of the starting point of our
thought, is probably due to the dying excitement
of processes but a moment since vividly aroused;

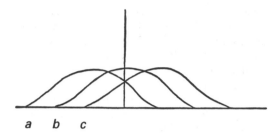

Figure 1.1

so the sense of the whither, the foretaste of the
terminus, must be due to the waxing excitement
of tracts or processes whose psychical correlative
will a moment hence be the vividly present feature
of our thought. Represented by a curve, the neu-
rosis underlying consciousness must at any moment be like this:

Let the horizontal in figure 1.1 be the line of
time, and let the three curves beginning at *a*, *b*,
and *c* respectively stand for the neural processes
correlated with the thoughts of those three letters.
Each process occupies a certain time during
which its intensity waxes, culminates, and wanes.
The process for *a* has not yet died out, the process
for *c* has already begun, when that for *b* is culminating. At the time-instant represented by the
vertical line all three processes are *present*, in
the intensities shown by the curve. Those before
c's apex *were* more intense a moment ago; those
after it *will be* more intense a moment hence. If I
recite *a*, *b*, *c*, then, at the moment of uttering *b*,
neither *a* nor *c* is out of my consciousness altogether, but both, after their respective fashions,
"mix their dim lights" with the stronger *b*, because their processes are both awake in some
degree.

It is just like "overtones" in music: they are not
separately heard by the ear; they blend with the
fundamental note, and suffuse it, and alter it;
and even so do the waxing and waning brain-
processes at every moment blend with and suffuse
and alter the psychic effect of the processes which
are at their culminating point.

The "Topic" of the Thought

If we then consider the *cognitive function* of different states of mind, we may feel assured that the difference between those that are mere "acquaintance" and those that are "knowledges-*about*" is reducible almost entirely to the absence or presence of psychic fringes or overtones. Knowledge *about* a thing is knowledge of its relations. Acquaintance with it is limitation to the bare impression which it makes. Of most of its relations we are only aware in the penumbral nascent way of a "fringe" of unarticulated affinities about it. And, before passing to the next topic in order, I must say a little of this sense of affinity, as itself one of the most interesting features of the subjective stream.

Thought may be equally rational in any sort of terms. *In all our voluntary thinking there is some* TOPIC or SUBJECT about which all the members of the thought revolve. Relation to this topic or interest is constantly felt in the fringe, and particularly the relation of harmony and discord, of furtherance or hindrance of the topic. Any thought the quality of whose fringe lets us feel ourselves "all right," may be considered a thought that furthers the topic. Provided we only feel its object to have a place in the scheme of relations in which the topic also lies, that is sufficient to make of it a relevant and appropriate portion of our train of ideas.

Now we may think about our topic mainly in words, or we may think about it mainly in visual or other images, but this need make no difference as regards the furtherance of our knowledge of the topic. If we only feel in the terms, whatever they be, a fringe of affinity with each other and with the topic, and if we are conscious of approaching a conclusion, we feel that our thought is rational and right. The words in every language have contracted by long association fringes of mutual repugnance or affinity with each other and with the conclusion, which run exactly parallel with like fringes in the visual, tactile, and

other ideas. The most important element of these fringes is, I repeat, the mere feeling of harmony or discord, of a right or wrong direction in the thought.

If we know English and French and begin a sentence in French, all the later words that come are French; we hardly ever drop into English. And this affinity of the French words for each other is not something merely operating mechanically as a brain-law, it is something we feel at the time. Our understanding of a French sentence head never falls to so low an ebb that we are not aware that the words linguistically belong together. Our attention can hardly so wander that if an English word be suddenly introduced we shall not start at the change. Such a vague sense as this of the words belonging together is the very minimum of fringe that can accompany them, if "thought" at all. Usually the vague perception that all the words we hear belong to the same language and to the same special vocabulary in that language, and that the grammatical sequence is familiar, is practically equivalent to an admission that what we hear is sense. But if an unusual foreign word be introduced, if the grammar trip, or if a term from an incongruous vocabulary suddenly appear, such as "rat-trap" or "plumber's bill" in a philosophical discourse, the sentence detonates as it were, we receive a shock from the incongruity, and the drowsy assent is gone. The feeling of rationality in these cases seems rather a negative than a positive thing, being the mere absence of shock, or sense of discord, between the terms of thought.

Conversely, if words do belong to the same vocabulary, and if the grammatical structure is correct, sentences with absolutely no meaning may be uttered in good faith and pass unchallenged. Discourses at prayer-meetings, reshuffling the same collection of cant phrases, and the whole genus of penny-a-line-isms and newspaper-reporter's flourishes give illustrations of this. "The birds filled the tree-tops with their morning song, making the air moist, cool, and pleasant," is a sentence I remember reading once in a report of

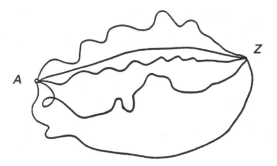

Figure 1.2

some athletic exercises in Jerome Park. It was probably written unconsciously by the hurried reporter, and read uncritically by many readers.

We see, then, that it makes little or no difference in what sort of mind-stuff, in what quality of imagery, our thinking goes on. The only images *intrinsically* important are the halting-places, the substantive conclusions, provisional or final, of the thought. Throughout all the rest of the stream, the feelings of relation are everything, and the terms related almost naught. These feelings of relation, these psychic overtones, halos, suffusions, or fringes about the terms, may be the same in very different systems of imagery. A diagram (figure 1.2) may help to accentuate this indifference of the mental means where the end is the same. Let *A* be some experience from which a number of thinkers start. Let *Z* be the practical conclusion rationally inferrible from it. One gets to this conclusion by one line, another by another; one follows a course of English, another of German, verbal imagery. With one, visual images predominate; with another, tactile. Some trains are tinged with emotions, others not; some are very abridged, synthetic, and rapid; others, hesitating and broken into many steps. But when the penultimate terms of all the trains, however differing *inter se*, finally shoot into the same conclusion, we say, and rightly say, that all the thinkers have had substantially the same thought. It would probably astound each of them beyond measure to be let into his neighbor's mind and to find how different the scenery there was from that in his own.

The last peculiarity to which attention is to be drawn in this first rough description of thought's stream is that—Consciousness is always interested more in one part of its object than in another, and welcomes and rejects, or chooses, all the while it thinks.

The phenomena of selective attention and of deliberative will are of course patent examples of this choosing activity. But few of us are aware how incessantly it is at work in operations not ordinarily called by these names. Accentuation and Emphasis are present in every perception we have. We find it quite impossible to disperse our attention impartially over a number of impressions. A monotonous succession of sonorous strokes is broken up into rhythms, now of one sort, now of another, by the different accent which we place on different strokes. The simplest of these rhythms is the double one, tick-tóck, tick-tóck, tick-tóck. Dots dispersed on a surface are perceived in rows and groups. Lines separate into diverse figures. The ubiquity of the distinctions, *this* and *that*, *here* and *there*, *now* and *then*, in our minds is the result of our laying the same selective emphasis on parts of place and time.

But we do far more than emphasize things, and unite some, and keep others apart. We actually *ignore* most of the things before us. Let me briefly show how this goes on.

To begin at the bottom, what are our very senses themselves . . . but organs of selection? Out of the infinite chaos of movements, of which physics teaches us that the outer world consists, each sense-organ picks out those which fall within certain limits of velocity. To these it responds, but ignores the rest as completely as if they did not exist. Out of what is in itself an undistinguishable, swarming *continuum*, devoid of distinction or emphasis, our senses make for us, by attending to this motion and ignoring that, a world full of contrasts, of sharp accents, of abrupt changes, of picturesque light and shade.

If the sensations we receive from a given organ have their causes thus picked out for us by the conformation of the organ's termination, Attention, on the other hand, out of all the sensations yielded, picks out certain ones as worthy of its notice and suppresses all the rest. We notice only those sensations which are signs to us of *things* which happen practically or aesthetically to interest us, to which we therefore give substantive names, and which we exalt to this exclusive status of independence and dignity. But in itself, apart from my interest, a particular dust-wreath on a windy day is just as much of an individual *thing*, and just as much or as little deserves an individual name, as my own body does.

And then, among the sensations we get from each separate thing, what happens? The mind selects again. It chooses certain of the sensations to represent the thing most *truly*, and considers the rest as its appearances, modified by the conditions of the moment. Thus my table-top is named *square*, after but one of an infinite number of retinal sensations which it yields, the rest of them being sensations of two acute and two obtuse angles; but I call the latter *perspective* views, and the four right angles the *true* form of the table, and erect the attribute squareness into the table's essence, for aesthetic reasons of my own. In like manner, the real form of the circle is deemed to be the sensation it gives when the line of vision is perpendicular to its center—all its other sensations are *signs* of this sensation. The real sound of the cannon is the sensation it makes when the ear is close by. The real color of the brick is the sensation it gives when the eye looks squarely at it from a near point, out of the sunshine and yet not in the gloom; under other circumstances it gives us other color-sensations which are but signs of this—we then see it looks pinker or bluer than it really is. The reader knows no object which he does not represent to himself by preference as in some typical attitude, of some normal size, at some characteristic distance, of some standard tint, etc., etc. But all these essential characteristics, which together form for us the genuine ob-

jectivity of the thing and are contrasted with what we call the subjective sensations it may yield us at a given moment, are mere sensations like the latter. The mind chooses to suit itself, and decides what particular sensation shall be held more real and valid than all the rest.

Next, in a world of objects thus individualized by our mind's selective industry, what is called our "experience" is almost entirely determined by our habits of attention. A thing may be present to a man a hundred times, but if he persistently fails to notice it, it cannot be said to enter into his experience. We are all seeing flies, moths, and beetles by the thousand, but to whom, save an entomologist, do they say anything distinct? On the other hand, a thing met only once in a lifetime may leave an indelible experience in the memory. Let four men make a tour in Europe. One will bring home only picturesque impressions—costumes and colors, parks and views and works of architecture, pictures and statues. To another all this will be non-existent; and distances and prices, populations and drainage-arrangements, door- and window-fastenings, and other useful statistics will take their place. A third will give a rich account of the theaters, restaurants, and public halls, and naught beside; whilst the fourth will perhaps have been so wrapped in his own subjective broodings as to be able to tell little more than a few names of places through which he passed. Each has selected, out of the same mass of presented objects, those which suited his private interest and has made his experience thereby.

If now, leaving the empirical combination of objects, we ask how the mind proceeds *rationally* to connect them, we find selection again to be omnipotent.... [w]e shall see that all Reasoning depends on the ability of the mind to break up the totality of the phenomenon reasoned about, into parts, and to pick out from among these the particular one which, in the given emergency, may lead to the proper conclusion. The man of genius is he who will always stick in his bill at the right point, and bring it out with the right element—

"reason" if the emergency be theoretical, "means" if it be practical—transfixed upon it.

If now we pass to the aesthetic department, our law is still more obvious. The artist notoriously selects his items, rejecting all tones, colors, shapes, which do not harmonize with each other and with the main purpose of his work. That unity, harmony, "convergence of characters," as M. Taine calls it, which gives to works of art their superiority over works of nature, is wholly due to *elimination*. Any natural subject will do, if the artist has wit enough to pounce upon some one feature of it as characteristic, and suppress all merely accidental items which do not harmonize with this.

Ascending still higher, we reach the plane of Ethics, where choice reigns notoriously supreme. An act has no ethical quality whatever unless it be chosen out of several all equally possible. To sustain the arguments for the good course and keep them ever before us, to stifle our longing for more flowery ways, to keep the foot unflinchingly on the arduous path, these are characteristic ethical energies. But more than these; for these but deal with the means of compassing interests already felt by the man to be supreme. The ethical energy *par excellence* has to go farther and choose which *interest* out of several, equally coercive, shall become supreme. The issue here is of the utmost pregnancy, for it decides a man's entire career. When he debates, Shall I commit this crime? choose that profession? accept that office, or marry this fortune?—his choice really lies between one of several equally possible future Characters. What he shall *become* is fixed by the conduct of this moment. Schopenhauer, who enforces his determinism by the argument that with a given fixed character only one reaction is possible under given circumstances, forgets that, in these critical ethical moments, what consciously *seems* to be in question is the complexion of the character itself. The problem with the man is less what act he shall now resolve to do than what being he shall now choose to become.

Taking human experience in a general way, the choosings of different men are to a great extent the same. The race as a whole largely agrees as to what it shall notice and name; and among the noticed parts we select in much the same way for accentuation and preference, or subordination and dislike. There is, however, one entirely extraordinary case in which no two men ever are known to choose alike. One great splitting of the whole universe into two halves is made by each of us; and for each of us almost all of the interest attaches to one of the halves; but we all draw the line of division between them in a different place. When I say that we all call the two halves by the same names, and that those names are "*me*" and "*not-me*" respectively, it will at once be seen what I mean. The altogether unique kind of interest which each human mind feels in those parts of creation which it can call *me* or *mine* may be a moral riddle, but it is a fundamental psychological fact. No mind can take the same interest in his neighbor's *me* as in his own. The neighbor's me falls together with all the rest of things in one foreign mass against which his own *me* stands out in startling relief. Even the trodden worm, as Lotze somewhere says, contrasts his own suffering self with the whole remaining universe, though he have no clear conception either of himself or of what the universe may be. He is for me a mere part of the world; for him it is I who am the mere part. Each of us dichotomizes the Cosmos in a different place.

2 The Cartesian Theater and "Filling In" the Stream of Consciousness

Daniel C. Dennett

Cartesian Materialism

The idea of a special center in the brain is the most tenacious bad idea bedeviling our attempts to think about consciousness. This idea is so prevalent that I will give it a name: *Cartesian Materialism*. This is the view you arrive at when you discard Descartes's dualism but fail to discard the imagery of a central (but material) theater in the mind where "it all comes together."

The pineal gland would be one candidate for such a Cartesian Theater, but there are others that have been suggested—the anterior cingulate, the reticular formation, various places in the prefrontal lobes. Cartesian materialism is the view that there is a crucial finish line or boundary somewhere in the brain, marking a place where the order of arrival equals the order of "presentation" in experience because *what happens there* is what you are conscious of.

Perhaps no one today explicitly endorses Cartesian materialism. Many theorists would insist that they have explicitly rejected such an obviously bad idea. But as we shall see, the persuasive imagery of the Cartesian Theater keeps coming back to haunt us—laypeople and scientists alike—even after its ghostly dualism has been denounced and exorcized. And there are a variety of ostensibly compelling reasons for that.

Most important of these is our personal, introspective appreciation of the "unity of consciousness," which impresses on us the distinction between "in here" and "out there." The naive boundary between "me" and "the outside world" is my skin (and the lenses of my eyes) but, as we learn more and more about the way events in our own bodies can be inaccessible "to us," the great outside encroaches. "In here" I can try to raise my arm, but "out there," it has "fallen asleep" or is paralyzed, it won't budge; my lines of communication from wherever *I* am to the neural machinery controlling my arm have been tampered with. And if my optic nerve were somehow severed, I wouldn't expect to go on seeing even though my eyes were still intact. Having visual experiences is something that apparently happens *inboard* of my eyes, somewhere in between my eyes and my voice when I tell you what I see.

In short, we must stop thinking of the brain as if it had such a single functional summit or central point. This is not an innocuous shortcut; it's a bad habit. In order to break this bad habit of thought, we need to explore some instances of the bad habit in action, but we also need a good image with which to replace it.

Introducing the Multiple Drafts Model

Here is a first version of the replacement, the Multiple Drafts model of consciousness. I expect it will seem quite alien and hard to visualize at first—that's how entrenched the Cartesian Theater idea is. According to the Multiple Drafts model, all varieties of perception—indeed, all varieties of thought or mental activity—are accomplished in the brain by parallel, multitrack processes of interpretation and elaboration of sensory inputs. Information entering the nervous system is under continuous "editorial revision."

These editorial processes occur over large fractions of a second, during which time various additions, incorporations, emendations, and overwritings of content can occur, in various orders. We don't directly experience what happens on our retinas, in our ears, on the surface of our skin. What we actually experience is a product of many processes of interpretation—editorial processes, in effect. They take in relatively raw and one-sided representations, and yield collated, revised, enhanced representations, and they take place in the streams of activity occurring in various parts of the brain. This much is recognized by virtually

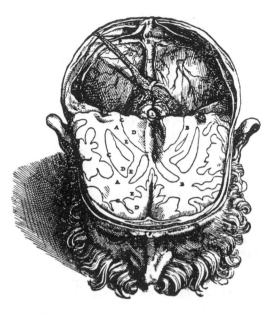

Figure 2.1
Descartes had the idea that the brain *did* have a center: the pineal gland, which served as the gateway to the conscious mind. The pineal gland is the only organ in the brain that is in the midline, rather than paired, with left and right versions. It is marked *L* in this diagram by the great sixteenth-century anatomist Vesalius. Smaller than a pea, it sits in splendid isolation on its stalk, attached to the rest of the nervous system just about in the middle of the back of the brain. Since its function was quite inscrutable (it is still unclear what the pineal gland does), Descartes proposed a role for it: in order for a person to be conscious of something, traffic from the senses had to arrive at this station, where it thereupon caused a special—indeed, magical—transaction to occur between the person's material brain and immaterial mind. Source: Dennett (1991), p. 104.

all theories of perception, but now we are poised for the novel feature of the Multiple Drafts model: Feature detections or discriminations *only have to be made once*. That is, once a particular "observation" of some feature has been made, by a specialized, localized portion of the brain, the information content thus fixed does not have to be sent somewhere else to be *re*-discriminated by some "master" discriminator. In other words, discrimination does not lead to a re-*presentation* of the already discriminated feature for the benefit of the audience in the Cartesian Theater—for there is no Cartesian Theater.

These spatially and temporally distributed content-fixations in the brain are precisely locatable in both space and time, but their onsets do *not* mark the onset of consciousness of their content. It is always an open question whether any particular content thus discriminated will eventually appear as an element in conscious experience, and it is a confusion, as we shall see, to ask *when* it becomes conscious. These distributed content-discriminations yield, over the course of time, something *rather like* a narrative stream or sequence, which can be thought of as subject to continual editing by many processes distributed around in the brain, and continuing indefinitely into the future. This stream of contents is only rather like a narrative because of its multiplicity; at any point in time there are multiple "drafts" of narrative fragments at various stages of editing in various places in the brain.

Probing this stream at different places and times produces different effects, precipitates different narratives from the subjcet. If one delays the probe too long (overnight, say), the result is apt to be no narrative left at all—or else a narrative that has been digested or "rationally reconstructed" until it has no integrity. If one probes "too early," one may gather data on how early a particular discrimination is achieved by the brain, but at the cost of diverting what would otherwise have been the normal progression of the multiple stream.

Most important, the Multiple Drafts model avoids the tempting mistake of supposing that there must be a single narrative (the "final" or "published" draft, you might say) that is canonical—that is the *actual* stream of consciousness of the subject, whether or not the experimenter (or even the subject) can gain access to it. Instead of such a single stream (however wide), there are multiple channels in which specialist circuits try, in parallel pandemoniums, to do their various things, creating Multiple Drafts as they go.

Thumbnail Sketch

Let me now recapitulate the Multiple Drafts model of consciousness in a Thumbnail Sketch. Here is my theory so far:

There is no single, definitive "stream of consciousness," because there is no central Headquarters, no Cartesian Theater where "it all comes together" for the perusal of a Central Meaner. Instead of such a single stream (however wide), there are multiple channels in which specialist circuits try, in parallel pandemoniums, to do their various things, creating Multiple Drafts as they go. Most of these fragmentary drafts of "narrative" play short-lived roles in the modulation of current activity but some get promoted to further functional roles, in swift succession, by the activity of a virtual machine in the brain. The seriality of this machine (its "von Neumannesque" character) is not a "hard-wired" design feature, but rather the upshot of a succession of coalitions of these specialists.

While everyone agrees that there is no single point in the brain, reminiscent of Descartes's pineal gland, the implications of this have not been recognized, and are occasionally egregiously overlooked. For instance, incautious formulations of "the binding problem" in current neuroscientific research often presuppose that there must be some single representational space in the brain (smaller than the whole brain) where the results of all the various discriminations are put into registration with each other—marrying the sound track to the film, coloring in the shapes, filling in the blank parts. There are some careful formulations of the binding problem(s) that avoid this error, but the niceties often get overlooked.

This tendency to think of consciousness as *the end of the line* is indeed one of the occupational hazards of neuroscience. It is like forgetting that the end product of apple trees is not apples—it's more apple trees. Here, for instance, is a hypothesis hazarded by Francis Crick and Christof Koch:

We have suggested that one of the functions of consciousness is to present the result of various underlying computations and that this involves an attentional mechanism that temporarily binds the relevant neurons together by synchronizing their spikes in 40 hz oscillations. (Crick and Koch, 1990, p. 272)

So a function of consciousness is to *present the results of underlying computations*—but to whom? The Queen? Crick and Koch do not go on to ask themselves the Hard Question: *And then what happens?* ("And then a miracle occurs?") Once their theory has shepherded something into what they consider to be the charmed circle of consciousness, it stops. It doesn't confront the problem about the tricky path from (presumed) consciousness to behavior, including, especially, introspective reports.

Filling In

There is yet another tenacious idea that emerges as a byproduct of the implicit commitment to the Cartesian Theater model: the idea of *filling in*. This idea is based on the misguided assumption that *after* the brain has arrived at a discrimination or judgment, it *re-presents* the material on which its judgment is based, for the enjoyment of the audience in the Cartesian Theater, filling in the missing details.

The question of whether the brain "fills in" in one way or another is not a question on which introspection by itself can bear, for introspection provides us—the subject as well as the "outside" experimenter—only with the content of representation, not with the features of the representational medium itself. For evidence about the medium, we need to conduct further experiments.[1]

Consider how the brain must deal with wallpaper, for instance. Suppose you walk into a

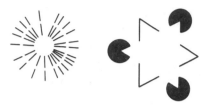

Figure 2.2
A closely related phenomenon of interest is that of "subjective contours." Look at the two shapes in this figure. Do you see a white circle with a circumventing ring around it on the left, and a white triangle superimposed on an inverted triangle with black borders on the right? This is a familiar illusion. There are no white figures on your retinal image, in addition to the black lines. This phenomenon, too, involves no "filling in" by the brain to produce the seemings of the white figures. It simply results from a brain circuit specializing in shape being misled to distinguish particular bounded regions: the two shapes with their "subjective contours." Source: Dennett (1991), p. 351.

room and notice that the wallpaper is a regular array of hundreds of identical sailboats, or—let's pay homage to Andy Warhol—identical photographic portraits of Marilyn Monroe. In order to identify a picture as a portrait of Marilyn Monroe, you have to foveate the picture: the image has to fall on the high-resolution foveae of your eyes. But it is well known that human *parafoveal* vision (served by the rest of the retina) does not have very good resolution; you can't even identify a jack of diamonds held at arm's length. Yet we know that if you were to enter a room whose walls were papered with identical photos of Marilyn Monroe, you would "instantly" see that this was the case. You would see in a fraction of a second that there were "lots and lots of identical, detailed, focused portraits of Marilyn Monroe." Since your eyes saccade four or five times a second at most, you could foveate only one or two Marilyns in the time it takes you to jump to the conclusion *and thereupon to see* hundreds of identical Marilyns. We know that parafoveal vision *could not* distinguish Marilyn from various Marilyn-shaped blobs, but nevertheless, what you

see is *not* wallpaper of Marilyn-in-the-middle surrounded by various indistinct Marilyn-shaped blobs.

Now, is it possible that the brain takes one of its high-resolution foveal views of Marilyn and reproduces it, as if by photocopying, across an internal mapping of the expanse of wall? That is the only way the high-resolution details you used to identify Marilyn could "get into the background" at all, since parafoveal vision is not sharp enough to provide it by itself. I suppose it is possible in principle, but the brain almost certainly does not go to the trouble of doing *that* filling in! Having identified a single Marilyn, and having received no information to the effect that the other blobs are not Marilyns, it jumps to the conclusion that the rest are Marilyns, and labels the whole region "more Marilyns" without any further rendering of Marilyn at all.

Of course it does not seem that way to you. It seems to you as if you are actually seeing hundreds of identical Marilyns. And in one sense you are: there are, indeed, hundreds of identical Marilyns out there on the wall, and you're seeing them. What is not the case, however, is that there are hundreds of identical Marilyns represented in your brain. Your brain just somehow represents that there are hundreds of identical Marilyns, and no matter how vivid your impression is that you see all that detail, the detail is in the world, not in your head.

Why don't we normally see the blind spot? The brain doesn't have to "fill in" for the blind spot, since the region in which the blind spot falls is already labeled (e.g., "plaid" or "Marilyns" or just "more of the same"). If the brain received contradictory evidence from some region, it would abandon or adjust its generalization, but not getting any evidence from the blind spot region is not the same as getting contradictory evidence. The absence of confirming evidence from the blind spot region is no problem for the brain; since the brain has no precedent of getting information from that gap of the retina, it has not developed any epistemically hungry agencies demanding to

Figure 2.3
What is it like to have a scotoma, a blind spot in one's visual field? It might seem that this is already familiar to all of us, for we all have blind spots in our visual fields corresponding to the places on our retinas where there are no rods or cones because the optic nerve exits the eyeball there. A normal blind spot, or optic disk, is not small: it blanks out a circle with a diameter of about 6 degrees of visual angle. Close one eye and look at the cross, holding the page about six inches from your eyes. One of the "blind spot" disks should disappear. (It may take some adjustment of the distance from the page to make the effect happen. Keep looking straight at the cross.) Why don't you normally notice this gap in your visual field? In part because you have two eyes, and one eye covers for the other; their blind spots do not overlap. But even with one eye closed, you won't notice your blind spot under most conditions. Why not? Since your brain has never had to deal with input from this area of your retina, it has devoted no resources to dealing with it. There are no homunculi responsible for receiving reports from this area, so when no reports arrive, there is no one to complain. *An absence of information is not the same as information about an absence.* In order for you to see a hole, something in your brain would have to respond to a contrast: *either* between the inside and outside edge—and your brain has no machinery for doing that at this location—*or* between before and after: now you see the disk, now you don't. (That's how the disappearing black disk alerts you to your blind spot.)
Source: From Dennett (1991), p. 324.

be fed from that region. Among all the homunculi of vision, not a single one has the role of coordinating information from that region of the eye, so when no information arrives from those sources, no one complains. The area is simply neglected. In other words, all normally sighted people "suffer" from a tiny bit of "anosognosia."[2] We are unaware of our "deficit"—of the fact that we are receiving no visual information from our blind spots.

The blind spot is a spatial hole, but there can be temporal holes as well. The smallest are the gaps that occur while our eyes dart about during sac-

cades. We don't notice these gaps, but they don't have to be filled in *because* we're designed not to notice them. The temporal analogues of scotomata might be the "absences" that occur during petit mal epileptic seizures. These are noticeable by the sufferer, but only by inference: they can't "see the edges" any more than you can see the edges of your blind spot, but they can be struck, retrospectively, by discontinuities in the events they have experienced.

The fundamental flaw in the idea of "filling in" is that it suggests that the brain is providing something when in fact the brain is ignoring something. And this leads even very sophisticated thinkers to make crashing mistakes, perfectly epitomized by Edelman: "One of the most striking features of consciousness is its continuity" (Edelman 1989, p. 119). This is utterly wrong. One of the most striking features of consciousness is its *dis*continuity—as revealed in the blind spot, and saccadic gaps, to take the simplest examples. The discontinuity of consciousness is striking because of the *apparent* continuity of consciousness. Neumann (1990) points out that consciousness may in general be a gappy phenomenon, and as long as the temporal edges of the gaps are not positively perceived, there will be no sense of the gappiness of the "stream" of consciousness. As Minsky puts it, "Nothing can *seem* jerky except what is *represented* as jerky. Paradoxically, our sense of continuity comes from our marvelous *insensitivity* to most kinds of changes rather than from any genuine perceptiveness" (Minsky 1985, p. 257).

Notes

This essay is put together based on various excerpts from Dennett (1991) by Güven Güzeldere. Thanks to Amy Friedman for secretarial assistance.

1. For instance, Roger Shepard's initial experiments with the mental rotation of cube diagrams showed that it certainly *seemed* to subjects that they harbored roughly continuously rotating representations of the shapes they were imagining, but it took further experiments,

probing the actual temporal properties of the underlying representations, to provide (partial) confirmation of the hypothesis that they were actually doing what it seemed to them they were doing. (See Shepard and Cooper, 1982.)

2. Total or partial loss of ability to recognize or to acknowledge one's own bodily defect or illness.

References

Crick, F. and Koch, C. (1990). "Towards a Neurobiological Theory of Consciousness," *Seminars in the Neurosciences*, 2, pp. 262–275.

Edelman, G. (1989). *The Remembered Present: A Biological Theory of Consciousness*. New York: Basic Books.

Minsky, M. (1985). *The Society of Mind*. New York: Simon & Schuster.

Neumann, O. (1990). "Some Aspects of Phenomenal Consciousness and Their Possible Functional Correlates," presented at the conference "The Phenomenal Mind—How Is It Possible and Why Is It Necessary?" Zentrum für Interdisziplinäre Forschung, Bielefeld, Germany, May 14–17.

Shepard, R. and Cooper, L. (1982). *Mental Images and Their Transformations*. Cambridge, MA: MIT Press, a Bradford Book.

3 The Robust Phenomenology of the Stream of Consciousness

Owen Flanagan

Can the way consciousness seems withstand pressure from theorizing about the way it really is, its underlying causal structure, its place in the mind as a whole, and its place in nature? Is the phenomenology in competition with the facts?

One might think that the phenomenology is true as phenomenology, as a description of how things seem from a point of view that tries to be both naive, in the sense of not bringing a load of theory to bear, but also reflective enough to notice things, like the network features of consciousness, as well as the fringe and its role, that do not reveal themselves in any simple and straightforward way in experience. One might nonetheless think that phenomenology does more harm than good when it comes to developing a proper theory of consciousness, since it fosters certain illusions about the nature of consciousness. I will focus my discussion by reflecting briefly on three issues: the continuity question, the binding problem, and the idea that mind is massively parallel rather than serial.

Continuity

One alleged illusion that the phenomenology might be accused of fostering is the idea that consciousness is continuous, when in fact it is not. Daniel Dennett, ever the gadfly, thinks that it is a "crashing mistake" to think that one of the most striking features of consciousness is its continuity. "This is utterly wrong. One of the most striking features of consciousness is its *dis*continuity—as revealed in the blind spot, and saccadic gaps, to take the simplest examples. The discontinuity of consciousness is surprising because of the *apparent* continuity of consciousness. . . . Consciousness may in general be a very gappy phenomenon, and as long as the temporal edges of the gaps are not positively perceived, there will be no sense of the gappiness of the 'stream' of consciousness" (Dennett 1991, 356).

Here is a good place to focus again on the tension between the subjective and the objective and on a certain ambiguity in the idea of the nature of consciousness. Dennett accepts that consciousness is apparently continuous, despite the existence of temporal gaps, changes in focus within and between modalities, and so on. So consciousness feels like a stream. This is its subjective side. But objectively, there is evidence of gaps and qualitative contrast. James acknowledged this. Viewed subjectively, consciousness is streamlike. Viewed objectively, it is less streamlike. Which is the truth? James thought that both can be true. I think he is right.

Both can be true because they have points of view built in. Phenomenologically, consciousness is a stream. Objectively, it is less streamlike. Interesting research problems fall out of the apparent tension between the two stories. Suppose that neuroscientists discover that consciousness is in fact realized like a movie reel consisting of individual images, the moments of consciousness, with small separations between them, the gaps. It is not clear that this would or should have any impact on what we say about how consciousness seems from a first-person point of view. What we have is the interesting problem of explaining how the streamlike quality so dominates ordinary awareness when the brain processes subserving it are so gappy. It isn't that we have an illusion to be explained. There is no mistake or illusion involved in claiming that consciousness feels streamlike. Again, the point of view is built in. The interesting question is why subjective consciousness is insensitive, if it is, to certain things about itself, objectively construed. Eventually we want a fine-grained answer of the sort we can give for how other discrete things, e.g., movies, give a continuous impression. Giving a continuous impression may well be what the system is designed to do. In that case there is no mistake in thinking that consciousness seems streamlike. It does because it is designed to feel that way.

Relatedly, consider the cascading saccadic eye movements. It is very impressive that the brain smooths over and ignores the visual leaping about of our eyes, and we will want a fine-grained explanation of how the brain does this. The mood at the start of inquiry should not be one of disappointment in the powerlessness of consciousness to reveal the way the brain works. Given the role of consciousness in "steering a nervous system grown too complex to regulate itself," it would be bad evolutionary design if consciousness were an accurate detector of all the neural goings-on. Its job is not to do neuroscience!

So we can accept that consciousness is not a sensitive detector of nonstreamlike features of brain processes without abandoning the idea that it is subjectively streamlike. We can also accept that our consciousness of the external world is gappy without doing harm to the claim that consciousness has a subjective streamlike character. Consciousness does not pick up all the information in the world. There are the visual blindspots, and there is much that we simply fail to consciously notice. But who would have thought otherwise? There are all sorts of interesting research questions about why we notice what we notice, about the architecture and baseline sensitivities of the sensory modalities, and about sensory compensation. But the fact that there are things in the world we miss at each and every moment has no direct consequences for the streamlike quality of consciousness. We must be careful, as James says, not to infer gaps in the conscious stream from gaps in what we know about things in the world.

That said, it is a very interesting question how we ought to conceive of cases of divided consciousness. William James was impressed by our ability to split consciousness and to attend to two different things and perform two different acts at once, though we are unaware at the time that we are doing so. Consciousness *may be split into parts which coexist but mutually ignore each other*" (James 1890, 206). Are such cases, cases in which there are two distinct streams running

simultaneously in parallel, or is there simply a single complex stream? One possibility is that a single attentional mechanism switches back and forth between two tasks at blazing speed. The mind somehow sequesters each task-solving sequence so that each seems to take place in a stream of its own, running in apparent parallel with the other stream, when in fact there is an objectively choppy serial switchback mechanism at work. The development of better theories about brain structure and function, about attention, perception, and motor activity, will help us to answer questions about apparent split streams. This is a case where the phenomenology is unclear in its deliverances and where we can imagine discoveries about underlying processes changing what we are inclined to say about the way things seem from a first person point of view.

In sum, I don't see that the phenomenological stream needs to foster any illusions. The National Science Foundation should not fund neuroscientists who want to use expensive equipment to find the stream. But they should fund researchers who want to explain the various discrepancies between the way consciousness seems and the way it is from the objective point of view. There is at this point in time no objective phenomenon that warrants giving up the streamlike phenomenology.

Binding

The stream of consciousness is, among other things, a stream of perceptions. I see the yellow tennis ball. I see your face and hear what you say. I see and smell the bouquet of roses. The binding problem arises by paying attention to how these coherent perceptions arise. There are specialized sets of neurons that detect different aspects of objects in the visual field. The color and motion of the ball are detected by different sets of neurons in different areas of the visual cortex (the medial temporal lobe and V4, respectively). Binding seeing and hearing, or seeing and smelling, is even more complex, since multimodal perception involves labor in different areas of the cortex, and when audition is involved, in areas of the paleo-cortex as well. The problem is how all this individually processed information can give rise to a unified percept. The answer would be simple if there were a place where all the outputs of all the processors involved delivered their computations at the same time, a faculty of consciousness, as it were. But the evidence suggests that there is no such place. There is simply lots of activity in the relevant areas, with resonance spreading near and far.

The binding problem is a puzzle, a deep problem, in cognitive neuroscience. But I don't see that it touches the claim that consciousness is a stream. (Wundt discovered in the 1880s that the *felt* simultaneity of seeing and smelling a rose is sometimes detectably sequential, even by the very person who feels them to be simultaneous!) Indeed, the facts that consciousness is streamlike and that its contents are unified perceptions make the binding problem a problem. Binding occurs. The question is whether it occurs by all the computations of special purpose processors finding a path to some yet to be discovered central headquarters (see Baars 1988 for an argument for a central "blackboard," a global workplace, realized in the extended reticular-thalamic activating system) or whether a certain level of synchronous oscillatory patterns in the relevant pathways simply produces perceptual binding without ever joining up, so that "timing is binding." Rather than standing in the way of this research, the phenomenology of the stream motivates explanatory work designed to explain how disparate processors can give rise to felt perceptual unity.

Parallelism

Daniel Dennett, we have seen, accepts that consciousness seems streamlike or continuous but thinks that it is a crashing mistake to think that it really is so. I tried above to show how we could save the truth of a streamlike phenomenol-ogy from Dennett's challenge. Consciousness is streamlike, and it is an important research problem to explain how and why it is this way phenomenologically, despite the fact that the physiological and brain processes that subserve consciousness are not streamlike in many respects.

One argument against the stream metaphor that I have not considered directly is based on the idea that the architecture of mind is massively parallel and that consciousness itself involves "parallel pandemoniums." Without even being sure what parallel pandemoniums are, it seems pretty clear that if "parallel pandemoniums" is the right metaphor for consciousness, the metaphor of the stream must go. The two metaphors are not compatible.

Dennett provides a thumbnail sketch of his theory of consciousness in these words:

There is no single, definitive "stream of consciousness," because there is no central Headquarters, no Cartesian Theater where "it all comes together" for the perusal of a Central Meaner. Instead of such a single stream (however wide) there are multiple channels in which specialist circuits try, in parallel pandemoniums, to do their various things, creating Multiple Drafts as they go. Most of these fragmentary drafts of "narrative" play short-lived roles in the modulation of current activity but some get promoted to further functional roles, in swift succession, by the activity of a virtual machine in the brain. The seriality of this machine (its "von Neu-mannesque" character) is not a "hard-wired" design feature, but rather the upshot of a succession of coalitions of these specialists. (1991, 253–254)

There is a lot going on in this passage. Indeed, this passage is an attempt to sketch Dennett's whole theory of consciousness. It deserves the treatment of a Talmudic exegete, whereas I can offer only some brief remarks on the main point of controversy: whether parallel architecture spells doom for the idea of a conscious stream. My view is that is does not.

First, notice that the quote ends with an acknowledgment of the seriality of consciousness, "its 'von Neumannesque' character," whereas it begins with a denial that there is a "single, definitive 'stream of consciousness.'" The quote is largely given over to defending a theory of mind in which most of the processing is carried out by a system of specialized processors often working in parallel. On Dennett's view, the system of "specialist circuits" is involved in the never ending process of performing "micro takes" on various matters that call on their powers. Only some takes become conscious. This idea is widely accepted (Calvin 1990, 1991; Baars 1988; Johnson-Laird 1983, 1988; Rumelhart and McClelland 1986). There is agreement that most mental processing is unconscious and occurs in parallel. There is also agreement that consciousness is serial or streamlike in quality (this despite our insensitivity to certain nonstreamlike features of the physiological processes that subserve consciousness, the saccades of the eye, for example). What there is disagreement about is whether the qualitative seriality, the streamlike feel of consciousness, is supported by an architectural feature of mind that is in fact really serial or whether the system consists of parallel processors from top to bottom that nonetheless have the capacity to produce the streamlike phenomenology. This is an interesting and complicated empirical question, as yet unsolved. But the main point is that the parties to this debate accept the same first-person phenomenology and treat it as a feature of our mental life in need of explanation.

Second and relatedly, since Dennett accepts that consciousness seems serial and streamlike, the complaint in the opening sentence that "there is no single, definitive 'stream of consciousness'" must rest exclusively on the *"no single, definitive"* part of the sentence, since the streamlike, von Neumannesque character of consciousness—what Dennett elsewhere refers to as its "Joycean character"—is accepted as a legitimate characterization at the end of the passage.

Third, the reason offered for doubting the existence of a single and definitive stream is dubious at best. It is "because there is no central Headquarters, no Cartesian Theater where 'it all comes together' for the perusal of a Central Meaner."

But the advocate of the Jamesian or Joycean stream has no need for such weird homunculi. The idea that consciousness has a streamlike quality is unfairly linked to these weird homunculi, and is dragged into the battle designed to destroy the ideas of a Cartesian theater, a central headquarters, and a central meaner. The aim is to defend the multiple-drafts model of mind. This is a credible model of mental processing. But it endangers the idea of the conscious stream not one bit.

Imagine a tailor fitting you for a new suit. He circles you. At what point in his perusal does the tailor achieve a single, definitive grasp of how you look in the suit? The right answer is at no point. The tailor looks, looks again, sizes you up, and forms an opinion about how you look, what needs adjustment, and so on. The tailor is creating drafts as he circles. Each step results in a revision of the previous draft. This continues until he is finished marking fabric and tells you to change back to your street clothes. So far, so good.

However, there being no single, definitive image of what you look like to the tailor is compatible with there being a single, definitive stream-of-consciousness segment for the tailor as he fits you. This single, definitive stream segment is constituted by whatever phenomenal events occurred to the tailor as he circled you (these needn't even mostly have been about you and the suit). To be sure, if the phone had rung or another customer had asked the whereabouts of the tie rack during your fitting, the tailor's stream segment would have been different (the phone and the customer correspond to different probes that change the character of the stream [see Dennett 1991, 113]). But these counterfactual possibilities weigh not a bit against the idea of a single and definitive stream. They simply show that what character a stream has is incredibly sensitive to small perturbations.

It may well be that the various nonconscious parallel processors involved in giving rise to the conscious stream "are multiple channels in which specialist circuits try, in parallel pandemoniums, to do their various things, creating Multiple Drafts as they go." But all the drafts that reach awareness become part of the singular, definitive stream of consciousness. Still, most of the representations and contents created in the pandemonium of nonconscious information processing never make phenomenal appearances.

The idea of multiple drafts is useful as a metaphor for the nonconscious information processing of mind. It is also useful as a way of describing how thinking, sizing things up, occurs *within* the stream of consciousness. However, when it is used as a metaphor for the conscious stream, it is fully consistent with the idea that there is a singular, definitive stream. The singular, definitive stream is the stream of phenomenal experience that the person actually has, realizes, or undergoes (whether she can remember each and every awareness is irrelevant). When the idea of multiple drafts is used to describe nonconscious parallel processing, the issue of the stream does not arise, so ncither does the question of whether the stream is singular and definitive.

In sum, the phenomenology of the stream is robust. The reality of a conscious stream is not incompatible with anything that the science of the mind thus far needs to say. Discontinuities in the neural underpinnings of conscious awareness, the binding problem, and massive parallelism neither undermine nor compete with the description of consciousness as a stream. They make more compelling the need for an explanation of how the stream emerges from neural processes that are anything but streamlike, at least at certain levels. But no one ever thought that consciousness was diaphanous, that we could see right through to its underlying nature and causal structure.

References

Baars, B. J. (1988). *A Cognitive Theory of Consciousness*. Cambridge: Cambridge University Press.

Calvin, W. H. (1990). *The Cerebral Symphony: Seashore Reflections on the Structure of Consciousness*. New York: Bantam.

———. (1991). *The Ascent of Mind: Ice Age Climate and the Evolution of Intelligence*. New York: Bantam.

Dennett, D. C. (1991). *Consciousness Explained*. Boston: Little, Brown.

James, William. (1890). *The Principles of Psychology*. 2 vols. New York: Dover, 1950.

Johnson-Laird, P. N. (1983). *Mental Models*. Cambridge: Harvard University Press.

———. (1988). *The Computer and the Mind: An Invitation to Cognitive Science*. Cambridge: Harvard University Press.

Rumelhart, D., J. McClelland, and the PDP Research Group. (1986). *Parallel Distributed Processing: Explorations in the Microstructure of Cognition*. 2 vols. Cambridge: MIT Press.

II CONSCIOUSNESS, SCIENCE, AND METHODOLOGY

4 Prospects for a Unified Theory of Consciousness or, What Dreams Are Made Of

Owen Flanagan

What are the prospects for a unified theory of consciousness? This is the question. It is a question that needs to be asked but about which I feel a certain ambivalence. The ambivalence comes from the fact that it seems like a bad idea to speculate too much about the future history of science, and because the question of whether there can be a unified theory of consciousness invites such speculation. On the other hand, this is a period of renewal in the scientific study of consciousness and some vision of the shape of theory is needed at such times. But I posed the question so I'll give my answer right away since my ambivalence about the question will surface and submerge itself as I proceed.

The answer is this: the prospects for a theory of consciousness are not bad and the prospects for a *unified* theory are not bad either—but they depend a great deal on the sort of unity one hopes for or demands. So is the glass half empty or half full, you ask. I recommend the half-full attitude. Be an optimist about the prospects for a theory of consciousness—not because the prospects for such a theory are so certain, but because optimism will make trying to solve this very hard problem seem worth the effort.

My aims in this essay are first, to exemplify and defend the method I proposed in *Consciousness Reconsidered* (1992) for tackling the problem of consciousness, what I call "the natural method," and second to respond to three different objections to the very idea that there could be a theory, especially a unified theory of consciousness. These objections are "the hodgepodge objection," "the heterogeneity objection," and "the superficiality objection." The example of dreams is used throughout as illustrative of distinctive scientific and philosophical concerns and as a good example of one of the multifarious types of conscious experience.

No Hodgepodges Allowed

Let me begin with three claims:

1. *Consciousness exists.* I mean this claim to be as innocent as possible, so it is probably better to put it this way: there exist conscious mental states, events, and processes, or, if you like, there are states, events, and processes that have the property of being conscious.

2. *Consciousness has depth, hidden structure, hidden and possibly multiple functions, and hidden natural and cultural history.* Consciousness has a first-personal phenomenal surface structure. But from a naturalistic point of view, the subjective aspects of consciousness do not exhaust the properties of consciousness. Part of the hidden structure of conscious mental states involves their neural realization. Conscious mental states supervene on brain states. These brain states are essential aspects or constituents of the conscious states, as are the phenomenal aspects of these states. But of course nothing about neural realizations is revealed at the phenomenal surface, not even that there is such realization. The phenomenal surface often hints at or self-intimates the causal role of conscious states; indeed it often seems as if we place certain conscious intentions onto the motivational circuits in order to live as we wish. But the phenomenology leaves us clueless as to how these conscious intentions actually get the system doing what it does; and of course, experience intimates nothing about the causal origins and evolutionary function, if there are any, for the different kinds of consciousness.

3. *Conscious mental states, processes, events— possibly conscious supervisory faculties, if there are any—are heterogeneous in phenomenal kind.* Again I mean this claim to be innocent and uncontroversial. 'Consciousness' is a superordinate term meant to cover all mental states, events, and

processes that are *experienced*—all the states that there is *something it is like for the subject of them to be in*. So, for example, sensory experience is a kind in the domain of consciousness which branches out into the types of experience familiar in the five sensory modalities. Each of these branches further, so that, for example, visual experience branches off from sensory experience and color experiences branch off from it. My experience of red, like yours, is a token color experience—a token of the type red-sensation. So sensory experience divides into five kinds and then branches and branches again and again as our taxonomic needs require. But of course consciousness covers far more than sensory experience. There is, in the human case, linguistic consciousness, and there is conscious propositional attitude thought which *seems* heavily linguistic but may or may not be; there are sensory memories, episodic memories, various types of self-consciousness, moods, emotions, dreams, and much else besides.

The first two claims—that consciousness exists *and* that it has depth and hidden structure—suggest the need for a theory. We should have theories for what exists, for what is real, and this is especially so when what interests us is ubiquitous and has heretofore hidden structure, hidden function, and a mysterious natural (and cultural) history.

But the third claim—*the heterogeneity claim*—has led many to express skepticism about the prospects for a theory, certainly for a *unified* theory of consciousness. But heterogeneity *in itself* is not a good basis for skepticism.

Consider elementary particle physics. Here heterogeneity of particle types reigns to a degree that surpasses normal capacities to count types. But elementary particle physics flourishes; heterogeneity of particle types does not thwart it.[1] Or to take a different example: the periodic table just is a table of the heterogeneous element-types—102, the last time I looked—that constitute chemistry. So elementary particle physics and chemistry exist and provide theoretical cohesion to heterogeneous kinds in their domain of inquiry. These examples are sufficient, I think, to show that heterogeneity of the phenomena in the domain-to-be-explained has *in itself* no bearing on whether theory can be developed for that domain. The inference from the premise that there are zillions of different kinds of elementary particles, heterogeneous in structure and function, to the conclusion that there can be no elementary particle physics yields a false conclusion because the implicit premise about heterogeneity thwarting theory development is false. The point is that the heterogeneity of forms of consciousness in itself should not worry us as we proceed to try to develop a theory of consciousness.

Some naturalists are skeptical about the prospects for a theory of consciousness not simply because of heterogeneity but because of the *kind* of heterogeneous array that the superordinate term 'consciousness' names—it names a heterogeneous hodgepodge (Wilkes 1988a, 1988b). A "hodgepodge," according to the dictionary on my desk, is a "heterogeneous mixture often of incongruous and ill-suited elements." Patricia Churchland compares 'consciousness' to the kind 'dirt' or the kind 'things-that-go-bump-in-the-night' (1983, 1988). Kathleen Wlikes (1988b, p. 33) thinks that 'conscious phenomena' is more like the arbitrary set consisting of "all the words with 'g' as the fourth letter" than it is like a superordinate category such as 'metal', 'mammal', 'fish', or like a subcategory of such a superordinate category: 'gold', 'whale', 'flounder'.

The problem is not with heterogeneity as such but with the hodgepodginess of the heterogeneous array. Perhaps one can develop a scientific theory for a heterogeneous set of phenomena, especially if the phenomena constitute a natural kind, but one cannot develop a scientific theory for a hodgepodge.

Wilkes's argument turns on the conviction that in order for a superordinate category to be nonarbitrary it must display a certain coherence, but that 'conscious phenomena' fail to display the required coherence. "What sort of coherence? Well, even though most of the interesting laws may concern only the subclasses, there might be some laws that are interestingly—nontrivially—true of all the subclasses; or even if this is not so, the laws that concern the subclasses may have significant structural analogy or isomorphism" (Wilkes 1988b, pp. 33–34).

We can put Wilkes's concern in terms of the two examples I have used so far. The heterogeneous types of elementary particle physics and chemistry have shown themselves to have a certain theoretical unity as evidenced by certain cross-kind similarities. For example, the kinds on the periodic table are typed according to atomic number, atomic weight, specific gravity, melting point, and boiling point—in some cases these are not yet known; and in the case of elementary particle physics typing is based on characteristic mass and quantum properties such as charge and spin. Furthermore, the phenomena-in-question adhere to a set of coherent laws—the laws of quantum physics in one case; the periodic law in the other case.[2] Chemistry and elementary particle physics are in reasonably good shape because they unify heterogeneous phenomena that are interestingly embedded in connected layers of laws of nature—this making them non-hodge-podgy.[3] We do not think celestial mechanics is suspect because of the heterogeneity of the composition, size, and gravitational force of bodies in our solar system. Nor do we think that the astronomical variety of subatomic particles, within the three main classes, forecloses the possibility of quantum theory. A theory of consciousness will in the end be part of a unified theory of the mind. This is compatible with the theory making generalizations suited to whatever deep local idiosyncracies exist. Physics tells us that bodies at extremely far distances from each other traveling close to the speed of light are subject to regularities very different from objects moving around our little sphere-like home. It would be no more surprising and no more damaging to the success of the science of the mind if it tells us that visual

consciousness obeys very different laws and is subserved by different neural mechanisms than is conscious reflection on one's love life. In fact this is exactly what we expect.

One thing worth noticing is that if this correctly characterizes the criterion of being non-hodge-podgy, then there is no requirement that a theory must be unified at the most general or highest level, since neither chemistry nor physics are at present, and possibly not even in principle, unified at that level. The important question for us is whether the category and the subcategories that constitute the kind 'consciousness' show signs, taken together or individually, of being a hodge-podge.

Wilkes (1988a) writes that "Scientific research, it would seem, can manage best if it ignores the notion of consciousness . . . 'consciousness' . . . is a term that groups a thoroughly heterogeneous bunch of psychological phenomena [and] is un-suited *per se* for scientific or theoretical purposes" (pp. 192–196).

But Wilkes cannot mean that heterogeneity dashes hopes for a theory of consciousness; she must be thinking that consciousness is a hodge-podge. According to Wilkes some set of phenomena is a hodgepodge if it lacks a certain kind of coherence. In particular, the demarcation criterion distinguishing phenomena-suited-for-respectable-theory and those not so suited rests on this idea quoted above that "even though most of the interesting laws may concern only the subclasses, there might be some laws at least that are interestingly—non-trivially—true of all the subclasses; or even if this is not so, the laws that concern the subclasses may have significant structural analogy or isomorphism" (Wilkes, 1988b, pp. 33–34).

I am not positive exactly what the standard here is, especially the last part. What exactly counts as "significant structural analogy or isomorphism?" Imagine, contrary to the truth, that all learning was governed by the laws of classical conditioning and the laws of operant conditioning. If this were so, we should want to say that a theory of learning exists. But the grounds would not be that all the types of learning were governed by some *single* high-level principle. It would be that there are laws governing each subclass, which taken together explain all learning. One might cite the additional fact that the relevant laws display a certain structural analogy or isomorphism, for example, they are stimulus-response laws. But analogies are a dime a dozen and any imaginative mind can see them most anywhere. What would make the imagined account of learning a theory of learning and a complete one at that would revolve around the fact that our taxonomy of a non-arbitrary domain of inquiry was exhaustive *and* our two sets of laws explain everything in need of explanation. I find it hard to imagine anyone worrying about a lack of structural analogy or isomorphism between two sets of explanatory laws *if* the relevant explanatory work got done.

As for the first part of Wilkes's criterion—that a set of phenomena are suited for a theory if in addition to special laws governing the subclasses there are laws that unify some, possibly all, the subclasses—it is worth noticing that there is no unified field theory in physics *and* no certainty whatsoever that one exists. To me this suggests that the proposal is too stringent for certain well-developed scientific theories.[4]

How to Naturalize Consciousness

If we hold more reasonable standards of unity and of lawlikeness (see Cummins 1983), I see no basis in the current state of consciousness studies for thinking the skeptical hodgepodgists right. There will undoubtedly be revision of the typologies with which we begin as scientific inquiry proceeds, but the evidence—both phenomenological and non-phenomenological—suggests even at this very early stage that conscious phenomena display coherence.

In *Consciousness Reconsidered* (1992), I ask by what method is consciousness to be studied. I propose that we try the most natural strategy— what I call *the natural method*. Start by treating three different lines of analysis with equal respect. Give *phenomenology* its due. Listen carefully to what individuals have to say about how things seem.[5] Also, let the psychologists and cognitive scientists have their say. Listen carefully to their descriptions about how mental life works, and what jobs, if any, consciousness has in its overall economy. When I say let the psychologists and cognitive scientists have their say, I mean also to include amateurs—let folk wisdom be put out on the table along with everything else. Finally, listen carefully to what the neuroscientist say about how conscious mental events of different sorts are realized, and examine the fit between their stories and the phenomenological and psychological stories.

The object of the natural method is to see whether and to what extent the three stories can be rendered coherent, meshed, and brought into reflective equilibrium, into a state where theory and data fit coherently together. The only rule is to treat all three—the phenomenology, the psychology, and the neuroscience—with respect. Any a priori decision about which line of analysis "gets things right" or "has the last word" prejudges the question of whether different analyses might be legitimate for different explanatory pur-

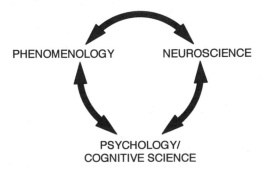

Figure 4.1
The natural method

poses and, in fact, compatible with each other, or at least capable of peaceful coexistence. As theory develops analyses at each level are subject to refinement, revision, or rejection.[6]

I should emphasize here a feature of the natural method that I did not emphasize in the book: this is that in the end what counts toward our theory of consciousness is everything we know from every and any source worth paying attention to. Besides the troika of phenomenology, psychology, and neuroscience, evolutionary biology and cultural and psychological anthropology will also be crucial players. There are, to the best of my knowledge, no very good theories about why conscious experientially sensitive hominids should have been favored over merely informationally sensitive ones, and although it is pretty clear that sensational consciousness—that is, phenomenal awareness in the sensory modalities—comes with the human genome, it is not clear that, for example, moral self-consciousness does. Moral self-consciousness, like the ability to play chess or basketball, is allowed by our genes, but it was hardly selected for.

In any case, one possibility is that in addition to their phenomenological unity, (many) conscious events types will be given an adaptationist evolutionary account—even while lacking certain kinds of unity at the psychological and neuroscientific levels. Embedding consciousness into theories of evolution (biological and cultural), thinking about different forms of consciousness in terms of their ecological role, and in terms of the mechanisms of drift, adaptive selection, and free-riding, will be an important part of understanding what consciousness is, how it works, and what, if anything, it is good for.

How Dreams Are like Being Awake

The specific example I want to try the natural method on in this chapter is dreams. Much of what I know about dreams I have learned from Allan Hobson's writings and from conversation with him. His theory, AIM, (activation, inhibition, modulation), is a robust and powerful one. Despite the existence of such a powerful theory as AIM, dreams are fodder for skeptics about the prospects for a theory of consciousness for a number of reasons. One route to skepticism is simple and straightforward. Common sense says that 'conscious' involves, among other things, being awake. But dreaming takes place during sleep, and, thus, by the distinguished deliverances of conceptual analysis, dreams cannot be conscious experiences. But common wisdom also says that dreams are experiences that take place during sleep, so our commonsense taxonomy of 'consciousness' is worse than a hodgepodge; it is riddled with inconsistency from the start.

There is a more sophisticated line of attack suggested in different ways and with different degrees of conviction by Norman Malcolm (1959) and Daniel Dennett (1978). This line sets aside the unsettling linguistic facts linking 'being conscious' with 'being awake' and focuses primarily on the received view that dreams are *experiences* that take place during sleep. To be sure, people give reports of experiences they allege to have had during sleep. But surely if one is in a sufficiently skeptical mood this does not remotely prove that the dream report is in fact about experience that took place during sleep, rather than a combined confabulation-misremembering accompanying waking. Remember, people also insist that they have visited certain places before or been in certain situations before only to discover that they are wrong. Déjà vu experiences just are claims to experiences that did not in fact occur. There are, one might say, déjà vu experiences but they are not truly déjà vu—you were not here before and this did not happen to you before. It seems that way, it just is not so.

Dennett calls attention to the possibility (also suggested by Malcolm) that so-called dreams *may* occur while awake or while waking up and not, as most everyone thinks, during REM (rapid eye movement) sleep at all. Sure, this is possible. But why think it more than merely possible?

Malcolm's position was verificationist: dreams line up with verbal reports people sometimes give in the morning, so that is all we can say that dreams are. Dennett (in this case) rejects the verificationist line, and points instead to certain kinds of dreams as support for the skeptical view of dreaming. Dennett reports this dream: "I searched long and far for a neighbor's goat; when at last I found her she bleated *baa-a-a*—and I awoke to find her bleat merging perfectly with the buzz of an electric alarm clock I had not used or heard for months" (1978, p. 135). One way to explain such dreams, but at high cost as Dennett points out, is to think that powers of *precognition* are operative—the dream-narrating mechanism prepares the narrative to fit with the alarm it knows is about to go off!

Even true believers in the theory that dreams are experiences that take place while sleeping think that most every dream report contains either more *or* less than was experienced or *both* more and less than was experienced in the dream state. On most every view, dream reports are putrid evidence about *what was experienced* while asleep, even if we accept that they provide reliable evidence that *something* was experienced while sleeping.

In any case, let us apply the natural method to the case of dreams, and in particular to the question "are dreams experiences?," to see where it leads. We know that most people, not having read Malcolm or Dennett, will report with confidence that they have dreamt while asleep. They will also say certain things about the content of their dreams. These reports are composed of part phenomenology and part folk wisdom (i.e., the reports are partly provoked by the "wisdom" that people dream while asleep). There are also psychological theories about dreams—the psychoanalytic theory being the best known, if not the most well-respected.[7] The nice thing about the psychoanalytic view is that it can easily be expressed in terms of the sort of functional-flow chartology admired in cognitive science: as sleep ensues repressor mechanisms loosen their grip on receptacles filled with wishes, strong socially unacceptable wishes squirm out and find their way to symbolic encoders that work up an "experienced" story that gives the disguised wish some sort of satisfying release, which "experienced" story is routed then (imperfectly) far away from waking memory.

Now, although Freud certainly thought that dreams are experiences, his theory is compatible with the view that dreams are not experiences—at least not ones taking place during sleep. That is, take all the phenomenological reports of dreams, treat them as displaying manifest content which yields in interpretation to latent content revealing what wish was being fulfilled. All this, as well as the associated view of why dreams are good for you, is compatible with a version of the skeptics' view, namely, a version that says that dreams are disguised wishes we happen to give (or think to ourselves) in the morning. Or to put it another way, dream reports reflect experiences, but not ones that take place while sleeping, rather one's experiences embedded in awake thoughts or reports.

The upshot so far is this: despite the widespread acceptance of the view that dreams are experiences that take place during REM sleep, the case is not remotely closed. And one consequence of its not being closed is that we do not have a really decisive reply to the skeptic, and lacking that, we do not know whether dreams fall under the concept of 'consciousness' or not. And this can be taken as evidence that the very taxonomy of the domain-to-be-explained is ill-defined. If we do not even know what falls under the concept of 'consciousness,' we can hardly be expected to build a coherent theory for it.

This is why the physiological and neuroscientific data are so important. These data both constrain and illuminate the phenomenology and the psychology and they provide an additional line of evidence against the skeptic. If there is to be a theory of consciousness we will want eventually to know how, or in what ways, conscious mental states are realized. It has been suggested

recently that subjective awareness is linked to oscillation patterns in the 40-Hz range in the relevant groups of neurons, that is, neurons involved
in a certain decoding task "synchronize their
spikes in 40Hz oscillations" (Crick and Koch
1990, p. 272). Oscillations of 40 Hz have been
found in single neurons and neural nets in the
retina, olfactory bulb, in the thalamus, and neocortex.

Recently, Rodolfo Llinás, Ribary, and Paré
have produced strong evidence that such oscillation patterns characterize REM sleep. Llinás
and Ribary (1993, p. 2078) report that "during the
period corresponding to REM sleep (in which a
subject if awakened reports dreaming), 40Hz oscillation patterns similar in distribution phase and
amplitude to that observed during wakefulness is
observed." The second finding of significance
they express this way: "during dreaming 40Hz
oscillations are not reset by sensory input ... We
may consider the dreaming condition a state of
hyperattentiveness in which sensory input cannot
address the machinery that generates conscious
experience." Within Hobson's theory, the 40-Hz
oscillations pertain to (A) activation level, while
the tuning out of external stimuli is explained by
the mechanisms of input-output gating (I).

The main point for present purposes is that the
reason dreams seem like conscious experiences is
because they *are* conscious experiences and they
are like awake conscious experiences in certain
crucial respects.[8]

Llinás and Ribary suggest this unifying hypothesis: 40-Hz activity in the non-specific system
comprised of the thalamocortical loop provides
the temporal binding of contentful states that involve 40-Hz oscillations in the areas devoted to
particular modalities. That is, the neural system
subserving a sensory modality provides the *content* of an experience and the non-specific system
consisting of resonating activity in the thalamus
and cortex provides "the *temporal binding* of such
content into a single cognitive experience evoked
either by external stimuli or, intrinsically during
dreaming" (1993, p. 2081). Llinás and Paré write

"*it is the dialogue between the thalamus and the
cortex that generates subjectivity*" (1991, p. 532).
Ah, science!

These data and hypotheses, in light of other
data and theory, increase the credibility of the
claim linking REM sleep with vivid experiences.
Whether it is really true that dreams are experiences depends, of course, on whether it is true that
40-Hz oscillations turn out to be a marker, a
constituent component, or a cause (which one
they are is, of course, very important) of vivid
conscious experiences. The point is that the neuroscientific data push credible theory in a certain
direction. If these data bring us closer to the answer to one question they open a host of others,
suggesting occasional answers—a sure sign of a
progressive research program.

For example, one might wonder whether 40-Hz
oscillation patterns will turn out to be necessary
or sufficient for experience or enable us to differ-
entiate different kinds of experiences. This is a
hard question. Oscillation patterns of 40 Hz are
like dust; there is always some to be found. This
suggests the possibility that alive human beings
might always be in some experiential state or
other, that is, that we are never wholly unconscious—if, that is, 40-Hz patterns are sufficient
for experience. If this sounds like an incredible
prospect, it is relevant that persons awakened
from NREM (non-rapid eye movement) sleep
often report having experiences—albeit experiences lacking the vivacity of post-REM reports.
And sleeptalking and sleepwalking are well
known to take place during NREM sleep (pos-
tural muscles are turned off during REM sleep)
and it is obscure whether, or in what precise sense,
sleepwalkers and sleeptalkers are experiential
blanks. *Globality* of 40-Hz activity may turn out
to be the relevant feature of robust conscious experiences, not the mere presence or absence of
some 40-Hz activity (Llinás and Paré 1991, p. 527).

We will also want to know why, despite involving vivid experience, dreams involve shutdowns
of the attentional, motor, and memory systems and
insensitivity to disturbance by external stimuli.

Here, as Allan Hobson, has pointed out, under the rubric of (M)odulation (specifically demodulation) ratios of neurochemicals of various sorts play the major role. The point can be put this way: 40-Hz oscillation patterns might explain the similarity between dreams and waking states while input-output gating and demodulation explain the main differences.

There is some neurophysiological evidence that auditory stimuli are *slightly discriminated* during REM sleep which would help explain how events in the external world are embedded in dream content, and might take some of the edge off Dennett's alarm clock worry (Llinás and Paré 1991, p. 522). Some other interesting facts are these: humans with pontine lesions do not have muscular atonia during dreams and are those very people one reads about who play linebacker with their dressers and endanger their spouses on a nightly basis. These people are not bad, they are doing what the rest of us would be doing if the relevant brain area were not effective at shutting the motor system down.

There are interesting convergences of neuroscientific and phenomenological data in other areas as well. For example, the parts of the brain that reveal robust activity on positron emission tomography (PET), magnetic resonance imaging (MRI), or on magnetoencephalogram (MEG) or similar devices suggest that "mentation during dreaming operates on the same anatomical substrate as does perception during the waking state" (Llinás and Paré 1991, p. 524).[9]

The Superficiality Objection

So what does the case of dreams show? It shows something, I think, about the nature of consciousness, or about the nature of one kind of consciousness, or, if you like, about the similarities and differences between two kinds of consciousness. It also shows some of the power of the natural method. Specifically, it shows that phenomenological facts and neurophysiological facts can be brought into reflective equilibrium in

certain cases. Phenomenologically, REM dreams and awake consciousness are very different in certain respects. But they also possess phenomenological commonalities, and these together with certain commonalities at the neural level, suggest that they are *two kinds of consciousness*. They are a heterogeneous dyad but hardly a hodgepodge, hardly an ill-suited or incongruous dyad.

The case of dreams also carries some weight against the objection that even if consciousness is not a hodgepodge, its only interesting feature is the *superficial* shared phenomenological feature of being experienced. This is not so, since in the case of dreams and awake states, the phenomenological similarities and differences gain some explanation at the neural level. Furthermore, certain psychological facts, for example, why noises in the external world are sometimes incorporated into dream narratives, are also explained by bringing neural facts to bear; in particular, the brain detects, but will not normally wake up for, noises in the external environment during REM sleep.

Nonetheless, one might worry that this case is exceptional. And indeed it might be. We know that there exists an important class of cases where phenomenal similarity is not subserved by similarity at the micro level. For example, the phenomenal property of "wetness" is multiply realized. There is, after all, H_2O which is wet and heavy water, D_2O, which is wet. Perhaps consciousness is like this: at the phenomenal level there is the shared property, but this shared property is subserved by all manner of different types of brain processes. I have acknowledged this possibility. I do not see that it harms the prospects for a theory of consciousness as I have been conceiving it. But one might imagine the examples where phenomenal similarity is unsupported by similarities at lower levels being used to press the worry that the shared property of being experienced really is too *superficial* to guide theory or to make us optimists about the prospects for a theory of consciousness.

Patricia Churchland gives an example from the history of science designed to feed the superficiality worry.[10] She reminds us how the commonsense concept of 'fire' has fared as science has progressed:

'Fire' was used to classify not only burning wood but also the activity on the sun and various stars (actually fusion), lightning (actually electrically induced incandescence), the Northern lights (actually spectral emission), and fire-flies (actually phosphorescence). As we now understand matters, only some of these things involve oxidation, and some processes which do involve oxidation, namely rusting, tarnishing, and metabolism, are not on the 'Fire' list. (1988, p. 285)

Churchland concludes that "the case of fire illustrates both how the intuitive classification can be re-drawn, and how the new classification can pull together superficially diverse phenomena once the underlying theory is available." This is true and important.

It has been suggested that we imagine a person in an earlier time—a philosophical ancestor of mine, perhaps—saying something like this: "No matter how science goes, we will still be able to talk of a theory of fire." Even if the constituents and causes of the different sorts of fire turn out to be physically very different, the theory of fire can still be constituted by gathering together all the interesting truths "about the class of phenomena that possess the shared property of being fire."[11]

It is possible that Churchland might want to read my position as analogous to this far-seeing fire sage. So I need to be clear that I accept the true and important point that phenomenological similarity, in and of itself,—even when it is similarity of *experience itself*, or experience *as such*, and not similarity of *thing experienced*—resolves nothing about the hidden nature and deep structure of the phenomenally similar stuff. Indeed, the very asking of the question—are dreams experiences?—concedes the possibility that, surprising as it might seem, science could force us to drop dreams from the class of experiences in the way it forced us to drop what goes on in the tails of fire-flies from the fire list. One can imagine two ex-

tremist views. One view would be that there is verbal behavior associated with waking or being awake that "sounds" to third parties like experiential reports about sleeping mentation, but which are—remember, we are at the skeptical extreme—just some narrative noise an awake person produces. To keep skepticism heightened, think of *all* parties involved—those producing dream narratives, and those they speak to, including themselves in soliloquy, convinced by the standard theory that the *narrative reports* are of experiences that occurred while sleeping, but that this is false. Another extreme hypothesis would be that dreams are experienced, contentwise, roughly as reported. The dreams that are remembered occur, however (very rapidly), while one is awake or as one awakes. Neither view is remotely incoherent.

The point is that dreams might have gone off the consciousness list (or changed status on the list) as inquiry proceeded in the same way the lightning bugs were removed from the list-of-things-on-fire (if anyone really believes they were once on the list). But the present discussion shows that, in fact, things are going in the other direction—science is helping to secure the place of dreams as experiences, not to make us remove dreams from the class of experiences. It could have worked out the other way (it still might), but thus far it has not. So our commonsense concept of consciousness is open to revision, to being "redrawn." How consciousness is conceived depends almost completely on how the science of the mind progresses.[12]

The best evidence against the critics who suspect that 'consciousness' names too superficial a phenomenon to play a useful role in scientific explanation or prediction involves deploying the natural method in cases like that of dreams and, in addition, pointing to the existence of predictive and explanatory generalizations that place conscious mental events in important causal roles. For example: there are important functional differences between people with phenomenal awareness in certain domains and those without.

Suitably motivated persons with normal sight naturally carry out voluntary actions toward seen things. When thirsty, we step over to the water fountain we see to our right. However, blind-sighted persons, who are identically motivated and who process information about the very same things in the visual field, do not naturally or efficiently carry out the suitable actions toward the "seen" things. There are also the differential abilities of amnesiacs to form integrated self-concepts and to create and abide a consistent narratively constructed self-model. And persons incapable of experiencing certain qualia, for example, color-blind persons, show all sorts of functional differences from non-color-blind persons. Check out their wardrobes.[13]

This evidence suggests that there exist true counterfactual generalizations in the domain of consciousness. Some of these generalizations will relate phenomena at the psychological level, for example, persons with qualia of kind q do x in circumstances c but persons without qualia q (but who are otherwise identical) fail to do x in c. Other generalizations will link phenomenological and psychological level processes with brain processes, for example, (1) people with damage to the speech centers and, in particular, to the left brain interpreter, will have trouble generating the narratively constructed self; (2) people with certain kinds of frontal lobe damage will have trouble formulating plans and intentions; other kinds of frontal lobe damage will obstruct links between consciously formulated action plans and actually carrying out the plans.

Given that these sorts of generalizations already exist and have been corroborated, it follows that there are laws which conscious mental life answers to. To be sure, the laws are pitched to the heterogeneous multiplicity of events and processes that possess the shared property of being experienced. But taken together I see no reason to say that they are not part of an emerging theory of consciousness, one basic insight of which is that consciousness is heterogeneous.

Conscious phenomena constitute legitimate explananda and conscious events play explanatory roles in certain well-grounded generalizations. In broad strokes there are two ways one might imagine building a theory of consciousness. Gathering together whatever scientific truths there are about this set of phenomena will constitute one way of building a theory of consciousness. Especially in the early stages, building such a theory might amount to the gathering together of all the interesting truths about the class of phenomena that possess the shared feature of being experienced. If dreams, for example, turned out not to be experiences, they would no longer be taxonomized as conscious, and would fall out of the theory so conceived. But they—no longer dreams but now "mere dream reports," or alleged dreams—would still require an explanation within our overall theory of mind. A theory of consciousness built in this way, around the shared phenomenological feature where it *really* resides, would crosscut our theories of perception, memory, and learning. Or, to put it differently, the theory of consciousness, such as it was, would contain generalizations that also show up within these special theories.

A second, related possibility is that we might forego altogether a specially demarcated space for *the* theory of consciousness, allowing instead all the true generalizations about conscious mental life to occur within the special theories.[14] The idea is that the interesting facts and generalizations about consciousness might be gathered under the rubric of the special theories of perception, memory, learning, and so on. Presumably this would happen—and it is a very reasonable prospect—if the most interesting generalizations of the science of the mind weave together conscious and unconscious processes and their neural realizations in accordance with *what, from a functional point of view, the system is doing*. Since perceiving and remembering, and the like, are things we *do*, whereas consciousness may be *a way we are* or one of the *ways* we perceive, remember, and so on, it is easy to imagine embedding most of what needs to be said about consciousness into the special theories.

Whichever shape a theory of consciousness takes—the first way as a theory of consciousness itself, or the second way as a "theory" in which what is true of consciousness gets said, possibly without much ado or fanfare, within all the necessary special theories—it will be part of the larger, more systematic theory of the mind as a whole. *The really important thing is that there can be a science of the mind.* So long as consciousness is given its place within such a theory it matters little whether it is explained in terms of a theory devoted exclusively to it, or whether it is just explained period (i.e., within the accounts given to domains like memory, problem solving, etc.).[15]

The best strategy is to get on with the hard work of providing the right fine-grained analysis of conscious mental life and to see where it leads. It will be our proudest achievement if we can demystify consciousness. Consciousness exists. It would be a mistake to eliminate talk of it because its semantic past is so bound up with ghostly fairy tales or because it names such a multiplicity of things. The right attitude is to deliver the concept from its ghostly past and provide it with a credible naturalistic analysis. I have tried to say a bit about how this might be done—indeed about how it is already being done. So dream on about a naturalistic account of consciousness and rest assured that your dream does not reveal some impure philosophical or scientific wish or fantasy.

Notes

I was fortunate to have received valuable comments on earlier versions of this chapter at both the Wake Forest conference on my book, *Consciousness Reconsidered*, and the Carnegie Mellon conference on Scientific Approaches to the Study of Consciousness. I am especially grateful to David H. Sanford, Allin Cottrell, Bob McCauley, George Graham, Allan Hobson, Marcel Kinsbourne, Ralph Kennedy, and David Galin, and Herbert Simon for their helpful comments. Ken Winkler and Robert Brandon also helped on an early draft. The current version of this paper was delivered at Carnegie-Mellon University in June 1993 and appears in Cohen, J., and Schooler, J. (Eds.), *Scientific Approaches to the Question of Consciousness: 25th Carnegie Symposium on Cognition.* Hillside, NJ: Erlbaum. (1996).

1. Of course, many elementary particle physicists worry about this lack of unity at the highest level.

2. The periodic law says that the physical and chemical properties of the elements depend on atomic structure and thus are, for the most part, periodic functions of their atomic numbers.

3. The idea is that a prima facie hodgepodge can turn out not to the a real hodgepodge if laws of nature unify the phenomena.

4. According to Brandon's (1990) account of evolutionary theory, it is not unified in Wilkes's strong sense. Evolutionary theory is unified by certain principles of probability theory, but not by any overarching contingently true generalization—this even though the principles of natural selection, drift, and so on instantiate the relevant probability principles.

5. At the Wake Forest colloquium on my book, *Consciousness Reconsidered*, May 7–9, 1993, there was spirited debate about the status of phenomenology. Bob McCauley argued persuasively that it provides data and that its pronouncements as pronouncements about how things really are must yield to explanation at the other levels. Even claims about how things *seem* can change as our views about how things are change. The case of dreams is a case in point. If we ever came to have really good theoretical reasons for thinking that dreams were not experiences, they might well seem less like experiences. It is hard to imagine giving up the idea that there are perceptual experiences since such experiences take place in the specious present (or so it strongly seems); but even dreamers will admit that they are remembering both the alleged experience and the content of the alleged experience. Since we allow false remembering, the intuition that dreams are experiences could yield if theoretical reasons deemed the sense that dream experiences had occurred misbegotten memories, akin to déjà vu experiences.

6. At the Carnegie-Mellon conference Clark Glymour proposed that theory should be as biologically constrained as possible, and he expressed the worry that cognitive information-processing models often fail to

attend to biological realism. I quite agree with the normative point. But our present knowledge of the brain is thin and often hard to interpret. Sometimes it is often hard to know what the neuroscientific data are or mean and thus hard to know how they should contrain our theories. For example, many effective antidepressants work by affecting norepinephrine or serotonin levels, absorption rates, and so on. But in many cases neither the Food and Drug Administration (FDA), nor the pharmaceutical companies know exactly how these drugs work. Judgments about what they do at the psychological level, what some of their phenomenological and physiological side effects are, as well as assessments about overall safety and effectiveness, are made without anything approaching complete understanding at the level of brain chemistry.

7. There is also, as I have noted, J. Allan Hobson's (1988), more credible and brain-based theory of dreams.

8. So being awake and REM sleep both involve 40-Hz oscillations. This might seem neat since both being awake and being in REM sleep are thought to be experiential states, to involve a type of conscious experience. NREM sleep, on the other hand, is often thought to be a state of unconsciousness—a state in which there is nothing it is like to be in it. But this is dead wrong. NREM sleep is experientially rich (see chapter). Forty-hertz oscillations may not turn out to be a marker of experience or they may be necessary or sufficient, or both; it is too early to know. One worry for the 40-Hz necessary condition hypothesis is this: the mentation occurring during NREM sleep when measured by electroencephalogram (EEG) does not appear to involve the 40-Hz oscilliations despite involving mentation. So 40-Hz oscillations may be a reliable marker of certain kinds of conscious mentation but not necessary for all mentation (see Steriade, M., McCormick, D.A., and Sejnowski, T. J. 1993. "Thalamocortical Oscillations in the Sleeping and Aroused Brain," *Science*, 262:679–685). On the other hand, when measured with MEG, one does find 40-Hz oscillations, but much attenuated in amplitude and we do not pick up much in the way of amplitude modulations.

9. This helps explain why prosopagnosiacs do not report dreaming of faces and why people with right parietal lobe lesions who cannot see the left side of the visual field report related deficits in their dream imagery Llinás and Paré, (1991, p. 524). On the other hand, it tells us something about memory that visual imagery sustains itself better in both the dreams and the awake experiences of people who develop various kinds of blindness in later life.

10. It is often and reasonably said that science proceeds best when there are very specific research problems to be addressed. For example, the double helix structure of DNA solved the "copying problem" in genetics. It was well understood by the time Watson and Crick came along that inheritance takes place, but there was no postulated mechanism that was up to the specific task of replication. DNA solved this problem. One problem with the scientific study of consciousness is that there are still open taxonomic questions (e.g., the one about dreams discussed here) about which states are conscious and which are not—even questions about whether there is any shared phenomenological feature, as I assume, and thus anything at all that really falls under the concept. But some good questions (about dreams, about automatic behaviors, about deficits of consciousness, about neural underpinnings of various conscious states) are opening up and getting attention.

11. See Cottrell, A. 1993. "Tertium Datur? Reflections on Owen Flanagan's *Consciousness Reconsidered*." Presented at Wake Forest conference, Winston-Salem, NC, May 1993.

12. Indeed, it would be very surprising if different kinds of consciousness were not realized in different ways. The individuation of conscious events at the neural level will undoubtedly entail tracing complex neural maps originating at different points on the sensory periphery and at different places within the system itself and traversing all sorts of neural terrain. This will be true even if all the events mapped share a physical property such as having the same oscillatory frequency. It would also be surprising if the neural underpinnings of certain kinds of conscious states were not also essential components of certain nonconscious states, but not of other kinds of conscious states. For example, it might be that the areas of the brain that light up during ordinary visual awareness, or when we are solving problems in geometry, also light up when we turn over during sleep, but never light up when we are listening to music with our eyes closed. And perhaps there is a deep reason why the relevant area lights up in the conscious and nonconscious cases it lights up in. Imagine that the area is a necessary component of all spatial analysis, so it is activated when one is wide awake and trying to prove the Pythagorean theorem, and when one is sound asleep but

computing information about edges and distances in order to keep from falling out of bed. In cases like this our theory of consciousness is interweaved, as it must be, with theories of unconscious processing.

But such results would in no way undermine the idea that conscious phenomena are legitimate explananda for which, and possibly with which, to build theory. It is to be expected that the development of the science of the mind will reveal deep and surprising things about the phenomena with the shared property of being experienced. Such discoveries might include the discovery that there are greater similarities in certain respects between certain phenomena that possess the shared property and those that do not, than among all those with the shared phenomenal property. The neural spatial analyzer would be such an example. But this could happen while at the same time important generalizations are found to obtain among all or most of the disparate events that possess the shared property.

13. Color blindness is an interesting example because there is reason to believe that the conscious deficit is caused, as it were, by low-level processing problems in the visual system. Still, it is not implausible to think that it is the deficit at the qualitative level that is the proximate cause of difficulties in color coordination in the color-blind person's wardrobe.

14. Herbert Simon has indicated to me that he favors, as I do, the second approach. It does seem to best represent what is in fact happening in the science of the mind.

15. Not to be frivolous, one might imagine the choice between collecting all and only Mickey Mantle cards vs. collecting New York Yankees cards (even assuming a complete set of the Yankees would yield a complete Mantle set). Mantle is, as a matter of fact, essentially embedded in the history of the Yankees. But the Yankees—a somewhat different version—could have done without number 7. Whether number 7 could have done without the Yankees is more obscure. The point though is a straightforward one about interest relativity. We design baseball and scientific collections within fairly broad constraints, some of which we create and all of which we interpret.

References

Brandon, R. (1990). *Adaptation and Environment.* Princeton, NJ: Princeton University Press.

Churchland, P. S. (1983). "Consciousness: The Transmutation of a Concept," *Pacific Philosophical Quarterly, 64,* 80–93.

——— (1988). "Reduction and the Neurobiological Basis of Consciousness" in Marcel, A. J. and E. Bisiach (Eds.) *Consciousness in Contemporary Science.* Oxford: Oxford University Press.

Crick, F., and Koch, C. (1990). "Towards a Neurobiological Theory of Consciousness," *Seminars in the Neurosciences, 2,* 263–275.

Cummins. (1983). *Psychological Explanation.* Cambridge, MA: MIT Press.

Dennett, D. (1978). *Brainstorms.* Cambridge, MA: MIT Press.

Flanagan, O. (1992). *Consciousness Reconsidered.* Cambridge, MA: The MIT Press.

Hobson, J. A. (1988). *The Dreaming Brain.* New York: Basic Books.

Llinás, R. R., and Paré, D. (1991). "Commentary of Dreaming and Wakefulness," *Neuroscience, 44,* 521–535.

Llinás, R. and Ribary, U. (1993). "Coherent 40-Hz oscillation characterizes dream state in humans," *Proceedings of the National Academy of Sciences of the United States of America, 90,* 2078–2081.

Malcolm, N. (1959). *Dreaming.* London: Routledge & Kegan Paul.

Marcel, A. J., and Bisiach E., (Eds.) (1988). *Consciousness in Contemporary Science.* Oxford: Oxford University Press.

Wilkes, K. V. (1988a). "———, yìshì, duh, um, and consciousness." In A. J. Marcel, and E. Bisiach (Eds.), *Consciousness in Contemporary Science.* Oxford: Clarendon Press.

——— (1988b). *Real People: Personal Identity without Thought Experiments.* Oxford: Oxford University Press.

5 Consciousness, Folk Psychology, and Cognitive Science

Alvin I. Goldman

Defining Consciousness

What is standardly meant in ordinary usage by the word "conscious"? One use of "conscious" is applied to a person's *total* state. A person is conscious, in this sense, if he or she is in a generalized condition of alertness or arousal: being awake rather than asleep or in a coma. This sense of "conscious," however, may be derivative from a primary or core sense of "conscious" in which it applies to *partial* psychological states (or perhaps processes or representations), such as individual beliefs, plans, or emotions. A partial psychological state is conscious if and only if it involves phenomenal awareness, that is, subjective experience or feeling. Given the notion of a conscious partial state, we can say that a person's generalized condition at a given moment is conscious if and only if he possesses at least one conscious partial state at that time. There is also a third sense of "conscious": consciousness *of* a particular object or event. This third sense can also be analyzed in terms of the core sense sketched above. To be conscious *of* an object, x, is to be in some (partial) state of phenomenal awareness which includes a representation of x. In other words, x is the referent or "intentional object" of a conscious state or representation.

Let us concentrate on the core sense of "conscious." The definition suggested above seems reasonably accurate but not terribly illuminating. "Awareness" is just an approximate synonym of "conscious," and so is "phenomenal." Not much progress is made by providing these synonyms. Is there a definition that gets outside this circle of unrevealing synonyms, while still confining itself to the ordinary grasp of the concept (rather than shifting to the psychological mechanisms of consciousness or its neurological basis)?

Attempts at definition might try to define consciousness (semi-) operationally, by reference to the sort of behavior that would provide public or external evidence for consciousness. For example, one might try do define a conscious state as a state available for verbal report. This proposal, unfortunately, has many defects. Verbal reportability is not a necessary condition for a state to be conscious. First, individuals with speech impairments such as global aphasia may be unable to report their inner states, but this does not render those states unconscious. Similarly, the right hemisphere of a split-brain patient might have awareness although its disconnection from the verbal left hemisphere precludes verbal report. Second, some states of awareness may be too brief, too confused, or too temporally removed from report possibilities to link up with the apparatus of verbal report. Dreams, for example, are episodes of awareness. Yet at the time of dreaming there seems to be no engagement with verbal apparatus. Dreams also commonly suffer from a degree of confusion and evanescence that make them difficult if not impossible to report. Third, no satisfactory definition of consciousness should automatically exclude animals from having states of consciousness, which the verbal reportability definition does. Although it is not certain that animals are conscious, it is surely an intelligible possibility despite their evident lack of report capability. So report capability cannot be required by consciousness. Finally, verbal reportability is not a *sufficient* condition for consciousness. Machines and robots might be capable of reporting their internal states, but intuitively this would not suffice to confer awareness on those states.

A second approach is to try to define consciousness in terms of its *function*, for example, informational accessibility. An example of this approach is the "global workspace" idea of Bernard Baars (1988) and others. A conscious representation, on this view, is one whose message is "broadcast" to the system as a whole, not just to some local or specialized processors. This idea of global broadcast may accurately describe a notable characteristic of human consciousness as studied by cognitive science, but it is unlikely to capture the ordinary grasp of the consciousness concept. Surely ordinary people do not understand consciousness as a set of messages posted on a large blackboard for all cognitive subsystems to read (Baars 1988, p. 87), since the picture of the mind as a collection of intercommunicating subsystems is not part of our naive conceptual repertoire. A similar point holds for other traits of consciousness described by Baars. For example, he notes that consciousness in human beings is typically reserved for messages that are "informative" in the technical sense of reducing uncertainty. When uncertainty is already (close to) zero, messages tend to be removed from consciousness; the most obvious example is the loss of awareness of repeated stimuli in stimulus habituation. But clearly this correlation between consciousness and informativeness is not something generally recognized by ordinary people, so it is not part of the naive understanding of consciousness. Moreover, one can readily conceive of a system in which uninformative or "redundant" thoughts remain vividly conscious. Thus, informativeness can hardly be viewed as an essential property of consciousness as commonly understood. In similar fashion we may note that the combination of global broadcast and informativeness is not sufficient for consciousness. We can easily conceive of a (nonhuman) system in which informative representations are distributed to all subsystems yet those representations are totally devoid of phenomenal awareness. Baars lists further properties of consciousness, but I doubt that even these, in conjunction with the first two, suffice for phenomenal consciousness.

A third general approach is to try to define consciousness in terms of self-knowledge, self-monitoring, or higher-order reflection. For a state S to be conscious, it might be proposed, the possessor of S must have another state that is conscious or aware *of* S at the time of its occurrence. Observe, however, that this formulation uses the term "conscious" in defining itself, obviously not terribly satisfactory. Such objectionable circularity can be avoided if we substitute "belief," "thought," or some other term referring to an informational state. This yields something of the following sort: "State S of a system is conscious if and only if the system possesses a "higher-order" belief that it is in S;" or perhaps " . . . if and only if the system has another informational state that monitors S." Such proposals are endorsed by philosophers such as David Armstrong (1968), David Rosenthal (1986, 1990, 1993), and William Lycan (1987), as well as psychologists like Philip Johnson-Laird (1988a, 1988b).

Does the higher-order belief or monitoring state required by this proposal itself have to be conscious? If the proposal is so intended, then we are still appealing to the consciousness of a higher-order state to confer consciousness on a first-order state, which leaves the circularity unremedied. It also generates an infinite regress, since each nth-level state must be rendered conscious by an $n + 1$st-level state. Suppose instead that the higher-order belief need not be conscious (it is generally assumed in cognitive science that belief per se, although it requires intentionality or aboutness, need not involve consciousness). Under that construal, clearly stated in Rosenthal (1993), the definition does not get things right. Couldn't there be a robot or "zombie" that totally lacks phenomenal awareness or subjective feeling but nonetheless has higher-order beliefs about its other internal states? In fact, we need not appeal to thought experiments to make this point. Real human beings have nonconscious representational states that are monitored by other nonconscious states. This objection is lodged by Anthony Marcel (1988, p. 140), who observes that we nonconsciously edit nonconscious speech production decisions and motor intentions. Since higher-order monitoring takes place in these nonconscious domains of cognition, the monitoring relationship is by no means sufficient for consciousness. In addition to these counterexamples, the underlying idea here is puzzling. How could possession of a meta-state confer subjectivity or feeling on a lower-level state that did not otherwise possess it? Why would being an intentional object or referent of a meta-state confer consciousness on a first-order state? A rock does not become conscious when someone has a belief about it. Why should a first-order psychological state become conscious simply by having a belief about it?

It is noteworthy that each of the failed attempts thus far examined offers a *relational* definition of consciousness. Each tries to explain the consciousness of a state in terms of some relation it bears to other events or states of the system: (1) its expressibility in verbal behavior, (2) the transmission of its content to other states or locations in the system, or (3) a higher-order state which reflects on the target state. The failure of such proposals leads one to suspect (although of course it does not prove) that no relational proposal will succeed. Of course, conscious states could still possess significant causal/functional relations to other cognitive events; it is just that consciousness is not *definable* by such relational characteristics. Our ordinary understanding of awareness or consciousness seems to reside in features that conscious states have in themselves, not in relations they bear to other states.

Call this sort of thesis about the ordinary understanding of consciousness: *intrinsicalism.* One way intrinsicalists defend their position is through inverted spectrum arguments. They try to produce conceptual "dissociations" between the intrinsic quality of awareness or experience and its functional-relational properties, thereby showing that the former are not simply equivalent to the latter. The traditional inverted spectrum argument tries to show that functional (relational) similarity can in principle be accompanied by qualitative (intrinsic) diversity. Two people, or the same person at different times, might have functionally identical states, i.e., states that interact equivalently with all inputs and outputs, and yet have different experiential "feels" to them, or no feels at all. A second type of conceptual dissociation is presented in Ned Block's (1990) dis-

cussion of the "Inverted Earth" example. Block demonstrates that qualitative or intrinsic similarity can in principle be accompanied by functional diversity. Two people, or the same person at different times, might have qualitatively identical states that are functionally-relationally diverse.[1]

For reasons such as this, Block (1991, 1992, 1993) holds that at least one sense of "consciousness" refers to an intrinsic (rather than a relational) property, called *phenomenal consciousness*. He distinguishes this from a second sense of consciousness, *access consciousness*, which picks out, roughly, a state's capacity for rational control of speech and/or behavior. A very similar distinction is drawn by Edoardo Bisiach (1988). John Searle (1992) denies that so-called access consciousness is a bona fide concept of consciousness at all (a worry also expressed by Bisiach), and our earlier discussion supports these doubts. Even Block, who defends access consciousness as a legitimate sense of "consciousness," does not take it as a substitute for phenomenal consciousness. Our own discussion strongly suggests that only the phenomenal notion of consciousness is the one intended in common usage.

We have not managed to define phenomenal consciousness except through unilluminating synonyms, but this does not necessarily show that anything is amiss. Not all words in the language (perhaps very few) can have "reductive" definitions. There must be exits from the circle of purely verbal definitions. Moreover, definitional problems are regularly encountered with many fundamental concepts, such as "truth" and "existence," which consistently resist nontrivial definition. Finally, it should not be surprising that the meanings of some words, especially those addressed here, should be attached largely to subjective experience rather than behavioral criteria. Why shouldn't words like "conscious," "aware," and "feeling" be associated in common understanding with subjectively identifiable conditions rather than behavioral events? The contrast between awareness and unawareness, for example, might be learned as follows. Someone asks whether you are aware of a certain humming noise. You now notice this noise for the first time and contrast your new state of awareness (*of* the noise) with your prior state of unawareness. There are also degrees of awareness—e.g., being dimly aware, vividly aware, etc.—that provide clues to the meaning. So why shouldn't the intended meanings be located primarily in subjective experience rather than behavioral dispositions, for example.[2]

Challenges to the Folk-Psychological Concept of Consciousness

Thus far I have probed the commonsense understanding of consciousness and sought to cast doubt on purely relational accounts of its meaning. (This is not meant to exclude the possibility—indeed, virtual certainty—that the neural substrate of consciousness involves relational dimensions.) However, our treatment of the ordinary understanding of consciousness might be viewed as having little or no scientific significance. Why should the scientific study of consciousness pay any heed to folk-psychological understanding? Doesn't the latter need to be supplanted by scientific constructs with fundamentally different contours? The "raw feels" or "qualia" of folk psychology may be unsustainable in a fully mature scientific materialism. Doubts of this sort have been expressed by many writers, including four contributors to a prominent collection of papers on consciousness in contemporary science (Marcel and Bisiach 1988). Their doubts are examined in this section.

Patricia S. Churchland (1988) gives one forceful expression of such worries (also see P. S. Churchland 1983). She offers a scenario in which "consciousness" might "go the way of 'caloric fluid' or 'vital spirit'" (P. S. Churchland 1988, p. 277). She does not exclude other possible scenarios, even a smooth reduction of consciousness to neurobiological phenomena. But she seems to lean toward the "outright replacement of the old folk notion of consciousness with new and better large-scale concepts" (p. 302). Although she does not use the word, she apparently contemplates the *elimination* of consciousness, just as the propositional attitudes (belief, desire, etc.) might be eliminated (see P. M. Churchland 1981, 1988; P. S. Churchland 1986). Eliminativism seems to be implied by the analogy with caloric fluid and vital spirit, although it may not be her intent. (Another interpretation will be considered later.) In any case, let us examine the arguments and see what conclusions they support.

One reconstruction of Churchland's reasoning might proceed as follows. Consciousness is a theoretical concept, which means it is implicitly defined by a network of putative laws. In this case the laws are ones that ordinary folk allegedly accept and regard as essential to consciousness. If these laws are in fact false, there is no phenomenon that instantiates, exemplifies, or realizes this concept. Churchland offers several examples of such concept-impregnating but factually false laws. It is generally assumed to be dead obvious, she says, that if someone can report on some visual aspect in the environment then he must be consciously aware of it. But blindsight reveals the falsity of this assumption. Second, says Churchland, it is generally assumed that the conscious self is an unanalyzable unity, that is, if the self reports a conscious experience, there is no other part of the self that could be unaware of that experience. But commissurotomized subjects falsify this assumption. Third, it is part of the very concept of consciousness that if one is not having visual experiences then one is aware that one is not having visual experiences. But denial syndromes, such as blindness denial (Anton's syndrome), falsify this generalization. Fourth, it is part of the conventional wisdom that what we are in control of we are also conscious of. But this is refuted by somnambulism: successful negotiation of the environment during *nonconscious* sleep.

These phenomena would indeed undercut the ordinary concept of consciousness if the folk accepted the assumptions Churchland imputes to them. But do they? That has not been established. How do ordinary folk react when they are initially told about blindsight. Do they conclude that blindsighted subjects must be consciously aware of what they are reporting (or guessing)? That is not how I responded when I originally heard descriptions of blindsight. What is the evidence that other ordinary folk would so respond? Do ordinary people believe that the self is an unanalyzable unity, that is, that there could not be one part of a self with awareness of a certain experience and another part lacking such awareness? Unity of the mind is, of course, a metaphysical doctrine advanced by philosophers (e.g., Descartes), but is it systematically assumed by ordinary folk? Usually a resolute empiricist, here Churchland provides no evidence about what ordinary folk assume. What about the putative assumption that consciousness and control go hand in hand, which somnambulism allegedly refutes? Somnambulism is hardly an esoteric phenomenon. If it were capable of refuting the existence of consciousness as it is commonly understood, why would that refutation not have been appreciated long ago? Are ordinary folk of the mistaken persuasion that sleep-walkers are aware during their nightly excursions? Churchland provides no evidence in support of this contention. Thus, it remains questionable whether the cited requirements on consciousness are really imposed by ordinary folk. If not, then the ordinary concept of consciousness is not overthrown by the so-called denormalizing facts she adduces.

There is a less radical view in Churchland's discussion. Elsewhere in the article she claims merely that consciousness is not a "natural kind" (see P. S. Churchland 1988, pp. 284 ff, and P. M. Churchland 1985). It is not a "unitary" phenomenon but a class of phenomena whose subclasses may be amenable to diverse neurobiological explanations. Neuroscience may eventually find little use for the consciousness construct and prefer to draw classifications rather differently. This idea is also advanced by a second contributor to

the Marcel and Bisiach volume: Kathleen Wilkes (1988).

I find the denial of natural-kind status a much more congenial point, especially when it is recognized that it does not entail the *nonexistence* of consciousness. Observe, for comparison, that there are plenty of terms in ordinary language, for example, "bush" or "bug," which do not pick out natural kinds as judged by scientific concerns, but still delineate a genuinely existing set of objects (cf. Flanagan 1992, p. 22). Scientists may not find "bush" or "bug" particularly useful classifications; they do not comprise botanically or biologically unitary categories. It does not follow that there are no bushes or bugs. Furthermore, John Dupré (1993) argues persuasively that scientific taxonomies do not normally give us insight into "essences," and are as messy as nonscientific classifications. Applied to the present domain, this would raise doubts about the assumption that neurobiological classifications convey the "real essences" of the mind-brain. Nonetheless, if Churchland only means to make the weaker claim (about consciousness), viz., that it is not a natural kind, we may have no serious disgreement.[3]

A third contributor to the Marcel and Bisiach volume, Alan Allport, expresses his doubts about consciousness in somewhat similar language as Churchland's: "... there is no unitary entity of 'phenomenal awareness'—no unique process or state, no *one*, coherently conceptualizable phenomenon for which there could be a single, conceptually coherent theory" (Allport 1988, p. 161). Allport says that he does not mean to deny the reality of phenomenal awareness, just as he does not deny the reality of *life* or *understanding*, which he regards as analogously disunified. Nonetheless, he seems to make a stronger claim than mere disunity when he denies that phenomenal awareness is *coherently* conceptualizable. A more radical interpretation is also invited when Allport endorses Daniel Dennett's (1988) eliminativist position about qualia in the latter's contribution to the volume. Allport says: "I find his [Dennett's] analysis, or rather his demolition of this incoherent notion, refreshing, and indeed liberating. *What* qualia, indeed?" (p. 162).

A prime source of Allport's difficulties with the concept of consciousness is his insistence on behavioral criteria. By "criterion" Allport refers to a procedure for telling whether the concept in question applies in a particular case. He presumes that if there is a unitary phenomenon picked out by a concept, there must be a unitary method of verifying the concept's applicability in all cases. A need for different criteria speaks against the unity of the phenomenon. But this methodological viewpoint conflicts with fairly standard treatments in the philosophy of science, which has long since given up the requirement or indeed desirability of unique operational criteria for theoretical concepts. For example, Carl Hempel writes:

[C]onsiderations of systematic import militate strongly against the proliferation of concepts called for by the maxim that different operational criteria determine different concepts. And indeed, in scientific theorizing we do not find the distinction between numerous different concepts of length (for example), each characterized by its own operational definition. Rather, physical theory envisages one basic concept of length and various more or less accurate ways of measuring lengths in different circumstances. Theoretical considerations will often indicate within what domain a method of measurement is applicable, and with what accuracy. (Hempel 1966, pp. 94–95).

In this spirit, all we should expect in the present domain are a variety of tests or indicators of awareness that may be applicable in different contexts, and may not always be wholly accurate, depending on different cognitive tasks confronting subjects or impairments from which they suffer. When Allport finds a multiplicity of criteria of awareness—ones that appeal to voluntary action, to memory, and to confidence of report (Cheesman and Merikle 1985)—he should not despair or infer the disunity of the phenomenon. True, the phenomenon *may* turn out to be disunified, but this does not follow from the necessity for multiple, noncoinciding criteria. To elaborate

on Hempel's length example, it is evidently impossible to measure astronomical lengths and subatomic lengths by the same operations, but it is still a unitary concept of length. Nor will it always transpire that two usable criteria always coincide. As we saw in the first section, verbal reportability may normally be a good test of awareness but it will obviously yield an inappropriate outcome when there are speech impairments or restricted access to the verbal subsystems.

Allport also errs in restricting criteria of consciousness to behavior; evidence may equally come from the neural direction. If a neural substrate of consciousness can be tentatively identified, it might be used to resolve problematic cases where behavioral criteria differ. We shall see examples of this shortly. Thus, it is wise to expect relevant evidence for consciousness to come from multiple sources, in accord with the general theoretical posture sketched in the passage from Hempel. Precisely this methodology is urged by Owen Flanagan (1992). Start by treating three different lines of analysis, he says, with equal respect, viz., phenomenology, psychology, and neuroscience.

Listen carefully to what individuals have to say about how things seem. Also, let the psychologists and cognitive scientists have their say. Listen carefully to their descriptions about how mental life works, and what jobs if any consciousness has in its overall economy. Finally, listen carefully to what the neuroscientists say about how conscious mental events of different sorts are realized, and examine the fit between their stories and the phenomenological and psychological stories. The object of the ... method is to see whether and to what extent the three stories can be rendered coherent, meshed, and brought into reflective equilibrium. (Flanagan 1992, p. 11).

Flanagan gives three examples of how his method of seeking coherence or meshing would work. I shall exposit one of his examples and then add one of my own.

In studies of dichotic listening, subjects are interviewed and give us a phenomenology. They tell us what they heard in the attended channel and insist that they heard nothing in the unattended channel. But we know that they are in fact influenced by, say, linguistic material that is presented in the unattended channel. One possible explanation of these results is to say that subjects are never conscious, or aware, of the sentences presented in the unattended channel, although the cognitive system is sensitive to this material. A second interpretation is that the material in the unattended channel is conscious for only an instant. The brevity of the conscious episode explains why it cannot be remembered, although it was in fact consciously experienced.

Could there be a motivated choice between the two interpretations? Brain science, says Flanagan, may here prove useful. Francis Crick and Christof Koch (1990), for example, have suggested that (visual) subjective awareness is linked to oscillation patterns in the 40–70 Hz range in the relevant groups of neurons; that is, neurons involved in a certain decoding task synchronize their spikes in 40- to 70-Hz oscillations. The 40-Hz patterns can be sustained for very short periods of time in which case there is rapid memory decay, or they can resonate for several seconds in which case they become part of working memory, give rise to more vivid phenomenology, and are more memorable. Suppose this hypothesis (or something in a similar vein) turns out to be corroborated across sensory modalities and that short term 40- to 70-Hz oscillations are observed to occur when the sentence in the unattended channel is presented. Combining present theories of short-term and working memory with such a finding would lend support to the second hypothesis that the sentence in the unattended channel makes a conscious, but unmemorable, appearance.

Another illustration (not discussed by Flanagan) of the attempt to "triangulate" on the phenomenon of conscious awareness through phenomenology, psychology, and neuroscience is given by Daniel Schacter (1989). Schacter first discusses consciousness in connection with the contrast between explicit and implicit memory, where explicit memory is roughly "memory with consciousness" while implicit memory refers to situations in which previous experiences facilitate performance on tests that do not involve any conscious memory for these experiences. Schacter then turns to studies of brain-damaged patients with specific perceptual and cognitive deficits. In a wide range of cases patients have access to knowledge of which they are unaware. Amnesic patients are a well-known case, but other types of brain damage also yield conditions in which patients show implicit knowledge of stimuli that they cannot consciously perceive, identify, recognize, or understand. Prosopagnosic patients have difficulties recognizing familiar faces and report no (conscious) familiarity with the faces of family, relatives, and friends. Despite the absence of conscious familiarity, however, data indicate that these patients do have implicit knowledge of facial familiarity. Blindsight patients are another well-known case, in which patients can gain access implicitly to information that does not inform conscious visual experience. Similar dissociations are observed in the syndrome of alexia without agraphia, in visual object agnosia, in Broca's and Wernicke's aphasia, and in studies of interhemispheric transfer in split-brain patients.

Schacter stresses two key points concerning these data. First, similar patterns of results have been observed across different patient groups, experimental tasks, types of information, and perceptual/cognitive processes. Second, the failures to gain access to consciousness are selective or domain-specific. Patients do not have difficulty gaining conscious access to information outside the domain of their specific impairment. Building on this evidence, Schacter suggests a framework that posits a distinct subsystem called the Conscious Awareness System (CAS), which interacts with modular mechanisms that process and represent various types of information. In cases of neuropsychological impairment, specific processing and memory modules are *selectively disconnected* from the conscious system, thereby resulting in a domain-specific deficit of conscious experience. CAS serves three functions in this framework. First, its activation is necessary for the subjective feeling of remembering, knowing, or perceiving. Second, CAS is a "global data base" that integrates the output of modular processes. Third, CAS sends outputs to an executive system that is involved in the regulation of attention and initiation of such voluntary activities as memory search, planning, and so forth. Finally, moving to neuroanatomical possibilities, Schacter draws on work by Dimond (1976) and Mesulam and colleagues (especially Mesulam 1983, 1985) to suggest that regions of parietal cortex have precisely the pattern of interconnections that would be necessary if they constituted part of a larger system with the properties and functions of CAS. Schacter's proposals, then, are an illustration of Flanagan's method of "triangulation" on the phenomenon of consciousness.

Daniel Dennett (1988) is a fourth contributor to the Marcel and Bisiach volume who voices grave doubts about consciousness, at least phenomenal consciousness. Dennett's specific target is the notion of qualia, and his view is bluntly eliminativist: "contrary to what seems obvious at first blush, there simply are no qualia at all" (Dennett 1988, p. 74; also see Dennett 1991, chap. 12, "Qualia Disqualified"). Dennett's arguments, like Allport's, center around the problem of verification. Both in this article and in later treatments (Dennett 1991; Dennett and Kinsbourne 1992), he presents cases where it is allegedly impossible to determine whether or when phenomenal awareness has occurred. His eliminativist conclusion about qualia is primarily based on such verificational indeterminacies.[4] Since one cannot *tell* which qualia story is correct, there is no true story about qualia at all; in other words, phenomenal consciousness, as ordinarily understood, is an illusion.

In the 1988 paper, "Quining Qualia," Dennett uses the example of a coffee-taster who thinks that he no longer has the same taste qualia from Maxwell House coffee as he used to get when he joined the company 6 years earlier. The question is whether his taste qualia have really changed or whether his standards of judgment or perhaps his memory have changed. Dennett argues that there is a fundamental verificational indeterminacy among these (ostensibly) competing hypotheses. In later publications (Dennett 1991; Dennett and Kinsbourne 1992) he presents the example of a man who briefly glimpses a lady without glasses run by and shortly afterward remembers her as wearing glasses. There are two alternative stories. The "Orwellian" story says that there was a phenomenal experience of a lady with no glasses followed by contamination of this experience by a previous memory of a woman with glasses. (This story is "Orwellian" because history is rewritten.) The "Stalinesque" story says that no such phenomenal experience occurred. Dennett's claim is that there is no way to distinguish between these competing stories either "from the inside" (by the observer himself) or "from the outside," and he appears to conclude that there are no genuine facts concerning the putative phenomenal experience at all. A third such example concerns "metacontrast." A subject gets a short (30 ms) presentation of a disk which is immediately followed by a doughnut whose inner border is just where the outside of the disk was. If the setup is right, the subject reports having seen only the doughnut. However, there is evidence that information about the disk is represented in the brain. For example, subjects are better than chance at guessing whether there were one or two stimuli. An Orwellian story would say that the subject has a conscious experience of *both* the disk and the doughnut, but that the latter wipes out the conscious memory of the disk. The Stalinesque story is that the disk is subjected to *pre*conscious processing, but that consciousness of it is prevented by the doughnut stimulus that follows. So the Orwellian and Stalinesque stories disagree about whether there was a brief flicker of consciousness of the disk that the subject does not remember. Dennett argues that there could be no matter of fact as between these two stories, because they cannot be discriminated.

There are several problems with these lines of argumentation. First a philosophical point. Even if it were true that nobody, including the subject, could subsequently determine which of the two stories is right, why does it follow that there is no matter of fact? It may be impossible now for anyone to get decisive evidence about the ornaments (if any) that Julius Caesar wore on his toga when he was slain. It hardly follows that there is no true fact of the matter, independent of our verification. Second, Dennett claims that the experience would "feel the same" on either account (Dennett 1991, p. 123). As Block (1993) points out, however, this assertion is just false, or at least question begging. If there is such a thing as phenomenal experience, there will *be* a slight subjective difference between a brief flicker of consciousness of the disk and no brief flicker. Such a flicker may go too quickly, though, for the subject to be able to *detect* or *report* it. (Notice that "detecting" is a matter of judging or believing, which should not be equated with the flicker of visual consciousness itself.) Third, Dennett is overhasty in claiming that there could be no scientific evidence favoring one story over the other (Flanagan 1992; Block 1993). Again, suppose we find evidence from normal contexts (where there are no perceptual or memory tricks) for the Crick-Koch hypothesis that consciousness is related to the 40- to 70-Hz neural oscillation, or for another Crick-Koch hypothesis that consciousness is fundamentally connected to activity in the larger pyramidal neurons in layer 5 of the neocortex. If we had converging evidence from normal cases to support some such hypothesis, we could use neural information to resolve the phenomenal facts of the case in metacontrast.[5] Whereas Dennett expresses doubts about the resolving power of brain science at this level of grain, I would echo Flanagan's motto, "Never say never" (Flanagan 1992, pp. 14–15).

Intrinsic Qualities and Self-Attribution

In the previous section I rebutted various attempts to cast the folk psychology of consciousness in a bad (or dim) light. In this section I move from defense to offense. I offer positive reasons for taking phenomenal consciousness seriously, appealing to the deployment of folk psychology itself considered as a datum of scientific psychology. It is uncontroversial that naive subjects attribute mental states to themselves, using ordinary mental terms like "believe," "want," "plan," "itch," and so forth. I shall argue that the best explanation of this cognitive-linguistic activity is the genuine occurrence of events of phenomenal consciousness which are categorized in intrinsic rather than relational terms. The argument sketched here is developed at greater length elsewhere (Goldman 1993).

Consider the old joke about two behaviorists. Just after making love, the first says to the second: "It was great for you, but how was it for me?" Why is this funny? Contrary to behaviorism, there seems to be an informational asymmetry in the knowledge of mental states that favors first-person over third-person knowledge rather than the reverse. People seem to have a different, and better, form of access to their own mental states than to the states of others. Such "privileged access" need not be perfectly reliable or infallible, but it seems to be *usually* reliable. Indeed, why is verbal reportability a normally reliable indicator of conscious states if not for the fact that people can ordinarily report the existence and content of their (current) conscious states correctly?

The privileged access thesis, of course, has its dissenters. In recent psychological literature, Alison Gopnik (1993) claims that people make inferences to their own mental states using the same theory they use to infer mental states in others. While denying that she is a behaviorist, she agrees with behaviorists that there is no informational asymmetry between first- and third-person mental attributions.

Unfortunately, Gopnik and other psychologists offer few details about the inferential processes that might underpin self-attributions. For possible details of such an account, the best place to look is the philosophical doctrine of functionalism. Philosophical functionalism holds that ordinary people understand each common mental-state descriptor to pick out a distinctive "functional role," that is, a set of causal-functional relations to stimulus inputs, behavioral outputs, and other mental states.[6] If this is correct, then the task of categorizing one's own mental states must involve deciding which functional roles are instantiated by one's current states. How might this task be executed?

Consider the descriptor "thirsty." According to functionalists, the meaning of "thirsty" is (partly) given by the following properties: (1) it is a state that tends to be caused by not drinking for a while; (2) it is a state that tends to cause a desire to drink. These two conditions are part of the distinctive functional role for thirst. What kind of state is a "desire to drink"? This is understood (among other things) as a state which, when coupled with a belief that a container of potable liquid is in one's hand, will cause one to bring the container to one's lips and drink. Notice that the posited understandings are purely *relational*, ultimately relating the states in question to peripheral inputs and outputs. They make no reference or commitment to any phenomenal character of the state. So functionalism is attractive to a qualia-skeptic or a qualophobe.

If functionalism were correct, what inferential procedures could a person use who is trying to decide whether he/she is currently thirsty or currently desires to drink? Since being thirsty is a state that is understood in terms of its relations to inputs, outputs, and other states, presumably one would classify a present target state by trying to determine what inputs preceded it or what outpts and/or other inner states followed it. In the case of the thirst concept, one might try to recall whether one had not drunk anything recently, or one might wait to see whether the target state is followed by a desire to drink. Insofar as inputs and outputs are the pieces of evidence available, functionalism does not differ from (philosophical) behaviorism. Only the addition of relations to other *internal* states differentiates functional-

ism from behaviorism. How much this helps functionalism remains to be seen.

Is it really plausible that people execute tasks of mental self-ascription in the fashion required by functionalism? There are three sorts of difficulties. First consider the case of a morning headache. You wake up to a distinctive sensation state and immediately classify it as a headache. However, you do not recall anything that might have caused it. You do not remember a bout of drinking, a long session of rock music, or anything analogous. So you do not infer the "headache" classification from knowledge of earlier inputs that are typical causes of headaches. Nor have you yet performed any action, such as taking an aspirin, that might help you identify your state as a headache. Is there some other *internal* state you identify which prompts the "headache" classification? Perhaps you notice a desire to get rid of the state. But this would not distinguish a headache from other unwanted states, like aches in other areas or even thirst. Furthermore, you may well identify the headache *before* you identify this desire. Finally, appeal to the desire simply transfers the difficulty to *that* state: How do you classify that state as a desire to be rid of the initial state? At this point, let us just label the current problem as the problem of *insufficient evidence*. If one could use only relational information of the sort considered thus far, it is doubtful that the classification task could be executed accurately, either at all or as rapidly as it is in fact executed.

Perhaps we have been unfair to functionalism. Our discussion of the morning headache case seemed to assume that only *actual* events or states preceding or following the target state are usable as evidence for its classification. But functionalism would not restrict relevant evidence to actual events or states. Functionalism says that the identity of a state depends on its subjunctive properties, for example, on the behavior or other internal states that it *would* produce. So perhaps one classifies mental states, including morning headaches, by their subjunctive properties. But this introduces a second problem for the functionalist model: *ignorance of subjunctive properties*. How can a person tell which subjunctive properties a current state has? Suppose you do not in fact believe that you are currently holding a container of potable liquid. How can you tell that if you did have such a belief, it would combine with the current state to cause you to bring the container to your lips and drink? Yet that is just the kind of subjunctive information you need to have, according to functionalism, to classify a current state as a desire to drink.

It may be replied that we often *do* have requisite subjunctive information, however that is obtained. In the morning headache case, for example, you probably would know that the state in question is one that would cause you to take an aspirin; and this is something you would know even before you actually got out of bed and went to the medicine cabinet. The problem, however, is *how* you would know this. Wouldn't you know it by first classifying the state as a headache and then coming to the conclusion that you should take an aspirin? If this is right, then you do not use the subjunctive information in order to classify. Quite the reverse: you use classification information to infer subjunctive properties.

A third problem for the functionalist model is at least as severe as the preceding ones. This difficulty arises from two central features of functionalism: (1) the type-identity of a token mental state depends on the type-identity of the states related to it (its "relata") and (2) the type-identity of many of the relata (viz., other internal states) depends in turn on *their* relata. To identify a state as an instance of thirst, for example, one might need to identify one of its effects as a desire to drink. Identifying a particular effect as a desire to drink, however, requires one to identify its relata, many of which would also be internal states whose identities are a matter of their relata, and so on. Complexity ramifies very quickly. There is a clear threat of *combinatorial explosion*: too many other internal states need to be type-identified in order to identify the initial state.

In light of these difficulties, it appears that our classification routines must not use only subjunctive information or causal-relational information of the kind functionalism suggests. Rather, our systems must rely on some properties of the target state that are *categorical* (rather than dispositional) and *intrinsic* to the state, that is, properties the states have in themselves rather than in virtue of their relations to other states. What might these categorical and intrinsic properties be?

There seem to be two candidates to fill this role: (1) neural properties and (2) qualitative or phenomenal properties. Every sensation state has some neural properties, and these might be categorical and intrinsic. (Notice that a neural property could be intrinsic to a state as a whole even though it involves relations among constituent neuronal structures, just as temperature is an intrinsic property of an entire volume of gas even though it involves relations among component molecules.) But neural properties are not the sort of properties to which the classification system has access. Certainly the untrained person has no "personal" access to neural properties and knows nothing whatever about them. Could there be "subpersonal" access to these properties? It goes without saying that neural events are involved in the relevant information processing; all information processing in the brain is, at the lowest level, neural processing. The question, however, is whether the *contents* (meanings) *encoded* by these neural events are contents *about* neural properties, from which subjunctive properties can be inferred. This seems quite implausible.

Obviously a great deal of information processing does occur at subpersonal levels within the organism. When the processing is purely subpersonal, though, it seems that no verbal labels are generated that are recognizably "mental." All sorts of homeostatic activities occur in which information is transmitted about levels of certain fluids or chemicals, for example, glucose. But we have no folk-psychological labels for these events or activities. Similarly, the pupillary response changes continuously in response not only to changes in illumination, but also to the hedonic value of environmental stimuli (Weiskrantz 1988). But there are no mentalistic labels for events concerning pupillary states, apparently because these states are not registered in awareness. Our spontaneous mental naming system does not seem to have access to purely subpersonal information. Only when physiological or neurological events give rise to conscious sensations, such as thirst, felt heat, and the like, or to other conscious mental events, does a primitive verbal label get introduced or applied.

We seem to be left, then, with qualitative or phenomenal properties, that is, qualia, as the intrinsic properties that permit mentalistic classification. As we argued earlier, these are indeed categorical, intrinsic properties that can be detected or monitored "directly" (although not necessarily infallibly). Thus, it looks as if the most promising psychological model of how one's own mental states are classified is by detecting phenomenal properties of these states, for example, the "itchiness" of an itch or the "headachy" quality of a headache. (More fully, microcomponents of such phenomenal properties may also be utilized. See Goldman 1993.) If this is right, phenomenal awareness has an essential role to play in explaining the execution of a very common cognitive task.

This discussion has focused on the phenomenon of verbal self-ascription of mental states. But the argument might equally be based on a purely internal and nonverbal activity, what Lawrence Weiskrantz (1988) calls a "monitoring" response. Weiskrantz suggests that blindsight patients (at least many of them) are disconnected from a monitoring system. If *we* had to discriminate between highly distinctive vertical and horizontal gratings, as blindsight patients are asked to do, we could press one of two keys appropriately to indicate "horizontal" or "vertical." But we would also typically have no difficulty in pressing a third key that indicated that we were "seeing" and not "guessing." This is where we would differ, says Weiskrantz, from the blindsight patient, whose third-key response would be "guessing." The best model of this difference is that there is an *extra* state that we are monitoring—a phenomenal or qualitative state—which the blindsight patients do not have at all (or have only in a limited or diminished form). These patients do have implicit informational states, but these are of a different sort and cannot be monitored in quite the same way. That is why blindsight patients (at least initially) regard the discrimination questions they are asked as a pointless game.

One question that arises at this juncture is whether the foregoing account could be extended from sensations (including perceptual states) to the self-ascription of so-called propositional attitudes: thinking, wanting, doubting, intending, and so on. Philosophers of mind often maintain that only sensations have phenomenal properties. If this were so, the account sketched above would not explain self-application of nonsensational mental descriptors. The prospects for the indicated extension, however, are reasonably good. First, as a terminological matter, we should be prepared to use the terms "phenomenal" and "qualitative" for states with any sort of subjective feel, not just sensory qualities. Next, consider the feeling of familiarity associated with (consciously) recognized faces. In addition to the purely visual quality of seeing a familiar face, there is an additional quality of "seeming familiar." The latter quality is what prosopagnosics presumably lack, although they fully enjoy the visual dimension of seeing faces. Thus, above and beyond the purely sensory (e.g., visual) feeling, there seems to be such a thing as nonsensory feeling. This might hold for feelings of remembering in general, and it is not outlandish to suggest that there are distinctive ways it feels to *believe* something rather than *desire* it, to *hope* for something rather than *dread* it, and so forth (Goldman 1993; Flanagan 1992, pp. 67–68).

It is sometimes argued that if qualia exist, they have no functional or causal role to play in cognition (Jackson 1982). That is not the position advocated here. As the foregoing arguments indicate, phenomenal states do have causal consequences: they often produce verbal self-attributions, and, purely internally, they trigger monitoring activity.[7] (According to Weiskrantz, this activity is also responsible for integrating and linking one's thoughts.) Our earlier arguments for the conclusion that qualia are not merely equvalent to functional states should not be confused with the thesis that qualia have no functional properties at all. Qualia are not equivalent to functional states because (1) the chosen functional states could ("logically") exist without qualia (Block 1980) and (2) the same qualia could play different roles in other people, or in people differently situated than we are. But in *us* they do in fact play specific functional roles of the kinds sketched above (among others, no doubt). Similarly, our earlier criticisms of the self-monitoring definition of consciousness do not conflict with the present endorsement of Weiskrantz's idea that conscious states are peculiarly available for monitoring. Our earlier criticisms were only aimed at the thesis that the concept of consciousness is *exhausted by*, or to be *identified with*, higher-level monitoring. Rejection of this thesis does not conflict with the claim that, in us, consciousness of a state makes it readily and distinctively available for monitoring. Since phenomenal properties do play a significant functional-causal role in our psychological systems, they deserve to be recognized by cognitive science, not thrown in the trash-bin of theoretically worthless constructs.[8]

Notes

1. Block's argument runs as follows. Suppose there is a Twin Earth which resembles Earth in all respects but two. First, the colors of all objects are complementary to those on Earth: the sky is yellow, grass is red, and so forth. Second, the color vocabulary of its residents is inverted. They call their sky "blue" (although it is yellow), their grass "green" (although it is red), and so forth. Now consider the following example (I only present the *inter*personal version of the case, although the *intra*personal version is equally compelling). Suppose you are a member of a pair of identical twins born

on Earth. You grow up normally on Earth, but your twin is taken immediately after birth to live on Inverted Earth and has color-inverting lenses inserted into his eyes. The qualiative character of the twin's visual awareness is identical to yours, but the two of you are "functionally" very different. Blue objects are what prompt you to call them "blue," but yellow objects (as Earthians would describe them) are what cause your twin to call them "blue." Thus qualitative identities are not matched by functional identities.

Block worries about the following criticism that might be made of his argument. Although a "long-arm" version of functionalism, in which the inputs and outputs are external objects or events, does not work, perhaps a "short-arm" version of functionalism will work, in which the relevant inputs and outputs are physiological states internal to the organism. This maneuver cannot succeed if we are concerned with the *ordinary understanding* of awareness properties, as we are in this section of the chapter. The ordinary person's understanding of awareness or qualitative properties could not arise from physiological events known only to scientific specialists.

Functionalists often try another stratagem for capturing qualitative characteristics in functional, that is, relational, terms. They suggest that it is part of the meaning of a mental term like "pain" that pain typically gives rise to beliefs that one is in pain (Shoemaker 1975). This proposal faces a problem of circularity, however (Hill 1993). One cannot fully appreciate the content that the definition confers on "pain" unless one understands the expression "believe that one is in pain." But since the meaning of "believe that one is in pain" itself depends on the meaning of "pain," it appears that the definition entails that one cannot grasp the meaning of "pain" unless one has *already* grasped its meaning.

2. This approach is sometimes thought to founder on the alleged impossibility of a "private language" or "learning by inner ostension" (Wittgenstein 1953), on which there is an immense philosophical literature. But all of this literature (in my opinion) is controversial and open to challenge. Furthermore, much of it antedates or neglects developments in cognitive science, which may well cast doubt on some of its presuppositions.

3. One further reason for interpreting Churchland this noneliminativist way is that when she writes that consciousness might go the way of caloric fluid or vital spirit, she puts quotation marks around these terms. This is the philosopher's standard way of indicating that

the topic is the words rather than the entities. What Churchland may mean, then, is that the ordinary *term* "consciousness" may be abandoned in favor of scientifically preferable vocabulary, from which it does not follow that consciousness is denied existence in the fashion in which caloric fluid and vital spirit are (now) denied existence. Furthermore, some of her more recent writing gives little hint of eliminativism vis-à-vis consciousness. For example, Churchland and Ramachandran (1993) seems decidedly realist in spirit.

4. Another strand of Dennett's argument is that qualia are alleged by philosphers to have a mix of properties such as ineffability, infallibility, unanalyzability, and so forth, which are not jointly realizable. As Flanagan (1992, chap. 4) points out, however, one can retain the qualia construct without admitting the whole mix of properties that assorted philosophers have imputed to them. As Flanagan says, quine (i.e., eliminate) the properties—or some of them, at any rate—but leave the real qualia alone.

5. Although Dennett endorses the radically revisionary claim that there is no phenomenal or qualitative consciousness, he tries to soften this message by replacing it with a more "cognitive" form of consciousness, constituted exclusively by beliefs or judgments (see his "multiple drafts" account of consciousness, where a "draft" is just a momentary judgment). A good specimen of this strategy is his treatment of the "filling in" of the blind spot. Instead of agreeing that the brain provides a "qualitative" visual representation to fill in the blind spot, Dennett claims that it just produces a *belief*: "more of the same" (Dennett 1991, pp. 354–355). This hypothesis is rendered extremely dubious by both psychophysical and physiological studies. This is convincingly shown in Churchland and Ramachandran (1993).

6. For a good formulation of functionalism, and different varieties thereof, see Block (1980). The relevant version of functionalism here is *analytic* or *commonsense* functionalism as opposed to *scientific* functionalism (or "psychofunctionalism"). In Goldman (1993) I call the present type of functionalism *representational* functionalism, meaning that people represent mental-state words in terms of functional roles.

7. Although I wish to advocate the causal efficacy of phenomenal states or properties, I do not pretend to have worked out the metaphysical details of such a position.

8. An initial version of this paper was presented as an invited address to the August 1992 meeting of the

American Psychological Association in Washington, DC, under the title "Consciousness and the Concept of Mind." I am grateful to John Kihlstrom for that invitation and for numerous helpful suggestions on the earlier draft. I have also benefited from discussion by Alfred Kaszniak, John Kihlstrom, Merrill Garrett and others in Kaszniak's seminar on the neuropsychology of consciousness at the University of Arizona.

References

Allport, A. (1988). What concept of consciousness? In A. J. Marcel and E. Bisiach (Eds.), *Consciousness in contemporary science*. Oxford: Oxford Univ. Press.

Armstrong. D. M. (1968). *A materialist theory of the mind*. New York: Humanities Press.

Baars, B. J. (1988). *A cognitive theory of consciousness*. Cambridge: Cambridge Univ. Press.

Bisiach, E. (1988). The (haunted) brain and consciousness. In A. J. Marcel and E. Bisiach (Eds.). *Consciousness in contemporary science*. Oxford: Oxford Univ. Press.

Block, N. (1980). Troubles with functionalism. In N. Block (Ed.), *Readings in philosophy of psychology* (Vol. 1). Cambridge, MA: Harvard Univ. Press.

——— (1990). Inverted earth. In J. Tomberlin (Ed.), *Philosophical perspectives: 4. Action theory and philosophy of mind*. Atascadero, CA: Ridgeview Publishing Co.

——— (1991). Evidence against epiphenomenalism. *Behavioral and Brain Sciences* 14, 670–672.

——— (1992). Begging the question against phenomenal consciousness. *Behavioral and Brain Sciences* 15, 205–206.

——— (1993). Review of *Consciousness explained. Journal of Philosophy* 90, 181–193.

Cheesman, J., and Merikle, P. M. (1985). Word recognition and consciousness. In D. Besner, T. G. Waller, and G. E. MacKinnon (Ed.), *Reading research: Advances in theory and practice* (Vol. 5). New York: Academic Press.

Churchland, P. M. (1981). Eliminative materialism and the propositional attitudes. *Journal of Philosophy* 78, 67–90.

——— (1985). On the speculative nature of our self-conception: A reply to some critics. In J. MacIntosh and D. Copp (Eds.), *New essays in the philosophy of mind*, supplemental volume of the *Canadian Journal of Philosophy*, 157–173.

—— (1988). *Matter and consciousness.* Cambridge, MA: MIT Press.

Churchland. P. S. (1983). Consciousness: The transmutation of a concept. *Pacific Philosophical Quarterly* 64, 80–93.

—— (1986). *Neurophilosophy: Toward a unified science of the mind/brain.* Cambridge, MA: MIT Press.

—— (1988). Reduction and the neurobiological basis of consciousness. In A. J. Marcel and E. Bisiach (Eds.), *Consciousness in contemporary science.* Oxford: Oxford Univ. Press.

Churchland, P. S., and Ramachandran, V. S. (1993). Filling in: Why Dennett is wrong. In B. Dahlbom (Ed.), *Dennett and his critics.* Oxford: Blackwell.

Crick, F., and Koch, C. (1990). Towards a neurobiological theory of consciousness. *Seminars in the Neurosciences* 2, 263–275.

Dennett, D. C. (1988). Quining qualia. In A. J. Marcel and E. Bisiach (Eds.), *Consciousness in contemporary science.* Oxford: Oxford Univ. Press.

—— (1991). *Consciousness explained.* Boston: Little, Brown.

Dennett, D. C., and Kinsbourne, M. (1992). Time and the observer: The where and when of consciousness in the brain. *Behavioral and Brain Sciences* 15, 183–201.

Dimond, S. J. (1976). Brain circuits for consciousness. *Brain, Behavior, and Evolution* 13, 376–395.

Dupré, J. (1993). *The disorder of things: Metaphysical foundations of the disunity of science.* Cambridge, MA: Harvard Univ. Press.

Flanagan, O. (1992). *Consciousness reconsidered.* Cambridge, MA: MIT Press.

Goldman, A. I. (1993). The psychology of folk psychology. *Behavioral and Brain Sciences* 16, 15–28.

Gopnik, A. (1993). How we know our minds: the illusion of first-person knowledge of intentionality. *Behavioral and Brain Sciences* 16, 1–14.

Hempel, C. G. (1966). *Philosophy of natural science.* Englewood Cliffs, NJ: Prentice-Hall.

Hill, C. S. (1993). Qualitative characteristics, type materialism and the circularity of analytic functionalism. *Behavioral and Brain Sciences* 16, 50–51.

Jackson, F. (1982). Epiphenomenal qualia. *Philosophical Quarterly* 32, 127–136.

Johnson-Laird, P. N. (1988a). *A computational analysis of consciousness.* In A. J. Marcel and E. Bisiach (Eds.), *Consciousness in contemporary science.* Oxford: Oxford Univ. Press.

—— (1988b). *The computer and the mind.* Cambridge, MA: Harvard Univ. Press.

Lycan, W. G. (1987). *Consciousness.* Cambridge. MA: MIT Press.

Marcel, A. J. (1988). Phenomenal experience and functionalism. In A. J. Marcel and E. Bisiach (Eds.), *Consciousness in contemporary science.* Oxford: Oxford Univ. Press.

Marcel, A. J., and Bisiach, E. (Eds.) (1988). *Consciousness in contemporary science.* Oxford: Oxford Univ. Press.

Mesulum, M.-M. (1983). The functional anatomy and hemispheric specialization for directed attention—The role of the parietal lobe and its connectivity. *Trends in Neuroscience* 6, 384–387.

—— (1985). Attention, confusional states, and neglect. In M.-M. Mesulum (Ed.), *Principles of behavioral neurology.* Philadelphia: Davis.

Rosenthal, D. M. (1986). Two concepts of consciousness. *Philosophical Studies* 49, 329–359.

—— (1990). *A theory of consciousness.* ZIF Report No. 40, Zentrum für Interdisziplinäre Forschung, Bielefeld, Germany.

—— (1993). Thinking that one thinks. In M. Davies and G. W. Humphreys (Eds.), *Consciousness.* Oxford: Blackwell.

Schacter, D. (1989). On the relation between memory and consciousness: Dissociable interactions and conscious experience. In H. L. Roediger and F. I. M. Craik (Eds.), *Varieties of memory and consciousness.* Hillsdale, NJ: Erlbaum.

Searle, J. (1992). *The rediscovery of the mind.* Cambridge, MA: MIT Press.

Shoemaker, S. (1975). Functionalism and qualia. *Philosophical Studies* 27, 291–315.

Weiskrantz, L. (1988). Some contributions of neuropsychology of vision and memory to the problem of consciousness. In A. J. Marcel and E. Bisiach (Eds.), *Consciousness in contemporary science.* Oxford: Oxford Univ. Press.

Wilkes, K. V. (1988). ——, yishi, duh, um, and consciousness. In A. J. Marcel and E. Bisiach (Eds.), *Consciousness in contemporary science.* Oxford: Oxford Univ. Press.

Wittgenstein, L. (1953). *Philosophical investigations.*

6 Can Neurobiology Teach Us Anything about Consciousness?

Patricia Smith Churchland

Introduction

Human nervous systems display an impressive roster of complex capacities, including the following: perceiving, learning and remembering, planning, deciding, performing actions, as well as the capacities to be awake, fall asleep, dream, pay attention, and be aware. Although neuroscience has advanced spectacularly in this century, we still do not understand in satisfying detail how any capacity in the list emerges from networks of neurons.[1] We do not completely understand how humans can be Conscious, but neither do we understand how they can walk, run, climb trees or pole-vault. Nor, when one stands back from it all, is awareness intrinsically more mysterious than motor control. Balanced against the disappointment that full understanding eludes us still, is cautious optimism, based chiefly on the nature of the progress behind us. For cognitive neuroscience has already passed well beyond what skeptical philosophers once considered possible, and continuing progress seems likely.

In assuming that neuroscience can reveal the physical mechanisms subserving psychological functions, I am assuming that it is indeed the brain that performs those functions—that capacities of the human mind are in fact capacities of the human brain. This assumption and its concomitant rejection of Cartesian souls or spirits or "spooky stuff" existing separately from the brain is no whimsy. On the contrary, it is a highly probable hypothesis, based on evidence currently available from physics, chemistry, neuroscience and evolutionary biology. In saying that physicalism is a hypothesis, I mean to emphasize its status as an empirical matter. I do not assume that it is a question of conceptual analysis, a priori insight, or religious faith, though I appreciate that not all philosophers are at one with me on this point.[2]

Additionally, I am convinced that the right strategy for understanding psychological capacities is essentially reductionist, by which I mean, broadly, that understanding the neurobiological mechanisms is not a frill but a necessity. Whether science will finally succeed in reducing psychological phenomena to neurobiological phenomena is, needless to say, yet another empirical question. Adopting the reductionist strategy means trying to explain the macro levels (psychological properties) in terms of micro levels (neural network properties).

The fundamental rationale behind this research strategy is straightforward: if you want to understand how a thing works, you need to understand not only its behavioral profile, but also its basic components and how they are organized to constitute a system. If you do not have the engineering designs available for reference, you resort to reverse engineering—the tactic of taking apart a device to see how it works.[3] Insofar as I am trying to discover macro-to-micro explanations, I am a reductionist. Because many philosophers who agree with me on the brain-based nature of the soul nonetheless rail against reductionism as ridiculous if not downright pitiful, it may behoove me to begin by explaining briefly what I do and, most emphatically, do *not* mean by a reductionist research strategy.[4]

Clearing away the "negatives" first, may I say that I do *not* mean that a reductionist research strategy implies that a *purely bottom-up strategy* should be adopted. So far as I can tell, no one in neuroscience thinks that the way to understand the nervous systems is first to understand everything about the basic molecules, then everything about every neuron and every synapse, and to continue ponderously thus to ascend the various levels of organization until, at long last, one arrives at the uppermost level—psychological processes (figure 6.1). Nor is there anything in the history of science that says a research strategy is

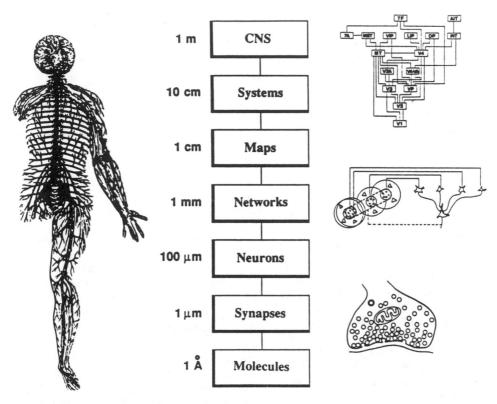

Figure 6.1
Schematic illustration of levels of organization in the nervous system. The spatial scales at which anatomical organization can be identified vary over many orders of magnitude. Icon to the left depicts the "neuron man," showing the brain, spinal cord, and peripheral nerves. Icons to the right represent structures at distinct levels: (*top*) a subset of visual areas in visual cortex; (*middle*) a network model proposing how ganglion cells could be connected to "simple" cells in visual cortex; and (*bottom*) a chemical synapse. (From Churchland and Sejnowski 1992).

reductionist only if it is purely bottom-up. That characterization is straw through and through. The research behind the classical reductionist successes—explanation of thermodynamics in terms of statistical mechanics; of optics in terms of electromagnetic radiation; of hereditary transmission in terms of DNA—certainly did not conform to any purely bottom-up research directive.

So far as neuroscience and psychology are concerned, my view is simply that it would be wisest to conduct research on many levels simultaneously, from the molecular, through to networks, sys-

tems, brain areas, and of course behavior. Here, as elsewhere in science, hypotheses at various levels can *co-evolve* as they correct and inform one another.[5] Neuroscientists would be silly to make a point of ignoring psychological data, for example, just as psychologists would be silly to make a point of ignoring all neurobiological data.

Second, by "reductionist research strategy" I do not mean that there is something disreputable, unscientific or otherwise unsavory about high level descriptions or capacities per se. It seems fairly obvious, to take a simple example, that certain rhythmic properties in nervous systems are network properties resulting from the individual membrane traits of various neuron types in the network, together with the way the set of neurons interact. Recognition that something is the face of Arafat, for another example, almost certainly emerges from the responsivity profiles of the neurons in the network plus the ways in which those neurons interact. "Emergence" in this context is entirely non-spooky and respectable, meaning, to a first approximation, "property of the network." Determining precisely what the network property is, for some particular feat, will naturally take quite a lot of experimental effort. Moreover, given that neuronal behavior is highly nonlinear, the network properties are *never* a simple "sum of the parts." They are some function—some *complicated* function—of the properties of the parts. High-level capacities clearly exist, and high-level descriptions are therefore needed to specify them.

Wherefore eliminative materialism, then? Because the existing characterization of the human brain's high-level capacities, embodied in what, for want of a better term, is referred to as "folk psychology," may well be reconfigured as time and cognitive neuroscience proceed. This too is an empirical hypothesis, and one for which empirical support already exists. Reconfiguration is already underway for such categories as "memory," "attention" and "reasoning."[6]

The possibility of nontrivial revision and even replacement of existing high-level descriptions by 'neurobiologically harmonious' high level categories is the crux of what makes eliminative materialism *eliminative*.[7] By 'neurobiologically harmonious' categories, I mean those that permit coherent, integrated explanations from the whole brain on down through neural systems, big networks, micronets, and neurons. Only the straw man is so foolish as to claim that there are no high-level capacities, that there are no high-level phenomena.[8] In its general aspect, my point here merely reflects this fact: in a profoundly important sense we do not understand exactly what, at

its higher levels, the brain really does. Accordingly, it is practical to earmark even our fondest intuitions about mind/brain function as revisable hypotheses rather than as transcendental absolutes or introspectively given certainties. Acknowledgment of such revisability makes an enormous difference in how we conduct psychological and neurobiological experiments, and in how we interpret the results.

Naysaying the Neurobiological Goal

Over the last several decades, a number of philosophers have expressed reservations concerning the reductionist research goal of discovering the neurobiological mechanisms for psychological capacities, including the capacity to be conscious. Consequently, it may be useful to consider the basis for some of these reservations in order to determine whether they justify abandoning the goal, or whether they should dampen our hopes about what might be discovered about the mind/brain. I shall here consider three main classes of objection. As a concession to brevity, my responses shall be ruthlessly succinct, details being sacrificed for the sake of the main gist.

The Goal Is Absurd (Incoherent)

One set of reasons for dooming the reductionist research strategy is summed up thus: "I simply cannot imagine that seeing blue or the feeling of pain, for example, could consist in some pattern of activity of neurons in the brain," or, more bluntly, "I cannot imagine how you can get awareness out of meat." There is sometimes considerable filler between the "it's unimaginable" premise and the "it's impossible" conclusion, but so far as I can tell, the filler is typically dust which cloaks the fallacious core of the argument.[9]

Given how little in detail we currently understand about how the human brain "en-neurons" any of its diverse capacities, it is altogether predictable that we should have difficulty imagining the neural mechanisms. When the human scientific community was comparably ignorant of such matters as valence, electron shells, and so forth, natural philosophers could not imagine how you could explain the malleability of metals, the magnetizability of iron, and the rust resistance of gold, in terms of underlying components and their organization. Until the advent of molecular biology, many people thought it was unimaginable, and hence impossible, that to be a living thing could consist in a particular organization of "dead" molecules. "I cannot imagine," said the vitalists, "how you could get *life* out of *dead* stuff."

From the vantage point of considerable ignorance, failure to imagine some possibility is only that: a failure of imagination—one psychological capacity amongst others. It does not betoken any metaphysical limitations on what we can come to understand, and it cannot predict anything significant about the future of scientific research. After reflecting on the awesome complexity of the problem of thermoregulation in homeotherms such as ourselves, I find I cannot imagine how brains control body temperature under diverse conditions. I suspect, however, that this is a relatively uninteresting psychological fact about me, reflecting merely my current state of ignorance. It is not an interesting metaphysical fact about the universe nor even an epistemological fact about the limits of scientific knowledge.

A variation of the "cannot imagine" proposal is expressed as "we can never, never know ...," or "it is impossible to ever understand ... " or "it is forever beyond science to show that...." The idea here is that something's being impossible to conceive says something decisive about its empirical or logical impossibility. I am not insisting that such proposals are never relevant. Sometimes they may be. But they are surprisingly highhanded when science is in the very early stages of studying a phenomenon.

The sobering point here is that assorted "a priori certainties" have, in the course of history, turned out to be empirical duds, however obvious and heartfelt in their heyday. The impossibility that space is non-Euclidean, the impossibility that in real space parallel lines should converge, the impossibility of having good evidence that some events are undetermined, or that someone is now dreaming, or that the universe had a beginning—each slipped its logical noose as we came to a deeper understanding of how things are. If we have learned anything from the many counterintuitive discoveries in science it is that our intuitions can be wrong. Our intuitions about ourselves and how we work may also be quite wrong. There is no basis in evolutionary theory, mathematics, or anything else, for assuming that prescientific conceptions are essentially scientifically adequate conceptions.

A third variation on this "nay, nay, never" theme draws conclusions about how the *world must actually be*, based on *linguistic properties* of certain central categories in current use to describe the world. Permit me to give a boiled-down instance: "the category 'mental' is remote in meaning—means something completely different—from the category 'physical'. It is absurd therefore to talk of the brain seeing or feeling, just as it is absurd to talk of the mind having neurotransmitters or conducting current." Allegedly, this categorial absurdity undercuts the very possibility that science could discover that feeling pain is activity in neurons in the brain. The epithet "category error" is sometimes considered sufficient to reveal the naked nonsense of reductionism.

Much has already been said on this matter elsewhere,[10] and I shall bypass a lengthy discussion of philosophy of language with three brief points. (1) It is rather far-fetched to suppose that intuitions in the philosophy of language can be a reliable guide to what science can and cannot discover about the nature of the universe. (2) Meanings *change* as science makes discoveries about what some macro phenomenon *is* in terms of its composition and the dynamics of the underlying structure. (3) Scientists are unlikely to halt their research when informed that their hypotheses and theories "sound funny" relative to current usage. More likely, they will say this: "the theories might sound funny to you, but let me teach the background science that makes us think the theory is true. Then it will sound less funny." It may be noted that it sounded funny to Copernicus' contemporaries to say the Earth is a planet and moves; it sounded funny to say that heat is molecular motion or that physical space is non-Euclidean or that there is no absolute "downness." And so forth.

That a scientifically plausible theory sounds funny is a criterion only of its not having become common coin, not of its being wrong. Scientific discoveries that a certain macro phenomenon is a complex result of the micro structure and its dynamics are typically surprising and typically sound funny—at first. Obviously none of this is positive evidence that we can achieve a reduction of psychological phenomena to neurobiological phenomena. It says only that sounding funny does not signify anything, one way or the other.

The Goal Is Inconsistent with "Multiple Realizability"

The core of this objection is that if a macro phenomenon can be the outcome of more than one mechanism (organization and dynamics of components), then it cannot be identified with any one mechanism, and hence the reduction of the macro phenomenon to *the* (singular) underlying micro phenomenon is impossible. This objection seems to me totally uninteresting to science. Again, permit me to ignore important details and merely to summarize the main thrust of the replies.

1. Explanations, and therefore reductions, are domain relative. In biology, it may be fruitful first to limn the general principles explaining some phenomenon seen in diverse species, and then figure out how to account for the interspecies differences, and then, if desirable, how to account for differences across individuals within a given

species. Thus the general principles of how hearts or stomachs work are figured out, perhaps based on studies of a single species, and particularities can be resolved thereafter. Frog hearts, macaque hearts and human hearts work in essentially the same general way, but there are also significant differences, apart from size, that call for comparative analyses. Consider other examples: (a) from the general solution to the copying problem that emerged from the discovery of the fundamental structure of DNA, it was possible to undertake explorations of how differences in DNA could explain certain differences in the phenotype; (b) from the general solution to the problem of how neurons send and receive signals, it was possible to launch detailed exploration into the differences in responsivity profiles of distinct classes of neuron.[11]

2. Once the mechanism for some biological process has been discovered, it may be possible to invent devices to mimic those processes. Nevertheless, invention of the technology for artificial hearts or artificial kidneys does not obliterate the explanatory progress on actual hearts and actual kidneys; it does not gainsay the reductive accomplishment. Again, the possibility that hereditary material of a kind different from DNA might be found in things elsewhere in the universe does not affect the basic scaffolding of a reduction on this planet. Science would have been much the poorer if Crick and Watson had abandoned their project because of the abstract possibility of Martian hereditary material or artificial hereditary material. In fact, we do know the crux of the copying mechanism *on Earth*—namely, DNA, and we do know quite a lot about how it does its job. Similarly, the engineering of artificial neurons and artificial neural nets (ANNs) facilitates and is facilitated by neurobiological approaches to how real neurons work; the engineering undertakings do not mean the search for the basic principles of nervous system function is misguided.

3. There are always questions remaining to be answered in science, and hence coming to grasp

the general go of a mechanism, such as the discovery of base-pairing in DNA, ought not be mistaken for the utopian ideal of a complete reduction—a complete explanation. Discoveries about the general go of something typically raise hosts of questions about the *detailed* go of it, and then about the details of the *details*. To signal the incompleteness of explanations, perhaps we should eschew the expression "reduction" in favor of "reductive contact." Hence we should say the aim of neuroscience is to make rich reductive contact with psychology as the two broad disciplines co-evolve. I have experimented with this recommendation myself, and although some philosophers warm to it, scientists find it quaintly pedantic. In any case, "reductive contact" between molecular biology and macrobiology has become steadily richer since 1953, though many questions remain. Reductive contact between psychology and neuroscience has also become richer, especially in the last decade, though it is fair to say that by and large the basic principles of how the brain works are poorly understood.

4. What, precisely, are supposed to be the progammatic sequelae to the multiple realizability argument? Is it that neuroscience is *irrelevant* to understanding the nature of the human mind? Obviously not. That neuroscience is *not necessary* to understanding the human mind? One cannot, certainly, deny that it is remarkably useful. Consider the discoveries concerning sleep, wakeness, and dreaming; the discoveries concerning split brains, humans with focal brain lesions, the neurophysiology and neuroanatomy of the visual system, and so on. Is it perhaps that we should not get our hopes up too high? What, precisely, is "too high" here? Is it the hope that we shall discover the general principles of how the brain works? Why is that too high a hope?

The Brain *Causes* Consciousness

Naysaying the reductionist goal while keeping dualism at arm's length is a maneuver requiring great delicacy. John Searle's strategy (Searle 1992) is to say that although the brain *causes* conscious states, any identification of conscious states with brain activities is unsound. Traditionally, it has been opined that the best the reductionist can hope for are *correlations* between subjective states and brain states, and although correlations can be evidence for causality they are not evidence for identity. Searle has tried to bolster that objection by saying that whereas *a/b* identifications elsewhere in science reveal the reality behind the appearance, in the case of awareness, the reality and the appearance are inseparable—there is no reality to awareness except what is present in awareness. There is, therefore, no reduction to be had.

Synoptically, here is why Searle's maneuver is unconvincing: he fails to appreciate why scientists opt for identifications when they do. Depending on the data, cross-level identifications to the effect that *a* is *b* may be less troublesome and more comprehensible scientifically than supposing thing *a* causes separate thing *b*. This is best seen by example.[12]

Science as we know it says electrical current in a wire is not caused by moving electrons; it *is* moving electrons. Genes are not caused by chunks of base pairs in DNA; they *are* chunks of base pairs (albeit sometimes distributed chunks). Temperature is not caused by mean molecular kinetic energy; it *is* mean molecular kinetic energy. Reflect for a moment on the inventiveness required to generate explanations that maintain the *nonidentity* and causal dependency of (a) electric current and moving electrons, (b) genes and chunks of DNA, and (c) heat and molecular motion. Unacquainted with the relevant convergent data and explanatory successes, one may suppose this is not so difficult. Enter Betty Crocker.

In her microwave oven cookbook, Betty Crocker offers to explain how a microwave oven works. She says that when you turn the oven on, the microwaves excite the water molecules in the food, causing them to move faster and faster. Does she, as any high school science teacher knows she should, end the explanation here, perhaps noting, "increased temperature just *is* increased kinetic energy of the constituent molecules?" She does not. She goes on to explain that because the molecules move faster, they bump into each other more often, which increases the friction between molecules, and, as we all know, friction causes heat. *Betty Crocker still thinks heat is something other than molecular KE; something caused by but actually independent of molecular motion.*[13] Why do scientists not think so too?

Roughly, because explanations for heat phenomena—production by combustion, by the sun, and in chemical reactions; of conductivity, including conductivity in a vacuum, the variance in conductivity in distinct materials, etc.—are *vastly* simpler and more coherent on the assumption that heat *is* molecular energy of the constituent molecules. By contrast, trying to make the data fit with the assumption that heat is some other thing *caused by* speeding up molecular motion is like trying to nail jelly to the wall.

If one is bound and determined to cleave to a caloric thermodynamics, one might, with heroic effort, pull it off for oneself, though converts are improbable. The cost, however, in coherence with the rest of scientific theory, not to mention with other observations, is extremely high. What would motivate paying that cost? Perhaps an iron-willed, written-in-blood, resolve to maintain unsullied the intuition that heat "*is what it is and not another thing.*" In retrospect, and knowing what we now know, the idea that anyone would go to exorbitant lengths to defend the "heat intuition" seems rather a waste of time.

In the case at hand, I am predicting that explanatory power, coherence and economy will favor the hypothesis that awareness just *is* some pattern of activity in neurons. I may turn out to be wrong. If I am wrong, it will not be because an introspectively-based intuition is immutable, but because the science leads us in a different direction. If I am right, and certain patterns of brain activity *are* the reality behind the experience, this fact does not in and of itself change my experience

and suddenly allow me (my brain) to view my brain as an MR scanner or a neurosurgeon might view it. I shall continue to have experiences in the regular old way, though in order to understand the neuronal reality of them, my brain needs to *have* lots of experiences and undergo lots of learning.

Finally, barring a jump to the dualist's horse, the idea that there has to be a bedrock of subjective "appearance" on which reality/appearance discoveries must ultimately rest is faintly strange. It seems a bit like insisting that "down" cannot be relative to where one is in space; down is down. Or like insisting that time cannot be relative, that either two events happen at the same time or they don't, and that's that. Humans are products of evolution; nervous systems have evolved in the context of competition for survival—in the struggle to succeed in the four F's: feeding, fleeing, fighting, and reproduction. The brain's model of the external world enjoys improvement through appreciating various reality/appearance distinctions—in short, through common critical reason and through science. In the nature of things, it is quite likely that the brain's model of its internal world also allows for appearance/reality discoveries. The brain did not evolve to know the nature of the sun as it is known by a physicist, nor to know itself as it is known by a neurophysiologist. But, in the right circumstances, it can come to know them anyhow.[14]

The Problem Is Beyond Our Feeble Intelligence

Initially, this claim appears to be a modest acknowledgment of our limitations. In fact, it is a powerful prediction based not on solid evidence, but on profound ignorance (McGinn 1990). For all we can be sure now, the prediction might be correct, but equally, it might very well be false. How feeble is our intelligence? How difficult is the problem? How could you possibly know that solving the problem is beyond our reach, no matter how science and technology develop? Inasmuch as it is not known that the brain is more complicated than it is smart, giving up on the attempt to find out how it works would be disappointing. On the contrary, as long as experiments continue to produce results that contribute to our understanding, why not keep going?[15]

Tracking Down the Neural Mechanisms of Consciousness

Finding a Route In

In neuroscience there are many data at higher levels relevant to consciousness. Blindsight, hemineglect, split brains, anosognosia (unawareness of deficit), for starters, are powerful constraints to guide theoretical reflection. Careful studies using scanning devices such as magnetic resonance imaging (MRI) and positron emission tomography (PET) have allowed us to link specific kinds of functional losses with particular brain regions.[16] This helps narrow the range of structures we consider selecting for preliminary micro exploration.

For example, the hippocampus might have seemed a likely candidate for a central role in consciousness because it is a region of tremendous convergence of fibers from diverse areas in the brain. We now know, however, that bilateral loss of the hippocampus, though it impairs the capacity to learn new things, does not entail loss of consciousness. At this stage, ruling something out is itself a valuable advance. We also know that certain brain stem structures such as the locus cereleus (LC) are indirectly necessary, but are not part of the mechanism for consciousness. LC does play a nonspecific role in arousal, but not a specific role in awareness of particular contents, such as awareness at a moment of the color of the morning sky rather than the sound of the lawn sprinklers. The data may be fascinating in its own right, but the question remains: how can we get from an array of intriguing data to genuine explanations of the basic mechanism? How can we get *started*?

In thinking about this problem, I have been greatly influenced by Francis Crick. His basic approach is straightforward: if we are going to solve the problem, we should treat it as a scientific problem to be tackled in much the way we tackle other difficult scientific problems. As with any scientific mystery, what we want is a revealing experimental entry. We want to find a thread which, when pulled, will unloose a whole lot else. To achieve that, we need to devise testable hypotheses that can connect macro effects with micro dynamics.

Boiled down, what we face is a constraint satisfaction problem: find psychological phenomena that (a) have been reasonably well studied by experimental psychology, (b) are circumscribed by lesion data from human patients as well as data from precise animal microlesions, (c) are known to be related to brain regions where good neuroanatomy and neurophysiology has been done and (d) where we know quite a lot about connectivity to other brain regions. The working assumption is that if a person is aware of a stimulus, his brain will be different in some discoverable respect from the condition where he is awake and attentive but unaware of the stimulus. An auspicious strategy is to hunt down those differences, guided by data from lesion studies, PET scans, magnetoencephalograph (MEG) studies, and so forth. Discovery of those differences, in the context of neurobiological data generally, should aid discovering a theory of the mechanism.

The central idea is to generate a theory constrained by data at many levels of brain organization—sufficiently constrained so that it can be put to meaningful tests. Ultimately a theory of consciousness will need to encompass a range of processes involved in awareness, including attention and short-term memory. Initially, however, it may target a subset, such as integration across space and across time. Whether the theory falls to falsifying evidence or whether it survives tough tests, we shall learn something. That is, either we shall have ruled out specific possibilities—a fine prize in the early stages of understanding—or we can go on to deepen and develop the theory further—an even finer prize. In any case, the trick is to generate testable, meaty hypotheses rather than loose, frothy hypotheses susceptible only to experiments of fancy. The trick is to make some real progress.

Visual Awareness

What plausible candidates surface from applying the constraint satisfaction procedure? Interestingly, the choices are quite limited. Although metacognition, introspection, and awareness of emotions, for example, are indeed aspects of consciousness, either we do not have good lesion data to narrow the search space of relevant brain regions, or the supporting psychophysics is limited, or both. Consequently, these processes are best put on the back burner for later study.

Visual awareness, by contrast, is a more promising candidate. In the case of vision, as Crick points out, there is a huge literature in visual psychophysics to draw upon, there is a rich literature of human and animal lesion studies, and relative to the rest of the brain, a lot is known about the neuroanatomy and neurophysiology of the visual system, at least in the monkey and the cat. Visual phenomena such as filling in, binocular rivalry, seeing motion, seeing stereoptic depth, and so forth might reward the search for the neurobiological differences between being aware and not being aware in the awake, attentive animal. This may get us started, and I do emphasize *started*.

The Crick Hypothesis

Immersed in the rich context of multi-level detail, Crick has sketched a hypothesis concerning the neuronal structures he conjectures make the salient differences, depending on whether the animal is or is not visually aware of the stimulus.[17] Integration of representations across spatially distributed neural networks—the unity in apperception, so to speak—is thought to be accomplished by temporal 'binding', namely synchrony

in the output responses of the relevant neurons. Very crudely, Crick's suggestion is that (1) for sensory awareness, such as visual awareness, the early cortices are pivotal (e.g., visual areas V1, V2; somatosensory areas S1, S2 etc.). This makes sense of lesion data, as well as recent PET data (Kosslyn et al. 1993) and single cell data (Logothetis and Schall 1989). (2) Within the early sensory cortical areas, pyramidal cells in layer 5 and possibly layer 6, play the key role.

What good is this idea? Part of its appeal is its foothold in basic structure. In biology, the solution to difficult problems about mechanism can be greatly facilitated by identification of critical structures. Crudely, if you know "what," it helps enormously in figuring out "how." On its own, the Crick hypothesis can be only a small piece of the puzzle. If we are lucky, however, it, or something like it, may be a *key* piece of the puzzle. This is not the time for a fuller discussion of this hypothesis. Suffice it to say that true or false, the Crick hypothesis provides a bold illustration of how to approach a problem so tricky it is often scrapped as unapproachable.

The Llinás Hypothesis

Another promising entry route is suggested by the differences—phenomenological and neurobiological—between sleep/dreaming/wakeness (SDW) states.[18] This entry point is attractive first because there is the familiar and dramatic loss of awareness in deep sleep, which is recovered as we awake, and is probably present also during dreaming. The phenomenon is highly available in lots of different subjects and across many species. Second, MEG and EEG techniques reveal global brain features characteristic of different states. Human and animal lesion data are important, especially as they concern deficits in awareness during wakeness. Here again I note the significance of research on blindsight, hemineglect (tendency to be unaware of stimuli in various modalities on the left side of the body), simultanagnosia (inability to see several things simultaneously), anosognosia (unawareness of deficits such as paralysis, blinds, garbled speech and so forth).

Third, we have learned a great deal from abnormalities in and manipulation of the SDW cycle and the link to specific brain properties. Fourth, some of the global changes in state in the SDW cycle seen by macro techniques have been linked by micro techniques to interactions between specific circuits in the cortex and subcortical circuits, especially circuits in several key structures in the thalamus. Fifth, and more specifically, MEG data reveal a robust 40 Hz waveform during wakeness and dreaming.[19] The definition and amplitude is much attenuated during sleep, and the amplitude is modulated during wakeness and dreaming. Analysis of the waveform by MEG reveals it to be a traveling wave, moving in the anterior to posterior direction in the brain, covering the distance in about 12 to 13 *milliseconds*. Cellular data suggest that these dynamical properties emerge from particular neural circuits and their dynamical properties.

What does all this add up to? Based on these data, and mindful of the various high-level data, Rodolfo Llinás and colleagues (1991,1993) have hypothesized that the fundamental organization subserving consciousness and the shifts seen in the SDW pattern are pairs of coupled oscillators, each of which connects thalamus and cortex, but each connects distinct cell populations via its own distinctive connectivity style (figure 6.2). One oscillator 'family' connects neurons in a thalamic structure known as the intralaminar nucleus, a bagel-shaped structure whose neurons reach to the upper layers of cortex to provide a highly regular fan-like coverage of the entire cortical mantle. The other oscillator 'family' connects neurons in thalamic nuclei for modality-specific information (MS nuclei) originating, for example, in the retina or the cochlea, with modality-specialized cortical areas (e.g., V2, S2). During deep sleep, the intralaminar neurons projecting to the cortex cease their 40 Hz behavior.

During deep sleep and dreaming, external signals to the cortex are gated by the reticular nucleus of the thalamus.

Ever so crudely, the idea is that the second oscillator 'family' provides the content (visual, somatosensory, etc.) while the first provides the integrating context. In deep sleep the oscillators are decoupled; in dreaming they are coupled but the MS oscillating circuit is largely nonresponsive to external signals from the periphery; in wakeness, the oscillators are coupled, and the MS circuit is responsive to external signals.

What are the effects of lesions to the intralaminar thalamic structure (bagel)? The main profile of small unilateral lesions is neglect (unawareness) of all stimuli originating in the opposite body side. Bilateral lesions result in "inanition," meaning roughly that the patient initiates no behavior and responds very poorly, if at all, to sensory stimuli or questions. Animal studies show much the same profile.

Lesions to modality-specific regions of the thalamus, by contrast, lead to modality-specific losses in awareness—visual awareness, for example, will be lost, but awareness of sounds, touches, etc. can be normal. Intriguingly, the MEGs of Alzheimer's patients who have degenerated to a state of inanition show a dilapidated 40 Hz waveform when it exists at all. Obviously these data are not decisive, but at least they are consistent with the hypothesis.

Do the Llinás hypothesis and the Crick hypothesis fit together? Minimally, they are consistent. Additionally, they are mutually supporting at the neuron and network levels. One encouraging point is this: the two families of oscillators (MS and intralaminar) richly connect to each other mainly in *cortical layer 5* (see figure 6.2). From what we can tell now, those connections seem to be the chief means whereby the oscillators are coupled. The possibility entertained here is that the temporal synchrony Crick hypothesizes in neurons carrying signals about external stimuli may be orchestrated by the intralaminar-cortical circuit. Connections between brain stem structures and the intralaminar nucleus could have a role in modulating arousal and alertness.

Many questions now suggest themselves. For example, how do the pivotal structures for aware-

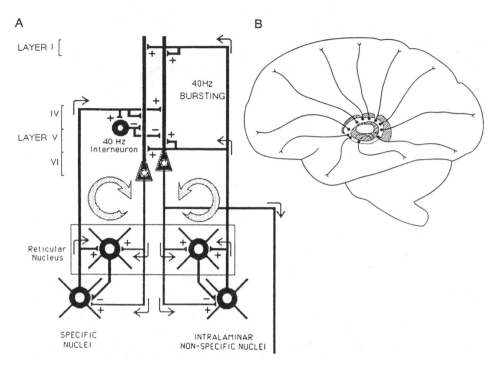

Figure 6.2

Schematic diagram of the circuits between the thalamus and the cerebral cortex proposed to serve temporal binding. (*A*) Diagram of two different types of circuit connecting thalamus and cortex. On the left, specific sensory nuclei or motor nuclei of the thalamus project to layer IV of cortex, producing cortical oscillations by direct activation and feed-forward inhibition via 40-Hz inhibitory interneurons. Collaterals of these projections produce thalamic feedback via the reticular nucleus (a kind of rind covering the thalamus). The return pathway (circular arrow with stipple) re-enters this loop to specific and reticular nuclei via layer VI cells. On the right, the second loop shows nonspecific intralaminar nuclei projecting to layer I of cortex, and giving collaterals to the reticular nucleus. Layer V cells return oscillation to the reticular and the intralaminar nuclei, establishing a second resonant loop. The conjunction of the specific and nonspecific loops is proposed to generate temporal binding. Connectivity between the loops is seen chiefly in layer V. (*B*) Schematic diagram showing the intralaminar nucleus as a circular neuronal mass (stipple shading). Other parts of the thalamus are shown in hatched shading. The intralaminar nucleus projects widely across the cortex, to layer I. (From Llinás and Ribary 1993)

ness interface with behavior? (Or as Dennett would ask, "what happens next?")[20] More specifically, what are the connections between the intralaminar nucleus and motor structures, and between layer 5 of sensory cortices and motor structures; do the projections from the intralaminar nucleus to the cingulate cortex have a role in attention? These are questions motivated by independent data. Convergence of hypotheses is of course encouraging, but it is well to remember that it can also encourage us down the proverbial garden path. Wisdom counsels guarded optimism.

Concluding Remarks

Viewing matters from the mystery side of a phenomenon, solutions can seem impossible, and perhaps even unwanted. On the understanding side, however, solutions seem almost obvious and hard to miss. Why, one might wonder, did it take so long to figure out what the elements are? How could someone as brilliant as Aristotle miss the plausibility in Aristarchus' idea that the Earth was a sphere moving around the sun? The deeper truths are all too easy to miss, of course, just as it is all too easy for us to miss whatever it is that explains why animals sleep and dream, and what autism is. The problems for neuroscience and experimental psychology are hard, but as we inch our way along and as new techniques increase noninvasive access to global brain processes in humans, intuitions change. What seems obvious to us was hot and surprising news only a generation earlier; what seems confounding to our imagination is routinely embraceable by the new cohort of graduate students. Who can tell with certainty whether or not all our questions about consciousness can eventually be answered? In the meantime, it is rewarding to see progress—to see some questions shift status from Mysteries We Can Only Contemplate in Awe, to Tough Problems We Are Beginning to Crack.

Notes

Presidential Address delivered before the Sixty-Seventh Annual Pacific Division Meeting of The American Philosophical Association in San Francisco, California, March 26, 1993.

1. See our discussion in *The Computational Brain*, Churchland and Sejnowski (1992).

2. For concordant opinions, see also Francis Crick (1994); Paul Churchland (1989); Daniel Dennett (1991); Owen Flanagan (1992); William G. Lycan (1987); John Searle (1993).

3. As P. S. Churchland and T. J. Sejnowski argued in (1989).

4. For an outstanding discussion of reductionism that includes many of the complexities I am not worrying too much about here, see Schaffner (1993).

5. P. S. Churchland (1986), *Neurophilosophy*.

6. See Churchland and Sejnowski (1992); Paul M. Churchland 1993b.

7. Or, as we have preferred but decided not to say "what makes revisionary materialism *revisionary*" (P. S. Churchland 1987). See also P. M. Churchland (1993). For a related but somewhat different picture, see Bickle (1992).

8. Ibid. See also P. M. Churchland and P. S. Churchland (1990).

9. For example, Colin McGinn (1990).

10. See, for example, Feyerabend (1981).

11. See also Owen Flanagan (1992, 1995).

12. In the following discussion, the ideas are mostly owed to Paul Churchland (1993a). For this discussion, see "Betty Crocker's Theory of the Mind: A Review of John Searle's *The Rediscovery of the Mind*." *London Review of Books*. (1995).

13. Paul Churchland made this discovery in our kitchen about eight years ago. It seemed to us a bang-up case of someone's not really understanding the scientific explanation. Instead of thinking the thermodynamic theory through, Betty Crocker just clumsily grafts it onto an old conception as though the old conception needed no modification. Someone who thought electricity was *caused* by moving electrons would tell a comparable Betty Crocker story: "voltage forces the electrons to move through the wire, and as they do so, they cause static electricity to build up, and sparks

then jump from electron to electron, on down the wire."
When I regale audiences of scientists with Betty's
"microwave" explanation, the mirth is audible.

14. See P. M. Churchland (1993b).

15. See Daniel Dennett's convincing and more detailed discussion of McGinn's naysaying (Dennett 1991).

16. See especially H. Damasio and A. R. Damasio (1990); H. Damasio (1991); A. R. Damasio (1994); Farah (1993).

17. This point is made in Crick and Koch (1990) and in Crick (1994).

18. See also my discussion in P. S. Churchland (1988).

19. See Llinás and Paré (1991).

20. Dennett (1992).

References

Bickle, J. (1992). "Revisionary physicalism." *Biology and Philosophy*. 7:411–430.

Churchland, P. M. (1988). *Matter and Consciousness*, 2nd Edition. Cambridge, Mass.: MIT Press.

Churchland, P. M. (1993a). "Betty Crocker's theory of the mind: A review of *The Rediscovery of the Mind*, by John Searle." *London Review of Books*, (1995).

Churchland, P. M. (1993b). "Evaluating our self conception." Mind and Language. (In press).

Churchland, P. M. and P. S. Churchland (1990). "Intertheoretic reduction: A neuroscientist's field guide." *Seminars in the Neurosciences*. 4:249–256.

Churchland, P. S. (1986). *Neurophilosophy*. Cambridge, Mass.: MIT Press.

Churchland, P. S. (1987)."Replies to Comments. Symposium on Patricia Smith Churchland's *Neurophilosophy*." *Inquiry*. 29:241–72.

Churchland, P. S. (1988). "Reduction and the neurobiological basis of consciousness." In: *Consciousness in Contemporary Science*. Ed. A. J. Marcel and E. Bisiach. 273–304.

Churchland, P. S. and T. J. Sejnowski (1989). "Brain and cognition." In: *Foundations of Cognitive Science*. Ed. M. Posner. Cambridge, Mass.: MIT Press. 245–300.

Churchland, P. S. and T. J. Sejnowski (1992). *The Computational Brain*. Cambridge, Mass.: MIT Press.

Crick, F. H. C. (1994). *The Astonishing Hypothesis*. New York: Scribner's and Sons.

Crick, F. H. C. and C. Koch (1990). "Towards a neurobiological theory of consciousness." *Seminars in the Neurosciences*. 4:263–276.

Damasio, A. R. (1994). *Descartes' Error*. New York: Simon and Schuster.

Damasio, H. "Neuroanatomy of frontal lobe in vivo: A comment on methodology." In: *Frontal Lobe Function and Dysfunction*. Ed. H. Levin, H. Eisenberg, and A. Benton. New York: Oxford University Press. 92–121.

Damasio, H. and A. R. Damasio (1990). The neural basis of memory, language and behavioral guidance: advances with the lesion method in humans. *Seminars in the Neurosciences*. 4:277–286.

Dennett, D. C. (1991). *Consciousness Explained*. Boston: Little, Brown and Co.

Farah, M. J. (1993). "Neuropsychological inference with an interactive brain: A critique of the "locality assumption'." *Behavioral and Brain Sciences*. (In press).

Feyerabend, P. K. (1981). *Philosophical Papers*. Vols. 1 and 2. Cambridge: Cambridge University Press.

Flanagan, O. (1992) *Consciousness Reconsidered*. Cambridge, Mass.: MIT Press.

Flanagan, O. (1996). "Prospects for a unified theory of consciousness, or, what dreams are made of." In: *Scientific Approaches to the Question of Consciousness: 25th Carnegie Symposium on Cognition*. Ed. J. Cohen and J. Schooler. Hillsdale, N.J.: L. Erlbaum. Reprinted as chapter 4 of this book.

Kosslyn, S. M., N. M. Alpert, W. L. Thompson, V. Maljkovic, S. B. Weise, C. F. Chabris, S. E. Hamilton, S. L. Rauch, and F. S. Buoanno. "Visual mental imagery activated topographically organized visual cortex: PET investigations." *Journal of Cognitive Neuroscience*. 5:263–287.

Llinás R. R. and D. Paré (1991). "Of dreaming and wakefulness." *Neuroscience* 44:521–535.

Llinás R. R. and U. Ribary (1993). Coherent 40-Hz oscillation characterizes dream state in humans. *Proceedings of the National Academy of Sciences*. 90:2078–2081.

Logothetis, N. and J. D. Schall. (1989). Neural correlates of subjective visual perception *Science*. 245:753–761.

Lycan W. G. (1987). *Consciousness*. Cambridge, Mass.: MIT Press.

McGinn, C. (1990). *The Problem of Consciousness*. Oxford: Blackwells.

Schaffner, K. F. (1993). "Theory structure, reduction, and disciplinary integration in biology. *Biology and Philosophy*. 8:319–348.

Searle, J. R. (1992). *The Rediscovery of the Mind*. Cambridge, Mass.: MIT Press.

7 Time and the Observer: The Where and When of Consciousness in the Brain

Daniel C. Dennett and Marcel Kinsbourne

I'm really not sure if others fail to perceive me or if, one fraction of a second after my face interferes with their horizon, a millionth of a second after they have cast their gaze on me, they already begin to wash me from their memory: forgotten before arriving at the scant, sad archangel of a remembrance.
—Ariel Dorfman, *Mascara*, 1988

When scientific advances contradict "common sense" intuitions, the familiar ideas often linger on, not just outliving their usefulness but even confusing the scientists whose discoveries ought to have overthrown them. Diagnosed here is a ubiquitous error of thinking that arises from just such a misplaced allegiance to familiar images, illustrated with examples drawn from recent work in psychology and neuroscience. Although this is a "theoretical" chapter, it is addressed especially to those who think, mistakenly, that they have no theories and no need for theories. We show how uncontroversial facts about the spatial and temporal properties of information-bearing events in the brain require us to abandon a family of entrenched intuitions about "the stream of consciousness" and its relation to events occurring in the brain.

In Section 1, we introduce two models of consciousness, the standard Cartesian Theater and our alternative, the Multiple Drafts model, briefly describing four phenomena of temporal interpretation that raise problems for the standard model. Two of these, drawn from the research of Libet, have been extensively debated on methodological grounds, but concealed in the controversy surrounding them are the mistaken assumptions we expose. In Section 2, we diagnose these intuitive but erroneous ideas and exhibit their power to create confusion in relatively simple contexts. We demonstrate the superiority of the Multiple Drafts model of consciousness by showing how it avoids the insoluble problems faced by versions of the Cartesian Theater. In Section 3, we show how covert allegiance to the Cartesian Theater has misled interpreters of Libet's phenomena and how the Multiple Drafts model avoids these confusions.

1 Two Models of Consciousness

1.1 Cartesian Materialism: Is There a "Central Observer" in the Brain?

Wherever there is a conscious mind, there is a *point of view*. A conscious mind is an observer who takes in the information that is available at a particular (roughly) continuous sequence of times and places in the universe. A mind is thus a *locus of subjectivity*, a thing it is like something to be (Farrell 1950; Nagel 1974). What it is like to be that thing is partly determined by what is available to be observed or experienced along the trajectory through space-time of that moving point of view, which for most practical purposes is just that: a *point*. For instance, the startling dissociation of the sound and appearance of distant fireworks is explained by the different transmission speeds of sound and light, arriving *at the observer* (at that point) at different times, even though they left the source simultaneously. But if we ask where precisely in the brain that point of view is located, the simple assumptions that work so well on larger scales of space and time break down. It is now quite clear that there is no single point in the brain where all information funnels in, and this fact has some far from obvious consequences.

Light travels much faster than sound, as the fireworks example reminds us, but it takes longer for the brain to process visual stimuli than to process auditory stimuli. As Pöppel (1985/1988) has pointed out, thanks to these counterbalancing differences, the "horizon of simultaneity" is *about* 10 meters: Light and sound that leave the same point about 10 meters from the observer's sense organs produce neural responses that are "centrally available" at the same time. Can we make this figure more precise? There is a problem. The problem is not just measuring the distances from the external event to the sense organs, or the transmission speeds in the various media, or allowing for individual differences. The more fundamental problem is deciding what to count as the "finish line" in the brain. Pöppel obtained his result by comparing behavioral measures: mean reaction times (button-pushing) to auditory and visual stimuli. The difference ranges between 30 and 40 msec, the time it takes sound to travel approximately 10 meters (the time it takes light to travel 10 meters is only infinitesimally different from zero). Pöppel used a peripheral finish line—external behavior—but our natural intuition is that the *experience* of the light and sound happens *between* the time the vibrations strike our sense organs and the time we manage to push the button to signal that experience. And it happens somewhere *centrally*, somewhere in the brain on the excited paths between the sense organ and muscles that move the finger. It seems that if we could say exactly *where* the experience happened, we could infer exactly *when* it happened. And vice versa: If we could say exactly when it happened, we could infer where in the brain conscious experience was located.

This picture of how conscious experience must sit in the brain is a natural extrapolation of the familiar and undeniable fact that *for macroscopic time intervals*, we can indeed order events into the categories "not yet observed" and "already observed" by locating the observer and plotting the motions of the vehicles of information relative to that point. But when we aspire to extend this method to explain phenomena involving very short intervals, we encounter a *logical* difficulty: If the "point" of view of the observer is spread over a rather large volume in the observer's brain, the observer's own subjective sense of sequence and simultaneity *must* be determined by something other than a unique "order of arrival" because order of arrival is incompletely defined until we specify the relevant destination. If A beats B to

one finish line but B beats A to another, which result fixes subjective sequence in consciousness (cf. Minsky 1985, p. 61)? Which point or points of "central availability" would "count" as a determiner of *experienced* order, and why?

Consider the time course of normal visual information processing. Visual stimuli evoke trains of events in the cortex that gradually yield content of greater and greater specificity. At different times and different places, various "decisions" or "judgments" are made: More literally, parts of the brain are caused to go into states that differentially respond to different features, for example, first mere onset of stimulus, then shape, later color (in a different pathway), motion, and eventually object recognition. It is tempting to suppose that there must be some place in the brain where "it all comes together" in a multimodal representation or display that is *definitive* of the content of conscious experience in at least this sense: The temporal properties of the events that occur in that particular locus of representation determine the temporal properties—of sequence, simultaneity, and real-time onset, for instance—of the subjective "stream of consciousness." This is the error of thinking we intend to expose. Where does it all "come together"? The answer, we propose, is nowhere. Some of the contentful states distributed around in the brain soon die out, leaving no traces. Others do leave traces, on subsequent verbal reports of experience and memory, on "semantic readiness" and other varieties of perceptual set, on emotional state, behavioral proclivities, and so forth. Some of these effects—for instance, influences on subsequent verbal reports—are at least symptomatic of consciousness. But there is no one place in the brain through which all these causal trains must pass to deposit their contents "in consciousness" (see also Damasio 1989).

The brain must be able to "bind" or "correlate" and "compare" various separately discriminated contents, but the processes that accomplish these unifications are themselves distributed, not gathered at some central decision point, and as a result, the "point of view of the observer" is spatially smeared. If brains computed at near the speed of light, as computers do, this spatial smear would be negligible. But given the relatively slow transmission and computation speeds of neurons, the spatial distribution of processes creates significant temporal smear—ranging, as we shall see, up to several hundred milliseconds—within which range the normal commonsense assumptions about timing and arrival at the observer need to be replaced. For many tasks, the human capacity to make conscious discriminations of temporal order drops to chance when the difference in onset is on the order of 50 msec (depending on stimulus conditions), but this variable threshold is the result of complex interactions, not a basic limit on the brain's capacity to make the specialized order judgments required in the interpretation and coordination of perceptual and motor phenomena. We need other principles to explain the ways *subjective temporal order* is composed, especially in cases in which the brain must cope with rapid sequences occurring at the limits of its powers of temporal resolution. As usual, the performance of the brain when put under strain provides valuable clues about its general modes of operation.

Descartes, early (1662) to think seriously about what must happen inside the body of the observer, elaborated an idea that is superficially so natural and appealing that it has permeated our thinking about consciousness ever since and permitted us to defer considering the perplexities—until now. Descartes decided that the brain *did* have a center: the pineal gland, which served as the gateway to the conscious mind. This was the only organ in the brain that was in the midline, rather than paired, with left and right versions. The pineal looked different, and because its function was then quite inscrutable (and still is), Descartes posited a role for it: For a person to be conscious of something, traffic from the senses had to arrive at this station, where it thereupon caused a special—indeed magical—transaction to occur between the person's material brain and immaterial mind. When the conscious mind then decided on a course of bodily action, it sent a message back "down" to the body via the pineal gland. The pineal gland, then, is like a theater in which information is displayed for perusal by the mind.

Descartes' vision of the pineal's role as the turnstile of consciousness (we might call it the Cartesian bottleneck) is hopelessly wrong. The problems that face Descartes' interactionistic dualism, with its systematically inexplicable traffic between the realm of the material and the postulated realm of the immaterial, were already well appreciated in Descartes' own day, and centuries of reconsideration have only hardened the verdict: The idea of the Ghost in the Machine, as Ryle (1949) aptly pilloried it, is a nonsolution to the problems of mind. But whereas materialism of one sort or another is now a received opinion approaching unanimity,[1] even the most sophisticated materialists today often forget that once Descartes' ghostly *res cogitans* is discarded, there is no longer a role for a centralized gateway, or indeed for any *functional* center to the brain. The brain itself is Headquarters, the place where the ultimate observer is, but it is a mistake to believe that the brain has any deeper headquarters, any inner sanctum, arrival at which is the necessary or sufficient condition for conscious experience.

Let us call the idea of such a centered locus in the brain *Cartesian materialism*, because it is the view one arrives at when one discards Descartes' dualism but fails to discard the associated imagery of a central (but material) theater where "it all comes together." Once made explicit, it is obvious that this is a bad idea, not only because, as a matter of empirical fact, nothing in the functional neuroanatomy of the brain suggests such a general meeting place, but also because positing such a center would apparently be the first step in an infinite regress of too-powerful homunculi. If all the tasks Descartes assigned to the immaterial mind have to be taken over by a "conscious" *sub*system, its own activity will either be systematically mysterious or decomposed into the activity of further subsystems that begin to duplicate the tasks of the "nonconscious" parts of the whole brain. Whether or not anyone explicitly endorses Cartesian materialism, some ubiquitous assumptions of current theorizing presuppose this dubious view. We show that the persuasive imagery of the Cartesian Theater, in its materialistic form, keeps reasserting itself, in diverse guises, and for a variety of ostensibly compelling reasons. Thinking in its terms is not an innocuous shortcut; it is a bad habit. One of its most seductive implications is the assumption that a distinction can *always* be drawn between "not yet observed" and "already observed." But, as we have just argued, this distinction *cannot* be drawn once we descend to the scale that places us within the boundaries of the spatiotemporal volume in which the various discriminations are accomplished. Inside this expanded "point of view," spatial and temporal distinctions lose the meanings they have in broader contexts.

The crucial features of the Cartesian Theater model can best be seen by contrasting it with the alternative we propose, the Multiple Drafts model:

All perceptual operations, and indeed all operations of thought and action, are accomplished by multitrack processes of interpretation and elaboration that occur over hundreds of milliseconds, during which time various additions, incorporations, emendations, and overwritings of content can occur, in various orders. Feature-detections or discriminations *have to be made only once*. That is, once a localized, specialized "observation" has been made, the information content thus fixed does not have to be sent somewhere else to be *rediscriminated* by some "master" discriminator. In other words, it does not lead to a re-*presentation* of the already discriminated feature for the benefit of the audience in the Cartesian Theater. How a localized discrimination contributes to, and what effect it has on the prevailing brain state (and thus awareness) can change from moment to moment, depending on what else is going on in the brain. Drafts of

experience can be revised at a great rate, and no one is more correct than another. Each reflects the situation at the time it is generated. These spatially and temporally distributed content-fixations are themselves precisely locatable in both space and time, but their onsets do *not* mark the onset of awareness of their content. It is always an open question whether any particular content thus discriminated will eventually appear as an element in conscious experience. These distributed content-discriminations yield, over the course of time, something *rather like* a narrative stream or sequence, subject to continual editing by many processes distributed around in the brain, and continuing indefinitely into the future (cf. Calvin's [1990] model of consciousness as "scenario-spinning"). This stream of contents is only rather like a narrative because of its multiplicity; at any point in time there are multiple "drafts" of narrative fragments at various stages of "editing" in various places in the brain. Probing this stream at different intervals produces different effects, elicits different narrative accounts from the subject. If one delays the probe too long (overnight, say) the result is apt to be no narrative left at all—or else a narrative that has been digested or "rationally reconstructed" to the point that it has minimal integrity. If one probes "too early," one may gather data on how early a particular discrimination is achieved in the stream, but at the cost of disrupting the normal progression of the stream. Most important, the Multiple Drafts model avoids the tempting mistake of supposing that there must be a single narrative (the "final" or "published" draft) that is canonical— that represents the *actual* stream of consciousness of the subject, whether or not the experimenter (or even the subject) can gain access to it.

The main points at which this model disagrees with the competing tacit model of the Cartesian Theater may be summarized:

1. Localized discriminations are *not* precursors of re-*presentations* of the discriminated content for consideration by a more central discriminator.

2. The objective temporal properties of discriminatory states may be determined, but they do *not* determine temporal properties of subjective experience.

3. The "stream of consciousness" is *not* a single, definitive narrative. It is a parallel stream of conflicting and continuously revised contents, no one narrative thread of which can be singled out as canonical—as the true version of conscious experience.

The different implications of these two models will be exhibited by considering several puzzling phenomena that seem at first to indicate that the mind "plays tricks with time." (Other implications of the Multiple Drafts model are examined at length in Dennett 1991).

1.2 Some "Temporal Anomalies" of Consciousness

Under various conditions people report experiences in which the temporal ordering of the elements in their consciousness, or the temporal relation of those elements to concurrent activity in their brains, seems to be anomalous or even paradoxical. Some theorists (Libet 1982, 1985a; Popper and Eccles 1977) have argued that these temporal anomalies are proof of the existence of an immaterial mind that interacts with the brain in physically inexplicable fashion. Others (Goodman 1978; Libet 1985b), although eschewing any commitment to dualism, have offered interpretations of the phenomena that seem to defy the accepted temporal sequence of cause and effect. Most recently, another theorist (Penrose 1989—see also multiple book review in *Behavioral and Brain Sciences [BBS]* 13 (4) 1990) has suggested that a materialistic explanation of these phenomena would require a revolution in fundamental physics. These radical views have been vigorously criticized, but the criticisms have overlooked the possibility that the appearance of anomaly in these cases results from conceptual errors that are so deeply anchored in everyday

thinking that even many of the critics have fallen into the same traps. We agree with Libet and others that these temporal anomalies are significant, but we hold a different opinion about what they signify.

We focus on four examples, summarized below. Two, drawn from the work of Libet, have received the most attention and provoked the most radical speculation, but because technical criticisms of his experiments and their interpretation raise doubts about the existence of the phenomena he claims to have discovered, we begin with a discussion of two simpler phenomena whose existence has not been questioned but whose interpretation raises the same fundamental problems. We use these simpler cases to illustrate the superiority of the Multiple Drafts model to the traditional Cartesian Theater model, and then apply the conclusions drawn in the more complicated setting of the controversies surrounding Libet's work. Our argument is that even if Libet's phenomena were not known to exist, theory can readily account for the possibility of phenomena of this pseudo-anomalous sort, and even predict them.

Color Phi

Many experiments have demonstrated the existence of apparent motion, or the phi phenomenon (Kolers and von Grünau 1976; see also Kolers 1972; van der Waals and Roelofs 1930; and the discussion in Goodman 1978). If two or more small spots separated by as much as 4 degrees of visual angle are briefly lit in rapid succession, a single spot will seem to move. This is the basis of our experience of motion in motion pictures and television. First studied systematically by Wertheimer (1912; for a historical account, see Kolers 1972; Sarris 1989), phi has been subjected to many variations; one of the most striking is reported in Kolers and von Grünau (1976). The philosopher Nelson Goodman had asked Kolers whether the phi phenomenon would persist if the two illuminated spots were different in color, and if so, what would happen to the color of "the " spot as "it" moved? Would the illusion of motion disappear, to be replaced by two separately flashing spots? Would the illusory "moving" spot gradually change from one color to another, tracing a trajectory around the color wheel? The answer, when Kolers and von Grünau performed the experiments, was striking: The spot seems to begin moving and then to change color abruptly *in the middle of its illusory passage* toward the second location. Goodman wondered: "How are we able. . . . to fill in the spot at the intervening place-times along a path running from the first to the second flash *before that second flash occurs?*" (1978, p. 73; the same question can be raised about any phi, but the color-switch in midpassage vividly brings out the problem). Unless there is precognition, the illusory content cannot be created until *after* some identification of the second spot occurs in the brain. But if this identification of the second spot is already "in conscious experience" would it not be too late to interpose the illusory color-switching-while-moving scene between the conscious experience of spot 1 and the conscious experience of spot 2? How does the brain accomplish this sleight-of-hand? Van der Waals and Roelofs (1930) proposed that the intervening motion is produced retrospectively, built only after the second flash occurs, and "projected backwards in time" (Goodman 1978, p. 74), a form of words reminiscent of Libet's "backwards referral in time." But what does it mean that this experienced motion is "projected backwards in time"?

The Cutaneous "Rabbit"

The subject's arm rests cushioned on a table, and mechanical square-wave tappers are placed at two or three locations along the arm, up to a foot apart (Geldard and Sherrick 1972; see also Geldard 1977; Geldard and Sherrick 1983, 1986). A series of rhythmical taps is delivered, for example, 5 at the wrist followed by 2 near the elbow and then 3 more on the upper arm. These taps are de-

livered with interstimulus intervals of between 50 and 200 msec. So a train of taps might last less than a second, or as long as two or three seconds. The astonishing effect is that the taps seem to the subjects to travel in regular sequence over equidistant points up the arm—as if a little animal were hopping along the arm. Now *how did the brain know* that after the 5 taps on the wrist there were going to be some taps near the elbow? The experienced "departure" of the taps from the wrist begins with the second one, yet in catch trials in which the later elbow taps are never delivered, all five wrist taps are felt at the wrist in the expected manner. The brain obviously cannot "know" about a tap at the elbow until after it happens. Perhaps, one might speculate, the brain delays the conscious experience until after all the taps have been "received" and then, somewhere upstream of the seat of consciousness (whatever that is), *revises* the data to fit a theory of motion, and sends the edited version on to consciousness. But would the brain always delay response to one tap in case more came? If not, how does it "know" when to delay?

"Referral Backwards in Time"

Since Penfield and Jasper (1954) it has been known that direct electrical stimulation of locations on the somatosensory cortex can induce sensations on corresponding parts of the body. For instance, stimulation of a point on the left somatosensory cortex can produce the sensation of a brief tingle in the subject's right hand. Libet compared the time course of such cortically induced tingles to similar sensations produced in the more usual way, by applying a brief electrical pulse to the hand itself (Libet 1965, 1981, 1982, 1985a; Libet et al. 1979; see also Churchland 1981a, 1981b; Dennett 1979; Honderich 1984; Popper and Eccles 1977). He argued that although in each case it took considerable time (approximately 500 msec) to achieve "neuronal adequacy" (the stage at which cortical processes culminate to yield a conscious experience of a tingle), when the hand itself was stimulated, the experience was "automatically.... referred backwards in time."

Most strikingly, Libet reported instances in which a subject's left *cortex* was stimulated *before* his left *hand* was stimulated, something one would tend to expect to give rise to two felt tingles: First right hand (cortically induced) and then left hand. In fact, however, the subjective report was reversed: "first left, then right." Even in cases of simultaneous stimulation, one might have thought, the left-hand tingle should be felt second, because of the additional distance (close to a meter) nerve impulses from the left hand must travel to the brain.

Libet interprets his results as raising a serious challenge to materialism: "A dissociation between the timings of the corresponding 'mental' and 'physical' events would seem to raise serious though not insurmountable difficulties for the ... theory of psychoneural identity" (1979, p. 222). According to Eccles, this challenge cannot be met:

This antedating procedure does not seem to be explicable by any neurophysiological process. Presumably it is a strategy that has been learnt by the self-conscious mind ... the antedating sensory experience is attributable to the ability of the self-conscious mind to make slight temporal adjustments, i.e., to play tricks with time. (Popper and Eccles 1977, p. 364)

Subjective Delay of Consciousness of Intention

In other experiments, Libet asked subjects to make "spontaneous" decisions to flex one hand at the wrist while noting the position of a revolving spot (the "second hand" on a clock, in effect) at the precise time they formed the intention (Libet 1985a, 1987, 1989; see also the accompanying commentaries). Subjects' reports of these subjective simultaneities were then plotted against the timing of relevant electrophysiological events in their brains. Libet found evidence that these "conscious decisions" lagged between 350 and 400 msec behind the onset of "readiness potentials" he was able to record from scalp electrodes,

which, he claims, tap the neural events that determine the voluntary actions performed. He concludes that "cerebral initation of a spontaneous voluntary act begins unconsciously" (1985a, p. 529). That one's consciousness might lag behind the brain processes that control one's body seems to some an unsettling and even depressing prospect, ruling out a real (as opposed to illusory) "executive role" for "the conscious self." (See the discussions by many commentators in *BBS*: Eccles 1985; Mortenson 1985; Van Gulick 1985; and in Pagels 1988, pp. 233ff; and Calvin 1990, pp. 80–81. But see, for a view close to ours, Harnad 1982.)

In none of these cases would there be prima facie evidence of any anomaly were we to forgo the opportunity to record the subjects' *verbal reports* of their experiences and subject them to semantic analysis. No sounds appear to issue from heads before lips move, nor do hands move before the brain events that purportedly cause them, nor do events occur in the cortex in advance of the stimuli that are held to be their source. Viewed strictly as the internal and external behavior of a biologically implemented control system for a body, the events observed and clocked in the experiments mentioned exhibit no apparent violations of everyday mechanical causation—of the sort to which Galilean/Newtonian physics provides the standard approximate model. Libet said it first: "It is important to realize that these subjective referrals and corrections are apparently taking place at the level of the *mental* 'sphere'; they are not apparent, as such, in the activities at neural levels" (1982, p. 241).

Put more neutrally (pending clarification of what Libet means by the "mental 'sphere' "), only through the subjects' verbalizations about their subjective experiences do we gain access to a perspective from which the anomalies can appear.[2] Once their verbalizations (including communicative button-pushes, etc.; Dennett 1982), are interpreted as a sequence of speech acts, their *content* yields a time series, *the subjective sequence of the stream of consciousness.* One can then attempt to put this series into registration with another time series, *the objective sequence of observed events in the environment and in the nervous system*. It is the apparent failures of registration, holding constant the assumption that causes precede their effects, that constitute the supposed anomalies (cf. Hoy 1982).

One could, then, "make the problems disappear" by simply refusing to take introspective reports seriously. Although some hearty behaviorists may cling comfortably to the abstemious principle, "Eschew content!" (Dennett 1978), the rest of us prefer to accept the challenge to make sense of what Libet calls "a primary phenomenological aspect of our human existence in relation to brain function" (1985a, p. 534).

The reports by subjects about their different experiences ... were not theoretical constructs but empirical observations.... The method of introspection may have its limitations, but it can be used appropriately within the framework of natural science, and it is absolutely essential if one is trying to get some experimental data on the mind-brain problem. (Libet 1987, p. 785)

In each example an apparent dislocation in time threatens the *prima facie* plausible thesis that our conscious perceptions are caused by events in our nervous systems, and our conscious acts, in turn, cause events in our nervous systems that control our bodily act. To first appearances, the anomalous phenomena show that these two standard causal links cannot be sustained unless we abandon a foundational—some would say a logically necessary—principle: *Causes precede their effects*. It seems that in one case (subjective delay of awareness of intention), our conscious intentions *occur too late* to be the causes of their bodily expressions or implementations, and in the other cases, percepts *occur too early* to have been caused by their stimuli. The vertiginous alternative, that something in the brain (or "conscious self") can "play tricks with time" by "projecting" mental events backwards in time, would require us to abandon the foundational principle that causes precede their effects.

There is a widespread conviction that no such revolutionary consequence follows from any of these phenomena, a conviction we share. But some of the influential arguments that have been offered in support of this conviction persist in a commitment to the erroneous presuppositions that made the phenomena appear anomalous in the first place. These presuppositions are all the more insidious because although in their overt, blatant forms they are roundly disowned by one and all, they creep unnoticed back into place, distorting analysis and blinding theory-builders to other explanations.

2 The Models in Action: Diagnosing the Tempting Errors

2.1 The Representation of Temporal Properties versus the Temporal Properties of Representations

The brain, as the control system responsible for solving a body's real-time problems of interaction with the environment, is under significant time pressure. It must often arrange to modulate its output in light of its input within a time window that leaves no slack for delays. In face, many acts can be only *ballistically* initiated; there is no time for feedback to adjust the control signals. Other tasks, such as speech perception, would be beyond the physical limits of the brain's machinery if they did not use ingenious anticipatory strategies that feed on redundancies in the input (Libermann 1970).

How, then, does the brain keep track of the temporal information it manifestly needs? Consider the following problem: Because the toe-brain distance is much greater than the hip-brain distance, or the shoulder-brain distance or the forehead-brain distance, stimuli delivered simultaneously at these different sites will arrive at Headquarters in staggered succession, if travel-speed is constant along all paths. How (one might be tempted to ask) does the brain "ensure central simultaneity of representation for distally simultaneous stimuli"? This encourages one to hypothesize some "delay loop" mechanism that could store the early arrivers until they could be put "in synch" with the latecomers, but this is a mistake. The brain should not solve *this* problem, for an obvious engineering reason: It squanders precious time by committing the full range of operations to a "worst case" schedule. Why should important signals from the forehead (for instance) dawdle in the anteroom just because there might someday be an occasion when concurrent signals from the toes need to be compared to (or "bound to") them?

The brain sometimes uses "buffer memories" to cushion the interface between its internal processes and the asynchronous outside world (Neisser 1967; Newell et al. 1989; Sperling 1960), but there are also ways for the brain to use the temporal information it needs without the delays required for imposing a master synchrony. The basic design principle is well illustrated in an example in which a comparable problem is confronted and (largely) solved, though on a vastly different temporal and spatial scale.

Consider the communication difficulties faced by the far-flung British Empire before the advent of radio and telegraph, as illustrated by the Battle of New Orleans. On January 8, 1815, 15 days after the truce was signed in Belgium, more than a thousand British soldiers were killed in this needless battle. We can use this debacle to see how the system worked. Suppose on Day 1 the treaty is signed in Belgium, with the news sent by land and sea to America, India, Africa. On Day 15 the battle is fought in New Orleans, and news of the defeat is sent by land and sea to England, India, and so on. On Day 20, too late, the news of the treaty (and the order to surrender) arrives in New Orleans. On Day 35, let's suppose, the news of the defeat arrives in Calcutta, but the news of the treaty doesn't arrive there until Day 40 (via a slow overland route). To the commander-in-chief in Calcutta, the battle would "seem" to have been fought before the treaty was signed—were it not

for the practice of dating letters, which permits him to make the necessary correction.

These communicators solved their problems of communicating information about time by embedding representations of the relevant time information in the *content* of their signals, so that the arrival time of the signals themselves was *strictly irrelevant* to the information they carried. A date written at the head of a letter (or a dated postmark on the envelope) gives the recipient information about when it was sent, information that survives any delay in arrival.[3] This distinction between time represented (by the postmark) and time of representing (the day the letter arrives) is an instance of a familiar distinction between content and vehicle, and although the details of this particular solution are not available to the brain's communicators (because they don't "know the date" when they send their messages), the general principle of the content/vehicle distinction is relevant to information-processing models of the brain in ways that have not been well appreciated.[4]

In general, we must distinguish features of representings from the features of representeds (Neumann 1990); someone can shout "softly, on tiptoe" at the top of his lungs, there are gigantic pictures of microscopic objects and oil paintings of artists making charcoal sketches. The top sentence of a written description of a standing man need not describe his head, nor the bottom sentence his feet. To suppose otherwise is confusedly to superimpose two different spaces: The representing space and the represented space. The same applies to time. Consider the *spoken phrase*, "a bright, brief flash of red light." The beginning of *it* is "a bright" and the end of it is "red light." Those portions of that speech event are not themselves representations of onsets or terminations of a brief red flash (cf. Efron 1967, p. 714). No informing event in the nervous system can have zero duration (any more than it can have zero spatial extent), so it has an onset and termination separated by some amount of time. If it *represents* an event in experience, then the event it represents must itself have nonzero duration, an onset, a middle, and a termination. But there is no reason to suppose that the beginning of the representing represents the beginning of the represented.[5]

Similarly, the representing by the brain of "A before B" does not have to be accomplished by first:

a representing of A,

followed by:

a representing of B.

"B after A" is an example of a (spoken) vehicle that represents A as being before B, and the brain can avail itself of the same freedom of temporal placement. What matters for the brain is not necessarily *when* individual representing events happen in various parts of the brain (as long as they happen in time to control the things that need controlling!) but their *temporal content*. That is, what matters is that the brain can proceed to control events "under the assumption that A happened before B" whether or not the information that A has happened enters the relevant system of the brain and gets recognized as such before or after the information that B has happened. (Recall the commander-in-chief in Calcutta: First he is informed of the battle, and then he is informed of the truce, but because he can extract from this the information that the truce came first, he can act accordingly.) Systems in various locations in the brain can, in principle, avail themselves of similar information-processing, and that is why fixing the exact time of onset of some representing element in some place in the brain does not provide a temporal landmark relative to which other elements *in the subjective sequence* can—or must—be placed.

How are temporal properties really inferred by the brain? Systems of "date stamps" or "postmarks" are not theoretically impossible (Glynn 1990), but there is a cheaper, less foolproof but biologically more plausible way: by what we might call *content-sensitive settling*. A useful analogy would be the film studio where the sound track is "synchronized" with the film. The various segments of audio tape may by themselves have lost all their temporal markers, so that there is no simple, mechanical way of putting them into apt registration with the images. But sliding them back and forth relative to the film and looking for convergences will usually swiftly home in on a "best fit." The slap of the slateboard at the beginning of each take provides a double saliency, an auditory and a visual clap, to slide into synchrony, pulling the rest of the tape and the frames into position at the same time. But there are typically so many points of mutually salient correspondence that this conventional saliency at the beginning of each take is just a handy redundancy. Getting the registration right depends on the *content* of the film and the tape, but not on sophisticated analysis of the content. An editor who knew no Japanese would find synchronizing a Japanese soundtrack to a Japanese film difficult and tedious but not impossible. Moreover, the temporal order of the stages of the process of putting the pieces into registration is independent of the content of the product; the editor can organize scene three before organizing scene two, and in principle could even do the entire job running the segments "in reverse."

Quite "stupid" processes can do similar jiggling and settling in the brain. The computation of depth in random-dot stereograms (Julesz 1971) is a spatial problem for which we can readily envisage temporal analogues. If the system receives stereo pairs of images, the globally optimal registration can be found without first having to subject each data array to an elaborate process of feature extraction. There are enough lowest-level coincidences of saliency—the individual dots in a random dot stereogram—to dictate a solution. In principle, then, the brain can solve some of its problems of temporal inference by such a process, drawing data not from left and right eyes, but from whatever information-sources are involved in a process requiring temporal judgments. (See Gallistel, 1990, especially pp. 539–49, for a discussion of the requirements for "spatiotemporal specification.")

Two important points follow from this. First, such temporal inferences can be drawn (such temporal discriminations can be made) by comparing the (low-level) *content* of several data arrays, and this real time process need not occur in the temporal order that its product eventually represents. Second, once such a temporal inference has been drawn, which may be *before* high-level features have been extracted by other processes, it does not have to be drawn again! There does not have to be a *later* representation in which the high-level features are "presented" in a real time sequence for the benefit of a second sequence-judger. In other words, having drawn inferences from these juxtapositions of temporal information, the brain can go on to represent the results in any format that fits its needs and resources—not necessarily a format in which "time is used to represent time."

There remains a nagging suspicion that whereas the brain may take advantage of this representational freedom for other properties, it cannot do so for the property of temporal sequence. Mellor explicitly enunciates this assumption, deeming it too obvious to need support:

Suppose for example I see one event *e* precede another, *e**. I must first see *e* and then *e**, my seeing of *e* being somehow recollected in my seeing of *e**. That is, my seeing of *e* affects my seeing of *e**: This is what makes me—rightly or wrongly—see *e* precede *e** rather than the other way round. But seeing *e* precede *e** means seeing *e* first. So the causal order of my perceptions of these events, by fixing the temporal order I perceive them to have, fixes the temporal order of the perceptions themselves.... The striking fact ... should be noticed, namely that perceptions of temporal order need temporally ordered perceptions. *No other property or relation has to be thus embodied in perceptions of it* [our emphasis]: perceptions of shape and colour, for example, need not themselves be correspondingly shaped or coloured. (Mellor 1981, p. 8)

We believe this is false, but there is something right about it. Because the fundamental function of representation in the brain is to control behavior in real time, the timing of representings is *to some degree* essential to their task, in two ways. First, the timing may, at the outset of a perceptual process, be *what determines the content*. Consider how to distinguish a spot moving from right to left from a spot moving from left to right on a motion picture screen. The *only* difference between the two may be the temporal order in which two frames (or more) are projected. If the brain determines "first A, then B" the spot is seen as moving in one direction; if the brain determines "first B, then A" the spot is seen as moving in the opposite direction. The discrimination is, then, as a matter of logic, based on the brain's capacity to make a temporal order judgment of a particular level of resolution. Motion picture frames are usually exposed at the rate of 24 per second, and so the visual system can resolve order between stimuli that occur within about 50 msec. This means that the actual temporal properties of signals—their onset times, their velocity in the system, and hence their arrival times—must be accurately controlled until such a discrimination is made. But once it is made locally by some circuit in the visual system (even as peripherally as the ganglion cells of the rabbit's retina!—Barlow and Levick 1965), the content "from left to right" can then be sent, in a temporally sloppy way, anywhere in the brain where this directional information might be put to use. This way one can explain the otherwise puzzling fact that at interstimulus intervals at which people are unable to perform above chance on temporal order judgments, they perform flawlessly on other judgments that logically call for the same temporal acuity. Thus Efron (1973) showed that subjects could easily distinguish sounds, flashes, and vibrations that differed only in the order in which two component stimuli occurred at a fraction of the interstimulus interval at which they can explicitly specify their order.

A second constraint on timing has already been noted parenthetically above: It does not matter in what order representations occur so long as they occur in time to contribute to the control of the appropriate behavior. The function of a representing may depend on meeting a *deadline*, which is a temporal property of the vehicle doing the represent*ing*. This is particularly evident in such time-pressured environments as the imagined Strategic Defense Initiative. The problem is not how to make computer systems represent, accurately, missile launches, but how to represent a missile launch accurately during the brief time while one can still do something about it. A message that a missile was launched at 6:04:23.678 A.M. EST may accurately represent the time of launch forever, but its utility may utterly lapse at 6:05 A.M. EST. For any task of control, then, there is a *temporal control window* within which the temporal parameters of representings may in principle be moved around ad lib.

The deadlines that limit such windows are not fixed, but rather depend on the task. If, rather than intercepting missiles, you are writing your memoirs or answering questions at the Watergate hearings (Neisser 1981), you can recover the information you need about the sequence of events in your life to control your actions in almost any order, and you can take your time drawing inferences.

These two factors explain what is plausible in Mellor's claim, without supporting the invited conclusion that all perceptions of temporal order must be accomplished in a single place by a process that observes *seriatim* a succession of "perceptions" or other representations. Once the perceptual processes *within* an observer have begun to do their work, providing the necessary discriminations, there is no point in undoing their work to provide a job for a yet more interior observer.

Causes must precede effects. This fundamental principle ensures that temporal control windows are bounded at both ends: by the earliest time at which information could arrive in the system, and by the latest time at which information could contribute causally to the control of a particular behavior. Moreover, the principle applies to the multiple distributed processes that achieve such control. Any particular process that requires information from some source must indeed wait for that information; it can't get there till it gets there. This is what rules out "magical" or precognitive explanations of the color-switching phi phenomenon, for example. The content *green spot* cannot be attributed to any event, conscious or unconscious, until the light from the green spot has reached the eye and triggered the normal neural activity in the visual system up to the level at which the discrimination of green is accomplished. Moreover, all content reported or otherwise expressed in subsequent behavior must have been "present" (in the relevant place in the brain, but not necessarily in consciousness) in time to have contributed causally to that behavior. For instance, if a subject in an experiment says "dog" in response to a visual stimulus, we can work backwards from the behavior, which was clearly controlled by a process that had the content *dog* (unless the subject says "dog" to every stimulus, or spends the day saying "dog dog dog ..." etc.) And since it takes on the order of 100 msec to execute a speech intention of this sort, we can be quite sure that the content *dog* was present in (roughly) the language areas of the brain by 100 msec before the utterance. Working from the other end, we can determine the earliest time the content *dog* could have been computed or extracted by the visual system from the retinal input, and even, perhaps, follow its creation and subsequent trajectory through the visual system and into the language areas.

What would be truly anomalous (indeed a cause for lamentations and the gnashing of teeth) would be if the time that elapsed between the *dog*-stimulus and the "dog"-utterance were less than the time physically required for this content to be established and moved through the system. No such anomalies have been uncovered, however. It is only when we try to put the sequence of events thus detectable in the objective processing stream into registration with the subject's subjective sequence *as indicated by what the subject subsequently says* that we have any sign of anomaly at all.

2.2 Orwellian and Stalinesque Revisions: The Illusion of a Distinction

Now let us see how the two different models, the Cartesian Theater and Multiple Drafts, deal with the presumed anomalies, starting with the simpler and less controversial phenomena. The Cartesian Theater model postulates a place within the brain where what happens "counts"; that is, it postulates that the features of events occurring within this functionally definable boundary (whatever it is) are definitive or constitutive features of conscious experience. (The model applies to all features of subjective experience, but we are concentrating on temporal features.) This implies that all revisions of content accomplished by the brain can be located relative to this place, a deeply intuitive—but false—implication that can be illustrated with a thought experiment.

Suppose we tamper with your brain, inserting in your memory a bogus woman wearing a hat where none was (e.g., at the party on Sunday). If on Monday, when you recall the party, you remember her, and can find no internal resources for so much as doubting the veracity of your memory, we could all agree that you never *did* experience her; that is, not at the party on Sunday. Of course, your subsequent experience of (bogus) recollection can be as vivid as may be, and on Tuesday we can certainly agree that you have had vivid conscious experiences of there being a woman in a hat at the party, but the *first* such experience, we would insist, was on Monday, not Sunday (although it doesn't seem this way to you). (See Figure 7.1)

We lack the power to insert bogus memories by neurosurgery, but sometimes our memories play tricks on us, so what we cannot yet achieve surgically happens in the brain on its own. Sometimes

we seem to remember, even vividly, experiences that never occurred. We might call such post-experiential contaminations or revisions of memory *Orwellian*, recalling George Orwell's chilling vision of the Ministry of Truth in *1984*, which busily rewrote history and thus denied access to the (real) past to all who followed.

Orwellian revision is one way to fool posterity. Another is to stage show trials, carefully scripted presentations of false testimony and bogus confessions, complete with simulated evidence. We might call this ploy *Stalinesque*. Notice that if we are usually sure which mode of falsification has been attempted on us, the Orwellian or the Stalinesque, this is just a happy accident. In any *successful* disinformation campaign, were we to wonder whether the accounts in the newspapers were Orwellian accounts of trials that never happened at all, or true accounts of phony show trials that actually did happen, we might be unable to tell the difference. If *all* the traces—newspapers, videotapes, personal memoirs, inscriptions on gravestones, living witnesses, and so on—have been either obliterated or revised, we will have no way of knowing which sort of fabrication happened: a fabrication *first*, culminating in a staged trial whose accurate history we now have before us, or *after* a summary execution, history-fabrication covering up the deed. No trial of any sort *actually* took place.

The distinction between reality and (subsequent) appearance, and the distinction between Orwellian and Stalinesque methods of producing misleading archives, work unproblematically in the everyday world, at macroscopic time scales. One might well think these distinctions apply unproblematically *all the way in*. That is the habit of thought that produces the cognitive illusion of Cartesian materialism. We can catch it in the act in a thought experiment that differs from the first one in nothing but time scale.

Suppose a long-haired woman jogs by. About one second *after* this, a subterranean memory of some earlier woman—a short-haired woman with glasses—contaminates the memory of what

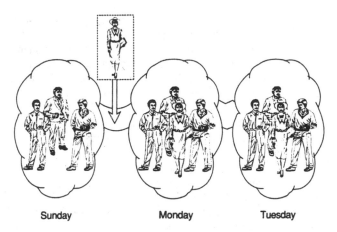

Figure 7.1
Post-experiential memory tampering

you have just seen: When asked a minute later for details of the woman you just saw, you report, sincerely but erroneously, that she was wearing glasses. Just as in the previous case, we are inclined to say that your original *visual* experience, as opposed to the memory of it seconds later, was *not* of a woman with glasses. But because of the subsequent memory-contaminations, it seems to you exactly as if at the first moment you saw her, you were struck by her eyeglasses. An Orwellian, postexperiential revision has happened: There was a fleeting instant, before the memory contamination took place, when it *didn't* seem to you she had glasses. For that brief moment, the *reality* of your conscious experience was a long-haired woman *without* eyeglasses, but this historical fact has become inert; it has left no trace, thanks to the contamination of memory that came one second after you glimpsed her.

This understanding of what happened is jeopardized by an alternative account, however. Your subterranean earlier memories of that short-haired woman with the glasses could just as easily have contaminated your experience *on the upward path*, in the processing of information that occurs "prior to consciousness" so that you actually

hallucinated the eyeglasses from the very beginning of your experience. In that case, your obsessive memory of the woman with glasses would be playing a Stalinesque trick on you, creating a "show trial" for you to experience, which you then accurately recall at later times, thanks to the record in your memory. To naive intuition these two cases are as different as can be. Told the first way (figure 7.2), you suffer no hallucination at the time the woman jogs by, but suffer subsequent memory-hallucinations: You have false memories of your actual ("real") experience. Told the second way (figure 7.3), you hallucinate when she runs by, and then accurately remember that hallucination (which "really did happen in consciousness") thereafter. Surely these are distinct possibilities, no matter how finely we divide up time?

No. Here the distinction between perceptual revisions and memory revisions that works so crisply at other scales is not guaranteed application. We have moved into the foggy area in which the subject's point of view is spatially and temporally smeared, and the question *Orwellian or Stalinesque?* (post-experiential or pre-experiential) need have no answer. The boundary between

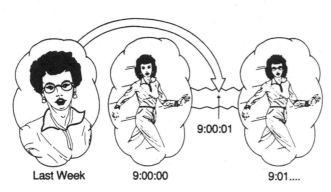

Figure 7.2
Orwellian revision

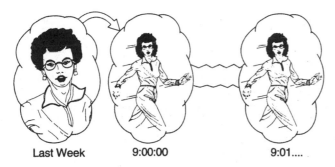

Figure 7.3
Stalinesque show trial

perception and memory, like most boundaries between categories, is not perfectly sharp, as has often been noted.

There is a time window that began when the long-haired woman jogged by, exciting your retinas, and ended when you expressed—to yourself or someone else—your eventual conviction that she was wearing glasses. At some time during this interval, the content *wearing glasses* was spuriously added to the content *long-haired woman*. We may assume (and might eventually confirm in detail) that there was a brief time when the content *long-haired woman* had already been discriminated in the brain but *before* the content *wearing glasses* had been erroneously "bound" to

it. Indeed, it would be plausible to suppose that this discrimination of a long-haired woman was what triggered the memory of the earlier woman with the glasses. What we would not know, however, is whether this spurious binding was before or after the fact—the presumed fact of "actual conscious experience." Were you first conscious of a long-haired woman without glasses and then conscious of a long-haired woman with glasses, a subsequent consciousness that wiped out the memory of the earlier experience, or was the very first instant of conscious experience already spuriously tinged with eyeglasses? If Cartesian materialism were correct, this question would have to have an answer, even if we—and you—could not

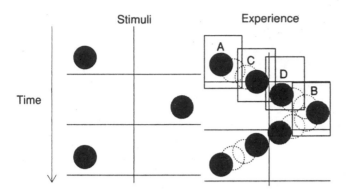

Figure 7.4
Frames C and D inserted in the editing room

determine it retrospectively by any test, for the content that "crossed the finish first" was either *long-haired woman* or *long-haired woman with glasses.* But what happens to this question if Cartesian materialism is incorrect (as just about everyone agrees)? Can the distinction between pre-experiential and post-experiential content revisions be maintained?

An examination of the color phi phenomenon shows that it cannot. On the first trial (i.e., without conditioning), subjects *report* seeing the color of the moving spot switch in midtrajectory from red to green—a report sharpened by Kolers's ingenious use of a pointer device which subjects retrospectively-but-as-soon-as-possible "superimposed" on the trajectory of the illusory moving spot; such pointer locations had the content: "The spot changed color right about *here*" (Kolers and von Grünau 1976, p. 330). Recall Goodman's (1978, p. 73) expression of the puzzle: "How are we able . . . to fill in the spot at the intervening place-times along a path running from the first to the second flash *before that second flash occurs?*"

Consider, first, a Stalinesque mechanism: In the brain's editing room, located before consciousness, there is a delay, a loop of slack like the "tape delay" used in broadcasts of "live" programs, which gives the censors in the control room a few seconds to bleep out obscenities before broadcasting the signal. *In the editing room,* first frame A, of the red spot, arrives, and then, when frame B, of the green spot, arrives, some interstitial frames (C and D) can be created and then spliced into the film (in the order A, C, D, B) on its way to projection in the theater of consciousness. By the time the "finished product" arrives at consciousness, it already has its illusory insertion.

Alternatively, there is the hypothesis of an Orwellian mechanism: Shortly after the awareness of the first spot *and* the second spot (with no illusion of apparent motion at all), a revisionist historian of sorts, in the brain's memory-library receiving station, notices that the unvarnished history of this incident doesn't make enough sense, so he "interprets" the brute events, red-followed-by-green, by making up a narrative about the intervening passage, complete with midcourse color change, and installs this history, incorporating his glosses, frames C and D (in figure 7.4), in the memory library for all future reference. Because he works fast, within a fraction of a second—the amount of time it takes to frame (but not utter) a verbal report of what you have experienced—the record you rely on, stored in the library of memory, is already contaminated. You *say* and *believe* that you saw the illusory motion and color change, but that is really a memory hallucination, not an accurate recollection of your original awareness.

How could we see which of these hypotheses is correct? It might seem that we could rule out the Stalinesque hypothesis quite simply, because of the delay in consciousness it postulates. In Kolers and von Grünau's experiment, there was a 200 msec difference in onset between the red and green spot, and since, *ex hypothesi*, the *whole experience* cannot be composed by the editing room until after the content *green spot* has reached the editing room, consciousness of the initial red spot will have to be delayed by at least that much. (If the editing room sent the content *red spot* up to the theater of consciousness immediately, before receiving frame B and then fabricating frames C and D, the subject would presumably experience a gap in the film, a noticeable delay of around 200 msec between A and C.)

Suppose we ask subjects to press a button "as soon as you experience a red spot." We would find little or no difference in response time to a red spot alone versus a red spot followed 200 msec later by a green spot (in which case the subjects report color-switching apparent motion). This could be because there is *always* a delay of at least 200 msec in consciousness, but aside from the biological implausibility of such a squandering of time, there is the evidence from many quarters that responses under conscious control, although slower than such responses as reflex blinks, occur with close to the minimum latencies that are physically possible; after subtracting the demonstrable travel times for incoming and outgoing pulse trains, and the response preparation time, there is little time left over in "central processing" in which to hide a 200 msec delay. So the responses had to have been initiated before the discrimination of the second stimulus, the green spot. This would seem overwhelmingly to favor the Orwellian, post-experiential mechanism: As soon as the subject *becomes conscious* of the red spot, he initiates a button-press. *While that button press is forming*, he becomes conscious of the green spot. *Then* both these experiences are wiped from memory, replaced in memory by the revisionist record of the red spot moving over and then turning green halfway across. He readily and sincerely (but mistakenly) reports having seen the red spot moving toward the green spot before changing color.

If the subject were to insist that he really was conscious from the very beginning of the red spot moving and changing color, the Orwellian theorist would firmly explain to him that he is wrong; his memory is playing tricks on him; the fact that he pressed the button when he did is conclusive evidence that he was conscious of the (stationary) red spot before the green spot had even occurred. After all, his instructions were to press the button *when he was conscious of* a red spot. He must have been conscious of the red spot about 200 msec before he could have been conscious of it moving and turning green. If that is not how it seems to him, he is simply mistaken.

The defender of the Stalinesque (pre-experiential) alternative is not defeated by this, however. Actually, he insists, the subject responded to the red spot *before* he was conscious of it! The directions to the subject (to respond to a red spot) had somehow trickled down from consciousness into the editing room, which *unconsciously* initiated the button-push before sending the edited version (frames ACDB) up to consciousness for "viewing." The subject's memory has played no tricks on him; he is reporting exactly what he was conscious of, unless he insists that he pushed the button after consciously seeing the red spot; his "premature" button-push was unconsciously (or preconsciously) triggered (cf. Velmans 1991).

Where the Stalinesque theory postulates a button-pushing reaction to an *unconscious* detection of a red spot, the Orwellian theory postulates a *conscious* experience of a red spot that is immediately obliterated from memory by its sequel. So here is the rub: We have two different models of what happens in the phi phenomenon: one posits a Stalinesque "filling in" on the upward, pre-experiential path, and the other posits an Orwellian "memory revision" on the downward, post-experiential path, and *both* of them are consistent with *whatever* the subject says or thinks or remembers. Note that the inability to distinguish these two possibilities does not apply only to the *outside observers* who might be supposed to lack some private data to which the subject had "privileged access." You, as a subject in a phi phenomenon experiment, *could not* discover anything in the experience from your own first-person perspective that would favor one theory over the other; the experience would "feel the same" on either account. As the interstimulus interval is lengthened subjects pass from seeing apparent motion to seeing individual stationary flashes. There is an intermediate range of intervals where the phenomenology is somewhat paradoxical: You see the spots as two stationary flashes *and* as one thing moving. This sort of apparent motion is readily distinguishable from the swifter, smoother sort of apparent motion of cinema, for instance, but your capacity to make *this* discrimination is not relevant to the dispute between the Orwellian and the Stalinesque theorist. They agree that you can make this discrimination under the right conditions; what they disagree about is how to describe the cases of apparent motion that you *can't* tell from real motion—the cases in which you really (mis-)*perceive* the illusory motion. To put it loosely, in these cases is your memory playing tricks with you, or are just your eyes playing tricks with you? You can't tell "from the inside."

We can see the same indistinguishability even more clearly when we see how the two different models handle the well-studied phenomenon of *metacontrast* (for a review, see Breitmeyer 1984). If a stimulus is flashed briefly on a screen and then followed, after a brief interstimulus interval, by a second "masking" stimulus, subjects *report* seeing only the second stimulus. (And if you put yourself in the subject's place you will see for youself; you will be prepared to swear that there was only one flash.) The standard description of such phenomena is that the second stimulus

somehow *prevents conscious experience* of the first stimulus (in other words, it somehow waylays the first stimulus on its way to consciousness). But people can nevertheless do much better than chance if required to guess whether there were two stimuli. This only shows once again that stimuli can have their effects on us without our being conscious of them. This standard line is, in effect, the Stalinesque model of metacontrast: The first stimulus never gets to play on the stage of consciousness; it has whatever effects it has entirely unconsciously. But we have just uncovered a second, Orwellian model of metacontrast: Subjects are indeed conscious of the first stimulus (which would "explain" their capacity to guess correctly) but their memory of this conscious experience is almost entirely obliterated by the second stimulus (which is why they deny having seen it, in spite of their tell-tale better-than-chance guesses).[6]

Both the Orwellian and the Stalinesque version of the Cartesian Theater model can deftly account for *all* the data—not just the data we already have, but the data we can imagine getting in the future. They both account for the verbal reports: One theory says they are innocently mistaken whereas the other says they are accurate reports of experienced "mistakes." (A similar verdict is suggested in the commentaries of Holender 1986; see especially Dixon 1986; Erdelyi 1986; Marcel 1986; Merikle and Cheesman 1986.) They agree about just where in the brain the mistaken content enters the causal pathways; they just disagree about whether that location is preexperiential or post-experiential. They both account for the nonverbal effects: One says they are the result of unconsciously discriminated contents while the other says they are the result of consciously discriminated but forgotten contents. They agree about just where and how in the brain these discriminations occur; they just disagree about whether to interpret those processes as happening inside or outside the charmed circle of consciousness. Finally, they both account for the subjective data—whatever is obtainable "from the first-person-perspective"—because they agree about how it ought to "feel" to subjects: Subjects should be unable to tell the difference between misbegotten experiences and immediately mis-remembered experiences. So, in spite of first appearances, there is really only a verbal difference between the two theories (cf. Reingold and Meri-kle 1990). They tell exactly the same story except for where they place a mythical Great Divide, a point in time (and hence a place in space) whose *fine-grained* location is nothing that subjects can help them locate, and whose location is also neutral with regard to all other features of their theories. This is a difference that makes no difference.

Consider a contemporary analogy. With the advent of word-processing and desktop publishing and electronic mail, we are losing the previously quite hard-edged distinction between pre-pub-lication editing, and post-publication correction of "errata." With multiple drafts in electronic circulation, and with the author readily making revisions in response to comments received by electronic mail, calling one of the drafts the can-onical text—the text of "record," the one to cite in one's own publications—becomes a somewhat arbitrary matter. Often most of the intended readers, the readers whose reading of the text matters, read only an early draft; the "published" version is archival and inert. If it is important ef-fects we are looking for, then most if not all the important effects of writing a text are now spread out over many drafts, not postponed until after publication. It used to be otherwise; virtually all of a text's important effects happened *after* ap-pearance in a book or journal and *because of* its making such an appearance. All the facts are in, and now that the various candidates for the "gate" of publication can be seen no longer to be functionally important, if we feel we need the distinction at all, we will have to decide arbitra-rily what is to count as publishing a text. There is no natural summit or turning point in the path from draft to archive.

Similarly—and this is the fundamental im-plication of the Multiple Drafts model—if one wants to settle on some moment of processing in the brain as the moment of consciousness, this has to be arbitrary. One can always "draw a line" in the stream of processing in the brain, but there are no functional differences that could motivate de-claring all prior stages and revisions unconscious or preconscious adjustments and all subsequent emendations to the content (as revealed by recol-lection) to be post-experiential memory-contami-nation. The distinction lapses at close quarters.

Another implication of the Multiple Drafts model, in contrast to the Cartesian Theater, is that there is no need—or room—for the sort of "filling in" suggested by frames C and D of figure 7.4. Discussing Kolers' experiment, Goodman notes that it "seems to leave us a choice between a retrospective construction theory and a belief in clairvoyance" (1978, p. 83). What then is "ret-rospective construction"?

Whether perception of the first flash is thought to be *delayed or preserved or remembered* [our emphasis], I call this the retrospective construction theory—the theory that the construction perceived as occurring be-tween the two flashes is accomplished not earlier than the second.

It seems at first that Goodman does not choose between a Stalinesque theory (perception of the first flash is delayed) and an Orwellian theory (the perception of the first flash is preserved or re-membered), but his Orwellian revisionist does not merely adjust judgments; he *constructs* material to *fill* in the gaps: "Each of the intervening places along a path between the two flashes is filled in ... with one of the flashed colors rather than with successive intermediate colors" (Goodman 1978, p. 85). What Goodman overlooks is the possi-bility that the brain doesn't actually have to go to the trouble of "filling in" anything with "con-struction," for no one is looking. As the Multiple Drafts model makes explicit, once a discrimina-tion has been made once, it does not have to be made again; the brain just adjusts to the conclusion that is drawn, making the new interpretation of the information available for the modulation of subsequent behavior. Recall the commander-in-chief in Calcutta; he just had to *judge* that the truce came before the battle; he didn't also have to mount some sort of pageant of "historical reconstruction" to watch, in which he receives the letters in the "proper" order.

Similarly, when Goodman (1978) proposes that "the intervening motion is produced retrospectively, built only after the second flash occurs, and projected backwards in time," this suggests ominously that a final film is made and then run through a magical projector whose beam somehow travels backwards in time onto the mind's screen. Whether or not this is just what Van der Waals and Roelofs (1930) had in mind when they proposed "retrospective construction," it is presumably what led Kolers (1972, p. 184) to reject their hypothesis, insisting that all construction is carried out in "real time." Why, though, should the brain bother to "produce" the "intervening motion"? Why not just conclude that there was intervening motion, and encode that "retrospective" content into the processing stream? This would suffice for it to seem to the subject that intervening motion had been experienced.

Our Multiple Drafts model agrees with Goodman that retrospectively the brain creates the content (the judgment) that there was intervening motion, and this content is then available to govern activity and leave its mark on memory. But our model claims that the brain does not bother "constructing" any representations that go to the trouble of "filling in" the blanks. That would be a waste of time and (shall we say?) *paint*. The judgment is *already in*, so the brain can get on with other tasks![7]

Goodman's "projection backwards in time," like Libet's "backwards referral in time," is an equivocal phrase. It might mean something modest and defensible: A *reference to some past time* is included in the content. On this reading it could be a claim like, "This novel takes us back to an-

cient Rome," which almost no one would interpret in a metaphysically extravagant way, as claiming that the novel was some sort of time travel machine. This is the reading that is consistent with Goodman's other views, but Kolers apparently took it to mean something metaphysically radical: that there was some actual projection of one thing at one time to another time. As we shall see, the same equivocation bedevils Libet's interpretation of his phenomena.

The model of the Cartesian Theater creates artifactual puzzle questions that cannot be answered, whereas for our model these questions cannot meaningfully arise. This can be seen by applying both models to other experiments that probe the limits of the distinction between perception and memory. A normally sufficient, but not necessary, condition for having experienced something is subsequent verbal report, and this is the anchoring case around which all the puzzle cases revolve. Suppose that although one's brain has registered—that is, responded to—(some aspects of) an event, something intervenes between that internal response and a subsequent occasion for verbal report. If there was no time or opportunity for an initial overt response of any sort, and if the intervening events prevent later overt responses (verbal or otherwise) from incorporating reference to some aspect(s) of the first event, this creates a puzzle question: Were they never consciously perceived, or have they been rapidly forgotten?

Consider the familiar span of apprehension. Multiple letters are simultaneously briefly exposed. Some are identified. The rest were certainly seen. The subject insists they were there, knows their number, and has the impression that they were clearcut and distinct. Yet he cannot identify them. Has he failed "really" to perceive them, or has he rapidly "forgotten" them? Or consider an acoustic memory span test, administered at a rapid rate, for example, 4 items a second, so that the subject perforce cannot respond till the acoustic event is over. He identifies some, not others. Yet, subjectively he heard all of them clearly and equally well. Did he not genuinely perceive or did he forget the rest?

And if, under still more constricted circumstances such as metacontrast, the subject even lacks all conviction that the unrecallable items *were there*, should we take this judgment as conclusive grounds for saying he did not experience them, even if they prove to have left other contentful traces on his subsequent behavior? If there is a Cartesian Theater, these questions demand answers, because what gets into the theater and when is supposedly determinate, even if the boundaries appear fuzzy because of human limitations of perception and memory.

Our Multiple Drafts model suggests a different perspective on these phenomena. When a lot happens in a short time, the brain may make simplifying assumptions (for a supporting view, see Marcel 1983). In metacontrast, the first stimulus may be a disc and the second stimulus a ring that fits closely outside the space where the disc was displayed. The outer contour of a disc rapidly turns into the inner contour of a ring. The brain, initially informed just that something happened (something with a circular contour in a particular place), swiftly receives confirmation that there was indeed a ring, with an inner and outer contour. Without further supporting evidence that there was a disc, the brain arrives at the conservative conclusion that there was only a ring. Should we insist that the disc was experienced because *if the ring hadn't intervened* the disc would have been reported? Our model of how the phenomenon is caused shows that there is no motivated way of settling such border disputes: Information about the disc was briefly in a functional position to contribute to a later report, but this state lapsed; there is no reason to insist that this state was inside the charmed circle of consciousness until it got overwritten, or contrarily, to insist that it never quite achieved this state. Nothing discernible to "inside" or "outside" observers could distinguish these possibilities.

In color phi, the processes that calculate that the second spot is green and that there is motion proceed roughly simultaneously (in different parts of the brain) and eventually contribute to the process that concludes that the red spot moved over and abruptly turned green on the way. That conclusion is achieved swiftly enough, in the standard case, to overwhelm or replace any competing contents before they can contribute to the framing of a report. So the subject says—and believes—just what Kolers and von Grünau report, *and that is what the subject was conscious of*. Was the subject *also* conscious a fraction of a second earlier of the stationary red spot? Ask him. If the interstimulus interval is made somewhat longer, there will come a point where the subject *does* report an experience of first a stationary red spot, then a green spot, and then a *noticeably retrospective* sense that the red spot ("must have") moved over and changed color. This experience has—as the subject will tell you—a quite different phenomenology. Apparent motion is experienced under such conditions, but it is obviously different from ordinary motion, and from swifter varieties of apparent motion. How is it different? The subject notices the difference! In this case it does seem to him as if he only later "realized" that there had been motion. But in cases in which this retrospective element is lacking it is still the case that the discrimination of motion-with-color-change is achieved after the colors and locations of the spots were discriminated—and there is no later process of "filling in" required.

In the cutaneous "rabbit," the shift in space (along the arm) is recorded over time by the brain. The number of taps is also recorded. Although in physical reality the taps were clustered at particular locations, the simplifying assumption is that they were distributed regularly across the space-time extent of the experience. The brain relaxes into this parsimonious though mistaken interpretation *after* the taps are registered, and this has the effect of wiping out earlier (partial) interpretations of the taps, but some side effects of those interpretations (e.g., the interpretation that there were five taps, that there were more than two taps, etc.) may live on.

Although different attributes are indeed extracted by different neural facilities at different rates (e.g., location vs. shape vs. color), and although if asked to respond to the presence of each one in isolation we would do so with different latencies, we perceive events, not a successively analyzed trickle of perceptual elements or attributes. As Efron remarks:

There are no grounds for an a priori assumption that the specificity of our awareness of an object of perception, or an aspect of that object, gradually increases or grows following the moment of its onset from the least specific experience to some maximally specific experience.... We do not, when first observing an object with central vision, fleetingly experience the object as it would appear with the most peripheral vision, then as it would appear with less peripheral vision.... Similarly, when we shift our attention from one object of awareness to another, there is no experience of "growing" specificity of the new object of awareness—we just perceive the new object. (1967, p. 721)

Is there an "optimal time of probing"? On the plausible assumption that after a while such narratives degrade rather steadily through both fading of details and self-serving embellishment (what I ought to have said at the party tends to turn into what I did say at the party), one can justify probing "as soon as possible" after the stimulus sequence of interest. At the same time, one wants to avoid interfering with the phenomenon by a premature probe. Because perception turns imperceptibly into memory, and "immediate" interpretation turns imperceptibly into rational reconstruction, there is no single, all-context summit on which to direct one's probes. Any probe may elicit a narrative (or narrative fragment), and any such elicited narrative determines a "time line," a subjective sequence of events from the point of view of an observer. This time line may then be compared with other time lines, in particular with the objective sequence of events occurring in the brain of that observer. For the reasons discussed, these two time lines may not superimpose themselves in orthogonal registra-

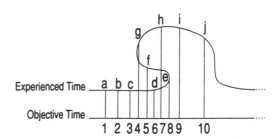

Figure 7.5
Superimposition of subjective and objective sequences

tion. There may be order differences that induce kinks. (See figure 7.5.)

There is nothing metaphysically extravagant or challenging about this failure of registration (Snyder 1988). It is no more mysterious or contracausal than the realization that the individual scenes in movies are often shot out of sequence, or that when you read the sentence, "Bill arrived at the party after Sally, but Jane came earlier than either of them," you learn of Bill's arrival before you learn of Jane's earlier arrival. The space and time of the representing is one frame of reference; the space and time of what the representing represents is another. But this metaphysically innocuous fact does nevertheless ground a fundamental metaphysical category: When a portion of the world comes in this way to compose a skein of narratives, that portion of the world is an observer. That is what it is for there to be an observer in the world, a something it is like something to be.

3   The Libet Controversies Re-examined

3.1   Libet's Experiments Allegedly Showing "Backwards Referral"

Libet's experiments with direct cortical stimulation have provoked a great deal of discussion and speculation, in spite of the fact that they involved very few subjects, were inadequately controlled, and have not been replicated (Churchland 1981a, 1981b). No doubt they have attracted this unusual attention, in spite of their serious technical flaws because, according to Libet, they demonstrate "two remarkable temporal factors":

1. *There is a substantial delay before cerebral activities*, initiated by a sensory stimulus, *achieve "neuronal adequacy"* for eliciting any resulting conscious sensory experience.

2. After neuronal adequacy is achieved, the *subjective timing* of the experience *is (automatically) referred backwards in time*, utilizing a "timing signal" in the form of the initial response of the cerebral cortex to the sensory stimulus (1981a, p. 182).

The "timing signal" is the primary evoked potential in the cortex 10 to 20 msec after peripheral stimulation. Libet suggests that the backwards referral is always "to" the timing signal.

Libet's model is Stalinesque: various editing processes occur prior to the moment of "neuronal adequacy," at which time a finished film is projected. How is it projected? Here Libet's account vacillates between an extreme view and a moderate view (cf. Honderich 1984):

a. *Backwards projection*: It is projected backwards in time to some Cartesian Theater where it actually runs in synch with the primary evoked potentials. (The primary evoked potentials, as "timing signals," serve rather like the slateboard used in film-making, showing the projector exactly how far back in time to project the experience.)

b. *Backwards referral*: It is projected in ordinary time, but it carries something like a postmark, reminding the viewer that these events must be understood to have occurred somewhat earlier. (In this case the primary evoked potentials serve simply as dates, which might be *represented* on the Cartesian screen by a title, "On the eve of the Battle of Waterloo" or "New York City, Summer, 1942.")

Libet's own term is "referral" and he defends it by reminding us of the "long recognized and accepted" phenomenon of spatial referral, which might suggest the moderate reading. But because he also insists that this backwards referral is "remarkable" and a challenge to the theory of "psychoneural identity," he invites the extreme interpretation.[8] And his interpretation is further supported by a passage at the close of Libet (1981):

There is experimental evidence for the view that the subjective or mental "sphere" could indeed "fill in" spatial and temporal gaps. How else, for example, could one view that already mentioned enormous discrepancy *that is known to exist* between a subjective visual image and the configuration of neuronal activities that gives rise to the experience of the image? (p. 196)[9]

Let us consider the details. "Neuronal adequacy," which Libet estimates to require up to 500 msec of cortical activity, is determined by seeing how late, following initial stimulation, a direct cortical stimulation can interfere with the consciousness subsequently reported. Beyond that critical interval, a direct cortical stimulus would be reported by the subject to be a *subsequent* experience. (Having arrived too late for incorporation by the editing room into the "final print" of the first stimulus experience, it would appear in the next installment.) Libet's data suggest a tremendously variable editing window: "The conditioning cortical stimulus could be started more than 500 msec following the skin pulse and still modify the skin sensation, although in most cases retroactive effects were not observed with S-C intervals greater than 200 msec" (1981, p. 185). Libet is careful to define neuronal adequacy in terms of effects on subsequent unhurried verbal report: "The subject was asked to report, within a few seconds after the delivery of each pair of ... stimuli" (1978, p. 195), and he insists that "the timing of a subjective experience must be distinguished from that of a behavioral response (such as in reaction time), which might be made before conscious awareness develops" (1978, p. 193).

This proviso permits him to defend a rival interpretation of Churchland's data. Churchland (1981a) attempted to discredit Libet's claim about the long rise time to "neuronal adequacy" for consciousness by asking subjects in an experiment to say "go" as soon as they were conscious of such a skin stimulus as those used by Libet. She reported a mean response time over 9 subjects of 358 msec, which, she argued, showed that the subjects must have achieved neuronal adequacy by the 200 msec mark at the latest (allowing time for the production of a verbal response). Libet's reply is Stalinesque: A verbal reaction can be unconsciously initiated. "There is nothing magical or uniquely informative when the motor response is a vocalization of the word 'go' instead of the more usual one of a finger tapping a button.... The ability to detect a stimulus and to react to it purposefully, or be psychologically influenced by it, without any reportable conscious awareness of the stimulus, is widely accepted" (Libet 1981, pp. 187–88). And to the objection, "But what did Churchland's subjects think they were doing, if not saying, as requested, just when they were conscious of the stimulus?" Libet could give the standard Stalinesque reply: They did indeed eventually become conscious of the stimulus, but by then, their verbal report had already been initiated.[10]

For this reason Libet rejects such reaction time studies as Churchland's as having "an uncertain validity as a primary criterion of a subjective experience" (1981, p. 188). He favors letting the subject take his time: "The report is made unhurriedly within a few seconds after each trial, allowing the subject to introspectively examine his evidence" (p. 188). How, then, can he deal with the rival prospect that this leisurely pace gives the Orwellian revisionist in the brain plenty of time to replace the *veridical* memories of consciousness with *false* memories? "Reporting after the trial of course requires that processes of short-term memory and recallability be operative, but

this presents no difficulty for subjects with no significant defects in these abilities" (p. 188).

This begs the question against the Orwellian, who is prepared to explain a variety of effects as the result of *normal* misremembering or hallucinatory recall, in which a prior, real event in consciousness is obliterated and replaced by subsequent memories. (For related discussions, see Allport 1988, pp. 171–76; Bisiach 1988, pp. 110–12.) Has Libet let the stew cook too long, or has Churchland sampled it too soon? If Libet wants to claim a *privileged* status for his choice of probe time, he must be prepared to combat the counterarguments.

Libet comes close to pleading *nolo contendere*: "Admittedly, a report of relative timing order cannot, in itself, provide an indicator of the 'absolute' time (clock-time) of the experience: As suggested, there is no known method to achieve such an indicator" (1981, p. 188). This echoes his earlier remark that there seemed to be "no method by which one could determine the absolute timing of a subjective experience" (Libet et al. 1979, p. 193). What Libet misses, however, is the possibility that this is because there is no such moment of absolute time (cf. Harnad, unpublished, 1989).

Churchland too fails to distinguish time represented from time of representing, in her critcisms (1981a, 1981b): "The two hypotheses differ essentially on just when the respective sensations *were felt* [our emphasis]," (1981a, p. 177) and "even if it be supposed that the sensations arising from the simultaneous skin and LM [medial lemniscus] sensations are *felt at exactly the same time* [our emphasis], the delay in neuronal adequacy for skin stimuli may well be an artifact of the setup" (1981b, p. 494).

Suppose that all such artifacts were eliminated, and *still* the sensations are "felt at exactly the same time." Will this mean that there is a time *t* such that stimulus 1 is felt at *t* and stimulus 2 is felt at *t* (the anti-materialist prospect) or only that stimulus 1 and stimulus 2 are felt as (experienced as) simultaneous? Churchland doesn't discourage the inference that Libet's findings, if vindicated, would wreak havoc (as he claims) on materialism. Elsewhere, however, she correctly notes that "intriguing as temporal illusions are, there is no reason to suppose there is something preternatural about them, and certainly there is nothing which distinguishes them from spatial illusions or motion illusions as uniquely bearing the benchmark of a nonphysical origin" (1981a, p. 178). This could only be the case if temporal illusions were phenomena in which *time was misrepresented*; if the *misrepresenting* take place at the "wrong" times, something more revolutionary is afoot.

Where does this leave Libet's experiments with cortical stimulation? As an interesting but inconclusive attempt to establish something about *how the brain represents temporal order*. Primary evoked potentials may somehow serve as specific reference-points for neural representations of time, although Libet has not shown this, as Churchland's technical criticisms make clear. Alternatively, the brain keeps its representations of time more labile. We don't represent seen objects as existing on the retina, but rather as various distances in the external world. Why should the brain not also represent events as happening *when* it makes the most "ecological" sense for them to happen? When we are engaged in some act of manual dexterity, "fingertip time" should be the standard; when we are conducting an orchestra, "ear time" might capture the registration. "Primary cortical time" might be the default standard (rather like Greenwich Mean Time for the British Empire)—a matter, however, for further research.

The issue has been obscured by the fact that both proponent and critic have failed to distinguish consistently between time of representing and time represented. They talk past each other, with Libet adopting a Stalinesque position and Churchland making the Orwellian countermoves, both apparently in agreement that there is a fact of the matter about exactly when (in "absolute" time as Libet would put it) a conscious experience happens.[11]

3.2   Libet's Claims about the "Subjective Delay" of Consciousness of Intention

The concept of the absolute timing of an experience is exploited in Libet's later experiments with "conscious intentions," in which he seeks to determine their absolute timing experimentally by letting the subjects, who alone have direct access (somehow) to their experiences, do *self-timing*. He asked subjects to look at a clock (a spot of light circling on an oscilloscope) *while* they experience consciously intending, and to make a judgment about the position on the clock of the spot at the onset of intention, a judgment they can later, at their leisure, *report*.

Libet is clearer than most of his critics about the importance of keeping content and vehicle distinguished: "One should not confuse *what* is reported by the subject with *when* he may become introspectively aware of what he is reporting" (Libet 1985a, p. 559). He recognizes (p. 560), moreover, that a judgment of simultaneity need not itself be simultaneously arrived at or rendered; it might mature over a long period of time (consider, for instance, the minutes it may take the stewards at the race track to develop and then examine the photo-finish picture on which they eventually base their judgment of the winner of a dead heat).

Libet gathered data on two time series: (1) the objective series, which includes the timing of the external clock and the salient neural events: the readiness potentials (RPs) and the electromyograms (EMGs), and (2) the subjective series (as later reported), which consists of mental imagery, memories of any preplanning, and, crucially, of a single benchmark datum for each trial: a simultaneity judgment of the form: *My conscious intention (W) began simultaneously with the clock spot in position P.*

Libet seems to have wanted to approximate the elusive *acte gratuit* discussed by the existentialists (e.g., Gide 1948; Sartre 1943), the purely motiveless—and hence in some special sense "free"—choice, and as several commentators have pointed out (Breitmeyer 1985; Bridgeman 1986;

Danto 1985; Jung 1985; Latto 1985) such highly unusual actions (what might be called acts of deliberate pseudorandomness) are hardly paradigms of "normal voluntary acts" (Libet 1987, p. 784). But has he in any event isolated a variety of conscious experience, however characterized, that can be absolutely timed by such an experimental design?

He claims that when conscious intentions to act (at least of his special sort) are put into registration with the brain events that actually initiate the acts, there is an offset: Consciousness of intention lags 300–500 msec behind the relevant brain events. This does look ominous to anyone committed to the principle that "our conscious decisions" *control* our bodily motions. It looks as if *we* are located in Cartesian theaters where we are shown, with a half-second tape delay, the *real* decision-making that is going on *elsewhere* (somewhere *we* aren't). We are not quite "out of the loop" (as they say in the White House), but because our access to information is thus delayed, the most we can do is intervene with last-moment "vetoes" or "triggers." One who accepts this picture might put it this way: "Downstream from (unconscious) command headquarters, I take no real initiative, am never in on the birth of a project, but do exercise a modicum of executive modulation of the formulated policies streaming through my office."

This picture is compelling but incoherent. For one thing, such a "veto" would itself have to be a "conscious decision," it seems, and hence ought to require its own 300–500 msec cerebral preparation—unless one is assuming outright Cartesian dualism (see MacKay 1985, who makes a related point). Setting that problem aside, Libet's model, as before, is Stalinesque, and the obvious Orwellian alternative is raised by Jasper (1985), who notes that both epileptic automatism and behaviors occurring under the effect of such drugs as scopolamine show that "brain mechanisms underlying awareness may occur without those which make possible the recall of this awareness in memory afterward." Libet concedes that this

"does present a problem, but was not experimentally testable" (p. 560).[12]

Given this concession, is the task of fixing the absolute *micro*timing of consciousness ill-conceived? Neither Libet nor his critics draw that conclusion. Libet, having carefully distinguished content from vehicle—*what* is represented from *when* it is represented—nonetheless tries to draw inferences from premises about what is represented to conclusions about the absolute timing of the representing in consciousness (cf. Salter 1989). Wasserman (1985) sees the problem: "The time when the external objective spot occupies a given clock position can be determined easily, but this is not the desired result." But he then falls into the Cartesian trap: "What is needed is the time of occurrence of the internal brain-mind representation of the spot."

"*The* time of occurrence" of the internal representation? Occurrence where? There is essentially continuous representation of the spot (representing it to be in various different positions) in various different parts of the brain, starting at the retina and moving up through the visual system. The brightness of the spot is represented in some places and times, its location in others, and its motion in still others. As the external spot moves, all these representations change, in an asynchronous and spatially distributed way. Where does "it all come together at an instant in consciousness"? Nowhere. Wasserman correctly points out that the task of determining where the spot was at some time in the subjective sequence is itself a voluntary task, and initiating it presumably takes some time. This is difficult not only because it is in competition with other concurrent projects (as stressed by Stamm 1985, p. 554), but also because it is unnatural—a conscious judgment of temporality of a sort that does not normally play a role in behavior control, and hence has no natural meaning in the sequence. The process of interpretation that eventually fixes the judgment of subjective simultaneity is itself an artifact of the experimental situation, and *changes the task*, therefore telling us nothing of interest about the actual timing of normal representational vehicles anywhere in the brain.

Stamm likens the situation to Heisenbergian uncertainty: "Self-monitoring of an internal process interferes with that process, so that its precise measurement is impossible" (p. 554). This observation betrays a commitment to the mistaken idea that *there is* an absolute time of intersection, "precise measurement" of which, alas, is impossible for Heisenbergian reasons (see also Harnad 1989). This could only make sense on the assumption that there is a particular privileged place where the intersection matters.

The all too natural vision that we must discard is the following: Somewhere deep in the brain an act-initiation begins; it starts out as an unconscious intention, and slowly makes its way to the theater, picking up clarity and power as it goes, and then, at an instant, t, it bursts on stage, where a parade of visual spot-representations are marching past, having made their way slowly from the retina, getting clothed with brightness and location as they moved. The audience or I is given the task of saying which spot-representation was "on stage" exactly when the conscious intention made its bow. Once identified, this spot's time of departure from the retina can be calculated, as well as the distance to the theater and the transmission velocity. That way we can determine the exact moment at which the conscious intention occurred in the Cartesian Theater.

Some have thought that although that particular vision is incoherent, one does not need to give up the idea of absolute timing of experiences. There is an alternative family of models for the onset of consciousness that avoids the preposterousness of the Cartesian-centered brain. Couldn't consciousness be a matter not of arrival at a point but rather a matter of a representation exceeding some threshold of activation over the whole cortex or large parts thereof? On this model, an element of content becomes conscious at some time t, not by entering some functionally defined and anatomically located system, but by changing state right where it is: by acquiring some property or by having the intensity of one of its properties boosted above some criterial level.

The idea that content becomes conscious not by entering a subsystem, but by the brain's undergoing a state change of one sort or another has much to recommend it (see, e.g., Crick and Koch 1990; Kinsbourne 1988; Neumann 1990). Moreover the simultaneities and sequences of such mode-shifts can presumably be measured by outside observers, providing, in principle, a unique and determinate sequence of contents attaining the special mode. But this is still the Cartesian Theater if it is claimed that the real ("absolute") timing of such mode shifts is definitive of subjective sequence. The imagery is different, but the implications are the same. Conferring the special property that makes for consciousness at an instant is only half the problem; discriminating that the property has been conferred at that time is the other, and although scientific observers with their instruments may be able to do this with microsecond accuracy, how is the brain to do this? We human beings do make judgments about simultaneity and sequence among elements of our own experience, some of which we express, so at some point or points in our brains the corner must be turned from the actual timing of representations to the representation of timing. This is a process that takes effort in one way or another (Gallistel 1990), and wherever and whenever these discriminations are made, thereafter the temporal properties of the representations embodying those judgments are not constitutive of their content.

Suppose that a succession of widely spread activation states, with different contents, sweeps over the cortex. The actual, objectively measured simultaneities and sequences in this broad field are of no functional relevance *unless they can also be accurately detected by mechanisms in the brain*. What would make *this* sequence the stream of consciousness if the brain could not discern the sequence? What matters, once again, is not the temporal properties of the representing, but the temporal properties *represented*, something determined by how they are "taken" by subsequent processes in the brain.

3.3 Grey Walter's Experiment: A Better Demonstration of the Central Contention of the Multiple Drafts Model

It was noted above that Libet's experiment created an artificial and difficult judgmental task that robbed the results of the hoped-for significance. This can be brought out more clearly by comparing it to a similar experiment by Grey Walter (1963), with patients in whose motor cortex he had implanted electrodes. He wanted to test the hypothesis that certain bursts of recorded activity were the initiators of intentional actions, so he arranged for each patient to look at slides from a carousel projector. The patient could advance the carousel at will, by pressing the button on the controller. (Note the similarity to Libet's experiment: This was a "free" decision, timed only by an endogenous rise in boredom, or curiosity about the next slide, or distraction, or whatever.) Unbeknownst to the patient, however, the controller button was a dummy, not attached to the slide projector at all. What actually advanced the slides was the amplified signal from the electrode implanted in the patient's motor cortex.

One might suppose that the patients would notice nothing out of the ordinary, but in fact they were startled by the effect, because it seemed to them as if the slide projector was anticipating their decisions. They reported that just as they were "about to" push the button, but before they had actually decided to do so, the projector would advance the slide—and they would find themselves pressing the button with the worry that it was going to advance the slide twice! The effect was strong, according to Grey Walter's account, but apparently he never performed the dictated follow-up experiment: introducing a variable delay element to see how large a delay had to be incorporated into the triggering to eliminate the "precognitive carousel" effect.

An important difference between Grey Walter's and Libet's designs is that the judgment of temporal order that leads to surprise in Grey Walter's experiment is part of a normal task of behavior monitoring. In this regard it is like the temporal order judgments by which our brains distinguish moving left-to-right from moving right-to-left, rather than "deliberate, conscious" order judgments. The brain in this case has set itself to "expect" visual feedback on the successful execution of its project of advancing the carousel, and the feedback arrives earlier than expected, triggering an alarm. This could show us something important about the actual timing of content vehicles and their attendant processes in the brain, but it would not, contrary to first appearances, show us something about the "absolute timing of the conscious decision to change the slide."

Suppose, for instance, that an extension of Grey Walter's experiment showed that a delay as long as 300 msec (as implied by Libet) had to be incorporated into the implementation of the act in order to eliminate the subjective sense of precognitive slide-switching. What such a delay would in fact show would be that expectations set up by a decision to change the slide are tuned to expect visual feedback 300 msec later, and to report back with alarm under other conditions. The fact that the alarm eventually gets interpreted in the subjective sequence as a perception of misordered events (change before button push) shows nothing about *when* in real time the consciousness of the decision to press the button first occurred. The sense the subjects reported of not quite having had time to "veto" the initiated button push when they "saw the slide was already changing" is a natural interpretation for the brain to settle on (eventually) of the various contents made available at various times for incorporation into the narrative. Was this sense already there at the first moment of consciousness of intention (in which case the effect requires a long delay to "show time" and is Stalinesque) or was it a retrospective reinterpretation of an otherwise confusing *fait accompli* (in which case it is Orwellian)? This question should no longer seem to demand an answer.

4 Conclusion

The Multiple Drafts model has many other implications for scientific theories of consciousness (Dennett 1991), but our main conclusion in this chapter is restricted to temporal properties of experience: The representation of sequence in the stream of consciousness is a product of the brain's interpretative processes, not a direct reflection of the sequence of events making up those processes. Indeed, as Jackedoff has pointed out to us, what we are arguing for in this essay is a straightforward extension to the experience of time of the common wisdom about the experience of space; the representation of space in the brain does not always use space-in-the-brain to represent space, and the representation of time in the brain does not always use time-in-the-brain. It may be objected that the arguments presented here are powerless to overturn the still obvious truth that our experiences of events occur in the very same order that we experience them to occur. If someone thinks the thought, "One, two, three, four, five," his thinking "one" occurs before his thinking "two" and so forth. The example docs illustrate a thesis that is true in general and does indeed seem unexceptioned, so long as we restrict our attention to psychological phenomena of "ordinary," macroscopic duration. But the experiments we selected for discussion are concerned with events that were constricted by unusually narrow time-frames of a few hundred milliseconds. At this scale, we have argued, the standard presumption breaks down.

It might be supposed, then, that we are dealing only with special cases. These limiting cases may interestingly reveal how the brain deals with informational overload, but, one might suggest, they are unrepresentative of the brain's more usual manner of functioning. The contrary is the case, however, as might be anticipated, in view of the brain's well-known propensity for applying a limited number of basic mechanisms across a wide range of situations. The processes of editorial revision that are dramatically revealed in the time-pressured cases continue indefinitely as the brain responds to the continued demands of cognition and control. For instance, as time passes after an event has occurred, that event may be recalled to episodic memory, but to an ever more limited extent. After some days, an occurrence that may have unrolled over minutes or more is remembered within as restricted a time frame as those we have been discussing. Such memories present not as randomly blurry or depleted versions but as internally coherent, simplified renderings of what are taken to be the most important elements. Temporal succession is typically an early victim of this reorganization of the event, sacrificed in favor of (apparently) more useful information (as instanced in the phi phenomenon).

We perceive—and remember—perceptual events, not a successively analyzed trickle of perceptual elements or attributes locked into succession as if pinned into place on a continuous film. Different attributes of events are indeed extracted by different neural facilities at different rates, (e.g., locations versus shape versus color) and people, if asked to respond to the presence of each one in isolation, would do so with different latencies, depending on which it was, and on other well-explored factors. The relative timing of inputs plays a necessary role in determining the information or content of experience, but it is not obligatorily tied to any stage or point of time during central processing. How soon we can respond to one in isolation, and how soon to the other, does not exactly indicate what will be the temporal relationship of the two in percepts that incorporate them both.

There is nothing theoretically amiss with the goal of acquiring precise timing information on the mental operations or informational transactions in the brain (Wasserman and Kong 1979). It is indeed crucial to developing a good theory of the brain's control functions to learn exactly when and where various informational streams converge, when "inferences" and "matches" and "bindings" occur. But these temporal and spatial details do not tell us directly about the contents of consciousness. The temporal sequence *in consciousness* is, within the limits of whatever temporal control window bounds our investigation, purely a matter of the content represented, not the timing of the representing.

Acknowledgments

The original draft of this chapter was written while the authors were supported by the Rockefeller Foundation as Scholars in Residence at the Bellagio Study Center, Villa Serbelloni, Bellagio, Italy, April, 1990. We are grateful to Kathleen Akins, Peter Bieri, Edoardo Bisiach, William Calvin, Patricia Churchland, Robert Efron, Stevan Harnad, Douglas Hofstadter, Tony Marcel, Odmar Neumann, Jay Rosenberg, and David Rosenthal for comments on subsequent drafts.

Notes

1. A philosophical exception is Vendler (1972, 1984) who attempts to salvage Cartesian dualism. A scientific exception is Eccles (e.g., Popper and Eccles 1977).

2. What about the prospect of a solitary Robinson Crusoe scientist who performs all these experiments wordlessly on himself? Would the anomalies be apparent to this lone observer? What about reconstructing these experiments with languageless animals? Would we be inclined to interpret the results in the same way? Would we be justified? These are good questions, but their answers are complicated, and we must reserve them for another occasion.

3. Such a "postmark" can be in principle added to a vehicle of content at any stage of its journey; if all materials arriving at a particular location come from the same place, by the same route at the same speed, their "departure time" from the original destination can be retroactively stamped on them, by simply subtracting a constant from their arrival time at the way station. This is an engineering possibility that is probably used by the brain for making certain automatic adjustments for standard travel times.

4. "The essence of much of the research that has been carried out in the field of sensory coding can be distilled into a single, especially important idea—any candidate code can represent any perceptual dimension; there is no need for an isomorphic relation between the neural and psychophysical data. Space can represent time, time can represent space, place can represent quality, and certainly, nonlinear neural functions can represent linear or nonlinear psychophysical functions equally well" (Uttal 1979). This is a widely acknowledged idea, but, as we will show, some theorists (mis-)understand it by tacitly reintroducing the unnecessary "isomorphism" in a dimly imagined subsequent translation or "projection" in consciousness.

5. Cf. Pylyshyn 1979: "No one ... is disposed to speak *literally* of such physical properties of a mental event as its color, size, mass, and so on—though we *do* speak of them as *representing* (or having the experiential content of) such properties. For instance, no one would not properly say of a thought (or image) that it was large or red, but only that it was a thought *about* something large or red (or that it was an image *of* something large or red). ... It ought to strike one as curious, therefore, that we speak so freely of the *duration* of a mental event."

6. P. S. Churchland (1981a, p. 172) notes a difference between "masking in the usual sense" and "blanking in short term memory," which perhaps is an allusion to these two possibilities, but does not consider how one might distinguish between them.

7. Consider the medio-temporal region of the cortex (MT), which responds to motion (and apparent motion). Suppose then that some activity in MT *is* the brain's concluding that there was intervening motion. There is no further question, on the Multiple Drafts model, of whether this is a pre-experiential or post-experiential conclusion. It would be a mistake to ask, in other words, whether this activity in MT was a "reaction to a conscious experience" (by the Orwellian historian) as opposed to a "decision to represent motion" (by the Stalinesque editor).

8. See also his dismissal of MacKay's suggestion of a more moderate reading (Libet 1981, p. 195, 1985b, p. 568).

9. Libet's final summation in 1981, on the other hand, was inconclusive: "My own view ... has been that the

temporal discrepancy creates relative difficulties for identity theory, but that these are not insurmountable" (p. 196). Presumably they would be undeniably insurmountable on the backwards *projection* interpretation, and Libet later (1985b, p. 569) describes these difficulties in a way that seems to require the milder reading: "Although the delay-and-antedating hypothesis does not separate the actual time of the experience from its time of neuronal production, it does eliminate the necessity for simultaneity between the *subjective timing* of the experience and the actual clock-time of the experience." Perhaps Eccles's enthusiastic support for a radical, dualistic interpretation of the findings has misdirected the attention of Libet (and his critics) from the mild thesis he sometimes defends.

10. In an earlier paper, Libet conceded the possibility of Orwellian processes and supposed there might be a significant difference between unconscious mental events and conscious-but-ephemeral mental events: "There may well be an immediate but ephemeral kind of experience of awareness which is not retained for recall at conscious levels of experience. If such experiences exist, however, their content would have direct significance only in later unconscious mental processes, although, like other unconscious experiences, they might play an indirect role in later conscious ones" (1965, p. 78).

11. Harnad (1989) sees an insoluble problem of measurement, but denies our contention that there is no fact of the matter: "Introspection can only tell us when an event *seemed* to occur, or which of two events *seemed* to occur first. There is no independent way of confirming that the real timing was indeed as it seemed. Incommensurability is a methodological problem, not a metaphysical one." So Harnad asserts what we deny: that among the real timings of events in the brain is a "real timing" of events *in consciousness*.

12. In a later response to a similar suggestion of Hoffman and Kravitz (1987) Libet asks the rhetorical question, "Are we to accept the primary evidence of the subjects' introspective report (as I do), or are we going to insist that the subject had a conscious experience which he himself does not report and would even deny having had?" (1987, p. 784). This is another expression of Libet's a priori preference for a Stalinesque position.

References

Allport, A. (1988) What concept of consciousness? In: *Consciousness in contemporary science*, ed. A. J. Marcel and E. Bisiach. Cambridge University Press (Cambridge).

Barlow, H. B., and Levick, W. R. (1965) Mechanisms of pattern selectivity in retina. *Journal of Physiology* 178:477.

Bisiach, E. (1988) The haunted brain and consciousness. In: *Consciousness in contemporary science*, ed. A. J. Marcel and E. Bisiach. Cambridge University Press (Cambridge).

Breitmeyer, B. G. (1984) *Visual masking*. Clarendon Press.

———. (1985) Problems with the psychophysics of intention. *Behavioral and Brain Sciences* 8:539–40.

Bridgeman, B. (1985) Free will and the functions of consciousness. *Behavioral and Brain Sciences* 8(2):540.

Calvin, W. (1990) *The cerebral symphony: Seashore reflections on the structure of consciousness*. Bantam.

Churchland, P. S. (1981a) On the alleged backwards referral of experiences and its relevance to the mind-body problem. *Philosophy of Science* 48:165–81.

———. (1981b) The timing of sensations: Reply to Libet. *Philosophy of Science* 48:492–97.

Crick, F., and Koch, C. (1990) Towards a neurobiological theory of consciousness. In: *Seminars in the neurosciences*, 2:263–75, ed. A. R. Damasio. W. B. Saunders.

Damasio, A. R. (1989) Time-locked multiregional retroactivation: A systems level proposal for the neural substrates of recall and recognition. *Cognition* 33:25–62.

Danto, A. (1985) Consciousness and motor control. *Behavioral and Brain Sciences* 8:540–41.

Dennett, D. C. (1978) Skinner skinned. In: *Brainstorms: Philosophical essays on mind and psychology*, ed. D. C. Dennett. Bradford Books.

———. (1979) [review of K. R. Popper and J. C. Eccles 1977.] *Journal of philosophy* 76:91–97.

———. (1982) How to study human consciousness empirically. *Synthese* 53:159–80.

———. (1991) *Consciousness explained*. Little, Brown.

Descartes, R. (1662) *Traite de l'homme*. Paris.

———. (1662/1972) *Treatise on man*. Translated by T. S. Hall. Harvard University Press.

Dixon, M. F. (1986) On private events and brain events. *Behavioral and Brain Sciences* 9:29–30.

Dorfman, A. (1988) *Mascara*. Viking.

Eccles, J. C. (1985) Mental summation: The timing of voluntary intentions by cortical activity. *Behavioral and Brain Sciences* 8:542–43.

Efron, R. (1967) The duration of the present. *Proceedings of the New York Academy of Science* 138:713–29.

———. (1973) Conservation of temporal information by perceptual systems. *Perception and Psychophysics* 14:518–30.

Erdelyi, M. H. (1986) Experimental indeterminacies in the dissociation paradigm of subliminal perception. *Behavioral and Brain Sciences* 9(1):30–31.

Farrell, B. A. (1950) Experience. *Mind* 59:170–98.

Gallistel, C. R. (1990) *The organization of learning.* MIT Press.

Geldard, F. A. (1977) Cutaneous stimuli, vibratory and saltatory. *Journal of Investigative Dermatology* 69:83–87.

Geldard, F. A., and Sherrick, C. E. (1972) The cutaneous "rabbit": A perceptual illusion. *Science* 178:178–79.

———. (1983) The cutaneous saltatory area and its presumed neural base. *Perception and Psychophysics* 33:299–304.

———. (1986) Space, time and touch. *Scientific American* 254:90–95.

Gide, A. (1948) *Journal des faux monnayeurs.* Gallimard.

Glynn, I. M. (1990) Consciousness and time. *Nature* 348:477–79.

Goodman, N. (1978) *Ways of worldmaking.* Harvester.

Grey Walter, W. (1963) Presentation to the Ostler Society, Oxford University, Oxford, England.

Harnad, S. (1982) Consciousness: An afterthought. *Cognition and Brain Theory* 5:29–47.

———. (1989) Editorial commentary [on Libet 1985a]. *Behavioral and Brain Sciences* 12:183.

———. (unpublished) Conscious events cannot be localized in time.

Hawking, S. (1988) *A brief history of time.* Bantam.

Hoffman, R. E., and Kravitz, R. E. (1987) Feedforward action regulation and the experience of will. *Behavioral and Brain Sciences* 10:782–83.

Holender, D. (1986) Semantic activation without conscious identification in dichotic listening, parafoveal vision, and visual masking: A survey and appraisal. *Behavioral and Brain Sciences* 9:1–23.

Honderich, T. (1984) The time of a conscious sensory experience and mind-brain theories. *Journal of Theoretical Biology* 110:115–29.

Hoy, R. C. (1982) Ambiguities in the subjective timing of experiences debate. *Philosophy of Science* 49:254–62.

Jasper, H. H. (1985) Brain mechanisms of conscious experience and voluntary action. *Behavioral and Brain Sciences* 8(4):543–44.

Jules, B. (1971) *Foundations of cyclopean perception.* University of Chicago Press.

Jung, R. (1985) Voluntary intention and conscious selection in complex learned action. *Behavioral and Brain Sciences* 8(4):544–45.

Kinsbourne, M. (1988) Integrated field theory of consciousness. In: *Consciousness in contemporary science,* ed. A. J. Marcel and E. Bisiach. Oxford University Press (Oxford).

———. (in preparation) The distributed brain basis of consciousness.

Kolers, P. A. (1972) *Aspects of motion perception.* Pergamon Press.

Kolers, P. A., and von Grünau, M. (1976) Shape and color in apparent motion. *Vision Research* 16:329–35.

Latto, R. (1985) Consciousness as an experimental variable: Problems of definition, practice, and interpretation. *Behavioral and Brain Sciences* 8:545–46.

Libermann, A. M. (1970) The grammar of speech and language. *Cognitive Psychology* 1:301–23.

Libet, B. (1965) Cortical activation in conscious and unconscious experience. *Perspectives in Biology and Medicine* 9:77–86.

———. (1978) Neuronal vs. subjective timing for a conscious sensory experience. In: *Cerebral correlates of conscious experience,* ed. P. A. Buser and A. Rougeul-Buser. Elsevier/North Holland Biomedical Press.

———. (1981) The experimental evidence for subjective referral of a sensory experience backwards in time: Reply to P. S. Churchland. *Philosophy of Science* 48:182–97.

———. (1982) Brain stimulation in the study of neuronal functions for conscious sensory experiences. *Human Neurobiology* 1:235–42.

———. (1985a) Unconscious cerebral initiative and the role of conscious will in voluntary action. *Behavioral and Brain Sciences* 8:529–66.

————. (1985b) Subjective antedating of a sensory experience and mind-brain theories: Reply to Honderich (1984). *Journal of Theoretical Biology* 114:563–70.

————. (1987) Are the mental experiences of will and self-control significant for the performance of a voluntary act? *Behavioral and Brain Sciences* 10:783–86.

————. (1989) The timing of a subjective experience. *Behavioral and Brain Sciences* 12:183–85.

Libet, B., Wright, E. W., Feinstein, B., and Pearl, D. K. (1979) Subjective referral of the timing for a conscious sensory experience: A functional role for the somatosensory specific projection system in man. *Brain* 102:193–224.

MacKay, D. M. (1985) Do we "control" our brains? *Behavioral and Brain Sciences* 8(4):546–47.

Marcel, A. J. (1983) Conscious and unconscious perception: An approach to the relations between phenomenal experience and perceptual process. *Cognitive Psychology* 15:238–300.

————. (1986) Consciousness and processing: Choosing and testing a null hypothesis. *Behavioral and Brain Sciences* 9(1):40–41.

Mellor, H. (1981) *Real time*. Cambridge University Press (Cambridge).

Merikle, P. M., and Cheesman, J. (1986) Consciousness is a "subjective" state. *Behavioral and Brain Sciences* 9(1):42.

Minsky, M. (1985) *The society of minds*. Simon & Schuster.

Mortenson, C. (1985) Conscious decisions. *Behavioral and Brain Sciences* 8:548–49.

Nagel, T. (1974) What is it like to be a bat? *Philosophical Review* 83:435–45.

Neisser, U. (1967) *Cognitive Psychology*. Appleton-Century-Crofts.

————. (1976) *Cognition and reality*. Freeman.

————. (1981) John Dean's memory: A case study. *Cognition* 9:1–22.

Neumann, O. (1990) Some aspects of phenomenal consciousness and their possible functional correlates. Presented at the conference, The phenomenal mind—how is it possible and why is it necessary? Center for Interdisciplinary Research (ZiF), Bielefeld, May 14–17.

Newell, A., Rosenbloom, P. S., and Laird, J. E. (1989) Symbolic architectures for cognition. In: *Foundations of cognitive science*, ed. M. Posner. MIT Press.

Pagels, H. (1988) *The dreams of reason*. Simon & Schuster.

Penfield, W., and Jasper, H. (1954) *Epilepsy and the functional anatomy of the human brain*. Little, Brown.

Penrose, R. (1989) *The Emperor's new mind: Concerning computers, minds, and the laws of physics*. Oxford University Press (Oxford).

Pöppel, E. (1985) *Grenzen des Bewusstseins*. Deutsche Verlags-Anstal. (Translated as *Mindworks: Time and conscious experience*. Harcourt Brace Jovanovich, 1988.)

Popper, K. R., and Eccles, J. C. (1977) *The self and its brain*. Springer-Verlag.

Pylyshyn, Z. (1979) Do mental events have durations? *Behavioral and Brain Sciences* 2(2):277–78.

Reinhold, E. M., and Merikle, P. M. (1988) Using direct and indirect measures to study perception without awareness. *Perception and Psychophysics* 44:563–75.

————. (1990) On the inter-relatedness of theory and measurement in the study of unconscious processes. *Mind and Language* 5:9–28.

Ringo, J. L. (1985) Timing volition: Questions of what and when about W. *Behavioral and Brain Sciences* 8(4):550–51.

Ryle, G. (1949) *The concept of mind*. Hutchison.

Salter, D. (1989) Voluntary process and the readiness potential: Asking the right questions. *Behavioral and Brain Sciences* 12(1):181–82.

Sarris, V. (1989) Max Wertheimer on seen motion: Theory and evidence. *Psychological Research* 51:58–68.

Sartre, J. P. (1943) *L'être et le néant*. Gallimard.

Snyder, D. M. (1988) On the time of a conscious peripheral sensation. *Journal of Theoretical Biology* 130:253–54.

Sperling, G. (1960) The information available in brief visual presentation. *Psychological Monographs* 74, no. 11.

Stamm, J. S. (1985) The uncertainty principle in psychology. *Behavioral and Brain Sciences* 8(4):553–54.

Uttal, W. R. (1979) Do central nonlinearities exist? *Behavioral and Brain Sciences* 2(2):286.

Van der Waals, H. G., and Roelfs, C. O. (1930) Optische Scheinbewegung. *Zeitschrift für Psychologie und Physiologie des Sinnesorgane* 114:241–88. (Also [1931] 115:91–190.)

Van Gulick, R. (1985) Conscious wants and self-awareness. *Behavioral and Brain Sciences* 8:555–56.

Velmans, M. (1991) Is human information processing conscious? *Behavioral and Brain Sciences* 14(4):651–669.

Vendler, Z. (1972) *Res cogitan.* Cornell University Press.

————. (1984) *The matter of minds.* Clarendon Press.

Wasserman, G. S. (1985) Neural/mental chronometry and chronotheology. *Behavioral and Brain Sciences* 8(4):556–60.

Wasserman, G. S., and Kong, K. L. (1979) Absolute timing of mental activities. *Behavioral and Brain Sciences* 2(2):243–304.

Welch, R. B. (1978) *Perceptual modification: Adapting to altered sensory environments.* Academic Press.

Wertheimer, M. (1912) Experimentelle studied über das Sehen von Bewegung. *Zeitschrift für Psychologie* 61: 161–265.

8 Begging the Question against Phenomenal Consciousness

Ned Block

Dennett and Kinsbourne's (D & K's) argument [in Chapter 7] hinges on the unmentioned and unargued assumption that there is no such thing as phenomenal consciousness. Those readers who believe in phenomenal consciousness should not find the argument convincing.

What Is Phenomenal Consciousness?

There is a great chasm among theorists about the mind: On one side are those who accept a concept of consciousness distinct from any cognitive or information processing or functional notion; on the other side are those who reject any such concept. Dennett (1991) gives a book-length argument against a noncognitive conception, drawing on, among other things, the raw materials of this target article, but there is no such argument in the target article.

The concept of consciousess at issue attracts descriptions like "raw feel," "immediate phenomenological quality," and Nagel's (1974) "what it is like." This is the concept of consciousness that leads us to speak of an "explanatory gap": At this stage in the relevant sciences we have no idea how the neural substrate of my pain can explain why my pain feels like *this* rather than some other way or no way at all. This is the concept of consciousness that gives rise to the famous "inverted spectrum" hypothesis—things we both call "green" look to you the way things we both call "red" look to me—and the "absent qualia qualia" hypothesis, the idea that there could be a machine that was computationally like us, but was nonetheless a phenomenally unconscious zombie. Note that these conundra are *routes* to phenomenal consciousness—they do not constitute it. One can accept phenomenal consciousness without accepting any of them because our fundamental access to phenomenal consciousness derives from our acquaintance with it.[1]

Of course, those who accept phenomenal consciousness do not disparage other concepts of consciousness. We can speak of information as conscious in the sense that it is inferentially promiscuous (Stich 1978), that is, it is easily available to be used as a premise in reasoning and in formulating plans, and it is available for reporting. (For example, information that is repressed is not inferentially promiscuous.) Or we can speak of a state as conscious in the sense that it is accompanied by a thought to the effect that one is having that state (Armstrong 1968; Rosenthal 1986). Or we can speak of a state as conscious in the sense that one can monitor it or have internal soliloquies about it.

The Question Begged

The point of the "multiple drafts" metaphor is that with the various forms of electronic quasi-publishing now flourishing, we may one day (though clearly not yet) have a situation in which any decision as to which of the many versions is to be counted as "the publication" will be arbitrary. D & K write that since a perception of an event is spread over the brain in space and therefore in time, labeling any of the stages or revisions 'conscious' would be similarly arbitrary. *But what if some of the brain representations of an event making up this spatio-temporal volume are phenomenally conscious whereas others are not?* It is surely *non*arbitrary to label those phenomenally conscious events as 'conscious'. D & K's claim that it is arbitrary to select some representations as conscious is plausible only if one swallows their unmentioned irrealism about phenomenal consciousness. Only if there is *no such thing* as phenomenal consciousness would it be arbitrary to ascribe "it" to one representation rather than another.

If there is such a thing as phenomenal consciousness, then presumably this fact will be reflected at the neural level. Perhaps there will be differences between those brain representations that are phenomenally conscious and those that are not of the sort that Crick and Koch (1990), have proposed. The D & K argument depends on supposing that the Crick and Koch research project is a confusion, a search for something that does not exist, but we are given no argument to this effect.

Note that the D & K arguments against Cartesian materialism (even assuming that they are successful) cast no doubt on the reality of phenomenal consciousness. The hypothesis I just mentioned, to the effect that some perceptual representations of an event are conscious whereas others are not, makes no commitment to there being any single place where all phenomenally conscious events live. Perhaps there are phenomenally conscious events in many different areas of the brain. No one endorses Cartesian materialism, but many of us endorse phenomenal consciousness. Note also that one who accepts phenomenal consciousness can also accept all sorts of borderline cases between consciousness and nonconsciousness, and other sorts of indeterminacies of consciousness; perhaps some of the stages of perceptual processing will be like phenomenally conscious events in some ways but not in others. Antirealists often try to stick realists with one or another version of the law of the excluded middle: "If there is such a thing as phenomenal consciousness, then every question about it has a definite yes or no answer." Is phenomenal event A before phenomenal event B? If one event contains the other, there will be no yes-or-no answer.

Orwellian versus Stalinist Accounts

D & K repeatedly write that "nothing discernible to 'inside' or 'outside' observers could distinguish" Orwellian from Stalinist options (sec. 2.2). Both claims are false if phenomenal consciousness exists, as I will now argue.

"Inside"

On the Orwellian story about the lady who runs by, for example, there is a phenomenal experience of a lady with long hair and no glasses. On the Stalinist story, there is no such phenomenal experience. The difference between *some* such phenomenal experience and *no* such phenomenal experience is an "inside" difference if there ever was one. What D & K appear to mean by something discernible "inside" is something discernible in the subject's *judgments*. But to assume that the subjective is exhausted by judgments is to beg the question against phenomenal consciousness, which, if it exists, is *not* just a matter of judgments.

The question-begging nature of the argument is summed up by the following lines about the Orwellian/Stalinist disagreement: "... they both account for the subjective data—whatever is obtainable 'from the first person perspective'—because they agree about how it ought to 'feel' to subjects" (sec. 2.2). On the contrary, the Orwellian and Stalinist theories do *not* agree about how things feel to the subject; the Orwellian accepts the phenomenally conscious experience of a lady with long hair and no glasses; the Stalinist rejects it. What the Orwellian and the Stalinist agree on is the subject's *judgments not on what he feels*.

D & K may wish to retreat to the position that one cannot use introspection as a source of data to decide between Orwellian and Stalinist theories of one's own experiences. This is not something that believers in phenomenal consciousness should dispute, since we believe that our privileged access, such as it is, extends to our experiences themselves, but does not make our memories of them infallible. If we want to decide between Orwellian and Stalinist accounts, we will need to appeal to science, and to this matter we now turn.

"Outside"

The D & K claim that "outside" observers could never tell the difference between Orwellian and

Stalinist hypotheses is equally question-begging. If the presence or absence of phenomenal consciousness is the presence or absence of a real property, ingenious experimenters will presumably find a way to get an experimental handle on it. (See Potter 1975 and 1976, for the beginnings of a line of evidence for an Orwellian stance.) D & K say that the Orwellian and the Stalinist can agree on where the mistaken content enters the causal pathway; they just disagree about whether the content prior to the point at which the mistaken content is introduced is phenomenally conscious or not. They conclude that "this is a difference that makes no difference." (sec. 2.2). But it makes no difference only on the assumption that there are no real facts about phenomenal consciousness, an assumption which the target paper does not state or support.

One crude approach to telling the difference between at least some Orwellian and Stalinist pairs of hypotheses is this: In some cases, the Orwellian postulates a change in memory representation not accepted by the Stalinist. (See for example, the case of Chase and Sanborn in Dennett 1988.) In such cases, if the relevant memory system could be independently isolated and found not to change, that would support the Stalinist. I tried this out on Dennett (he mentioned that it was independently suggested by P. S. Churchland); his initial response was that we could not rely on any independent identification of the relevant memory system. If D & K want to pursue this line of thought, they owe us a reason to believe that standard scientific procedures cannot succeed in making such an independent identification. The hypothesis that the earth is flat can be insulated from data by the ad hoc postulation of special forces that make a disk look like a sphere, for example. Why should we believe that standard scientific criteria cannot possibly distinguish between Orwellian and Stalinist hypotheses?

Another line of empirical investigation would be to isolate the neurological nature of phenomenal consciousness itself as in the Crick and Koch project mentioned earlier. Again, D & K owe us a reason to think that this cannot be done.

Their eliminativism is also indicated by their claim that it makes no sense to speak of a brief flash of consciousness that vanishes without a trace. Real things are always vanishing without a trace. Quine observes that often there is no substantive difference between eliminativism and deflationism. But often there is a difference. The ideas that consciousness is just judgment, or just computation, or just sentences in the head are all deflationist but realist: there can be brief flashes of these things that vanish without a trace. D & K's "consciousness" that cannot vanish without a trace is not real.

Mellor, Churchland, and Harnad

D & K correctly point out that the temporal order of outside events needn't be represented by the temporal order of inside events. This Kantian point (Kant distinguished apprehension of succession from succession of apprehension) is certainly correct. D & K accuse P. S. Churchland, and somewhat less directly, S. Harnad and H. Mellor, of confusing order of representeds with order of representings. In my view, the quotations that they give from Churchland and Harnad show no signs of such a confusion, but rather just a commitment to the reality of phenomenal consciousness. I suggest you look at the quotations (sec. 3.1) to see for yourself.

The Mellor quotation (sec. 2.1) raises a more complex question. In addition to more ordinary phenomenal experiences, we sometimes have phenomenal experience of *relations* among some of our phenomenal experiences, relations that involve "co-consciousness" of the experiences. Choosing a nontemporal example, we may experience one pain as more intense than another pain in part by experiencing both pains. The more complex question is this: Can we be conscious of the intensity relation between two pains (including co-consciousness of the two pains) without the two pains themselves having the intensity relation? Of course, I can judge that the headache was more intense than the backache without ever being co-conscious at all of the two pains. But the issue here is not one of judgments, but of experience of relations among experiences. Mellor takes a stand on this issue for the special case of temporal relations. D & K treat this view with scorn, even linking it to "the invited conclusion that all perceptions of temporal order must be accomplished in a single place" (sec. 2.1). Their tacit rejection of phenomenal consciousness influences their interpretation of those who accept it, and so they see Cartesian materialism lurking under every bush.

Cartesian Modularism

In concentrating on Cartesian materialism, a view that D & K concede probably no one holds explicitly, they ignore a far more interesting view that is a genuine object of contention. The more interesting view is Cartesian modularism, the claim that there is a *system* for phenomenal consciousness. In talking of Cartesian materialism, D & K usually interpret "place" as *physical place*, but occasionally they talk as if they want "place" to cover *functional* place as well (sec. 1.1). They don't elaborate, but on the functional understanding of Cartesian materialism it would be Cartesian modularism, the view that all conscious events occur in a single system. Then, however, the neurophysiological evidence D & K give against there being an actual place in the brain where all phenomenally conscious events occur would have no relevance. What does spatiotemporal spread have to do with Cartesian modularism?

I explore Cartesian modularism elsewhere (Block 1995), but briefly, it is an interesting fact that the following co-occur:

1. Phenomenally conscious events.

2. Events that have access to inferentially promiscuous reasoning processes.

3. Events that guide action and speech.

This co-occurrence, along with many other considerations, suggests a model in which there is a single system or group of closely connected systems that subserve these functions. Schacter (1989) puts forward such a model; critics of phenomenal consciousness should take it seriously.[2]

Notes

1. See Shoemaker (1981) on the inverted spectrum; Block (1978) on absent qualia; Nagel (1974) and Levine (1983) on the explanatory gap. See van Gulick (forthcoming) and Flanagan (1991) for general treatments. Note that I do not share McGinn's (1991) skepticism about the scientific investigation of phenomenal consciousness (though in other respects our positions are similar). Note also that although the concept of consciousness is not identical to any functional or information-processing concept, that does not preclude an identification of the property of consciousness (as opposed to the concept) from being identified with a functional or information-processing property. The property/concept distinction cannot be clarified here. See Loar (1990).

2. I am grateful to Michael Antony, Paul Boghossian, Stevan Harnad, and Stephen White for comments on an earlier draft.

References

Armstrong, David (1968). *A Materialist Theory of Mind* Routledge: London.

Block, Ned (1978). "Troubles with Functionalism." In W. Lycan, ed., *Mind and Cognition*. Oxford: Blackwell. 1990.

Block, Ned (1991). "Evidence Against Epiphenomenalism" *Behavioral and Brain Sciences* 14, 14:670–672.

Block, Ned (1995). "On a Confusion about a Function of Consciousness." *Behavioral and Brain Sciences* 18, 2:227–247.

Crick, F. and Koch, C. (1990). "Towards a neurobiological theory of consciousness." *Seminars in the Neurosciences* 2:263–275.

Dennett, Daniel (1988). "Quining Qualia." In A. J. Marcel and E. Bisiach, *Consciousness in Contemporary Society*. Cambridge: Cambridge University Press.

Dennett, Daniel (1991). *Consciousness Explained*. Boston: Little Brown.

Flanagan, Owen (1991). "Consciousness," chapter 8 of *The Science of the Mind*, Second Edition. Cambridge: MIT Press.

Levine, Joseph (1983). "Materialism and Qualia: The Explanatory Gap." *Pacific Philosophical Quarterly* 64: 354–361.

Loar, Brian (1990). "Phenomenal States." In J. Tomberlin, ed., *Philosophical Perspectives, 4: Action Theory and Philosophy of Mind*. Atascadero, CA: Ridgeview.

McGinn, Colin (1991). *The Problem of Consciousness*. Oxford: Blackwell.

Nagel, T. (1974). "What is it Like to be a Bat?" *Philosophical Review* 83:435–450.

Potter, M. (1975). "Meaning in Visual Search," *Science* 187:965–966.

Potter, M. (1976). "Short-Term Conceptual Memory for Pictures," *Journal of Experimental Psychology: Human Learning and Memory* 2, 5:509–522.

Rosenthal, David (1986). "Two Concepts of Consciousness," *Philosophical Studies* 49, 3.

Schacter, D. (1989). "On the Relation Between Memory and Consciousness: Dissociable Interactions and Conscious Experience." In H. L. Roediger III and F. I. M. Craik, eds., *Varieties of Memory and Consciousness: Essays in Honor of Endel Tulving*. Hillsdale, NJ: Erlbaum.

Shoemaker, Sidney (1981). "The Inverted Spectrum." *The Journal of Philosophy* 74, 7.

Stich, S. (1978). "Autonomous Psychology and the Belief-Desire Thesis." *The Monist* 61, 573–591.

Van Gulick, Robert (forthcoming). "Understanding the Phenomenal Mind: Are We All Just Armadillos?" In M. Davies and G. Humphreys, ed., *Consciousness: Psychological and Philosophical Essays*. Oxford: Blackwell.

9 Time for More Alternatives

Robert Van Gulick

Dennett and Kinsbourne (D & K) argue in favor of their Multiple Drafts (MD) model of consciousness and against what they call the Cartesian Theater model by showing that the former is able to explain various facts about the subjective timing of experience that remain anomalous on the latter. They make a convincing case against the Cartesian Theater, but they are less than clear about just what the MD model entails and about exactly which aspects of it are supposed to be supported by their arguments.

There are four main sorts of problems.

1. To what extent is the Cartesian Theater a straw man whose defeat confers little credit on the MD model? That is, what other alternatives are there?

2. In particular can one accommodate the temporal data on a model that is not so antirealist or indeterministic about the stream of consciousness?

3. Are there possible sources of evidence to decide questions about the content of conscious experience beyond those that D & K consider?

4. Can the phenomena to which D & K appeal support the general conclusions they want to draw or are they special cases of only limited relevance?

Let me deal briefly with each of these in turn.

D & K intend the Cartesian Theater as a model not only of historical Cartesianism but also of the Cartesian materialism they find implicit and widespread in current thinking about the mind. The theater metaphor is that of a place where "it all comes together," a materialist version of the Cartesian bottleneck between mind and body. The notion of *place* is understood quite literally as a spatial location; the view as D & K put it is that if we knew *when*, on the inward pathway of the stimulus, experience occurred, then we could say *where* it occurred, and vice versa. Whatever the historical facts, it seems unfair to saddle current friends of consciousness with the view that it occurs at a distinct spatial location in the brain. The distinction between conscious and unconscious processing can be significant and fairly clear even if consciousness does not occur at a special place. Conscious states differ from unconscious ones in the processes they involve, not in where they occur. Consciousness may well be a more or less global brain state involving the simultaneous activation and interaction of many different brain regions and systems of representation; being spatially "smeared" in D & K's sense does not rule out a clear divide between conscious and unconscious stages of processing and awareness. Other features of the Cartesian Theater seem to unburden it unfairly also. As D & K present it, the model requires an observer who is all-seeing and all-knowing regarding the perfectly determinate projections on the screen of the inner theater. What is projected there can never be fuzzy or indeterminate, and though the observer may succumb to rapid loss of memory, he can never fail to notice anything on the screen before him at the instant of its presence. Such strong commitments make the Cartesian Theater an easy model to defeat, but again it is not clear that those who want to be more realist about consciousness than the MD model allows need to buy into such strong commitments.

Thus, turning to our second point, what might an alternative model look like? One possibility is to distinguish as conscious those representations and states of awareness that have phenomenal properties and structure; my present conscious visual awareness of the computer screen on which I am writing would be a good example. Such states need not be locally realized; indeed, the rich informational structure of phenomenal representation (e.g., when I am visually aware of the computer I am also aware of what it is and of its myriad relations to other sorts of items) would probably require the simultaneous interaction of many brain regions and representational systems. Since such states would involve global, integrative activity in many subsystems, and would have phenomenal properties, we can call this alternative the Global Integrative Phenomenal State (or GIPS) model of consciousness. Like the MD model it denies that there is any central homunculus or any special location in which consciousness takes place. But unlike the MD model, it takes seriously the distinction between phenomenal and non-phenomenal representation; not all drafts and not all representations or content fixations count as conscious (nor is the difference just a matter of whether they can be reported, a criterion that would make all the mental states of nonhuman animals nonconscious). On the GIPS model, questions about a person's state of consciousness at a given moment are questions about the content of her phenomenal representations.

Can the GIPS model handle the data about subjective timing without anomaly? I think it can. Consider the color phi. The GIPS explanation would be more or less of the sort D & K call Stalinesque. Apparent motion in phenomenal consciousness would result when the interstimulus interval was shorter than that of the integrative interactions producing the phenomenal representation (note that representation need not be a completely independent downstream product of earlier representation as opposed to being a stabilized cooperative activation of them). The resultant lag (of 200 ms or less) need not be biologically implausible, as D & K claim given

1. that it is so important to be aware of motion,

2. that the relevant integrative processes (not unlike what D & K call content-sensitive settling) will take some time, and

3. that it is possible to make automatic or reflex responses prior to and in the absence of conscious phenomenal awareness, as D & K themselves note.

The third of these facts can also explain why the lag or delay is not manifest in reaction time tests. Since the role of phenomenal awareness does not seem to be to trigger automatic responses but to provide a representation capable of planning and guiding flexible and variable responses, a delay of a few hundred milliseconds to carry out the integration generating such representations need not have any costly consequences.

The GIPS model would also favor the standard or Stalinesque explanation of meta-contrast or backward masking experiments. The mask prevents the initial brief stimulus from being integrated into phenomenal representation. D & K argue that the Orwellian and Stalinesque accounts disagree about "a difference that makes no difference." Their position is based on a quasi-verificationist claim that the two versions can equally account for all the imaginable data. But (coming now to our third point), it seems that there could be evidence relevant to settling the dispute. D & K consider first person introspective evidence and third person evidence of verbal and nonverbal behavior. But there is also the possibility of third person neurological evidence, which at least in the future might be evaluated in terms of a theory of the neural basis of phenomenal experience that could tell us whether or not the masked stimulus even briefly generated what we independently knew to be the neural correlate of phenomenal representation of the relevant stimulus. Utopian hopes? Perhaps so. But in the absence of any principled reasons to rule out such a possibility a priori, it teems premature to conclude that the dispute is devoid of content.

In their summary D & K acknowledge that some critics may accuse them of overgeneralizing from special cases (the fourth sort of problem). And they admit with their mental counting example that in typical macroscopic cases our experiences occur in the temporal order in which we experience them to occur. They nonetheless claim that the special cases are representative of the brain's normal manner of functioning. However, the reasons they cite in favor of this claim seem somewhat beside the point. They appeal to the fact that our memories of past events tend to be in the form of internally coherent simplified descriptions that frequently lose or misrepresent details of temporal sequence. This is undeniably true and it is consistent with their view of the mind as continuously trying to spin consistent and coherent scenarios, but it leaves untouched the central claim that in our *perceptual experience* of events (as opposed to our memories of such events) we experience the sequence of events by experiencing them in that sequence. The claim of Mellor's (1981) that D & K dispute is entirely about the *perceptual experience* of succession, and it seems untouched with respect to macroscopic perception. Facts about memory consolidation seem irrelevant to the issue.

Thus I don't think D & K can be said to have dislodged or dealt adequately with the view that phenomenal consciousness involves what Kant called intuitions, that is, continuous sensuous manifolds of time and space within which phenomenal objects and events are presented. Kant and a multitude of others may have been wrong in supposing that conscious experience requires such manifolds, but that remains to be shown. The GIPS model draws a clear distinction between phenomenal and non-phenomenal representation, and thus in the end it must provide some account of the structure of phenomenal space and time. The Multiple Drafts model as I understand it would give little or no weight to the phenomenal/nonphenomenal distinction and might thus avoid giving any such account. In order to avoid that burden, however, it must make its case for rejecting the distinction and I don't think that case has yet been made.

Reference

Mellor, H. (1981). *Real Time*. Cambridge: Cambridge University Press.

III THE PSYCHOLOGY AND NEUROPSYCHOLOGY OF CONSCIOUSNESS

10 Contrastive Phenomenology: A Thoroughly Empirical Approach to Consciousness

Bernard J. Baars

The study ... of the distribution *of consciousness shows it to be exactly such as we might expect in an organ added for the sake of steering a nervous system grown too complex to regulate itself ...*
—William James

For many years after James penned The Principles of Psychology ... *most cognitive scientists ignored consciousness, as did almost all neuroscientists. The problem was felt to be either purely 'philosophical' or too elusive to study experimentally ... In our opinion, such timidity is ridiculous.*
—Francis H. C. Crick and Christof Koch

Natural Contrasts Between Conscious and Unconscious Processes

Human beings are all mind-brain philosophers, whether we know it or not. More than any other discipline, philosophers are aware how much each of us is run by beliefs that are unconscious at the time they shape our thoughts and actions. Ask people about their own freedom of action, and they will claim some type of free-will mentalism. Ask them about taking a physical aspirin for a mental headache, and they will smoothly switch to dualism. Ask college students whether their minds can be understood in terms of neurons, and they will probably agree to physicalistic reductionism. Each of these positions involves a cluster of beliefs, most of which are unconscious most of the time. Becoming a philosopher or psychologist is, in many ways, a process of rethinking explicitly what we already believe implicitly.

Beliefs about free will can be either conscious or not; but even if they are currently unconscious, we can often infer from derivative statements that they are active as presuppositions. One could suggest a set of rules for making such unconscious beliefs conscious, and vice versa. For example, it is roughly true that unconscious belief sets, when they lead to severe contradictions, can be made conscious simply by repeatedly calling attention to the contradictions. Conversely, when presupposed beliefs are not challenged they will tend to fade from consciousness, though they continue silently to shape our thinking.

It is natural under these circumstances to view beliefs as either unconscious (largely inaccessible at any given time) or conscious (or readily accessible). This chapter suggests that it is the *contrast* between similar conscious and unconscious beliefs that is the key to gathering evidence relevant to consciousness.

These points may seem obvious to some. What is not obvious is that by contrasting similar conscious and unconscious mental representations in beliefs, perception, selective attention, imagery, and the like, *we can gather a set of sound empirical constraints on the distinctive properties of consciousness as such.* This is a generally applicable technique to define empirical constraints which any complete theory of conscious experience must meet. We have called this approach contrastive phenomenology (CP), and the principle is to treat consciousness as a variable, which can be studied if we hold content as constant as possible, and look at the degree of consciousness as the variable of interest. If we assume in the first few paragraphs above that free-will assumptions can be either conscious or unconscious, and if we can specify the evidence for each, we can then try to specify precisely what the differences are between the two. One major difference, it appears, is that conscious beliefs create access to new decisions, revisions of the beliefs, and the like (see Block 1995). Unconscious presupposed beliefs are not nearly as flexible and accessible.

Treating Consciousness as a Variable

In the history of science the ability to newly conceive of something as a variable often creates a breakthrough. When Newton was able to imagine space without friction and with very little gravity, contrary to Aristotelian physics, he could write that "an object in motion continues in motion." But on earth there is no such thing as frictionless low-gravity space. It required a great act of imagination to treat friction and gravity as variables with zero points. The same sort of leap of imagination made all the difference in understanding oxygen as the crucial component of the atmosphere, in the discovery of the Kelvin scale of absolute temperature, and so on.

Contrastive phenomenology aims to do just that with respect to consciousness. It is not a new idea in science. To understand consciousness we need to compare at least its presence and absence, with other factors as well-controlled as possible. Only then can we ask, "What is the difference between the two?" Only then can we deal with the issue of consciousness *as such*.

Some Informal Examples

You, the reader, are now conscious of words in your visual focus, but not of the detailed syntactic and semantic analyses which your nervous system is performing with silent expertise at this very moment. On reading the word "focus" in the last sentence you were very probably unaware of its alternative meanings—*Webster's Dictionary* cites nine definitions—even though in a different sentence context you would instantly grasp a different conscious meaning. You are not now conscious of a thought or image that came to mind just a few moments ago; of a sound or sight that could be perceived at this very instant, were it not for the fact that reading this sentence competes against it; of the feeling of your clothing, the color mix of the ambient light, that monotonous background noise, your current social status, or any other constant, highly predictable information. These currently unconscious thoughts, images, and events can often be made conscious "at will," unlike the syntactic and semantic processes mentioned above.

These examples illustrate the sense of the word "consciousness" we aim for in this paper: that is,

focal consciousness of easily described events. According to Natsoulas (1978), "it is difficult to emphasize sufficiently the fundamental importance of consciousness in this sense. It is arguably our most basic concept of consciousness, for it is implicated in all the other senses."

The cognitive framework suggests that behavioral and brain observations can be used to infer underlying explanatory constructs (Baars 1986). There have been those who argue that psychologists should not be permitted to infer theoretical constructs at all (e.g., Skinner 1974; Ryle 1949), but they are in a dwindling minority. Given our current metatheory, cognitive theories typically postulate some system that performs information processing—the internal manipulation of representations.[1] This approach has proved fruitful with dozens of topics including perception, memory, language, and mental imagery. As brain hypotheses have become more testable in recent years, we talk increasingly in terms of neural processes, but for our purposes either the neural or cognitive language will do. The question in this chapter is whether conscious and unconscious processes can be usefully treated as constructs in such a theoretical language.

Several modern brain and cognitive proposals about conscious experience have appeared so far. Some stress the close connection with limited-capacity mechanisms like selective attention and working memory (e.g., Posner and Rothbart 1991; Mandler 1975, 1984; Baddeley 1993). Others relate conscious experience to executive functions and the control of action (e.g., Shallice 1972, 1978; Norman and Shallice 1986; Hilgard 1992). A third set emphasizes the integrative capacity of awareness. For instance, Marcel (1983a) has suggested that conscious experience involves "an attempt to make sense of as much data as possible at the most functionally useful level.... [It] requires a constructive act whereby perceptual hypotheses are matched against information recovered from memory and serves to structure and synthesize information recovered from different domains." Finally, some recent theories suggest

Table 10.1
Perception as Input Representation

Conscious cases

1. Percepts: Conscious input representations

Comparable unconscious cases

1. Stimuli low in intensity or duration, and masked stimuli
2. Preperceptual input processing
3. Habituated input representation
4. Unaccessed interpretations of ambiguous input
5. Contextual constraints on the interpretation of conscious percepts
6. Expectations about specific stimuli

modern versions of the traditional "theater of the mind," in which consciousness operates as a focus of multiple expert networks in the brain, to combine and distribute information needed to coordinate a large, unconscious, distributed society of unconscious networks (e.g., Baars 1983, 1988; Damasio and Damasio 1994; Schacter 1990; McClelland 1986).

My own work has two emphases, first on evidence, second on theoretical efforts to account for the evidence. This chapter presents the first, the accumulation of evidence using the method of contrastive phenomenology.[2] The theoretical effort, called Global Workspace (GW) theory, suggests a modern theater of consciousness based on a large set of psychological and neurobiological contrasts (Baars 1983, 1988, 1993; Newman and Baars 1993; Baars 1996). Conceptually, GW theory emerged from the long series of Unified Theories of Cognition developed by Allan Newell, Herbert Simon, John Anderson, and their coworkers (e.g., Newell and Simon 1972; Newell 1992; Anderson 1983). In these models "working memory" corresponds metaphorically to the stage of a theater in a distributed collection of expert systems. GW theory applies the theater architecture to the issue of conscious experience, quite different from standard interpretations of the working memory construct, though both are part of the limited capacity system. The theory has been worked out in considerable detail over

the last decade, and can incorporate all of the current proposals (cited above) in a single integrated framework (see Baars 1988; 1996 for details).

Five sets of phenomena

CP compares two events that are similar except for the consciousness factor, so that we can hone in on just those elements that are uniquely associated with personal experience. This course follows William James's recommendation that we consider the *distribution* of consciousness in attempting to understand its workings (see epigraph). It is basically a generalization of the experimental method.

We will touch on five empirical domains where contrastive analysis can be applied, including perception, attention, mental imagery, memory and learning, and spontaneous problem-solving. In each case we will find that the conscious components stand out clearly in contrast to well-established unconscious comparison cases.

Perception as Input Representation[3]

There is little disagreement that "perception" involves conscious input representation. Even a radical behaviorist like B. F. Skinner suggested that consciousness is associated with "stimulus control" (1974). Since the advent of cognitive psychology, perception has come to be widely viewed as the process of representing the world (Neisser 1967; Rock 1983). But the converse does not necessarily hold—not all kinds of input representation are conscious (e.g., Libet 1977; Marcel 1983a, 1983b; Baars 1988).

We know of several types of unconscious input-representation. One obvious case where we experience a sensory stimulus "fading out of consciousness" involves a decrease in the intensity or duration of a stimulus below some minimum threshold. This topic has been studied thoroughly since the 1860s under the heading of the absolute psychophysical threshold, and a great deal is known about it. There is a vast literature on subliminal effects, revived by Marcel's classic 1983 experiment showing that an unconscious word, which could not be reported, would still "prime" the processing of a related word. For example, a word like "book" presented just below the threshold of conscious perception will still influence the recognition time for a related word like "paper." This would only be possible if the unconscious word activates the meaning of "book" sufficiently to affect related words like "paper," "novel," "Bible," and so on. Marcel's work created a new consensus that subthreshold words are still semantically represented (Marcel 1983; Dixon 1981; Shevrin and Dickman 1980). It is well known that conscious words easily trigger wide semantic activation of related words, so that we have a matched pair of events, one conscious and the other not, which both involve semantic activation of individual words. (There is, however, evidence that unconscious word-*pairs* cannot be integated into meaningful phrases [Greenwald 1992]. This suggests a major difference between conscious and unconscious presentation of words.)

Even an above-threshold stimulus is processed unconsciously for a fraction of a second before becoming conscious. There are many sources of evidence for such preconscious stimulus processing. For instance, studies of cortical electrical

activity in brain surgery suggest that activity in the primary sensory projection area may take hundreds of milliseconds before becoming conscious (Libet, Alberts, Wright, and Feinstein 1967; Libet 1977).

Many events in the world are locally ambiguous. Virtually all words in English have multiple meanings, as a glance at a dictionary will verify. The word "will" in the last sentence is ambiguous, but no reader is likely to realize that, because normally only a single meaning of multivalent events becomes conscious at any given time. Nevertheless, there is much evidence that unconscious meanings of ambiguous events are activated in normal processing. In seeing a visual scene, local information, such as may be acquired in a single eye fixation, can also be highly ambiguous (Gregory 1966; Rock 1983). Such local ambiguities must be resolved in a larger framework representing the visual scene or the linguistic message at a higher level (Neisser 1967; Baars 1983, 1988).

When input information is degraded, people often begin to perform conscious hypothesis-testing. A good example of this occurs in reading upside-down words, one that the reader can explore simply by turning this page upside down. You will soon notice yourself actively testing conscious hypotheses about words and letters— "Is that a *b* or a *d*?" "Is that word 'may' or 'way'?" Such hypothesis-testing may be a conscious analogue of a preconscious process that normally takes place quickly, automatically, and unconsciously. Again, we have comparable conscious and unconscious mental events, more grist for the mill of contrastive analysis.

Is a habituated stimulus, one that has faded from consciousness because we have gotten used to it, still represented in the nervous system? Our feeling of the chair once we have been sitting for a while, the ambient light and noise level, one's orientation to gravity, and indeed all the multifarious sources of predictable stimulation tend to be unconscious. Nevertheless, it is generally believed that the nervous system continues to represent habituated stimuli even after they have faded from consciousness. Sokolov (1963) developed a persuasive set of arguments for this position, based upon the occurrence of an Orienting Response (OR) whenever people or animals are confronted with a novel stimulus; it is the "surprise response." (The OR consists of a large set of central and peripheral physiological events which the nervous system uses to prepare the body for rapid action. In humans, we can be pretty sure that a surprising event that triggers an OR is conscious.)

Suppose you hear the sound of a refrigerator pump—a series of noise bursts of a certain duration, spectral distribution, onset and offset envelope, location in space, cycle time, and so on. If the sound is not painfully loud, people will lose awareness of it rather quickly, but they will tend to become conscious of the noise again as soon as any parameter of the sound changes: The noise can become louder or softer, the time between the noise bursts can change, the intensity envelope can change, or the noise bursts can just stop. Any of these changes will trigger a new OR, just as we may become aware of the noisy refrigerator as soon as the noise stops. To explain this pattern, Sokolov argues, we can only assume that there is a "model of the stimulus" against which the unconscious stimulus is matched; as long as the match fits reasonably well, one does not become conscious of the noise; only when there is a *mismatch in any parameter* of the sound do we produce another OR. This suggests that predictable sources of stimulation continue to be represented in the nervous system, even after they fade from consciousness.

While Sokolov's arguments have been widely accepted, some critics object that specific neural nets might produce the same results, thereby avoiding the notion that the nervous system "represents" the stimulus. From a cognitive perspective, this implies a misunderstanding of the argument. The claim that the nervous system continues to represent all stimulus parameters after habituation does not imply that there is no specific neural substrate able to trigger another OR; rather, these are two different levels of theory, which it is useful to keep separate. One does not need to believe in "strong functionalism" (e.g., Dennett 1991) to take the position that we can usefully specify a psychological level of analysis, even without knowing the precise neural basis. In this "weakly functional" sense, *everybody*, including neurobiologists interested in mental processes, begins by postulating some reasonable level of psychological analysis that can be rigorously defined without a complete neural reduction (e.g., Crick 1994; Edelman 1989).

It seems safe to conclude that habituated stimulus processing is representational, though unconscious. This contrast provides one more empirical boundary that any adequate theory of conscious perception must explain.

Contextual Constraints on Perception

Perceptual experiences are constrained by numerous factors that are not conscious. Perhaps the most famous demonstration of such unconscious constraints was devised by Adelbert Ames (1953) who noted that the rectangular walls, floor, and ceiling of a normal "carpentered" room actually project trapezoids, not rectangles, onto the retina. Any single retinal projection can be interpreted as the result of an infinite set of trapezoids placed at different angles to the eye. But in Western culture we are exposed almost exclusively to rectangular walls, floors, and ceilings, and we interpret any consistent set of joined trapezoids to be box-shaped with rectangular sides. Hence the "Ames distorted room," which actually consists of joined trapezoidal surfaces, but is perceived as an ordinary rectangular room. And because we assess height in a carpentered environment by implicit comparison with the presumed constant height of the walls, people in an Ames room will appear to grow and shrink dramatically as they walk from one end of the trapezoidal wall to the other. In this way our

Table 10.2
Imagery and Inner Speech as Input Simulation

Conscious cases

1. Retrieved images and inner speech
2. Currently rehearsed item in working memory
3. Sensory memory (iconic and echoic)

Comparable unconscious cases

1. Unrecalled memories of images and inner speech
2. Currently unrehearsed items in working memory
3. Long-term memory representations needed to process sensory memory

conscious experience of size is dramatically shaped by unconscious "presuppositions" about the space in which we live. Numerous other examples can be cited (Rock 1983). Contextual constraints on perception and comprehension are the rule, not the exception (Baars 1988, chapters 4 and 5).

Stimulus Expectations

Expectations about the world are clearly representations of some sort. Syntax and semantics create such strong expectations that we can often spontaneously fill in a missing _____ in a sentence. Or, as T. S. Eliot noted, we can walk down a dark staircase and expect another step when there is none, and be shocked at the result. The ability to detect matches and mismatches with respect to one's expectations is itself an argument for the representational nature of expectations. We can immediately detect a violation of an expectation, in any dimension of an expected stimulus or predictable action. We can therefore apply the Sokolov argument (above) here as well—if the nervous system can detect a *change* in *any* dimension of an event, it must have a representation of all the mismatchable parameters.[4] Unlike percepts and images, expectations have no qualia—no figure-ground properties, color, texture, no discrete beginning or end, nor any other perceptual qualities.

Stimulus expectations behave in other ways like percepts and images: they are representa-
tional, they correspond to some part of the world, they help to resolve ambiguities, are internally consistent—yet they are not *objects* of conscious experience. This point is rarely made, but it seems well-grounded and theoretically significant.

Imagery and Inner Speech

Consider a second example of contrastive analysis: the comparison of conscious images with comparable unconscious representations. "Images" are broadly defined to mean *internally generated* quasi-perceptual events that occur in the absence of external input. They can occur in any sensory modality, although humans have a penchant for visual imagery, inner speech, and emotional feelings. Images can be viewed as "simulated percepts." Visual images resemble visual percepts in a number of respects (Finke 1980), and many of the same assessment tasks can be used for both perception and imagery—people can indicate with their hands the size of the imagined "visual field," for example, drawing a space with the size and shape of the true visual field.

Conscious Aspects of Imagery and Inner Speech

We are conscious of more than external events. We can re-experience this morning's breakfast, autobiographical events in the past, and our own inner speech. People sometimes have hallucina-

Table 10.3
Attention as Input Selection

Conscious cases

1. Attended streams of stimulation
2. Previously unattended events interrupting the attended stream
3. Conscious events involved in directing attention voluntarily
4. Attention drawn to new or changed stimuli

Comparable unconscious cases

1. Wholly unattended streams of events
2. Unattended input affecting the interpretation of attended input
3. Events controlling involuntary attention
4. Predictable repetitions of stimuli (see table 10.1)

---

tions, and we all have dreams. Over the past few decades a large and reliable research literature has emerged in visual imagery, so that now a great deal is known about it (Paivio 1971; Cooper and Shepard 1973; Kosslyn and Schwartz 1981). Imagery in other sense modalities, inner speech, and feelings associated with emotion have seen much less research, but it is hard to see any principled reason why one could not investigate these domains with the same kind of solid results.

Comparable Unconscious Aspects of Imagery and Inner Speech

Where is our image of this morning's breakfast before we bring it back to mind? If it is accurate, it must in some sense still be represented in long-term memory. And because we generally produce such an image in the same sensory modality in which it was originally experienced, in most cases we can be reasonably sure that the image, though unconscious, still has visual features. This suggests that there are very good unconscious analogues to conscious visual images, permitting us to use the two phenomena for a contrastive analysis.

A particularly interesting case of "unconscious visual images" exists in highly practiced imagery. Cooper and Shepard (1973) already noted that subjects who are skilled in their classic mental

rotation task often report losing awareness of their own processes. Nevertheless, the unconscious "image" continues to rotate at the same rate, as shown by a very reliable linear function between the degrees of imagined rotation and reaction time, matching to sample, and the like. Similarly, Pani (1982) has shown that mental images needed to match a visual shape become less consciously available with practice, but can reemerge when the task is made more difficult.

Any adequate theory of conscious experience should be able to explain why visual images are sometimes conscious, while comparable "visual" representations are not conscious, whether that is due to forgetting, habituation, or automaticity in the task.

Attention as Input Selection

"Everybody knows what attention is," wrote William James in a famous passage. "It is the taking possession by the mind, in clear and vivid form, of one out of what seem several simultaneously possible objects or trains of thought. Focalization, concentration of consciousness are of its essence." As often as this passage is cited in cognitive books and papers, we rarely see an effort to really deal with its implications for consciousness. Attention and consciousness are not the same, if James is to be taken seriously. It seems that attention involves systems that create *access* to consciousness (Posner 1994; Baars 1988). Since the 1950s attention has been treated as a selective function, which is fine as far as it goes, but consciousness, the end product of selective attention, has been ignored until quite recently (Broadbent 1958; Norman 1976; Neisser 1976). Thus in three decades of cognitive studies of selective attention, we have managed to evade James's central point, which is that *paying attention to some event results in its becoming focally conscious* (see Baars 1988, 1996).

Attended versus Unattended Messages

In the prototype experiments by Broadbent (1958) and others, a subject wearing earphones is listening to two different stories, one in each ear. Material in the "attended" ear is conscious, and if the subject tracks the conscious flow of information adequately, the "unattended" ear is unconscious, except perhaps for some awareness of an incomprehensible voice in the unattended channel. If we can show that both ears are processing language to some level of representation, we can compare the conscious and unconscious flow of processing as a contrastive analysis.

There is considerable evidence that the unconscious channel is processed to quite a high level, at least including semantics. A loud noise in the unattended channel can interrupt consciousness of the attended stream. Further, biologically or personally significant stimuli in the unattended ear (such as one's own name) can interrupt the conscious stream, even when they are not particularly loud. This strongly suggests that words such as one's own name are processed to quite a high level—at least the lexicon—even unconsciously. How else could the brain "know" whether to interrupt the ongoing flow of conscious information? Unconscious information can also influence the interpretation of attended words, even without interrupting the attended flow. MacKay (1973) reported that the interpretation of an am-

biguous word in the conscious stream can be changed when a disambiguating word is presented unconsciously at the same moment in time. For example, the word "bank" in the sentence "They were walking near the bank" can be interpreted either as the edge of a river or as a financial institution. If simultaneously with "bank" one presents the word "money" or "water" in the unconscious stream, the conscious interpretation of "bank" will shift toward the unconscious word. Both the interruption and the disambiguation experiment suggest that linguistic information in the unconscious stream must be processed to quite a high level, at least to the point of semantic representation.

Once we know that attended and unattended streams both process linguistic information, we can proceed to analyze the contrasts. One interesting finding is that learning does not seem to occur in the unattended channel, although individual words can apparently be analyzed. For example, one can repeat the same word 35 times in the unconscious channel, without any improvement in recall (Norman 1976). This result is generally consistent with other findings, such as the fact that subliminal presentation of single words, which is known to influence subsequent conscious processes, fails when more than one word is presented (Greenwald 1992). This makes a great deal of sense if we view consciousness as our major integrative capacity. Unconscious processing then may allow identification of highly predictable and overlearned events, such as single words, but not of new and unpredictable combinations of words.

Voluntary versus Involuntary Control of Attention

We can ask someone to switch to the unconscious channel voluntarily. Our request to listen to the other channel obviously creates a conscious event for the subject, which is translated into a voluntary action. The contrastive case is getting someone's attention without volition by presenting a loud noise, the name of the subject, and a variety

Table 10.4
Learning and Memory Contrasts

Conscious cases

1. Novel actions (learning to ride a bicycle)
1'. De-automatized actions (e.g., actions when the bicycle breaks down)
2. Stimuli presented in an implicit learning paradigm
3. Recalled autobiographical and lexical memories
4. Sensory memories (iconic and echoic)
5. Currently rehearsed items in working memory

Comparable unconscious cases

1. Automatic actions (skilled and predictable bicycling)
2. Abstract rules in implicit learning
3. Autobiographical and lexical memories before recall, skill memory, implicit memory
4. Long-term information required to interpret sensory memories
5. Currently nonrehearsed items in working memory

of other significant stimuli. These attention-getting stimuli will interrupt the conscious stream of information without the subject's intention or foreknowledge. In sum, conscious events seem to precede voluntary control of attention, while involuntary switches of attention require no such conscious processing.

Learning and Memory Contrasts

Developing Automaticity with Practice

It is commonly observed that when we begin learning a difficult skill, we may be conscious of many details; after skill acquisition we are conscious of much less; and if the skill is disrupted in some way, we become conscious of some missing ingredient. Indeed, Langer and Imber (1979) have shown that subjects learning a simple coding task cannot retrieve the number of steps in the task once it has become automatic, although this is quite easy before automatization of the task. This suggests that conscious involvement may help to integrate new information, but that it is not required for the smooth, routine execution of complex tasks. When automatic execution of a skilled

task is disrupted, as in reading upside-down words, the opposite occurs: we tend to become more conscious of the details of the task (Baars 1988).

Implicit Learning of Miniature Grammars

Subjects who are given a set of stimuli (such as playing cards or strings of words) generated by a simple "grammar," unconsciously infer the underlying grammar, as shown by successful recognition of novel cases generated by the same set of rules (Franks and Bransford 1971; Reber 1993). Because humans routinely learn rule-systems without being able to state the rules, this finding has implications for a great deal of everyday learning. It is one among many indications that consciousness helps to focus many unconscious resources upon significant events (Baars 1983, 1988). This kind of learning does not require an intention to learn; it takes place as long as people are paying attention to the set of stimuli provided.

Immediate Memory: Sensory Memories

Immediately after a bright visual stimulus we can experience a rapidly fading image of stimulus.

Table 10.5
Spontaneous Problem-solving

Conscious cases

Stage of problem definition (first stage)

Aha! experience (final stage)

Comparable unconscious cases

Incubation (intermediate stage)

Implicit constraints on the problem outcome

Automatic components of problem-solving

Memory for task instructions is available but not conscious during the process

(The three stages may repeat many times for any given problem.)

Such fast sensory memories are generally interpreted as a momentary representation which can be further processed by other parts of the cognitive apparatus. In a classic experiment, Sperling (1960) showed that immediately after seeing a 4×3 matrix of visual symbols we can access many more symbols than we can report. Neisser (1967) and Atkinson and Shiffrin (1968) suggest that information from the sensory information stores is transferred to short-term memory, and may in turn be encoded into long-term memory.

Immediate Memory: Working Memory

In a typical working memory (WM) experiment, subjects are given a series of unrelated words, letters, or numbers, and asked to recall them shortly afterward. If the items are mentally rehearsed, WM content will top out quite predictable at 7 ± 2 items of any kind. A great deal is known of the resulting memory patterns, but little attention has been given to the fact that during the retention interval, *only the currently rehearsed item is conscious at any single moment*. Thus WM is closely associated with conscious experience, though not identical to it (Baddeley 1993).

Note that what constitutes an "item" in WM depends completely on long-term memory information. Consider the following sixteen numbers: 4, 9, 9, 1, 0, 0, 9, 1, 6, 7, 7, 1, 6, 6, 0, 1. Being more than 7 ± 2 numbers, it exceeds the capacity of

WM. But reading the sequence backward helps dramatically, because the backward series only contains four well-known "chunks": 1066, 1776, 1900, and 1994. Suddenly the number series is well within WM limits. But our knowledge about the famous years 1066, etc., resides in long-term memory. We probably learned those years a long time ago. Of course the knowledge that resides in long-term memory, and which shapes our ability to chunk the WM sequence, is unconscious before it is brought to bear on the problem. Again, there is a natural contrast between our unconscious knowledge about certain years when it resides in long-term memory, and when it is retrieved (conscious), so that we can chunk the information in WM.

Spontaneous Problem-Solving

Most thinking is inexplicit. Entirely conscious problem-solving, such as working out a mental arithmetic problem in full detail, is extraordinarily rare. Rather, we tend to solve problems "spontaneously": to be conscious of the problem for some time, unconscious of it at some intermediate stage, and conscious again of the solution of the problem.

These are the famous phenomena of problem incubation and the Aha! experience (Köhler 1929). It is the pattern that is generally reported in creative mathematical work, in he experience of "having" a poem, in scientific problem-solving, and the like. In these cases one is conscious of the stage of problem-definition, but not of the incubation stage, in which the problem is presumably moving toward solution. Finally the problem "comes to mind" again, and the solution is clear. In complex problems we need to be conscious as well of intermediate steps on the road to a solution.

This pattern again invites a contrastive analysis, since the events that are conscious continue to shape problem-solving after it has become unconscious. However, the pattern extends far beyond the classic accounts of creative problem-solving in mathematics, science, or literature. It is typical of many more common mental processes, as follows.

Word-Retrieval and Question-Answering

We may be conscious of an incomplete sentence, unconscious of the process of retrieving the missing word, and conscious again of the right word when it comes to mind. Similarly, if someone asks a question, we are conscious of the question, usually not of searching for an answer, and conscious again of the answer. While the time periods involved in these common tasks are much shorter than in truly creative problem-solving, the conscious-unconscious-conscious pattern seems the same.

Recall from Long-Term Memory

The same may be said of recall processes. We can retrieve the image of a flag, but the process whereby we do so is utterly opaque. Free association and other memory tasks have the same character.

Perceptual Reorganization

We can see two interpretations of an ambiguous cube, but we rarely have insight into the process that brings us from one to the other. We may be solving a visual puzzle or trying to understand a sentence spoken in a heavy dialect; in either case, we are conscious of some early information, often seeming complex and difficult to organize, but this early organization is succeeded by a second, simpler experience without any awareness of the intermediate processes.

Thus the conscious-unconscious-conscious pattern of problem-solving is very general indeed. It can be found in symbolic computation such as mental arithmetic; in minor everyday problem-solving, like question-answering; in recall, action planning, and execution; and in perceptual reorganization.

One intriguing possibility is that James's "stream of consciousness," which appears as a series of rather arbitrary "flights and perches" of the mind on different topics, actually consists of an interwoven series of such conscious-unconscious-conscious triads. It may be that we are continuously acting to solve many overlapping problems, in which unconscious mechanisms attempt to resolve issues posed consciously, returning their answers to consciousness again; the conscious answers may, in turn, provide the input for another unconscious problem-solving session. Such spontaneous intertwining of problem-related thoughts is often observed with "thinking out loud" procedures (Singer and Kolligian 1987). It suggests that problem-solving may be going on without our "metacognitive" awareness that our thoughts are in fact purposeful.

Summary and Conclusions

What can we conclude overall? First, that criterial facts about consciousness can be specified without either evading the issue, or requiring that we first solve the mind-body problem. Second, that a great deal of reliable empirical information on conscious experience is already at hand, based on decades of research under other labels. Further, that the pattern of phenomena is sufficiently complex and non-obvious to make it extremely unlikely that it is merely dictated by social convention (e.g., Wilkes 1988). And finally, that even the atheoretical approach we have taken in this chapter yields some generalizations about conscious experience, thereby placing strong constraints on any reasonable theory.

Notes

An earlier version of this chapter appeared in Baars (1986, 1994). The current version has undergone significant revisions and additions to reflect more recent findings and theory. It is further elaborated in Baars, (1996).

1. Some connectionists argue that the notion of mental representation should be replaced by a state of adaptation. However, any representation already exists in an adaptive medium, such as neural tissue or computer chips. A usable adaptive medium maintains a flexible but robust isomorphism between a representation and the represented event. Thus the notion of representation already requires adaptiveness. Adaptation and representation are two views of the same elephant.

2. Contrastive phenomenology has also been applied fruitfully to the comparison of conscious and unconscious functional capabilities, to the issue of volition and "self."

3. The same analysis can be applied to abstract concepts. Conscious concepts are not the same as images, but often have prototypical images associated with them. This issue is discussed in considerable detail in Baars (1988).

4. In a curious sense, the Sokolov model of the stimulus *is* an expectation, though, unlike other expectations, it represents the unconscious, habituated stimulus rather than a conscious input.

References

Ames, A. Jr. (1953). "Reconsideration of the Origin and Nature of Perception." In S. Ratner (Ed.), *Vision and Action*. New Brunswick, NJ: Rutgers University Press.

Anderson, J. R. (1983). *The Architecture of Cognition*. Cambridge, MA: Harvard University Press.

Atkinson, R. C. and Shiffrin, R. M. (1968). "Human memory: A Proposed System and Its Control Processes." In K. W. Spence and J. T. Spence (Eds.), *Advances in the Psychology of Learning and Motivation: Research and Theory*, Vol. 2. New York: Academic Press.

Baars, B. J. (1983). "Conscious Contents Provide the Nervous System with Coherent, Global Information." In R. Davidson, G. Schwartz, and D. Shapiro (Eds.), *Consciousness and Self-Regulation*, Vol. 3, pp. 45–76. New York: Plenum Press.

Baars, B. J. (1985). "What is a Theory of Consciousness a Theory Of? The Search for Criterial Constraints on Theory." *Imagination, Cognition and Personality*, 6(10), 3–23.

Baars, B. J. (1986). *The Cognitive Revolution in Psychology*. New York: Guilford.

Baars, B. J. (1988). *A Cognitive Theory of Consciousness*. London: Cambridge University Press.

Baars, B. J., (Ed.) (1992). *Experimental Slips and Human Error: Exploring the Architecture of Volition*, pp. 289–316. New York: Plenum Press.

Baars, B. J. (1993). "Why Volition Is a Foundation Issue for Psychology." *Consciousness and Cognition, 2*, 281–309.

Baars, B. J., (1996). *In the Theater of Consciousness: the Workspace of the Mind*. New York: Oxford University Press.

Baars, B. J., Cohen, J., Bower, G. H., and Berry, J. W. (1992). "Some Caveats on Testing the Freudian Slip Hypothesis: Problems in Systematic Replication." In Baars, B. J. (Ed.) (1992).

Baddeley, A. D. (1976). *The Psychology of Memory*. New York: Basic Books.

Baddeley, A. (1993). "Working Memory and Conscious Awareness." In A. F. Collins and M. A. Conway (Eds.), *Theories of Memory*. Hove, UK: Erlbaum.

Block, N. (1995). "On a Confusion About a Function of Consciousness." *Behavioral and Brain Sciences*, 18:2, June, 227–288.

Broadbent, D. E. (1958). *Perception and Communication*. New York: Pergamon.

Cooper, L. A., and Shepard, R. N. (1973). Chronometric Studies of the Rotation of Mental Images." In W. G. Chase (Ed.), *Visual Information Processing*. New York: Academic Press.

Crick, F. C. H. (1994). *The Astonishing Hypothesis: The Scientific Search for the Soul*. New York: Scribner.

Crick, F. C. H., and Koch, C. (1992). "The Problem of Consciousness." *Scientific American, 267*(3), 152–160.

Damasio, A. R., and Damasio, H. "Cortical Systems for Concrete Knowledge: The Convergence Zone Framework." In Christof Koch and Joel L. Davis, Eds., *Large-Scale Neuronal Theories of the Brain.* Cambridge, MA: MIT Press.

Dennett, D. (1991). *Consciousness Explained.* Boston: Little, Brown.

Dixon, N. F. (1981). *Preconscious Processes.* New York: Wiley.

Edelman, G. (1989). *The Remembered Present: A Biological Theory of Consciousness.* New York: Basic Books.

Erdelyi, M. (1974). "A New Look at the New Look: Perceptual Defense and Vigilance." *Psychological Review, 81,* 1–25.

Ericsson, K. A., and Simon, H. A. (1984/1993) *Protocol Analysis: Verbal Reports as Data.* Cambridge, MA: MIT Press.

Finke, R. (1980). "Levels of Equivalence in Imagery and Perception." *Psychological Review, 87*(2), 113–132.

Franks, J. J., and Bransford, J. D. (1971). "Abstraction of Visual Images." *Journal of Experimental Psychology, 90*(1), 65–74.

Greenwald, A. (1992). "New Look 3, Unconscious Cognition Reclaimed." *American Psychologist, 47*(6), 766–779.

Gregory, R. L. (1966). *Eye and Brain: The Psychology of Seeing.* New York: Harper and Row.

Herbart, J. F. (1824/1961). "Psychology as a Science, Newly Founded on Experience, Metaphysics, and Mathematics." Reprinted in T. Shipley (Ed.), *Classics in Psychology,* pp. 22–50. New York: Philosophical Library.

Hilgard, E. R. (1992). "Divided Consciousness and Dissociation." *Consciousness and Cognition, 1*(1), 16–32.

Hochberg, J. (1964). *Perception.* Englewood Cliffs, NJ: Prentice-Hall.

Hull, C. L. (1937). "Mind, Mechanism, and Adaptive Behavior. *Psychological Review, 44,* 1–32.

James, W. (1890/1984). *The Principles of Psychology.* New York: Holt. Reprinted by Harvard University Press.

Köhler, W. (1929). *Gestalt Psychology.* New York: Liveright.

Kosslyn, S. M., and Schwartz, S. P. (1981). "Empirical Constraints on Theories of Visual Mental Imagery." In J. Long and A. D. Baddeley (Eds.), *Attention and Performance,* Vol. 9, pp. 214–260. Hillsdale, NJ: Erlbaum.

Langer, E. J., and Imber, L. G. (1979). "When Practice makes Imperfect: Debilitating Effects of Overlearning." *Journal of Personality and Social Psychology, 37*(11), 2014–2024.

Libet, B. (1978). "Neuronal vs. Subjective Timing for a Conscious Sensory Experience. In P. A. Buser and A. Rougeul-Buser (Eds.), *Cerebral Correlates of Conscious Experiences: INSERM Symposium No. 6,* pp. 69–82. Amsterdam: Elsevier.

Libet, B., Alberts, W. W., Wright, E. W., and Feinstein, B. (1967). "Responses of Human Somatosensory Cortex to Stimuli Below Threshold for Conscious Sensation. *Science, 158,* 1597–1600.

Logothetis, N. D., and Schall, J. D. (1989). "Neuronal Correlates of Subjective Visual Perception." *Science, 245,* 761–763.

MacKay, D. G. (1966). "To End Ambiguous Sentences." *Perception and Psychophysics, 1,* 426–436.

MacKay, D. G. (1973). "Aspects of a Theory of Comprehension, Memory and Attention." *Quarterly Journal of Experimental Psychology: General, 110,* 341–462.

MacKay, D. G. (1992). "Errors, Ambiguity, and Awareness in Language Perception and Production." In B. J. Baars (Ed.), *Experimental Slips and Human Error: Exploring the Architecture of Volition,* pp. 39–67. New York: Plenum Press.

Mandler, G. A. (1975). "Consciousness: Respectable, Useful, and Probably Necessary." In R. Solso (Ed.), *Information Processing and Cognition: The Loyola Symposium.* Hillsdale, NJ: Erlbaum.

Mandler, G. (1984). *Mind and Body: Psychology of Emotion and Stress.* New York: Norton.

Mangan, B. (1993). "Taking Phenomenology Seriously: The 'Fringe' and Its Implications for Cognitive Research." *Consciousness and Cognition, 2*(2), 89–108.

Marcel, A. J. (1983a). "Conscious and Unconscious Perception: Experiments on Visual Masking and Word Recognition." *Cognitive Psychology, 15,* 197–237.

Marcel, A. J. (1983b). "Conscious and Unconscious Perception: An Approach to Relations Between Phenomenal Experience and Perceptual Processes." *Cognitive Psychology, 15,* 238–300.

McClelland, J. L. (1986). "The Programmable Blackboard Model of Reading. In D. E. Rumelhart, J. L. McClelland, and PDP-Research-Group (Eds.), *Parallel Distributed Processing: Explorations in the Microstructure of Cognition*, pp. 122–169. Cambridge, MA: MIT Press.

Miller, G. A. (1962). *Psychology: The Science of Mental Life*. New York: Harper and Row.

Nagel, T. (1980). "What Is It Like to Be a Bat? In N. Block (Ed.), *Readings in the Philosophy of Science*, *1*, pp. 159–170. Cambridge, MA: Harvard University Press.

Natsoulas, T. (1982). "Conscious Perception and the Paradox of 'Blindsight'. In G. Underwood, *Aspects of Consciousness*, *3*, pp. 79–110. Hillsdale, NJ: Erlbaum.

Neisser, U. (1967). *Cognitive Psychology*. New York: Appleton-Century-Crofts.

Neisser, U. (1976). *Cognition and Reality*. San Francisco: W. H. Freeman.

Newell, A. (1990). *Unified Theories of Cognition*. Cambridge, MA: Harvard University Press.

Newell, A. (1992). "SOAR as a Unified Theory of Cognition: Issues and Explanations." *Behavioral and Brain Sciences*, *15*(3), 464–492.

Newell, A., and Simon, H. A. (1972). *Human Problem-Solving*. Englewood Cliffs, NJ: Prentice-Hall.

Newman, J., and Baars, B. J. (1993). "A Neural Attentional Model for Access to Consciousness: A Global Workspace Perspective." *Concepts in Neuroscience*, *4*(2), 255–290.

Nisbett, R. E., and Wilson, T. D. (1977). Telling More Than We Can Know: Verbal Reports on Mental Processes." *Psychological Review*, *84*, 231–259.

Norman, D. A. (1976). *Memory and Attention*. New York: Wiley.

Norman, D. A., and Shallice, T. (1986). "Attention and Action: Willed and Automatic Control of Behavior." In R. Davidson, G. E. Schwartz, and D. Shapiro (Eds.), *Consciousness and Self-Regulation*, Vol. 4. New York: Plenum.

Paivio, A. (1971). *Imagery and Verbal Processes*. New York: Holt, Rinehart.

Pani, J. R. (1982). "A functionalist Approach to Mental Imagery." Presented at the 23rd Annual Psychonomic Society Meeting, Chicago, IL. November 10–12, 1982.

Posner M. I. (1994). "Attention: The Mechanisms of Consciousness." *Proceedings of the National Academy of Sciences of the United States of America*, *91*(16): 7398–7403.

Posner, M. I., and Rothbart, M. K. (1991). "Attentional Mechanisms and Conscious Experience." In A. D. Milner and M. D. Rugg (Eds.), *The Neuropsychology of Consciousness*, pp. 91–112. New York: Academic Press.

Reber, A. S., Kassin, S. M., Lewis, S., and Cantor, G. (1980). "On the Relationship Between Implicit and Explicit Modes in the Learning of a Complex Rule Structure." *Journal of Experimental Psychology: Human Learning and Memory*, *6*(5), 492–502.

Rock, I. (1983). *The Logic of Perception*. Cambridge, MA: MIT Press.

Ryle, G. (1949). *The Concept of Mind*. London: Hutchinson.

Schacter, D. L. (1990). "Toward a Cognitive Neuropsychology of Awareness: Implicit Knowledge and Anosognosia." *Journal of Clinical and Experimental Neuropsychology*, *12*(1), 155–178.

Shallice, T. (1972). "Dual Functions of Consciousness." *Psychological Review*, *79*(5), 383–393.

Shallice, T. (1978). "The Dominant Action System: An Information-processing Approach to Consciousness." In K. S. Pope and J. L. Singer (Eds.), *The Stream of Consciousness: Scientific Investigations into the Flow of Experience*. New York: Plenum.

Shevrin, H., and Dickman, S. (1980). "The Psychological Unconscious: A Necessary Assumption for All Psychological Theory." *American Psychologist*, *35*(5), 421–434.

Singer, J. L., and Kolligian, J. (1987). "Personality: Developments in the Study of Private Experience." *Annual Review of Psychology* 38:533–574.

Skinner, B. F. (1974). *About Behaviorism*. New York: Knopf.

Snodgrass, M., Shevrin, H., and Kopka, M. (1994). "The Mediation of Intentional Judgments by Unconscious Perception." *Consciousness and Cognition*, *2*(3), 169–193.

Sokolov, E. N. (1963). *Perception and the Orienting Reflex*. New York: Macmillan.

Sperling, G. (1960). "The Information Available in Brief Conscious Presentations." *Psychological Monographs*, *74*, No. 11.

Swinney, D. (1979). "Lexical Access During Sentence Comprehension. (Re)consideration of context effects." *Journal of Verbal Learning and Verbal Behavior, 18*, 645–660.

Weiskrantz, L. (1988). *Blindsight. A Case Study and Its Implications*. Oxford, UK: Oxford University Press.

Wilkes, K. V. (1988). ———, yishi, duh, um, and consciousness. In A. J. Marcel and E. Bisiach (Eds.), *Consciousness in Contemporary Science*. Oxford: Clarendon Press.

11 Visual Perception and Visual Awareness after Brain Damage: A Tutorial Overview

Martha J. Farah

1 Introduction and Goals

Perception and awareness of perception are normally inextricably related. Most people would say that one has not perceived something if one is not consciously aware of that thing. Yet recent findings in neuropsychology are forcing us to revise this notion of the relation between perception and conscious awareness. Brain-damaged people may manifest considerable knowledge of stimuli, or of particular properties of stimuli, of which they deny any conscious perceptual experience. Although these findings challenge the intuitive idea that part and parcel of perceiving something is being aware of it, they also offer an empirical means of understanding the relations between the neural systems underlying perception and conscious awareness.

Four neuropsychological syndromes involving apparent dissociations between vision and awareness of vision have been documented in some detail: blindsight, covert recognition of faces in prosopagnosia, unconscious perception of extinguished or neglected stimuli, and implicit reading in pure alexia. Although any one of these syndromes could, on its own, be the topic of a whole chapter or even a whole book, I will consider each one in much less detail here. Rather than provide exhaustive reviews, my goals for this tutorial are to review representative findings about each syndrome, to lay out the different possible mechanistic explanations of each of the dissociations in patient performance, to consider the implications of each of the mechanistic accounts for the relation between conscious awareness and neural information processing, to weigh the different accounts against the available evidence, to examine the relations among the different syndromes, and to consider the broader implications of these findings for the functional and neural systems underlying conscious awareness.

2 Brain Mechanisms and Conscious Awareness: What Kind of Relation?

Before proceeding towards these goals, I will offer a general framework for discussing the different ways in which conscious awareness has been related to brain states in neuropsychology. I will distinguish between three broad types of accounts.

Consciousness as the Privileged Role of Particular Brain Systems

The most straightforward account of the relation between consciousness and the brain is to conceive of particular brain systems as mediating conscious awareness. The great-grandfather of this type of account is Descartes's theory of mind-body interaction through the pineal gland. Patterns of brain activity impinging on the pineal gland, unlike patterns of activity in other parts of the brain, were consciously experienced. The most direct and influential descendant of this tradition is the DICE (dissociated interactions and conscious experience) model of Schacter, McAndrews, and Moscovitch (1988) (fig. 11.1). Although they do not propose a localization for the conscious awareness system (CAS), their account does suppose that there is some brain system or systems, the CAS, separate from the brain systems concerned with perception, cognition, and action, whose activity is necessary only for conscious experience. Within this framework, unconscious perception can be explained very simply in terms of a disconnection between perceptual systems and the CAS.

The brain systems that play a privileged role in mediating conscious awareness could also carry out other functions as well. For example, Gazzaniga (1988) attributes many of the differences between what one would call conscious and unconscious behavior to the involvement of left

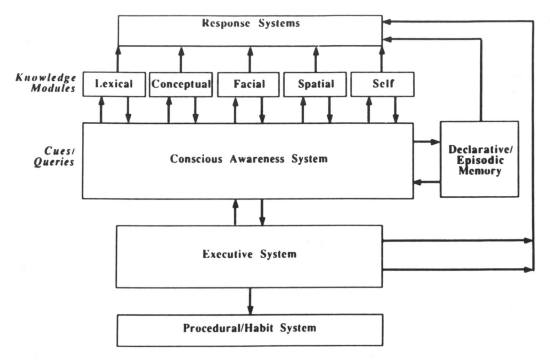

Figure 11.1
The DICE (dissociated interactions and conscious experience) model of Schacter, McAndrews, and Moscovitch (1992).

hemisphere interpretive mechanisms, closely related to speech. Thus, unconscious perception could be explained as the failure of a perceptual representation to access critical areas of the left hemisphere. For brevity, this first class of accounts will be referred to as *privileged role* accounts, because only certain systems play a role in mediating conscious awareness.

Consciousness as a State of Integration among Distinct Brain Systems

In contrast, the next two types of approach attempt to explain the relations between conscious and unconscious information processing in terms of the dynamic states of brain systems rather than in terms of the enduring roles of particular brain systems themselves. Kinsbourne's (1988) inte-

grated field theory will be taken as the index case of the approach that emphasizes integration as the underlying basis of conscious awareness. According to Kinsbourne, conscious awareness is a brain state in which the various modality-specific perceptions, recollections, current actions, and action plans are mutually consistent. Normally, the interactions among these disparate brain systems automatically bring the ensemble into an integrated state, continually updated to reflect the current information available in all parts of the brain. However, anatomical disconnection can prevent integration, as in split-brain patients who may have two separate awarenesses, or damage to one system may weaken its influence on the global brain state, thus preventing it from updating the contents of awareness, as in neglect patients who remain unaware of stimuli in their neglected hemifield. Thus, unconscious perception could be explained by either disconnection of or damage to the perceptual system, preventing it from participating in the integrated patterns of activity over the rest of the brain.

Related accounts have been proposed by Crick and Koch (1990) and by Damasio (1990). Crick and Koch limit themselves to the issue of visual awareness and equate this phenomenon with the binding together of the different, separately represented visual properties of a stimulus (e.g., color, shape, depth, motion) into a single integrated percept. They call upon the work of Singer and colleagues (Gray and Singer 1989), who found synchronization of the oscillations of neuronal activity within visual cortex for different parts of the same representation of a stimulus. Such synchrony provides an attractive solution to the so-called binding problem, which arises when multiple objects are present and the features of different objects must be distinguished. For example, if color and orientation were separately represented features, then without some way to "bind" the features of an object, a red vertical bar and a green horizontal bar would be indistinguishable from a red horizontal and a green vertical bar. Crick and Koch suggest that synchronization across visual areas could enable both binding and conscious awareness of stimuli. Damasio has proposed a similar identification of binding with conscious awareness. The type of binding he discusses operates across different modality-specific representations of an object rather than within the visual system, as in Crick and Koch's account. In the remainder of the chapter, accounts of this second type will be referred to as *integration* accounts.

Consciousness as a Graded Property of Neural Information Processing

Information representation in neural networks is not all or none, such that a stimulus must either be represented within the visual system or not. Rather, it may be partially represented, as a result of either impoverished input or damage to the network itself. The third view of the relation between brain mechanisms and conscious awareness is based on the observation that, in normal and in brain-damaged subjects, there is a correlation between the "quality" of the perceptual representation and the likelihood of conscious awareness. Experiments on subliminal perception in normal subjects invariably dissociate perception and awareness by using very brief, masked stimulus presentations, by dividing attention, or by embedding the stimulus to be perceived in a high level of noise. In other words, to reduce the likelihood of conscious awareness in normal subjects, one must use experimental manipulations known to degrade the quality of the perceptual representation. Similarly, one could argue that in many, if not all, of the neuropsychological syndromes in which visual perception has been dissociated from conscious awareness, patients' visual performance reflects a degree of impairment in visual perception per se, not merely the stripping away of conscious experience from a normal percept (Farah, Monheit, and Wallace 1991; Farah, O'Reilly, and Vecera 1993; Wallace and Farah 1992). Consciousness may be associated only with the higher-quality end of the continuum of degrees of representation. This type of account will be referred to as a *quality of representation* account.

These different types of explanation are not necessarily mutually exclusive. For example, if a particular part of the brain were needed to enable the activity of widespread regions to become integrated, there would be a sense in which both the first type of explanation and the second were correct. Alternatively, if a representation in one part of the brain were degraded, it might be less able to participate in an integrated state with other parts of the brain, in which case both the second and third types of explanation would be correct. Nevertheless, many of the explanations to be considered in this chapter exemplify just one of these categories, and the proposed three-category framework helps make clear the relations among the different explanations to be considered, even in the hybrid cases.

Finally, it should be noted explicitly what these three types of approach cannot explain and are not intended to explain. None of these accounts offers any insight into the question of what consciousness is, above and beyond its hypothesized dependence on a certain brain system, or state of integration, or quality of representation. Nor do they tell us why a certain brain system, state of integration, or quality of representation should be necessary for consciousness. Nevertheless, they are not vacuous or question begging. Although they do not answer metaphysical questions about consciousness, they are substantive claims about the neural correlates of conscious experience.

3 Blindsight

Blindsight refers to the preserved visual abilities of patients with damage to primary visual cortex, for stimuli presented in regions of the visual field formerly represented by the damaged cortex. The first documentation of this phenomenon was made by Poppel, Held, and Frost (1973), who found that patients with large scotomata could move their eyes to the location of a light flash presented in the scotomatous region of their visual field. Although the eye movements were not highly accurate, they were better than would be expected by chance and were not accompanied by any conscious visual experience according to patients' reports.

Representative Findings

Shortly after this initial report, Weiskrantz and his colleagues undertook extensive and rigorous investigations of what they termed "blindsight" (Weiskrantz, Sanders, and Marshall 1974; Weiskrantz 1986). They were able to demonstrate a much greater degree of preserved visual function in some of their subjects than in the initial series.

Case D.B., in particular, was the subject of many investigations in which the abilities to point to stimulus locations, to detect movement, to discriminate the orientation of lines and gratings, and to discriminate shapes such as X's and O's were found to be remarkably preserved. Figure 11.2 shows the results of an early study of localization by pointing in this patient. Over subsequent years, a number of different patients with blindsight have been studied in different laboratories (Weiskrantz 1990). The pattern of preserved and impaired abilities has been found to vary considerably from case to case. Detection and localization of light and detection of motion are invariably preserved to some degree. In addition, many patients can discriminate orientation, shape, direction of movement, and flicker. Color vision mechanisms appear to be preserved in some cases, as indicated by Stoerig and Cowey's (1990) findings (fig. 11.3). Normal subjects show a characteristic profile of spectral sensitivity, that is, different intensity thresholds for detection of light of different wavelengths. Although subjects with blindsight showed overall higher thresholds for above-chance detection, their spectral sensitivity functions had the same shape, indicating preserved functioning of opponent-process color mechanisms, despite no conscious awareness of color (or even light) perception.

An interesting new source of data on blindsight comes from the use of indirect measures of the subject's visual information processing capabilities in the blind field. Marzi et al. (1986) showed that subjects with blindsight, like normal subjects, respond more quickly in a simple reaction time task when there are two stimuli instead of one and that this is true even when the second stimulus falls in the blind field. Rafal et al. (1990) studied the effects of a second stimulus in the blind field on the speed with which hemianopic subjects could make a saccade to a stimulus in their normal field. With their task, a second stimulus was found to inhibit the saccade. Like the facilitation of manual reaction time found by Marzi et al., this inhibition shows that

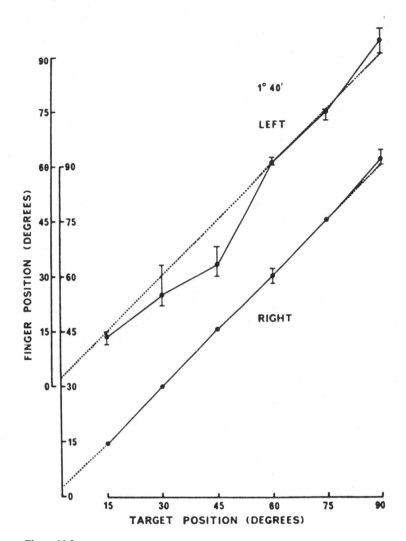

Figure 11.2
Average finger-reaching responses to targets at different positions in left (blind) and right visual field for case D.B. Bars show range of responses. From Weiskrantz et al. (1974).

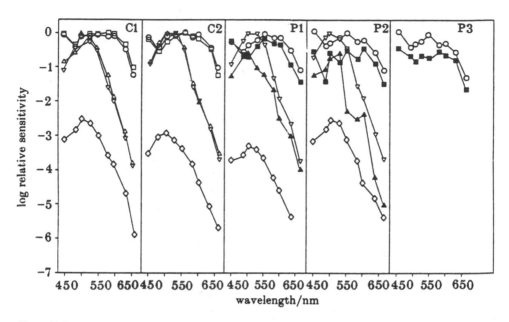

Figure 11.3
Relative spectral sensitivity of normal subjects (C) and patients with blindsight (P). From Stoerig and Cowey (1990).

the stimulus was perceived, in that it influenced performance. Significantly, Rafal et al. found this effect only when the second stimulus was presented to the temporal half of the retina, that is, to the half of the retina that projects to the superior colliculus. The projections from the retina to the cortical visual system are symmetrical, with equal connectivity between each hemiretina and the lateral geniculate nucleus (LGN).

Awareness of Perception

Just as the particular set of visual abilities and level of performance vary from patient to patient, so does the nature of patients' subjective report. Some subjects claim to be guessing on the basis of no subjective sense whatsoever. These include the subjects whose highly systematic data are shown in figures 11.2 and 11.3. In other studies, patients report some "feeling" that guides their responses, but the feeling is not described as specifically vis-

ual in nature. For example, patients will state that they felt the onset of a stimulus or felt it to be in a certain location. Shape discriminations between circles and crosses are made on the basis of "jagged" versus "smooth" feelings, which are nevertheless not subjectively visual. Some subjects may occasionally report specifically visual sensations, such as "dark shadows," particularly for very intense or salient stimuli. In his 1986 book, Weiskrantz includes descriptions of the subjective reports of his subjects, as well as the objective data collected from them in a variety of studies.

Explanations of Blindsight

The mechanism of blindsight has been a controversial topic. Some researchers have argued that the phenomenon is mediated, directly or indirectly, by residual functioning of primary visual cortex and should therefore be considered an artifact. Even for researchers who reject the artifact explanation, the mechanism of blindsight has not been settled decisively, and there remain at least two different types of account.

Campion, Latto, and Smith (1983) presented the most comprehensive and influential critique of blindsight, alleging that it is no different from normal vision in being mediated by primary visual cortex, either indirectly, by light from the scotomatous region of the visual field reflecting off other surfaces into regions of the visual field represented by intact primary visual cortex, or directly, by residual functioning of lesioned areas of primary visual cortex. The latter idea is an example of a quality of representation account. They supported their arguments with experiments involving both hemianopic subjects, whose blindsight performance was correlated with conscious awareness, and normal subjects, presenting stimuli to the natural blind spot and assessing the degree to which scattered light was sufficient for various visual judgments. More recently, Fendrich, Wessinger, and Gazzaniga (1992) showed that what appeared to be a small island of functional primary visual cortex in one subject could support above-chance detection and even shape discrimination, despite the subject's belief that he was guessing in these tasks. The hypothesis of primary visual cortex mediation of blindsight meets several difficulties in accounting for the totality of the empirical data now available on blindsight. For example, it is difficult to see how scattered light would enable case D.B. to perceive black figures on a bright background or how this account could explain the qualitative differences in his performance within his natural blind spot and his acquired blind region. Unlike Fendrich et al.'s subject, the blindsight performance of most subjects is not sharply limited to a small patch of the blind field. Residual functioning of spared cortex is clearly not a possibility for hemidecorticate subjects, and yet they too show a wide range of blindsight abilities. Finally, recall the results of Rafal et al. (1990) on inhibition of saccades by stimuli presented to the blind field. This result

has the important property of demonstrating subcortical mediation of blindsight by a positive finding, nasal-temporal asymmetries, rather than by the negation of possibilities for primary visual cortex involvement. Although it is possible that some of the abilities classified in some patients as blindsight do derive from spared striate cortex, the available data seem to suggest that additional mechanisms play an important role too.

Other than spared primary visual cortex, what other neural systems might mediate the preserved abilities in blindsight? Initially, the answer was thought to be the so-called subcortical visual system, which consists of projections from the retina to the superior colliculus, and on to the pulvinar and cortical visual areas. This is an instance of a privileged role account, in that both cortical and subcortical visual systems are hypothesized to mediate various types of visual information processing but the mediation of visual awareness is taken to be the privileged role of the cortical visual system. Although it might at first seem puzzling that both visual systems mediate vision but only one mediates awareness thereof, the puzzle may be more apparent than real. There is, after all, much neural information processing that operates outside the realm of conscious awareness— for example, body temperature regulation. According to the hypothesis of subcortical mediation of blindsight, at least some of the neural information processing of visual representations also operates without conscious awareness. Perhaps the reason this seems strange at first, and in fact engendered such extreme skepticism in some quarters, is that we use the phrase "visual perception" in two ways: to process representations of visual stimuli within our nervous systems and to become aware of visually transduced stimuli. According to the subcortical mediation hypothesis, both visual systems mediate visual perception in the first sense, whereas only the cortical visual system mediates visual perception in the second sense.

There is evidence in favor of the subcortical mediation hypothesis for at least some blindsight abilities. The close functional similarities between the known specializations of the subcortical visual system and many of the preserved abilities in blindsight, such as detection and localization of onsets and moving stimuli (Schiller and Koerner 1971), constitute one source of evidence. In addition, the nasal-temporal asymmetries found in Rafal et al.'s (1990) study are indicative of collicular mediation.

Recently, however, Cowey and Stoerig (1989) have suggested that the so-called cortical visual system, which projects from the retina to cortex by way of the LGN, may also contribute to blindsight. They marshaled evidence, from their own experiments and other research, of a population of cells in the LGN that project directly to extrastriate visual cortex and could therefore bring stimulus information into such areas as V4 and MT in the absence of primary visual cortex. This type of mechanism fits most naturally with the quality of representation hypotheses. According to this account, many of the same visual association areas are engaged in blindsight as in normal vision. What distinguishes normal vision and visual performance without awareness is that in the latter, only a subset of the normal inputs arrives in extrastriate visual cortex. The remaining inputs are both fewer in number and lacking whatever type of processing is normally accomplished in primary visual cortex. Consciousness of the functioning of extrastriate visual areas may occur only when these areas are operating on more complete and more fully processed visual representations. Evidence for this hypothesis is still preliminary. Although the anatomical connections between the LGN and the extrastriate visual areas have been shown to exist, their functional significance in blindsight has not been fully established. A systematic comparison between the blindsight abilities of patients with circumscribed striate lesions and with hemidecortication (which removes extrastriate visual areas as well) should reveal the functional role of the LGN-to-extrastriate projections in blindsight.

In sum, although some dissociations between visual performance and subjective awareness may be mediated by spared primary visual cortex, it seems fairly clear that the range of abilities documented in blindsight does not result from degraded normal vision (where "normal" means relying on primary visual cortex). It is also clearly not a single homogeneous phenomenon. At the level of preserved visual abilities, subjective experience, and neural mechanisms, there is apparently much variation from subject to subject. An important research goal in this area would be to establish correspondences among these three levels of individual difference as a means of characterizing the functional and experiential roles of different components of the visual system. In the meantime, we can discern two main types of mechanism that may account for the dissociations between visual abilities and conscious awareness in blindsight: subcortical visual mechanisms and direct projections from the LGN to extrastriate areas.

4   Covert Recognition of Faces in Prosopagnosia

Prosopagnosia is an impairment of face recognition following brain damage, which can occur relatively independently of impairments in object recognition and is not caused by impairments in lower-level vision or memory. In some cases of prosopagnosia, there is a dramatic dissociation between the loss of face recognition ability as measured by standard tests of face recognition, as well as patients' own introspections, and the apparent preservation of face recognition when tested by certain indirect tests.

Representative Findings

Covert recognition in prosopagnosia has been demonstrated using psychophysiological measures such as skin conductance response (SCR) and indirect behavioral measures. In the first clear demonstration of covert recognition, Bauer (1984) presented a prosopagnosic patient with a series of photographs of familiar faces. While viewing each face, the patient heard a list of names read aloud, one of them the name of the person in the photograph. For normal subjects, the SCR is greatest to the name belonging to the pictured person. Bauer found that although the prosopagnosic patient's SCRs to names were not as strongly correlated with the names as a normal subject's would be, they were nevertheless significantly correlated. In contrast, the patient performed at chance levels when asked to select the correct name for each face. In a different use of the SCR measure, Tranel and Damasio (1985) and Tranel, Damasio, and Damasio (1988) showed that prosopagnosic patients had larger SCRs to familiar faces than to unfamiliar faces, although their overt ratings of familiarity versus unfamiliarity did not reliably discriminate between the two.

Bruyer et al. (1983) pioneered the use of a paired-associate face-name relearning task as a way of demonstrating covert recognition in prosopagnosia. Their patient was asked to learn to associate the facial photographs of famous people with the names of famous people. When the pairing of names and faces was correct, the patient required fewer learning trials than when it was incorrect, suggesting that the patient did possess some knowledge of the people's facial appearance. Unfortunately, this demonstration of covert recognition is not as meaningful as it could be, because the subject was only mildly prosopagnosic. However, several more severe prosopagnosic patients have recently been tested in the face-name relearning task, and some have shown the same pattern of faster learning of correct than incorrect face-name associations, despite little or no success at the overt recognition of the same faces. For example, De Haan, Young, and Newcombe (1987b) documented consistently faster learning of face-name and face-occupation pairings in their prosopagnosic subject, even when the stimulus faces were selected from among those that the patient had been unable to identify in a pre-experiment stimulus screening test.

Evidence of covert recognition has also come from reaction time tasks in which the familiarity of identity of faces is found to influence processing time. In a visual identity match task with simultaneously presented pairs of faces, de Haan, Young, and Newcombe (1987b) found that a prosopagnosic patient was faster at matching pairs of previously familiar faces than unfamiliar faces, as is true of normal subjects. In contrast, he was unable to name any of the previously familiar faces.

In another reaction time (RT) study, De Hann, Young, and Newcombe (1987b; also see 1987a) found evidence that photographs of faces could evoke covert semantic knowledge of the depicted person, despite the inability of the prosopagnosic patient to report such information about the person when tested overtly. Their task was to categorize a printed name as belonging to an actor or a politician as quickly as possible. On some trials an irrelevant (i.e., to be ignored) photograph of an actor's or politician's face was simultaneously presented (fig. 11.4). Normal subjects are slower to categorize the names when the faces come from a different occupation category relative to a no-photograph baseline. Although their prosopagnosic patient was severely impaired at categorizing the faces overtly as belonging to actors or politicians, he showed the same pattern of interference from different-category faces.

A related finding was reported by Young, Hellawell, and De Haan (1988) in a task involving the categorization of names as famous or nonfamous. Both normal subjects and a prosopagnosic patient showed faster RTs to the famous names when the name was preceded by a picture of a semantically related face (e.g., the name "Diana Spencer" preceded by a picture of Prince Charles) than by an unfamiliar or an unrelated face. Furthermore, the same experiment was carried out with printed names as the priming stimulus, so that the size of the priming effect with

Figure 11.4
Examples of stimuli from De Haan, Young, and Newcombe's (1987a) study. The name of the politician is presented with his own face (*top*), with the face of another politician, Peter Walker (*middle*), or with the face of a nonpolitician, Michael Aspel (*bottom*).

faces and names could be compared. The prosopagnosic patient's priming effect from faces was not significantly different from the priming effect from names. However, the patient was able to name only two of the twenty face prime stimuli used.

Awareness of Perception

Prosopagnosic patients who manifest covert recognition appear to lack the subjective experience of recognition, at least for many of the faces for which they show covert recognition. These patients may occasionally recognize a face overtly, that is, assign it the correct name and express a degree of confidence that they know who the person is. However, this happens rarely, and the dissociation between covert recognition and awareness of recognition holds for many faces that they fail to identify and for which they report no sense of familiarity.

Explanations of Covert Face Recognition

Several competing explanations have been offered for the dissociation between overt and covert recognition of faces in prosopagnosia. The oldest, and still predominant, explanation is that the face recognition system is intact in these patients but has been prevented from conveying information to other brain mechanisms necessary for conscious awareness. In one of the earliest reports of the dissociation, De Haan, Young, and Newcombe (1987a) described their subject's prosopagnosia as involving a "loss of awareness of the products of the recognition system rather than . . . a breakdown in the recognition system per se." Perhaps the most explicit and general statement of this view was made recently by De Haan, Bauer, and Greve (1992), who proposed the model shown in figure 11.5. According to their model, the face-specific visual and mnemonic processing of a face (carried out within the "face processing module") proceeds normally in covert recognition, but the results of this process cannot

access the "conscious awareness system" because of a lesion at location 1. This account clearly falls into the privileged role category; it entails a specific brain system needed for conscious awareness, separate from the brain systems needed to carry out perception and cognition. Indeed these authors cite the DICE model as an important source of inspiration for their model.

A second type of explanation was put forth by Bauer (1984), who suggested that there may be two neural systems capable of face recognition, only one of which is associated with conscious awareness. According to Bauer, the ventral cortical visual areas, which are damaged in prosopagnosic patients, are the location of normal conscious face recognition. The dorsal visual areas are hypothesized to be capable of face recognition as well, although they do not mediate conscious recognition but, instead, affective responses to faces. Covert recognition is explained as the isolated functioning of the dorsal face system, as diagrammed in figure 11.6. Like the account depicted in figure 11.5, this account also fits into the general category of consciousness as a privileged property of particular brain systems. However, this account does not feature a neural system whose primary function is to enable conscious awareness, like the "conscious awareness system" of DICE and figure 11.3. Rather, this account is more analogous to theorizing about the subcortical visual system in blindsight, in that two systems are postulated, each carrying out related but distinct functions, and only one of which is endowed with conscious awareness.

Tranel, Damasio, and Damasio (1988) interpret covert recognition as the normal activation of visual face representations, which is prevented by the patients' lesions from activating representations in other areas of the brain, such as representations of the people's voices in auditory areas, affective valences in limbic areas, and names in language areas. This interpretation is therefore of the second type described in section 2, in that it requires an integration of active

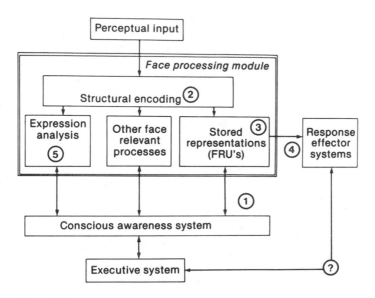

Figure 11.5
Functional architecture of face recognition and awareness. Covert face recognition is attributed to a lesion at location 1. From De Haan, Bauer, and Greve (1992).

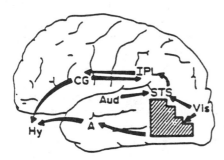

Figure 11.6
Diagram of the two hypothesized face recognition pathways. From Bauer (1984).

representations across different brain areas in order for conscious awareness to occur; we cannot be consciously aware of an isolated, modality-specific representation. A similar idea was recently embodied in a computer simulation of semantic priming effects, in which covert recognition was modeled as a partial disconnection

separating intact visual recognition units from the rest of the system (Burton et al. 1991) (fig. 11.7).

The last account of the mechanism by which overt and covert recognition are dissociated is that covert recognition reflects the residual processing capabilities of a damaged but not obliterated visual face recognition system. My colleagues and I have argued that lower-quality visual information processing is needed to support performance in tests of covert recognition (e.g., to show savings in relearning, and the various RT facilitation and interference effects) relative to the quality of information processing needed to support normal overt recognition performance (e.g., naming a face, sorting faces into those of actors and politicians). This account falls into the third category reviewed, in that the difference between face recognition with and without conscious awareness is the quality of representations activated by the face.

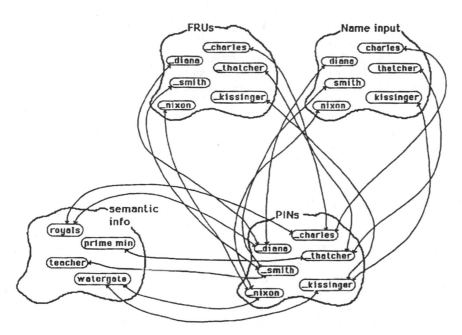

Figure 11.7
Model of face recognition proposed by Burton et al. (1991), in which covert recognition is stimulated by attenuating connections between FRUs (face recognition units) and PIUs (personal identity units).

What evidence is available to distinguish among these hypotheses? In general, prosopagnosics are impaired in their perception of faces, although this impairment may be subtle enough to require chronometric measures to detect (Farah 1990). To take an example from the body of research under discussion, the prosopagnosic subject studied by De Haan, Young, and Newcombe (1987b) was both slower and considerably less accurate than normal subjects in the face matching task. This is not what one would expect assuming that the underlying impairment in prosopagnosia occurs downstream from visual face recognition processes. However, this assumption is central to all of the explanations reviewed so far, with the exception of the dual-route account of Bauer (1984) and our degraded systems hypothesis. Of course, brain-damaged patients often have deficits in more than

one functional system, so in principle it is possible that problems with face matching are distinct from prosopagnosia.

If covert recognition reflects the normal functioning of a preserved face recognition system, then, in addition to normal face perception, we should also find normal levels of covert recognition, as opposed to merely partial preservation of recognition. The issue here is analogous to that in amnesia research of whether nondeclarative memory measures such as priming are truly normal in amnesic patients. Much research has been devoted to answering this question, and the finding that such patients are normal in at least some measures of nondeclarative memory has played an important role in theorizing about the functional organization of memory (e.g., see Squire 1992). Unfortunately, the data needed to test the analogous prediction for prosopagnosics are not

available. In some cases, data from normal subjects would be impossible to obtain, as when
famous faces and names are retaught with either
the correct or incorrect pairings. In other cases,
the problem of comparing effect sizes on different
absolute measures arises. In both the SCR and
RT paradigms, covert recognition is measured
by differences between the dependent measures
in two conditions (e.g., familiar and unfamiliar
faces). Unfortunately, patients' SCRs are invariably weaker than those of normal subjects (Bauer
1986), and their RTs are longer (De Haan,
Young, and Newcombe 1987b). It is difficult to
know how to assess the relative sizes of differences when the base measures are different. For
example, is an effect corresponding to a 200-ms
difference between RTs on the order of 2 sec bigger than, comparable to, or smaller than an effect
corresponding to a 100-ms difference between
RTs of less than a second?

The study that comes closest to allowing a direct comparison of covert recognition in patients
and normal subjects is the priming experiment
of Young, Hellawell, and de Haan (1988). Recall
that they found equivalent effects of priming name
classification for their prosopagnosic patient with
either photographs or names of semantically related people. Of course, this fact alone does not
imply that the face-mediated priming was normal, because the priming in this task might normally be larger than name-mediated priming.
They devised an ingenious way to address this
problem. They refer back to an earlier experiment, reported in the same article, in which normal subjects were tested with both face primes
and name primes. The normal subjects also
showed equivalent amounts of priming in the two
conditions. Unfortunately, the earlier experiment
differed in several ways from the latter, which
could conceivably shift the relative sizes of the
face-mediated and name-mediated priming effects: normal subjects in the earlier experiment
performed only 30 trials each, whereas the prosopagnosic patient performed 240 trials; items
were never repeated in the earlier experiment,

whereas they were in the later one; the type of
prime was varied among subjects in the earlier
experiment, whereas the patient received both
types; different faces and names were used in the
two experiments; and the primes were presented
for about half as long in the earlier experiment as
in the later one. Ideally, to answer the question of
whether this prosopagnosic patient shows normal
priming from faces, a group of normal control
subjects should be run through the same experiment as the patient. Finally, as if empirical progress in this area is not difficult enough, there is an
inherent ambiguity in one of the possible outcomes to such an experiment. Just as the finding
of normal perception would disconfirm a quality
of representation account but the finding of impaired perception is not decisive against the privileged role and integration accounts, so a finding
of subnormal levels of covert recognition would
disconfirm the privileged role and integration accounts, but the finding of normal covert recognition would not be decisive against the quality of
representation account. This is because the covert
measures might have lower ceilings than overt
measures of recognition, that is, they might work
equally well with intact or partly degraded representations. Parametric study of the relations between covert and overt performance in normal
subjects would determine whether this is true.

In sum, most of the current explanations of
covert recognition assume both normal face perception and normal covert recognition in prosopagnosics, but neither assumption is empirically
supported at present. When tested rigorously,
face perception is not normal. However, this
result should not be taken as decisive evidence
against this class of hypotheses, because the perceptual impairments could be due to functionally
distinct lesions from those causing the prosopagnosia. As to the question of whether covert
recognition is truly normal, appropriate tests
have not yet been carried out. When and if they
are, a finding of impaired covert recognition
would be immediately interpretable, but a finding
of normal covert recognition would require fur-

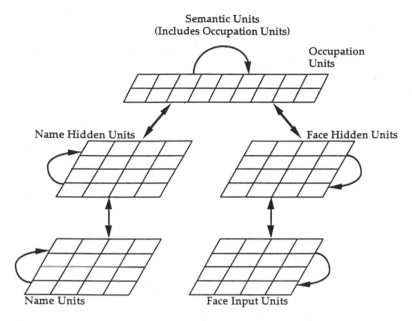

Semantic Units
(Includes Occupation Units)

Occupation
Units

Name Hidden Units

Face Hidden Units

Name Units

Face Input Units

Figure 11.8
Model of face recognition proposed by Farah, O'Reilly, and Vecera (1993), in which covert recognition is simulated by damaging either face input units or face hidden units.

ther scaling studies with normal subjects to determine whether the normalcy is due to a ceiling effect.

Bauer's (1984) dual-route version of a privileged role explanation has not been subject to any direct tests. Its most distinctive prediction concerns the difference between face recognition for enabling appropriate affective responses and face recognition for other purposes. Consistent with this prediction is Greve and Bauer's (1990) finding that a prosopagnosic patient rated previously seen faces as more likeable, just as normal subjects tend to do. However, most findings of covert recognition have little to do with affective responses, instead engaging implicit knowledge of names or occupations, and this seems inconsistent with the dual-route hypothesis.

Turning to the quality of representation account of covert recognition, is there any independent evidence that a degraded, but not obliterated,

face recognition system would lead to a dissociation between overt and covert recognition? In one study, Wallace and Farah (1992) showed that savings in face-name relearning can be obtained with normal subjects who are trained on a set of face-name associations and then allowed to forget these associations over a 6-month interval. Presumably normal forgetting does not involve the diverting of intact information from conscious awareness but rather the degradation of representations (albeit in a different way from prosopagnosia).

Probably the strongest evidence for this view, however, is computational. Farah, O'Reilly, and Vecera (1993) trained a neural network to associate "face" patterns with "semantic" patterns and to associate these, in turn, with "name" patterns (fig. 11.8). We found that at levels of damage to the face representations that led to poor or even chance performance in overt tasks, the network showed all of the behavioral covert recognition effects reviewed above: it relearned correct associations faster than novel ones, it completed the visual analysis of familiar faces faster than unfamiliar, and it showed priming and interference from the faces on judgments about names (fig. 11.9).

Why should this be? To answer this question requires a brief digression into neural network models. In these models, representations consist of a pattern of activation over a set of highly interconnected neuronlike units. The extent to which the activation of one unit causes an increase or decrease in the activation of a neighboring unit depends on the weight of the connection between them. For the network to learn that a certain face representation goes with a certain name representation, the weights among units in the network are adjusted so that presentation of either the face pattern in the face units or the name pattern in the name units causes the corresponding other pattern to become activated. Upon presentation of the input pattern, all of the units connected with the input units will begin to change their activation in accordance with the activation value of the units to which they are connected and the weights on the connections. As activation propagates through the network, a stable pattern of activation eventually results, determined jointly by the input activation and the pattern of weights among the units of the network.

Our account of covert face recognition is based on the following key idea: the set of the weights in a network that cannot correctly associate patterns because it has never been trained (or has been trained on a different set of patterns) is different in an important way from the set of weights in a network that cannot correctly associate patterns because it has been trained on those patterns and then damaged. The first set of weights is random with respect to the associations in question, whereas the second is a subset of the necessary weights. Even if it is an inadequate subset for

performing the association, it is not random; it has embedded in it some degree of knowledge of the associations. Hinton and colleagues (Hinton and Sejnowski 1986; Hinton and Plaut 1987) have shown that such embedded knowledge can be demonstrated when the network relearns, suggesting the findings of savings in relearning face-name associations may be explained in this way. In general, consideration of the kinds of tests used to measure covert recognition suggests that the covert measures would be sensitive to this embedded knowledge. The most obvious example is that a damaged network would be expected to relearn associations that it originally knew faster than novel associations because of the nonrandom starting weights. Less obvious, but confirmed by our simulations, the network would settle faster when given previously learned inputs than novel inputs, although the pattern into which it settles is not correct, because the residual weights come from a set designed to create a stable pattern from that input. Finally, to the extent that the weights continue to activate partial and subthreshold patterns over the nondamaged units in association with the input, these resultant patterns could prime (contribute activation toward) the activation of patterns by intact routes.

The general implication of these ideas is that as a neural network is increasingly damaged, there might be a window of damage in which overt associations between patterns (e.g., faces and names) would be extremely poor, while the kinds of performance measures tapped by the covert tasks might remain at high levels.

In conclusion, the mechanism by which overt and covert face recognition are dissociated has not been established. All three types of explanation outlined in section 2 have been advanced to account for covert recognition in prosopagnosia. Many of the explanations would appear to run aground on evidence of perceptual impairment in prosopagnosia because they maintain that the locus of impairment is postperceptual. However, the perceptual impairments could conceivably be distinct but associated impairments. The quality of representation explanation has the advantage of accounting for these perceptual impairments, and of accounting for performance in three types of covert recognition task, and is therefore favored here. However, a decisive resolution to the issue of mechanism will require much more careful, quantitative analyses of covert recognition, analogous to the work that established the normalcy of nondeclarative learning in amnesics. Further computational work would also be helpful to account for more fine-grained features of the empirical data and to generate new predictions that could be tested with patients.

5 Unconscious Perception in Neglect and Extinction

Neglect is a disorder of spatial attention that generally follows posterior parietal damage and results in patients' failure to report or even orient to stimuli occurring on the side of space contralateral to the lesion. Patients with neglect need not be hemianopic (blind in the affected side of space), although they may behave as if they are. Simple hemianoppia is distinguishable from neglect in that a hemianopic patient will search, with eye and head movements, for contralateral stimuli, whereas a patient with neglect, hemianopic or not, will fail to do so. Extinction is often viewed as a mild form of neglect. It also occurs predominantly in parietal-damaged patients but results in difficulty with contralateral stimuli only when an ipsilateral stimulus is presented at the same time.

The behavior of patients with neglect and extinction suggests that they do not perceive neglected and extinguished stimuli. However, evidence is beginning to accumulate showing that, in at least some cases, considerable information about neglected and extinguished stimuli is extracted by patients. As with covert recognition in

prosopagnosia, this information is generally detectable only using indirect tests.

Representative Findings

Evidence for unconscious perception comes from two general types of experimental paradigms: those employing brief, bilateral stimulus presentations, to produce extinction in patients with full visual fields and either extinction alone or extinction and neglect; and those employing single stimuli in central vision, with no limitation on viewing time, in patients with neglect. (A relatively complete review of research in this area can be found in Wallace 1994.)

The first suggestion that patients with extinction may see more of the extinguished stimulus than is apparent from their conscious verbal report came from Volpe, LeDoux, and Gazzaniga (1979). They presented four right-parietal–damaged extinction patients with pairs of visual stimuli, including drawings of common objects and three-letter words, one in each hemifield. On each trial, subjects were required to perform two types of task: to state whether the two stimuli shown were the same or different and to name the stimuli. Figure 11.10 shows the stimuli and results from a typical trial. As would be expected, the subjects did poorly at overtly identifying the stimuli on the left. Two subjects failed to name any of the left stimuli correctly, and the other two named fewer than half. In view of this, their performance on the same/different matching task was surprising. Although this task also requires perception of the left stimulus, subjects achieved between 88 percent and 100 percent correct. More recently, the same dissociation between identification of the left stimulus and cross-field same/different matching was obtained with parietal-damaged neglect patients whose attentional impairment is so severe that contralesional stimuli may fail to be identified even in the absence of a simultaneously occurring ipsilesional stimulus (Karnath and Hartje 1987; Karnath 1988).

A.

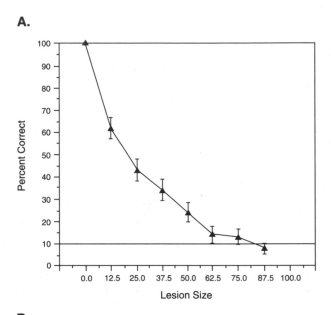

B.

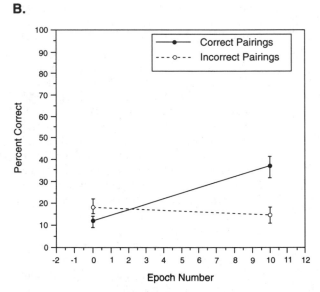

Figure 11.9
Selected results from the model of Farah, O'Reilly, and Vecera (1993). *A.* Performance of model in 10-alternative forced-choice naming task after different amounts of damage to face hidden units. *B.* Relearning correct and incorrect face-name associations after removal of 75 percent of face -hidden units. *C.* Speed of perception of familiar and unfamiliar faces after different amounts of damage to face hidden units. *D.* Effect of faces with same or different occupation on time to categorize a name according to occupation, after different amounts of face-hidden unit damage.

C.

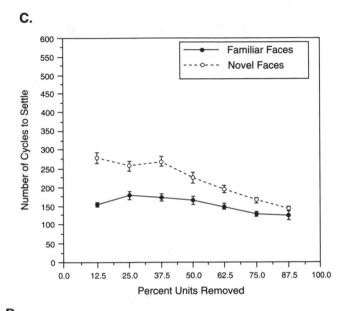

D.

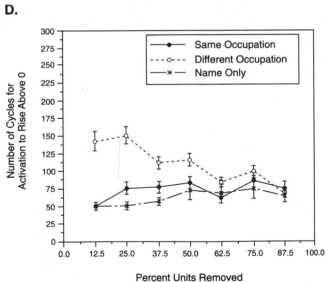

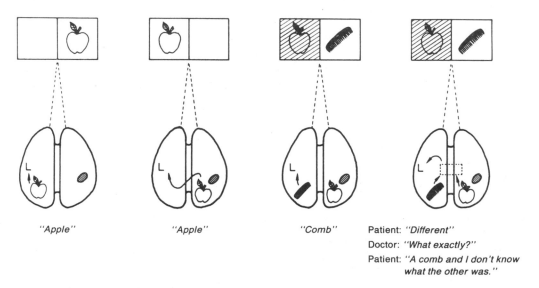

"Apple"   "Apple"   "Comb"   Patient: *"Different"*
                                                  Doctor: *"What exactly?"*
                                                  Patient: *"A comb and I don't know
                                                            what the other was."*

Figure 11.10
Typical trials from the experiment of Volpe, LeDoux, and Gazzaniga (1979), showing extinction of the left stimulus
with preserved same/different matching.

Farah, Monheit, and Wallace (1991) noted that the dissociation between naming and same/ different matching could, in principle, be explained by the differing demands these tasks make on the quality of the representation of the left stimulus. Consider the example of the comb and apple, shown in figure 11.10. If only partial stimulus information were picked up on the left— for example, the perception that there is something roundish and light-colored—this would be sufficient to enable fairly accurate same/different judgments. However, there are so many roundish, light-colored objects in the world that this partial perception would be of no help in naming the stimulus on the left. We performed two experiments to test the hypothesis that the differential amounts of stimulus information required for same/different matching and overt identification is what causes the dissociation between them. First, we degraded the left side of the display with a translucent mask and repeated Volpe, LeDoux, and Gazzaniga's experiment with normal sub-

jects. This manipulation was not intended as a simulation of extinction but rather as test of our hypothesis concerning the quality of visual information needed in the two kinds of task. Merely depriving normal subjects of some information from the left stimulus produced the same dissociation in normal subjects that Volpe, LeDoux, and Gazzaniga observed in patients with extinction. Second, we repeated the paradigm with extinction patients in its original form, and replicated the original finding, and also in an altered from, in which the overt identification task was administered in a forced-choice format. The purpose of this alteration was to enable us to equate the same/different trials and identification trials for the amount of information needed from the left stimulus. We did this by yoking trials from the two conditions, such that if there was a same/ different trial with a triangle and a square, there was an identification trial in which one of these stimuli was presented on the left and the subject was asked, "Did you see a triangle or a square?"

When same/different matching and identification were equated for their demands on the quality of the subjects' representations of the left stimuli, the dissociation vanished. We concluded that the task of same/different matching and identification differ significantly in their demands on the quality of visual representation. This implies that the results of Volpe, LeDoux, and Gazzaniga are consistent with extinction's affecting perception per se and do not require us to conclude that perception is normal and only postperceptual access to conscious awareness is impaired by extinction. Specifically, our results suggest that extinction results in partial, low-quality perceptual representations of stimuli.

Berti et al. (1992) extended these findings in a different direction, with a study of one patient who showed extinction following a temporal lobectomy. The goal of their study was to determine the level of processing to which extinguished stimuli were encoded. In Volpe, LeDoux, and Gazzaniga's (1979) study, stimuli were either physically identical or entirely different, and subjects could therefore make accurate responses on the basis of relatively early perceptual representations, were they of high or low quality. Berti et al. included pairs of pictures that were physically different but depicted either the same object from a different view or different-looking exemplars of the same type of object, such as two different cameras, and they instructed their subject to say "same" if the two stimuli had the same name. If extinguished stimuli are encoded to early levels of visual perception prior to object constancy but do not make any contact with stored object representations or meaning, then the subject should perform well only when the two stimuli are physically identical. In contrast, if extinguished stimuli are encoded to the level of meaning, then the subject should be able to say, for example, that two different cameras are the same. In fact, this is what was found, implying that extinguished stimuli are not only registered at some early level of visual processing but that they re-

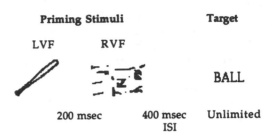

Priming Stimuli **Target**

LVF RVF

BALL

200 msec 400 msec Unlimited
ISI

Figure 11.11
Sequence of stimuli from a typial trial in the experiment of McGlinchy-Berroth et al. (1993).

ceive perceptual and even conceptual processing, despite subjects' inability to report specifically what they saw.

A recent study by McGlinchey-Berroth et al. (1993) showed semantic priming by neglected pictures in a lexical decision task. On each trial of this experiment, subjects with left neglect viewed a picture in one hemifield, followed by a letter string in central vision to which they made a "word"/"nonword" response (fig. 11.11). When the picture was semantically related to the word, "word" responses were faster, even when the picture had been presented on the left side of the display. Perhaps most striking about this result is that the amount of priming did not differ significantly between left- and right-field stimuli. Although this might appear to imply that the amount of semantic priming from neglected stimuli is quantitatively normal, such a conclusion is not warranted because normal subjects show greater left- than right-field semantic priming (Chiarello 1988). In fact, this asymmetry was visible in the control subjects in McGlinchy-Berroth et al.'s experiment.

The finding of preserved semantic priming by left-field stimuli must also be interpreted in the context of the degree of neglect for left-field stimuli. McGlinchey-Berroth et al. conducted a second experiment in which the degree of neglect for left stimuli was assessed in a delayed matching task. Patients were indeed poor at matching a left stimulus picture with a central one presented shortly after, achieving on average only 56 percent correct. However, they were also surprisingly poor at performing the same task with stimuli presented on the right, achieving on average only 74 percent correct, raising the worry that performance in this matching task was limited by difficulties other than neglect and that not all left stimuli would therefore necessarily have been neglected in the priming task.

Unconscious perception of neglected stimuli has also been investigated under conditions of nontachistoscopic viewing in central vision. Sieroff, Pollatsek, and Posner (1988) analyzed the reading capabilities of patients with neglect and found that letters falling in the neglected regions of the visual field (as assessed by poor naming of letters in nonword letter strings) could nevertheless be used to identify familiar words. For example, patients might read *table* correctly, but read *taspi* as "f-o-s-p-i" or "s-p-i," misperceiving or omitting the letters on the left. Sieroff, Posner, and Pollatsek argue against the possibility that patients were simply guessing the letters on the left sides of words by pointing out that words and nonwords were intermixed in their experiments, and patients did not often guess words when shown the nonword letter strings. Although these authors were not specifically concerned with the issue of conscious awareness in neglect, their findings seem to imply that the leftmost letters were unconsciously perceived and therefore available to the word recognition system, despite patients' inability to report the letters.

Marshall and Halligan (1988) described a patient with neglect who evinced a consistent preference for a picture of a normal house over a picture of the same house with flames coming from the left side, despite her inability to say how (or even whether) the two stimuli differed. This pattern of performance is consistent with the hypothesis that neglected stimuli are perceived and understood, at least to the degree that they can evoke an affective response, without being accessible to the mechanisms of conscious verbal report.

In further research, by Bisiach and Rusconi (1990), who tested four patients with four pairs of drawings, the striking finding of Marshall and Halligan (1988) was not replicated. Often patients displayed no consistent preference. Perhaps more revealing, when patients did have a preference, it was not necessarily in the normal, rational direction. For example, the only patients who showed a preference with the house stimuli preferred the burning house! Bisiach and Rusconi queried their subjects as to the reasons for their preferences and found that the reasons fell into two categories: real but minor differences on the right sides of the stimulus materials, and confabulated differences, such as alleged differences in the layouts of the houses or the numbers of rooms. These confabulations are not uninteresting; they suggest that patients with neglect may detect differences on the left that they cannot describe verbally, instead evoking confabulations. However, the results of Bisiach and Rusconi do suggest that Marshall and Halligan's case was probably responding to some minor difference on the right side of the stimulus pair or to some dimly perceived difference on the left, rather than to the unconscious realization that one of the houses was on fire and would therefore be a dangerous place to live.

Awareness of Perception

Patients with neglect and extinction generally report no awareness of having seen stimuli that they fail to detect or of having recognized stimuli that they fail to identify. One measure of the extent to which the subjects were not aware of their own perceptions in the studies reviewed here is their tendency to remark on the silliness or absurdity of answering questions about stimuli on the left, or choosing between a pair of stimuli identical except for a feature on the left (Marshall and Halligan 1988; Volpe, LeDoux, and Gazzaniga 1979). Such tasks would indeed seem silly if one were not aware of a stimulus on the left or of the difference between the paired stimuli. It should be noted, however, that the ways in which awareness of perception was formally operationalized in these studies was not to ask the subjects whether they detected a stimulus. Rather, the most common means was verbal identification of the stimulus. This was used in the studies of same/different matching ability and in the studies of letter perception within word and non-word letter strings. Although Volpe, LeDoux, and Gazzaniga stated that their subjects sometimes denied seeing any stimulus at all on the left, no systematic data are reported on detection; they contrasted same/different matching performance only with naming. Other tasks intended to assess conscious awareness of stimulus identity included the delayed matching task of McGlinchy-Berroth et al. and the same/different judgment of Marshall and Halligan. In contrast to the research on covert recognition in prosopagnosia, research on unconscious perception in neglect and extinction has not drawn a clear and principled line between tasks that require overt conscious awareness of perception and tasks considered to be indirect tests of unconscious perception. The fact that same/different matching was considered an indirect test of unconscious perception by Volpe, LeDoux, and Gazzaniga and a test of overt conscious perception by Marshaal and Halligan is symptomatic of this problem.

Explanations of Perceptual Dissociations in Patients with Neglect and Extinction

The earliest and most straightforward interpretation of the dissociation between perception and awareness in patients with neglect and/or extinction was offered by Volpe, LeDoux, and Gazzaniga. They suggested that extinction in their subjects consisted of "a breakdown in the flow of information between conscious and nonconscious mental systems. The stimulus comparison task in our study appears to have been carried out at a postperceptual, preverbal level, with only the resultant comparison entering consciousness." This account clearly falls into the privileged rote category, because consciousness is being attributed

to certain systems and not others. Although the authors are not very explicit on the point, it appears from the quotation just cited and another reference to "some level of neuronal processing which allows for verbal description, if not conscious awareness" that the system required for consciousness is closely related to the language system (Gazzaniga 1988).

An alternative interpretation of the kinds of dissociations reviewed here has been offered by Kinsbourne (1988). Rather than viewing consciousness as a property of some neural systems and not others, he considers it a state of integration among different neural systems. According to this view, neglect does not divert percepts from conscious awareness by somehow preventing their transmission to another system that is required for consciousness. Rather, it weakens or degrades the representation of the stimulus, such that the representation does not have sufficient influence over the other, concurrent, patterns of activity in the brain to create a new global brain state into which the stimulus representation is integrated. This contrasts with the integration account of covert face recognition by Damasio (1990), according to which the percept is normal but disconnected from other systems. A related interpretation seems to be advocated by Bisiach (1992). He rejects the notion of a single central locus of consciousness, which he identifies with Cartesianism and the homunculus, and calls our attention to the possibility of numerous parallel mechanisms linking stimuli and responses.

The dissociations reviewed earlier can also be explained by a quality of representation account. According to this type of account, extinction and neglect result in poor-quality perceptual representations, which supply input, albeit degraded input, to higher levels of conceptual and linguistic processing. This type of account is similar to Kinsbourne's integration account; both emphasize the degradation of perception and consequent weakening of the influence of neglected and extinguished percepts on other parts of the system. The accounts differ in emphasis in that the integration account stresses the lessening of influence on the rest of the system, whereas the quality of representation account stresses the existence of the residual influence.

The available data provide some constraints on possible mechanisms but do not discriminate decisively among them. The privileged role account of Volpe, LeDoux, and Gazzaniga can be distinguished from the others in that it hypothesizes normal perception, with the impairment occurring downstream, whereas the other accounts hinge on an impairment in perception per se. The finding of Farah, Monheit, and Wallace (1991) that same/different matching was dissociated from identification only by virtue of the demands on visual perception is more consistent with the integration and quality of representation accounts than with the privileged role account.

It might appear that several of the other findings described earlier are inconsistent with the hypothesis that perception is impaired. For example, McGinchy-Berroth et al.'s subjects showed semantic priming from left field stimuli; Sieroff, Pollatsek, and Posner's subjects could use letters from neglected regions of the field to read words; and Berti et al.'s subject could match extinguished stimuli on the basis of conceptual rather than structural equivalence. However, as noted earlier, neural representation is not all or none, and it is probably not necessary for the visual system to have completed its processing of a stimulus and to have derived a high-quality representation in order for it to pass some information on to subsequent levels of processing. A degraded or incomplete visual representation will therefore presumably activate, to some degree, conceptual and semantic representations.

The possibility of semantic priming by words that are poorly perceived is well established in the cognitive psychology literature. Marcel (1983) and others have shown that subliminal tachistoscopic presentations of words can prime judgments about subsequent supraliminal words. The most natural and direct interpretation of the effect of limiting the exposure duration of a word and following it with a mask is that the perceptual processing of the word is impaired.[1] Therefore, we should not infer that if a word or picture can semantically prime subsequent stimulus processing, that it must have been perceived normally.

A mechanistic explanation of how poor-quality perceptual representations could produce priming at semantic levels is suggested by the covert face recognition model of Farah, O'Reilly, and Vecera (1993). In our model the locus of damage was visual, and the quality of the visual representations was such that multiple-choice naming was poor or at chance. However, the model showed semantic priming. This was because the patterns of activation reaching semantic levels of representation contained partial, noisy, and subthreshold information about the semantic identity of the stimulus. The resultant pattern in semantics would, on average, be more consistent with the semantics of that stimulus, or a semantically related stimulus, than with an unrelated stimulus, and hence tended to have a net facilatory effect on the semantic representation of identical or related stimuli, relative to unrelated stimuli. However, because much of this priming effect was caused by subthreshold activation in the semantics units, the semantic representations engendered by the poor-quality visual input were not, themselves, able to activate response representations such as names. This suggests a reason why indirect tests may be more sensitive to the residual capabilities of damaged systems: such tests generally require that residual knowledge affect the processing of a probe stimulus within the perceptual and semantic layers, as opposed to requiring that knowledge to be propagated through additional levels of representation for an overt response. The model of Farah, O'Reilly, and Vecera is sufficiently simple and generic that it is equally relevant to priming in neglect as in prosopagnosia.

The ability of neglect patients to use letters on the left sides of words to read, despite their inability to identify letters in equivalent spatial positions in nonword letter strings, is another phenomenon that might at first seem to imply that perception has been spared. However, like semantic priming, it has been explained in terms of impaired perception and interactions among graded representations. Mozer and Behrmann (1990) present a computer simulation in which an impairment of spatial attention results in impoverished stimulus information reaching stored word knowledge. By a completion-like process characteristic of distributed neural networks, the good-quality information from the right side of the word and the stored word structure combine with the poor-quality information from the left side of the word to "complete" or "clean up" the perceptual representation of the left side. Behrmann et al. (1990) present additional data from patients that support this account. Brunn and Farah (1991) demonstrated that the top-down effects of stored word representations on perception include an attenuation of the neglect during word reading. For example, patients named more colors, of different colored letters, when the letters made words than when they made nonwords. This implies that the preserved letter perception of Sieroff, Pollatsek, and Posner's neglect patients with words may not have been a case of preserved perception despite neglect but of a lessening of the neglect.

There are no independent demonstrations that conceptual matching of the kind documented by Berti et al. (1992) could be accomplished on the basis of impaired visual percepts. However, the same general principles invoked by Farah, O'Reilly, and Vecera (1992) and Mozer and Behrmann (1990) suggest that this finding, too, can be explained without hypothesizing normal visual perception and semantic representation, deprived of access to other brain systems necessary for conscious awareness. With the relatively light demands on representational quality made by the same/different matching task (Farah, Monheit, and Wallace 1991) and the additional constraints provided by a limited stimulus set, it seems at least possible that a poor-quality visual representation could be used to make reasonably

accurate judgments of the kind made by Berti et al.'s subject. In addition, Berti et al. point out that perception of the extinguished stimulus on "same" trials may have been semantically primed by the ipsilesional stimulus.

In sum, we find ourselves in roughly the same position with respect to explanations of unconscious perception in neglect and extinction as we did with explanations of covert face recognition. The current body of empirical knowledge is of great interest and utility in establishing certain important qualitative conclusions: that patients can be unable to report the identity of a neglected or extinguished stimulus but still manifest a fair degree of perceptual and even semantic knowledge about it. Yet these results are ambiguous with respect to the mechanisms by which neglect and extinction have these effects. The hypothesis that neglect and extinction spare perceptual and semantic processing, and affect only subsequent processing by some other system that plays a privileged role in mediating conscious awareness, seems inconsistent with the finding that perception is not normal in neglect and extinction (Farah, Monheit, and Wallace 1991). Demonstrations of semantic processing in neglect and extinction have not provided the kind of careful quantitation of effect sizes needed to determine whether semantic processing is normal or merely partially preserved. Thus, there is no decisive evidence in favor of the privileged role account and a small amount of evidence against it.

The available data appear compatible with the view of Kinsbourne (1988), Bisiach (1992), and Farah, Monheit, and Wallace (1991), that the effect of neglect and extinction is to degrade perceptual representation and thus attenuate its influence on the integrated state of the cognitive system as a whole. This conclusion could be strengthened, or disconfirmed, by further quantitative empirical studies of the degree of preservation of implicit processing and by computational simulations of a fuller range of the experimental paradigms used to demonstrate unconscious perception in neglect and extinction.

6 Implicit Reading in Pure Alexia

Patients with pure alexia are impaired at reading, despite being able to write normally and understand spoken words. To the extent that they can read at all, they appear to do so in a letter-by-letter fashion, spelling the word to themselves before they can recognize it. There are three main hypotheses about the cause of pure alexia and letter-by-letter reading:

1. Disconnection account: Visual input from the occipital cortices is unable to access left hemisphere language representations because of some combination of visual cortical damage and disconnection, and at most one letter at a time can be transmitted by alternative routes (e.g., Geschwind, 1965).

2. Word form hypothesis: Reading-specific knowledge of visual word structure has been destroyed, or is partly disconnected from earlier levels of visual representation such as letter representations, so that word recognition must proceed letter by letter, without the benefit of larger-scale word structure (e.g., Warrington and Shallice 1980).

3. Visual impairment hypothesis: The ability to encode multiple visual shapes of any sort rapidly and accurately, including but not limited to letters in words, is impaired, so that the most reliable strategy is to read letter by letter (e.g., Farah and Wallace 1991).

What the three hypotheses have in common is that there is some capacity essential for reading—linguistic knowledge in general, word forms in particular, or the ability to encode multiple visual shapes—that incoming visual information cannot gain access to because of either the loss of that capacity or disconnection from it. These analyses suggest that patients' oral reading abilities reflect their comprehension abilities, and indeed the everyday behavior and clinical test performance of pure alexics suggest that they cannot understand words that they fail to decipher by letter-by-letter reading.

This belief was first called into question by Landis, Regard, and Serrat (1980) in a case study of a patient recovering from surgery for a left occipital tumor. The patient was a pure alexic, and when tested within a week of the surgery, was unable to read words that were flashed for only 30 ms in a tachistoscope. However, he was able to point to objects in the room whose names had been presented in this manner. Unfortunately, he was tested with relatively few words on that day, and when retested a week later, he had lost his ability to point to the words' referents, even though his explicit reading performance had improved.

Representative Findings

Subsequent studies have examined the implicit reading of pure alexics more thoroughly. Patterson and Kay (1982) reported several unsuccessful attempts to elicit evidence of comprehension of briefly presented unread words in their pure alexic subjects. Shortly after, Grossi et al. (1984) presented evidence of disproportionately preserved picture-word matching in one case of pure alexia, and Shallice and Saffran (1986) described a comprehensive investigation of implicit word recognition and comprehension in another pure alexic. Shallice and Saffran's subject was able to perform lexical decision with relatively high accuracy on letter strings that were presented for 2 sec, which was too quickly for him reliably to identify the words explicitly. The subject was best at recognizing high-frequency words, and the closer the resemblance was between non-words and words, the harder it was for him to reject the non-words. For high-frequency words, he was able to classify 90 percent as words, and false-alarmed to only 38 percent of the pseudowords derived from the high-frequency words by changing one or two letters. An interesting exception to his generally good lexical decision ability was that he was unable to discriminate appropriately and inappropriately affixed words, for example, calling *applaudly* a word. Shallice and Saffran also demonstrated that their subject was able to make reasonably accurate semantic categorizations of words presented too briefly to be read. For example, he correctly classified 94 percent of unread place names as in or out of Europe, 93 percent of unread people's names as authors or politicians, and 87 percent of unread concrete nouns as living or nonliving.

Coslett and Saffran (1989) replicated and extended these findings with four new cases of pure alexia. Like Shallice and Saffran (1986), they found effects or word frequency on lexical decision and an insensitivity to affixes. They also found better lexical decision performance for concrete and imageable words and for content words, in general, relative to functors. In a subsequent study, Coslett and Saffran (1994) report that they tested one of their subjects on rhyme/nonrhyme judgments with written words and found that he performed at chance. Perhaps their most striking finding is that their subjects performed the implicit reading tasks more accurately with extremely brief exposures of the words, such as 250 ms, than with exposures of 2 sec. They interpret this in terms of the different strategies needed for implicit and explicit reading. Explicit letter-by-letter reading is incompatible with the strategy needed for implicit reading. Coslett and Saffran were able to foil subjects' attempts at letter-by-letter reading by using extremely short exposure durations and thereby enabled the alternative strategy to be expressed. This is consistent with Landis, Regard, and Serrat's original case study, in which implicit reading was lost as explicit reading improved. It also suggests a reason that Patterson and Kay not have detected any preserved implicit reading in their subjects: in attempting to maximize the chances of eliciting implicit reading in their subjects, they used words that were most likely to be recognized explicitly— that is, very short words and words that had been successfully read explicitly.

Awareness of Perception

Although patients' reports of their subjective experiences are not reported in great detail in most cases, there is a suggestion of some variability among cases. Whereas Landis, Regard, and Serrat and Coslett and Saffran's subjects generally complained of not even being able to see the stimuli clearly when they were manifesting implicit reading, Shallice and Saffran's subject was able to give rather detailed descriptions of how he performed the lexical decision and semantic categorization tasks. For lexical decision, he described "a process of looking at the whole length of the word and finding a combination of letters that can't be right, or looking at the whole word and seeing that it looked sensible." For semantic categorization, he reported getting a "first impression" of each word and, with a particular category in mind, deciding whether he "feels the first flash is right." Karen Klein and I have studied a similar patient, R.H., and with the help of Coslett and Saffran replicated all of their findings with him. In terms of his implicit reading performance, he seems to differ from their subjects only in that he is able to perform implicit reading at any exposure duration and never needs prompting to abandon the letter-by-letter reading strategy (at which he is extremely poor). Like Shallice and Saffran's subject, R.H. seems quite aware of the information he gleans during implicit reading and is reasonably confident of his responses.

From this very small and sketchy empirical base, I would tentatively suggest that for pure alexics who are able to abandon the letter-by-letter strategy and manifest implicit reading at relatively long exposure durations, there is no dissociation between the information that has been processed in implicit reading and awareness of having processed that information. The striking dissociation in these cases is between knowing the specific word presented and knowing its lexical status and semantic category. However, this dissociation does not have any direct implications for the relation between word perception and awareness thereof. Only when exposure durations must be extremely short, for subjects who would otherwise persist in letter-by-letter reading, do subjects manifest knowledge in their implicit reading performance that they themselves are not aware of possessing. Under these circumstances, however, the dissociation between performance and awareness may be attributable to the same mechanisms as subthreshold perception in normal subjects, with thresholds being higher for brain-damaged subjects.

Explanations of Implicit Reading

Because it is not clear whether implicit reading necessarily involves a dissociation between subjects' experience of reading and their performance, it is equally unclear whether explanations of making reference to the neural mechanisms of conscious awareness will have any relevance to the phenomena of implicit reading. Nevertheless, some of the proposed explanations can be applied either to performance/awareness dissociations or simply to accounting for the surprising pattern of performance in these patients.

Recall that several account of pure alexia exist and that they have in common some hypothesized capacity that is necessary for reading and is either damaged or disconnected from early visual representations of words. The capacity in question has been hypothesized to be language in general, word from knowledge in particular, or the ability to encode multiple visual shapes rapidly, and in all cases is assumed to be localized to the left hemisphere. The different accounts of implicit reading can be differentiated from one another with respect to the role played by these left hemisphere mechanisms.

The DICE model has been applied to implicit reading and suggests that implicit reading is simply normal reading, drawing as usual on the critical left hemisphere–mediated processing, deprived of access to other systems necessary for

conscious awareness (Schacter, McAndrews, and Moscovitch 1988). This is an example of a privileged role account.

Implicit reading has also been explained by a quality of representation account. Shallice and Saffran (1986) suggested that "lexical decision above chance but well below normal levels; recognition of morphemes but insensitivity to the appropriateness of their combination; limited access to semantic information [and] the failure to identify the stimulus explicitly, could conceivably be explained in terms of decreased levels of activation within the system that normally subserves explicit identification."

Finally, Shallice and Saffran also discuss the possibility that implicit reading reflects the operation of right hemisphere reading mechanisms, a view that Coslett and Saffran (1989) later endorsed. This constitutes a different type of privileged role account according to which the normal left hemisphere component of the reading system is uniquely endowed with the ability to mediate conscious awareness of reading (if the account is to be applied to awareness) and with the more fine-grained semantic distinctions and syntactic and morphological capabilities found to be lacking in implicit reading.

How does the available evidence adjudicate among these alternatives? The DICE model does not provide an explanation of the peculiarities of implicit reading with regard to part of speech, morphology, and concreteness, and so on, and is therefore not a very satisfactory account of the phenomenon. In contrast, the right hemisphere hypothesis seems particularly well-suited to explaining these findings. On the basis of independent evidence with split-brain patients and with normal subjects, the right hemisphere appears to be better at reading high-frequency and concrete words, and to be ignorant of morphology (see, e.g., Baynes 1990 for a review). The right hemisphere is also believed to be deficient at deriving phonology from print, consistent with the inability of one of Coslett and Saffran's subjects to make rhyme judgments on pairs of printed words, which Klein and I also observed with our implicit reader.

It is not clear exactly how well the hypothesis of a degraded reading system accounts for these phenomena. On the basis of general properties of neural network models, one might well expect higher-frequency words to be better preserved, on the basis of more initial learning. One might also predict greater preservation of concrete and imageable words, especially with the assumption that such words have more associated semantic attributes (Plaut and Shallice 1993). On these points, the quality of representation approach does well in accounting for some of the features of implicit reading. In contrast, the more regular mapping between orthography and phonology, relative to the mapping between orthography and semantics, would seem to predict the relative preservation of phonological judgments relative to semantic ones, just the opposite of what is observed, on grounds similar to the prediction concerning frequency effects: to the extent that sets of similar-looking words have similar-sounding pronunciations, the learning accomplished for each one will also generalize toward the others. Finally, the finding that shorter exposure durations lead to better implicit reading in at least some patients is awkward for a quality of representation account.

In sum, there is a good deal of relatively fine-grained information about implicit reading concerning the effects of different stimulus properties, instructions, and tasks, and these enable us to evaluate the different explanations of the phenomena that have been put forward. Pending some counterintuitive results concerning the modes of failure in damaged reading networks, the available evidence seems most consistent with right hemisphere mediation of implicit reading. However, dissociated awareness is not an essential aspect of implicit reading, and the mechanism of implicit reading is therefore not necessarily relevant to the neural bases of visual awareness.

7 General Conclusions

The goal of this final section is to review and compare the different syndromes in terms of the ways in which conscious awareness has been operationalized and the mechanisms that seem most likely to account for dissociated awareness, and to consider what general conclusions might follow about the relations between perception and conscious awareness.

Awareness and the Likely Mechanisms of Its Dissociation from Perceptual Performance in the Four Syndromes

There is a range of ways that the absence of patients' conscious awareness has been demonstrated in the four different syndromes reviewed here. Within the literature on blindsight, there are two common types of introspective report. Subjects often claim that they are guessing on the basis of no subjective experience, with resulting very low confidence. In other instances, subjects say that they are answering based on an experience but not one that they would classify as visual. Occasionally a specifically visual experience is reported. Prosopagnosic subjects are, of course, aware of when they are viewing a face. But they typically report no sense of familiarity when they view a face, perform poorly when trying to identify faces, and have low confidence in their identifications. In neglect and extinction, subjects may fail even to report detecting a stimulus. However, the only systematically collected data on awareness in the experiments demonstrating unconscious perception measure the ability to make various explicit judgments of such stimuli. Nevertheless, these data suggest a dissociation between awareness and performance, as explicit performance is poor, and confidence is generally low. Finally, in implicit reading, the dissociation that holds for all patients is between the ability to report a specific word and the ability to make judgments about the lexicality and semantic category of the word, not the dissociation between word perception and awareness of that perception. For two cases, at least, subjects are aware of the information they are using to make these judgments, and they have confidence in their answers. In sum, the four syndromes constitute a heterogeneous group from the point of view of awareness.

The four syndromes also appear to be heterogeneous from the point of view of mechanism. I will tentatively suggest that the groupings of the syndromes according to the status of awareness in each syndrome correspond with the groupings one might impose on the basis of the currently most likely mechanisms. For example, in blindsight, there appear to be two main types of subjective report, depending on the patient and task. There are also two main types of mechanism that have been proposed, without any intended mutual exclusivity. There is evidence consistent with both subcortical mediation of some blindsight abilities, and extrastriate cortical mediation of others, interpretable with privileged role and quality of representation accounts, respectively. Whether these two mechanisms can, in fact, be placed in correspondence with the two types of subjective experience is an empirical question for which I know of no direct evidence.

Covert face recognition in prosopagnosia and unconscious perception of stimuli in neglect and extinction are similar in that subjects are generally unaware of those aspects of the stimulus for which they manifest unconscious knowledge. The mechanisms responsible for the dissociations observed in these two syndromes are not well established because of a dearth of evidence capable of discriminating among them. However, both syndromes currently seem explainable in terms of a quality of representation account or, equivalently, in terms of the version of Kinsbourne's (1988) integration account that postulates a failure of integration due to low-quality representation. In prosopagnosia the poor quality of the representations is due to a loss of stored perceptual knowledge of faces, whereas in neglect and

extinction it is due to a more dynamic processing failure of the attention system.

Implicit reading seems distinct from all of the foregoing dissociations, both in terms of subjects' conscious awareness of the information they are able to extract from stimuli and in terms of mechanism. Unless word presentations are so brief that subjects report not seeing the words, implicit reading is accompanied by awareness of the information gleaned from the words. Although the issue of mechanism is far from settled, currently the right hemisphere reading hypothesis, a type of privileged role hypothesis, appears more plausible than a quality of representation hypothesis.

General Implications

One general conclusion that should be abundantly clear is that the four different syndromes reviewed here are unlikely to share a common explanation. Although there is a family resemblance among them, a close inspection reveals that the kinds of perceptual abilities and forms of experience that are preserved and impaired are not uniform. If we are still inclined to characterize them as demonstrating perception in the absence of conscious awareness (which seems reasonable to me, at least for the first three), then we may need to consider the possibility that the relation between conscious awareness and neural systems is itself not explicable by just one type of account. For example, we might conclude that enabling conscious awareness is a privileged role of certain cortical regions and that within these regions, a certain quality of representation is also necessary (thus denying consciousness to both the normal-quality functioning of the superior colliculus and the impaired functioning of cortical face representations).

Among all of the syndromes, there is none for which visual perception, in its totality, has been convincingly demonstrated to be normal or near normal. Therefore, there is no reason to view these syndromes as consisting of normal perception with conscious awareness merely stripped away. This, in turn, should deprive theories like DICE of their basic motivation: to explain a straightforward dissociation between perception and awareness of perception. Although the results of future research could reverse this situation, at present we lack evidence of such a straightforward dissociation. There is currently no evidence for a dedicated conscious awareness system, distinct from the systems that perform specific perceptual or cognitive functions.

The study of perception and awareness in brain-damaged patients is fairly new, particularly for syndromes other than blindsight, and our empirical knowledge of them is still rudimentary. Alan Allport urged in his 1988 article, "*What Concept of Consciousness?*," that researchers in this area do more conceptual analysis of their subject matter. This is certainly a highly desirable goal, especially with a subject matter that so tempts us to cross and confuse explanatory domains, such as the personal and subpersonal and the empirical and metaphysical. To this wise advice I would like to add a plea for more humble old empirical analysis as well. Are levels of performance on implicit perceptual tasks, in these various syndromes normal? Is performance on explicit tasks poor but above chance, or truly at chance by a reasonably powerful test? How do these measures relate to the likelihood of reporting some awareness of the visual information being tested? What additionally can we discover about the more fine-grained charateristics of unconscious visual performance that might provide further constraints on mechanistic explanations (e.g., the part-of-speech effects in implicit reading, the relative sizes of interference and facilitation in priming by faces in prosopagnosia and neglected stimuli in parietal-damaged patients, or the nasal/temporal asymmetries in blindsight)? These questions must be answered if we are to distinguish among the different accounts of the syndromes reviewed here and thereby distinguish their asso-

ciated views of the neural correlates of conscious awareness.

Notes

The writing of this chapter was supported by ONR grant N00014-93-I0621, NIMH grant R01 MH48274, NIH career development award K04-NS01405, and a grant from the McDonnell-Pew Program in Cognitive Neuroscience. I thank several colleagues who read an early draft of this chapter and made many helpful suggestions: Tom Carr, Max Coltheart, David Finkelstein, Morris Moscovitch, and Larry Weiskrantz.

1. This interpretation has been questioned by Marcel, among others, because of the preservation of semantic processing. This reasoning appears to be based on the assumption that impairment in visual processing is inconsistent with evidence of semantic processing. The simulation results described in the next paragraph demonstrate that this assumption need not be true.

References

Allport, A. (1988). What concept of consciousness? In A. J. Marcel and E. Bisiach (Eds.), *Consciousness in contemporary science*. Oxford: Clarendon Press.

Bauer, R. M. (1984). Autonomic recognition of names and faces in prosopagnosia: A neuropsychological application of the guilty knowledge test. *Neuropsychologia*, 22, 457–469.

Bauer, R. M. (1986). The cognitive psychophysiology of prosopagnosia. In H. D. Ellis, M. A. Jeeves, F. Newcombe, and A. Young (Eds.), *Aspects of face processing*. Dordrecht: Martinus Nijhoff.

Bauer, R. M., and Trobe, J. D. (1984). Visual memory and perceptual impairments in prosopagnosia. *Journal of Clinical Neuro-ophthalmology*, 4, 39–46.

Baynes, K. (1990). Language and reading in the right hemisphere: Highways or byways of the brain? *Journal of Cognitive Neuroscience*, 2, 159–179.

Behrmann, M., Moscovitch, M., Black, S. E., and Mozer, M. (1990). Perceptual and conceptual mechanisms in neglect dyslexia. *Brain*, 113, 1163–1183.

Berti, A., Allport, A., Driver, J., Dienes, Z., Oxbury, J., and Oxbury, S. (1992). Levels of processing for visual stimuli in an "extinguished" field. *Neuropsychologia*, *30*, 403–415.

Bisiach, E. (1992). Understanding consciousness: Clues from unilateral neglect and related disorders. In A. D. Milner and M. D. Rugg (Eds.), *The neuropsychology of consciousness*. San Diego: Academic Press.

Bisiach, E., and Rusconi, L. L. (1990). Break-down of perceptual awareness in unilateral neglect. *Cortex, 26*, 643–649.

Brunn, J. L., and Farah, M. J. (1991). The relation between spatial attention and reading: Evidence from the neglect syndrome. *Cognitive Neuropsychology, 8*, 59–75.

Bruyer, R., Laterre, C., Seron, X., Feyereisne, P., Strypstein, E., Pierrard, E., and Rectem, D. (1983). A case of prosopagnosia with some preserved covert remembrance of familiar faces. *Brain and Cognition, 2*, 257–284.

Burton, A. M., Young, A. W., Bruce, V., Johnston, R. A., and Ellis, A. W. (1991). Understanding covert recognition. *Cognition, 39*, 129–166.

Campion, J., Latto, R., and Smith, Y. M. (1983). Is blindsight an effect of scattered light, spared cortex, and near-threshold vision? *Behavioral and Brain Sciences, 3*, 423–447.

Chiarello, C. (1988). *Right hemisphere contributions to lexical semantics*. Berlin: Springer-Verlag.

Coslett, H. B., and Saffran, E. M. (1989). Evidence for preserved reading in "pure alexia." *Brain, 112*, 327–359.

Coslett, H. B., and Saffran, E. M. (1994). Mechanisms of implicit reading in alexia. In M. J. Farah and G. Ratcliff (eds.), *The neuropsychology of high-level vision: collected tutorial essay*. Hillsdale, NJ: Erlbaum Associates.

Cowey, A., and Stoerig, P. (1989). Projection patterns of surviving neurons in the dorsal lateral geniculate nucleus following discrete lesions of striate cortex: Implications for residual vision. *Experimental Brain Research, 75*, 631–638.

Crick, F., and Koch, C. (1990). Function of the thalamic reticular complex: The searchlight hypothesis. *Seminars in the Neurosciences, 2*, 263–275.

Damasio, A. R. (1990). Synchronous activation in multiple cortical regions: A mechanism for recall. *Seminars in the Neurosciences, 2*, 287–296.

De Haan, E. H. F., Bauer, R. M., and Greve, K. W. (1992). Behavioral and physiological evidence for cov-

ert recognition in a prosopagnosic patient. *Cortex, 28*, 77–95.

De Haan, E. H. F., Young, A. W., and Newcombe, F. (1987a). Faces interfere with name classification in a prosopagnosic patient. *Cortex, 23*, 309–316.

De Haan, E. H. F., Young, A. W., and Newcombe, F. (1987b). Face recognition without awareness. *Cognitive Neuropsychology, 4*, 385–415.

Farah, M. J. (1990). *Visual agnosia: Disorders of object recognition and what they tell us about normal vision*. Cambridge, MA: MIT Press/Bradford Books.

Farah, M. J., Monheit, M. A., and Wallace, M. A. (1991). Unconscious perception of "extinguished" visual stimuli: Reassessing the evidence. *Neuropsychologia, 29*, 949–958.

Farah, M. J., O'Reilly, R. C., and Vecera, S. P. (1993). Dissociated overt and covert recognition as on emergent property of lesioned attractor networks. *Pychological Review, 100*, 571–588.

Farah, M. J., and Wallace, M. A. (1991). Pure alexia as a visual impairment: A reconsideration. *Cognitive Neuropsychology, 8*, 313–334.

Fendrich, R., Wessinger, C. M., and Gazzaniga, M. S. (1992). Residual vision in a scotoma: Implications for blindsight. *Science, 258*, 1489–1491.

Gazzaniga, M. S. (1988). Brain modularity: Towards a philosphy of conscious experience. In A. J. Marcel and E. Bisiach (Eds.), *Consciousness in contemporary science*, Oxford: Clarendon Press.

Geschwind, N. (1965). Disconnexion syndromes in animals and man. Part II. *Brain, 88*, 585–645.

Gray, C. M., and Singer, W. (1989). Stimulus specific neuronal oscillations in the orientation columns of cat visual cortex. *Proceedings of the National Academy of Science, 86*, 1698–1702.

Greve, K. W., and Bauer, R. M. (1990). Implicit learning of new faces in prosopagnosia: An application of the mere exposure paradigm. *Neuropsychologia, 28*, 1035–1041.

Grossi, D., Fragassi, N. A., Orsini, A., De Falco, F. A., and Sepe, O. (1984). Residual reading capacity in a patient with alexia without agraphia. *Brain and Language, 23*, 337–348.

Hinton, G., and Plaut, D. C. (1987). Using fast weights to beblur old memories. *Proceedings of the Ninth Annual Meeting of the Cognitive Science Society*, Hillsdale, NJ: Erlbaum Associates.

Hinton, G. E., and Sejnowski, T. J. (1986). Learning and relearning in Boltzmann machines. In D. E. Rumelhart and J. L. McClelland (Eds.), *Parallel distributed processing: explorations in the microstructure of cognition.* Cambridge, MA: MIT Press.

Karnath, H. O. (1988). Deficits of attention in acute and recovered visual hemineglect. *Neuropsychologia, 26,* 27–43.

Karanath, H.-O., and Hartje, W. (1987). Residual information processing in the neglected visual half-field. *Journal of Neurology, 234,* 180–184.

Kinsbourne, M. (1988). Integrated field theory of consciousness. In A. J. Marcel and E. Bisiach (Eds.), *Consciousness in contemporary science.* Oxford: Clarendon Press.

Landis, T., Regard, M., and Serrat, A. (1980). Iconic reading in a case of alexia without agraphia caused by brain tumor: A tachistoscopic study. *Brain and Language, 11,* 45–53.

Marcel, A. J. (1983). Conscious and unconscious perception: Experiments on visual masking and word recognition. *Cognitive Psychology, 15,* 197–237.

Marshall, J. C., and Halligan, P. W. (1988). Blindsight and insight in visuospatial neglect. *Nature, 336,* 766–767.

Marzi, C. A., Tassinari, C., Aglioti, S., and Lutzemberger, L. (1986). Spatial summation across the vertical meridian in hemianopics: A test of blindsight. *Neuropsychologia, 24,* 749–758.

McGlinchey-Berroth, R., Milberg, W. P., Verfaellie, M., Alexander, M., and Kilduff, P. T. (1993). Semantic processing in the neglected visual field: Evidence from a lexical decision task. *Cognitive Neuropsychology, 10,* 79–108.

Mozer, M. C., and Behrmann, M. (1990). On the interaction of selective attention and lexical knowledge: A connectionist account of neglect dyslexia. *Journal of Cognitive Neuroscience, 2,* 96–123.

Patterson, K. E., and Kay, J. (1982). Letter-by-letter reading: Psychological descriptions of a neurological syndrome. *Quarterly Journal of Experimental Psychology, 34*A, 411–441.

Plaut, D. C., and Shallice, T. (1993). Deep dyslexia: A case study of connectionist neuropsychology. *Cognitive Neuropsychology, 10,* 377–500.

Poppel, E., Held, R., and Frost, D. (1973). Residual visual functions after brain wounds involving the central visual pathways in man. *Nature, 243,* 2295–2296.

Rafal, R., Smith, J., Krantz, J., Cohen, A., and Brennan, C. (1990). Extrageniculate vision in hemianopic humans: Saccade inhibition by signals in the blind field. *Science, 250,* 118–121.

Schacter, D. L., McAndrews, M. P., and Moscovitch, M. (1988). Access to consciousness: Dissociations between implicit and explicit knowledge in neuropsychological syndromes. In L. Weiskrantz (Ed.), *Thought without language.* Oxford: Oxford University Press.

Schiller, P. H., and Koerner, F. (1971). Discharge characteristics of single units in superior collicus of the alert rhesus monkey. *Journal of Neurophysiology, 36,* 920–936.

Shallice, T., and Saffran, E. (1986). Lexical processing in the absence of explicit word identification: Evidence from a letter-by-letter reader. *Cognitive Neuropsychology, 3,* 429–458.

Sieroff, E., Pollatsek, A., and Posner, M. I. (1988). Recognition of visual letter strings following injury to the posterior visual spatial attention system. *Cognitive Neuropsychology, 5,* 427–449.

Squire, L. (1992). Memory and the hippocampus: A synthesis of findings from rats, monkeys and humans. *Psychological Review, 99,* 195–231.

Stoerig, P., and Cowey, A. (1990). Wavelength sensitivity in blindsight. *Nature, 342,* 916–918.

Tranel, D., and Damasio, A. R. (1985). Knowledge without awareness: An autonomic index of facial recognition by prosopagnosics. *Science, 228,* 1453–1454.

Tranel, D., Damasio, A. R., and Damasio, H. (1988). Intact recognition of facial expression, gender, and age in patients with impaired recognition of face identity. *Neurology, 38,* 690–696.

Volpe, B. T., LeDoux, J. E., and Gazzaniga, M. S. (1979). Information processing of visual stimuli in an "extinguished" field. *Nature, 282,* 722–724.

Wallace, M. A. (1994). Unconscious perception in neglect and extinction. In M. J. Farah and G. Ratcliff (Eds.), *The neuropsychology of high-level vision: Collected tutorial essays.* Hillsdale, NJ: Erlbaum Associates.

Wallace, M. A., and Farah, M. J. (1992). Savings in relearning face-name associations as evidence for "covert recognition" in prosopagnosia. *Journal of Cognitive Neuroscience, 4,* 150–154.

Warrington, E. K., and Shallice, T. (1980). Word-form dyslexia. *Brain, 103,* 99–112.

Weiskrantz, L. (1986). *Blindsight: A case study and implications.* Oxford: Oxford University Press.

Weiskrantz, L. (1990). Outlooks for blindsight: Explicit methodologies for implicit processes. *Proceedings of the Royal Society of London,* B239, 247–278.

Weiskrantz, L., Sanders, M. D., and Marshall, J. (1974). Visual capacity in the hemianopic visual field following a restricted occipital ablation. *Brain, 97,* 709–728.

Young, A. W., Hellawell, D., and De Haan, E. H. F. (1988). Cross-domain semantic priming in normal subjects and a prosopagnosic patient. *Quarterly Journal of Experimental Psychology, 38A,* 297–318.

12 Understanding Consciousness: Clues from Unilateral Neglect and Related Disorders

Edoardo Bisiach

... if we did not have phenomenal experience we would not have a concept of consciousness at all.
—Anthony J. Marcel

Suspicion about consciousness as an object of scientific inquiry is rooted in the cultural prejudice due to which we regard physics as the paradigm of science *par excellence*. This prejudice may lead us to legislate away subjective experience from the scientific domain—a solution with which I have formerly sympathized (Bisiach 1988)—or vice versa (e.g., Nagel 1974), depending on where the emphasis is laid. Alternatively, it may induce outright denial of the subjectivity of consciousness, as exemplified by Rorty's statement, "The problem is not to take account of the special difficulty raised by the 'inside'-character of consciousness, but to convince people that there is no reason to grant that persons have more of an inside than particles" (Rorty 1982, p. 183).

Not many people, I surmise, are likely to be persuaded by Rorty. In fact, although I would hardly describe myself as having inside experience of the particles that constitute the complex physical system I am, I strongly oppose defining as "fictional" or "eliminable" the inside experience inherent in some states and processes of that system. This does not imply regarding that experience as a mysterious non-physical accompaniment of those states and processes. That experience is *my* "point of view." That's the way it is. The bat, I presume has its own (Nagel 1974; chapter 32). Why on earth should they be "eliminated?"

People who resist programmatic repudiation of their own consciousness may legitimately develop a specific scientific interest in it. They may enquire as to how phenomenal experience is structured; what distinguishes conscious from nonconscious states and processes *besides* subjective experience, that is, in neural and/or information processing terms; what conditions determine access to, and recess from, that experience; how conscious and nonconscious states and processes interact; and

so forth. The case of blindsight (Weiskrantz 1986) has been very instrumental in disciplining the urge and clarifying the scope of scientific inquiry on consciousness.

Recognizing consciousness as a proper object of scientific inquiry entails extending the paradigm of science beyond the standards of traditional physics. So what? It has often been claimed that the study of the mind is an "immature" discipline, but it would be more accurate to view it as the most problematic and least explored frontier of science, and it is probably our general conception of science that needs further maturation.

1 Methodological Issues

After having sanctioned, at least in principle, the project of studying one's own consciousness empirically, something should be said about tactics, expectations, and boundary conditions, while bearing in mind that it would be a mistake to be too prescriptive and exacting at the start. The only method I can envisage is the ascription of *phenomenal experience* to an observed individual, by analogy with the phenomenal experience of the observer. Commonplace as it might appear at first sight, this move is exceptional in science: what it affords, indeed, is neither an anthropomorphic metaphor nor a theoretical construct. It is not a metaphor because what is ascribed is meant to apply literally to the recipient. It is not a theoretical construct because the *observer's* consciousness is not such, and to the extent that the ascription of phenomenal experience to the observed individual *is not simply intended to explain his or her behavior*. What the move consists in, is the *hypothetical ascription* to another individual of a property, that the observer asserts to be real of him- or herself on the basis of inside information. This is the first step one must make in an attempt to gain insight into *one's own* conscious mentality and, secondarily, into that of other people. The transaction may be reversed, as it were, in the sense of the observer's hypothetical self-ascription of the behavior displayed by the observed individual, so that the question becomes what would it be like to be me, if I displayed such behavior. An advantage of this reversal of perspective is that it tallies with the condition in which I would *directly* learn about my consciousness if I were a subject, for example, of Marcel's (1983) experiments on non-conscious priming. While this condition can be realized, granting phenomenal experience to other people is the only possibility we are given to learn *indirectly* about consciousness when we study the consequences of brain lesions (unless we were *ourselves* suffering from dysfunctions such as blindsight or unilateral neglect). Trying to figure out what it would be like to be the person whose behavior we are studying, is not the "first step in the operationalist sleight of hand" (Searle 1980, p. 451). On the contrary, it prevents that step and its unavoidable consequence, namely, the replacement of consciousness by a conventional, impoverished, and more or less rigid substitute such as a piece of behavior or some putative functional components of the cognitive machinery (see Shallice 1988, p. 401, for a catalogue of proposals for such components, as well as for his own account). On the other hand, no matter how problematic and tricky it might be, reference to the observer's phenomenal experience obviates the need for the "objective" criteria in the absence of which sceptical conclusions are drawn about consciousness as a proper object of empirical investigation (e.g., by Allport, 1988).

The move I am advocating has obvious disadvantages. First of all, it could be claimed that it misses "the real thing," that is, what it would actually be like to be the observed individual (or what it would actually be like to be oneself as subject of the observed behavior). To the extent to which it is qualia-related, this claim is a truism with which it would be otiose to bother, because it misses the point altogether. There is no way in which a natural science of consciousness could have anything to do with qualia. Whatever experimental manipulations of its own brain processes a gifted bat could devise, they would not tell it the whole story about why being a bat is like what it is. There cannot be a science of those aspects of phenomenal experience that are manipulated in thought experiments such as qualia inversion. Our problem is to understand what, *besides* such aspects, distinguishes conscious activities of a system, in themselves and with respect to any other activity of the same system.

A more serious disadvantage of the move at issue is its being based, as it were, upon introspection by proxy. This is a severe handicap, considering the halo of disrepute surrounding direct introspection itself. For those who are not frightened away from the outset, this means investing a great deal of labor in an intricate trigonometry of the mind while still not being in a position to form a correct estimate of the validity of its results; it also requires the utmost caution in assessing such results. 'Introspection', to make things worse, is a potentially misleading term. On the one hand, it may induce questionable linguistic constructs (such as 'consciousness of consciousness' or 'reflexive consciousness') that suggest an enigmatic higher order consciousness rather than the mundane act of conscious thinking about conscious experience. On the other hand, it may be misused or misunderstood as meaning (fallible) self-interpretation. I use the term 'introspection' in the sense of bona fide self-witnessing and I think that what can first of all be expected from a scientific approach to consciousness is a closer view of what is being witnessed and a better estimate of the veridicality of its report.

2 The General Content of Consciousness and Its Spatiotemporal Structure

As regards what is self-witnessed, we must make a distinction between externally driven (i.e., perceptual) and internally driven phenomenal experience, such as mental images and thought. The first kind of experience is strictly constrained by, and anchored to, the properties of the perceived environment. The second is conceivable inherent in the largely parallel activities of a network of "fuzzy-jittery" neuronal assemblies whose surfacing in consciousness is *enthymematic*, in the sense that it leaves out a great deal of what gives meaning to what we are aware of. This is what makes internally driven experience almost impossible to describe except when we endeavor to entertain a relatively stable mental image or crystallize an idea into the format of inner speech. The notion of *fuzzy-jittery cell assemblies* is an admittedly vague expansion of Hebb's (1949) seminal proposal. Roughly, the term is intended to capture and combine four ideas;

1. The huge expanse of the busy neural network in which representational activity is implemented and which is beyond any realistic hope of panoramic assessment by neurophysiological means.

2. The imprecise correspondence of a cell assembly involved in thinking about a certain object to the cell assembly activated during perception of that object.

3. The co-occurrence of different cell assemblies, some of which may have segments of the relevant circuitry in common.

4. The instability of endogenous clusters of neural representational activity.

Phenomenal correlates of points 1–4 are suggested to be the sketchiness and possible overlap of the fleeting conscious experiences resulting from endogenous neural activity at any given instant. As an explanatory construct, the notion of fuzzy-jittery cell assemblies has the obvious problem of being too versatile. It is hoped that its main virtue may be that of warning against some models of the brain's representational activities, offered by AI-inspired theorists, that are often too clear-cut and rationalistic inasmuch as they relate more to the final product than to the process of thought.

Both kinds of phenomenal experience, perceptual and internally driven, are spatio-temporal. They are spatial in two senses: *phenomenological* and *information processing*. In the phenomenological sense, their sensory or sensory-like content extends in an egocentric space; a space that is likely to be represented by the brain in an analogue medium (Bisiach and Berti, 1987). Within this space, consciousness may either be focal or (borrowing the term from Kinsbourne 1988) panoramic, or focal with a panoramic periphery. In the information processing sense, phenomenal experience has spatial structure insofar as it is most likely to be assembled from activities distributed among centralized processors. These processors work more or less in parallel, following a complex interactive schedule by which, no matter how stabilized it might appear in a short interval of time, the content of consciousness is continually restructured.

In saying that conscious experience is the result of processing distributed in neural space, I do not simply refer to the horizontal separation of the various sensory modalities, nor to the fact that, within single modalities, there are spatially organized neural maps conforming to spatial and even to non-spatial features of environmental stimuli (see, e.g., Merzenich and Kaas 1980, as regards the distribution of intensity- and pitch-sensitive cells in the auditory cortex). I refer in particular to the vertical organization along the input-output axis that offers the possibility of sensory-premotor interaction in the generation of conscious experience. The dependence of consciousness on such an interaction is theoretically most significant and is suggested, by way of example, by the effect of response modality on awareness of sensory stimuli. This effect may give rise to phenomena that, unlike other phenomena of interference such as backward masking, are not explicable in terms of a modulation of incoming information at a response-independent preconscious level, and therefore question any pre-theoretical intuition of consciousness as a flat interface dividing efferent from afferent processes.

Neuropsychological investigation offers several examples of such an effect. In right brain–damaged patients, awareness of contralesional visual stimuli may to a variable extent be impaired by damage to visual pathways or due to the dysfunction(s) underlying unilateral neglect of space. So far, it is often impossible to assess the contribution of each of these factors to the disorder. However, it has been found that awareness of contralesional stimuli may appear more impaired if manual choice-reactions, rather than verbal responses, are used to monitor detection (Bisiach et al. 1989). In our tachistoscopic experiment patients had to react to elementary visual stimuli—200-ms illumination of a single diode in either hemifield, or of two diodes, one in each hemifield—either by verbally reporting the number of stimuli, or by pressing a key if they had perceived a single stimulus, witholding their response to double stimuli and on blank trials. Whatever may be the correct explanation of the reduced rate of detection of contralesional stimuli we recorded in right brain–damaged patients—both in conditions of single and in conditions of double simultaneous stimulation—when a manual as opposed to verbal response was required, this result shows that the different ways in which sensory information has to be processed in order to result in different kinds of intentional activity may differently affect access to consciousness.

A further example is provided by another experiment in right brain–damaged subjects suffering from unilateral neglect (Bisiach et al. 1990a). It is well known that such patients usually bisect horizontal lines to the right of the objective midpoint. In our experiment, we asked patients to execute the task by means of a pulley device operating in two different conditions: a congruent (canonical) condition in which a pointer was *directly* moved from either end of the line to its subjective midpoint, and a non-congruent condition in which the pointer was *indirectly* moved along the line by a hand movement *in the opposite direction*. The amount of the rightward bisection error was found to decrease, to an extent varying

among patients, in the non-congruent as opposed to the congruent condition. We interpreted the result as revealing two different factors of neglect, respectively related to input analysis and premotor programming. The latter corresponds to Watson et al.'s (1978) concept of 'directional hypokinesia', that is, reluctance to carry out actions toward the contralesional side of egocentric space. More precisely, we concluded that in the congruent condition of the task perceptual and premotor factors contributed to displacing the subjective midpoint in the same direction, that is, rightward, whereas in the non-congruent condition the rightward displacement of the subjective midpoint resulting from faulty perceptual analysis was to a variable degree counteracted by the inertness of the leftward hand-movement required to move the pointer rightward. Here too, phenomenal experience appears to be influenced by variables that relate to premotor programming of intentional actions, that is, to a stage traditionally conceived to be later than the representation in consciousness of sensory information on the basis of which actions are initiated. We found the premotor component of the dysfunction to be relatively more pronounced in patients whose lesions extended to the frontal lobe, or to subcortical structures held to have motor functions, than in patients with exclusively retrorolandic lesions. As regards neglect, this is in agreement with a distinction conjectured by Watson et al. (1978) and Mesulam (1981). As regards consciousness, this differentiation affords a glimpse of the anatomical arrangement of the distributed mechanism by which input and output stages of information processing interactively frame perceptual judgments.

A dependence of perceptual awareness on response mechanisms is also suggested by the results of a recent investigation by Tegnér and Levander (1991). Eighteen patients with left neglect were asked to execute a variant of Albert's (1973) cancellation task in which the subject has to cross out with a pencil a number of short lines drawn on a sheet of paper. Patients had to perform first in the canonical condition, and then in a condition in which the visual array was left-to-right inverted by means of a 90° mirror device, while direct view of their hand and of the sheet of paper was prevented by a bench. In this condition, the subject's hand must operate on the left side of the sheet of paper to cross out the lines he sees on the right side of the visual display, and vice versa. In the canonical condition, as usual, the patients only crossed out lines lying on the right side. The inverted condition revealed three different patterns of behavior. Ten patients only crossed out the lines they could *see* on their right; to do that their (right) hand had to cross the midline and work on the left side of the sheet of paper. Their neglect was therefore interpreted as being due to *perceptual* factors. Four patients, on the contrary, only crossed out lines lying on the right of the sheet of paper (as they had done in the canonical condition), although those lines were seen through the mirror as lying on the left side. In these patients neglect appeared thus to be due to a (broadly conceived) *premotor* dysfunction. The remaining four patients, in the mirror-inverted condition, only crossed out the lines in the middle. Their performance was interpreted by the authors as being caused both by perceptual and premotor factors of neglect. In agreement with our results, Tegnér and Levander found evidence of 'directional hypokinesia' only in patients whose lesion involved the frontal lobe or the basal ganglia.

Perhaps "directional hypokinesia" is also responsible for the fact, observed by Halligan and Marshall (unpublished; cited by Allport 1988), that a neglect patient may seem unaware of the full extent of the horizontal line he is asked to bisect, whereas he seems to be aware of it when he has to use that same line as the base of an imaginary square of which he is asked to draw the right-hand (vertical) side.

There are still other examples of the role of response mechanisms in gating access to consciousness in patients with unilateral neglect. Joanette et al. (1986) and Halligan and Marshall

(1989) described patients whose ability to detect left-side stimuli was more impaired when they had to respond with their right hand than when they had to respond with their left.

Finally, an impressive demonstration of the influence of response factors on reports of visual stimuli in blindsight has been given by Zihl and Von Cramon (1980). Their study was replicated and expanded both in blindsight and normal subjects by Marcel (1990). In his Experiment 2, Marcel asked his patient GY to react either by blinking or by pressing a button with his right forefinger, or by saying "yes" when he "felt" that a light had come on in his blind field. Blink responses were found to be more sensitive than finger responses; verbal responses were least sensitive. Similar results were obtained in two normal subjects by using near-threshold visual stimuli.[1]

The data so far reviewed suggest that conscious experience of external stimuli cannot be separated from, and is affected by, the whole situation in which they are perceived, including any response to such stimuli (no matter whether spontaneous or, as in most experimental conditions, complying with instructions). If so, we must conclude that the mechanisms by which conscious experience of a relatively complex situation is achieved are indeed widely distributed in neural space and subdivided into several processors. None of these, so far as we know from observation of brain-damaged subjects, centralizes in itself the role of conscious homunculus.

The division of preconscious labor among several processors with no sole gateway to consciousness entails a relativity of the timing of consciousness as well as the possibility of ongoing rearrangement of what is being experienced. In normal people, a rearrangement of this kind is suggested by the results of an unpublished experiment by Cumming, cited by Allport (1988). In that experiment, a row of five letters was presented to the subjects. The letters flashed one after another in rapid sequence and in a spatio-temporal order such as to produce masking of the letters in the second and fourth locations in the row. Subjects had to press one key if a target letter was present and another key if it was not. Under time pressure, when the target letter was in a masked position subjects on some occasions correctly responded by pressing the "present" key and then apologized for what they believed was an error. The phenomenon is similar to the abortive movement which, under conditions of double simultaneous stimulation, I observed some brain-damaged patients to make toward the stimulus undergoing extinction before indicating the location of the antagonist stimulus. In both cases, however, the problem arises as to whether the subjects had responded on the basis of a fleeting sensory experience or had produced a non-consciously triggered reaction.

The kind of problems arising from the diachronic structure of conscious experience is illustrated by the following example. In an experiment done some years ago (Bisiach et al. 1985), patients with left hemineglect had to react to single 200-ms illuminations of red or green diodes in either visual hemifield by pressing a lit response-key of the same color with their right forefinger. There were four response keys, one red and one green on each side of the apparatus which lay in front of the patient. On each trial, two keys of different colors, one on the left and one on the right, came on simultaneously with the flash of light and remained lit until one of them was pressed. Stimuli were flashed during visual fixation on the center of the frontal panel of the apparatus; after their appearance, the patient was free to move his eyes in any direction. There were four stimulus-response conditions, two spatially uncrossed and two crossed, with 16 trials for each of them (left-side stimuli requiring left-side response; left-side stimuli requiring right-side response; etc.). Catch trials in which the response keys were turned on in the absence of any stimulus were interspersed among regular trials. The rate of correct reactions to left (contralesional) stimuli was found to be more severely reduced when the response was required on the left-side

key than when required on the right-side key. Reactions to stimuli appearing in the right visual hemifield (i.e., in the hemifield unaffected by the brain lesion) were almost errorless when the response was required on the right side; when it was required on the left side, however, the patients made many errors. The latter were mainly due to an erroneous ipsilateral response, either to the unlit key of the correct color or to the lit key of the incorrect color, but in several instances the patients gave no response at all, as if they had not perceived the stimulus in the *intact* visual field.

This paradoxical phenomenon was most evident in patient FS, who had a lesion involving the frontal lobe and anterior subcortical structures. Whereas his performance was errorless on trials in which right-side stimuli required responses to the right, on the 16 trials on which he should have reacted to the same type of stimuli by pressing the left key, FS gave only one correct response. On several such occasions he asserted, as he did on catch trials, that no stimulus had appeared. Given his correct performance on trials with right-hand stimuli requiring responses to the right side of the panel, it is plausible to assert that he had been phenomenally aware of those stimuli, at least for a brief interval, also when he denied the occurrence of some of them in trials requiring responses to the left side. What is not possible to say is whether any trace of phenomenal experience persisted at the moment when he uttered his denial. Perhaps, all conscious memory of the stimulus had been suppressed by inhibitory processes caused by not having found the appropriate response-key on the preferred side. Alternatively, his denial could have been confabulated, as suggested by Shallice (1988, p. 398) over a preserved phenomenal experience of the stimulus. It is worth noting that a paradoxical denial of stimuli present on the *ipsilesional* side of egocentric space has also been found by Tegnér and Levander in the above mentioned study. Those of their patients who showed 'directional hypokinesia', after having crossed out in the mirror-inverted condition only the lines which lay on their right but were seen on their left, denied the presence of further lines, thus ignoring those which were present on the right side of the visual array.

If one considers these puzzling data, Allport's (1988) doubts about the possibility of giving a full answer to some questions about consciousness appear justified. Nevertheless, it is evident that this sceptical conclusion is drawn from data that tell us a great deal about what phenomenal experience consists of.

3   Unity and Disunity of Consciousness

One may still feel inclined to play down the import of the distributed origin of phenomenal experience suggested by the data reviewed above and claim that what really matters is the coherence of that experience. However, the unity that at first glance distinguishes most of everyday phenomenal experience breaks down progressively if we take into consideration the transition from illusions to delusions and other more dramatic dissociations, some of which, though of marginal occurrence, are not of a pathological nature. A touch of dissociation is already present in common perceptual illusions, where phenomenal experience may peacefully coexist with the conscious belief in its lack of veridicality. The dissociation becomes much more impressive when an illusion overwhelms a belief of which the rationality is still acknowledged by the subject. I have two favourite examples. One is the patient mentioned by Hécaen (1972), who remarked on her inability to be convinced by her own sight that the upper limb joined to the left side of her body belonged to her. The other is LA-O, a patient of mine. Shortly after the onset of a right hemisphere lesion, while taking for granted the ownership of her left shoulder, she inferred that the left upper arm was also her (because it was attached to her left shoulder), but was unsure about her elbow and lower arm and firmly refused to admit that the left hand was part of her body. During recovery, she seemed to entertain con-

temporaneously opposing doxastic attitudes toward the same proposition, as can be observed in patients recovering from schizophrenia: averments of true and false beliefs about the ownership of her left upper limb appeared in close temporal proximity and were equally suffixed, as it were, with a short-lived look of tense puzzlement.

It might be objected that what occurs in such instances is not a split of phenomenal awareness but an alternation of normal and abnormal experiences which does not undermine the notion of the unity of consciousness. There are, however, situations in which the dissociability of phenomenal experience seems undeniable. Dreams, indeed, are sometimes experienced as real and unreal at the same time, as happens when one finds solace in the *arrière-pensée* that the terrifying event one is involved in is in fact a dream. A double awareness, in dreaming, may sometimes be likened to two different characters on the stage. This is exemplified by the following personal anecdote. I once dreamt that I was being told by my teacher Alexsandr Romanovich Luria that a certain patient had undergone an intracarotid sodium amytal test a few days earlier at the Burdenko Neurosurgical Institute. "Which side?", I asked. Alexsandr Romanovich hesitated an instant and then answered, somewhat dryly: "Both sides, of course." On which I felt ashamed of my silly question: *of course*, I "remembered" patients always undergo sodium amytal injection on both sides when a test is required.

The above example, however, demonstrated that, even when under particular circumstances the content of awareness reveals the disunity of its source, a great deal of integration may be achieved through mechanisms we are still very far from knowing. In my dream, a mechanism of some sort had done the job of the playwright, giving coherence to incompatible pieces of cognitive activity through the expedient of dramatization, that is, by meaningfully dividing between two individuals what would have been incoherent in one. In an old-time party game, a haphazard cluster of words may directly combine or be edited into surrealist prose such as "*Le cadavre exquis goûtera le vin nouveau.*" Likewise, when the elements of what is going to be the content of phenomenal experience swarm from the endogenous activity of the nervous system in a disorderly way, they might be integrated by the intervention, as it were, of the brain's editorial staff. In the awareness of the external world, the coherence of phenomenal experience largely reflects the coherence of the environment; a slight amount of retouching is evident in phenomena such as the visual completion occurring in the blind spot, the phoneme restoration effect (Warren 1970), or intriguing illusions (reviewed by Dennett and Kinsbourne 1991) such as the color changes during illusory movement or the "cutaneous rabbit" phenomenon. In the case of internally generated experiences, on the other hand, coherence is probably achieved with reference to a model set by previous exposure to the environment and through induction; this leaves much room for inventiveness but imposes constraints, vestiges of which are retained even in dreaming and schizophrenia. Conformity with such a model is likely to require a great deal of pruning and readjusting of preconscious activity, whereas it may admit nonveridical intrusions in the recollection of previous experiences. At any rate, the process of coherent cross-integration of phenomenal experience does not require a mind within the mind— let alone a mind above the mind—any more than a resident architect is required for the shaping of a cluster of H_2O molecules into a snow crystal. The result of this process may be a more or less complete temporary relaxation achieved through a distributed counterbalance of different competing representations arising within the expanse of the neural network. The fact that in wakefulness thought processes are radically different from those occurring in dreaming suggests that there are progressive levels of cross-integration. This, however, does not imply the endorsement of an intelligent homunculus responsible for the highest level: (relative) rationality may still be conceived

to result from a virtual machine distributed across a vast expanse of the cerebral cortex.

4 Levels of Processing of Conscious Representations

The foregoing attempt to clarify what it means for phenomenal experience to have spatio-temporal structure and to dispel homuncular preconceptions still leaves unanswered the question as to what level of processing characterizes the representation of individual contents of consciousness. This aspect of the problem has been discussed at length by Jackendoff (1987). If I understand it correctly, his *Intermediate-Level Theory of Consciousness* states that: (a) the contents of phenomenal experience are sensory-specific; (b) as regards perceptual awareness, their structure is neither an unelaborated neural reproduction of the most peripheral stimulation pattern, nor a "central" (categorical and amodal) interpretation of that same pattern. In other words, the contents of phenomenal experience consist of parsed and selected information preserving the instant, modality-specific properties of objects in a singular, definite orientation with respect to the sensory surface. Thus, for example, phenomenal awareness of a word is held by Jackendoff to correspond to the phonological structure of that word, rather than to its acoustic spectrum or to its meaning, and phenomenal awareness of a visual object to Marr's concept of "$2\frac{1}{2}$-D sketch" of that object, rather than to a "3-D model" of the latter. I largely subscribe to Jackendoff's views, to which, however, I will add a few comments.

It is true that, in the normal case, we are not separately conscious of, for example, the intermediate product of the dedicated processors that in the case of vision analyze in parallel single features of objects such as shape, location, color, and motion. However, when damage to all but one of such processors leaves a single feature being processed, awareness of that isolated feature is still possible, as for example in patient BRA, studied by Warrington (1985, and personal communication). While being severely impaired as regards visual acuity, shape perception, and visual location due to brain infarctions incurred during open-heart surgery, BRA was fully aware of the color of an object though unable to attribute definite shape or location to that "feeling" of color.

As regards the lack of any phenomenal experience of more abstract structures such as types or categories, even within single sensory domains, this might be due to the fact that such conceptual entities, as opposed to tokens, have no existence in the brain, except as procedures available to *catalogue* or *generate*, when required, modality-specific instances of any category through activation of determinate cell assemblies. The application of procedures of this kind to incoming sensory information might underlie capabilities such as perceptual constancies and intersensory matching. Their endogenous activation might give rise to mental images, dreams, and hallucinations. Jackendoff argues that if phenomenal experience of a *pereceived* token went beyond the intermediate-level structure (which, in the case of vision, would be something like Marr's "$2\frac{1}{2}$-D sketch") we would not be conscious of a seen cube as something different from a felt cube. But this might be due to the fact that, whatever might be the ultimate structural level of conscious percepts, our being conscious of a seen cube as something different from a felt cube depends on lower-level structures being organized into, *but not superseded by*, higher-level structures. On the other hand, there is no earmark left by earlier sensory processing upon the contents of phenomenal awareness, on the basis of which to explain why an imagined or hallucinated cube is experienced as seen or felt rather than amodal. Activities of the mind underlying uninstantiated concepts such as 'cubeness' do not figure, *per se*, among the contents of phenomenal experience. We may know them, as it were, by *our own* description, rather than by acquaintance. This is why I would

qualify such activities as 'abstracting' (rather than 'abstract') and 'generative', and call them 'procedures' involved in the construction of the contents of phenomenal experience, rather than 'structures' (in order to avoid confusion with that which is being constructed).

Finally, granted that what Jackendoff calls "intermediate-level structure" is the skeleton of what we experience, the question remains open as to the extent to which such a structure can be teased apart from what goes beyond it, that is, from the unavoidable experiential halo aroused by associations of any kind. As soon as I happen to hear "If" played by Art Tatum, my experience differs in important respects from what it would be if I were born in the 1960s.

Within the specific scope of this chapter, however, the main problem is whether reaching an "intermediate-level structure" is a sufficient condition for access to consciousness or, if it is not, what else is needed. Do "nonconscious" masked primes in experiments such as those of Marcel (1983) and Allport et al. (1985) fail to access consciousness despite having been processed up to an intermediate-level structure or do they immediately recede from it, without leaving any trace, as a consequence of backward masking? To what extent are neglect patients nonconscious of stimuli lying on the side of space contralateral to their lesioned hemisphere when their behavior shows that such stimuli are processed up to the level at issue?

My patient EB, who suffered from right brain damage, was apparently unaware of the left side of written words and pronounceable non-words, so that, for example, she read STAGIONE (season) or RAGIONE (reason) or CARNAGIONE (complexion); yet she would correctly name the letters composing the left side of unpronounceable non-words such as XRTMNGIONE, although stimuli belonging to the three categories were randomly interleaved (Bisiach et al, 1990b). Did the left side of words and pronounceable nonwords have short-lived permanence in consciousness, or did they have no access to it at all? These questions seem to take for granted that access to consciousness is an all-or-nothing step. Probably it is not. In the case of EB we had an observable input, that is, the written word, and an observable output, that is, the spoken word. What was in between is conjectural. Earlier stages of visual processing were evidently unimpaired, as demonstrated by her ability to react differently to pronounceable and unpronounceable strings of letters. Yet, when she read real words and pronounceable nonwords the output did not match the input. A possible explanation of EB's behavior is that what occurred in her head was the wrong construction of an incremental hypothesis about the input. Due to the dysfunction underlying her hemineglect, that hypothesis was eventually dominated by the right side of the input, thus giving rise to phenomena of neglect or completion, unless an interrupt was brought about by the strangeness of an unpronounceable string of letters. However, given the data, we cannot say anything definite about EB's phenomenal experience during the process leading up to the output, all the more so because there is no reason to believe that processes of that kind are linear. All we can say is that, as in the case of nonconscious priming, information that has reached a relatively advanced stage of cognitive processing may not have access to (or permanence in) consciousness.

In unilateral neglect a dissociation between graphemic and word awareness may even be found. Whereas we have no definite evidence about conscious experience of the content of the graphemic buffer as regards EB's neglect and completion dyslexia, RB, a neglect patient described by Hillis and Caramazza (1990), was at least temporarily aware of graphemes in the word-segment undergoing neglect or completion; invited to read words (e.g., VILLAGE), he would first spell them correctly and, immediately after, make a neglect or completion error in reporting the whole word (MILEAGE).

Patients suffering from unilateral neglect may provide further evidence about the possible lack of consciousness of visual information the processing of which has reached what Jackendoff calls "intermediate level." This evidence comes from simple experiments in which two drawings are shown, one above the other, differing in a conspicuous detail on the left (neglected) side. When it is established that the patient is unable to detect that difference, he is invited to indicate his preference for one of the two drawings. If he objects to the silliness of being asked to opt for one of two identical drawings, it is necessary to induce him to choose. The preference test is repeated a number of times, with one of the two drawings placed at random above or below the other. In the original experiment by Marshall and Halligan (1988), the drawings were outlines of two houses, of which one had bright red flames on the left side; asked which house she would prefer to live in, the patient, despite having found the two pictures identical, consistently chose the non-burning house. We attempted to replicate Marshall and Halligan's results in four patients, with three additional pairs of drawings (Bisiach and Rusconi 1990; see fig. 12.1). The preference test was not always possible, either because some patients were able to indicate the relevant difference in a pair, or because they were not able to identify some of the drawings. When it was possible, the result was not always in agreement with that obtained by Marshall and Halligan. Of the three patients who were asked to show their preference for one of the two houses, one gave inconsistent responses and two consistently preferred the burning house. On the contrary, the unbroken glass was consistently preferred by the two patients who could be tested with that pair. The pot containing flowers was also preferred in all trials by the only patient to whom that test could be given. Our patients offered spontaneous comments on their choices, which appeared in some instances to be made on the basis of real (though negligible) differences on the right side of two paired drawings. In other instances, however, the alleged difference was clearly confabulated. The extent of the confabulation was impressive when it referred, for example, to the different number of windows or the different layout of the two houses. Taken together, the results suggest that infor-

Figure 12.1
From Bisiach and Rusconi 1990.

In an attempt to force the patients to find the relevant difference existing between the two drawings of each pair, we asked them to trace the contour of each drawing with the tip of their right forefinger. Altogether, we were able to collect the results of 10 administrations of this tracing task. In one instance, the procedure was effective in revealing the differing detail to the patient; its effectiveness was dubious in two, but in the remaining seven the correct execution of the task was of no help. Hard to believe as it might appear, a patient could slide his fingertip through the flames without noticing them, or trace the contour of the left side of the broken glass without realizing that it was broken.

The phenomenon we observed on the tracing task is most significant because it reveals a severe disorder in the very area to which the patient's gaze is directed. The patients never lost sight of the path their finger had to follow; not even when that path was half concealed, as was the case with the drawing in which flames were superimposed on the outline of the house. Nevertheless, they seemed unaware of the left-side differences they came across in tracing the contour of the drawings, even when—as in the case of the two houses or of the two flowerpots—such differences lay, for an interval of time, to the *right* of the moving fingertip. This finding suggests that neglect, in some instances, may be related to the (observer-relative) left side of a visual object, rather than to retinotopic co-ordinates, or other self-centered co-ordinates, independent of the content of the visual field.

It is well known that people can engender variable gradients of spatial attention independent of the line of their gaze. Therefore, and in agreement with Kinsbourne's theory (1987), neglect patients' *covert* attention is likely to be polarized toward the ipsilesional side of the visual field and to decrease—with a more or less continuous gradient—toward the fixation point and beyond, reaching its minimum in the most contralesional area. Some experiments by Posner and associated (Posner et al. 1982) indeed suggest that in unilateral neglect covert attention cannot easily be

mation about a prominent detail, the presence of which is not acknowledged by the patient, may influence his appraisal of the configuration in which that detail is located. In some instances, information about that detail appears to be processed up to the level at which meaning is captured.

5   Breakdown of Awareness of Stimuli in Central Vision

Our replication of Marshall and Halligan's (1988) study was supplemented by a very elementary task from which we obtained unexpected results.

disengaged from the ipsilesional side when conative attention should be addressed to a more contralesional area. In left hemineglect, this may explain the paradoxical extinction of a parafoveal stimulus in the right (unaffected) half-field, when a more peripheral (i.e., rightward) stimulus is simultaneously presented in *that* half-field (Bisiach and Geminiani 1991). Accordingly, it may be conjectured that an inability to disengage covert attention from the right side of a drawing might cause extinction-like phenomena as regards left-side details even when such details come into central vision. Obviously, however, an extinction hypothesis cannot explain the patients' failure to discover any left-side difference in a pair of drawings even when the difference lies in a contour they are able to trace. On the other hand, the failure can hardly be interpreted as being due to a faulty comparison depending on a disorder of visual memory restricted to contralesional space: in the pictures of the burning house, the broken glass, and the torn banknote, indeed, the differing details were anomalies worthy of attention in their own right.

Although what we have learned from blindsight warns against forming rash opinions as regards the amount of phenomenal experience of sensory information guiding willed movements, it would seem preposterous to assert that an unfamiliar outline could be traced by the patient's finger with no perceptual awareness of the edge along which the finger has to proceed. It seems more reasonable to suggest that *mindful* processing of the right side of a visual object shaded, in our patients, into *absent-minded* processing of the left side, where sensory information would fail to achieve integration into a fully fledged conscious representation. This might also be the case when the object is the patient's own body. A common explanation would thus apply to our findings relative to the tracing task and to the puzzling instances in which neglect patients deny their hemiplegia even when they look at the examiner's demonstration of its presence.

A similar phenomenon is likely to affect perception of the whole environment. This is strongly suggested by what Crowne et al. (1981) found in the monkey after unilateral frontal eye-field ablation. Before fully recovering from the effects of the operation, the monkeys reacted to menacing stimuli approaching from either side by retreating to the opposite side of the cage. However, if two such stimuli were simultaneously presented, one on each side, the avoidance reaction appeared only to the ipsilesional stimulus, so that the animal retreated near to the contralesional. (Preoperatively, double stimulation caused double avoidance and the monkey would retreat to the middle of the cage.) "Frequently," the authors reported, "the operated monkeys would turn their heads briefly to look at the proximate threat object, but immediately returned to regard the distal threat. These contralateral-gaze glances were not accompanied by shifts in position in the cage" (p. 179). This is all the more significant because when the monkey looked at the contralesional threat the ipsilesional was out of sight, thus ruling out any explanation in terms of *sensory* competition. Evidently, however, the ipsilesional threat was not out of mind, otherwise the monkeys would have reacted to the contralesional as they would if it had been presented alone. Full awareness of the contralesional threat thus appeared to be barred by competition at a higher representational level.

6 Unilateral Distortion of the Content of Subjective Experience

The contralesional disorder of representational activity appearing as a consequence of damage to crucial areas of one side of the brain may not only manifest itself in the form of the more or less complete eclipse from consciousness of one side of egocentric space (within one or more domains of representational content) that characterizes unilateral neglect in the strict acceptance of the term. Productive phenomena such as pathological completion, confabulation, and somatoparaphrenia (Gerstmann 1942) may also emerge. For reasons that are still unknown, such productive phenomena are most infrequent as regards the content of far extrapersonal space, although some patients claim, for example, that the side opposite to the hospital environment they correctly perceive on their right belongs to their home and behave in accordance with this claim (e.g., by calling for members of the family they assume to be there). In near extrapersonal space, pathological completion of one side of perceived words and drawings is much more frequent, but the imported portion is, as a rule, totally compatible with what is correctly reported from the other side. It is worth noting that in this case the phenomenon seems to be the result, as it were, of conceptual confabulation rather than of sensory completion; this, at least, is the impression one gets from the reading disorders of my patient EB and patient RB of Hillis and Caramazza (1990). Processes of a different kind are likely to underlie the paradoxical leftward displacement of the subjective midpoint observed in neglect patients when they bisect very short lines (Halligan and Marshall 1988; Tegnér et al. 1990). One of these patients reported seeing a "shadow-line" extending leftward from the line he had to bisect (Tégner, personal communication).

Productive misrepresentation of the contralesional side is much more frequent in bodily space. Its implications for the study of neural correlates of consciousness have been discussed elsewhere (Bisiach and Geminiani 1991) and I will not deal with them here, except to attenuate my former opposition to a psychodynamic interpretation of unawareness and denial of neurological disorders such as hemiplegia and hemianopia, and to make a cursory remark on the impetus, as it were, of contents that are gated from consciousness in these pathological conditions.

I still believe that at the root of unawareness or denial of hemiplegia and hemianopia lies a dysfunction of the brain's representational activity circumscribed to one side of the body, rather than the concealment of extremely disturbing evidence. However, I agree that, at least as regards denial of hemiplegia and disavowal of the paralyzed limbs, part of the patient's behavior reflects the need to come to terms with the pathological representation of one side of his or her body. That is to say that the contents of the patient's consciousness corresponding to manifestations ranging from "personification" of the paralyzed limbs (Critchley 1955) to the most abstruse forms of somatoparaphrenia are likely to combine active and reactive components; the former being the direct product of the lesion of a critical area of the neural network, the latter issuing from the spared areas of that same network.

An issue that has so far been neglected is whether and to what extent the phenomenal experience and the behavior of the patients who are oblivious of neurological disorders, or utterly deny them, is influenced by contents that find no access to conscious representation. Although its assessment requires further data and reflection, this issue is worth attention, given the results of investigations in normal subjects that demonstrate different utilization of sensory input depending on whether or not its content reaches consciousness (Marcel 1980). Contents held in incommunicado might still influence phenomenal experience in patients showing unilateral neglect and related disorders. Such nonconscious contents, rather than an (originally) content-free emotional attitude caused by the lesion, might be responsible for the phenomena of levophobia that can sometimes be observed in patients with left hemineglect and/or misrepresentaton. Misoplegia (Critchley 1953), that is, hatred for the paralyzed limbs, is a well-known instance of levophobia. The latter, however, can also manifest itself in regard to the extrapersonal environment, for example, when the patients assert a dislike for things on their left, or simply behave as if they felt such a dislike.

7 Conclusions

In this chapter, I have argued—against the Cartesian tradition (Fig. 12.2)—that there is no

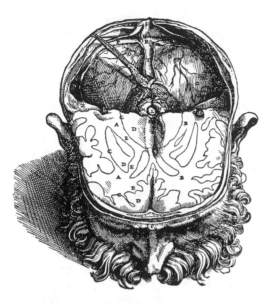

Figure 12.2
The pineal gland (L) in Vesalius's *De Humani Corporis Fabrica* (1543).

definite brain center for conscious experience (sections 2 and 3). Clinical and experimental data collected in patients suffering from unilateral spatial neglect and related disorders, indeed, suggest that conscious experience rests entirely on a virtual mechanism distributed over brain circuits that are still very poorly understood. This distribution, however, seems to be both horizontal (across and within sensory modalities) and vertical, insofar as conscious experience appears to be shaped not only by afferent occurrences but also by the kinds of actions that happen to be undertaken on the basis of such occurrences. The spread of such mechanisms in neural space entails the possibility of local failures and the dissociability of conscious experience into contrasting states. Clinical neurology provides dramatic examplex of both kinds of disorder: the former is evident in the (cognitively irremediable) lack of awareness of one side of space or of the consequences of a brain lesion; among those most

suggestive of the latter are the mirror-reversal of the lack of awareness of one side of visual space found by Tegnér and Levander and the doxastic doubleness that may affect particular beliefs on a background of normal cognitive activities (Bisiach and Geminiani 1991).

In section 4, I touched on the issue of the level of processing and representational contents (as regards the conscious/nonconscious dichotomy) and argued that patients may be apparently unaware of what lies on the side opposite to the brain lesion despite its having been processed up to a high level, even to the level, perhaps, at which meaning is captured. It might be objected that neglect and pathological completion of the contralesional side of visual stimuli could be the result of a false revision of earlier conscious veridical percepts, as suggested by the correct reading of the left side of unpronounceable nonwords by my patient EB; an "Orwellian" revision, as Dennett (1991) would put it. The validity of this conjecture, however, is seriously questioned by the finding that neglect patients may adequately react to features of stimuli of which they seem to be totally unaware even *while* they focus attention on those features: such patients may in fact be quite consistent in "liking" the drawing of an unbroken glass better than that of a broken one while being unable to tell the difference between the two of them even when they trace the contour of the broken edge (section 5). All in all, there seem to be at present no available data about the precise way in which conscious and nonconscious representational structures might differ.

Finally, I raised (without even attempting to answer it) the question as to whether anomalous experiences about the contents of the contralesional side of personal and extrapersonal space might be an effect of nonconsciously processed features of such contents (section 6). This, I believe, is one of the main tasks left for future investigation.

Another fundamental task for future investigation is to ascertain to what extent the failure underlying unilateral neglect and misrepresentation is due to structural unavailability (or subversion, or disconnection) of the representational medium, to withdrawal of processing resources from it, or to its inhibition by competing brain processes. Firmer grounds will be available for comprehensive theories of the brain mechanisms of conscious representation, in proportion to the development of our knowledge of the mechanisms underlying neglect and related disorders, as well as those that underlie their compensation.

Let us now turn to the crucial issue (section 1). To what extent do the data reviewed in this chapter contribute to an understanding of consciousness? If we select each time just one of the possible operational definitions of consciousness (e.g., the ability to report verbally the contents of our mental processes), then it is clear that such data tell us a great deal. Conflicting conclusions, however, seem to be reached if we refer to different operational definitions, since we have confronted instances in which what is verbally reported fails to be witnessed by nonverbal responses (Bisiach et al. 1989) and instances in which the opposite is true (e.g., Marcel 1990). But here indeed seems to lie the main moral we can draw from the corpus of empirical data so far collected: any intuition to the contrary notwithstanding, consciousness is far from being unitary.

The aim stated at the beginning of the chapter, however, was somewhat more ambitious. It made explicit reference to the understanding of phenomenal experience, rather than of an operationalized consciousness. Now there are, as we have seen, extreme instances in which trying to make inferences about the phenomenal experience of a patient may seem to be hopeless, given the degree of incoherence of the observed behavior. Such is the case, for example, as regards the delayed denial of visual stimuli in the unaffected field by patient FS (Bisiach et al. 1985), or the denial of lines lying in the unaffected visual field by Tegnér and Levander's patients showing "directional hypokinesia." There is much less difficulty as regards the different rates of perceptual report that characterize different kinds of response. Here, the observed behavior may be quite similar to that of normal subjects tested with near-threshold stimuli. In this case, the evaluation of data in terms of phenomenal experience is much safer and any residual doubt could be cleared up by first-person experience. Between these two extremes lies an area of uncertainty where reference to phenomenal experience, no matter how utopian in its aims, might at least guide retreat to an intelligent, non-eliminative operationalism.

Acknowledgments

The preparation of this chapter has greatly benefited from my participation in the workshop on Human Consciousness and the Brain. I gratefully acknowledge my debt to Dan Dennett who organized the workshop, the small group of participants who contributed in making it productive and pleasurable, and the Rockefeller Foundation, who gave us magnificent hospitality at the Villa Serbelloni in Bellagio at the end of March, 1990. David Milner, Mick Rugg, and the Russell Trust/ Wellcome Trust Symposium gave me the incentive to lay down, for what they are worth, some of the ideas that have grown out of my work with brain-damaged patients. Joe Bogen, Ray Jackendoff, and Tony Marcel made very valuable comments on a preliminary draft; I hope I have not misinterpreted them in the final version.

Note

1. It must be noted that Marcel used *simple* nonverbal reactions, whereas we (Bisiach et al. 1989) used *choice* nonverbal responses. This may explain why nonverbal indicators of perceptual awareness were more sensitive than verbal indicators in his experiments and less sensitive in ours (cf. the interpretation we gave in our paper).

References

Albert, M. L. (1973). A simple test of visual neglect. *Neurology*, 23, 658–664.

Allport, D. A. (1988). What concept of consciousness? In A. J. Marcel and E. Bisiach (eds), *Consciousness in Contemporary Science*. Oxford: Clarendon Press.

Allport, D. A., Tipper, S. P., and Chmiel, N. R. J. (1985). Perceptual integration and postcategorical filtering. In M. I. Posner and O. S. M. Marin (eds), *Attention and Performance XI*. Hillsdale NJ: Erlbaum.

Bisiach, E. (1988). The (haunted) brain and consciousness. In A. J. Marcel and E. Bisiach (eds), *Consciousness in Contemporary Science*. Oxford: Clarendon Press.

Bisiach, E., and Berti, A. (1987). Dyschiria. An attempt at its systemic explanation. In M. Jeannerod (ed.), *Neurophysiological and Neuropsychological Aspects of Spatial Neglect*, Amsterdam: North-Holland.

Bisiach, E., and Geminiani, G. (1991). Anosognosia related to hemiplegia and hemianopia. In G. P. Prigatano and D. L. Schacter (eds), *Awareness of Deficit after Brain Injury*, pp. 17–39. New York: Oxford University Press.

Bisiach, E., and Rusconi, M. L. (1990). Break-down of perceptual awareness in unilateral neglect. *Cortex*, 26, 643–649.

Bisiach, E., Berti, A., and Vallar, G. (1985). Analogical and logical disorders underlying unilateral neglect of space. In M. I. Posner and O. S. M. Marin (eds), *Attention and Performance XI*. Hillsdale NJ: Erlbaum.

Bisiach, E., Vallar, G., and Geminiani, G. (1989). Influence of response modality on perceptual awareness of contralesional visual stimuli. *Brain*, 112, 1627–1636.

Bisiach, E., Geminiani, G., Berti, A., and Rusconi, M. L. (1990a). Perceptual and premotor factors of unilateral neglect. *Neurology*, 40, 1278–1281.

Bisiach, E., Meregalli, S., and Berti, A. (1990b). Mechanisms of production control and belief fixation in human visuospatial processing: clinical evidence from unilateral neglect and misrepresentation. In M. L. Commons, R. J. Herrnstein, S. M. Kosslyn and D. B. Mumford (eds), *Quantitative Analyses of Behavior. Vol. IX: Computational and Clinical Approaches to Pattern Recognition and Concept Formation*. Hillsdale NJ: Erlbaum.

Critchley, M. (1953). *The Parietal Lobes*. London: Hafner Press.

Critchley, M. (1955). Personification of paralyzed limbs in hemiplegics. *British Medical Journal*, 2, 284–286.

Crowne, D. P., Yeo, C. H., and Steele Russell, I. (1981). The effects of unilateral frontal eye field lesions in the monkey: Visual-motor guidance and avoidance behaviour. *Behavioural Brain Research*, 2, 165–187.

Dennett, D. (1991). *Consciousness Explained*. Boston: Little, Brown.

Dennett, D. and Kinsbourne, M. (1991). Time and the observer. *Behavioral and Brain Sciences*, 15, 183–247.

Gerstmann, J. (1942). Problems of imperception of disease and of impaired body territories with organic lesions. *Archives of Neurology and Psychiatry*, 48, 890–913.

Halligan, P. W. and Marshall, J. C. (1988). How long is a piece of string? A study of line bisection in a case of neglect. *Cortex*, 24, 321–328.

Halligan, P. W. and Marshall, J. C. (1989). Laterality of motor response in visuospatial neglect: A case study. *Neuropsychologia*, 27, 1301–1307.

Hebb, D. O. (1949). *Organization of Behavior*. New York: Wiley.

Hécaen, H. (1972). *Introduction à la Neuropsychologie*. Paris: Larousse.

Hillis, A. and Caramazza, A. (1990). The effects of attentional deficits on reading and spelling. In A. Caramazza (ed.), *Cognitive Neuropsychology and Neurolinguistics: Advances in Models of Cognitive Function and Impairment*. Hillsdale NJ: Erlbaum.

Jackendoff, R. (1987). *Consciousness and the Computational Mind*. Cambridge MA: MIT Press.

Joanette, Y., Brouchon, M., Gauthier, L. and Samson, M. (1986). Pointing with left vs right hand in left visual field neglect. *Neuropsychologia*, 24, 391–396.

Kinsbourne, M. (1987). Mechanisms of unilateral neglect. In M. Jeannerod (ed.), *Neurophysiological and Neuropsychological Aspects of Spatial Neglect*. Amsterdam: North-Holland.

Kinsbourne, M. (1988). Integrated field theory of consciousness. In A. J. Marcel and E. Bisiach (eds), *Consciousness in Contemporary Science*. Oxford: Clarendon Press.

Marcel, A. J. (1980). Conscious and preconscious recognition of polysemous words: Locating the selective effects of prior verbal context. In R. S. Nickerson (ed.), *Attention and Performance VIII*. Hillsdale NJ: Erlbaum.

Marcel, A. J. (1983). Conscious and unconscious perception: Experiments on visual masking and word recognition. *Cognitive Psychology*, 15, 197–237.

Marcel, A. J. (1988). Phenomenal experience and functionalism. In A. J. Marcel and E. Bisiach (eds), *Consciousness in Contemporary Science*. Oxford: Clarendon Press.

Marcel, A. J. (1990). Slippage in the unity of consciousness, or, to what do perceptual speech acts refer? Poster presented at Russell Trust Symposium, St Andrews, Scotland, September 1990.

Marshall, J. C. and Halligan, P. W. (1988). Blindsight and insight in visuo-spatial neglect. *Nature*, 336, 766–767.

Mesulam, M.-M. (1981). A cortical network for directed attenton and unilateral neglect. *Annals of Neurology*, 10, 309–325.

Merzenich, M. M. and Kaas, J. H. (1980). Principles of organization of sensoriperceptual systems in mammals. *Progress in Psychobiology and Physiological Psychology*, 9, 1–41.

Nagel, T. (1974). What is it like to be a bat? *Philosophical Review*, 83, 435–450.

Posner, N. I., Cohen, Y. and Rafal, R. D. (1982). Neural systems control of spatial orienting. *Philosophical Transactions of the Royal Society. B*, 298, 187–198.

Rorty, R. (1982). Comments on Dennett. *Synthese*, 53, 181–187.

Searle, J. R. (1980). Minds, brains and programs. *Behavioral and Brain Sciences*, 3, 417–457.

Shallice, T. (1988). *From Neuropsychology to Mental Structure*. New York: Cambridge University Press.

Tegnér, R. and Levander, M. (1991). Through a looking glass. A new technique to demonstrate directional hypokinesia in unilateral neglect. *Brain*, in press.

Tegnér, R., Levander, M. and Caneman, G. (1990). Apparent right neglect in patients with left visual neglect. *Cortex*, 26, 455–458.

Vesalius, A. (1543). *De Humani Corporis Fabrica*. Basel: J. Oporinus.

Warren, R. M. (1970). Perceptual restoration of missing speech sounds. *Science*, 167, 392–393.

Warrington, E. K. (1985). Visual deficits associated with occipital lobe lesions in man. *Pontificiae Academiae Scientiarum Scripta Varia*, 54, 247–261.

Watson, R. T., Miller, B. D. and Heilman, K. M. (1978). Nonsensory neglect. *Annals of Neurology*, 3, 505–508.

Weiskrantz, L. (1986). Blindsight. *A Case Study and Implications*. Oxford: Clarendon Press.

Zihl, J. and Von Cramon, D. (1980). Registration of light stimuli in the cortically blind hemifield and its effect on localization. *Behavioural Brain Research*, 1, 287–298.

13 Modularity and Consciousness

Tim Shallice

1 The Relevance of Modeling Consciousness

There is an even more severe conceptual difficulty for the modular view of mind than how it can operate efficiently. The efficiency problem can at least be posed in a "mechanistic" framework closely related to the framework in which "modularity" itself is expressed. A more complex issue is why the human cognitive-processing system, which is apparently modular, should have the property of being conscious, unlike most modular systems—for example, present-day complex machines.

The obvious strategy within a modular approach is to identify some aspects of the operation of some particular module—say, its input—as conscious experience. However, one is then faced with the question of what could be so special about the processing in that module as to give its input such exceptional status. No real progress appears to have been made. One appears merely to be taking the first step on the road to infinite regress.

The situation is worse than it appears. Not only is there no apparent line of attack on how and why a modular system might be conscious, but an explanation of consciousness within the conceptual framework of modularity would probably need to be "functionalist" (Putnam 1960). In other words, consciousness would correspond to some "system-level" property (i.e., information-processing characteristic), of the brain and not to some aspect of its material constituents. In wait for any explanation of this form that might be produced, there already lie the prepared tank traps of philosophical criticism. Attempting to refute a functionalist explanation is at present a popular enterprise for philosophers (e.g., Block 1980; Searle 1980).[1]

There is a simple and basically behaviorist response to these types of conceptual difficulty.

Worry about consciousness has historically been a snare and a delusion in psychology. What, it might be asked, is so special about the system-level of explanation of human thought that it needs to incorporate consciousness? After all, a number of philosophical positions on consciousness are in conflict with the idea that consciousness has any particular relation to an information-processing level of explanation of cognition. Consciousness has been conceived of as a property of non-material entities, as in classical dualism, of more molecular constituents of the brain, such as matter itself, and also of persons (e.g., Strawson, 1959), all in conflict with any priority for an information-processing explanation. Why should cognitive psychology and neuropsychology not progress as nicely as, say, neurophysiology without being concerned about consciousness?

The obvious response is that consciousness exists. Historically, there have been other phenomena as basic and obvious that in their time have been as inexplicable as the existence of consciousness or were explained in a way antithetical to modern scientific thought. Life is an obvious example, but planetary motions or fire would be others. It seems ahistorical to assume that consciousness is some freak phenomenon totally resistant to a scientific account. Yet for such an explanation to be achieved, the existence of awareness must be interpretable in terms of some scientific level of explanation of human cognition or of the more basic processes that are required for it to operate. No progress has been made in linking consciousness with concepts relevant to these more basic processes, those of physics, biology, or physiology.[2] The conceptual framework that cognitive psychology offers is tantalizingly different. The names of its subject areas—memory, attention, perception, and so on—come from terms denoting mental states. In its practice, cognitive psychology even requires that subjects understand such terms in order to carry out the instructions of experiments, and it uses procedures that require subjects to comment on their mental states (see, e.g., Ericcson and Simon 1985).

The most convincing concrete support for the need to understand consciousness in system terms would be provided by the existence of unexpected phenomena within the domain of system-level explanations of human cognition that are best describable in terms of consciousness. Consciousness would then become part of the scientific phenomena requiring explanation and not just a philosophical luxury. In fact, two of the neuropsychological phenomena that have created general interest in recent years—blindsight and the split-brain—have been compelling for this very reason.[3] They will be considered in the following sections, together with lesser known neuropsychological phenomena relating to knowledge without awareness.

This argument has an Achilles heel. It can be reversed. Bisiach (1988) has recently claimed that there are neuropsychological phenomena that show the limitations of consciousness as a scientific concept. These phenomena have led him to argue that "we may have to learn to live together with the idea that some of the questions set by commisurotomy [the split-brain operation], blindsight, unilateral neglect of space etc. will remain forever unanswerable." His arguments will be considered in section 5.

2 Blindsight

One of the most commonplace observations in neurology is the existence of a scotoma, a loss of visual capacity over a certain region of the visual field. It is known that it can arise from lesions to the striate cortex (area 17) (Holmes 1918; Teuber, Battersby, and Bender, 1960). In its most extreme form, the patient has *no* visual experience of anything in that area of the field; in other cases, the patient can be aware of stimuli, but only when they move or flicker (Riddoch 1917). One of the most interesting developments in modern neuropsychology has been the discovery of an unexpected potential in some patients for the visual processing of stimuli presented in a scotoma.

The initial investigation was made by Pöppel, Held, and Frost (1973). They studied four patients, each of whom had a visual-field defect involving at least one quadrant of the visual field. The patients were tested along an axis in one of the quadrants in which they were totally blind. A brief flash was presented, together with a tone. When the patients heard the tone, their task was to move their eyes to the position in the visual field where they guessed the flash had been presented. The patients could make a voluntary eye movement in the general direction of a stimulus projected into the scotoma, even though they denied seeing the stimulus. All four subjects showed a slight tendency to move the eyes farther when the flash was presented 25° eccentrically than when it was presented 10° eccentrically. Pöppel et sults across subjects in a rather arbitrary fashion. Although the correspondence between stimulus and response positions was above chance, there was only a weak correlation in three of the four patients.

A more extensive study of an individual patient, DB, was made the following year by Weiskrantz, Warrington, Sanders, and Marshall (1974). As blindsight is a condition that does not manifest itself in an identical way in different patients, it is worth considering one prototypic patient in more detail. DB is by general consent the prototypic patient.

DB had had an arteriovenous malformation in the right occipital pole removed at the age of 26. The initial experiments on his blindsight were conducted in the year following the operation. At the time they were carried out, he had no visual experience in the left visual field, except for a crescent of preserved vision at the periphery of the upper quadrant. All experiments at that time were performed on the horizontal meridian in order to remain in the entirely blind part of the field.

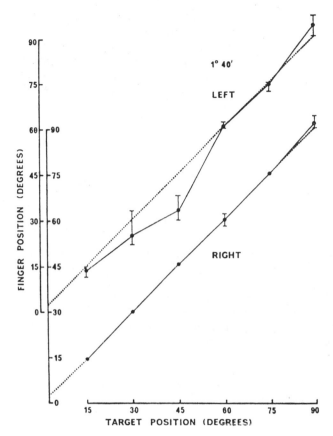

Figure 13.1
Mean finger-reaching responses to stimuli flashed to different positions in the sighted (*right*) and blind (*left*) half-fields of DB. The left results are plotted against the upper of the two scales. Reprinted from Weiskrantz, Warrington, Sanders, and Marshall (1974); *Brain 97:* 714; by permission of Oxford University Press.

The procedure adopted by Pöppel et al. (1973) was also used with DB. In locating a light turned on in different positions in his blind field by means of a voluntary eye movement, DB showed only a non-significant trend towards matching his eye movement to the light position. However, when the response of making a voluntary eye movement was replaced by one of the reaching to the position of the light with a finger, he was remarkably accurate (see figure 13.1).[4] In addition, DB could discriminate a long horizontal from a

long vertical line exposed in the lower quadrant of the blind half-field at over 97% accuracy, even for an exposure duration of less than 100 msec. Any unreliability of fixation is not therefore a relevant factor. DB could also discriminate a circle from a cross at 90% accuracy. Moreover, he showed an acuity threshold using gratings in his blind half-field that was no more than double that obtained in his normal sighted field.

When the stimulus crossed the border of his scotoma, he was very reliable about reporting it.

Otherwise, throughout these experiments, DB reported having no visual experience. When repeatedly pressed, he said at times that he had a "feeling" about a stimulus pointing in a particular direction or that it was "smooth" (the circle) or "jagged" (the cross). He repeatedly, though, stressed that he had no sensation of seeing and that he was always guessing.

Since these experiments were done, a number of related studies have been carried out (e.g., Perenin and Jeannerod 1978; Barbur, Ruddock, and Waterfield 1980; Zihl 1980).[5] None of the patients reported in these studies is as clear a case of blindsight as DB. These authors do, though, agree on two conclusions. The first is that there are patients who can use visual information for a number of purposes, such as reaching to a point, without any visual experience being available to guide the act. Second, it is believed that these functions depend not on information transmitted from the retina via the lateral geniculate to the visual cortex, but on information transmitted by other pathways, probably including one that involves a subcortical structure—the superior colliculus.

In a critical review article, Campion, Latto, and Smith (1983) have challenged both these conclusions. They have argued that all the phenomena claimed for blindsight can be attributed to one or other of two processes. The first is that light from the target might have spread to portions of the retina unrelated to the scotoma as a result of reflection off structures external to the eye or off ones within the eye, such as the retina itself (the "scattering" hypothesis). The second is that there may be spared, if abnormally functioning, tissue within the cortical region mediating visual analysis of the area of the field covered by the scotoma (the "residual striate vision" hypothesis). In addition, they argued that the phenomenological accounts given by the patients are inconsistent and irrelevant.

Light scattering within the eye is a far from negligible phenomenon (see, e.g., Bartley 1941). The weight that Campion et al. gave to this effect

as an explanation of blindsight is based on two types of experiments they carried out on normal subjects.[6] One experiment attempted to mimic the reaching results shown in figure 13.2 using the blind field of a simulated hemianopia in a normal subject. Both the left eye and the right visual field of the right eye of the subject were occluded. Targets were then presented to the subject's right visual field. This meant that the subject could not see the targets directly, so that any detection would have to depend on scattered light. Localization ability under these conditions was described as "very accurate," but it is clearly less impressive than that of DB. Campion et al. also reported experiments on normal subjects on the detection of stimuli projected onto the blind spot using this as an analogue of a scotoma. They held that any intact capacity in this situation must also depend on the use of scattered light. However, as Barbur and Ruddock (1983) pointed out, there are great differences in degree of scatter between the blind-spot situation, in which stimuli must be very close to the intact field, and those in which stimuli are projected well into a hemianopic field.[7]

A variety of additional arguments have been given to counter the scattered-light claims.[8] Two particularly compelling ones are available with DB. First, Weiskrantz (1986) pointed out that DB was able to detect *black* stimuli on a white ground—for instance, in the *X* versus *O* discrimination—and that the testing of acuity used a grating with light intensity modulated sinusoidally. Indeed, with the latter technique, acuity could be *better* in part of the blind field than in more peripheral parts of the sighted field, although this was never the case for form discrimination. It is very hard to see how these findings could be explained by scattered light.

A second procedure devised by Weiskrantz (1988) used the fact that a stimulus projected onto the blind spot in the *blind* field would not produce a neural response to light. However, light would be reflected to other parts of the retina. Therefore, if DB were using scattered light, he should have

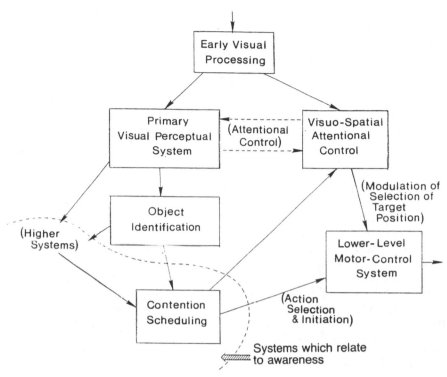

Figure 13.2
Functionalist model of subsystems involved in reaching to objects detected by normal or blindsight vision. It is presupposed that the visuo-spatial attentional control system is also linked to the system controlling the direction of action.

been able to detect the stimulus. DB could not detect a stimulus projected onto the blind spot in the blind field at above chance level when it could be detected well in other parts of the field defect. DB's blindsight would appear to be a real phenomenon.

The other line of criticism made by Campion et al. (1983) remains more problematic. They claimed that there is no strong evidence that the blindsight phenomenon can be attributed to the operation of operation of subsystems not involved in conscious perception. Thus they point out that over time, DB's scotoma reduced in size (see Weiskrantz 1980) and that parts of the field previously used for blindsight testing functioned

normally later. This, they argued, suggests recovery of function of parts of the visual cortex and hence is compatible with blindsight having been mediated earlier by the visual cortex operating in a damaged but not totally impaired fashion.

What this account fails to explain is the close match between what DB can and, more critically, cannot do and how monkeys perform after striate cortex lesions. DB, in particular, could not perform above chance on any pattern-discrimination test that could not be mediated by a simple sensory cue, such as orientation (Weiskrantz 1988). Thus he could not carry out the simple discrimination of a square from a rectangle.... Moreover, the functions that have been shown to return in the monkey after visual cortex lesions, although not to the same level as before the operation—spatial localization, orientation detection, spatial frequency discrimination, and very simple shape discrimination (see Pasik and Pasik 1982)—are those that can be carried out by DB in a scotoma (see Weiskrantz 1980). Overall, the idea that "blindsight" depends on a processing route that involves structures other than the visual cortex seems most plausible.

Finally, how do these behavioral and anatomical issues relate to questions of awareness? Campion et al. (1983) advocated the standard behaviorist position that as there is no way of verifying the fidelity of the report of personal experiences, reports of phenomenal experience should not be a part of scientific psychology. The inappropriateness of using reports of experience as scientific evidence was, they claimed, shown by the way that the reports given by blindsight patients in test sessions are very heterogenous.

The reports given by these patients, when light is presented to their impaired field, do differ. They appear to fall into three classes. DB, for instance, showed a variation in what he experienced within his scotoma (Warrington, personal communication). In one part, which he called the "dead" part of his field, he never had any form of experience. His responses were complete guesses. A second type of experience, that mentioned earlier, occurred in another part of the blind field. When pressed, he admitted some form of awareness of the stimulus, but it was not described as a *visual* awareness. Thus he reported feelings like a "feeling of smoothness" for the *O* in the *X* versus *O* discrimination. Similarly, two of Zihl's (1980) subjects reported that they could "feel" the correspondence between target and eye position.

It is noteworthy that in the scattered-light experiments performed by Campion et al. (1983) on the blind spot of normal subjects, the subjective reports were not of these two types. Subjects reported instead some form of *visual* experience. A "halo of light" was perceived, and the experience of the light "waxed and waned." Reports of

visual experience do also occur with blindsight subjects; such reports constitute the third type of experience described by the patients. Often, they arise when intense light sources like flash bulbs are used (e.g., Perenin and Jeannerod 1978), where light scatter might indeed be producing the experience. Occasionally, visual experiences can occur in these patients with lower intensity stimuli. For instance, DB's scotoma reduced in size in the years after he was initially tested, and within the reduced scotoma, he now acknowledged *seeing* something under certain condition—namely, when moving stimuli were used.

It is now clear that the difference in visual experience between normal subjects and blindsight patients is not an absolute one. Nor is it predictable under what conditions any given subject will have a visual experience (see Weiskrantz 1980), although moving stimuli and, particularly, the beginning or end of movement seem to be the most likely conditions to produce it. Yet good performance on tasks that use visual input in the absence of *visual* experience occurs reliably across tasks and across blindsight patients. It is not reported in scattered-light experiments in normal subjects. The heterogeneity of experiential reports of blindsight patients is therefore no grounds for ignoring their most surprising characteristic. The absence of *visual* experience when a response can be made to a visually presented stimulus is a phenomenon that requires explanation.[9]

It is clear that blindsight is not an artifact. Certain types of judgments or actions can be based on input processes that differ from those involved in normal object identification. Most critically for the argument of this chapter, these judgments are not associated with a visual experience.

Our everyday intuition is that a reaching action requires an awareness of what one is trying to touch or grasp. The study of blindsight shows that this is not necessarily so. Moreover, this unexpected fact about awareness is tightly linked to one about processing systems; the absence of visual awareness seems to occur when the standard input to the visual cortex is not available. It seems anomalous to ban such phenomena concerned with awareness from science, while the rest of the patient's behavior is admitted. If one does attempt to link accounts of awareness and scientific conceptual systems, a functionalist framework—a system-level one—provides a natural starting place for a phenomenon of this sort. In the case of blindsight, it seems most plausible that information transmitted from the input is failing to arrive at some higher level subsystem, but the subsystems to which it can arrive are sufficient to effect appropriate reaching behavior. It is simple to assume that it is the failure of the input to arrive at these higher level subsystems that is responsible for the patient's lack of visual awareness of the stimulus (figure 13.2).

3 Knowledge without Awareness

An issue that has been vigorously debated over the past 30 years in cognitive psychology is whether semantic processes can take place for stimuli of which the subject does not become aware. During the 1950s, there was great interest in whether it was more difficult to recognize a taboo word than a control word—so-called perceptual defense. By the 1960s, workers in the field had split into two non-communicating camps. One group believed that the effects are artifacts (e.g., Eriksen 1960). The other argued that the effects are real (e.g., Dixon 1971) and arise from subconscious identification of the taboo word before it can be consciously identified. During the 1970s, new paradigms were developed. The most popular were concerned with whether there could be any effect on the processing of a subsequent word from the rapid presentation of a word that was followed virtually immediately by a pattern mask, so that the subject had no awareness of it. The most widely supported position is that the masked word can facilitate recognition of an associate that follows it (e.g., Marcel 1983a, 1983b). However, again, as with perceptual defense, critics have attacked the phenomenon on methodological grouds, claiming it to be an artifact (see,

e.g., Holender 1986; see also Cheesman and Merikle 1985).

Can neuropsychology shed any light on the controversy? Recently, Tranel and Damasio (1985) reported a study of autonomic responses (galvanic skin response, or GSR) in two patients who did not recognize the stimuli presented to them. The patients were "prosopagnosics"; in other words, they had a specific difficulty in recognizing faces.[10] Tranel and Damasio investigated the GSRs to faces that would have been familiar to the patients if they had not been prosopagnosic. The faces of three types of people were used in the study: family members of the patients, famous people, and hospital personnel who under normal circumstances the patients would have learned to recognize while in hospital. These faces were interspersed with unknown faces and shown one at a time to the patients at intervals of 20 sec. The GSR response was recorded. Afterwards, they were shown the faces again and had to rate them for familiarity under a scale of 1 (familiar) to 5 (unfamiliar). Subject 1 recognized no faces and yet showed a significantly higher GSR reading to those that, but for her prosopagnosia, would have been familiar. Subject 2 failed to recognize only the faces of people she had met since her illness. However, for these faces, she, too, showed a significantly greater GSR than for faces of people she had not met.

A closely related study was carried out by Bauer (1984). De Haan, Young, and Newcombe (1987) have shown analogous effects using entirely psychological procedures. They found that semantic-category judgments about printed names showed interference from distracting faces in a different category in a prosopagnosic patient who could not explicitly identify the faces.

Tranel and Damasio (1985) explained their findings in terms of a four-stage theory of face perception:

1. Early visual processes.

2. Matching the face to a template; the function of this stage is similar to the perceptual-classification stage of Warrington and Taylor (1978)

or the pictogens of Seymour (1979) in object perception.

3. The activating of multi-modal associations.

4. Read-out of the evoked associations, which permits a conscious experience of familiarity and verbal report or non-verbal matching of the stimulus.

They held that the impairment lies in stage 3, and on their account, awareness of whose face it is requires stage 3 so the impairment leads to a loss of awareness. Stages 1 and 2 were held to be relatively intact in their patient, so that the GSR response can be triggered. They were not specific about how it is triggered, but Bauer (1984) argued that this is because GSR activation requires a different route from stage 2 onwards. This is a parallel account to that given for blindsight (see figure 13.2). Awareness depends on input reaching certain higher level systems, and some other responses are based on a diverging proc essing route.

All these findings on prosopagnosia have a family resemblance to semantic access phenomena.... Thus in semantic access dyslexia, the patient has no explicit knowledge of what the stimulus is and yet can make certain correct semantic decisions about it. An account that has been given for these phenomena is that the preserved function requires a weaker or more noisy input reaching critical systems than does explicit identification; explicit identification requires inhibition of competing possibilities as well as activation of the representation of the stimulus itself (Shallice and Saffran 1986; see also Shallice and McGill 1978). A similar explanation could be given for the prosopagnosia phenomenon. Reduced activation at Tranel and Damasio's (1985) Stage 3 would be sufficient to produce a GSR response, but insufficient for conscious identification of the stimulus. Whichever interpretation is accepted, the phenomenon itself offers a neuropsychological parallel to experiments on normal subjects that are held to show uncon-

scious semantic priming (e.g., Marcel 1983a, 1983b; Cheeseman and Merikle 1985). Moreover, both of the two explanations are basically system-level ones. They fit well with a functionalist perspective.

4 The Split-Brain Patient and Dual Consciousness

One of the most widely known neuropsychological syndromes is that of the split-brain patient. It is the condition produced by a rarely carried out operation in which the corpus callosum and the anterior commissure—the fiber tracts that link the hemispheres—are sectioned for the relief of intractable epilepsy (see, e.g., Gazzaniga and Le Doux 1978). This syndrome has become famous because its implications seem so dramatic. The operation was widely interpreted in the 1960s and 1970s as resulting in two relatively normal hemispheres being present in the same skull but each disconnected from the other. It was generally believed that by using appropriate input and output processes, one could study the operation of the normal right hemisphere in isolation from its partner. Moreover, it was widely believed that the operation resulted in two conscious entities being present within the same body.

The first of these beliefs no longer seems plausible according to Gazzaniga (1983a), the investigator with probably the greatest experience of these patients. By 1983, at least four series of split-brain patients had been described. In the original series, studied by Akelaitis and his colleagues (see Geschwind 1965), no remarkable behavioral problems or capacities were noted. The second series of 11 patients, that of Bogen and Vogel (1962)—the California series—was dramatically different. At least two patients, NG and LB, showed evidence of considerable language ability in their right hemispheres, a finding at variance with earlier views of right hemisphere function. It therefore became widely believed that the normal right hemisphere has considerable language capacities.

Evidence for the existence of language abilities in the right hemisphere had been obtained in a variety of ways. The most elegant and reliable procedure used a device developed by Zaidel (1975), which occludes one-half of the visual field while allowing prolonged viewing of the display with the other half-field. The Peabody test—a word-picture matching test—was carried out with the word presented auditorily and the four pictures presented to the patient's left visual field and so to the right hemisphere. NG had a raw score of 82 and LB, of 103 (Zaidel 1976). These scores indicate that the right hemispheres of these patients had comprehension skills equivalent to those of children of mental ages of 11 and 16.

The other two series, though, show that these results are not typical of split-brain patients. A later East Coast series, carried out by Wilson, consisted of 28 patients, and an additional patient has been operated on by Rayport in the Midwest (see Gazzaniga 1983a). Of these 29 patients, Gazzaniga stated that only 3 (PS$_2$, VP, and JW) show clear evidence of language processing in the right hemisphere. He concluded that right hemisphere language in split-brain patients can be attributed in almost every case to left hemisphere brain damage occurring at an early age, at which time language capacities can transfer better to the right hemisphere.

This was disputed by Zaidel (1983b), who argued that LB and NG are not atypical as far as the California series is concerned. He said that "all of these patients have by now shown evidence of right hemisphere language" (p. 544), but quoted no specific findings. Gazzaniga (1983b) assumed that Zaidel was referring to the six most studied patients in the California series. He retorted skeptically, "We look forward to examining the data finally acquired from patients in whom the existence of right hemisphere language resisted empirical demonstration for over 15 years" (p. 548). If someone who worked extensively with both the major series of split-brain patients—the

California one in the 1960s and the East Coast one in the 1970s and 1980s—considers that right hemisphere language is a rare abnormality in such patients and objective evidence is not available to disprove him, then the safest conclusion is to accept the conservative position. This implies that the most widely studied split-brain patients can tell us little about the capacities of the normal right hemisphere.

The split-brain syndrome bears on a second issue. Indeed, it is for this second reason that the syndrome has been so widely discussed. The anatomical separation of the two hemispheres has been held to result in the presence of two conscious entities in the same body (Sperry 1968, 1984). As far as the wider implications of this claim are concerned, it is not critical whether the right hemisphere cognitive systems in the most widely studied split-brain patients are or are not normal. For there is no reason to assume that before their operation, such patients differed from normal subjects in how unitary was their experience of the world.

What evidence, though, is there that the "right hemisphere" of a split-brain patient like NG is conscious? As the right hemisphere of the classical split-brain patients produces no language, no evidence can be obtained through report about whether it experiences the world. The standard argument is to list a set of capacities for the right hemisphere and to infer from them that the right hemisphere must be aware. So Sperry (1984) stated:

The mental performance of this hemisphere after commissurotomy has been found repeatedly to be superior and dominant to that of the speaking hemisphere in a series of nonverbal, largely spatial tests.... Examples include the copying of designs, reading faces [sic], fitting forms into molds, discrimination and recall of nondescript tactual and visual forms, spatial transformations and transpositions, judging whole circle size from a small arc, grouping series of different sized and shaped blocks into categories, perceiving whole plane forms from a collection of parts and intuitive apprehension of geometrical properties. (p. 666) [11]

He concluded that "after watching repeatedly the superior performance of the right hemisphere in tests like the above, one finds it most difficult to think of this half of the brain as being only an automaton lacking in conscious awareness" (p. 666).

This is undoubtedly the natural assumption of those who work with split-brain patients, but one can hardly take what observers assume as a strong form of evidence. An observer, watching a mute blindsight patient reaching towards a spot of light would, for instance, if ignorant of the literature, assume that the patient could see the light. The work discussed in section 13.3 and that on action lapses in normals indicate that our intuitive assumptions of what cognitive processing is possible without awareness is not solidly based. Does this mean that one can hold a position like that advocated by Eccles (1965) and MacKay (1966b) that the right hemisphere in split-brain subjects is some form of non-conscious automaton?

Consider, as one example, the study of Zaidel, Zaidel, and Sperry (1981) on the performance of the right and left hemispheres of two classic split-brain patients, NG and LB, on a standardly used non-verbal reasoning test—Progressive Matrices. The test was carried out using the device developed by Zaidel (1975). The task was done first with the left visual field and left hand, to assess the capacity of the right hemisphere. A week later, it was performed with the right visual field and right hand, to assess the capacities of the left hemisphere. Finally, a week after that, it was carried out with free vision. Both patients did as well or nearly as well with their right hemisphere as with their left. Indeed, with his right hemisphere, LB scored at a level equivalent to an 11-year-old child. To perform correctly on this test, the relation between two items has to be abstracted and then extrapolated so as to infer the third item in a progression; finally, the result must be matched to one of a set of possible answers. The processes involved are far more demanding than, say, those used in picture-word matching

Table 13.1

Mental-age equivalents of performance on Progressive Matrices of two split-brain patients given input to right visual field, to left visual field, and bilaterally

	Input		
	Right field	Left field	Bilateral
NG	7.9	7.9	8.2
LB	>14	11.3	>14

From Zaidel, Zaidel, and Sperry (1981)

in the number of components, the level of abstraction, and the involvement of more than the operation of a routine schema. If this level of performance could be obtained unconsciously, then it would be really difficult to argue that consciousness is not an epiphenomenon. Given that it is not, it is therefore very likely, if not unequivocally established, that the split-brain right hemisphere is aware.

If one does accept that the split-brain right hemisphere can be conscious, then this has created much difficulty for some philosophical positions.[12] Thus the philosopher Nagel (1971) has argued, referring to split-brain patients,

If we decide that they definitely had two minds, then it would be problematical why we didn't conclude on anatomical grounds that everyone has two minds, but that we don't notice it except in these odd cases because most pairs of minds in a single body run in perfect parallel due to the direct communication between the hemispheres which provide their anatomical base. (p. 409)

This, he pointed out, would be a *reductio ad absurdum* position because the unitariness of mind derives directly from our own experience. Another philosopher—Puccetti (1973)—has grasped the nettle and claimed that normal subjects are indeed two distinct conscious entities. On Puccetti's approach, the left hemisphere self is unaware of the other and so considers mind to be unitary. The right hemisphere self, however, "has known the true state of affairs from a very tender age. It has known this because beginning at age two or three it heard speech emanating from the common body" (Puccetti 1981, p. 97).

That two fairly self-contained processing systems inhabit the same body in normal people is a common, but quite unjustified, extrapolation from split-brain research. In the normal person, processing in the two hemispheres is frequently complementary.... The different processes involved in simple tasks like reading a word in script or recognizing a picture taken from an unusual angle or copying a drawing can involve different hemispheres. Any conscious experience limited to one hemisphere would be quite unlike the one we have.

A system-level, or functionalist, approach to consciousness provides a very simple answer to these philosophical puzzles. As Kinsbourne (1974a) pointed out, the conceptual difficulties over split-brain conscious experience are not basically different from those arising from any other major disconnection syndrome or from what normal subjects experience over short intervals of time when carrying out two fairly demanding tasks simultaneously.[13] If consciousness is some, as yet unspecified, property of the system-level organization of cognition, then the split-brain operation has the effect of creating two separate, if peculiarly functioning, systems where originally the subsystems operated as a co-ordinated whole.

To flesh out this argument, one would need to specify what these system-level properties might be so that it is clear why before the separation, they apply to one system and after the operation, to two. Before discussing this issue, it is necessary to consider certain views on consciousness that derive directly from neuropsychological research. The first—that of Le Doux, Wilson, and Gazzaniga (1979)—derives directly from split-brain research, particularly from work with three East Coast patients with some capacity both to comprehend and to produce language in both hemispheres (see Gazzaniga, Holtzman, Deck, and Lee 1985).

Le Doux, Wilson, and Gazzaniga were interested in responses made by the left hemisphere to a stimulus presented to the left visual field and so to the right hemisphere. In the test situation used, two stimuli were presented simultaneously, one to each visual field. The subject's task was to select those two pictures out of an array of eight that were semantically related to the two stimuli presented. One picture had to be selected with either hand. Thus if a snow scene was presented to the right visual field and a chicken claw to the left, the left hand is supposed to choose a shovel and the right hand, a chicken. Split-brain patients PS_2 and VP are said to be able to perform this task.

Of particular relevance to Le Doux, Wilson, and Gazzaniga's theory is what the left hemisphere said about responses presumed to be generated by the right hemisphere. When in the example just given PS_2 was asked what he saw, he replied, "I saw a claw and I picked the chicken and you have to clean out the chicken shed with a shovel." From examples such as this, Gazzaniga and Le Doux (1978) have developed the following "metaphor":

Our sense of subjective awareness arises out of our dominant left hemisphere's unrelenting need to explain actions taken from any one of a multiplicity of mental systems that dwell within us.... These systems, which coexist with the language system, are not necessarily in touch with language processes prior to a behavior. Once actions are taken, the left, observing these behaviors, constructs a story as to the meaning, and this in turn becomes part of the language system's understanding of the person. (Gazzaniga, 1983a, p. 536)

The argument is inadequate. Assume that the evidence obtained by Gazzaniga and Le Doux does indeed support the idea that if an action is produced and the left hemisphere systems responsible for language production have no information about the causal antecedents of the action, then a rationalization will tend to be produced to account for the action. To generalize from the split-brain patient to the normal subject, one has to assume that for the normal subject, too, there is usually no information about the causal antecedents of an action available to the cognitive system. The idea that one acted from an "intention" would need to be a delusion.

To make this position plausible, the normal cognitive system must contain some functional analogue of the disconnection of the split-brain system or some other means by which part of the overall system might operate independently of the rest to produce actions that have causes "unknown" to the rest of the system. Gazzaniga offers no evidence that this is generally the case or that "a cognitive system that strives for consistency and order in the buzzing chaos of behaviors that are constantly being produced by the total organism" (p. 536) is indeed what is responsible for our sense of subjective awareness. For he does not show that a "buzzing chaos of behaviors" is an appropriate way to characterize human action. Indeed, it is a classical position about consciousness (James 1890) that it is the product of a mechanism that has come about in evolution to prevent just such a "buzzing chaos" from existing. The behavior of split-brain patients can be a misleading guide to normal function in more ways than one!

5 Bisiach's Critique

The three types of phenomena discussed so far in this chapter are paradoxical from a lay view of consciousness. They are, though, easily explicable on functionalist theories of consciousness. Two other types of neuropsychological observation—also paradoxical to the lay perspective—have been used by Bisiach et al. (1985) to argue more subtly against attempting to explain conscious experience in scientific terms.

Bisiach et al. begin their argument with an aspect of unilateral neglect . . . —the patient's denial of any deficit. Denial of deficit, anosognosia, can also occur for other syndromes, such as cortical blindness or aphasia. It is far from universal in the syndromes in which neglect is observed, but when

it occurs, it can be dramatic. Take, for instance, the hemiplegic patient described by Bisiach, Meregalli, and Berti (1985):

E (Holding one of his fingers in the patient's right visual field) Seize my finger with your left hand. . . . Well? Can't you move your left hand at all?

P . . . . Just give me time to proceed from thought to action.

E Why don't you need time to proceed from thought to action when you use your right hand? Maybe you *can't* move your left hand?

P I can move it perfectly. Only, there are sometimes illogical reactions in behavior; some positive and some negative. . . .

E (Placing the patient's left hand between his own hands) Whose hands are these?

P Your hands.

E How many of them?

P Three.

E Ever seen a man with *three* hands?

P A hand is the extremity of an arm. Since you have three arms you must have three hands. (Bisiach, Meregalli, and Berti, 1985, unpublished)

Bisiach, Luzzatti, and Perani (1979) have argued that dementia is not a sufficient explanation for such denial of symptoms. It would not account, they say, for phenomena like the classic one of Anton (1899), where the patient denied being cortically blind even though she was vividly aware of much milder dysphasic difficulties. Instead, Bisiach and his colleagues argue that all *expectations* concerning the damaged function can be lost as a result of relatively local damage as well as the perceptual processing itself.

Why else would the evidence of other senses have so little effect? Bisiach and Berti (1987) say,

In severe cases, any effort to beset the patient and force him to admit and critically evaluate his pathological conditions is doomed to failure; either the patient eludes the problem altogether, or he cuts short and shelters his cognitive disorder by arguments of which a confrontation would be in vain. . . . This seems to entail that consciousness is *inherent* in the representational activity of

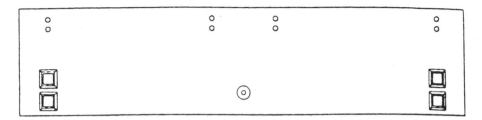

Figure 13.3
The apparatus used with patient FS. There are pairs of lights (one red, one green) at four positions in the upper half of the apparatus. The stimulus flash was the illumination of one of these eight lights. The response was to press one of the four response panels in the lower half, two of which lighted up on a trial. Subjects always used their unimpaired hand (i.e., the one ipsilateral to the lesion). Reprinted from Bisiach, Berti, and Vallar (1985); *Attention and Performance 11:* 240; by permission of Erlbaum.

these analog structures, both as referring to the monitoring of these activities and as referring to their control ... no further mechanisms for consciousness seem to exist, either in the form of a unitised hierarchically superimposed component of the cognitive machinery or emerging from the whole of cognitive activities of the brain.

Here Bisiach and Berti are attacking the idea of consciousness as an all-seeking homunculus. The critique of functionalist theories of consciousness is taken further in Bisiach (1988), where he uses some observations of Bisiach, Berti, and Vallar (1985). In the experiment described in this study, subjects were asked to respond manually to the red or green colour of a 200-msec light flash presented to the left or right half-field. The subjects had four panels to press, two for each side (figure 13.3). On any trial, two would light up on different sides—one red and one green—and the subject had to press the lighted panel of the same color as the flash.

In his interpretation of the results, Bisiach (1988) discussed the observations made on a patient, FS, who had an extensive right frontal lesion. Of particular interest were the responses FS made when the flash was to the right half-field, which projects to the undamaged left hemisphere. In a preliminary experiment in which he just had to name the color, FS was completely accurate

with this stimulus in this situation. This was also the case in the main experiment, when FS had to respond to the color by pressing one of the right-side keys. If, however, the response to the right-field stimulus had to be with a left-side key, FS made no response on 8 out of 16 trials. More critically, on several occasions, he spontaneously stated that no stimulus had occurred.

Bisiach (1988) considered the possibility that FS did not become aware of the stimulus until he made a response, but argued that this suggestion is implausible because we are normally aware of many stimuli to which we make no response. So he continued that it seems more sensible to hold that "denial of supra-threshold stimuli ... would be better interpreted as an inhibitory effect of the action made which suppresses or overrides any experience of the stimulus after its fleeting appearance in consciousness, and prevents recovery of episodic memory of it."

Given the other anosognosia phenomena he had investigated, denial is a natural explanation for Bisiach of why his right frontal patient FS said that no stimulus had occurred on some of the trials on which he failed to respond.[14] The purpose of Bisiach's argument is not, though, to establish a denial explanation. The conclusion he draws "is that in trying to explain neuropsychological disorders we cannot turn from the Spinozian 'inner perspective' of the mental events

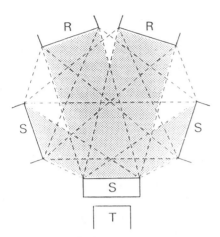

Figure 13.4
A purposefully tendentious and highly simplified model of the organization of the cognitive system developed to illustrate a theoretical argument about consciousness. *T* are sensory transducers, *S*, higher level sensory processes, *R*, response organization systems. From Bisiach, Mergalli, and Berti (1985).

lived by our subjects to the functionalist level."[15] Instead, he believes that we should be concerned with the information-processing properties that allow such processes as reflection or intersubjective communication to occur, but not with their relation to "inner experiences." "raw feels," or the like.

Bisiach's argument that it makes little sense to speculate on the inner experience of a patient like FS seems apt. Indeed, in the spirit of his argument, one might even say that "inner experience" is not an appropriate phrase to use of FS's state during the episodes that he discussed. However, it is not valid to extrapolate and assume that all phenomenal experience is irrelevant for science or that it is invalid to attempt to explain an abstraction based on it—consciousness—in scientific terms.

As far as the reporting of phenomenal experience is concerned, it is useful for science only if its subject has concepts that, at least roughly, cap-

ture it and when the complex mechanisms of abstraction, categorization, memory, and language required to articulate it are intact. These mechanisms function effectively in many psychological experiments on normal subjects (see Ericcson and Simon 1985). They can be presumed to be intact in, say, blindsight patients and in Tranel and Damasio's (1985) prosopagnosic patient. They may well, however, be impaired in FS. Thus Bisiach's argument about FS could be valid, and the phenomenal experience of other subjects still be of value for science.

This defense does not, however, help as far as Bisiach's deeper objections about anosognosia are concerned. Denial phenomena have led Bisiach, Meregalli, and Berti (1985) to propose the following "purposefully tendentious" model (figure 13.4). In the model, the T components are sensory transducers, the S are multi-level sensory processors that carry out both perceptual and representational activities, and the R are response systems. The essence of the model is its modularity, the relative segregation of S-R paths, and the absence of a superordinate general-purpose module for detecting and controlling failures in the system. Neglect arises on this view because a certain level of operation of S is responsible not only for the processing of the stimulus, but also expectations concerning it. Such a model provides no reasonable correspondence for consciousness, for there is no element that controls and no unitariness in its processing.

How, then, can anosognosic denial be explained? The position developed by Bisiach and his colleagues is that the locus of the impairment is close to that of the sensory processors themselves. To make this type of position more concrete, it is useful to consider a phenomenon discovered by Gregory (personal communication). He constructed a self-luminant outline cube. It is possible to invert the cube as one would a Neckar cube so that in the dark what appears to be its near face is actually the far one. Gregory then asks the subject to rotate the cube. The visual and kinaesthetic cues are now in conflict because they suggest that the cube is rotating in diametrically opposed ways. Either one observes a strange visual distortion of the cube or, alternatively, the object remains a cube but one's wrist feels as though it were breaking. The power of "unconscious inference" is so great that one or the other percept, which would otherwise be clear, cannot survive. The outputs of the two perceptual modules—visual and tactile—have to produce representations of the world, which are consistent.

An analogous explanation can be given for denial in anosognosia. If the mechanisms that mediate perceptual "unconscious inference" are intact, but part of the perceptual subsystems—because they are damaged—give a grossly distorted reading, the preceptual-inference system has to resolve the discrepancy. Knowledge is no help. In Gregory's example, one knows that one is seeing a real cube inverted like a Neckar cube, but one still feels one's wrist breaking. So for Bisiach, Meregalli, and Berti's patient, it may be that the knowledge that the doctor attempts to induce in the patient cannot shift the operation of the "unconscious inference" mechanism. Its output continues to register the position of the arm as elsewhere than in the doctor's hands.

How do these positions on anosognosic denial relate to the conceptual framework of contention-scheduling and Supervisory Systems? On the surface the model and the conceptual framework seem diametrically opposed. Yet the opposition is more apparent than real. The distributed procesing that characterizes the model of Bisiach and his colleagues, is, in fact, present in the schemata that are selected in contention scheduling and in the modules on which they are implemented.

The denial phenomenon, itself, is compatible with the idea that perceptual subsystems, including spatial representations, are "impenetrable"—to use Pylyshyn's (1980) term—to higher systems. It does not, however, rule out the possibility that a general-purpose Supervisory System exists, especially one that activates *schemata* not modules.

The way that schemata utilize modules would not be known to the Supervisory System; it does not need to know because if one schema is activated, any incompatible one will be automatically inhibited. So why should the Supervisory System be in a position to know what is happening to modules when they are damaged? As the use of Helmholtz's views on unconscious inference should make clear, the position being developed is entirely compatible with consciousness corresponding to the operation of some higher level processing system that has access only to the outputs of the perceptual system.

6 Conclusion

Neuropsychological research is not, then, in conflict with the need to explain consciousness scientifically. It is entirely compatible with a functionalist solution of the body-mind dilemma. Over the past 15 years, a wide variety of theories for an information-processing correspondence for consciousness have been offered by cognitive psychologists. It has been identified with the operation of a high-level processing system, as in my early idea that it corresponded to the input that selects which action-system (action or thought schema) is dominant and sets its goal for that particular operation (Shallice 1972). Related positions are Posner and Klein's (1973) view that it corresponds to a limited-capacity processing system and Johnson-Laird's (1983) suggestion that it corresponds to the operating system of a computer. It has been identified with a system analogous to the Supervisory System by MacKay (1966a), Luria (1969), Marshall and Morton (1978), and Mandler (1975, 1985). It has been held to correspond to the contents of a short-term store by Atkinson and Shiffrin (1971), the input to the speech system by Dennett (1969), the contents of a globally distributed data-base by Baars (1983), the recovery of synthesized percepts by Marcel (1983b), and the functions carried out by the hippocampus by O'Keefe (1985)!

It is natural to view these as competing hypotheses, although their very variety suggests that little progress is being made. One could, however, ask whether neuropsychological research can help to choose between them. At present, it seems to offer relatively little in this respect. From a neuropsychological perspective, it can, for instance, be argued that short-term stores are various and specific and lowly in function, and so their contents are not satisfactory candidates for a correspondence with consciousness. One can point out that no syndrome has yet been characterized as damage to a globally distributed database. Yet this still leaves many alternatives. However, to a considerable extent, it can contribute little because the theories themselves are too vaguely specified and so difficult to falsify.

I will take a different tack, ... [making] two basic assumptions. First—and here there are echoes of Fodor's (1983) position—there are many subsystems with internal mechanisms and even outputs that are "unknown" to higher systems. Second—and here there is a resemblance to Bisiach's view—it seems likely there is no single higher-level system that directly controls the operation of the lower level modules. There are a variety of higher level systems, and *control* is too strong a term to describe their relation to lower level subsystems. The higher level systems influence the activation of schemata, each of which, in its specific way, will, if selected, determine which modules will be operative and modulate their activities. On the present approach, these control systems include contention scheduling, the Supervisory System, episodic memory processing, and the language system.

My position is to reject a common denominator in the theories listed earlier, the attempt to identify any particular subsystem—or, better, its output or some other aspect of its processing—with consciousness. Instead, I would argue that another aspect of the operation of our information-processing system holds the key. The processes of willed action, of reflection, of re-

membering, and of speaking about something do not involve identical subsystems or even the same control system, but it is normal for these control systems to operate in an integrated way. The output of episodic memory, say, feeds the Supervisory System, which feeds the language system or contention scheduling; alternatively, the activities of contention scheduling are fed to episodic memory and the Supervisory System (figure 13.5). Consider the information that is successively represented, in different forms, in different control systems in such a process. By comparison with the other types of information being processed at the same time in various special-purpose modules, this information would be both much more widely accessible and especially important for present and future activities. If the organism also has sufficient powers of abstraction to attempt to categorize its internal states, the distinction between the two types of information would be a key aspect of the concepts that it employs to understand itself. The conscious/non-conscious contrast would correspond to the distinction between the two types of information.[16]

If the process that corresponds to having a conscious experience is one that necessarily involves more than one control system, then it is apparent why each of two theorists could take a different control system and produce a plausible argument about why the properties of conscious experience map with what is happening in the particular control system that he or she chose. Also, there will be rare occasions in normal subjects or frequent occasions in rare patients when the control systems operate in an uncoordinated fashion. Patient FS of Bisiach, Berti, and Vallar (1985) may well be an example. In these cases, the adjective *conscious* could not be unambiguously applied. For instance, it might happen that the language system could, say, be controlled by the Supervisory System, but a strong input to episodic memory could be coming from contention scheduling. The person would then be unable to remember what had been said because of what

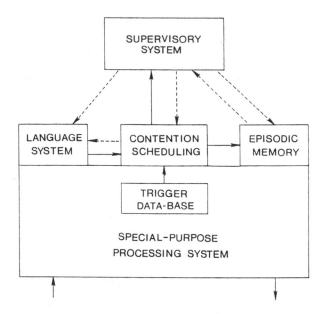

Figure 13.5
The four subsystems or processes hypothesized to have a relation with awareness (those extensively interconnected by arrows). Solid arrows represent obligatory transmission operations; dashed arrows are optional (i.e., under the control of the Supervisory System).

else was being done. One such occasions, there would be no clear answer to the question of whether one is conscious of what one was saying or doing. As an example, in the course of an action-lapse, the operations of contention scheduling and the Supervisory System are in conflict. It would not be appropriate to say of people in this situation either that they are conscious of how they are acting or that they are not.[17]

Whatever the merit of this particular approach to consciousness, neuropsychology's most fundamental contribution to our understanding of human cognition, however, is to provide by far the strongest evidence for its modular basis. The conception of the organization of the cognitive system as composed of specialized subsystems in turn offers few openings for a concept like consciousness. Yet neuropsychology, with a phenomenon like blindsight, seems to require that consciousness be included within science. Neuro-

psychological research thus poses a deep conceptual problem in an acute fashion.

The discussion in this chapter has strayed increasingly far from the more solid aspects of cognitive neuropsychological research. In a way, though, these issues concerning consciousness are typical of modern cognitive neuropsychology. The phenomena that have been uncovered are stunningly counterintuitive, challenging many of our most standard assumptions about the mechanisms underlying cognition. Thirty years ago, except for certain seemingly outdated schools of neurologists, the modular view of the cognitive system that cognitive neuropsychology offers would have seemed as implausible as that provided by Gall. The answers that have been given for the variety of phenomena discovered and documented over many aspects of perception, language, memory, and cognition may not survive. The range of conceptual problems that these phenomena pose will, however, remain. When they can be adequately answered, psychology will have become a science.

Notes

1. The most critical issue is how functionalism accounts for so-called qualia, or "raw-feels"—that is, the *redness* of red, the experience of pain and, so on. I prefer to think of the relationship between information processing explanations and accounts of experience as analogous to the relation between two different maps of the *same* part of the world; neither map need be totally deducible from the other, but there will be many correspondences (see Shallice 1972). In my view, the best strategy as far as the philosophical problems are concerned is to assume, hopefully, that any paradoxes represent an intellectual eddy that can be safely neglected, if *positive* evidence for a functionalist position can be obtained. There are precedents for such intellectually psychopathic behavior. Darwin, in his theorizing on evolution, was quite at a loss to account for the similarity among the flora of South America, Africa, and Australia, which should, on the theory, mean that the three regions were close together. The phenomenon became comprehensible only with the development of the theory of continental drift.

2. Indeed, one might almost say that consciousness viewed from the perspective of those levels of explanation is becoming more paradoxical! Thus Libet, Wright, Feinstein, and Pearl (1979) and Libet, Gleason, Wright, and Pearl (1983) have discovered counterintuitive phenomena concerning correlations between evoked potential recordings and reported experience. This led them to the paradoxical conclusion that the subjective timing of experiences is "retroactively antedated." (For criticisms of this claim, see Bisiach 1988) For discussion of the more general issue of whether the existence of consciousness should be interpretable in terms of a scientific conceptual framework, see the articles in Marcel and Bisiach (1988), which take conflicting positions.

3. For related phenomena in cognitive psychology, see Marcel (1983a, 1983b) and Groeger (1984, 1986).

4. This was so for all but the smallest diameter light spot used.

5. The patients reported in the studies are often collectively referred to as having "blindsight." However, the tests that have been carried out by the different authors vary considerably, and the patients themselves are also rather heterogeneous. Thus the patients of Perenin and Jeannerod (1978) had had a whole hemisphere removed at operation, while DB had most of his right hemisphere including post-striate visual regions intact. This heterogeneity means that it is premature to treat their visual impairments as exemplars of the same underlying functional syndrome. The argument will therefore primarily be based on DB, with other patients referred to in a secondary fashion.

6. Campion, Latto, and Smith (1983) also carried out two experiments on three hemianopic patients. However, the results, even given their assumptions, did not clearly support their position that "blindsight" results are artifacts.

7. These differences are not just quantitative. Light from stimuli projected onto the blind spot can be detected, whichever way it scatters. When a patient has a hemianopia, only scatter towards the intact field is relevant. The findings of experiments on stimuli projected onto the blind spot are to be treated cautiously, especially if accurate measurement of fixation is not made. Thus Bartley (1941) found that in this situation, "a great variety of results ... occurred, and that by deliberately shifting slightly from the original good fixation in which the direct illumination undoubtedly fell within the bounds of the optic disc [i.e., the blind spot], the variety of results reported by different observers will be repeated" (p. 106). In the experiments conducted by Campion et al. (1983), deviations of fixation of 1°, sufficient to bring the stimulus to the edge of the sighted field for two of the three subjects, could not be reliably detected by the procedure adopted to check fixation position.

8. Barbur, Ruddock, and Waterfield (1980) attempted to calculate the amount of scattering of light from the blind to the sighted field that would be needed to produce the "blindsight" results they obtained from a hemianopic patient, G. They deduced that the stimulus light would need to scatter 15 times its own energy into the sighted field to be detected, which is obviously impossible.

9. To argue that the phenomenon is only analogous to effects that occur in normal subjects with near-threshold stimuli only substitutes one experiential phenomenon that requires explanation for another. The two situations are probably qualitatively different.

10. For a review of this syndrome, see Damasio, Yamada, Damasio, Corbett, and McKee (1980) and Bauer and Rubens (1985). In one case, the impairment occurred from bilateral occipital lobe strokes; in the other, from herpes simplex encephalitis. It is stated that patient 1 was normal on tests of language, intellect, and visual perception. For patient 2, it is rather obscurely stated that "language abilities are intact and her visual perception is compatible with normal recognition of faces learned before the onset of her illness" (Tranel and Damasio, 1985, p. 1454). Unfortunately, no quantitative data are given on these points. However, it does not seem too likely that other deficits unrelated to the prosopagnosia influence the results.

11. Sperry (1984) continues at this point, "the literature is still scattered but see reviews" (p. 666), and then gives five references, four of which are to reviews of the older split-brain literature of the 1960s. In fact, descriptions of methodologically adequate quantitative experiments are very rare in the split-brain literature until the 1970s.

12. One way of avoiding the difficulties is to adopt a suggestion of Kinsbourne (1974b), that a function of the corpus callosum is to maintain the activation level of both hemispheres at reasonable levels. Without it, he argued, only one hemisphere, at most, can be reasonably activated by mid-brain structures. It seems unlikely that this is always true. It would not, for instance, seem possible on this account to explain "cross-cueing," where one hemisphere detects the inner response of the other. For instance, Gordon (1974) described, but did not document, a split-brain patient who could name a picture of a common object flashed to the right hemisphere, "The patient's eyes rove about until he sees some square shape or cubic object. As he stares the left hemisphere picks up the cue and guesses 'box'" (p. 145). Another phenomenon that would present difficulties is the perception of chimeric figures: two half-faces joined down the middle so that a different half-face is presented to each visual field and analyzed by each hemisphere. If the patient has to point with the left hand to a match of one half-face (the left visual one) or to give the name of the other verbally, then the subject can perform either task and can do so fairly accurately, even though the task that has to be performed is not known until after the stimulus is presented (Levy, Trevarthen, and Sperry 1972). Both half-faces must therefore have been registered in their respective hemispheres.

13. For a discussion of the phenomenology of carrying out two demanding tasks simultaneously, see Spelke, Hirst, and Neisser (1976).

14. In favor of an explanation of this type is the way that right frontal patients are the group most likely to confabulate and to produce an association of ideas rather than an appropriate response.

15. Bisiach's (1988) arguments are concerned with the irrelevance for science of the nature of a subject's phenomenal experience; he does not, however, reject the use of phenomenal reports. His is basically a "double aspect" theory of mind.

16. This is a descendant of William James's (1890) idea that consciousness is an organ, added for the sake of steering a nervous system too complex to handle itself.

17. There are various surprising consequences of this position. For instance, one cannot determine a precise time at which a conscious experience occurs; thus paradoxes like those described by Libet et al. (1983) (footnote 2) would be dissolved. Also, if one considers an organism that has a rudimentary form of contention scheduling but no other control systems, it would be inappropriate to say *either* that it had consciousness or that it did not have it. One of the requirements for consciousness—the existence of a scheduling control system—would be present, but the other requirement—that the information that "dominated" that system was represented on other control systems—would not hold. The arguments presented in this section are given in more detail in Shallice (1988).

References

Anton, G. (1899). Ueber die Selbstwahrnemung der Herderkrankugen des Gehrins durch den Kranken bei Rindenblindheit und Rindentaubheit. *Archiv für Psychiatrie und Nervenkrankheiten* 32, 86–127.

Atkinson, R. C., and Shiffrin, R. M. (1971). The control of short-term menory. *Scientific American* 224, 82–90.

Baars, B. J. (1983). Conscious contents provide the nervous system with coherent global information. In R. J. Davidson, G. E. Schwartz, and D. Shapiro (eds.), *Consciousness and self-regulation* (Vol. 3). New York: Plenum Press.

Barbur, J. L., and Ruddock, K. H. (1983). The analysis of scattered light effects in hemianopic and normal vision. *Behavioral and Brain Sciences* 6, 448–449.

Barbur, J. L., Ruddock, K. H., and Waterfield, V. A. (1980). Human visual response in the absence of the geniculo-calcarine projection. *Brain* 103, 905–928.

Bartley, S. H. (1941). *Vision*. New York: Van Nostrand.

Bauer, R. M. (1984). Autonomic recognition of names and faces in prosopagnosia: A neuropsychological application of the guilty knowledge test. *Neuropsychologia* 22, 457–469.

Bauer, R. M., and Rubens, A. B. (1985). *Agnosia*. In K. M. Heilman and E. Valenstein (eds.), *Clinical neuropsychology* (2d ed.). New York: Oxford University Press.

Bisiach, E. (1988). The (haunted) brain and consciousness. In A. J. Marcel and E. Bisiach (eds.), *Consciousness in contemporary science*. Oxford: Oxford University Press.

Bisiach, E. and Berti, A. (1987). "Dyschiria. An attempt at its systematic explanation. In *Neurophysiological and neuropsychological aspects of spatial neglect*, pp. 183–201. Amsterdam: North-Holland.

Bisiach, E., Berti, A., and Vallar, G. (1985). Analogical and logical disorders underlying unilateral neglect of space. In M. I. Posner and O. S. M. Marin (eds.), *Attention and performance* (Vol. 11). Hillsdale, NJ: Erlbaum.

Bisiach, E., Luzzatti, C., and Perani, D. (1979). Unilateral neglect of representational schema and consciousness. *Brain* 102, 609–618.

Bisiach, E., Meregalli, S., and Berti, A. (1985, June). *Mechanisms of production-control and belief-fixation in human visuospatial processing: Clinical evidence from hemispatial neglect*. Paper presented at the Eighth Symposium on Quantitative Analyses of Behavior, Cambridge, MA.

Block, N. (1980). Troubles with functionalism. In N. Block (ed.), *Readings in the philosophy of psychology* (Vol.1). Cambridge, MA: Harvard University Press.

Bogen, J. E., and Vogel, P. J. (1962). Cerebral commissurotomy in man. *Bulletin of Los Angeles Neurological Society* 27, 169–172.

Campion, R. L., Latto, R., and Smith, Y. M. (1983). In blindsight and effect of scattered light, spared cortex and near-threshold vision. *Behavioral and Brain Sciences* 6, 423–486.

Cheesman, J., and Merikle, P. M. (1985). Word recognition and consciousness. In D. Besner, T. G. Waller, and G. E. MacKinnon (eds.), *Reading research: Advances in theory and practice* (Vol. 5). New York: Academic Press.

Damasio, A. R., Yamada, T., Damasio H., Corbett, J., and McKee, J. (1980). Central achromatopsia: Behavioral, anatomic and physiological aspects. *Neurology* 30, 1064–1071.

De Haan, E. H. F., Young, A., and Newcombe, A. (1987). Face recognition without awareness. *Cognitive Neuropsychology* 4, 385–415.

Dennett, D. C. (1969). *Content and consciousness*. London: Routledge.

Dixon, N. F. (1971). *Subliminal perception: The nature of a controversy*. London: McGraw-Hill.

Eccles, J. C. (1965). *The brain and the unity of conscious experience*. Nineteenth Authur Stanley Eddington Memorial Lecture. Cambridge: Cambridge University Press.

Ericsson, K. A., and Simon, H. A. (1985). *Protocol analysis: Verbal reports as data*. Cambridge, MA: MIT Press.

Eriksen, C. W. (1960). Discrimination and learning without awareness. *Psychological Review* 67, 279–300.

Fodor, J. A. (1983). *The modularity of mind*. Cambridge, MA: MIT Press.

Gazzaniga, M. S. (1983a). Right hemisphere language following bisection: A 20-year perspective. *American Psychologist* 38, 525–537.

———. (1983b) Reply to Levy and to Zaidel. *American Psychologist* 38, 547–549.

Gazzaniga, M. S., Holtzman, J. D., Deck, M. D. F., and Lee, B. C. P. (1985). MRI assessment of human callosal surgery with neuropsychological correlates. *Neurology* 35, 1763–1766.

Gazzaniga, M. S., and Le Doux, J. E. (1978). *The integrated mind*. New York: Plenum Press.

Geschwind, N. (1965). Disconnection syndromes in animals and man. *Brain* 88, 237–294, 585–644.

Gordon, H. W. (1974). Olfaction and cerebral separation. In M. Kinsbourne and W. L. Smith (eds.), *Hemisphere disconnection and cerebral function*. Springfield, IL: Thomas.

Groeger, J. A. (1984). Evidence of unconscious semantic processing for a forced error situation. *British Journal of Psychology* 75, 305–314.

———. (1986). Predominant and non-predominant analysis: Effects of level of presentation. *British Journal of Psychology* 77, 109–116.

Holender, D. (1986). Semantic activation without conscious identification in dichotic listening, parafoveal vision, and visual masking: A survey and appraisal. *Behavioral and Brain Sciences* 9, 1–66.

Holmes, G. (1918). Disturbances of visual orientation. *British Journal of Ophthalmology* 2, 449–468.

James, W. (1890). *The principles of psychology.* New York: Holt.

Johnson-Laird, P. N. (1983). *Mental models.* Cambridge: Cambridge University Press.

Kinsbourne, M. (1974a). Cerebral control and mental evolution. In M. Kinsbourne and W. L. Smith (eds.), *Hemisphere disconnection and cerebral function.* Springfield, IL: Thomas.

———. (1974b). Lateral interactions in the brain. In M. Kinsbourne and W. L. Smith (eds.), *Hemisphere disconnection and cerebral function.* Springfield, IL: Thomas.

Le Doux, J. E., Wilson, D. H., and Gazzaniga, M. S. (1979). Beyond commissurotomy: Clues to consciousness. In M. S. Gazzaniga (ed.), *Handbook of behavioral neurobiology* (Vol. 2). New York: Plenum Press.

Levy, J., Trevarthen, C., and Sperry, R. W. (1972). Perception of bilateral chimeric figures following hemisphere disconnection, *Brain* 95, 61–78.

Libet, B., Gleason, C. A., Wright, E. W., and Pearl, D. K. (1983). Time of conscious intention to act in relation to onset of cerebral activity (readiness-potential): The unconscious initiation of a freely voluntary act. *Brain* 106, 623–642.

Libet, B., Wright, E. W., Feinstine, B., and Pearl, D. K. (1979). Subjective referral of the timing of a conscious sensory experience: A functional role for the somatosensory specific projection system. *Brain* 102, 193–224.

Luria, A. R. (1969). Frontal lobe syndromes. In P. J. Vinken and G. W. Bruyn (eds.), *Handbook of clinical neurology* (Vol. 2). Amsterdam: North-Holland.

MacKay, D. M. (1966a). Cerebral organisation and the conscious control of action. In J. C. Eccles (ed.), *Brain and conscious experience.* Heidelberg: Springer Verlag.

———. (1966b). Discussion of Dr. Sperry's paper. In J. C. Eccles (ed.), *Brain and conscious experience.* Heidelberg: Springer Verlag.

Mandler, G. (1975). *Mind and emotion.* New York: Wiley.

———. (1985). *Cognitive psychology: An essay in cognitive science.* Hillsdale, NJ: Erlbaum.

Marcel, A. J. (1983a). Conscious and unconscious perception: Experiments on visual masking and word recognition. *Cognitive Psychology* 15, 197–237.

———. (1983b). Conscious and unconscious perception: An approach to the relations between phenomenal experience and perceptual processes. *Cognitive Psychology* 15, 238–300.

Marcel, A. J., and Bisiach, E. (eds.). (1988). *Consciousness in contemporary science.* Oxford: Oxford University Press.

Marshall, J. C., and Morton, J. (1978). On the mechanics of Emma. In A. Sinclair, R. J. Jarvella, and W. J. M. Levelt (eds.), *Child's conception of language.* Berlin: Springer.

Nagel, T. (1971). Brain bisection and the unity of conscious experience. *Synthese* 22, 396–413.

O'Keefe, J. (1985). Is consciousness the gateway to the hippocampal cognitive map: A speculative essay on the neural basis of mind. In D. Oakley (ed.), *Brain and mind.* London: Methuen.

Pasik, P., and Pasik, T. (1982). Visual functions in monkeys after total removal of visual cerebral cortex. In W. D. Neff (ed.), *Contribution to sensory physiology* (Vol. 7). New York: Academic Press.

Perenin, M. T., and Jeannerod, M. (1978). Visual function within the hemianopic field following early cerebral hemidecortication in man: I. Spatial localisation. *Neuropsychologia* 16, 1–13.

Pöppel, E., Held, R., and Frost, D. (1973). Residual visual function after brain wounds involving the central visual pathways in man. *Nature* 243, 295–296.

Posner, M. I., and Klein, R. M. (1973). On the functions of consciousness. In S. Kornblum (ed.), *Attention and performance* (Vol. 4). New York: Academic Press.

Puccetti, R. (1973). Brain bisection and personal identity. *British Journal for the Philosophy of Science* 24, 339–355.

——— (1981). The case for mental duality: Evidence from split-brain data and other considerations. *Behavioral and Brain Sciences* 4, 93–123.

Putnam, H. (1960). Minds and machines. In S. Hook (ed.), *Dimensions of mind.* New York: New York University Press.

Pylyshyn, Z. W. (1980). Computation and cognition: Issues in the foundation of cognitive science. *Behavioral and Brain Sciences* 3, 111–169.

Riddoch, G. (1917). Dissociation of visual perception due to occipital injuries with special reference to appreciation of movement. *Brain* 40, 15–57.

Searle, J. (1980). Minds, brains and programs. *Behavioral and Brain Sciences* 3, 417–457.

Seymour, P. H. K. (1979). Human visual cognition: a study in experimental cognitive psychology. London: Collier Macmillan.

Shallice, T. (1972). Dual functions of consciousness. *Psychological Review* 79, 383–393.

———. (1988). Information-processing models of consciousness: Possibilities and problems. In A. J. Marcel and E. Bisiach (eds.), *Consciousness in contemporary science*. Oxford: Oxford University Press.

Shallice, T., and McGill, J. (1978). The origins of mixed errors. In J. Requin (ed.), *Attention and performance* (Vol. 7). Hillsdale, NJ: Erlbaum.

Shallice, T., and Saffran, E. M. (1986). Lexical processing in the absence of explicit word identification: Evidence from a letter-by-letter reader. *Cognitive Neuropsychology* 3, 429–458.

Spelke, E., Hirst, W., and Neisser, U. (1976). Skills of divided attention. *Cognition* 4, 205–230.

Sperry, R. W. (1968). Mental unity following surgical disconnection of the cerebral hemispheres. *Harvey Lectures Series* 62, 293–323.

———. (1984). Consciousness, personal identity and the divided brain. *Neuropsychologia* 22, 661–673.

Strawson, P. F. (1959). *Individuals*. London: Methuen.

Teuber, H. L., Battersby, W. S., and Bender, M. B. (1960). *Visual field defects after penetrating missile wounds of the brain*. Cambridge, MA: Harvard University Press.

Tranel, E., and Damasio, A. R. (1985). Knowledge without awareness: An autonomic index of facial recognition by prosopagnosics. *Science* 228, 1453–1454.

Warrington, E. K., and Taylor, A. M. (1978). Two categorical stages of object recognition. *Perception* 7(6), 695–705.

Weiskrantz, L. (1980). Varieties of residual experience. *Quarterly Journal of Experimental Psychology* 32, 365–386.

———. (1986). *Blindsight*. Oxford: Clarendon Press.

———. (in press). Residual vision in a scotoma: A follow-up study in "form" discrimination. *Brain*.

Weiskrantz, L., Warrington, E. K., Sanders, M. D., and Marshall, J. (1974). Visual capacity of the hemianopic field following a restricted occipital ablation. *Brain* 97, 709–728.

Zaidel, E. (1975). A technique for presenting lateralised visual input with prolonged exposure. *Visual Research* 15, 283–289.

———. (1976). Auditory vocabulary in the right hemisphere following brain bisection and hemidecortication. *Cortex* 12, 191–211.

———. (1983b). A response to Gazzaniga: Language in the right hemisphere, convergent perspectives. *American Psychologist* 38, 542–546.

Zaidel, E., Zaidel, D. W., and Sperry, R. W. (1981). Left and right intelligence: Case studies of Raven's Progressive Matrices following brain bisection and hemi-decortication. *Cortex* 17, 167–186.

Zihl, J. (1980). "Blindsight": Improvememt of visually guided eye movements by systematic practice in patients with cerebral blindness. *Neuropsychologia* 18, 71–77.

14 Towards a Neurobiological Theory of Consciousness

Francis Crick and Christof Koch

Introduction

It is remarkable that most of the work in both cognitive science and the neurosciences makes no reference to consciousness (or "awareness"), especially as many would regard consciousness as the major puzzle confronting the neural view of the mind and indeed at the present time it appears deeply mysterious to many people. This attitude is partly a legacy of behaviorism and partly because most workers in these areas cannot see any useful way of approaching the problem. In the last few years several books have appeared[1-4] that address the question directly but most of these[1-3] have been written largely from a functional standpoint and so have said rather little about neurons and other machinery of the brain.

We suggest that time is now ripe for an attack on the neural basis of consciousness. Moreover, we believe that the problem of consciousness can, in the long run, be solved only by explanations at the neural level. Arguments at the cognitive level are undoubtedly important but we doubt whether they will, by themselves, ever be sufficiently compelling to explain consciousness in a convincing manner. Attempting to infer the internal structure of a very complex system using a "black-box" approach (i.e., manipulating the input variables while observing the output of the system) will never lead to unique answers. In short, such methods are not by themselves powerful enough ever to solve a problem, though they are good enough to suggest tentative solutions.

Our basic idea is that consciousness depends crucially on some form of rather short-term memory and also on some form of serial attentional mechanism. This attentional mechanism helps sets of the relevant neurons to fire in a coherent semi-oscillatory way, probably at a frequency in the 40–70 Hz range, so that a temporary global unity is imposed on neurons in many different parts of the brain. These oscillations then activate short-term (working) memory. In the later parts of the chapter we shall be mainly concerned with visual awareness.

Before approaching the problem in detail, it seems sensible to describe our general approach to consciousness and to decide what aspects of it are best left on one side.

Prolegomenon to the Study of Consciousness

We make two basic assumptions. The first is that there is something that requires a scientific explanation. There is general agreement that we are not conscious of all the processes going on in our heads, though exactly which might be a matter of dispute. While we are aware of many of the results of perceptual and memory processes, we have only limited access to the processes that produce this awareness (e.g., "How did I come up with the first name of my grandfather?"). In fact, some psychologists[5] have argued that we have only very limited introspective access to the origins of even higher order cognitive processes. It seems probable, however, that at any one moment some active neuronal processes correlate with consciousness, while others do not. What are the differences between them?

The second assumption is tentative: that all the different aspects of consciousness, for example, pain and visual awareness, employ a basic common mechanism or perhaps, a few such mechanisms. If we understand the mechanisms for one aspect, we will have gone most of the way to understanding them all. Paradoxically, consciousness appears to be so odd and, at first sight, so difficult to understand that only a rather special explanation is likely to work. The general nature of consciousness may be easier to discover than more mundane operations, such as shape-from-shading, that could, in principle, be explained in many different ways. Whether this is really true remains to be seen.

The following topics will be left on one side or our attitude to them stated without further discussion, for experience has shown that otherwise much time can be frittered away in fruitless argument about them.

1. Everyone has a rough idea of what is meant by consciousness. We feel that it is better to avoid a precise definition of consciousness because of the dangers of premature definition. Until we understand the problem much better, any attempt at a formal definition is likely to be either misleading or overly restrictive, or both.

2. Arguments about what consciousness is for are probably premature, although such an approach may give a few hints about its nature. It is, after all, a bit surprising that one should worry too much about the function of something when we are rather vague about what it is.

3. We shall assume that some species of animals, and in particular the higher mammals, possess some of the essential features of consciousness, but not necessarily all. For this reason, appropriate experiments on such animals may be relevant to finding the mechanisms underlying consciousness.

3.1. From this it follows that a language system (of the type found in humans) is not essential for consciousness. That is, one can have the key features of consciousness without language. This is not to say that language may not enrich consciousness considerably.

3.2. We consider that it is not profitable at this stage to argue about whether "lower" animals, such as octopus, *Drosophila*, or nematodes, are conscious. It is probable, though, that consciousness correlates to some extent with the degree of complexity of any nervous system.

4. There are many forms of consciousness, such as those associated with seeing, thinking, emotion, pain and so on. We shall assume that self-consciousness, that is the self-referential aspect of

consciousness, is merely a special case of consciousness and is better left on one side for the moment. Volition and intentionality will also be disregarded and also various rather unusual states, such as the hypnotic state, lucid dreaming and sleep walking, unless they turn out to have special features that make them experimentally advantageous.

5. No neural theory of consciousness will explain everything about consciousness, at least not initially. We will first attempt to construct a rough scaffold, explaining some of the dominant features, and hope that such an attempt will lead to more inclusive and refined models.

6. There is also the problem of qualia.[6] Some argue that certain aspects of consciousness (such as whether the red I see is the same as the red you see), being essentially private, cannot in principle be addressed by any objective, scientific study. We feel that this difficult issue is, for the moment, best left on one side. Our present belief is that it *may* prove possible, in the fullness of time, to make it plausible that you see red as I do (assuming that psychophysical tests suggest you do). To decide whether one *can* make a plausible case or not we shall need to know the exact neural correlate in a human brain of seeing red. Whatever the outcome, we believe that any adequate theory of consciousness should explain how we see color at all.

This outlines the framework within which we will address the problem of consciousness. We next ask what psychology can tell us about the phenomenon.

The Cognitive Approach

The most effective way to approach the problem of consciousness would be to use the descriptions of psychologists and cognitive scientists and attempt to map different aspects of their models onto what is known about the neuroanatomy and neurophysiology of the brain. Naturally we have attempted to do this but have not found it as useful as one might hope, although such models do point to the importance of attention and short-term memory and suggest that consciousness should have easy access to the higher, planning levels of the motor system.

A major handicap is the pernicious influence of the paradigm of the von Neumann digital computer. It is a painful business to try to translate the various boxes labeled "files," "CPU," "character buffer," and so on occurring in psychological models, each with its special methods of processing, into the language of neuronal activity and interaction. This is mainly because present-day computers make extensive use of precisely detailed pulse-coded messages. There is no convincing evidence that the brain uses such a system and much to suggest that it does not. For these reasons we will not attempt to comment in detail on these psychological models but only make rather general remarks.

Johnson-Laird[1] proposes that the brain is a complex hierarchy of largely parallel processors —an idea that is almost certainly along the right lines—and that there is an operating system at the top of the hierarchy. He considers the conscious mind to correspond to this operating system. Thus the mechanism of consciousness expresses the results of some of the computations the brain makes but not the details of how they were done. If there is an operating system of this type it is not easy at the moment to see any particular brain area in which it is located.[7] Johnson-Laird also lays emphasis on self-reflection and self-awareness, topics that we have decided to leave on one side.

An alternative view, due to Jackendoff[2] is that consciousness is not associated with the highest levels in the hierarchy but with the intermediate levels. He arrives at this point of view by considering in detail the language system, the visual system and the music system. His arguments are certainly suggestive, though not completely compelling.

Both authors emphasize the intimate relationship between consciousness and working memory. They also both envisage a serial process (that we may loosely identify as attention) on top of the parallel processes. Thus clearly we shall have to consider the mechanisms of attention and of working memory.

The type of memory that will be of most interest to us is short-term memory, whether it be very short (a fraction of a second; sometimes called "iconic" memory[8] if it is visual) or short-term memory proper (meaning a few seconds), sometimes called working memory.[9,10] These are so important that we shall take up each of these subjects later. It does not seem essential for consciousness that the brain should be able to put anything into the long-term episodic memory system,[11] since people with certain brain damage (to be discussed below) cannot lay down new episodic memories but appear in all other respects to be fully conscious. Procedural memory,[11] that is, that part of memory responsible for highly automated procedures, such as typing or swimming, is probably largely unconscious.

Consciousness appears to be a process that is fairly immediate. In other words, it does not take too long to become conscious of, at least, straightforward things. Exactly how long is not clear, but figures somewhere in the 50–250 ms time range might be reasonable, rather than a few seconds.

General Neurobiological Aspects

When

When is an animal conscious? This turns out not to be a straightforward problem. It seems likely that the essential features of consciousness are probably not usually present in slow-wave sleep, nor under a deep anaesthetic. Rapid Eye Movement (REM) or dreaming sleep is another matter. It seems to us that a limited form of consciousness often occurs in REM sleep. Although cognition is not completely normal and memories cannot be put into the long-term store, nevertheless dreams seem to have some of the attributes of consciousness. Whether there are any experimental advantages in studying REM sleep to help us understand consciousness remains to be seen. At the moment we do not see any.

The really difficult case is that of rather light anaesthesia or states induced by modern receptor-specific anaesthetic agents.[12] It seems likely that in some such states the brain is at least partly conscious. This would not matter were it not for the large amount of experimentation on mammals in this state. We return to this problem later.

Where

Where in the brain are the neural correlates of consciousness? One of the traditional answers—that consciousness depends on the reticular activating system in the midbrain—is misleading. Certainly the relevant parts of the brain need to be activated in various ways, but this is a little like believing that the characteristic part of a television set is its electrical supply. It is more likely that the operations corresponding to consciousness occur mainly (though not exclusively) in the neocortex and probably also in the paleocortex, associated with the olfactory system, since local damage to the cerebral cortex often removes particular aspects of consciousness (as, for example, in face agnosia).

The hippocampal system (the allocortex) is a little more complicated. A person with complete bilateral damage to the hippocampal system, and to all the higher order association cortices that are connected with it, appears to have most aspects of consciousness[13] (including short-term conjunctions over at least three modalities) so the hippocampal system is unlikely to be essential. But it could be argued that what goes on in the normal hippocampus does indeed reach consciousness, so it may be important to consider in detail the inputs and outputs of the hippocampal system.

Structures in the midbrain or hindbrain, such as the cerebellum, are probably not essential for consciousness. It remains to be seen whether certain other structures, such as the thalamus, the basal ganglia and the claustrum, all intimately associated with the neocortex, are closely involved in consciousness. We shall include these structures together with the cerebral cortex as "the cortical system."

Split Brains

The study of persons with "split brains" gives us information about some of the pathways that are (or are not) involved in consciousness. It is a well-established fact[14] that for persons whose corpus callosum—the massive fiber bundle connecting the two cortical hemispheres—has been cut, the left-hand side of the brain (for right-handed people) is not aware of the activity in the visual system taking place on the right side, whereas in a normal person it is. (We leave on one side the somewhat controversial matter as to whether the right side, on its own, is as conscious as the left side.) This strongly suggests that some of the information associated with consciousness can traverse the normal corpus callosum. It also suggests that such information, with the exception of some emotional states, cannot be transmitted from one side of the cortex to the other by the subcortical pathways that remain intact in this operation.

Blindsight

It now seems generally agreed that blindsight is a genuine phenomenon.[15] Certain people with cortical blindness can point fairly accurately to the position of objects in their blind visual field, while denying that they see anything. It was previously suspected that the neural pathway was subcortical, through the superior colliculus, but this has recently been brought into question.[16] The motor output appears to be voluntary and the subject is certainly aware what movements he is making. It is now an urgent matter to decide experimentally, by comparative work on humans and monkeys, exactly which neural pathways are used in blindsight, since this information may suggest which neural pathways are used for consciousness and which not.

We shall not discuss here other cases in which people respond to a stimulus such as an auditory or visual cue, but claim to be unaware of the stimulus (for example, subliminal perception and priming,[17,18] and also galvanic skin responses[19]). Such stimuli may affect ongoing mental processes, including higher order processes, without being registered in working or long-term memory.

Neuronal Firing

What is the general character of neural behaviors associated, or not, with consciousness? We think it plausible that consciousness in some sense requires neuronal activity, in which we include not only neurons that fire action potentials but also non-spiking neurons such as amacrine cells.

Our basic hypothesis at the neural level is that it is useful to think of consciousness as being correlated with a special type of activity of perhaps a subset of neurons in the cortical system. Consciousness can undoubtedly take different forms, depending on which parts of the cortex are involved, but we hypothesize that there is one basic mechanism (or a few such) underlying them all. At any moment consciousness corresponds to a particular type of activity in a transient set of neurons that are a subset of a much larger set of potential candidates. The problem at the neural level then becomes:

1. Where are these neurons in the brain?

2. Are they of any particular neuronal type?

3. What is special (if anything) about their connections?

4. What is special (if anything) about the way they are firing?

Visual Awareness

At this point we propose to make a somewhat arbitrary personal choice. Since we hypothesize that there is a basic mechanism for consciousness that is rather similar in different parts of the brain (and, in particular, in different parts of the neocortex), we propose that the visual system is the most favorable for an initial experimental approach. The visual system has several well-known advantages as an experimental system for investigating the neuronal basis of consciousness. Unlike language, it is fairly similar in man and the higher primates. There is already much experimental work on it, both by psychophysicists and by neuroscientists. Moreover we believe that it will be easier to study than the more complex aspects of consciousness associated with self-awareness. From now on, then, we shall discuss not consciousness in all its aspects but visual awareness and only the awareness that does not involve the laying down of long-term episodic memory. Johnson-Laird[1] has called this "bare awareness," which does indeed convey the idea that it is simpler than self-awareness. Although here we mainly consider visual perception, many of the processes we discuss are also likely to be used in visual imagery.

The Mammalian Visual System

The visual system of mammals is complex and we only give an outline description. In the macaque monkey there are many distinct visual areas in the neocortex, perhaps as many as two dozen.[20] One reason for these multiple areas is that to handle all activity in one single very large neural net, with everything connected to everything else, would make the brain both cumbersome and prohibitively large. Loosely speaking these areas are connected in several hierarchies, with the processing within any one area being largely parallel (see figure 14.1). There are also many back projections (and some cross connections) between cortical areas, and also from the cortex back to the thalamus, the functions of all of which are unknown.

The dominant output of the retina projects—through the lateral geniculate nucleus of the thalamus—to the primary visual cortex at the back of the brain. This area has neurons responding to fairly simple features (such as an oriented edge) occupying a tiny part of the visual field.

The neurons in the higher cortical areas respond to more complex features, e.g., aspects of faces, and their receptive fields cover much larger areas. The different cortical areas respond, in general, to different features. For example, the neurons in area MT are mostly interested in motion and depth, those in area V4 in color and shape, and those in 7a in position in space relative to the head or the body. *So far no single area has been found whose neurons correspond to everything we see.* How is it, then, that we seem to have a single coherent visual picture of the scene before us?

The obvious suggestion is that at any one time the relevant neurons in many cortical areas cooperate together to form some sort of global activity and that this global activity corresponds to visual awareness. This is the hypothesis that we shall try to fill out with psychological and neurobiological details.

Convergence Zones

Which particular cortical areas contribute directly to visual awareness? For example, is the first visual area, V1, closely involved? Damasio[7] has also suggested that many cortical areas take part at any moment at several different levels. It is probably significant that Damasio arrived at this idea largely from considering the detailed effects of various types of brain damage, evidence rarely used by other theorists. He suggests that the synchronous activity in the various cortical areas

is coordinated by feedback projections from "convergence zones."

What exactly convergence zones means in neural terms is somewhat obscure. We suggest that convergence zones may mainly refer to the neurons (or a subset of them) that project "backwards" (see figure 14.1), such as those that project from the second visual area back to the first one. Thus the term zones may turn out to convey a somewhat misleading impression, since such neurons may be sprinkled fairly uniformly through certain layers of the neocortex. Nevertheless the basic idea is a valuable one. It points to the possibility that, in addition, convergence zones may also exist in other places, such as the thalamus or the claustrum. (The claustrum[21] is a thin sheet of cells located just below the neocortex of the insula. It receives axons from almost all cortical areas and, in return, projects back to them. Its caudal region is largely visual.)

One would certainly expect areas near to the hippocampus, such as the inferotemporal region, as well as those near to the higher levels of the motor system to be closely involved in visual awareness. How far awareness is directly correlated with every neocortical level of the visual system remains uncertain, as is the involvement of the thalamus, although certain parts of it, such as its reticular nucleus[22] and the pulvinar,[23] may be involved with attention.

Binding and Selective Visual Attention

The Binding Problem

There are an almost infinite number of possible, different objects that we are capable of seeing. There cannot be a single neuron, often referred to as a grandmother cell, for each one. The combinatorial possibilities for representing so many objects at all different values of depth, motion, color, orientation and spatial location are simply too staggering. This does not preclude the existence of sets of somewhat specialized neurons

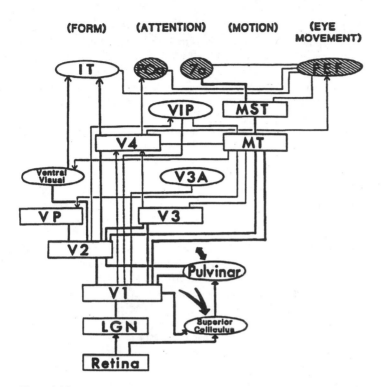

Figure 14.1

Some of the major cortical and sub-cortical visual areas in the macaque monkey. Major pathways are indicated by bold lines, minor pathways by thin lines; dashed lines weak or uncertain. The shaded ellipsoids correspond to high-level visual-motor areas. Most cortical areas project back to the superior colliculus as well as to the different maps in the pulvinar, which is part of the thalamus. Furthermore, every forward projection has usually an equally strong, if not stronger, back-projection associated with it (not shown). These feedback pathways usually terminate outside cortical layer IV, while the forward projection terminates most densely in this layer. Areas related to the control and expression of visual attention include the superior colliculus and the pulvinar, as well as areas POa and 7a, part of the posterior parietal cortex. Abbreviation: FEF—frontal eye fields; IT—inferior temporal lobe; LGN—lateral geniculate nucleus; MT, MST—motion-processing areas; V1—primary visual area; V2–4—higher-order visual processing areas; VIP—ventral interparietal area; VP—ventral posterior. The figure is from D. Van Essen and J. Maunsell, personal communication. For more information, see ref. 20.

responding to very specific and ecological highly significant objects, such as the neurons responding to aspects of faces in inferotemporal cortex of primates.[24]

It seems likely that at any moment any individual object in the visual field is represented by the firing of a *set* of neurons. This would not cause any special problem if the members of the set were in close proximity (implying that they probably interact somewhat), received somewhat similar inputs and projected to somewhat similar places. But because any object will have different characteristics (form, color, motion, orientation) that are processed in several different visual areas, it is highly reasonable to assume that seeing any one object often involves neurons in many different visual areas. The problem of how these neurons temporarily become active as a unit is often described as "the binding problem." As an object seen is often also heard, smelled, or felt, this binding must also occur across different sensory modalities.

Our experience of perceptual unity thus suggests that the brain in some way binds together, in a mutually coherent way, all those neurons actively responding to different aspects of a perceived object. In other words, if you are currently paying attention to a friend discussing some point with you, neurons in area MT that respond to the motion of his face, neurons in V4 that respond to its hue, neurons in auditory cortex that respond to the words coming from his face and possibly the memory traces associated with recognition of the face all have to be "bound" together, to carry a common label identifying them as neurons that jointly generate the perception of that specific face.

Types of Binding

Binding can be of several types. In a sense a neuron responding to an oriented line can be considered to be binding a set of points. The inputs to such a neuron are probably determined by

genes and by developmental processes that have evolved due to the experience of our distant ancestors. Other forms of binding, such as that required for the recognition of familiar objects such as the letters of a well-known alphabet, may be acquired by frequently repeated experience; that is, by being overlearned. This probably implies that many of the neurons involved have as a result become strongly connected together. (Recall that most cortical neurons have many thousands of connections and that initially many of these may be weak.) Both these types of binding are likely to have a large but limited capacity. These are the types of binding with which Damasio[7] is mainly concerned.

The binding we are especially concerned with is a third type, being neither epigenetically determined nor overlearned. It applies particularly to objects whose exact combination of features may be quite novel to us. The neurons actively involved are unlikely all to be strongly connected together, at least in most cases. This binding must arise rapidly. By its very nature it is largely transitory and must have an almost unlimited potential capacity although its capacity at any one time may be limited. If a particular stimulus is repeated frequently, this third type of transient binding may eventually build up the second, overlearned type of binding.

The Role of Attention

This form of transient binding probably depends on a serial attentional mechanism, sometimes called the spotlight of attention.[25,28] It is thought by some to concentrate on one place in the visual field after another, possibly moving every 60 ms or so. It is faster than eye-movements (another, slower, form of attention), and can work across different spatial scales. We suggest (the idea goes back to the last century)[29] that what reaches visual awareness is usually the result of this attentional step—in other words, *that awareness and attention are intimately bound together*. Note that although the results of attention are postulated to reach consciousness the attentional mechanisms themselves are probably largely unconscious.

Short-Term Memory

It has long been argued that awareness is not only associated with attention but also with some form of short-term memory. We have to distinguish two forms, iconic and working memory.

Iconic memory is similar to a sensory input buffer, storing information mainly at a precategorical level, i.e., in terms of simple visual primitives such as orientation or movement, although it may also involve more complex features, such as familiar words. It has a very large capacity but decays very quickly, perhaps in half a second or less.[8] Working memory, in contrast, may last for seconds;[9,10] it seems to have a rather limited capacity (a figure often quoted is seven items),[30] is different for different modalities and seems to use a much more abstract representation (postcategorical memory). It can be prolonged by rehearsal, as when one rehearses a telephone number. We suspect that it is this form of memory that is strongly activated in the binding process.

Neural Basis of Short-Term Memory

The neural basis of these two forms of memory is much understudied. Three broad types of mechanisms might underlie either iconic or working memory, either singly or in combination:

(i) the strength of certain synapses is temporarily increased or decreased;

(ii) a neuron keeps on firing for some time due mainly to its intrinsic biophysical properties;

(iii) a neuron keeps on firing mainly due to extrinsic circuit properties ("reverberatory circuits").

Intracellular recordings show that the cell bodies of retinal ganglion cells remain depolarized for 200 ms or longer following a very brief flash of light within their receptive field.[31] How neurons further in the system express a transient memory remains to be seen. In a memory task in which a trained monkey had to discriminate and retain individual features of compound stimuli, about 15 percent of the neurons in inferotemporal cortex continued to fire for 10–20 s after the stimulus.[32] The mechanism producing (and terminating) this sustained firing is unknown. It is not yet known whether this firing is oscillatory or not. It may not have to be oscillatory, since a task can be remembered well enough without one being vividly conscious of it all the time.

A phenomenon that may correspond to the first mechanism was discovered many years ago at the neuromuscular junction and called post-tetanic potentiation. This is not to be confused with the much studied long-term potentiation (LTP)[33] that has a longer time course. The terminology for these short-lasting changes has now become more complicated,[34,35] with effects variously labelled facilitation (with two time constants of decay, of 50 ms and 300 ms), augmentation (7 s) and potentiation (30 s to minutes). There is also depression (5 s). We shall refer to all these collectively as "short-term synaptic modification." Note that the decay times are in general in the same range as the times required for the decay of working memory. Short-term modification has also been observed in the hippocampus and, in one case, in the neocortex. These temporary changes in synaptic strength can be surprisingly large (see figures 11 and 13 in ref. 33).

Hebbian or Non-Hebbian?

The causes of the various aspects of short-term modification are not fully understood but many of them seem to result from calcium accumulation in the presynaptic terminal[34,35] and are not influenced by activity in the postsynaptic cell. For this reason they are probably all non-Hebbian[36] in character. ("Hebbian" means that the alteration in synaptic strength depends on activity, at about the same time, in both the presynaptic and the postsynaptic cell.) Non-Hebbian implies that the change is not (to a first approximation) just at an individual synapse but at all the synapses associated with that particular presynaptic cell, so that the "unit of change" is the presynaptic cell, not a single synapse. Such changes may form part of the neuronal basis of (short-term) priming.[17]

Von der Malsburg[37] in 1981 postulated on theoretical grounds a fast (fraction of a second) mechanism for increased synaptic efficiency, having a broadly Hebbian[36] character. So far this transient Hebbian alteration to synaptic strength has not been observed, although if it existed it would provide very considerable theoretical advantages.

We know almost nothing concerning the anatomical localization of iconic and working memory, except that (as discussed above)[13] the hippocampal system need not be present in order to remember for short times. Both iconic and working memory are likely to be distributed throughout the appropriate cortical areas, with auditory events transiently stored in auditory cortices, visual events in the visual cortices, and so on. No case of a person who is conscious but has lost all forms of short-term memory has been reported.

Neuronal Oscillations

It has often been hypothesized, in particular by von der Malsburg,[37] that in neural terms binding means the temporarily correlated firing of the neurons involved. In other words, neurons in different parts of cortex responding to the currently perceived object fire action potentials at about the same time. The main theoretical requirement is for correlated firing. It now seems theoretically plausible that this is most easily implemented using oscillations. There are many oscillations known in the cortex, among them the α-rhythm and the θ-rhythm of the hippocampus. Experimental work on "γ-oscillations" in mammalian

olfactory cortex[38,39] and in the visual cortex[40-46] indicates that an important mechanism may involve neurons firing in semisynchrony at a frequency in the 40–70 Hz range (at least in the cat) (see figure 14.2). In the visual cortex, only a proportion of the active neurons fire in this way. Most of the neurons that do oscillate appear to be complex cells rather than simple cells, so that very few are found in cortical layer IV.[45]

It has been shown[41] in cat primary visual cortex that in many cases two neurons some distance apart, but both responding to a particular moving bar, can show frequency-locked oscillations with no measurable phase shift in their cross-correlations. More tellingly, the activity of two relevant neurons, some 7 mm apart, showed[41] more highly correlated oscillations (at about 50 Hz) to a single moving bar than did the same two neurons stimulated by two shorter, separate, moving bars. That is, the correlation was much greater in response to an obviously single object than to a pair of somewhat distinct objects. The activity of the relevant neurons in both the first and second visual areas has also been shown to be correlated.[44] We shall refer to these neuronal oscillations as the 40 Hz oscillations, though the frequency on any one occasion is not very precise and can vary between 35 and 75 Hz.

Most of these experiments have been done on lightly anaesthetized cats whose exact state of awareness is unknown but as similar oscillations have also been seen in neurons in alert cats,[46] they are unlikely to be merely an artifact of the anaesthetic.

A Sketch of a Theory

The role of the oscillations in binding may be as follows. Objects in the visual field give rise to appropriate responses in the appropriate cortical areas. Visual attention now has to select one of these objects at a particular location. Exactly how this works is not yet known. One possible solution[25,28,47] is that the brain has some sort of topographic saliency map that codes for the conspicuousness of locations in the visual field in terms of generalized center-surround operations. This map would derive its input from the individual feature maps and give a very "biased" view of the visual environment, emphasizing locations where objects differed in some perceptual dimension, i.e., color, motion, depth, from objects at neighboring locations. Where this map might be located is unclear but parts of the thalamus,[22,23] such as the pulvinar, might be involved. (Note that the pulvinar receives a projection from the superior colliculus, an area that could be thought of as having a saliency map for eye movements.)

Once a particular salient location has been selected, probably by a winner-take-all mechanism, the information associated with it must be activated by referring back to the individual feature maps. The various parts of the visual thalmus are well suited to influence the behavior of neurons in those parts of the neocortex from which they receive information and to which they project back. Some such feedback pathways then activate or synchronize the oscillations at the corresponding locations in areas such as V1, V4, and MT, so that a coherent set of features is bound. Of course, the system has to decide, using the categorical knowledge stored in the connections, exactly which neurons must oscillate together to produce a veridical representation of the object being attended to. This is probably not an easy task. These are the problems that concern much theoretical work in cognitive science and computational neuroscience. It is well known that making sense of our perceptual inputs is an "ill-posed" problem and much "computation" must be done to produce veridical solutions.

It seems likely that, for one reason or another, certain neurons in the cortical areas involved tend to oscillate at around 40 Hz. This could make it easier to activate such oscillations quickly. The effect of the 40 Hz oscillations is probably greater than the same amount of random firing for two reasons: first, because spikes arriving at a neuron

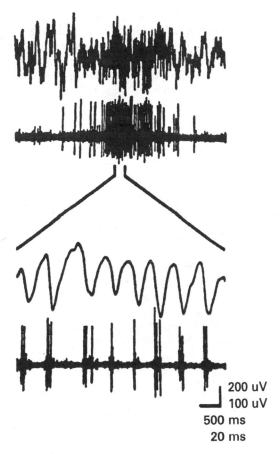

200 uV
100 uV
500 ms
20 ms

Figure 14.2
The local field potential (upper trace) and multiunit activity (second trace) recorded from an electrode in the first visual area of an adult cat in response to an optimally oriented light bar moving across the receptive field. The third and fourth traces show a corresponding part of the first and second ones (respectively) on an expanded time scale. Note the presence of rhythmic oscillations (35–45 Hz). The multiunit activity occurs near the peak negativity of the local field potential. Reproduced by permission, from ref. 42.

simultaneously will produce a larger effect at the soma; and second, because the 40 Hz oscillations may promote 40 Hz "resonances" elsewhere.

To be effective the phases of the relevant neurons must be synchronized. A recent mathematical analysis[48] shows that a set of oscillating neurons can very quickly be frequency- as well as phase-locked if there is a centralized feedback unit. On the other hand phase-locking is much slower and more difficult to achieve if the interactions have to pass over long chains of interneuronal connections.

As there has probably been strong evolutionary pressure to produce appropriate phase-locking as quickly as possible, it may be a general principle that all phase-locking interactions use only pathways with as few links as possible; these may be within a cortical area, between cortical areas (in adjacent levels in the hierarchy) or to and from one or more global coordinating regions, such as the thalamus or the claustrum.

We suggest that one of the functions of consciousness is to present the result of various underlying computations and that this involves an attentional mechanism that temporarily binds the relevant neurons together by synchronizing their spikes in 40 Hz oscillations. These oscillations do not themselves encode additional information, except in so far as they join together some of the existing information into a coherent percept. We shall call this form of awareness "working awareness." We further postulate that *objects for which the binding problem has been solved are placed into working memory*. In other words, some or all of the properties associated with the attended location would automatically be remembered for a short time. One very attractive possibility, with no experimental support, is that the 40 Hz oscillations themselves preferentially activate the mechanisms underlying working memory and possibly other longer term forms of memory as well.

The likelihood that only a few simultaneous, distinct oscillations can exist happily together might explain,[49] in a very natural way, the well-known limited capacity of the attentional system. The 40 Hz oscillations may also be an important element in laying down and improving stored, categorical information, because at any moment they represent the brain's consensus as to what it is seeing.

Fleeting Awareness

Can a spotlight of attention, moving over the visual field from one "salient" location to the next, explain the perceptual richness of our environment? Would such a mechanism not lead to a sort of "tunnel vision," in which the currently attended location appears in vivid detail with its associated perceptual attributes while everything else is invisible? We suggest, very tentatively, that this richness may be mediated by another form of awareness that is very transient, being associated with iconic memory and having a very large capacity at any one time. This form, that we propose to call "fleeting awareness," we expect not to solve the *ad hoc* binding problem (as working awareness does) but to embody "features" that are bound only epigenetically or by overlearning. Attention can then focus on a subset of relevant items within iconic memory for further processing. Because fleeting awareness is very transient it may be especially difficult to study. Whether it really exists remains to be seen.

Experimental Problems

To understand working awareness it seems clear that experimental studies of three somewhat different phenomena are needed. The first is the 40 Hz oscillations, and indeed all other oscillations and any other kinds of coherent firing. In what cortical areas are oscillations found, especially in alert animals? What is their natural history: when do they occur? How long do they take to set up? How long does any one of them last? Are there, simultaneously, several different frequencies and/or phases? Are they indeed mainly correlated with objects? Do they solve the well-known figure-ground problem? Do they ever occur in the thalamus or the basal ganglia? Is the claustrum[21] involved? It is ideally placed to help synchronize neurons in different places.

The second is attention. Are any of the oscillations associated with it? How does the mechanism work in neural terms? It is already known that neurons in area V4[50] and in the parietal region[51] in the macaque monkey are influenced by attention. Evidence on humans with brain damage implicates parts of the thalamus in certain aspects of attention,[22] as do certain experiments on monkeys,[23] but we need to know much more about how attention works neurobiologically.

The third is the neural basis of both iconic and working memory. These are neglected subjects that urgently demand an experimental attack. If there are reverberating circuits, where are they? Under what circumstances do they oscillate? Are there special mechanisms within certain neurons that make it easy for them to continue firing? How widely is the short-term synaptic modification mechanism distributed? What are its characteristics in different places? Is there any sign of a Hebbian form of modification? What exactly are the biochemical and biophysical mechanisms[34,35] underlying it? In addition we need to relate the neural activity to psychological observations.

We plan to discuss these experimental questions more fully in a later paper and to offer some tentative answers based on more detailed theoretical arguments.

Some Experimental Approaches

There are at least three possible methods of directly approaching working awareness. One is to exploit the process known as rivalry, an example of which is the two alternative ways of viewing the well-known Necker cube drawing. Here the visual input is constant but the percept varies from one interpretation to the other. A form of rivalry that is easier to study neurophysiologically

is binocular rivalry, where one eye is given one constant visual input and the other a constant but rivalrous one. An example studied by John Allman and his colleagues (personal communication) involved projecting a small horizontal grating into one eye of a macaque monkey and a small vertical one into the other eye so that their visual fields overlap. In the same circumstances people see first one grating and then the other, the two percepts alternating every second or so. Detailed psychophysical studies on both monkeys and humans, where the monkeys signaled the change by pressing one of two keys, give fairly similar results, so it is reasonable to assume that the monkey has an awareness of the changing precepts. Most neurons in the first visual area fire in response to the constant visual input and do not change but the firing of others tends to change with the monkey's apparent percept. A similar experiment involving horizontal gratings moving either upwards (in one eye) or downwards (in the other) produces a similar variety of responses in area MT of the monkey.[52,53]

The second approach,[54] using cats, is to let the animal view the same set of visual signals first while it is awake and then again when it is in slow-wave sleep. The neurons studied were mainly in the first visual area. The general result is that the response of any given neuron is broadly the same in the two conditions but neurons in the lower layers are often markedly less active in slow-wave sleep. This was confirmed by experiments in which activity was monitored histochemically using deoxyglucose. (Note that all this was done before the 40 Hz oscillations were discovered.) Both these types of experiments are obviously in their infancy but they certainly suggest that visual awareness can be directly approached by suitably designed experiments.

A third approach to working awareness would be to study the effect of anaesthetics on awareness and recall in humans and on neuronal responses in monkey under similar conditions. Surprisingly, no reliable means exists today to test whether a patient is unconscious during modern anaesthetic procedures,[12] which usually includes muscle relaxants to block voluntary and involuntary movements. Even the EEG is no reliable indicator of depth of anaesthesia, as it is often not distinguishable from that of a sleeping person. It has been claimed, however, that the disappearance of a 40 Hz wave in the auditory evoked potential correlates with loss of consciousness under anesthesia.[55] Four to six cycles of such an oscillation, with a period of about 25 ms, can be seen following stimulation by a single or a series of sharp clicks.[56] More work on this is obviously very desirable.

Much useful information can also be obtained by careful studies on humans with brain damage who have selective impairment of different aspects of visual perception[7,57] and especially of attention and binding.

Conclusion

Our tentative theory, most of the elements of which have already been proposed by others, is a program for research rather than a detailed model.

What are the essential features of visual awareness? The first requirement is for a form of running short-term memory, an idea that is certainly more than 100 years old.[29] We postulate two distinct forms of this running memory, a very transient iconic one that records built-in visual features and a working memory that lasts for a somewhat longer time and can also store combinations of features. We presume that parts of iconic memory form the basis of working memory.

The information about a single object is distributed about the brain. There has, therefore, to be a way of imposing a temporary unity on the activities of all the neurons that are relevant at that moment. (Incidentally we see no reason at all why this global unity should require fancy quantum effects.) The achievement of this unity may be assisted by a fast attentional mechanism, the exact nature of which is not yet understood. This mechanism is postulated to concentrate on one object at a time, choosing by a winner-take-all process the next object that appears to it to be the most salient. The required unity takes the form of the relevant neurons firing together in semi-synchrony, probably at a frequency in the 40–70 Hz range. We tentatively suggest that this activates the appropriate parts of the working-memory system. The neural basis of this memory system is at the moment obscure, although the transient alteration of synaptic strengths is one likely mechanism.

There is also much neural activity in the visual system that does not reach full awareness. Much of this corresponds to the computations needed to arrive at the best interpretation of all the incoming information that is compatible with the stored, categorical information acquired in the past. It is this "best interpretation" of which we become aware.

Why, then, is consciousness so mysterious? A striking feature of our visual awareness (and of consciousness in general) is that it is very rich in information, even if much of it is retained for only a rather brief time. Not only can the system switch rapidly from one object to another, but in addition it can handle a very large amount of information in a coherent way at a *single moment*. We believe it is mainly these two abilities, combined with the very transient memory systems involved, that has made it appear so strange. We have no experience (apart from the very limited view provided by our own introspection) of machines having complex, rapidly changing and highly parallel activity of this type. When we can both construct such machines and understand their detailed behavior, much of the mystery of consciousness may disappear.

Acknowledgments

We thank John Allman, Bernard Baars, Patricia Churchland, Paul Churchland, Antonio Damasio, Charles Gray, Bela Julesz, Dan Kammen, Georg Kreisel, and Leslie Orgel for helpful comments on earlier versions of the manuscript and thank Jennifer Altman especially for extensive improvements to the submitted manuscript.

F. C. is supported by the J. W. Kieckhefer Foundation. C. K. is supported by the Air Force Office of Scientific Research, a Presidential Young Investigator Award from NSF and by the James S. McDonnell Foundation.

References

1. Johnson-Laird, P. N. (1988). *The Computer and the Mind*. Harvard Univ Press, Cambridge, MA.

2. Jackendoff, R. (1987). *Consciousness and the Computational Mind*. MIT Press, Cambridge, MA.

3. Baars, B. J. (1988). *A Cognitive Theory of Consciousness*. Cambridge Univ Press, Cambridge, UK.

4. Edelman, G. R. (1989). *The Remembered Present*. Basic Books, New York.

5. Nisbett, R. E., and Wilson, T. D. (1977). Telling more than we can know: Verbal reports on mental processes. *Psych Rev* 84:231–259.

6. Churchland, P. M. (1985). Reductionism, qualia and the direct introspection of brain states. *J Philos* 82:8–28.

7. Damasio, A. R. (1989). The brain binds entities and events by multiregional activation from convergence zones. *Neural Computat* 1:123–132.

8. Coltheart, M. (1983). Iconic memeory. *Philos Trans R Soc Lond B* 302:283–294.

9. Baddeley, A. (1986). *Working Memory*. Oxford Univ Press, Oxford.

10. Phillips, W. A. (1983). Short-term visual memory. *Philos Trans R Soc Lond B* 302:295–309.

11. Tulving, E. (1985). Memory and consciousness. *Can J Psychol* 26:1–12.

12. Kulli, J., and Koch, C. (1991). Does anesthesia cause loss of consciousness? *Trends Neurosci* 14:6–10.

13. Damasio, A. R., Eslinger, P. J., Damasio, H, Van Hoesen, G. H., and Cornell, S. (1985). Multimodal amnesic syndrome following bilateral temporal and basal forebrain damage. *Arch Neurol* 42:252–259.

14. Geschwind, N., and Galaburda, A. M. (1986). *Cerebral Lateralization*. MIT Press, Cambridge, MA.

15. Weiskrantz, L. (1986). *Blindsight*. Oxford Univ Press, Oxford.

16. Stoerig, P., and Cowey, A. (1989). Wavelength sensitivity in blindsight. *Nature* 324:916–918.

17. Tulving, E., and Schacter, D. L. (1990). Priming and human memory systems. *Science* 247:301–306.

18. Kihlstrom, J. F. (1987). The cognitive unconscious. *Science* 237:1445–1452.

19. Tranel, D., and Damasio, A. R. (1985). Knowledge without awareness: An autonomic index of facial recognition by prosopagnosics. *Science* 228:1453–1454.

20. Van Essen, D. (1985). Functional organization of primate visual cortex. In *Cerebral Cortex*, vol. 3, *Visual Cortex* (Peters, A., and Jones, E. G., eds.), pp. 259–329. Plenum Press, New York.

21. Sherk, H. (1986). The claustrum and the cerebral cortex. In *Cerebral Cortex*, vol. 5, *Sensory-Motor Areas and Aspects of Cortical Connectivity* (Jones, E. G., and Peters, A., eds), pp. 467–499. Plenum Press, New York.

22. Rafal, R. D., and Posner, M. I. (1987). Deficits in human visual spatial attention following thalamic lesions. *Proc Natl Acad Sci USA* 84:7349–7353.

23. Petersen, S. E., Robinson, D. L., and Morris, J. D. (1987). Contributions of the pulvinar to visual spatial attention. *Neuropsychologia* 25:97–105.

24. Desimone, R., and Ungerleider, L. G. (1989). Neural mechanisms of visual processing in monkeys. In *Handbook of Neuropsychology*, vol. 2 (Damasio, A. R., ed), pp. 267–299. Elsevier, Amsterdam.

25. Treisman, A. (1988). Features and objects: the fourteenth Bartlett Memorial Lecture. *Q J Exp Psychol* 40A(2):201–237.

26. Julesz, B. (1981). Textons, the elements of texture perception, and their interactions. *Nature* 290:91–97.

27. Posner, M. I. (1986). *Chronometirc Explorations of Mind*. Oxford Univ Press, Oxford, UK.

28. Wolfe, J. M., Cave, K. R., and Franzel, S. L. (1989). Guided search: An alternative to the feature integration model for visual search. *J Exp Psychol* 15:419–433.

29. James, W. (1981). *The Principles of Psychology*. Harvard Univ Press, Cambridge, MA.

30. Miller, G. A. (1956). The magical number seven, plus or minus two: Some limits on our capacity for processing information. *Psychol Rev* 63:81–97.

31. Baylor, D. A., and Fettiplace, R. (1979). Synaptic drive and impulse generation in ganglion cells of turtle retina. *J Physiol Lond* 288:107–127.

32. Fuster, J. M., and Jervey, J. P. (1981). Inferotemporal neurons distinguish and retain behaviorally relevant features of visual stimuli. *Science* 212:952–955.

33. Brown, T. H., Ganong, A. H., Kairiss, E. W., Keenan, C. L., and Kelso, S. R. (1989). Long-term potentiation in two synaptic systems of the hippocampal brain slice. In *Neural Models of Plasticity* (Byrne, J. H., Berry, W. O., eds), pp. 266–306. Academic Press, New York.

34. Magleby, K. L. (1987). Short-term changes in synaptic efficacy. In *Synaptic Function* (Edelman, G. M., Gall, W. E., Cowan, W. M., eds.), pp. 21–56. Wiley, New York.

35. Zucker, R. S. (1989). Short-term synaptic plasticity. *Ann Rev Neurosci* 12:13–31.

36. Brown, T. H., Kairiss, E. W., and Keenan, C. L. (1990). Hebbian synapses: Biophysical mechanisms and algorithms. *Ann Rev Neurosci* 13:475–511.

37. Von der Malsburg, C., and Schneider, W. (1986). A neural cocktail-party processor. *Biol Cybern* 54:29–40.

38. Freeman, W. J. (1978). Spatial properties of an EEG event in the olfactory bulb and cortex. *Electroencephalogr and Clin Neurophysiol* 44:586–605.

39. Wilson, M. A., and Bower, J. M. (1990). Cortical oscillations and temporal interactions in a computer simulation of piriform cortex. *J Neurophysiol*.

40. Freeman, W. J., and van Dijk, B. W. (1987). Spatial patterns of visual cortical fast EEG during conditioned reflex in a rhesus monkey. *Brain Res* 422:267–276.

41. Gray, C. M., König, P., Engel, A. K., and Singer, W. (1989). Oscillatory responses in cat visual cortex exhibit inter-columnar synchronization which reflects global stimulus properities. *Nature* 338:334–337.

42. Gray, C. M., and Singer, W. (1989). Stimulus-specific neuronal oscillations in orientation columns of cat visual cortex. *Proc Natl Acad Sci USA* 86:1698–1702.

43. Eckhorn, R., and Reitboeck, H. J. (1989). Stimulus-specific synchronizations in cat visual cortex and their possible role in visual pattern recognition. In *Synergetics of Cognition*, Springer Series in Synergetics, vol. 43 (Haken, H., ed.), pp. 99–111. Springer, Heidelberg.

44. Eckhorn, R., Bauer, R., Jordan, W., Brosch, M., Kruse, W., Munk, M., and Reitboeck, H. J. (1988). Coherent oscillations: A mechanism of feature linking in the visual cortex? *Biol Cybern* 60:121–130.

45. Gray, C. M., Engel, A. K., König, P., and Singer, W. (1992). Synchronization of oscillatory neuronal responses in cat striate cortex: temporal properties. *Visual Neuroscience* 8:337–347.

46. Gray, C. M., Raether, A., and Singer, W. (1989). Stimulus-specific intercolumnar interactions of oscillatory neuronal resposes in the visual cortex of alert cats. *Soc Neurosci Abstr* 15:320.4.

47. Koch, C., and Ullman, S. (1985). Shifts in selective visual attention: Towards the underlying neural circuitry. *Human Neurobiol* 4:219–227.

48. Kammen, D. M., Holmes, P. J., and Koch, C. (1989). Cortical architecture and oscillations in neuronal networks: Feedback versus local coupling. In *Models of Brain Function* (Cotterill, R. M. J., ed.), pp. 273–884. Cambridge Univ Press, Cambridge.

49. Stryker, M. P. (1989). Is grandmother an oscillation? *Nature* 338:297–298.

50. Spitzer, H., Desimone, R., and Moran, J. (1988). Increased attention enhances both behavior and neuronal performance. *Science* 240:338–240.

51. Andersen, R. A. (1987). Inferior parietal lobule function in spatial perception and visuomotor integration. In *Handbook of Physiology: The Nervous System V* (Mountcastle, V. B., Plum, F. S., and Geiger, S. R., eds), pp. 483–518. American Physiol Society, Bethesda, MD.

52. Logothetis, N. K., and Schall, J. D. (1989). Neuronal correlates of subjective visual perception. *Science* 245:761–763.

53. Myerson, J., Miezin, F., and Allman, J. (1981). Binocular rivalry in macaque monkeys and humans: A comparative study in perception. *Behav Anal Lett* 1:149–159.

54. Livingstone, M. S., and Hubel, D. H. (1981). Effects of sleep and arousal on the processing of visual information in the cat. *Science* 291:544–561.

55. Madler, C., and Pöppel, E. (1987). Auditory evoked potentials indicate the loss of neuronal oscillations during general anaesthesia. *Naturwiss* 74:S.42.

56. Galambos, R., Makeig, S., and Talmachoff, P. J. (1981). A 40-Hz auditory potential recorded from the human scalp. *Proc Natl Acad Sci USA* 78:2643–2647.

57. Marcel, A. J. (1983). Conscious and unconscious perception: An approach to the relations between phenomenal experience and perceptual processes. *Cog Psych* 15:238–300.

IV CONSCIOUSNESS AND CONTENT

15 Consciousness and Content

Colin McGinn

Naturalism in the philosophy of mind is the thesis that every property of mind can be explained in broadly physical terms.[1] Nothing mental is physically mysterious. There are two main problems confronting a naturalistically inclined philosopher of mind. There is, first, the problem of explaining consciousness in broadly physical terms: in virtue of what does a physical organism come to have conscious states? And, second, there is the problem of explaining representational content—intentionality—in broadly physical terms: in virtue of what does a physical organism come to be intentionally directed toward the world? We want to know how consciousness depends upon the physical world; and we want to know, in natural physical terms, how it is that thoughts and experiences get to be *about* states of affairs. We want a naturalistic account of subjectivity and mental representation.[2] Only then will the naturalist happily accept that there are such things as consciousness and content.

Recent years have witnessed a curious asymmetry of attitude with respect to these two problems. While there has been much optimism about the prospects of success in accounting for intentionality, pessimism about explaining consciousness has deepened progressively. We can, it is felt, explain what makes a mental state have the content it has; at least there is no huge barrier of principle in the way of our doing so. But, it is commonly conceded, we have no remotely plausible account of what makes a mental state have the phenomenological character it has; we do not even know where to start. Books and articles appear apace offering to tell us exactly what mental aboutness consists in, while heads continue to be shaken over the nature of consciousness. Indeed, standard approaches to content tend simply to ignore the problem of consciousness, defeatedly postponing it till the next century. True, there are those rugged souls who purport to see no difficulty of principle about consciousness; but

among those who do appreciate the difficulty there coexists much optimism about content. This is curious because of the apparently intimate connection between consciousness and content: intentionality is a property precisely of conscious states, and arguably only of conscious states (at least originally). Moreover, the content of an experience (say) and its subjective features are, on the face of it, inseparable from each other. How then can we pretend that the two problems can be pursued quite independently? In particular, how can we prevent justified pessimism about consciousness spreading to the problem of content? If we cannot say, in physical terms, what makes it the case that an experience is *like* something for its possessor, then how can we hope to say, in such terms, what makes it the case that the experience is *of* something in the world—since what the experience is like and what it is of are not, prima facie, independent properties of the experience? That is the question I shall be addressing in this chapter.

I mean to be considering a broad family of naturalistic theories of intentionality here; the tension just mentioned does not arise from one sort of theory alone. There are currently a number of theories to choose from: causal theories, functionalist theories, computational theories, teleological theories.[3] Take any of these and ask yourself whether that theory accounts satisfactorily for consciousness: does it, specifically, provide sufficient conditions for being in a conscious state? If it does not, then the question must be faced how it can be an adequate explanation of content *for* conscious states. Consider, for instance, teleological theories (my own favorite). This type of theory identifies the content of a mental state with (roughly) its world-directed biological function. A desire state has a content involving *water*, say, just if that state has the function of getting the organism to obtain water. A perceptual experience represents squareness, say, just if its function is to indicate (covary with) the presence of square things in the environment. But now these contents serve to fix the phenomenological aspects of the states in question, what it is like subjectively to be in them; yet the theory itself seems neutral on the question of consciousness. Certainly the teleological descriptions of the states seem insufficient to confer conscious subjective features on them. *Any* naturalistic theory of the kinds currently available looks to be inadequate as an account of what makes a mental state have a particular *conscious* content, a specific phenomenology. Yet phenomenology seems configured by content.[4]

This question is especially pressing for me, since I have come to hold that it is literally impossible for us to explain how consciousness depends upon the brain, even though it does so depend.[5] Yet I also believe (or would like to believe) that it is possible for us to give illuminating accounts of content.[6] Let me briefly explain my reasons for holding that consciousness systematically eludes our understanding. Noam Chomsky distinguishes between what he calls "problems" and "mysteries" that confront the student of mind.[7] Call that hopeful student S, and suppose S to be a normal intelligent human being. Chomsky argues that S's cognitive faculties may be apt for the solution of some kinds of problem but radically inadequate when it comes to others. The world need not in all of its aspects be susceptible of understanding by S, though another sort of mind might succeed where S constitutionally fails. S may exhibit, as I like to say, *cognitive closure* with respect to certain kinds of phenomena: her intellectual powers do not extend to comprehending these phenomena, and this as a matter of principle.[8] When that is so Chomsky says that the phenomena in question will be a perpetual mystery for S. He suspects that the nature of free choice is just such a mystery for us, given the way our intellects operate. That problem need not, however, be intrinsically harder or more complex than other problems we can solve; it is just that our cognitive faculties are skewed

away from solving it. The structure of a knowing mind determines the scope *and limits* of its cognitive powers. Being adept at solving one kind of problem does not guarantee explanatory omniscience. Human beings seem remarkably good (surprisingly so) at understanding the workings or the physical world—matter in motion, causal agents in space—but they do far less well when it comes to fathoming their own minds. And why, in evolutionary terms, should they be intellectually equipped to grasp how their minds ultimately operate?

Now I have come to the view that the nature of the dependence of consciousness on the physical world, specifically on the brain, falls into the category of mysteries for us human beings, and possibly for all minds that form their concepts in ways constrained by perception and introspection. Let me just summarize why I think this; a longer treatment would be needed to make the position plausible. Our concepts of the empirical world are fundamentally controlled by the character of our perceptual experience and by the introspective access we enjoy to our own minds. We can, it is true, extend our concepts some distance beyond these starting-points, but we cannot prescind from them entirely (this is the germ of truth Kant recognized in classical empiricism). Thus our concepts of consciousness are constrained by the specific form of our own consciousness, so that, we cannot form concepts for quite alien forms of consciousness possessed by other actual and possible creatures.[9] Similarly, our concepts of the body, including the brain, are constrained by the way we perceive these physical objects; we have, in particular, to conceive of them as spatial entities essentially similar to other physical objects in space, however inappropriate this manner of conception may be for understanding how consciousness arises from the brain.[10] But now these two forms of conceptual closure operate to prevent us from arriving at concepts for the property or relation that intelligibly links consciousness to the brain. For, first, we cannot grasp other forms of consciousness, and so we cannot grasp the theory that explains these other forms: that theory must be general, but *we* must always be parochial in our conception of consciousness. It is as if we were trying for a general theory of light but could only grasp the visible part of the spectrum. And, second, it is precisely the perceptually controlled conception of the brain that we have which is so hopeless in making consciousness an intelligible result of brain activity. No property we can ascribe to the brain on the basis of how it strikes us perceptually, however inferential the ascription, seems capable of rendering perspicuous how it is that damp gray tissue can be the crucible from which subjective consciousness emerges fully formed. That is why the feeling is so strong in us that there has to be something *magical* about the mind-brain relation. There must *be* some property of the brain that accounts non-magically for consciousness, since nothing in nature happens by magic, but no form of inference from what we perceive of the brain seems capable of leading us to the property in question. We must therefore be getting a partial view of things. It is as if we were trying to extract psychological properties themselves from our awareness of mere physical objects; or again, trying to get normative concepts from descriptive ones. The problem is not that the brain lacks the right explanatory property; the problem is that this property does not lie along any road we can travel in forming our concepts of the brain. Perception takes us in the wrong direction here. We feel the tug of the occult because our methods of empirical concept formation are geared toward properties of kinds that cannot in principle solve the problem of how consciousness depends upon the brain. The situation is analogous to the following possibility: that the ultimate nature of matter is so different from anything we can encounter by observing the material world that we simply cannot ever come to grasp it. Human sense organs are tuned to certain kinds of properties the world may instantiate, but it may be that the theoretically basic properties are not ones that can be reached by starting from perception

and workings outward; the starting point may point us in exactly the wrong direction. Human reason is not able to travel unaided in just any theoretical direction, irrespective of its basic input. I think that honest reflection strongly suggests that nothing *we* could ever empirically discover about the brain *could* provide a fully satisfying account of consciousness. We shall either find that the properties we encounter are altogether on the wrong track or we shall illicitly project traits of mind into the physical basis.[11] In particular, the essentially spatial conception we have, so suitable for making sense of the non-mental properties of the brain, is inherently incapable of removing the sense of magic we have about the fact that consciousness depends upon the brain. We need something radically different from this but, given the way we form our concepts, we cannot free ourselves of the conceptions that make the problem look insoluble. Not only, then, is it *possible* that the question of how consciousness arises from the physical world cannot be answered by minds constructed as ours are, but there is also strong positive reason for supposing that this is actually the case. The centuries of failure and bafflement have a deep souce: the very nature of our concept-forming capacities. The mind-body problem is a "mystery" and not merely a "problem."

The foregoing is only intended to provide a flavor of the reasons I should give for abject pessimism over the problem of consciousness. My question in this chapter concerns the consequences of such pessimism for the problem of content. Must we suppose likewise that intentionality is closed to our theoretical understanding, that the correct naturalistic theory treats of properties that lie outside the area of reality we can comprehend? Or is there some way to stop the mystery of consciousness spreading to content? Before considering some possible suggestions on how to contain the mystery, let me focus the tension a bit more sharply.

Consider conscious perceptual experiences, such as my now seeing a scarlet sphere against a blue background. We can say, following Thomas Nagel and others, that there is something it is like to have such experiences; they have a subjective aspect.[12] That is to say, there is something it is like *for the subject* of such experiences: subjective aspects of experience involve a reference to the subject undergoing the experience—this is what their *subject*ivity consists in. But we can also say that perceptual experiences have a world-directed aspect: they present the world in a certain way, say as containing a scarlet sphere against a blue background. This is their representational content, what states of affairs they are *as of.* Thus perceptual experiences are Janus-faced: they point outward to the external world but they also present a subjective face to their subject: they are of something other than the subject and they are like something for the subject. But these two faces do not wear different expressions: for what the experience is like is a function of what it is of, and what it is of is a function of what it is like. Told that an experience is as of a scarlet sphere you know what it is like to have it; and if you know what it is like to have it, then you know how it represents things. The two faces are, as it were, locked together. The subjective and the semantic are chained to each other. But then it seems that any conditions necessary and sufficient for the one aspect will have to be necessary and sufficient for the other. If we discover what gives an experience the (full) content it has, then we will have discovered what gives it its distinctive phenomenology; and the other way about. But now we are threatened with the following contraposition: since we cannot give a theory of consciousness we cannot give a theory of content, since to give the latter would *be* to give the former (at least in the case of conscious experiences). Accordingly, theories of content are cognitively closed to us: we cannot say in virtue of what an experience has the content it has. Suppose, for example, that we favored some sort of causal theory of perceptual content: content is fixed by regular causal connections between experiences and properties instantiated in the surrounding world, say being

scarlet or spherical.[13] Such causal facts would be deemed sufficient for having the kind of content in question. But if this content fixes the subjective side of the experience—what it is like for the subject—then we are committed, it seems, to holding that such causal facts are sufficient for this subjective side also. For what fixes content fixes qualia. But these causal conditions seem manifestly insufficient for subjectivity, intuitively, and the claim contradicts the closure I said I concede. Intentionality has a first-person aspect, and this seems impossible to capture in the naturalistic terms favored by causal theories and their ilk.[14] If consciousness is a mystery, then so must its content be. So the challenge runs.

How, if at all, can we escape this argument? One response would be not to try: accept that intentionality is inexplicable by us but insist that it is not inherently mysterious or inconsistent with what we know of the physical world. This would be to extend to content the treatment I should propose for consciousness. About consciousness I should say that there is no objective miracle in how it arises from the brain; it only seems to us that there is because of the veil imposed by cognitive closure. We project our own limitations on to nature, thus making nature appear to contain supernatural facts. In reality, there is no metaphysical mind-body problem; there is no *ontological* anomaly, only an epistemic hiatus. The psychophysical nexus is no more intrinsically mysterious than any other causal nexus in the body, though it will always strike *us* as mysterious. This is what we cal call a "nonconstructive" solution to the problem of how consciousness is possible. But if that solution removes the basic philosophical problem, as I think it does, then we can say the same about intentionality. We do not need to be able to produce a constructive solution to "Brentano's problem" in order to convince ourselves that there is no inherent mystery in the phenomenon of intentionality; we can rest secure in the knowledge that *some* property of the physical world explains that phenomenon in an entirely natural way—though we cannot ever discover what that property is.[15] To the omniscient intellect of God intentionality in a physical organism is no more remarkable than digestion is. Thus there is no pressure toward eliminativism about content arising from the fact that *we* can never make content (physically) comprehensible to ourselves; any more than a minded creature who is constitutionally unable to grasp the correct theory of digestion has to deny that anything ever gets digested. So we can, according to this response, solve the philosophical problem of intentionality without actually *specifying* the correct theory.

I do not think this nonconstructive response can be rejected on general grounds, since I believe it applies to the case of consciousness. But I think it is implausibly extreme in the case of content; for we can, I believe, produce naturalistic theories of content that provide substantial illumination as to its workings. It is not as if the theories now available strike us as just hopelessly misguided, as telling us nothing whatever about the nature of intentionality. Whereas I do think that the usual theories of consciousness (e.g., functionalism) do not even begin to make a dent in our incomprehension. Thus it seems to me that teleological theories, in particular, promise to shed a good deal of light on the roots of intentionality; they provide real insight. Who can deny that the vast amount of work devoted to the nature of reference and belief in the last twenty or so years has added significantly to our understanding of their nature? Something, I venture to suggest, has been learned. So it cannot be that the whole nature of intentionality is hidden from us, that we simply cannot form the kinds of concepts that would shed light on it. The question is how to square this apparent illumination with extreme pessimism about consciousness. How is such illumination *possible*, given that we are completely in the dark about consciousness?

At this point it is natural to pin one's hopes on what I shall call the "insulation strategy." The insulation strategy proposes radically to separate the two theories: in particular, it proposes to do the theory of content in complete isolation from the theory of consciousness. How might this insulation of theories be made plausible? The obvious first move is to switch theoretical attention to (so-called) subpersonal content, the kind that exists without benefit of consciousness. We attribute content of a sort to machines and to subconscious processes in the nervous system; and this kind of content might be thought to be explicable without bringing in consciousness. It is true that content is also possessed by conscious states, but this is only a contingent truth about content, a dispensable accretion. Then once we have a theory for subpersonal content we can extend it to conscious content, simply by adding in the fact that the content is conscious. In principle, this strategy insists, the conditions necessary and sufficient for content are *neutral* on the question whether the bearer of the content happens to be a conscious state. Indeed, the very same range of contents that are possessed by conscious creatures could be possessed by creatures without a trace of consciousness. Consciousness is simply a further fact, super-added; it is not itself in any way constitutive of content. This contingency claim might then be bolstered by the consideration that the outstanding problem in the naturalistic theory of content—namely, accounting for the possibility of error or misrepresentation—does not seem to require invoking consciousness: it is not the fact that a state is conscious that makes it susceptible to error and hence semantic evaluation. We do not ascend from mere natural indication or nomic dependence to full-blown truth and falsity by ensuring that there is something it is like to be in the state in question. Subjectivity is not what creates the possibility of error. Hence subjective features lie quite outside the proper domain of the theory of content.

There are two problems with this suggestion. The first is tactical: we do not want the possibility of a theory of content to depend upon the particular conception of the relation between content and consciousness that the suggestion assumes. One view, by no means absurd, is that *all* content is originally of conscious states. There is no (un-derivative) intentionality without consciousness. (Brentano's thesis was that all consciousness is intentional: this "converse Brentano thesis" is that all intentionality is conscious—or somehow derivative from consciousness.) Our attributions of content to machines and cerebral processes is, on this view, dependent or metaphorical or in-strumental; there would be no content in a world without consciousness. Accordingly, we labor under an illusion if we think we can *complete* the theory of content without even mentioning that contentful states are associated with conscious-ness. There is no ofness without likeness. When we think we are conceiving of content in the ab-sence of consciousness we are really treating a system *as if* it were conscious, while simulta-neously denying that this is what we are up to.

Now it is not that I myself agree with this ex-treme thesis of dependence; I have yet to see a convincing argument for the claim that any kind of representation worthy of the name requires consciousness. But I should agree that the possi-bility of subpersonal content of *some* kind does not serve to insulate the two theories when it comes to the kind of content distinctively pos-sessed by conscious states. And this brings us to the second point. There may indeed be two spe-cies of content, personal and subpersonal, but this does not show that the personal kind lacks dis-tinctive properties that tie it essentially to con-sciousness. I doubt that the self-same *kind* of content possessed by a conscious perceptual ex-perience, say, could be possessed independently of consciousness; such content seems essentially conscious, shot through with subjectivity. This is because of the Janus-faced character of conscious content: it involves presence to the subject, and hence a subjective point of view. Remove the in-ward-looking face and you remove something in-tegral—what the world *seems* like to the subject. Just as there are two types of "meaning," natural and non-natural, so there seem to be two types of content, conscious and nonconscious; the sub-jective perspective creates, as it were, a new and special kind of content. This is why what an ex-perience is as of already contains a phenomeno-logical fact—how the subject is struck in having the experience. So we cannot hope to devise an exhaustive theory of the nature of conscious con-tent which remaining neutral on whether such content is conscious. Content distinctions confer subjective distinctions. Experiential content is es-sentially phenomenological.

I suspect that the insulation strategy is fueled by a conception of consciousness that we can call the "medium conception": consciousness is to its content what a medium of representation is to the message it conveys. Compare sentences, spoken or written. On the one hand, there is their sound or shape (the medium); on the other, their mean-ing, the proposition they express. We can readily envisage separate studies of these two properties of a sentence, neither presupposing the other. In particular, we could have a theory of the content of sentences that was neutral as to their sound or shape. The meaning could vary while the sound or shape stayed constant, and there could be var-iations in sound or shape unaccompained by var-iations in meaning. Message and medium can vary along independent dimensions. Suppose, then, that we try to think of perceptual experience in this way: subjective features are analogous to the sound or shape of the sentence, content to its meaning. The content is *expressed* in a particular conscious medium but we can in principle sepa-rate the properties of the medium from the message it carries. What it is like to have the ex-perience is thus fixed by intrinsic features of the medium, whereas what the experience is about is fixed by certain extrinsic relations to the world. According to this conception, then, the absolute intractability of consciousness need not infect the theory of content in the slightest. Consciousness is to bc conceived, in effect, as a mysterious medium in which something relatively mundane is (con-tingently) embedded.

I think the medium conception is the kind of view which, once clearly articulated, sheds what-ever attractions it may have initially possessed. In effect, it tries to treat perceptual experience as if its phenomenology were analogous to that of (non-representational) bodily sensations: content comes from subtending this intrinsic phenomenology with causal or other relations to the world, these relations being strictly orthogonal to that intrinsic phenomenology. Or again, it tries to conceive of experiential content as if it operated like truth or veridicality: whether a belief is true or an experience veridical is not a phenomenological property of the state in question, so that any theory of what confers these properties need not encroach on consciousness itself. A causal account of veridicality, for example, is not, and is not intended as, an account of what gives an experience the representational content it has (what it is as of). *If* we could think of content itself as lying in this way "outside" of phenomenology, then we could indeed insulate the two theories. But, as I have insisted, this attempted extrusion of the subjective from the semantic just does not work. The content of an experience simply does contribute to what it is like to have it, and indeed it is not at all clear that anything else does. A visual experience, for example, presents the world to the subject in specific ways, as containing spatially disposed objects of various shapes and colors, and this kind of "presentation-to" is constitutive of what it is like to have visual experience. It is true, of course, that different sense-modalities may present the same kinds of environmental feature, for example, shape or texture—as with sight and touch—but the subjectively distinct experiences that present these features also present *other* features. It is not that sight and touch present precisely the *same* range of features yet differ phenomenologically, so that we need something like a medium conception to capture the difference; it is rather that they overlap in the features they present at certain points but are disjoint at others—notably, in the secondary qualities they present. These differences in the range of contents available to different types of experience seem enough to capture the obvious phenomenological differences in the experiences associated with different senses. Bats perceive different secondary qualities from us when they employ their echolocation sense; it is not that they perceive precisely the same qualities and embed them in a different (non-representational) medium. But even if there were subjective distinctions that could not be captured in terms of distinctions of content, this would not help the insulation strategy, since there are too many subjective distinctions that *are* generated by distinctions of content. The difference between a visual experience of red and a visual experience of green just is a difference in what it is like to have these two types of experience. The case is quite unlike the difference between a veridical and an hallucinatory experience, or a true belief and a false one. Content, we might say, is *internal* to phenomenology; the link here is anything but contingent.

If this is right, then we cannot suppose that the theory of content simply has nothing to do with the nature or constitution of consciousness. Since distinctions of content can constitute (or contribute toward) distinction of phenomenology, we cannot totally insulate the theory of the former from the theory of the latter; we must admit that a correct theory of content will deliver resources sufficient to capture subjective features of conscious states. But if we are convinced that no naturalistic theory of the kinds available to us can explain conscious features, then we are again in a state of tension. Either we can explain features of consciousness ("qualia") naturalistically or we cannot explain content naturalistically. The fate of the one theory seems yoked to the fate of the other. Yet I, for one, should like to believe that we can make progress with content, while accepting that consciousness is beyond us. Where then can I turn to have this tension relieved?

Instead of attempting to insulate the two theories entirely, I want to suggest that we limit the scope of the theory of content. We should accept that there is a part or aspect of intentionality that our theories do not and probably cannot capture, but we should also hold that there is a part or aspect that they do have some prospect of illiminating. There is *partial* cognitive closure with respect to content: we can naturalize certain properties of the total phenomenon but we cannot naturalize all of its properties (though, as I said earlier, all the properties are in themselves entirely natural). And this will imply that there are *some* features of consciousness—subjective features—that we can treat naturalistically. There is a feasible branch of the theory of content that delivers an account of certain phenomenological facts: but this falls short of a full explanation of conscious intentionality.

Let me distinguish two questions. The first is the question what *individuates* contents: what accounts for identity and difference between contents; what makes a content of this rather than that? We classify experiences according to what they represent, and the question is what principles underlie these classifications. The second question concerns the *nature* of content: what does it consist in for a creature to have intentional states at all; what makes a creature enjoy mental "directedness" on the world in the fires place? Thus, we can ask what natural facts make a creature an intentional being, and then we can ask what natural facts *target* this intentionality in specific ways? The question of nature is the more fundamental question: it asks what this directedness, grasping, apprehension, encompassing, reaching out ultimately consists in. It wants to know by virtue of what natural facts the mind is endowed with the power to "point" beyond itself. The question of individuation takes this for granted and enquires how the intentional capacity picks up the particular objects and properties it does. *Given* that consciousness has the power to "lasso" things in the world, what determines the direction of its throw? Putting it in terms of linguistic intentionality or reference: we can ask what makes a physical organism capable of referring (the act itself), and we can ask how it is that this act is tied down to particular objects and properties. "What is reference?" is one question; "How does reference get targeted this way rather than that?" is another question.

Now, assuming this distinction is sufficiently clear, I can state my proposal: the *nature* of intentionality is congnitively closed to us but the *individuation* of intentional contents is in principle open. We can say what makes a content of this rather than that but we cannot say what the relation of intentionality itself consists in. We cannot specify, in naturalistic (i.e., broadly physical) terms, the essential nature of the conscious mental act of apprehending states of affairs, but we can say in such terms what distinguishes one such act from another. Let me now try to defend this proposal. First I shall explain why the proposal is consistent. Then I shall defend the pessimistic part of the proposal. Finally I shall urge a qualified optimism about the question of content individuation.

The proposal is consistent because we do not need to fathom the nature of the intentional *act* in order to provide constraints on the identity conditions of instances of the act. I can tell you what distinguishes referring to redness from referring to greenness without being able to tell you what referring is *au fond*. The direction of reference may be constrained by relations with which reference itself cannot literally be *identified*. An analogy from action theory may help here. We can ask what distinguishes different kinds of world-directed bodily action without asking what the nature of intentional action in general is. Thus I can tell you what distinguishes intentionally kicking a brick from intentionally kicking a cat— there are different objects on the end of my toe— without having to explain what intentional action is in general. Consider, then, causal theories of mental aboutness. I can tell you, in terms of causal history, what distinguishes thinking about London from thinking about Neo York—there are different cities as the causal origin of these thoughts—without having to venture on the question what mental aboutness is to start with. The causal relations in question make these thoughts home in on certain objects, but we do not need to infer that mental aboutness is reducible to these relations. I do not have to be able to explain or analyze the act of grasping itself in order to be able to lay down laws that fix what is grasped. I don't have to be able to provide a naturalistic account of the intentional *structure* of consciousness in order to be in a position to pin down what gives that structure the specific content it has. Specific content is, as it were, the "logical product" of the intentional capacity and the natural relations that target that capacity in particular ways; the capacity is not reducible to the relations. In view of this distinction of questions, we have to be very careful when we offer what we are pleased to call a "theory of intentionality/reference." Suppose we favor causal theories of perceptual content: content is individuated by regular causal links between experiences and properties instantiated in the subject's environment. It is tempting to suggest that such links give us the very nature of perceptual representation, that the conscious act of enjoying an experience as of a scarlet sphere against a blue background is analyzable as a special kind of causal relation. But if I am right this is not what we should say. Rather, we should say that causal relations tie the intentional structure of perceptual experience down to specific states of affairs but that such relations do not constitute the very nature of that structure. Intentional directedness is not exhaustively analyzable as a causal relation, however complex. And similarly for teleological theories. Neither do we need to suppose this in order to find a point for naturalistic theories of content; we need rather to locate their legitimate area of application some way short of a full account of what it is stand in intentional relations to things.

The pessimism about the essential nature of intentionality can be motivated in two ways. First we can simply deduce it from pessimism about consciousness: if consciousness cannot be explained (by us) naturalistically, in broadly physical terms, then neither can the constitutive structures of consciousness. The intentionality of experiences and thoughts belongs with the subjective "feel" of sensations: neither admits of objective physical explanation. But, second, we can also generate a mood of pessimism more directly: we can ask ourselves whether it really seems plausible that any of the standard theories capture the complete nature of conscious intentionality. In the case of sensations we have a strong sense that standard naturalistic theories, for example, reductive functionalism, omit something essential—the "feel" of the sensation. And I think our intuitions about intentionality parallel our intuitions about sensations: it really does seem that causal or teleological theories omit something essential in the intentional relation as it occurs in consciousness. They do not capture that phenomenological feature we describe (somewhat metaphorically) as grasping, apprehending, reaching out, taking in, and so forth. There is an *internality* about the relation between an experience and its object that seems hard to replicate in terms of "external" causal or teleological relations. Presence *to* the subject of the object of his experience seem not exhaustively explicable in terms of such natural relations. These kinds of relations hold, after all, between all sorts of things, not just brains and items in their environment, and it seems unsatisfactory to try to assimilate conscious intentional directedness to these ordinary relations. Conscious intentionality is more special than this sort of account suggests. (This is, of course, why Brentano claimed that intentionality is what distinguishes minds from mere physical objects.) Naturalistic theories fail to do justice to the *uniqueness* of conscious intentionality. Nothing we know about the brain, including its relations to the world, seems capable of rendering unmysterious the capacity of conscious states to "encompass" external state of affairs.[16] I think this is a very primitive intuition, by which I suspect many of us have been struck at some point in our philosophical lives. How *can* our minds reach out to the objects of experience? What is it about our brains, and their location in the world, that could possibly explain the way consciousness *arcs out* into the world? Consciousness seems to extend an invisible hand into the world it represents (if I may put it so): how on earth could my *brain* make that possible? No ethereal prehensile organ protrudes from my skull! Phenomenologically, we feel that the mind "lays hold" of things out there, mentally "grasps" them, but we have no physical model of what this might consist in. We flounder in similes. It is precisely our perplexity about this question that makes it seem to us that there could be a creature whose brain had all the same natural properties and relations as ours and yet enjoyed no such conscious arcing out. For none of the natural properties and relations we come across seems to add up to what we know from the first-person point of view of conscious aboutness. It is thus reasonable to suspect that cognitive closure is operative here. Somehow we are not keyed in to the kinds of natural fact that actually underlie intentionality—as we are not to consciousness in general. Something about our make-up explains how consciousness can reach out into the world in the way it does, but we seem constitutionally blind to what that something is.

Cautious optimism is possible, however, since we do not need to explain everything about intentionality in order to be able to say something illuminating about it. And I think it is undeniable that illuminating things have been said about content in recent years; all is not darkness. Teleological theories, in particular, seem to me to contain valuable insights. The question is *what* precisely has been illuminated. And my suggestion is that these naturalistic theories should be seen as contributions to the indiveduation conditions of mental states: they tell us what differentiates one kind of intentional state from another: they tell us how intentional states collect their specific content. They may also tell us something about the natural antecedents of conscious intentionality—what basci natural relations got transformed by consciousness into genuine content. First there were preconscious states with certain functions relating them to things in the world; then consciousness built upon

this natural foundation to produce the intertional relation. The "intentional arc" is not reducible to this foundation but it takes its rise from it. So there is room for naturalistic apeculation about where intentionality came from, if not what it ultimately consists in. We can pursue these more modest questions without having to take on the full explanatory task of reducing intentionality to something we can understand, something broadly physical. In fact, something like this perspective is already implicit in much work on reference and content. It is not invariably assumed that causal theories (say) give us the real nature of the reference relation, that they successfully analyze the capacity to refer; rather, they tell us how that capacity gets targeted, what constrains the direction of acts of reference.[17] So we can be grateful for this kind of illumination without insisting that it be spread across the whole phenomenon.

Yet there is a residual puzzle. We have resisted the insulation strategy, arguing that content colors consciousness. Differences of content do determine differences of subjectivity; "ofness" fixes "like-ness." But this staining of subjectivity by reference does imply that we can provide a naturalistic theory of subjective distinctions, since we can say in naturalistic terms what individuates the content of experience. Here we have an objective handle on to the constitution of the subjective. An experience as of a red square thing is subjectively distinct from an experience as of a green triangular thing, in virtue of the fact that different kinds of objects are represented; and this distinction can be captured, we have agreed, in terms of natural relations that these experiences stand in to the properties represented—say, teleological relations. So it looks as though we are committed to accounting for *some* features of consciousness naturalistically; not *all* phenomenological facts are closed to us. I think this does indeed follow: there are some features of consciousnes whose natural explanation, in broadly physical terms, is in principle available to us. Our concept-forming capacities afford us partial access to the natural basis of these subjective features of consciousness.

But this is puzzling because one would expect the closure to be total: how can it be impossible for us to explain how consciousness arises from the physical world and yet not so very difficult to account naturalistically for distinctions *within* consciousness? Why should the general phenomenon of consciousness be so recalcitrant to natural explanation while specific determinations of consciousness yield to naturalistic account? It's puzzling. Even where consciousness is not mysterious it is mysterious why it is not mysterious!

This puzzle should be set beside another. A moderate externalist about content will hold that objective properties, for example, being square, enter into the identity of contentful states; they occur as 'constituents' of content.[18] Thus objective properties penetrate experiences in ways that fix their phenomenology. Again, the subjective is invaded by the objective. Combining this act of colonization with the previous one we get a double dependence of the subjective on the objective: objective items figure as 'constituents' of subjective states, so shaping their phenomenology, *and* these states collect those objective 'constituents' by way of objective natural relations—say, biological function. What now begin to look mysterious is the way consciousness is so resistant to objective physical reduction and yet is so permeated by the objective and physical. Consciousness, as it were, appropriates the objective while holding itself aloft from it; it takes the physical in but it refuses to be ruled by it. And, oddly enough, it is just this capacity to "incorporate" the physically objective, to bring it within consciousness, that the physical brain seems so inadequate to.[19] The puzzles multiply. But then the more you think about consciousness the more puzzling it comes to seem. It is comforting to reflect that from God's point of view, that is, the point of view of Nature, there is no inherent mystery about consciousness at all. The impression of mystery derives from our own incurable cognitive poverty, not from the objective world in which consciousness exists. There is no real magic in the link between mind and matter,

however incapable we are of seeing how the trick is performed. Cold comfort, perhaps, but whoever said that the nature of the mind should be fully accessible to those with a mind?[20]

Notes

This paper was read to the British Academy on 29 November 1988 and was published in the *Proceedings*, LXXIV, 1988, 219–39. Published with permission.

1. This is the standard contemporary view of naturalism. See, e.g., Jerry Fodor, *Psychosemantics* (The MIT Press: Cambridge, Mass., 1987), chapter 4. I do not say that it is my view of what it takes to be a good naturalist. As will become clear, I think we can view the mind naturalistically without being able to offer broadly physical explanations of its powers. (I say 'broadly physical' in order to include biological properties and higher-order causal properties, as well as the properties directly treated in physics.) An alternative way of putting the naturalistic demand is this: explain why it is that the mental is supervenient on the physical, given that it is. The general motive behind such naturalism is the avoidance of some sort of radical 'emergence' of the mental with respect to the physical. See Thomas Nagel, "Panpsychism," *Mortal Questions* (Cambridge University Press, 1979), on why emergence is to be avoided.

2. A third, and connected, problem is explaining how a physical organism can be subject to the norms of rationality. How, for example, does *modus ponens* get its grip on the causal transitions between mental states? This question is clearly connected with the question about intentionality, since rationality (as we ordinarily understand it) requires intentionality (the converse thesis is less obvious). But it is not so clear how closely connected are the problems of rationality and consciousness: can the former exist without the latter? If we find consciousness theoretically daunting (as I argue we should), then we should hope that reationality can be separated from it. There is a general question here: how much of the mind can be explained without being able to explain consciousness? This, as I suggest later, is the same as the question how much of the mind can be explained.

3. For discussions of these approaches see: Jerry Fodor, *Psychosemantics* (The MIT Press: Cambridge, Mass., 1987); Fred Dretske, *Knowledge and the Flow of Information* (The MIT Press: Cambridge, Mass., 1988);

Hilary Putnam, *Representation and Reality* (The MIT Press: Cambridge, Mass., 1988); Ruth Millikan, *Language, Thought and Other Biological Categories* (The MIT Press: Cambridge, Mass., 1984); Colin McGinn, *Mental Content* (Basil Blackwell: Oxford, 1989).

4. My focus in this chapter is on the content of perceptual experiences, mental states for which the notion of a subjective phenomenology is best suited. But essentially the same questions arise for thoughts, mental states for which the notion of what it is like to have them seems strained at best (thoughts are not inherently "qualia-laden"). Thoughts are conscious, of course, and the question, what confers this consciousness, is equally pressing for them as it is for experiences. Moreover, the content of thoughts looks even more closely tied to their conscious features than in the case of experiences; so it is even harder to see how we could pull apart the theory of content for thoughts and the theory of what gives thoughts their conscious aspect. What more is there to the specific way a thought is present in the stream of consciousness than its having the particular content it has?

5. See my "Can we Solve the Mind-Body Problem?" *Mind* 98:349–366. Reprinted in this volume as chapter 33.

6. See my *Mental Content* (Basil Blackwell: Oxford, 1989). The present chapter is an attempt to reconcile the optimism of that book with the pessimism of the chapter cited above.

7. See his *Reflections on Language* (Pantheon Books: New York, 1975), chapter 4.

8. Cf. Fodor's notion of 'epistemic boundedness': *The Modularity of Mind* (The MIT Press: Cambridge, Mass., 1983), Part V.

9. Nagel discusses this in *The View From Nowhere* (Oxford University Press, 1986), chapter. 2.

10. That is, our natural perception-based sense of similarity underestimates the objective difference there must be between brains and other physical objects, if brains are to be (as they are) the basis of consciousness. To God, brains seem *sui generis*, startlingly different from other physical objects. His sense of similarity, unlike ours, does justice to the uniqueness we know the brain must possess. (Compare the fallibility of our natural sense of similarity with respect to natural kinds.)

11. This latter tendency gives rise to illusions of understanding. We think we are seeing how consciousness depends upon the brain when all we are doing is reading consciousness into the physical basis. This tendency is particularly compelling when the brain is conceived as a computer: thinking of neurons as performing computations, we are tempted to credit them with conscious states (or proto-conscious states). Then it seems easy enough to see how neurons could generate consciousness. But, of course, this just pushes the question back (as well as being false): for how do these conscious properties of neurons arise from their physical nature? (Panpsychism now threatens.) If we are to describe physical processes computationally, then we must be clear that this does not involve consciousness—and then it will also be clear that we cannot get consciousness out of such descriptions. Either we presuppose what we should be explaining or we find ourselves as far away as ever from our explanandum.

12. Thomas Nagel, "What is it Like to be a Bat?," *Mortal Questions* (Cambridge University Press, 1979); Brian Farrell, "Experience," *Mind* 1950.

13. This kind of theory is defended by (among others) Tyler Burge, "Individualism and Psychology," *Philosophical Review*, January 1986. I criticize such views in *Mental Content* (Basil Blackwell: Oxford, 1989).

14. Such theories stress the third-person perspective: how we determine what someone else is referring to or thinking about. But we must not forget the perspective of the subject: how he experiences the intentional directedness of his mental states. It is the same stress on the third-person perspective that makes the likes of functionalism about sensations seem more adequate than it ought to seem.

15. Here, then, is a possible response to Hartry Field's demand that truth and reference be reducible if they are to be respectable: see his "Mental Representation," in Ned Block (ed.), *Readings in Philosophy of Psychology* (Harvard University Press: Cambridge, Mass., 1981). We need to distinguish being able to *give* a reduction from knowing that a reduction *exists*—in order not to rule out the possibility that the reduction can be specified only in a science that is congitively inaccessible to us. We cannot infer elimination from irreducibility *by us*. Nor can we simply *assume* that the correct naturalistic account of intentionality employs "broadly physical" notions, if this means that these notions do not extend our present physical concepts beyond what is intelligible to us. In a word, we must not be dogmatic conceptual conservatives. The correct reduction (if that is the right word) might not be recognizable by us as correct. (I take this to be an expression of realism.)

16. Two thinkers who have recognized the mysterious-seeming nature of meaning and reference are Thomas Nagel and Ludwig Wittgenstein. Nagel draws attention to the way meaning seems to be able to "take in" much more of the world than its basis in the particular doings and undergoings of speakers could permit: it can reach across vast stretches of space and time; it has a universality or generality that transcends the particular actions and experiences of speakers; it determines indefinitely many uses of language, past and future, as correct or incorrect. See his *What Does It All Mean?* (Oxford University Press, 1987), chapter 5. Wittgenstein, for his part, speaks of "the mysterious relation of the object and its name," and he says of the "mental activities" of wishing and believing that "for the same reason [they] have something mysterious and inexplicable about them": *The Blue and Brown Books* (Basil Blackwell: Oxford, 1958), pp. 172–3. Wittgenstein's idea, though, is that this sense of mystery arises from a (correctable) mistake: "A primitive philosophy condenses the whole usage of the name into the idea of a relation, which thereby becomes a mysterious relation" (p. 173). I am inclined to agree with him about the aura of mystery, but I doubt that it can be dispelled in the way he suggests, namely by reminding ourselves of how we actually use names or ascribe propositional attitudes. I do not think a deflationary response of this kind is adequate to the problem.

17. This seems the right way to interpret Saul Kripke's remarks about naming and reference in *Naming and Necessity* (Basil Blackwell: Oxford, 1980). Kripke disavows any intention of analyzing or reducing the relation of reference, offering us only a "picture" of how reference operates; but he does give us substantive constraints on *which* object is being referred to by the use of a name—the object which lies at the origin of the "causal chain" of uses that historically lead up to the use in question. Nor is there anything in the kind of closure I acknowledge to preclude descriptive work in the theory of reference: distinguishing the different kinds of referential device, articulating the modes of identification that underlie uses of these different devices, showing how sense and reference are related in different cases, and so forth. Nothing I say undermines the viability and usefulness of, say, Gareth Evans's work in *The Varieties of Reference* (Oxford University Press, 1982). What I am doubting is the possibility of a certain kind of explanatory enterprise: giving a broadly physical account of the very nature of the reference re-lation. We can prune the pretensions of causal theories (say) without declaring them completely out of a job.

18. For a discussion of this see my *Mental Content* (Basil Blackwell: Oxford, 1989). I set aside here the question of how secondary qualities enter into the content of experience. If these are subjectively constituted, then there is a sense in which the subjective gets turned back on itself when colors (say) penetrate the content of color epxerience. Still, colors are properties of external objects, so color experience—like shape experience—does reach out to the world beyond the subject. We may wonder whether the ultimate explanation of why we perceive secondary qualities as all is one of those questions about consciousness whose answer is forever closed to us. That would certainly account for my struggles to explain it in *The Subjective View* (Oxford University Press, 1983).

19. Genuine externalism therefore requires us to reject the more obvious kinds of physicalism, since the brain cannot incorporate the external in the way the mind can. We have no physical model of how consciouseness can lay hold of the physical world in the peculiar way it does.

20. I am grateful for comments to Thomas Nagel, Simon Blackburn, and various members of an Oxford discussion group.

16 Externalism and Experience

Martin Davies

In this chapter, I shall defend externalism for the contents of perceptual experience. A perceptual experience has representational properties; it presents the world as being a certain way. A visual experience, for example, might present the world to a subject as containing a surface with a certain shape, lying at a certain distance, in a certain direction; perhaps a square with sides about 30 cm, lying about one meter in front of the subject, in a direction about 20 degrees to the left of straight-ahead.

There are two views that we might take about these representational, or semantic, properties of experiences. On the one hand, we might hold that the content of a perceptual experience is just the content of the judgment that the subject would make if he or she took the experience at face value. In that case, perceptual content is the same kind of content as the content of judgment and belief; and externalism about perceptual content is just the same as externalism about belief content. On the other hand, we might hold that perceptual content is a distinct kind of content, different from belief content. In that case, arguments for externalism about belief content cannot automatically be transposed into arguments for externalism about perceptual content.

I shall be adopting this second view: externalism concerning perceptual content requires separate argument. That argument comes in the fifth section of this paper. The first section offers a little more clarification of what is distinctive about perceptual content, while the second section characterizes the externalist's claim. The third section sets out in more detail what is required of an externalist argument, and the fourth section explains a dilemma that the externalist is liable to face—a dilemma that I try to avoid in the fifth section. The sixth and final section raises the question whether externalist perceptual content should be conceived of as a representational superstructure erected upon a sensational substrate.

1 Perceptual Content

On the view that I am adopting here, the perceptual content of an experience is a kind of *non-conceptual* content. What this means is that a subject can have an experience with a certain perceptual content without possessing the concepts that would be used in specifying the content of that experience. Indeed, the philosophical category of perceptual content applies equally to the experiences of normal adult human beings, who are deployers of a rich repertoire of concepts, and to the experiences of human infants and certain other creatures, who arguably are not deployers of concepts at all. Enjoying experiences with perceptual content does not require the possession of concepts; *a fortiori*, it does not require the employment of such concepts as may be possessed by the experiencer.

Because the perceptual content of an experience is a kind of non-conceptual content, it must be distinguished from the content of any judgment that might be made if the experience is taken at face value. An experience may present the world to a subject as containing something square in front of her; and the subject may take that experience at face value and judge that there is, indeed, something square in front of her. Making the judgment requires possession and employment of the concept of being square; but merely undergoing the experience does not.

This is not to deny that there is a close connection between the non-conceptual content of experiences and possession of observational concepts such as the concept of being square. Thus, Christopher Peacocke says (1989, p. 5):

We can consider the case of a possession condition for a relatively observational concept. It is plausible that such a possession condition will link mastery of the concept in question to the nonconceptual representational contents of the thinker's perceptual experience.

Possession of those concepts requires a certain answerability of judgments to the perceptual content of experiences. As Colin McGinn says (1989, p. 60), "to have the concept *square* just is to apply it on the basis of experiences as of square things." But it is the notion of perceptual content (of experiences *as of* ...) that comes first in the order of philosophical explanation, and is then appealed to in an account of what it is to possess a concept such as the concept of being square.

To help fix the idea of non-conceptual perceptual content, we can note here that Peacocke offers *scenario content* as just such a kind of content. Here is what he says to introduce scenario content (1992, pp. 61–2):

I suggest that one basic form of representational content should be individuated by specifying which ways of filling out the space around the perceiver are consistent with the representational content's being correct. The idea is that the content involves a spatial *type*, the type being that under which fall precisely those ways of filling the space around the subject that are consistent with the correctness of the content.

And here is the point that scenario content is non-conceptual (1992, p. 63):

There is no requirement at this point that the conceptual apparatus used in specifying a way of filling out the space be an apparatus of concepts used by the perceiver himself. Any apparatus we want to use, however sophisticated, may be employed in fixing the spatial type, however primitive the conceptual resources of the perceiver with whom we are concerned.

We can also use the notion of scenario content to illustrate two further features of perceptual content. The first is that perceptual content abstracts from the identities of the particular objects that may be perceived: perceptual content is *not object-involving*. The second is that, despite the fact that it is not object-involving, perceptual content determines correctness conditions: perceptual content is *fully representational*. (We should note that, in Peacocke's account, a further layer of perceptual content—*protopropositional content*— is introduced, to mark distinctions between per-

ceived axes of symmetry, for example (1992, p. 77). Possession of the concept of being square then requires answerability of judgments—that a presented object is square—to the protopropositional content, rather than simply the scenario content, of experiences. This is an important complication. But protopropositional content retains the three features that we have noted: it is non-conceptual, it is not object-involving, and it is fully representational.)

Finally in this section, we can achieve some further clarification of the present use of the idea of non-conceptual perceptual content by looking back at the introduction of the notion by Gareth Evans (1982). In fact, Evans introduces the notion of non-conceptual content in two slightly different contexts: unconscious information processing, and perceptual experiences. In the first case, he says (1982, p. 104, n. 22):

When we attribute to the brain computations whereby it localizes the sounds we hear, we *ipso facto* attribute to it representations of the speed of sound and of the distance between the ears, without any commitment to the idea that it should be able to represent the speed of light or the distance between anything else.

The point here is that when we talk about "the information-processing that takes place in our brains" we attribute representational properties—contents involving speed and distance, for example—to states of the brain, without any requirement that conditions for the possession of concepts should be met. In the second case, he says (1982, pp. 226–7):

In general, we may regard a perceptual experience as an informational state of the subject: it has a certain *content*—the world is represented a certain way—and hence it permits of a non-derivative classification as *true* or *false*. ...

The informational states which a subject acquires through perception are *non-conceptual*, or *non-conceptualized*.

And, in a remark that appears to apply to both cases, he recommends that we "take the notion of *being in an informational state with such-and-such a content* as a primitive notion for philosophy, rather than . . . attempt to characterize it in terms of belief" (1982, p. 123).

Now, the notion of non-conceptual content does, indeed, have an important philosophical role to play in both these contexts. In the first case—that of unconscious information processing—it can figure in an account of *tacit knowledge* of rules, for example (Davies 1989; Crane 1992b, pp. 156–7). But it is, of course, the second case that primarily concerns us here; and the question that we need to ask is this. What, according to Evans, distinguishes the second case—the non-conceptual content of perceptual experiences—from the first case—the non-conceptual content of unconscious informational states?

We can see the answer to this question very clearly, if we consider what Evans says about the spatial element in the non-conceptual content of perceptual states. First, spatial content requires links to spatial behavior: "we must say that having spatially significant perceptual information consists at least partly in being disposed to do various things" (1982, p. 155). But the connections between informational states and appropriate behavior could be in place even while there was no conscious subject, and so no perceptual experiences. So, for the non-conceptual content of perceptual experiences, something more is required (1982, p. 158):

we arrive at conscious perceptual experience when sensory input is not only connected to behavioural dispositions . . . but also serves as the input to a *thinking, concept-applying, and reasoning system.*

Crucially, Evans equates a conscious subject with a thinking subject; he equates the consciousness of perceptual experiences with a kind of accessibility of the non-conceptual content of those experiences to the system of conceptualized judgment and belief formation (1982, p. 227):

In the case of [concept-exercising and reasoning] organisms, the internal states which have a content by virtue

of their phylogenetically more ancient connections with the motor system also serve as input to the concept-exercising and reasoning system. Judgements are then *based upon* (reliably caused by) these internal states; when this is the case we can speak of the information being "accessible" to the subject, and, indeed, of the existence of conscious experience.

For Evans, then, we only find experiences with perceptual content where we also have a thinker. Where there is no thinker, there is no conscious experience; and the perceptual states with non-conceptual content are like the informational states that enable a blindsight patient to "guess" correctly the direction of a light source (1982, p. 158).

This element of Evans's account is not preserved in the use that I am making of the idea of non-conceptual perceptual content. I would not, myself, impose such a strict standard for perceptual experience, since it closes some questions about the notion of consciousness which I would prefer to leave open. In particular, it seems to be implicit in Evans's account that the *phenomenal* consciousness of perceptual experiences is best understood as a kind of *access* consciousness. (For this distinction, see Block 1990, 1991, 1992, 1993, 1995; and for further discussion, see Davies and Humphreys 1993.) As our understanding of consciousness improves, we may come to regard that as the correct position. But, pending such an improved understanding, I would prefer to leave room for the possibility of a creature that does not attain the full glory of conceptualized mentation, yet which enjoys conscious experiences with non-conceptual content—experiences that play a role in the explanation of the creature's spatial behavior.

Despite this difference from Evans over the notion of conscious experience, however, the key idea about perceptual content remains (1982, p. 159):

It is not necessary, for example, that the subject possess the egocentric *concept* "to the right" if he is to be able to have the experience of a sound as being to the right. I am not requiring that the content of conscious experience itself be conceptual content.

With so much by way of clarification of the notion of perceptual content, we can now turn to a second preliminary matter: what is needed to establish externalism.

2 The Externalist Claim

My aim is to establish a *modal* externalist claim. I shall introduce that claim by contrasting externalist claims with corresponding *individualist* claims, and by drawing a distinction between modal and *constitutive* claims in each case.

Here, to begin with, is a statement of *constitutive individualism* (Burge 1986, pp. 3–4):

Individualism is a view about how kinds are correctly individuated, how their natures are fixed. . . . According to individualism about the mind, the mental natures of all a person's or animal's mental states (and events) are such that there is no necessary or deep individuative relation between the individual's being in states of those kinds and the individual's physical or social environments.

I take this to mean that the most fundamental philosophical account of what it is for a person or animal to be in the mental states in question does not need to advert to that individual's physical or social environment, but only to what is going on within the spatial and temporal boundaries of the creature.

Suppose for a moment that that were right— that constitutive individualism were correct—and imagine that some individual x is in some mental state S. Imagine, too, that y is a duplicate of x in the same, or in another, possible situation. Then, the constitutive account of what it is for x to be in mental state S will be satisfied equally by y, since that account adverts only to features that x and y have in common as duplicates. So, if the constitutive individualist claim were correct for mental state S, then that state would be preserved

across duplicates, whether in the same, or in different, possible situations.

In short, the constitutive individualist claim about a family of mental states or properties entails *modal individualist* claims about those states or properties—claims to the effect (Burge 1986, p. 4) that they

could not be different from what they are, given the individual's physical, chemical, neural, or functional histories, where these histories are specified non-intentionally and in a way that is independent of physical or social conditions outside the individual's body.

Such a modal individualist claim is a claim about supervenience: the mental states or properties in question supervene upon physical, chemical, neural, or functional states or properties. More specifically, it is a claim of *local supervenience*, since it says that the mental states or properties of an individual are fixed by what goes on—physically, chemically, neurally, or functionally— within the boundaries of that individual's body. If a mental state or property of an individual x is locally supervenient, then any other individual y that is a duplicate of x (is the same from the skin inward) shares that state or property.

I speak of modal individualist claims in the plural, because supervenience claims vary in strength along modal dimensions. What is principally at issue here is a *modally strong* local supervenience claim of the form: If x has mental property F in possible world w_1, and y is a duplicate in w_2 of x (in w_1), then y has F in w_2. It is important to distinguish this modally strong claim from a claim that is restricted to counterfactual duplicates of *actual* individuals, and also from a claim that concerns only duplicates within the *same* possible world: If x has intentional property F in possible world w, and y is a duplicate in w of x, then y has F in w. (For a taxonomy of supervenience claims, and a map of their entailment relations, see McFetridge 1985. In his notation, the modally strong claim concerns (XYWW′) supervenience; and the claim about counterfactual duplicates of actual individuals concerns

(XYAW) supervenience. The claim about duplicates within the same possible world concerns (XYWW) supervenience.)

Just as the various modal individualist claims are entailed by constitutive individualism, so also the negations of those modal claims entail the following statement of *constitutive externalism*:

According to *externalism* about the mind, the mental natures of at least some of a person's or animal's mental states (and events) are such that *there is a* necessary or deep individuative relation between the individual's being in states of those kinds and the individual's physical or social environments.

I take this to mean that the most fundamental philosophical account of what it is for a person or animal to be in the mental states in question does advert to that individual's physical or social environment, and not only to what is going on within the spatial and temporal boundaries of the creature.

Constitutive externalism is entailed by the negation of the modally strong local supervenience claim; and it is this relatively modest modal externalist claim for which I shall be arguing in the case of perceptual content. My aim is to provide an example in which duplicates x and y, embedded in possible circumstances w_1 and w_2 respectively, differ in respect of the non-conceptual contents of their perceptual experiences.

---

3 The Task for an Externalist Argument

Because the conceptual content of judgments and beliefs is different in kind from the perceptual content of experiences, externalist arguments about the one cannot necessarily be used to defend externalist claims about the other. In this section, I shall outline the task that confronts the externalist about perceptual content. The three main points that need to be made correspond to the three features of perceptual content that we noted in section 1: it is non-conceptual, it is not object-involving, and it is fully representational.

First, some celebrated externalist arguments about belief content (e.g., Burge 1979) are designed to show that the contents of certain beliefs depend in part upon the *social* context of the believer. In these arguments, a modal externalist claim is defended by way of examples in which the social environment differs as between the possible worlds w_1 and w_2.

Such social externalist arguments about belief content often seem to depend upon the social character of public language meaning—a dependence mediated by a presumed close tie between, on the one hand, belief content itself and, on the other hand, the linguistic meaning of expressions and reports of belief. But, because perceptual content is non-conceptual content, it is not so plausible that it is dependent upon the subject's membership in a speech community. Indeed, perceptual content is reasonably assumed to be independent of public language (cf. Burge 1986, p. 26). So, we shall not expect to find social externalist arguments about perceptual content.

This independence of perceptual content from linguistic meaning has other consequences, too. Many familiar "Twin Earth" arguments for externalism in the case of belief content—environmental as well as social—go in step with arguments for the externalism of meaning. Indeed, the line of argument began with meaning (Putnam 1975), and was then transposed to belief (see McGinn 1989, p. 31). In the case of perceptual content, a different argumentative strategy is required.

Of course, in the case of belief content—particularly the contents of *de re* beliefs—there are environmental externalist arguments that proceed directly, rather than via externalism about meaning. But—this is the second point that needs to be made—because perceptual content is not object-involving, externalism about perceptual content cannot be established by arguments analogous to externalist arguments about *de re* beliefs.

If I look at an apple, Fido, and think, "That apple is rotten," and you look at a numerically distinct but qualitatively indistinguishable apple, Fifi, and think, "That apple is rotten," then—be we ever so similar internally—our beliefs have different contents in virtue of our being related to different apples. My belief, concerning Fido, to the effect that it is rotten, is a belief whose correctness depends upon how things are with Fido: whether Fido is indeed a rotten apple. Your belief, in contrast, is one whose correctness is indifferent to how things are with Fido, but depends instead upon how things are with Fifi. In that sense, the contents of our beliefs are object-involving. As a result, it is easy to generate a modal externalist example just by varying the object of belief as between the possible worlds w_1 and w_2. But this strategy is not available in the case of perceptual content.

We introduced the idea that perceptual content is not object-involving in the context of Peacocke's account of scenario content in terms of ways of filling out the space around the subject. We can now connect the idea with the thought that the perceptual content of experience is a phenomenological notion: perceptual content is a matter of how the world *seems* to the experiencer (Evans 1982, p. 154; McGinn 1989, p. 66). If perceptual content is, in this sense, 'phenomenological content' (McGinn, *ibid.*) then, where there is no phenomenological difference for the subject, there is no difference in perceptual content. So, if two objects are genuinely indistinguishable for a subject, then a perceptual experience of the one has the same content as a perceptual experience of the other. This is in sharp contrast to the case of belief content, since the intuition about the content of *de re* beliefs concerning Fido and Fifi carries over to the case of two beliefs held by a single subject.

While perceptual content is not object-involving, it is still fully representational: the content of a perceptual experience determines a condition for correctness, or truth. One way to see how perceptual content can be truth conditional, although not object-involving, is to take perceptual

content to be existentially quantified content. A visual experience may present the world as containing *an* object of a certain size and shape, lying at a certain distance from the subject, in a certain direction. It matters not at all to that existentially quantified content of a subject's experience whether, for example, it is Fido or Fifi that she is looking at.

The third point that needs to be made is that, because perceptual content is fully representational although not object-involving, the individualist about perceptual content is in a very different position from the individualist about belief content.

In the case of object-involving belief content, there are familiar proposals to factor the content into two components. There is one component that the content of my belief about Fido has in common with the content of your belief about Fifi; and there is another component that is not shared—a component that determines the involvement of the particular apple Fido in the correctness conditions of my belief (e.g., McGinn 1982). The first component—the *narrow* content of the belief—is supposed to be locally supervenient, and so preserved across actual and counterfactual duplicates. But it does not, by itself, determine truth conditions, since what is in common between your belief and mine does not, by itself, specify whether the correctness of my belief turns upon how things are with Fido or upon how things are with Fifi. The second component is a matter of how things are in my environment. More specifically, the second component concerns causal relations between my brain and a particular object in my environment, namely Fido.

In the context of a dual component, or two factor, proposal of this kind, the individualist typically concedes an externalist claim for the truth conditional content of beliefs, but says that, for serious explanatory purposes, attention should be restricted to narrow content. Thus, the individualist about belief content recommends the employment of a kind of content that is locally supervenient, but is not fully representational (Fodor 1986; 1987, chapter 2).

Because of the differences between perceptual content and belief content—especially, because perceptual content is not object-involving—it is open to the individualist about perceptual content, in contrast, to say that experiences have content that is both locally supervenient and fully representational. Indeed, I shall take it that the individualist makes just this bolder claim, and that this is what the externalist has to argue against.

In order to establish his case, the externalist is obliged to produce a persuasive example with the following structure. First, in some possible situation w_1—perhaps the actual situation—a subject x has an experience with a certain existentially quantified content. For example, it might be an experience as of a square object of a certain size (cf. McGinn 1989), or an experience as of a shadow of a certain size and shape (cf. Burge 1986, 1988a). Second, a duplicate subject y in some other possible situation w_2 has an experience which, despite everything being the same from the skin inward, does not have that same content. This is all that is required to refute the modally strong claim of local supervenience, and establish the modest modal externalist claim.

But the externalist may choose to go further by trying to make it plausible, not merely that the duplicate's experience does not have the same content as the original subject's experience, but also that the duplicate's experience has some specific alternative content. It might be that the duplicate's experience is as of a round object, instead of as of a square object, or that the duplicate's experience is as of a crack, instead of as of a shadow.

4   Two Individualist Stances and a Dilemma for the Externalist

Given a putative externalist example with this structure, the individualist may adopt one of two possible stances. The individualist who adopts a *conservative* stance toward an example accepts the externalist's specification of the content of the experience in the original possible situation (say, the actual situation). But the individualist then rejects the externalist's claim that the experience of the duplicate in the alternative possible situation does not have that same content. Thus, for example, an individualist adopting a conservative stance may accept that an actual subject has an experience as of a shadow; but the individualist then insists that the duplicate subject's experience is also as of a shadow, despite the environmental differences.

The individualist who adopts a *revisionary* stance toward an example does not accept the externalist's specification of the content of the experience in the original possible situation. Thus, for example, an individualist adopting a revisionary stance might agree that, *if* an actual subject's experience is as of a shadow, then the experience of a duplicate may differ in content. But the individualist insists that the specification of the content of the actual subject's experience—as of a shadow—is unmotivated. The experiences of both the actual subject and the duplicate subject should be assigned some more inclusive content—perhaps: as of a shadow-or-crack.

Robert Matthews illustrates how to adopt each kind of stance in response to versions of Tyler Burge's (1986, 1988a) example of the shadows and cracks. In Burge's story, an individual P normally perceives Os (shadows of a certain small size) as Os, but occasionally misperceives a C (a similarly sized crack) as an O. In a counterfactual situation (1988a, pp. 75–6):

there are no visible Os ... [and] ... the visual impressions caused by and explained in terms of Os in the actual situation are counterfactually caused by and explained in terms of Cs—relevantly sized cracks. The cracks are where the shadows were in the actual case.

In the actual situation, the subject P sees shadows as shadows and occasionally sees a crack as a shadow. Concerning the counterfactual situation,

Burge makes a bolder and a more cautious claim. The bolder claim is that, "Counterfactually, ... P sees Cs as Cs" (1988a, p. 76); that is, the duplicate sees cracks as cracks. The more cautious claim is just that the duplicate does not see the cracks as shadows (1988b, p. 95):

[N]othing in the argument depends on attributing any specific perceptual states to the organism in the counterfactual situation. All that is important is that it be plausible that the counterfactual perceptual states are different from those in the actual situation. So the question about whether ... the organism perceives cracks as cracks in the counterfactual situation is not directly relevant to the argument.

This latter claim reflects just how little is dialectically required of the externalist. He only has to make it plausible that the subject in the counterfactual situation differs from the subject in the actual situation to the extent of not seeing the cracks as shadows.

Matthews demonstrates a conservative individualist stance as follows. In Burge's illustration, "we may imagine that the sort of entities being perceived are very small and are not such as to bear on the individual's success in adapting to the environment" (1988a, p. 75). But suppose instead, says Matthews (1988, p. 83):

that the shadows and cracks in question are important to the organism's adaptive success, e.g., that the shadows are important sources of shade for the organism during the heat of the day, and that the cracks are large enough that the organism risks injury if it should fall into them.

In the actual situation, then, the organism will go toward whatever is seen as a shadow, and avoid whatever is seen as a crack; the type of experience that is normally produced by shadows will be connected to dispositions to produce certain bodily movements. It is built into Burge's example that behavioral dispositions are the same in the counterfactual situation as in the actual situation. So, likewise in Matthews's variant, the same connections to bodily movements will be present in the duplicate in the counterfactual situation in which there are cracks where the shadows were.

Now, the externalist is supposed to make it plausible that the duplicate sees cracks as cracks, or at least not as shadows. But (Matthews, 1988, p. 83):

If in the counterfactual environment the organism repeatedly fell into the cracks when during the heat of the day it sought shelter from the sun, we would surely conclude that in this environment the organism perceives cracks as shadows, or at least not as cracks.

The behavior consequent upon the organism's visual experiences in the counterfactual situation supports the attribution of the very same content as in the actual situation. (If the individualist is adopting a conservative stance, then it is not adequate merely to argue that the organism does not see cracks as cracks; he must maintain that the organism sees cracks as shadows.)

Matthews shows how to adopt a revisionary stance in response to Burge's original version of his illustration in which no particularly adaptive behavior is produced as a result of the type of experience that is normally caused in the actual situation by shadows. In this case (Matthews, 1988, p. 83):

Burge has provided no reason for supposing that in the counterfactual environment the organism perceives cracks as cracks. Of course, there is no reason to suppose that in the counterfactual environment the organism perceives cracks as shadows, but it hardly follows from this that it perceives cracks as cracks. Given that the organism does not discriminate cracks from shadows ... one could as well argue that this organism perceives cracks and shadows as instances of one and the same type of entity.

An organism may perceive O's in the actual environment and C's in the counterfactual environment, not as O's or C's, but rather as instances of an objective type that includes both O's and C's.

If the behavior that is consequent upon a type of experience is equally appropriate to a shadow and to a crack, then we have no compelling reason to say that the experience is as of a shadow or that it is as of a crack. Just as we now lack a reason to say that the duplicates's experience is as of a shadow, so also we lack a reason for claiming that the experience of the organism in the actual situation is as of a shadow. Rather, we should say that both actual and counterfactual experiences are as of a shadow-or-crack. Thus the revisionary individualist stance. (For a detailed development of this revisionary stance, see Segal 1989. For a rejection of adopting the stance toward Burge's example, see Davies 1991; and for a rejoinder, see Segal 1991.)

What lesson should we draw from the individualist's adoption of one or the other of these stances towards the externalist's examples? One lesson concerns causal covariance theories of perceptual content.

Externalism is easy to establish if we take as a premise a covariance theory of content. For, according to such a theory, if the (predominant) causal antecedents of a type of experience are changed as between the actual and counterfactual situations, then the content of experiences of that type is changed, too.

But, causal covariance theories do not merely entail externalism. Covariance theories are pure input-side theories that nowhere advert to output factors such as behavior. Consequently, they impose constraints upon putative externalist examples; particularly, upon pairs of examples that differ only in the behavioral consequences of experiences, and not in the causal antecedents of experiences. If two examples differ in that way, then they should agree in the content they assign to the organism's actual experience and in the content they assign to the duplicate's experience in the counterfactual situation.

Matthews's adoption of a conservative individualist stance exploits this consequence, and thereby casts doubt upon covariance theories. For Matthews's variant of the example of the shadows and cracks differs from Burge's own version of his illustration only in the causal consequences of experiences. Yet, it is markedly less plausible to say that the duplicate sees cracks as cracks in Matthews's variant than it is in Burge's original version.

This certainly counts against causal covariance theories of perceptual content. But it does not count straightforwardly against externalism unless the externalist is committed to a covariance theory; that is, unless the externalist is committed to saying that a difference in causal antecedents is sufficient for a difference in content. Is the externalist so committed?

Matthews seems to see such a commitment in Burge: "we consider a modification of Burge's example that *should*, but does not, *leave his conclusion intact*" (1988, p. 82; emphasis added). But Burge himself stresses that he is not committed to any sufficient condition for an experience to have a particular content (1988b, p. 93); and, so far from opting for a covariance theory, he regards evolutionary factors, for example, as relevant to the attribution of perceptual content (e.g., 1986, p. 40). In any case, it is clear that a causal covariance theory of content is not an essential requirement in an externalist argument. For, to rebut the modally strong claim of local supervenience, all that the externalist has to show is that there are some environmental differences between situations w_1 and w_2—however thoroughgoing—that suffice for a difference of perceptual content between duplicates x in w_1 and y in w_2.

Objections to covariance theories of content are not automatically objections to externalism. But still, the inadequacy of covariance theories serves to highlight the fact that attributions of perceptual content—particularly, contents involving shape and distance properties—are partly answerable to the subject's behavior; and this fact presents the externalist with something of a dilemma.

For, either the subject in the actual situation produces behavior that is particularly appropriate to the supposed content of her experience, or else she does not. If she does, and that behavior perseveres into the counterfactual situation, then the individualist may adopt a conservative stance, insisting that the duplicate subject's experience has that same content. If she does not, then the individualist may adopt a revisionary stance, maintaining that the specification of content for the actual subject's experience is unmotivated.

This dilemma is particularly pressing for the externalist who sets out to show just what Burge aims to show with his example of the shadows and the cracks; namely, that perceptual content does not supervene upon internal constitution *plus behavioral dispositions* (1986, p. 39; 1988a, p. 69). But it is important to notice that this is strictly speaking more than the externalist is obliged to demonstrate. The externalist is allowed to have the duplicate's behavioral dispositions differ from those of the actual subject, to the extent that this is consistent with the two being duplicates.

This may appear to be a negligible degree of freedom for the externalist since, surely, the basis of behavioral dispositions is to be found inside the skin. But, if behaviour is itself characterized externalistically, then the production of behavior of a certain type depends both upon what happens inside the skin—nerve firings, muscle contractions, and the like—and upon environmental factors. In principle, behavior—externalistically characterized—can be varied even while everything inside the skin remains the same.

The externalist carries the day if, taking advantage of this freedom, he can construct a persuasive example against which neither a conservative nor a revisionary individualist stance can plausibly be adopted.

---

5 Externalism Vindicated

In this section, my aim is to provide—at least in outline—a persuasive externalist example. I shall first present the example in schematic form, and then sketch an instantiation of the schema by giving a twist to an example of McGinn's (1989, pp. 63–8).

5.1 A Schematic Example

First, in some possible situation w_1—let us say, the actual situation—a subject x enjoys experiences with perceptual content. On the input side, perceptual states of intrinsic type T covary with the distal occurrence of visual property O. (We might think of O as a shape property, say, being square, or a distance property, say, being one meter away, or a direction property, say, being 20 degrees to the left of straight-ahead.) On the output side, the behavior of type B that is consequent upon internal states of type T is particularly appropriate to O's occurrence. Thus, the input side—distal antecedents—and the output side—behavioral consequences—are in harmony; and we can suppose that evolutionarily this is no accident. We may assume that in securing covariation between T and O, the subject's visual system is doing just what it is supposed to do. Aspects or components of the visual system have been selected for their having the consequence that internal states of type T covary with occurrences of property O.

Even without a detailed theory of perceptual content, it does not seem illegitimate to suppose that, by elaborating these input-side, output-side, and teleological factors, we can make it plausible that the subject sees Os as Os; that is, that in the actual situation the perceptual states of type T are experiences as of an O.

Second, in some other possible situation w_2—a counterfactual situation—there is a duplicate y of x. This counterfactual situation is different from the actual situation in respect of the environment and perhaps also the laws of nature. As a result of these differences, distal occurrences of visual property C produce just the same retinal array as do occurrences of O in the actual situation. Consequently, perceptual states of the intrinsic type T covary with the occurrence of C, rather than of O. (We might think of C as a different shape property, say, being round, or a different distance property, say, being 75 cm away, or a different direction property, say, being 30 degrees to the left of straight-ahead.)

Because y has the same internal constitution as x, states of type T have just the same internal consequences, such as nerve firings and muscle contractions, as in the actual situation. But, environmental differences in—as it might be—gravity or friction conspire to produce trajectories for y's body that are quite different from those carved out by x's body in the actual situation. Thus, input-output harmony is preserved: the behavior of type D that is counterfactually consequent upon internal states of type T is distinctively appropriate to C's occurrence, rather than to O's. Furthermore, y's visual system is doing just what it is supposed to do. The ancestors of y have led full and happy lives and had lots of babies in part because internal states of type T covary with occurrences of C.

Once again, even without a constitutive theory of perceptual content to hand, it seems reasonable to suppose that we can make it plausible that the duplicate subject sees Cs as Cs; that is, that in the counterfactual situation the states of type T are experiences as of a C. *A fortiori*, we can make it plausible that those states are not experiences as of an O; and this latter claim is all that is needed to rebut local supervenience.

An example of this form cannot, of course, be used to demonstrate that perceptual content fails to supervene on internal constitution *plus* behavioral dispositions. For although we can plausibly vary perceptual content as between the actual and the counterfactual situation, we also vary behavioral dispositions if these are externalistically characterized in terms of bodily trajectories. But, just as it stands, a persuasive example of this form carries the day against individualism. For it presents a difference of perceptual content between duplicates; and that is enough to establish all that the externalist is dialectically obliged to establish, namely that (Burge 1986, p. 4):

A person's intentional states and events could (counterfactually) vary, even as the individual's physical,

functional (and perhaps phenomenological) history ... is held constant.

Whether it is possible to modify such an example so as to vary perceptual content while keeping the behavioral dispositions the same is a subsidiary question that is not my main concern here.

5.2 Percy

The example to which I shall, in the next subsection, give a twist is actually used by McGinn (1989, pp. 58–94) to argue *against* what he calls *strong externalism* for perceptual content. McGinn's target is the thesis that the difference between an experience of something looking square and an experience of something looking round is "a matter of a difference in how those experiences relate to instantiations of squareness and roundness" (1989, p. 63). In essence, what McGinn aims to rebut is a causal covariance theory of perceptual content.

To this end, McGinn constructs an example. In the actual situation, internal state S1 of the subject Percy is caused by square things and internal state S2 is caused by round things. In the counterfactual situation, Percy's internal constitution and behavioral dispositions are just as in the actual situation, but as a result of environmental differences, state S1 is produced by round things and state S2 is produced by square things. On a particular occasion in the counterfactual situation, Percy is in state S1. Is the perceptual content of his experience that there is a square thing before him or that there is a round thing before him? Is the experience as of something square or as of something round?

The strong externalist must say that the content of the experience in the imagined case is individuated in terms of the distal causes of state S1 in the counterfactual situation; thus the content of Percy's experience is that there is a round thing before him. McGinn, in contrast, argues that in the counterfactual situation Percy is doomed to misperceive round things as square. In support of this view, McGinn points to the fact that Percy's behavior, consequent upon his being in internal state S1, is appropriate to the presence of a square thing—for behavioral dispositions are preserved across the actual and counterfactual situations. He makes it plausible that, where there is dislocation between the facts of covariance on the input side and the facts of behavior on the output side, output-side factors should dominate in the ascription of perceptual content (1989, p. 66): "So when it comes to a competition between action and environment, in the fixation of perceptual content, action wins."

Furthermore, McGinn points out, this judgment about the content of Percy's experiences is backed up by teleological elements that plausibly belong in a theory of perceptual content (1989, pp. 66–7):

We naturally want to say that the *purpose* of his moving in a square path is to negotiate square objects successfully, that this is the *function* of his moving like that.
... if Percy's functional properties are preserved [in the counterfactual situation], so too will be the content of ... his perceptual states. That is, if his squarewise movements have the function precisely of negotiating square things, then the perceptual states that lead to these movements will partake of this function and have their contents fixed accordingly.

We shall surely agree with McGinn in rejecting strong externalism here. In effect, he is adopting a conservative individualist stance toward a particular example; and his attitude toward Percy in the counterfactual situation is much like Matthews's attitude toward the creatures who keep falling into the cracks.

But, McGinn's argument does not, of course, show that individualism is correct for perceptual content; it does not establish a modally strong claim of local supervenience. Nor does McGinn set out to defend individualism, as we have defined that doctrine. So, there is nothing inconsistent in adapting McGinn's example in the service of externalism.

In fact, the issue of externalism—in the sense of the denial of local supervenience—lies somewhat off to one side from McGinn's main concerns. For, in his thought experiments, McGinn includes behavioral dispositions among the internal factors that are to be held constant across actual and counterfactual scenarios (1989, p. 2). But, as we have seen, if behavioral dispositions are characterized externalistically in terms of bodily trajectories, then they can vary even while all that is inside the skin stays the same. This point will be crucial when we come to give a twist to the example of Percy.

Before we move on, however, it is tempting to pause briefly and ask whether the example of Percy makes it plausible that perceptual content supervenes upon internal constitution *plus behavioral dispositions*. There are grounds for supposing that it does not. In the counterfactual situation we have Percy (or a duplicate) moving squarewise in response to round things; and McGinn makes it plausible that the character of the behavior is more important for perceptual content than are the distal antecedents. This intuition is particularly strong when the function of the behavior is preserved along with its spatial character. Nevertheless, it does seem possible that, where there is a sufficiently hopeless breakdown of harmony between input-side and output-side factors, we may be entitled to withhold all attributions of perceptual content (Fricker 1991, p. 141). Consequently, there could be an example of duplicates, sharing their behavioral dispositions, yet differing in that one has experiences with perceptual content and the other does not.

5.3 Percy with a Twist

Let us slightly vary McGinn's example. In the counterfactual situation we now find, not Percy himself, but a duplicate with a very different evolutionary history. This creature's ancestors survived to reproduce in part because their behavior was appropriate to the distal causes of their perceptual experiences. In this imaginary scenario, internal state S1 is produced by distal round things, as in McGinn's example; but the behavior consequent upon the creature's being in S1 is now appropriate to the presence of round things, and not to the presence of square things.

What is being imagined here is not that walking a square trajectory is the best way of avoiding a round object. Rather, we suppose that environmental differences have the consequence that the same nerve firings and muscle contractions as in the actual situation result in a quite different bodily trajectory. In particular, the goings-on inside the skin which in the actual situation lead to a square trajectory now have a round trajectory as their upshot. This happy agreement of input-side, output-side, and teleological factors makes it plausible that, when Percy's duplicate is in state S1, he has an experience as of a round thing. *A fortiori*, it is implausible that the duplicate misperceives round things as square; and this is all that the externalist argument strictly requires.

What we have here is, of course, just an instantiation of our schematic example, with the shape properties of being square and being round now playing the roles of O and C. And what goes for shape properties surely goes equally—or even more so—for distance and direction properties. But, perhaps some individualist critic will deny that this is a persuasive externalist example, on the grounds that the departures from actuality required by the substitution of circles for squares are wildly science fictional.

It is unclear that this is an effective individualist response, since the whole discussion has been carried out in the domain of thought experiments; and, in the face of the individualist's modally strong claim of local supervenience, it is surely legitimate to consider counterfactual situations that are also counternomic. Certainly Burge is explicit that, "Since examples usually involve shifts in optical laws, they are hard to fill out in great detail" (1986, p. 42). But, perhaps we can do something to reduce the wildness.

Instead of considering squares in the actual situation, let us consider ellipses. In particular, let us consider ellipses that are slightly elongated along the (gravitational) vertical axis. Our perceiver Percy sees these ellipses as ellipses—as witness input-side, output-side, and teleological factors surrounding his internal state S1. In addition, in the actual situation, Percy sees round things as round (and is then in internal state S2).

In the counterfactual situation, we imagine that the retinal arrays—and consequent internal state S1—that are actually produced by these vertically elongated ellipses are instead produced by circles; and behavior is squashed along the vertical axis so that input-output harmony is preserved. Furthermore, we imagine all this to be the result of evolution. Percy's duplicate is as well adapted to this counterfactual situation as Percy is to the actual situation.

The plausible externalist claim about this example is that, when Percy's duplicate is in the same internal state S1 that Percy is in when he has an experience as of a vertically elongated ellipse, the duplicate's experience is as of a round thing. *A fortiori*, the duplicate's experience is not as of an ellipse; and this is all that the externalist argument strictly requires.

It is as well to enter two clarificatory comments about this example. The first concerns axes of symmetry. Since an ellipse has just two axes of symmetry while a circle has infinitely many, someone might ask how many axes of symmetry Percy's duplicate sees circles as having. This is a question about the representational properties of the duplicate's perceptual experiences. (It is a matter of protopropositional content: Peacocke 1992, p. 77.) So, it would be begging the question against externalism if someone were to insist that the duplicate must see circles as having just two axes of symmetry. Nevertheless, it is open to the externalist to allow that Percy's duplicate sees circles as having only vertical and horizontal axes of symmetry, just as Percy sees ellipses as having only two axes of symmetry. For it is not uncommon for subjects to see shapes as having fewer axes of symmetry than they really have. For example, a square has four axes of symmetry, but when seen as a square it is seen as having two axes of symmetry (intersecting the sides), and when seen as a diamond it is seen as having a different two (intersecting the corners).

The second clarificatory comment concerns the simplifying assumptions that are implicit in the example. The duplicate's behavior is supposed to be squashed along the (gravitational) vertical axis, in virtue of some environmental difference in, say, gravity or friction. But, there is an implicit assumption here, to the effect that the range of Percy's behavioral interactions with ellipses is very limited. This does not undermine the dialectical purpose of the example of Percy and his duplicate. But it does suggest that it will be difficult to provide an externalist example relating to the experiences of shape that are enjoyed by creatures whose interactions with the world are as complex and sophisticated as ours are (see Davies 1993).

So much, then, for what I claim to be (a sketch of) a simple but persuasive externalist example involving shape properties. (It is a straightforward matter to produce similar examples involving distance or direction properties.) Can either a conservative or a revisionary individualist stance be adopted toward the example of Percy and his duplicate? Neither looks plausible.

The individualist who adopts a conservative stance toward the example accepts the externalist's specification of the content of the experience that Percy enjoys when he is in internal state S1. It is an experience as of a vertically elongated ellipse (or as of a square, in the first version of the example). But the individualist then insists that the experience of Percy's duplicate has that same content; that the duplicate misperceives round things as elliptical, despite producing behavior that is distinctively appropriate to the occurrence of roundness. Given the convergence of input-side, output-side, and teleological factors in the example, the conservative individualist stance appears quite unmotivated.

But a revisionary individualist stance looks even less attractive. To adopt this stance is to deny that Percy's actual experience is as of an ellipse, and to say that the experiences of both Percy—in the actual situation—and his duplicate—in the counterfactual situation—should be assigned some more inclusive content, such as: as of an ellipse-or-circle. But, if that is the content of Percy's actual experience when he is in state S1, then why does he execute behavior that is particularly appropriate to vertically elongated ellipses? And what is the content of his experience when he is in state S2 (produced by round things)? In short, the adoption of a revisionary individualist stance is problematic for the intentional explanation of Percy's behavior (see Davies 1991).

Thus is externalism concerning perceptual content vindicated. But the vindication leaves us with a puzzle about the phenomenology of perceptual experience. This puzzle is the topic of my final section.

---

6   Perceptual Content and Phenomenology

Our externalist conclusion that perceptual content is not locally supervenient—that it does not strongly modally supervene upon the internal state of the subject—appears to be inconsistent with the conjunction of two antecedently plausible propositions about phenomenology.

The first of these two propositions is that perceptual content is a matter of how things seem to the conscious subject. Thus, for example, McGinn insists (1989, p. 63):

Let us be clear that we are considering a phenomenological notion here: conscious seemings, states there is something it is like to have. . . .

So we are considering properties of organisms that determine the form of their subjectivity, . . .

Perceptual content is a matter of how the world is presented to the conscious subject as being arranged.

The second proposition is that experience has a phenomenal character that is supervenient upon the internal state of the subject. The intuition here is that neither the nature of the distal antecedents, nor the shape of the consequent trajectory, nor the course of evolutionary history, is a determinant of the subjective nature—the "what it is like"—of sensory experience. According to this second proposition, what it is like, phenomenally, to be Percy is just the same as what it would be like to be Percy's duplicate.

If perceptual content is a phenomenological notion—as the first proposition says—then the inescapable conclusion appears to be that perceptual content supervenes upon whatever the phenomenal character of the subject's experience supervenes upon. But then, by the second proposition, perceptual content turns out to supervene upon internal constitution—in contradiction with our externalist conclusion.

The first proposition says that the way the world is presented to the subject is a matter of phenomenology; perceptual content supervenes on phenomenal character. The second proposition says that phenomenology is locally supervenient: phenomenal character supervenes upon internal consititution. The clash with externalism then appears to be a consequence of an undeniable principle: the transitivity of supervenience.

But, we can see our way to one possible resolution of the puzzle if we are more careful about the notion of supervenience that is at work in the first proposition about phenomenology.

6.1   A Resolution: Kinds of Supervenience

In section 2, we noted that supervenience claims vary in strength along modal dimensions, and we distinguished "across worlds" (XYWW') supervenience—which has been our principal concern in this paper—from, for example, "within a world" (XYWW) supervenience. So, the question to ask is: What kind of supervenience is involved in the first plausible proposition about phenomenology (perceptual content supervenes upon phenomenal character)?

We are certainly committed to the claim that perceptual content is a phenomenological notion. Indeed, we have already used that claim (in section 16.3) to support the idea that perceptual content is not object-involving. As McGinn says (1989, p. 63), "Looking square is subjectively distinct from looking round": where there is a difference of perceptual content, there must be some difference in the phenomenal character of the experiences. Supervenience is surely in the offing here. But, in order to honor the phenomenologicality of perceptual content, we only need this supervenience to apply within an individual subject, in a single possible world. If there is no phenomenal difference between two experiences in the life of a given subject, then those experiences have the same perceptual content.

From this "within a subject, within a world" (XXWW) supervenience claim—however modally strong may be the supervenience claim in the second proposition about phenomenology— no amount of transitivity will take us to the denial of our externalist conclusion. In short, the apparent puzzle is generated by a failure to distinguish between the modally modest supervenience that is used in the first proposition about phenomenology and the modally strong supervenience that is at issue in the debate between individualism and externalism.

The distinction between kinds of supervenience claim yields a resolution of the puzzle about externalism and phenomenology by trading upon another distinction; namely, that between the perceptual content of an experience and its intrinsic phenomenal character. Perceptual content is a matter of representational properties of experience, while intrinsic phenomenal character is conceived of as being non-representational.

Given the distinction between perceptual content and phenomenal character, the externalist about perceptual content can accept both the propositions about phenomenology. He accepts the first proposition by saying that, for the experiences of a given subject, a difference of perceptual content requires a difference in intrinsic phenomenal character. Within a subject, and within a world, a representational difference requires a non-representational difference. He accepts the second proposition by saying that the (non-representational) intrinsic phenomenal character of an experience really is strongly modally locally supervenient: it is preserved across actual and counterfactual duplicates.

His externalism then commits him to the possibility of a difference of perceptual content between the experiences of (actual and counterfactual) duplicates; that is—by the second proposition—to the possibility of a difference of perceptual content even while intrinsic phenomenal character is preserved. Across subjects, and across worlds, a representational difference does not require a non-representational difference. Indeed, this possibility is explicitly recognized in Burge's expression of modal externalism (1986, p. 4; emphasis added):

A person's intentional states and events could (counterfactually) vary, even as the individual's physical, functional (*and perhaps phenomenological*) history ... is held constant.

But, before we rest content with this resolution of the puzzle, we should ask ourselves whether we want to take on this commitment to the intrinsic phenomenal character of experience.

6.2 Sensational Properties of Experience

The idea of a level of intrinsic phenomenal character, intermediate between internal physical constitution and perceptual content, is the idea of perceptual experience as having a sensational (non-representational) substrate upon which the representational superstructure of perceptual content is erected. Appealing to this intermediate level so as to resolve the puzzle about externalism and phenomenology commits us to there being a sensational difference corresponding to every representational difference within the experience of a given subject. That commitment goes well beyond the mere acknowledgment that perceptual experiences have sensational as well as representational properties.

Certainly some who reject the idea of a sensational substrate take the further step of rejecting sensational properties altogether. Thus, McGinn points out (1989, p. 75) "obscurities and problems" that beset the view that recognizes (1989, p. 73):

a prerepresentational yet intrinsic level of description of experiences: that is, a level of description that is phenomenal yet noncontentful ...

and accompanies this with the strong claim that "perceptual experience has none but representational properties (at least so far as consciousness is concerned)" (1989, p. 75). But, it is surely an option to acknowledge the existence of some non-representational properties of experience without embracing the idea of a sensational substrate.

The distinction between representational and sensational (intrinsic but not representational) properties of experience is the focus of earlier work by Peacocke (1983, chapter 1). There, he offers examples that are intended to show that there could be pairs of experiences with the same sensational properties but different representational properties, and other examples that are intended to show the converse—that there could be pairs of experiences with the same representational properties but different sensational properties. Now, one of the background assumptions of that earlier work is that perceptual content is conceptual content (1983, p. 19):

[N]o one can have an experience with a given representational content unless he possesses the concepts from which that content is built up.

As a consequence, many of the lessons drawn from the examples do not carry over into the framework of Peacocke's own later work, and of this paper, where non-conceptual content is recognized. (See Crane 1992a, for a helpful discussion of these differences.) For example, in the earlier work, grouping phenomena are described in terms of sensational properties (1983, pp. 24–5); in the later work, they are described in terms of protopropositional content (1992, p. 79), which is a kind of non-conceptual content, cutting somewhat more finely than scenario content.

Nevertheless, there is still enough in those examples to make it plausible that perceptual experiences have sensational, as well as representational, properties. In particular, the example of monocular and binocular viewing of the same scene—in a case where the scene provides sufficiently many cues that there is no loss of depth information when only one eye is used (1983, p. 13)—seems to provide a pair of experiences that present the space around the subject as being filled out in just the same way. Yet the two experiences are phenomenologically different. What it is like to have the monocular experience is not just the same as what it is like to have the binocular experience, even though the experiences have the same perceptual content.

Certainly, not everyone is persuaded by this example (e.g., Tye 1991, p. 130; 1992, p. 174). Further discussion would be warranted. But the important point for present purposes is that acknowledging the existence of some sensational properties, on the basis of examples such as this one, is very far from embracing the idea of a sensational substrate. It would take a massive leap to move from a modest non-representational difference between monocular and binocular viewing of the same scene to a host of non-representational properties subvening under the myriad representational properties of every perceptual experience.

6.3 A Question About Phenomenal Character

If we do make that leap then, as we have seen, we can resolve the puzzle about externalism and phenomenology. That is, we can accept the modal externalist claim, along with the two plausible propositions about phenomenology. (We might even take the possibility of resolving the puzzle in this way as an argument for making the leap; see Davies 1992, pp. 42–4.) But, we then face a further

problematic question. For, if perceptual content can vary—as between duplicates in different possible worlds—while intrinsic phenomenal character remains the same, then we are bound to ask whether the correlation between sensational and representational properties is relatively constrained or relatively unconstrained. Just how different might be the representational superstructures erected upon one and the same non-representational substrate?

If the correlation between sensational substrate and representational superstructure is relatively constrained, then it must be governed by some theoretical principles. But, it is far from obvious where the required constraining principles might issue from. On the other hand, to the extent that the relation is unconstrained, we are left entertaining scarcely intelligible hypotheses, along the lines that I, or a duplicate, might enjoy an experience with just the same intrinsic phenomenal character as my visual experience now, yet with utterly different representational properties. Neither option is very inviting.

I do not say, definitively, that there is no way to answer this question about the correlation between sensational substrate and representational superstructure. Perhaps some constraining principles will be forthcoming, for example. But, I do say that the question is problematic; that the problem it poses is no less daunting than the original puzzle concerning externalism and the two propositions about phenomenology. Confronted with the problematic question, we should hesitate over a commitment to a sensational substrate—to the intrinsic phenomenal character of experience.

As a result, we should reconsider the second proposition about phenomenology; namely, the proposition that there is a level of phenomenal description of perceptual experience that is (modally strongly) supervenient upon the internal state of the subject. We can accept that perceptual experiences have some sensational properties (on the basis of such examples as monocular and binocular viewing of the same scene); and, indeed, we can suppose that these non-representational properties are strongly modally locally super- venient. But, it is at best an open question whether such sensational properties constitute a subvening basis upon which the representational properties of experience are variously supported in actual and counterfactual situations.

Suppose that we give up the idea of a non- representational underpinning for every repre- sentational property of experience. Then we can still make something of the first proposition about phenomenology: perceptual content is a phenomenological notion. We no longer say that perceptual content supervenes (within a subject, within a world) upon something that is supposed to be more fundamentally phenomenal: the non- representational intrinsic phenomenal character of experience. Instead, we say that perceptual content is itself irreducibly an aspect of what it is like to have a perceptual experience. But the second proposition about phenomenology has to be given up. Given externalism, what it is like to have a perceptual experience—now regarded as shot through with perceptual content—is not wholly independent of causal antecedents, con- sequent trajectory, and evolutionary history. It is not supervenient (across subjects, across worlds) upon the internal state of the subject. If we give up the idea of a sensational substrate, then there is an important difference here between externalist and individualist conceptions of the subjective nature of sensory experience.

In the first five sections of this chapter, I argued in favor of externalism about perceptual content. Now, in this final section, we see that, once ex- ternalism is accepted, we may well have to give up the idea that experience has any (strongly mo- dally) locally supervenient level of phenomenal description.

Acknowledgments

This chapter is a descendant of "Perceptual Con- tent and Local Supervenience" (Davies 1992), which appeared in the *Proceedings of the Aristo- telian Society*, Volume 92. I am grateful to the Aristotelian Society for permission to re-use sub- stantial parts of that paper. While many of the differences are presentational, there has also been a substantive change in my views about the sen- sational properties of experiences (section 3 of Davies 1992, and section 6 of the present chap- ter). For more on these themes, see Davies (1993).

Some of the early work toward the paper was carried out at the Australian National University in 1990 and at MIT in 1991. I am grateful to ANU, the British Academy, MIT, and the Rad- cliffe Trust for financial support. Thanks to David Bell, Tyler Burge, Frank Jackson, Greg McCulloch, Christopher Peacocke, Gabriel Segal, Tom Stoneham, Stephen Williams, and especially Ned Block, for comments and con- versations.

References

Block, N. 1990. "Consciousness and Accessibility." *Be- havioral and Brain Sciences*, vol. 13, pp. 596–8.

Block, N. 1991. "Evidence Against Epiphenomena- lism." *Behavioral and Brain Sciences*, vol. 14, pp. 670–2.

Block, N. 1992. "Begging the Question Against Phenomenal Consciousness." *Behavioral and Brain Sciences*, vol. 15, pp. 205–6.

Block, N. 1993. Review of D. C. Dennett, *Conscious- ness Explained. Journal of Philosophy*, vol. 90, pp. 181– 93.

Block, N. 1995. "On a Confusion about a Function of Consciousness." *Behavioral and Brain Sciences*, vol. 18, pp. 227–87.

Burge, T. 1979: "Individualism and the Mental." In P. A. French, T. E. Uehling and H. K. Wettstein (eds.), *Midwest Studies in Philosophy, Volume 4: Studies in Metaphysics*, Minneapolis: University of Minnesota Press, pp. 73–121.

Burge, T. 1986. "Individualism and Psychology." *Philosophical Review*, vol. 95, pp. 3–45.

Burge, T. 1988a: "Cartesian Error and the Objectivity of Perception." In R. H. Grimm and D. D. Merrill (eds.), *Contents of Thought*, Tucson, AZ.: University of Arizona Press, pp. 62–76. Also in P. Pettit and J. McDowell (eds.), *Subject, Thought, and Context*, Oxford: Oxford University Press, 1986.

Burge, T. 1988b. "Authoritative Self-Knowledge and Perceptual Individualism." In R. H. Grimm and D. D. Merrill (eds.), *Contents of Thought*, Tucson, AZ.: University of Arizona Press, pp. 86–98.

Crane, T. 1992a. "Introduction." In T. Crane (ed.), *The Contents of Experience: Essays on Perception*, Cambridge: Cambridge University Press, pp. 1–17.

Crane, T. 1992b. "The Nonconceptual Content of Experience." In T. Crane (ed.), *The Contents of Experience: Essays on Perception*, Cambridge: Cambridge University Press, pp. 136–57.

Davies, M. 1989. "Tacit Knowledge and Subdoxastic States." In A. George (ed.), *Reflections on Chomsky*, Oxford: Basil Blackwell, pp. 131–52.

Davies, M. 1991. "Individualism and Perceptual Content." *Mind*, vol. 100, pp. 461–84.

Davies, M. 1992. "Perceptual Content and Local Supervenience." *Proceedings of the Aristotelian Society*, vol. 92, pp. 21–45.

Davies, M. 1993. "Aims and Claims of Externalist Arguments." In E. Villanueva (ed.) *Philosophical Issues Volume 4: Naturalism and Normativity*, Atascadero, CA.: Ridgeview Publishing Company, pp. 227–49.

Davies, M. and Humphreys, G. W. 1993. "Introduction." In M. Davies and G. W. Humphreys (eds.), *Consciousness: Psychological and Philosophical Essays*, Oxford: Blackwell Publishers, pp. 1–39.

Dennett, D. 1988. "Quining Qualia." In A. J. Marcel and E. Bisiach (eds.), *Consciousness in Contemporary Science*, Oxford: Oxford University Press. Reprinted in W. G. Lycan (ed.), *Mind and Cognition: A Reader*, Oxford: Basil Blackwell, 1990, pp. 519–47.

Evans, G. 1982. *The Varieties of Reference*. Oxford: Oxford University Press.

Fricker, E. 1991. "Content, Cause and Function" (Critical Notice of McGinn, *Mental Content*), *Philosophical Books*, vol. 32, pp. 136–44.

Fodor, J. 1986. "Individualism and Supervenience." *Proceedings of the Aristotelian Society*, supplementary volume 60, pp. 235–62.

Fodor, J. 1987. *Psychosemantics*. Cambridge MA.: MIT Press.

McFetridge, I. G. 1985. "Supervenience, Realism, Necessity." *Philosophical Quarterly*, vol. 35, pp. 246–58.

Reprinted in *Logical Necessity and Other Essays*, London: Aristotelian Society, 1990, pp. 75–90.

McGinn, C. 1982. "The Structure of Content." In A. Woodfield (ed.), *Thought and Object*, Oxford: Oxford University Press, pp. 207–259.

McGinn, C. 1989. *Mental Content*. Oxford: Basil Blackwell.

Matthews, R. J. 1988. "Comments (on Burge 1988a)." In R. H. Grimm and D. D. Merrill (eds.), *Contents of Thought*, Tucson, AZ.: University of Arizona Press, pp. 77–86.

Peacocke, C. 1983. *Sense and Content*. Oxford: Oxford University Press.

Peacocke, C. 1989. "What Are Concepts?" In P. A. French, T. E. Uehling and H. K. Wettstein (eds.), *Midwest Studies in Philosophy, Volume 14: Contemporary Perspectives in the Philosophy of Language II*, Notre Dame, IN: University of Notre Dame Press, pp. 1–28.

Peacocke, C. 1992. *A Study of Concepts*. Cambridge, MA.: MIT Press.

Putnam, H. 1975. "The Meaning of 'Meaning.'" In *Philosophical Papers, Volume 2: Mind, Language and Reality*, Cambridge, Cambridge University Press, pp. 215–71.

Segal, G. 1989. "Seeing What Is Not There". *Philosophical Review*, vol. 98, pp. 189–214.

Segal, G. 1991. "Defence of a Reasonable Individualism". *Mind*, vol. 100, pp. 485–94.

Tye, M. 1991. *The Imagery Debate*. Cambridge, MA.: MIT Press.

Tye, M. 1992. "Visual Qualia and Visual Content." In T. Crane (ed.), *The Contents of Experience: Essays on Perception*, Cambridge: Cambridge University Press, pp. 158–76.

17 A Representational Theory of Pains and Their Phenomenal Character

Michael Tye

The fundamental assumption of cognitive psychology is that the mind is a *representational system* which mediates between sensory inputs and behavioral outputs. The primary task for the cognitive psychologist is one of explaining how the various cognitive capacities operate by reference to the structure of the salient parts of this representational system. The explanations offered are both functional and decompositional: they decompose the relevant capacities into their basic representational components and show how those components function together to produce the capacities. Theories are evaluated by how well they account for the behavior observed in psychological experiments and, at the lowest level, by how well they fit with knowledge gleaned from neurophysiology about the physical bases of the capacities.

Philosophers have usually assumed that pain cannot lie within the domain of cognitive psychology. Pains, it has been supposed, are not like images or memories or visual percepts: they have no representational content. So, there can be no explanation of the desired sort. To understand the various facets of pain, we need to look elsewhere, perhaps to the realm of neurophysiology. Cognitive psychology cannot help us. This, I now believe, is a mistake: pains *do* have representational content. So, the view that pain is not a proper object of study for cognitive psychology is not well founded.

My discussion begins with an old objection to the token identity theory in connection with afterimages, and a modern response to it which has become widely accepted. This response, I maintain, is unsatisfactory, as it stands. But, with one key revision, it is, I believe, defensible, and it has ramifications for our understanding of pain. In particular, it points to the conclusion that pains have representational content, as does at least one other facet of our everyday conception of pain. In the third section of the paper, I consider the question of what sorts of representations pains are most plausibly taken to be. Are they sentences in an inner language, like beliefs and desires, on the usual computational conception of the latter states? Or are they representations of a different sort? I suggest that a sentential approach is difficult to reconcile with some of the neuropsychological data on pain, and I make an alternative proposal. Pains, I propose, are representations of the same general sort as mental images: they are arrays to which descriptive labels are appended. So, pain, I urge, is a proper object of study of cognitive psychology. In the final section, I take up some questions concerning the phenomenal character of pain.

I

In the 1950s J. J. C. Smart (1959) raised the following objection to the identity theory for sensations: Afterimages are sometimes yellowy-orange; brain processes cannot be yellowy-orange. So afterimages are not brain processes. The reply that Smart himself made to the objection was to deny that afterimages exist, there really being, in Smart's view, only experiences of *having* afterimages, which are not themselves yellowy-orange.

Another less radical response is available on behalf of the identity theory. It is on this response that I wish to focus here. Why not say that in predicating color words of images we are not attributing to them the very same properties that we attribute to external objects via our use of color language. So, afterimages are not literally green or blue in the way that grass or the sky have one or the other of these features. Now it is no longer obviously true that brain processes cannot be yellowy-orange in the relevant sense.

The obvious problem that this response faces is that of explaining how it is that color vocabulary is applied at all to afterimages, given that they do not really have the appropriate colors. One solution proposed by Ned Block is to say that color words are used elliptically for expressions like "real-blue-representing," "real-green-representing." and so on, in connection with images generally. (Block 1983, esp. p. 518). In my view, this solution has a number of important virtues.[1] For one thing, brain processes can certainly represent colors. So, the identity theory is no longer threatened. For another, as Block has noted (Block 1983, pp. 516–517), terms like "loud" and "high-pitched" are standardly applied directly to oscilloscope readings used in connection with the graphical representations of sounds. In this context, these terms evidently do not name real sounds made by the readings. One possibility, then, is that they pick out representational properties such as loud-representing and high-pitched–representing. If this is so, then there already exists an established usage of terms that conforms to the one alleged to obtain in the case of color terms and afterimages.

There is a serious difficulty, however. Mental images are not literally square any more than they are literally blue. So, extending the above proposal to shape, we get that a blue, square afterimage is simply an afterimage that is square-representing and also blue-representing. But intuitively this seems too weak. Surely, a blue, square image cannot represent different things as blue *and* square. Unfortunately, nothing in the above proposal rules this out. "Blue," then, in application to afterimages, does not mean "blue-representing." Likewise "square."

This difficulty is not peculiar to images. Precisely the same problem can be raised in connection with oscilloscope readings. The way out, I suggest, is to appreciate that there is nothing elliptical about the meanings of terms like "blue" or "loud" in the above contexts. Instead it is the contexts themselves that need further examination. Let me explain.

The contexts "Hopes for an *F*" and "Hallucinates a *G*" are typically intensional. Thus, I can hope for eternal life and hallucinate a pink elephant, even though there are no such things.

Similarly, I can hope for eternal life without hoping for eternal boredom, even if in reality the two are the same. It seems evident that the terms substituting for "*F*" and "*G*" in these contexts retain their usual meanings. The above peculiarities are due to the fact that hoping and hallucinating are representational states, and to the special character of representation itself.

Now precisely the same peculiarities are present in the case of the context "an *F* image," where "*F*" is a color or shape term. Thus, in a world in which nothing is really triangular, I can still have a triangular image. Also, if I have a red image, intuitively it does not follow that I have an image the color of most fire engines even given that most fire engines are red. The explanation, I suggest, is straightforward: an *F* image is an image that *represents that something* is *F*.[2]

Likewise, an *F*, *G* image is an image *which represents that something* is both *F* and *G*. My suggestion, then, is that there is nothing elliptical or peculiar about the meanings of the terms "*F*" and "*G*" in the context "An *F*, *G* image." Rather the context itself is an intensional one, having a logical structure which reflects the representational character of images generally.

It may still be wondered why we *say* that the image itself is *F* and *G*, for example, blue and square. This is, I suggest, part of a much broader usage. Frequently when we talk of representations, both mental and nonmental, within science and in ordinary life, we save breath by speaking as if the representations themselves have the properties of the things they represent. In such cases, in saying of a representation that it is *F*, what we mean is that it represents that something is *F*. So, when it is said of some given oscilloscope reading that it is loud and high-pitched, what is being claimed is that loud and high-pitched are features that the reading represents some sound as having. "Loud" and "high-pitched" mean what they normally do here. The context itself is intensional.

The above proposal solves the problem of the blue, square image. Here the image represents that something is both blue and square, not merely that something is blue *and* that something is square.[3]

The claim that afterimages are representational, I might add, does not entail or presuppose that creatures cannot have afterimages unless they also have the appropriate concepts (at least as "concept" is frequently understood). Having the concept *F* requires, on some accounts, having the ability to use the linguistic term '*F*' correctly. On other accounts, concept possession requires the ability to represent in thought and belief that something falls under the concept. But afterimages, like other perceptual sensations, are not themselves thoughts or beliefs; and they certainly do not demand a public language. They are, if you like, nondoxastic or nonconceptual representations.

The broad picture I have here very briefly is this. Processes operating upon proximal stimuli generate certain sorts of visual representations via mechanical procedures. Categorizations of various sorts occur along the way. Visual sensations are representations that form the outputs of this early modular processing, and stand ready to produce conceptual responses via the action of higher-level cognitive processing of one sort or another. So, visual sensations feed into the conceptual system, without themselves being a part of that system.

In admitting that afterimages are nonconceptual representations, I am not thereby granting that they do not really have *intentional* content, that they are representations of a nonintentional sort. In my view, intentionality does not require concepts. As I use the term "intentionality," the key features are representation (and hence the possibility of *mis*representation) along with the possibility of substitution failures in the associated linguistic contexts. These features, I have argued, are present in the case of afterimages. So, afterimages are intentional. Those philosophers who want to insist that there cannot be full-blooded intentionality without concepts (or that intentionality is restricted to the central

executive) are entitled to their use of the term. But any disagreement here is, I suggest, purely verbal. Nothing of substance hangs upon which usage is adopted.

We are now ready to turn to the case of pain.

II

It is often supposed that terms applied to pain that also apply to physical objects do not have their ordinary meanings. Ned Block, who takes this view, says the following:

There is some reason to think that there is a systematic difference in meaning between certain predicates applied to physical objects and the same predicates applied to mental particulars. Consider a nonimagery example: the predicate _____ in _____. This predicate appears in each premise and the conclusion of this argument:

The pain is in my fingertip.
The fingertip is in my mouth.
Therefore, the pain is in my mouth.

This argument is valid for the "in" of spatial enclosure..., since "in" in this sense is transitive. But suppose that the two premises are true in their *ordinary* meanings.... The conclusion obviously does not follow, so we must conclude that "in" is not used in the spatial enclosure sense in all three statements. It certainly seems plausible that "in" as applied in locating pains differs in meaning systematically from the standard spatial enclosure sense. (Block 1983, p. 517)

This seems to me quite wrong. There is no more reason to adopt the strange position that "in" does not mean spatial enclosure in connection with pain than there is to say that "orange" in connection with images has a special meaning. With the collapse of the latter view, the former becomes unstable. And the inference Block cites does *not* establish his claim. To see this, consider the following inference:

I want to be in City Hall
City Hall is in a ghetto
Therefore, I want to be in a ghetto.

The term "in" has the same meaning in both premises and the conclusion. But the argument is invalid: I might want to be in City Hall to listen to a particular speech, say, without thereby wanting to be in a ghetto. The same is true, I suggest, in the case of Block's example, and the explanation is the same. In both the first premise and the conclusion, the term "in" appears in an intensional context. Just as when we say that an image is blue, we are saying that it represents that something is blue, so when we say that a pain is in my fingertip, we are saying that it represents that something is in my fingertip.

It is perhaps worth noting here that the invalidity of the inference involving pain has nothing to do with the fact that mouths are cavities of a certain sort, and hence items whose ontological status might itself be questioned. If I have a pain in my fingertip, and I slit open a small portion of my leg, into which I then thrust my finger, still it does not follow that I have a pain in my leg. Suppose, for example, that my leg has been anesthetized. In this case, I feel a pain in my finger, but not in my leg.

Nor does it help to say that what the inference failure really shows is that pains themselves are ontologically suspect. For even if it were true that there are no pains, only people who are pained, still this gives us no account of why the inference fails. After all, if "in" means inside, and I am pained in my fingertip, then I am also pained in my mouth, assuming my fingertip is in my mouth.

That there is a hidden intensionality in statements of pain location is confirmed by our talk of pains in phantom limbs. We allow it to be true on occasion that people are subject to pains in limbs that no longer exist. How can this be? Answer: You can have a pain in your left leg even though you have no left leg, just as you can search for the Fountain of Youth. Again the context is intensional: specifically, you have a pain that represents that something is in your left leg.[4]

Of course, there is some temptation to say that if you do not have a left leg, then you cannot really have a pain in it. But that is no problem for my proposal. For there is a *de re* reading of the context, namely that to have a pain in your left leg is for your left leg to be such that you have a pain in *it*. Now a left leg *is* required.

But does not a pain in the leg represent more than just that something is in the leg? To answer this question, it is necessary to make some more general remarks about pain. To have a pain is to feel a pain, and to feel a pain is to experience pain. Thus, if I have a pain, I undergo a token experience of a certain sort. This token experience is, I suggest, the particular pain I have.

The identification of pains with token experiences explains why no one else could feel the *particular* pain I am feeling, and moreover why pains are necessarily owned by *someone* or other. Token experiences are events (in the broad sense, which includes token states), and, in general, events are individuated in part via the objects which undergo them. So, laughs cannot exist unowned, and neither can screams. Likewise, killings, births, and explosions. In each of these cases, there must be a subject for the event: a killer, a creature that is born, an object that explodes. Moreover, the subject is essentially related to the event. No one else can die my death or laugh my laugh, although, of course, someone else can certainly undergo qualitatively very similar deaths or laughs.

Now pain experiences, if they are anywhere, are in the head. But in the case of a pain in the leg, what the pain experience tracks, when everything is functioning normally, is tissue damage in the leg. So, a pain in the leg, I suggest, is a token sensory experience which represents that something in the leg is damaged.[5]

So far I have said nothing directly about the painfulness of pains. How is this feature of pains to be accounted for within the above proposal? To begin with, it should be noted that we often speak of bodily damage as painful. When it is said that a cut in a finger or a burn or a bruise is painful or hurts, what is meant is (roughly) that it is *causing* a feeling, namely the very feeling the person is undergoing, and that this feeling elicits an immediate dislike for itself together with anxiety about, or concern for, the state of the bodily region where the disturbance feels located.

Of course, pains do not themselves normally cause feelings that cause dislike: they *are* such feelings, at least in typical cases. So, pains are not painful in the above sense. Still, they are painful in a slightly weaker sense: they typically elicit the *cognitive* reactions described above.[6] Moreover, when we introspect our pains we are aware of their sensory contents as painful. This is why if I have a pain in my leg I am intuitively aware of something in my leg as painful (and not in my head, which is where, in my view, the experience itself is). My pain represents damage in my leg, and I then cognitively classify that damage as painful (via the application of the concept *painful* in introspection).

So, in normal circumstances, a person who has a pain in a leg and who reports that something in her leg is painful is not under any sort of illusion. But a man who reports to his doctor that he has a pain in his left arm is in a different situation, if it is discovered that the real cause of his pain lies in his heart. Such a man has a pain in his left arm—he undergoes a sensory experience that represents to him damage there—but there really is nothing wrong *in his left arm*. What is painful is a disturbance happening in his heart.

There is one objection worth mentioning here. Perhaps it will be said that a person who experiences a pain in a certain bodily part need not be aware *that* there is such-and-such tissue damage inside the relevant part. Such a proposal is too complicated to fit the phenomenology of pain experiences (or many such expriences).

This objection is not compelling. Pains, in my view, are *sensory* representations of tissue damage. To feel a pain, one need not have the resources to conceptualize what the pain represents (see note 5). One need not be able to say or think that such-and-such tissue damage is occurring. Still, the content of the pertinent sensory representation is what gives the pain its phenomenal character.

In my view, the intentionalist treatment I have proposed can be extended to pains of more specific sorts. A twinge of pain is a pain that represents a mild, brief disturbance. A throbbing pain is one that represents a rapidly pulsing disturbance. Aches represent disorders that occur *inside* the body, rather than on the surface. These disorders are represented as having volume, as gradually beginning and ending, as increasing in severity and then slowly fading away (cf. Armstrong 1962). The volumes so represented are not represented as precise or sharply bounded. This is why aches do not feel to have precise locations, unlike pricking pains, for example. A stabbing pain is one that represents sudden damage over a particular well-defined bodily region. This region is represented as having volume (rather than being two-dimensional), as being the shape of something sharp-edged and pointed (like that of a dagger).[7] In the case of a pricking pain, the relevant damage is represented as having a sudden beginning and ending on the surface or just below, and as covering a very tiny area. A racking pain is one that represents that the damage involves the stretching of internal body parts (e.g., muscles).

In each of these cases, the subject of the pain undergoes a sensory representation of a certain sort of bodily disturbance. The disturbances vary with the pains. Consider, for example, a pricking pain in the leg. Here, it seems phenomenologically undeniable that pricking is experienced *as* a feature tokened within the leg, and not as an intrinsic feature of the experience itself. What is experienced as being pricked is a part of the surface of the leg. This is nicely accounted for by the above proposal. It should also be noted that since pricking pains do not represent pins, my account does not have the implausible consequence that creatures who live in worlds without pins cannot have pricking sensations or that in these worlds creatures undergoing such sensations are misrepresenting what is going on in them.

Pains, I conclude, like afterimages, have representational content. Unlike images, however, they have bodily locations (in the representational sense I have elucidated).[8] So, although pains, in my view, are really constituted by physical processes in the head, it is also true to say that they can occur anywhere in the body.[9]

III

The language of thought hypothesis is an empirical hypothesis about how the representational contents of mental states are, in fact, encoded in the head. It is not an a priori philosophical analysis. So, it is not intended to cover the contents of mental states of all actual and possible creatures. In its most general form, it concerns the coding of *all* actual mental contents. The basic thesis, stemming from the computer model of mind, is that such contents are encoded in symbol-structures in an inner language.

In the case of the so-called propositional attitudes—that is, those mental states like belief and desire whose contents are standardly expressed in "that" clauses—it has typically been supposed that the relevant symbol-structures are sentences (Fodor 1975, 1978). The apparent need to acknowlege inner sentences in an account of the propositional attitudes (hereafter the PAs) derives from several different sources.

To begin with, the PAs are systematic: there are intrinsic connections between certain thoughts. Consider, for example, the thought that the boy is chasing the dog and the thought that the dog is chasing the boy. Anyone who has the capacity to think the former thought also has the capacity to think the latter and vice versa. Secondly, the PAs are productive: we have the capacity, it seems, to think indefinitely many thoughts and to think thoughts we have never thought before. The PAs are also fine-grained: I can think that you know something important without thinking that you justifiably and truly believe something important, even if the correct analysis of "know" is "justifiably and truly believe." Finally, the PAs have truth-values: my belief that the English pound is worth less than two years ago in dollars is either true or false.

Facts exactly parallel to these obtain in the case of sentences in public languages. According to adherents to the language of thought hypothesis, these parallels are best explained by supposing that the PAs themselves have a sentence-like structure.[10]

What sorts of representations, then, are pains? Are they too inner sentences? It may be tempting to suppose that if they have representational content, as I have urged, and if the language of thought hypothesis is true, then they must *must* be sentences. This would be much too quick, however. For a commitment to an inner language within which cognition occurs is not a commitment to sentences in each and every case of mental representation. After all, computers—symbol manipulators, par excellence—operate on all sorts of symbol structures (e.g., lists, sentences, arrays); and, to mention one example, there are well-known theories of mental imagery which fall within the computational approach, but which reject the thesis that images are sentences.[11] Moreover, it is certainly not obvious that the language of thought hypothesis in its unrestricted form is true. Perhaps some mental representations are not coded in our heads in linguistic symbols at all.

A simple appeal to the general language of thought hypothesis does not justify the claim that pains are sentences. Do the considerations adduced above in connection with the PAs support the sententialist view of pains? It might be held that, to some extent, they do. There are some systematic connections between pains: the capacity to feel a burning pain in the leg and (at the same or another time) a stinging pain in the arm seem connected to the capacity to feel a stinging pain in the leg and a burning pain in the arm. Moreover, if pains are representations, then they can misrepresent.[12] So, there is a sense in which some pains may be characterized as false: what they represent is not, in fact, the case.

It must be admitted that these considerations are not very compelling, however. Systematic connections between pains are limited and can easily be accounted for on a model of pains as maps, for example. And the possibility of misrepresentation does not *require* that pains be true or false, any more than the fact that maps or paintings are sometimes inaccurate requires that they be true or false.

Are there any pieces of evidence which count against a sententialist view of pain? It seems to me that there are. We know that in visual perception, the retinal image is reconstructed in the visual cortex so that in a quite literal sense adjacent parts of the cortex represent adjacent parts of the retinal image. There is, then, an orderly topographic projection of the retinal image onto the brain. This has been established from experiments in which a recording electrode is placed inside the visual cortex. Greater neural activity is picked up by the electrode when light is shone onto a particular spot on the retina. Moving the electrode a little results in the continued registration of greater activity only if light is directed onto an adjacent part of the retina.

Topographic organization of this sort is also found in the somatosensory cortex. There is, for example, an orderly topographic representation of the surface of the human body that is dedicated to touch. Here adjacent regions of the body surface are projected onto adjacent regions of the cortex. Enhanced activity in one of the relevant cortical regions represents that the region of body surface projected onto it is being touched. Some relatively small portions of the body, for example, the hands and face, provide input to more neurons than do some relatively large portions, for example, the trunk. This is why, when two separate points on the face are touched, the shortest distance between the points at which both can be felt is much less than the shortest distance when points are on the trunk are touched.

There are further representations of the human body in the somatosensory cortex that are similarly structured. It has been established that the experience of pain is associated with activity in this cortex.[13] Now the fact that the somatosensory cortex is topograpically organized and that it is the primary locus of pain raises doubts about the sentential view of pain. For sentences do not have the requisite maplike representational structure.[14]

My suggestion, then, is is that pains themselves are topographic or maplike representations. More specifically, I hold that pains are patterns of active cells occurring in topographically structured three-dimensional arrays to which descriptive labels are attached. This proposal may be unpacked as follows.

For each pain, there is an array made up of cells corresponding to irregularly sized portions of the body, with adjacent cells representing adjacent body regions.[15] Each cell, when active, may be conceived of as representing that something painful is occurring at the corresponding body region. The irregularity of the grain in the array is partly responsible, I suggest, for variations in our experience of pain when the same degree of damage occurs in different bodily regions of the same size (e.g., the face versus the torso).

Since the cells within the pain array itself are individually concerned only with arbitrary body regions, there is no representation in the array of natural body parts. Segmentation of the body regions into such parts occurs via inspection processes that examine patterns of active cells in the array, and assess them, on the basis of their location, as pains in arms, legs, and so forth. It is here that descriptive labels that represent the relevant body parts are appended to the array. I speculate that further labels are introduced for global features of the represented damage via further routines that mechanically work over the array and extract at least *some* of the relevant information from its contents. For example, in the case of a stabbing pain, we may suppose that there is a sudden pattern of activity in the array, beginning at a part of the array representing a narrow region of body surface and extending in the proper temporal sequence to cells representing adjacent deeper internal regions (so that a roughly dagger-shaped volume is marked out). The relevant computational routines process this activity and assign an appropriate descriptive term.[16] In the case of a stinging pain, we may suppose that certain cells in the array representing contiguous regions of body surface along a narrow band are strongly activated, more or less simultaneously, for a brief period of time. This activity generates a computational response, and the relevant term again affixed. Whether these suppositions are along the right lines is a matter for investigation by cognitive psychology.

This crude model is, of course, very sketchy indeed. What it gives us, I suggest, is an alternative way of thinking about pains as representations, one which seems to me more promising than the purely sentential view. Pains, I believe, represent in something like the way that maps represent that contain additional descriptive information for salient items ("treasure buried here," "highest mountain on island"). In this respect, they are very like mental images, as I conceive them.

There is strong evidence that images and visual percepts share a medium which has been called "the visual buffer." This medium is functional in character: it consists of a large number of cells, each of which is dedicated to representing, when filled, a tiny patch of surface at a particular location in the visual field. For visual percepts and afterimages, the visual buffer is filled, in normal cases, by processes that operate on information contained in the light striking the eyes. For mental images (other than afterimages), the visual buffer is filled by generational processes that act on information stored in long-term memory about the appearances of objects and their spatial structure.

Images and percepts, I have argued elsewhere, are interpreted symbol-filled patterns of cells in the visual buffer. The symbols within each cell represent at least some of the following local features: presence of a patch of surface, orientation of the surface, color, texture, and so on. Interpretations are affixed to the patterns of filled cells in the form of descriptions that provide a more specific content, for example, whether the imaged object is a circle or a square, or, in more complex cases, a duck or a rabbit. I have elaborated this view in detail in another work (Tye 1991). So, I shall not pursue it here. I conjecture that bodily sensations generally, perceptual experiences, and imagistic experiences all have their contents encoded in arrays of the sort I have described.

I should perhaps emphasize here a point I made earlier in connection with afterimages. On my view, although the processes responsible for filling the arrays in both bodily and perceptual sensation do not essentially require belief or thought, they certainly involve categorization. Consider, for example, the sorts of categorization that go on in very early vision, for example, the detection of edges and the computation of distance away—categorizations that are relevant to how the visual buffer is filled. These categorizations are automatic. They do not demand that the creature have beliefs or thoughts about the properties of visual stimuli that are represented in such categorizations. Much the same is true, I maintain, in the case of bodily sensations. So nothing in the proposed account entails that a very small child or an animal could not feel pain. Their relative conceptual impoverishment does not preclude them from undergoing processing and representations of the sort necessary to fill some portion of the appropriate array.

What about the descriptive labels that are appended to the arrays? Is thought or belief involved here? Again I am inclined to suppose that in at least *some* cases, the further categorizations that take place here do so without the essential involvement of concepts (understood as involving a public language or thought). Consider, for example, the case of simple shapes in perceptual experience. Nothing looks square to me, unless the appropriate processes have operated upon the filled cells in the visual buffer and categorized them as representing a square shape.[17] But it is not necessary that I think (or believe) of the object I am seeing that it is square. Indeed, I need not have any thought (or belief) at all about the real or apparent features of the seen object.

Perhaps it will now be said that it is not clear how the model I have outlined accommodates the well-established fact that pain is susceptible to top-down influences. For example, in one experiment, joggers were found to run faster in a lovely wooded area than on a track. Apparently, they experienced less pain in their arms and legs while viewing the trees and flowers, and as a result, ran at a quicker pace (Pennebaker and Lightner 1980). There is also the interesting case of some Scottish terriers raised in restricted environments. Upon being released, Melzack tells us, they behaved as follows:

They were so frisky and rambunctious that inevitably someone would accidentally step on their tails. But we didn't hear a squeak from them. In their excitement, they would also bang their heads with a resounding smack on the building's low water pipes and just walk away. I was curious, and lit a match to see how they would respond to the flame. They kept sticking their noses in it, and though they would back off as if from a funny smell, they did not react as if hurt. (Quoted in Warga 1987)

Anxiety, by contrast, increases the experience of pain, as, for example, when one compares a present injury with some past one.

These facts about pain are no threat to the proposal I have made. They may be explained by supposing that the pain receptor pathway in the spinal column leading to the somatosensory cortex has a gate in it that is controlled by input from the higher brain centers (the gate control theory) (Melzack and Wall 1965). When this gate is partly closed, less information gets through and the feeling of pain diminishes. As it opens further, more information is enabled to pass. Anxiety, excitement, joy, concentration, and other higher-level activities affect the orientation of the gate. So, the fact that the experience of pain is, *in the above sense*, cognitively penetrable presents no real difficulty for my proposal.

Still, there is one very important feature of pain on which I have as yet made only a couple of passing comments: its phenomenal character. In what does the phenomenal character of pain consist? What is the relationship of phenomenal character to representational content?

These are questions I shall address in the final section. My concern so far has been simply to establish the thesis that pains have representational content and to make plausible my contention that pains, like images, are a proper object of study for cognitive psychology. Whether pains have phenomenal features that cannot be representationally or intentionally grounded is a further issue (just as in the case of mental images).

IV

It is usually held that pains have intrinsic, introspectively accessible properties that are wholly nonintentional and that are *solely* responsible for their phenomenal character. Such properties are often called qualia, although the term is sometimes used in a broader way to refer to subjective or phenomenal features, however they are analyzed or understood. As a general view about the phenomenal character of pain, this view seems to me clearly mistaken.

Consider the following case. As I write, I have a backache. There is something it is like for me to be the subject of this backache. What it is like to be the subject of this backache is, of course, the same as what it is like to be the subject of this backache. But what it is like to be the subject of this backache is not the same as what it is like to be me, even though I am the subject of this backache. Why not?

The answer, I suggest, is that the "what it is like" context is intensional. Co-referential expressions cannot always be safely substituted without change of truth-value. What creates the intensional context is the intentional nature of phenomenal character or "feel." The specific phenomenal character of a state—what it is like to undergo it—is none other than the state's intentional content, or more accurately, in my view, an aspect of that content.

Consider again the above case of a backache. The qualities I experience (and strongly dislike) are experienced *as* features instantiated in some region of my back and not as intrinsic features of my experience. Since it could be the case that there really is nothing wrong with my back, the qualities need not be actual features of my back. Rather they are features my experience *represents* as being tokened in my back (e.g., the feature of being such and such a sort of disturbance). Moreover, these features are not intrinsic properties of my experience that I mistakenly project onto part of my body. There is no general error embedded in pain experiences.

Now the phenomenal character of my pain intuitively is something that is given to me via introspection of *what* I experience in having that pain. But what I experience is what my experience represents. So, phenomenal character is representational.

Perhaps it will be denied that the qualities I experience when I have a backache are apparently located in my back. But this is certainly what introspection strongly suggests. When I turn my gaze inwards and try to focus my attention on *intrinsic* features of my pain experience in such a case, features the experience has in itself apart from what it represents, I do not seem to come across any. I always seem to end up attending to what I am experiencing *in my back*. Careful introspection reveals only further aspects of *that*, further aspects of my experience's representational or intentional content. The experience itself is transparent.[18] Why? The answer, I suggest, is that my experience has no *introspectible* features that distinguish it from other experiences over and above those implicated in its content. So, the specific phenomenal character of my experience—itself something that is introspectibly accessible—is identical with, or contained within, its overall intentional content.

Still, if the distinctive phenomenal character of pains is an aspect of their intentional content, just which aspect is this? What is *phenomenal content*? This is a complex question which I take up fully in my book (Tye 1995). In this chapter, I can make only some very schematic remarks.

In my view, phenomenal content is abstract, nonconceptual, intentional content that is poised for use by the cognitive centers. The claim that contents relevant to phenomenal character of pains (and other sensory experiences) must be *poised* is to be understood as requiring that these contents attach to the output representations of the relevant sensory module(s) and stand ready and in position to make a direct impact on the belief/desire system.[19]

This view entails that no belief could have phenomenal character. A content is classified as phenomenal only if it is nonconceptual and poised. Beliefs are not nonconceptual; and they are not appropriately poised. They lie within the conceptual arena, rather than providing inputs to it. Beliefs are not sensory representations at all (although on given occasions they may certainly be accompanied by such representations).

The claim that the contents relevant to phenomenal character must be *abstract* is to be understood as demanding that no concrete objects enter into these contents. The reason for this requirement is straightforward. Whether or not you have a left leg, you can feel a pain in your left leg; and in both cases, the phenomenal character of your experience can be exactly the same. So, the existence of that particular leg is not required for the given phenomenal character. What matters rather is the conjunction of general features or properties the experience represents. The experience nonconceptually represents that there are such and such co-instantiated locational and nonlocational features, and thereby it acquires its phenomenal character.

The claim that the contents relevant to phenomenal character must be *nonconceptual* is to be understood as saying that the general features entering into these contents need not be ones for which their subjects possess matching concepts. I have already made some remarks pertinent to this requirement.

Exactly which features represented by pains are elements of their phenomenal contents? There is no a priori answer. Empirical research is necessary. The relevant features will be the ones represented by the output representations of the sensory module for pain. We might call features that are so represented in connection with the outputs of the various sensory modules "*observational features.*" Since the receptors associated with the modules and the processing that goes on within them vary, features that are observational for one module need not be observational for another.[20] What gets outputted obviously depends upon what gets inputted, and how the module operates. In my view, it is the representation of a certain class of observational features by our pain experiences, and the role that they play, which gives pains their phenomenal character.

Many questions remain here, of course, not the least of which concern the supervenience of phenomenal character upon what is in the head, and the issue of absent qualia (Tye 1995). But I hope that I have said enough to show that a wholly representational approach to pains is a promising one.[21]

Notes

This chapter is reprinted, with substantial revisions, from *Philosophical Perspectives*, volume 9, edited by J. Tomberlin (Northridge, CA: Ridgeview, 1995), pp. 223–240.

1. These virtues led me to accept the proposal until very recently. See Tye 1991.

2. There is, I might add, a possible *de re* reading of this context as follows: *F*-ness is such that an *F* image represents that something has *it*. Now, from "I have a red image" and "Red is the color of most fire engines," "I have an image the color of most fire engines" *may* be inferred.

3. I might add that, in my view, a necessary condition of any image representing that something is both *F* and *G* is that it represent that something is *F*. So, if I have an *F*, *G* image, I must have an *F* image. The argument for

the premise here is straightforward: In having a blue, square image, I experience blue *as* a feature of something or other, a feature co-instantiated with square. *What* I experience, in part, is *that* something is blue. So, my image, in part, represents that something is blue.

4. Phantom limb pain shows that pains do not essentially involve relations between persons and parts of their bodies. This seems to me a decisive objection to the relational view presented in Aune 1967, p. 130.

5. In my view, the representation of damage here is nonconceptual. So, I can certainly see that my leg is damaged without feeling any pain there. In the case of seeing-that, my state involves a belief about damage (and hence the exercise of concepts).

6. According to pain researchers, people who have been given prefrontal lobotomies, or certain other treatments, often report that they feel pain but that they do not mind it or that it does not really bother them (see Melzack 1961, 1973). These reports, even if taken at face value, are compatible with the proposal in the text. For clearly such cases are abnormal.

7. I do not mean to suggest here that one cannot have a stabbing pain unless one has the concept of a dagger. Pains, to repeat, are non-conceptual sensory representations.

8. I deny that so-called psychological pains, for example, pains of regret or embarrassment, are really pains. I think it plausible to hold that such states are labeled 'pains' because, like (normal) pains, people are aversive to them. But this usage of 'pain' is, I suggest, metaphorical or analogical. This is not to deny, of course, that real pains may have psychological causes. Embarrassment may certainly *cause* burning facial pain (see Stephens and Graham 1987, p. 413).

9. The constitution relation is weaker than the relation of identity. *A* can be constituted by *B* even though *A* and *B* differ in some of their modal properties (Tye 1992).

10. For a detailed development of the above points concerning systematicity and productivity, see Fodor and Pylyshyn (1988).

11. One such theory is Stephen Kosslyn's Pictorialism (Kosslyn 1980).

12. Cases of misrepresentation are not rare. Pains in the upper left arm are often due to disturbances in the heart.

13. This is not to deny that other neural regions also play a role in some pain experiences. In particular there

are pain pathways which terminate in both the posterior parietal cortex and the superior frontal cortex.

14. For a discussion of the representational differences between sentences, pictures, and maps, see Tye 1991.

15. The characteristics of arrays are examined further in Tye 1991.

16. It need not be assumed that the proper temporal sequence referred to in the last sentence of the text *necessarily* corresponds to the real-world temporal sequence. The fact that the inspection routines treat the activity in one cell C as representing a later bodily disturbance than the activity in another cell C' does not necessitate an implementation via an arrangement in which C is active after C'. For some illuminating comments on the representation of time which can be brought to bear upon this point, see Dennett 1991, chapter 6.

17. For one possible sketch of these processes, see Marr 1982.

18. Transparency has been discussed by a number of philosophers. See, for example, Harman (1990).

19. This is developed further in Tye 1995 and 1996. For a discussion of some differences between Block's conception (this volume) of what it is for a state to be poised and my own, see Tye 1996.

20. Moreover, in classifying a feature as observational, I am not supposing that it has that status for all possible species of creatures. Observationality, in my view, is relative to creatures with a certain sort of sensory equipment. Thus, some features that are observational for us might not be for other possible creatures (and vice versa).

21. I would like to thank Ned Block, Gabriel Segal, and especially Sydney Shoemaker for helpful comments.

References

Armstrong, D. (1962). *Bodily Sensations* London: Routledge and Kegan Paul.

Aune, B. (1967). *Knowledge, Mind, and Nature*. New York: Random House.

Block, N. (1983). "Mental Pictures and Cognitive Science," *Philosophical Review, 93*, 499–542.

Dennett, D. (1991). *Consciousness Explained*. Boston: Little, Brown.

Fodor, J. (1975). *The Language of Thought*. New York: Thomas Crowell.

Fodor, J. (1978). "Propositional Attitudes," *Monist, 61*, 501–523.

Fodor, J., and Pylyshyn, Z. (1988). "Connectionism and Cognitive Architecture: A Critical Analysis," *Cognition, 28*, 3–71.

Harman, G. (1990). "The Intrinsic Quality of Experience." In J. Tomberlin (Ed.), *Philosophical Perspectives*, vol. 4. Northridge, CA: Ridgeview.

Kosslyn, S. 1980. *Image and Mind*. Cambridge, MA: Harvard University Press.

Marr, D. (1982). *Vision*. San Francisco: W. H. Freeman.

Melzack, R. (1961). "The Perception of Pain," *Scientific American, 204*.

Melzack, R. (1973). "How Acupuncture Can Block Pain," *Impact of Science on Society, 23*, 1–8.

Melzack, R., and Wall, P. (1965). "Pain Mechanisms: A New Theory," *Science, 150*, 971–979.

Pennebaker, J., and Lightner, J. (1980). "Competition of Internal and External Information in an Exercise Setting," *Journal of Personality and Social Psychology, 39*, 165–174.

Smart, J. (1959). "Sensations and Brain Processes," *Philosophical Review, 68*, 141–156.

Stephens, L. and Graham, G. (1987). "Minding Your P's and Q's: Pain and Sensible Qualities," *Nous, 21*, 395–406.

Tye, M. (1991). *The Imagery Debate*, Cambridge, MA: MIT Press.

Tye, M. (1992). "Naturalism and the Mental," *Mind, 101*, 421–441.

Tye, M. (1995). *Ten Problems of Consciousness*, Cambridge, MA: MIT Press.

Tye, M. (1996). "The Function of Consciousness," *Nous*, 30.

Warga, C. (1987). "Pain's Gatekeeper," *Psychology Today*, August, pp. 51–56.

18   Sensation and the Content of Experience: A Distinction

Christopher Peacocke

Nothing is more fundamental to understanding the content of psychological states than sense experience....

But experience is not merely of instrumental interest. Having an experience is a psychological state in its own right, and one that raises many puzzles. How can senses as intrinsically different as sight and touch both serve as sources of knowledge about the spatial layout of our environment? Is the ancient tradition correct which holds that some concepts, those of secondary qualities, are more intimately related to experience than those of primary qualities? If so, must we acquiesce in the circular view that being red is to be explained in terms of looking red?[1]

... The present chapter develops some claims and distinctions needed ... for the discussion of those questions.... As such, it has the character of a prelude. Nevertheless, it too has a venerable subject, one that would have been discussed by a classical British empiricist under the heading "Sensation and Perception." My claim in this chapter will be that concepts of sensation are indispensable to the description of the nature of any experience. This claim stands in opposition to the view that, while sensations may occur when a subject is asked to concentrate in a particular way on his own experience, or may occur as by-products of perception, they are not to be found in the mainstream of normal human experience, and certainly not in visual experience. But first we need to clarify the issues.

Historically, the distinction between putative perceptual experiences and sensations has been the distinction between those experiences which do in themselves represent the environment of the experiencer as being a certain way, and those experiences which have no such representational content. A visual perceptual experience enjoyed by someone sitting at a desk may represent various writing implements and items of furniture as having particular spatial relations to one another and to the experiencer, and as themselves having

various qualities; a sensation of small, by contrast, may have no representational content of any sort, though of course the sensation will be of a distinctive kind. The representational content of a perceptual experience has to be given by a proposition, or set of propositions, which specifies the way the experience represents the world to be. To avoid any ambiguity, I will use the phrase "content of experience" only for the representational content of an experience, and never for a type of sensation: many past writers followed the opposite practice and used "object" or "meaning" for representational content. Corresponding to the historical distinction between sensation and perception, we can draw a distinction between sensational and representational properties of experience. Representational properties will be properties an experience has in virtue of features of its representational content; while sensational properties will be properties an experience has in virtue of some aspect—other than its representational content—of what it is like to have that experience.[2]

The content of an experience is to be distinguished from the content of a judgment caused by the experience. A man may be familiar with a perfect *trompe l'oeil* violin painted on a door, and be sure from his past experience that it is a *trompe l'oeil*: nevertheless his experience may continue to represent a violin as hanging on the door in front of him. The possibility of such independence is one of the marks of the content of experience as opposed to the content of judgment. One of the earliest writers to state a distinction between sensation and perceptual experience, Thomas Reid, introduced it in terms which require that perceptual experience implies belief in the content of the experience.[3] In fact, we need a threefold distinction between sensation, perception, and judgment, to formulate the issues precisely.

This independence of the contents of judgment and experience does not mean that judgments cannot causally influence the content of experiences. In some cases they do. You may walk into your sitting-room and seem to hear rain falling outside. Then you notice that someone has left the stereo system on, and realize that the sound you hear is that of applause at the end of a concert. It happens to many people that after realizing this, the sound comes to be heard as applause: the content of experience is influenced by that of judgment. All the independence claim means is that this need not happen.

Among the many current uses of the term "information," there is one in particular from which the present notion of representational content should be distinguished. There is a sense in which a footprint contains the information that a person with a foot of such-and-such shape and size was at the location of the footprint earlier; and in which a fossil may contain the information that there was an organism of a certain kind at its location in the past. This is a clear and important use of "informational content," and it seems that it is, very roughly, to be explained along these lines (the details will not matter for us); x's being F at t has the informational content that there was something standing in R to x at some earlier time t' and which was then G, iff in normal circumstances an object's being F at some particular time is causally, and perhaps differentially explained by there existing at some earlier time an object standing in R to it and which was then G.[4] An experience, or more strictly the occurrence to someone of an experience of a certain type at a certain time, will certainly have informational content in this sense. But informational content differs from representational content in at least four respects. First, the informational content of a visual experience will include the proposition that a bundle of light rays with such-and-such physical properties struck the retina; nothing like this will be in the representational content of the experience. Second, there are cases in which the representational content and the informational content of an experience are incompatible. This will be so for experiences of geometrical illusions. Such experiences are normally differentially ex-

plained by the presence of objects with properties incompatible with those they are represented by the experience as having. Third, though both informational content and representational content are specified by "that" clauses, the contents are of different kinds. A specification of informational content is completely referentially transparent in genuine singular term position: this property it inherits from the corresponding transparency of "causally explains." In the representational content of an experience, on the other hand, objects are presented under perceptual modes of presentation. (This contrast applies not only to singular term position, but also to predicate position. We shall later wish to distinguish properties from modes of presentation of properties, and when that distinction is drawn, it will appear that only the properties themselves, and not properties under modes of presentation, enter causal explanations.) Finally, it is in the nature of representational content that it cannot be built up from concepts unless the subject of the experience himself has those concepts: the representational content is the way the experience presents the world as being, and it can hardly present the world as being that way if the subject is incapable of appreciating what that way is. Only those with the concept of a sphere can have an experience as of a sphere in front of them, and only those with spatial concepts can have experiences which represent things as distributed in depth in space.

By emphasizing these differences, I do not mean to exclude the possibility that possession of representational content can be analyzed in terms of informational content (whether this is so is a complex and difficult matter). The present point is just that any such analysis would not consist in an identity. So when I argue that all experiences have nonrepresentational properties, this is *not* a claim to the effect that the intrinsic properties of experience are not determined by their informational content. It is rather a claim about the range of intrinsic properties themselves.

Those who say that sensation has almost no role to play in normal, mature human experience, or at least in normal human visual experience, commonly cite as their ground the fact that all visual experiences have some representational content. If this is indeed a fact, it shows that no human visual experience is a pure sensation. But it does not follow that such experiences do not have sensational properties. It is one thing to say that all mature visual experiences have representational content, another thing to say that no such experience has intrinsic properties (properties which help to specify what it is like to have the experience) explicable without reference to representational content. To assert that all experiences have sensational properties is not necessarily to return to the views of Wundt and his followers.[5] My aim is just to argue that every experience has some sensational properties, and I will concentrate on visual experience as the most challenging case. We can label those who dispute this view, and hold that all intrinsic properties of mature human visual experiences are possessed in virtue of their representational content, "extreme perceptual theorists."

Again, we need to sharpen the dispute. One way to do so is to introduce for consideration what I will call the *Adequacy Thesis* (AT). The AT states that a complete intrinsic characterization of an experience can be given by embedding within an operator like "it visually appears to the subject that ... " some complex condition concerning physical objects. One component of the condition might be that there is a black telephone in front of oneself and a bookshelf a certain distance and direction to one's left, above and behind which is a window. Such contents can equally be the contents of perceptual or hallucinatory experiences.[6] The content need not be restricted to the qualitative properties of objects, their spatial relations to one another and to the location of the experiencer. It can also concern the relations of the objects and the experiencer to some environmental dimension: the experience of being in a tilted room is different from that of being in the same room when it is upright and the experiencer's body is tilted. Or again, a visual experience as of everything around one swinging to one's left can be distinguished from the visual experience as of oneself revolving rightwards on one's vertical axis. The specification of content may also need in some way to make reference to individuals whom the subject of the experience can recognize: a visual experience can represent Nixon as giving a speech in front of one. The representational content of a visual experience seems always to contain the indexical notions "now" and "I," and almost always "here" and "there." ... It should be emphasized that the propositional contents available to the defender of the AT are not all restricted to those features of experience which do not result from unconscious cognitive processing. If there are indeed unconscious mechanisms analogous, say, to inference in the production of experience, then certainly many features of the representational content of an experience will result from the operation of these mechanisms. The important point about representational content, as the notion is used here, is not its freedom from processing but its simultaneous possession of two features. The first is that the representational content concerns the world external to the experiencer, and as such is assessable as true or false. The second feature is that this content is something intrinsic to the experience itself—any experience which does not represent to the subject the world as being the way that this content specifies is phenomenologically different, an experience of a different type. It is quite consistent with these two features that the presence of experiences with a given representational content has been caused by past experience and learning. What one must not do is to suppose that such explanations show that representational content is a matter of judgment caused by some purer experience: even when an experience has a rich representational content, the judgment of the subject may still endorse or reject this content.

The extreme perceptual theorist is committed to the AT. For if the AT is false, there are intrinsic features of visual experience which are not captured by representational content. My initial strategy in opposition to the extreme perceptual theorist will be to argue against the AT by counterexamples. There is no obvious defender of the AT whose views one can take as a stalking horse, no doubt partly because the sensational/representational distinction seems not to have been sufficiently sharply formulated. There are, though, strong hints of the thesis in Hintikka. He writes, "The appropriate way of speaking of our spontaneous perceptions is to use the same vocabulary and the same syntax as we apply to the objects of perception ... *all* there is [in principle] to perception [at this level of analysis] is a specification of the information in question" (Hintikka's emphasis). He is not here using "information" in the sense of informational content, for he writes of the information that our perceptual systems give *us*.[7]

There are at least three types of example which are *prima facie* evidence against the AT. I will give all three before discussing ways in which the extreme perceptual theorist might try to account for each type, for any satisfactory account must accommodate all three types. The point in giving these examples is not to cite newly discovered phenomena—on the contrary, all the phenomena are familiar. The point is rather to consider their bearing on the correct conception of the representational and sensational properties of experience. Any novelty lies in claims about this bearing.

Since I shall be arguing by counterexample, the extreme perceptualist's reasons for his view will not initially affect the argument. But his views do not come from nowhere, and if the counterexamples are sound, the extreme perceptualist's reasons for his views must be insufficient: insofar as there are true beliefs amongst his reasons, those beliefs cannot carry him all the way to his extreme perceptualism. The extreme perceptualist's main motivation is likely to be the thought that if the AT is false, then there are intrinsic features of an experience which are unknowable by anyone not actually having that experience. This thought may be backed by the following superficially plausible argument. We can tell what kind of ex-

perience someone has if we know his desires and intentions, and find that he is disposed to act in such-and-such ways when he takes his experience at face value. If, for instance, he wants to travel to a certain place, and takes the shortest available route even though this is not on a straight line, we can come to have reason to believe that he perceives an obstacle on the most direct route: this hypothesis could be inductively confirmed. But it seems that techniques of this sort could only ever reveal representational properties of the subject's experience: for the technique consists in checking that he acts in ways appropriate to the world being as his experience represents it. If this is the only way in which we could come to know the intrinsic properties of another's experiences, the nonrepresentational properties of another's experiences would be unknowable. If the counterexamples below are correct, there must be a gap in this argument. Though the massive general topic of our understanding of consciousness in others is beyond the scope ... [here], I will try to indicate at suitable points how we might know of the sensational properties of others' experiences.

There is one last preliminary. Our perceptual experience is always of a more determinate character than our observational concepts which we might use in characterizing it. A normal person does not, and possibly could not, have observational concepts of every possible shade of color, where shades are individuated by Goodman's identity condition for qualia.[8] Even concepts like "yellow ochre" and "burnt sienna" will not distinguish every such shade; and in any case not everyone has such concepts. Thus if the extreme perceptualist is not to be mistaken for trivial reasons, the most that he can maintain is this: the intrinsic properties of a visual experience are exhausted by a specification of its representational content together with some more specific determination of the properties mentioned in that content. I will not trade on this qualification.

Here then are the examples:

(1) Suppose you are standing on a road which stretches from you in a straight line to the hori-

zon. There are two trees at the roadside, one a hundred yards from you, the other two hundred. Your experience represents these objects as being of the same physical height and other dimensions; that is, taking your experience at face value you would judge that the trees are roughly the same physical size, just as in the *trompe l'oeil* example, without countervailing beliefs you would judge that there is a violin on the door; and in this case we can suppose that the experience is a perception of the scene around you. Yet there is also some sense in which the nearer tree occupies more of your visual field than the more distant tree. This is as much a feature of your experience itself as is its representing the trees as being the same height. The experience can possess this feature without your having any concept of the feature or of the visual field: you simply enjoy an experience which has the feature. It is a feature which makes Rock say that the greater size of the retinal image of the nearer tree is not without some reflection in consciousness, and may be what earlier writers such as Ward meant when they wrote of differences in extensity.[9] It presents an initial challenge to the Adequacy Thesis, since no veridical experience can represent one tree as larger than another and also as the same size as the other. The challenge to the extreme perceptual theorist is to account for these facts about size in the visual field without abandoning the AT. We can label this problem "the problem of the additional characterization."

The problem of the additional characterization does not arise only for size in the visual field, or for properties such as speed of movement in the visual field which are defined in terms of it. It can arise for colors and sounds. Imagine you are in a room looking at a corner formed by two of its walls. The walls are covered with paper of a uniform hue, brightness and saturation. But one wall is more brightly illuminated than the other. In these circumstances, your experience can represent both walls as being the same color: it does not look to you as if one of the walls is painted with brighter paint than the other. Yet it is equally an aspect of your visual experience itself

that the region of the visual field in which one wall is presented is brighter than that in which the other is presented. An example of the same type of phenomenon involving hearing might be this. You see two cars at different distances from yourself, both with their engines running. Your experience can represent the engines as running equally loudly (if you are searching for a quiet car, your experience gives you no reason to prefer one over the other); but again it seems undeniable that in some sense the nearer car sounds louder.

(2) All these illustrations of the problem of the additional characterization were in some way related to the duality of representational properties and properties of the two-dimensional visual field, but they were not cases in which the additional characterization apparently omitted by representational properties was something which could vary even though representational content is held constant. Yet there are also examples of this, examples in which a pair of experiences in the same sense-modality have the same representational content, but differ in some other intrinsic respect. Suppose you look at an array of pieces of furniture with one eye closed. Some of the pieces of furniture may be represented by your experience as being in front of others. Imagine now that you look at the same scene with both eyes. The experience is different. It may be tempting to try to express this difference by saying that some chairs now appear to be in front of others, but this cannot suffice: for the monocular experience also represented certain objects as being in front of others. Taking your monocular experience at face value, you would judge that some pieces of furniture are in front of others: objects do not suddenly seem to be at no distance from you when you close one eye. The experiential difference between monocular and binocular vision is independent of the double images of unfocused objects produced by binocular vision. The extra way depth is indicated in binocular vision is present when you look into a child's stereoscope, and there need not be any double

images when you do.[10] (There are not many examples of this phenomenon with the other senses, but one such might be this. A stereophonic recording of a wave breaking sounds quite different from a monaural recording, even if one cannot locate aurally the various directions of the components of the whole sound.)

The situation in the visual example is more complex than it may at first seem. The complexity can be brought out by reflecting that there are pairs of experiences which differ in the way in which the experiences of monocular and binocular vision of an ordinary scene differ, and in which only the binocular experience contains any dimension of depth. Consider two arrays of dots, one a random array and the other random except in some region in which the dots are arranged as they are in the corresponding region of the first array, but slightly displaced to take account of binocular disparity. These are the Julesz random-dot patterns.[11] When viewed with two eyes, some dots are seen as being in front of others: when the arrays are seen with only one eye, there is no impression of depth. There are two different attitudes one could take to this example. One, incompatible with what we have so far said, would be that the example shows that though there is indeed an additional way in which depth is represented in binocular as opposed to monocular vision, the extra feature is purely representational; and it is this additional purely representational feature which is present in binocular vision of the random-dot patterns. The second attitude is that even in the random-dot case, the difference between monocular and binocular vision is both sensational and representational. This is the attitude for which I shall argue.

On the second attitude, there is a sensational property which in normal human experience is indeed associated with the representation of depth. If it is granted that visual field properties are sensational, we already have other examples of such association, since in normal humans perceiving an ordinary scene, the visual field properties are associated with a representational content. The difference between the two attitudes lies in the fact that according to the first, it ought to be impossible to conceive of cases in which the alleged sensational property is present, but in which a representation of certain objects as being behind others in the environment is absent. According to the second attitude, this ought to be conceivable.

But it does seem to be conceivable. It could be that there is a being for whom visual experience is in certain respects like the experience enjoyed by a congenitally blind user of a tactile-vision substitution system (TVSS).[12] A TVSS consists of a television camera, the output of which is connected to a two-dimensional array of vibrating rods on the user's back. After using the TVSS for a short time, the congenitally blind subject has intrinsically spatial sensations resulting from the vibrations, sensations which are not those of pressure or vibration on his back, and which are reported to be quite unlike those of touch. These sensations are arranged in a two-dimensional space, and they do not seem to the experiencer to be of objects in the space around him. That is, the space of the sensations is not experienced as bearing any spatial relations to the physical space in which the experiencer is located.[13] The subjects report that the sensations are not as of anything "out there." Now it seems that we can also conceive, at least as a logical possibility, of such sensations (perhaps resulting from the output of two cameras) existing in a three-dimensional space, which is nevertheless still not experienced as the space around the perceiver. Finally, it seems that we can conceive of someone's visual experience being like that of the subject in his hypothetical three-dimensional case: someone with tactile experience of the world around him and suddenly given stereoscopic vision of unfamiliar objects (such as small blobs randomly distributed in three-dimensional space) could conceivably be so. Here then a sensational third dimension would be present; but there would be no representation of depth in the sense that the experience itself represents some things as being further away than others in the forward direction in the physical space in which the experiencer is located. There is, then, a dangerous ambiguity in the term "depth." It is indeed true that whenever the extra feature which distinguishes binocular from monocular vision is present, there will be an impression of depth; but since on the sense in which this must be so, depth is a sensational property, the point cannot be used to argue that the difference between monocular and binocular vision is purely representational.[14]

(3) The third type of problem is illustrated by the switching of aspects under which some object or array of objects is seen. Consider an example in which a wire framework in the shape of a cube is viewed with one eye and is seen first with one of its faces in front, the face parallel to this face being seen as behind it, and is then suddenly seen, without any change in the cube or alteration of its position, with that former face now behind the other. The successive experiences have different representational contents. The first experience represents a face ABCD as nearer oneself than the face EFGH; the later experience represents the presence of a state of affairs incompatible with its being nearer. Yet there seems to be some additional level of classification at which the successive experiences fall under the same type; indeed that something like this is so seems to be a feature of the experience of a switch in aspect—as Wittgenstein writes, "I *see* that it has not changed."[15] We have here another example of apparently nonrepresentational similarities between experiences.

The challenge to the extreme perceptual theorist is to explain how there can be nonrepresentational similarities between experiences without giving up the AT. He might propose simply to introduce a new classification of visual experience by means of a content which still conforms to the spirit of the AT, but which relates to some time just before the occurrence of the experience: the content would presumably be that the scene around oneself has not altered. But this view ignores the fact that, in normal circumstances,

with memory errors aside, the presence of the impression that the scene has or has not altered surely depends on the character of the successive experiences. If we just added this new type of experience to our characterizations, we would still have to say on what properties of successive experiences its presence or absence depends. This suggestion also fails to cope with an aspect switch accompanied by loss of memory of the earlier experience: for here there need be no impression that the scene has not altered. Finally, the suggestion does not capture the nonrepresentational similarity between the experiences of two different subjects looking at the cube, one seeing a certain face in front, the other seeing it as behind. It is not only between successive experiences of a single person that there are nonrepresentational similarities. We do then have a third type of problem for the extreme perceptual theorist.

Why have I chosen to use the example of monocular vision of a three-dimensional wire frame to make these points, rather than the traditional duck-rabbit figure? The reason lies in this: when a subject undergoes an aspect switch while looking at that figure, there is nothing which is seen first as a duck, and then as a rabbit—rather, something is seen first as a representation of a duck, and then is seen as a representation of a rabbit. But then what is so seen, an arrangement of lines on paper, remains constant in the representational content of the successive experiences. So the example does not serve the purpose of showing that there can be nonrepresentational similarities between experiences, since someone who denies that could simply say that in this example the component of representational content concerning the arrangement of the lines on paper remains constant, and accounts for the similarity. In the example of the wire cube, this reply is not available: for after the aspect switch, the wires do not all seem to be in the same relative positions as before.[16]

A natural reaction of the extreme perceptual theorist to examples of these three types is to claim that all the statements whose truth seems to conflict with the Adequacy Thesis can be translated into statements which do not attribute to experiences any features going beyond those countenanced by the AT.[17] Let us consider this translational response as applied to size in the visual field and the two trees on the road. It might be suggested that the statement, "The nearer tree takes up more of the visual field," could be approximately translated by the counterfactual, "For any plane perpendicular to the subject's line of sight and lying between him and the two trees, a larger area of that place would have to be made opaque precisely to obscure the nearer tree than would have to be made opaque precisely to obscure the more distant tree." It is not clear how the translational response could be implemented in the second kind of example; but does it succeed even for the first kind?

Of what is this translational suggestion offered as an explanation? A first possibility is that it might be offered as an explanation of why we use the same spatial vocabulary as applies to extended objects in space in connection with the visual field. As an explanation of this it is satisfying, and can be extended to such relations as *above* and *next to* in the visual field. But the defender of the AT needs more than this. If this account of the content of experience is to be adequate, he needs this suggestion to supply an account of what it means to say that one object is larger than another in the subject's visual field. This is the second possibility. As a meaning-giving account, the suggestion seems quite inadequate. When we reflect on the possibility that light rays might bend locally, or that the experiencer might have astigmatism, it seems clear that the counterfactual which is alleged to translate the statement, "The nearer tree takes up more of the visual field than the further tree," is in general neither necessary nor sufficient for the truth of that statement. There is also an objection of principle to a counterfactual analysis of an intrinsic property of experience. Whether one object is larger than another in the subject's visual field is a property of his experience in the actual world, be counterfacutal circumstances as they may. An account of size in the visual field should make it dependent only upon the actual properties of the experience itself.

The distinction between the acceptable and the unacceptable components of the translational view can be explained in terms of a partial parallel with Kripke's distinction between fixing the referent of an expression and giving its meaning.[18] Kripke noted that though one may fix the reference of a proper name "Bright" by stipulating that it is to refer to the man who invented the wheel, nevertheless the sentence, "It might have been that Bright never invented the wheel," is true. Now to understand this last sentence, we have to have some grasp of the possibility of a person who actually meets a condition failing to meet it. Similarly, experiences of such a type that the nearer tree is large in the visual field than the further do actually meet the condition that more of the previously mentioned plane must be obscured precisely to block perception of the nearer tree. This condition fixes the type of the experience, but this type might have failed to meet that condition, just as it might have been that Bright was less inventive. What the translational defender of the extreme perceptual view fails to supply is any account of sameness of experience which allows for the possibility that the type of experience which in fact meets his translational condition fails to do so.

A different strategy in defense of the Adequacy Thesis would be to expand the range of representational contents. It would be conceded that the three types of example make trouble for the AT if we confine ourselves to representational contents of the sorts already considered; but there would be no difficulty, it may be said, if for instance we included in representational content the angle subtended by an object. Such is the view of Rock, who regards perceived visual angle and perceived objective size as simply different aspects of perception. He follows the practice of calling experiences of the former type "proximal mode experiences" and writes, "Proximal mode experiences are best thought of as perceptions rather than sensations."[19] Despite his important contributions on the issues of this section, Rock's views here are open to criticism. As we emphasized, it is a conceptual truth that no one can have an experience with a given representational content unless he possesses the concepts from which that content is built up: an experience cannot represent the world to the subject of experience as being a certain way if he is not capable of grasping what that way is. This conceptual point entails that adding contents concerning the visual angle to representational content to save the AT is illegitimate: for an unsophisticated perceiver who does not have the concept of subtended angle it is nevertheless true that one object takes up more of his visual field than another, just as it does for a more sophisticated theorist.[20] This criticism would equally apply to a view once endorsed by Boring, who, after asking what "observation would demonstrate" that a subject is perceiving the size of his own retinal image, continued: "For a man to perceive the size of his own retinal images his perception of size must remain invariant under all transformations that leave the size of the retinal images invariant."[21] If this is a sufficient condition, it is one that can be met by a man who has never heard of a retina. It would also involve a fundamental overdeterminacy of the representational content of experience, since transformations that leave the size of the retinal image invariant will equally leave suitable cross-sections of the light rays in a given plane within the eye unaltered in area, and by Boring's lights this could equally be taken as the content of the perception. These problems result from trying to construe a sensational property, size in the visual field, as a representational property.

It will help at this point if we introduce a simple piece of notation. If a particular experience e has the familiar sensational property which in normal circumstances is produced by a white object (such as a tilted plate) which would be precisely obscured by an opaque elliptical region (r, say) of the imagined interposed plane, let us express this fact in the notation "elliptical$'$ (r, e) and white$'$ (r, e)." These primed predicates "elliptical" and "white" should not be confused with their unprimed homonyms. In using the notation, we are not thereby saying that experiences have color properties or spatial properties. With this apparatus we can express what would more traditionally have been expressed by saying, "There is a yellow elliptical region of the visual field next to a white square region." Thus, using logical notation:

$\exists r \exists s$(elliptical$'$ (r, e) & yellow$'$ (r, e)
& square$'$ (s, e) & white$'$ (s, e) & next$'$ (r, s)).[22]

We said earlier that the means by which these expressions containing primes have been introduced serves only to fix which properties they pick out. The point of invoking Kripke's distinction between fixing the referent and giving the meaning was to emphasize a modal point: that we can conceive of circumstances in which, for example, a tilted plate does not produce an elliptical region of the visual field. But the phrase "it fixes the referent rather than gives the meaning" is potentially misleading: it may suggest that there is more to understanding "red$'$" than knowing that it is the sensational property of the visual field in which a red thing is presented in normal circumstances. But there is not more than this. Anyone who knows what it is like to have an experience as of something red and has the concept of the visual field knows what it is like to have an experience which is red$'$ (relative to some region). In this respect the means by which we have fixed which property "red$'$" refers to does indeed play a special role in understanding that primed predicate. It would be equally true to say that the property of being red$'$ is that property of the visual field normally produced by the presence of an object with such-and-such physical reflectance properties. This description would not convey understanding of "red'," except in the presence of additional knowledge of which sensational property it is that meets the physically specified condition.

The sensational properties of an experience, like its representational properties, have reliable and publicly identifiable causes. We argued that the property of being presented in a large region of the visual field cannot be identified with the property of being represented as subtending a large visual angle: but nevertheless the fact that an object does subtend a large visual angle does causally explain its presentation in a large region of the visual field. This explanatory fact is one which concerns the physical spatial relations of the perceiver to the physical objects in his environment. Nor is it true that the sensational properties of an experience cannot explain a subject's behavior. We can conceive of someone who does indeed want to obscure precisely certain objects by attaching opaque surfaces to a glass plane which is perpendicular to his line of sight. At first, he may have to learn from experience with several particular objects what shape of surface to place on the plane. But it seems clear that we can also imagine that his learning successfully transfers to shapes quite different from those cases in which he learned which shape to choose, and that he comes to need not more than his ordinary visual experience in order to make a selection of the shape. At this stage, the sensational properties of his experience would have to be cited in the explanation of why he chooses one shape rather than another to obscure precisely some particular kind of object seen for the first time behind the glass. It is not clear that the sensational properties of experience are in principle any more problematic epistemologically than are the representational properties (which are, certainly, problematic enough).

These points about sensational properties have been tailored to the first type of example offered

against the Adequacy Thesis. But they apply equally to the second: they apply *pari passu* if we introduce a primed relation "behind" and fix its reference in terms of the physical conditions which normally produce the sensational property it stands for—the conditions for binocular vision of objects at different depths. I suggest that in the third kind of case, nonrepresentational similarity of experiences consists in sameness or similarity of sensational properties. In all the standard cases of switches of aspect, the successive experiences have the same primed sensational properties, those fixed in terms of the imagined interposed plane. Such identity of sensational properties is also not confined to successive experiences of one individual. This explanation of the third type of case also generalizes to an example with which it is hard to reconcile the AT. A person can have the experience of waking up in an unfamiliar position or place, and his experience initially has a minimal representational content. The content may be just that there are surfaces at various angles to him, without even a rough specification of distances. Suddenly, everything falls into place, and he has an experience with a rich representational content: he sees that nothing has altered in the scene in the sense in which one sees this when experiencing an aspect switch with the wire cube. Again, the primed sensational properties of the successive experiences are identical.

If this treatment of the examples is correct, then neither one of representational content and sensational properties determines the other. The cases of change of aspect show that sensational properties do not determine representational content, while the case of binocular vision of depth shows that representational content in a given sense-modality does not determine sensational properties. Concepts of both types are needed for a full description.[23]

Sensational properties are ubiquitous features of visual experiences: indeed it seems impossible to conceive of an experience devoid of all sensational properties. This is one reason why the visual properties which have been argued here to be sensational should be distinguished from the early Gibsonian conception of the visual field. Concepts of the Gibsonian visual field apply not to ordinary visual experience, but only to a special kind of experience we can have when we adopt the attitude a painter adopts to his experience. "By adopting the appropriate attitude, one can have either kind of visual experience.... The visual field is a product of the chronic habit of civilized men of seeing the world as a picture.... The visual field is a picture-like phenomenal experience at a presumptive phenomenal distance from the eyes, consisting of perspective size-impressions."[24] Gibsonian visual field experiences can occur only to those who have the concept of a planar representation of the environment. It would perhaps be open to a Gibsonian to hold that the pictorial attitude and the special experiences it produces merely emphasize features already present in ordinary visual experience. This is indeed the position I have been defending, but on such a defense the account of the nature of these features cannot make essential reference to pictorial representation.

Where do the phenomena to which the Gestalt psychologists referred with the label "grouping" fall within this classification? One such phenomenon is given by the fact that we see the array

as three columns of dots rather than as four rows. Two points make it plausible to classify grouping phenomena as generally sensational properties of experience. One is that it is manifested simply in the exercise of experientially based discriminative capacities. Someone who perceives the array grouped into three columns will find this array subjectively more similar to

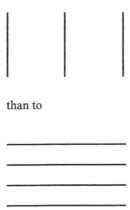

than to

Instances of a three-place relation of comparative subjective similarity can be manifested in experientially based discriminative reactions. Quine emphasized this point in *The Roots of Reference*,[25] and in this he was in agreement with the experimental techniques of the Gestalt psychologists themselves.[26] A second reason for saying that grouping properties are sensational rather than representational is that they are found in experiences which have no representational properties. In listening to the rhythms produced by a solo drum player, each sound is grouped with some but not with other sounds.[27] It is true that in our initial example, the very description of the case "seen as three columns rather than four rows" seems to suggest that we are concerned with a representational, not a sensational, property: the concept of a column enters the content. But this is because experiences with a particular sensational property also have, in normal mature humans, a certain representational property. Many of the examples given by Gestalt psychologists are ones in which there are distinctive grouping properties, groupings in particular curves and shapes, and in which the subject of the experience has no concept in advance with which to pick out the curve or shape in question.[28]

Grouping phenomena do, however, raise two closely related problems for what I have so far said about the category of sensational properties.

In some cases we can perceive one and the same array as differently grouped in successive experiences. This array

```
o     o     o     o

●     ●     ●     ●

o     o     o     o

●     ●     ●     ●

o     o     o     o

●     ●     ●     ●
```

can be seen as either rows or columns.[29] The first problem now is this: we earlier said that in switches of aspect the sensational properties of the successive experiences remained constant. But now, in the case of switches of grouping, we are distinguishing switches *within* the class of sensational properties of experience according to the account so far given. No doubt aspect—and grouping—switches are to be distinguished, but the impression after a switch of either type that nothing has altered seems to have a similar basis; yet the account seems to leave no room for saying that it does. That is the first problem. The second problem, now that grouping is included as a sensational property, is how the particular sensational properties an experience may possess are to be explained. For the primed properties of the successive experiences, for someone who views our most recent array and undergoes a switch of grouping, may be identical; and yet their sensational properties are different.

A full treatment of these problems would give a detailed theory of the types of sensational properties and the relations between them. Here I will just note a distinction which can be applied to the problem. The facts about grouping show that many different types of experience may be pro-duced in normal circumstances by a given pattern of light on the imagined frontal glass plane. We can capture the nonrepresentational differences between these types by using again the fact that if an experience has a particular grouping, it will be subjectively more similar to a second experience with different primed properties than it is to a third. There are at least two levels of classification of visual experience in sensational terms: a basic level, at which terms for the properties have their references fixed by means of the imagined frontal glass plane; and a second level, determined by different possible patterns of comparative subjective similarity between experiences falling under these basic types. The difference between the case in which a given array is seen to be grouped in columns and the case in which it is seen to be grouped in rows is captured at this second level. The difference remains a difference within the class of sensational properties.

Notes

1. For a clear statement of this last problem, see B. Williams, *Descartes: The Project of Pure Enquiry* (London: Penguin, 1978), pp. 243–4.

2. Brian O'Shaughnessy in *The Will: A Dual Aspect Theory* (Cambridge: CUP, 1980) says that experiences with content are the causal consequences of sensations (vol. 1, pp. 172–3; vol. 2, pp. 68–74 and 139–42). I have set up the issues in such a way that sensational properties, if they exist, are properties of the very same thing, the experience, which has representational properties. That some properties of the experience are causally responsible for others would be an empirical psychological hypothesis, and one which involves simultaneous causation. O'Shaughnessy also writes, as I do not, of seeing sensations. Despite these differences and others noted later, much of what O'Shaughnessy says about sensation is congenial and complementary to the main theses of this chapter, in particular his emphasis on the inseparability of sensation from experience and on the nonconceptual character of sensation.

3. Essay II (ch. XVI) of *Essays on the Intellectual Powers of Man* (Edinburgh: Thin, 1895), p. 312: "sensation, taken by itself, implies neither the conception

nor the belief of any external object.... Perception implies an immediate conviction and belief of something external—something different both from the mind that perceives, and from the act of perception."

4. For differential explanation, see Ch. 2 of my *Holistic Explanation* (Oxford: OUP, 1979).

5. W. Wundt, *Outlines of Psychology* (Leipzig: Engelmann, 1907).

6. If we are to be strict, the attribution of a common existential content to perceptual and hallucinatory experience is too crude. There is a sense in which, as one incompetently says, a hallucination presents a *particular* nonexistent object, and so has more than a general existential content. (This can be important in explaining such sentences as, "He hallucinated a cup; he believed it to be medieval, and tried to pick it up; later he came to think it a fake.") To capture this the common content of perception and hallucination could be given by specifying perceptual *types* of modes of presentation of objects, types which do not in every context determine an object.

7. "Information, Causality and the Logic of Perception," in *The Intentions of Intentionality and Other New Models for Modality* (Dordrecht: Reidel, 1975), pp. 60–2.

8. *The Structure of Appearance* (Indianapolis: Bobbs-Merrill, 1966), p. 290.

9. I. Rock. "In Defense of Unconscious Inference," in *Stability and Constancy in Visual Perception* (New York: Wiley, 1977), ed. W. Epstein; J. Ward, *Psychological Principles* (Cambridge: CUP, 1920).

10. In *The Perception of the Visual World* (Boston: Houghton Mifflin, 1950); J. J. Gibson says of the impression of distance in depth in binocular vision that "You can reduce the distance somewhat by closing one eye" (p. 42). Even if this is in fact true in all cases, it cannot be definitional of the distinctive impression produced by depth in binocular vision: one can imagine that closing one eye eliminates this impression even though as a result nothing looks closer than it did before.

11. B. Julesz, "Texture and visual perception," *Scientific American*, February 1965.

12. P. Bach-y-Rita *et al.*, "Vision Substitution by Tactile Image Projection," *Nature* 221 (1969), 963–4; G. Guarniero, "Experience of tactile vision," *Perception* 3 (1974), 101–4.

13. Cp. Guarniero, p. 104: "By this time objects had come to have a top and a bottom; a right side and a left; but no depth—they existed in an ordered two-dimensional space, the precise location of which has not yet been determined."

14. My position here is incompatible with that of O'Shaughnessy, *The Will*, vol. 1, pp. 171–3, where he argues that (in my terminology) depth is never a sensational property. He offers three reasons, the first two of which aim to show that "concepts play a causal role in the genesis of visual depth experience." The first reason is that "*any* visual depth experience depends upon one's seeing one's visual depth sensations *as* contributing the color of physical items situated at some distance from one." This begs the question by presuming that the third dimension in the space of the sensations must represent to the experiencer depth in the physical space around him. The text above gives an imagined counterexample to this claim of necessary coincidence. The second reason given is that "two visual fields of sensations could be internally indistinguishable and yet thanks to the diverse concepts and beliefs of their owners cause different *veridical* visual depth impressions." But when there are stereoscopic depth impressions resulting from binocular vision, the three-dimensional visual field properties are not compatible with different depth impressions, at least in respect of the distribution in three dimensions of the surface actually seen. O'Shaughnessy's third reason is that his view is corroborated by the optical facts; but he considers only the bundle of light rays reaching a single eye. In the nature of the case, monocular vision is insufficient for stereopsis; and the optical facts when we consider binocular vision not only make depth as a sensational property intelligible, but also explain why the property should peter out at greater distances.

15. *Philosophical Investigations* (Oxford: Blackwell, 1958), p. 193; cp. also *Remarks on the Philosophy of Psychology* (Oxford: Blackwell, 1980), vol. 1, section 33.

16. The possibility of the notion of representation itself entering the content of an experience would allow one to give this explanation of the difference between seeing one area as figure and another as ground: the whole is seen as a representation in which the former area is represented as being in front of the latter.

17. In effect, some philosophers reacted this way to Gibson's use in his earlier writings of the concept of the visual field; D. W. Hamlyn for instance wrote, "the

properties which Gibson ascribes to the visual field are all logically derivative from those ascribable to the visual world." See "The Visual Field and Perception," *Proceedings of the Aristotelian Society*, supplementary volume 31 (1957) at p. 121. (I should add that Hamlyn later changed his mind on this question.)

18. *Naming and Necessity* (Oxford: Blackwell, 1980).

19. "In Defense of Unconscious Inference," p. 349, and also in his *Introduction to Perception* (New York: Macmillan, 1975), pp. 39, 47, 56.

20. Even if the perceiver does have the concept of the subtended angle and it enters the representational content of his experience, it is not clear that the suggestion works. For it would rule out *a priori* the following possibility. There is someone who suffers from unsystematic distortion in a particular region of his visual field. He knows this, and after a time objects presented in that region of his visual field are no longer presented as being as determinate in size in the way those presented elsewhere are so represented. If this is possible, then an object may be presented outside the distorting region, and be presented as subtending a certain angle, and it may occupy the same size of region of the visual field as an object in the distorting region which is not presented as subtending any particular angle.

21. "Visual Perception and Invariance," *Psychological Review* 59 (1952), 141–8, at p. 145.

22. The visual field sensational properties caused by an object can of course be influenced by the properties of the other objects perceived: geometrical illusions again illustrate the point. A more complex means of introducing the primed properties would take account of this relativity.

23. A listener hearing an earlier version of this chapter drew my attention to David Lewis's unduly neglected "Percepts and Color Mosaics in Visual Experience," *Philosophical Review* 75 (1966), 357–68. Lewis's notion of experiences which are modification-equivalent and his claims concerning it are clearly close to what I would call the relation of having the same sensational properties and the claim that sensational properties are distinct from representational properties. But readers wishing to compare his views with those of this chapter should note that Lewis's percept and my representational content are not to be identified. He writes of percepts which are pure percepts of color mosaic and nothing else (p. 363): such experiences do not in my sense have representational content. Like the early experiences of the TVSS

user, they do not represent the world in the environment of the subject as being a particular way. Correspondingly they are not directly assessable as veridical or otherwise. (Less direct relations of correspondence could, though, be defined.)

24. J. J. Gibson, "The Visual Field and the Visual World," *Psychological Review* 59 (1952), 149–51.

25. La Salle, Illinois: Open Court, 1974.

26. W. Köhler, *Gestalt Psychology* (New York: Liveright, 1947), Ch. 5.

27. Compare also hearing a chord as an augmented fourth rather than as a diminished fifth. Someone can have this experience without having the concept of an augmented fourth. His hearing it that way is necessarily linked to the resolutions of that chord which sound right to him. If it is true that different groupings are sensational properties, any proposal to include both grouping phenomena and switches in the aspect under which an object is perceived under the common label of "organization in experience," needs some positive justification. Note also that the fact that there seems to be a conceptual distinction between grouping and seeing something as an instance of a particular concept may underlie Wittgenstein's otherwise somewhat obscure remark in his discussion of seeing-as—that one has to distinguish "purely optical" aspects from those "*mainly determined by thoughts and associations*": see *Remarks on the Philosophy of Psychology* vol. 1, sections 970, 1017.

28. For sample illustrations, see Köhler, op. cit. and Rock, *Introduction to Perception*.

29. The array is after Rock, *Introduction to Perception*.

V FUNCTION OF CONSCIOUSNESS

Conscious Inessentialism and the Epiphenomenalist Suspicion

Owen Flanagan

Conscious Inessentialism

Consciousness did not have to evolve. It is conceivable that evolutionary processes could have worked to build creatures as efficient and intelligent as we are, even more efficient and intelligent, without those creatures being subjects of experience. Consciousness is not essential to highly evolved intelligent life. This claim is true and important. However, from the fact that consciousness is inessential to highly evolved intelligent life, it does not follow that it is inessential to our particular type of intelligent life.

Conscious inessentialism is the view that for any intelligent activity *i* performed in any cognitive domain *d*, even if *we* do *i* consciously, *i* can in principle be done nonconsciously. Conscious inessentialism does not follow from the true claim about the possibility of intelligent life absent consciousness. It does not follow because there are certain intelligent activities that would not be the intelligent activities they are if they were not done consciously. Consciousness is partly constitutive of these intelligent activities. Take an action like lying. Telling a lie essentially involves a conscious intention to mislead. The intelligent activity called "misleading" could be done by a well-programmed robot. But misleading is not lying. Lying is an intelligent activity that requires consciousness. Not all our intelligent actions essentially involve consciousness, but many do— telling the truth, lying, thinking in words, and self-reflection come to mind as examples. The same point holds on the input side. Greeting a friend requires that one consciously perceives a particular human individual as that friend. Prosopagnosiacs don't see faces as faces and thus don't visually recognize friends as friends. When a prosopagnosiac greets a friend, it is because he has recognized that individual as a friend through a nonvisual modality, usually hearing.

One might agree that consciousness enters essentially into the characterization of some kinds of perception and action but still wonder whether consciousness does any work in these cases where it is partly constitutive of the intelligent activity in question. So what that some perception is conscious or that some types of actions are the actions they are only if done consciously. Perhaps the intelligent kernel involved in conscious perception and conscious action can occur without consciousness. Or to put the point differently, consciousness might be essential to how we characterize and individuate the exercise of certain human capacities without playing any interesting causal role in the exercise of these very capacities. Having an appendix is an essential property of *Homo sapiens*. We cannot give a true and complete characterization of human anatomy without bringing in the appendix. But the appendix plays no functional, causal role in human life (it can, however, play a dysfunctional role). Perhaps conscious inessentialism can be defeated as a claim about how intelligent mental activity must be described. But its falsehood is compatible with the truth of a different claim, the claim that consciousness lacks causal power.

The Epiphenomenalist Suspicion

The thesis of conscious inessentialism is not the only source of trouble. There is also the epiphenomenalist suspicion, the suspicion that although consciousness exists and enters into the characterization of some human actions, it plays a relatively inconsequential role in mental life, akin to the ineffectual, often misled, and ever belatedly informed public-relations office for a large organization. The analogy with the public-relations officer is significant. It suggests that consciousness is not the proverbial ghost in the machine but rather a dispensable cog in the machine.

I take the epiphenomenalist suspicion seriously. Consciousness might be essential to our natures without being centrally involved in the causal fray. I have suggested at several points that we take seriously the idea that conscious experience involves neuronal groups locking into synchronous or semisynchronous oscillatory patterns in the 40–hertz range (Crick and Koch 1990). Seeing a red square involves a 40–hertz lock on the spiking patterns in the visual areas subserving color and shape detection. There may be no place where the patterns meet up, marry, and bind. Getting the right neuronal groups into synchrony and keeping them in synchrony for a short time may be sufficient for the experience.

This hypothesis, attractive as it may be, is fully compatible with epiphenomenalism. Consider this analogy. Seeing a red square is to the brain as the whistling pot is to the water boiling within it. Immediately after the brain detects a red square and gets on with whatever it intends to do with the information that a red square is there, it goes into this funny oscillatory state that persists for a few seconds and subserves the experience of seeing a red square. This oscillatory pattern does nothing useful. It is so smooth and predictable that the brain is able more or less to ignore it. Eventually it disappears into outer space. Likewise, immediately after the water starts boiling, the pot whistles. The whistling is a set of sound waves caused by the boiling. The whistling indicates that boiling is taking place, but it has no (interesting) effect on the boiling. When the boiling stops, the whistling rapidly, but not simultaneously, dissipates. The sound waves that constitute the whistling spread into sounds of silence.

The likening of consciousness to escaping steam—both are real, but both are relatively inconsequential—is an epiphenomenalist favorite. William James (1890, 135) quotes Thomas Huxley's startling version of epiphenomenalism:

The consciousness of brutes would appear to be related to the mechanism of their body simply as a collateral product of its working, and to be completely without any power of modifying that working, as the steam-whistle which accompanies the work of a locomotive engine is without influence upon its machinery. Their volition, if they have any, is an emotion indicative of physical changes, not a cause of such changes.... The soul stands to the body as the bell of a clock to the works, and consciousness answers to the sound which the bell gives out when it is struck.... To the best of my judgment, the argumentation which applies to brutes holds equally good of men.... We are conscious automata.

James aptly refers to the epiphenomenalist position as the "inert spectator" view of the mind or the "conscious automaton" theory. The steam whistle is a physical effect of the work of the steam engine. Furthermore, it has physical effects. It adds moisture to the surrounding air and sound waves escape. But these effects are minor and of no consequence as far as the subsequent states of the steam engine go. Epiphenomenalism is the thesis that conscious experience has the same incidental relation to the whole person as the steam whistle has to the locomotive engine. To be sure, consciousness, like the whistle, makes itself noticed. But being noticeable, or even noisy, are different from being effectively involved in the real action. Or, so the epiphenomenalist suggests.

To James, as to most contemporary philosophers, psychologists, and laypersons, such a view seems preposterous. Consciousness is more like the steam engine that powers the locomotive and produces the steam than like the quaint but terminal toot. James calls epiphenomenalism an "unwarrantable impertinence." Against the epiphenomenalist he musters the commonsense evidence that we often bring about what we in fact mentally intend. He then joins this evidence to evolutionary theory, arguing that it is "inconceivable that consciousness should have nothing to do with a business [to] which it so faithfully attends." According to James, Darwin taught us that species-specific characteristics are selected for because they confer some survival advantage on the organisms that possess them. But consciousness cannot enhance an individual's survival advantage "without being in some way efficacious and influencing the course of his bodily history."

This sort of argument is now viewed with skepticism. Selection works over populations of genes. Species survive and proliferate when their members possess genes that lead to differential reproductive success. To be sure, well-adapted organisms make it. But being well adapted is not the same as being optimally adapted. Furthermore, selection isn't fussy about every single trait. Traits that are neutral and even some that marginally reduce reproductive success can sneak in as free riders in satisfactorily designed species (Gould and Lewontin 1979). The color of blood is widely thought to be an example of a trait that was not directly selected for, as is the structure of the human chin.

Could consciousness, despite its faithful attention to the life of the organism that houses it, be more like the nosey housekeeper who keeps an overzealous eye on the goings-on in the mansion and gossips about those goings-on to outsiders than like the master of the mansion who really runs the show? Maybe. Neo-Darwinian theory does not rule the possibility out of court. We need some arguments against epiphenomenalism.

Some Arguments from Design

It is possible, even on the neo-Darwinian picture I have recommended, that consciousness does little work, or at least that it does less work that we standardly give it credit for. To be sure, our species would not have survived if we had not been quick to respond to harmful stimuli. The natural temptation, therefore, is to think that conscious sensitivity to painful and dangerous things was directly selected for. The trouble with this sort of facile adaptationism is that some species that have survived much longer than we have detect when danger lurks but are conscious of nothing. Scallops, for example, get out of the way of potential predators without experiencing them as such, and when they fail to do so, they get eaten alive, quite possibly without experiencing pain.

It is possible that we survived as a species because we were unconsciously responsive (informationally sensitive) to harmful and useful stimuli, for example, the appearance of a predator or a mate. And it is possible that the capacities to *experience* fear and lust, pleasure and pain simply came on board as free riders at some later time and play no important psychological role even now, save whatever role is played by letting ourselves and others know how we feel. The standard view is this:

(1) Hot stimulus on hand → feeling of pain → withdrawal of hand

The epiphenomenalist suggests that the real picture is this:

(2) Hot stimulus on hand ⟨ feeling of pain
withdrawal of hand

I will not try to allay all the fears that motivate the epiphenomenalist suspicion. In part, this is because I think that the causal role of consciousness has been overrated, and thus that the suspicion is healthy to a degree. Furthermore, the epiphenomenalist suspicion is extraordinarily hard to dispel. Take the case of pain. The usual hypothesis is that the experience of pain plays a functional role mediating a response to a potentially harmful stimulus. The epiphenomenalist hypothesis is that the experience of pain is just a very noticeable added attraction of the causal fray—all sparkle, glitter, and noise—that in fact does no useful work. One might think that the first hypothesis easily defeats the second, since individuals who are otherwise normal but who lack pain receptors on their skin are in constant danger of being scalded, of hemorrhaging, of losing fingers, limbs, and life. It can be argued, however, that these people are dysfunctional not because they do not experience pain but because they lack the receptors that, besides getting people to remove their hands and so forth, from harmful objects, also typically give rise to feelings of a certain sort. The idea that conscious experiences are all sparkle, glitter, and noise is not crazy. I think it is false, but it is not *obviously* false.

The epiphenomenalist suspicion, even if untenable in its extreme from, is a useful corrective to views that overstate the role of consciousness in mental life. It is only in the last century that the idea that consciousness is definitive of the mental has yielded. Even if we no longer believe that consciousness is involved in all mental activity, we tend to think that when it is involved, it is centrally involved. Consciousness itself impels us to overestimate its causal role in mental life. That said, I want to allay worries about epiphenomenalism somewhat.

One credible way to argue for the claim that some trait has been directly selected for because of its adaptive value is to show that it occurs in different species that are not closely related. The force of this sort of argument comes from the idea that "really useful features tend to be reinvented by evolution. Photoreceptors have been independently invented over 40 times in various invertebrate lineages: partway out a branch on the tree of species, photoreception will appear and persist. Powered flight was invented at least three times after the insects did it: by the flying dinosaurs, by the bats, and by the birds (not to mention all the jumping spiders, gliding mammals, 'flying' fish, even a snake that glides between tropical treetops)" (Calvin 1991, 30). If one believes that there is something it is like to be a snake, a salamander, a fish, a bird, a bat, a dolphin, and that these creatures lie in different lineages from *Homo sapiens*, then there is some gain to the idea that endowing subjective consciousness is a matter of good evolutionary design.

Even if one is unwilling to impute consciousness to creatures other than *Homo sapiens* or thinks that the bloodlines of all these creatures have a single common source, there is still an opening based on properties of our own species design. Subjective consciousness is well connected to certain mental processors. This is why one can have an isolated deficit in subjective consciousness. For example, one can be blind or color blind or deaf or unable to recognize faces, and so on (you name a possible defect of consciousness and it seems to exist; see Shallice 1988).

This provides the basis for the following argument from design. Just as frequent appearance of a trait in many different species is evidence that the trait is a good solution to certain engineering problems faced again and again by Nature, so too the fact that a trait or capacity has been hooked onto many distinct mental systems in one species is evidence that the trait or capacity serves a purpose.

Memory is functional. One view is that we have one general-purpose memory system that stores information from a variety of processors. Another view is that there are multiple memory systems, with each memory system suited for remembering events processed by the system, the sensory modality, to which it is attached. Like memory, consciousness is depicted in two main ways by mind scientists. Often consciousness is portrayed as a single integrative, domain-nonspecific "faculty" that receives input from all the sensory modules and from the declarative memory system (the system that retains propositional information about facts and events). At other times consciousness is viewed as the name for all the different types of awareness attached, as it were, to each distinct sensory module and to the declarative memory system. In the first case, Nature had to invent the faculty and then work at wiring it to the sensory modules and to memory. In the second case, Nature had to do for consciousness what it did for wings and photoreceptors. It invented consciousness time and again for many distinct modules. In either case, consciousness has been hooked onto many distinct mental systems. Furthermore, the hook-ups are not random. Most of what goes on in our head is consciously inaccessible. What is consciously accessible is primarily just what we have the most need to know about: conditions in the sensory environment, and past facts, and events. This gives some support to the idea that our conscious capacities were selected for because of their adaptive value. The argument is not decisive, but it has some credibility and provides some argumentative leverage against the suspicious epiphenomenalist.

A different sort of argument from design comes less from evolutionary considerations than from consideration of certain phenomenological features of consciousness and the types of neural structures that might subserve these phenomenological features. Coordinating the phenomenological and neural considerations helps us see that the brain, in being designed to display conscious states, is also designed in a way that quite possibly endows these states with a functional role. What are the phenomenological features I have in mind? Consciousness is multimodal, involving the discrimination of many different types of states, things, and events, and it is loud and noisy. It broadcasts what it knows. In the first instance, these broadcasts are to the system itself, for one's self only. What consciousness knows or represents at any given time often consists of disparate kinds of information. I am now aware of the computer on which I am writing, I hear its buzz, I hear music in the background, I smell and taste my coffee, and I see the trees in autumn colors outside my window. What the conscious mind knows is presented in "a connected and orderly flow ... which represents the myriad connections within the represented world. If we consider what sort of pattern of brain activity would be required as the neural substrate for such representations and their interactions, it would seem that of necessity it would also have to satisfy the conditions of broadcasting information. Conscious phenomenal representations because of their highly integrated and multimodal content require rich associative networks of activation as their basis" (Van Gulick 1991).

The epiphenomenalist thinks the noisy broadcasts of consciousness are like the noisy work of the printer that produces the text already written and filed away in the computer. The alternative is that broadcasting is internal to the ongoing activity of the brain. Since many conscious states are global in the sense that they involve synthesis of many different types of contents, the most plausible inference is that these states involve interpenetrating and/or synchronous processing in many different neural areas (Smolensky 1988). If that is right, then the broadcasts are realized in the system and available to it as it modifies, coordinates, and plans its next moves (Baars 1988). To be sure, we broadcast what we know to the outside when we say what is on our mind. Furthermore, speaking is always conscious (Rosenthal 1990). But we are conscious when we do not emit external broadcasts. The suspicious epiphenomenalist must explain how such consciousness can be realized in myriad brain structures without its content also being available to the brain structures it interacts with for subsequent information processing. The brain hardly seems like a system that doesn't listen to itself.

An Experiment in Epiphenomenalism

Whether epiphenomenalism is true is ultimately an empirical question, although it is notoriously hard to think of decisive tests for or against it. In regard to the epiphenomenalist suspicion, consider this widely discussed experiment of Benjamin Libet (1985). Libet's experiment has been thought by some to prove dualism and by others to secure the case for materialism. I am interested in it only as it relates to the issue of epiphenomenalism. The experiment works as follows: First, subjects are hooked up to electroencephalographs, which measure "the readiness potential" in the cortical area thought to subserve hand movement, and to electromyographs, which measure onset of activity in the hand muscles.

Second, subjects are told to spontaneously flex their right hand whenever they feel like it. They are also told "to pay close introspective attention to the instant of the onset of the urge, desire, or decision to perform each such act and to the correlated position of a revolving spot on a clock face (indicating 'clock time'). The subject is also instructed to allow such acts to arise 'spontaneously,' without deliberately planning or paying attention to the 'prospect' of acting in advance" (Libet 1985, 530).

The findings were these: First, in cases where subjects experience no preplanning, the consciousness of an intention to flex occurs abut 350 milliseconds after the onset of the readiness potential and about 200 milliseconds before muscle activation. Second, in cases where the subjects reported a feeling of preplanning, of getting ready to spontaneously flex a few seconds before they flexed, the subjects still were able to distinguish this preplanning stage from the immediately following urge to flex. The finding that the readiness potential precedes conscious intention or urge, which precedes muscle movement, was confirmed. Libet writes, "Onsets of RP regularly begin at least several hundred ms before reported times for awareness of any intention to act in the case of acts performed ad lib. It would appear, therefore, that some neuronal activity associated with the eventual performance of the act occurs before any (recallable) conscious initiation or intervention.... This leads to the conclusion that cerebral initiation of the kind studied ... can and does usually begin *unconsciously*" (1985, 536). Libet asks, "If the brain can initiate a voluntary act before the appearance of conscious intention, that is, if the initiation of the specific performance of the act is by unconscious processes, is there any role for conscious function?" He answers, "Conscious control can be exerted before the final motor outflow to select or control volitional outcome. The volitional process, initiated unconsciously, can either be consciously permitted to proceed to consummation in the motor act or be consciously 'vetoed'" (1985, 536–537).

Libet argues that so long as there is veto power, conscious triggering would be redundant. That is, the mind allows the action to proceed to consummation unless it has reason to stop it. So long as it can stop a motor movement before it occurs, it does not need to actively trigger it.

This experiment is interesting, but one wonders why it generates such surprise and why it is taken by many to be so deflationary, so bad for consciousness. In the first place, the strong evidence that subjects can consciously veto flexion in the 200 ms between the urge or intention to flex and the response indicates that consciousness can play an important functional role in this particular motor routine. So consciousness is hardly shown to be epiphenomenal by this experiment. Second, it is hard to see what causes surprise at the fact that brain processes precede conscious experience, unless it is, as I suspect, a lurking Cartesian intuition that in voluntary action our conscious intentions are prime movers, themselves unmoved (except possibly by prior intentions).

From a naturalistic perspective, this intuition, familiar as it is, gives rise to a set of deep illusions to be avoided at all costs. According to the naturalist, only some neural activity is conscious. All conscious processes occur in complex causal networks in which they both supervene on certain neural processes and are caused by and cause other mental processes (also supervenient on the neural), some of which are conscious but most of which are not. It would be completely unexpected if all the causal antecedents of conscious mental processes were themselves conscious. In other words, conscious mental processes emerge out of the neural processes that give rise to them. It would be absurd to expect these emergent conscious neural processes to precede the neural processes they arise from.

Analogously, frozen water supervenes on collections of water molecules whose mean molecular kinetic energy has slowed to 32 degrees Fahrenheit. Freezing is caused by water reaching that temperature. But getting to that temperature involves a process of cooling, and it would be absurd to expect the frozen water to antedate the process that brings it about.

In addition to misunderstanding the nature of emergent properties, the picture of the mind as conscious of all that goes on in it falls prey to a further difficulty. It involves a very inefficient design. The "buzzing confusion" that James (probably incorrectly) thought constituted the experiential world of the infant would be our lot for life if we were aware of everything happening in our nervous system!

Third, there is a problem with the interpretation of the experiment. The experiment and most of the discussion about it ask us to picture the experiment this way (Libet 1985 and accompanying commentary):

(3) Readiness potential (500 ms) → conscious awareness of urge to flex (200 ms) → flexion

The trouble with this way of conceptualizing things is that it leaves out of view the fact that the subjects are first asked *to make a conscious effort* to let flexion occur spontaneously. To do so, the subjects have to load from conscious awareness an instruction to perform a certain complex task. Perhaps the instruction could be given subliminally to comatose patients or to normal persons in deep sleep. The fact is that in the actual experiment the instructions are given to fully conscious individuals who agree to comply with the experimental instructions and who make an effort to do so. How we load such instructions and get ourselves to do such things is completely closed off to introspection (to mine, anyway). But the power of complex intentions or plans to be carried out once the initial steps have been taken is made vivid in cases where individuals suffer petit mal seizures while driving to some destination and then, while unconscious, complete the drive to that destination! Once they have reached the destination, they just stop, unless they come out of the the seizure-induced sleeplike state.

It is a matter of utmost importance that Libet's experiment begins with a discussion of the task and the conscious agreement on the part of the subject to perform as instructed. The right picture, then, is this:

(4) Conscious awareness of instructions → conscious self-instruction to comply (minutes later) → readiness potential (500 ms) → conscious awareness of urge to flex (200 ms) → flexion

The upshot is that conscious processes are not epiphenomenal, even on (3), the narrow description of the experimental situation. Conscious processes serve as the middle link in a three-term chain, and they have the power to inhibit (or veto) the motor response being readied, if the agent so desires. It may be that occurrence of the awareness of the urge to flex 200 ms before flexion is not part of the cause of flexion in the case where flexion is allowed to go forward. But the fact that flexion can be stopped by a conscious veto strongly suggests that awareness of the impending flexion plays the role of broadcasting information about the system that the system can then use to change its course. On (4), the wide description, conscious processes appear at two different stages: first, when instructions are given and the effort to comply is made; second, when the instructions loaded at the first step are actually carried out.

I conclude that Libet's results, far from offering solace to the suspicious epiphenomenalist, are precisely the sort of results one would expect if one believes that conscious processes are subserved by nonconscious neural activity, and that conscious processes play variable but significant causal roles at various points in different cognitive domains.

Teleological Functionalism, Epiphenomenalism, and Defects of Consciousness

Teleological functionalism conceives of most mental capacities, both conscious and unconscious, as typically playing some adaptive role for the systems that have them (Lycan 1981, 1987; Van Gulick 1988, 1990). The words "most" and "typically" are important. The biological functions of objectless moods, especially bad ones, are fairly obscure. Perhaps they never had any. It is easier to tell a story about the emergence of emotions that gives them a role in enhancing fitness. This is compatible with certain emotional displays being less functional now than they were originally. Further, much of what we are conscious of is culturally transmitted. The learning capacities that subserve the acquisition of knowledge are clearly adaptive. But the details of what we learn and how we use the information we acquire, e.g., about how to make weapons, may or may not be functional in the short or long run. Finally, many of our conscious capacities, for example, to do arithmetic or geometry, were probably not directly selected for. They are the fortuitous outgrowths of combining our linguistic capacities and our capacities for abstraction with our abilities to individuate objects, estimate quantities, and display spatial savvy in manipulating objects and moving about the world.

In any case, there is evidence from both normal individuals and individuals with certain defects of consciousness that this hypothesis that consciousness has a function, that it generally serves a purpose, is true. Max Velmans (1992) argues for epiphenomenalism by arguing that there are cases in which choice, memory, learning, and novel responses occur without consciousness. But the fact that consciousness is not necessary for certain capacities to be exercised does not remotely imply that it serves no function when it is involved. There is ample evidence that consciousness facilitates performance on many activities, despite being not absolutely necessary for these activities (see Van Gulick 1992, for an effective response to Velmans 1992).

There are two main ways that information gets into our head and becomes available for reasoning, action guidance, and reporting. First, there are episodes of experiential sensitivity. I learned about the governmental system of checks and balances in third grade. The nun who taught and tested me on this made me vividly aware of how

the system works. Since then I have often used that information in reasoning, acting (e.g., voting), and reporting, but usually only as implicit background. Second, there are cases of subliminal or implicit learning. In these cases, knowledge is acquired, but normal phenomenal awareness is prevented or for some other reason fails to occur (Schacter 1989, 359). The latter sort of cases require the postulation of modes of knowledge acquisition that do not require phenomenal consciousness. We really do gain information unaware.

It is worth emphasizing that many experiments indicate that knowledge *acquired* without awareness is accessed and deployed somewhat less well than knowledge acquired with awareness (Dixon 1987, 752–754; Schacter 1989, 359). One explanation is that phenomenal awareness involves attention, and attention secures better treatment by the keepers of the gates of memory.

Even if some knowledge can be acquired without awareness, it remains an open question as to how much is acquired without awareness and how well it can be acquired without awareness. It is useful to distinguish between the role of phenomenal awareness in acquiring knowledge and in deploying that knowledge. There is a sense in which well-honed activities, like the tennis stroke of a proficient player, are automatic. But it is important to watch the slide from automatic to unconscious. Activities, such as sports play by proficient players, driving, eating, and the like, are not performed unconsciously, as is sometimes suggested. It is a commonplace that excellent athletes were once coached. While being coached, they were phenomenally aware of the instructions they received, as well as the visual trajectory of the ball, the feel of the racquet, and so on. Once the body learns to do what has been described and subtle adjustments are made on the basis of experience, the instructions appropriately recede into the cognitive background (if they didn't recede from occurrent consciousness, they would actually interfere with performance). Reaching a stage of proficiency in tennis involves continuous phenomenologically robust experience of the ball's trajectory, of the visual surround, of the racquet's feel, and so on. The true idea that one eventually goes on "automatic pilot" can give rise to the mistaken thought that one consciously disassociates oneself from the play. The mistaken thought arises from the fact that the experiences are eventually mostly sensory and tactile-kinaesthetic, not verbal or thoughtlike.

One could try gaining all the information a good coach gives via techniques of subliminal perception. But there is good reason to think that to the extent that consciousness is kept out of the learning environment, acquisition and performance will suffer somewhat, although it is notoriously difficult to control for consciousness in subjects who are not brain damaged, especially if the task is something like listening to tennis tapes while asleep. Let me and twin me receive instruction from the same coach, twin me subliminally, me in the normal way, and let us both practice the same amount. Bet on me in the match. If learning many tasks is superior when there is conscious loading of information and instruction about how to perform the task, relative to when the information and instructions are given subliminally, then the case for a functional role for consciousness scores some points.

There are other results relevant to the function of consciousness that come from persons with brain damage. The neurologically impaired individuals I now consider have inner lives, but their inner lives differ from those of normal persons in a variety of ways. These differences in conscious mental life cause certain functional deficits, and permit certain inferences about the role of consciousness in normal persons. Consider the following cases.

First, there are the blindsighted persons I have mentioned several times. Blindsighted persons have damage to the striate cortex (area V1) and therefore claim not to see objects in certain portions of the visual field, usually on one side. The evidence indicates that although such individuals are consciously insensitive to stimuli in the blind field, they are informationally sensitive to these stimuli. This shows up in a variety of ways. If blindsighted persons hear an ambiguous word (for example, "bank" or "palm") and have been primed in the blind field with another word relevant to the interpretation of the heard word ("money"/"river" or "hand"/"tree"), they favor the interpretation tied to the word shown in the blind field. Blindsighted persons do far less well at this task than sighted people, but their responses are better than the chance level one would expect with the truly blind.

Furthermore, if a blindsighted individual is asked to say what object is on her blind side, she says she does not know. But if told to reach for what is there "preparatory adjustments of the wrist, fingers, and arm are suited much better than chance to the shape, orientation, size, location, and distance of the objects" (Marcel 1988, 136).

The evidence of semantic disambiguation and preparatory hand movements indicates that blindsighted persons are informationally sensitive to things they are not conscious of. Their being in certain unconscious intentional states—unconsciously knowing that there is a glass of water rather than a ball to their right or knowing that "money" was flashed in the blind field—best explains their better than chance performance.

The fact remains that blindsighted persons claim to know nothing about the goings-on in their blindfield. They are wrong in this. But we have to press them to get them to show what they know. The case is altogether different with normal persons, and this difference is crucial from a functional point of view. Conscious awareness of a word that favors a particular interpretation, for example, river *bank* over money *bank*, leads to better performance on disambiguation tasks than does mere informational sensitivity to the helpful clue. Conscious awareness of a water fountain to my right will lead me to drink from it if I am thirsty. But the thirsty blindsighted person will make no move toward the fountain unless pressed to do so. The inference to the best explanation is that conscious awareness of the environment facilitates semantic comprehension and adaptive motor actions in creatures like us.

In his brief on behalf of epiphenomenalism, Velmans (1992) cites impressive performance rates of blindsighted persons in tasks involving guessing whether Xs or Os are appearing in the blindfield. As impressive as rates of 27 out of 30 are for blindsighted persons, they are not impressive compared to normal subjects, who will never make mistakes detecting Xs or Os.

Persons with memory deficits provide a different sort of example. Sadly, amnesiacs are commonplace. Some have a good grasp of their life before some time but lack the capacity to remember new things. Victims of Korsakoff's syndrome, advanced Alzheimer patients, and persons who have suffered certain kinds of traumatic brain injury cannot remember anything from one second to the next. Often people who can't remember what has happened to them or what they did in the near or distant past still comprehend language, can speak, and have no trouble with routinized motor tasks, such as walking, reaching successfully for things, cooking a meal, and using bathroom facilities.

Depending on the nature and extent of the amnesia, amnesiacs are functionally impaired in different ways. One well-studied amnesiac, H. M., has acquired certain skills. H. M. can mirror read, and he knows how to do the Tower of Hanoi puzzle. However, H. M. is not aware that he knows how to do the Tower of Hanoi puzzle. Each time the puzzle is brought to him, he claims never to have seen it before. But his performance has improved over the years from that of a normal beginner to that of a fairly proficient player. Each time H. M. does the puzzle, his performance starts close to the level he previously reached. He does not begin at the point of someone his age who truly does not know how to do the puzzle. H. M. is epistemically impaired with respect to the Tower of Hanoi puzzle but less so than a patient who not only said he never saw the puzzle before but also always returned to a beginner's performance level. Such a patient would be both experientially insensitive and informationally insensitive. He might work on the Tower of Hanoi puzzle, but the information about how to do it would not sink in or it would not stick. In H. M.'s case the knowledge sinks in and sticks. But he believes certain falsehoods, namely, that he has never seen the puzzle before and that he has no idea of how to do it. H. M.'s epistemic impairment involves an inability to consciously remember certain things.

H. M.'s problems are more than epistemic, of course. He belongs to a class of persons who have identity disorders. There are identity disorders (such as multiple personality disorder) that, as best as we can now determine, have nothing directly to do with neurological deficits. But I will concentrate here on identity disorders linked to neurologically based amnesia since these are best suited to displaying the multifarious types and roles of subjective consciousness. Cases of severe loss of autobiographical memory involve incapacities to constitute and reconstitute one's sense of identity, of who one is, of where one is coming from and where one is going. John Locke, in the second edition of his *An Essay Concerning Human Understanding* (1694), most famously linked the first-person sense of identity with conscious memory: "As far as this consciousness can be extended backwards to any past action or thought, so far reaches the identity of that person." From a subjective point of view, I am who I remember myself being.

In *The Man with the Shattered World: The History of a Brain Wound* (1972), A. R. Luria, the great Russian neuropsychologist, tells the story of Zazetsky, a soldier who suffered massive damage to the left occipito-parietal region of his brain. Subsequent to being shot, Zazetsky lived in a visually chaotic world; the right side of both his body and the external world were not there for him. He suffered profound incapacities to understand and produce language, and he had lost his memory. Most of his past was a blank.

Zazetsky eventually showed clear evidence of possessing an enormous amount of information about his own past. His first problem was accessing the information about himself and his life. He had to figure out a way to express the information he had inside himself so that he could see it again. His second problem was to consciously reappropriate this information, to recover it as the right description of his self. Zazetsky succeeded in many respects at solving the first problem. But the second remained in large measure intractable. That is, despite his possession of a great deal of information about his life and success at experiencing certain "memories *as memories*" at the moment of recollection (Marcel 1988, 125), Zazetsky's brain damage prevented him from drawing this information together into an experientially robust sense of his self. This inability appears in turn to have been at the root of his difficulty in carrying out a normal life plan after his tragic injury.

There are cases in which the loss of autobiographical memory involves the complete destruction or erasure of all the relevant information. There is nothing there—no permanent file, no well-honed set of distributed neural activity—to gain access to or to reactivate. The memories constitutive of one's past self and deeds are gone, never to return. Zazetsky's case, like H. M.'s on the Tower of Hanoi puzzle, was not like this. The information was still in there, and Zazetsky each day for almost three decades tried to get it out and thereby regain his identity.

How did he do this? Well, especially in the early stages, conscious effort was to no avail. The breakthrough came when Zazetsky made a fortuitous discovery. Luria writes,

A discovery he made one day proved to be the turning point: writing could be very simple. At first he proceeded just as little children do when they first learn to write—he had tried to visualize each letter in order to form it. Yet he had been writing for almost twenty years and as such did not need to employ the same methods as a child, to think about each letter and consider what strokes to use. For adults, writing is an automatic skill, a series of built-in movements, which I call "kinetic melodies." (1972, 72)

The next step was to convince Zazetsky to let his writing flow automatically, to let the "kinetic melodies" emerge, not worrying about what he was writing or whether it made sense. In fact, it did make sense, and gradually over the course of twenty-five years, Zazetsky produced what Luria called an "archeological study of his memory."

Once the wound had healed, Zazetsky was able to remember his childhood fairly well. But the years after that were not there for him. As Zazetsky wrote automatically but with extreme difficulty, a life began to appear on paper. Zazetsky was able to recognize certain things he wrote as true of himself, and he was able with extreme effort to order the narrative into something approximating its right temporal sequence. The saddest irony is that although each piece of Zazetsky's autobiography was consciously reappropriated by him each time he hit upon a veridical memory in writing, he himself was never able to fully reappropriate, to keep in clear and continuous view, to live with, the self he reconstructed in the three thousand pages he wrote. His memory impairment was deep and abiding. Furthermore, many grammatical constructions, including many of those he himself was able to produce on paper, were exceedingly hard for him to decipher, and even harder to keep in mind over time. Tragically, Zazetsky, to some significant degree, was kept from regaining himself and from reconstituting himself in the first-person way that Locke thought was necessary if one is to have an identity.

Cases like Zazetsky's provide further evidence for functional deficits that are deficits of consciousness in some important respects and are rooted in underlying neurological problems. Zazetsky is at loose ends, he feels aimless, and his life lacks meaning. He cannot find his self. Much of the information about his self is inside Zazetsky. Indeed, he has externalized many of the most salient parts of his self in his monumental autobiography. He is simply unable to consciously reappropriate the whole story and own it. He has problems of identity and meaning, and these are rooted in problems of self-consciousness.

Zazetsky's quest to reconstruct and reappropriate his self—to locate an identity constituted by a particular history, a direction, and a set of identity-conferring likes, dislikes, roles, and commitments—is a universal one. Formulating complex intentions and life plans and carrying them out require the capacity to hold in subjective consciousness certain salient aspects (but obviously not every aspect) of one's past, character, and plans. Zazetsky can access information about all these things. What he cannot do is to hold this information in subjective view and, with this sense of where he is coming from and where he is going, move forward in living his life.

Zazetsky's tragedy consists in part in the fact that he knows what is wrong. His knowledge of his disability and his intact frontal lobes enable him to formulate an unambiguous and straightforward plan. He will fight on and try to regain his self, but he will not succeed, because the damage he has suffered undermines his abilities to coordinate impressions and memories from different sensory modalities, to tap memory, to hold onto his memories as memories, and to deploy the linguistic system in reliable ways. Zazetsky's ability to hold himself and his experience together in a mindful way is a casualty to the shrapnel that has indifferently slashed the neuronal connections in the posterior occipito-parietal regions of his left cerebral hemisphere. Zazetsky's conscious capacities are (partly) maimed. His dysfunction is rooted in certain defects of consciousness.

Blocking Teleological Functionalism

For several years now I have been especially fond of arguments of the sort just produced as ways of dispelling the epiphenomenalist suspicion. There are all sorts of cases of neurological deficits linked with deficits in subjective consciousness, and in many of these cases the incapacitation of subjective consciousness seems to explain some fur-

ther incapacity. Zazetsky can't get on with his life because, although he can in some sense reconstruct who he is, he cannot hold that image firmly in view and move on as *that* person. Blindsighted patients never initiate activity toward the blindfield because they lack subjective awareness of things in that field. Prosopagnosiacs don't consciously recognize familiar faces. Thus they don't rush to greet long-lost friends, even though their hearts go pitter-patter when they see them (Pascal was right: the heart often knows what the mind does not).

Recently Ned Block (1995) has caused me to worry about the form of the argument (chap. 20). Although Block thinks that epiphenomenalism is probably false, he does not think standard arguments based on cases like blindsight show it to be false. Block's argument goes like this:

1. We can distinguish between two kinds of consciousness: phenomenal, what-it-is-like, consciousness (consciousness$_p$), and access consciousness (consciousness$_a$). Access consciousness "has to do with information flow not qualia. The idea is that some—but not all—of the information that gets into our heads becomes (1) in Stich's (1978) sense 'inferentially promiscuous', i.e., easily available as premise in reasoning, and (2) available for guiding action and (3) available for reporting."

2. A person who is knocked unconscious by a blow to the head is not conscious$_a$, but if she is seeing stars or dreaming, she is conscious$_p$. Consciousness$_a$ without consciousness$_p$ is also conceptually possible, although there may be no actual cases of it. "However when people talk about robots being unconscious zombies, they mean [they lack] consciousness$_p$ rather than consciousness$_a$. . . . The robot zombies are envisioned to have mechanisms of reasoning and guiding action and reporting that process information about the world."

3. The distinction between consciousness$_p$ and consciousness$_a$ is useful in describing such syndromes as prosopagnosia. "We can give descrip-

tions of prosopagnosia in both phenomenal terms and cognitive or intentional terms (related to access), and both get at something important about the syndrome. Phenomenally speaking, we can say that prosopagnosiacs fail to have a feeling of familiarity when looking at familiar faces. . . . We can also characterize the syndrome cognitively: they don't know just from looking at people which ones are familiar, or who they are. They lack the usual visual access to information about which people are their friends and relations."

4. We can apply the distinction between consciousness$_p$ and consciousness$_a$ to expose a fallacy in the "reasoning to the effect that since a thirsty blindsighter doesn't reach for the glass of water in his blind field, we can reasonably suppose that it is the lack of consciousness that is to blame. And thus the function of consciousness lies in part in its role in initiating behavior."

5. The problem is this: "If it is consciousness$_a$ we are talking about, this reasoning is trivially right. If the information that there is a glass of water in front of me is to be put together with the information that this water can be used to quench my thirst, so as to guide action, these items must be conscious$_a$. After all, being available for inference and guiding action are part of what makes information conscious$_a$. . . . And it is equally obvious that this reasoning *cannot* simply be *assumed* to apply to consciousness$_p$. True, the blindsight patient is not conscious$_p$ of the glass of water, but consciousness$_p$ of the glass of water would not help in initiating action unless it brought consciousness$_a$ of the glass with it. The blindsight patient has *neither* consciousness$_a$ nor consciousness$_p$ of the glass, whereas the normal person who sees the glass and drinks has *both* consciousness$_a$ and consciousness$_p$ of the glass. The obvious facts of the case tell us nothing about the relation between consciousness$_a$ of the glass and consciousness$_p$ of the glass, for example, whether one causes the other, and if so, which cause which. . . . These points seem entirely obvious once one accepts the distinction between consciousness$_a$ and consciousness$_p$."

6. In sum, the argument for the causal efficacy of consciousness is an argument for the causal efficacy of consciousness$_p$. But cases such as blindsight do not show that consciousness$_p$ is causally efficacious. The sighted person has both consciousness$_p$ and consciousness$_a$, and the blindsighted person lacks both. It is entirely possible, therefore, that it is the lack of consciousness$_a$ that is at the root of the difference and that the lack of consciousness$_p$ is irrelevant.

Block's point is that arguments against epiphenomenalism fail to keep the two kinds of consciousness apart. Unless this is done, we won't be able to disentangle whether it is access consciousness or phenomenal consciousness (or neither or both) that accounts for the differences between sighted and blindsighted persons.

Phenomenal Access

My reply to Block's argument is based on the premise that we should not accept any sharp distinction between the two kinds of consciousness. This is not to deny that it is useful in cases such as prospagnosia to distinguish between the feeling of the condition and the type of information not picked up because of the deficit. But from both a terminological point of view and from a point of view that tries to do justice to the relevant phenomena, we are better off with the distinction I have drawn between informational sensitivity, which involves access to information without phenomenal awareness, and experiential sensitivity, which involves both phenomenal feel and access to information, than we are with Block's distinction between the two kinds of consciousness. If I am right that the distinction is less credible than Block makes it out to be, then the points that "seem entirely obvious once one accepts the distinction between consciousness$_a$ and consciousness$_p$" will seem less obvious, and the arguments linking deficits in subjective awareness with action deficits will look less problematic than Block maintains.

According to my preferred distinction between experiential sensitivity and informational sensitivity, some states we go into have qualitative or phenomenal feel to them, and some labor in our minds without possessing such feel. Phenomenal feel necessarily involves access to whatever it is we feel. This access may be epistemically impoverished, as in the case of the prosopagnosiac or the case of Block's character who is seeing stars. But all cases of phenomenal awareness, even if the awareness has no propositional content, are cases in which the agent has access to information about what state he is in. If, for example, I am in a good mood, I am in a state that, strictly speaking, is not of or about anything. But I can report that I am in that state, it makes a difference to how I act, and so on. The prosopagnosiac may not be able to say that this person before him is his friend Jane, but he will have access to and be able to report on *whatever* is phenomenally available to him, for example, "There is a person in front of me." Phenomenal consciousness always involves access to whatever we are phenomenally aware of. We are experientially sensitive to what we are phenomenally aware of.

However, there are things to which we are informationally sensitive but not experientially sensitive. It happens that things we barely notice or do not notice at all sometimes have detectable impacts on thought and behavior. Knowledge without awareness is a well-known phenomenon. I think it best to think of knowledge without awareness as unconscious, period. But if one insists on Block's distinction, then knowledge without awareness is unconscious$_p$; it involves informational but not experiential sensitivity. Block thinks that knowledge without awareness is unconscious$_a$, but I don't see how Block can avoid construing knowledge without awareness as conscious$_a$. After all, such knowledge involves access to information, and this information plays a role in inference, reporting, and action. States that can be shown to play a significant cognitive role without making a phenomenal appearance should be conscious$_a$ on Block's view, unless he im-

plicitly assumes that conscious$_a$ events must *also* be conscious$_p$.

Block wants implicit or subliminal-learning, what I call informational sensitivity and contrast with experiential sensitivity, to be unconscious$_a$, not conscious$_a$. However, if we adopt Block's terminology, we are better off thinking of the blindsighted person as unconscious$_p$ but conscious$_a$, since he has some access to the information in his blind field. The same is true of the prosopagnosiac; remember the prosopagnosiac's heart goes pitter-patter when his beloved appears. My next move is predictable. Since the blindsighted person is conscious$_a$ in the blindfield but unconscious$_p$, it is his lack of phenomenal access that explains the problem. Actually, the situation is more complicated than this. Strictly speaking, I should say something like this: The information the blindsighted person has may be degraded. This may be part of the reason that the information does not reach phenomenal awareness. Or it may be that the information is not degraded but simply untransmissible due to the nature of the lesion in V1. In either case the inference to the best explanation is that if the information were to become phenomenally conscious, performance would improve.

In effect, the case isn't one where because both consciousness$_p$ and consciousness$_a$ are lacking, and we can't tell which one causes the problem. Only consciousness$_p$ is clearly lacking; consciousness$_a$, in Block's sense, is not. That is, the most natural way to describe the case in Block's terminology is to say that the blindsighted person possesses zero subjective awareness and is therefore unconscious$_p$ but conscious$_a$ to some degree. The task is to explain why being conscious$_a$, in the ways he is conscious$_a$, is insufficient to generate the normal sorts of linguistic identifications and bodily movements. If this is the right way to think about matters, then the idea that phenomenal consciousness is what helps explain the case looks more promising, for contrary to what Block says, the blindsighted person is not correctly characterized as unconscious$_a$. By what we know from the knowledge-without-awareness literature and about what the blindsighted person has access to, there is some plausibility in inferring that the lack of phenomenal awareness of the blindfield at every stage of processing partly explains the inability to bring the knowledge the system possesses into awareness and into normal, high-quality play in inference, reporting, and action. In a telling remark Block says that consciousness$_a$ without consciousness$_p$ is "conceptually possible" but "perhaps not actual." My suggestion is that it is actual. His imaginary case of a zombie shows the conceptual possibility, the case of blindsight shows its actuality.

Can the Epiphenomenalist Explain Everything That the Teleological Functionalist Can Explain?

Block is attracted to a general view that posits a consciousness$_p$ module that feeds the executive system responsible for issuing high-quality reports and sensibly guiding actions. The blindsighted person has some information about the blindfield, but this information is stuck in the peripheral modules. Forced guesses can tune in the executive because the person hears her own guesses and receives reports about how she is doing. But by and large the information is locked up in the peripheral modules. For people with normal sight, the information from the peripheral modules passes through the consciousness$_p$ module and into the executive. Thus normal reasoning, reporting, and action can occur.

According to this model, it is not the absence of consciousness$_p$ that directly causes poor performance or its presence that directly causes good performance. Good performance depends on whether or not information gets into the executive system, and it gets into the executive system only if it goes through the consciousness$_p$ module. The absence of consciousness$_p$ is an indication that the executive is not able to play its executive role, and the presence of consciousness$_p$ is an indication that it is able to play its executive role.

It would not be profitable to get embroiled in a debate over this specific theoretical model. The point I want to emphasize is that if the model is true, it would help the argument against epiphenomenalism. The support comes from the fact that on the proposed model, the consciousness$_p$ module plays a role in driving the executive. The model implies that the blindsighted person is dysfunctional because information is locked in the peripheral modules. If the information about the visual field were to get to the executive, it would be routed first through the consciousness$_p$ module, and consciousness$_p$ would thereby play an important causal role in the complex process that gives rise to reasoning, reporting, and action.

The suspicious epiphenomenalist has a counterproposal at the ready. The consciousness$_p$ module does not feed the executive. Rather, the executive informs the consciousness$_p$ module about what it has been up to. (See Velmans 1992, for a version of this hypothesis where focal attentive processing takes the role of the executive.) In the cases of blindsight the executive hasn't been up to anything, so phenomenal consciousness receives no reports.

The suspicious epiphenomenalist can also give an account of why I beat twin me at tennis, even though we have received identical coaching, I while fully conscious, my twin subliminally. The reason I beat twin me is that my executive system was properly tapped and that of twin me wasn't. The evidence for this is straightforward. According to the epiphenomenalist, executive activity causes (but is not caused by) phenomenal awareness (which causes nothing else). I can report the coaching techniques I have been taught because my executive system was activated and caused me to be aware of what I was taught. My twin lacks phenomenal awareness about how to play tennis (although he does many of the right things). This shows that subliminal coaching did not activate his executive system. Had it been activated, his executive system would have issued a phenomenal report, a report as inconsequential to the ability to play tennis well as the toot of the train's whistle is to its ability to continue full steam ahead, but a report nonetheless.

The epiphenomenalist is most resourceful. But the fact that the epiphenomenalist can explain certain data with a model that endows nonconscious parts of the system with executive powers and depicts phenomenal consciousness as a mental cul de sac does not mean that the view is credible overall. Epiphenomenalism is a coherent view. But it lacks credibility when considered in light of plausible theoretical commitments discussed earlier that emanate from neuroscience and evolutionary biology.

The biggest problem the epiphenomenalist faces is explaining how, given the massive connectivity of the brain, *any* feature as common, well-structured, and multimodal as phenomenal consciousness could supervene on certain neural processes without having interesting and important causal effects in other parts of the neural network. We know that different kinds of phenomenal experiences are processed in different parts of the brain. The epiphenomenalist will need to show that there is a cul de sac in each of the relevant areas where phenomenal consciousness is stopped dead in its tracks so that it makes no causal contribution to other neural events. This, I suggest, is a research program destined to fail. The brain doesn't work that way.

The second problem the epiphenomenalist faces is explaining why phenomenal consciousness is out of touch with so much of what goes on in the brain but is hooked up to the sensory modules and to declarative memory, that is, memory for facts and events. Our species' success and our personal survival depend on successful commerce with the external world. This requires being in touch with the present state of the environment and drawing inductive inferences based on the past. In theory, we could have evolved so as to succeed in being in touch and drawing the right inferences without phenomenal consciousness. But the fact is that we did evolve with phenomenal consciousness. Furthermore, phenomenal consciousness is hooked up to exactly the systems

processing the information that, from the point of view of wise evolutionary design, it has most need to know about if it is to make a significant contribution to the life of the organism in which it occurs.

The experiments and data discussed in this chapter must be considered in light of a general theoretical commitment to massive neural connectivity, to a picture of consciousness as distributed (a single faculty might be locked up and do no interesting work, but it is extremely implausible that widely distributed conscious activity plays no significant causal role at any of the distributed sites), and to the evolutionary rationale for the structure and function of consciousness. In light of these credible theoretical commitments, the experiments and data discussed in this chapter weigh on the side of conceiving of phenomenal consciousness as playing multifarious causal roles.

I conclude that subjective awareness plays a role in our mental lives. But exactly what role it plays, how important it is in fixing informational content, in what domains it is important, how it figures in remembering, what its relation is to attention (possibly it is a species of attention, or attention is a species of it), whether it is constitutive of certain kinds of sensation and memory, or whether it receives output from the sensory modules and memory—all these are unsettled questions. Until they are settled, the precise roles of subjective awareness will remain unclear, as will its relative importance in the multifarious domains of mental life. This will leave the suspicious epiphenomenalist with many openings to raise his skeptical question. But, as far as I can see, all current and potential disputes between the epiphenomenalist and his opponents are matters to be settled in empirical court. I have shown how we already possess some theory and evidence that, taken together, bears on the question of the role of subjective consciousness. At this point in a five-set tennis match, the teleological functionalist leads the suspicious epiphenomenalist two games to one, up 15-love in the fourth game of the first set. There is still a long way to go, the day is hot, and both players have their strengths. I can't see the epiphenomenalist winning. But it will be a good fight, and there are lessons to be learned by those overzealous fans of consciousness who have historically overrated its power and ability to get to every place on the court.

References

Baars, B. J. (1988). *A Cognitive Theory of Consciousness*. Cambridge: Cambridge University Press.

Block, N. (1995). "On a Confusion about a Function of Consciousness" (with open peer commentary). *Brain and Behavioral Sciences*, 18: 2, 227–287.

Calvin, W. H. (1991). *The Ascent of Mind: Ice Age Climate and the Evolution of Intelligence*. New York: Bantam.

Crick, Francis, and Christof Koch. (1990). "Towards a Neurobiological Theory of Consciousness." *Seminars in the Neuroscience* 2:263–275.

Dixon, N. F. (1987). "Subliminal Perception." In R. Gregory, *The Oxford Companion to Mind*. Oxford: Oxford University Press.

Gould, S. J., and R. Lewontin. (1979). "The Spandrels of San Marco and the Panglossian Paradigm: A Critique of the Adaptationist Programme." *Proceedings of the Royal Society of London*, Series B, 205.

Gregory, R, ed. (1987). *The Oxford Companion to Mind*. Oxford: Oxford University Press.

James, William. (1890). *The Principles of Psychology*. 2 vols. New York: Dover, 1950.

Libet, B. (1985). "Unconscious Cerebral Initiative and the Role of Conscious Will in Voluntary Action." *Behavioral and Brain Sciences* 8:529–566.

Locke, John. (1690). *An Essay Concerning Human Understanding*. Ed. P. H. Nidditch. 2nd ed., 1694. 5th ed., 1706. Oxford: Oxford University Press, 1975.

Luria, A. R. (1972). *The Man with the Shattered World*. Cambridge: Harvard University Press, 1987.

Lycan, W. (1981). "Form, Function, and Feel." *Journal of Philosophy* 78:23–49.

———. (1987). *Consciousness*. Cambridge: MIT Press.

Marcel, A. J. (1988). "Phenomenal Experience and Functionalism." In *Consciousness in Contemporary Science*, ed. A. J. Marcel and E. Bisiach. Oxford: Oxford University Press.

Rosenthal, David. (1990). "Why Are Verbally Expressed Thoughts Conscious?" ZIF report no. 32, Research Group on Mind and Brain, University of Bielefeld, Germany.

Schacter, D. (1989). "On the Relation between Memory and Consciousness: Dissociable Interactions and Conscious Experience." In *Varieties of Memory and Consciousness: Essays in Honour of Endel Tulving*, ed. Henry L. Roediger III and F. I. M. Craik. Hillsdale, N. J.: L. Erlbaum.

Shallice, T. (1988). *From Neuropsychology to Mental Structure*. Cambridge: Cambridge University Press.

Smolensky, Paul. (1988). "On the Proper Treatment of Connectionism." *Behavioral and Brain Sciences* 11:1–23.

Stich, S. 1978. "Autonomous Psychology and the Belief-Desire Thesis." *Monist* 61.

Van Gulick, R. 1988. "A Functionalist Plea for Self-Consciousness." *Philosophical Review* 97, no. 2:149–181.

———. (1990). "What Difference Does Consciousness Make?" *Philosophical Topics* 17:211–230.

———. 1992. "Consciousness May Still Have a Processing Role to Play." *Brain and Behavioral Sciences*. 14.4, pp. 699–700.

Velmans, M. 1992. "Is Human Information Processing Conscious?" *Brain and Behavioral Sciences*. 14:651–669.

On a Confusion about a Function of Consciousness

Ned Block

1 Introduction

The concept of consciousness is a hybrid or better, a mongrel concept: the word "consciousness" connotes a number of different concepts and denotes a number of different phenomena. We reason about "consciousness" using some premises that apply to one of the phenomena that fall under "consciousness," other premises that apply to other "consciousnesses," and we end up with trouble. There are many parallels in the history of science. Aristotle used "velocity" sometimes to mean average velocity and sometimes to mean instantaneous velocity; his failure to see the distinction caused confusion (Kuhn 1964). The Florentine experimenters of the seventeenth century used a single word (roughly translatable as "degree of heat") for temperature and for heat, generating paradoxes. For example, when they measured "degree of heat" by whether various heat sources could melt paraffin, heat source A came out hotter than B, but when they measured "degree of heat" by how much ice a heat source could melt in a given time, B was hotter than A (Wiser and Carey 1983). These are very different cases, but there is a similarity, one that they share with the case of "consciousness." The similarity is: very different concepts are treated as a single concept. I think we all have some tendency to make this mistake in the case of "consciousness."

Though the problem I am concerned with appears in many lines of thought about consciousness, it will be convenient to focus on one of them. My main illustration of the kind of confusion I'm talking about concerns reasoning about the *function* of consciousness. But the issue of the function of consciousness is more of the *platform* of this chapter than its topic. Because this chapter attempts to expose a confusion, it is primarily concerned with reasoning, not with data. Long stretches of text without data may make some readers uncomfortable, as will my fanciful thought-experiments. But if you are interested in consciousness, if I am right you can't afford to lose patience. A stylistic matter: because this paper will have audiences with different concerns, I have adopted the practice of putting items that will mainly be of technical interest to part of the audience in endnotes. Endnotes can be skipped without losing the thread. I now turn to blindsight and its role in reasoning about a function of consciousness.

Patients with damage in primary visual cortex typically have "blind" areas in their visual fields. If the experimenter flashes a stimulus in one of those blind areas and asks the patient what he saw, the patient says "Nothing." The striking phenomenon is that some (but not all) of these patients are able to "guess" reliably about certain features of the stimulus, features having to do with motion, location, direction (e.g., whether a grid is horizontal or vertical). In "guessing," they are able to discriminate some simple forms; if they are asked to grasp an object in the blind field (which they say they can't see), they can shape their hands in a way appropriate to grasping it, and there are some signs of color discrimination. Interestingly, visual acuity (as measured, e.g., by how fine a grating can be detected) increases further from where the patient is looking in blindsight, the opposite of normal sight. (Blindsight was first noticed by Poppel et al. 1973, and there is now a huge literature on this and related phenomena. I suggest looking at Bornstein and Pittman 1992 and Milner and Rugg 1992).

Consciousness in some sense is apparently missing (though see McGinn 1991, p. 112, for an argument to the contrary), and with it, the ability to deploy information in reasoning and rational control of action. For example, Tony Marcel (1986) observed that a thirsty blindsight patient would not reach for a glass of water in his blind field. (One has to grant Marcel some "poetic license" in this influential example, since blindsight patients appear to have insufficient form perception in their blind fields to pick out a glass of water.) It is tempting to argue (Marcel 1986, 1988; Baars 1988; Flanagan 1991, 1992; van Gulick 1989) that since consciousness is missing in blindsight, consciousness must have a function of somehow enabling information represented in the brain to be used in reasoning, reporting, and rationally guiding action. I mean the "rationally" to exclude the "guessing" kind of guidance of action that blindsight patients *are* capable of in the case of stimuli presented to the blind field. (The intended contrast is that between guidance by reason and guidance by inclination; I don't mean to say that the blindsight patient is irrational.) The idea is that when a representation is not conscious—as in the blindsight patient's blindfield perceptual representations—it can influence behavior behind the scenes, but only when the representation is conscious does it play a rational role; and so consciousness must be involved in promoting this rational role.

A related argument is also tempting: Robert van Gulick (1989) and John Searle (1992) discuss Penfield's observations of epileptics who have a seizure while walking, driving, or playing the piano. The epileptics continue their activities in a routinized, mechanical way despite, it is said, a total lack of consciousness. Searle says that since both consciousness and also flexibility and creativity of behavior are missing, we can conclude that a function of consciousness is to somehow promote flexibility and creativity. These two arguments are the springboard for this chapter. Though some variants of this sort of reasoning have merit, they are often given more weight than they deserve because of a persistent fallacy involving a conflation of two very different concepts of consciousness.

The plan of the chapter is as follows: in the next section, I will briefly discuss some other syndromes much like blindsight, and I will sketch one model that has been offered for explaining these syndromes. Then, in the longest part of the chapter I will distinguish the two concepts of consciousness whose conflation is the root of the fallacious arguments. Once that is done, I will sketch what is wrong with the target reasoning and also what is right about it, and I will conclude with some remarks on how it is possible to investigate empirically what the function of consciousness is without having much of an idea about the scientific nature of consciousness.

2 Other Syndromes and Schacter's Model

To introduce a second blindsight-like syndrome, I want to first explain a syndrome that is not like blindsight: prosopagnosia (*prosop* = face, *agnosia* =neurological deficit in recognizing). Prosopagnosics are unable visually to recognize their closest relatives—even pictures of themselves—though usually they have no trouble recognizing their friends via their voices, or, according to anecdotal reports, visually recognizing people by recognizing characteristic motions of their bodies. Although there is wide variation from case to case, prosopagnosia is compatible with a high degree of visual ability, even in tasks involving faces.

One patient who has been studied by my colleagues in the Boston area is LH, a Harvard undergraduate who emerged from a car accident with very localized brain damage that left him unable to recognize even his mother. His girlfriend began to wear a special ribbon so that he would know who she was. Now, years later, he still cannot identify his mother or his wife and children from photographs (Etcoff et al. 1991). Still, if shown a photo and asked to choose another photo of the same person from a set of, say, five photos presented simultaneously with the original, LH can do almost as well as normal people despite differences between the target and matching photos in lighting, angle, and expression.

Now we are ready for the analog of blindsight. The phenomenon appears in many experimental paradigms, but I will mention only this: It has recently been discovered (by Sergent and Poncet 1990) that some prosopagnosics are very good at "guessing" as between two names in the same occupational category ("Reagan" and "Bush") of a person whose face they claim is unfamiliar. (See Young and de Haan 1993 and Young 1994a, 1994b for a description of these phenomena.) Interestingly, LH, the patient mentioned above, does not appear to have "covert knowledge" of the people whose faces he sees, but he does appear to have "covert knowledge" of their facial expressions (Etcoff et al. 1992).

Many such phenomena in brain-damaged patients have now been explored using the techniques of cognitive and physiological psychology. Further, there are a variety of such phenomena that occur in normals, you and me. For example, suppose that you are given a string of words and asked to count the vowels. This can be done so that you will have no conscious recollection or even recognition of the words and you will be unable to "guess" which words you have seen at a level above chance. However, if I give you a series of word-stems to complete according to your whim, your likelihood of completing "rea-" as "reason" is greater if "reason" is one of the words that you saw, even if you don't recall or recognize it as one of the words you saw. [1]

Recall that the target reasoning, the reasoning I will be saying is importantly confused (but also importantly right) is that since, when consciousness is missing, subjects cannot report or reason about the nonconscious representations or use them to guide action, a function of consciousness is to facilitate reasoning, reporting, and guiding action. This reasoning is *partially* captured in a model suggested by Daniel Schacter (1989; see also Schacter et al. 1988) in a paper reviewing phenomena such as the ones described above. Figure 20.1 is derived from Schacter's model.

The model is only partial (i.e., it models some aspects of the mind, but not others), and so may be a bit hard to grasp for those who are used to seeing inputs and outputs. Think of the hands and feet as connected to the Response System box, and the eyes and ears as connected to the specialized modules. (See Schacter 1989, for some indication of how these suggestions are oversimple.) The key feature of the model is that it contains a box for something called "phenomenal consciousness"; I'll say more about phenomenal consciousness later, but for now, let me just say that phenomenal consciousness is experience; what makes a state phenomenally conscious is that there is something "it is like" (Nagel 1974) to be in that state. The model dictates that the phenomenal consciousness module has a function: it is the gateway between the special purpose "knowledge" modules and the central Executive System that is in charge of direct control of reasoning, reporting, and guiding action. So a function of consciousness on this model includes integrating the outputs of the specialized modules and transmitting the integrated contents to mechanisms of reasoning and control of action and reporting.

I will be using this model as a focus of discussion, but I hope that my endorsement of its utility as a focus of discussion will not be taken as an endorsement of the model itself. I have no commitment to a single executive system or even to a phenomenal consciousness module. One can accept the idea of phenomenal consciousness as distinct from any cognitive or functional or intentional notion while frowning on a modular treatment of it. Perhaps, for example, phenomenal consciousness is a feature of the whole brain.

Many thinkers will hate any model that treats phenomenal consciousness as something that could be accomplished by a distinct system.[2] I call that feature Cartesian Modularism, by analogy to the Cartesian Materialism of Dennett and Kinsbourne (1992a), the view that consciousness occupies a literal place in the brain. Modules are individuated by their function, so the point of the box's place between the specialized modules and the Executive System is to indicate that there is a single system that has the function of talking to the specialized modules and integrating their

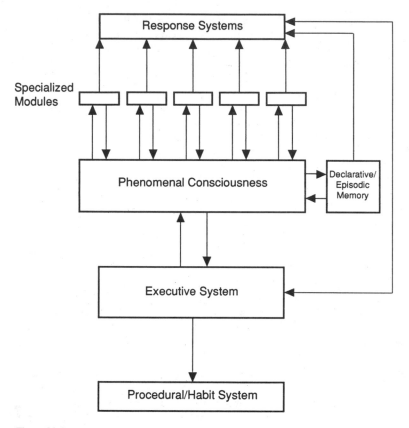

Figure 20.1

outputs, and talking to the Executive System, passing on information from the specialized modules. But there is an additional point in *calling* that system the phenomenal consciousness system, namely to say that phenomenal consciousness is somehow involved in performing that function. The idea is that phenomenal consciousness *really does* something: it is involved somehow in powering the wheels and pulleys of access to the Executive System. This is a substantive claim, one that is distinct from the claims that phenomenal consciousness is *correlated* with that information-processing function, or that phenomenal consciousness should be *identified* with that information-processing function. The

idea is that phenomenal consciousness is distinct (at least conceptually) from that information-processing function, but is part of the implementation of it.

Martha Farah (see chapter 11) criticizes this model on the ground that we don't observe patients whose blindsight-like performance is up to the standard of normal vision. Blindsight and its analogs are always degraded in discriminatory capacity. Her assumption seems to be that if there is a phenomenal consciousness module, it could simply be bypassed without decrement in performance; and the fact that this is not observed is taken as reason to reject the phenomenal consciousness module. She appears to think that if there is a phenomenal consciousness module, then phenomenal consciousness *doesn't do any information processing* (except, I guess, for determining reports of phenomenal consciousness), for otherwise why assume that it could be bypassed without decrement in performance. But why assume that phenomenal consciousness doesn't do any information processing? For example, phenomenal consciousness might be like the water in a hydraulic computer. You don't expect the computer to just work normally without the water. Even if there could be an electrical computer that is isomorphic to the hydraulic computer but works without water, one should not conclude that the water in the hydraulic system does nothing. I will return to this issue later.

One reason that many philosophers would hate Cartesian Modularist models is that such models may be regraded as licensing the possibility of "zombies," creatures which have information processing that is the same as ours but which have no phenomenal consciousness. If the phenomenal consciousness module could be replaced by a device that had the same information-processing effects on the rest of the system, but without phenomenal consciousness, the result would be a zombie. My view is that we now know so little about the scientific nature of phenomenal consciousness and its function that we cannot judge whether the same function could be performed by an ersatz phenomenal consciousness module—that is, whether an ersatz phenomenal consciousness module could inject its representations with ersatz conscious content that would affect information processing the same way as real conscious content. There is much of interest to be said about this idea and its relation to other ideas that have been mentioned in the literature, but I have other fish to fry, so I leave the matter for another time.

The information-processing function of phenomenal consciousness in Schacter's model is the ground of the concept of consciousness that I will mainly be contrasting with phenomenal consciousness, what I will call "access-consciousness." A perceptual state is access-conscious roughly speaking if its content—what is represented by the perceptual state—is processed via that information-processing function, that is, if its content gets to the Executive System, whereby it can be used to control reasoning and behavior.

Schacter's model is useful for my purposes both because it can be used to illustrate the contrast between phenomenal and access-consciousness and because it allows us to see one possible explanation of the "covert knowledge" syndromes just described. This explanation (and also Schacter's model) are certainly incomplete and no doubt wildly oversimple at best, but it is nonetheless useful to see the rough outlines of how an account might go. In addition, there is an association between Schacter's model and the target reasoning—though as we shall see there is another processing model that perhaps better embodies the target reasoning.

Consider a blindsight patient who has just had a vertical line displayed in his blind field. "What did you see?" "Nothing," says the patient. "Guess as between a vertical and a horizontal line," says the experimenter. "Vertical," says the patient, correctly. Here's story about what happened. One of the specialized modules is specialized for spatial information; it has some information about the verticality of the stimulus. The pathways between this specialized module and the phenomenal consciousness system have been damaged, creating the "blind field," so the patient has no phenomenally conscious experience of the line, and hence his Executive System has no information about whether the line is vertical or horizontal. But the specialized module has a direct connection to the Response System, so when the subject is given a binary choice, the specialized module can somehow directly affect the response. Similarly, there is a specialized module for face information, which can have some identifying information about the face that has been presented to a prosopagnosic. If the prosopagnosia is caused by damage in the link between the face module and the phenomenal consciousness system, then that prevents the identifying face information from being phenomenally conscious, and without phenomenal consciousness, the Executive System does not get the information about the person behind the face. When the prosopagnosic guesses as between "Reagan" and "Bush," the face module somehow directly controls the response. (It is assumed that the face module has information about people—e.g., their names—linked to representations of their faces.) It is interesting in this regard that the patients who do best in these experiments are the ones judged to be the most "passive" (Marcel 1983, p. 204; Weiskranz 1988). One can speculate that in a laid-back subject, the Executive does not try out a guessing strategy, and so peripheral systems are more likely to affect the response.

Alexia is a neurological syndrome whose victims can no longer read a word "at a glance," but can only puzzle out what word they have seen at a rate of, for example, a second per letter. Nonetheless, these subjects often show various kinds of understanding of the meanings of words that have been flashed far too briefly for them to read in their laborious way. The idea, once again, is that one of the specialized modules is specialized for lexical information, and this module has information about words that the subject cannot consciously read. This information somehow affects responses. Landis et al. (1980) report that such a patient actually became worse at "guesses" having to do with the meanings of "unread" words as his explicit reading ability improved (Young and de Haan 1993). Again, perhaps once the Executive has more information, it "takes over," preventing peripheral systems from controlling responses. Coslett and Saffran (1994) report that alexics did worse at "guessing" words with longer exposures. An exposure of 250 ms was better than an exposure of 2 sec. Again, longer exposures may give the Executive System a chance to try to read letter by letter.

Schacter's model and the explanation I have just sketched are highly speculative; my purposes in appealing to them are heuristic.

3 Two Concepts of Consciousness

First, consider phenomenal consciousness, or P-consciousness, as I will call it. Let me acknowledge at the outset that I cannot define P-consciousness in any remotely noncircular way. I don't consider this an embarrassment. The history of reductive definitions in philosophy should lead one not to expect a reductive definition of anything. But the best one can do for P-consciousness is in some respects worse than for many other things because really all one can do is *point* to the phenomenon (cf. Goldman 1993a). Nonetheless, it is important to point properly. John Searle, acknowledging that consciousness cannot be defined noncircularly, defines it as follows:

> By consciousness I simply mean those subjective states of awareness or sentience that begin when one wakes in the morning and continue throughout the period that one is awake until one falls into a dreamless sleep, into a coma, or dies or is otherwise, as they say, unconscious. (This comes from Searle 1990b; there is a much longer attempt along the same lines in his 1992, p. 83ff.)

I will argue that this sort of pointing is flawed because it points to too many things, too many different consciousnesses.

So how should we point to P-consciousness? Well, one way is via rough synonyms. As I said, P-consciousness is experience. P-conscious properties are experiential properties. P-conscious states are experiential states, that is, a state is P-conscious if it has experiential properties. The totality of the experiential properties of a state are "what it is like" to have it. Moving from synonyms to examples, we have P-conscious states when we see, hear, smell, taste, and have pains. P-conscious properties include the experiential properties of sensations, feelings, and perceptions, but I would also include thoughts, wants, and emotions.[3] A feature of P-consciousness that is often missed is that differences in intentional content often make a P-conscious difference. What it is like to hear a sound as coming from the left differs from what it is like to hear a sound as coming from the right. P-consciousness is often representational. (See Jackendoff 1987; van Gulick 1989; McGinn 1991, chapter 2; Flanagan, 1992, chapter 4; Goldman 1993b.) So far, I don't take myself to have said anything terribly controversial. The controversial part is that I take P-conscious properties to be distinct from any cognitive, intentional, or functional property. (Cognitive = essentially involving thought; intentional properties = properties in virtue of which a representation or state is about something; functional properties = e.g., properties definable in terms of a computer program. See Searle 1983 on intentionality; see Block 1980, 1994, for better characterizations of a functional property.) But I am trying hard to limit the controversiality of my assumptions. Though I believe that functionalism about P-consciousness is false, I will be trying not to rely on that view.[4]

It is of course P-consciousness rather than access-consciousness or self-consciousness that has seemed such a scientific mystery. The magazine *Discover* (November, 1992) devoted an issue to the ten great unanswered questions of science, such as "What is Consciousness?," "Does Chaos Rule the Cosmos?," and "How Big is the Universe?" The topic was P-consciousness, not, for example, self-consciousness.

By way of homing in on P-consciousness, it is useful to appeal to what may be a contingent property of it, namely the famous "explanatory gap." To quote T. H. Huxley (1866), "How it is that anything so remarkable as a state of consciousness comes about as a result of irritating nervous tissue, is just as unaccountable as the appearance of Djin when Aladdin rubbed his lamp." Consider a famous neurophysiological theory of P-consciousness offered by Francis Crick and Christof Koch: namely, that a synchronized 35- to 75-hertz neural oscillation in the sensory areas of the cortex is at the heart of phenomenal consciousness. No one has produced the concepts that would allow us to explain why

such oscillations might be the physiological basis of phenomenal consciousness.

However, Crick and Koch have offered a sketch of an account of how the 35- to 75-hertz oscillation might contribute to a solution to the "binding problem." Suppose one simultaneously sees a red square moving to the right and a blue circle moving to the left. Different areas of the visual cortex are differentially sensitive to color, shape, motion, and so forth, so what binds together redness, squareness, and rightward motion? That is, why don't you see redness and blueness without seeing them as belonging with particular shapes and particular motions? And why aren't the colors normally seen as bound to the wrong shapes and motions? Representations of colors, shapes, and motions of a single object are supposed to involve oscillations that are in phase with one another but not with representations of other objects. But even if the oscillation hypothesis deals with the informational aspect of the binding problem (and there is some evidence against it), how does it explain *what it is like to see something as red in the first place*—or for that matter, as square or as moving to the right? Why couldn't there be brains functionally or physiologically just like ours, including oscillation patterns, whose owners' experience was different from ours or who had no experience at all? (Note that I don't say that there *could be* such brains. I just want to know *why not*.) And why is it a 35- to 75-hertz oscillation—as opposed to some other frequency—that underlies experience? If the synchronized neural oscillation idea pans out as a solution to the binding problem, no doubt there will be some answer to the question of why *those* frequencies, as opposed to, say 110 hertz, are involved. But will that answer explain why 110-hertz oscillations don't underlie experience? No one has a clue how to answer these questions.[5]

The explanatory gap in the case of P-consciousness contrasts with our relatively good understanding of cognition. We have two serious research programs into the nature of cognition, the classical "language of thought" paradigm, and the connectionist research program. Though no doubt there are many ideas missing in our understanding of cognition, we have no difficulty seeing how pursuing one or both of these research programs could lead to an adequate theoretical perspective on cognition. But it is not easy to see how current approaches to P-consciousness *could* yield an account of it. Indeed, what passes for research programs on consciousness just *is* a combination of cognitive psychology and explorations of neuropsychological syndromes that contain no theoretical perspective on what P-consciousness actually is.

I mentioned the explanatory gap partly by way of pointing at P-consciousness: *that's* the entity to which the mentioned explanatory gap applies. Perhaps this identification is contingent; at some time in the future, when we have the concepts to conceive of much more about the explanation of P-consciousness, this may not be a way of picking it out. (See McGinn 1991, for a more pessimistic view.)

What I've been saying about P-consciousness is of course controversial in a variety of ways, both for some advocates and some opponents of some notion of P-consciousness. I have tried to steer clear of some controversies, for example, controversies over inverted and absent qualia; over Jackson's (see chapter 32) Mary (the woman who is raised in a black and white room, learning all the physiological and functional facts about the brain and color vision, but nonetheless discovers a new fact when she goes outside the room for the first time and learns what it is like to see red); and even Nagel's view (see chapter 32) that we cannot know what it is like to be a bat.[6] Even if you think that P-consciousness as I have described it is an incoherent notion, you may be able to agree with the main point of this chapter, which is that a great deal of confusion arises as a result of confusing P-consciousness with something else. Not even the concept of what time it is now on the sun is so confused that it cannot itself be confused with something else.

4 Access-Consciousness

I now turn to the nonphenomenal notion of consciousness that is most easily and dangerously conflated with P-consciousness: access-consciousness. I will characterize access-consciousness, give some examples of how it is at least possible to have access-consciousness without phenomenal consciousness and vice versa, and then go on to the main theme of the paper, the damage done by conflating the two.

A is access-consciousness. A state is A-conscious if it is poised for direct control of thought and action. To add more detail, a representation is A-conscious if it is poised for free use in reasoning and for direct "rational" control of action and speech. (The "rational" is meant to rule out the kind of control that obtains in blindsight.) An A-state is one that consists in having an A-representation. I see A-consciousness as a cluster concept in which reportability is the element of the cluster that has the smallest weight even though it is often the best practical guide to A-consciousness.[7]

The interest in the A/P distinction arises from the battle between two different conceptions of the mind, the biological and the computational. The computational approach supposes that all of the mind (including consciousness) can be captured with notions of information processing, computation and function in a system. According to this view (often called functionalism by philosophers), the level of abstraction for understanding the mind is one that allows multiple realizations, just as one computer can be realized electrically or hydraulically. Their bet is that the different realizations don't matter to the mind, generally, and to consciousness specifically. The biological approach bets that the realization does matter. If P = A, the information processing side is right. But if the biological nature of experience is crucial, then realizations *do* matter, and we can expect that P and A will diverge.

Although I make a firm distinction between A-consciousness and P-consciousness, I also want to insist that they interact. For example, what perceptual information is being accessed can change figure to ground and conversely, and a figure-ground switch can affect one's phenomenal state. For example, attending to the feel of the shirt on your neck, accessing those perceptual contents, switches what was in the background to the foreground, thereby changing one's phenomenal state. (See Hill 1991, pp. 118–126; Searle 1992.)

I will suggest that A-consciousness plays a deep role in our ordinary 'consciousness' talk and thought. However, I must admit at the outset that this role allows for substantial indeterminacy in the concept itself. In addition, there are some loose ends in the characterization of the concept which cannot be tied up without deciding about certain controversial issues, to be mentioned below.[8] My guide in making precise the A-consciousness/P-consciousness distinction is to avoid trivial cases of A without P and P without A. The target reasoning (in one form) says that the blindsight patient lacks consciousness of stimuli in the blind field, and that is why he does not use information he actually has about these stimuli, so the function of consciousness must be to harness information for use in guiding action. (Maybe the blindsight patient does not lack P-consciousness of these stimuli, but the target reasoning supposes it, it is independently plausible, and I will consider later what happens if this assumption is wrong. For example, Cowie and Stoerig (1992) point out that the removal of primary visual cortex in these patients disrupts the Crick and Koch 40-Hz oscillations. That is some reason to believe that the blindsight patient lacks P-consciousness of the stimuli.) I will be pointing out that something *else* is also problematic in blindsight that can equally well be blamed for the blindsight patient's failure, namely the machinery of A-consciousness. Of course, the missing P-consciousness may be responsible for the missing A-consciousness; no fallacy is involved in that hypothesis. Rather, the fallacy is *sliding* from an obvious function of A-consciousness to an unobvious function of P-consciousness.

I will mention three main differences between P-consciousness and A-consciousness. The first point, *put crudely*, is that P-conscious content is phenomenal, whereas A-conscious content is representational. It is of the essence of A-conscious content to play a role in reasoning, and only representational content can figure in reasoning. The reason this way of putting the point is crude is that many phenomenal contents are *also* representational. So what I really want to say is that it is in virtue of its phenomenal content or the phenomenal aspect of its content that a state is P-conscious, whereas it is in virtue of its representational content, or the representational aspect of its content, that a state is A-conscious.[9]

(In the last paragraph, I used the notion of P-conscious *content*. The P-conscious content of a state is the totality of the state's experiential properties, what it is like to be in that state. One can think of the P-conscious content of a state as the state's experiential "value" by analogy to the representational content as the state's representational "value." In my view, the content of an experience can be both P-conscious and A-conscious; the former in virtue of its phenomenal feel and the latter in virtue of its representational properties.)

A closely related point: A-conscious states are necessarily transitive; A-conscious states must always be states of consciousness *of*. P-conscious states, by contrast, sometimes are and sometimes are not transitive. P-consciousness, as such, is not consciousness of. (I'll return to this point in a few paragraphs.)

Second, A-consciousness is a functional notion, and so A-conscious content is system-relative: what makes a state A-conscious is what a representation of its content does in a system. P-consciousness is not a functional notion.[10] In terms of Schacter's model, content gets to be P-conscious because of what happens *inside* the P-consciousness module. But what makes content A-conscious is not anything that could go on *inside* a module, but rather informational relations *among* modules. Content is A-conscious in virtue of (a representation with that content) reaching the Executive System, the system that is in charge of rational control of action and speech, and to that extent, we could regard the Executive module as the A-consciousness module. But to regard *anything* as an A-consciousness module is misleading, because what makes an A-conscious representation A-conscious is its causal relations to other representations.

A third difference is that there is such a thing as a P-conscious *type* or *kind* of state. For example the feel of pain is a P-conscious type—every pain must have that feel. But any particular token thought that is A-conscious at a given time could fail to be accessible at some other time, just as my car is accessible now, but will not be later when my wife has it. A state whose content is informationally promiscuous now may not be so later.

The paradigm P-conscious states are sensations, whereas the paradigm A-conscious states are "propositional attitude" states like thoughts, beliefs, and desires, states with representational content expressed by "that " clauses. (E.g., the thought that grass is green.) However, as I said, thoughts often are P-conscious and perceptual experiences often have representational content. For example, a perceptual experience may have the representational content *that there is a red square in front of me*. Even pain typically has *some* kind of representational content. Pains often represent something (the cause of the pain? the pain itself?) as somewhere (in the leg). A number of philosophers have taken the view that the content of pain is *entirely* representational. (See Dretske 1994; Shoemaker 1994; Tye 1995.) I don't agree with this view, so I certainly don't want to rely on it here, but I also don't want to make the existence of cases of P-consciousness without A-consciousness any kind of trivial consequence of an idiosyncratic set of definitions. To the extent that representationalism of the sort just mentioned is plausible, one can regard a pain as A-conscious if its representational content is inferentially promiscuous, and so forth. Alternatively, we could take the A-conscious content

of pain to consist in the content that one has a pain or that one has a state with a certain phenomenal content.[11]

Note that the notion of *poised* in the characterization of A-consciousness is intermediate between actual use in reasoning, and so forth, and mere availability for use. You may have learned in elementary school that the sun is 93 million miles from the earth, and a representation of this fact is therefore available for use if re-activated, but that level of access doesn't make it either P-conscious or A-conscious. And if we required actual use, then there could not be a brief episode of A-consciousness which is wiped out by death, as could happen with P-consciousness. The whole idea of A-consciousness is to capture an information processing analog of P-consciousness, and that is the basis of the definition.

There is a familiar distinction, alluded to above, between 'consciousness' in the sense in which we speak of a state as being a conscious state (intransitive consciousness) and consciousness *of* something (transitive consciousness). (See, e.g., Rosenthal 1986. Humphrey (1992) mentions that the intransitive usage is much more recent, only 200 years old.) It is easy to fall into an identification of P-consciousness with intransitive consciousness and a corresponding indentification of access-consciousness with transitive consciousness. Such an identification is oversimple. As I mentioned earlier, P-conscious contents can be representational. Consider a perceptual state of seeing a square. This state has a P-conscious content that represents something, a square, and thus it is a state of P-consciousness *of* the square. It is a state of P-consciousness of the square even if it doesn't represent the square *as* a square, as would be the case if the perceptual state is a state of an animal that doesn't have the concept of a square. Since there can be P-consciousness *of* something, P-consciousness is not to be identified with intransitive consciousness.

Here is a second reason why the transitive/intransitive distinction cannot be identified with the A-consciousness/P-consciousness distinction: The *of*-ness required for transitivity does not guarantee that a content be utilizable by a *consuming* system at the level required for A-consciousness. For example, a perceptual state of a brain-damaged creature might be a state of P-consciousness of, say, motion, even though connections to reasoning and rational control of action are damaged so that the state is not A-conscious. In sum, P-consciousness can be consciousness of, and consciousness of need not be A-consciousness.[12]

Those who are uncomfortable about P-consciousness should pay close attention to A-consciousness because it is a good candidate for a reductionist identification with P-consciousness.[13]

A-Consciousness Without P-Consciousness

Since the main point of this chapter is that these two concepts of consciousness are easily confused, it will pay us to consider conceptually possible cases of one without the other. Actual cases will be more controversial.

First, I will give some examples of A-consciousness without P-consciousness. If there could be a full-fledged phenomenal zombie, say a robot computationally identical to a person, but whose silicon brain did not support P-consciousness, that would do the trick. I think such cases conceptually possible, but this is very controversial, and I am trying to avoid controversial assumptions. (See Shoemaker 1975, 1981.)

But there is a less controversial kind of case, a very limited sort of partial zombie. Consider the blindsight patient who "guesses" that there is an X rather than an O in his blind field. Taking his word for it (for the moment), I am assuming that he has no P-consciousness of the X. As I mentioned, I am following the target reasoning here, but as I will point out later, my own argument does not depend on this assumption. I am certainly *not* assuming that lack of A-consciousness guarantees lack of P-consciousness—that is, I am

not assuming that if you don't say it you haven't got it.

The blindsight patient also has no X-representing A-conscious content, because although the information that there is an X affects his "guess," it is not available as a premise in reasoning (until he has the quite distinct state of hearing and believing his own guess), or for rational control of action or speech. Recall Marcel's point that the thirsty blindsight patient would not reach for a glass of water in the blind field. So the blindsight patient's perceptual or quasi-perceptual state is unconscious in the phenomenal *and* access senses (*and* in the monitoring senses to be mentioned below, too).

Now imagine something that may not exist, what we might call *super-blindsight*. A real blindsight patient can only guess when given a choice from a small set of alternatives (X/O; horizontal/vertical, etc.). But suppose—interestingly, apparently contrary to fact—that a blindsight patient could be trained to prompt himself at will, guessing what is in the blind field without being told to guess. The super-blindsighter spontaneously says "Now I know that there is a horizontal line in my blind field even though I don't actually see it." Visual information from his blind field simply pops into his thoughts in the way that solutions to problems we've been worrying about pop into our thoughts, or in the way some people just know the time or which way is north without having any perceptual experience of it. The super-blindsighter himself contrasts what it is like to know visually about an X in his blind field and an X in his sighted field. There is something it is like to experience the latter, but not the former, he says. It is the difference between *just knowing* and knowing via a visual experience. Taking his word for it, here is the point: the content that there is an X in his visual field is A-conscious but not P-conscious. The super-blindsight case is a very limited partial zombie.[14]

Of course, the super-blindsighter has a *thought* that there is an X in his blind field that is *both* A-conscious and P-conscious, but I am not talking about the thought. Rather, I am talking about the state of his perceptual system that gives rise to the thought. It is this state that is A-conscious without being P-conscious.[15]

Is there *actually* such a thing as super-blindsight? Humphrey (1992) describes a monkey (Helen) who despite *near* total loss of the visual cortex could nonetheless act in a somewhat visually normal way in certain circumstances, without any "prompting." One reason to doubt that Helen is a case of super-blindsight is that Helen may be a case of *sight*. There was some visual cortex left, and the situations in which she showed unprompted visual discrimination were ones in which there was no control of where the stimuli engaged her retina. Another possibility mentioned by Cowie and Stoerig (1992—attributed to an unpublished paper by Humphrey), is that there were P-conscious sensory events, though perhaps auditory in nature. Helen appeared to confuse brief tones with visual stimuli. Cowie and Stoerig propose a number of ways of getting information out of monkeys that are close to what we get out of blindsighted humans. Weiskrantz (1992) mentions that a patient GY sometimes knows that there is a stimulus (though not what it is) without, he says, seeing anything. But GY also seems to be having some kind of P-conscious sensation. (See Cowie and Stoerig 1992.)

The (apparent) nonexistence of super-blindsight is a striking fact, one that a number of writers have noticed. Indeed, it is the basis for the target reasoning. After all, what Marcel was in effect pointing out was that the blindsight patients, in not reaching for a glass of water, are not super-blindsighters. As I mentioned, Farah (see chapter 11) says that blindsight (and blind perception generally) turns out always to be degraded. In other words, blind perception is never super-blind perception.[16]

I don't know whether there are any actual cases of A-consciousness without P-consciousness, but I hope that I have illustrated their conceptual possibility.

P-Consciousness Without A-Consciousness

Consider an animal that you are happy to think of as having P-consciousness for which brain damage has destroyed centers of reasoning and rational control of action, thus preventing A-consciousness. It certainly seems *conceptually possible* that the neural bases of P-consciousness systems and A-consciousness systems be distinct, and if they are distinct, then it is possible, at least conceptually possible, for one to be damaged while the other is working well. Evidence has been accumulating for twenty-five years that the primate visual system has distinct dorsal and ventral subsystems. Though there is much disagreement about the specializations of the two systems, it does appear that much of the information in the ventral system is much more closely connected to P-consciousness than information in the dorsal system (Goodale and Milner 1992). So it may actually be possible to damage A-consciousness without P-consciousness and conversely.[17]

Further, one might suppose (Rey 1983, 1988; White 1987) that some of our own subsystems— say each of the two hemispheres of the brain— might themselves be separately P-conscious. Some of these subsystems might also be A-consciousness, but other subsystems might not have sufficient machinery for reasoning or reporting or rational control of action to allow their P-conscious states to be A-conscious; so if those states are not accessible to another system that does have adequate machinery, they will be P-conscious but not A-conscious.

Here is another reason to believe in P-consciousness without A-consciousness: Suppose that you are engaged in intense conversation when suddenly at noon you realize that right outside your window, there is—and has been for some time—a pneumatic drill digging up the street. You were aware of the noise all along, one might say, but only at noon are you *consciously aware* of it. That is, you were P-conscious of the noise all along, but at noon you are both P-conscious *and* A-conscious of it. Of course, there is a very similar string of events in which the crucial event at noon is a bit more intellectual. In this alternative scenario, at noon you realize not just that there is and has been a noise, but also that *you are now and have been hearing* the noise. In this alternative scenario, you get "higher-order thought" as well as A-consciousness at noon. So on the first scenario, the belief that is acquired at noon is that there is and has been a noise, and on the second scenario, the beliefs that are acquired at noon are the first one plus the belief that you are and have been hearing the noise. But it is the first scenario, not the second, that interests me. It is a good case of P-consciousness without A-consciousness. Only at noon is the content of your representation of the drill *poised* for use in rational control of action and speech. (Note that A-consciousness requires being poised, not merely available for use.)

In addition, this case involves a natural use of "conscious" and "aware" for A-consciousness and P-consciousness, respectively. "Conscious" and "aware" are more or less synonymous, so calling the initial P-consciousness "awareness" makes it natural to call the later P-consciousness plus A-consciousness "conscious awareness." Of course I rely here on introspection, but when it comes to P-consciousness, introspection is an important source of insight.[18] This case of P-consciousness without A-consciousness exploits what William James (1890) called "secondary consciousness" (at least I think it does; James scholars may know better), a category that he may have meant to include cases of P-consciousness without attention.[19]

I have found that the argument of the last paragraph makes those who are distrustful of introspection uncomfortable. I agree that introspection is not the last word, but it is the first word, when it comes to P-consciousness. The example shows the conceptual distinctness of P-consciousness from A-consciousness and it also puts the burden of proof on anyone who would

argue that as a matter of empirical fact they come to the same thing.

The difference between different concepts of consciousness gives rise to different types of *zombie*. We have already encountered the phenomenal zombies that appear in science-fiction and philosophers' examples—the familiar computers and robots that think but don't feel. Their states are A-conscious, but not P-conscious. However, our culture also acknowledges the concept of voodoo zombies and zombies in *Night of the Living Dead*. If we find that voodoo zombies are cognitively or affectively diminished, say without will, rather than phenomenally diminished, we would not decide that they were not zombies after all. And on seeing the next installment in the "Living Dead" series, we would not feel that our concept of a zombie had been toyed with if it turned out that there is something it is like for these zombies to eat their relatives. (They say "yumm!") No doubt we have no very well formed zombie-concept, but the considerations just mentioned motivate the view that a zombie is something that is mentally dead in one respect or another, and the different respects give rise to different zombies.

Kathleen Akins (1993) has argued against the distinction between a phenomenal and a representational aspect of experience. She asks the reader to look around his or her office, noting what it is like to have that experience. Then she challenges the reader to imagine that "a bat's consciousness is just like that—the feel of the scene is exactly the same—except, of course, all those visual sensations mean something quite different to the bat. They represent quite different properties. Imagine that!" She goes on to say, "The problem is that you cannot imagine that, no matter how hard you try" (p. 267). Of course, she is right that you cannot imagine that. But the explanation of this fact is not that there is no distinction between the P-conscious and representational aspects of experience. The explanation is that, as I said earlier, many representational

differences themselves *make* a P-conscious difference. To repeat the example given earlier, what it
is like to hear a sound as coming from the left is
different from what it is like to hear a sound as
coming from the right. Or suppose that you are
taken to what appears to be a town from the Old
West; then you are told that it is a backdrop for a
film and that what appear to be buildings are
mere fronts. This representational difference can
make a difference in what the buildings look like
to you. A visual experience as of a facade differs
from a visual experience as of a building, even if
the retinal image is the same. Or consider the difference in what it is like to hear sounds in French
before and after you have learned the language
(McCullough 1993).

Flanagan (1992) criticizes my notion of A-
consciousness, suggesting that we replace it with
a more liberal notion of informational sensitivity
that counts the blindsight patient as having
access-consciousness of the stimuli in his blind
field. The idea is that the blindsight patient has
some access to the information about the stimuli
in the blind field, and that amount of access is
enough for access consciousness. Of course the
notion of A-consciousness that I have framed is
just one of a family of access notions. But there is
more than a verbal issue here. The real question
is what good is A-consciousness as I have framed
it in relation to the blindsight issue? The answer
is that in blindsight, the patient is supposed to
lack "consciousness" of the stimuli in the blind
field. My point is that the blindsighter lacks both P-
consciousness and a kind of access, and that these
are easily confused. This point is not challenged
by pointing out that the blindsight patient also
has a lower level of access to this information.

The kind of access that I have built into A-
consciousness plays a role in theory outside of this
issue and in daily life. Consider the Freudian
unconscious. Suppose I have a Freudian unconscious desire to kill my father and marry my
mother. Nothing in Freudian theory requires that
this desire be P-unconscious; for all Freudians
should care, it might be P-conscious. What is the

key to the desire being Freudianly unconscious is
that it come out in slips, dreams, and the like, but
not be freely available as a premise in reasoning
(in virtue of having the unconscious desire) and
that it not be freely available to guide action and
reporting. Coming out in slips and dreams *makes
it conscious in Flanagan's sense*, so that sense of
access is no good for capturing the Freudian idea.
But it must be unconscious in my A-sense. If I can
just tell you that I have a desire to kill my father
and marry my mother (and not as a result of
therapy), then it isn't an unconscious state in
Freud's sense. Similar points can be made about
a number of the syndromes talked about above.
For example, prosopagnosia is a disorder of
A-consciousness, not P-consciousness and not
Flanagan's informational sensitivity. We count
someone as a prosopagnosic even when he or she
is able to guess at a better than chance level whom
the face belongs to, so that excludes Flanagan's
notion. Further, P-consciousness is irrelevant,
and that excludes P-consciousness as a criterion.
It isn't the presence or absence of a feeling of familiarity that defines prosopagnosia, but rather
the patient not knowing whose face he is seeing or
whether he knows that person.

To see this, consider the Capgras delusion, a
syndrome in which patients claim that people
they know (usually relatives) have been replaced
by doubles who look just like them. (There is a
closely related syndrome, reduplicative paramnesia, in which patients claim that they are in a
hospital which is a duplicate of another hospital
that they have been in.) Young (1994c) suggests
that perhaps what is going on in this syndrome
is that a patient recognizes, for example, his
mother, but he has no feeling of familiarity, so
he thinks that perhaps his mother is a victim of
something out of "Invasion of the Body Snatch-
ers." (Actually, it is interesting to note that victims of Capgras syndrome almost never call the
FBI or do any of the things someone might do
if he really thought his mother was replaced by
an extraterrestrial duplicate.) Suppose that this is
right. Notice that this patient is not thereby a

prosopagnosic. He recognizes his mother's face, he can learn to recognize new faces, and so forth. So loss of the P-conscious feeling of familiarity is not sufficient for prosopagnosia.[20]

I am now just about finished justifying and explaining the difference between P-consciousness and A-consciousness. However, there is one objection I feel I should comment on. The contrast between P-consciousness and A-consciousness was in part based on the distinction between representational and phenomenal content. Put crudely, I said, the difference was that P-conscious content is phenomenal, whereas A-conscious content is representational. I said this was crude because many phenomenal contents are also representational. Some will object that phenomenal content just *is* a kind of representational content. (Dretske 1994, and Tye 1994, forthcoming, take this line; Shoemaker 1994 has a more moderate version. The representational/phenomenal distinction is discussed in Jackson 1977, Shoemaker 1981, and Peacocke 1983.) My reply is first that phenomenal content need not be representational at all (my favorite example is the phenomenal content of orgasm). Second, suppose I have an auditory experience as of something overhead, and simultaneously have a visual experience as of something overhead. I'm imagining a case where one has an impression only of where the thing is without an impression of other features. For example, in the case of the visual experience, one catches a glimpse of something overhead without any impression of a specific shape or color. (So the difference cannot be ascribed to further representational differences.) The phenomenal contents of both experiences represent something as being overhead, but not in virtue of a common phenomenal quality of the experiences. Note that the point is *not* just that there is a representational overlap without a corresponding phenomenal overlap (as is said, e.g., in Pendlebury 1992). That would be compatible with the following story (offered to me by Michael Tye): phenomenal content is just one kind of representational content, but these experiences overlap in nonphenomenal representational content. The point, rather, is that there is a modal difference that isn't at all a matter of representation, but rather is a matter of how those modes of representation feel. Or so I would argue. The look and the sound are both *as of something overhead*, but the two phenomenal contents represent this via different phenomenal qualities. (There is a line of thought about the phenomenal/representational distinction that involves versions of the traditional "inverted spectrum" hypothesis. (See Shoemaker 1981b, 1993; Block 1990a.))

I am finished sketching the contrast between P-consciousness and A-consciousness. In the remainder of this section, I will briefly discuss two cognitive notions of consciousness, so that they are firmly distinguished from both P-consciousness and A-consciousness. Then in the next section, I will examine some conflations of P-consciousness and A-consciousness, so if you don't feel you have a perfect grasp of the distinction, you have another chance.

Self-Consciousness

By this term, I mean the possession of the concept of the self and the ability to use this concept in thinking about oneself. A number of higher primates show signs of recognizing that they see themselves in mirrors. They display interest in correspondences between their own actions and the movements of their mirror images. By contrast, dogs treat their mirror images as strangers at first, slowly habituating. In one experimental paradigm, experimenters painted colored spots on the foreheads and ears of anesthetized primates, watching what happened. Chimps between ages 7 and 15 usually try to wipe the spot off (Povinelli 1994; Gallup 1982). Monkeys do not do this, according to published reports as of 1994. Human babies don't show similar behavior until the last half of their second year. Perhaps this is a test for self-consciousness. (Or perhaps it is only a test for understanding mirrors; but what is involved in understanding mirrors if not that it is oneself one is seeing?) But even if monkeys and dogs have no self-consciousness, no one should deny that they have P-conscious pains, or that there is something it is like for them to see their reflections in the mirror. P-conscious states often seem to have a "me-ishness" about them, the phenomenal content often represents the state as a state of me. But this fact does not at all suggest that we can reduce P-consciousness to self-consciousness, since such "me-ishness" is the same in states whose P-conscious content is different. For example, the experience as of red is the same as the experience as of green in self-orientation, but the two states are different in phenomenal feel.[21]

The word "conscious" is often used to mean self-consciousness though often one sees some allusion to P-consciousness. For example, a Time-Life book on the mind (1993) says: "No mental characteristic is so mysterious and elusive—or so fundamentally human—as consciousness, the self-awareness that attends perceiving, thinking, and feeling."

Monitoring Consciousness

The idea of consciousness as some sort of internal monitoring takes many forms. One notion is that of some sort of inner perception. This could be a form of P-consciousness, namely P-consciousness of one's own states or of the self. Another notion is often put in information-processing terms: internal scanning. And a third, metacognitive notion, is that of higher-order thought: a conscious state in this sense is a state accompanied by a thought to the effect that one is in that state. The thought must be arrived at nonobservationally and noninferentially. Otherwise, as Rosenthal points out, the higher-order thought definition would get the wrong result for the case in which I come to know about my anger by inferring it from my own behavior.[22] Given my liberal terminological policy, I have no objection to any of these notions as notions of consciousness. Where I balk is at attempts to identify P-consciousness with any of these cognitive notions.

To identify P-consciousness with internal scanning is just to grease the slide to eliminativism

about P-consciousness. Indeed, as Georges Rey (1983) has pointed out, ordinary laptop computers are capable of various types of self-scanning, but as he also points out, no one would think of their laptop computer as "conscious" (using the term in the ordinary way, without making any of the distinctions I've introduced). Since, according to Rey, internal scanning is essential to consciousness, he concludes that the concept of consciousness is incoherent. The trouble here is the failure to make distinctions of the sort I've been making. Even if the laptop has "internal scanning consciousness," it nonetheless lacks P-consciousness.[23]

The concepts of consciousness which this paper is mainly about (P-consciousness and A-consciousness) differ in their logics from the consciousnesses just mentioned, self-consciousness and monitoring consciousness. A distinction is often made between the sense of 'conscious' in which a person or other creature is conscious and the sense in which a state of mind is a conscious state. What it is for there to be something it is like to be me, that is for me to be P-conscious, is for me to have one or more states that are P-conscious. If a person is in a dreamless sleep, and then has a P-conscious pain, he is to that extent P-conscious. For P-consciousness, it is states that are primary. In the case of self-consciousness and reflective consciousness, however, creature consciousness is basic. What it is for a pain to be reflectively conscious is, for example, for the person whose pain it is to have another state that is about that pain. And it is creatures who can think about themselves. It is not even clear what a self-conscious state would *be*. A-consciousness is intermediate between P on the one hand and self and monitoring consciousness on the other. No state is A-conscious in virtue of its intrinsic properties; what makes it A-conscious is what it controls. But it is not clear that a whole creature is necessary for A-consciousness.

Perhaps you are wondering why I am being so terminologically liberal, counting P-consciousness, A-consciousness, monitoring consciousness, and self-consciousness all as types of consciousness. Oddly, I find that many critics wonder why I would count *phenomenal* consciousness as consciousness, whereas many others wonder why I would count *access* or *monitoring* or *self*-consciousness as consciousness. In fact two reviewers of this chapter complained about my terminological liberalism, but for incompatible reasons. One reviewer said: "While what he uses ["P-consciousness"] to refer to—the "what it is like" aspect of mentality—seems to me interesting and important, I suspect that the discussion of it under the heading "consciousness" is a source of confusion ... he is right to distinguish access-consciousness (which is what I think deserves the name "consciousness") from this." Another reviewer said: "I really still can't see why access is called ... access-consciousness? Why isn't access just ... a purely information processing (functionalist) analysis?" This is not a merely verbal matter. In my view, all of us, despite our explicit verbal preferences, have some tendency to use "conscious" and related words in both ways, and our failure to see this causes a good deal of difficulty in thinking about "consciousness." This point will be illustrated below.

I've been talking about different concepts of consciousness and I've also said that *the* concept of consciousness is a mongrel concept. Perhaps, you are thinking, I should make up my mind. My view is that "consciousness" is actually an ambiguous word, though the ambiguity I have in mind is not one that I've found in any dictionary. I started the paper with an analogy between "consciousness" and "velocity," and I think there is an important similarity. One important difference, however, is that in the case of "velocity," it is easy to get rid of the temptation to conflate the two senses. With "consciousness," there is a tendency toward "now you see it, now you don't." I think the main reason for this is that P-consciousness presents itself to us in a way that makes it hard to imagine how a conscious state could fail to be accessible and self-reflective, so it is easy to

fall into habits of thought that do not distinguish these concepts.[24]

The chief alternative to the ambiguity hypothesis is that there is a single concept of consciousness that is a *cluster concept*. For example, a prototypical religion involves belief in supernatural beings, sacred and profane objects, rituals, a moral code, religious feelings, prayer, a world view, an organization of life based on the world view, and a social group bound together by the previous items (Alston 1967). But for all of these items, there are actual or possible religions that lack them. For example, some forms of Buddhism do not involve belief in a supreme being and Quakers have no sacred objects. It is convenient for us to use a concept of religion that binds together a number of disparate concepts whose referents are often found together.

The distinction between ambiguity and cluster concept can be drawn in a number of equally legitimate ways that classify some cases differently. That is, there is some indeterminacy in the distinction. Some might even say that *velocity* is a cluster concept because for many purposes it is convenient to group average and instantaneous velocity together. I favor tying the distinction to the clear and present danger of conflation, especially in the form of equivocation in an argument. Of course, this is no analysis, since equivocation is definable in terms of ambiguity. My point, rather, is that one can make up one's mind about whether there is ambiguity by finding equivocation hard to deny. I will give some examples of conflations in what follows, and there is, I claim, a real-life case of equivocation on the senses of 'consciousness' that I have distinguished in an argument in Dennett (1991).[25]

When I called *consciousness* a mongrel concept I was not declaring allegiance to the cluster theory. Rather, what I had in mind was that an ambiguous word often corresponds to an ambiguous mental representation, one that functions in thought as a unitary entity and thereby misleads. These are mongrels. I would also describe *velocity* and *degree of heat* (as used by the Florentine experimenters of the seventeenth century) as mongrel concepts. This is the grain of truth in the cluster-concept theory.

5 Conflations

Conflation of P-consciousness and A-consciousness is ubiquitous in the burgeoning literature on consciousness, especially in the literature on syndromes like blindsight. Nearly every article I read on the subject by philosophers and psychologists involves some confusion. For example, Baars (1988) makes it abundantly clear that he is talking about P-consciousness. "What is a theory of consciousness a theory of? In the first instance ... it is a theory of the nature of experience. The reader's private experience of *this* word, his or her mental image of yesterday's breakfast, or the feeling of a toothache—these are all contents of consciousness" (p.14). Yet his theory is a "global workspace" model of A-consciousness. Shallice (1988a, 1988b) says he is giving an account of "phenomenal experience," but actually gives an information-processing theory of A-consciousness. (His 1988b is about an "information-processing model of consciousness.") Mandler (1985) describes consciousness in P-conscious terms like "phenomenal" and "experience" but gives a totally cognitive account appropriate to A-consciousness. Edelman's (1989) theory is also intended to explain P-consciousness, but it seems a theory of access-consciousness and self-consciousness; see Chalmers (1996). Kosslyn and Koenig (1992) say, "We will address here the everyday sense of the term ["consciousness"]; it refers to the phenomenology of experience, the feeling of red and so forth" (pp. 431–433; I am indebted to Michael Tye for calling this quotation to my attention). But then they give a "parity check" theory that seems more of a theory of monitoring consciousness or A-consciousness.

One result of conflating P-consciousness with other consciousnesses is a tendency to regard ideas as plausible that should be seen as way out

on a limb. For example, Johnson-Laird (1988, pp. 360–361) talks of consciousness, using terms like "subjective experience." He goes on to hypothesize that consciousness is a matter of building models of the self and models of the self building models of itself, and so on. This hypothesis has two strikes against it, as should be obvious if one is clear about the distinction between P-consciousness and self-consciousness. Dogs and babies may not build such complex models, but the burden of proof is surely on anyone who doubts that they have P-consciousness.

Another example: In a discussion of phenomena of implicit perception, Kihlstrom et al. (1992) make it clear that the phenomena concern P-consciousness: "In the final analysis, consciousness is a phenomenal quality that may accompany perception ..." (p. 42). But they claim that self-consciousness is precisely what is lacking in implicit perception: "This connection to the self is just what appears to be lacking in the phenomena of implicit perception.... When contact occurs between the representation of the event—what might be called the "fact node" and the representation of oneself—what might be called the 'self-node,' the event comes into consciousness" (p. 42). But again, as we go down the phylogenetic scale we may well encounter creatures that are P-conscious but have no "self-node," and the same may be true of the very young of our own species. What should be announced as a theory that conflicts with common sense, that P-consciousness arises from representing the self, can appear innocuous if one is not careful to make the distinctions among the consciousnesses.

Andrade (1993) makes it clear that the concern is P-consciousness. For example, "Without consciousness, there is no pain. There may be tissue damage, and physiological responses to tissue damage, but there will not be the phenomenological experience of pain" (p. 13). Considering work on control by a central Executive System, Andrade (correctly, I think) takes the dominant theories to "identify" consciousness with central executive control. "Current psychological theories identify consciousness with systems that coordinate lower-level information processing." But there are two very different paths to such an identification: (1) conflating P-consciousness with A-consciousness and theorizing about A-consciousness in terms of the systems Andrade mentions, (2) clearly distinguishing P-consciousness from A-consciousness and hypothesizing that the mechanisms that underlie the latter give rise to the former. I doubt that any objective reader of this literature will think that the hypothesis of path 2 is often very likely.

In the writings of some psychologists, assimilation of P-consciousness to A-consciousness is a product of the (admirable) desire to be able to *measure* P-consciousness. Jacoby et al. (1992) assimilate P-consciousness to A-consciousness for that reason. Their subject matter is perception without "subjective experience," in normal perceivers in conditions of divided attention or degraded presentations. In other words, perception without P-consciousness, what is often known as subliminal perception. They note that it is very difficult to disentangle conscious perception from unconscious perception because no one has conceived of an experimental paradigm that isolates one of these modes. "We avoid this problem," they say, "by inferring awareness ["subjective experience"—N. B] from conscious control and defining unconscious influences as effects that cannot be controlled" (p. 108). The effect of this procedure is to definitionally disallow phenomenal events that have no effect on later mental processes and to definitionally type phenomenal events by appeal to judgments made on the basis of them. "Subjective experience," they say, "results from an attribution process in which mental events are interpreted in the context of current circumstances" (p. 112). I am reminded of an article in the sociology of science that I once read that defined the quality of a scientific paper as the number of references to it in the literature. Operational definitions do no good if the result is measuring something *else*.

Schacter (1989) is explicit about what he means by 'consciousness' (which he often calls 'conscious awareness'), namely P-consciousness. He mentions that the sense he has in mind is that of "phenomenal awareness ... 'the running span of subjective experience'" (quoting Dimond 1976), and consciousness in his sense is repeatedly contrasted with information-processing notions. Nonetheless, in an effort to associate the "Conscious Awareness System" (what I call the phenomenal consciousness system in my labeling of his model in figure 20. 1) with the inferior parietal lobes, he says that lesions in this area

have also been associated with confusional states, which are characterized by disordered thought, severe disorientation, and a breakdown of selective attention—in short, a global disorder of conscious awareness ... Several lines of evidence indicate that lesions to certain regions of the parietal lobes can produce disorders of conscious awareness. First, global confusional states have been reported in right parietal patients.... Second, the syndrome of anosognosia—unawareness and denial of a neuropsychological deficit—is often associated with parietal damage.... Anosognosic patients ... may be unaware of motor deficits ... perceptual deficits ... and complete unawareness can be observed even when the primary deficit is severe. (1988, p. 371)

Here, Schacter reverts to a use of 'consciousness' and 'awareness' in a variety of cognitive senses. Disordered thought, disorientation, and a breakdown of selective attention are not primarily disorders of P-consciousness. Further, anosognosia is primarily a defect in A-consciousness, not P-consciousness. Anosognosia is a neurological syndrome that involves an inability to acknowledge or have access to information about another neurological syndrome. A patient might have anosognosia for, say, his prosopagnosia while complaining incessantly about another deficit. Young (1994a) describes a woman who was a painter before becoming prosopagnosic. Looking at portraits she had painted, trying to figure out whom they represented, she laboriously figured out whom each painting was of, reasoning out loud about the person's apparent age, sex, and any significant objects in the picture, plus her verbal memories of the portraits that she had painted. When the experimenter commented on her porsopagnosia, she said that she "had recognized them," and did not think that there was anything odd about her laborious reasoning.[26]

The crucial feature of anosognosia about prosopagnosia is that the patient's access to information about her own inability to recognize faces is in some way blocked. She cannot report this inability or reason about it or use information about it to control her action. In addition to this A-consciousness problem, there may also be some defect of P-consciousness. Perhaps everyone looks familiar or no one looks familiar, or perhaps there are no visual feelings of familiarity that are distinct from feelings of unfamiliarity. Whatever the answer to the issue of familiarity, this issue of P-consciousness is not crucial to the syndrome, as is shown by the fact that we confidently ascribe anosognosia on the basis of the patient's cognitive state—the lack of knowledge of the deficit—without knowing what defects of P-consciousness may or may not be involved. Further, the same defects of P-consciousness could be present in a *non-anosognosic* prosopagnosic without discrediting the patient's status as non-anosognosic. One can imagine such a person saying, "Gosh, I don't recognize anyone—in fact, I no longer have a visual sense of the difference between familiar and unfamiliar faces." This would be prosopagnosia *without* anosognosia. To take anosognosia as primarily a defect of P-consciousness is a mistake.[27]

I don't think these conflations cause any real problem in Schacter's theorizing, but as a general rule, if you want to get anywhere in theorizing about X you should have a good pretheoretical grip on the difference between X and things that are easily confused with it.

Daniel Dennett (1986, 1991) provides another example of conflation of a number of concepts of consciousness. (See Block 1993.) I will focus on

Dennett's claim that consciousness is a cultural construction. He theorizes that "human consciousness (1) is too recent an innovation to be hard-wired into the innate machinery, (2) is largely the product of cultural evolution that gets imparted to brains in early training" (1991, p. 219). Sometimes he puts the point in terms of memes, which are ideas such as the idea of the wheel or the calendar. Memes are the smallest cultural units that replicate themselves reliably, viz., cultural analogs of genes. In these terms then, Dennett's claim is that "human consciousness is *itself* a huge complex of memes" (1991, p. 210). This view is connected with Dennett's idea that you can't have consciousness without having the concept of consciousness. He says consciousness is like love and money in this regard, though in the case of money, what is required for one to have money is that *someone* have the concept of money (1991, p. 24; 1986, p. 152).

I think the reason Dennett says "largely" the product of cultural evolution is that he thinks of consciousness as the software that operates on genetically determined hardware that is the product of biological evolution. Though consciousness requires the concept of consciousness, with consciousness as with love, there is a biological basis without which the software could not run.

Now I hope it is obvious that P-consciousness is not a cultural construction. Remember, we are talking about P-consciousness itself, not the concept of P-consciousness. The idea would be that there was a time at which people genetically like us ate, drank, and had sex, but there was nothing it was like for them to do these things. Further, each of us would have been like that if not for specific concepts we acquired from our culture in growing up. Ridiculous! Of course, culture *affects* P-consciousness; the wondrous experience of drinking a great wine takes training to develop. But culture affects feet too; people who have spent their lives going barefoot in the Himalayas have feet that differ from those of people who have worn tight shoes 18 hours a day. We mustn't confuse the idea that culture *influences* consciousness with the idea that it (largely) creates it.

What about A-consciousness? Could there have been a time when humans who are biologically the same as us never had the contents of their perceptions and thoughts poised for free use in reasoning or in rational control of action? Is this ability one that culture imparts to us as children? Turning to Dennett's doctrine that you can't be conscious without having the concept of consciousness: Could it be that until we acquired the concept of *poised for free use in reasoning or in rational control of action*, none of our perceptual contents were A-conscious? Again, there is no reason to take such an idea seriously. Very much lower animals are A-conscious, presumably without any such concept.

A-consciousness is as close as we get to the official view of consciousness in *Consciousness Explained* (Dennett 1991) and in later writings, for example, Dennett (1993). The official theory of Dennett (1991) is the Multiple Drafts Theory, the view that there are distinct parallel tracks of representation that vie for access to reasoning, verbalization, and behavior. This seems a theory of A-consciousness. Dennett (1993) says "Consciousness is cerebral celebrity—nothing more and nothing less. Those contents are conscious that persevere, that monopolize resources long enough to achieve certain typical and 'symptomatic' effects—on memory, on the control of behavior, and so forth" (p. 929). Could it be anything other than a biological fact about humans that some brain representations persevere enough to affect memory, control behavior, and so forth? So on the closest thing to Dennett's official kind of consciousness, the thesis (that consciousness is a cultural construction) is no serious proposal.

What about monitoring consciousness? No doubt there was a time when people were less introspective than some of us are now. But is there any evidence that there was a time when people genetically like us had no capacity to think or express the thought that one's leg hurts? To be able to think this thought involves being able to think that one's leg hurts, and that is a higher-order thought of the sort that is a plausible candidate for monitoring consciousness (Rosenthal 1986). Here for the first time we do enter the realm of actual empirical questions, but without some very powerful evidence for such a view, there is no reason to give it any credence. Dennett gives us not the slightest hint of the kind of weird evidence that we would need to begin to take this claim seriously, and so it would be a disservice to so interpret him.

What about self-consciousness? I mentioned Gallup and Povinelli's "mark test" evidence (the chimp tries to wipe off a mark on its face seen in a mirror) that chimps are self-conscious. An experiment in this vein that Dennett actually mentions (1991, p. 428), and mentions positively, is that a chimp can learn to get bananas via a hole in its cage by watching its arm on a closed circuit TV whose camera is some distance away (Menzel et al. 1985). The literature on the topic of animal self-consciousness is full of controversy. (See Heyes 1993, Mitchell 1993a, 1993b; Gallup and Povinelli 1993; de Lannoy 1993; Anderson 1993; Byrne 1993.) I have no space to do justice to the issues, so I will have to make do with just stating my view: I think the weight of evidence in favor of minimal self-consciousness on the part of chimps is overwhelming. By minimal self-consciousness I mean the ability to think about oneself in some way or other—that is, no particular way is required. Many of the criticisms of the mark test actually presuppose that the chimp is self-conscious in this minimal sense. For example, it is often suggested that chimps that pass the mark test think that they are seeing another chimp (e.g., Heyes 1993), and since the chimp in the mirror has a mark on its forehead, the chimp who is looking wonders whether he or she does too. But in order for me to wonder whether *I* have a mark on my forehead, I have to be able to think about myself. In any case, Dennett does not get into these issues (except, as mentioned, to favor chimp self-consciousness), so it does not appear that he has this interpretation in mind.

So far, on all the consciousness I have mentioned, Dennett's thesis turns out to be false. But there is a trend: of the concepts I considered, the first two made the thesis silly, even of animals. In the case of monitoring consciousness, there is a real empirical issue in the case of many types of mammals, and so it isn't completely silly to wonder about whether people have it. Only in the last case, self-consciousness, is there a serious issue about whether chimps are conscious, and that suggests that we might get a notion of self-consciousness that requires some cultural elements. In recent years, the idea of the self as a federation of somewhat autonomous agencies has become popular, and for good reason. Nagel (1971) made a good case on the basis of split-brain data, and Gazzaniga and LeDoux (1978) and Gazzaniga (1985) have added additional considerations that have some plausibilty. And Dennett has a chapter about the self at the end of the book that gives similar arguments. Maybe what Dennett is saying is that nonfederal self-consciousness, the ability to think of oneself as not being such a federation (or more simply, federal self-consciousness) is a cultural construction.

But now we have moved from falsity to banality. I'm not saying that the proposal that we are federations is banal. What is banal is that the having and applying a sophisticated concept such as being a federation (or not being a federation) requires a cultural construction. Consider chairman self-consciousness, the ability to think of oneself as chairman, as the one who guides the department, the one who has the keys, and so forth. It is a banality that a cultural construction is required in order for a person to think of himself in that way, and the corresponding point about federal self-consciousness is similarly banal.

The great oddity of Dennett's discussion is that throughout he gives the impression that his theory is *about P-consciousness*, though he con-

cedes that what he says about it conflicts with our normal way of thinking about consciousness. This comes out especially strongly in an extended discussion of Julian Jaynes's (1976) book which he credits with a version of the view I am discussing, namely, that consciousness is a cultural construction which requires its own concept. He says (Dennett, 1986):

Perhaps this is an autobiographical confession: I am rather fond of his [Jaynes's] way of using these terms ['consciousness', 'mind', and other mental terms]; I rather like his way of carving up consciousness. It is in fact very similar to the way that I independently decided to carve up consciousness some years ago.

So what then is the project? The project is, in one sense, very simple and very familiar. It is bridging what he calls the "awesome chasm" between mere inert matter and the inwardness, as he puts it, of a conscious being. Consider the awesome chasm between a brick and a bricklayer. There isn't, in Thomas Nagel's (1974) famous phrase, anything that it is like to be a brick. But there is something that it is like to be a bricklayer, and we want to know what the conditions were under which there happened to come to be entities that it was like something to be in this rather special sense. That is the story, the developmental, evolutionary, historical story, that Jaynes sets out to tell. (Dennett 1986, p. 149)

In sum, Dennett's thesis is trivially false if it is construed to be about P-consciousness, as advertised. It is also false if taken to be about A-consciousness which is Dennett's official view of consciousness. But if taken to be about a highly sophisticated version of self-consciousness, it is banal. That's what can happen if you talk about consciousness without making the sorts of distinctions that I am urging.

In talking about failure to see the distinction, I have concentrated on cases in which points having to do with one kind of consciousness are applied to another. But far more commonly, they are not distinguished from one another sufficiently for one to know which consciousness any given claim is about. Crick and Koch (1990) and Crick (1994), for example, usually seem to be talking about P-consciousness. Crick (p. 9) speaks of the issue of explaining "the redness of red or the painfulness of pain." But often, P-consciousness and A-consciousness are just mixed together with no clear indication of which is at issue.

6 The Fallacy of the Target Reasoning

We now come to the denouement of the paper, the application of the P-consciousness/A-consciousness distinction to the fallacy of the target reasoning. Let me begin with the Penfield-Van Gulick-Searle reasoning. Searle (1992) adopts Penfield's (1975) claim that during petit mal seizures, patients are "totally unconscious." Quoting Penfield at length, Searle describes three patients who, despite being "totally unconscious," continue walking or driving home or playing the piano, but in a mechanical way. Van Gulick (1989) gives a briefer treatment, also quoting Penfield. He says, "The importance of conscious experience for the construction and control of action plans is nicely illustrated by the phenomenon of automatism associated with some petit mal epileptic seizures. In such cases, electrical disorder leads to a loss of function in the higher brain stem.... As a result the patient suffers a loss of conscious experience in the phenomenal sense although he can continue to react selectively to environmental stimuli" (p. 220). Because Van Gulick's treatment is more equivocal and less detailed, and because Searle also comments on my accusations of conflating A-consciousness with P-consciousness, I'll focus on Searle. Searle says:

The epileptic seizure rendered the patient *totally unconscious*, yet the patient continued to exhibit what would normally be called goal-directed behavior.... In all these cases, we have complex forms of apparently goal-directed behavior without any consciousness. Now why could all behavior not be like that? Notice that in the cases, the patients were performing types of actions that were habitual, routine and memorized ... normal, human, conscious behavior has a degree of flexibility and creativity that is absent from the Penfield cases of the unconscious driver and the unconscious pianist. *Con-sciousness adds powers of discrimination and flexibility even to memorized routine activities.... one of the evolutionary advantages conferred on us by consciousness is the much greater flexibility, sensitivity, and creativity we derive from being conscious.* (1992, pp. 108–109, italics mine)

Searle's reasoning is that consciousness is missing, and with it, flexibility, sensitivity, and creativity, so this is an indication that a function of consciousness is to add these qualities. Now it is completely clear that the concept of consciousness invoked by both Searle and van Gulick is P-consciousness. Van Gulick speaks of "conscious experience in the phenomenal sense," and Searle criticizes me for supposing that there is a legitimate use of "conscious" to mean A-conscious: "Some philosophers (e.g., Block, "Two Concepts of Consciousness") claim that there is a sense of this word that implies no sentience whatever, a sense in which a total zombie could be 'conscious'. I know of no such sense, but in any case, that is not the sense in which I am using the word" (1992, p. 84). But neither Searle nor van Gulick nor Penfield gives any reason to believe that P-consciousness is missing or even diminished in the epileptics they describe. The piano player, walker, and the driver don't cope with new situations very well, but they do show every sign of *normal sensation*. For example, Searle, quoting Penfield, describes the epileptic walker as "thread[ing] his way" through the crowd. Doesn't he *see* the obstacles he avoids? Suppose he gets home by turning right at a red wall. Isn't there something it is like for him to see the red wall— and isn't it different from what it is like for him to see a green wall? Searle gives no reason to think the answer is no. Because of the very inflexibility and lack of creativity of the behavior they exhibit, it is the *thought processes* of these patients (including A-consciousness) that are most obviously deficient; no reason at all is given to think that their P-conscious states lack vivacity or intensity. Of course, I don't claim to know what it is really like for these epileptics; my point is rather that for the argument for the function of P-consciousness to have any force, a case would have to be made that P-consciousness is *actually* missing, or at least diminished. Searle argues: P-consciousness is missing; so is creativity; therefore the former lack explains the latter lack. But no support at all is given for the first premise, and as we shall see, it is no stretch to suppose that what's gone wrong is that the ordinary mongrel notion of consciousness is being used; it wraps P-consciousness and A-consciousness together, and so an obvious function of A-consciousness is illicitly transferred to P-consciousness.[28]

Searle and Van Gulick base their arguments on Penfield's claim that a petit mal seizure "converts the individual into a mindless automaton" (Penfield 1975, p. 37). Indeed, Penfield repeatedly refers to these patients as "unconscious," "mindless," and as "automata." But what does Penfield *mean*? Searle and Van Gulick assume that Penfield means P-consciousness, since they adopt the idea that that is what the term means (though as we shall see, Searle himself sometimes uses the term to mean A-consciousness). Attending to Penfield's account, we find the very shifting among different concepts of consciousness that I have described here, but the dominant theme by far involves thinking of the patients as cognitively rather than phenomenally deficient during petit mal seizures. Here is Penfield's summary of the description of the patients:

In an attack of automatism the patient becomes suddenly unconscious, but, since other mechanisms in the brain continue to function, he changes into an automaton. He may wander about, confused and aimless. Or he may continue to carry out whatever purpose his mind was in the act of handing on to his automatic sensory-motor mechanism when the highest brain-mechanism went out of action. Or he follows a stereotyped, habitual pattern of behavior. In every case, however, the automaton can make few, if any decisions for which there has been no precedent. *He makes no record of a stream of consciousness.* Thus, he will have complete amnesia for the period of epileptic discharge.... In general, if new decisions are to be made, the automaton cannot make them. In such a circumstance, he may become completely unreasonable and uncontrollable and even dangerous. (Penfield 1975, p. 38–40, italics mine)

In these passages, and throughout the book, the dominant theme in descriptions of these patients is one of deficits in thinking, planning, and decision making. No mention is made of any sensory or phenomenal deficit.[29]

My interpretation is supported by a consideration of Penfield's theoretical rationale for his claim that petit mal victims are unconscious. He distinguishes two brain mechanisms, "(a) the *mind's mechanism* (or highest brain mechanism); and (b) the *computer* (or automatic sensory-motor mechanism)" (p. 40, Penfield's italics). The mind's mechanism is most prominently mentioned in connection with planning and decision making, for example, "the highest brain mechanism is the mind's executive." When arguing that there is a soul that is connected to the mind's mechanism, he mentions only cognitive functions. He asks whether such a soul is improbable, and answers, "It is not so improbable, to my mind, as is the alternative expectation—that the highest brain mechanism should itself understand, and reason, and direct voluntary action, and decide where attention should be turned and what the computer must learn, and record, and reveal on demand" (p. 82). Penfield's soul is a cognitive soul.

By contrast, the computer is devoted to *sensory* and motor functions. Indeed, he emphasizes that the mind only has contact with sensory and motor areas of the cortex via controlling the computer, which itself has direct contact with the sensory and motor areas. Since it is the mind's mechanism that is knocked out in petit mal seizures, the sensory areas are intact in the "automaton."

Searle (1990b) attempts (though of course he wouldn't accept this description) to use the idea of degrees of P-consciousness to substitute for A-consciousness. I will quote a chunk of what he says about this. (The details of the context don't matter.)

By consciousness I simply mean those subjective states of awareness or sentience that begin when one wakes in the morning and continue throughout the period that one is awake until one falls into a dreamless sleep, into a coma, or dies or is otherwise, as they say, unconscious.

I quoted this passage earlier as an example of how a characterization of consciousness can go wrong by pointing to too many things. Searle means to be pointing to P-consciousness. But A-consciousness and P-consciousness normally occur together when one is awake, and both are normally absent in a coma and a dreamless sleep—so this characterization doesn't distinguish them.

On my account, dreams are a form of consciousness, ... though they are of less intensity than full blown waking alertness. Consciousness is an on/off switch: You are either conscious or not. Though once conscious, the system functions like a rheostat, and there can be an indefinite range of different degrees of consciousness, ranging from the drowsiness just before one falls asleep to the full blown complete alertness of the obsessive.

Degrees of P-consciousness are one thing, obsessive attentiveness is another—indeed the latter is a notion from the category of A-consciousness, not P-consciousness.

There are lots of different degrees of consciousness, but door-knobs, bits of chalk, and shingles are not conscious at all.... These points, it seems to me, are misunderstood by Block. He refers to what he calls an "access sense of consciousness." On my account there is no such sense. I believe that he ... [confuses] what I would call peripheral consciousness or *inattentiveness* with total unconsciousness. It is true, for example, that when I am driving my car "on automatic pilot" I am not paying much attention to the details of the road and the traffic. But it is simply not true that I am totally unconscious of these phenomena. If I were, there would be a car crash. We need therefore to make a distinction between the *center of my attention, the focus of my consciousness* on the one hand, and the *periphery* on the other.... There are lots of phenomena right now of which I am peripherally conscious, for example the feel of the shirt on my neck, the touch of the computer keys

at my finger-tips, and so on. But as I use the notion, none of these is unconscious in the sense in which the secretion of enzymes in my stomach is unconscious. (All quotations from Searle 1990b, p. 635, italics mine)

The first thing to note is the *contradiction*. Earlier, I quoted Searle saying that a "totally unconscious" epileptic could nonetheless drive home. Here, he says that if a driver was totally unconscious, the car would crash. The sense of 'conscious' in which the car would crash if the driver weren't conscious is *A-consciousness*, not P-consciousness. P-consciousness *all by itself* wouldn't keep the car from crashing—the P-conscious contents have to be put to use in rationally controlling the car, *which is an aspect of A-consciousness*. When Searle says the "totally unconscious" epileptic can nonetheless drive home, he is talking about P-consciousness; when he says the car would crash if the driver were totally unconscious, he is talking mainly about A-consciousness. Notice that it will do no good for Searle to say that in the quotation of the last paragraph, he is talking about creature-consciousness rather than state-consciousness. What it is for a person to be P-unconscious is for his states (all or the relevant ones) to lack P-consciousness. Creature P-consciousness is parasitic on state P-consciousness. Also, it will do him no good to appeal to the conscious/conscious of distinction. (The epilectics were "totally unconscious," but if he were "unconscious of " the details of the road and traffic the car would crash.) The epileptics were "totally unconscious" and therefore, since Searle has no resource of A-consciousness, he must say that the epilectics were totally unconscious *of* anything. So he is committed to saying that the epilectic driver can drive despite being totally unconscious of anything. And that contradicts the claim that I quoted that if Searle were totally unconscious of the details of the road and traffic, then the car would crash. If Searle says that someone who is totally unconscious can nonetheless be conscious of something, that would be a backhanded way of acknowledging the distinction.

The upshot is that Searle finds himself drawn to using 'consciousness' in the sense of A-consciousness, despite his official position that there is no such sense. Despite his official ideology, when he attempts to deploy a notion of degrees of P-consciousness he ends up talking about A-consciousness—or about both A-consciousness and P-consciousness wrapped together in the usual mongrel concept. Inattentiveness just *is* lack of A-consciousness (though it will have effects on P-consciousness). Thus, he may be right about the inattentive driver (note, the inattentive driver, not the petit mal case). When the inattentive driver stops at a red light, presumably there is something it is like for him to see the red light—the red light no doubt looks red in the usual way, that is, it appears as brightly and vividly to him as red normally does. But since he is thinking about something else, perhaps he is not using this information very much in his reasoning nor is he using this information to control his speech or action in any sophisticated way—that is, perhaps his A-consciousness of what he sees is diminished. (Of course, it can't be totally gone or the car would crash.) Alternatively, A-consciousness might be normal, and the driver's poor memory of the trip may just be due to failure to put contents that are both P-conscious and A-conscious into memory; my point is that to the extent that Searle's story is right about *any* kind of consciousness, it is right about A-consciousness, not P-consciousness.

Searle's talk of the center and the periphery is in the first instance about kinds of or degrees of access, not "degrees of phenomenality." You may recall that in introducing the A/P distinction, I used Searle's example of attending to the feel of the shirt on the back of one's neck. My point was that A-consciousness and P-consciousness interact: bringing something from the periphery to the center can *affect* one's phenomenal state. The attention makes the experience more fine-grained, more intense (though a pain that is already intense needn't become more intense when one attends to it). There is a phenomenal difference between figure and ground, though the perception of the colors of the ground can be just as intense as those of the figure, or so it seems to me. Access and phenomenality often interact, one bringing along the other—but that shouldn't make us blind to the difference.

Though my complaint is partly verbal, there is more to it. For the end result of deploying a mongrel concept is wrong reasoning about a function of P-consciousness.

Let me turn now to a related form of reasoning used by Owen Flanagan (1992, pp. 142–145). Flanagan discusses Luria's patient Zazetsky, a soldier who lost the memories of his "middle" past—between childhood and brain injury. The information about his past is represented in Zazetsky's brain, but it only comes out via "automatic writing." Flanagan says, "The saddest irony is that although each piece of Zazetsky's autobiography was consciously reappropriated by him each time he hit upon a veridical memory in writing, he himself was never able to fully reappropriate, to keep in clear and continuous view, to live with, the self he reconstructed in the thousand pages he wrote." Flanagan goes on to blame the difficulty on a defect of consciousness, and he means P-consciousness: "Zazetsky's conscious capacities are (partly) maimed. His dysfunction is rooted in certain defects of consciousness" (pp. 144–145). But Zazetsky's root problem appears to be a difficulty in A-consciousness, though that has an effect on self-consciousness and P-consciousness. The problem seems to be that the memories of the middle past are not accessible to him in the manner of his memories of childhood and recent past. To the extent that he knows about the middle past, it is as a result of reading his automatic writing, and so he has the sort of access we have to a story about someone else. The root difficulty is segregation of information, and whatever P-conscious feelings of fragmentation he has can be taken to result from the segregation of information. So there is nothing in this case that suggests a function of P-consciousness.

Let us now move to the line of thought mentioned at the outset about how the thirsty blindsight patient doesn't reach for the glass of water in the blind field.[30] (This line of thought appears in Marcel 1986, 1988; Van Gulick 1989 [though endorsed equivocally]; and Flanagan 1989.) The reasoning is that (1) consciousness is missing, (2) information that the patient in some sense possesses is not used in reasoning or in guiding action or in reporting, so (3) the function of consciousness must be to somehow allow information from the senses to be so used in guiding action (Marcel 1986, 1988). Flanagan (1992) agrees with Marcel: "Conscious awareness of a water fountain to my right will lead me to drink from it if I am thirsty. But the thirsty blindsighted person will make no move towards the fountain unless pressed to do so. The inference to the best explanation is that conscious awareness of the environment facilitates semantic comprehension and adaptive motor actions in creatures like us." And: "Blindsighted patients never initiate activity toward the blindfield because they lack subjective awareness of things in that field" (Flanagan 1992, pp. 141–142; the same reasoning occurs in his 1991, p. 349). Van Gulick (1989) agrees with Marcel, saying, "Subjects never initiate on their own any actions informed by perceptions from the blind field. The moral to be drawn from this is that information must normally be represented in phenomenal consciousness if it is to play any role in guiding voluntary action" (p. 220).

Bernard Baars argues for eighteen different functions of consciousness on the same ground. He says that the argument for these functions is "that loss of consciousness—through habituation, automaticity, distraction, masking, anesthesia, and the like—inhibits or destroys the functions listed here."[31]

Schacter (1989) approvingly quotes Marcel, using this reasoning to some extent in formulating the model of figure 20.1 (though as I mentioned, there is a model that perhaps more fully embodies this reasoning; see below). The P-consciousness module has the function of integrating information from the specialized modules, injecting them with P-conscious content, and of sending these contents to the system that is in charge of reasoning and rational control of action and reporting.

This is the fallacy: In the blindsight patient, both P-consciousness and A-consciousness of the glass of water are missing. There is an obvious explanation of why the patient doesn't reach for the glass in terms of the information about it not reaching mechanisms of reasoning and rational control of speech and action, the machinery of A-consciousness. (If we believe in an Executive System, we can explain why the blindsight patient does not reach for the water by appealing to the claim that the information about the water does not reach the Executive System.) More generally, A-consciousness and P-consciousness are almost always present or absent together, or rather this seems plausible. This is, after all, *why* they are folded together in a mongrel concept. A function of the mechanisms underlying A-consciousness is completely obvious. If information from the eyes and ears did not get to mechanisms of control of reasoning and of rational control of action and reporting, we would not be able to use our eyes and ears to guide our action and reporting. But it is just a mistake to slide from a function of the machinery of A-consciousness to any function at all of P-consciousness.

Of course, it could be that the lack of P-consciousness is itself responsible for the lack of A-consciousness. If *that* is the argument in any of these cases, I do not say "fallacy." The idea that the lack of P-consciousness is responsible for the lack of A-consciousness is a bold hypothesis, not a fallacy. Recall, however, that there is some reason to ascribe the opposite view to the field as a whole. The discussion earlier of Baars, Shallice, Kosslyn and Koenig, Edelman, Johnson-Laird, Andrade, and Kihlstrom et al. suggested that to the extent that the different consciousnesses are distinguished from one another, it is often thought that P-consciousness is a product of (or is identical to) cognitive processing. In this climate of opinion, if P-consciousness and A-consciousness were clearly distinguished, and something like the opposite of the usual view of their relation advanced, we would expect some comment on this fact, something that does not appear in any of the words cited.

The fallacy, then, is jumping from the premise that "consciousness" is missing—without being clear about what kind of consciousness is missing—to the conclusion that P-consciousness has a certain function. If the distinction were seen clearly, the relevant possibilities could be reasoned about. Perhaps the lack of P-consciousness causes the lack of A-consciousness. Or perhaps the converse is the case: P-consciousness is somehow a product of A-consciousness. Or both could be the result of something else. If the distinction were clearly made, these alternatives would come to the fore. The fallacy is failing to make the distinction, rendering the alternatives invisible.

Note that the claim that P-consciousness is missing in blindsight is just an assumption. I decided to take the blindsight patient's word for his lack of P-consciousness of stimuli in the blind field. Maybe this assumption is mistaken. But if it is, then the fallacy now under discussion reduces to the fallacy of the Searle-Penfield reasoning: if the assumption is wrong, if the blindsight patient *does* have P-consciousness of stimuli in the blind field, then *only* A-consciousness of the stimuli in the blind field is missing, so *of course* we cannot draw the mentioned conclusion about the function of P-consciousness from blindsight.

I said at the outset that although there was a serious fallacy in the target reasoning, there was also something importantly right about it. What is importantly right is this. In blindsight, both A-consciousness and P-consciousness (I assume) are gone, just as in normal perception, both are present. So blindsight is yet another case in which P-consciousness and A-consciousness are both present or both absent. Further, as I mentioned earlier, cases of A-consciousness without P-consciousness, such as the super-blindsight patient I described earlier, do not appear to exist. Training

of blindsight patients has produced a number of phenomena that look a bit like super-blindsight, but each such lead that I have pursued has fizzled. This suggests an intimate relation between A-consciousness and P-consciousness. Perhaps there is something about P-consciousness that greases the wheels of accessibility. Perhaps P-consciousness is like the liquid in a hydraulic computer (as mentioned earlier in connection with Farah's criticism), the means by which A-consciousness operates. Alternatively, perhaps P-consciousness is the gateway to mechanisms of access as in Schacter's model, in which case P-consciousness would have the function Marcel et al. mention. Or perhaps P-consciousness and A-consciousness even amount to much the same thing empirically even though they differ conceptually, in which case P-consciousness would also have the aforementioned function. Perhaps the two are so entwined together that there is no empirical sense to the idea of one without the other.

Indeed, there are many striking cases in which P-consciousness and A-consciousness come and go together. Kosslyn (1980) reports an imagery scanning experiment in which subjects were asked to zoom in on one location of an imaged map to the point where other areas of the map "overflow." The parts of the imaged map that lose P-consciousness are no longer readily accessible. (Kosslyn, in conversation) Cooper and Shepard (1973) note that practice in imagery tasks result in images no longer being conscious even though they are still there and are rotating, as shown by their function in reaction time experiments. From their description, one can see that the images lose both P-consciousness and A-consciousness. Baars (1994) mentions this (as an example of something else) and another such case.

Compare the model of figure 20.1 (Schacter's model) with those of figures 20.2 and 20.3 The model of figure 20.2 is just like Schacter's model except that the Executive System and the P-consciousness system are collapsed together. We might call the hypothesis that is embodied in it the Collapse Hypothesis.[32] Figure 20.3 is a variant

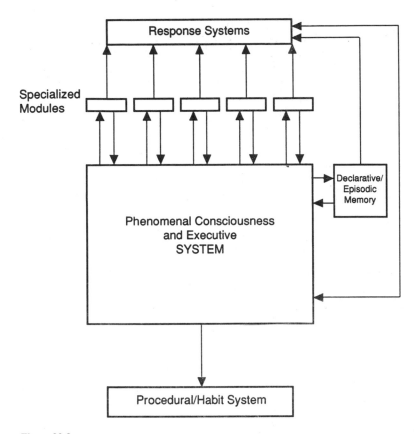

Figure 20.2

on Schacter's model in which the Executive module and the P-consciousness module are reversed. Schacter's model clearly gives P-consciousness a function in controlling action. Model 3 clearly gives it no function. Model 2 can be interpreted in a variety of ways, some of which give P-consciousness a function, others of which do not. If P-consciousness is literally identical to some sort of information processing, then P-consciousness will have whatever function that information processing has. But if P-consciousness is, say, a by-product of and supervenient on certain kinds of information processing (something that could also be represented by Model 3), then P-consciousness will in that respect at least have no

function. What is right about the Marcel et al. reasoning is that some of the explanations for the phenomenon give P-consciousness a role; what is wrong with the reasoning is that one cannot immediately conclude from missing "consciousness" to P-consciousness having *that* role.

7 Can We Distinguish among the Models?

I'm finished with the point of the chapter, but having raised the issue of the three competing models, I can't resist making some suggestions for distinguishing among them. My approach is one that takes introspection seriously, that is, that we

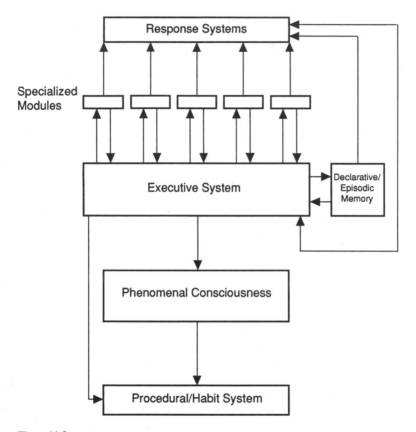

Figure 20.3

take seriously our impressions of how things seem to us. Famously, introspection is unreliable about some matters—for example, what cognitive processes underlie our choices (Nisbett and Wilson, 1977; Jacoby, Toth, Lindsay, and Debner 1992). But it would be foolish to conclude that we can afford to ignore our own P-conscious experience in studying P-consciousness.

One phenomenon that counts against the Collapse Hypothesis (fig. 20.2) is the familiar phenomenon of the solution to a difficult problem just popping into P-consciousness. If the solution involves high-level thought, then it must be done by high-level reasoning processes that are not P-conscious. (They aren't A-conscious either, since one can't report or base action on the intermediate stages of such reasoning.) There will always be disputes about famous cases (e.g. Kekulé's discovery of the benzene ring in a dream), but we should not be skeptical about the idea that though the results of thought are both P-conscious and A-conscious, much in the way of the intermediate stages are neither. If we assume that all high-level reasoning is done in the Executive System, and that Model 2 is committed to all Executive processes being P-conscious, then Model 2 is incompatible with solutions popping into P-consciousness. Of course, alternative forms of Model 2 that do not make these assumptions may not make any such predictions.

(Do cases of the sort mentioned count as A-conscious without being P-conscious? No, or rather, probably not. We would have A-consciousness without P-consciousness if we had a representation somewhere in the system [say in a perceptual module] that was never P-conscious, but which is sent to the Executive System and becomes A-conscious. That is what was supposed to happen in super-blindsight. But what may be going on in these cases of a solution "popping into consciousness" is a case of problem-solving machinery whose workings are not privy to either P- or A-consciousness producing a solution whose representation is simultaneously A- and P-conscious. Certainly, we have no reason to think that there is any representation of the solution which is A-conscious but not P-conscious, although we could find out that this is true.)

I think there are a number of phenomena that, if investigated further, might lead to evidence for P-consciousness without A-consciousness and thus provide some reason to reject Model 2 in favor of Schacter's model (figure 20.1). (I also think that these phenomena, if investigated further, might yield some reason to reject Model 3 in favor of Model 1, but I cannot go into that here.) I repeat: the phenomena I am about to mention don't show anything on their own. I claim only that they are intriguing and deserve further work.

One such phenomenon—or perhaps I should describe it as an idea rather than a phenomenon—is the hypothesis, already mentioned, that there could be animals whose P-conscious brain processes are intact, but whose A-conscious brain processes are not. Another is the case mentioned earlier of states of P-consciousness that go on for some time without attention and only become A-conscious with the focusing of attention. (See also Hill 1991).

Sperling (1960) flashed arrays of letters (e.g., 3 by 3) to subjects for brief periods (e.g., 50 milliseconds). Subjects typically said that they could see all or most of the letters, but they could report only about half of them. Were the subjects right in

saying that they could see all the letters? Sperling tried signaling the subjects with a tone. A high tone meant the subject was to report the top row, a medium tone indicated the middle row, and so forth. If the tone was given immediately after the stimulus, the subjects could usually get all the letters in the row, whichever row was indicated. But once they had named those letters, they usually could name no others. This experiment is taken to indicate some sort of raw visual storage, the "icon." But the crucial issue for my purposes is what it is like to be a subject in this experiment. My own experience is that I see all or almost all the letters, and this is what other subjects describe (Baars 1988, p. 15). Focusing on one row allows me to report what letters are in that row (and only that row) and again this is what other subjects report. Here is the description that I *think* is right and that I need for my case: I am P-conscious of all (or almost all—I'll omit this qualification) the letters at once, that is, jointly, and not just as blurry or vague letters, but as specific letters (or at least specific shapes), but I don't have access to all of them jointly, all at once. (I would like to know whether others describe what it is like in this way, but the prejudice against introspection in psychology tends to keep answers to such questions from the journals.) One item of uncertainty about this phenomenon is that responses are serial; perhaps if some parallel form of response were available the results would be different. Ignoring that issue, the suggestion is that I am P-conscious, but not A-conscious, of all jointly.[33]

It may be that some evidence for P-consciousness without A-consciousness can be derived from phenomena involving hypnosis. Consider the phenomenon known as hypnotic analgesia in which hypnosis blocks a patient's access to pain, say from an arm in cold water or from the dentist's drill. Pain must be P-conscious, it might be said, but access is blocked by the hypnosis, so perhaps this is P- without A-consciousness? But what reason is there to think that there is any pain at all in cases of hypnotic analgesia? One reason is that there are the normal psychophysiological indications that would be expected for pain of the sort that would be caused by the stimulus, such as an increase in heart rate and blood pressure (Melzack and Wall 1988; Kihlstrom et al. 1992). Another (flakier) indication is that reports of the pain apparently can be elicited by Hilgard's "hidden observer" technique in which the hypnotist tries to make contact with a "hidden part" of the person who knows about the pain (Hilgard 1986; Kihlstrom 1987). The hidden observer often describes the pain as excruciating and also describes the time course of the pain in a way that fits the stimulation. Now there is no point in supposing that the pain is not P-conscious. If we believe the hidden observer, there is a pain that has phenomenal properties, and phenomenal properties could not be P-unconscious.

One way to think about this situation is that we have different persons sharing some part of one body. The pain is both P-conscious and A-conscious to the system that reports as the "hidden observer." This system doesn't dominate the control of behavior, but since it can report, it can control behavior under some circumstances. This reasoning is supported by the idea that if there is a P-conscious state in me that I don't have access to, then that state is not *mine* at all. Turning now to a different way of thinking about what is going on: There is one system, *the person*, who has some sort of dissociation problem. There is P-conscious pain in there somewhere, but the person, himself or herself, does not have access to that pain, as shown by the failure to report it, and by the failure to use the information to escape the pain. Only on this latter view would we have P- without A-consciousness.

A phenomenon that could lead to evidence of P-consciousness with diminished A-consciousness has to do with persistent reports over the years of P-conscious events under general anesthesia. Patients wake up and say that the operation hurt. (A number of doctors have told me that this is why doctors make a point of giving patients intravenous valium, an amnestic, to wipe out patients' memory of the pain. If the patients don't re-

member the pain, they won't sue.) So far, it seems we might have both P- and A-consciousness under anesthesia. However, general anesthesia is thought to suppress reasoning power in subanesthetic doses (Kihlstrom 1987; see also Ghoneim et al. 1984), thus plausibly interfering with Executive function and A-consciousness. I know of no reports that would suggest diminished P-consciousness. If P-consciousness were diminished much more than A-consciousness, for example, we could perhaps have analogs of superblindsight. The patient might report events but not having seen or heard them. So if there are P-conscious states under general anesthesia, they may be states of more or less normal P-consciousness with diminished A-consciousness.

Further, Crick and Koch (1990) mention that the aforementioned neural oscillations persist under light general anesthesia. Kihlstrom and Schacter (1990), Kihlstrom and Couture (1992), and Ghoneim and Block (1993) conclude that the phenomenon depends in ways that are not understood on details of the procedure and the anesthetic cocktail, but there do appear to be some methods that show some kind of memory for events under anesthesia. Bennett et al. (1988) gave some patients under anesthesia suggestions to lift their index fingers at a special signal, whereas other patients were told to pull their ears. Control groups were given similar procedures without the suggestions. The result: the experimental group exhibited the designated actions at a much higher rate than controls. Of course, even if these results hold up, they don't show that the patients *heard* the suggestions under anesthesia. Perhaps what took place was some sort of auditory analog of blindsight (with no A- or P-consciousness).

An item of more use for present purposes comes from a study done on pilots during WWII by a pair of American dentists (Nathan 1985; Melzack and Wall 1988). The unpressurized cabins of the time caused pilots to experience sensations that as I understand it amount to some sort of re-creation of the pain of previous dental work. The mechanism appeared to have to do with stimulation of the sinuses caused by the air pressure changes. The dentists coined the term "aerodontalgia" for this phenomenon. The dentists were interested in the relation of aerodontalgia to general and local anesthetic. So they did dental work on patients using combinations of general and local anesthetics. For example, they would put a patient under general anesthesia, and then locally anesthetize one side of the mouth, and then drill or pull teeth on both sides. The result (with stimulation of the nasal mucosa in place of the sinus stimulation caused by pressure changes): they found re-creation of pain of previous dental work only for dental work done under general anesthesia, not for local anesthesia, whether or not the local was used alone or together with general anesthesia. Of course, there may have been no pain at all under general anesthesia, only memories of the sort that would have been laid down if there had been pain. But if you hate pain, and if both general and local anesthesia make medical sense, would *you* take the chance on general anesthesia? At any rate, the tantalizing suggestion is that this is a case of P-consciousness without A-consciousness.

The form of the target reasoning discussed misses the distinction between P-consciousness and A-consciousness and thus jumps from the fact that consciousness in some sense or other is missing simultaneously with missing creativity or voluntary action to the conclusion that P-consciousness functions to promote the missing qualities in normal people. But if we make the right distinctions, we can investigate non-fallaciously whether any such conclusion can be drawn. Model 2 would identify P-consciousness with A-consciousness, thus embodying an aspect of the target reasoning. But Model 2 is disconfirmed by the apparent fact that much of our reasoning is neither P-conscious nor A-conscious, as suggested by the phenomenon of the answer to problems "popping" into P- and A-consciousness. I have made further suggestions for

phenomena that may provide examples of P-consciousness without A-consciousness, further disconfirming Model 2.

My purpose in this chapter has been to expose a confusion about consciousness. But in reasoning about it I raised the possibility that it may be possible to find out something about the function of P-consciousness without knowing very much about what it is. Indeed, learning something about the function of P-consciousness may help us in finding out what it is.[34]

Notes

Reprinted with some changes from *The Behavioral and Brain Sciences*, *18*, 2, 1995, with permission of the author and Cambridge University Press.

1. See Bowers and Schacter (1990), and Reingold and Merikle (1990). The phenomenon just mentioned is very similar to phenomena involving "subliminal perception," in which stimuli are degraded or presented very briefly. Holender (1986) harshly criticizes a variety of "subliminal perception" experiments, but the experimental paradigm just mentioned and many others, are in my judgment free from the problems of some other studies. Another such experimental paradigm is the familiar dichotic listening experiments in which subjects wear headphones in which different programs are played to different ears. If they are asked to pay attention to one program, they can report only superficial features of the unattended program, but the unattended program influences interpretation of ambiguous sentences presented in the attended program. See Lackner and Garrett (1973).

2. See, for example, Dennett, and Kinsbourne's (1992b) scorn in response to my suggestion of Cartesian Modularism. I should add that in Dennett's more recent writings, Cartesian materialism has tended to expand considerably from its original meaning of a literal place in the brain at which "it all comes together" for consciousness. In reply to Shoemaker (1993) and Tye (1993), both of whom echo Dennett's (1991) and Dennett and Kinsbourne's (1992a) admission that no one really is a proponent of Cartesian materialism, Dennett (1993) says, "Indeed, if Tye and Shoemaker want to see a card-carrying Cartesian materialist, each may look in the mirror ..." See also Jackson (1993a).

3. But what is it about thoughts that makes them P-conscious? One possibility is that it is just a series of mental images or subvocalizations that make thoughts P-conscious. Another possibility is that the contents themselves have a P-conscious aspect independently of their vehicles. See Lormand, forthcoming.

4. I say both that P-consciousness is not an intentional property and that intentional differences can make a P-conscious difference. I also say that P-conscious properties are often representational. My view is that although P-conscious content cannot be reduced to or identified with intentional content, P-conscious contents often have an intentional aspect, and also P-conscious contents often represent in a primitive non-intentional way. A perceptual experience can represent space as being filled in certain ways without representing the object perceived as falling under any concept. Thus, the experiences of a creature which does not possess the concept of a donut or a torus could represent space as being filled in a donut-like way. Intentional representation is representation under concepts, so the creature that represents space as being filled in a donut-like way without any concept of that shape has representational content without intentional content. See Davies (1992, 1995), Peacocke (1992), and finally Evans (1982), in which the distinction between conceptualized and non-conceptualized content is first introduced.

5. My diagnosis is that initially Crick and Koch didn't distinguish solving the binding problem from explaining P-consciousness, but to the extent that they did distinguish, they hypothesized that the solution to the former problem would also solve the latter. Levine (1983) coined the term "explanatory gap," and has elaborated the idea in interesting ways; see also his (1993). Van Gulick (1993) and Flanagan (1992, p. 59) note that the more we know about the connection between (say) hitting middle C on the piano and the resulting experience, the more we have in the way of hooks on which to hang something that could potentially close the explanatory gap. Some philosophers have adopted what might be called a deflationary attitude toward the explanatory gap. See Levine (1993), Jackson (1993), Chalmers (1996), Byrne (1993), and Block (1994).

6. I know some will think that I invoked inverted and absent qualia a few paragraphs above when I described the explanatory gap as involving the question of why a creature with a brain which has a physiological and functional nature like ours couldn't have different experience or none at all. But the spirit of the question as I

asked it allows for an answer that explains why such creatures cannot exist, and thus there is no presupposition that these are real possibilities. Levine (1983, 1993) stresses that the relevant modality is epistemic possibility.

7. This is an improvement over the definition of A-consciousness in the original version of this paper.

8. I have been using the P-consciousness/A-consciousness distinction in my lectures for many years, but it only found its way into print in my "Consciousness and Accessibility" (1990b), and my (1991, 1992, 1993). My claims about the distinction have been criticized in Searle (1990b, 1992) and Flanagan (1992)—I reply to Flanagan below; and there is an illuminating discussion in Humphreys and Davies (1993b), a point of which will be taken up in a note to follow. See also Levine's (1994) review of Flanagan which discusses Flanagan's critique of the distinction. See also Kirk (1992) for an identification of P-consciousness with something like A-consciousness.

9. Some may say that only fully conceptualized content can play a role in reasoning, be reportable, and rationally control action. If so, then non-conceptualized content is not A-conscious.

10. However, I acknowledge the empirical possibility that the scientific nature of P-consciousness has something to do with information processing. We can ill afford to close off empirical possibilities, given the difficulty of solving the mystery of P-consciousness. Cf. Loar (1990).

11. On my view, there are a number of problems with the first of these suggestions. One of them is that perhaps the representational content of pain is too primitive for a role in inference. Arguably, the representational content of pain is nonconceptualized. After all, dogs can have pain and one can reasonably wonder whether dogs have the relevant concepts at all. But there is a better suggestion. Davies and Humphreys (1993b) discuss a related issue. Applying a suggestion of theirs about the higher-order thought notion of consciousness to A-consciousness, we could characterize A-consciousness of a state with nonconceptualized content as follows: such a state is A-conscious if, in virtue of one's having the state, its content would be inferentially promiscuous and poised for rational control of action and speech if the subject were to have had the concepts required for that content to be a conceptualized content. The idea is to bypass the inferential disadvantage of nonconceptualized content by thinking of its accessi-

bility counterfactually—in terms of the rational relations it would have if the subject were to have the relevant concepts. See Lormand (forthcoming) on the self-representing nature of pain.

12. Later in this chapter I introduce the distinction between creature consciousness and state consciousness. In those terms, transitivity has to do primarily with creature consciousness, whereas in the case of P-consciousness and A-consciousness, it is state consciousness that is basic. See the discussion at the end of this section.

13. The distinction has some similarity to the sensation/perception distinction; I won't take the space to lay out the differences. See Humphrey (1992) for an interesting discussion of the latter distinction.

14. Tye (1994) argues (on the basis of neuropsychological claims) that the visual information processing in blindsight includes no processing by the object recognition system or the spatial attention system, and so is very different from the processing of normal vision. This point does not challenge my claim that the super-blindsight case is a very limited partial zombie. Note that super-blindsight, as I describe it, does not require object recognition or spatial attention. Whatever it is that allows the blindsight patient to discriminate an X from an O and a horizontal from a vertical line will do. I will argue later that the fact that such cases do not exist, if it is a fact, is important. Humphrey (1992) suggests that blindsight is mainly a motor phenomenon—the patient is perceptually influenced by his own motor tendencies.

15. If you are tempted to deny the existence of these states of the perceptual system, you should think back to the total zombie just mentioned. Putting aside the issue of the possibility of this zombie, note that on a computational notion of cognition, the zombie has all the same A-conscious contents that you have (if he is your computational duplicate). A-consciousness is an informational notion. The states of the super-blindsighter's perceptual system are A-conscious for the same reason as the zombie's.

16. Actually, my notion of A-consciousness seems to fit the data better than the conceptual apparatus she uses. Blindsight isn't always more degraded in any normal sense than sight. Weiskrantz (1988) notes that his patient DB had better acuity in some areas of the blind field (in some circumstances) than in his sighted field. It would be better to understand her "degraded" in terms of lack of access.

Notice that the super-blindsighter I have described is just a little bit different (though in a crucial way) from the ordinary blindsight patient. In particular, I am not relying on what might be thought of as a full-fledged quasi-zombie, a super-duper-blindsighter whose blindsight is every bit as good, functionally speaking, as his sight. In the case of the super-duper-blindsighter, the only difference between vision in the blind and sighted fields, functionally speaking, is that the quasi-zombie himself regards them differently. Such an example will be regarded by some (though not me) as incoherent—see Dennett (1991), for example. But we can avoid disagreement about the super-duper-blindsighter by illustrating the idea of A-consciousness without P-consciousness by appealing only to the super-blindsighter. Functionalists may want to know why the super-blindsight case counts as A-conscious without P-consciousness. After all, they may say, if we have really high-quality access in mind, the super-blindsighter that I have described does not have it, so he lacks both P-consciousness and really high-quality A-consciousness. The super-duper-blindsighter, on the other hand, has both, according to the functionalist, so in neither case, the objection goes, is there A-consciousness without P-consciousness. But the disagreement about the super-duper-blindsighter is irrelevant to the issue about the super-blindsighter, and the issue about the super-blindsighter is merely verbal. I believe in the possibility of a quasi-zombie like the super-duper-blindsighter, but the point I am making here does not depend on it. There is no reason to frame notions so as to muddy the waters with unnecessary conflicts. One could put the point by distinguishing three types of access: (1) really high-quality access, (2) medium access, and (3) poor access. The actual blindsight patient has poor access, the super-blindsight patient has medium access, and the super-duper-blindsight patient—as well as most of us—has really high-quality access. The functionalist identifies P-consciousness with A-consciousness of the really high-quality kind. I am defining 'A-consciousness'—and of course, it is only one of many possible definitions—in terms of medium access. Defining 'A-consciousness' in terms of low-quality access would make blindsight patients cases of A without P. Defining 'A-consciousness' in terms of the rich information of high-quality access would render the kind of vision you have when you close your eyes lightly (and can still tell whether the lights are on) as P without A. My concern is to make gaps between P and A as interesting as possible.

17. Thus, there is a conflict between this physiological claim and the Schacter model which dictates that destroying the P-consciousness module will prevent A-consciousness.

18. There is a misleading aspect to this example—namely that to the extent that "conscious" and "aware" differ in ordinary talk, the difference goes in the opposite direction.

19. Of course, even those who don't believe in P-consciousness at all, as distinct from A-consciousness, can accept the distinction between a noise that is A-conscious and a noise that is not A-conscious. There is a more familiar situation which illustrates the same points. Think back to all those times when you have been sitting in the kitchen when suddenly the compressor in the refrigerator goes off. Again, one might naturally say that one was aware of the noise, but only at the moment in which it went off was one consciously aware of it. A point on the other side: perhaps habituation stems P-consciousness of the noise; perhaps what happens at the moment it goes off is that one is P-conscious of the change only.

20. Whether loss of a feeling of familiarity is a necessary condition of prosopagnosia is a more complex issue. Perhaps it will suffice to say that in the case of prosopagnosics, there may be no fact of the matter as to whether they are experiencing familiarity, yet we still count them as prosopagnosics. See the discussion of anosognosia below.

21. See White (1987) for an account of why self-consciousness should be firmly distinguished from P-consciousness, and why self-consciousness is more relevant to certain issues of value.

22. The pioneer of these ideas in the philosophical literature is David Armstrong (1968, 1980). William Lycan (1987) has energetically pursued self-scanning, and David Rosenthal (1986, 1993), Peter Carruthers (1989, 1992), and Norton Nelkin (1993) have championed higher-order thought. See also Natsoulas (1993). Lormand (forthcoming) makes some powerful criticisms of Rosenthal.

23. To be fair to Rey, his argument is more like a dilemma: for any supposed feature of consciousness, either a laptop of the sort we have today has it or else you can't be sure you have it yourself. So in the case of P-consciousness, laptops don't have it, and we are sure we do, so once we make these distinctions, his argument loses plausibility.

24. This represents a change of view from Block (1994), wherein I said that 'consciousness' ought to be ambiguous rather than saying it is now ambiguous.

25. See Block (1993).

26. Interestingly, she was in many respects much worse at many face-perception tasks than LH (the prosopagnosic mentioned earlier)—she couldn't match photographs of faces, for example. I have noticed that people who know little about anosognosia tend to favor various debunking hypotheses. That is, they assume that the experimenters have made one or another silly mistake in describing the syndrome, because, after all, how could anyone fail to notice that they can't recognize faces, or worse, that they are blind. See Young et al. (1993) for a good debunking of the debunking hypotheses.

27. The same considerations show that prosopagnosia itself is a defect of A-consciousness, not P-consciousness.

28. There is an additional problem in the reasoning that I won't go into except here. There is a well-known difficulty in reasoning of the form: X is missing; the patient has lost the ability to do blah-blah; therefore a function of X is to facilitate blah-blahing. In a complex system, a loss may reverberate through the system, triggering a variety of malfunctions that are not connected in any serious way with the function of the missing item. An imperfect but memorable example (that I heard from Tom Bever) will illustrate: the Martians want to find out about the function of various Earthly items. They begin with the Pentagon, and focus in on a particular drinking fountain in a hall on the third floor of the north side of the building. "If we can figure out what that is for," they think, "we can move on to something more complex." So they vaporize the drinking fountain, causing noise and spurting pipes. Everyone comes out of their offices to see what happened, and the Martians conclude that the function of the fountain was to keep people in their offices. The application of this point to the petit mal case is that even if I am right that it is A-consciousness, not P-consciousness, that is diminished or missing, I would not jump to the conclusion that A-consciousness has a function of adding powers of discrimination, flexibility, and creativity. Creativity, for example, may have its sources in the un-A-conscious, requiring powers of reasoning and control of action and reporting only for its expression.

29. Indeed, in the italicized passage above there is an implicit suggestion that perhaps there are P-conscious events of which no record is made. I could only find one place in the book where Penfield says anything that might be taken to contradict this interpretation: "Thus, the automaton can walk through traffic as though he were aware of all that he hears and sees, and so continue on his way home. But he is aware of nothing and so makes no memory record. If a policemen were to accost him he might consider the poor fellow to be walking in his sleep" (1975, p. 60). But to properly understand this, we need to know what he means by "awareness," and what he thinks goes on in sleep. Judging by Penfield's use of synonyms, by "awareness" he means something in the category of the higher-order thought analyses or the self-consciousness sense. For example, in discussing his peculiar view that ants are conscious, he seems to use 'conscious' and 'aware' to mean self-aware (pp. 62, 105, 106). Further, he makes it clear that although the mind is shut off during sleep, the sensory cortex is quite active.

30. A similar line of reasoning appears in Shevrin (1992); he notes that in subliminal perception, we don't fix the source of a mental content. Subliminal percepts aren't conscious, so consciousness must have the function of fixing the source of mental contents.

31. Baars (1988, p. 356). Though Baars is talking about the function of "conscious experience," he does have a tendency to combine P-consciousness with A-consciousness under this heading.

32. The Collapse Hypothesis should not be confused with Marcel's (1988, pp. 135–7) Identity Hypothesis, which hypothesizes that the processing of stimuli is identical with consciousness of them. As Marcel points out, blindsight and similar phenomena suggest that we can have processing without consciousness.

33. I am imdebted to Jerry Fodor here.

34. I would like to thank Tyler Burge, Susan Carey, David Chalmers, Martin Davies, Wayne Davis, Bert Dreyfus, Owen Flanagan, Güven Güzeldere, Paul Horwich, Jerry Katz, Leonard Katz, Joe Levine, David Rosenthal, Jerome Schaffer, Sydney Shoemaker, Stephen White, and Andrew Young for their very helpful comments on earlier versions of this paper. I have been giving this paper at colloquia and meetings since the fall of 1990, and I am grateful to the many audiences which have made interesting and useful comments, especially the audience at the conference on my work at the University of Barcelona in June, 1993.

References

Akins, K. (1993). A bat without qualities. In Davies and Humphreys (1993a).

Alston, W. (1967). Religion. In *The Encyclopedia of Philosophy*. Macmillan/Free Press, 140–145.

Anderson, J. (1993). To see ourselves as others see us: a response to Mitchell. *New Ideas in Psychology* 11, 3:339–346.

Andrade, J. (1993). Consciousness: current views. In Jones, 1993.

Armstrong, D. M. (1968). *A Materialist Theory of Mind*. Humanities Press.

———. What is consciousness? In *The Nature of Mind*. Ithaca, NY: Cornell University Press.

Baars, B. J. (1988). *A Cognitive Theory of Consciousness*. Cambridge: Cambridge University Press.

Baars, B. J. (1994). A thoroughly empirical approach to consciousness. *Psyche* (the email journal).

Block, N. (1980). What is functionalism? In N. Block (ed), *Readings in the Philosophy of Psychology*, vol 1. Cambridge, MA: Harvard University Press.

——— (1990a). Inverted earth. In J. Tomberlin (ed.), *Philosophical Perspectives*, vol. 4. Atascadero, CA: Ridgeview.

——— (1990b). Consciousness and accessibility. *Behavioral and Brain Sciences* 13:596–598.

——— (1991). Evidence against epiphenomenalism. *Behavioral and Brain Sciences* 14(4):670–672.

——— (1992). Begging the question against phenomenal consciousness. *Behavioral and Brain Sciences* 15, 205–206.

——— (1993). Review of D. Dennett, *Consciousness Explained. The Journal of Philosophy* 90, 4:181–193.

——— (1994). "Consciousness," "Functionalism," "Qualia." In S. Guttenplan (ed). *A Companion to Philosophy of Mind*. Oxford: Blackwell.

Bowers, J., and Schacter, D. (1990). Implicit memory and test awareness. *Journal of Experimental Psychology: Learning, Memory and Cognition* 16:3:404–416.

Bornstein, R., and Pittman, T. (1992). *Perception without Awareness*. New York: Guilford Press.

Byrne, A. (1993). *The Emergent Mind*, Ph.D. thesis, Princeton University, Princeton, NJ.

Byrne, R. W. (1993). The meaning of 'awareness': a response to Mitchell. *New Ideas in Psychology* 11, 3:347–350.

Carruthers, P. (1989). Brute experience. *Journal of Philosophy* 86.

——— (1992). Consciousness and concepts. *Proceedings of the Aristotelian Society, Supplementary Volume* 66, 40–59.

Chalmers, D. J. (1996). *The Conscious Mind*. Oxford: Oxford University Press.

Churchland, P. S. (1983). Consciousness: the transmutation of a concept. *Pacific Philosophical Quarterly* 64:80–93.

——— (1986). Reduction and the neurobiological basis of consciousness. In Marcel and Bisiach (1988).

Cooper, L., and Shepard, R. (1973). Chronometric studies of the rotation of mental images. In W. G. Chase (ed), *Visual Information Processing*. New York: Academic Press.

Coslett, H., and Saffran, E. (1994). Mechanisms of implicit reading in alexia. In *The Neuropsychology of High-Level Vision*, M. Farah and G. Ratcliff, eds. Hillside, NJ: Erlbaum.

Cowie, A., and Stoerig, P. (1992). Reflections on blindsight. In Milner and Rugg (1992).

Crick, F., and Koch, C. (1990). Towards a neurobiological theory of consciousness. *Seminars in the Neurosciences* 2:263–275.

Crick, F. (1994). *The Astonishing Hypothesis*. New York: Scribners.

Davies, M., and Humphreys, G. (1993a). *Consciousness*. Oxford: Blackwell.

——— (1993b). Introduction. In Davies and Humphreys (1993a), 1–31.

Davies, M. (1992). Perceptual content and local supervenience. *Proceedings of the Aristotelian Society* 92:21–45.

——— (1995). Externalism and experience. In A. Clark, J. Exquerro, J. Larrazabal (eds), *Categories, Consciousness and Reasoning*. Dordrecht, Netherlands: Kluwer.

de Lannoy, J. (1993). Two theories of a mental model of mirror self-recognition: a response to Mitchell. *New Ideas in Psychology* 11, 3:337–338.

Dennett, D. (1986). Julian Jaynes' software archeology. *Canadian Psychology* 27, 2:149–154.

——— (1991). *Consciousness Explained*. Boston: Little Brown.

——— (1993). The message is: there is no medium. In *Philosophy and Phenomenological Research* 3:4.

Dennett, D., and Kinsbourne, M. (1992a). Time and the observer: the where and when of consciousness in the brain *Behavioral and Brain Sciences* 15:183–200.

——— (1992b). Escape from the Cartesian theater. *Behavioral and Brain Sciences* 15:234–248.

Dimond, S. (1976). Brain circuits for consciousness. *Brain, Behavior and Evolution* 13:376–395.

Dretske, F. (1993). Conscious experience. *Mind* 102, 406:263–284.

Dupre, J. (1981). Natural kinds and biological taxa. *Philosophical Review* 90:66–90.

Edelman, G. (1989). *The Remembered Present: A Biological Theory of Consciousness*. New York: Basic Books.

Etcoff, N. L., and Freeman, R., and Cave, K. Can we lose memories of faces? Content specificity and awareness in a prosopagnosic. *Journal of Cognitive Neuroscience* 3, 1.

Etcoff, N. L., and Magee, J. J. (1992). Covert recognition of emotional expressions. *Journal of Clinical and Experimental Neuropsychology* 14:95–96.

Evans, G. (1982). *The Varieties of Reference*. Oxford University Press.

Flanagan, O. (1991). *The Science of the Mind*, 2nd ed. Cambridge, MA: MIT Press.

——— (1992). *Consciousness Reconsidered*. Cambridge, MA: MIT Press.

Gallup, G. (1982). Self-awareness and the emergence of mind in primates. *American Journal of Primatology* 2:237–248.

Gallup, G., and Povinelli, D. Mirror, mirror on the wall, which is the most heuristic theory of them all? A response to Mitchell. *New Ideas in Psychology* 11, 3:327–335.

Ghoneim, M., Hinrichs, J., and Mewaldt, S. (1984). Dose-response analysis of the behavioral effects of diazepam: 1. Learning and memory. *Psychopharmacology* 82:291–295.

Ghoneim, M., and Block, R. (1993). Learning during anesthesia. In Jones, 1993.

Goldman, A. (1993a). The psychology of folk psychology *The Behavioral and Brain Sciences* 16:1:15–28.

——— (1993b). Consciousness, folk psychology and cognitive science. *Consciousness and Cognition* 2:3.

Goodale, M., and Milner, D. (1992). Separate visual pathways for perception and action. *Trends in Neurosciences* 15, 20–25.

Harman, G. (1990). The intrinsic quality of experience. In J. Tomberlin (ed.), *Philosophical Perspectives*, vol. 4. Atascadero, CA: Ridgeview.

Heyes, C. (1993). Reflections on self-recognition in primates, *Animal Behavior*

Hilgard, E. (1986). *Divided Consciousness*, 2nd ed. New York: John Wiley.

Holender, D. (1986). Semantic activation without conscious identification in dichotic listening, parafoveal vision, and visual masking: a survey and appraisal. *Behavioral and Brain Sciences* 9:1–66.

Hill, C. (1991). *Sensations: A Defense of Type Materialism*. Cambridge: Cambridge University Press.

Humphrey, N. (1992). *A History of the Mind*. New York: Simon & Schuster.

Huxley, T. H. (1866). *Lessons in Elementary Psychology* 8, p. 210. Quoted in Humphrey, (1992).

Jackendoff, R. (1987). *Consciousness and the Computational Mind*. Cambridge, MA: MIT Press

Jackson, F. (1977). *Perception*. Cambridge: Cambridge University Press.

—— (1993a). Appendix A (for philosophers). In *Philosophy and Phenomenological Research* 3:4.

—— (1993b). 'Armchair metaphysics'. In J. O'Leary-Hawthorne and M. Michael (eds), *Philosophy in Mind*. Dordrecht, Netherlands: Kluwer.

Jacoby, L., Toth, J., Lindsay, D., and Debner, J. (1992). Lectures for a layperson: methods for revealing unconscious processes. In Bornstein and Pittman (1992).

James, W. (1890/1950). *The Principles of Psychology*, 2 vols. New York: Dover.

Jaynes, J. (1976). *The Origin of Consciousness in the Breakdown of the Bicameral Mind*. Boston: Houghton-Mifflin.

Jones, J. G. (1993). *Depth of Anesthesia*. Boston: Little Brown.

Kihlstrom, J. (1987). The cognitive unconscious. *Science* 237:1445–1452.

Kihlstrom, J., and Schacter, D. (1990). Anaesthesia, amnesia, and the cognitive unconscious. In B. Bonke (ed), *Memory and Awareness in Anaesthesia*. Swets and Zeitlinger.

Kihlstrom, J., Barnhardt, T., and Tataryn, D. (1992). Implicit perception. In Bornstein and Pittman (1992).

Kihlstrom, J., and Couture, L. (1992). Awareness and information processing in general anesthesia. *Journal of Psychopharmacology* 6(3) 410–417.

Kirk, R. (1992). Consciousness and concepts. *Proceedings of the Aristotelian Society, Supplementary Volume* 66:23–40.

Kosslyn, S. (1980). *Image and Mind*. Cambridge: Harvard University Press.

Kosslyn S. and Koenig, O. (1992). *Wet Mind: The New Cognitive Neuroscience*. New York: Free Press.

Kuhn, T. (1964). A function for thought experiments. In *Melanges Alexandre Koyre* Vol 1. Hermann: 307–334.

Lackner, J., and Garrett, M. (1973). Resolving ambiguity: effects of biasing context in the unattended ear. *Cognition* 1:359–372.

Landis, T., Regard, M., and Serrat, A. (1980). Iconic reading in a case of alexia without agraphia caused by a brain tumour: a tachistoscopic study. *Brain and Language* 11, 45–53.

Levine, J. (1983) Materialism and qualia: the explanatory gap. *Pacific Philosophical Quarterly* 64:354 361.

—— (1993). One leaving out what it is like. In Davies and Humphreys (1993a).

—— (1994) Review of Owen Flanagan's *Consciousness Reconsidered*. In *The Philosophical Review* 103, 353–356.

Loar, B. (1990). Phenomenal properties. In J. Tomberlin (ed), *Philosophical Perspectives*, vol 4. Atascadero, CA: Ridgeview.

Lormand, E. (forthcoming). What qualitative consciousness is like.

Lycan, W. (1987). *Consciousness*. Cambridge, MA: MIT Press.

Mandler, G. (1985). *Cognitive Psychology*, chapter 3. Hillside, NJ: Erlbaum.

McGinn, C. (1991). *The Problem of Consciousness*. Oxford: Blackwell.

—— (1993). Consciousness and cosmology: hyperdualism ventilated. In Davies and Humphreys (1993a).

Marcel, A. J. (1983). Conscious and unconscious perception: An approach to relations between phenomenal experience and perceptual processes. *Cognitive Psychology* 15:238–300.

——— (1986). Consciousness and processing: choosing and testing a null hypothesis. *The Behavioral and Brain Sciences* 9:40–41.

——— (1988). Phenomenal experience and functionalism. In Marcel and Bisiach (1988).

Marcel, A. J., and Bisiach, E. (eds) (1988). *Consciousness in Contemporary Science*. Oxford: Oxford University Press.

McCullough, G. (1993). The very idea of the phenomenological. *Proceedings of the Aristotelian Society* 93: 39–58.

Melzack, R., and Wall, P. (1988). *The Challenge of Pain*, 2nd edition. London: Penguin.

Menzel, E., Savage-Rumbaugh, E., Lawson, J. (1985). Chimpanzee (*Pan troglogdytes*) spatial problem solving with the use of mirrors and televised equivalents of mirrors. *Journal of Comparative Psychology* 99:211–217.

Milner, B., and Rugg, M. (1992). (eds). *The Neuropsychology of Consciousness*. New York: Academic Press.

Mitchell, R. W. (1993a). Mental models of mirror self-recognition: two theories. In *New Ideas in Psychology* 11:295–325.

——— (1993b). Recognizing one's self in a mirror? A reply to Gallup and Povinelli, de Lannoy, Anderson, and Byrne. In *New Ideas in Psychology* 11:351–377.

Moscovitch, M., Goshen-Gottstein, Y., Vriezen, E. (1994). "Memory without conscious recollection: a tutorial review from a neuropsychological perspective." In Umilta and Moscovitch, 1994.

Nagel, T. (1974) What is it like to be a bat? *Philosophical Review* chapter 32.

Nagel, T. (1979). *Mortal Questions*. Cambridge: Cambridge University Press.

——— (1986). *The View from Nowhere*. Oxford: Oxford University Press.

Nathan, P. (1985). Pain and nociception in the clinical context. *Philosophical Transactions of the Royal Society of London. Series B: Biological Sciences* 308:219–226.

Natsoulas, T. (1993). What is wrong with the appendage theory of consciousness? *Philosophical Psychology* 6, 2: 137–154.

Nelkin, N. (1993). The connection between intentionality and consciousness. In Davies and Humphreys (1993a).

Nisbett, R., and Wilson, T. (1977). Telling more than we can know: verbal reports on mental processes, *Psychological Review* 84, 231–259.

Peacocke, C. (1983). *Sense and Content*. Oxford: Oxford University Press.

——— (1992). *A Study of Concepts*. Cambridge, MA: MIT Press.

Pendlebury, M. (1992) Experience, theories of. In J. Dancy and E. Sosa, *A Companion to Epistemology*. Oxford: Blackwell.

Penfield, W. (1975). *The Mystery of the Mind: A Critical Study of Consciousness and the Human Brain*. Princeton, NJ: Princeton University Press.

Plourde, G. (1993). Clinical use of the 40-Hz auditory steady state response. In Jones (1993).

Povinelli, D. (1994). What chimpanzees know about the mind. In *Behavioral Diversity in Chimpanzees*. Cambridge, MA: Harvard University Press.

Putnam, H. (1975). The meaning of 'meaning'. In Putnam's *Mind, Language and Reality*. Cambridge, MA: Cambridge University Press.

Reingold, E., and Merikle, P. (1993). Theory and measurement in the study of unconscious processes. In Davies and Humphreys (1993a).

Rey, G. (1983). A reason for doubting the existence of consciousness. In *Consciousness and Self-Regulation*, vol 3. R. Davidson, G. Schwartz, D. Shapiro (eds). New York: Plenum.

——— (1988) A question about consciousness. In *Perspectives on Mind*, H. Otto and J. Tuedio (eds). Dordrecht: Reidel.

Rosenthal, David (1986). Two concepts of consciousness. *Philosophical Studies* 49:329–359.

——— (1993). Thinking that one thinks. In Davies and Humphreys (1993a).

Schacter, D. (1989). On the relation between memory and consciousness: dissociable interactions and conscious experience. In: H. Roediger and F. Craik (eds), *Varieties of Memory and Consciousness: Essays in Honour of Endel Tulving*. Hillside, NJ: Erlbaum.

Searle, J. (1983). *Intentionality*. Cambridge: Cambridge University Press.

——— (1990a). Consciousness, explanatory inversion and cognitive science. *Behavioral and Brain Sciences* 13:4:585–595.

——— (1990b). Who is computing with the brain? *Behavioral and Brain Sciences* 13, 4:632–642.

—— (1992). *The Rediscovery of the Mind*. Cambridge, MA: MIT Press.

Sergent, J., and Poncet, M. (1990). From covert to overt recognition of faces in a prosopagnosic patient. *Brain* 113:989–1004.

Shallice, T. (1988a). *From Neuropsychology to Mental Structure*. Cambridge: Cambridge University Press.

—— (1988b). Information-processing models of consciousness: possibilities and problems. In Marcel and Bisiach (1988).

Shevrin, H. (1992). Subliminal perception, memory and consciousness: cognitive and dynamic perspectives. In Bornstein and Pittman (1992).

Shoemaker, S. (1975). Functionalism and qualia. *Philosophical Studies* 27:291–315.

—— (1981a) Absent qualia are impossible—a reply to Block. *The Philosophical Review* 90, 4:581–599.

—— (1981b). The inverted spectrum. *The Journal of Philosophy* 74, 7:357–381.

—— (1993). Lovely and suspect ideas. In *Philosophy and Phenomenological Research*. 3, 4:905–910.

—— (1994). Phenomenal Character, *Nous* 21–38.

Sperling, G. (1960). The information available in brief visual presentations. *Psychological Monographs* 74, 11.

Stich, S. (1978). Autonomous psychology and the belief-desire thesis. *The Monist* 61, 573–591.

Time-Life (1993). *Secrets of the Inner Mind: Journey Through the Mind and Body*. New York: Time-Life Books.

Tye, M. (1991). *The Imagery Debate*. MIT Press

—— (1993). Reflections on Dennett and consciousness. In *Philosophy and Phenomenological Research* 3, 4.

—— (1994). Blindsight, the absent qualia hypothesis and the mystery of consciousness. In *Philosophy and Cognitive Science*. C. Hookway and D. Peterson (eds), *Royal Institute of Philosophy Supplement*: 34. Cambridge: Cambridge University Press.

—— (1995). A representational theory of pains and their phenomenal character. In J. Tomberlin (ed), *Philosophical Perspectives* 9: Atascadero, CA: Ridgeview.

Umilta, C., and Moscovitch, M. (1994). *Attention and Performance XV*. Cambridge, MA: MIT Press

Van Gulick, R. (1989). What difference does consciousness make? *Philosophical Topics* 17, 1:211–230.

—— (1993). Understanding the phenomenal mind: are we all just armadillos? In Davies and Humphreys (1993a).

Weiskrantz, L. (1986). *Blindsight*. Oxford: Oxford University Press

—— (1988). Some contributions of neuropsychology of vision and memory to the problem of consciousness. In Marcel and Bisiach (1988).

—— (1992). Introduction: Dissociated issues. In B. Milner and M. Rugg (1992).

White, S. L. (1987) What is it like to be an homunculus. *Pacific Philosophical Quarterly* 68:148–174.

—— (1991). Transcendentalism and its discontents. In White, S. L. *The Unity of the Self*, Cambridge, MA: MIT Press.

Wiser, M. and Carey, S. (1983) When heat and temperature were one. In D. Gentner and A. Stevens (eds) *Mental Models*. Hillside, NJ: Erlbaum.

Young, A. W. (1994a). Covert recognition. In M. Farah and G. Ratcliff (eds) *The Neuropsychology of Higher Vision: Collected Tutorial Essays*. Hillside, NJ: Erlbaum.

—— (1994b). Neuropsychology of awareness. In M. Kappinen and A. Revonsuo (eds), *Consciousness in philosophy and cognitive neuroscience*. Hillside, NJ: Erlbaum.

—— (1994c). Recognition and reality. In E. M. R. Critchley (ed). *Neurological boundaries of Reality*: Farrand Press.

Young, A. W., and De Haan, E. (1993). Impairments of Visual Awareness. In Davies and Humphreys (1993a).

21 The Path Not Taken

Daniel C. Dennett

Block amply demonstrates that there is ubiquitous confusion among researchers about consciousness, and he is right to locate a major source of the confusion in the spectrum of differences he attempts to tame with his purported distinction between P-consciousness and A-consciousness. That distinction may start out seeming quite intuitive. Indeed, Block relies heavily on appeals to our intuitions to hold it in place until he can get it properly defined and defended, but once that effort gets underway, he runs into a swarm of difficulties from which there is apparently no escape. I for one found it difficult to keep track of the tangle of objections and counterobjections, exemptions, caveats and promissory notes, and will be interested to see if other commentators can find their way into, and back out of, the maze Block has created.

There is an alternative, much more direct path that Block ignores, perhaps because it is deeply counterintuitive at first blush: the varieties of consciousness he thinks he sees falling under P-consciousness and A-consciousness can all be accommodated under the two rough *quantitative* headings of *richness of content* and *degree of influence*. Some episodes of mental life have impoverished contents, whereas others are so rich in content—so full of information about the perceived world, for instance—that one has the sense that no practical description or catalog could do justice to them. The latter—and they are the normal, everyday episodes of consciousness—Block would declare to be instances of P-consciousness because they are, shall we say, *phenomenologically impressive*. The former, such as actual (as opposed to imaginary) cases of blindsight, have such vanishingly little content that subjects standardly deny that they are conscious of any content at all, though forced-choice guessing famously demonstrates that there was some content at work there after all, capable of influencing some choices, but unable to serve as the cue or prompt for rational action (Weiskrantz 1986). Can such simple differences of quantity, not quality, do justice to the variety of phenomena? Don't we need something altogether different—*qualia* (or their absence)—as well? I have said no, and have defended this claim at length (Dennett 1991), but it was apparently too drastic a stroke for some readers to accept—or in the case of Block, to be recognized as a serious alternative to be dealt with at all. Yet now Block has done my theory a fine service: nothing could make my admittedly counterintuitive starting point easier to swallow than Block's involuntary demonstration of the pitfalls one must encounter if one turns one's back on it and tries to take his purported distinction seriously.

The main trouble with Block's attempt to motivate two independent dividing lines (where I would put differences in degree) is that in the normal run of things, his two kinds of consciousness run together, as he himself acknowledges several times. He cannot provide clear examples of A-consciousness without P-consciousness or P-consciousness without A-consciousnesss, and although he claims that both are "conceptually possible," it is unclear what this comes to. Moreover, if these two sorts of consciousness are conceptually independent, as Block insists, then he is not entitled to several claims he makes about P-consciousness. Consider, for instance, his discussion of the phenomenon in which the solution to a difficult problem suddenly comes to you without conscious thought. He surmises that the "high-level reasoning processes" by which you solve such a problem are not P-conscious (in addition to not being A-conscious). How does he know this? How could he know this, or even deem this more probable than not? He notes—but is apparently not embarrassed by—a similar problem with his account of blindsight. "Note that the claim that P-consciousness is missing in blindsight is just an assumption. I decided to take the blindsight patient's word for his lack of P-consciousness of stimuli in the blind field" (sect. 6, para. 21). But taking the subject's word is using the best criterion for A-consciousness as one's sole evidence of P-consciousness. Block himself demonstrates thereby that the very idea of a sort of consciousness independent of access is incoherent.

Although Block discusses my theory of consciousness at some length, his discussion always leans on the presupposition that his putative distinction is in place. My theory of consciousness is stranded, he concludes, between being trivially false (if a theory of P-consciousness), nontrivially false (if a theory of "just" A-consciousness), and banal if a theory of "a highly sophisticated version of self-consciousness" (sect. 5, last para.). Because I not only decline to draw any such distinction but argue at length against any such distinction, Block's critique is simply question-begging. I may be wrong to deny the distinction, but this could not be shown by proclaiming the distinction, ignoring the grounds I have given for denying it, and then showing what a hash can be made of ideas I have expressed in other terms, with other presuppositions. If Block thinks his distinctions is too obvious to need further defense, he has missed the whole point of my radical alternative. This is a fundamental weakness in the strategy Block employs, and it vitiates his discoveries of "fallacies" in the thinking of other theorists as well. Those of us who are not impressed by his candidate distinction are free to run the implication in the other direction: since our reasoning is not fallacious after all, his distinction must be bogus.

What would a good test of the two different starting points be? Look at their treatment of a particular phenomenon—for example, blindsight—from a neutral point of view. In my own discussion of blindsight (Dennett 1991, pp. 332–43) I argued that if a patient could be trained to treat blindsight stimuli as self-cuing or prompting, this would amount to *restoring* the patient's consciousness of events in the scotoma, the only remaining difference between such experience and normal vision being the relative poverty of the content of what could be gleaned from the scotoma. Relative poverty of content—not "absence

of qualia" or lack of P-consciousness—was a non-optional hallmark of blindsight, I claimed. To drive the point home, I asked counterfactually, what we would conclude if we encountered someone who *claimed* to suffer from blindsight of a strange high-content variety—correctly "guessing" not just the words written on a page placed in the putative scotoma, for example, but their typeface and color, for instance. I claimed this would stretch our credulity beyond the limit; we would not and should not take somebody's word that they were "just guessing" in the absence of all consciousness (all P-consciousness, in Block's terms) in such a case. Block, interestingly, thinks otherwise. He does not refer to my discussion of blindsight, but coins the term "super-blindsight" to discuss much the same sort of imaginary case, and supposes without argument that in such a case we *would* credit the patient: "The superblindsighter himself contrasts what it is like to know visually about an X in his blind field and an X in his sighted field. There is something it is like to experience the latter, but not the former" (sect. 4.1, para. 5).

Now here we have a direct difference of implication between the two starting points—a useful point of contrast even if the cases are not likely to come up for empirical confirmation! But the issue is not yet joined if we imagine the case the way Block invites us to do, with the huge normal difference in richness of content between the sighted field and the scotoma or blind field. If our imaginary patient, like all actual blindsight patients yet studied, can identify the typeface, size, colors, and textures of the sighted-field X and its background, but can only identify that there is an X (as opposed to an O) in the blind field, this would be a large difference in richness of content that would account, on my view, for the patient's willingness to draw the sort of contrast Block imagines the superblindsighter to draw: it is "like something" to detect the X in the sighted field, and it isn't like anything to detect the X in the blind field.

For Block to put his claim about blindsight in direct competition with my alternative, he must control for richness of content, which I claim is the only other important variable; he must stipulate—in whichever way he chooses—that the richness in content is the same in both fields. The patient can tell us no more about the X in the sighted field than about the X in the blind field—either because the former is bizarrely impoverished or the latter is bizarrely rich. Take the latter case first: would you "take the subject's word," as Block says, that *it wasn't like anything at all* for him to come to know, swiftly and effortlessly, that there was a bright orange Times Roman italic X about two inches high, on a blue-green background, with a pale gray smudge on the upper right arm, almost touching the intersection? (That's a sample of the sort of richness of content normally to be gleaned from the sighted field, after all.) I for one would wonder what sort of lexical amnesia or madness had overcome anybody who could gather that much information from a glance and yet deny having any conscious visual experience. Alternatively, if all our imaginary patient can tell us about the X in the *sighted* field is that it was an X, not an O, I think most people would be baffled about what he could possibly mean by his insistence that nevertheless he had "P-consciousness" of the sighted field, but not of the blind field (in which he made the same discrimination).

Imaginary cases are of limited value in such theoretical explorations, but this time I think the flight of fancy nicely reveals how Block mislocates the issue. It is not that we others are "conflating" two sorts of consciousness; it is that he is inflating differences in degree into imaginary differences in kind.

References

Dennett, D. (1991). *Consciousness Explained.* Boston: Little Brown.

Weiskrantz, L. (1986). *Blindsight. Oxford*: Oxford University Press.

22 Availability: The Cognitive Basis of Experience?

David J. Chalmers

Block's distinction between access consciousness and phenomenal consciousness (or experience) is very useful. There is clearly a *conceptual* distinction here, as illustrated by the facts that: (1) one can imagine access without experience and vice versa; (2) access can be observed straightforwardly, whereas experience cannot; and, most important, (3) access consciousness seems clearly amenable to cognitive explanation, whereas phenomenal consciousness is quite perplexing in this regard. But the tight *empirical* link between the two phenomena deserves attention.

Bringing Access and Experience Closer Together

Block himself notes that P-consciousness and A-consciousness often occur together. This is no accident, as one can see by noting that a P-conscious experience is usually reportable, and that reportability implies accessibility of the corresponding information. Block does not think they always occur together, but I think that with appropriate modifications they might. One of the most interesting projects in this area is that of modifying the concept of A-consciousness in such a way as to make it plausible that A-consciousness (in the modified sense) and P-consciousness are perfect correlates.

A good start is the modified notion of *direct availability for global control*. That is, a content is A-conscious in the modified sense when it is directly available for use in directing a wide range of behaviors, especially deliberate behaviors. I am not sure how different this is from Block's definition: it plays down the role of rationality and reasoning (after all, impairments of rationality probably do not diminish phenomenal consciousness), it relegates verbal report to the status of a heuristic (as Block himself suggests), and there is another important difference that I will come to shortly. The restriction to *direct* availability

works to eliminate contents that can be retrieved with some work but that are not conscious.

To see how well this modified notion of A-consciousness correlates with P-consciousness, we need to see how it handles Block's examples in which one sort of consciousness occurs without the other. Block's examples of A-consciousness without P-consciousness are all mere conceptual possibilities (zombies and super blindsight, for example), so they are not relevant here, but to illustrate P-consciousness with A-consciousness he gives some real-world examples. One is Sperling's example in which all nine letters in a square array are experienced, but only three can be reported at a time. In this case, only three letter-representations are *accessed*, but it is nevertheless plausible that each of the nine was *available*, until the process of access destroyed their availability. This works because the modified notion of A-consciousness is dispositional—not access but accessibility is required. And it is plausible that all nine letter-representations are A-conscious in the modified sense. So even in this case, P-consciousness and modified A-consciousness occur together.

The case of the drilling noise in the background can be handled similarly. Here it seems reasonable to say that the information was directly available all along; it simply was not accessed. The case of experience under anesthesia (if this is actual) is trickier, but we might handle it by saying that in these cases the corresponding contents are *available* for global control; it is just that the control mechanisms themselves are mostly shut down. We might say that the information makes it to a location where it could have been used to direct behavior, had the motor cortex and other processes been functioning normally.

Other cases could be considered and further refinements could be made. A fuller account might flesh out the kind of availability required (perhaps a kind of high-bandwidth availability is required for experience, or at least for experience of any intensity) and might specify the relevant kind of control role more fully. Counterexamples are not threatening but helpful; they allow us to refine the definition further. The details can be left aside here; the point is that this project will lead to a functionally characterized property that might correlate perfectly with P-consciousness, at least in the cases with which we are familiar.

This property—something in the vicinity of direct availability for global control—could then be thought of as the information-processing correlate of P-consciousness, or as the cognitive basis of experience. There are some interesting consequences for the issues that Block discusses.

Empirical Work on Consciousness

Block notes that researchers on consciousness often start with an invocation of phenomenal consciousness but end up offering an explanation of A-consciousness and leaving P-consciousness to the side. The tight link between the two suggests that a somewhat more charitable interpretation is possible. If experience correlates with availability for global control, much of this work can be interpreted as seeking to *explain* A-consciousness, but trying to find a *basis* for P-consciousness. For example, Crick and Koch's (1990) oscillations are put forward because of a potential role in binding and working memory; that is, in integrating contents and making them available for control (working memory is itself an availability system, after all). If both the empirical hypothesis (oscillations subserve availability) and the bridging principle (availability goes along with experience) are correct, then the oscillations are a neural correlate of experience, which is just what Crick and Koch claim.

The same holds elsewhere. Shallice's "selector inputs" for "action systems" (1972) and his "Supervisory System" (1988a; 1988b) are clearly supposed to play a central role in availability and

control; if the empirical hypothesis is correct, these could reasonably be regarded as part of the basis for conscious experience. Similarly, the "global workspace" of Baars (1988), the "high-quality representations" of Farah (1994), the "temporally-extended neural activity" of Libet (1993), and many other proposals can be all be seen as offering mechanisms in the process whereby some contents are made available for global control. The common element is striking. Of course, it is an empirical question which of these proposals is correct (more than one might be, if they offer accounts of different parts of the process or descriptions at different levels). But insofar as these mechanisms play a role in the availability/control process, they are candidates to be neural or cognitive correlates of experience, which is often what the authors suggest (correlation is all that Farah and Libet claim; Shallice and Baars oscillate between "correspondence" and explanation).

The picture is this: (1) we know that availability goes along with experience; (2) we empirically discover that some mechanism plays the central role in the availability process. We may then conclude that the mechanism is part of the explanation of A-consciousness and part of the basis of P-consciousness. Of course, the story about the mechanism does not alone *explain* P-consciousness, as we still have not explained why availability always goes along with experience; we have simply taken for granted that it does. But if we are prepared to take the link between availability and experience as a kind of background assumption (perhaps for later explanation), this can provide a useful partial explanation of the contents of experience.

A Phenomenal Consciousness Module?

Interestingly, this analysis allows us to make some sense of the idea of a phenomenal consciousness module. *If* it turns out that there is a single system responsible for mediating the availability of certain contents for global control—something like Baars's global workspace or Shallice's supervisory system—then it might be plausible that the contents of that system correspond precisely to the contents of experience, and maybe we could call it a P-consciousness module. I do not think it is probable that there is such a module—more likely there are many different mechanisms by which contents become available for a control role—but at least the idea makes sense. But the *only* way there could be a "P-consciousness" module would be for it to be an availability/control module. If a module were dissociable from the relevant role in availability and control, the considerations above suggest that it would be dissociable from P-consciousness too.

In particular, there is something very strange about the idea of an "epiphenomenal" P-consciousness module (Block's figure 20.3). The main motivation for epiphenomenalism is surely that experience seems superfluous to any information processing; but Block's idea suggests an implausible epiphenomenalism *within* the information-processing story. Indeed, if the module has no effect on other processes, then we could lesion it with no external change (same reports, even), and no empirical evidence could support the hypothesis. Perhaps Block means to allow that the module has the very limited function of causing phenomenal reports, so that lesioning it eliminates remarks such as "I am having a blue sensation." But now either (1) remarks such as "There is a blue object," confident blue-directed behavior, and so on are all eliminated too—in which case the module had an important function after all—or (2) they are preserved (a kind of ultra-super-blindsight), implying an extraordinary independence between the pathways responsible for phenomenal report and those responsible for visual descriptions and normal visual processing. Given the remarkable coherence between visual descriptions and reports of visual experience, one presumes that they are tied more closely than this.

The Function of Consciousness?

The link between P-consciousness and (modified) A-consciousness makes the search for a function for P-consciousness even more hopeless. Given the correlation, *any* purported function for P-consciousness can be attributed to A-consciousness instead.

Only those who implausibly identify the *concept* of P-consciousness with that of (modified) A-consciousness have a way out. If one accepts the conceptual distinction, one will accept the conceivability of zombie functional isomorphs (made of silicon, say). To be consistent, one must then accept the conceivability of zombie *physical* isomorphs, as there is no more of a conceptual entailment from neural stuff to consciousness than there is from silicon stuff. From here, it is easy to see that P-consciousness gives me no functional advantage. After all, I am different from my zombie twin *only* in that I have P-consciousness and he does not, but we are functionally identical.

Block suggests that P-consciousness might "grease the wheels" of A-consciousness, but this cannot work. P-consciousness is redundant to the explanation of the physical mechanisms of A-consciousness, as the conceivability of the zombie shows: same physical mechanisms, same explanation of A-consciousness, no P-consciousness. The remaining option is to "identify" P-consciousness with modified A-consciousness (empirically but not conceptually), solving the problem by fiat. I think this sort of identification without explanation misunderstands the way that scientific identification works (see Chalmers 1996), but in any case it still leaves the concept of P-consciousness with no *explanatory* role in cognitive functioning. The independent concept of A-consciousness does all the work. I think it best to accept instead that phenomenal consciousness is distinct from any physical or functional property, and that it does not need to have a function to be central to our mental lives.

References

Baars, B. J. 1988. *A Cognitive Theory of Consciousness*. Cambridge: Cambridge University Press.

Chalmers, D. J. (1996). *The Conscious Mind: In Search of a Fundamental Theory*. New York: Oxford University Press.

Crick, F., and Koch, C. (1990). Towards a neurobiological theory of consciousness. *Seminars in the Neurosciences* 2:263–275.

Farah, M. J. 1994. Visual perception and visual awareness after brain damage: A tutorial overview. In C. Umilta and M. Moscovitch, eds., *Consciousness and Unconscious Information Processing: Attention and Performance 15*. Boston: MIT Press.

Libet, B. (1993). The neural time factor in conscious and unconscious events. In G. R. Bock and J. Marsh, eds., *Experimental and Theoretical Studies of Consciousness*, Ciba Foundation Symposium 174. Chichester: John Wiley and Sons.

Shallice, T. 1972. Dual Functions of Consciousness. *Psychological Review, 79*, 383–393.

Shallice, T. 1988a. *From Neuropsychology to Mental Structure*. Cambridge: Cambridge University Press.

Shallice, T. 1988b. Information-processing models of consciousness: Possibilities and problems. In A. Marcel and E. Bisiach, eds., *Consciousness in Contemporary Science*. Oxford: Oxford University Press.

23 Fallacies or Analyses?

Jennifer Church

Ned Block accuses several writers of a fallacy—the fallacy of equivocation. According to him, from premises about what is true of consciousness in one sense of the term, conclusions about an entirely different sense of consciousness are drawn. The two senses of consciousness at issue are "access-consciousness," understood as a state's "availability for use in reasoning and rationally guiding speech and action," and "phenomenal consciousness," understood as the "experiential" aspect of a state.

To demonstrate that a fallacy is committed, Block needs to convince us of two things: first, that there are indeed two separate concepts at issue, and second, that the shift from claims that employ one concept to claims that employ the other is not justified—as it might be, for example, by an argument to the effect that the two separate concepts actually pick out the same property. I am not sure that he has done either.

As Block himself reminds us, the concept of a "phenomenal" property is notoriously elusive, but he refuses to be embarrassed by this fact. Even those who suspect the concept of incoherence can, he claims, recognize that it is a *different* concept from that of "accessibility to reasoning, etc...." I am not sure what it means to judge that an incoherent concept (as opposed to each of its incompatible constituents) is different from some other concept; Block relies on examples (real and imaginary) to demonstrate the distinction, but it is doubtful that those who suspect incoherence can be persuaded in this way, since an incoherent concept, by definition, can have no referent. Most of the writers in question, however, seem to think that talk of phenomenal properties is merely a loose or imprecise way of talking about what is more carefully rendered in terms of various access relations. While I agree with Block in thinking that the shift from one way of talking to the other often occurs with very little by way of justification, I remain unconvinced that there is a conflation of two distinct senses of consciousness.

As I see it, the reasons for thinking that the concept of a "phenomenal" property is incoherent actually overlap with the reasons for thinking that the concept of phenomenal-consciousness and the concept of access-consciousness are indeed the same concept. To those of us with Kantian sympathies, anyway, it seems that a state cannot have a phenomenal property (or, equally, that it cannot count as an "experience", and there cannot be "something it is like" to be in that state), unless it is a certain way *for*, or *to* a subject. Which is to say, for a state to have a phenomenal property it must stand in a particular relation to the subject of that state. But, assuming that we have done away with the Cartesian idea of an insubstantial or homuncular self, a state can stand in some relation to the subject in that state only if it stands in some relation(s) to various *other* states of that subject. So if one insists, as most advocates of phenomenal properties do, that a state such as the state of pain has the phenomenal character that it does regardless of its relations with other states of the subject, one encounters a contradiction: the phenomenal properties of a state must be properties had in virtue of some relation between the state and a subject, yet they cannot be relational properties because they are supposed to be intrinsic to the states which have them. If, on the other hand, one accepts that phenomenal properties are relational properties, it seems plausible to suppose that the relevant relations are some sort of access relations—relations connecting the state to reasoning and to rational action, for example—since these are just the sort of connections that shape an organism into a subject. If these are not the access relations that constitute a subject, presumably some other access relations (memory access, for example) are, and it is these others that will be necessary for consciousness.

As I said, Block depends on examples to demonstrate the independence of phenomenal-consciousness and access-consciousness. But in addition to underestimating the problems posed by the charge of incoherence vis-à-vis phenomenal consciousness, he seems to underestimate the resources available to those who think phenomenal-consciousness *is* access-consciousness. Consider the example of a noise that I suddenly realize I have been hearing for the last hour. Block uses it to show that, prior to my realization, there is phenomenal-consciousness without access-consciousness—thus that the two types of consciousness are distinct. But the access*ibility* (i.e., the access *potential*) of the hearing experience is evident from the fact that I do eventually access it. Further, it seems that I *would* have accessed it sooner had it been a matter of greater importance—and thus, in a still stronger sense, it was accessible all along. Finally, it is not even clear that it was not *actually* accessed all along insofar as it rationally guided my behavior in causing me to speak louder, or move closer, and so forth. (Similar moves seem plausible in several of the other cases cited.)

Accessibility, like its close cousin verifiability, is a notoriously accommodating notion. For this reason among others, I am partial to analyses that emphasize actual rather than potential access—especially access by second-order thoughts, or what Block calls "reflective consciousness." But that is another story.

I have noted some reasons to wonder whether the concept of phenomenal-consciousness, if it is coherent, is really a different concept from that of access-consciousness. Even if one grants the distinction, however, one could maintain that they refer to the same property—just as the concept of water and the concept of H_2O may be thought to refer to the same property. Once one accepts such an identity, there will be no fallacy in supposing that what is true of access-consciousness must be true of phenomenal-consciousness as well—just as there is no fallacy in supposing that what is true of H_2O must be true of water as well. There are,

of course, complicated and controversial metaphysical debates (concerning the nature of properties, essences, and identity, to name a few) that have a bearing on this line of reasoning; and, like Block, I find that the reasoning of the cited writers is often unclear. If one is prepared to treat consciousness as a natural kind, however, then the fact that, in real life, phenomenal-consciousness and access-consciousness seem always to occur together may be treated as strong evidence in favor of the hypothesis that they are indeed one and the same thing.

At the end of his chapter, Block briefly entertains this possibility, remarking that phenomenal-consciousness and access-consciousness may "amount to much the same thing empirically even though they differ conceptually." He acknowledges that his imagined case of "super-blindsight" (where there is complete access-consciousness but no phenomenal-consciousness) never actually occurs, yet goes on to suggest the existence of real cases (such as Sperling's letter display experiment) where phenomenal-consciousness and access-consciousness do part company. Again, though, in my opinion he overestimates the power of examples because he underestimates both the need to defend the concept of phenomenal-consciousness against charges of incoherence, and the potential for endless accommodation by the concept of access-consciousness.

Tyler Burge

I want to develop some ideas about consciousness that derive from reflection on a distinction between phenomenal consciousness and access consciousness drawn by Ned Block.[1] I accept a version of such a distinction, and I think that Block's drawing it is a significant contribution. But I believe that Block has not drawn it quite right. I will maintain three primary points. First, access consciousness—indeed, any sort of consciousness—in an individual presupposes the existence of phenomenal consciousness in that individual. Second, the relevant notion of access consciousness is not captured by the idea of a state's being poised for use in rational activity, even if it is assumed that the individual is phenomenally conscious. The relations between access consciousness and phenomenal consciousness need detailed exploration. But access conscious states, and even events, need not themselves be phenomenally conscious. Third, although phenomenal qualities are individuated in terms of what it is like to feel or be conscious of them, one may have phenomenal states or events with phenomenal qualities that one is unconscious of. Thus, phenomenal qualities themselves do not guarantee phenomenal consciousness. To be phenomenally conscious, phenomenal states, or their phenomenal qualities, must be sensed or felt by the individual subject.

Block explicates phenomenally conscious states and properties as experiential states and properties. He says that the totality of experiential properties of a state are "what it is like" to have it. He notes that we have phenomenally conscious states when we exercise our senses or have pains. More generally, phenomenally conscious properties are said to be the "experiential" properties of sensations, feelings, perceptions, thoughts, wants, and emotions.[2] I do not believe that "experiential" coincides with "phenomenally conscious," but I will not press the point here. Ordinary pain and other sensations provide paradigms for phenomenally conscious states. And Block's use of the notions of sensed phenomenality or felt quality, and of "what it is like" to have a state, elicits recognition of a type of consciousness that is broadly familiar.

I will assume that phenomenal properties are distinct from intentional properties (in roughly Brentano's [1874] sense) and from functional properties. Moreover, by virtue of being phenomenal, a property is not necessarily either intentional or functional. I assume that there not only can be but are phenomenal properties that are not intentional. At least they need not indicate anything beyond themselves. These assumptions are not universally accepted. I state them here to clarify my discussion.

Some intentional states and events—some thoughts, for example—seem to have phenomenal states or properties as an essential aspect of their content. Thus, associated with the intentional content of typical perceptual judgments is a phenomenal element that is part of, or at least necessary to, the content—inseparable from the way of thinking, or mode of presentation, of the perceived entities. A normal visual judgment about a visually presented red surface would have a different content—or would be a different visual judgment—if the phenomenal aspect associated with the judgment were relevantly different (though the different visual judgment might still represent a red surface). Since I think that phenomenal consciousness is essential to individuating phenomenal properties, phenomenal consciousness seems to play a role in type individuating certain intentional contents—hence certain intentional states and events.

It is a multifaceted question whether phenomenal aspects of intentional content could have had, or could have been associated with, different intentional content. In many cases, the answer to this question is affirmative. One can imagine that the causal antecedents and cognitive use of given phenomenal aspects could have been different in such a way as to make for different intentional content. For example, it seems to me that the tactile feeling of cold—an essential element of the content of some tactile judgments about cold surfaces—could, in a different environment (perhaps with different neural wiring associating the sensations with different action, and with different conceptual training), have played a part in representing warmth in surfaces or any of various other physical properties. In such a case the phenomenal aspects of the tactile feeling would be the same, even though it is no longer a feeling of cold. This is one ground for distinguishing between phenomenal and intentional aspects of experience. At least in those perceptual judgments whose content involves phenomenal elements that make reference to entities in the environment of the thinker, there is always the possibility of some degree of referential flexibility for the phenomenal elements. In other cases, such flexibility is absent. Phenomenal elements surely have some sort of primacy in sensorily based thoughts about those very elements. Whether there are restrictions on the degree of representational flexibility in various other cases is an interesting question, which I leave open.

I believe that the notion of phenomenal consciousness is the core notion of consciousness. Any being that is not phenomenally conscious is not conscious in any sense. There are no zombies that lack phenomenal consciousness but are conscious in some further way. I will return to this point.

Block distinguishes phenomenal consciousness from access consciousness. He writes that a state is access conscious "if, in virtue of one's having the state, a representation of its content is ... poised to be used as a premise in reasoning, poised for *rational* control of action and poised for rational control of speech." He adds that the last condition is not necessary for access consciousness, despite its centrality for practical purposes.[3]

I will use the term "rational-access consciousness" for the sort of consciousness that I think Block is on to but does not correctly characterize.

I will begin with some points of agreement. Rational-access conscious states and events— paradigmatically thoughts—are necessarily intentional. Most such states refer or purport to refer to things beyond themselves. Phenomenally conscious states do not, as such, necessarily or essentially involve purported intentional relations to objects of reference beyond themselves. Rational-access consciousness is a consciousness of things through or by means of "conscious" thoughts, perceptions, and concepts.

Rational-access consciousness is not the same as phenomenal consciousness. One can have rational-access consciousness with respect to intentional states or events that lack any phenomenological types as essential elements. Conscious mathematical beliefs or thoughts are commonly examples. Rational-access consciousness is not simply phenomenal consciousness within content elements of certain intentional states or events. Further, rational-access consciousness of an intentional event need not have any essentially phenomenal aspects. As will emerge, I think that one can have rational-access consciousness with respect to an event but lack any phenomenal consciousness of that event.

Moreover, I think that one can have phenomenal consciousness of a given state but lack rational-access consciousness of it, as Block emphasizes. If one "sees stars" in a drunken stupor but cannot reason with or about that state, the images might be phenomenally conscious, but thoughts with or about such a state might be unconscious in the sense that they are not rationally accessible.

I hold with Block that access to central rational powers and rational activity of an individual is a necessary condition for a kind of consciousness having to do with rational access. But I believe, contrary to Block, that poised accessibility to central rational activity is not a sufficient condition for any sort of consciousness. No matter how accessible and no matter how poised for use in reasoning, rational control of action, or rational control of speech a thought may be, it can still fail to be conscious in every way. As noted, I think that a phenomenal zombie, no matter how freely rational, is not conscious in any sense.

A being that lacks phenomenal consciousness altogether could not be conscious in any way. It would not, for example, have imageless conscious thought. Phenomenal consciousness need not be part of a thought or of its articulation in order for the thought to be rational-access conscious. But there must be some phenomenal consciousness—some sensed or imaged what-it-is-like quality—in the individual for a thought to count as conscious in any sense. The individual may close his or her eyes and think imageless thoughts with a surround of subliminal, phenomenally conscious blackness. Or the individual might have some sort of super blindsight but have some other sensations or a capacity to articulate thoughts through phenomenal verbalizations. But lacking some such frame of phenomenal consciousness, one's thinking could not be conscious in any way. A phenomenal zombie has no consciousness—no matter how efficiently rational its behavior, verbalizations, and reasoning. I do not know how to defend this view. I do not know why it is true. But despite a literature replete with assumptions to the contrary, I find it compelling. I think that the view is a reflection of the fact that phenomenal consciousness is the core notion.

Thus, potential use is not the same as consciousness. If there is a distinctive sort of consciousness having to do with rational access, as I think there is, being poised for use in rational activity is not a sufficient condition for it, only a necessary condition. It is an empirical question, not a matter of conceptual analysis, whether intentional states or events that are poised for rational use are always, or in individual cases, conscious in any way.

Perhaps in a phenomenally conscious individual, being poised for use in central rational activity, and being poised for being brought into rational-access occurrently conscious thought, suffice for standing states, such as beliefs, to have, in one sense, rational-access consciousness. They are conscious proleptically, through their accessibility to being made occurrently conscious. But accessibility to use in central rational activity—even in a phenomenally conscious individual—does not suffice for an intentional event to be rational-access conscious.

Some of the nonphenomenal mental events that enter into our highest practical and theoretical reasoning, and that are as poised as possible for free interaction with other rationally controlled mental states and events, are not in fact conscious in any way. I may be imaging a rainy night in Salisbury while thinking about philosophy. I could bring the philosophical thoughts to consciousness at any moment, and they may be fully available to all other rational activity. But they could be unconscious—with my being unconscious in those moments of all the philosophical points my mind is working on—until I bring them to consciousness.

These are empirical suppositions. What seems clear is a more modest point: the supposition that thoughts might be freely accessible, even in a being that meets the general condition of being phenomenally conscious, but not be in the sort of actual occurrent relation that entails conscious thought is conceptually coherent. Accessibility is one thing; actual occurrent consciousness (of any kind) is another.

Thus, what makes rational-access conscious states and events conscious is not primarily their representational aspects nor their accessibility to rational activity. Similarly, I do not accept the view that rational-access consciousness is a functional notion. I am inclined to believe that no notion of consciousness is a fully functional notion. This is not so much a firmly held theoretical view as a conjectural inference from the intuitive failures of the various functionalist attempts to account for anything I mean by "consciousness."

I cannot pretend to have a clear reflective understanding of my notion of rational-access consciousness. But I will hazard some remarks that I hope will prove constructive. I will focus mainly on the rational-access consciousness of intentional events, such as thoughts or judgments. I have already indicated that I accept two necessary conditions. First, to be rational-access conscious, a state or event must be poised for use in the central rational operations of an individual (animal or person). Second, rational-access consciousness must maintain at least a general connection to phenomenal consciousness in the individual. I do not, however, believe that to be rational-access conscious, a state or event must be phenomenally conscious. The connection between the two kinds of consciousness is loose, though phenomenal consciousness often seems to be a factor in the consciousness of rational-access conscious events.

Because it seems to me that we phenomenally conscious beings might have unconscious thought that is fully rationally accessible (cf. the Salisbury example), I do not think that the two necessary conditions I have articulated are sufficient for rational-access consciousness. I do not have a full account. Instead of trying for one, I will canvass some examples of conscious thoughts. (I do not claim that any of these cases represents necessary conditions, though I assume they meet sufficient conditions, given that the two necessary conditions are satisfied.)

Thoughts type-individuated partly in terms of phenomenal elements, at least when these elements are phenomenally conscious, form one subclass of rational-access conscious thoughts. When such thoughts meet the condition of being accessible to the central rational activity of an individual, they are rational-access conscious. A visual judgment, or occurrent visual belief, that involves a sensation of a red surface will be rational-access conscious, assuming that the sensation is phenomenally conscious and that the rational-accessibility condition is met.

Verbally articulated thoughts also normally count as rational-access conscious, again assuming the necessary access condition is met. The relevant notion of articulation will often involve phenomenal consciousness again. Certainly when the symbols are verbalized through visual, auditory, or tactile symbol images that are phenomenally conscious, the thought expressed by the symbols is conscious. There are, of course, different theories about the relations between the symbols and the thought contents. On my view, the symbols are not usually identifiable with the content, nor are they normally essential elements of the content. They merely express something that is more abstract. In my view in such cases, no essential element of the thoughts or thought contents need be phenomenally conscious for the thoughts to be rational-access conscious. Yet the fact that the symbols that express the content are tokened by phenomenally conscious states seems sufficient to make the thoughts expressed by the symbols conscious (assuming as always that the general rational-accessibility condition is met).

Sometimes we seem to use shorthand in silent thought, with some phenomenal representation of a symbol standing for a whole thought (where we could articulate the thought immediately if called upon). Such thoughts seem to be typically rational-access conscious.

To be rational-access conscious through verbalization, a thought need not be phenomenally articulated or abbreviated. Often we verbalize our thoughts unreflectively and immediately in a public manner, without any prior phenomenally conscious inner articulation. Lacking special obstructions, articulated thoughts of this sort seem, given rational accessibility, to count as rational-access conscious, even if they briefly precede the articulation in time.

I think there are rational-access conscious thoughts that are neither symbolically articulated nor involve phenomenally conscious states as content-essential elements. These may be what used to be called "imageless thoughts." They bear perhaps the loosest relation to phenomenal consciousness. As I have indicated, some of our imageless unarticulated thoughts seem rationally accessible but not conscious in any sense (cf. the Salisbury example). What would make such thoughts rational-access conscious?

When one is aware of the occurrence of thoughts as they occur, and the thoughts have immediate accessibility to rational operations, then imageless unarticulated thoughts seem to count as rational-access conscious. (One may lack a conscious thought of their content.) The notion of awareness of the occurrence of thoughts obviously calls for further comment. It is not merely the occurrence of a higher-order thought; such higher-order thoughts might still be unconscious. But the relevant awareness of the occurrence of one's thoughts seems not always to involve phenomenal consciousness. I think that there are nonphenomenal sorts of conscious awareness of one's mental activity. For example, when one gets a solution to a problem, one may be consciously aware of the event of one's getting it, yet lack any phenomenal marker for the thought or (so far) any articulation of the solution. One "just knows" one has a conclusion.

I do not think that one must be aware of the occurrence of a thought in order for it to be rational-access conscious. One might be phenomenally conscious of some marker of the subject matter and then go on thinking, in an appropriately controlled, guiding way, without making further use of such individual elements of consciousness or event awareness. Or the nonphenomenal awareness may attach to the general process of thinking, involving some general guiding by the individual of the stages of the process, without awareness of particular occurrences within the process. I do not know how to provide a satisfying generalization. Clearly these matters are in need of further exploration and articulation.

Whether there are further major types of rational-access consciousness, whether I have correctly characterized conscious imageless thought (as far as that characterization goes), and what further necessary conditions apply to rational-access consciousness seem thoroughly open questions. What is clear is that rational-access consciousness cannot count as a type of consciousness unless there is more to it than being poised for rational operations, even if these occur within a frame of phenomenal consciousness. Often this "something more" derives from some specific connection between the thought and some element of phenomenal consciousness. I have suggested that this is not always so.

Some of the interest of the notion of rational-access consciousness is that it is connected to the notions of rationality and agency. Availability to the central executive powers of a higher animal or person is surely connected to what it is to be an individual agent—and, with the right associated abilities, to what it is to be a person. It seems correct and insightful of Block to have separated this type of consciousness, associated with access to higher-order cognitive abilities, from the ontogenetically more basic type of consciousness associated with phenomenal field and feel.

Let me return now to phenomenal consciousness. Phenomenal consciousness seems to play a role in typing some kinds of mental states and events, whereas rational-access consciousness does not. A given belief, and perhaps a given token thought event, could go into and out of rational-access consciousness and remain the same state or event. Further, whether an intentional state or event bears an access relation to central rational powers does not seem essential to being what it is, at least in most cases. But phenomenal consciousness is fundamental to typing phenomenal properties, and phenomenal properties are fundamental to typing phenomenal mental states and events. The way a pain feels is essential or basic to what pain, and what a pain, is. The same is true with other sensations and feelings. I think nothing could be a pain, a token event of pain, and lack the what-it-is-likeness or characteristic feel or phenomenal properties that individuate pain. As I have noted, phenomenal properties also seem to be part of the type individuation of certain thoughts, for example, certain perceptual judgments, whose content seems necessarily associated with phenomenal states.

It would be easy to infer from this point that phenomenal states and events must be phenomenally conscious at every moment of their existence, but I do not think that this is so. It seems to me that phenomenal states can be phenomenally unconscious. Pains that are not felt at all because of some distraction or other obstruction are sometimes examples. They may remain pains even though they are not felt, not conscious for the individual, at some times.

What it is like to feel pain, pain's phenomenal quality, is essential to the type and token individuation of pains. A pain essentially has phenomenal qualities at every moment. But pains and other sensations can be phenomenally unconscious—not actually felt by their possessor—at a given time. I distinguish what-it-is-likeness (phenomenality) from what it is occurrently like for the individual (phenomenal consciousness). Phenomenality is individuated, necessarily, in terms of how such a state actually feels to individuals. But states with phenomenal qualities need not be felt at all times by an individual who has them.

Of course, one must distinguish subliminal unattended-to conscious feeling from lack of all feeling, or unconsciousness. If a pain is not felt at all at some time by the individual who has it, it is not conscious for the individual at that time. And the idea of a pain that is conscious but not conscious for any individual seems incoherent. Some individual subject (however rudimentary the individual's cognitive or sensory capacities) must be associated with a conscious state.[4]

It would be a mistake to respond to these points by claiming that putative cases of unconscious phenomenal states are always cases of phenomenally conscious events that are rational-access unconscious. An unfelt pain is not the same as a felt pain that is not accessible to rational operations. I have endorsed the idea that a subject might sense sensations but be unable to access them for rational operations. These would be cases of phenomenal consciousness without rational-access consciousness. But it also seems possible that there are sensations that are temporarily not felt or sensed by the individual—sensations that have no phenomenal consciousness for the individual. This is not a lack of rational access, and it is not a lack of higher-order thought or belief. It is a lack of sensing or feeling or imaging by the individual. Such sensations might or might not be accessible (by other means than being phenomenally conscious with respect to them) to central rational operations. There seems no conceptual reason that a phenomenal event could not be unfelt (hence phenomenally unconscious), even while it remained fully accessible to rational operations, by some other means.

Unfelt sensations remain sensations (phenomenal states) because there is a way that it is like to feel them, and they are individuated in terms of their qualitative features; and because they meet empirical criteria of sensibility and sensation continuity. In most cases, the onset of a pain feels different from the bringing to consciousness of a pain that has been unconscious. And there are rough criteria for when a pain remains the same even when it comes into or goes out of consciousness. Some of these criteria are commonsensical; some may result from further empirical discovery.

For those who do not believe that phenomenal states necessarily have representational properties, there is a further reason for not assimilating unconscious phenomenal states to conscious phenomenal states that are rational-access unconscious. Sensations that are not representational are trivially noncandidates for being rational-access conscious. I think that those sensations too could be either (phenomenally) conscious or unconscious for certain periods of time. In those cases one cannot match the difference with a difference between the sensations' being phenomenally conscious and rational-access unconscious. Nor does it seem that putative cases of unconscious phenomenal states are always cases of unattended-to phenomenally conscious states. One could attend to phenomenally unconscious states (by other means than feeling them) and fail to attend to states that are still phenomenally though subliminally conscious.

Phenomenal states, with phenomenal qualities, may be unconscious through more than mere lack of attention (though distraction can be one source of their lack of consciousness). It seems to me empirically possible and certainly conceptually possible that the cases involving hypnosis for suppressing pain and those involving epileptics who have "blanked out" but succeed in driving a car may turn out to be cases in which limited use is made of information that is phenomenally registered but unavailable to both phenomenal and rational-access consciousness. It may be that there is no feeling of a pain (a pain that is nevertheless present) for the hypnotic. There may be no way that it is actually and occurrently like for the epileptic to drive the car. Perhaps what enables the epileptic to operate is the phenomenally registered information (which has phenomenal what-it-is-like qualities that are simply not actually felt by the individual), operating through limited unconscious mental and sensory-motor procedures. But the phenomenal states and the information might be in no sense conscious. In these cases, it would not be mere distraction of attention, or lack of rational access, that accounts for the individual's failure to feel or be conscious with respect to the phenomenal states. Again, what is important for my purposes is not whether these empirical conjectures are correct but that the distinctions mark conceptual possibilities.

Unfelt pains or other sensations must be susceptible to phenomenal consciousness, if attentional or other obstructions to consciousness were removed. And what it is like for one to feel them, to be conscious with respect to them, is part of what individuates them as pains or other sensations. But to be a sensation or other state with phenomenal qualities does not entail that it is phenomenally conscious at every moment.

The mere fact that a token of a kind of state or event can go unconscious and remain the same token does not show that consciousness does not help to type-individuate that kind of thing. It is an interesting and difficult question to explain these issues of individuation in more depth and detail.

Distinguishing phenomenal consciousness and rational-access consciousness is important to understanding how different types or aspects of consciousness feature in the fundamental notions of mentality, agency, and personhood. Such understanding will be deepened when it is liberated from ideological and programmatic preoccupations with materialism and functionalism that have dominated the revival of philosophical interest in consciousness.

Notes

1. Ned Block, chapter 20, this volume.

2. Ibid.

3. Ibid.

4. I am tempted by the idea that phenomenal consciousness is at bottom a transitive relation between a subject and a state or event. Although the phenomenal quality of phenomenally conscious states does not as such represent anything, there may be some relation of sensing or feeling (not of higher-order thought or belief) between the individual and the phenomenal state or event that is intrinsic to phenomenal consciousness. Similarly, phenomenal states, when conscious, may in some sense indicate themselves reflexively. They are sensed by way of themselves. I am aware that this "act-object picture" is objectionable to some philosophers. I am not committed to it except as a prima facie feature of surface grammar. But I think that surface grammar is often hard to rearrange convincingly for metaphysical purposes. As far as epistemology is concerned, I certainly do not maintain that sensations are the fundamental objects of perception, when, for example, we are perceiving physical objects by way of sensations.

Reference

Brentano, F. (1874). *Psychology from an Empirical Standpoint*. Original in German. Leipzig.

Robert Van Gulick

In part I of "Understanding the Phenomenal Mind: Are We All Just Armadillos?" (see chapter 35), I discussed two families of arguments designed to show that phenomenal consciousness poses a special difficulty for the materialist view of mind: the so-called Knowledge Argument and the Explanatory Gap Argument. I showed that neither in fact presents a significant obstacle to materialism. Here in part II I will examine a third family of arguments, those that appeal to the alleged possibility of absent qualia. Such arguments are typically directed against the functionalist thesis that mental states can be type-individuated on the basis of the causal functional relations they bear to each other and to the inputs and outputs of the relevant system. The standard and by now all too familiar absent qualia claim is that given *any* functionally specified organizational structure, it is always possible (at least in principle) to construct realizations of that structure which we have every reason to believe possess *no qualia*—realizations such as Ned Block's nation of China example in which the functional role of each state is filled by a distinct member of the population of China (Block 1980). It is claimed that the bizarre construction would realize the relevant functional organization, though it is absurd to believe that the *overall construction*, as opposed to its *individual personal parts*, actually has any qualia or phenomenal properties.

This line of argument has been much discussed and criticized, at times in subtle and successful ways (e.g., by Sidney Shoemaker 1975, 1981). But I wish to offer a not very subtle criticism—the argument is *question begging*. Consider how it might look on reconstruction.

A3   The Absent Qualia Argument

P1. Any functional model of mental organization will be capable of being realized by systems lacking qualia (or phenomenal properties). The Absent Qualia Claim.

P2. A model M of some feature of the world F explains F (or what F is) only if nothing could be a realization of M without being F.

Therefore

C3. Functionalism cannot explain (what) phenomenal mentality (is).

The reasoning is valid, but its premises are problematic. One might object to the claim of its second premise that nothing short of a logically or metaphysically sufficient condition counts as an adequate explanation. But the real problem is premise 1. How can the anti-functionalist know *a priori* that *any future* functionalist theory will allow for absent qualia realization? The absent qualia claim is made plausible only by construing functionalism as restricted to a highly abstract sort of *computationalism*, which requires of its realizations only that they mirror in the *temporal or causal order of their states* the sequence relations specified in the functional model. There is a widespread but mistaken belief that in constructing his model the functionalist cannot appeal to any relations among states other than that of *simple causation* (by which I mean causing, inhibiting, or contributing to the joint causation of). So construed it would seem that a realization by the population of China would always be possible; all we need to do is make sure that each person goes "on" and "off" in a way that mirrors the sequence of states in the model. But the functionalist need not and should not accept any such restriction on his theorizing; his job is to characterize the relations that hold among mental states, processes, and properties without regard for the austere constraints of purely computational relations or relations of simple causation.

Once such constraints are rejected, the absent qualia claim no longer seems obvious. What we need to determine is whether there are functional relations into which phenomenal states can enter but nonphenomenal states cannot. The burden of proof may lie with the functionalist to show that there are such relations by coming forward with a specific theory about the roles played by phenomenal states, but his attempts cannot be rendered dead before arrival by *a priori* appeals to inevitable absent qualia realizations.

The Functional Role of Phenomenal States—A First Attempt

One way to investigate this question is to consider the psychological roles played by phenomenal states in humans (Van Gulick 1989). Which of our human psychological abilities, if any, are dependent on our having conscious phenomenal experience? This way of asking the question has its limits. Even if it should be that certain psychological processes cannot operate *in humans* in the absence of experience, it would not follow that phenomenal experience is a necessary condition *in general* for those psychological processes or abilities. The "necessity" may be only a *contingent fact* about how those processes are *realized in us* and nothing more.

That said, let us consider a few abilities that seem *de facto* to require conscious phenomenal experience in humans. In a recent article Tony Marcel (1988) mentions at least four such abilities. Two concern respects in which human subjects suffer a total (or nearly total) loss of function as the result of losing some aspect of their capacity for phenomenal experience:

1. Loss of the ability to initiate actions with respect to parts of the world lost from conscious experience though still in some sense perceived (as in cases of blindsight with respect to objects located within the blind field of a hemianopic patient).

2. Loss of ability to form an integrated self-concept in amnesic patients as the result of losing the capacity for episodic memory (i.e., memory of past conscious experiences as such).

Two others concern less pathological limitations:

3. The inability to learn new nonhabitual tasks without conscious awareness of task instructions.

4. The inability to form plans of action without conscious thought.

One might ask, "What if anything do these various cases of dependency on phenomenal experience *have in common*? "A skeptical or deflationary answer would be that they share nothing in common, or nothing more than the brute fact that the particular human representation systems that underlie or subserve those abilities just happen *accidentally* to involve representations with phenomenal content. I think, we should resist such a deflationary strategy; at least we should not embrace it until we have made a thorough effort to find some psychologically interesting explanation of *why* the relevant abilities seem to require conscious phenomenal experience in humans.

In his discussion Marcel at least implicitly suggests that all four abilities require not merely consciousness but some form of *self-consciousness* since the mental states that figure in the relevant psychological processes are all *reflexive* and *metacognitive in content*. That is, all the relevant processes require awareness or knowledge about some aspect of one's own mental or psychological organization or activity.

Ability 4:   Both planning and control of plan execution require knowledge of one's goals and their relative priority, as well as knowledge of one's mental capacities and resources and the ability to monitor the ongoing operation of those resources in the course of execution. All of which, as Philip Johnson-Laird (1983, 1988) has argued, involves having a model of oneself.

Ability 2:   The lack of personal integration noted in amnesic patients could well result from the inability to construct and update such a self-model.

Ability 3:   The inability to acquire new nonhabitual task behaviors might be a result of the failure of the same systems involved in action planning.

Ability 1:   And even the fact that hemianopic patients do not initiate voluntary actions toward objects in the blind field might be explained on this basis as a deficit in the representation of the *world-in-relation-to-self* that is employed by the action planning system.

While I think there may be something interestingly right about this suggestion, I find it less than satisfying as an answer to the question of *why* the relevant abilities in humans all seem to require conscious phenomenal experience. The proposed explanation is that they all involve reflexive meta-cognition (or meta-psychological knowledge.) But left unanswered is the question of why such meta-cognition should require phenomenal awareness. Meta-cognitive awareness is a straightforwardly functional process, and one should be able to build such self-directed control and its associated iterative mental states into an organized system without having to give it anything like phenomenal awareness.

One could fall back on a *unitary version* of the *brute fact explanation* by arguing that all the relevant abilities involve higher order meta-cognition and its associated model of the self, and then claiming that it is *just a brute fact* that the self-model in humans involves phenomenal awareness. The final explanation would still terminate in a brute fact, but it would replace four independent brute fact terminations with one making it less *ad hoc*.

I am still inclined to hope for more. The account in terms of functionally defined self-monitoring and self-control offers both *too little* and *too much* to explain the role of phenomenal consciousness. *Too little* because it seems one could get the higher-order cognition without phenomenal experience, *too much* because it is doubtful that such sophisticated meta-cognitive processes are present in all the nonhuman animals which we believe to have some form of phenomenal consciousness (Nelkin 1993).

The Functional Role of Phenomenal States—A Second and more Speculative Attempt

We may gain some insight if we take a somewhat different perspective on the proposal to analzyze self-consciousness in terms of reflexive meta-cognition. Most accounts of meta-cognition postulate a set of explicit higher-order processes that are distinct from the lower-level cognitive processes they monitor and control. However, as I have argued elsewhere (Van Gulick 1988) meta-cognitive understanding can also be implicitly embodied in the very processes that operate on lower-level representations. In particular, a system can be said to possess information about (or understand) the intentional content of its own internal representations, insofar as its internal operations with respect to those representations are specifically adapted to their content.

In brief this involves two steps. First one gives a basically functionalist account of what it is to possess information (or understand) some fact in terms of having a capacity to specifically modify one's behavior in a way which adapts it to that fact, and then applies that general account of understanding to the special case of understanding facts about the intentional content of one's own internal system of representation (Van Gulick 1988).

If we expand our account of meta-cognition to cover such cases, we can introduce a notion which may help explain what is special about phenomenal representations. The notion is that of *semantic transparency* and concerns the extent to which a system can be said to understand the content of the internal symbols or representations on which it operates. The basic idea is that the greater the extent to which the system's use of a representation reflects an understanding of its content the more the representation can be said to be *semantically transparent* to the system. The relevant behavior by the system will consist in part of behaviors connecting the symbols with the outside world through input and output relations, but will also include behaviors relating symbols to each other in ways sensitive to their content. The important point is that the understanding is embedded in the organization of the system, that is, in how it is organized to relate symbols to its input, output, and each other.

Phenomenal representations, of the sort associated with normal conscious experience, involve a very high degree of semantic transparency. Indeed, they are so transparent that we typically "look" right through them. Our experience is the experience of a world of familiar objects—of desks, chairs, coffee cups, and beech trees. Moreover this transparency is to some extent an *immediately experienced feature of our conscious life*. On the whole when we have a conscious experience, we know what we are conscious of (though there are exceptions such as infants, persons newly sighted after a lifetime of congenital blindness, or patients suffering from visual agnosia). The phenomenal representations that are constructed or activated in conscious experience are normally transparent to us. We know what they represent in virtue of our capacity to instantaneously and effortlessly connect those representations with other semantically related representations.

My understanding that part of my visual field represents the presence of a telephone is in part a matter of my ability to rapidly connect that representation with a host of others concerning the structure, function, and use of a telephone. It is the awareness of these transitions among representations in the seemingly continuous flow of experience that provides the phenomenal or subjective experience of understanding, our conscious feeling that we know what we are thinking about.

A bit of care is needed here. I am not claiming that a system's being able to make such automatic and rapid transitions is in itself sufficient to guarantee that it has a subjective phenomenal life and that there is *something that it is like to be* that system. I am assuming that human beings have a subjective life and making the more modest claim that our *subjective experience of understanding* is

to be accounted for in terms of the connections and transitions that our underlying organization allows us to make within our experience.

We are now in a position to pose two last why questions, which are perhaps the most interesting and the most difficult, though I can at present supply only some sketchy and speculative suggestions in answer. The questions are these.

1. *Why* do phenomenal representations (normally) involve a high degree of semantic transparency? and

2. *Why* do we humans use representations with phenomenal properties to construct our self-model?

I suggest we take quite seriously the Kantian notion that our conscious phenomenal experience is the experience of a world—a world of objects. Conscious experience involves more than just being in states that represent or refer to objects and their properties. In some sense, which is hard to articulate, it involves there *being* a world of objects *inherent* in the representation. Or perhaps one should say it inherently involves an interdependent structure of conscious subject and world of objects set over against one another, since, as Kant taught us, the notions of subject and object are interdependent correlatives within the structrue of experience. One might say that conscious phenomenal experience involves the construction of a model of the would that in some sense itself *is a world*, but is so only from the subjective perspective of the self, which in turn exists only as a feature of the organization of experience. The problem is to give some account of the objectivity and concreteness of phenomenal objects, that is, to give some account of the fact that we *experience* them as concrete, independent, and objective.

How might trying to solve this problem help with our two questions?

With respect to our first question, the semantic transparency of phenomenal representation might be explained as a consequence of the fact that such representations are *of a world* in the strong sense we have been considering. Part of what makes a world a world in that sense is the density of relations and connections among the objects which are simultaneously the *constituents* of which that world is composed and also *constituted as* the objects that they are by their relations within that world. Put another way, the (experienced) objectivity of phenomenal objects consists in part of the enormous diversity of the perspectives from which they are accessible from within the representation. Any phenonenal object is delimited and defined within the representation in large part through the relations that it bears to other objects, which are in turn defined in part by the relations that they bear to it. It is in part the density of these interdefining relations that gives phenonemal objects their "thickness," their objectivity. The fact that the phenomemal representation of objects involves such dense and interdependent relations might help to account for its high degree of semantic transparency; any phenomenal representation of an object would of necessity also be a representation of its myriad relations within its world.

Solving our problem and explaining the sense in which conscious phenomenal representations are objective and *of a world* may also help to explain the importance and role of qualia such as colors. As we learned long ago from *The Critique of Pure Reason*, conscious experience requires the presence of an *intuition* in the Kantian sense of the term, that is, a *continuous sensuous manifold*, whether it be the spatial manifold of perception or the merely temporal manifold of inner sense. Without such a particular manifold there is no way in which objects can be present as particular things. Thus the "thing-liness" of phenomenal experience, the sense in which objects are present to us in experience as real and concrete requires that there be such an intuition or sensuous manifold within the structure of experience. Indeed in clinical cases in which there is a loss of part of the sensuous manifold, reports of patients indicate (directly, or indirectly by omission) that it is sub-

jectively as if a portion of *the world itself* has been lost. Consider this autobiographical comment by Oliver Sacks

I didn't care to tell Nurse Sulu that she was bisected and half of her was missing. And then suddenly with a most enormous and wonderful relief, I realized I was having one of my migraines. I had completely lost my visual field to the left, and with this as would sometimes happen, the sense that there was (or ever had been, or could be) any world on the left. (1984, p. 97)

Qualia might then be understood as properties by which regions of such manifolds are differentiated and by which objects as particulars are delimited and located within them.

We can thus begin to see a route by which qualia might be connected with semantic transparency via the fact that phenomenal representations are *of a world* in the strong sense we have been discussing. As we noted just above, part of what makes a representation *of a world* in the relevant sense is the density of relations among objects that it specifies. In particular, such a representation should specify in very great detail the spatio-temporal relations holding among arbitrary pairs of objects within the represented world, that is, it should carry a rich and easily accessed store of information about how any represented object is spatio-temporally related to other objects in the represented world, with perhaps some falling off of detail or precision as we move from an object's immediate neighbors to objects at a greater distance.

Sensuous manifolds provide a medium well suited for the representation of such rich and easily accessed spatio-temporal information. They have a continuous structure isomorphic to the spatio-temporal domains they are used to represent. Thus by using qualia to delimit regions of such manifolds as representing objects, it is possible to implicitly represent a large stock of information about the relative spatio-temporal relations of those objects.

Indeed, following a suggestion by the ethologist Konrad Lorenz (1973), it is plausible to suppose that the phenomenal representation of space appeared evolutionarily with the transition from organisms whose system of spatial representation was linked to the guidance of specific behavior patterns (such as taxes) to those with a general representation of space capable of being used to guide a wide range of behaviors in flexible and open-ended ways. Both ants and birds acquire and make use of spatial information. Insofar as the ability of ants to acquire and make use of spatial information is restricted to a fairly narrow range of stimulus/response mechanisms, there is little reason to think that they have a general and central representation of space; in contrast it is hard to imagine how birds could do without one.

What then have we shown with respect to our first question? I hope to have shown that insofar as the phenomenal mode of representation is *of a world* in the strong sense and involves a sensuous manifold of representation, it is particularly well suited for the construction of representations with a high degree of semantic transparency. I have not argued that phenomenal representation is either necessary or sufficient for a high degree of semantic transparency. It may be possible for active representational systems to achieve a high degree of semantic transparency using non-phenomenal representations; though phenomenal representations provide *one* design solution to the problem of achieving high semantic transparency, they need not be the *only* solution. And conversely, it seems possible for phenomenal representations to lack a high degree of semantic transparency as seems to be the case with the visual experiences of those with visual agnosia. Such agnosia appears to result from damage to the association cortex which prevents the establishment of a normal rich network of connections to representations in other modalities; the fact that the agnosic cannot connect the representations in his visual system with those in other systems leaves him in a state of not understanding his visual experiences. For him they become semantically opaque.

Consider in this regard the hypothesis offered by Baars (1988) that one of the functions of consciousness is to "broadcast" information throughout the nervous system and make that information widely available. Here again there are possibilities for explaining in a more than brute fact way *why* phenomenal representations play the functional roles they do. As we noted above part of the objectivity of phenomenal representation consists in the density and diversity of ways in which objects are represented. Objects within the phenomenal model are represented from many perspectives and in many different modalities which nonetheless harmonize and "agree." Conscious phenomenal awareness thus likely involves large-scale higher-order patterns of brain activity spanning many different sensory and representational modalities providing a very rich set of active associative links. Thus it becomes quite reasonable to think of conscious awarenss as identical with (or at least part of) the process by which information is broadcast. Because of their highly integrated and multimodal content, conscious phenomenal representations require rich associative networks of activation as their basis. Thus any type of brain activity able to serve as the neural substrate for phenomenal representations would seem of necessity also able to fulfill the function of "broadcasting information." Some recent hypotheses about the neurological substrate of consciousness (Flohr 1992) seem to support just such a link.

With respect to our second question let me make three very brief suggestions.

1. Phenomenal representation probably predates the advent of meta-cognitive self-models in evolutionary development. Since it has the high degree of semantic transparency that is desirable in constructing a self-model, it may have been "recruited" for that application.

2. We should not forget the Kantian point that the conscious self is implicitly represented in the structure of conscious experience. Thus con-

structing a model of the self of the sort used in meta-cognitive process is in part a matter of making *explicit* what is at least partly *implicit* in the phenomenal mode of representation.

3. Third is the fact that having a model of the self of the sort that is lost in amnesics seems to require the presence of an intuition in the Kantian sense, that is, a sensuous manifold, within which the self can be constructed or located as a self. It need not be a spatial intuition; for Kant it was merely temporal. But it seems that some sort of intuition is required, some structure with particularity, within which the isolated units of experience can be unified into the experiences of a single self. Again the phenomenal mode of representation satisfies the design requirement for the self-model. The intuition of continuous time associated with phenomenal experience provides the required intuition within which to carry out the construction of a unified self. For amnesics it is not merely the self that is truncated and compressed into the present moment; it is time itself that shrinks.

Conclusions

The absent qualia argument, like the arguments discussed earlier in part I, does not provide a necessarily insurmountable obstacle to functionalistic materialism. Only when we have developed adequate theories of the structure and organization of phenomenal consciousness will we be in a position to say without begging the question whether or not nonphenomenal representations (*absent qualia*) can play the same functional roles as phenomenal representations. The ultimate outcome of such theorizing remains an empirical question not open to *a priori* answer. As we saw above, there are reasonable prospects for articulating the structure of the phenomenal color space (part I), for linking semantic transparency with phenomenal objectivity, and for showing why phenomenal representations serve an information broadcasting role within the nervous system.

Thus there is at least some reason to think that future theorizing will banish absent qualia.

Notes

1. This chapter is the second half of "Understanding the phenomenal mind: Are we all just armadillos?" which was originally published in *Consciousness—A Mind and Language Reader*, edited by Martin Davies and Glynn Humphries, Oxford: Basil Blackwell, 1992. That paper was divided and slightly revised to form two independent parts at the request of the editors of this volume. An earlier version of the complete paper was presented at the conference on The Phenomenal Mind: How is it Possible? Why is it Necessary? held at the Center for Interdisciplinary Studies (ZIF), Bielefeld University, Bielefeld, Germany, May 1990. Part II is a revised version of material originally published in "What difference does Consciousness make?" (Van Gulick 1989). I am grateful to Martin Davies who encouraged me to include them in the Blackwell's volume and offered many acute criticisms from which I benefited in making revisions.

References

Block, Ned (1980) "Troubles with functionalism" in *Readings in the Philosophy of Psychology*, Vol. 1, N. Block (ed.) Harvard University Press, Cambridge, MA, 268–305.

Churchland, Paul (1985) "Reduction, qualia and the direct introspection of brain states," *Journal of Philosophy*, 2–28.

Flohr, Hans (1992) "Qualia and brain processes," in *Emergence or Reduction?* A. Beckermann, H. Flohr, and J. Kim (eds.), de Gruter, New York 220–38.

Hardin, C. L. (1988) *Color for Philosophers*, Hackett Publishers, Indianapolis, IN.

Jackson, Frank (1982) "Epiphenomenal qualia," *American Philosophical Quarterly*, 127–36.

Jackson, Frank (1986) "What Mary didn't know," *Journal of Philosophy*, 291–95.

Johnson-Laird, Philip (1983) *Mental Models*, Cambridge University Press, Cambridge.

Johnson-Laird, Philip (1988) "A computational analysis of consciousness" in *Consciousness in Contemporary*

Science, A. Marcel and E. Bisiach (eds.), Oxford University Press, Oxford, 357–68.

Levine, Joseph (1983) "Materialism and qualia: the explanatory gap," *Pacific Philosophical Quarterly*, 354–61.

Lewis, David (1983) "Postscript to 'Mad pain and martian pain'" in D. Lewis *Philosophical Papers*, Vol. 1, Oxford University Press, Oxford.

Lewis, David (1988) "What Experience Teaches, *Proceedings of the Russellian Society of the University of Sidney*, reprinted in *Mind and Cognition*, W. Lycan (ed.), Basil Blackwell Publishers, Oxford 1990, 499–519.

Loar, Brian (1990) "Phenomenal properties" in *Philosophical Perspectives*, Vol. 4, *Action Theory and Philosophy of Mind*, J. Tomberlin (ed.), Ridgeview Publishing, Atascadero, CA, 81–108.

Lorenz, Konrad (1973) *Behind the Mirror*, Harcourt Brace Jovanovich, New York.

Lycan, William (1990) "What is the subjectivity of the mental?" in *Philosophical Perspectives*, Vol. 4, *Action Theory and Philosophy of Mind*, J. Tomberlin (ed.), Ridgeview Publishing, Atascadero, CA, 109–30.

Marcel, Anthony (1988) "Phenomenal experience and functionalism" in *Consciousness in Contermporary Science*, A. Marcel and E. Bisiach (eds.), Oxford University Press, Oxford, 121–58.

McGinn, Colin (1989) "Can we solve the mind-body problem?," *Mind*, 349–66.

Nagel, Thomas (1974) "What is it like to be a bat?", *Philosophical Review*, 435–50.

Nelkin, Norton (1993) "The connection between intentionality and consciousness" in *Consciousness*, M. Davies and G. Humphreys (eds.), Basil Blackwell Publishers, Oxford, 224–39.

Nemirow, Lawrence (1980) Review of T. Nagel *Mortal Questions, Philosophical Review*, 475–76.

Nemirow, Lawrence (1990) "Physicalism and the cognitive role of acquaintance" in *Mind and Cognition*, W. Lycan (ed.), Basil Blackwell Publishers, Oxford, 490–99.

Tye, Michael (1986) "The subjectivity of experience," *Mind*, 1–17.

Sacks, Oliver (1984) *A Leg To Stand On*, Summit Books, New York.

Shoemaker, Sidney (1975) "Functionalism and qualia," *Philosophical Studies*, 291–315.

Shoemaker, Sidney (1981) "The inverted spectrum," *Journal of Philosophy*, 74, 357–81.

Shoemaker, Sidney (1981a) "Absent qualia are impossible—a reply to Block," *Philosophical Review*, 581–99.

Van Gulick, Robert (1985) "Physicalism and the subjectivity of the mental," *Philosophical Topics*, 51–70.

Van Gulick, Robert (1988a) "A functionalist plea for self-consciousness," *Philosophical Review*, 149–81.

Van Gulick, Robert (1988b) "Consciousness, intrinsic intentionality and self-understanding machines" in *Consciousness in Contemporary Science*, E. Bisiach and A. Marcel (eds.), Oxford University Press, Oxford, 78–100.

Van Gulick, Robert (1989) "What difference does consciousness make?," *Philosophical Topics*, 211–30.

VI METAPHYSICS OF CONSCIOUSNESS

26 The Identity Thesis

Saul A. Kripke

Identity theorists have been concerned with several distinct types of identifications: of a person with his body, of a particular sensation (or event or state of having the sensation) with a particular brain state (Jones's pain at 06:00 was his C-fiber stimulation at that time), and of *types* of mental states with the corresponding *types* of physical states (pain is the stimulation of C-fibers). Each of these, and other types of identifications in the literature, present analytical problems, rightly raised by Cartesian critics, which cannot be avoided by a simple appeal to an alleged confusion of synonymy with identity. I should mention that there is of course no obvious bar, at least (I say cautiously) none which should occur to any intelligent thinker on a first reflection just before bedtime, to advocacy of some identity theses while doubting or denying others. For example, some philosophers have accepted the identity of particular sensations with particular brain states while denying the possibility of identities between mental and physical *types*.[1] I will concern myself primarily with the type-type identities, and the philosophers in question will thus be immune to much of the discussion; but I will mention the other kinds of identities briefly.

Descartes, and others following him, argued that a person or mind is distinct from his body, since the mind could exist without the body. He might equally well have argued the same conclusion from the premise that the body could have existed without the mind.[2] Now the one response which I regard as plainly inadmissible is the response which cheerfully accepts the Cartesian premise while denying the Cartesian conclusion. Let "Descartes" be a name, or rigid designator, of a certain person, and let "*B*" be a rigid designator of his body. Then if Descartes were indeed identical to *B*, the supposed identity, being an identity between two rigid designators, would be necessary, and Descartes could not exist without *B* and *B* could not exist without Descartes. The case

is not at all comparable to the alleged analogue, the identity of the first Postmaster General with the inventor of bifocals. True, this identity obtains despite the fact that there could have been a first Postmaster General even though bifocals had never been invented. The reason is that "the inventor of bifocals" is not a rigid designator; a world in which no one invented bifocals is not *ipso facto* a world in which Franklin did not exist. The alleged analogy therefore collapses; a philosopher who wishes to refute the Cartesian conclusion must refute the Cartesian premise, and the latter task is not trivial.

Let "*A*" name a particular pain sensation, and let "*B*" name the corresponding brain state, or the brain state some identity theorist wishes to identify with *A*. *Prima facie*, it would seem that it is at least logically possible that *B* should have existed (Jones's brain could have been in exactly that state at the time in question) without Jones feeling any pain at all, and thus without the presence of *A*. Once again, the identity theorist cannot admit the possibility cheerfully and proceed from there; consistency, and the principle of the necessity of identities using rigid designators, disallows any such course. If *A* and *B* were identical, the identity would have to be necessary. The difficulty can hardly be evaded by arguing that although *B* could not exist without *A*, *being a pain* is merely a contingent property of *A*, and that therefore the presence of *B* without pain does not imply the presence of *B* without *A*. Can any case of essence be more obvious than the fact that *being a pain* is a necessary property of each pain? The identity theorist who wishes to adopt the strategy in question must even argue that *being a sensation* is a contingent property of *A*, for *prima facie* it would seem logically possible that *B* could exist without any sensation with which it might plausibly be identified. Consider a particular pain, or other sensation, that you once had. Do you find it at all plausible that *that very sensation* could have existed without being a sensation, the way a certain inventor (Franklin) could have existed without being an inventor?

I mention this strategy because it seems to me to be adopted by a large number of identity theorists. These theorists, believing as they do that the supposed identity of a brain state with the corresponding mental state is to be analyzed on the paradigm of the contingent identity of Benjamin Franklin with the inventor of bifocals, realize that just as his contingent activity made Benjamin Franklin into the inventor of bifocals, so some contingent property of the brain state must make it into a pain. Generally they wish this property to be one statable in physical or at least "topic-neutral" language, so that the materialist cannot be accused of positing irreducible non-physical properties. A typical view is that *being a pain*, as a property of a physical state, is to be analyzed in terms of the "causal role" of the state,[3] in terms of the characteristic stimuli (e.g., pinpricks) which cause it and the characteristic behavior it causes. I will not go into the details of such analyses, even though I usually find them faulty on specific grounds in addition to the general modal considerations I argue here. All I need to observe here is that the "causal role" of the physical state is regarded by the theorists in question as a contingent property of the state, and thus it is supposed to be a contingent property of the state that it is a mental state at all, let alone that it is something as specific as a pain. To repeat, this notion seems to me self-evidently absurd. It amounts to the view that the *very pain I now have* could have existed without being a mental state at all.

I have not discussed the converse problem, which is closer to the original Cartesian consideration—namely, that just as it seems that the brain state could have existed without any pain, so it seems that the pain could have existed without the corresponding brain state. Note that *being a brain state* is evidently an essential property of *B* (the brain state). Indeed, even more is true: not only being a brain state, but even being a brain state of a specific type is an essential property of

B. The configuration of brain cells whose presence at a given time constitutes the presence of *B* at that time is essential to *B*, and in its absence *B* would not have existed. Thus someone who wishes to claim that the brain state and the pain are identical must argue that the pain *A* could not have existed without a quite specific type of configuration of molecules. If *A* = *B*, then the identity of *A* with *B* is necessary, and any essential property of one must be an essential property of the other. Someone who wishes to maintain an identity thesis cannot simply *accept* the Cartesian intuitions that *A* can exist without *B*, that *B* can exist without *A*, that the correlative presence of anything with mental properties is merely contingent to *B*, and that the correlative presence of any specific physical properties is merely contingent to *A*. He must explain these intuitions away, showing how they are illusory. This task may not be impossible; we have seen above how some things which appear to be contingent turn out, on closer examination, to be necessary. The task, however, is obviously not child's play, and we shall see below how difficult it is.

The final kind of identity, the one which I said would get the closest attention, is the type-type sort of identity exemplified by the identification of pain with the stimulation of C-fibers. These identifications are supposed to be analogous with such scientific type-type identifications as the identity of heat with molecular motion, of water with hydrogen hydroxide, and the like. Let us consider, as an example, the analogy supposed to hold between the materialist identification and that of heat with molecular motion; both identifications identify two types of phenomena. The usual view holds that the identification of heat with molecular motion and of pain with the stimulation of C-fibers are both contingent. We have seen above that since "heat" and "molecular motion" are both rigid designators, the identification of the phenomena they name is necessary. What about "pain" and "C-fiber stimulation?" It should be clear from the previous discussion that "pain" is a rigid designator of the type, or phenomenon, it designates: if something is a pain it is essentially so, and it seems absurd to suppose that pain could have been some phenomenon other than the one it is. The same holds for the term "C-fiber stimulation," provided that "C-fibers" is a rigid designator, as I will suppose here. (The supposition is somewhat risky, since I know virtually nothing about C-fibers, except that the stimulation of them is said to be correlated with pain.[4] The point is unimportant; if "C-fibers" is not a rigid designator, simply replace it by one which is, or suppose it used as a rigid designator in the present context.) Thus the identity of pain with the stimulation of C-fibers, if true, must be *necessary*.

So far the analogy between the identification of heat with molecular motion and pain with the stimulation of C-fibers has not failed; it has merely turned out to be the opposite of what is usually thought—both, if true, must be necessary. This means that the identity theorist is committed to the view that there could not be a C-fiber stimulation which was not a pain nor a pain which was not a C-fiber stimulation. These consequences are certainly surprising and counterintuitive, but let us not dismiss the identity theorist too quickly. Can he perhaps show that the apparent possibility of pain not having turned out to be C-fiber stimulation, or of there being an instance of one of the phenomena which is not an instance of the other, is an illusion of the same sort as the illusion that water might not have been hydrogen hydroxide, or that heat might not have been molecular motion? If so, he will have rebutted the Cartesian, not, as in the conventional analysis, by accepting his premise while exposing the fallacy of his argument, but rather by the reverse—while the Cartesian argument, given its premise of the contingency of the identification, is granted to yield its conclusion, the premise is to be exposed as superficially plausible but false.

Now I do not think it likely that the identity theorist will succeed in such an endeavor. I want to argue that, at least, the case cannot be interpreted as analogous to that of scientific identification of the usual sort, as exemplified by the

identity of heat and molecular motion. What was the strategy used above to handle the apparent contingency of certain cases of the necessary *a posteriori*? The strategy was to argue that although the statement itself is necessary, someone could, *qualitatively* speaking, be in the same epistemic situation as the original, and in such a situation a *qualitatively* analogous statement could be false. In the case of identities between two rigid designators, the strategy can be approximated by a simpler one: Consider how the references of the designators are determined; if these coincide only contingently, it is this fact which gives the original statement its illusion of contingency. In the case of heat and molecular motion, the way these two paradigms work out is simple. When someone says, inaccurately, that heat might have turned out not to be molecular motion, what is true in what he says is that someone could have sensed a phenomenon in the same way we sense heat, that is, feels it by means of its production of the sensation we call "the sensation of heat" (call it "*S*"), even though that phenomenon was not molecular motion. He means, additionally, that the planet might have been inhabited by creatures who did not get *S* when they were in the presence of molecular motion, though perhaps getting it in the presence of something else. Such creatures would be, in some qualitative sense, in the same epistemic situation as we are; they could use a rigid designator for the phenomenon that causes sensation *S* in them (the rigid designator could even be "heat"), yet it would not be molecular motion (and therefore not heat!), which was causing the sensation.

Now can something be said analogously to explain away the feeling that the identity of pain and the stimulation of C-fibers, if it is a scientific discovery, could have turned out otherwise? I do not see that such an analogy is possible. In the case of the apparent possibility that molecular motion might have existed in the absence of heat, what seemed really possible is that molecular motion should have existed without being *felt as heat*, that is, it might have existed without producing the sensation S, the sensation of heat. In the appropriate sentient beings is it analogously possible that a stimulation of C-fibers should have existed without being felt as pain? If this is possible, then the stimulation of C-fibers can itself exist without pain, since for it to exist without being *felt as pain* is for it to exist without there *being any* pain. Such a situation would be in flat-out contradiction with the supposed necessary identity of pain and the corresponding physical state, and the analogue holds for any physical state which might be identified with a corresponding mental state. The trouble is that the identity theorist does not hold that the physical state merely *produces* the mental state, rather he wishes the two to be identical and thus *a fortiori* necessarily co-occurrent. In the case of molecular motion and heat there is something, namely, the sensation of heat, which is an intermediary between the external phenomenon and the observer. In the mental-physical case no such intermediary is possible, since here the physical phenomenon is supposed to be identical with the internal phenomenon itself. Someone can be in the same epistemic situation as he would be if there were heat, even in the absence of heat, simply by feeling the sensation of heat; and even in the presence of heat, he can have the same evidence as he would have in the absence of heat simply by lacking the sensation S. No such possibility exists in the case of pain and other mental phenomena. To be in the same epistemic situation that would obtain if one had a pain *is* to have a pain; to be in the same epistemic situation that would obtain in the absence of a pain *is* not to have a pain. The apparent contingency of the connection between the physical state and the corresponding brain state thus cannot be explained by some sort of qualitative analogue as in the case of heat.

We have just analyzed the situation in terms of the notion of a qualitatively identical episetemic situation. The trouble is that the notion of an epistemic situation qualitatively identical to one in which the observer had a sensation S simply *is* one in which the observer had that sensation. The

same point can be made in terms of the notion of what picks out the reference of a rigid designator. In the case of the identity of heat with molecular motion the important consideration was that although "heat" is a rigid designator, the reference of that designator was determined by an accidental property of the referent, namely the property of producing in us the sensation S. It is thus possible that a phenomenon should have been rigidly designated in the same way as a phenomenon of heat, with its reference also picked out by means of the sensation S, without that phenomenon being heat and therefore without its being molecular motion. Pain, on the other hand, is not picked out by one of its accidental properties; rather it is picked out by the property of being pain itself, by its immediate phenomenological quality. Thus pain, unlike heat, is not only rigidly designated by "pain" but the reference of the designator is determined by an essential property of the referent. Thus it is not possible to say that although pain is necessarily identical with a certain physical state, a certain phenomenon can be picked out in the same way we pick out pain without being correlated with that physical state. If any phenomenon is picked out in exactly the same way that we pick out pain, then that phenomenon *is* pain.

Perhaps the same point can be made more vivid without such specific reference to the technical apparatus in these lectures. Suppose we imagine God creating the world; what does He need to do to make the identity of heat and molecular motion obtain? Here it would seem that all He needs to do is to create the heat, that is, the molecular motion itself. If the air molecules on this earth are sufficiently agitated, if there is a burning fire, then the earth will be hot even if there are no observers to see it. God created light (and thus created streams of photons, according to present scientific doctrine) before He created human and animal observers; and the same presumably holds for heat. How then does it appear to us that the identity of molecular motion with heat is a substantive scientific fact, that the mere creation of molecular motion still leaves God with the additional task of making molecular motion into heat? This feeling is indeed illusory, but what *is* a substantive task for the Deity is the task of making molecular motion felt as heat. To do this He must create some sentient beings to insure that the molecular motion produces the sensation S in them. Only after he has done this will there be beings who can learn that the sentence "Heat is the motion of molecules" expresses an *a posteriori* truth in precisely the same way that we do.

What about the case of the stimulation of C-fibers? To create this phenomenon, it would seem that God need only create beings with C-fibers capable of the appropriate type of physical stimulation; whether the beings are conscious or not is irrelevant here. It would seem, though, that to make the C-fiber stimulation correspond to pain, or be felt as pain, God must do something in addition to the mere creation of the C-fiber stimulation; He must let the creatures feel the C-fiber stimulation as *pain*, and not as a tickle, or as warmth, or as nothing, as apparently would also have been within His powers. If these things in fact are within His powers, the relation between the pain God creates and the stimulation of C-fibers cannot be identity. For if so, the stimulation could exist without the pain; and since "pain" and "C-fiber stimulation" are rigid, this fact implies that the relation between the two phenomena is not that of identity. God had to do some work, in addition to making the man himself, to make a certain man be the inventor of bifocals; the man could well exist without inventing any such thing. The same cannot be said for pain; if the phenomenon exists at all, no further work should be required to make it into pain.

In sum, the correspondence between a brain state and a mental state seems to have a certain obvious element of contingency. We have seen that identity is not a relation which can hold contingently between objects. Therefore, if the identity thesis were correct, the element of contingency would not lie in the relation between the mental and physical states. It cannot lie, as in the case of heat and molecular motion, in the relation between the phenomenon (heat = molecular motion) and the way it is felt or appears (sensation S), since in the case of mental phenomena there is no "appearance" beyond the mental phenomenon itself.

Here I have been emphasizing the possibility, or apparent possibility, of a physical state without the corresponding mental state. The reverse possibility, the mental state (pain) without the physical state (C-fiber stimulation), also presents problems for the identity theorists which cannot be resolved by appeal to the analogy of heat and molecular motion.

I have discussed similar problems more briefly for views equating the self with the body, and particular mental events with particular physical events, without discussing possible countermoves in the same detail as in the type-type case. Suffice it to say that I suspect that the considerations given indicate that the theorist who wishes to identify various particular mental and physical events will have to face problems fairly similar to those of the type-type theorist; he too will be unable to appeal to the standard alleged analogues.

That the usual moves and analogies are not available to solve the problems of the identity theorist is, of course, no proof that no moves are available. I certainly cannot discuss all the possibilities here. I suspect, however, that the present considerations tell heavily against the usual forms of materialism. Materialism, I think, must hold that a physical description of the world is a *complete* description of it, that any mental facts are "ontologically dependent" on physical facts in the straightforward sense of following from them by necessity. No identity theorist seems to me to have made a convincing argument against the intuitive view that this is not the case.[5]

Notes

1. Thomas Nagel and Donald Davidson are notable examples. Their views are very interesting, and I wish I could discuss them in further detail. It is doubtful that

such philosophers wish to call themselves "materialists." Davidson, in particular, bases his case for his version of the identity theory on the supposed *impossibility* of correlating psychological properties with physical ones.

The argument against token-token identification and the text *does* apply to these views.

2. Of course, the body *does* exist without the mind, and presumably without the person, when the body is a corpse. This consideration, if accepted, would already show that a person and his body are distinct. (See David Wiggins, "On Being at the Same Place at the Same Time," *Philosophical Review*, Vol. 77 (1968), pp. 90–5.) Similarly, it can be argued that a statue is not the hunk of matter of which it is composed. In the latter case, however, one might say instead that the former is "nothing over and above" the latter; and the same device might be tried for the relation of the person and the body. The difficulties in the text would not then arise in the same form, but analogous difficulties would appear. A theory that a person is nothing over and above his body in the way that a statue is nothing over and above the matter of which it is composed, would have to hold that (necessarily) a person exists if and only if his body exists and has a certain additional physical organization. Such a thesis would be subject to modal difficulties similar to those besetting the ordinary identity thesis, and the same would apply to suggested analogues replacing the identification of mental states with physical states. A further discussion of this matter must be left for another place. Another view which I will not discuss, although I have little tendency to accept it and am not even certain that it has been set out with genuine clarity, is the so-called functional state view of psychological concepts.

3. For example, David Armstrong, *A Materialist Theory of the Mind*, London and New York, 1968; see the discussion review by Thomas Nagel, *Philosophical Review* 79 (1970), pp. 394–403; and David Lewis, "An Argument for the Identity Theory," *The Journal of Philosophy*, pp. 17–25.

4. I have been surprised to find that at least one able listener took my use of such terms as "correlated with," "corresponding to," and the like as already begging the question against the identity thesis. The identity thesis, so he said, is not the thesis that pains and brain states are correlated, but rather that they are identical. Thus my entire discussion presupposes the anti-materialist position that I set out to prove. Although I was surprised to hear an objection which concedes so little intelligence to the argument, I have tried especially to avoid the term "correlated' which seems to give rise to the objection. Nevertheless, to obviate misunderstanding, I shall explain my usage. Assuming, at least *arguendo*, that scientific discoveries have turned out so as not to refute materialism from the beginning, both the dualist and the identity theorist agree that there is a correlation or correspondence between mental states and physical states. The dualist holds that the "correlation" relation in question is irreflexive; the identity theorist holds that it is simply a special case of the identity relation. Such terms as "correlation" and "correspondence" can be used neutrally without prejudging which side is correct.

5. Having expressed these doubts about the identity theory in the text, I should emphasize two things: first, identity theorists have presented positive arguments for their view, which I certainly have not answered here. Some of these arguments seem to me to be weak or based on ideological prejudices, but others strike me as highly compelling arguments which I am at present unable to answer convincingly. Second, rejection of the identity thesis does not imply acceptance of Cartesian dualism. In fact, my view above that a person could not have come from a different sperm and egg from the ones from which he actually originated implicitly suggests a rejection of the Cartesian picture. If we had a clear idea of the soul or the mind as an independent, susbsistent, spiritual entity, why should it have to have any necessary connection with particular material objects such as a particular sperm or a particular egg? A convinced dualist may think that my views on sperms and eggs beg the question against Descartes. I would tend to argue the other way; the fact that it is hard to imagine me coming from a sperm and egg different from my actual origins seems to me to indicate that we have no such clear conception of a soul or self. In any event, Descartes' notion seems to have been rendered dubious ever since Hume's critique of the notion of a Cartesian self. I regard the mind-body problem as wide open and extremely confusing.

Reductionism and the Irreducibility of Consciousness

John R. Searle

The view of the relation between mind and body that I have been putting forward is sometimes called "reductionist," sometimes "antireductionist." It is often called "emergentism," and is generally regarded as a form of "supervenience." I am not sure that any one of these attributions is at all clear, but a number of issues surround these mysterious terms, and in this chapter I will explore some of them.

Emergent Properties

Suppose we have a system, S, made up of elements $a, b, c \ldots$ For example, S might be a stone and the elements might be molecules. In general, there will be features of S that are not, or not necessarily, features of $a, b, c \ldots$ For example, S might weigh ten pounds, but the molecules individually do not weigh ten pounds. Let us call such features "system features." The shape and the weight of the stone are system features. Some system features can be deduced or figured out or calculated from the features of $a, b, c \ldots$ just from the way these are composed and arranged (and sometimes from their relations to the rest of the environment). Examples of these would be shape, weight, and velocity. But some other system features cannot be figured out just from the composition of the elements and environmental relations; they have to be explained in terms of the causal interactions among the elements. Let's call these "causally emergent system features." Solidity, liquidity, and transparency are examples of causally emergent system features.

On these definitions, consciousness is a causally emergent property of systems. It is an emergent feature of certain systems of neurons in the same way that solidity and liquidity are emergent features of systems of molecules. The existence of consciousness can be explained by the causal interactions between elements of the brain at the micro level, but consciousness cannot itself be deduced or calculated from the sheer physical structure of the neurons without some additional account of the causal relations between them.

This conception of causal emergence, call it "emergent1," has to be distinguished from a much more adventurous conception, call it "emergent2." A feature F is emergent2 iff F is emergent1 and F has causal powers that cannot be explained by the causal interactions of $a, b, c \ldots$ If consciousness were emergent2, then consciousness could cause things that could not be explained by the causal behavior of the neurons. The naive idea here is that consciousness gets squirted out by the behavior of the neurons in the brain, but once it has been squirted out, it then has a life of its own.

... On my view consciousness is emergent1, but not emergent2. In fact, I cannot think of anything that is emergent2, and it seems unlikely that we will be able to find any features that are emergent2, because the existence of any such features would seem to violate even the weakest principle of the transitivity of causation.

Reductionism

Most discussions of reductionism are extremely confusing. Reductionism as an ideal seems to have been a feature of positivist philosophy of science, a philosophy now in many respects discredited. However, discussions of reductionism still survive, and the basic intuition that underlies the concept of reductionism seems to be the idea that certain things might be shown to be *nothing but* certain other sorts of things. Reductionism, then, leads to a peculiar form of the identity relation that we might as well call the "nothing-but" relation: in general, A's can be reduced to B's, iff A's are nothing but B's.

However, even within the nothing-but relation, people mean so many different things by the notion of "reduction" that we need to begin by making several distinctions. At the very outset it is important to be clear about what the relata of the relation are. What is its domain supposed to be: objects, properties, theories, or what? I find at least five different senses of "reduction"—or perhaps I should say five different kinds of reduction—in the theoretical literature, and I want to mention each of them so that we can see which are relevant to our discussion of the mind-body problem.

1. *Ontological reduction.* The most important form of reduction is ontological reduction. It is the form in which objects of certain types can be shown to consist in nothing but objects of other types. For example, chairs are shown to be nothing but collections of molecules. This form is clearly important in the history of science. For example, material objects in general can be shown to be nothing but collections of molecules, genes can be shown to consist in nothing but DNA molecules. It seems to me this form of reduction is what the other forms are aiming at.

2. *Property ontological reduction.* This is a form of ontological reduction, but it concerns properties. For example, heat (of a gas) is nothing but the mean kinetic energy of molecule movements. Property reducitons for properties corresponding to theoretical terms, such as "heat," "light," etc., are often a result of theoretical reductions.

3. *Theoretical reduction.* Theoretical reductions are the favorite of theorists in the literature, but they seem to me rather rare in the actual practice of science, and it is perhaps not surprising that the same half dozen examples are given over and over in the standard textbooks. From the point of view of scientific explanation, theoretical reductions are mostly interesting if they enable us to carry out ontological reductions. In any case, theoretical reduction is primarily a relation between theories, where the laws of the reduced theory can (more or less) be deduced from the laws of the reducing theory. This demonstrates that the re-duced theory is nothing but a special case of the reducing theory. The classical example that is usually given in textbooks is the reduction of the gas laws to the laws of statistical thermodynamics.

4. *Logical or definitional reduction.* This form of reduction used to be a great favorite among philosophers, but in recent decades it has fallen out of fashion. It is a relation between words and sentences, where words and sentences referring to one type of entity can be translated without any residue into those referring to another type of entity. For example, sentences about the average plumber in Berkeley are reducible to sentences about specific individual plumbers in Berkeley; sentences about numbers, according to one theory, can be translated into, and hence are reducible to, sentences about sets. Since the words and sentences are *logically* or *definitionally* reducible, the corresponding entities referred to by the words and sentences are *ontologically* reducible. For example, numbers are nothing but sets of sets.

5. *Causal reduction.* This is a relation between any two types of things that can have causal powers, where the existence and a fortiori the causal powers of the reduced entity are shown to be entirely explainable in terms of the causal powers of the reducing phenomena. Thus, for example, some objects are solid and this has causal consequences: solid objects are impenetrable by other objects, they are resistant to pressure, etc. But these causal powers can be causally explained by the causal powers of vibratory movements of molecules in lattice structures.

Now when the views I have urged are accused of being reductionist—or sometimes insufficiently reductionist—which of these various senses do the accusers have in mind? I think that theoretical reduction and logical reduction are not intended. Apparently the question is whether the causal reductionism of my view leads—or fails to lead—to ontological reduction. I hold a view of mind/

brain relations that is a form of causal reduction, as I have defined the notion: Mental features are caused by neurobiological processes. Does this imply ontological reduction?

In general in the history of science, successful causal reductions tend to lead to ontological reductions. Because where we have a successful causal reduction, we simply redefine the expression that denotes the reduced phenomena in such a way that the phenomena in question can now be identified with their causes. Thus, for example, color terms were once (tacitly) defined in terms of the subjective experience of color perceivers; for example, "red" was defined ostensively by pointing to examples, and then real red was defined as whatever seemed red to "normal" observers under "normal" conditions. But once we have a causal reduction of color phenomena to light reflectances, then, according to many thinkers, it becomes possible to redefine color expressions in terms of light reflectances. We thus carve off and eliminate the subjective experience of color from the "real" color. Real color has undergone a property ontological reduction to light reflectances. Similar remarks could be made about the reduction of heat to molecular motion, the reduction of solidity to molecular movements in lattice structures, and the reduction of sound to air waves. In each case, the causal reduction leads naturally to an ontological reduction by way of a redefinition of the expression that names the reduced phenomenon. Thus, to continue with the example of "red," once we know that the color experiences are caused by a certain sort of photon emission, we then redefine the word in terms of the specific features of the photon emission. "Red," according to some theorists, now refers to photon emissions of 600 nanometers. It thus follows trivially that the color red is nothing but photon emissions of 600 nanometers.

The general principle in such cases appears to be this: Once a property is seen to be *emergent1*, we automatically get a causal reduction, and that leads to an ontological reduction, by redefinition if necessary. The general trend in ontological reductions that have a scientific basis is toward greater generality, objectivity, and redefinition in terms of underlying causation.

So far so good. But now we come to an apparently shocking asymmetry. When we come to consciousness, we cannot perform the ontological reduction. Consciousness is a causally emergent property of the behavior of neurons, and so consciousness is causally reducible to the brain processes. But—and this is what seems so shocking—a perfect science of the brain would still not lead to an ontological reduction of consciousness in the way that our present science can reduce heat, solidity, color, or sound. It seems to many people whose opinions I respect that the irreducibility of consciousness is a primary reason why the mind-body problem continues to seem so intractable. Dualists treat the irreducibility of consciousness as incontrovertible proof of the truth of dualism. Materialists insist that consciousness must be reducible to material reality, and that the price of denying the reducibility of consciousness would be the abandonment of our overall scientific world view.

I will briefly discuss two questions: First, I want to show why consciousness is irreducible, and second, I want to show why it does not make any difference at all to our scientific world view that it should be irreducible. It does not force us to property dualism or anything of the sort. It is a trivial consequence of certain more general phenomena.

Why Consciousness Is an Irreducible Feature of Physical Reality

There is a standard argument to show that consciousness is not reducible in the way that heat, etc., are. In different ways the argument occurs in the work of Thomas Nagel (1974), Saul Kripke (1971), and Frank Jackson (1982). I think the argument is decisive, though it is frequently misunderstood in ways that treat it as merely epistemic and not ontological. It is sometimes treated as an epistemic argument to the effect that, for example, the sort of third-person, objective knowledge we might possibly have of a bat's neurophysiology would still not include the first-person, subjective experience of what it feels like to be a bat. But for our present purposes, the point of the argument is ontological and not epistemic. It is a point about what real features exist in the world and not, except derivatively, about how we know about those features.

Here is how it goes: Consider what facts in the world make it the case that you are now in a certain conscious state such as pain. What fact in the world corresponds to your true statement, "I am now in pain"? Naively, there seem to be at least two sorts of facts. First and most important, there is the fact that you are now having certain unpleasant conscious sensations, and you are experiencing these sensations from your subjective, first-person point of view. It is these sensations that are constitutive of your present pain. But the pain is also caused by certain underlying neurophysiological processes consisting in large part of patterns of neuron firing in your thalamus and other regions of your brain. Now suppose we tried to reduce the subjective, conscious, first-person sensation of pain to the objective, third-person patterns of neuron firings. Suppose we tried to say the pain is really "nothing but" the patterns of neuron firings. Well, if we tried such an ontological reduction, the essential features of the pain would be left out. No description of the third-person, objective, physiological facts would convey the subjective, first-person character of the pain, simply because the first-person features are different from the third-person features. Nagel states this point by contrasting the objectivity of the third-person features with the what-it-is-like features of the subjective states of consciousness. Jackson states the same point by calling attention to the fact that someone who had a complete knowledge of the neurophysiology of a mental phenomenon such as pain would still not know what a pain was if he or she did not know

what it felt like. Kripke makes the same point when he says that pains could not be identical with neurophysiological states such as neuron firings in the thalamus and elsewhere, because any such identity would have to be necessary, because both sides of the identity statement are rigid designators, and yet we know that the identity could not be necessary. This fact has obvious epistemic consequences: my knowledge that I am in pain has a different sort of basis than my knowledge that you are in pain. But the antireductionist point of the argument is ontological and not epistemic.

So much for the antireductionist argument. It is ludicrously simple and quite decisive. An enormous amount of ink has been shed trying to answer it, but the answers are all so much wasted ink. But to many people it seems that such an argument paints us into a corner. To them it seems that if we accept that argument, we have abandoned our scientific world view and adopted property dualism. Indeed, they would ask, what is property dualism but the view that there are irreducible mental properties? In fact, doesn't Nagel accept property dualism and Jackson reject physicalism precisely because of this argument? And what is the point of scientific reductionism if it stops at the very door of the mind? So I now turn to the main point of this discussion.

Why the Irreducibility of Consciousness Has No Deep Consequences

To understand fully why consciousness is irreducible, we have to consider in a little more detail the pattern of reduction that we found for perceivable properties such as heat, sound, color, solidity, liquidity, etc., and we have to show how the attempt to reduce consciousness differs from the other cases. In every case the ontological reduction was based on a prior causal reduction. We discovered that a surface feature of a phenomenon was caused by the behavior of the elements of an underlying microstructure. This is true both in the cases in which the reduced phenomenon was a matter of subjective appearances, such as the "secondary qualities" of heat or color; and in the cases of the "primary qualities" such as solidity, in which there was both an element of subjective appearance (solid things feel solid), and also many features independent of subjective appearances (solid things, e.g., are resistant to pressure and impenetrable by other solid objects). But in each case, for both the primary and secondary qualities, the point of the reduction was to carve off the surface features and redefine the original notion in terms of the causes that produce those surface features.

Thus, where the surface feature is a subjective appearance, we redefine the original notion in such a way as to exclude the appearance from its definition. For example, pretheoretically our notion of heat has something to do with perceived temperatures: Other things being equal, hot is what feels hot to us, cold is what feels cold. Similarly with colors: Red is what looks red to normal observers under normal conditions. But when we have a theory of what causes these and other phenomena, we discover that it is molecular movements causing sensations of heat and cold (as well as other phenomena such as increases in pressure), and light reflectances causing visual experiences of certain sorts (as well as other phenomena such as movements of light meters). We then *redefine* heat and color in terms of the underlying causes of both the subjective experiences and the other surface phenomena. And in the redefinition we eliminate any reference to the subjective appearances and other surface effects of the underlying causes. "Real" heat is now defined in terms of the kinetic energy of the molecular movements, and the subjective feel of heat that we get when we touch a hot object is now treated as just a subjective appearance caused by heat, as an effect of heat. It is no longer part of real heat. A similar distinction is made between real color and the subjective experience of color. The same pattern works for the primary qualities: Solidity is defined in terms of the vibratory movements

of molecules in lattice structures, and objective, observer-independent features, such as impenetrability by other objects, are now seen as surface effects of the underlying reality. Such redefinitions are achieved by way of carving off all of the surface features of the phenomenon, whether subjective or objective, and treating them as effects of the real thing.

But now notice: The actual pattern of the facts in the world that correspond to statements about particular forms of heat such as specific temperatures is quite similar to the pattern of facts in the world that correspond to statements about particular forms of consciousness, such as pain. If I now say, "It's hot in this room," what are the facts? Well, first there is a set of "physical" facts involving the movement of molecules, and second there is a set of "mental" facts involving my subjective experience of heat, as caused by the impact of the moving air molecules on my nervous system. But similarly with pain. If I now say, "I am in pain," what are the facts? Well, first there is a set of "physical" facts involving my thalamus and other regions of the brain, and second there is a set of "mental" facts involving my subjective experience of pain. So why do we regard heat as reducible and pain as irreducible? The answer is that what interests us about heat is not the subjective appearance but the underlying physical causes. Once we get a causal reduction, we simply redefine the notion to enable us to get an ontological reduction. Once you know all the facts about heat—facts about molecule movements, impact on sensory nerve endings, subjective feelings, etc.—the reduction of heat to molecule movements involves no new *fact* whatever. It is simply a trivial consequence of the redefinition. We don't first discover all the facts and then discover a new fact, the fact that heat is reducible; rather, we simply redefine heat so that the reduction follows from the definition. But this redefinition does not eliminate, and was not intended to eliminate, the subjective experiences of heat (or color, etc.) from the world. They exist the same as ever.

We might not have made the redefinition. Bishop Berkeley, for example, refused to accept such redefinitions. But it is easy to see why it is rational to make such redefinitions and accept their consequences: To get a greater understanding and control of reality, we want to know how it works causally, and we want our concepts to fit nature at its causal joints. We simply redefine phenomena with surface features in terms of the underlying causes. It then looks like a new discovery that heat is *nothing but* mean kinetic energy of molecule movement, and that if all subjective experiences disappeared from the world, real heat would still remain. But this is not a new discovery; it is a trivial consequence of a new definition. Such reductions do not show that heat, solidity, etc., do not really exist in the way that, for example, new knowledge showed that mermaids and unicorns do not exist.

Couldn't we say the same thing about consciousness? In the case of consciousness, we do have the distinction between the "physical" processes and the subjective "mental" experiences, so why can't consciousness be redefined in terms of the neurophysiological processes in the way that we redefined heat in terms of underlying physical processes? Well, of course, if we insisted on making the redefinition, we could. We could simply define, for example, "pain" as patterns of neuronal activity that cause subjective sensations of pain. And if such a redefinition took place, we would have achieved the same sort of reduction for pain that we have for heat. But, of course, the reduction of pain to its physical reality still leaves the subjective experience of pain unreduced, just as the reduction of heat left the subjective experience of heat unreduced. Part of the point of the reductions was to carve off the subjective experiences and exclude them from the definition of the real phenomena, which are now defined in terms of those features that interest us most. But where the phenomena that interest us most are the subjective experiences themselves, there is no way to carve anything off. Part of the point of the reduction in the case of heat was to distinguish between

the subjective appearance on the one hand and the underlying physical reality on the other. Indeed, it is a general feature of such reductions that the phenomenon is defined in terms of the "reality" and not in terms of the "appearance." But we can't make that sort of appearance-reality distinction for consciousness because consciousness consists in the appearances themselves. *Where appearance is concerned we cannot make the appearance-reality distinction because the appearance is the reality.*

For our present purposes, we can summarize this point by saying that consciousness is not reducible in the way that other phenomena are reducible, not because the pattern of facts in the real world involves anything special, but because the reduction of other phenomena depended in part on distinguishing between "objective physical reality," on the one hand, and mere "subjective appearance," on the other; and eliminating the appearance from the phenomena that have been reduced. But in the case of consciousness, its reality is the appearance; hence, the point of the reduction would be lost if we tried to carve off the appearance and simply defined consciousness in terms of the underlying physical reality. In general, the pattern of our reductions rests on rejecting the subjective epistemic basis for the presence of a property as part of the ultimate constituent of that property. We find out about heat or light by feeling and seeing, but we then define the phenomenon in a way that is independent of the epistemology. Consciousness is an exception to this pattern for a trivial reason. The reason, to repeat, is that the reductions that leave out the epistemic bases, the appearances, cannot work for the epistemic bases themselves. In such cases, the appearance is the reality.

But this shows that the irreducibility of consciousness is a trivial consequence of the pragmatics of our definitional practices. A trivial result such as this has only trivial consequences. It has no deep metaphysical consequences for the unity of our overall scientific world view. It does not show that consciousness is not part of the ultimate furniture of reality or cannot be a subject of scientific investigation or cannot be brought into our overall physical conception of the universe; it merely shows that in the way that we have decided to carry out reductions, consciousness, by definition, is excluded from a certain pattern of reduction. Consciousness fails to be reducible, not because of some mysterious feature, but simply because by definition it falls outside the pattern of reduction that we have chosen to use for pragmatic reasons. Pretheoretically, consciousness, like solidity, is a surface feature of certain physical systems. But unlike solidity, consciousness cannot be redefined in terms of an underlying microstructure, and the surface features then treated as mere effects of real consciousness, without losing the point of having the concept of consciousness in the first place.

So far, the argument of this chapter has been conducted, so to speak, from the point of view of the materialist. We can summarize the point I have been making as follows: The contrast between the reducibility of heat, color, solidity, etc., on the one hand, and the irreducibility of conscious states, on the other hand, does not reflect any distinction in the structure of reality, but a distinction in our definitional practices. We could put the same point from the point of view of the property dualist as follows: The apparent contrast between the irreducibility of consciousness and the reducibility of color, heat, solidity, etc., really was *only* apparent. We did not really eliminate the subjectivity of red, for example, when we reduced red to light reflectances; we simply stopped calling the subjective part "red." We did not eliminate any subjective phenomena whatever with these "reductions"; we simply stopped calling them by their old names. Whether we treat the irreducibility from the materialist or from the dualist point of view, we are still left with a universe that contains an irreducibly subjective physical component as a component of physical reality.

To conclude this part of the discussion, I want to make clear what I am saying and what I am not saying. I am not saying that consciousness is not a strange and wonderful phenomenon. I think, on the contrary, that we ought to be amazed by the fact that evolutionary processes produced nervous systems capable of causing and sustaining subjective conscious states. ... Consciousness is as empirically mysterious to us now as electromagnetism was previously, when people thought the universe must operate entirely on Newtonian principles. But I am saying that once the existence of (subjective, qualitative) consciousness is granted (and no sane person can deny its existence, though many pretend to do so), then there is nothing strange, wonderful, or mysterious about its *irreducibility*. Given its existence, its irreducibility is a trivial consequence of our definitional practices. Its irreducibility has no untoward scientific consequences whatever. Furthermore, when I speak of the irreducibility of consciousness, I am speaking of its *irreducibility according to standard patterns of reduction*. No one can rule out a priori the possibility of a major intellectual revolution that would give us a new— and at present unimaginable—conception of reduction, according to which consciousness would be reducible.

Supervenience

In recent years there has been a lot of heavy going about a relationship between properties called "supervenience" (e.g., Kim 1979, 1982; Haugeland 1982). It is frequently said in discussions in the philosophy of mind that the mental is supervenient on the physical. Intuitively, what is meant by this claim is that mental states are totally dependent on corresponding neurophysiological states in the sense that a difference in mental states would necessarily involve a corresponding difference in neurophysiological states. If, for example, I go from a state of being thirsty to a state of no longer being thirsty, then there must have been some change in my brain states corresponding to the change in my mental states.

On the account that I have been proposing, mental states are supervenient on neurophysiological states in the following respect: Type-identical neurophysiological causes would have type-identical mentalistic effects. Thus, to take the famous brain-in-the-vat example, if you had two brains that were type-identical down to the last molecule, then the causal basis of the mental would guarantee that they would have the same mental phenomena. On this characterization of the supervenience relation, the supervenience of the mental on the physical is marked by the fact that physical states are causally sufficient, though not necessarily causally necessary, for the corresponding mental states. That is just another way of saying that as far as this definition of supervenience is concerned, sameness of neurophysiology guarantees sameness of mentality; but sameness of mentality does not guarantee sameness of neurophysiology.

It is worth emphasizing that this sort of supervenience is *causal* supervenience. Discussions of supervenience were originally introduced in connection with ethics, and the notion in question was not a causal notion. In the early writings of Moore (1922) and Hare (1952), the idea was that moral properties are supervenient on natural properties, that two objects cannot differ solely with respect to, for example, their goodness. If one object is better than another, there must be some other feature in virtue of which the former is better than the latter. But this notion of moral supervenience is not a causal notion. That is, the features of an object that make it good do not *cause* it to be good, they rather *constitute* its goodness. But in the case of mind/brain supervenience, the neural phenomena cause the mental phenomena.

So there are at least two notions of supervenience: a constitutive notion and a causal notion. I believe that only the causal notion is important for discussions of the mind-body problem. In this respect my account differs from the usual accounts of the supervenience of the mental on the physical. Thus Kim (1979, especially p. 45ff.) claims that we should not think of the relation of neural events to their supervening mental events as causal, and indeed he claims that supervening mental events have no causal status apart from their supervenience on neurophysiological events that have "a more direct causal role." "If this be epiphenomenalism, let us make the most of it," he says cheerfully (p. 47).

I disagree with both of these claims. It seems to me obvious from everything we know about the brain that macro mental phenomena are all caused by lower-level micro phenomena. There is nothing mysterious about such bottom-up causation; it is quite common in the physical world. Furthermore, the fact that the mental features are supervenient on neuronal features in no way diminishes their causal efficacy. The solidity of the piston is causally supervenient on its molecular structure, but this does not make solidity epiphenomenal; and similarly, the causal supervenience of my present back pain on micro events in my brain does not make the pain epiphenomenal.

My conclusion is that once you recognize the existence of bottom-up, micro to macro forms of causation, the notion of supervenience no longer does any work in philosophy. The formal features of the relation are already present in the causal sufficiency of the micro-macro forms of causation. And the analogy with ethics is just a source of confusion. The relation of macro mental features of the brain to its micro neuronal features is totally unlike the relation of goodness to good-making features, and it is confusing to lump them together. As Wittgenstein says somewhere, "If you wrap up different kinds of furniture in enough wrapping paper, you can make them all look the same shape."

References

Hare, R. M. (1952). *The Language of Morals*. Oxford: Oxford University Press.

Haugeland, J. (1982). "Weak Supervenience." *American Philosophical Quarterly* 19, 1:93–104.

Jackson, F. (1982). "Epiphenomenal Qualia." *Philosophical Quarterly* 32:127–136.

Kim, J. (1979). "Causality, Identity and Supervenience in the Mind-Body Problem." *Midwest Studies in Philosophy* 4:31–49.

———— (1982). "Psychophysical Supervenience." *Philosophical Studies* 41, 1:51–70.

Kripke, S. A. (1971). "Naming and Necessity." In D. Davidson and G. Harman (eds.), *Semantics of Natural Language*, pp. 253–355, 763–769. Dordrecht: Reidel.

Moore, G. E. (1922). *Philosophical Studies*. London: Routledge and Kegan Paul.

Nagel, T. (1974). "What Is It Like to Be a Bat?" *Philosophical Review* 4, 83, 435–450.

28 A Question about Consciousness

Georges Rey

I

For my part, when I enter most intimately upon what I call *myself*, I always stumble upon some particular perception or other, of heat or cold, light or shade, love or hatred, pain or pleasure.... Were all my perceptions removed by death, and could I neither think, nor feel, nor see, nor love, nor hate, after the dissolution of my body, I should be entirely annihilated, nor do I conceive what is further requisite to make me a perfect non-entity. [Hume 1739/1965, Vol. 1, p. 6]

In this well-known passage, Hume raises a particular kind of criticism against a primitive notion of the soul. That criticism might be put this way: once we attend to the full details of our mental lives, the notion of a simple soul, of some piece of our mentation that remains unchanged through all changes of our lives seems unacceptably crude and simplistic. It has no place in the ultimate story about ourselves. We would seem merely to be imposing it upon the really quite diverse portions of our lives in an effort to underwrite metaphysically the special concern we feel towards our futures and our pasts.[1]

I shall not be concerned with the correctness of Hume's criticism, or with whether there might be some line of defense of the primitive view. Rather, I shall be concerned with whether a very similar kind of criticism mightn't also be raised against our ordinary notion of consciousness. Consciousness has received a great deal of press recently, both popular and professional. It is once again a serious object of study in psychology and psychobiology,[2] and one even finds it figuring in accounts of quantum mechanics.[3] For all the interest of the notion, however, it is none too clear what, if anything, is being researched or appealed to in such accounts. On the one hand, consciousness is supposed to be (at least in one's own case) the most obvious thing in the world; on the other, no one seems to be able to say anything very illuminating about it.

Like Hume, I propose to examine the notion of consciousness in the light of the actual details of our mental life, or what we seem so far to know about those details. Unlike Hume, however, I shall not restrict my attention merely to introspection (much less "perceptions"), nor, like many of Hume's followers, to an analysis of our ordinary talk, although I shall not ignore these either. What I shall do is consider some plausible theories about the nature of human mentation that are available in recent psychology, psychobiology, and artificial intelligence, and attempt to determine approximately where consciousness, as we ordinarily conceive it, might fit in. I think we shall find, as Hume did with at least the primitive notion of the soul, that it appears not to fit. The most plausible theoretical accounts of human mentation presently available appear not to need, nor to support, many of the central claims about consciousness that we ordinarily maintain. One could take this as showing that we are simply mistaken about a phenomenon that is nevertheless quite real, or, depending upon how central these mistakes are, that consciousness may be no more real than the simple soul exorcised by Hume.

This latter conclusion would, of course, be extraordinarily puzzling. Among ordinary beliefs about consciousness, none seems more powerful or more certain than that we each know immediately in our own case, in a special way that is immune to any serious doubt, that we *are* conscious. "I see clearly that there is nothing which is easier for me to know than my own mind," remarked Descartes (1641/1911, Vol. I, p. 157). Thought being "whatever is in us in such a way that we are immediately conscious of it," he took as one of his certainties his "clear and distinct idea" of himself as a "thinking thing" (1641/1911, Vol. 1, p. 190). Someone today might put it thus: "No matter what your theories and instruments might say, you cannot provide me any reason to doubt that I am conscious right here now."

I shall call this view about the infallibility of first-person present-tense beliefs about consciousness the "Cartesian Intuition." It is particularly this intuition about consciousness that I think turns out to be problematic in the light of present theories. I shall provide reasons for doubting that oneself is conscious, and, then, since first-person infallibility seems to be so central to the ordinary notion, I shall argue that that doubt, in conjunction with those theories, further provides reason for thinking that nothing is conscious. But, of course, few of us are going to be persuaded in this (or any?) way to give up a belief in consciousness. The question about consciousness that I want to raise, then, is this: how are we to understand our insistence on the existence of consciousness given that we cannot find a place for it in any reasonable theory of the world? My strategy will be as follows. I will discuss various mental phenomena and some reasonable theories that have been advanced to explain them. I shall then consider in each case the plausibility of regarding each particular phenomenon, with or without the others, as a candidate for the role of consciousness. In each case, I shall consider whether the phenomenon could occur *un*consciously. I think that in a surprising number of cases we will find that they can.

Judgments about these matters, however, can often be distorted by what might be called "ghostly" intuitions: our judgments about mental states can often be affected by a belief in a background condition that mysteriously presupposes consciousness and so cannot explain it. This belief may take the form of an explicit commitment to a dualistic "ghost in the machine"; but it may also appear in subtler forms in purely materialistic approaches. Too often the ghost is replaced by an equally obscure "complexity" in the machine: "Of course," declares the thoroughly modern materialist, "we are machines, but"—and here he waves his hands towards properties as fabulously mysterious as any conceived by the dualist—"we are very, very complex ones." I call this view "facile materialism." (It appears in other guises, sometimes, as in John Searle's (1980, 1983, 1984)

appeals to some crucially unspecified "biology" in our brains.) Until we begin to explain the *specific* kinds of complexity, biology, or special substances that are relevant to mental phenomena, such appeals only serve as ways to evade the mind/body problem, not solve it.

I shall consider these ghostly intuitions in due course. However, to avoid contamination by them in our consideration of candidate analyses of consciousness, I shall consider in each case the plausibility of regarding an *existing machine* that exhibited the candidate phenomenon, in a fashion that we can understand, as thereby conscious. I think that we shall find such proposals unacceptable, just as Hume would have found unacceptable proposals to identify a particular perception, or a cluster of them, with his soul. This reluctance to identify consciousness with any particular mental operations, or with any combination of them, I shall take to be evidence of a defect with the notion of consciousness similar to the defect Hume found with the notion of a soul.

Someone, of course, might insist that the term "consciousness" be defined before we undertake such an investigation so that there might be a reasonable way to evaluate the proposals I shall consider. But that approach would misconstrue the problem. Part of the question I mean to raise is that we really don't have any good definition of "consciousness." We have a wide variety of usages of the term and its related forms,[4] each of which can be assimilated to or distinguished from the others, depending upon the purposes at hand. Whether they can be assimilated into a single or several different definitions seems to me a problem that is inseparable from forming a general theory of the mind.[5] But those who want to insist upon definitions can regard that follows as so many efforts to provide one, with a reason in each case to reject it.

II

One of the soundest reasons for taking a particular description of an object seriously is that the object obeys laws in which the description figures. Amoebas, for example, can be regarded as literally alive, since they obey many of the laws of living things. Similarly, an object can be regarded as literally possessing a mental life insofar (and perhaps only insofar) as it obeys psychological laws. Now, to be sure, given the still adolescent state of psychology as a science, there really aren't any fully developed psychological laws available. But there are law sketches (cf. Hempel 1965, pp. 423–425). Among them, few seem to be more central and basic than those that attempt to capture what might be called the "Rational Regularities": these are the regularities among a creature's states whereby they instantiate the steps of inductive[6], deductive, and practical reasoning. So far, the best explanation[7] of such remarkable capacities seems to be one that postulates mental processes in the animals whereby they are able to perform at least rudimentary inductions and deductions, and are able to base their behavior upon some one or other form of practical reasoning: for example, they generally act in ways that they believe will best secure what they most prefer.[8] It is these regularities that justify us in ascribing beliefs and preferences to anything at all: were an object not to satisfy them, neither in its behavior nor (more importantly) in its internal processing, it would be difficult to see any reasonable basis for such ascription, and insofar as an object does satisfy them, there would seem to be a very firm basis indeed. They certainly seem to form the basis we ordinarily employ in ascribing beliefs and preferences and other mental states to people and animals in the many useful and sometimes insightful ways we do. They are a central part of what Max Weber (1922/ 1980) called "Verstehen" or "empathic" explanation, and of what many recent philosophers have come to call "intentional explanation," the creatures (or, more generally, the systems) whose behavior is in this way explained being "intentional systems" (Dennett 1971/1978).

I don't mean to suggest that we yet fully understand this form of explanation, much less all the behavior of the explicands. Notoriously, there is the problem of the "intentionality" of the mental idioms: the beliefs and preferences that enter into these rational relations are "about" things that seem (e.g., physically) quite unrelated to them—my beliefs about Socrates are quite remote from and unlike Socrates—and often about "things," such as Santa Claus or the largest prime, that don's exist at all. And then there is the problem simply of specifying clearly wherein the rationality of our thought consists. These problems are among the hardest in philosophy.

For all their difficulty, however, there have been some advances. Philosophers have noticed that both the intentionality and rationality of thought suggests that thought involves relations to *representations*, for example, sentences, or some other kind of structured intermediary between the agent and the world. Such postulation explains the familiar failures of coreferential substitution associated with intensionality, and at the same time provides a suitable vehicle for the kinds of *formal* theories of reasoning familiar from the study of logic.[9] At any rate, Harman (1973), Fodor (1975), Field (1978), and Stich (1983) have postulated just such a system of representation, a "language of thought," encoded and computed upon in the nervous systems of psychological beings, as a way to explain their intentional rationality. Putting their point a little perversely, we might say that intentionality and rationality—the two properties that seem peculiar to psychological beings—are to be explained by a surprising hypothesis: *thinking is spelling* (and transformations thereof).

I shall not be concerned here with whether or not this hypothesis is actually true for human beings. It will be enough for our purposes that this hypothesis provides a *possible* explanation of thought, one possible way that something could manage to satisfy the rational regularities. For, if that's true, then regardless of how people actually *do* manage to think, any system that could consistently spell and transform strings of symbols according to certain rules would still, by its resulting satisfaction of those regularities, qualify as a thinking thing.

The "Language of Thought" hypothesis suggests, then, the possibility in principle of constructing a machine that could think. Surprisingly, this is not so remote a possibility in practice either. In particular, it would seem entirely feasible (although, for reasons I shall come to, not awfully worthwhile) to render an existing computing machine intentional by providing it with a program that would include the following:

1. the alphabet, formation, and transformation rules for quantified modal logic with indexicals, e.g., David Kaplan's "Logic of Demonstratives," as the system's Language of Thought;

2. the axioms for a system of inductive logic, and an abductive system of hypotheses, with a "reasonable" function for selecting among them for a given input;

3. the axioms for decision theory, whit some set of basic preferences;

4. in addition to the usual keyboard, various transducers (e.g., a television camera) for supplying inputs to(2);

5. devices (e.g., printers, mechanical hands) that permit the machine to realize its outputs (e.g., its "most preferred" basic act descriptions).

The machine would operate roughly as follows. The input supplied by (4) would produce "observation" sentences that would be checked against comparable deductive consequences of the hypotheses provided by (2); hypotheses would be selected whose consequences "best matched" the observation sentences; those hypotheses in turn would serve as input to (3), where, on the basis of them, the given preferences, and the decision-theoretic functions, a "most preferred" basic act description would be generated, and then be executed by (5).

Someone might wonder how such a machine could have genuine intentionality, how, for example, the sentences being entertained by the machine could be "about" anything.[10] There are a number of strategies for answering this question (see Rey 1997). For purposes here Stampe's (1977) will suffice. He proposes to regard sentence meaning as a species of natural meaning. Just as the n rings in a tree trunk "mean" the tree is n years old because, under ideal condition, the n rings are produced as a causal consequence of the tree's being that old, so would a sentence selected by our machine mean that a certain state of affairs obtains because, under ideal conditions, it would be produced as a causal consequence of those states of affairs. Thus, '(Ex) Sx, h, n' might mean for the machine, "There is a square in front of me now," because under ideal conditions—good lighting, direct placement of the stimulus before the transducer—it would select that sentence (putting it, for example, in what Schiffer (1980) has called a "yes" box) as a causal consequence of there being a square directly in front of it. The sentences of such a machine would be "about" the states of affairs that would, under ideal circumstances, cause the machine to select them. [11] We might call these causal regularities "ideal detection regularities."

Satisfying ideal detection regularities by means of (1)–(5) is a way that the machine could obey the Rational Regularities, complete with intentionality. We would certainly be able to explain and predict its worldly behavior and internal states on the basis of those regularities. It would be natural to say that the reason it did or will do such and such is that it believes this and most prefers that; for example, that the reason that it pushed the button is that it most preferred putting the pyramid atop the cube, and thought that pushing the button was the best way of doing so. We would, that is, find it natural to adopt towards it what Dennett (1971/1978) has called "the intentional stance." Unlike Dennett, however, I see no reason not to take the resulting ascription of beliefs and preferences entirely *literally*. For, again, what better reason to take a description of an object seriously than that the object obeys laws into which that description essentially enters? We would seem to have the best reason in the world therefore for regarding the computer so programmed as a genuine thinking thing.

Caveat emptor: for all its rationality and intentionality, there is also every reason to think that such a machine would, at least for the foreseeable future, be colossally stupid. We need to distinguish two senses of "AI": artificial *intelligence* and artificial *intentionality*. A machine can exhibit the latter without exhibiting very much of the former. And this is because artificial intentionality requires only that it obey rational and ideal detection regularities, performing intelligently under ideal conditions, e.g., situations in which the light is good and the stimuli are presented squarely in front. Intelligence requires doing well under *non*-ideal conditions as well, when the light is bad and the views skewed. But performing well under varied conditions is precisely what we know existing computers tend not to do.[12] Decreasingly ideal cases require increasingly clever inferences to the best explanation in order for judgments to come out true; and characterizing such inferences is one of the central problems confronting artificial intelligence—to say nothing of cognitive psychology and traditional philosophy of science. We simply don't yet know how to spell out the "reasonable" of the proposed program's clause (2). Philosophers have made some suggestions that, within narrow bounds, are fairly plausible (e.g., statistical and Bayesian inferences, principles of simplicity, conservatism, entrenchment), but we know that they aren't even approximately adequate yet.

But, meager though the suggestions might be, the proposed inductive principles, within bounds, are not unreasonable. Existing programs are, I submit, adequate to satisfy ideal detection regularities for a wide range of concepts (e.g., mathematical and geometric concepts, concepts of material objects, and many of their basic properties). In suitably restricted environments, and particularly in conjunction with the relatively better understood deductive and practical regularities of (1) and (3), they provide a rich basis for serious explanation and prediction of our computer's states and behaviors in terms of its preferences and beliefs. Limited rationality, to a point, is still rationality. I see no reason to think that we can't right now devise programs like (1)–(5) that would get us to that point (which is not to say that, given the system's general stupidity, it would actually be worth doing).[13]

For purposes here, what the practical possibility of this machine does is to underscore a point that has been gradually emerging from a century's work in psychology: that, contrary to the spirit of Descartes, the letter of Locke, most of the definitions in the O.E.D., and the claims of many theorists down to the present day, *consciousness must involve something more than mere thought*. However clever a machine programmed with (1)–(5) might become, counting thereby as a thinking thing, it would not also count thereby as conscious. There is, first of all the fact that no one would seriously regard it as conscious.[14] But, secondly, in support of this intuition, there is now substantial evidence of systems of at least the richness of (1)–(5) that are clearly unconscious. Besides the standard clinical literature regarding peoples' unconscious beliefs and motives, there are a large number of "self-attribution" experiments detailing different ways in which people engage in elaborate thought processes of which they are demonstrably unaware. Subjects in these experiments have been shown to be sensitive to such factors as cognitive dissonance (Festinger 1957), expectation (Darley and Berschied 1967), numbers of bystanders (Latané and Darley 1970), pupillary dilation (Hess 1975), positional and "halo" effects (Nisbett and Wilson 1977), and subliminal cues in problem solving and semantic disambiguation (Maier 1931, Zajonc 1968, Lackner and Garrett 1972). Instead of noticing these factors, however, subjects often "introspect" material independently shown to be irrelevant, and, even when explicitly asked about the relevant material, deny that it played any role. These factors, though, clearly played a role in the regularities that determined the subjects' actions.

Thus, whatever consciousness turns out to be, it will need to be distinguished from the thought processes we ascribe on the basis of rational regularities.

How easily this can be forgotten, neglected, or missed altogether can be seen from proposals about the nature of consciousness current in much of psychobiological literature. The following is representative:[15]

Modern views ... regard human conscious activity as consisting of a number of components. These include the reception and processing (recoding) of information, with the selection of its most important elements and retention of the experience thus gained in the memory; enunciation of the task or formulation of an intention, with the preservation of the corresponding modes of activity, the creation of a pattern or model of required action, and production of the appropriate program (plan) to control the selection of necessary actions; and finally the comparison of the results of the action with the original intention ... with correction of the mistakes made. (Luria 1976).

What is astonishing about such proposals is that they are all more or less satisfiable by almost *any* information processing system. Precisely what modern computers are designed for is to receive, process, unify, and retain information; create (or "call") plans, patterns, models, subroutines to control their activity; and, to compare the results of its action with its original intention in order to adjust its behavior to its environment—this latter process is exactly what the "feedback" mechanisms that Wiener (1954) built into homing rockets are for! Certainly most of the descriptions in these proposals are satisfied by any recent game-playing program (see, e.g., Berliner 1980). And if genuine "modalities," "thoughts," "intentions," "perceptions," or "representations" are wanted, then I see no reason to think that programming the machine with (1)–(5) wouldn't suffice,[16] but without rendering anything a whit more conscious.

Something more is required. There are many proposals that have been or might be made, but what is disturbing about all of the ones I have encountered is that they seem to involve either very trivial additions to (1)–(5), or absolutely no additions whatsoever. I'll consider some of the more plausible ones.

A natural extension of the notion of an intentional system has elsewhere been developed by Dennett (1978) into what we might call the notion of an "n-order intentional system." A "first-order" intentional system is one that has beliefs and preferences merely by virtue of obeying rational regularities. A "second-order" intentional system is one that not only has beliefs and preferences by virtue of obeying such regularities, but in particular has beliefs and preferences *about* beliefs and preferences. It might, for example, engage in deliberately deceptive behavior, attempting to satisfy its own preferences by manipulating the beliefs and preferences of some other system. An "n-order" intentional system is simply a generalization of these notions: it has beliefs and preferences about beliefs and preferences about beliefs and preferences ... to any arbitrary degree, n, of such nestings.

This might be regarded as a promising suggestion about the nature of consciousness until one considers some work in computer science of Brown (1974) and Schmidt and D'Addami (1973). They have devised a program called the "Believer System" that essentially exploits the Rational Regularities as a basis for explaining the behavior of people who figure in some simple stories. For example, from descriptions of someone gathering together some logs and rope and subsequently building a raft, the program constructs (by iterations of means-ends reasoning) the motive that the agent wanted to build a raft, and imputes to him a plan to the effect that gathering together some logs and rope was the best available means of doing so. The program is hardly very imaginative. But then neither are we much of the time when we ascribe beliefs and preferences to each other on what I have argued above seems to be the very same basis.

The perhaps surprising moral of this research would seem to be that, if a system is intentional at all, it is a relatively small matter to render it n-order intentional as well. One would simply allow the program at some juncture to access itself in such a fashion that it is able to ascribe this very same "Believer System" to the agent as part of that agent's plan. Given that every time it reached that juncture it would be able to further access itself in this way, it would be able to ascribe such ascriptions, and such ascriptions of such ascriptions, indefinitely, to a depth of nesting limited only by its memory capacity. We might call this extension of the "Believer System:"

6. The Recursive Believer System.

It is the paradigm of the kind of program that is realizable on existing machines. Given that the Rational Regularities afford a sufficient basis for the ascription of beliefs and preferences in the first place, a machine programmed with (1)–(6) would be capable of having beliefs and preferences about beliefs and preferences to an arbitrary degree of nesting. That is to say, it would be relatively easy to program an existing machine to be n-order intentional.

Someone might protest that being seriously n-order intentional—and maybe intentional at all—requires not merely having objective attitudes, but also having attitudes essentially about oneself, attitudes *de se*. For example, it's not enough that I might believe that *Georges Rey* is presently thinking certain things; I need to be able to think that *I* am presently doing so. What's wanted is a special way of referring to oneself as we do in English when we use 'I'; what, for example, Chisholm (1981, p. 24)[17] calls the "emphatic reflexive." I see no reason, however, why we mightn't endow our computer with this form of reference. We need simply constrain the use of a specific variable in the program's Language of Thought (e.g., 'i') so it functions as an internal name of the receiver of the inputs, the entertainer of the thoughts, and the instigator of the actions of the machine, but specifically controlled by rules for these roles. Imposing such constraints is already available by virtue of Kaplan's Logic of Demon-

stratives included in our clause (1). As a result of using such a language, the machine would, for example, when directly stimulated by a square and observing '(Ex) Sx, h, n' ("There's square here now"), be able to conclude '(Ex) (Sx, h, n & Pi, x)' ("and I perceive it"); and similarly for others of its beliefs, preferences, decisions and actions.

Would such a machine programmed with a suitably indexicalized recursive believer system be conscious? Human consciousness is often thought to consist in self-awareness.[18] A number of writers (e.g., Rosenthal 1984, Smith 1986) have recently defended such a hypothesis. But, in view of the relatively small addition that (6) makes to (1)–(5), it is hard to see why we should believe it. Moreover, Dennett (1976/1978, pp. 279–280) himself remarks on a number of cases in which the presence of nested reasonings does not at all require consciously entertaining them. On the contrary, people seem to be quite poor at consciously entertaining merely second-order intentions: for example, it is unlikely that people are consciously aware of the kinds of intentions Grice (1957) and Schiffer (1972) claim underlie communication. Or consider an example of a "reciprocal perspective' that Laing, Phillipson, and Lee (1966) find so crucial in explaining domestic interactions:

From the point of view of the subject, the starting point is often between the second and third order level of perspective. Jill thinks that Jack thinks that she does not love him, that she neglects him, that she is destroying him, and so on, although she says she does not think she is doing any of these things . . . She may express fears lest he think that she thinks he is ungrateful to her for all that she is doing, when she wants him to know that she does *not* think that he thinks that she thinks he thinks she does not do enough. (pp. 30–31)

Such deeply nested intentions probably affect our behavior efficiently only so long as we are *not* struggling to make ourselves conscious of them. In any case, the authors discuss examples of Rorschach and intelligence tests in which, they say, responses were often affected by unconscious reciprocal perspectives (1966, pp. 42–44). But, if Jill's thought that Jack's thought about her thoughts can be unconscious, why should her thoughts about *her own* thoughts *have* to be conscious? Why should consciousness be *required* to pop up only at that level and not at more complex ones?[19] In view of the complexity of peoples' actual unconscious thoughts, and the simplicity of the machine I have described, it would certainly be surprising were nested intentionality of self-consciousness to provide the condition on consciousness we are seeking.

III

Throughout my discussion of human cases so far, I have been relying on the reportability of a stimulus or mental state as a necessary condition for consciousness (of that stimulus or state). Elsewhere, Dennett (1969) advances this as a criterion of consciousness, or at least of what he calls "awareness$_1$"—A is aware$_1$ that p at time t if and only if p is the content of A's speech center at time t—as opposed to "awareness$_2$" which involves contents ascribed to explain the agent's rational behavior generally.[20] To avoid too close an association with specifically *speech* mechanisms, it would probably be better to put p into the machine's language of thought, and have it stored in a special "buffer memory" used as a source of avowals and other speech acts.[21] We might further require that the sentences in this location include second-order emphatic reflexive self-ascriptions of psychological states (the internal translations of, e.g., "I think the light is on" or "I'd like some lemonade"), which would be available to be translated into the agent's natural language. Would such an arrangement be sufficient for consciousness?

Existing computers already have the capacity to report in a public language—e.g., programming languages—upon at least some of their own internal states. Increasingly, these languages resemble fragments of English; and in some cases large portions of English are parsed and used for communication between machine and user (for an amusing example, there is Weizenbaum's [1965] notorious ELIZA program, designed to provide the responses of a Rogerian psychotherapist). Now, to be sure, capturing full English is difficult: its syntax is intricate and not obviously separable from its semantics, which is not obviously separable from the worldly wisdom of English speakers, an understanding of which, as mentioned earlier, is beyond the means of present artifical intelligence.[22] Pending progress there, one probably wouldn't have a very stimulating or far-ranging conversation with any existing machine. But one could probably do as well with regard at least to introspection as one does with the vast majority of human beings. All one would need to do is supplement the program that includes (1)–(6) with:

7. a fragment af English adequate to describe/ express the mental states entered in executing (1)-(6), descriptions which are produced as a reliable consequence of being in those states.

We might simply include with (1)–(6) a specific instruction to temporarily store in a special buffer a description (in the Language of Thought) of (most[23]) every mental state the machine enters immediately after entering it. This would be compiled into the English supplied by (7) whenever an avowal or introspective report was requested or otherwise motivated. Since by clause (6) the machine is already n-order intentional, it could respond to such requests with just the sort of nested intentions that Grice and Schiffer have argued are essential to human linguistic communication. The syntax and semantics needed for communication of at least these kinds of introspective reports would seem to be quite managably limited, and isolable from the as yet unmanagable syntax and semantics of complete English. Conversing with the machine would be like talking with as extremely unimaginative, but unusually self-percetpive human being, who knew mostly only about his own psychological states. I submit that would count as conversing with a full-fledged introspector nonetheless.

So, would a machine programmed with (1)–(7) be conscious? It is hard to see why. As I've said, versions of (7) are already being run on existing computers. If one were inclined to think (1)–(6) insufficient, then adding (7) would amount to little more than running (1)–(6) on an existing machine with an odd, special purpose compiler. Most any computer in the country could be made conscious in this way in about a week!

There are further mechanisms and processes to which we might turn. Attention and short-term memory might seem promising. Humans appear to be able to concentrate their cognitive processing in one area or modality of stimulation often to the near exclusion of others. There has been a good deal of research in this regard on "short term memory" (Miller 1956), on the nature of selective filtering of signals (Kahnemann 1973), and on the relation of such filtering to feedback and "feed-forward" (or plan-related) processing (Pribram 1980). Some writers, noting the association of these roles with consciousness, have suggested that they be taken as constitutive of it. Thus, Piaget (176) writes:

If a well-adapted action requires no awareness, it is directed by sensori-motor regulations which can then automate themselves. When on the contrary an active regulation becomes necessary, which presupposes intentional choices between two or several possibilities, there is an awareness in function of these needs themselves. (p. 41)

The trouble with these sorts of processes as candidates for consciousness is that they don't make any further demands whatsoever on a machine of the sort we've been considering. Machines with suitable memory necessarily have a limited number of work addresses into which material from long-term storage, as well as some of the present inputs to the system, can be placed for short term, "on line" processing. That the capacity of these addresses is limited, and that the selection of content for them is contingent upon the plan (or program) being implemented, which in turn is sensitive to feedback, goes without saying. Certainly any machine equipped to deal with (1)–(7) would need to be designed in such a fashion: there is, for example, the buffer memory we included to execute (7). Such centralized work addresses might well be precisely the place at which high-level decisions in a program—e.g., whether or not to continue a particular sub-routine, whether to call a new one—might be made, causing the machine to make "intentional choices between two or several possibilities," to "formulate new goals," and thereby to "modify its habitual action patterns."[24] But where in any of this is there any need of consciousness? Again, if this were sufficient for consciousness, then practically every computer in the country would be conscious already!

"But," the reader may be anxious to ask, "What about *sensations*? Surely a device capable of them would thereby qualify as conscious." Here, to be sure, the issues are a little complicated; but not, I fear, in the end very helpful. First of all, in clause (3) of our program we've already allowed for transducers that would convert, e.g., electromangetic wave forms into signals that would issue in "observation sentences" in the system's language of thought. Given the apparent modularity of perception and observation (see Fodor 1983), we should suppose that the sentences issuing here are in a special vocabulary, involving predicates whose use is heavily constrained in wasys analogous to the constraints on essential indexicals like "I." Just as I can believe *I* am in Maryland only under specific compuional circumstances, so I can believe I am seeming to see *red* only when I am in fact receiving specific signals from (or into) my visual module. Insofar as these signals might be responsible, by means of the inductive processing involved in (2), for confirming and disconfirming hypotheses about the lay of the land and the probable shape of things to come, it would be reasonable to regard the process as at least a *functional* equivalent of visual perception.

We might also include under (3) sensors that would signal to the machine the presence of certain kinds of damage to its surface or parts of its interior. These signals could be processed in such a way as to cause in the machine a sudden, extremely high preference assignment, to the implementation of any sub-routine that the machine believed likely to reduced that damage and/or the further reception of such signals, that is, it would try to get itself out of such states. The states produced in this way would seem to constitute a functional equivalent of pain. Insofar as these processes could, either by mistake or by program design, be self-induced, the machine would be subject to the functional equivalents of hallucinations and its own deliberate imaginings.

But, of course, it is the sensations—the colors, the pains, the hallucinations—*themselves* that are important, not mere "functional equivalents" of them. Most of us would pretty surely balk at claiming that a machine that ran on (1)–(7) alone should be regarded as *really* having the experience of red just because it has a transducer that emits a characteristic signal, with some of the usual cognitive consequences, whenever it is stimulated with red light. But I'm not sure what entitles us to our reservations.[25] For what else is there? In particular, what else is there that we are so sure is there and essential in our own case? How do we know *we* "have the experience of red" over and above our undergoing just some such process as I have described in this machine? What more do we do than enter a specific cognitive state when certain of our transducers are stimulated with red light? How do we know *we* "have the experience of red" over and above our undergoing just such a process as I have described in this machine?[26] Certainly it's not because we have some well-confirmed theory of sense experience that distinguishes us!

Whether or not it's especially well-confirmed, something like a theory with a long tradition to

it claims that we have some sort of "privileged access" to such experiences, "direct, incorrigible" knowledge of their qualitative feel.[27] Now, it's not entirely clear how this claim is to be made out. If it is the claim that believing one is having a sensation entails one's having it, then we would be forced to concede that the machine I've described really does have them after all. What with its transducers, inductions, and nested self-ascriptions, it would acquire sensory beliefs that it *seemed* to see red; and that would be difficult to distinguish from the belief that it's having a red sensation (cf. Sellars 1956). Someone could of course object that the entailment—this privileged access—holds only for us, not for machines. But we should then entitled to know why. Or do we have privileged access not only to our sensations, but to the fact of our privileged access as well? I forbear from following out the question-begging regress this line of reasoning suggests.

Several philosophers have recently proposed that the qualitative character of our sensations is tied not merely to our cognitive structure, but to our physiology as well (see Block 1978, Searle 1981, Jackson 1982, and Maloney 1985). Elsewhere, (Rey 1980) I have argued that one thing that may distinguish us from any machines yet envisaged are many of our emotions. For there is strong psychobiological evidence that the capacity for, for example, depression, anger, and fear depends upon the presence in our brains of certain hormones and neuro-regulators (e.g., norepinepherine, testosterone), or at least upon certain as yet unknown properties of those substances.[28] We have no reason to believe that, whatever those properties turn out to be, they will be available in existing computational hardware. To the contrary, given the extraordinarily high level of functional abstraction on which cognitive processes can be defined, it would be a surprising coincidence if they were.[29]

I think it would be rash to clutch at these emotions and their associated hormones and neuro-regulators as providing the conditions of consciousness that we are seeking: our feelings (e.g., anger, grief) are, after all, not always conscious, nor are moments without feeling unconscious. However, perhaps a similar dependence upon non-cognitive properties of our bodies and brains is essential to our having sensations and qualitative states. This dependence would have to be spelled out and justified. At the moment, it is to my knowledge utterly obscure how we might do that, much less precisely what those properties might be.

However, any such appeal to a non-cognitive condition is open to the following difficulty. Call the further non-cognitive condition, be it neurophysiological or otherwise, condition K. It would follow from the psychological theories we have been considering, together with an insistence on K, that it would be *metaphysically* possible[30] for someone to *believe* she is in a particular sensory state without actually being in it: for it would be metaphysically possible for her to be in the position of our computer, satisfying (1)–(7) without satisfying K. But this amounts to an extraordinary contribution to anesthesiology. For it would then be open to surgeons, or others adept at dealing with K, to eliminate K without disturbing a patient's cognitions. A patient might undergo an operation fully believing that she was in intense pain and very much preferring she wasn't, but be reassured by the surgeon that nevertheless, lacking K, she wasn't actually experiencing any sensations at all. She only thought she was. (I remind the reader that this is precisely the position in which we were willing to leave our computer, helplessly programmed with merely (1)–(7). This consequence seems clearly unacceptable; and so therefore does appeal to condition K.[31]

IV

This last argument can be expanded and applied to the problem of consciousness itself. Just as it seems perfectly possible to program an existing machine to believe it's in pain and experiencing

other sensory states, so does it seem to be possible to program it to believe it's conscious. It might come to believe this, as we often seem to do, simply as a consequence of being perceptually functional: for example, it might automatically (be disposed to) enter a sentence 'Ci' into the aforementioned "attention" buffer whenever any other sensory sentence is already there. We can even suppose it has many of the beliefs about consciousness that we have: for example, that it's a state that something is in if it's perceptually functional, moreover, a state that something is in if it thinks it is; a state, indeed, that something can never be given any reason to doubt it's in. That is, we could provide our machine with:

8. The Cartesian Intuition

The machine could think and print out, "I see clearly that there is nothing easier for me to know than my own mind," and proceed to insist that "no matter what your theory and instruments might say, they can never give me reason to think that I am not conscious here, now." After all, such beliefs are relatively simple second-order ones, easily specified by means of (6).

If someone now replies that we've only provided the machine with the functional equivalent of consciousness, we may ask, as we did in the case of sensory experiences, what more is required? In particular, what further properties other than those provided by (1)–(8) can we reasonably demand as a necessary condition on consciousness? As in the case of sensory experiences, we would seem to be faced with the problem of appealing to what might be called "arcane" conditions: that is, conditions, like the supposed physiological condition K, about whose presence or absence a person is entirely fallible. But if a person is not infallible about a necessary condition for her consciousness then she is not infallible about her consciousness itself.[32] This is a consequence for which our ordinary notion of consciousness is, I submit, radically unprepared.

Surprisingly enough, this argument can be deployed against the very appeals that are supposed to save consciousness from materialism: for example, dualistic substances, contra-causal freedom, spontaneous creativity, and the like. I won't consider these conditions in detail here. Suffice it to say that they are all clearly independent of (1)–(8) and are about as arcane as conditions can get: not even our best scientific theories are in a position to establish whether they obtain. Quite apart from whether such conditions actually make sense, there is the serious epistemological question of how in the world people are supposed to tell whether they've got what it takes. A particularly appealing arcane condition that nicely illustrates this point is *life*. Requiring it as necessary for consciousness initially seems to capture many of our intuitions, and would explain why we balk at ascribing consciousness to the machines I have imagined, and perhaps to any machine at all.[33] Maybe if something realizing (1)–(8) were also alive, our reluctance to regard it as conscious would diminish.

There are, however, a number of problems with this condition. In the first place, one has to be careful to distinguish 'life' in the biological sense, from "life" in the sense that is merely synonymous with "consciousness" (as in "life after death," which in the first sense would be self-contradictory). Obviously, it is only the first sense that presents a substantial condition. Once we focus on the condition, however, it is by no means clear that people generally regard it as a condition on consciousness. Many people do think of consciousness ("life" in the second sense) after death as at least a possibility, and of many apparently non-biological beings (angels, gods)[34] as being conscious. Moreover, I don't think their judgments about something's being conscious would change merely as result of learning that that thing wasn't biological.[35] Indeed, are we really *so* certain—as certain as we are that they are conscious—that we and our close friends actually are alive? We seem to know this only in the usual "external" way in which we know about other theoretical facts of the world—mostly by taking other peoples' word for it. Perhaps future research will reveal that some of us *are* artifacts, machines, cleverly constructed at MIT out of fleshlike plastics and surreptitiously slipped to our parents the day they say we were born. Surely if we were to discover this about ourselves we would not think it showed that we were not conscious. Thus, even life is too arcane a condition to require for consciousness, if consciousness is to be something of which we are infallibly aware.

Of course, if life or some other arcane condition is not essential to consciousness, then perhaps one ought after all to regard a computer programmed with (1)–(8) as conscious. However, for all my faith in the mechanical duplicability of the other specific aspects of mentation that I have discussed, I must confess that I find myself unable to do so. I am unnerved, and I find most other people unnerved, by the possibility of these machines—not, mind you, by the possibility of any machine being conscious, since we are hardly in a position to speculate about such dimly imagined possibilities, but by the possibility of *existing* machines, programmed merely by (1)–(8), being so. It simply seems impossible to take their mental life all that seriously: to feel morally obliged (not) to treat them in certain ways (not to unplug them, not to frustrate their preferences, not to cause them pain). It's as though they lack a certain "inner light," an inner light that we tend to think awakens our otherwise unconscious bodies and bathes many of our thoughts and feelings in such a glow as to render them immediately accessible to our inner, introspective eye and somehow of some intrinsic moral worth. We see this light each of us only in our own case; we are only able to "infer" it, however uncertainly, in the case of other human beings (and perhaps some animals); and we are unwilling to ascribe it to any machine.[36]

As I draw this familiar picture out and compare it with the details of our mental lives that I have considered, it seems to me appallingly crude, as simplistic a conception of human psychology as the idea of a soul is as an account of personal identity. Just what sort of thing is this "inner light" supposed to be? What possibly could be its source? How is it "perceived," necessarily each in his own case, not possibly by any other? What is its relation to attention, reasoning, nested intentions, problem solving, decision making, memory? Somehow, these *detailed* questions seem inappropriate, a little like asking of a Fundamentalist, "Just how did God go about creating the world in six days?" "How did His saying 'Let there be light!' bring about there being light?" Indeed, just as the Fundamentalist seems to believe in his account of the world independently of scientific research, so do we seem to believe in our consciousness and the machine's lack of it independently of any reasonable arguments.[37]

Perhaps the problem is better seen the other way around: once we have accounts of the various processes I have mentioned, *what is added by consciouess?* What further light does this inner light shed upon our minds? What phenomena is unexplained without it? Perhaps there is something. But, perhaps too, as Hume found in the case of personal identity, there is nothing more, and it would be wrong-headed to identify consciousness with any of these actual processes, singly or together. None of them play particularly the moral role that consciousness traditionally is supposed to play. There would seem to be no actual thing or process (or even "function"[38]) that our past usages have been "getting at" (cf. Putnam 1975). That would seem to afford at least one reason for doubting that the term refers, that is, it would give a reason for doubting there really is such a thing as consciousness at all.

This doubt, however, is pernicious. Once we allow it, it would seem that the concept of consciousness no longer has a hold. Although arguments about necessary conditions for the application of a concept are difficult in general to defend, it would seem that, if we abandon the Cartesian Intuition, we've lost what little hold on the notion of consciousness that we have. But if the truth of the Cartesian Intuition is a necessary condition on the applicability of the notion of consciousness, then the *mere possibility* of a

machine of the sort I have described not being conscious entails that the there is no such thing as consciousness.

We should be clear about precisely what the consequences would be were we to give up our belief in consciousness. It would by no means entail any extravagant Behavioristic or Eliminitivist claim that no mental terms at all are scientifically respectable, much less that none of them succeeded in referring. I have used mental terms throughout my descriptions of the capacities of people and machines, and I doubt very much that they could ever be reasonably eliminated. But one needn't be committed thereby to *every* pre-scientific mentalistic term, or to finding for every such term some post-scientific equivalent. Some terms may simply have to go, as "angels" did in an account of planetary motion, and as "the soul" does in our account of our personal identities. Nor would one be committed to abandoning the term in ordinary talk. If the term "conscious" is only meant to indicate that a person is, say, awake and capable of intentional, attended activity on which she might be able to report, then the term is clearly harmless enough. I think it is often used in this way: it would seem to be the usage underlying such claims as those of Moruzzi (1966) and Penfield (1975) that locate consciousness merely in the activation of the reticular formation. We need only notice that, according to such usage, a computer programmed with just clauses (1)–(5), if my earlier arguments are correct, would qualify as conscious too.

In view of the doubts that I have raised here, what are we to make of our beliefs about consciousness? In a famous passage, Wittgenstein (1953/1967, p. 97e) writes: "only of a living human being can one say: it has sensations ... is conscious or unconscious," and, more recently, Karl Pribram (1976, p. 298) innocently remarks, "I tend to view animals, especially furry animals, as conscious—not plants, not inanimate crystals, not computers. This might be called the "cuddliness criterion." I don't see any *justification* in these claims; they seem, in Block's (1978) phrase, arbitrarily chauvanistic, "speciesist." But they may accurately describe the pattern of our ascriptions, unjustifiable though that pattern may be. We may be strongly inclined to think of ourselves and our biological kin in a special way that we are not disposed to think of machines, or at least not machines that don't look and act like us. Should a machine look and act as human beings normally do—indeed, should we discover that one of us *is* a machine—then we *would* think of it in the same way. We might, of course, try to justify this disposition by behaviorism (and I think this accounts for much of the attraction of that otherwise bankrupt theory), or, failing that, we might try to find some inner condition that would mark the distinction that we want. We are tempted, I think, to try to ground the difference that is so vivid to us in the kind of metaphysical difference that the traditional picture of consciousness suggests, and to claim for it a certainty to which we feel introspection naturally entitles us. (On the extent to which introspection may be susceptible to this sort of imposition, see Nisbett and Wilson 1977.) But then we find, as I have found in this chapter, that no such inner condition exists. In all theoretically significant ways we seem to be indistinguishable from the "mere machines" from which we nevertheless insist upon distinguishing ourselves.

If some story like this were true, perhaps all we could do is acquiesce to our apparently arbitrary biases. We would need to abandon the attempt to find for them any false metaphysical buttressing in some special condition of consciousness, just as we need to abandon the attempt to find such buttressing for our personal identities in same special soul. In both cases, of course, the consequences for moral theory would be disappointing: we would have trouble justifying the special concern we feel towards people and animals, just as we have trouble justifying the special concern we feel toward our futures and our pasts (cf. Parfit 1971a, 1971b). Human reason would turn out to have the peculiar fate, that in one species of its beliefs it would be burdened by questions that it would not

be able to ignore, but which it would never be able satisfactorily to answer.

Postscript

Since the appearance of this essay eight years ago, I have expanded on a number of its ideas in articles that the interested reader may want to consult (See Rey 1997 for an expansion of the argument as a whole).

In section III, I make a passing analogy between sensation experiences and first-person reflexive thoughts that I have since developed at length (Rey 1992, 1993, 1997, chap. 11). Similar suggestions have been independently developed by Lycan (1990) and Leeds (1992).

In section IV, I failed to emphasize what I briefly mention in its antepenultimate paragraph: that I have no argument against what might be called a "weak" notion of consciousness, which involves, for example, merely wakefulness, attention, or reportability, and is of obvious utility to psychology. The only problem with such a weak notion is that if the rest of my argument is correct, it applies equally well to the suitably programmed computer. The notion whose application I am doubting is a "stronger" one, intended to distinguish us from such machines.

Brian Loar has complained to me that the argument in section IV seems excessively epistemic, in ways reminiscent of positivism and the passages of the later Wittgenstein to which I allude. Although the possibility of first-person skepticism that I emphasize is a disturbing consequence of the considerations I marshal, the ultimate argument against (strong) consciousness that I am raising does not rest on it alone. Rather, my point is that such a property is explanatorily otiose: it plays no more role in any warranted account of the world than do angels or absolute space. We have no non-question-begging reason to postulate such properties. As I argue in Rey 1994, 1996, 1997, chap. 11, it is this metaphysical insight—that such consciousness would be like "a wheel that can be turned though nothing else moves with it" (Wittgenstein 1953: §271)—that lies buried amid Wittgenstein's admittedly far too epistemic discussions of "private languages" and the like.

Elsewhere (Rey 1993, 1994, 1996, and 1997: chap. 11), I develop the suggestions of the last two paragraphs of section IV: that our notion of (strong) consciousness involves a projection of our ineluctable (perhaps weakly conscious) reactions to the appearances of our conspecifics and things that look like them. I argue that it is this projection that underlies our insistence on what Wittgenstein rightly noted was the poor "picture" of the "inner" modeled on the "outer" that has so many of us in its grip.

Notes

This chapter is a slightly revised version of Rey (1986), which was a substantial revision of (1983a). Although details could be changed and updated, none would affect the general strategy or conclusions. Intermediate drafts have served as bases for talks at the Universities of Arizona, Illinois, Belgrade, Ljubljana, Graz, and Vienna, at Bates College, at the 1984 Dubrovnik Conference in the Philosophy of Science, and at the filozofski fakultet, Zadar (Croatia). I am indebted to these audiences for their hospitality and stimulating responses. I am also grateful to the National Endowment for the Humanities and the Fulbright Commission for financial support, and to Louise Antony, Ned Block, Richard Davidson, Joe Levine, Gary Matthews, Elizabeth Robertson, Michael Slote, and Eleanor Saunders for helpful discussions and suggestions.

1. For more recent developments of the Humean argument, see Parfit (1971a), and for replies, Lewis (1976) and Rey (1976).

2. See many of the essays in, e.g., Eccles (1966); Globus, Maxwell, and Savodnik (1976); Schwartz and Shapiro (1976); Davidson and Davidson (1980); and Davidson, Schwartz, and Shapiro (1983).

3. See, e.g., Wigner (1967, 1982) and Wheeler (1982).

4. The Oxford English Dictionary lists ten definitions of "conscious," seven of "consciousness," on the latter of which Natsoulas (1978) expanded, although Ryle (1949) considered only seven for both.

5. That the business of providing definitions of even commonly used words is not an entirely *a priori* activity, but may go hand in hand with the development of a theory of their referents seems a natural corollary of recent discussions of reference in Putnam (1970, 1975) and Kripke (1972/1980). I develop this in relation to concept identity in Rey (1983b, 1985, 1997: 1.5).

6. I shall use "inductive" here very broadly so as to include not only principles of enumeration, but also any "reasonable" relations between evidence and explanatory hypotheses, especially those associated with "abduction," "analysis-by-synthesis," and "inference to the best explanation"; see, e.g., Peirce (1901/1955). MacKay (1951), Harman (1965), Chomsky (1972).

7. Behaviorists thought they had a better one that didn't advert to any mental terms at all. I take for granted the standard criticisms of that view, as found in, e.g., Chomsky (1959), Taylor (1963), Dennett (1978, Pt. 2, sec. 4, pp. 53-70), Gleitman (1981: Ch. 5), many of which I summarize in Rey (1984).

8. I discuss practical reason and its status as a law of thought in Rey (1987). See also, e.g., Horgan and Woodward (1985); and Elster (1986).

9. The properties of a sentential model that seem to me to recommend it are its capabilities of (a) expressing structured propositions; (b) capturing rational relations into which attitudes enter; (c) individuating attitudes sufficiently finely to distinguish ones containing, e.g., synonymous descriptions, co-referential names, and indexicals (cf. Burge 1978; Kripke 1979; Bealer 1982; Ch. 3); (d) explaining how attitudes can be causally efficacious; and (e) allowing different roles and access relations for different attitudes. It is difficult to imagine any sort of representation other than a sentence that can perform all these roles (e.g., *images* certainly couldn't).

10. This seems to be the main issue bothering Searle (1980) in his well-known example of the "Chinese Room." In Rey (1986), I discuss this and related issues that I think are confounded in Searle's discussion. The Stampe (1977) proposal that I advocate here and there has also been advanced in slightly different form by Dretske (1981), Stalnaker (1984), and Fodor (1987).

11. This is not the place to defend such a theory of meaning in detail. Suffice it to say that (a) I intend it only as a *sufficient* condition of meaning: there may be other ways that meaning may arise, but should something be able to operate as described, its states would seem to play the role that meaningful states seem ordinarily to play and (b) such a basis figures in a variety of

theories of meaning, from truth-conditional proposals of Wittgenstein (1920) and Davidson (1967), to possible world proposals of Stalnaker (1984), to discrimination proposals one finds in the work of Behaviorists like Quine (1960: Ch. 2) and even in Searle (1983: 177). The proposal is plausibly confined to the primitive predicates of a language, the semantics of logical particles relying on their inferential roles, and that of complex expressions on standard recursions (capturing Searle's (1984) "aspectual shape").

12. I have in mind here the "frame problem" currently vexing work in artificial intelligence (see McCarthy and Hayes 1969, and Dennett 1984 for useful discussion). Although I disagree with many of the ways Dreyfus (1972) proposes for thinking about the problem, I do think it a merit of his book that it anticipated many aspects of it, particularly what Fodor (1983) has called the "globality" and "Quinity" of central belief fixation. In distinguishing artificial intentionality from artificial intelligence. I hope I've made it plain that none of this discussion depends on a solution to these problems.

13. Some, e.g., Lucas (1961, 1968), have argued that it is a consequence of the Gödel Incompleteness theorem that the human mind is no machine; so, the machine I am imagining would necessarily fall short of human mentation. The short answer to this argument is that it presumes human minds are consistent. Aside from the vast implausibility of *that* claim generally, the mechanist may also reply that, if indeed we can decide the formally undecidable sentence, we do it only on pain of inconsistency. See Lewis (1969, 1979) for longer answers, and Cherniak (1986) for an excellent discussion of the "minimal rationality" that needs to be required of us, and consequently of any machine.

14. In considering here and below the consciousness of machines programmed in this and other ways, I shall be citing what I take to be ordinary pre-theoretic intuitions about the notion of consciousness.

15. For similar, but less complex proposals by leading neurophysiologists, see Moruzzi (1966), Knapp (1976), John (1976). Wilks (1984: 123) makes the criticism I make here of such proposals in computer science of, e.g., Sayre (1976).

16. One might argue that *genuine* thoughts, intentions, perceptions presuppose consciousness at least as a background condition. But they would need to account for the explanatory power, adumbrated above, that such ascription seems to possess without it. In any case

we would still be entitled to an answer to the question being addressed in this paper, that of precisely wherein this presupposition consists.

17. See also Casteneda (1968), Anscombe (1975), Perry (1979).

18. Where being "self-aware" or "self-conscious" doesn't merely verbally entail consciousness. That is, to avoid begging the question, these expressions must be used merely for emphatic reflexive propositional attitudes.

19. What is wanted here to clinch the case are experimentally controlled examples à la Nisbett and Wilson (1977) of the effects of specifically *second*-order emphatic reflexive thoughts that the agent is unable to express. Unfortunately, Laing et al. (1966) don't provide any, and I've been so far unable to find any studies that do (Gur and Sackheim (1979) in their interesting work on self-deception provide some, but inconclusive evidence in this regard). However, it's hard to believe that this isn't simply an accident due to the disinterest of psychologists in specific philosophical theses. It's not at all difficult to imagine plausible psychoanalytical explanations adverting to second-order thoughts that the agent is repressing: e.g., someone might unconsciously *think* that he *wants* to murder his father, and because he can't bear to admit this, neither the thought nor the want is permitted to enter consciousness; the unconscious thought explains, though, his "free floating" feelings of guilt, which the unconscious want by itself would fail to do.

Another objection to second-order views like Rosenthal's and Smith's is that they conflate an agent's being conscious *of* a thought with that thought's *being conscious*: an "educated neurotic" might eagerly accept Freudian theory, and ascribe to himself all manner of unconscious motives that he becomes "conscious of", without them becoming thereby conscious. The "buffer memory" I propose below, and discuss in detail in Rey (1987) affords a way to deal with this problem in a way that is not committed to second-order attitudes.

20. See also Wilks (1984, 122), who endorses a similar criterion, citing Danto (1960).

21. Dennett (1978a, 156) himself makes such a proposal, one that, incidentally, permits ascribing consciousness to animals and to the humanly inarticulate. In Rey (1987) I develop this proposal in some detail, distinguishing "avowed" from "central" attitudes, and arguing that the distinction is important to us in a

number of ways, for example, as a basis for an account of akrasia and self-deception. I am inclined to think that the proposal does capture a "weak" notion of consciousness, i.e., consciousness as we apply it to human beings and perhaps some animals (see below); but it would seem to fail to capture the full, ordinary notion insofar as it is equally applicable to existing desk top computers which few people would seriously regard as conscious for a moment.

22. The problem here is *not* that raised by Searle's "Chinese Room," concerning whether anyone following *any* program could be said to understand Chinese. *That* problem is solved simply by considering richer (particularly recursive semantic) programs than Searle considers, as well as by avoiding fallacies of division. See Rey (1986, sec. I).

23. So that the machine won't spend all of its time merely brooding over increasingly nested beliefs, a limit would need to be placed on the nestings generated by (6), particularly as it might interact with (7).

24. Bealer (1982, 247) claims that "attending, concentrating, meditating, contemplating" do not have "mechanically recognizable functions." I fail to see why the mechanical operations described here wouldn't essentially suffice.

25. Searle (1981) argues that, since someone could follow a computer program like the one I am sketching without feeling pain, a machine running on such a program wouldn't feel pain either. This, of course, is simply another version of his "Chinese Room" argument, and would seem to be guilty of the same fallacy of division that advocates of the "systems" reply have deplored, and which I have further criticized in Rey (1986). Briefly, the person following a program corresponds to a computer's central processing unit, which no more needs to share properties of the entire system than Ronald Reagan needs to share the properties of the United States.

26. The important (im)possibility of scepticism about one's own present sensations that I shall be considering in what follows was, I believe, first raised by Wittgenstein (1953/1967, 243–315) in his famous "private language argument." Shoemaker (1975/1984, 189–190) in a passage that was the inspiration for much that I have written here, takes the impossibility of such scepticism to be an argument for functionalism, a specific version of which I am developing in this paper. I think Shoemaker is right in regarding functionalism as the only

plausible account of mental states that preserves first-person privileges. Unfortunately it seems to do so at the cost of third person attributions of such states to a computer of the sort I am describing.

27. See, e.g., Descartes (*Meditations*, II), Locke (*Essay*, IV, 2), Hume (*Treatise*, I, iv, 2), Ayer (1956, 55), Malcolm (1963, 85), Chisholm (1981, 79–81). For a useful survey of these and other versions of privileged access, see Alston (1971). For interesting experimental data undermining the privileges even in the human case, see Hilgard (1977).

28. I am no longer confident that that claim is plausible. It now seems to me that all that is necessary are all the probably very subtle cognitive effects of the hormones and neuroregulators (e.g., beliefs about how one's body feels, the timing of cognitive processes). If this were true, then the appeal to physiology here would be even less plausible than I argue it to be below.

29. Lycan (1981) has pointed out that in general one would expect our various psychological faculties to be characterizable on many different levels of functional abstraction from the basic physical properties of the brain.

30. That is, it is possible within the world(s) described by the psychological laws being considered here. It is important that the possibility here is not merely epistemic but metaphysical, Were it only epistemic, it could be dismissed as due merely to ignorance, as many previous arguments, e.g., against materialism reasonably have been, cf. Maloncy (1985: 32).

31. I say "unacceptable," not "false," I leave open as part of the puzzle I am raising whether one is entitled to move from the former to the latter.

32. By 'x is infallible about p' here I intend no claim about *knowledge*, but only 'it is impossible for x to think or believe that p when not-p': this latter is closed under logical implication even if 'x knows p' isn't. For purposes of contrast with "arcane" conditions. I'm also presuming here that the agent is *cognitively* fully normal, thinking that (s)he/it is conscious clearly and confidently, not in the way one might do when asleep or in some other cognitively marginal state.

33. Recent proponents of life as a condition on consciousness include Wittgenstein (1953/1967, p. 97e), Ziff (1959), Cook (1969), Gareth Matthews (1977).

34. Why shouldn't the computer I am imagining have the status of an angel, a god, a ghost, or some other non-biological, but still psychological agent?

35. It is some indictment of our ordinary notion of consciousness that we seem to have contradictory intuitions about its application, our judgments about something's consciousness being sensitive to the way in which we encounter it. Described from the "bottom up," i.e., imagining first a non-biological machine, and then a program that would realize various human mental abilities, we are disinclined to regard it as conscious; but proceeding from the "top down" and discovering that close friends, or we ourselves, are just such machines seems to elicit the opposite verdict. I suspect this has to do with the ways in which our understanding of people and animals are "triggered" by certain patterns of stimulation (cf. the penultimate paragraph of this essay).

36. The image of consciousness as an inner light is advanced in many places, perhaps most recently in Smith (1986). Even Wittgenstein, so critical of traditional pictures of the mind, compares "turning my attention to my own consciousness" to the glance of someone "admiring the illumination of the sky and drinking in the light" (1953/1967, 124). Other passages in Wittgenstein, e.g., sec. 308, do suggest, however, a version of the eliminativist proposal being avocated here. The peculiar amalgamation of epistemology and ethics that the traditional image involves is explored at some length by Richard Rorty (1979:42–69), when he discusses what he regards as the traditional belief in "Our Glassy Essence," a term he draws from Shakespeare and Peirce. The view I am entertaining in this chapter might be called "eliminativist" with respect to consciousness, although (token ontologically) "reductionist," with regard to the propositional attitudes.

37. Cf. Wittgenstein (1953/1967: p. 178e): "My attitude towards him is an attitude towards a soul. I am not of the *opinion* that he has a soul."

38. James (1912) also denied the existence of consciousness, although he went on to explain that he meant "only to deny that the word stands for an entity, but to insist most emphatically that it does stand for a function" (p. 4). When I say there may be no such thing, I mean no such thing *whatsoever*.

References

Alston, W. (1971). "Varieties of Privileged Access." *American Philosophical Quarterly* 8(3), pp. 223–241.

Anscombe, G. (1975). "The First Person." In *Mind and Language*, Edited by S. Guttenplan, Oxford: Oxford Univ. Press, pp. 45–66.

Ayer, A. J. (1956). *The Problem of Knowledge*. London: Macmillan.

Bealer, G. (1982). *Quality and Concept*. New York: Oxford University Press.

Berliner, H. (1980). "Computer Backgammon." *Scientific American* 242(6), pp. 64–85.

Block, N. J. (1978). "Troubles with Functionalism." In *Readings in the Philosophy of Psychology*, vol. 2. Edited by N. Block. Cambridge: Harvard University Press.

Brown, G. (1974). "The Believer System." Technical Report RUCBM-TR-34. Department of Computer Science, Rutgers University.

Burge, T. (1978). "Belief and Synonymy." *Journal of Philosophy* 75(3), March, pp. 119–138.

Castenada, H. (1968). "On the Logic of Attributions of Self-Knowledge to Others." *Journal of Philosophy* 65, pp. 439–456.

Cherniak, C. (1986). *Minimal Rationality*. Cambridge: MIT Press/Bradford Books.

Chisholm, R. M. (1981). *The First Person*. Minneapolis: University of Minnesota Press.

Chomsky, N. (1959). Review of Skinner's *Verbal Behavior*. *Language* 35, pp. 26–58.

———. (1972). *Language and Mind* (enlarged edition). New York: Harcourt Brace Jovanovich.

Cook, J. (1969). "Human Beings." In *Studies in the Philosophy of Wittgenstein*, pp. 117–151. Edited by P. Winch. New York: Humanities Press.

Danto, A. (1961). "On Consciousness in Machines." In *Determinism and Freedom in the Age of Modern Science*. Edited by S. Hook. New York: Collier.

Darley, J. M., and E. Berscheid (1967). "Increased Liking as a Result of the Anticipation of Personal Contact." *Human Relations* 20, pp. 29–40.

Davidson, D. (1967). "Truth and Meaning." *Synthese*, 17, pp. 304–323.

Davidson, J., and R. Davidson, eds. (1980). *The Psychobiology of Consciousness*. New York: Plenum Press.

Davidson, R., G. Schwartz, and D. Shapiro, eds. (1983). *Consciousness and Self-Regulation* vol. 3. New York: Plenum Press.

Dennett, D. (1969). *Content and Consciousness*. London: Routledge & Kegan Paul.

———. (1971/1978). "Intentional Systems." *Journal of Philosophy* 68, pp. 87–106.

———. (1978). *Brainstorms: Philosophical Essays on Mind and Psychology.* Cambridge: MIT Press/Bradford Books.

———. (1984). "Cognitive Wheels: The Frame Problem of AI." In *Minds, Machines and Evolution.* Edited by C. Hookway. Cambridge: Cambridge University Press.

Descartes, R. (1641/1911). "Meditations on First Philosophy (with Replies and Objections)." In *The Philosophical Works of Descartes.* Edited by E. S. Haldane and G. R. T. Ross. London: Cambridge University Press.

Dretske, F. (1981). *Knowledge and the Flow of Information.* Cambridge: MIT Press/Bradford Books.

Dreyfus, H. (1972). *What Computers Can't Do,* revised edition. New York: Harper and Row.

Eccles, J. C., ed. (1966). *Brain and Conscious Experience.* Berlin: Springer Verlag.

Elster, J., ed. (1986). *Rational Choice.* New York: New York University Press.

Festinger, L. (1957). *Cognitive Dissonance.* Stanford: Stanford University Press.

Field, H. (1978). "Mental Representation." In *Readings in the Philosophy of Psychology,* vol. 2. Edited by N. Block. Cambridge: Harvard University Press.

Fodor, J. A. (1975). *The Language of Thought.* New York: Crowell.

———. (1983). *The Modularity of Mind.* Cambridge: MIT Press.

———. (1987). *Psychosemantics.* Cambridge: MIT Press.

Gleitman, H. (1981). *Psychology.* New York: Norton & Co.

Globus, G., G. Maxwell, and I. Savodnik, eds. (1976). *Consciousness and the Brain.* New York: Plenum Press.

Grice, H. P. (1957). "Meaning." *Philosophical Review* 66, pp. 337–388.

Gur, R., and H. Sackheim (1979). "Self-Deception: A Concept in Search of a Phenomenon." *Journal of Personality and Social Psychology* 37(2).

Harman, G. (1965). "Inference to the Best Explanation." *Philosophical Review* 74, pp. 88–95.

———. (1973). *Thought.* Princeton: Princeton University Press.

Hempel, C. (1965). *Aspects of Scientific Explanation and Other Essays in the Philosophy of Science.* New York: Free Press.

Hess, R. (1975). "The Role of Pupil Size in Communication." *Scientific American* 233(5), pp. 110–118.

Hilgard, E. (1977). *Divided Consciousness: Multiple Controls in Human Thought and Action.* New York: Wiley & Sons.

Horgan, T. and Woodward, J. (1985), "Folk Psychology is Here to Stay." *Philosophical Review* 94, 2, pp. 197–225.

Hume, D. (1739/1965). *A Treatise of Human Nature,* Edited by L. A. Selby-Bigge. Oxford: Clarendon.

Jackson, F. (1982). "Epiphenomenal Qualia." *Philosophical Quarterly* 32, pp. 127–136.

James, W. (1912). "Does Consciousness Exist?" In *Essays in Radical Empiricism and Pluralistic Universe.* Edited by R. B. Perry. New York: Dutton.

John, E. (1976). "A Model of Consciousness." In *Consciousness and Self-Regulation,* Vol. 1. Edited by G. Schwartz and D. Shapiro. New York: Plenum.

Kahneman, D. (1973). *Attention and Effort.* Englewood Cliffs: Prentice-Hall.

Knapp, P. (1976). "The Mysterious 'Split': A Clinical Inquiry into Problem of Consciousness and Brain." In *Consciousness and the Brain.* Edited by G. Globus, G. Maxwell, and I. Savodnik. New York: Plenum Press.

Kripke, S. A. (1972/1980). *Naming and Necessity.* Cambridge: Harvard University Press.

———. (1979). "A Puzzle about Belief." In *Meaning and Use,* pp. 239–283. Edited by A. Margalit. Dordrecht: Reidel.

Lackner, J. R., and M. Garrett (1972). "Resolving Ambiguity: Effects of Biasing Context in the Unattended Ear." *Cognition* 1.

Laing, R., H. Phillipson, and A. Lee (1966). *Interpersonal Perception: A Theory and Method of Research.* London: Ravistock.

Latané, B., and J. M. Darley (1970). *The Unresponsive Bystander: Why Doesn't He Help?* New York: Appleton-Century-Crofts.

Leeds, S. (1992). "Qualia, Awareness and Sellars." *Nous,* pp. 303–329.

Lewis, D. (1969). *Convention: A Philosophic Study.* Cambridge: Harvard University Press.

———. (1976). "Survival and Identity." In *The Identities of Persons*, pp. 1–40. Edited by A. Rorty. Berkeley: University of California Press.

———. (1979). "Lucas against Mechanism II." *Canadian Journal of Philosophy* 9, pp. 373–376.

Lucas, J. (1961). "Minds, Machines, and Gödel." *Philosophy* 36, pp. 112–137.

———. (1968). "Satan Stultified: A Rejoiner to Paul Beneceraff." *Monist* 52, pp. 45–48.

Luria, A. (1976). "The Human Brain and Conscious Activity." In *Consciousness and Self-Regulation*, vol. 1. Edited by F. Schwartz and D. Shapiro. New York: Plenum Press.

Lycan, W. (1981). "Form, Function, and Feel." *Journal of Philosophy* 78(1), pp. 24–50.

———. (1990). "What Is the 'Subjectivity of the Mental'?" In J. Tomberlin, ed., *Philosophical Perspectives*, Vol. 4: *Action Theory and the Philosophy of Mind*. Atascadero, CA: Ridgview.

McCarthy, J., and P. Hayes (1969). "Some Philosophical Problems from the Standpoint of Artificial Intelligence." In *Machine Intelligence*, Vol. 4, pp. 463–502. Edited by B. Meltzer and D. Michie. Edinburgh: Edinburgh University Press.

MacKay, D. (1951). "Mind-Like Behavior in Artifacts." *British Journal for the Philosophy of Science* 2, pp. 105–121.

Maier, N. (1931). "Reasoning in Humans: II. The Solution of a Problem and Its Appearance in Consciousness." *Journal of Comparative Psychology* 12, pp. 181–194.

Malcolm, N. (1963). *Knowledge and Certainty*. Englewood Cliffs: Prentice-Hall.

Maloney, J. (1985). "About Being a Bat." *Australasian Journal of Philosophy*, 63(1), pp. 26–47.

Matthews, G. (1977). "Consciousness and Life." *Philosophy* 52, pp. 13–26.

Miller, G. (1956). "The Magic Number Seven Plus or Minus Two: Some Limits on Our Capacity for Processing Information." *Psychological Review* 63, pp. 81–97.

Moruzzi, G. (1966). "Functional Significance of Sleep with Particular Regard to the Brain Mechanisms Underlying Consciousness." In J. C. Eccles, ed., *Brain and Conscious Experience*. Berlin: Springer Verlag.

Natsoulas, T. (1978). "Consciousness." *American Psychologist* 12, pp. 906–914.

Nisbett, R., and T. Wilson (1977). "Telling More Than We Can Know." *Psychological Review*, pp. 231–259.

Parfit, D. (1971a). "Personal Identity." *Philosophical Review* 80(1), pp. 3–28.

———. (1971b). "On the Importance of Self-Identity." *Journal of Philosophy*, pp. 683–690.

Peirce, C. S. (1901/1955). "Abduction and Induction." In *Philosophical Writings of Peirce*, pp. 150–156. Edited by J. Buchler. New York: Dover.

Penfield, W. (1975). *The Mystery of the Mind*. Princeton: Princeton University Press.

Perry, J. (1979). "The Problem of the Essential Indexical." *Nous* 13, pp. 3–21.

Piaget, J. (1976). *The Child and Reality: Principles of Genetic Epistemology*. New York: Penguin.

Pribram, K. (1976). "Problems Concerning the Structure of Consciousness." In G. Globus, G. Maxwell, and I. Savodnik, eds., *Consciousness and the Brain*. New York: Plenum Press.

Putnam, H. (1970/1975). "Is Semantics Possible?" In his *Collected Papers*, Vol. 3, pp. 139–152. Cambridge: Cambridge University Press.

———. (1975). "The Meaning of Meaning." In in his *Collected Papers*, Vol. 3, pp. 215–271. Cambridge: Cambridge University Press.

Quine, W. V. (1960). *Word and Object*. Cambridge: MIT Press.

Rey, G. (1976). "Survival." In *The Identities of Persons*, pp. 41–66. Edited by A. Rorty. Berkeley: University of California Press.

———. (1980). "Functionalism and the Emotion." In *Explaining Emotions*. Edited by A. Rorty. Berkeley: University of California Press.

———. (1983a). "A Reason for Doubting the Existence of Consciousness." In *Consciousness and Self-Regulation*, Vol. 3. Edited by R. Davidson, G. Schwartz, and D. Shapiro. New York: Plenum.

———. (1983b). "Concepts and Stereotypes." *Cognition* 15, pp. 237–262.

———. (1984). "Ontology and Ideology of Behaviorism and Mentalism." Commentary on B. F. Skinner, "Behaviorism at Fifty." *Behavioral and Brain Sciences* 7(4), pp. 640–641.

———. (1985). "Concepts and Conceptions: A Reply to Smith, Medin, and Rips." *Cognition* 19.

———. (1986). "What's Really Going On is Searle's Chinese Room." *Philosophical Studies.*

———. (1987). "Beliefs, Avowals, Akrasia, and Self-Deception." In *Perspectives on Self-Deception.* Edited by A. Rorty and B. MacLaughlin. Berkeley: University of California Press.

———. (1992). "Sensational Sentences." In *Consciousness.* Edited by M. Davies and G. Humphysies. Oxford: Blackwell.

———. (1993). "Sensational Sentences Switched." *Philosophical Studies.* Special issue.

———. (1994). "Wittgenstein, Computationalism and Qualia." In *Philosophy and the Cognitive Sciences*, pp. 61–74. Edited by R. Casati and G. White. Vienna: Hölder-Pichler-Tempsky.

———. (1996). "Towards a Projectivist Account of Conscious Experience." Ferdinand-Schöningh-Verlag. (German version "Annäherung an eine projectivistische Theorie bewuBten Erlebens" published by same, 1995.)

———. (1997). *Contemporary Philosophy of Mind: A Contentiously Classical Approach.* Oxford: Blackwell.

Rorty, T. (1979). *Philosophy and the Mirror of Nature.* Princeton: Princeton University Press.

Rosenthal, D. (1984). "Armstrong's Casual Theory of the Mind." In *D. M. Armstrong*, pp. 79–120. Edited by R. Bogdan. Dordrecht: Reidel.

Ryle, G. (1949). *The Concept of Mind.* London: Hutchinson.

Sayre, K. (1976). *Cybernetics and the Philosophy of Mind.* Atlantic Highlands, NJ: Humanities Press.

Schiffer, S. (1972). *Meaning.* Oxford: Oxford University Press.

———. (1980). "Truth and the Theory of Content." In *Meaning and Understanding.* Edited by H. Parrett and J. Bourveresse. Berlin: de Gruyter.

Schmidt, C., and G. D'Addami (1973). "A Model of the Common Sense Theory of Intention and Personal Causation." In *Proceedings of the Third International Joint Conference on Artificial Intelligence.* Standford: Stanford University Press.

Schwartz, G., and D. Shapiro, eds. (1976). *Consciousness and Self-Regulation*, Vol. 1. New York: Plenum Press.

Searle, J. R. (1980). "Minds, Brains, and Programs." *Behavioral and Brain Sciences* 3, pp. 417–457.

———. (1981). "Analytic Philosophy and Mental Phenomena." In *Midwest Studies in Philosophy*, Vol. 6. Edited by P. French, T. Uehling, and H. Wettstein. Minneapolis: University of Minnesota Press.

———. (1983). *Intentionality: An Essay in the Philosophy of Mind.* Cambridge: Cambridge University Press.

———. (1984). "Intentionality and Its Place in Nature." *Synthese* 61, pp. 3–16.

Shoemaker, S. (1975). "Functionalism and Qualia." *Philosophical Studies* 27, pp. 291–315.

Smith, D. W. (1986). "The Structure of (Self-)Consciousness." *Topoi.*

Stalnaker, R. (1984). *Inquiry.* Cambridge: MIT Press/Bradford Books.

Stampe, D. (1977). "Towards a Causal Theory of Linguistic Representation." In *Midwest Studies in Philosophy II: Studies in the Philosophy of Language*, pp. 42–63. Edited by H. Wettstein and T. Uehling. Morris: University of Minnesota Press.

Stich, S. P. (1983). *From Folk Psychology to Cognitive Science: The Case Against Belief.* Cambridge: MIT Press/Bradford Books.

Taylor, C. (1963). *The Explanation of Behavior.* London: Routledge & Kegan Paul.

Weber, M. (1922/1980). "The Nature of Social Action." In *Weber: Selections in Translation.* Edited by W. G. Runciman. Cambridge: Cambridge University Press.

Weizenbaum, J. (1965). "ELIZA—A Computer Program for the Study of Natural Language Communication Between Men and Machine." *Communication of the Association for Computing Machinery* 9(1), pp. 36–45.

Wheeler, E. (1982). "Bohr, Einstein, and the Strange Lesson of the Quantum." In *Mind in Nature*, pp. 1–30. Edited by R. Elvee. San Francisco: Harper and Row.

Wiener, N. (1954). *The Human Use of Human Beings.* Garden City, NY: Doubleday.

Wigner, E. (1967). "Remarks on the Mind-Body Question." In *Symmetries and Reflections*, pp. 171–184. Bloomington: Indiana University Press.

———. (1982). "The Limitation of the Validity of Present Day Physics." In *Mind in Nature*, pp. 118–133. Edited by R. Elvee. San Francisco: Harper and Row.

Wilks, Y. (1984). "Machines and Consciousness." In *Minds, Machines and Evolution.* Edited by C. Hookway. Cambridge: Cambridge University Press.

Wittgenstein, L. (1920/1967). *Tractatus Logico-Philo-sophicus*. Translated by D. Pears and B. McGuiness. London: Routledge & Kegan Paul.

————. (1953/1967). *Philosophical Investigations*. Translated by G. E. M. Anscombe. 3d edition. Oxford: Blackwell.

Zajonc, R. (1968). "The Attitudinal Effects of Mere Exposure." *Journal of Personality and Social Psychology* 8.

Ziff, P. (1964). "The Feelings of Robots." In *Minds and Machines*, pp. 98–103. Edited by A. R. Anderson. Englewood Cliffs, NJ: Prentice-Hall.

29

Finding the Mind in the Natural World

Frank Jackson

Conceptual analysis played a prominent role in the defense of materialism mounted by the Australian materialists and their American ally David Lewis. It was how they found a place for the mind within the material world. The leading idea is encapsulated in the following argument schema:

1. Mental state M = occupant of functional role F (By conceptual analysis)
2. Occupant of role F = brain state B (By science)

Therefore, M = B (By Transitivity)

This schema gives the role of conceptual analysis in the Australian defense. But it does not tell us why conceptual analysis *had* to have a role in the defense. Indeed, the schema positively invites the thought that conceptual analysis was not needed. For to get the conclusion that M = B, all that is needed is the truth of the two premises. It is not necessary that one of them be a conceptual truth. And I think, speaking more generally, that the Australian materialists left it unclear why materialists need to do some conceptual analysis. Nevertheless, I think that they were right that materialists need to do some conceptual analysis. This paper is a defense of this view. In a nutshell my argument will be that only by doing some conceptual analysis can materialists find a place for the mind in their naturalistic picture of the world. In a final section we will note the implications of our discussion for the knowledge argument.

In arguing for the necessity of conceptual analysis I am swimming against the tide. Current orthodoxy repudiates the role of conceptual analysis in the defense of materialism for at least three reasons. First, materialism is a doctrine in speculative metaphysics. And, runs the first reason, though conceptual analysis has a role in the philosophy of language and the study of concepts, it has no essential role when our subject is what

the world is, at bottom, like. The second reason is that the history of conceptual analysis is the history of failure. For any proffered analysis someone clever always finds a counterexample. The final reason turns on the claim that we have learned from Hilary Putnam and Saul Kripke about the necessary *a posteriori*, and that tells us that there can be necessary connections that, precisely by virtue of being *a posteriori*, are not revealed by or answerable to conceptual analysis. The materialist should, according to this line of thought, hold that the connection between the mental and the material or physical is a necessary *a posteriori* one, and so not a matter accessible via conceptual analysis. During the course of the discussion we will see how to reply to each of these objections to the need for conceptual analysis in the defense of materialism.

The first step in our defense of the materialists' need for conceptual analysis is to note that materialism is a piece of what I will call serious metaphysics, and that, like any piece of serious metaphysics, it faces the location problem.

The Location Problem

Metaphysics is about what there is and what it is like. But it is concerned not with any old shopping list of what there is and what it is like. Metaphysicians seek a comprehensive account of some subject matter—the mind, the semantic, or, most ambitiously, everything—in terms of a limited number of more or less fundamental notions. Some who discuss the debate in the philosophy of mind between dualism and monism complain that *each* position is equally absurd. We should be *pluralists*. Of course we should be pluralists in some sense or other. However, if the thought is that any attempt to explain it all, or to explain it all as far as the mind is concerned, in terms of some limited set of fundamental ingredients is mistaken in principle, then it seems to me that we are being, in effect, invited to abandon serious metaphysics in favor of drawing up big lists. And we know we can do better than that. At least some of the diversity in our world conceals an underlying identity of ingredients. The diversity is a matter of the same elements differently selected and arranged. But if metaphysics seeks comprehension in terms of limited ingredients, it is continually going to be faced with the problem of location. Because the ingredients *are* limited, some putative features of the world are not going to appear explicitly in the story told in the favored terms. The question then will be whether the features nevertheless figure *implicitly* in the story. Serious metaphysics is simultaneously discriminatory and putatively complete, and the combination of these two facts means that there is bound to be a whole range of putative features of our world up for either elimination or location.

What then is it for some putative feature to have a place in the story some metaphysic tells in its favored terms? One answer is for the feature to be *entailed* by the story told in the favored terms. Perhaps the story includes information about mass and volume in so many words, but nowhere mentions density by name. No matter—density facts are entailed by mass and volume facts. Or perhaps the story in the favored terms says that many of the objects around us are nothing but aggregations of molecules held in a lattice-like array by various intermolecular forces. Nowhere in the story in the favored terms is there any mention of solidity. Should we then infer that nothing is solid, or at any rate that this particular metaphysic is committed to nothing being solid? Obviously not. The story in the favored terms will, we may suppose, tell us that these lattice-like arrays of molecules *exclude* each other, the intermolecular forces being such as to prevent the lattices encroaching on each others' spaces. And *that* is what we understand by solidity. That is what it takes, according to our concept, to be solid. Or at least it is near enough. Perhaps prescientifically we might have been tempted to insist that being solid required being everywhere dense

in addition to resisting encroachment. But resisting encroachment explains the stubbing of toes quite well enough for it to be pedantic to insist on anything more in order to be solid. Hence, solidity gets a location or place in the molecular story about our world by being entailed by that story, and we see this by asking ourselves about our concept of solidity in the sense of asking what it takes to be solid.

Thus, one way materialists can show that the psychological has a place in their world view is by showing that the psychological story is entailed by the story about the world told in the materialists' favored terms. We will see, however, that it is not just one way; it is the one and only way.

Completeness and Supervenience

Materialism is the very opposite of a "big list" metaphysics. It is highly discriminatory, operating in terms of a small set of favored particulars, properties, and relations, typically dubbed "physical"—hence, its other name, "physicalism"; and it claims that a complete story, or anyway a complete story of everything contingent, including everything psychological, about our world can in principle be told in terms of these physical particulars, properties, and relations alone. Only then is materialism interestingly different from dual attribute theories of mind.

Now what, precisely, is a complete story? We can make a start by noting that one particularly clear way of showing *incompleteness* is by appeal to independent variation. What shows that three coordinates do not provide a complete account of location in space-time is that we can vary position in space-time while keeping any three coordinates constant. Hence, an obvious way to approach completeness is in terms of the lack of independent variation. But, of course, lack of independent variation is supervenience: position in space-time supervenes on the four coordinates. So the place to look when looking for illumination regarding the sense in which materialism claim to be complete, and, in particular, to be complete with respect to the psychological, is at various supervenience theses.[1]

Now materialism is not just a claim about the completeness of the physical story concerning certain individuals or particulars in our world. It claims completeness concerning the world itself, concerning, that is, the total way things are. Accordingly, we need to think of the supervenience base as consisting of possible worlds—complete ways things might be. We need, accordingly, to look to *global* superevenience theses, an example of which is

(I)   Any two possible worlds that are physical duplicates (physical property, particular and relation for physical property, particular and relation identical) are duplicates *simpliciter*.

But (I) does not capture what the materialists have in mind. Materialism is a claim about *our* world, the actual world, to the effect that its physical nature exhausts all its nature, whereas (I) is a claim about worlds in general. A more restricted supervenience thesis in which our world is explicitly mentioned is:

(II)   Any world that is a physical duplicate of our world is a duplicate *simpliciter* of our world.

However, materialists can surely grant that there is a possible world physically exactly like ours but which contains as an *addition* a lot of mental life sustained in non-physical stuff, as long as they insist that this world is not our world. Consider the view of those theists that hold that materialism is the correct account of earthly existence but it leaves out of account the afterlife. When we die our purely material psychology is reinstated in purely non-physical stuff. Surely materialists can grant that these theists are right about some world, some way things might be, as long as they insist that it is *not* our world, not the way things actually are. Hence, materialists are not committed to (II).

The trouble with (II) is that it represents materialists' claims as more wide-ranging than they in fact are. What we need is something like (II) but that limits itself to worlds more nearly like ours, or at least more nearly like ours on the materialists' conception of what our world is like. I suggest

(III)   Any world that is a *minimal* physical duplicate of our world is a duplicate *simpliciter* of our world.

What is a minimal physical duplicate? Think of a recipe for making scones. It tells you what to do, but not what *not* to do. It tells you to add butter to the flour but does not tell you not to add whole peppercorns to the flour. Why not? Part of the reason is that no one would think to add them unless explicitly told to. But part of the reason is logical. It is impossible to list all the things *not* to do. There are indefinitely many of them. Of necessity the writers of recipes rely on an intuitive understanding of an implicitly included "stop" clause in their recipes. A minimal physical duplicate of our world is what you would get if you used the physical nature of our world (including of course its physical laws) as a recipe in this sense for making a world.

We arrived at (III) by eliminating alternatives. But we can give a positive argument for the conclusion that the materialist is committed to (III). Suppose that (III) is false; then there is a difference in nature between our world and some minimal physical duplicate of it. But then either our world contains some nature that the minimal physical duplicate does not, or the minimal physical duplicate contains some nature that our world does not. The second is impossible because the extra nature would have to be non-physical (as our world and the duplicate are physically identical), and the minimal physical duplicate contains no non-physical nature by definition. But if our world contains some nature that the duplicate does not, this nature must be non-physical (as our world and the duplicate are physically identical). But then materialism would be false, for our world would contain some non-physical nature. Hence, if (III) is false, materialism is false—that is to say, materialism is committed to (III).

From (III) to Entry by Entailment

Given that (III) follows from materialism, there is a straightforward and familiar argument to show that if materialism is true, then the psychological story about our world is entailed by the physical story about our world.

We can think of a statement as telling a story about the way the world is, and as being true inasmuch as the world is the way the story says it is. Let Θ be the statement which tells the rich, complex, and detailed physical story that is true at the actual world and all and only the minimal physical duplicates of the actual world, and false elsewhere. Let Π be any true statement entirely about the psychological nature of our world: Π is true at our world, and every world at which Π is false differs in some psychological way from our world. If (III) is true, every world at which Θ is true is a duplicate *simpliciter* of our world, and so *a fortiori* a psychological duplicate of our world. But then every world at which Θ is true is a world at which Π is true—that is, Θ entails Π.

We have thus derived what we might call the *entry by entailment thesis*. A putative psychological fact has a place in the materialists's world view if and only if it is entailed by the physical story about the world. The one and only way of getting a place is by entailment.

From Entry by Entailment to Conceptual Analysis

How does entry by entailment show the importance of conceptual analysis? If Θ entails Π, what makes Θ true also makes Π true (at least when Θ and Π are contingent). But what makes Θ true is the physical way our world is. Hence, the materialist is committed to each and every psychological statement being made true by a purely physical way our world is. But it is the very business of conceptual analysis to address which matters framed in terms of one set of terms and concepts are made true by which matters framed in a different set of terms and concepts. For instance, when we seek an analysis of knowledge in terms of truth, belief, justification, causation, and so on, we seek an account of how matters described in terms of the latter notions make true matters described in terms of the former. When we seek an account of reference, we seek an account of the kinds of causal and descriptive facts which make it true that a term names an object. When and if we succeed, we will have an account of what makes it true that "Moses" names in terms of, among other things, causal links between uses of the word and Moses himself. And so on and so forth.

How could the *a priori* reflections on, and intuitions about, possible cases so distinctive of conceptual analysis be relevant to, for instance, the causal theory of reference? Well, the causal theory of reference is a theory about the conditions under which, say, "Moses" refers to a certain person. But that is nothing other than a theory about the possible situations in which "Moses" refers to that person, and the possible situations in which "Moses" does not refer to that person. Hence, intuitions about various possible situations—the meat and potatoes of conceptual analysis—are bound to hold center stage. (This is particularly true when the test situations cannot be realized. We cannot, for instance, make Twin Earth to check empirically what we would say about whether XYZ is water.)

The alternative is to *invent* our answers. Faced with the question, say, of whether the physical way things are makes true the belief way things are, we could *stipulate* the conditions under which something counts as a belief in such a way as to ensure that there are beliefs, or, if we preferred, that there are no beliefs. But that would not bear on whether beliefs according to *our* concept have a place in the materialists' picture of things, only on whether beliefs according to the stipulated concept have a place. In order to address the question of whether beliefs as we understand them have a place, what else can we do but consult and be guided by our honed intuitions about what counts as a belief? Would it be better to invent, or to go by what seems *counter* intuitive?

I should emphasize, though, that a sensible use of conceptual analysis will allow a limited but significant place for *a posteriori* stipulation. We mentioned earlier the example of finding a place for solidity in the molecular picture of our world, and the fact that what the molecular picture vindicates is the existence of solid bodies according to a conception of solidity cashed out in terms of mutual exclusion rather than in terms of the conjunction of mutual exclusion and being everywhere dense. For our day-to-day traffic with objects, it is the mutual exclusion that matters, and accordingly it is entirely reasonable to rule that mutual exclusion is enough for solidity. The role of conceptual analysis of *K*-hood is not always to settle on a nice, neat, *totally a priori* list of necessary and sufficient conditions for being a *K*—indeed, that is the task that has so often been beyond us. It is rather to guide us in dividing up the cases that *clearly* are *not* cases of a *K*, from the cases that a principle of charity might lead us to allow as cases of a *K*. Then, armed with this information, we are in a position to address the question of whether some inventory of fundamental ingredients, does, or does not, have a place for *K*s.

I should also emphasize that the contention is not that *a priori* reflection on possible cases gives us new information, let alone some sort of infallible new information, about what the world is like. The reflection is *a priori* in the sense that we are not consulting our intuitions about what would *happen* in certain possible cases—it is not like the famous thought experiments in science—rather we are consulting our intuitions about how to *describe* certain possible cases. And what we learn (in the sense of making explicit) is not something new about what the world is like, but something about how, given what the world is like as described in one set of terms, it should be described in some other set of terms. Perhaps the point is clearest in the example about finding

solidity in the molecular account of the objects around us. Reflection on our concept of solidity tells us that the molecular account includes solidity, but it does not tell us that solidity is an *addition* to what appears in the molecular account of objects, let alone an infallible one.

The Objection from the Necessary *a Posteriori*

It might well be urged that the argument given above from (III) to the conclusion that Θ entails Π is undermined by the existence of necessary *a posteriori* truths. The objection can be put in two different ways. Consider

Over 60 percent of the Earth is covered by H_2O. Therefore, over 60 percent of the Earth is covered by water.

One way of putting the objection is that although every world where the premise is true is a world where the conclusion is true, the argument is not valid because the premise does not entail the conclusion in the relevant sense. It is not possible to move *a priori* from the premise to the conclusion. The premise fixes the conclusion without entailing it, as it is sometimes put. Likewise, for all we have shown by the considerations based on (III), Θ fixes Π but does not entail it.

This way of putting the objection makes it sound like a quarrel over terminology. It invites the response of distinguishing entailment *simpliciter*, the notion cashed out simply in terms of being necessarily truth-preserving, from *a priori* or, as it is sometimes called, *conceptual*, entailment, the latter being the notion tied to *a priori* deducibility. But the real objection, of course, is that the necessarily truth-preserving nature of the passage from "Over 60 percent of the Earth is covered by H_2O" to "Over 60 percent of the Earth is covered by water" is not one that can in principle be revealed by conceptual analysis. Reflection on, and intuitions about, possible cases and concepts, unless supplemented by the *a posteriori* information that water is H_2O, will get you nowhere. Materialists, it seems, can allow that (III) forces them to admit a necessarily truth-preserving passage from Θ to Π, without allowing a role for conceptual analysis. They can simply insist that the entailment from Θ to Π is an *a posteriori* one.

We will see, however, that acknowledging the necessary *a posteriori* does not alter matters in any essential respects as far as the importance of conceptual analysis goes. The argument to this conclusion turns on a negative claim about the nature of the necessity possessed by the necessary *a posteriori*, and a consequent view about the role of conceptual analysis, in the sense of intuitions about possibilities, in the detection of the necessary *a posteriori*.

The Necessity of the Necessary *a Posteriori*

There are two different ways of looking at the distinction between necessary *a posteriori* statements like "Water = H_2O" and necessary *a priori* ones like "$H_2O = H_2O$" (all necessary modulo worlds where there is no water, of course). You might say that the latter are analytically or conceptually or logically (in some wide sense not tied to provability in a formal system) necessary, whereas the former are *metaphysically* necessary, meaning by the terminology that we are dealing with two senses of "necessary" in somewhat the way that we are when we contrast logical necessity with nomic necessity. One this approach, the reason the necessity of water's being H_2O is not available *a priori* is that its necessity is not the kind that is available *a priori*.

I think, as against this view, that it is a mistake to hold that the necessity possessed by "Water = H_2O" and "If over 60 percent of the Earth is covered by H_2O, then over 60 percent of the Earth is covered by water" is different from that possessed by "Water = water" and "If over 60 percent of the Earth is covered by H_2O, then over 60 percent of the Earth is covered by H_2O." Just as Quine insists that numbers and tables exist in

the very same sense, I think that we should insist that water's being H_2O and water's being water are necessary in the very same sense.

My reason for holding that there is one sense of necessity here relates to what it was that convinced us that "Water = H_2O" is necessarily true. What convinced us were the arguments of Saul Kripke and Hilary Putnam about how to *describe* certain possibilities, rather than arguments about what is possible *per se*. Kripke and Putnam convinced us that a world where XYZ plays the water role—that is, satisfies enough of (but how much is enough is vague): filling the oceans, being necessary for life, being colorless, being called "water" by experts, being of a kind with the exemplars we are acquainted with, and so on—did not warrant the description "world where water is XYZ," and the stuff correctly described as water in a counterfactual world is the stuff—H_2O—which fills the water role in the actual world. The key point is that the right way to describe a counterfactual world sometimes depends in part on how the actual world is, and not solely on how the counterfactual world is in itself. The point is not one about the space of possible worlds in some newly recognized sense of "possible," but instead one about the role of the actual possible world in determining the correct way to describe certain counterfactual possible worlds—in the sense of "possible" already recognized.

All this was, it seems to me, an exercise in conceptual analysis. We had an old theory about the meaning of "water," namely, that it meant "that which fills the water role," a theory that was refuted by appealing to our intuitions about how to describe possible worlds in which something different from that which actually fills the water role fills the water role. We became convinced of a new theory—again by reflection on possible cases, the meat and potatoes of conceptual analysis—according to which "water" is a rigid designator of the stuff that fills the water role in the actual world. At no time did we have to recognize a new sort of possibility, only a new way for something in some counterfactual situation to count as a *K*, namely, by virtue not solely of how things are in that counterfactual situation, but in part in virtue of how things actually are.

If this is right, the inference

Over 60 percent of the Earth is covered by H_2O. Therefore, over 60 percent of the Earth is covered by water.

is not an example of an *a posteriori* entailment that shows the irrelevance of conceptual analysis to the question of whether an *a posteriori* entailment holds. For it is conceptual analysis that tells us, in light of the fact that H_2O fills the water role, that the entailment holds.

Two-Dimensionalism and the Knowledge Argument

I have argued that materialists must hold that the complete story about the physical nature of our world given by Θ entails everything about our psychology, and that such a position cannot be maintained independently of the results of conceptual analysis. But it is quite another question whether they must hold that Θ *a priori* entails everything about our psychology, including its phenomenal side, and so quite another question whether they must hold that it is in principle possible to deduce from the full physical story alone what it is like to see red or smell a rose—the key assumption in the knowledge argument that materialism leaves out *qualia*. I will conclude by noting how the two dimensional treatment of the necessary *a posteriori*—the obvious treatment of the necessary *a posteriori* for anyone sympathetic to the view that such necessity is not a new sort of necessity—means that materialists are committed to the *a priori* deducibility of the phenomenal from the physical.

If the explanation of the *a posteriori* nature of the necessary *a posteriori* does not lie in the special necessity possessed, where does it lie? Two-dimensionalists insist that the issue is an issue about sentences, and not about propositions, or at least not propositions thought of as sets of possible worlds. For, by the conclusion that we are not dealing with a new sort of necessity, the set of worlds where water is water is the very same set as the set where water is H_2O, and so, by Leibniz's Law, there is no question of the proposition that water is water differing from the proposition that water is H_2O in that one is, and one is not, necessary *a posteriori*. Their contention is that there are sentences such that the proposition expressed by them depends on the context of utterance.[2] We understand them in that we know how the proposition expressed depends on the context, but if we do not know the relevant fact about the context, we will not know the proposition expressed. (In Robert Stalnaker's terminology, we know the propositional concept but not the proposition; in David Kaplan's, we know the character but not the content.[3]) Consider "Over 60 percent of the Earth is covered by water." Because "water" is a rigid designator whose reference is fixed by "the stuff that fills the water role," someone who does not know what that stuff is does not know which proposition the sentence expresses, but they understand the sentence by virtue of knowing how the proposition expressed depends on how things actually are, and, in particular, this being the relevant contextual matter in this case, on what actually fills the water role. The explanation of the necessary *a posteriori* status of "If over 60 percent of the Earth is covered by H_2O, then over 60 percent of the Earth is covered by water" then runs as follows. The proposition expressed by the sentence "Over 60 percent of the Earth is covered by H_2O," is the same as the proposition expressed by "Over 60 percent of the Earth is covered by water," and so the *proposition* expressed by the conditional sentence is *a priori* and necessary. But consistent with what is required to count as understanding the conditional *sentence*, it is contingent and *a posteriori* that it expresses a necessary *a priori* proposition.

I should emphasize that this does not mean that people who fully understand a sentence like

"Over 60 percent of the Earth is covered by water" but do not know that water is H_2O do not, in some perfectly natural sense, know the conditions under which what they are saying is true.[4] True, full understanding of the sentence does not in itself yield which proposition is expressed by the sentence, but knowledge of the way in which the proposition expressed depends on context, combined with knowledge of the truth conditions of the various propositions, does enable them to say when the sentence they produce is true. For their knowledge about how the proposition expressed depends on context together with the conditions under which the various propositions are true is given in the following array:

If H_2O fills the water role, then "Over 60 percent of the Earth is covered by water" expresses a proposition that is true iff over 60 percent of the Earth is covered by H_2O.

If XYZ fills the water role, then "Over 60 percent of the Earth is covered by water" expresses a proposition that is true iff over 60 percent of the Earth is covered by XYZ.

If——fills the water role, then "Over 60 percent of the Earth is covered by water" expresses a proposition that is true iff over 60 percent of the Earth is covered by——.

For each distinct, context-giving, antecedent, a distinct proposition is expressed by the sentence. Nevertheless, simple inspection of the array shows that the sentence is true iff over 60 percent of the Earth is covered by the stuff that fills the water role. That is the sense in which the fully understanding producer of the sentence knows when the sentence is true.[5]

Now, to return to the main plot, although understanding alone does not necessarily give the proposition expressed by certain sentences—that is, how they can be necessary and yet this fact be in principle not accessible to understanding plus acumen alone, that is, how they can be necessary a posteriori—understanding alone does give us the way the proposition expressed depends on

context; and that fact is enough for us to move a priori from, for example, sentences about the distribution of H_2O combined with the right context-giving sentences, to information about the distribution of water. Consider, for instance, a supplementation of our earlier inference:

1. Over 60 percent of the Earth is covered by H_2O.

2. H_2O fills the water role.

3. Therefore, over 60 percent of the Earth is covered by water.

Although, as noted earlier, the passage from (1) to (3) is necessarily truth-preserving but a posteriori, being an a posteriori entailment, the passage from (1) and (2), to (3) is a priori. And it is so because, although our understanding of "Over 60 percent of the Earth is covered by H_2O" does not in itself yield the proposition expressed by the sentence, it yields how the proposition depends on context, and (2) gives that context. Sentence (2) gives the relevant fact about how things are "outside the head." We did not know that (1) entailed (3) until we learned (2), because we did not, and could not, have known that (1) and (3) express the same proposition until we learned (2). But as soon as we learn (2), we have the wherewithal, if we are smart enough, to move a priori to (3).

The point, then, is that the necessary a posteriori nature of "Water = H_2O" does not mean that the fact that the H_2O way things are entails the water way things are is not answerable to our grasp of the relevant concepts plus acumen. It means, rather, that we need to tell a rich enough story about the H_2O way things are, a story that includes the crucial contextual information, before we can move from the H_2O way things are to the water way they are using our grasp of the concepts alone.

More generally, the two-dimensional way of looking at the necessary a posteriori means that even if the entailment the materialist is committed to from some physical story about the world to the full psychological story is *a posteriori*, there is still an *a priori* story tellable about how the story in physical terms about our world makes true the story in psychological terms about our world. Although understanding may not, even in principle, be enough to yield the proposition expressed by the physical story, understanding and logical acumen are enough to yield how the proposition expressed depends on context. But, of course, the context is, according to the materialist, entirely physical. The context concerns various matters about the nature of the actual world, and that nature is capturable in entirely physical terms according to the materialist. Hence, the materialist is committed to there being an *a priori* story to tell about how the physical way things are makes true the psychological way things are. But the story may come in two parts. It may be that one part of the story says which physical way things are, Θ_1, makes some psychological statement true, and the other part of the story, the part that tells the context, says which different physical way things are, Θ_2, makes it the case that it is Θ_1 that makes the psychological statement true. What will be *a priori* accessible is that Θ_1 and Θ_2 *together* make the psychological statement true.[6]

Notes

1. What follows is one version of a familiar story, see, e.g., Terence Horgan, "Supervenience and Microphysics," *Pacific Philosophical Quarterly*, 63, 1982, 29–43 and David Lewis, "New Work for a Theory of Universals," *Australasian Journal of Philosophy*, 61, 1983, 343–377.

2. I take it that what follows is a sketch of the approach suggested by the version of two-dimensionalism in Robert C. Stalnaker. "Assertion." In P. Cole (Ed.), *Syntax and Semantics*, Vol. 9. New York, Academic Press, 1978, pp. 315–332.

3. Stalnaker, *op. cit.*, and David Kaplan, "Dthat." In P. Cole (Ed.), *Syntax and Semantics*, Vol. 9, New York, Academic Press, 1978.

4. I am indebted here to David Lewis and David Chalmers.

5. This observation bears on the dispute about whether Earthians and Twin Earthians believe alike. Although the sentence "Water is plentiful" expresses different propositions in the mouths of the Earthians and the Twin Earthians, they agree about when the sentence is true, and so, in *that* sense agree in belief.

6. I am indebted to Lloyd Humberstone, David Chalmers, David Lewis, Michael Smith, and Philip Pettit.

30

Breaking the Hold: Silicon Brains, Conscious Robots, and Other Minds

John R. Searle

The view of the world as completely objective has a very powerful hold on us, though it is inconsistent with the most obvious facts of our experiences. As the picture is false, we ought to be able to break the hold. I don't know any simple way to do that. . . . In this chapter I want to describe some thought experiments that will challenge the accuracy of the picture. Initially the aim of the thought experiments is to challenge the conception of the mental as having some important internal connection to behavior.

To begin undermining the foundations of this whole way of thinking, I want to consider some of the relationships between consciousness, behavior, and the brain. Most of the discussion will concern conscious mental phenomena; but leaving out the unconscious at this point is not such a great limitation, because . . . we have no notion of an unconscious mental state except in terms derived from conscious states. To begin the argument, I will employ a thought experiment that I have used elsewhere (Searle 1982). This *Gedankenexperiment* is something of an old chestnut in philosophy, and I do not know who was the first to use it. I have been using it in lectures for years, and I assume that anybody who thinks about these topics is bound to have something like these ideas occur to him or her eventually.

Silicon Brains

Here is how it goes. Imagine that your brain starts to deteriorate in such a way that you are slowly going blind. Imagine that the desperate doctors, anxious to alleviate your condition, try any method to restore your vision. As a last resort, they try plugging silicon chips into your visual cortex. Imagine that to your amazement and theirs, it turns out that the silicon chips restore your vision to its normal state. Now, imagine further that your brain, depressingly, continues to deteriorate and the doctors continue to implant more silicon chips. You can see where the thought experiment is going already: in the end, we imagine that your brain is entirely replaced by silicon chips; that as you shake your head, you can hear the chips rattling around inside your skull. In such a situation there would be various possibilities. One logical possibility, not to be excluded on any a priori grounds alone, is surely this: you continue to have all of the sorts of thoughts, experiences, memories, etc., that you had previously; the sequence of your mental life remains unaffected. In this case, we are imagining that the silicon chips have the power not only to duplicate your input-output functions, but also to duplicate the mental phenomena, conscious and otherwise, that are normally responsible for your input-output functions.

I hasten to add that I don't for a moment think that such a thing is even remotely empirically possible. I think it is empirically absurd to suppose that we could duplicate the causal powers of neurons entirely in silicon. But that is an empirical claim on my part. It is not something that we could establish a priori. So the thought experiment remains valid as a statement of logical or conceptual possibility.

But now let us imagine some variations on the thought experiment. A second possibility, also not to be excluded on any a priori grounds, is this: as the silicon is progressively implanted into your dwindling brain, you find that the area of your conscious experience is shrinking, but that this shows no effect on your external behavior. You find, to your total amazement, that you are indeed losing control of your external behavior. You find, for example, that when the doctors test your vision, you hear them say, "We are holding up a red object in front of you; please tell us what you see." You want to cry out, "I can't see anything. I'm going totally blind." But you hear your voice saying in a way that is completely out of your control, "I see a red object in front of me." If we carry this thought experiment out to the limit, we get a much more depressing result than last time. We imagine that your conscious experience slowly shrinks to nothing, while your externally observable behavior remains the same.

It is important in these thought experiments that you should always think of it from the first-person point of view. Ask yourself, "What would it be like for me?" and you will see that it is perfectly conceivable for you to imagine that your external behavior remains the same, but that your internal conscious thought processes gradually shrink to zero. From the outside, it seems to observers that you are just fine, but from the inside you are gradually dying. In this case, we are imagining a situation where you are eventually mentally dead, where you have no conscious mental life whatever, but your externally observable behavior remains the same.

It is also important in this thought experiment to remember our stipulation that you are becoming unconscious but that your behavior remains unaffected. To those who are puzzled how such a thing is possible, let us simply remind them: As far as we know, the basis of consciousness is in certain specific regions of the brain, such as, perhaps, the reticular formation. And we may suppose in this case that these regions are gradually deteriorating to the point where there is no consciousness in the system. But we further suppose that the silicon chips are able to duplicate the input-output functions of the whole central nervous system, even though there is no consciousness left in the remnants of the system.

Now consider a third variation. In this case, we imagine that the progressive implantation of the silicon chips produces no change in your mental life, but you are progressively more and more unable to put your thoughts, feelings and intentions into action. In this case, we imagine that your thoughts, feelings, experiences, memories, etc., remain intact, but your observable external behavior slowly reduces to total paralysis. Eventually you suffer from total paralysis, even though

your mental life is unchanged. So in this case, you might hear the doctors saying,

The silicon chips are able to maintain heartbeat, respiration, and other vital processes, but the patient is obviously brain dead. We might as well unplug the system, because the patient has no mental life at all.

Now in this case, you would know that they are totally mistaken. That is, you want to shout out,

No, I'm still conscious! I perceive everything going on around me. It's just that I can't make any physical movement. I've become totally paralyzed.

The point of these three variations on the thought experiment is to illustrate the *causal* relationships between brain processes, mental processes, and externally observable behavior. In the first case, we imagined that the silicon chips had causal powers equivalent to the powers of the brain, and thus we imagined that they caused both the mental states and the behavior that brain processes normally cause. In the normal case, such mental states mediate the relationship between input stimuli and output behavior.

In the second case, we imagined that the mediating relationship between the mind and the behavior patterns was broken. In this case, the silicon chips did not duplicate the causal powers of the brain to produce conscious mental states, they only duplicated certain input-output functions of the brain. The underlying conscious mental life was left out.

In the third case, we imagined a situation where the agent had the same mental life as before, but in this case, the mental phenomena had no behavioral expression. Actually, to imagine this case we need not even have imagined the silicon chips. It would have been very easy to imagine a person with the motor nerves cut in such a way that he or she was totally paralyzed, while consciousness and other mental phenomena remained unaffected. Something like these cases exists in clinical reality. Patients who suffer from the Guillain-Barré syndrome are completely paralyzed, but also fully conscious.

What is the philosophical significance of these three thought experiments? It seems to me there is a number of lessons to be learned. The most important is that they illustrate something about the relationship between mind and behavior. What exactly is the importance of behavior for the concept of mind? *Ontologically speaking, behavior, functional role, and causal relations are irrelevant to the existence of conscious mental phenomemena. Epistemically*, we do learn about other people's conscious mental states *in part* from their behavior. *Causally*, consciousness serves to mediate the causal relations between input stimuli and output behavior; and from an *evolutionary* point of view, the conscious mind functions causally to control behavior. But *ontologically* speaking, the phenomena in question can exist completely and have all of their essential properties independent of any behavioral output.

Most of the philosophers I have been criticizing would accept the following two propositions:

1. Brains cause conscious mental phenomena.

2. There is some sort of conceptual or logical connection between conscious mental phenomena and external behavior.

But what the thought experiments illustrate is that these two cannot be held consistently with a third:

3. The capacity of the brain to cause consciousness is conceptually distinct from its capacity to cause motor behavior. A system could have consciousness without behavior and behavior without consciousness.

But given the truth of 1 and 3, we have to give up 2. So the first point to be derived from our thought experiments is what we might call "the principle of the independence of consciousness and behavior." In case number two, we imagined the circumstance in which the behavior was unaffected, but the mental states disappeared, so behavior is not a sufficient condition for mental phenomena. In case number three, we imagined the circumstance in which mental phenomena were present, but the behavior disappeared, so behavior is not a necessary condition for the presence of the mental either.

Two other points are illustrated by the thought experiments. First, the ontology of the mental is essentially a first-person ontology. That is just a fancy way of saying that every mental state has to be *somebody's* mental state. Mental states only exist as subjective, first-person phenomena. And the other point related to this is that, epistemically speaking, the first-person point of view is quite different from the third-person point of view. It is easy enough to imagine cases, such as those illustrated by our thought experiments, where from a third-person point of view, somebody might not be able to tell whether I had any mental states at all. He might even think I was unconscious, and it might still be the case that I was completely conscious. From the first-person point of view, there is no question that I am conscious, even if it turned out that third-person tests were not available.

Conscious Robots

I want to introduce a second thought experiment to buttress the conclusions provided by the first. The aim of this one, as with the first, is to use our intuitions to try to drive a wedge between mental states and behavior. Imagine that we are designing robots to work on a production line. Imagine that our robots are really too crude and tend to make a mess of the more refined elements of their task. But imagine that we know enough about the electrochemical features of human consciousness to know how to produce robots that have a rather low level of consciousness, and so we can design and manufacture conscious robots. Imagine further that these conscious robots are able to make discriminations that unconscious robots could not make, and so they do a better job on the production line. Is there anything incoherent in the above? I have to say that according to my "intuitions," it is perfectly coherent. Of course, it is science fiction, but then, many of the most important thought experiments in philosophy and science are precisely science fiction.

But now imagine an unfortunate further feature of our conscious robots: Suppose that they are absolutely miserable. Again, we can suppose that our neurophysiology is sufficient for us to establish that they are extremely unhappy. Now imagine we give our robotics research group the following task: Design a robot that will have the capacity to make the same discriminations as the conscious robots, but which will be totally unconscious. We can then allow the unhappy robots to retire to a more hedonically satisfying old age. This seems to me a well-defined research project; and we may suppose that, operationally speaking, our scientists try to design a robot with a "hardware" that they know will not cause or sustain consciousness, but that will have the same input-output functions as the robot that has a "hardware" that does cause and sustain consciousness. We might suppose then that they succeed, that they build a robot that is totally unconscious, but that has behavioral powers and abilities that are absolutely identical with those of the conscious robot.

The point of this experiment, as with the earlier ones, is to show that as far as the ontology of consciousness is concerned, behavior is simply irrelevant. We could have *identical behavior* in two different systems, one of which is conscious and the other totally unconscious.

Empiricism and the "Other Minds Problem"

Many empirically minded philosophers will be distressed by these two thought experiments, especially the first. It will seem to them that I am alleging the existence of empirical facts about the mental states of a system that are not ascertainable by any empirical means. Their conception of the empirical means for ascertaining the existence of mental facts rests entirely on the presupposition of behavioral evidence. They believe that the only evidence we have for attributing mental states to other systems is the behavior of those systems.

In this section ... part of my aim will be to show that there is nothing incoherent or objectionable in the epistemic implications of the two thought experiments I just described, but my primary aim will be to give an account of the "empirical" basis we have for supposing that other people and higher animals have conscious mental phenomena more or less like our own.

It is worth emphasizing at the beginning of the discussion that in the history of empirical philosophy and of the philosophy of mind, there is a systematic ambiguity in the use of the word "empirical", an ambiguity between an ontological sense and an epistemic sense. When people speak of empirical facts, they sometimes mean actual, contingent facts in the world as opposed to, say, facts of mathematics or facts of logic. But sometimes when people speak of empirical facts, they mean facts that are testable by third-person means, that is, by "empirical facts" and "empirical methods," they mean facts and methods that are accessible to all competent observers. Now this systematic ambiguity in the use of the word "empirical" suggests something that is certainly false: that all empirical facts, in the ontological sense of being facts in the world, are equally accessible epistemically to all competent observers. We know independently that this is false. There are lots of empirical facts that are not equally accessible to all observers. The previous sections gave us some thought experiments designed to show this, but we actually have empirical data that suggest exactly the same result.

Consider the following example.[1] We can with some difficulty imagine what it would be like to be a bird flying. I say "with some difficulty" because, of course, the temptation is always to imagine what it would be like *for us* if we were flying, and not, strictly speaking, what it is like for *a bird* to be flying. But now some recent research tells us that there are some birds that navigate by detecting the earth's magnetic field. Let us suppose that just as the bird has a conscious experience of flapping its wings or feeling the wind pressing against its head and body, so it also has a conscious experience of a feeling of magnetism surging through its body. Now, what is it like to feel a surge of magnetism? In this case, I do not have the faintest idea what it feels like for a bird, or for that matter, for a human to feel a surge of magnetism from the earth's magnetic field. It is, I take it, an empirical fact whether or not birds that navigate by detecting the magnetic field actually have a conscious experience of the detection of the magnetic field. But the exact qualitative character of this empirical fact is not accessible to standard forms of empirical tests. And indeed, why should it be? Why should we assume that all the facts in the world are equally accessible to standard, objective, third-person tests? If you think about it, the assumption is obviously false.

I said that this result is not as depressing as it might seem. And the reason is simple. Although in some cases we do not have equal access to certain empirical facts because of their intrinsic subjectivity, in general we have indirect methods of getting at the same empirical facts. Consider the following example. I am completely convinced that my dog, as well as other higher animals, has conscious mental states, such as visual experiences, feelings of pain, and sensations of thirst and hunger, and of cold and heat. Now why am I so convinced of that? The standard answer is because of the dog's behavior, because by observing his behavior I infer that he has mental states like my own. I think this answer is mistaken. It isn't just because the dog behaves in a way that is appropriate to having conscious mental states, but also because I can see that the causal basis of the behavior in the dog's physiology is relevantly like my own. It isn't just that the dog has a structure like my own and that he has behavior that is interpretable in ways analogous to the way that I interpret my own. But rather, it is in the combination of these two facts that I can see that the behavior is appropriate and that it has the ap-

propriate *causation* in the underlying physiology. I can see, for example, that these are the dog's ears; this is his skin; these are his eyes; that if you pinch his skin, you get behavior appropriate to pinching skin; if you shout in his ear, you get behavior appropriate to shouting in ears.

It is important to emphasize that I don't need to have a fancy or sophisticated anatomical and physiological theory of dog structure, but simple, so to speak, "folk" anatomy and physiology—the ability to recognize the structure of skin, eyes, teeth, hair, nose, etc., and the ability to suppose that the causal role that these play in his experiences is relevantly like the causal role that such features play in one's own experiences. Indeed, even describing certain structures as "eyes" or "ears" already implies that we are attributing to them functions and causal powers similar to our own eyes and ears. In short, though I don't have direct access to the dog's consciousness, nonetheless it seems to me a well-attested empirical fact that dogs are conscious, and it is attested by evidence that is quite compelling. I do not have anything like this degree of confidence when it comes to animals much lower on the phylogenetic scale. I have no idea whether fleas, grasshoppers, crabs, or snails are conscious. It seems to me that I can reasonably leave such questions to neurophysiologists. But what sort of evidence would the neurophysiologist look for? Here, it seems to me, is another thought experiment that we might well imagine.

Suppose that we had an account of the neurophysiological basis of consciousness in human beings. Suppose that we had quite precise, neurophysiologically isolable causes of consciousness in human beings, such that the presence of the relevant neurophysiological phenomena was both necessary and sufficient for consciousness. If you had it, you were conscious; if you lost it, you became unconscious. Now imagine that some animals have this phenomenon, call it "x" for short, and others lack it. Suppose that x was found to occur in all those animals, such as ourselves, monkeys, dogs, and so on, of which we feel quite confident that they are conscious on the basis of their gross physiology, and that x was totally absent from animals, such as amoebas, to which we do not feel inclined to ascribe any consciousness. Suppose further that the removal of x from any human being's neurophysiology immediately produced unconsciousness, and its reintroduction produced consciousness. In such a case, it seems to me we might reasonably assume that the presence of x played a crucial causal role in the production of consciousness, and this discovery would enable us to settle doubtful cases of animals either having or lacking conscious states. If snakes had x, and mites lacked it, then we might reasonably infer that mites were operating on simple tropisms and snakes had consciousness in the same sense that we, dogs, and baboons do.

I don't for a moment suppose that the neurophysiology of consciousness will be as simple as this. It seems to me much more likely that we will find a great variety of forms of neurophysiologies of consciousness, and that in any real experimental situation we would seek independent evidence for the existence of mechanical-like tropisms to account for apparently goal-directed behavior in organisms that lacked consciousness. The point of the example is simply to show that we can have indirect means of an objective, third-person, empirical kind for getting at empirical phenomena that are intrinsically subjective and therefore inaccessible to direct third-person tests.

It shouldn't be thought, however, that there is something second rate or imperfect about the third-person empirical methods for discovering these first-person subjective empirical facts. The methods rest on a rough-and-ready principle that we use elsewhere in science and in daily life: *same causes–same effects*, and *similar causes–similar effects*. We can readily see in the case of other human beings that the causal bases of their experiences are virtually identical with the causal bases of our experiences. This is why in real life there is no "problem of other minds." Animals provide a good test case for this principle because, of course, they are not physiologically identical with us, but they are in certain important respects similar. They have eyes, ears, nose, mouth, and so forth. For this reason we do not really doubt that they have the experiences that go with these various sorts of apparatus. So far, all these considerations are prescientific. But let us suppose that we could identify for the human cases exact causes of consciousness, and then could discover precisely the same causes in other animals. If so, it seems to me we would have established quite conclusively that other species have exactly the same sort of consciousness that we have, because we can presume that the same causes produce the same effects. This would not be just a wild speculation, because we would have very good reason to suppose that those causes would produce the same effects in other species.

In actual practice, neurophysiology textbooks routinely report, for example, how the cat's perception of color is similar to and different from the human's *and even other animals*. What breathtaking irresponsibility! How could the authors pretend to have solved the other cat's mind problem so easily? The answer is that the problem is solved for cats' vision once we know exactly how the cat's visual apparatus is similar to and different from our own and other species'.[2]

Once we understand the causal basis of the ascription of mental states to other animals, then several traditional skeptical problems about "other minds" have an easy solution. Consider the famous problem of spectrum inversion.... It is often said that, for all we know, one section of the population might have a red/green inversion such that though they make the same behavioral discriminations as the rest of us, the actual experiences they have when they see green, and which they call "seeing green", are experiences that we would, if we had them, call "seeing red, " and vice versa. But now consider: Suppose we actually found that a section of the population actually did have the red and green receptors reversed in such a way, and so connected with the rest of their visual apparatus, that we had overwhelming neurophysiological evidenced that though their molar discriminations were the same as ours, they actually had different experiences underlying them. This would not be a problem in philosophical skepticism, but a well-defined neurophysiological hypothesis. But then if there is no such section of the population, if all of the non-colorblind people have the same red/green perceptual pathways, we have solid empirical evidence that things look to other people the way they look to us. A cloud of philosophical skepticism condenses into a drop of neurocscience.

Notice that this solution to "the other minds problem," one that we use in science and in daily life, gives us sufficient but not necessary conditions for the correct ascription of mental phenomena to other beings. We would, as I suggested earlier in this chapter, need a much richer neurobiological theory of consciousness than anything we can now imagine to suppose that we could isolate necessary conditions of consciousness. I am quite confident that the table in front of me, the computer I use daily, the fountain pen I write with, and the tape-recorder I dictate into are quite unconscious, but, of course, I cannot *prove* that they are unconscious and neither can anyone else.

Summary

In this chapter I have so far had two objectives: First, I have tried to argue that as far as the ontology of the mind is concerned, behavior is simply irrelevant. Of course in real life our behavior is crucial to our very existence, but when we are examining the existence of our mental states as mental states, the correlated behavior is neither necessary nor sufficient for their existence. Second, I have tried to begin to break the hold of three hundred years of epistemological discussions of "the other minds problem," according to which behavior is the sole basis on which we know of the existence of other minds. This seems to me obviously false. It is only because of the *connection* between behavior and the causal structure of other organisms that behavior is at all relevant to the discovery of mental states in others.

A final point is equally important: except when doing philosophy, there really is no "problem" about other minds, because we do not hold a "hypothesis," "belief," or "supposition" that other people are conscious, and that chairs, tables, computers, and cars are not conscious. Rather, we have certain Background ways of behaving, certain Background capacities, and these are constitutive of our relations to the consciousness of other people. It is typical of philosophy that skeptical problems often arise when elements of the Background are treated as if they were hypotheses that have to be justified. I don't hold a "hypothesis" that my dog or my department chairman is conscious, and consequently the question doesn't arise except in philosophical debate.

Intrinsic, As-If, and Derived Intentionality

Before proceeding further, I need to introduce some simple distinctions that have been implicit in what I have said so far, but will need to be made explicit for what follows. To introduce these distinctions, let us consider the similarities and differences among the various sorts of truth-conditions of sentences that we use to ascribe intentional mental phenomena. Consider the similarities and differences among the following:

1. I am now thirsty, really thirsty, because I haven't had anything to drink all day.

2. My lawn is thirsty, really thirsty, because it has not been watered in a week.

3. In French, "j'ai grand soif" means "I am very thirsty."

The first of these sentences is used literally to ascribe a real, intentional mental state to oneself. If I utter that sentence, making a true statement, then there is in me a conscious feeling of thirst that makes that statement true. That feeling has intentionality because it involves a desire to drink. But the second sentence is quite different. Sentence 2 is used only metaphorically, or figuratively, to ascribe thirst to my lawn. My lawn, lacking water, is in a situation in which I would be thirsty, so I figuratively describe it *as if* it were thirsty. I can, by analogy, quite harmlessly say that the lawn is thirsty even though I do not suppose for a moment that it is literally thirsty. The third sentence is like the first in that it literally ascribes intentionality, but it is like the second and unlike the first in that the intentionality described is not intrinsic to the system.

The first sort of ascription ascribes *intrinsic* intentionality. If such a statement is true, there must really be an *intentional state in the object of the ascription*. The second sentence does not ascribe any intentionality at all, intrinsic or otherwise; it is merely used to speak figuratively or metaphorically. Therefore, I will say that the "intentionality" in the ascription is merely *as-if*, and not intrinsic. To avoid confusion, it is important to emphasize that *as-if* intentionality is not a kind of intentionality, rather a system that has *as-if* intentionality is as-if-it-had-intentionality. In the third case I literally ascribe intentionality to the French sentence, that is, the French sentence literally means what I say it does. But the intentionality in the French sentence is not intrinsic to that particular sentence construed just as a syntactical object. That very sequence might have meant something very different or nothing at all. *Speakers* of French can use it to express *their* intentionality. Linguistic meaning is a real form of intentionality, but it is not intrinsic intentionality. It is derived from the intrinsic intentionality of the users of the language.

We can summarize these points as follows: intrinsic intentionality is a phenomenon that humans and certain other animals have as part of their biological nature. It is not a matter of how they are used or how they think of themselves or how they choose to describe themselves. It is just a plain fact about such beasts that, for example, sometimes they get *thirsty* or *hungry*, they *see*

things, *fear* things, etc. All of the italicized expressions in the previous sentence are used to refer to intrinsic intentional state. It is very convenient to use the jargon of intentionality for talking about systems that do not have it, but that behave they did. I say about my thermostat that it *perceives* changes in the temperature; I say of my carburetor that it *knows* when to enrich the mixture; and I say of my computer that its *memory* is bigger than the *memory* of the computer I had last year. All of these attributions are perfectly harmless and no doubt they will eventually produce new literal meanings as the metaphors become dead. But it is important to emphasize that these attributions are psychologically irrelevant, because they do not imply the presence of any mental phenomena. The intentionality described in all of these cases is purely *as-if*.

Cases of the third sort are rendered interesting by the fact that that we often do literally endow nonmental phenomena with intentional properties. There is nothing metaphorical or *as-if* about saying that certain sentences *mean* certain things or certain maps are correct *representations of* the state of California or that certain pictures are *pictures of* Winston Churchill. These forms of intentionality are real, but they are derived from the intentionality of human agents.

I have been using the terminology of "intrinsic" for over a decade (see Searle 1980), but it is subject to certain persistent misunderstandings. In common speech "intrinsic" is often opposed to "relational." Thus the moon intrinsically has a mass, but is not intrinsically a satellite. It is only a satellite relative to the earth. In this sense of intrinsic, people who believe in intentional states with "wide content," that is content essentially involving relations to objects outside the mind, would be forced to deny that such intentional states are intrinsic, because they are relational. I don't believe in the existence of wide content (see Searle 1983, ch. 7), so the problem does not arise for me. The distinctions I am making now are independent of the dispute about wide and narrow content. So I am just stipulating that by "intrinsic intentionality" I mean the real thing as opposed to the mere appearance of the thing (*as-if*), and as opposed to derived forms of intentionality such sentences, pictures, etc. You do not have to accept my objections to wide content to accept the distinctions I am trying to make.

Another—amazing to me—misunderstanding is to suppose that by calling cases of the real thing "intrinsic" I am implying that they are somehow mysterious, ineffable, and beyond the reach of philosophical explanation or scientific study. But this is nonsense. I have right now many intrinsic intentional states, for example, and urge to go to the bathroom, a strong desire for a cold beer, and a visual experience of a lot of boats on the lake. All of these are *intrinsic* intentional states, in my sense, which just means they are the real thing and not just something more or less like the real thing (*as-if*), or something that is the result of somebody else's uses of or attitudes toward the thing (*derived*).[3]

I have seen efforts to deny these distinctions, but it is very hard to take the denials seriously. If you think that there are no principled differences, you might consider the following from the journal *Pharmacology*.

Once the food is past the chrico-pharyngus sphincter, its movement is almost entirely involuntary except for the final expulsion of feces during defecation. *The gastrointestinal tract is a highly intelligent organ that senses* not only the presence of food in the lumen but also its chemical composition, quantity, viscosity and adjusts the rate of propulsion and mixing by producing appropriate patterns of contractions. *Due to its highly developed decision making ability* the gut wall comprised of the smooth muscle layers, the neuronal structures and paracrine-endocrine cells *is often called the gut brain.* (Sarna and Otterson 1988, my italics)[4]

This is clearly a case of *as-if* intentionality in the "gut brain." Does anyone think there is no principled difference between the gut brain and the brain brain? I have heard it said that both sorts of cases are the same; that it is all a matter of taking an "intentional stance" toward a system. But just try in real life to suppose that the "perception" and the "decision making" of the gut brain are no different from that of the real brain.

This example reveals, among other things, that any attempt to deny the distinction between intrinsic and *as-if* intentionality faces a general reductio ad absurdum. If you deny the distinction, it turns out that everything in the universe has intentionality. Everything in the universe follows laws of nature, and for that reason everything behaves with a certain degree of regularity, and for that reason everything behaves *as if* it were following a rule, trying to carry out a certain project, acting in accordance with certain desires, etc. For example, suppose I drop a stone. The stone *tries* to reach the center of the earth, because it *wants* to reach the center of the earth, and in so doing it *follows the rule* $S = 1/2 \ gt^2$. The price of denying the distinction between intrinsic and *as-if* intentionality, in short, is absurdity, because it makes everything in the universe mental.

No doubt there are marginal cases. About grasshoppers or fleas, for example, we may not be quite sure what to say. And no doubt, even in some human cases we might be puzzled as to whether we should take the ascription of intentionality literally or metaphorically. But marginal cases do not alter the distinction between the sort of facts corresponding to ascriptions of intrinsic intentionality and those corresponding to *as-if* metaphorical ascriptions of intentionality. There is nothing harmful, misleading, or philosophically mistaken about *as-if* metaphorical ascriptions. The only mistake is to take them literally.

I hope the distinctions I have been making are painfully obvious. However, I have to report, from the battlefronts as it were, that the neglect of these simple distinctions underlies some of the biggest mistakes in contemporary intellectual life. A common pattern of mistake is to suppose that because we can make *as-if* ascriptions of intentionality to systems that have no intrinsic intentionality, that somehow or other we have discovered the nature of intentionality.[5]

Notes

1. In the style of Thomas Nagel's article, "What Is It Like to Be a Bat?"(1974).

2. For example, "As one might expect, cells whose receptive fields are specifically color-coded have been noted in various animals, including the monkey, the ground squirrel, and some fishes. *These animals, in contradistinction to the cat, possess excellent color vision* and an intricate neural mechanism for processing color" (Kuffler and Nicholls 1976, p. 25, my italics).

3. For an example of this misunderstanding, see P. M. and P. S. Churchland (1983).

4. I am indebted to Dan Rubermann for calling my attention to this article.

5. See, for example, Dennett (1987).

References

Churchland, P. M., and Churchland, P. S. (1983). "Stalking the Wild Epistemic Engine." *Nous* 17:5–18.

Dennett, D. C. (1987). *Intentional Stance*. Cambridge, MA: MIT Press.

Kuffler, S. W., and Nicholls, J. G. (1976). *From Neuron to Brain*. Sunderland, MA: Sinauer Associates.

Nagel, T. (1974.) "What Is It Like to Be a Bat?" *Philosophical Review* 4, 83:435–450.

Sarna, S. K., and Otterson, M. F. (1988). "Gastrointestinal Motility: Some Basic Concepts." *Pharmacology: Supplement* 36:7–14.

Searle, J. R. (1980). "Intrinsic Intentionality: Reply to Criticisms of Minds, Brains, and Programs." *Behavioral and Brain Sciences* 3:450–456.

———. (1982). "The Chinese Room Revisited: Response to Further Commentaries on 'Minds, Brains, and Programs." *Behavioral and Brain Sciences* 5, 2: 345–348.

———. (1983). *Intentionality: An Essay in the Philosophy of Mind*. Cambridge: Cambridge University Press.

31 The First-Person Perspective

Sydney Shoemaker

Some would say that the philosophy of mind without the first-person perspective, or the first-person point of view, is like *Hamlet* without the Prince of Denmark. Others would say that it is like *Hamlet* without the *King* of Denmark, or like *Othello* without Iago. I say both. I think of myself as a friend of the first-person perspective. Some would say that I am too friendly to it, for I hold views about first-person access and first-person authority that many would regard as unacceptably "Cartesian." I certainly think that it is essential to a philosophical understanding of the mental that we appreciate that there *is* a first-person perspective on it, a distinctive way mental states present themselves to the subjects whose states they are, and that an essential part of the philosophical task is to give an account of mind which makes intelligible the perspective mental subjects have on their own mental lives. And I do not think, as I think some do, that the right theory about all this will be primarily an "error theory." But I also think that the first-person perspective is sometimes rightly cast as the villain in the piece. It is not only the denigrators of introspection that assign it this role. Kant did so in the Paralogisms, seeing our vantage on our selves as the source of transcendental illusions about the substantiality of the self. And Wittgenstein's "private language argument" can be seen as another attempt to show how the first-person perspective can mislead us about the nature of mind.

My concern here is with the role of the first-person perspective in the distinctively philosophical activity of conducting thought experiments designed to test metaphysical and conceptual claims about the mind. In conducting such a thought experiment one envisages a putatively possible situation and inquires whether it really is possible and, if so, what its possibility shows about the nature of mind or the nature of mental concepts. Such envisaging can be done either from the "third-person point of view" or the "first-person point of view." In the one case, one

imagines seeing someone doing, saying, and undergoing certain things, and one asks whether this would be a case of something which has been thought to be philosophically problematic—for example, someone's having an unconscious pain. In the other case, one imagines being oneself the subject of certain mental states—imagines feeling, thinking, and so on, certain things—in a case in which certain other things are true, for example, one's body is in a certain condition, and asks what this shows about some philosophical claim about the relation of mind to body. The question I want to pursue is whether there is anything that can be established by such first-person envisagings that cannot be revealed just as effectively by third-person envisagings.

It is not difficult to see why first-person thought experiments have often been thought to be more revealing than third-person thought experiments. In a broad range of cases, first-person ascriptions of mental states are not grounded on evidence of any sort. It is natural to move from this to the claim that they are grounded on the mental states themselves, or on "direct acquaintance" with the mental states themselves. One can, apparently, have this knowledge without presuming anything about the connections between the mental states and the bodily states of affairs, behavioral or physiological, which serve as the evidence for our ascription of these same mental states to other persons. Thus the first-person perspective apparently gives one a freer rein than the third-person perspective in investigating, empirically, the connections between mental states of affairs and bodily ones. And so if we are concerned with what the possibilities are, with respect to these connections, imagining what we could discover from the first-person perspective seems potentially more revealing than imagining what we could discover from the third-person perspective.

There are a number of areas in the philosophy of mind in which first-person imaginings have played an important role in philosophical reflection. These include the issue of whether the identity over time of a person involves the identity of a body or brain, the issue of whether disembodied existence of persons is a possibility, the issue of whether "spectrum inversion" is a possibility, and the issue of whether mental states can be identical with physical states of bodies or with functional states realized in physical states of bodies. In many of these cases I agree with the possibility claims that first-person imaginings have been used to support. I think that personal identity does not require bodily identity or brain identity, and I think that spectrum inversion is a possibility. But I think that in these cases the possible states of affairs in question are ones that could be known to obtain from the third-person perspective. In any event, it is not these cases I shall be discussing here. My focus in the remainder of this talk will be on the bearing of first-person and third-person imaginings on physicalist views of mind, in particular the identity theory and functionalism.

My thoughts about this were partly inspired, or perhaps I should say provoked, by a recent argument of John Searle's, and my discussion will be in large part about that. But I will lead up to this by considering briefly what is perhaps the best known piece of philosophical imagining in recent times, namely Saul Kripke's assault, over twenty years ago, on the psychophysical identity theory.[1] Kripke claimed that for any given brain state that is a candidate for being identical with pain, one can imagine both being in pain without one's brain being in that state, and also not being in pain when one's brain is in that state. What was novel about Kripke's argument was of course not the claim that these states of affairs are imaginable, or the claim that they are possible, but certain other claims that licensed the inference from these imaginability and possibility claims to the conclusion that pain cannot be identical with any such brain state—most importantly, the claim that "pain" is a rigid designator, and the point that identity judgments involving rigid designators are necessarily true if true at all. But it

did seem central to his case, as he presented it, that the imagining was from the first-person point of view. When he speaks of the "epistemic situation" vis-à-vis pain, he is plainly speaking of the epistemic situation of the putative subject of pain. The claim that it is possible that there should be pain without C-fiber stimulation, or C-fiber stimulation without pain, seems to be grounded on the claim that one can imagine being in pain without there being any C-fiber stimulation occurring in one, and can imagine not being in pain when there is C-fiber stimulation occurring in one. Kripke was of course well aware that the inference from imaginability to possibility could be challenged, and he had very interesting things to say about this; but these do not bear on the issue of first-person versus third-person imagining that is our concern here.

Around the time Kripke presented this argument, other philosophers, most notably Hilary Putnam, were challenging the psychophysical identity theory in a way that also depended on the claim that for any given sort of brain state there could be pain in the absence of that brain state.[2] The arguments of these philosophers were in support of the view that pain is a functional state that is "multiply realizable." As originally presented, these arguments involved claims of nomological possibility rather than claims of metaphysical or logical possibility, and appealed to actual physiological differences between different species, for example, humans and mollusks, rather than to imaginings of purely hypothetical situations. But it is easy enough to convert them into arguments from imaginings that differ from Kripke's only in that the imaginings are from the third-person rather than the first-person perspective. One imagines finding creatures that manifestly experience pain, as is shown by their behavior and circumstances, but lack whatever brain state is the candidate for being identical with pain. One goes from there to the claim that it is possible for there to be pain unaccompanied by that brain state, and uses Kripke's claims about the necessity of identity and the rigidity of the concept of pain to argue from this that pain cannot be identical with that brain state.

There is certainly a difference in spirit between Kripke's argument and its third-person counterpart. The arguments appeal to different groups of philosophers, and annoy different groups of philosophers. But it is far from obvious, to say the least, that the first-person imaginings carry any more evidential weight, *vis-à-vis* the issue of psychophysical identity, than the third-person imaginings.[3]

But now recall that there were two parts to Kripke's claim. For any brain state that is a candidate for being pain, one can imagine being in pain without being in that brain state, *and* one can imagine being in that brain state without being in pain. If the second half of the claim can be made out, and if the inference from imaginability to possibility is accepted, we will have more than an argument against the identity theory—we will have an argument against the view that pain can be realized in, or implemented by, brain states, and against the view that pain supervenes on states of the brain. For the latter views, while allowing that pain, being "multiply realizable," can occur without any *given* brain state occurring, will hold that there are brain states, perhaps a large number of them, each of which is such that its occurrence is necessarily sufficient, although not necessary, for the occurrence of pain. If *every* brain state is such that one can imagine it occurring without pain occurring, and if imaginability here implies possibility, then all such views topple.

Can the imagining that leads to this result be done from the third-person point of view? Well, it's easy enough to imagine a case in which C-fiber stimulation is going on in someone and that person is not in pain. But C-fiber stimulation never was a very good candidate for being pain. The question should be whether it is true of each and every brain state that it can be imagined to occur without the subject being in pain. This will have to include brain states that are good candidates for being pain. What will make a brain state a good candidate? Well, the ideal candidate would be one that satisfies some description which we have reason to think only pain satisfies. If the first part of the Kripkean argument is successful, and it is established that for any given brain state it is possible for pain to occur without that brain state occurring, then no brain state is an ideal candidate in this sense. No brain state is an ideal candidate for being *identical* with pain—and here nothing less than an ideal candidate will do. But it is compatible with this that there are brain states that are good candidates for "being pain" in the sense of being realizations of pain. And presumably what this requires is that they play the causal role of pain—that they make the contribution to causing other things, including other mental states as well as behavior, that we believe pain to make, and are caused by the things that we take pain to be caused by.

There are of course ways and ways in which causal or functional roles can be described. Some ways make explicit reference to particular mental states—for example, part of the causal role of pain is causing the belief that one is in pain. A state having a causal role thus described cannot of course belong to something devoid of mental states. But I will assume here that the roles are described in "topic neutral" terms; this will permit us to consider the idea, rejected by functionalists but affirmed by philosophers such as John Searle, that for any causal or functional role there could be something that has a state playing that role without having any mental states at all.

Even if C-fiber stimulation did play the causal role of pain, it might do so only contingently. That is, it might do so in virtue of the fact that the brain is "wired" in a certain way, a way in which it could fail to be wired and still have C-fiber stimulation occur in it. It would then be only contingently an optimal candidate for being a realization of pain. In that case we could imagine discovering from the third-person perspective someone who was not in pain but in whom C-fiber stimulation was occurring—this would be a case in which the brain was wired up differently.

But now consider the state, call it "C-fiber-stimulation-plus," which consists in the brain's having C-fiber stimulation occurring in it *and* its being wired in such a way that C-fiber stimulation plays the causal role of pain (or what we believe to be the causal role of pain). Let's say here that, on the supposition we are making, C-fiber stimulation is an optimal candidate for being a *core* realization of pain, and C-fiber-stimulation-plus is an optimal candidate for being a *total* realization of pain. One can easily enough imagine from the third-person perspective a case in which someone is not in pain despite having in his brain what is an optimal candidate for being a core-realization of pain. But can one imagine from the third-person perspective a case in which someone is not in pain despite having in his brain an optimal candidate for being a total realization of pain?

I think that the answer is no. The reason is that playing the causal role of pain or at any rate playing what we have good reason to think is the causal role of pain will essentially involve producing precisely the kinds of behavior that serve as our-third-person basis for ascribing pain. We cannot be in a position to judge about someone *both* that she is not in pain *and* that she is in a state that influences her behavior in just the ways we think pain influences behavior. Of course, someone can be in pain when there is no behavioral evidence that she is, and when there is behavioral evidence that she is not—she may be successfully suppressing the manifestations of pain. And in such a case we will normally believe, mistakenly, that the person is not in pain. We might in such a case know that the person's brain is in the state C-fiber-stimulation-plus—and if we don't realize that this is an optimal candidate for being a total realization of pain, we may continue to believe that the person is not in pain while believing that she has in her brain what is in fact an optimal candidate for being a total realization of pain. But if we realize that it is an optimal candidate, we will have to believe that something, such as an effort to suppress tendencies to manifest pain behavior, is preventing it from having its

normal effect; and then we can no longer believe on the basis of the behavior that the person is not in pain.

So it seems that nothing we can imagine from the third-person perspective would entitle us to say that someone is not in pain despite instantiating what we acknowledge to be an optimal candidate for being a total realization of pain. And now we may seem to have a case in which a first-person imagining can achieve something no third-person imagining can achieve. For can't I imagine feeling no pain and yet finding, with the help of an autocerebroscope, that I am in state C-fiber-stimulation-plus, a state I know to be an optimal candidate for being a realization of pain?

One physicalist response to this would be to say that faced with such a case I ought to conclude that while it *seems* to me that I do not feel pain, the evidence of the autocerebroscope should persuade me that after all I do. This is not my response, and I count it as not sufficiently respecting the first-person perspective. While I am willing to allow that there are circumstances in which a sincere self-ascription of pain can be mistaken, I am not willing to allow that someone might be in excruciating pain and yet that it might seem to him, when he reflects in a calm and unflustered way on his state, that he feels no pain at all, and that it might continue to seem that way to him throughout the extended period during which the excruciating pain is supposed to last. And yet that is what would have to be possible if the seeming evidence of the autocerebroscope were overriding in such a case.

But we need to appreciate how bizarre our latest version of Kripke's example is. You are to imagine feeling no pain while having very good evidence that you are in a state that plays the causal role of pain. If you have such a state, you ought to be behaving, or disposed to behave, like someone who is in pain. Suppose you are. Then you should reply affirmatively if asked whether you are in pain. Suppose you do. How does this seem to you, from the inside? Does it seem like your own action, something you are intentionally doing? Will it seem to you that you are lying? But if you can imagine what we have already envisaged, surely you can also imagine that in addition to feeling no pain you have your normal desire to tell the truth. So is it instead that you try to say that you feel no pain, but hear coming from your mouth an avowal of excruciating pain? But if you are alienated from your verbal behavior in this way, presumably you will be similarly alienated from other kinds of behavior as well. You will have no intention of taking aspirin; but you will see your hand reaching for the medicine cabinet and removing the aspirin bottle. You will have no intention of seeing the doctor; but you will see your hand reaching for the telephone, and hear your voice making an appointment. And so on.

Before I discuss the implications of this feature of the case, I want to switch to a somewhat different example—a first-person thought experiment that is presented by John Searle in *The Rediscovery of Mind*.[4] I think that Searle's though experiment can usefully be viewed as a version of Kripke's, or rather, an elaboration of the extended version of the second half of Kripke's that we have just been considering. Searle is, of course, an outspoken and eloquent advocate of the first-person point of view.

Searle's example is a variation on the familiar one in which, in a series of operations, the parts of someone's brain are progressively replaced by silicon chips, until eventually the brain is entirely composed of silicon. The replacements are always such as to preserve the behavioral dispositions of the person, and the functional organization needed to sustain these. Searle's variation on the example is to invite the reader to imagine being the subject of this procedure, and to imagine the results from the inside. In his presentation of the case the procedure starts as a treatment for blindness due to deterioration of the brain, and is successful as long as the replacements are limited to the visual cortex. For my own expository purposes, I prefer to have the subject be someone who has bravely volunteered to be the subject of a

philosophical experiment—one designed to test the hypothesis that a creature with a brain having a certain functional organization, one that underwrites behavioral dispositions that enable it to pass the most stringent Turing test, will be conscious, no matter what the material composition of that brain.

One possible outcome of the experiment is that one finds that each successive replacement of gray stuff with silicon makes no difference to one's conscious life: "you continue to have all of the sorts of thoughts, experiences, memories, etc., that you had previously; the sequence of your mental life remains unaffected" (p. 66). Searle thinks that in fact it is "empirically absurd to suppose that we could duplicate the causal posers of neurons entirely in silicon," but says that this cannot be ruled out a priori.

He goes on to describe two other ways the experiment might turn out. One is that "as the silicon is progressively implanted into your dwindling brain, you find that the area of your conscious experience is shrinking, but that this shows no effect on your external behavior. You find, to your total amazement, that you are indeed losing control of your external behavior. You find, for example, that when the doctors test your vision, you hear them say, 'We are holding up a red object in front of you; please tell me what you see.' You want to cry out, 'I can't see anything. I'm going totally blind.' But you hear your voice saying in a way that is completely out of your control, 'I see a red object in front of me'" (pp. 66–7). Here, he says, "we are imagining a situation in which you are eventually mentally dead, where you have no conscious mental life whatever, but your externally observable behavior remains the same."

This second case is the main one I want to examine. But Searle also mentions a third possible outcome. This is that "the progressive implantation of the silicon chips produces no change in your mental life, but you are progressively more and more unable to put your thoughts, feelings, and intentions into action" (p. 67). Here your external behavior eventually ceases, and the doctors think you are dead. But you know better.

My focus, as I said, will be on the second case. Searle takes this to show how it could be known that a certain physical makeup, one consisting in assemblies of silicon chips, fails to support mentality and consciousness, even if it is the case that something having this makeup would be behaviorally and functionally indistinguishable from a normal human being. This is not explicitly presented as a possibility argument of the sort Kripke gives. But, plainly, if he can show what he thinks he shows, he thereby establishes at least the conceptual possibility of a mindless creature that passes the most stringent Turing test imaginable, and does so in virtue of having physical states that are from a functionalist point of view optimal candidates for being realizations of mental states.

Let the sad character in Searle's story, the one on the verge of extinction, be me. My situation, as imagined here, is much the same as it is if I imagine myself as the subject of the most recently considered version of the Kripke example. In both cases I am alienated from my behavior. In the Searle example I hear my voice engaged in conversations with others, conversations to which I am not myself a party, and—here I extend the example—I see my hand writing answers to questions on an IQ test, questions that I am, in my weakened state of mind, unable even to understand. The main difference between the two cases, besides the fact that in Searle's case my consciousness is waning, is that Searle's story contains an account of how I got into this mess— it is the result of my volunteering to be the subject of the philosophical experiment, and the infusions of silicon I subsequently underwent. From now on I will concentrate on Searle's version of the case, but my main points will apply to the earlier version as well.

Let me focus on the alienation from my behavior that this case involves. This amounts to a kind of alienation from my body. Indeed, its status as *my* body should seem problematic, from

my point of view, for by hypothesis I have no voluntary control over it, and it moves about, and spouts utterances, in defiance of my will. I do seem to see through its eyes and hear through its ears. But given my alienation from it, or rather, given that I am alienated from it *if* my experiences are veridical, shouldn't I be wondering whether these experiences *are* veridical? Notice that I lack the normal ways of checking to see whether things are as they appear—I cannot initiate tests of any sort, and I cannot consult with others. My situation seems rather like a bad dream. And of course, if it is a bad dream, or if I am not entitled to think it isn't, then I am not establishing what Searle has me establishing—that the behavior of my body is independent of such consciousness there is in it, and that very soon, when my consciousness has vanished completely, this body will be behaving as it is, passing the most stringent Turing tests, without there being any consciousness in it at all.

Admittedly, I would be rash to conclude, just on the basis of my alienation from my behavior, that I cannot trust my senses. What I am calling alienation from behavior occurs, although in a less dramatic way, in actual cases of paralysis, and we do not think that people in that condition should doubt their senses. But it would seem that I have reasons for doubting my senses over and above the fact that I have no voluntary control over the body I seem to be perceiving from. For if what my senses tell me is right, people are ascribing to me, on the basis of my behavior, mental states that I know I don't have. And these ascriptions are regularly being confirmed by my subsequent behavior. What is at stake here is the reliability of a well established practice of mental state ascription, one we rely on in all of our dealings with other people. Can I justifiably take it that my perceptual experiences are veridical in this instance? *If* they are then, it seems, *both* a well established practice is systematically issuing in mistaken mental state ascriptions in this case, *and* I am alienated from by behavior and body. That seems to me a reason for saying that I can't be justified in taking my perceptual experiences to be veridical. And if I can't, then in the imagined situation I do not establish what Searle thinks I do.

I am not going to rest my case on this point. But I think that it has some force. When first-person thought experiments seem to have philosophically interesting results, the content of the first-person imagining always has an "objective" as well as a "subjective" component. In the present case, the subjective component is my being in a certain mental condition, which includes my having certain sense-experiences—my seeming to see and hear certain things. The objective component is my body's being in a certain condition, and my being surrounded by people and instruments of which certain things are true. Normally, when the veridicality of sense experiences is in no way in question, it is unproblematic to move from saying that one imagines *seeming to see* such and such to saying that one imagines *seeing* such and such, and from there to saying that one imagines *such and such being the case*. But when what is in question is the relation between the mental states of a creature and the creature's bodily condition and situation, then the veridicality or otherwise of the creature's sense experiences is part of what is in question. Obviously, that my sense-experiences are veridical is not something I know "from the inside," in the way I know that I have them. This is not something about which I have "first-person authority." There is, to be sure, a presumption in favor of the assumption of veridicality. But there is also a presumption in favor of the assumption that our ordinary third-person ways of ascribing mental states are reliable. If, holding fixed the nature of my mental states over some interval, these two assumptions come into conflict, nothing that I know from the inside, nothing about which I have first-person authority, tips the balance in favor of the assumption that my perceptual experiences are veridical. Perhaps what we have is a standoff between the two assumptions. But I think that the fact that on the veridicality assumption I am alienated from the body from which I am supposed to be doing the perceiving

could reasonably be held to tip the balance against the veridicality assumption.

To see that the veridicality of experiences *can* be an issue in such cases, consider a modification of Searle's example in which the brain operations are replaced by something less invasive. For example, instead of a series of operations in which brain matter is replaced by silicon, they give me a series of *shampoos*! As before, we will try to suppose, each item in the series is followed by a diminution of consciousness, and I end up radically alienated from my body. But in this case, the behavior of my body in the final stages of the procedure stems from just the sorts of neural goings-on that such behavior stems from in normal cases. At any rate, this is how things seem to me. I doubt if anyone will want to maintain that this thought experiment shows, or even provides prima facie evidence, that the actual processes going on in our brains are not metaphysically sufficient for the mental states we take to be manifested by the behavior they produce. And I think that if things did seem to me as just imagined, it would be more reasonable for me to doubt my senses or memories than to conclude that a series of shampoos could destroy my mentality without affecting my brain or its influence on my behavior.

But let's return to Searle's example, with me again as the subject. As it happens, we do not have to choose between overriding the presumption that my sense experiences are veridical and overriding the presumption that our ordinary practice of third-person mental state ascription is reliable. For there is a way of honoring both presumptions. Assume that my sense experiences are veridical. Then I am radically alienated from the body I am perceiving from. Given its independence of my will, my claim that it is my body is a bit shaky. So maybe someone else has a less shaky claim on it. That is precisely what the third-person evidence indicates to others. The behavior of the body is such as to lead them to take it to be the body of a person having certain mental states, mental states that as a matter of fact are, except for the perceptual experiences among them, utterly different from my own. Nothing I know from the inside, nothing about which I have first-person authority, gives me any reason to reject this possibility.

Is this a possibility? Well, to begin with, there would seem to be no conceptual incoherence in the idea that two minds, or persons, or "consciousnessess," might simultaneously animate a single body, or at any rate have that body as the point of view from which they experience the world. This is what some have thought happens in split-brain cases, and what others have thought happens in cases of multiple personality; and while that view of those cases appears not to fit the actual facts, there are possible facts that it does fit. If we think about the features of these cases that make it tempting to speak of there being multiple persons, or multiple minds, in a single body, it is not difficult to envisage cases of which this would be the literally correct description.

But how do we apply this to Searle's example? As an example of an unsatisfactory application of it, let me quote my own response to Searle when he presented this example at a conference a year or two ago: "you seem to imply that . . . just after your consciousness fades out you have all the functional organization there without any mentality. Surely that's not warranted, because it's perfectly compatible with this that as you fade out someone else is coming in."[5] Daniel Dennett subsequently put the point in a similar way in his review of Searle's book.[6] Supposing that I am the subject of the series of operations, what this formulation suggests is that what the scientists were perhaps unwittingly doing in their series of operations was building in my skull a new person, one with a silicon brain, while gradually destroying the brain and person, namely me, that was there originally. As appropriate connections were established between the silicon brain and the nervous and motor systems, the new brain took over control of the body. The trouble with this version

of the story is that it is not compatible with a central feature of it, namely that throughout the series of replacements the behavior of my body was such that from a third-person point of view it appeared to be animated by a *single* person with normal mental abilities and normal consciousness, and exhibiting normal mental continuity over time. Yoking a waning mind to a waxing mind could hardly be expected to produce this result. What it should produce, instead, is conflicted behavior, dominated in the early parts of the interval by behavior showing mental decline, dominated during the later parts of it by behavior showing the opposite, and perhaps manifesting at various times behavior analogous to that of the split-brain monkey, reported by Tom Nagel, whose right and left hands had a tug of war over a nut.[7]

But there is a version of the story that is compatible with what we are supposed to imagine about the behavior of the body. It says that a single person animated the body throughout the interval, and that during the interval that person's brain was gradually reconstituted—it began as a normal human brain, and ended as a functionally equivalent silicon brain. It follows that if at the end of the story there was "in " the body a feeble mind that was not in control of it, then that was not the mind that was there at the outset. Or, putting it in terms of persons, the person who near the end found himself a mentally enfeebled prisoner in the body is not, although he *thinks* he is, the same as the person who at the beginning volunteered to undergo the series of operations. Perhaps the case could be construed as a case of "fission," in which both of the inhabitants of the body, the mentally enfeebled prisoner as well as the person who controls the body's behavior, have veridical "quasi-memories" corresponding to the life of the original person. But if so, it is unequal fission, and the "closest continuer," the person with the best claim to be the original possessor of the body, is the one who controls the body's behavior, not the mentally enfeebled prisoner.

Someone might object that I have here fallen into skepticism about memory, and about personal identity. Surely, it will be said, if someone remembers being the person who did such and such, that person has every reason to think that he is the person who did such and such. And if I imagine remembering being the person who did such and such, I have every reason to describe the imagined situation as one in which I am the person who did such and such.

But the point here is much the same as the point made earlier about sense perception. Normally one has no reason to distrust one's senses, and normally one has no reason to distrust one's memories. But in the thought experiment now under consideration we have mover very far from normal circumstances. And the content of the memory, insofar as it is first-person content, actually conflicts with the judgments of personal identity others would make on the basis of third-person evidence. Assuming that our subject can trust his senses to the extent of being entitled to think that the people about him really are saying the things they seem to be saying, this provides him with positive reasons for distrusting his memory. Conversely, if he trusts his memory this gives him a reason for distrusting his senses. What he cannot have good reason for believing is that *both* he is the person who volunteered to be the subject of the series of operations *and* he is in the envisaged situation, that is, is alienated from the behavior of "his" body in the way described. So the imaginability of being in the situation he knows he is in (certain things *seeming* to be the case) is not evidence for the possibility of someone's being in the situation whose possibility is in question (those things really *being* the case).

One upshot of this discussion is that some cases of imagining from the first-person perspective are problematic in a way that is not initially apparent. One imagines what purports to be a succession of events involving oneself. Each event in the succession is imagined "from the inside." If the imaginability of each event in the succession is unproblematic, it may seem that the imagi-

nability of the series of events is unproblematic. And if each event in the series is described in the first-person, it may seem that one has imagined oneself undergoing such a series of events. But if imaginability is to bear on possibility, we need to go slow here. First of all, we need to distinguish two senses in which one can imagine something from the "first-person point of view." This might mean simply imagining it "from the inside"—imagining some aspect of the life of a person as it might be experienced by that person. Or it might mean imagining *oneself* doing or undergoing such and such, where the imagining is again from the inside. Imagining from the first-person point of view in the first sense needn't involve imagining from the first-person point of view in the second sense. If I imagine the battle of Cannae as it might have been experienced by Hannibal, I do not thereby imagine *being* Hannibal—not, at any rate, in a sense in which the imaginability of something is at least prima facie evidence of its possibility. And if I imagine a series of personal episodes, imagining each from the point of view of the person involved and so imagining each from the inside, I do not thereby imagine myself, or any single person, being the subject of all of those episodes. It is tempting to say that I can simply stipulate that the subject of one of my imaginings is myself. And so I can, up to a point. But there are limits to what one can coherently stipulate. If I successively imagine how the President's State of the Union Address is being received by the different members of the Congress, in each case imagining the reception from the inside, I cannot *both* regard this as an imagining of a single series of events *and* stipulate that in each case the person imagined from the inside is myself—not, at least, if imaginability is to be evidence of possibility. Returning to the Searle example, I can imagine from the inside first the agreeing to be the subject of the experiment, and then the somewhat diminished mental condition of someone after the first operation, and then the somewhat more diminished mental condition of someone after the second operation, and so on. It is natural to describe this by saying that I imagine agreeing to be the subject, and then experiencing diminished consciousness after the first operation, and then experiencing a further diminished consciousness after the second operation, and then . . . and so on. But this implies, illegitimately, that it is one and the same person who is the subject of all of these imagined episodes. If I stipulate that I am the imagined person who initially agrees to submit to the series of operations, then I cannot, without begging the question, stipulate also that I am the imagined person who experiences the final stages of the extinction of his consciousness while observing the external behavior of the body to go on as before. And if I stipulate that the latter person is myself, then I cannot stipulate that the former person is. That is, I cannot make these stipulations if the description of what is imagined is not to beg the question by assuming the truth of the possibility claim it is supposed to support.

But let me stipulate now that I am the person with radically diminished consciousness who is totally without control of the body from which he experiences the world. And suppose that I am right in claiming that I would not, in these circumstances, be entitled to say that there is no consciousness behind the silicon-driven behavior of the body I am imprisoned in. So we agree that for all we know there is another mind in there who is running the show. If we let "Sydney" be the name of the person who agreed to undergo the series of operations, we agree that while it seems to me that I am Sydney, since I remember Sydney's life from the inside, there is good third-person evidence that Sydney is the man whose behavior is generated in the now largely silicon brain that now inhabits my skull. Still, it might be thought that I know at least that there is something wrong with the view that a person's mentality is determined by the functional organization of the person's brain or body. By hypothesis, the brain part replacements were all such as to preserve the relevant sorts of functional organization. And let's take this to mean that the functional organization throughout is such that

according to functionalism there is just one mind realized in the brain. It is ruled out, in other words, that there are two functional organizations there, one superimposed on the other, corresponding to the total mental states of two different persons. So, assuming functionalism, the mentality associated with this body ought to be that which others ascribe, on the basis of behavior, to the man they call "Sydney." And while I am not in a position to know directly that there is not this sort of mentality associated with the body, I am in a position to know that there is another sort of mentality, quite different from this, which is associated with it—namely the diminished consciousness, frustration and despair that I am now experiencing. This might seem to undermine the functionalist view, even if it does not undermine the reasons others have for thinking that Sydney, as they conceive him, exists. Like the third outcome Searle imagines for his thought experiment, this seems to support the claim, not that that there is no functional organization that is *sufficient* for the possession of the mental states in question (which is what the possibility of the second outcome was alleged to show), but that there is none that is *necessary* for this.

But I do not think that this argument fares any better than the earlier one. First of all, once we are this far into the realm of fantasy, multiple bodies for one mind are as much a possibility to be reckoned with as multiple minds for one body. Supposing that the autocerebroscope indicates that the functional states in question are not realized in the body from which I see, it remains a possibility that they are realized elsewhere. I do not think that there is anything I could observe that could assure me that *now*here, and in *no* way, are there instantiated functional states that could underwrite the mental states I know myself to have. Moreover—and here I revert to the "bad dream point" invoked earlier—if what I seem to observe did *seem* to assure me of this, I would have at least as much reason to doubt the veridicality of my sense experiences and/or memories as I did in the previous case in which a series of shampoos seemed to produce alienation from my own body. In fact, of course, it is unrealistic to suppose that I would have to choose between wholesale distrust of my senses and the rejection of functionalism; I might more reasonably conclude that the cerebroscope is on the blink.

But there is more to be said than this. For I submit that it is out and out incoherent, and not just highly implausible, to suppose that the testimony of my senses could establish the negative existential that nowhere, neither in the body I see from nor anywhere else, does there exist a realization of the appropriate functional states that could be a realization of my current mental states. For the testimony of my senses to establish that negative existential would be for me to come to know on the basis of my senses that my current mental states are not playing the functional roles that according to functionalism are constitutive of such states. But if I *know* something on the basis of my senses, this requires, surely, that my beliefs be modified by my sensory inputs, acting in concert with my background beliefs, in a way that conforms to certain principles of rationality. And that *is* for certain mental states, sense-experiences, and beliefs, to play functional roles that according to functionalism are constitutive of them. To the extent that knowledge requires rationality, and that what are held to be the defining functional roles of mental states are the causal roles constitutive of rationality, it is incoherent to claim that one could know that one's own mental states are not playing the defining causal roles. Admittedly, this argument by itself shows only that one could not know that there is a total lack of realization of the relevant functional states, not that one could not know that there is a partial such lack. But we have seen other reasons for denying that one could know even that.

Let's take stock. Searle has claimed that it is an *empirical question* whether beings with a physical makeup different from ours, for example, beings made of silicon, can have conscious mental lives of the sort we have.[8] I take it this means a question that could in principle be settled, empirically, in the negative. It is of course an empirical question whether creatures with such a physical makeup could be behaviorally like us, to the extent of being able to pass the most stringent Turing tests. And it seems entirely possible to me, as I am sure it does to Searle, that the answer to this question is no. To put the point in a functionalist way, it may well be that the evolutionary process that resulted in us came up with the only possible implementation of the functional organization that bestows our sorts of mental states, and the only possible physical organization that bestows our behavioral dispositions. But Searle thinks that even supposing that there are possible creatures whose physical makeup is very different from ours but who are behaviorally just like us, *and* have whatever functional makeup you like, it is an empirical question whether such creatures could have a conscious mental life like ours. Now it is very difficult to see how this empirical question, supposing that it is one, could be settled in the negative by an investigation from the third-person point of view. Obviously it is not to be settled by observing the behavior of the creatures, since the creatures whose mentality is in question are precisely those which can be counted on to pass every behavioral test with flying colors. Nor does it seem that it could be settled in the negative by investigating their internal makeup; the most that could be established in that way is that certain functional states are realized differently in them than in us, and not that those functional states do not bestow mentality. Searle thinks that for any functional organization, it is an empirical question whether creatures that have it have genuine mental states. It does appear that if *this* is an empirical question, and one that could in principle be settled in the negative, it is one that could only be so settled from the first-person point of view. No wonder, then, that Searle devised his first-person thought experiment. What I have shown, however, is that where the question cannot be settled in the negative from the third-person point of view, it also cannot be settled in the negative from the first-person point of view.

I suspect that some people will be unmoved by all this because they think that the third-person point of view is, right from the start, parasitic on the first-person point of view. This would be true if we know what the various mental states are "from our own case," and if our entitlement to ascribe them to others on the basis of behavior rests on something like the argument from analogy. This view, call it the analogical position, is one of the hardiest weeds in the philosophical garden. It has been sprayed, in this century, with everything from the verificationist theory of meaning to Wittgenstein's private language argument, and it keeps coming back, usually under assumed names. A wholesale assault on it would be a task for another occasion. But I think that the considerations I have raised provide part of the case against it. They bring out that the first-person point of view does not provide a perspective from which, starting with no assumptions about the relations between mental and physical states of affairs, and about the causal roles of mental states, one can proceed to investigate empirically what these relations and roles are, first discovering what they are in one's own case and then extrapolating inductively to the case of others. This is for three related reasons. First, one can discover nothing at all about bodies, or about physical states of affairs, without assuming the veridicality of one's sense experiences, and to assume that is to assume something about the relations between mental and physical states of affairs—relations that are constitutively bound up in what it is for a body to *be* the body of a particular person.[9] The truth of this assumption is certainly not something one can straightforwardly discover empirically from the first-person point of view. Second, some of the causal relations amongst mental states involved in rationality must hold as a condition of one's coming to know anything at all, and there is no sense to the idea that one might investigate empirically, by introspection, whether these hold in one's own case. Finally, the use of the first-person point of view to discover counterexamples to claims about

the sufficiency of bodily (or functional) states of affairs for mental states of affairs depends on the assumption that one is the sole inhabitant of one's body, and that assumption is not one whose truth one can discover empirically from the first-person point of view without relying on other assumptions about how the mental and physical realms are related.

The epistemology of modality is a large topic, and I have barely scratched the surface. But here, for whatever it is worth, is the moral I am inclined to draw. Where it seems that one can imagine discovering the realization of a putative possibility from the first-person perspective, one should always ask whether the seeming discovery could be confirmed from the third-person point of view. If one finds that it is impossible in principle that it should be, one should look to see whether the first-person thought experiment can be faulted in the ways I have tried to fault the first-person thought experiments here. I have not proven that the latter will always be the case. But I suspect that it will be.[10]

Notes

This chapter was delivered as the Presidential Address before the Ninetieth Annual Eastern Division Meeting of The American Philosophical Association in Atlanta, Georgia, December 29, 1993.

1. *Naming and Necessity*, Harvard University Press, 1972, pp. 144–155.

2. See, e.g., Putnam's "The Nature of Mental States," in his *Philosophical Paper*. Volume 2 (Cambridge: Cambridge University Press, 1975).

3. Someone might try to ground a difference in the fact that judgments about the pains of others are inferential and subject to error in ways in which judgments about one's own pains are not. This might seem a reason for saying that in the first-person thought experiment what one imagines knowing is that someone is *in pain* without there being any C-fiber stimulation going on, while in the third-person thought experiment what one imagines knowing is only that someone is *manifesting pain behavior* without there being any C-fiber stimulation going

on. But if one insists that the only imaginable states of affairs are ones to which one has an access that is non-inferential and not subject to error, then the first-person thought experiment is no better off than the third-person thought experiment; both require that one have access to whether there is C-fiber firing going on in one, and any access one has to that will be subject to error and, arguably, inferential in whatever sense one's access to the pains of others is inferential.

4. MIT Press, Cambridge, Mass., 1992.

5. See *Experimental and Theoretical Studies of Consciousness*, Ciba Foundation Symposium 174 (John Wiley & Sons, 1993), p. 73. Unaccountably, the published transcript has the word "representation" where I have put "organization."

6. *The Journl of Philosophy*, XC, 4, April 1993, p. 198.

7. See Nagel's "Brain Bisection and the Unity of Consciousness," *Synthese*, vol. 22, 1977.

8. See his "Minds, Brains and Programs," *The Behavioral and Brain Sciences* III, 3 (September 1980), 417–24.

9. See my "Embodiment and Behavior," in A. Rorty (ed.), *The Identities of Persons* (Berkeley: University of California Press, 1976), reprinted in my *Identity, Cause, and Mind*, Cambridge, 1984.

10. My thanks to Ned Block, Mark Crimmins, Carl Ginet, Chris Hill, Norman Kretzmann, Dick Moran, and Bob Stalnaker for their very helpful comments on earlier versions of this. All gave me good advice, not all of which I took.

VII SUBJECTIVITY AND EXPLANATORY GAP

32 What Is It Like to Be a Bat?

Thomas Nagel

Consciousness is what makes the mind-body problem really intractable. Perhaps that is why current discussions of the problem give it little attention or get it obviously wrong. The recent wave of reductionist euphoria has produced several analyses of mental phenomena and mental concepts designed to explain the possibility of some variety of materialism, psychophysical identification, or reduction.[1] But the problems dealt with are those common to this type of reduction and other types, and what makes the mind-body problem unique, and unlike the water-H_2O problem or the Turing machine–IBM machine problem or the lightning–electrical discharge problem or the gene-DNA problem or the oak tree–hydrocarbon problem, is ignored.

Every reductionist has his favorite analogy from modern science. It is most unlikely that any of these unrelated examples of successful reduction will shed light on the relation of mind to brain. But philosophers share the general human weakness for explanations of what is incomprehensible in terms suited for what is familiar and well understood, though entirely different. This has led to the acceptance of implausible accounts of the mental largely because they would permit familiar kinds of reduction. I shall try to explain why the usual examples do not help us to understand the relation between mind and body—why, indeed, we have at present no conception of what an explanation of the physical nature of a mental phenomenon would be. Without consciousness the mind-body problem would be much less interesting. With consciousness it seems hopeless. The most important and characteristic feature of conscious mental phenomena is very poorly understood. Most reductionist theories do not even try to explain it. And careful examination will show that no currently available concept of reduction is applicable to it. Perhaps a new theoretical form can be devised for the purpose, but such a solution, if it exists, lies in the distant intellectual future.

Conscious experience is a widespread phenomenon. It occurs at many levels of animal life, though we cannot be sure of its presence in the simpler organisms, and it is very difficult to say in general what provides evidence of it. (Some extremists have been prepared to deny it even of mammals other than man.) No doubt it occurs in countless forms totally unimaginable to us, on other planets in other solar systems throughout the universe. But no matter how the form may vary, the fact that an organism has conscious experience *at all* means, basically, that there is something it is like to *be* that organism. There may be further implications about the form of the experience; there may even (though I doubt it) be implications about the behavior of the organism. But fundamentally an organism has conscious mental states if and only if there is something that it is like to *be* that organism—something it is like *for* the organism.

We may call this the subjective character of experience. It is not captured by any of the familiar, recently devised reductive analyses of the mental, for all of them are logically compatible with its absence. It is not analyzable in terms of any explanatory system of functional states, or intentional states, since these could be ascribed to robots or automata that behaved like people though they experienced nothing.[2] It is not analyzable in terms of the causal role of experiences in relation to typical human behavior—for similar reasons.[3] I do not deny that conscious mental states and events cause behavior, nor that they may be given functional characterizations. I deny only that this kind of thing exhausts their analysis. Any reductionist program has to to be based on an analysis of what is to be reduced. If the analysis leaves something out, the problem will be falsely posed. It is useless to base the defense of materialism on any analysis of mental phenomena that fails to deal explicitly with their subjective character. For there is no reason to suppose that a reduction which seems plausible when no attempt is made to account for consciousness can be extended to include consciousness. Without some idea, therefore, of what the subjective character of experience is, we cannot know what is required of a physicalist theory.

While an account of the physical basis of mind must explain many things, this appears to be the most difficult. It is impossible to exclude the phenomenological features of experience from a reduction in the same way that one excludes the phenomenal features of an ordinary substance from a physical or chemical reduction of it—namely, by explaining them as effects on the minds of human observers.[4] If physicalism is to be defended, the phenomenological features must themselves be given a physical account. But when we examine their subjective character it seems that such a result is impossible. The reason is that every subjective phenomenon is essentially connected with a single point of view, and it seems inevitable that an objective, physical theory will abandon that point of view.

Let me first try to state the issue somewhat more fully than by referring to the relation between the subjective and the objective, or between the *pour-soi* and the *en-soi*. This is far from easy. Facts about what it is like to be an X are very peculiar, so peculiar that some may be inclined to doubt their reality, or the significance of claims about them. To illustrate the connection between subjectivity and a point of view, and to make evident the importance of subjective features, it will help to explore the matter in relation to an example that brings out clearly the divergence between the two types of conception, subjective and objective.

I assume we all believe that bats have experience. After all, they are mammals, and there is no more doubt that they have experience than that mice or pigeons or whales have experience. I have chosen bats instead of wasps or flounders because if one travels too far down the phylogenetic tree, people gradually shed their faith that there is experience there at all. Bats, although more closely related to us than those other species, nevertheless present a range of activity and a sensory apparatus so different from ours that the problem I want to pose is exceptionally vivid (though it certainly could be raised with other species). Even without the benefit of philosophical reflection, anyone who has spent some time in an enclosed space with an excited bat knows what it is to encounter a fundamentally *alien* form of life.

I have said that the essence of the belief that bats have experience is that there is something that it is like to be a bat. Now we know that most bats (the Microchiroptera, to be precise) perceive the external world primarily by sonar, or echolocation, detecting the reflections, from objects within range, of their own rapid, subtly modulated, high-frequency shrieks. Their brains are designed to correlate the outgoing impulses with the subsequent echoes, and the information thus acquired enables bats to make precise discriminations of distance, size, shape, motion, and texture comparable to those we make by vision. But bat sonar, though clearly a form of perception, is not similar in its operation to any sense that we possess, and there is no reason to suppose that it is subjectively like anything we can experience or imagine. This appears to create difficulties for the notion of what it is like to be a bat. We must consider whether any method will permit us to extrapolate to the inner life of the bat from our own case,[5] and if not, what alternative methods there may be for understanding the notion.

Our own experience provides the basic material for our imagination, whose range is therefore limited. It will not help to try to imagine that one has webbing on one's arms, which enables one to fly around at dusk and dawn catching insects in one's mouth; that one has very poor vision, and perceives the surrounding world by a system of reflected high-frequency sound signals; and that one spends the day hanging upside down by one's feet in an attic. Insofar as I can imagine this (which is not very far), it tells me only what it would be like for *me* to behave as a bat behaves.

But that is not the question. I want to know what it is like for a *bat* to be a bat. Yet if I try to imagine this, I am restricted to the resources of my own mind, and those resources are inadequate to the task. I cannot perform it either by imagining additions to my present experience, or by imagining segments gradually subtracted from it, or by imagining some combination of additions, subtractions, and modifications.

To the extent that I could look and behave like a wasp or a bat without changing my fundamental structure, my experiences would not be anything like the experiences of those animals. On the other hand, it is doubtful that any meaning can be attached to the supposition that I should possess the internal neurophysiological constitution of a bat. Even if I could by gradual degrees be transformed into a bat, nothing in my present constitution enables me to imagine what the experiences of such a future stage of myself thus metamorphosed would be like. The best evidence would come form the experiences of bats, if we only knew what they were like.

So if extrapolation from our own case is involved in the idea of what it is like to be a bat, the extrapolation must be incompletable. We cannot form more than a schematic conception of what it *is* like. For example, we may ascribe general *types* of experience on the basis of the animal's structure and behavior. Thus we describe bat sonar as a form of three-dimensional forward perception; we believe that bats feel some versions of pain, fear, hunger, and lust, and that they have other, more familiar types of perception besides sonar. But we believe that these experiences also have in each case a specific subjective character, which it is beyond our ability to conceive. And if there is conscious life elsewhere in the universe, it is likely that some of it will not be describable even in the most general experiential terms available to us.[6] (The problem is not confined to exotic cases, however, for it exists between one person and another. The subjective character of the experience of a person deaf and blind from birth is not accessible to me, for example, nor presumably is mine to him. This does not prevent us each from believing that the other's experience has such a subjective character.)

If anyone is inclined to deny that we can believe in the existence of facts like this whose exact nature we cannot possibly conceive, he should reflect that in contemplating the bats we are in much the same position that intelligent bats or Martians[7] would occupy if they tried to form a conception of what is was like to be us. The structure of their own minds might make it impossible for them to succeed, but we know they would be wrong to conclude that there is not anything precise that it is like to be us: that only certain general types of mental state could be ascribed to us (perhaps perception and appetite would be concepts common to us both; perhaps not). We know they would be wrong to draw such a skeptical conclusion because we know what it is like to be us. And we know that while it includes an enormous amount of variation and complexity, and while we do not possess the vocabulary to describe it adequately, its subjective character is highly specific, and in some respects describable in terms that can be understood only by creatures like us. The fact that we cannot expect ever to accommodate in our language a detailed description of Martian or bat phenomenology should not lead us to dismiss as meaningless the claim that bats and Martians have experiences fully comparable in richness of detail to our own. It would be fine if someone were to develop concepts and a theory that enabled us to think about those things; but such an understanding may be permanently denied to us by the limits of our nature. And to deny the reality or logical significance of what we can never describe or understand is the crudest form of cognitive dissonance.

This brings us to the edge of a topic that requires much more discussion than I can give it here: namely, the relation between facts on the one hand and conceptual schemes or systems of representation on the other. My realism about the subjective domain in all its forms implies a belief in the existence of facts beyond the reach of human concepts. Certainly it is possible for a human being to believe that there are facts which humans never *will* possess the requisite concepts to represent or comprehend. Indeed, it would be foolish to doubt this, given the finiteness of humanity's expectations. After all, there would have been transfinite numbers even if everyone had been wiped out by the Black Death before Cantor discovered them. But one might also believe that there are facts which *could* not ever be represented or comprehended by human beings, even if the species lasted forever—simply because our structure does not permit us to operate with concepts of the requisite type. This impossibility might even be observed by other beings, but it is not clear that the existence of such beings, or the possibility of their existence, is a precondition of the significance of the hypothesis that there are humanly inaccessible facts. (After all, the nature of beings with access to humanly inaccessible facts is presumably itself a humanly inaccessible fact.) Reflection on what it is like to be a bat seems to lead us, therefore, to the conclusion that there are facts that do not consist in the truth of propositions expressible in a human language. We can be compelled to recognize the existence of such facts without being able to state or comprehend them.

I shall not pursue this subject, however. Its bearing on the topic before us (namely, the mind-body problem) is that it enables us to make a general observation about the subjective character of experience. Whatever may be the status of facts about what it is like to be a human being, or a bat, or a Martian, these appear to be facts that embody a particular point of view.

I am not adverting here to the alleged privacy of experience to its possessor. The point of view in question is not one accessible only to a single individual. Rather it is a *type*. It is often possible to take up a point of view other than one's own, so the comprehension of such facts is not limited to one's own case. There is a sense in which phenomenological facts are perfectly objective: one person can know or say of another what the quality of the other's experience is. They are subjective, however, in the sense that even this objective ascription of experience is possible only for someone sufficiently similar to the object of ascription to be able to adopt his point of view—to understand the ascription in the first person as well as in the third, so to speak. The more different from oneself the other experiencer is, the less success one can expect with this enterprise. In our own case we occupy the relevant point of view, but we will have as much difficulty understanding our own experience properly if we approach it from another point of view as we would if we tried to understand the experience of another species without taking up *its* point of view.[8]

This bears directly on the mind-body problem. For if the facts of experience—facts about what it is like *for* the experiencing organism—are accessible only from one point of view, then it is a mystery how the true character of experiences could be revealed in the physical operation of that organism. The latter is a domain of objective facts *par excellence*—the kind that can be observed and understood from many points of view and by individuals with differing perceptual systems. There are no comparable imaginative obstacles to the acquisition of knowledge about bat neurophysiology by human scientists, and intelligent bats or Martians might learn more about the human brain than we ever will.

This is not by itself an argument against reduction. A Martian scientist with no understanding of visual perception could understand the rainbow, or lightning, or clouds as physical phenomena, though he would never be able to understand the human concepts of rainbow, lightning, or cloud, or the place these things occupy in our phenomenal world. The objective nature of the things picked out by these concepts could be apprehended by him because, although the concepts themselves are connected with a particular point of view and a particular visual phenomenology, the things apprehended from that point of view are not: they are observable from the point of view but external to it; hence they can be comprehended from other points of view also, either by the same organisms or by others. Lightning has an objective character that is not exhausted by its visual appearance, and this can be investigated by a Martian without vision. To be precise, it has a *more* objective character than is revealed in its visual appearance. In speaking of the move from subjective to objective characterization, I wish to remain noncommittal about the existence of an end point, the completely objective intrinsic nature of the thing, which one might or might not be able to reach. It may be more accurate to think of objectivity as a direction in which the understanding can travel. And in understanding a phenomenon like lightning, it is legitimate to go as far away as one can from a strictly human viewpoint.[9]

In the case of experience, on the other hand, the connection with a particular point of view seems much closer. It is difficult to understand what could be meant by the *objective* character of an experience, apart from the particular point of view from which its subject apprehends it. After all, what would be left of what it was like to be a bat if one removed the viewpoint of the bat? But if experience does not have, in addition to its subjective character, an objective nature that can be apprehended from many different points of view, then how can it be supposed that a Martian investigating my brain might be observing physical processes which were my mental processes (as he might observe physical processes which were bolts of lightning), only from a different point of view? How, for that matter, could a human physiologist observe them from another point of view?[10]

We appear to be faced with a general difficulty about psychophysical reduction. In other areas the process of reduction is a move in the direction of greater objectivity, toward a more accurate view of the real nature of things. This is accomplished by reducing our dependence on individual or species-specific points of view toward the object of investigation. We describe it not in terms of the impressions it makes on our senses, but in terms of its more general effects and of properties detectable by means other than the human senses. The less it depends on a specifically human viewpoint, the more objective is our description. It is possible to follow this path because although the concepts and ideas we employ in thinking about the external world are initially applied from a point of view that involves our perceptual apparatus, they are used by us to refer to things beyond themselves—toward which we *have* the phenomenal point of view. Therefore we can abandon it in favor of another, and still be thinking about the same things.

Experience itself, however, does not seem to fit the pattern. The idea of moving from appearance to reality seems to make no sense here. What is the analogue in this case to pursuing a more objective understanding of the same phenomena by abandoning the initial subjective viewpoint toward them in favor of another that is more objective but concerns the same thing? Certainly it *appears* unlikely that we will get closer to the real nature of human experience by leaving behind the particularity of our human point of view and striving for a description in terms accessible to beings that could not imagine what it was like to be us. If the subjective character of experience is fully comprehensible only from one point of view, then any shift to greater objectivity—that is, less attachment to a specific viewpoint—does not take us nearer to the real nature of the phenomenon: it takes us farther away from it.

In a sense, the seeds of this objection to the reducibility of experience are already detectable in successful cases of reduction; for in discovering sound to be, in reality, a wave phenomenon in air or other media, we leave behind one viewpoint to take up another, and the auditory, human, or animal viewpoint that we leave behind remains unreduced. Members of radically different species may both understand the same physical events in objective terms, and this does not require that they understand the phenomenal forms in which those events appear to the senses of members of the other species. Thus it is a condition of their referring to a common reality that their more particular viewpoints are not part of the common reality that they both apprehend. The reduction can succeed only if the species-specific viewpoint is omitted from what is to be reduced.

But while we are right to leave this point of view aside in seeking a fuller understanding of the external world, we cannot ignore it permanently, since it is the essence of the internal world, and not merely a point of view on it. Most of the neo-behaviorism of recent philosophical psychology results from the effort to substitute an objective concept of mind for the real thing, in order to have nothing left over which cannot be reduced. If we acknowledge that a physical theory of mind must account for the subjective character of experience, we must admit that no presently available conception gives us a clue how this could be done. The problem is unique. If mental processes are indeed physical processes, then there is something it is like, intrinsically,[11] to undergo certain physical processes. What it is for such a thing to be the case remains a mystery.

What moral should be drawn from these reflections, and what should be done next? It would be a mistake to conclude that physicalism must be false. Nothing is proved by the inadequacy of physicalist hypotheses that assume a faulty objective analysis of mind. It would be truer to say that physicalism is a position we cannot understand because we do not at present have any conception of how it might be true. Perhaps it will be thought unreasonable to require such a conception as a condition of understanding. After all, it might be said, the meaning of physicalism is clear enough: mental states are states of the body; mental events are physical events. We do not know *which* physical states and events they are, but that should not prevent us from understanding the hypothesis. What could be clearer than the words "is" and "are?"

But I believe it is precisely this apparent clarity of the word "is" that is deceptive. Usually, when we are told that *X* is *Y* we know *how* it is supposed to be true, but that depends on a conceptual or theoretical background and is not conveyed by the "is" alone. We know how both "*X*" and "*Y*" refer, and the kinds of things to which they refer, and we have a rough idea how the two referential paths might converge on a single thing, be it an object, a person, a process, an event, or whatever. But when the two terms of the identification are very disparate it may not be so clear how it could be true. We may not have even a rough idea of how the two referential paths could converge, or what kind of things they might converge on, and a theoretical framework may have to be supplied to enable us to understand this. Without the framework, an air of mysticism surrounds the identification.

This explains the magical flavor of popular presentations of fundamental scientific discoveries, given out as propositions to which one must subscribe without really understanding them. For example, people are now told at an early age that all matter is really energy. But despite the fact that they know what "is" means, most of them never form a conception of what makes this claim true, because they lack the theoretical background.

At the present time the status of physicalism is similar to that which the hypothesis that matter is energy would have had if uttered by a pre-Socratic philosopher. We do not have the beginnings of a conception of how it might be true. In order to understand the hypothesis that a mental event is a physical event, we require more than an understanding of the word "is." The idea of how a mental and a physical term might refer to the same thing is lacking, and the usual analogies with theoretical identification in other fields fail to supply it. They fail because if we construe the reference of mental terms to physical events on the usual model, we either get a reappearance of separate subjective events as the effects through which mental reference to physical events is secured, or else we get a false account of how mental terms refer (for example, a causal behaviorist one).

Strangely enough, we may have evidence for the truth of something we cannot really understand. Suppose a caterpillar is locked in a sterile safe by someone unfamiliar with insect metamorphosis, and weeks later the safe is reopened, revealing a butterfly. If the person knows that the safe has been shut the whole time, he has reason to believe that the butterfly is or was once the caterpillar, without having any idea in what sense this might be so. (One possibility is that the caterpillar contained a tiny winged parasite that devoured it and grew into the butterfly.)

It is conceivable that we are in such a position with regard to physicalism. Donald Davidson has argued that if mental events have physical causes and effects, they must have physical descriptions. He holds that we have reason to believe this even though we do not—and in fact *could* not—have a general psychophysical theory.[12] His argument applies to intentional mental events, but I think we also have some reason to believe that sensations are physical processes, without being in a position to understand how. Davidson's position is that certain physical events have irreducibly mental properties, and perhaps some view describable in this way is correct. But nothing of which we can now form a conception corresponds to it; nor have we any idea what a theory would be like that enabled us to conceive of it.[13]

Very little work has been done on the basic question (from which mention of the brain can be entirely omitted) whether any sense can be made of experiences' having an objective character at all. Does it make sense, in other words, to ask what my experiences are *really* like, as opposed to how they appear to me? We cannot genuinely understand the hypothesis that their nature is captured in a physical description unless we understand the more fundamental idea that they *have* an objective nature (or that objective processes can have a subjective nature).[14]

I should like to close with a speculative proposal. It may be possible to approach the gap between subjective and objective from another direction. Setting aside temporarily the relation between the mind and the brain, we can pursue a more objective understanding of the mental in its own right. At present we are completely unequipped to think about the subjective character of experience without relying on the imagination—without taking up the point of view of the experiential subject. This should be regarded as a challenge to form new concepts and devise a new method—an objective phenomenology not dependent on empathy or the imagination. Though presumably it would not capture everything, its goal would be to describe, at least in part, the subjective character of experiences in a form comprehensible to beings incapable of having those experiences.

We would have to develop such a phenomenology to describe the sonar experiences of bats; but it would also be possible to begin with humans. One might try, for example, to develop concepts that could be used to explain to a person blind from birth what it was like to see. One would reach a blank wall eventually, but it should be possible to devise a method of expressing in objective terms much more than we can at present, and with much greater precision. The loose intermodal analogies—for example, "Red is like the sound of a trumpet"—which crop up in discussions of this subject are of little use. That should be clear to anyone who has both heard a trumpet and seen red. But structural features of perception might be more accessible to objective description, even though something would be left out. And concepts alternative to those we learn in the first person may enable us to arrive at a kind of understanding even of our own experience which is denied us by the very ease of description and lack of distance that subjective concepts afford.

Apart from its own interest, a phenomenology that is in this sense objective may permit questions about the physical[15] basis of experience to assume a more intelligible form. Aspects of subjective experience that admitted this kind of objective description might be better candidates for objective explanations of a more familiar sort. But whether or not this guess is correct, it seems unlikely that any physical theory of mind can be contemplated until more thought has been given to the general problem of subjective and objective. Otherwise we cannot even pose the mind-body problem without sidestepping it.[16]

Notes

1. Examples are J. J. C. Smart, *Philosophy and Scientific Realism* (London, 1963); David K. Lewis, "An Argument for the Identity Theory," *Journal of Philosophy*, LXIII (1966), reprinted with addenda in David M. Rosenthal, *Materialism & the Mind-Body Problem* (Englewood Cliffs, N.J., 1971); Hilary Putnam, "Psychological Predicates" in Capitan and Merrill, *Art, Mind, & Religion* (Pittsburgh, 1967), reprinted in Rosenthal, *op. cit.,* as "The Nature of Mental States"; D. M. Armstrong, *A Materialist Theory of the Mind* (London, 1968); D. C. Dennett, *Content and Consciousness* (London, 1969). I have expressed earlier doubt in "Armstrong on the Mind," *Philosophical Review* LXXIX (1970), 394–403; "Brain Bisection and the Unity of Consciousness," *Synthèse*, 22 (1971); and a review of Dennett, *Journal of Philosophy*, LXIX (1972). See also Saul Kripke, "Naming and Necessity" in Davidson and Harman, *Semantics of Natural Language* (Dordrecht, 1972), esp. pp. 334–342; and M. T. Thornton, "Ostensive Terms and Materialism," *The Monist*, 56 (1972).

2. Perhaps there could not actually be such robots. Perhaps anything complex enough to behave like a person would have experiences. But that, if true, is a fact which cannot be discovered merely be analyzing the concept of experience.

3. It is not equivalent to that about which we are incorrigible, both because we are not incorrigible about experience and because experience is present in animals lacking language and thought, who have no beliefs at all about their experiences.

4. Cf. Richard Rorty, "Mind-Body Identity, Privacy, and Categories," *The Review of Metaphysics*, XIX (1965), esp. 37–38.

5. By "our own case" I do not mean just "my own case," but rather the mentalistic ideas that we apply unproblematically to ourselves and other human beings.

6. Therefore the analogical form of the English expression "what it is *like*" is misleading. It does not mean "what (in our experience) it *resembles*," but rather "how it is for the subject himself."

7. Any intelligent extraterrestrial beings totally different from us.

8. It may be easier than I suppose to transcend interspecies barriers with the aid of the imagination. For example, blind people are able to detect objects near them by a form of sonar, using vocal clicks or taps of a cane. Perhaps if one knew what that was like, one could by extension imagine roughly what it was like to possess the much more refined sonar of a bat. The distance between oneself and other persons and other species can fall anywhere on a continuum. Even for other persons the understanding of what it is like to be them is only partial, and when one moves to species very different from oneself, a lesser degree of partial understanding may still be available. The imagination is remarkably flexible. My point, however, is not that we cannot *know* what it is like to be a bat. I am not raising that epistemological problem. My point is rather that even to form a *conception* of what it is like to be a bat (and a fortiori to know what it is like to be a bat) one must take up the bat's point of view. If one can take it up roughly, or partially, then one's conception will also be rough or partial. Or so it seems in our present state of understanding.

9. The problem I am going to raise can therefore be posed even if the distinction between more subjective and more objective descriptions or viewpoints can itself be made only within a larger human point of view. I do not accept this kind of conceptual relativism, but it need not be refuted to make the point that psychophysical reduction cannot be accommodated by the subjective-to-objective model familiar from other cases.

10. The problem is not just that when I look at the '*Mona Lisa*,' my visual experience has a certain quality, no trace of which is to be found by someone looking into my brain. For even if he did observe there a tiny image of the '*Mona Lisa*,' he would have no reason to identify it with the experience.

11. The relation would therefore not be a contingent one, like that of a cause and its distinct effect. It would be necessarily true that a certain physical state felt a certain way. Saul ˙Kripke (*op. cit.*) argues that causal behaviorist and related analyses of the mental fail because they construe, e.g., "pain" as a merely contingent name of pains. The subjective character of an experience ("its immediate phenomenological quality" Kripke calls it [p. 340]) is the essential property left out by such analyses, and the one in virtue of which it is, necessarily,

the experience it is. My view is closely related to his. Like Kripke, I find the hypothesis that a certain brain state should *necessarily* have a certain subjective character incomprehensible without further explanation. No such explanation emerges from theories which view the mind-brain relation as contingent, but perhaps there are other alternatives, not yet discovered.

A theory that explained how the mind-brain relation was necessary would still leave us with Kripke's problem of explaining why it nevertheless appears contingent. That difficulty seems to me surmountable, in the following way. We may imagine something by representing it to ourselves either perceptually, sympathetically, or symbolically. I shall not try to say how symbolic imagination works, but part of what happens in the other two cases is this. To imagine something perceptually, we put ourselves in a conscious state resembling the state we would be in if we perceived it. To imagine something sympathetically, we put ourselves in a conscious state resembling the thing itself. (This method can be used only to imagine mental events and states—our own or another's.) When we try to imagine a mental state occurring without its associated brain state, we first sympathetically imagine the occurrence of the mental state: that is, we put ourselves into a state that resembles it mentally. At the same time, we attempt to perceptually imagine the non-occurrence of the associated physical state, by putting ourselves into another state unconnected with the first: one resembling that which we would be in if we perceived the non-occurrence of the physical state. Where the imagination of physical features is perceptual and the imagination of mental features is sympathetic, it appears to us that we can imagine any experience occurring without its associated brain state, and vice versa. The relation between them will appear contingent even if it is necessary, because of the independence of the disparate types of imagination.

(Solipsism, incidentally, results if one misinterprets sympathetic imagination as if it worked like perceptual imagination: it then seems impossible to imagine any experience that is not one's own.)

12. See "Mental Events" in Foster and Swanson, *Experience and Theory* (Amherst, 1970); though I don't understand the argument against psychophysical laws.

13. Similar remarks apply to my paper "Physicalism," *Philosophical Review* LXXIV (1965), 339–356, reprinted with postscript in John O'Connor, *Modern Materialism* (New York, 1969).

14. This question also lies at the heart of the problem of other minds, whose close connection with the mind-body problem is often overlooked. If one understood how subjective experience could have an objective nature, one would understand the existence of subjects other than oneself.

15. I have not defined the term "physical." Obviously it does not apply just to what can be described by the concepts of contemporary physics, since we expect further developments. Some may think there is nothing to prevent mental phenomena from eventually being recognized as physical in their own right. But whatever else may be said of the physical, it has to be objective. So if our idea of the physical ever expands to include mental phenomena, it will have to assign them an objective character—whether or not this is done by analyzing them in terms of other phenomena already regarded as physical. It seems to me more likely, however, that mental-physical relations will eventually be expressed in a theory whose fundamental terms cannot be placed clearly in either category.

16. I have read versions of this paper to a number of audiences, and am indebted to many people for their comments.

33 Can We Solve the Mind-Body Problem?

Colin McGinn

"How it is that anything so remarkable as a state of consciousness comes about as a result of initiating nerve tissue, is just as unaccountable as the appearance of the Djin, where Aladdin rubbed his lamp in the story..."
—Thomas Huxley

We have been trying for a long time to solve the mind-body problem. It has stubbornly resisted our best efforts. The mystery persists. I think the time has come to admit candidly that we cannot resolve the mystery. But I also think that this very insolubility—or the reason for it—removes the philosophical problem. In this chapter I explain why I say these outrageous things.

The specific problem I want to discuss concerns consciousness, the hard nut of the mind-body problem. How is it possible for conscious states to depend upon brain states? How can technicolor phenomenology arise from soggy gray matter? What makes the bodily organ we call the brain so radically different from other bodily organs, say the kidneys—the body parts without a trace of consciousness? How could the aggregation of millions of individually insentient neurons generate subjective awareness? We know that brains are the *de facto* causal basis of consciousness, but we have, it seems, no understanding whatever of how this can be so. It strikes us as miraculous, eerie, even faintly comic. Somehow, we feel, the water of the physical brain is turned into the wine of consciousness, but we draw a total blank on the nature of this conversion. Neural transmissions just seem like the wrong kind of materials with which to bring consciousness into the world, but it appears that in some way they perform this mysterious feat. The mind-body problem is the problem of understanding how the miracle is wrought, thus removing the sense of deep mystery. We want to take the magic out of the link between consciousness and the brain.[1]

Purported solutions to the problem have tended to assume one of two forms. One form, which we may call constructive, attempts to specify some natural property of the brain (or body) which explains how consciousness can be elicited from it. Thus functionalism, for example, suggests a property—namely, causal role—which is held to be satisfied by both brain states and mental states; this property is supposed to explain how conscious states can come from brain states.[2] The other form, which has been historically dominant, frankly admits that nothing merely natural could do the job, and suggests instead that we invoke supernatural entities or divine interventions. Thus we have Cartesian dualism and Leibnizian pre-established harmony. These "solutions" at least recognize that something pretty remarkable is needed if the mind-body relation is to be made sense of; they are as extreme as the problem. The approach I favor is naturalistic but not constructive: I do not believe we can ever specify what it is about the brain that is responsible for consciousness, but I am sure that whatever it is it is not inherently miraculous. The problem arises, I want to suggest, because we are cut off by our very cognitive constitution from achieving a conception of that natural property of the brain (or of consciousness) that accounts for the psychophysical link. This is a kind of causal nexus that we are precluded from ever understanding, given the way we have to form our concepts and develop our theories. No wonder we find the problem so difficult!

Before I can hope to make this view plausible, I need to sketch the general conception of cognitive competence that underlies my position. Let me introduce the idea of *cognitive closure*. A type of mind M is cognitively closed with respect to a property P (or theory T) if and only if the concept-forming procedures at M's disposal cannot extend to a grasp of P (or an understanding of T). Conceiving minds come in different kinds, equipped with varying powers and limitations, biases and blindspots, so that properties (or theories) may be accessible to some minds but not to others.

What is closed to the mind of a rat may be open to the mind of a monkey, and what is open to us may be closed to the monkey. Representational power is not all or nothing. Minds are biological products like bodies, and like bodies they come in different shapes and sizes, more or less capacious, more or less suited to certain cognitive tasks.[3] This is particularly clear for perceptual faculties, of course: perceptual closure is hardly to be denied. Different species are capable of perceiving different properties of the world, and no species can perceive every property things may instantiate (without artificial instrumentation anyway). But such closure does not reflect adversely on the reality of the properties that lie outside the representational capacities in question; a property is no less real for not being reachable from a certain kind of perceiving and conceiving mind. The invisible parts of the electromagnetic spectrum are just as real as the visible parts, and whether a specific kind of creature can form conceptual representations of these imperceptible parts does not determine whether they exist. Thus cognitive closure with respect to P does not imply irrealism about P. That P is (as we might say) *noumenal* with respect to M does not show that P does not occur in some naturalistic scientific theory T—it shows only that T is not cognitively accessible to M. Presumably monkey minds and the property of being an electron illustrate this possibility. And the question must arise as to whether human minds are closed with respect to certain true explanatory theories. Nothing, at least, in the concept of reality shows that everything real is open to the human concept-forming faculty—if, that is, we are realists about reality.[4]

Consider a mind constructed according to the principles of classical empiricism, a Humean mind. Hume mistakenly thought that human minds were Humean, but we can at least conceive of such a mind (perhaps dogs and monkeys have Humean minds). A Humean mind is such that perceptual closure determines cognitive closure, since "ideas" must always be copies of "impressions"; therefore the concept-forming system cannot transcend what can be perceptually presented to the subject. Such a mind will be closed with respect to unobservables; the properties of atoms, say, will not be representable by a mind constructed in this way. This implies that explanatory theories in which these properties are essentially mentioned will not be accessible to a Humean mind.[5] And hence the observable phenomena that are explained by allusion to unobservables will be inexplicable by a mind thus limited. But notice: the incapacity to explain certain phenomena does not carry with it a lack of recognition of the theoretical problems the phenomena pose. You might be able to appreciate problem without being able to formulate (even in principle) the solution to that problem (I suppose human children are often in this position, at least for a while). A Humean mind cannot solve the problems that our physics solves, yet it might be able to have an inkling of what needs to be explained. We would expect, then, that a moderately intelligent enquiring Humean mind will feel permanently perplexed any mystified by the physical world, since the correct science is forever beyond its cognitive reach. Indeed, something like this was precisely the view of Locke. He thought that our ideas of matter are quite sharply constrained by our perceptions and so concluded that the true science of matter is eternally beyond us—that we could never remove our perplexities about (say) what solidity ultimately is.[6] But it does not follow for Locke that nature is itself inherently mysterious; the felt mystery comes from our own cognitive limitations, not from any objective eeriness in the world. It looks today as if Locke was wrong about our capacity to fathom the nature of the physical world, but we can still learn from his fundamental thought—the insistence that our cognitive faculties may not be up to solving every problem that confronts us. To put the point more generally: the human mind may not conform to empiricist principles, but it must conform to *some* principles—and it is a substantive claim that these principles permit the solution of every problem we can formulate or sense. Total cognitive openness is not guaranteed for human beings and it should not be expected. Yet what is noumenal for us may not be miraculous in itself. We should therefore be alert to the possibility that a problem that strikes us as deeply intractable, as utterly baffling, may arise from an area of cognitive closure in our ways of representing the world.[7] That is what I now want to argue is the case with our sense of the mysterious nature of the connection between consciousness and the brain. We are biased away from arriving at the correct explanatory theory of the psychophysical nexus. And this makes us prone to an illusion of objective mystery. Appreciating this should remove the philosophical problem: consciousness does not, in reality, arise from the brain in the miraculous way in which the Djin arises from the lamp.

I now need to establish three things: (i) there exists some property of the brain that accounts naturalistically for consciousness; (ii) we are cognitively closed with respect to that property; but (iii) there is no philosophical (as opposed to scientific) mind-body problem. Most of the work will go into establishing (ii).

Resolutely shunning the supernatural, I think it is undeniable that it must be in virtue of *some* natural property of the brain that organisms are conscious. There just *has* to be some explanation for how brains subserve minds. If we are not to be eliminativists about consciousness, then some theory must exist which accounts for the psychophysical correlations we observe. It is implausible to take these correlations as ultimate and inexplicable facts, as simply brute. And we do not want to acknowledge radical emergence of the conscious with respect to the cerebral: that is too much like accepting miracles *de re*. Brain states cause conscious states, we know, and this causal nexus must proceed through necessary connections of some kind—the kind that would make the nexus intelligible *if* they were understood.[8] Consciousness is like life in this respect. We know that life evolved from inorganic matter, so we ex-

pect there to be some explanation of this process. We cannot plausibly take the arrival of life as a primitive brute fact, nor can we accept that life arose by some form of miraculous emergence. Rather, there must be some natural account of how life comes from matter, whether or not we can know it. Eschewing vitalism and the magic touch of God's finger, we rightly insist that it must be in virtue of some natural property of (organized) matter that parcels of it get to be alive. But consciousness itself is just a further biological development, and so it too must be susceptible of some natural explanation—whether or not human beings are capable of arriving at this explanation. Presumably there exist objective natural laws that somehow account for the upsurge of consciousness. Consciousness, in short, must be a natural phenomenon, naturally arising from certain organizations of matter. Let us then say that there exists some property P, instantiated by the brain, in virtue of which the brain is the basis of consciousness. Equivalently, there exists some theory T, referring to P, which fully explains the dependence of conscious states on brain states. If we knew T, then we would have a constructive solution to the mind-body problem. The question then is whether we can ever come to know T and grasp the nature of P.

Let me first observe that it is surely *possible* that we could never arrive at a grasp of P; there is, as I said, no guarantee that our cognitive powers permit the solution of every problem we can recognize. Only a misplaced idealism about the natural world could warrant the dogmatic claim that everything is knowable by the human species at this stage of its evolutionary development (consider the same claim made on behalf of the intellect of Cro-Magnon man). It *may* be that every property for which we can form a concept is such that *it* could never solve the mind-body problem. We *could* be like five-year-old children trying to understand Relativity Theory. Still, so far this is just a possibility claim: what reason do we have for asserting, positively, that our minds are closed with respect to P?

Longstanding historical failure is suggestive, but scarcely conclusive. Maybe, it will be said, the solution is just around the corner, or it has to wait upon the completion of the physical sciences. Perhaps we simply have yet to produce the Einstein-like genius who will restructure the problem in some clever way and then present an astonished world with the solution.[9] However, I think that our deep bafflement about the problem, amounting to a vertiginous sense of ultimate mystery, which resists even articulate formulation, should at least encourage us to explore the idea that there is something terminal about our perplexity. Rather as traditional theologians found themselves conceding cognitive closure with respect to certain of the properties of God, so we should look seriously at the idea that the mind-body problem brings us bang up against the limits of our capacity to understand the world. That is what I shall do now.

There seem to be two possible avenues open to us in our aspiration to identify P: we could try to get to P by investigating consciousness directly; or we could look to the study of the brain for P. Let us consider these in turn, starting with consciousness. Our acquaintance with consciousness could hardly be more direct; phenomenological description thus comes (relatively) easily. "Introspection" is the name of the faculty through which we catch consciousness in all its vivid nakedness. By virtue of possessing this cognitive faculty we ascribe concepts of consciousness to ourselves; we thus have "immediate access" to the properties of consciousness. But does the introspective faculty reveal property P? Can we tell just by introspecting what the solution to the mind-body problem is? Clearly not. We have direct cognitive access to one term of the mind—brain relation, but we do not have such access to the nature of the link. Introspection does not present conscious states *as* depending upon the brain in some intelligible way. We cannot therefore introspect P. Moreover, it seems impossible that we should ever augment our stock of introspectively ascribed concepts with the concept

P—that is, we could not acquire this concept simply on the basis of sustained and careful introspection. Pure phenomenology will never provide the solution to the mind-body problem. Neither does it seem feasible to try to extract P from the concepts of consciousness we now have by some procedure of conceptual analysis—any more than we could solve the life-matter problem simply by reflecting on the concept *life*.[10] P has to lie outside the field of the introspectable, and it is not implicitly contained in the concepts we bring to bear in our first-person ascriptions. Thus the faculty of introspection, as a concept-forming capacity, is cognitively closed with respect to P; which is not surprising in view of its highly limited domain of operation (*most* properties of the world are closed to introspection).

But there is a further point to be made about P and consciousness, which concerns our restricted access to the concepts of consciousness themselves. It is a familiar point that the range of concepts of consciousness attainable by a mind M is constrained by the specific forms of consciousness possessed by M. Crudely, you cannot form concepts of conscious properties unless you yourself instantiate those properties. The man born blind cannot grasp the concept of a visual experience of red, and human beings cannot conceive of the echolocatory experiences of bats.[11] These are cases of cognitive closure within the class of conscious properties. But now this kind of closure will, it seems, affect our hopes of access to P. For suppose that we were cognitively open with respect to P; suppose, that is, that we had the solution to the problem of how specific forms of consciousness depend upon different kinds of physiological structure. Then, of course, we would understand how the brain of a bat subserves the subjective experiences of bats. Call this type of experience B, and call the explanatory property that links B to the bat's brain P_1. By grasping P_1 it would be perfectly intelligible to us how the bat's brain generates B-experiences; we would have an explanatory theory of the causal nexus in question. We would be in possession of the same kind of understanding we would have of our own experiences if we had the correct psychophysical theory of them. But then it seems to follow that grasp of the theory that explains *B*-experiences would *confer* a grasp of the nature of those experiences: for how could we understand that theory without understanding the concept *B* that occurs in it? How could we grasp the *nature* of *B*-experiences without grasping the *character* of those experiences? The true psychophysical theory would seem to provide a route to a grasp of the subjective form of the bat's experiences. But now we face a dilemma, a dilemma which threatens to become a reduction: either we *can* grasp this theory, in which case the property *B* becomes open to us; or we *cannot* grasp the theory, simply because property *B* is *not* open to us. It seems to me that the looming reduction here is compelling: our concepts of consciousness just *are* inherently constrained by our own from of consciousness, so that any theory the understanding of which required us to transcend these constraints would *ipso facto* be inaccessible to us. Similarly, I think, any theory that required us to transcend the finiteness of our cognitive capacities would *ipso facto* be a theory we could not grasp—and this despite the fact that it might be needed to explain something we can see needs explaining. We cannot simply stipulate that our concept-forming abilities are indefinitely plastic and unlimited just because they would have to be to enable us to grasp the truth about the world. We constitutionally lack the concept-forming capacity to encompass all possible types of conscious state, and this obstructs our path to a general solution to the mind-body problem. Even if we could solve it for our own case, we could not solve it for bats and Martians. *P* is, as it were, too close to the different forms of subjectivity for it to be accessible to all such forms, given that one's form of subjectivity restricts one's concepts of subjectivity.[12]

I suspect that most optimists about constructively solving the mind-body problem will prefer to place their bets on the brain side of the relation.

Neuroscience is the place to look for property *P*, they will say. My question then is whether there is any conceivable way in which we might come to introduce *P* in the course of our empirical investigations of the brain. New concepts have been introduced in the effort to understand the workings of the brain, certainly: could not *P* then occur in conceivable extensions of this manner of introduction? So far, indeed, the theoretical concepts we ascribe to the brain seem as remote from consciousness as any ordinary physical properties are, but perhaps we might reach *P* by diligent application of essentially the same procedures: so it is tempting to think. I want to suggest, to the contrary, that such procedures are inherently closed with respect to *P*. The fundamental reason for this, I think, is the role of *perception* in shaping our understanding of the brain—the way that our perception of the brain constrains the concepts we can apply to it. A point whose significance it would be hard to overstress here is this: the property of consciousness itself (or specific conscious states) is not an observable or perceptible property of the brain. You can stare into a living conscious brain, your own or someone else's, and see there a wide variety of instantiated properties—its shape, color, texture, and so on—but you will not thereby *see* what the subject is experiencing, the conscious state itself. Conscious states are simply not, *qua* conscious states, potential objects of perception: they depend upon the brain but they cannot be observed by directing the senses onto the brain. You cannot see a brain state *as* a conscious state. In other words, consciousness is noumenal with respect to perception of the brain.[13] I take it this is obvious. So we know there *are* properties of the brain that are necessarily closed to perception of the brain; the question now is whether *P* is likewise closed to perception.

My argument will proceed as follows. I shall first argue that *P* is indeed perceptually closed; then I shall complete the argument to full cognitive closure by insisting that no form of *inference* from what is perceived can lead us to *P*. The argument for perceptual closure starts from the thought that nothing we can imagine perceiving in the brain would ever convince us that we have located the intelligible nexus we seek. No matter what recondite property we could see to be instantiated in the brain we should always be baffled about how it could give rise to consciousness. I hereby invite you to try to conceive of a perceptible property of the brain that might allay the feeling of mystery that attends our contemplation of the brain-mind link: I do not think you will be able to do it. It is like trying to conceive of a perceptible property of a rock that would render it perspicuous that the rock was conscious. In fact, I think it is the very impossibility of this that lies at the root of the felt mind-body problem. But why is this? Basically, I think, it is because the senses are geared to representing a spatial world; they essentially present things in space with spatially defined properties. But it is precisely *such* properties that seem inherently incapable of resolving the mind-body problem: we cannot link consciousness to the brain in virtue of spatial properties of the brain. There the brain is, an object of perception, laid out in space, containing spatially distributed processes; but consciousness defies explanation in such terms. Consciousness does not seem made up out of smaller spatial processes; yet perception of the brain seems limited to revealing such processes.[14] The senses are responsive to certain *kinds* of properties—those that are essentially bound up with space—but these properties are of the wrong sort (the wrong *category*) to constitute P. Kant was right, the form of outer sensibility is spatial; but if so, then P will be noumenal with respect to the senses, since no spatial property will ever deliver a satisfying answer to the mind-body problem. We simply do not understand the idea that conscious states might intelligibly arise from spatial configurations of the kind disclosed by perception of the world.

I take it this claim will not seem terribly controversial. After all, we do not generally expect that every property referred to in our theories should be a potential object of human perception:

consider quantum theory and cosmology. Unrestricted perceptual openness is a dogma of empiricism if ever there was one. And there is no compelling reason to suppose that the property needed to explain the mind-brain relation should be in principle perceptible; it might be essentially "theoretical", an object of thought, not sensory experience. Looking harder at nature is not the only (or the best) way of discovering its theoretically significant properties. Perceptual closure does not entail cognitive closure, since we have available the procedure of hypothesis formation, in which *un*observables come to be conceptualized.

I readily agree with these sentiments, but I think there are reasons for believing that no coherent method of concept introduction will ever lead us to P. This is because a certain principle of *homogeneity* operates in our introduction of theoretical concepts on the basis of observation. Let me first note that consciousness itself could not be introduced simply on the basis of what we observe about the brain and its physical effects. If our data, arrived at by perception of the brain, do not include anything that brings in conscious states, then the theoretical properties we need to explain these data will not include conscious states either. Inference to the best explanation of purely physical data will never take us outside the realm of the physical, forcing us to introduce concepts of consciousness.[15] Everything physical has a purely physical explanation. So the property of consciousness is cognitively closed with respect to the introduction of concepts by means of inference to the best explanation of perceptual data about the brain.

Now the question is whether P could ever be arrived at by this kind of inference. Here we must be careful to guard against a form of magical emergentism with respect to concept formation. Suppose we try out a relatively clear theory of how theoretical concepts are formed: we get them by a sort of analogical extension of what we observe. Thus, for example, we arrive at the concept of a molecule by taking our perceptual representations of macroscopic objects and conceiving of smaller scale objects of the same general kind. This method seems to work well enough for unobservable material objects, but it will not help in arriving at P, since analogical extensions of the entities we observe in the brain are precisely as hopeless as the original entities were as solutions to the mind-body problem. We would need a method that left the base of observational properties behind in a much more radical way. But it seems to me that even a more unconstrained conception of inference to the best explanation would still not do what is required: it would no more serve to introduce P than it serves to introduce the property of consciousness itself. To explain the observed physical data we need only such theoretical properties as bear upon those data, not the property that explains consciousness, which does not occur in the data. Since we do not need consciousness to explain those data, we do not need the property that explains consciousness. We shall never get as far away from the perceptual data in our explanations of those data as we need to get in order to connect up explanatorily with consciousness. This is, indeed, why it seems that consciousness is theoretically epiphenomenal in the task of accounting for physical events. No concept needed to explain the workings of the physical world will suffice to explain how the physical world produces consciousness. So if P is perceptually noumenal, then it will be noumenal with respect to perception-based explanatory inferences. Accordingly, I do not think that P could be arrived at by empirical studies of the brain alone. Nevertheless, the brain *has* this property, as it has the property of consciousenss. Only a magical idea of how we come by concepts could lead one to think that we can reach P by first perceiving the brain and then asking what is needed to explain what we perceive.[16] (The mind-body problem tempts us to magic in more ways than one.)

It will help elucidate the position I am driving toward if I contrast it with another view of the source of the perplexity we feel about the mind-brain nexus. I have argued that we cannot know which property of the brain accounts for consciousness, and so we find the mind-brain link unintelligible. But, it may be said, there is another account of our sense of irremediable mystery, which does not require positing properties our minds cannot represent. This alternative view claims that, even if we *now* had a grasp of P, we would *still* feel that there is something mysterious about the link, because of a special epistemological feature of the situation. Namely this: our acquaintance with the brain and our acquaintance with consciousness are necessarily mediated by distinct cognitive faculties, namely perception and introspection. Thus the faculty through which we apprehend one term of the relation is necessarily distinct from the faculty through which we apprehend the other. In consequence, it is not possible for us to use one of these faculties to apprehend the nature of the psychophysical nexus. No single faculty will enable us ever to apprehend the fact that consciousness depends upon the brain in virtue of property P. Neither perception alone nor introspection alone will ever enable us to witness the dependence. And this, my objector insists, is the real reason we find the link baffling: we cannot make sense of it in terms of the deliverances of a single cognitive faculty. So, even if we now had concepts for the properties of the brain that explain consciousness, we would still feel a residual sense of unintelligibility; we should still take there to be something mysterious going on. The necessity to shift from one faculty to the other produces in us an illusion of inexplicability. We might in fact have the explanation right now but be under the illusion that we do not. The right diagnosis, then, is that we should recognize the peculiarity of the epistemological situation and stop trying to make sense of the psychophysical nexus in the way we make sense of other sorts of nexus. It only *seems* to us that we can never discover a property that will render the nexus intelligible.

I think this line of thought deserves to be taken seriously, but I doubt that it correctly diagnoses our predicament. It is true enough that the problematic nexus is essentially apprehended by distinct faculties, so that it will never reveal its secrets to a single faculty; but I doubt that our intuitive sense of intelligibility is so rigidly governed by the "single-faculty condition". Why *should* facts only seem intelligible to us if we can conceive of apprehending them by one (sort of) cognitive faculty? Why not allow that we can recognize intelligible connections between concepts (or properties) even when those concepts (or properties) are necessarily ascribed using different faculties? Is it not suspiciously empiricist to insist that a causal nexus can only be made sense of by us if we can conceive of its being an object of a single faculty of apprehension? Would we think this of a nexus that called for touch and sight to apprehend each term of the relation? Suppose (*per impossible*) that we were offered *P* on a plate, as a gift from God: would we still shake our heads and wonder how that could resolve the mystery, being still the victims of the illusion of mystery generated by the epistemological duality in question? No, I think this suggestion is not enough to accounts for the miraculous appearance of the link: it is better to suppose that we are permanently blocked from forming a concept of what accounts for that link.

How strong is the thesis I am urging? Let me distinguish *absolute* from *relative* claims of cognitive closure. A problem is absolutely cognitively closed if no possible mind could resolve it; a problem is relatively closed if minds of some sorts can in principle solve it while minds of other sorts cannot. Most problems, we may safely suppose, are only relatively closed: armadillo minds cannot solve problems of elementary arithmetic but human minds can. Should we say that the mind-body problem is only relatively closed or is the closure absolute? This depends on what we allow as a possible concept-forming mind, which is not an easy question. If we allow for minds that form their concepts of the brain and consciousness in ways that are quite independent of perception and introspection, then there may be room for the idea that there are possible minds for which the mind-body problem is soluble, and easily so. But if we suppose that *all* concept formation is tied to

perception and introspection, however loosely, then no mind will be capable of understanding how it relates to its own body—the insolubility will be absolute. I think we can just about make sense of the former kind of mind, by exploiting our own faculty of a priori reasoning. Our mathematical concepts (say) do not seem tied either to perception or to introspection, so there does seem to be a mode of concept formation that operates without the constraints I identified earlier. The suggestion might then be that a mind that formed all of its concepts in this way—including its concepts of the brain and consciousness—would be free of the biases that prevent *us* from coming up with the right theory of how the two connect. Such a mind would have to be able to think of the brain and consciousness in ways that utterly prescind from the perceptual and the introspective—in somewhat the way we now (it seems) think about numbers. This mind would conceive of the psychophysical link in totally a priori terms. Perhaps this is how we should think of God's mind, and God's understanding of the mind-body relation. At any rate, something pretty radical is going to be needed if we are to devise a mind that can escape the kinds of closure that make the problem insoluble for us—if I am right in my diagnosis of our difficulty. *If* the problem is only relatively insoluble, then the type of mind that can solve it is going to be very different from ours and the kinds of mind we can readily make sense of (there may, of course, be cognitive closure here too). It certainly seems to me to be at least an open question whether the problem is absolutely insoluble; I would not be surprised if it were.[17]

My position is both pessimistic and optimistic at the same time. It is pessimistic about the prospects for arriving at a constructive solution to the mind-body problem, but it is optimistic about our hopes of removing the philosophical perplexity. The central point here is that I do not think we need to do the former in order to achieve the latter. This depends on a rather special understanding of what the philosophical problem consists in. What I want to suggest is that the nature of the psychophysical connection has a full and non-mysterious explanation in a certain science, but that this science is inaccessible to us as a matter of principle. Call this explanatory scientific theory T: T is as natural and prosaic and devoid of miracle as any theory of nature; it describes the link between consciousness and the brain in a way that is no more remarkable (or alarming) than the way we now describe the link between the liver and bile.[18] According to T, there is nothing eerie going on in the world when an event in my visual cortex causes me to have an experience of yellow—however much it seems to *us* that there is. In other words, there is no intrinsic conceptual or metaphysical difficulty about how consciousness depends on the brain. It is not that the correct science is compelled to postulate miracles *de re*; it is rather that the correct science lies in the dark part of the world for us. We confuse our own cognitive limitations with objective eeriness. We are like a Humean mind trying to understand the physical world, or a creature without spatial concepts trying to understand the possibility of motion. This removes the philosophical problem because it assures us that the entities *themselves* pose no inherent philosophical difficulty. The case is unlike, for example, the problem of how the abstract world of numbers might be intelligibly related to the world of concrete knowing subjects: here the mystery seems intrinsic to the entities, not a mere artefact of our cognitive limitations or biases in trying to understand the relation.[19] It would not be plausible to suggest that there exists a science, whose theoretical concepts we cannot grasp, which completely resolves any sense of mystery that surrounds the question how the abstract becomes an object of knowledge for us. In this case, then, eliminativism seems a live option. The *philosophical* problem about consciousness and the brain arises from a sense that we are compelled to accept that nature contains miracles—as if the merely metallic lamp (*lump*) of the brain could really spirit into existence the Djin of con-

sciousness. But we do not need to accept this: we can rest secure in the knowledge that some (unknowable) property of the brain makes everything fall into place. What creates the philosophical puzzlement is the assumption that the problem must somehow be scientific but that any science *we* can come up with will represent things as utterly miraculous. And the solution is to recognize that the sense of miracle comes from us and not from the world. There is, in reality, nothing mysterious about how the brain generates consciousness. There is no *metaphysical* problem.[20]

So far that deflationary claim has been justified by a general naturalism and certain considerations about cognitive closure and the illusions it can give rise to. Now I want to marshall some reasons for thinking that consciousness is actually a rather simple natural fact; objectively, consciousness is nothing very special. We should now be comfortable with the idea that our own sense of difficulty is a fallible guide to objective complexity: what is hard for us to grasp may not be very fancy in itself. The grain of our thinking is not a mirror held up to the facts of nature.[21] In particular, it may be that the extent of our understanding of facts about the mind is not commensurate with some objective estimate of their intrinsic complexity: we may be good at understanding the mind in some of its aspects but hopeless with respect to others, in a way that cuts across objective differences in what the aspects involve. Thus we are adept at understanding action in terms of the folk psychology of belief and desire, and we seem not entirely out of our depth when it comes to devising theories of language. But our understanding of how consciousness develops from the organization of matter is non-existent. But now, think of these various aspects of mind from the point of view of evolutionary biology. Surely language and the propositional attitudes are more complex and advanced evolutionary achievements than the mere possession of consciousness by a physical organism. Thus it seems that we are better at understanding some of the more complex aspects of mind than the

simpler ones. Consciousness arises early in evolutionary history and is found right across the
animal kingdom. In some respects it seems that
the biological engineering required for consciousness is less fancy than that needed for certain
kinds of complex motor behavior. Yet we can
come to understand the latter while drawing a
total blank with respect to the former. Conscious
states seem biologically quite primitive, comparatively speaking. So the theory T that explains
the occurrence of consciousness in a physical
world is very probably less objectively complex
(by some standard) than a range of other theories
that do not defy our intellects. If only we could
know the psychophysical mechanism it might
surprise us with its simplicity, its utter naturalness. In the manual that God consulted when
He made the earth and all the beasts that dwell
thereon the chapter about how to engineer consciousness from matter occurs fairly early on, well
before the really difficult later chapters on mammalian reproduction and speech. It is not the *size*
of the problem but its *type* that makes the mind-
body problem so hard for us. This reflection
should make us receptive to the idea that it is
something about the tracks of our thought that
prevents us from achieving a science that relates
consciousness to its physical basis: the enemy lies
within the gates.[22]

The position I have reached has implications
for a tangle of intuitions it is natural to have regarding the mind-body relation. On the one hand,
there are intuitions, pressed from Descartes to
Kripke, to the effect that the relation between
conscious states and bodily states is fundamentally contingent.[23] It can easily seem to us
that there is no necessitation involved in the dependence of the mind on the brain. But, on the
other hand, it looks absurd to try to dissociate the
two entirely, to let the mind float completely free
of the body. Disembodiment is a dubious possibility at best, and some kind of necessary supervenience of the mental on the physical has seemed
undeniable to many. It is not my aim here to adjudicate this longstanding dispute; I want simply

to offer a diagnosis of what is going on when one
finds oneself assailed with this flurry of conflicting
intuitions. The reason we feel the tug of contingency, pulling consciousness loose from its physical moorings, may be that we do not and cannot
grasp the nature of the property that intelligibly
links them. The brain has physical properties we
can grasp, and variations in these correlate with
changes in consciousness, but we cannot draw the
veil that conceals the manner of their connection.
Not grasping the nature of the connection, it
strikes us as deeply contingent; we cannot make
the assertion of a necessary connection intelligible
to ourselves. There *may* then be a real necessary
connection; it is just that it will always strike us
as curiously brute and unperspicuous. We may
thus, as upholders of intrinsic contingency, be
the dupes of our own cognitive blindness. On the
other hand, we are scarcely in a position to assert
that there *is* a necessary connection between the
properties of the brain we can grasp and states of
consciousness, since we are so ignorant (and irre-
mediably so) about the character of the connection. For all we know, the connection may be
contingent, as access to P would reveal if we
could have such access. The link between consciousness and property P is not, to be sure, contingent—virtually by definition—but we are not
in a position to say exactly how P is related to the
"ordinary" properties of the brain. It may be
necessary or it may be contingent. Thus it is that
we tend to vacillate between contingency and necessity; for we lack the conceptual resources to
decide the question definitively—or to understand the answer we are inclined to give. The
indicated conclusion appears to be that we can
never really know whether disembodiment is
metaphysically possible, or whether necessary
supervenience is the case, or whether spectrum
inversion could occur. For these all involve
claims about the modal connections between
properties of consciousness and the ordinary
properties of the body and brain that we can
conceptualize; and the real nature of these connections is not accessible to us. Perhaps P makes

the relation between C-fiber firing and pain necessary or perhaps it does not: we are simply not equipped to know. We are like a Humean mind wondering whether the observed link between the temperature of a gas and its pressure (at a constant volume) is necessary or contingent. To know the answer to that you need to grasp atomic (or molecular) theory, and a Humean mind just is not up to attaining the requisite theoretical understanding. Similarly, we are constitutionally ignorant at precisely the spot where the answer exists.

I predict that many readers of this chapter will find its main thesis utterly incredible, even ludicrous. Let me remark that I sympathize with such readers: the thesis is not easily digestible. But I would say this: if the thesis *is* actually true, it will still strike us as hard to believe. For the idea of an explanatory property (or set of properties) that is noumenal for us, yet is essential for the (constructive) solution of a problem we face, offends a kind of natural idealism that tends to dominate our thinking. We find it taxing to conceive of the existence of a real property, under our noses as it were, which we are built not to grasp—a property that is responsible for phenomena that we observe in the most direct way possible. This kind of realism, which brings cognitive closure so close to home, is apt to seem both an affront to our intellects and impossible to get our minds around. We try to think of this unthinkable property and understandably fail in the effort; so we rush to infer that the very supposition of such a property is nonsensical. Realism of the kind I am presupposing thus seems difficult to hold in focus, and any philosophical theory that depends upon it will also seem to rest on something systematically elusive.[24] My response to such misgivings, however, is unconcessive: the limits of our minds are just not the limits of reality. It is deplorably anthropocentric to insist that reality be constrained by what the human mind can conceive. We need to cultivate a vision of reality (a metaphysics) that makes it truly independent of our given cognitive powers, a conception that includes these powers as a proper part. It is just that, in the case of the mind-body problem, the bit of reality that systematically eludes our cognitive grasp is an aspect of our own nature. Indeed, it is an aspect that makes it possible for us to have minds at all and to think about how they are related to our bodies. This particular transcendent tract of reality happens to lie within our own heads. A deep fact about our own nature as a form of embodied consciousness is thus necessarily hidden from us. Yet there is nothing inherently eerie or bizarre about this embodiment. We are much more straightforward than we seem. Our weirdness lies in the eye of the beholder.

The answer to the question that forms my title is therefore "No and Yes."[25]

Notes

Previously published in *Mind*, Vol. xcviii, no. 891, July 1989, this article appears by permission of the publishers, Oxford University Press.

1. One of the peculiarities of the mind-body problem is the difficulty of formulating it in a rigorous way. We have a sense of the problem that outruns our capacity to articulate it clearly. Thus we quickly find ourselves resorting to invitations to look inward, instead of specifying precisely *what* it is about consciousness that makes it inexplicable in terms of ordinary physical properties. And this can make it seem that the problem is spurious. A creature without consciousness would not properly appreciate the problem (assuming such a creature could appreciate other problems). I think an adequate treatment of the mind-body problem should explain why it is so hard to state the problem explicitly. My treatment locates our difficulty in our inadequate conceptions of the nature of the brain and consciousness. In fact, if we knew their natures fully we would already have solved the problem. This should become clear later.

2. I would also classify panpsychism as a constructive solution, since it attempts to explain consciousness in terms of properties of the brain that are as natural as consciousness itself. Attributing specks of proto-consciousness to the constituents of matter is not supernatural in the way postulating immaterial substances or divine interventions is; it is merely extravagant. I shall here be assuming that panpsychism, like all other extant

constructive solutions, is inadequate as an answer to the mind-body problem—as (of course) are the supernatural "solutions." I am speaking to those who still feel perplexed (almost everyone, I would think, at least in their heart).

3. This kind of view of cognitive capacity is forcefully advocated by Noam Chomsky in *Reflections on Language*, Pantheon Books, 1975, and by Jerry Fodor in *The Modularity of Mind*, (The MIT Press: Cambridge, Mass., 1983.) Chomsky distinguishes between "problems," which human minds are in principle equipped to solve, and "mysteries," which systematically elude our understanding; and he envisages a study of our cognitive systems that would chart these powers and limitations. I am here engaged in such a study, citing the mind-body problem as falling on the side of the mysteries.

4. See Thomas Nagel's discussion of realism in *The View Form Nowhere* (Oxford University Press: Oxford, 1986), ch. 6. He argues there for the possibility of properties we can never grasp. Combining Nagel's realism with Chomsky-Fodor cognitive closure gives a position looking very much like Locke's in the *Essay Concerning Human Understanding*: the idea that our God-given faculties do not equip us to fathom the deep truth about reality. In fact, Locke held precisely this about the relation between mind and brain: only divine revelation could enable us to understand how "perceptions" are produced in our minds by material objects.

5. Hume, of course, argued, in effect, that no theory essentially employing a notion of objective causal necessitation could be grasped by our minds—and likewise for the notion of objective persistence. We might compare the frustrations of the Humean mind to the conceptual travails of the pure sound beings discussed in ch. 2 of P. F. Strawson's *Individuals*, (Methuen: London, 1959); both are types of mind whose constitution puts various concepts beyond them. We can do a lot better than these truncated minds, but we also have our constitutional limitations.

6. See the *Essay*, Book II, ch. 4. Locke compares the project of saying what solidity ultimately is to trying to clear up a blind man's vision by talking to him.

7. Some of the more arcane aspects of cosmology and quantum theory might be thought to lie just within the bounds of human intelligibility. Chomsky suggests that the causation of behavior might be necessarily mysterious to human investigators: see *Reflections on Lan-*

guage, p. 156. I myself believe that the mind-body problem exhibits a qualitatively different, and higher, level of mystery from this case (unless it is taken as an aspect of that problem).

8. Cf. Nagel's discussion of emergence in "Panpsychism," in *Mortal Questions* (Cambridge University Press: Cambridge, 1979). I agree with him that the apparent radical emergence of mind from matter has to be epistemic only, on pain of accepting inexplicable miracles in the world.

9. Despite his reputation for pessimism over the mind-body problem, a careful reading of Nagel reveals an optimistic strain in his thought (by the standards of the present chapter): see, in particular, the closing remarks of (see chapter 32) "What Is It Like to be a Bat?" Nagel speculates that we might be able to devise an "objective phenomenology" that made conscious states more amenable to physical analysis. Unlike me, he does not regard the problem as inherently beyond us.

10. This is perhaps the most remarkably optimistic view of all—the expectation that reflecting on the ordinary concept of pin (say) will reveal the manner of pain's dependence on the brain. If I am not mistaken, this is in effect the view of common-sense functionalists: they think that P consists in causal role, and that this can be inferred analytically from the concept of conscious states. This would make it truly amazing that we should ever have felt there to a mind-body problem at all, since the solution is already contained in our mental concepts. What optimism!

11. See Nagel, "What is it Like to be a Bat?" (chapter 32). Notice that the fugitive character of such properties with respect to our concepts has nothing to do with their "complexity"; like fugitive color properties, such experiential properties are "simple". Note too that such properties provide counter-examples to the claim that (somehow) rationality is a faculty that, once possessed, can be extended to encompass all concepts, so that if *any* concept can be possessed then *every* concept can.

12. It might be suggested that we borrow Nagel's idea of "objective phenomenology" in order to get around this problem. Instead of representing experiences under subjective descriptions, we should describe them in entirely objective terms, thus bringing them within our conceptual ken. My problem with this is that, even allowing that there could be such a form of description, it would not permit us to understand how the subjective aspects of experience depend upon the brain—which is

really the problem we are trying to solve. In fact, I doubt that the notion of objective phenomenology is any more coherent than the notion of subjective physiology. Both involve trying to bridge the psychophysical gap by a sort of stipulation. The lesson here is that the gap cannot be bridged just by applying concepts drawn from one side to items that belong on the other side; and this is because neither sort of concept could ever do what is needed.

13. We should distinguish two claims about the imperceptibility of consciousness: (i) consciousness is not perceivable by directing the senses onto the brain; (ii) consciousness is not perceivable by directing the senses anywhere, even toward the behavior that "expresses" conscious state. I believe both theses, but my present point requires only (i). I am assuming, of course, that perception cannot be unrestrictedly theory-laden; or that if it can, the infusions of theory cannot have been originally derived simply by looking at things or tasting them or touching them or . . .

14. Nagel discusses the difficulty of thinking of conscious processes in the spatial terms that apply to the brain in *The View From Nowhere*, pp. 50–1, but he does not draw my despairing conclusion. The case is exactly *un*like (say) the dependence of liquidity on the properties of molecules, since here we do think of both terms of the relation as spatial in character; so we can simply employ the idea of spatial composition.

15. Cf. Nagel: "it will never be legitimate to infer, as a theoretical explanation of physical phenomena alone, a property that includes or implies the consciousness of its subject," "Panpsychism," p. 183.

16. It is surely a striking fact that the microprocesses that have been discovered in the brain by the usual methods seem no nearer to consciousness than the gross properties of the brain open to casual inspection. Neither do more abstract "holistic" features of brain function seem to be on the right lines to tell us the nature of consciousness. The deeper science probes into the brain the more remote it seems to get from consciousness. Greater knowledge of the brain thus destroys our illusions about the kinds of properties that might be discovered by traveling along this path. Advanced neurophysiological theory seems only to deepen the miracle.

17. The kind of limitation I have identified is therefore not the kind that could be remedied simply by a large increase in general intelligence. No matter how large the frontal lobes of our biological descendants may become,

they will still be stumped by the mind-body problem, so long as they form their (empirical) concepts on the basis of perception and introspection.

18. Or again, no more miraculous than the theory of evolution. Creationism is an understandable response to the theoretical problem posed by the existence of complex organisms; fortunately, we now have a theory that renders this response unnecessary, and so undermines the theism required by the creationist thesis. In the case of consciousness, the appearance of miracle might also tempt us in a "creationist" direction, with God required to perform the alchemy necessary to transform matter into experience. Thus the mind-body problem might similarly be used to prove the existence of God (no miracle without a miracle-maker). We cannot, I think, refute this argument in the way we can the original creationist argument, namely by actually producing a nonmiraculous explanatory theory, but we can refute it by arguing that such a naturalistic theory must *exist*. (It is a condition of adequacy upon any account of the mind-body relation that it avoid assuming theism.) 70, 8:661–679.

19. See Paul Benacerraf, "Mathematical Truth," *Journal of Philosophy*, 1973, for a statement of this problem about abstract entities. Another problem that seems to me to differ from the mind-body problem is the problem of free will. I do not believe that there is some unknowable property Q which reconciles free will with determinism (or indeterminism); rather, the concept of free will contains internal incoherencies—as the concept of consciousness does not. This is why it is much more reasonable to be an eliminativist about free will than about consciounsess.

20. A test of whether a proposed solution to the mind-body problem is adequate is whether it relieves the pressure toward eliminativism. If the data can only be explained by postulating a miracle (i.e., not explained), then we must repudiate the data—this is the principle behind the impulse to deny that conscious states exist. My proposal passes this test because it allows us to resist the postulation of miracles; it interprets the eeriness as merely epistemic, thought deeply so. Constructive solutions are not the only way to relieve the pressure.

21. Chomsky suggests that the very faculties of mind that make us good at some cognitive tasks may make us poor at others; see *Reflections on Language*, pp. 155–6. It seems to me possible that what makes us good at the science of the purely physical world is what skews us

away from developing a science of consciousness. Our faculties bias us toward understanding matter in motion, but it is precisely this kind of understanding that is inapplicable to the mind-body problem. Perhaps, then, the price of being good at understanding matter is that we cannot understand mind. Certainly our notorious tendency to think of everything in spatial terms does not help us in understanding the mind.

22. I get this phrase from Fodor, *The Modularity of Mind*, p. 121. The intended contrast is with kinds of cognitive closure that stem from exogenous factors—as, say, in astronomy. Our problem with P is not that it is too distant or too small or too large or too complex; rather, the very structure of our concept-forming apparatus points us away from P.

23. Saul Kripke, *Naming and Necessity* (Basil Blackwell: Oxford, 1980). Of course, Descartes explicitly argued from (what he took to be) the essential natures of the body and mind to the contingency of their connection. If we abandon the assumption that we know these natures, then agnosticism about the modality of the connection seems the indicated conclusion.

24. This is the kind of realism defended by Nagel in ch. 6 of *The View From Nowhere*: to be is not to be conceivable by us. I would say that the mind-body problem provides a demonstration that there *are* such concept-transcending properties—not merely that there *could* be. I should also say that realism of this kind should be accepted precisely because it helps solve the mind-body problem; it is a metaphysical thesis that pulls its weight in coping with a problem that looks hopeless otherwise. There is thus nothing "epiphenomenal" about such radical realism: the existence of a reality we cannot know can yet have intellectual significance for us. Anti-realists are unable to solve the mind-body problem, in addition to their other troubles.

25. Discussions with the following people have helped me work out the ideas of this paper: Anita Avramides, Jerry Katz, Ernie Lepore, Michael Levin, Thomas Nagel, Galen Strawson, Peter Unger. My large debt to Nagel's work should be obvious throughout the paper: I would not have tried to face down the mind-body problem had he not first faced up to it.

34 On Leaving Out What It's Like

Joseph Levine

Among the reasons for doubting the adequacy of physicalist theories of the mind is the charge that such theories must "leave out" the qualitative, conscious side of mental life. One problem with evaluating this objection to physicalism is that it is not clear just what physicalist theories are being charged with. What is it for a theory to "leave out" a phenomenon? My project in this chapter is threefold: First, I want to clarify the anti-physicalist charge of "leaving out" qualia, distinguishing between a metaphysical and an epistemological reading of the objection. Second, I will argue that standard anti-physicalist conceivability arguments fail to show that physicalist theories "leave out" qualia in the metaphysical sense. But, third, I will also argue that these conceivability arguments do serve to establish that physicalist theories "leave out" qualia in the epistemological sense, because they reveal our inability to explain qualitative character in terms of the physical properties of sensory states. The existence of this "explanatory gap" constitutes a deep inadequacy in physicalist theories of the mind.[1]

The Metaphysical Reading

To begin, let us focus on the metaphysical reading of the phrase "leave out." In this sense, to say that a theory leaves out a certain phenomenon is to say that there are objects, events or properties to which the descriptive apparatus of the theory cannot refer. For instance, on Descartes's view, since the mind is composed of a non-physical, unextended substance, there is no way to use the predicates that apply to extended objects to refer to the mind. Property dualist views are similar in this respect. For a property dualist, there is no way of constructing descriptions using physical predicates[2] that apply to mental properties.

At least since Descartes, anti-physicalist arguments have taken roughly the following form. It is alleged that certain situations are imaginable, conceivable etc., and then a metaphysical conclusion is drawn. So, Descartes claims that from the fact that he can coherently conceive of the situation in which his body does not exist—for example, he may be deceived by an evil demon—and from the fact that he cannot conceive of the situation in which his mind does not exist (i.e., consistent with his having his current experiences), it follows that his body and his mind are not identical.

A look at the current state of the debate shows that anti-physicalist arguments have not advanced significantly beyond Descartes's. In particular, I want to focus on the two most prominent contemporary anti-physicalist arguments, those of Saul Kripke (1980) and Frank Jackson (1982).

Kripke's Argument

Kripke argues that there is an important asymmetry between purported mental-physical identity statements and those that derive from other scientific reductions. In both cases, if the identity statements are true, they are necessarily true. Also, in both cases, the identity statements involved appear contingent.[3] The asymmetry arises when we attempt to explain away their apparent contingency. Whereas the apparent contingency of other scientific identity statements can be explained away adequately, this cannot be done for mental-physical identity statements.

Suppose we compare a standard scientific identity statement like (1) below to a mental-physical identity statement like (2) below:

1. Water $= H_2O$
2. Pain $=$ the firing of C-fibers

Since neither statement is known *a priori*, they are both imaginably false. Yet, if they are true, they are necessarily true—they are not even possibly false. How do we reconcile the apparent contingency with the actual necessity? According to Kripke, this is easy to do in the case of (1). When we think we are imagining a situation in which water is not H_2O, in fact we are imagining a situation in which some substance which behaves superficially like water—but is not *water*—is not H_2O. On the other hand, a similar account will not work to explain the apparent contingency of (2), for to imagine a situation in which one is experiencing a state superficially like pain *just is* to imagine a situation in which one is experiencing pain. Conscious mental states are unlike external objects in that the standard distinction between how they appear and how they really are does not apply.

Many responses to Kripke's argument have appeared over the years. Early on it was pointed out that materialism does not entail the sort of type-type reductionism of the mental to the physical that is manifested in statements like (2). Rather, mental states are higher-order functional states, which can be realized, at least in principle, in a wide variety of physical systems. Hence, it is quite consistent with materialism that it is possible for one to experience pain and yet have no C-fibers whatever to fire.

However, functionalism itself has come under attack from Cartesian-style objections, particularly the inverted and absent qualia hypotheses.[4] The essence of these objections is that it seems perfectly imaginable that there could be creatures functionally alike who nevertheless differed in the qualitative character of their experiences; or, even worse, that there could be a creature functionally like ourselves who had no qualitative experiences at all. One line of response to either or both of these objections is to retreat to a physiological reductionist view with respect to qualia. That is, instead of identifying qualia with functional states, we identify them with the neurophysiological states that play the relevant functional roles in human beings, which would explain the possibility of both inverted and absent qualia.[5] Of

course, this just brings us back to where we started.

I favor another strategy in response to Kripke's argument. Suppose he's right that we can coherently imagine feeling pain without having C-fibers firing. What's more, suppose he's right that this coherently imagined scenario cannot be explained away in the manner in which we explain away imagining that water is not H_2O. Still, what is imaginable is an *epistemological* matter, and therefore what imagining pain without C-fibers does is establish the *epistemological* possibility that pain is not identical with the firing of C-fibers. It takes another argument to get from the *epistemological* possibility that pain is not the firing of C-fibers to the metaphysical possibility, which is what you need to show that pain isn't *in fact* identical to the firing of C-fibers.[6]

Kripke, following Descartes, seems to rely on the idea that when you have a really "clear and distinct" idea you have access to how things are, metaphysically speaking. If one believes in this sort of access to metaphysical facts, it then makes sense to use the Kripke test, by which I mean the test that determines whether the imagined scenario can be explained away appropriately, to determine whether one has hold of a genuine metaphysical possibility or not. So, in the water/H_2O case, Kripke shows that, as it were, when your idea is made properly clear and distinct, you see that what you are really entertaining is the thought that something that behaves like water is not H_2O. Notice that the situation satisfying this description is indeed metaphysically possible. Since the same move doesn't work for the pain/C-fibers case, we conclude that there is a metaphysically possible world in which pain isn't the firing of C-fibers.

But suppose we reject the Cartesian model of epistemic access to metaphysical reality altogether. One's ideas can be as clear and distinct as you like, and nevertheless not correspond to what is in fact possible. The world is structured in a certain way, and there is no guarantee that our ideas will correspond appropriately. If one follows this line of thought, then the distinction Kripke points out between the pain/C-fibers case and the water/H_2O case turns out to be irrelevant to the question of what is or is not metaphysically possible. Thus, for all we know, pain *just is* the firing of C-fibers or, if functionalism is right, the realization of a certain functional state.

Early identity theorists, in their response to Cartesian conceivability arguments, protested that they only intended their theory to be empirical, and therefore it was not subject to objections from what was conceivable or not.[7] Kripke correctly pointed out the error of that sort of response. Empirical or not, if they were making identity claims, then a consequence of their theory is that it is not possible for some mental state not to be identical to its physical or functional correlate. But the basis of Kripke's objection lies in a strict distinction between metaphysical and epistemological possibility. Once we appreciate that distinction, the physicalist can return to her original ploy, i.e., to say that metaphysical consequences cannot be drawn from considerations of what is merely conceivable. Thus, without an argument to the effect that what is metaphysically possible is epistemologically accessible, the Cartesian argument fails.

Jackson's Argument

A similar problem—that is, a reliance on the Cartesian model of epistemic access to metaphysical reality or, in other words, using epistemoloical premises to support a metaphysical conclusion—seems to infect Frank Jackson's well-known "knowledge argument" against materialism. Jackson takes the thesis of physicalism to be the claim that "all (correct) information is physical information" (Jackson 1982, p. 127). of course, his use of the notion of information here is already fraught with ambiguity as between matters epistemological and metaphysical, a point to which I will return shortly. His argument against physicalism revolves around examples like the following:

Mary is a brilliant scientist who is ... forced to investigate the world from a black and white room *via* a black and white television monitor. She specializes in the neurophysiology of vision and acquires ... all the physical information there is to obtain about what goes on when we see ripe tomatoes, or the sky, and use terms like "red," "blue," and so on....

What will happen when Mary is released from her black and white room or is given a color television monitor? Will she *learn* anything or not? It seems just obvious that she will learn something about the world and our visual experience of it. But then it is inescapable that her previous knowledge was incomplete. But she had *all* the physical information. *Ergo* there is more to have than that, and Physicalism is false. (Jackson 1982, p. 130)

There have been a number of replies to Jackson in the literature, and the sort of reply I am most interested in is exemplified by Horgan (1984). Horgan argues that Jackson is equivocating on the notion of "physical information." In one sense this might mean information expressed in terms used in the physical sciences. In another sense it might mean information about physical facts, processes, etc. It is only in the second sense that any reasonable physicalist is committed to the claim that all information is physical information. Of course, in this sense, the thesis could be better put by just saying that all token events and processes are physical events and processes—by which one means something like, they have a true description in the terms of the physical sciences. (Actually, I think any interesting doctrine of physicalism is committed to more than this, though it's difficult to pin down exactly how much more. At any rate, it doesn't affect the present point.) But no plausible version of physicalism is committed to the claim that all information is physical information in the first sense: in the sense that it is expressed in (or translatable into) the terms of the physical sciences.

What Mary's case shows, argues Horgan, is that there is information Mary acquires after leaving the room that isn't physical information in the first sense, but not that it isn't physical information in the second sense. Certainly, she may think something like,"Oh, so *this* is what red looks like." Her experience of *learning* something new shows that she now knows something she didn't know before. She now knows what it's like to see red, which she didn't know before. But it doesn't follow that her new information isn't physical information in the second sense: that is, that it isn't information about a physical event or process. On the contrary, the case of Mary typifies the phenomenon of there being several distinguishable ways to gain epistemic access to the same fact. One cannot infer from a variety of modes of access to a variety of facts being accessed.

A similar emphasis on the distinction between the epistemology and the metaphysics of the matter underlies the following sort of reply to Jackson. What the case of Mary shows is that one can know which physical (or functional) description a mental state satisfies without knowing what it's like to occupy that state. But of course! After all, in order to know what it's like to occupy a state one has actually to occupy it! All Mary's newly acquired knowledge amounts to is her new experience, which is indeed new, since she didn't have those experiences until leaving the room. So it remains perfectly possible that what she learns is what it's like to occupy a certain physico-functional state. There is no threat to physicalism here.

Two Metaphysical Anti-Physicalist Replies

The common thread in the responses to both Kripke and Jackson is that their thought experiments demonstrate only an epistemological divide between different modes of access to what may, for all we know, be the very same phenomenon. On the one hand, we have certain physico-functional descriptions of certain states occupied by psychological subjects. On the other hand, we have whatever descriptions are derived from one's first-hand experience of these states. If these thought experiments show that physicalism leaves

something out, it can't be in the sense that there are facts that physicalistic descriptions fail to pick out, since we have no argument to show that the two sorts of descriptions just cited do not refer to the same facts.

I will briefly consider two replies on behalf of the metaphysical anti-physicalist. First, perhaps Cartesian conceivability arguments can't demonstrate that qualia aren't physical states or processes, but they at least throw the burden of argument back onto the physicalist to show why we should think they are physical states or processes. The physicalist strategy presented above only opens a space for the physicalist hypothesis, but it doesn't give us any reason to believe it.

Fair enough. That's all it was intended to accomplish. The main burden of the physicalist argument is borne by considerations of causal interaction. If qualia aren't physical processes (or realized in physical processes), then it becomes very difficult to understand how they can play a causal role in both the production of behavior and the fixation of perceptual belief. Jackson himself admits the cogency of this argument, and therefore bites the bullet by endorsing epiphenomenalism. Those who don't find that bullet particularly appetizing must either show how the requisite mental-physical causal relations are possible on a dualist account or endorse physicalism.

The second reply on behalf of the metaphysical anti-physicalist goes like this.[8] Take some identity statement that is not epistemologically necessary, like (3) below:

3. The Morning Star = the Evening Star.

Though one might accept Kripke's claim that (3) is necessarily true if true at all, still one has to explain its apparent contingency. The way we do this is to say that what is contingent is that the very same heavenly body should appear where Venus does in the morning and also where it does in the evening. Notice that our explanation of the apparent contingency of (3) adverted to a real distinction between two of Venus's properties: namely, appearing at a certain heavenly location in the morning and appearing at a certain heavenly location in the evening. That is, we can explain the epistemological state of conceiving of the Morning Star and the Evening Star as two distinct objects, despite their identity, by reference to two distinct properties through which we have epistemic access to the one object.

Suppose one grants that the absent qualia argument does indeed establish at least the epistemological possibility that a qualitative state and a functional state are distinct, even though they are in fact identical. In order to explain how it is possible to conceive of this one state as two distinct states, we must assume that there are (at least) two "modes of presentation" under which we apprehend this one state. Let us call them the "first-person mode of presentation" and the "third-person mode of presentation." But now we seem committed to the claim that there are at least two distinct properties of the state corresponding to the two modes of access, akin to the two spatiotemporal properties of Venus by which we gain epistemic access to it in the morning and in the evening. If so, this shows that qualitative character, the property by which we identify a conscious state in the first-person mode of access, is distinct from the property of playing a certain functional role, the property by which we identify that conscious state in the third-person mode of access. So, we seem to be back to deriving a metaphysical conclusion from an epistemological premise, namely, that the property of having a certain qualitative character is distinct from the property of playing a certain functional role (or being in a certain neurophysiological state).[9]

The physicalist, however, can reply as follows. Certainly whenever we conceive of a single object in two distinct ways—sufficiently distinct ways, in fact, that we believe we are conceiving of two distinct objects—the object in question must possess (at least) two distinct properties that correspond to these different modes of presentation.

But whether or not we now have a problem for physicalism depends on which two district properties we find ourselves committed to. This requires some elaboration.

What the physicalist needs to maintain is that having a certain qualitative character is a physical or functional property. This reduction of qualitative character is necessary in order to account for the causal role that qualia play in the fixation of perceptual belief and the production of behavior. So, if the argument above could establish that having a certain qualitative character is a property distinct from a mental state's physical and functional properties, that would be the sort of metaphysical conclusion the anti-physicalist is after.

However, the argument above does not in fact establish the non-identity of having a certain qualitative character and any of a state's physical or functional properties. The argument begins with the premise that there must be two properties of the one state, providing two epistemic paths by which the subject conceives of that state, in order to account for the fact that it is epistemologically possible for someone to experience qualitative character without occupying the relevant physico-functional state. We can accept this premise and yet refuse to grant the conclusion—that having a certain qualitative character is irreducible to a state's physico-functional properties—by finding two other properties to provide the requisite epistemic paths. For instance, we can account for the conceivability of experiencing a certain quale without occupying the relevant physico-functional state by noting that the two relational properties, being thought of under the description "what I am now consciously experiencing" and being thought of under the description "the state that normally causes [such-and-such behavioral effects]," are not identical. However, there is no reason for the physicalist to claim that *these* two properties are identical, and therefore the argument above fails to mount a challenge to physicalism.

The Epistemological Reading

I have argued that on a metaphysical reading of "leave something out," Cartesian conceivability arguments cannot establish that physicalist theories of mind leave something out. However, there is also an epistemological sense of "leave something out," and it is in this sense that conceivability arguments, being epistemological in nature, can reveal a deep inadequacy in physicalist theories of mind.

For a physicalist theory to be successful, it is not only necessary that it provide a physical description for mental states and properties, but also that it provide an *explanation* of these states and properties. In particular, we want an explanation of why when we occupy certain physico-functional states we experience qualitative character of the sort we do. It's not enough for these purposes to explain the contribution of qualitative states to the production of behavior, or the fixation of perceptual belief; this is a job that a physicalist theory can presumably accomplish. (At least there is no reason stemming from conceivability arguments to suppose that it cannot.) Rather, what is at issue is the ability to explain qualitative character itself; why it is like what it is like to see red or feel pain.

Conceivability arguments serve to demonstrate the inability of physicalist theories to provide just this sort of explanation of qualitative character. To see this, consider again the disanalogy Kripke draws between statements (1) and (2) above. Kripke bases his argument on the fact that both statements appear contingent, and then distinguishes between them by pointing out that the apparent contingency of (1), but not of (2), can be explained away. My strategy is quite different. I see the disanalogy between the water/H_2O case and the pain/C-fibers case in the fact that there is an apparent *necessity* that flows from the reduction of water to H_2O, a kind of necessity that is missing from the reduction of pain to the firing of C-fibers.

The necessity I have in mind is best exemplified by considering statement (1′):

1′. The substance that manifests [such-and-such macro properties of water] is H_2O.

On Kripke's view, (1′) is in fact contingent, and it is the contingency of (1′) that explains the apparent contingency of (1). So, on his view, (1′) and (2) are on a par. Yet, it seems to me that there is an important difference between them. If we consider the apparent contingency that attaches to (2), we notice that it works in both directions: it is equally conceivable that there should exist a pain without the firing of C-fibers, and the firing of C-fibers without pain. However, the apparent contingency of (1′) only works in one direction. While it is conceivable that something other than H_2O should manifest the superficial macro properties of water, as Kripke suggests, it is not conceivable, I contend, that H_2O should fail to manifest these properties (assuming, of course, that we keep the rest of chemistry constant).

This difference between the two cases reflects an important epistemological difference between the purported reductions of water to H_2O and pain to the firing of C-fibers: namely, that the chemical theory of water explains what needs to be explained, whereas a physicalist theory of qualia still "leaves something out." It is because the qualitative character itself is left *unexplained* by the physicalist or functionalist theory that it remains conceivable that a creature should occupy the relevant physical or functional state and yet not experience qualitative character.

The basic idea is that a reduction should explain what is reduced, and the way we tell whether this has been accomplished is to see whether the phenomenon to be reduced is epistemologically necessitated by the reducing phenomenon, that is, whether we can see why, given the facts cited in the reduction, things must be the way they seem on the surface. I claim that we have this with the chemical theory of water but not with a physical or functional theory of qualia.

The robustness of the absent and inverted qualia intuitions is testimony to this lack of explanatory import.

Let me make the contrast between the reduction of water to H_2O and a physico-functional reduction of qualia more vivid. What is explained by the theory that water is H_2O? Well, as an instance of something that's explained by the reduction of water to H_2O, let's take its boiling point at sea level. The story goes something like this. Molecules of H_2O move about at various speeds. Some fast-moving molecules that happen to be near the surface of the liquid have sufficient kinetic energy to escape the intermolecular attractive forces that keep the liquid intact. These molecules enter the atmosphere. That's evaporation. The precise value of the intermolecular attractive forces of H_2O molecules determines the vapor pressure of liquid masses of H_2O, the pressure exerted by molecules attempting to escape into saturated air. As the average kinetic energy of the molecules increases, so does the vapor pressure. When the vapor pressure reaches the point where it is equal to atmospheric pressure, large bubbles form within the liquid and burst forth at the liquid's surface. The water boils.

I claim that given a sufficiently rich elaboration of the story above, it is inconceivable that H_2O should not boil at 212°F at sea level (assuming, again, that we keep the rest of the chemical world constant). But now contrast this situation with a physical or functional reduction of some conscious sensory state. No matter how rich the information processing or the neurophysiological story gets, it still seems quite coherent to imagine that all that should be going on without there being anything it's like to undergo the states in question. Yet, if the physical or functional story really explained the qualitative character, it would not be so clearly imaginable that the qualia should be missing. For, we would say to ourselves something like the following:

Suppose creature X satisfies functional (or physical) description F. I understand—from my functional (or physical) theory of consciousness—what it is about instantiating F that is responsible for its being. a conscious experience. So how could X occupy a state with those very features and yet *not* be having a conscious experience?

One might object at this point that my position presumes something like the deductive-nomological account of explanation, an account that is certainly controversial.[10] In fact, I quite openly endorse the view that explanations involve showing how the explanandum follows from the explanans. I believe that the deductive-nomological model, in analyzing explanation in terms of exhibiting a necessary connection between explanans and explanandum, is certainly on the right track.

I am not committed, however, to the view that all explanations take the form of the "covering law" model described by Hempel (1965) in his classic account of explanation. For instance, Robert Cummins (1983) has argued that some explanations take the form of "property theories," in which the instantiation of one sort of property is explained by reference to the instantiation of some other properties. So we might, for example, explain a certain psychological capacity by reference to the physico-functional mechanisms that underlie it. In such cases we are not explaining one event by citing initial conditions and subsuming it under a law, so it does not quite fit the traditional deductive-nomological model.

I have no problem with Cummins's objection to the covering law model. Yet even in his example—explaining how a psychological capacity is instantiated by reference to the underlying mechanisms—the element of necessity is there, even if there is no subsumption under laws. For it is clear that if citing the relevant underlying mechanisms really does explain how the psychological capacity in question is instantiated, then it would be inconceivable that some creature should possess these mechanisms and yet lack the capacity. If not, if we could conceive of a situation in which a creature possessed the relevant underlying mechanisms and yet didn't possess the capacity in question, then I would claim that we haven't adequately explained the presence of the capacity by reference to those mechanisms. For we are still left wondering what distinguishes the actual situation, in which the creature possesses the capacity, from those conceivable situations in which it (he/she) does not.

The Conceptual Basis of the Explanatory Gap

I have argued that there is an important difference between the identification of water with H_2O, on the one hand, and the identification of qualitative character with a physico-functional property on the other. In the former case the identification affords a deeper understanding of what water is by explaining its behavior. Whereas, in the case of qualia, the subjective character of qualitative experience is left unexplained, and therefore we are left with an incomplete understanding of that experience. The basis of my argument for the existence of this explanatory gap was the conceivability of a creature's instantiating the physico-functional property in question while not undergoing an experience with the qualitative character in question, or any qualitative character at all.

In order fully to appreciate the nature and scope of the problem, however, it is necessary to explore in more detail the basis of the explanatory adequacy of theoretical reductions such as that of water to H_2O, as well as the difference between these cases and the case of qualitative character. I can only being that project here, with the following admittedly sketchy account. We will see that an adequate account must confront deep problems in the theory of conceptual content, thus drawing a connection between the issue of intentionality and the issue of consciousness.

Explanation and Reduction

To begin with, it seems clear that theoretical reduction is justified principally on the basis of its explanatory power. For instance, what justifies the claim that water is H_2O anyway? Well, we might say that we find a preponderance of H_2O molecules in our lakes and oceans, but of course that can't be the whole story. First of all, given all the impurities in most samples of water, this may not be true. Second, if we found that everything in the world had a lot of H_2O in it—suppose H_2O were as ubiquitous as protons—we wouldn't identify *water* with H_2O. Rather, we justify the claim that water is H_2O by tracing the causal responsibility for, and the explicability of, the various superficial properties by which we identify water—its liquidity at room temperature, its freezing and boiling points, and so forth—to H_2O.

But suppose someone pressed further, asking why being causally responsible for this particular syndrome of superficial properties should be so crucial.[11] Well, we would say, *what else* could it take to count as water? But the source of this "what else" is obscure. In fact, I think we have to recognize an *a priori* element in our justification. That is, what justifies us in basing the identification of water with H_2O on the causal responsibility of H_2O for the typical behavior of water is the fact that our very concept of water is of a substance that plays such-and-such a causal role. To adopt Kripke's terminology, we might say that our pretheoretic concept of water is characterizable in terms of a "reference-fixing" description that roughly carves out a causal role. When we find the structure that in this world occupies that role, then we have the referent our concept.

But now how is it that we get an explanation of these superficial properties from the chemical theory? Remember, explanation is supposed to involve a deductive relation between explanans and explanandum. The problem is that chemical theory and folk theory don't have an identical vocabulary, so somewhere one is going to have to introduce bridge principles. For instance, suppose I want to explain why water boils, or freezes, at the temperatures it does. In order to get an explanation of these facts, we need a definition of "boiling" and "freezing" that brings these terms into the proprietary vocabularies of the theories appealed to in the explanation.

Well, the obvious way to obtain the requisite bridge principles is to provide theoretical reductions of these properties as well.[12] To take another example, we say that one of water's superficial properties is that it is colorless. But being colorless is not a chemical property, so before we can explain why water is colorless in terms of the molecular structure of water and the way that such structures interact with light waves, we need to reduce colorlessness to a property like having a particular spectral reflectance function. Of course, the justification for this reduction will, like the reduction of water to H_2O, have to be justified on grounds of explanatory enrichment as well. That is, there are certain central phenomena we associate with color, by means of which we pick it out, such that explaining those phenomena is a principal criterion for our acceptance of a theoretical reduction of color.

The picture of theoretical reduction and explanation that emerges is of roughly the following form. Our concepts of substances and properties like water and liquidity can be thought of as representations of nodes in a network of causal relations, each node itself capable of further reduction to yet another network, until we get down to the fundamental causal determinants of nature. We get bottom-up necessity, and thereby explanatory force, from the identification of the macroproperties with the microproperties because the network of causal relations constitutive of the micro level realizes the network of causal relations constitutive of the macro level. Any concept that can be analyzed in this way will yield to explanatory reduction.

Notice that on this view explanatory reduction is, in a way, a two-stage process. Stage 1 involves the (relatively? quasi?) *a priori* process of working the concept of the property to be reduced "into shape" for reduction by identifying the causal role for which we are seeking the underlying mechanisms. Stage 2 involves the empirical work of discovering just what those underlying mechanisms are.[13]

A Digression about Concepts

In order to clarify the sense in which it is inconceivable that something should be H_2O and not be water, I have had to slip into talking about concepts; even worse, talking about analyzing the contents of concepts. This is unfortunate for my position, since the whole topic of concepts is filled with controversy, and I do not yet see how to construct a theory of conceptual content that will do the work, briefly outlined above, that needs to be done. Let me briefly indicate where the problems lie.

In the literature on concepts and contents, various distinctions have emerged which are useful to our concerns here. First of all, we can distinguish between a concept's[14] "narrow content" and its "broad content."[15] A concept's broad content is its satisfaction conditions. This is the referential component of its content. The notion of narrow content is meant to capture that aspect of its content that is psychologically significant and independent of facts external to the subject. With regard to the famous Twin Earth example, narrow content is what my concept of water and my twin's concept of water have in common.

It is, of course, controversial whether or not it is narrow content that is relevant to the individuation of psychological states, or even whether there is such a thing as narrow content. However, I believe there is something psychologically significant that I and my twin have in common when we entertain the concept of water and, moreover, it is this aspect of our concept that seems relevant to the question of explanatory reduction. In will not defend this claim here, I will just presume it.

So, how do we characterize the narrow content of our concept of water? On one view, the "functional role" view,[16] narrow content is determined by the cluster of beliefs involving the concept of water that determine the inferential relations among them. On this view, to analyze the concept of water is just to present those central beliefs. Our concept of water is the concept of a substance that..., where statements about the typical behavior of water fill in the blank. On a functional role view, then, to say that our concept of water can be analyzed as the concept of a causal niche is just to say that the beliefs which go into the blank all involve the causal role of water.

Thus a functional role view of narrow content seems quite amenable to my needs. However, there are real problems with this view. In particular, there is the problem of holism. That is, if you change any element of the description of causal relations definitive of the concept, you change the concept. Now, in the course of scientific investigation, we can expect to revise our beliefs about these causal connections as we learn more about the phenomenon under investigation. If such changes counted as changing the concept, then it wouldn't be *water* we were learning about when we discovered that water was H_2O. This would seem to be an intolerable consequence.

There are three ways one might deal with this problem. First, just bite the bullet and admit that our concepts are hopelessly holistic. Second, attempt to distinguish those elements of the functional role that are essential to the concept from those that are accidental, so that only changes in the essential elements constitute changes in concept. Third, find a different theory of narrow content.

One might argue that biting the bullet is not as bad as it seems on the grounds that we are only talking about *narrow* content. So long as we are atomistic about reference, we can still make sense of the claim that two theories contain conflicting claims *about water*, since they are talking *about* the very same thing. However, what we are looking for here is a notion of conceptual content suitable for grounding the explanatory relation, and this is clearly a matter of narrow content. Unless we can build stability into the notions, it is unclear how to make sense of the idea that the chemical theory of water explains why water behaves the way it does.

The second sort of strategy has a sad history, and I do not see how to make it work. For any

element of the functional role you pick as essential, there always seems to be a story you can tell in which that element is missing and yet it seems intuitively right to claim that the subject still has the concept in question. As for a different theory of narrow content, the only one I know, that departs radically from the functional role theory, is Fodor's (1987) theory of narrow content as a function from contexts to broad contents. It is not at all clear to me how the notion of a conceptual content as the specification of a causal niche could be made to work on this view.

To sum up, there seems to be a need for a theory of conceptual content that both grounds explanatory reductions on the basis of some sort of functional/causal analysis of the requisite concepts, and yet does not entail holism. I do not have such a theory, and so must content myself with merely characterizing this desideratum on a theory yet to be developed.

Qualia Again

If we apply the same model of explanatory value to the theoretical reduction of qualia as we used for the reduction of water, then we need to look for a property that is being reduced and then a property, or set of properties, by which the to-be-reduced property is normally picked out. Of course, this raises a problem. When it comes to something like the qualitative character of a sensation of red, what other property could we point to to play the role of the reference-fixer? We seem to pick out this property by itself. The distinction between the property to be reduced and the properties by which we normally pick it out, or its superficial manifestation, seems to collapse. (Obviously this is connected to Kripke's point about the appearance/reality distinction not getting a hold in this case.)

There are, of course, other properties of qualia that we can expect a theoretical reduction to explain; namely, those properties associated with their causal role in mediating environmental stimuli and behavior. It is precisely on the grounds that a particular physico-functional property can explain the "behavior" of qualitative states that we would endorse an identification between a particular quale and that property. Furthermore, if that were all there were to our concept of qualitative character—as the analytical functionalist maintains—then there would be no difference between the theoretical reduction of water and of qualia with respect to explanatory success. But the very fact that one can conceive of a state playing that role and yet not constituting a qualitative experience shows, or at least so I have argued, that causal role is not all there is to our concept of qualitative character.

What seems to be responsible for the explanatory gap, then, is the fact that our concepts of qualitative character do not represent, at least in terms of their psychological contents, causal roles. Reduction is explanatory when by reducing an object or property we reveal the mechanisms by which the causal role constitutive of that object or property is realized. Moreover, this seems to be the only way that a reduction could be explanatory. Thus, to the extent that there is an element in our concept of qualitative character that is not captured by features of its causal role, to that extent it will escape the explanatory net of a physicalistic reduction.

Conclusion

I will conclude by drawing out another consequence of this discussion of the explanatory gap. It is customary to attack the mind-body problem by a divide-and-conquer strategy. On the one hand, there is the problem of intentionality. How can mere matter support meaning; how can a bit of matter be *about* something? On the other hand, there is the problem of consciousness, or, to be more specific, the problem of qualitative character. How can there be something it is like to be a mere physical system? By separating the two questions, it is hoped that significant progress can be made on both.

Certainly in recent years we have come to have a deeper understanding of the issues surrounding the question of intentionality, and this progress has been largely the result of divorcing the question of intentionality from the question of consciousness.[17] However, if I am right, there may be more of a connection between the problem of qualitative character and the problem of intentionality than it is fashionable now to suppose. It is not that one needs to be capable of experiencing qualia in order to bear intentional states, as Searle would have it. Rather, since the problem of qualitative character turns out to be primarily epistemological, the source of which is to be found in the peculiar nature of our cognitive representations of qualitative character, a theory of intentional content ought to explain what makes these representations so uniquely resistant to incorporation into the explanatory net of physical science.[18] Thus the problem of qualia threatens to enlarge into the problem of the mind generally.

Acknowledgments

An earlier version of this chapter was delivered at the conference on Mind, Meaning, and Nature, at Wesleyan University, March 31, 1989. The chapter was completed while I was holding a fellowship from the National Endowment for the Humanitites. I would also like to thank Louise Antony, David Auerbach, Martin Davies, and Georges Rey for helpful discussions and critical comments on earlier drafts.

Notes

1. See Levine (1983) where I first argued for the existence of an explanatory gap.

2. Of course, it is a non-trivial question to decide which predicates count as "physical" predicates, but for present purposes we need not attempt a precise explication of the notion.

3. As Kripke (1980, p. 154) puts it, there is a "certain obvious element of contingency" about such theoretical identity statements.

4. For extensive discussion of the absent and inverted gualia hypotheses, see Block and Fodor (1972); Block (1978, 1980); Horgan (1984); Shoemaker (1984, chs. 9, 14, and 15); Conee (1985); Levine (1989).

5. For various versions of this position, see Block (1978, 1980), Horgan (1984), and Shoemarker (1984).

6. Given that Kripke is largely responsible for drawing the philosophical world's attention to the distinction between epistemological possibility and metaphysical possibility, it might seem odd to accuse him of confusing the two in this case. I diagnose his mistake as follows. Since he believes that any state which appears painful is thereby a pain, he infers that there is no appearance/ reality distinction with respect to pain, and therefore epistemological and metaphysical possibility collapse in this case. But even if he's right that any state that appears to be a pain is a pain, he still has to justify the premise that it's possible for one to suffer even apparent pain without having one's C-fibers firing, and he can't do that, I contend, merely by noting that it *seems* possible.

7. See, for instance, Smart's (1959) reply to his "Objection 2."

8. This objection was suggested to me by a discussion in White (1986). The analogy to the Morning Star– Evening Star case is his.

9. As White expicitly acknowledges, a precursor of this objection can be found in Smart's (1959) famous "Objection 3."

10. For the classic presentation of the deductive-nomological model of explanation, see Hempel (1965, ch. 12).

11. Of course, it's possible to imagine situations in which we would accept a theory of water that nevertheless left many of its superficial properties unexplained. However, unless the theory explained at least some of these properties, it would be hard to say why we consider this a theory of *water*.

12. In some cases, for instance, with properties such as liquidity and mass, it might be better to think of their theoretical articulations in physical and chemical theory more as a matter of incorporating and refining folk theoretic concepts than as a matter of reducing them. But this is not an idea I can pursue here.

13. To a certain extent my argument here is similar to Alan Sidelle's (1989) defense of conventionalism, though I don't believe our positions coincide completely.

14. Some readers might find my speaking of a *concept's* content, as opposed to a *term's* content confusing. I am interested in the nature of our thoughts, not with their expression in natural language. For present purposes, we can think of a concept as a term in whatever internal, mental language is employed in our cognitive processing.

15. For the source of this distinction, see Putnam (1975). For further discussion of its significance for psychology, see Fodor (1987, ch. 3) and Burge (1986).

16. See Block (1986) for a defense of the functional role view.

17. For a dissenting opinion on the question of divorcing intentionality from consciousness, see Searle (1989).

18. See Rey (chapter 12) and Van Gulick (chapter 7) in Davies and Humphries for suggestive approaches to just this problem.

References

Block, N. (1978). Troubles with functionalism. In C. Wade Savage (ed.), *Perception and Cognition: Issues in the Foundations of Psychology*. Vol. 9, *Minnesota Studies in the Philosophy of Science*. Minneapolis: University of Minnesota Press.

———. (1980). Are absent qualia impossible? *Philosophical Review* 89, 257–74.

———. (1986). Advertisement for a semantics for psychology. In P. A. French, T. E. Uehling, Jr., and H. K. Wettstein (eds.), *Studies in the Philosophy of Mind*. Vol. 10, *Midwest Studies in Philosophy*. Minneapolis: University of Minnesota Press, 615–78.

Block, N., and Fodor, J. A. (1972). What psychological states are not. *Philosophical Review*, 81, 159–81.

Burge, T. (1986). Individualism and psychology. *Philosophical Review* 95, 3–46.

Conee, E. (1985). The possibility of absent qualia, *Philosophical Review* 94, 345–66.

Cummins, R. (1983). *The Nature of Psychological Explanation*. Cambridge, MA: MIT Press.

Davies, M., and Humphreys, G. (eds.). (1993). *Consciousness*. Oxford: Blackwell.

Fordor, J. A. (1987). *Psychosemantics: The Problem of Meaning in the Philosophy of Mind*. Cambridge, MA: MIT Press

Hempel, C. G. (1965). *Aspects of Scientific Explanation*. New York: Free Press.

Horgan, T. (1984). Functionalism, qualia, and the inverted spectrum. *Philosophy and Phenomenological Research* 44, 453–69.

Jackson, F. (1982). Epiphenomenal qualia. *Philosophical Quarterly* 32, 127–36.

Kripke, S. (1980). *Naming and Necessity*. Oxford: Blackwell.

Levine, J. (1983). Materialism and qualia: The explanatory gap. *Pacific Philosophical Quarterly* 64, 354–61.

———. (1989). Absent and inverted qualia revisited. *Mind and Language* 3, 271–87.

Putnam, H. (1975). The meaning of meaning. In K. Gunderson (ed.), *Language, Mind, and Knowledge*, 131–93. Minneapolis: University of Minnesota Press.

Rey, Georges (1993). Sensational sentences. In Davies, M., and Humphreys, G. (eds.) *Consciousness*, 240–57. Oxford: Blackwell.

Searle, J. (1989). Consciousness, unconsciousness, and intentionality. *Philosophical Topics* 17, 193–209.

Shoemaker, S. (1984). *Identity, Cause, and Mind*. Cambridge: Cambridge University Press.

Sidelle, A. (1989). *Necessity, Essence, and Individuation: A Defense of Conventionalism*. Ithaca: Cornell University Press.

Smart, J. J. C. (1959). Sensations and brain processes. *Philosophical Review* 68, 141–56.

Van Gulick, Robert (1993). Understanding the phenomenal mind: Are we all just armadillos? In Davies, M., and Humphreys, G. (eds.), *Consciousness*, 134–54. Oxford: Blackwell.

White, S. L. (1986). Curse of the qualia. *Synthese* 68.

VIII THE KNOWLEDGE ARGUMENT

35 Understanding the Phenomenal Mind: Are We All Just Armadillos? Part I: Phenomenal Knowledge and Explanatory Gaps

Robert Van Gulick

Do phenomenal mental states pose a special obstacle to materialism or functionalism? Three main families of arguments in the recent philosophical literature may seem to show that they do: the Knowledge Argument, the Explanatory Gap Argument, and the various versions of the Inverted and Absent Qualia Argument. I shall here discuss the first two of these and show that neither presents an insurmountable barrier to materialistic functionalism. Elsewhere, in part II, (chap. 25, this volume) I show the same for the third group of arguments.

Before turning to the arguments, let me issue one caveat about the use of the word "phenomenal." In much of the recent philosophical literature it has been used to refer exclusively to sensory qualia or so-called raw feels, such as the redness of which one is immediately aware when viewing a ripe tomato, or the taste of a fresh mango. Although I will myself spend some time discussing just such sensory qualia, I nonetheless believe it is a serious mistake to equate the phenomenal aspect of mind solely with such properties. We should not forget that the idea of the phenomenal structure of experience entered philosophical thought through Kant, who introduced it in the context of rejecting the sensational theory of experience associated with traditional empiricism. Phenomenal experience is not merely a succession of qualitatively distinguished sensory ideas, but rather the organized cognitive experience of a world of objects and of ourselves as subjects within that world.

Any adequate theory of the phenomenal aspect of mentality should take this richer Kantian concept into account. To focus exclusively on raw feels would be a mistake in at least two respects. First, it would provide too narrow a definition of what needs to be explained, and, secondly, I doubt that qualia and raw feels can themselves be understood in isolation from the roles they play within the richer Kantian structure of phenomenal experience.

The Knowledge Argument

Let us turn then to the Knowledge Argument. Its basic underlying assumption is that there is some knowledge about experience that can be acquired *only* by undergoing the relevant experience oneself. In the paradigm case, one can come to know what the character of phenomenal red is only by having a red experience. No *physical* knowledge of what goes on in the brain when one has a red experience would suffice. It is for this reason that Thomas Nagel believes that no human can ever know what it's like to be a bat (see chapter 32). Given our human inability to undergo experiences of the sort the bat has when sensing its surroundings by echo location, the relevant knowledge about bat-type experience is forever beyond us. The relevant facts about what its like to be a bat are cognitively inaccessible to us in the sense that we are incapable of even understanding them.

To see how this is supposed to lead to an antimaterialist conclusion, let us consider the knowledge argument as presented by Frank Jackson (1982,1986), certainly the most widely discussed anti-physicalist argument in the American philosophical world during the 1980's. Jackson offers the hypothetical case of Mary the super color scientist who has spent her entire life within a strictly black and white (and gray) environment (see chapter 36). Mary nonetheless (via television) has become the world's greatest expert on color perception and *ex hypothesi* she is said to know *everything physical* there is to know about what goes on in a normal perceiver when he perceives something red. Yet, Jackson argues, Mary does not know *everything* there is to know about having a red experience, a fact that he believes is obvious if we consider what would happen if Mary were released from her achromatic isolation and shown a ripe tomato for the first time. Jackson's claim is that Mary would come to know something that she didn't know before. But since *ex hypothesi* she already knew *everything physical* there was to know about seeing red, the knowledge or information she gains must be non-physical phenomenal information.

A1   The Knowledge Argument

P.1. Mary (before her release) knows *everything physical* there is to know about seeing red.

P.2. Mary (before her release) does not know *everything* there is to know about seeing red because she learns something about it on her release.

Therefore

C.3. There are some truths about seeing red that escape the physicalist story.

C.4. Physicalism is false and phenomenal properties cannot be explained as (or identified with) physical properties.

This argument has been regarded as a serious threat to physicalism. Indeed so ardent a physicalist and formidable a philosopher as David Lewis (see chapter 38) has held that if we admit that Mary really gains information when she first experiences red, then physicalism must be false. However, being regarded as a serious threat is not the same as being regarded as a sound argument, and a wide variety of critical objections have been raised against the knowledge argument. We can classify them into groups by use of a few diagnostic questions about Mary (figure 35.1). They are all variants of the question that riveted the Watergate investigations of Richard Nixon: *What* did she know and *when* did she know it?

Question 1:   Does Mary in fact learn anything or gain any knowledge when she first experiences red?

Most philosophers have been willing to concede that Mary does learn something, but Paul Churchland (1985) has argued that the claim is open to reasonable doubt. Remember that *ex-hypothesi* Mary knows *everything physical* there is

to know about what goes on in peoples' brains when they experience red. Since our present knowledge of the brain is so far short of what Mary would know, it is difficult to say what she would or would not be able to understand or anticipate. It seems at least possible that when Mary sees her first tomato (rather than expressing surprise) she might remark, "Ah yes, it is just as I expected it would be." Thus there is the possibility of undercutting the argument right at the start by simply rejecting its first premise. But let us follow most philosophers in conceding that Mary gains at least some knowledge and push on to question 2.

Question 2:   What sort of knowledge does Mary gain? Is it strictly *know-how* or does it include new *knowledge* of *facts, propositions* or *information*?

One reply to the knowledge argument, originally proposed by Lawrence Nemirow (1980, 1990) and championed by David Lewis (1983, 1988) is to hold that the only knowledge Mary gains is *know-how*; she gains no new knowledge of facts or propositions. According to this so-called *ability reply*, she gains only new practical abilities to recognize and imagine the relevant phenomenal properites. If the argument's second premise P. 1. is thus read as saying only that Mary gains new abilities (new know-how) then its conclusion C. 3. no longer follows. There need be no truths or information left out of the physicalist story or out of Mary's prior knowledge. The ability reply thus promises a quick and clean solution to the knowledge argument. But its viability depends on the plausibility of the claim that Mary gains no new knowledge of facts or propositions, and like many other philosophers I find that claim not very plausible. Part of what Mary gains is know-how, but that does not seem to be all she gains. There seems to be a fact about how phenomenal red appears that she apprehends only after her release.

Let us thus turn to a *similar*-sounding but *importantly different* question.

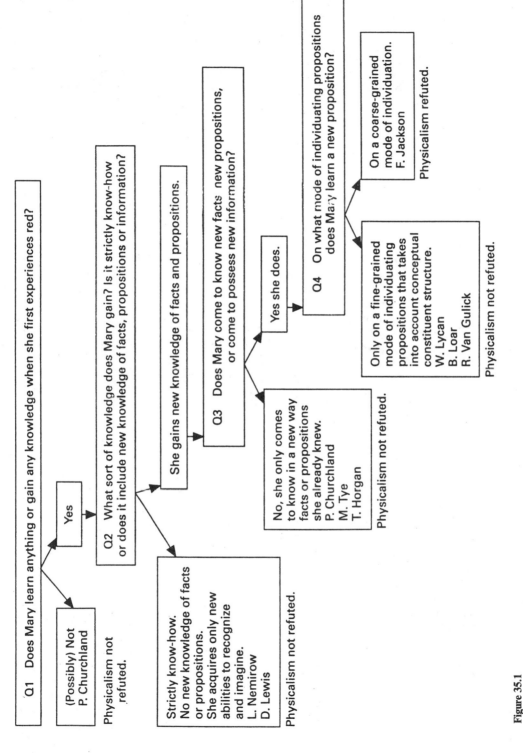

Figure 35.1
Classification of critical objections raised against the knowledge argument

Question 3:   Does Mary come to know *new facts, new propositions*, or come to possess *new information*?

The difference between questions 2 and 3 is a change in the scope of the word "new." In 2 it qualifies knowledge (new *knowledge*), but in 3 it qualifies the *object of knowledge* (knowledge of *new propositions* or *new facts*). The difference can be significant since there are philosophers who hold that Mary gains new knowledge only in the sense that she comes to know *in a new way* facts and propositions that she already knew. (Churchland 1985; Tye 1986) There are various options for unpacking the notion of knowing an old fact in a new way. Mary now knows *directly* by *introspection* what she knew before only *indirectly by inference*. Mary is now able to represent such facts to herself using a basic *biological* and *probably pre-linguistic system of representation* quite distinct from the *linguistic representations* she had to use to represent such facts in the past. Such differences in *mode of access* or *system of representation* might justify us in saying that Mary was now in a new epistemic state and might suffice to explain our inclination to accept the claim that Mary gains new knowledge. Read in this way premise 2 again fails to support the argument's conclusion; there need be no facts or propositions that Mary failed to know before her release and thus none that were left out by the physicalist story.

David Lewis (1988) has recently criticized such approaches as inadequate to account for the intuitive appeal of the knowledge argument. He argues that they make the sense in which Mary gains new knowledge from experiencing red no different from that in which she gains new knowledge about her brain when she learns Russian or Urdu and thus acquires a new system of representation. He finds it uncharitable to suppose the proponents of the knowledge argument have confused so innocuous a sense of "new knowledge" with any that would support their conclusion. Lewis' criticism strikes me as a bit

unfair insofar as the differences between Mary's linguistic and biological nonlinguistic systems for representing experiential states seem far greater than those between English and Russian and thus better able to account for our sense that Mary has gained new knowledge, *even if* she has not come to know a new proposition.

There is however one last question we need to ask, one which can allow us to concede even the strong claim that Mary learns a new proposition without being forced to an anti-physicalist conclusion.

Question 4:   *On what mode of individuating propositions* does Mary learn a new proposition? (That is what counts here as a new proposition?)

Propositions, like beliefs, can be individuated in a variety of fine- or coarse-grained ways. Coarse-grained propositions might be taken as functions from possible worlds to truth-values. On such a mode of individuation, the proposition that $5+7=12$ is the same proposition as the proposition that 38 is the square root of 1,444, they are both true in every possible world. And the proposition that water freezes at 32 degrees Fahrenheit is the same proposition as the proposition that H_2O freezes at 32 degrees Fahrenheit. However, one can use a more *fine-grained scheme* of individuation which treats propositions as having *constituent structure* composed of such things as *concepts* that must also match up if two propositions are to be identified.

Thus *even if* Mary has come to know a new proposition, that in itself need not undercut materialism *as long* as propositions are being individuated in a sufficiently fine-grained way. (Lycan 1990; Loar 1990) I find this reply to the knowledge argument quite attractive especially as developed in a recent paper by Brian Loar (1990). Indeed I have made a similar argument in the past in a reply to Thomas Nagel's argument regarding the individuation of facts (1985). Loar argues that Mary acquires a new concept, a concept that enters her cognitive repertoire in part on the basis of her newly acquired discriminative abilities. Thus using this new concept she is able to apprehend the truth of new propositions. Yet the addition of such a new proposition to her store of knowledge need not cause any concern to the physicalist insofar as the *property* to which her new concept refers can be just some property she referred to in the past by use of a *purely physical concept*, that is, a concept constructed within the resources of the physical sciences.

What then is the bottom line on the knowledge argument? Despite its widespread intuitive appeal and the air of mystification it produces about the explanatory elusiveness of phenomenal qualities, I think it's pretty clearly a *loser* as an argument against the possibility of giving a materialist explanation of phenomenal mentality. There are any number of points at which one can cut off the argument. Though I favor a Loar-type solution, I think each of the other replies provides a plausible place at which to draw the line against the anti-materialist attack. Please choose your favorite.

The Explanatory Gap Argument

Let us turn then to our second argument, the Explanatory Gap Argument. It aims at a more modest though still substantiative result. It does not try to show that materialism is *false*, but only that with respect to the phenomenal aspect of mind, materialism is in an important sense *unintelligible* or *incapable of being adequately comprehended*, at least by us humans. Thus Thomas Nagel writes, "We have at present no conception of how a single event or thing could have both physical and phenomenological aspects or how if it did they might be related" (1986, p. 47). Joseph Levine (1983) puts the point like this:

... there is more to our concept of pain than its causal role, there is how it feels; and what is left unexplained by the discovery of C-fiber firing (the standard philosophical candidate for the neural basis of pain, despite its total empirical implausibility) is why pain should feel the way it does! For there seems to be nothing about C-fiber firing that makes it naturally "fit" the phenomenal properties of pain, any more than it would fit some other set of phenomenal properties. Unlike its functional role, the identification of the qualitative side of pain with C-fiber firing (or some property of C-fiber firing) leaves the connection between it and what we identify it with completely mysterious. One might say it makes the way pain feels into merely a brute fact. (p. 358)

Levine maintains that psychophysical statements asserting such brute fact identities are unintelligible; they leave an explanatory gap that we have no idea how to fill.

In chapter 33 Colin McGinn argues that making the psychophysical link intelligible may be beyond our conceptual capacities. We humans should not with hubris assume that every fact about the natural world is within our cognitive capacity to comprehend. Just as monkeys are unable to comprehend the concept of an electron, and armadillos (those ugly armored ant-eating survivors of an earlier biological era that still inhabit Texas and points south) are not even up to the task of doing elementary arithmetic. So too we may all be armadillos when it comes to understanding the link between brain and phenomenal mentality. Or so McGinn suggests.

The explanatory gap argument is not an argument in the sense that the knowledge argument is. Its strength derives not from any path of deductive reasoning but rather from the intuitive appeal of its conclusion, which speaks to our bewilderment about how any physical story about the brain could ever explain phenomenal consciousness. Recall Wittgenstein holding his head in the *Philosophical Investigations* and saying, "THIS is supposed to be produced by a process in the brain!" (1953, p. 412).

Nonetheless, I want to consider one deductive reconstruction of the argument because I think it will help us see what needs to be done to defuse the intuitive appeal of the position. At one point, Joe Levine makes an approving reference to John Locke's seventeenth-century claim that sensory qualia are *arbitrary*.

The point I am trying to make was captured by Locke in his discussion of the relation between primary and secondary qualities. He states that the simple ideas which we experience in response to impingements from the external world bear no intelligible relation to the corpuscular processes underlying impingement and response. Rather the two sets of phenomena are stuck together in an arbitrary manner. (p. 359).

Immediately following this passage Levine attempts to support his point by appeal to a standard philosophical case of hypothetical spectrum inversion with red and green qualia switching causal roles in an otherwise normal subject. What is important here is the suggestion that basic ideas, such as color qualia, are *simples*. They have *no structure*, and since each one is what it is *sui generis*, it is hard to see how their connection to anything could fail to be anything but arbitrary. We might reconstruct the gap argument as A2.

A2 The Explanatory Gap Argument

P.1. Qualia such as phenomenal hues are basic simples; they have no structure.

Thus

C.2. Any links between such qualia and the organizational structure of their neural substrates must be arbitrary.

Thus

C.3. The links between qualia and their neural bases are unintelligible and present us with an unfillable explanatory gap.

Formulating the argument in this way suggests a possible line of reply, one that has in fact been made by Larry Hardin (1988). It is the first premise of A2 that we must reject. Hardin argues the phenomenal hues that philosophers such as Locke and Levine regard as *sui generis simples* are not in fact such, but rather elements within a highly organized and structured color space. Any attempt to invert them or interchange them *in undetectable ways* would have to preserve that structural organization. More impotant the articulation of an organized structure among color

qualia provides the basis for establishing *explanatory connections* between them and their neural substrates. The method is the familiar one of explaining higher-order organization in terms of underlying structure. Consider a few brief examples.

1. Some color qualia are phenomenally experienced as binary (e.g., orange and purple) and others as unary (e.g., red and blue) while other combinations are phenomenally impossible, (e.g., a color that is both red and green in the way purple is both red and blue.) This phenomenal organization is explained by appeal to the existence of two underlying opponent color channels, one subserving red/green discrimination and the other yellow/blue. Since red and green are mutually exclusive extreme outputs of the red/green channel they cannot be combined; binaries are always combinations of the outputs of the two distinct channels.

2. Some hues are experienced as *warm, positive*, and *advancing* (red and yellow) and others as *cool, negative*, and *receding* (green and blue). They have an affective dimension. The warm hues are those that result from increased stimulation in their respective channel, while the cool hues result from decreased stimulation.

3. Phenomenal yellow tends to be "captured" by phenomenal green in the sense that hues intermediate between yellow and green tend to be perceived as shades of green (rather than of yellow) far more quickly as one moves away from unary yellow than when one moves away from any other unary hue. This phenomenon has as yet no neural explanation. (All examples from Hardin 1988, pp. 134–42.)

The three examples allow us to make our two points. First, most (perhaps even all) of the hypothetical spectrum inversions considered by philosophers would disrupt the organization of the phenomenal color space in detectable ways. One cannot preserve structure while interchanging red with orange or with any other binary hue, nor by interchanging red with the cool hues of green or blue, nor red with yellow given the phenomenon of capture. Secondly and of more immediate relevance to the explanatory gap argument, the phenomenal color space is revealed to have a *complex organizational structure* that allows us to establish *explanatory* rather than simply brute fact connections between it and underlying neural processes.

Our critic may still reply that any explanations we produce will still leave something essentially qualitative unexplained. No matter how much structural organization we can find in the phenomenal realm and explain neurophysiologically, she will insist that the distinct redness of phenomenal red will not have been captured or explained by our theory. For though it may be impossible to map the hues of *our* color space in a way that rearranges them while making the change behaviorally undetectable by preserving all their organizational relations, it seems there could be other nonhuman creatures who had *alien qualia* quite unlike our own, but whose interrelations exactly mirrored those among our phenomenal hues (Shoemaker 1981). Red*, their correlate of red, would bear to green* and orange* the same relations that red bears to our phenomenal greens and oranges; yet red* would not be the same as red. If so, then something essentially qualitative would seem to have escaped our explanation (Shoemaker 1975, 1981a). We might have explained why a given brain process is identical with experiencing red rather than with experiencing orange but not why it is a case of experiencing red rather than red*.

This countercharge needs to be taken seriously, but I think we have altered the nature of the debate. The more one can articulate structure within the phenomenal realm, the greater the chances for physical explanation; without structure we have no place to attach our explanatory "hooks." There is indeed a residue that continues to escape explanation, but the more we can explain relationally about the phenomenal realm, the more the leftover residue shrinks toward zero. Though I admit that we are as yet a long way from that.

Conclusions

Neither of the arguments we have considered succeeds in giving a sound a priori reason for concluding that the phenomenal aspect of mind cannot be adequately explained in physical or functional terms. First the *knowledge argument* turns out to be vulnerable in a wide variety of ways. Second, as long as phenomenal properties are not thought of as basic simples, filling the *explanatory gap* between the phenomenal and the physical (or functional) remains an option by continuing the step-by-step process of articulating structure within the phenomenal realm and mapping it onto the structure of underlying nonphenomenal processes.

Notes

This chapter is the first half of "Understanding the Phenomenal Mind: Are We All Just Armadillos?" which was originally published in *Consciousness—A Mind and Language Reader*, edited by Martin Davies and Glynn Humphries, Basil Blackwell, Oxford, 1992. That chapter was divided and slightly revised to form two independent parts at the request of the editors of this volume. An earlier version of the complete paper was presented at the conference on The Phenomenal Mind: How Is It Possible? Why Is It Necessary? held at the Center for Interdisciplinary Studies (ZIF), Bielefeld University, Bielefeld, Germany, May 1990.

References

Block, Ned (1980) "Troubles with functionalism" in *Readings in the Philosophy of Psychology*, Vol. 1, N. Block (ed.) Harvard University Press, Cambridge, MA, 268–305.

Churchland, Paul (1985) "Reduction, qualia and the direct introspection of brain states," *Journal of Philosophy*, 2–28.

Flohr, Hans (in press) "Brain processes and consciousness: a new and specific hypothesis." *Philosophical Psychology*.

Hardin, C. L. (1988) *Color for Philosophers,* Hackett Publishers, Indianapolis, In.

Jackson, Frank (1982) "Epiphenomenal qualia," *American Philosophical Quarterly,* 127–36.

Johnson-Laird, Philip (1983) *Mental Models,* Cambridge University Press, Cambridge.

Johnson-Laird, Philip (1988) "A computational analysis of consciousness" in *Consciousness in Contemporary Science,* A. Marcel and E. Bisiach (eds.), Oxford University Press, Oxford, 357–68.

Levine, Joseph (1983) "Materialism and qualia: the explanatory gap," *Pacific Philosophical Quarterly,* 354–61.

Lewis, David (1983) "Postscript to 'Mad pain and martian pain'" in D. Lewis *Philosophical Papers,* Vol. 1, Oxford University Press, Oxford,

Lorenz, Konrad (1973) *Behind the Mirror,* Harcourt Brace Jovanovich, New York.

Lycan, William (1990) "What is the subjectivity of the mental?" in *Philosopical Perspectives,* Vol. 4. *Action Theory and Philosophy of Mind,* Ridgeview Publishing, Atascadero, CA, 109–30.

Marcel, Anthony (1988) "Phenomenal experience and functionalism" in *Consciousness in Contemporary Science,* A. Marcel and E. Bisiach (eds.), Oxford University Press, Oxford, 121–58.

Nemirow, Lawrence (1980) Review of T. Nagel *Mortal Questions, Philosophical Review,* 475–76.

Nemirow, Lawrence (1990) "Physicalism and the cognitive role of acquaintance" in *Mind and Cognition,* W. Lycan (ed.) Basil Blackwell Publishers, Oxford, 490–99.

Tye, Michael (1986) "The subjectivity of experience," *Mind,* 1–17.

Sacks, Oliver (1984) *A Leg To Stand On,* Summit Books, New York.

Shoemaker, Sidney (1975) "Functionalism and qualia," *Philosophical Studies,* 291–315.

Shoemaker, Sidney (1981a) "Absent qualia are impossible—a reply to Block," *Philosophical Review,* 581–99.

Van Gulick, Robert (1985) "Physicalism and the subjectivity of the mental," *Philosophical Topics,* 51–70.

Van Gulick, Robert (1988a) "A functionalist plea for self-consciousness," *Philosophical Review,* 149–81.

Van Gulick, Robert (1988b) "Consciousness, intrinsic intentionality and self-understanding machines" in *Consciousness in Contemporary Science,* E. Bisiach & A. Marcel (eds.), Oxford University Press, Oxford, 78–100.

Van Gulick, Robert (1989) "What difference does consciousness make?," *Philosophical Topics,* 211–30.

36 What Mary Didn't Know

Frank Jackson

Mary is confined to a black-and-white room, is educated through black-and-white books and through lectures relayed on black-and-white television. In this way she learns everything there is to know about the physical nature of the world. She knows all the physical facts about us and our environment, in a wide sense of 'physical' which includes everything in *completed* physics, chemistry, and neurophysiology, and all there is to know about the causal and relational facts consequent upon all this, including of course functional roles. If physicalism is true, she knows all there is to know. For to suppose otherwise is to suppose that there is more to know than every physical fact, and that is just what physicalism denies.

Physicalism is not the noncontroversial thesis that the actual world is largely physical, but the challenging thesis that it is entirely physical. This is why physicalists must hold that complete physical knowledge is complete knowledge simpliciter. For suppose it is not complete: then our world must differ from a world, $W(P)$, for which it is complete, and the difference must be in nonphysical facts; for our world and $W(P)$ agree in all matters physical. Hence, physicalism would be false at our world [though contingently so, for it would be true at $W(P)$].[1]

It seems, however, that Mary does not know all there is to know. For when she is let out of the black-and-white room or given a color television, she will learn what it is like to see something red, say. This is rightly described as *learning*—she will not say "ho, hum." Hence, physicalism is false. This is the knowledge argument against physicalism in one of its manifestations.[2] This note is a reply to three objections to it mounted by Paul M. Churchland.[3]

I Three Clarifications

The knowledge argument does not rest on the dubious claim that logically you cannot imagine what sensing red is like unless you have sensed red. Powers of imagination are not to the point. The contention about Mary is not that, despite her fantastic grasp of neurophysiology and everything else physical, she *could not imagine* what it is like to sense red; it is that, as a matter of fact, she *would not know*. But if physicalism is true, she would know; and no great powers of imagination would be called for. Imagination is a faculty that those who *lack* knowledge need to fall back on.

Second, the intensionality of knowledge is not to the point. The argument does not rest on assuming falsely that, if S knows that a is F and if $a = b$, then S knows that b is F. It is concerned with the nature of Mary's total body of knowledge before she is released: is it complete, or do some facts escape it? What is to the point is that S may know that a is F and *know* that $a = b$, yet arguably not know that b is F, by virtue of not being sufficiently logically alert to follow the consequences through. If Mary's lack of knowledge were at all like this, there would be no threat to physicalism in it. But it is very hard to believe that her lack of knowledge could be remedied merely by her explicitly following through enough logical consequences of her vast physical knowledge. Endowing her with great logical acumen and persistence is not in itself enough to fill in the gaps in her knowledge. On being let out, she will not say "I could have worked all this out before by making some more purely logical inferences."

Third, the knowledge Mary lacked which is of particular point for the knowledge argument against physicalism is *knowledge about the experiences of others*, not about her own. When she is let out, she has new experiences, color experiences she has never had before. It is not, therefore, an objection to physicalism that she learns *something* on being let out. Before she was let out, she could not have known facts about her experience of red, for there were no such facts to know. That physicalist and nonphysicalist alike can agree on. After she is let out, things change; and physicalism can happily admit that she learns this; after all, some physical things will change, for instance, her brain states and their functional roles. The trouble for physicalism is that, after Mary sees her first ripe tomato, she will realize how impoverished her conception of the mental life of *others* has been *all along*. She will realize that there was, all the time she was carrying out her laborious investigations into the neurophysiologies of others and into the functional roles of their internal states, something about these people she was quite unaware of. All along their experiences (or many of them, those got from tomatoes, the sky, ...) had a feature conspicuous to them but until now hidden from her (in fact, not in logic). But she knew all the physical facts about them all along; hence, what she did not know until her release is not a physical fact about their experiences. But it is a fact about them. That is the trouble for physicalism.

II Churchland's Three Objections

Churchland's first objection is that the knowledge argument contains a defect that "is simplicity itself" (p. 23). The argument equivocates on the sense of 'knows about'. How so? Churchland suggests that the following is "a conveniently tightened version" of the knowledge argument:

(1) Mary knows everything there is to know about brain states and their properties.

(2) It is not the case that Mary knows everything there is to know about sensations and their properties.

Therefore, by Leibniz's law,

(3) Sensations and their properties $\neq$ brain states and their properties. (p. 23)

Churchland observes, plausibly enough, that the type or kind of knowledge involved in premise 1 is distinct from the kind of knowledge involved in premise 2. We might follow his lead and tag the first 'knowledge by description', and the second 'knowledge by acquaintance'; but, what-

ever the tags, he is right that the displayed argument involves a highly dubious use of Leibniz's law.

My reply is that the displayed argument may be convenient, but it is not accurate. It is not the knowledge argument. Take, for instance, premise 1. The whole thrust of the knowledge argument is that Mary (before her release) does *not* know everything there is to know about brain states and their properties, because she does not know about certain qualia associated with them. What is complete, according to the argument, is her knowledge of matters physical. A convenient and accurate way of displaying the argument is:

(1)′ Mary (before her release) knows everything physical there is to know about other people.

(2)′ Mary (before her release) does not know everything there is to know about other people (because she *learns* something about them on her release).

Therefore,

(3)′ There are truths about other people (and herself) which escape the physicalist story.

What is immediately to the point is not the kind, manner, or type of knowledge Mary has, but *what* she knows. What she knows beforehand is ex hypothesi everything physical there is to know, but is it everything there is to know? That is the crucial question.

There is, though, a relevant challenge involving questions about kinds of knowledge. It concerns the *support* for premise 2′. The case for premise 2′ is that Mary learns something on her release, she acquires knowledge, and that entails that her knowledge beforehand (*what* she knew, never mind whether by description, acquaintance, or whatever) was incomplete. The challenge, mounted by David Lewis and Laurence Nemirow, is that on her release Mary does *not* learn something or acquire knowledge in the relevant sense. What Mary acquires when she is released is a certain representational or imaginative ability; it is knowledge how rather than knowledge that. Hence, a physicalist can admit that Mary acquires something very significant of a knowledge kind—which can hardly be denied—without admitting that this shows that her earlier factual knowledge is defective. She knew all *that* there was to know about the experiences of others beforehand, but lacked an ability until after her release.[4]

Now it is certainly true that Mary will acquire abilities of various kinds after her release. She will, for instance, be able to imagine what seeing red is like, be able to remember what it is like, and be able to understand why her friends regarded her as so deprived (something which, until her release, had always mystified her). But is it plausible that that is *all* she will acquire? Suppose she received a lecture on skepticism about other minds while she was incarcerated. On her release she sees a ripe tomato in normal conditions, and so has a sensation of red. Her first reaction is to say that she now knows more about the kind of experiences others have when looking at ripe tomatoes. She then remembers the lecture and starts to worry. Does she really know more about what their experiences are like, or is she indulging in a wild generalization from one case? In the end she decides she does know, and that skepticism is mistaken (even if, like so many of us, she is not sure how to demonstrate its errors). What was she to-ing and fro-ing about—her abilities? Surely not; her representational abilities were a known constant throughout. What else then was she agonizing about than whether or not she had gained factual knowledge of others? There would be nothing to agonize about if ability was *all* she acquired on her release.

I grant that I have no *proof* that Mary acquires on her release, as well as abilities, factual knowledge about the experiences of others—and not just because I have no disproof of skepticism. My claim is that the knowledge argument is a valid argument from highly plausible, though admittedly not demonstrable, premises to the conclusion that physicalism is false. And that, after all, is about as good an objection as one could expect in this area of philosophy.

Churchland's second objection (pp. 24/5) is that there must be something wrong with the argument, for it proves too much. Suppose Mary received a special series of lectures over her black-and-white television from a full-blown dualist, explaining the "laws" governing the behavior of "ectoplasm" and telling her about qualia. This would not affect the plausibility of the claim that on her release she learns something. So if the argument works against physicalism, it works against dualism too.

My reply is that lectures about qualia over black-and-white television do not tell Mary all there is to know about qualia. They may tell her some things about qualia, for instance, that they do not appear in the physicalist's story, and that the quale we use 'yellow' for is nearly as different from the one we use 'blue' for as is white from black. But why should it be supposed that they tell her everything about qualia? On the other hand, it is plausible that lectures over black-and-white television might in principle tell Mary everything in the physicalist's story. You do not need color television to learn physics or functionalist psychology. To obtain a good argument against dualism (attribute dualism; ectoplasm is a bit of fun), the premise in the knowledge argument that Mary has the full story according to physicalism before her release, has to be replaced by a premise that she has the full story according to dualism. The former is plausible; the latter is not. Hence, there is no "parity of reasons" trouble for dualists who use the knowledge argument.

Churchland's third objection is that the knowledge argument claims "that Mary could not even *imagine* what the relevant experience would be like, despite her exhaustive neuroscientific knowledge, and hence must still be missing certain crucial information" (p. 25), a claim he goes on to argue against.

But, as we emphasized earlier, the knowledge argument claims that Mary would not know what the relevant experience is like. What she could imagine is another matter. If her knowledge is defective, despite being all there is to know according to physicalism, then physicalism is false, whatever her powers of imagination.

Notes

I am much indebted to discussions with David Lewis and with Robert Pargetter.

1. The claim here is not that, if physicalism is true, only what is expressed in explicitly physical language is an item of knowledge. It is that, if physicalism is true, then if you know everything expressed or expressible in explicitly physical language, you know everything. *Pace* Terence Horgan, "Jackson on Physical Information and Qualia," *Philosophical Quarterly*, 34, 135 (April 1984): 147–152.

2. Namely, that in my "Epiphenomenal Qualia," *ibid.*, XXXII, 127 (April 1982): 127–136. See also Thomas Nagel, "What Is It Like to Be a Bat?," *Philosophical Review*, 83, 4 (October 1974): 435–450, and Howard Robinson, *Matter and Sense* (New York: Cambridge, 1982).

3. "Reduction, Qualia, and the Direct Introspection of Brain States." *The Journal of Philosophy*, (January 1985): 8–28. Future page references are to this paper.

4. See Laurence Nemirow, review of Thomas Nagel, *Mortal Questions, Philosophical Review* 89, 3 (July 1980): 473–477, and David Lewis, "Postscript to 'Mad Pain and Martian Pain'," *Philosophical Papers*, vol. 1 (New York: Oxford, 1983). Churchland mentions both Nemirow and Lewis, and it may be that he intended his objection to be essentially the one I have just given. However, he says quite explicitly (bottom of p. 23) that his objection does not need an "ability" analysis of the relevant knowledge.

37 Knowing Qualia: A Reply to Jackson

Paul M. Churchland

In a paper concerning the direct introspection of brain states (1985) I leveled three criticisms against Frank Jackson's "knowledge argument." At stake was his bold claim that no materialist account of mind can possibly account for all mental phenomena. Jackson has replied to those criticisms in his 1986. It is to those replies, and to the issues that prompted them, that the present chapter is directed. [Jackson's essay is chapter 36 in this book.]

The Persistent Equivocation

Jackson concedes the criticism I leveled at my own statement of his argument—specifically, that it involves an equivocation on "knows about"— but he insists that my reconstruction does not represent the argument he wishes to defend. I accept his instruction, and turn my attention to the summary of the argument he provides in section II of his paper (page 568, this volume). Mary, you will recall, has been raised in innocence of any color experience, but has an exhaustive command of neuroscience.

(1) Mary (before her release) knows everything physical there is to know about other people.

(2) Mary (before her release) does not know everything there is to know about other people (because she *learns* something about them on her release).

Therefore

(3) There are truths about other people (and herself) which escape the physicalist story.

Regimenting further, for clarity's sake, yields the following.

(1) $(x)[(Hx \,\&\, Px) \supset Kmx]$

(2) $(\exists x)[Hx \,\&\, \sim Kmx]$ (viz., "what it is like to see red")

Therefore

(3) $(\exists x)[Hx \,\&\, \sim Px]$

Here $m =$ Mary; $Kyx = y$ knows about x; $Hx = x$ is about persons; $Px = x$ is about something physical in character; and x ranges over "knowables," generously construed so as not to beg any questions about whether they are propositional or otherwise in nature.

Thus expressed, the argument is formally valid: the salient move is a *modus tollens* that applies the second conjunct of premise (2), "$\sim Kmx$," to the waiting consequent of premise (1), "Kmx." The questions now are whether the premises are jointly true, and whether the crucial notion "Kmx" is univocal in both of its appearances. Here I am surprised that Jackson sees any progress at all with the above formulation, since I continue to see the same equivocation found in my earlier casting of his argument.

Specifically, premise (1) is plausibly true, within Jackson's story about Mary's color-free upbringing, only on the interpretation of "knows about" that casts the object of knowledge as something propositional, as something adequately expressible in an English sentence. Mary, to put it briefly, gets 100 percent on every written and oral exam; she can pronounce on the truth of any given sentence about the physical characteristics of persons, especially the states of their brains. Her "knowledge by description" of physical facts about persons is without lacunae.

Premise (2), however, is plausibly true only on the interpretation of "knows about" that casts the object of knowledge as something nonpropositional, as something inarticulable, as something that is nontruth-valuable. What Mary is missing is some form of "knowledge by acquaintance," acquaintance with a sensory character, prototype, or universal, perhaps.

Given this prima facie difference in the sense of "knows about," or the kind of knowledge appearing in each premise, we are still looking at a prima facie case of an argument invalid by reason of equivocation on a critical term. Replace either of the "*K*"'s above with a distinct letter, as acknowledgment of the ambiguity demands, and the inference to (3) evaporates. The burden of articulating some specific and unitary sense of "knows about," and of arguing that both premises are true under that interpretation of the epistemic operator, is an undischarged burden that still belongs to Jackson.

It is also a *heavy* burden, since the resources of modern cognitive neurobiology already provide us with a plausible account of what the difference in the two kinds of knowledge amounts to, and of how it is possible to have the one kind without the other. Let me illustrate with a case distinct from that at issue, so as not to beg any questions.

Any competent golfer has a detailed representation (perhaps in his cerebellum, perhaps in his motor cortex) of a golf swing. It is a *motor* representation, and it constitutes his "knowing how" to *execute* a proper swing. The same golfer will also have a discursive representation of a golf swing (perhaps in his language cortex, or in the neighboring temporal and parietal regions), which allows him to describe a golf swing or perhaps draw it on paper. The motor and the discursive representations are quite distinct. Localized brain trauma, or surgery, could remove either one while sparing the other. Short of that, an inarticulate golf champion might have a superb representation of the former kind, but a feeble representation of the latter kind. And a physicist or sports physiologist might have a detailed and penetrating representation of the mechanics of a good swing, and yet be unable to duff the ball more than ten feet because he lacks an adequate *motor* representation, of the desired behavioral sequence, in the brain areas that control his limbs. Indeed, if our physicist is chronically disabled in his motor capacities, he may have no motor representation of a golf swing whatsoever. In one medium of representation, his representational achievements on the topic may be complete; while in another medium of representation, he has nothing.

A contrast between "knowing how" and "knowing that" is one already acknowledged in common sense, and thus it is not surprising that some of the earliest replies to Jackson's argument (Nemirow 1980; Lewis 1983) tried to portray its equivocation in these familiar terms, and tried to explicate Mary's missing knowledge solely in terms of her missing some one or more *abilities* (to recognize red, to imagine red, etc.). While the approach is well motivated, this binary distinction in types of knowledge barely begins to suggest the range and variety of different sites and types of internal representation to be found in a normal brain. There is no reason why we must be bound by the crude divisions of our prescientific idioms when we attempt to give a precise and positive explication of the equivocation displayed in Jackson's argument. And there are substantial grounds for telling a somewhat different story concerning the sort of nondiscursive knowledge at issue. Putting caution and qualification momentarily aside, I shall tell such a story.

In creatures with trichromatic vision (i.e., with three types of retinal cone), color information is coded as a pattern of spiking frequencies across the axonal fibers of the parvocellular subsystem of the optic nerve. That massive cable of axons leads to a second population of cells in a central body called the lateral geniculate nucleus (LGN), whose axonal projections lead in turn to the several areas of the visual cortex at the rear of the brain's cerebral hemispheres, to V1, V2, and ultimately to V4, which area appears to be especially devoted to the processing and representation of color information (Zeki 1980; Van Essen and Maunsell 1983; Hubel and Livingstone 1987). Human cognition divides a smooth continuum of color inputs into a finite number of prototypical categories. The laminar structure at V4 is perhaps the earliest place in the processing hierarchy to which we might ascribe that familiar taxonomy. A creature competent to make reliable color discriminations has there developed a representation of the range of familiar colors, a representation that appears to consist in a specific configuration of weighted synaptic connections meeting the millions of neurons that make up area V4.

That configuration of synaptic weights partitions the "activation space" of the neurons in area V4: it partitions that abstract space into a structured set of subspaces, one for each prototypical color. Inputs from the eye will each occasion a specific pattern of activity across these cortical neurons, a pattern or vector that falls within one of those subspaces. In such a pigeon holing, it now appears, does visual recognition of a color consist.... This recognition depends upon the creature possessing a prior representation—a learned configuration of synapses meeting the relevant population of cells—that antecedently partitions the creature's visual taxonomy so it can respond selectively and appropriately to the flux of visual stimulation arriving from the retina and LGN.

This distributed representation is not remotely propositional or discursive, but it is entirely real. All trichromatic animals have one, even those without any linguistic capacity. It apparently makes possible the many abilities we expect from color-competent creatures: discrimination, recognition, imagination, and so on. Such a representation is presumably what a person with Mary's upbringing would lack, or possess only in stunted or incomplete form. Her representational space within the relevant area of neurons would contain only the subspace for black, white, and the intervening shades of gray, for the visual examples that have shaped her synaptic configuration were limited to these. There is thus more than just a clutch of abilities missing in Mary: there is a complex representation—a processing framework that deserves to be called "cognitive"—that she either lacks or has in reduced form. There is indeed something she "does not know." Jackson's premise (2), we may assume, is thus true on these wholly materialist assumptions.

These same assumptions are entirely consistent with the further assumption that elsewhere in Mary's brain—in the language areas, for example—she has stored a detailed and even ex-

haustive set of discursive, propositional, truth-valuable representations of what goes on in people's brains during the experience of color, a set she has brought into being by the exhaustive reading of authoritative texts in a completed cognitive neuroscience. She may even be able to explain her own representational deficit, as sketched above, in complete neurophysical detail. Jackson's premise (1), we may thus assume, is also true on these wholly materialist assumptions.

The view sketched above is a live candidate for the correct story of sensory coding and sensory recognition. But whether or not it is true, it is at least a logical possibility. Accordingly, what we have sketched here is a consistent but entirely *physical* model (i.e., a model in which Jackson's conclusion is false) in which both of Jackson's premises are true under the appropriate interpretation. They can hardly entail a conclusion, then, that is inconsistent with physicalism. Their compossibility, on purely physicalist assumptions, resides in the different character and the numerically different medium of representation at issue in each of the two premises. Jackson's argument, to refile the charge, equivocates on "knows about."

Other Invalid Instances

An argument form with one invalid instance can be expected to have others. This was the point of a subsidiary objection in my 1985 paper: if valid, Jackson's argument, or one formally parallel, would also serve to refute the possibility of *substance dualism*. I did not there express my point with notable clarity, however, and I accept responsibility for Jackson's quite missing my intention. Let me try again.

The basic point is that the canonical presentation of the knowledge argument, as outlined above, would be just as valid if the predicate term "*P*" were everywhere replaced by "*E*." And the resulting premises would be just as plausibly true if

(1) "*E*" stood for "is about something ecto-plasmic in character" (where "ectoplasm" is an arbitrary name for the dualist's nonphysical sub-stance), and

(2) the story is altered so that Mary becomes an exhaustive expert on a completed *ectoplasmic* science of human nature.

The plausibility would be comparable, I sub-mit, because a long discursive lecture on the objective, statable, law-governed properties of ectoplasm, whatever they might be, would be exactly as useful, or use*less*, in helping Mary to *know-by-acquaintance* "what it is like to see red," as would a long discursive lecture on the ob-jective, statable, law-governed properties of the physical matter of the brain. Even if substance dualism were true, therefore, and ectoplasm were its heroic principal, an exactly parallel "knowl-edge argument" would "show" that there are some aspects of consciousness that must forever escape the *ectoplasmic* story. Given Jackson's antiphysicalist intentions, it is at least an irony that the same form of argument should inci-dentally serve to blow substance dualism out of the water.

Though I am hardly a substance dualist (and neither is Jackson), I do regard substance dualism as a theoretical possibility, one that might con-ceivably succeed in explicating the psychological ontology of common sense in terms of the under-lying properties and law-governed behavior of the nonmaterial substance it postulates. And I must protest that the parallel knowledge argument against substance dualism would be wildly un-fair, and for the very same reason that its analogue against physicalism is unfair: it would equivocate on "knows about." It would be no more effective against dualism than it is against materialism.

The parallel under examination contains a fur-ther lesson. If it works at all, Jackson's argument works against physicalism not because of some defect that is unique to physicalism; *it works be-*cause no amount of discursive knowledge, on any topic, will constitute the nondiscursive form of knowledge that Mary lacks*. Jackson's argument is one instance of an indiscriminately *antireduc-tionist* form of argument. If it works at all, an analogue will work against any proposed reduc-tive, discursive, objective account of the nature of our subjective experience, no matter what the re-ducing theory might happen to be. I see this as a further symptom of the logical pathology de-scribed earlier. Since the argument "works" for reasons that have nothing essential to do with physicalism, it should "work" against the ex-planatory aspirations of other ontologies as well. And so it "does." The price of embracing Jack-son's argument is thus dramatically higher than first appears. For it makes any scientific account of our sensory experience entirely impossible, no matter what the ontology employed.

A Genuinely Nonequivocal Knowledge Argument

We can appreciate the equivocation more deeply it we explore a version of Jackson's argument that does *not* equivocate on "knows about." The equivocation can quickly be closed, if we are de-termined to do so, and the results are revealing. Given that the problem is a variety in the possible forms of knowing, let us simply rewrite the argu-ment with suitable quantification over the rele-vant forms of knowing. The first premise must assert that, for any knowable *x*, and for any form *f* of knowledge, if *x* is about humans and *x* is physical in character, then Mary knows (*f*) about *x*. The second premise is modified in the same modest fashion, and the conclusion is iden-tical. Canonically,

(1′) $(x)(f)[(Hx \& Px) \supset K(f)mx]$
(2′) $(\exists x)(\exists f)[Hx \& \sim K(f)mx]$
Therefore
(3′) $(\exists x)[Hx \& \sim Px]$

This argument is also formally valid, and its premises explicitly encompass whatever variety there may be in forms of knowing. What can we say about its soundness?

Assume that Mary has had the upbringing described in Jackson's story, and thus lacks any knowledge-by-acquaintance with "what it is like to see red." Premise (2′) will then be true, as and for the reasons that Jackson's story requires. What will be the truth value of premise (1′) on these assumptions?

Premise (1′) is now a very strong claim indeed, much stronger than the old premise (1), and a materialist will be sure to insist that it is false. The reason offered will be that, because of her deprived upbringing, Mary quite clearly *lacks* one form of knowledge of a certain physical aspect of people. Specifically, she lacks a proper configuration of synaptic connections meeting the neurons in the appropriate area of her visual cortex. She thus lacks an appropriately partitioned activation vector space across those neurons, and therefore has no representation, at that site, of the full range of sensory coding vectors that might someday come from the retina and the LGN. In other words, there is something physical about persons (their color sensations, or identically, their coding vectors in their visual pathways), and there is some form of knowledge (an antecedently partitioned prelinguistic taxonomy), such that Mary lacks that form of knowledge of that aspect of persons. Accordingly, premise (1′) is false and the conclusion (3′) is not sustained.

From a materialist's point of view, it is obvious that (1′) will be false on the assumptions of Jackson's story. For that story denies her the upbringing that normally provokes and shapes the development of the relevant representation across the appropriate population of cortical neurons. And so, of course, there is a form of knowledge, of a physical aspect of persons, that Mary does not have. As just illustrated, the materialist can even specify that form of knowledge, and its objects, in neural terms. But this means that premise (1′), as properly quantified at last, is false. Mary

does *not* have knowledge of everything physical about persons, in every way that is possible for her. (That is why premise (2′) is true.)

There is, of course, no guarantee that the materialist's account of sensations and sensory recognition is correct (although the experimental and theoretical evidence for a view of this general kind continues to accumulate). But neither is Jackson in a position to insist that it must be mistaken. That would beg the very question at issue: whether sensory qualia form a metaphysically distinct class of phenomena beyond the scope of physical science.

To summarize, if we write a deliberately nonequivocal form of Jackson's argument, one that quantifies appropriately over all of the relevant forms of knowledge, then the first premise must almost certainly be false under the conditions of his own story. So, at any rate, is the materialist in a strong position to argue. Jackson's expressed hope for "highly plausible premises" is not realized in (1′). The original premise (1) was of course much more plausible. But it failed to sustain a valid argument, and it was plausible only because it failed to address all the relevant forms of knowledge.

Converting a Third-Person Account into a First-Person Account

My final objection to Jackson was aimed more at breaking the grip of the ideology behind his argument than at the argument itself. That ideology includes a domain of properties—the qualia of subjective experience—that are held to be metaphysically distinct from the objective physical properties addressed by orthodox science. It is not a surprise, then, on this view, that one might know all physical facts, and yet be ignorant of some domain of these nonphysical qualia. The contrast between what is known and what is not known simply reflects an antecedent metaphysical division in the furniture of the world.

But there is another way to look at the situation, one that finds no such division. Our capacity for recognizing a range of (currently) inarticulable features in our subjective experience is easily explained on materialist principles; the relevant sketch appears earlier in this chapter .... Our discursive inarticulation of those features is no surprise either, and signifies nothing about their metaphysical status.... Indeed, that veil of inarticulation may itself be swept aside by suitable learning. What we are now able spontaneously to report about our internal states and cognitive activities need not define the limit on what we might be able to report, spontaneously and accurately, if we were taught a more appropriate conceptual scheme in which to express our discriminations. In closing, let me again urge on Jackson this exciting possibility.

The intricacies of brain function may be subjectively opaque to us now, but they need not remain that way forever. Neuroscience may appear to be defective in providing a purely "third-person account" of mind, but only familiarity of idiom and spontaneity of conceptual response are required to make it a "first-person account" as well. *What makes an account a "first-person account" is not the content of that account, but the fact that one has learned to use it as the vehicle of spontaneous conceptualization in introspection and self-description.* We all of us, as children, learned to use the framework of current folk psychology in this role. But it is entirely possible for a person or culture to learn and use some other framework in that role, the framework of cognitive neuroscience, perhaps. Given a deep and practiced familiarity with the developing idioms of cognitive neurobiology, we might learn to discriminate by introspection the coding vectors in our internal axonal pathways, the activation patterns across salient neural populations, and myriad other things besides.

Should that ever happen, it would then be obvious to everyone who had made the conceptual shift that a completed cognitive neuroscience would constitute not a pinched and exclusionary picture of human consciousness, one blind to the subjective dimension of self, as Jackson's argument suggests. Rather, it would be the vehicle of a grand reconstruction and expansion of our subjective consciousness, since it would provide us with a conceptual framework that, unlike folk psychology, is at last equal to the kinematical and dynamical intricacies of the world within....

Real precedents for such a reformation can be drawn from our own history. We did not lose contact with a metaphysically distinct dimension of reality when we stopped seeing an immutable, sparkle-strewn quintessential crystal sphere each time we looked to the heavens, and began to see instead an infinite space of gas and dust and giant stars structured by gravitational attractions and violent nuclear processes. On the contrary, we now see far more than we used to, even with the unaided eye. The diverse "colors" of the stars allow us to see directly their absolute temperatures. Stellar temperature is a function of stellar mass, so we are just as reliably seeing stellar masses. The intrinsic luminosity or brightness of a star is tightly tied to these same features, and thus is also visually available, no matter how bright or faint the star may appear from Earth. Apparent brightness is visually obvious also, of course, and the contrast between the apparent and the intrinsic brightnesses gives you the star's rough distance from Earth. In this way is the character and three-dimensional distribution of complex stellar objects in a volume of interstellar space hundreds of light years on a side made visually available to your unaided eyes from your own back yard, given only the right conceptual framework for grasping it, and observational practice in using that framework. From within the new framework, one finds a systematic significance in experiential details that hitherto went largely or entirely unnoticed (compare Feyerabend 1963).

The case of inner space is potentially the same. We will not lose contact with a metaphysically distinct dimension of self when we stop introspecting inarticulable qualia, and start introspecting "instead" sensory coding vectors and sundry activation patterns within the vector spaces of our accessible cortical areas. As with the revolution in astronomy, the prospect is one we should welcome as metaphysically liberating, rather than deride as metaphysically irrelevant or metaphysically impossible.

References

Churchland, P. M. (1979). *Scientific Realism and the Plasticity of Mind*. Cambridge: Cambridge University Press.

————. (1981). "Eliminative Materialism and the Propositional Attitudes." *Journal of Philosophy* 78, no. 2:67–90.

————. (1985). "Reduction, Qualia, and the Direct Introspection of Brain States." *Journal of Philosophy* 82, no. 1:8–28.

Feyerabend, P. K. (1963). "How to Be a Good Empiricist." In B. Baumrin, ed., *Philosophy of Science*, vol. 2, pp. 3 19. New York: Interscience Publications.

Hubel, D. H., and Livingstone, M. S. (1987). "Segregation of Form, Color, and Stereopsis in Primate Area 18." *Journal of Neuroscience* 7:3378–3415.

Jackson, F. (1986). "What Mary Didn't Know." *Journal of Philosophy* 83, no. 5:291–295.

Lewis, D. (1983). "Postscript to 'Mad Pain and Martian Pain.'" *Philosophical Papers*, vol. 1. New York: Oxford.

Nemirow, L. (1980). Review of Thomas Nagel, *Mortal Questions. Philosophical Review* 89, no. 3:473–477.

Van Essen, D. C., and Maunsell, J. (1983). "Hierarchical Organization and Functional Streams in the Visual Cortex." *Trends in Neuroscience* 6:370–375.

Zeki, S. (1980). "The Representation of Colours in the Cerebral Cortex." *Nature* 284:412–418.

38   What Experience Teaches

David Lewis

Experience is the Best Teacher

They say that experience is the best teacher, and the classroom is no substitute for Real Life. There's truth to this. If you want to know what some new and different experience is like, you can learn it by going out and really *having* that experience. You can't learn it by being told about the experience, however thorough your lessons may be.

Does this prove much of anything about the metaphysics of mind and the limits of science? I think not.

Example: Skunks and Vegemite   I have smelled skunks, so I know what it's like to smell skunks. But skunks live only in some parts of the world, so you may never have smelled a skunk. If you haven't smelled a skunk, then you don't know what it's like. You never will, unless someday you smell a skunk for yourself. On the other hand, you may have tasted Vegemite, that famous Australian substance; and I never have. So you may know what it's like to taste Vegemite. I don't, and unless I taste Vegemite (what, and spoil a good example!), I never will. It won't help at all to take lessons on the chemical composition of skunk scent or Vegemite, the physiology of the nostrils or the taste-buds, and the neurophysiology of the sensory nerves and the brain.

Example: The Captive Scientist[1]   Mary, a brilliant scientist, has lived from birth in a cell where everything is black or white. (Even she herself is painted all over.) She views the world on black-and-white television. By television she reads books, she joins in discussion, she watches the results of experiments done under her direction. In this way she becomes the world's leading expert on color and color vision and the brain states produced by exposure to colors. But she doesn't know what it's like to see color. And she never will, unless she escapes from her cell.

Example: The Bat[2]   The bat is an alien creature, with a sonar sense quite unlike any sense of ours. We can never have the experiences of a bat; because we could not become bat-like enough to have those experiences and still be ourselves. We will never know what it's like to be a bat. Not even if we come to know all the facts there are about the bat's behavior and behavioral dispositions, about the bat's physical structure and processes, about the bat's functional organization. Not even if we come to know all the same sort of physical facts about all the other bats, or about other creatures, or about ourselves. Not even if we come to possess all physical facts whatever. Not even if we become able to recognize all the mathematical and logical implications of all these facts, no matter how complicated and how far beyond the reach of finite deduction.

Experience is the best teacher, in this sense: having an experience is the best way or perhaps the only way, of coming to know what that experience is like. No amount of scientific information about the stimuli that produce that experience and the process that goes on in you when you have that experience will enable you to know what it's like to have the experience.

... But Not Necessarily

Having an experience is surely one good way, and surely the only practical way, of coming to know what that experience is like. Can we say, flatly, that it is the only *possible* way? Probably not. There is a change that takes place in you when you have the experience and thereby come to know what it's like. Perhaps the exact same change could in principle be produced in you by precise neurosurgery, very far beyond the limits of present-day technique. Or it could possibly be produced in you by magic. If we ignore the laws of nature, which are after all contingent, then there is no necessary connection between cause and effect: anything could cause anything. For instance, the casting of a spell could do to you exactly what your first smell of skunk would do. We might quibble about whether a state produced in this artificial fashion would deserve the *name* "knowing what it's like to smell a skunk," but we can imagine that so far as what goes on within you is concerned, it would differ not at all.[3]

Just as we can imagine that a spell might produce the same change as a smell, so likewise we can imagine that science lessons might cause that same change. Even that is possible, in the broadest sense of the word. If we ignored all we know about how the world really works, we could not say what might happen to someone if he were taught about the chemistry of scent and the physiology of the nose. There might have been a causal mechanism that transforms science lessons into whatever it is that experience gives us. But there isn't. It is not an absolutely necessary truth that experience is the best teacher about what a new experience is like. It's a contingent truth. But we have good reason to think it's true.

We have good reason to think that something of this kind is true, anyway, but less reason to be sure exactly what. Maybe some way of giving the lessons that hasn't yet been invented, and some way of taking them in that hasn't yet been practiced, could give us a big surprise. Consider sight-reading: a trained musician can read the score and know what it would be like to hear the music. If I'd never heard that some people can sight-read, I would never have thought it humanly possible. Of course the moral is that new music isn't altogether new—the big new experience is a rearrangement of lots of little old experiences. It just might turn out the same for new smells and tastes *vis-à-vis* old ones; or even for color vision *vis-à-vis* black and white[4]; or even for sonar sense experience *vis-à-vis* the sort we enjoy. The thing we can say with some confidence is that we have no faculty for knowing on the basis of mere science lessons what some *new enough* experience would be like. But how new is "new enough?"— There, we just might be in for surprises.

Three Ways to Miss the Point

The First Way   A literalist might see the phrase "know what it's like" and take that to mean: "know what it resembles." Then he might ask: what's so hard about that? Why can't you just be told which experiences resemble one another? You needn't have had the experiences—all you need, to be taught your lessons, is some way of referring to them. You could be told: the smell of skunk somewhat resembles the smell of burning rubber. I have been told: the taste of Vegemite somewhat resembles that of Marmite. Black-and-white Mary might know more than most of us about the resemblances among color-experiences. She might know which ones are spontaneously called "similar" by subjects who have them; which gradual changes from one to another tend to escape notice; which ones get conflated with which in memory; which ones involve roughly the same neurons firing in similar rhythms; and so forth. We could even know what the bat's sonar experiences resemble just by knowing that they do not at all resemble any experiences of humans, but do resemble—as it might be—certain experiences that occur in certain fish. This misses the point. *Pace* the literalist, "know what it's like" does not mean "know what it resembles." The most that's true is that knowing what it resembles *may* help you to know what it's like. If you are taught that experience A resembles B and C closely, D less, E not at all, that will help you know what A is like—*if* you know already what B and C and D and E are like. Otherwise, it helps you not at all. I don't know any better what it's like to taste Vegemite when I'm told that it tastes like Marmite, because I don't know what Marmite tastes like either. (Nor do I know any better what Marmite tastes like for being told it tastes like Vegemite.) Maybe Mary knows enough to triangulate each color experience exactly in a network of resemblances, or in many networks of resemblance in different respects, while never knowing what any node of any network is like.

Maybe we could do the same for bat experiences. But no amount of information about resemblances, just by itself, does anything to help us know what an experience is like.

The Second Way   Insofar as I don't know what it would be like to drive a steam locomotive fast on a cold, stormy night, part of my problem is just that I don't know what experiences I would have. The firebox puts out a lot of heat, especially when the fireman opens the door to throw on more coal; on the other hand, the cab is drafty and gives poor protection from the weather. Would I be too hot or too cold? Or both by turns? Or would it be chilled face and scorched legs? If I knew the answers to such questions, I'd know much better what it would be like to drive the locomotive. So maybe "know what it's like" just means "know what experiences one has." Then again: what's the problem? Why can't you just be told what experiences you would have if, say, you tasted Vegemite? Again, you needn't have had the experiences   all you need, to be taught your lessons, is some way of referring to them. We have ways to refer to experiences we haven't had. We can refer to them in terms of their causes: the experience one has upon tasting Vegemite, the experience one has upon tasting a substance of such-and-such chemical composition. Or we can refer to them in terms of their effects: the experience that just caused Fred to say "Yeeuch!" Or we can refer to them in terms of the physical states of the nervous system that mediate between those causes and effects: the experience one has when one's nerves are firing in such-and-such pattern. (According to some materialists, I myself for one, this means the experience which is identical with such-and-such firing pattern. According to other materialists it means the experience which is realized by such-and-such firing pattern. According to many dualists, it means the experience which is merely the lawful companion of such-and-such firing pattern. But whichever it is, we get a way of referring to the experience.) Black-and-white Mary is in a position to refer to color-experiences

in all these ways. Therefore you should have no problem in telling her exactly what experiences one has upon seeing the colors. Or rather, your only problem is that you'd be telling her what she knows very well already! In general, to know what is the X is to know that the X is the Y, where it's not too obvious that the X is the Y. (Just knowing that the X is the X won't do, of course, because it is too obvious.) If Mary knows that the experience of seeing green is the experience associated with such-and-such pattern of nerve firings, then she knows the right sort of unobvious identity. So she knows what experience one has upon seeing green.

(Sometimes it's suggested that you need a "rigid designator": you know what is the X by knowing that the X is the Y only if "the Y" is a term whose referent does not depend on any contingent matter of fact. In the first place, this suggestion is false. You can know who is the man on the balcony by knowing that the man on the balcony is the Prime Minister even if neither "the Prime Minister" nor any other phrase available to you rigidly designates the man who is, in fact, the Prime Minister. In the second place, according to one version of Materialism (the one I accept) a description of the form "the state of having nerves firing in such-and-such a pattern" *is* a rigid designator, and what it designates is in fact an experience; and according to another version of Materialism, a description of the form "having some or other state which occupies so-and-so functional role" is a rigid designator of an experience. So even if the false suggestion were granted, still it hasn't been shown, without begging the question against Materialism, that Mary could not know what experience one has upon seeing red.)

Since Mary *does* know what experiences she would have if she saw the colors, but she *doesn't* know what it would be like to see the colors, we'd better conclude that "know what it's like" does not after all mean "know what experiences one has." The locomotive example was misleading. Yes, by learning what experiences the driver would have, I can know what driving the loco- motive would be like; but only because I already know what those experiences are like. (It matters that I know what they're like under the appro- priate descriptions—as it might be, the descrip- tion "chilled face and scorched legs." This is something we'll return to later.) Mary may know as well as I do that when the driver leans out into the storm to watch the signals, he will have the experience of seeing sometimes green lights and sometimes red. She knows better than I what ex- periences he has when signals come into view. She can give many more unobviously equivalent de- scriptions of those experiences than I can. But knowing what color-experiences the driver has won't help Mary to know what his job is like. It will help me.

The Third Way Until Mary sees green, here is one thing she will never know: she will never know that she is seeing green. The reason why is just that until she sees green, it will never be true that she is seeing green. Some knowledge is irre- ducibly egocentric, or *de se*.[5] It is not just knowl- edge about what goes on in the world; it is knowledge of who and when in the world one is. Knowledge of what goes on in the world will be true alike for all who live in that world; whereas egocentric knowledge may be true for one and false for another, or true for one at one time and false for the same one at another time. Maybe Mary knows in advance, as she plots her escape, that 9 a.m. on the 13th of May, 1997, is the mo- ment when someone previously confined in a black-and-white cell sees color for the first time. But until that moment comes, she will never know that she herself is then seeing color—because she isn't. What isn't true isn't knowledge. This goes as much for egocentric knowledge as for the rest. So only those of whom an egocentric proposition is true can know it, and only at times when it is true of them can they know it. That one is then seeing color is an egocentric proposition. So we've found a proposition which Mary can never know until she sees color—which, as it happens, is the very

moment when she will first know what it's like to see color! Have we discovered the reason why ex- perience is the best teacher? And not contingently after all, but as a necessary consequence of the logic of egocentric knowledge?

No; we have two separate phenomena here, and only some bewitchment about the "first-per- son perspective" could make us miss the differ- ence. In the first place, Mary will probably go on knowing what it's like to see green after she stops knowing the egocentric proposition that she's then seeing green. Since what isn't true isn't known she must stop knowing that proposition the moment she stops seeing green. (Does that only mean that we should have taken a different egocentric proposition: that one *has* seen green? No; for in that case Mary could go on knowing the proposition even after she forgets what it's like to see green, as might happen if she were soon recaptured.) In the second place, Mary might come to know what it's like to see green even if she didn't know the egocentric proposition. She might not have known in advance that her escape route would take her across a green meadow, and it might take her a little while to recognize grass by its shape. So at first she might know only that she was seeing some colors or other, and thereby finding out what some color-experiences or other were like, without being able to put a name either to the colors or to the experiences. She would then know what it was like to see green, though not under that description, indeed not under any de- scription more useful than "the color-experience I'm having now"; but she would not know the egocentric proposition that she is then seeing green, since she wouldn't know which color she was seeing. In the third place, the gaining of ego- centric knowledge may have prerequisites that have nothing to do with experience. Just as Mary can't know she's seeing green until she *does* see green, she can't know she's turning 50 until she *does* turn 50. But—I hope!—turning 50 does not involve some special experience. In short, though indeed one can gain egocentric knowledge that one is in some situation only when one is in it, that is not the same as finding out what an experience is like only when one has that experience.

We've just rejected two suggestions that don't work separately, and we may note that they don't work any better when put together. One knows what is the X by knowing that the X is the Y, where the identity is not too obvious; and "the Y" might be an egocentric description. So knowledge that the X is the Y might be irreducibly egocentric knowledge, therefore knowledge that cannot be had until it is true of one that the X is the Y. So one way of knowing what is the X will remain unavailable until it comes true of one that the X is the Y. One way that I could gain an unobvious identity concerning the taste of Vegemite would be for it to come true that the taste of Vegemite was the taste I was having at that very moment— and that would come true at the very moment I tasted Vegemite and found out what it was like! Is this why experience is the best teacher?—No; cases of gaining an unobvious egocentric identity are a dime a dozen, and most of them do not result in finding out what an experience is like. Suppose I plan ahead that I will finally break down and taste Vegemite next Thursday noon. Then on Wednesday noon, if I watch the clock, I first gain the unobvious egocentric knowledge that the taste of Vegemite is the taste I shall be having in exactly 24 hours, and thereby I have a new way of knowing what is the taste of Vegemite. But on Wednesday noon I don't yet know what it's like. Another example: from time to time I find myself next to a Vegemite-taster. On those occasions, and only those, I know what is the taste of Vegemite by knowing that it is the taste being had by the person next to me. But on no such occasion has it ever yet happened that I knew what it was like to taste Vegemite.

The Hypothesis of Phenomenal Information

No amount of the physical information that black-and-white Mary gathers could help her know what it was like to see colors; no amount of the physical information that we might gather about bats could help us know what it's like to have their experiences; and likewise in other cases. There is a natural and tempting explanation of why physical information does not help. That is the hypothesis that besides physical information there is an irreducibly different kind of information to be had: *phenomenal information*. The two are independent. Two possible cases might be exactly alike physically, yet differ phenomenally. When we get physical information we narrow down the physical possibilities, and perhaps we narrow them down all the way to one, but we leave open a range of phenomenal possibilities. When we have an experience, on the other hand, we acquire phenomenal information; possibilities previously open are eliminated; and that is what it is to learn what the experience is like.

(Analogy. Suppose the question concerned the location of a point within a certain region of the x-y plane. We might be told that its x-coordinate lies in certain intervals, and outside certain others. We might even get enough of this information to fix the x-coordinate exactly. But no amount of x-information would tell us anything about the y-coordinate; any amount of x-information leaves open all the y-possibilities. But when at last we make a y-measurement, we acquire a new kind of information; possibilities previously open are eliminated; and that is how we learn where the point is in the y-direction.)

What might the subject matter of phenomenal information be? *If* the Hypothesis of Phenomenal Information is true, then you have an easy answer: it is information about experience. More specifically, it is information about a certain part or aspect or feature of experience. But if the Hypothesis is false, then there is still experience (complete with all its parts and aspects and features) and yet no information about experience is phenomenal information. So it cannot be said in a neutral way, without presupposing the Hypothesis, that information about experience is phenomenal information. For if the Hypothesis is false and Materialism is true, it may be that all the information there is about experience is physical information, and can very well be presented in lessons for the inexperienced.

It makes no difference to put some fashionable new phrase in place of "experience." If instead of "experience" you say "raw feel" (or just "feeling"), or "way it feels," or "what it's like," then I submit that you mean nothing different. Is there anything it's like to be this robot? Does this robot have experiences?—I can tell no difference between the new question and the old. Does sunburn feel the same way to you that it does to me? Do we have the same raw feel? Do we have the same experience when sunburned?—Again, same question. "Know the feeling," "know what it's like"—interchangeable. (Except that the former may hint at an alternative to the Hypothesis of Phenomenal Information.) So if the friend of phenomenal information says that its subject matter is raw feels, or ways to feel, or what it's like, then I respond just as I do if he says that the subject matter is experience. Maybe so, *if* the Hypothesis of Phenomenal Information is true; but if the Hypothesis is false and Materialism is true, nevertheless there is still information about raw feels, ways to feel or what it's like; but in that case it is physical information and can be conveyed in lessons.

We might get a candidate for the subject matter of phenomenal information that is not just experience renamed, but is still tendentious. For instance, we might be told that phenomenal information concerns the intrinsic character of experience. A friend of phenomenal information might indeed believe that it reveals certain special, non-physical intrinsic properties of experience. He might even believe that it reveals the existence of some special non-physical thing or process, *all* of whose intrinsic properties are non-physical. But he is by no means alone in saying that experience has an intrinsic character. Plenty of us materialists say so too. We say that a certain color-experience is whatever state occupies a certain functional role. So if the occupant of that role (universally, or in the case of humans, or in the

case of certain humans) is a certain pattern of neural firing, then that pattern of firing *is* the experience) (in the case in question). Therefore the intrinsic character of the experience is the intrinsic character of the firing pattern. For instance, a frequency of firing is part of the intrinsic character of the experience. If we materialists are right about what experience is, then black-and-white Mary knows all about the intrinsic character of color-experience; whereas most people who know what color-experience is like remain totally ignorant about its intrinsic character.[6]

To say that phenomenal information concerns "qualia" would be tendentious in much the same way. For how was this notion introduced? Often thus. We are told to imagine someone who, when he sees red things, has just the sort of experiences that we have when we see green things, and vice versa; and we are told to call this a case of "inverted qualia." And then we are told to imagine someone queerer still, who sees red and responds to it appropriately, and indeed has entirely the same functional organization of inner states as we do and yet has no experiences at all; and we are told to call this a case of "absent qualia." Now a friend of phenomenal information might well think that these deficiencies have something to do with the non-physical subject matter of phenomenal information. But others can understand them otherwise. Some materialists will reject the cases outright, but others, and I for one, will make sense of them as best we can. Maybe the point is that the states that occupy the roles of experiences, and therefore *are* the experiences, in normal people are inverted or absent in victims of inverted or absent qualia. (This presupposes, what might be false, that most people are enough alike.) Experience of red—the state that occupies that role in normal people—occurs also in the victim of "inverted qualia," but in him it occupies the role of experience of green; whereas the state that occupies in him the role of experience of red is the state that occupies in normal people the role of experience of green. Experience of red and of green—that is, the occupants of those roles for normal people—do not occur at all in the victim of "absent qualia"; the occupants of those roles for him are states that don't occur at all in the normal. Thus we make good sense of inverted and absent qualia; but in such a way that "qualia" is just the word for role-occupying states taken *per se* rather than *qua* occupants of roles. Qualia, so understood, could not be the subject matter of phenomenal information. Mary knows all about them. We who have them mostly don't.[7]

It is best to rest content with an unhelpful name and a *via negativa*. Stipulate that "the phenomenal aspect of the world" is to name whatever is the subject matter of phenomenal information, if there is any such thing; the phenomenal aspect, if such there be, is that which we can become informed about by having new experiences but never by taking lessons. Having said this, it will be safe to say that information about the phenomenal aspect of the world can only be phenomenal information. But all we really know, after thus closing the circle, is that phenomenal information is supposed to reveal the presence of some sort of non-physical things or processes within experience, or else it is supposed to reveal that certain physical things or processes within experience have some sort of non-physical properties.

The Knowledge Argument

If we invoke the Hypothesis of Phenomenal Information to explain why no amount of physical information suffices to teach us what a new experience is like, then we have a powerful argument to refute any materialist theory of the mind. Frank Jackson (see note l) calls it the "Knowledge Argument." Arguments against one materialist theory or another are never very conclusive. It is always possible to adjust the details. But the Knowledge Argument, if it worked, would directly refute the bare minimum that is common to *all* materialist theories.

It goes as follows. First in a simplified form; afterward we'll do it properly. Minimal Materialism is a supervenience thesis: no difference without physical difference. That is: any two possibilities that are just alike physically are just alike *simpliciter*. If two possibilities are just alike physically, then no physical information can eliminate one but not both of them. If two possibilities are just alike *simpliciter* (if that is possible) then no information whatsoever can eliminate one but not both of them. So if there is a kind of information—namely, phenomenal information— that can eliminate possibilities that any amount of physical information leaves open, then there must be possibilities that are just alike physically, but not just alike *simpliciter*. That is just what minimal Materialism denies.

(Analogy. If two possible locations in our region agree in their x-coordinate, then no amount of x-information can eliminate one but not both. If, *per impossibile*, two possible locations agreed in all their coordinates, then no information whatsoever could eliminate one but not both. So if there is a kind of information—namely, y-information—that can eliminate locations that any amount of x-information leaves open, then there must be locations in the region that agree in their x-coordinate but not in all their coordinates.)

Now to remove the simplification. What we saw so far was the Knowledge Argument against Materialism taken as a necessary truth, applying unrestrictedly to all possible worlds. But we materialists usually think that Materialism is a contingent truth. We grant that there are spooky possible worlds where Materialism is false, but we insist that our actual world isn't one of them. If so, then there might after all be two possibilities that are alike physically but not alike *simpliciter*, but one or both of the two would have to be possibilities where Materialism was false. Spooky worlds could differ with respect to their spooks without differing physically. Our minimal Materialism must be a *restricted* supervenience thesis: within a certain class of worlds, which includes our actual world, there is no difference without physical difference. Within that class, any two possibilities just alike physically are just alike *simpliciter*. But what delineates the relevant class? (It is trivial that our world belongs to *some* class wherein there is no difference without physical difference. That will be so however spooky our world may be. The unit class of our world is one such class, for instance. And so is any class that contains our world, and contains no two physical duplicates.) I think the relevant class should consist of the worlds that have nothing wholly alien to this world. The inhabitants of such a non-alien world could be made from the inhabitants of ours, so to speak, by a process of division and recombination. That will make no wholly different kinds of things, and no wholly different fundamental properties of things.[8] Our restricted materialist supervenience thesis should go as follows: throughout the non-alien words, there is no difference without physical difference.

If the Hypothesis of Phenomenal Information be granted, then the Knowledge Argument refutes this restricted supervenience nearly as decisively as it refutes the unrestricted version. Consider a possibility that is eliminated by phenomenal information, but not by any amount of physical information. There are two cases. Maybe this possibility has nothing that is alien to our world. In that case the argument goes as before: actuality and the eliminated possibility are just alike physically, they are not just alike *simpliciter*; furthermore, both of them fall within the restriction to non-alien worlds, so we have a counterexample even to restricted supervenience. Or maybe instead the eliminated possibility does have something X which is alien to this world— an alien kind of thing, or maybe an alien fundamental property of non-alien things. Then the phenomenal information gained by having a new experience has revealed something negative: at least in part, it is the information that X is *not* present. How can that be? If there is such a thing as phenomenal information, presumably what it reveals is positive: the presence of something

hitherto unknown. Not, of course, something alien from actuality itself; but something alien from actuality as it is inadequately represented by the inexperienced and by the materialists. If Mary learns something when she finds out what it's like to see the colors, presumably she learns that there's *more* to the world than she knew before— not *less*. It's easy to think that phenomenal information might eliminate possibilities that are impoverished by comparison with actuality, but that would make a counterexample to the restricted supervenience thesis. To eliminate possibilities without making a counterexample, phenomenal information would have to eliminate possibilities less impoverished than actuality. And how can phenomenal information do that? Compare ordinary perceptual information. Maybe Jean-Paul can just *see* that Pierre is absent from the café, at least if it's a small café. But how can he just see that Pierre is absent from Paris, let alone from the whole of actuality?

(Is there a third case? What if the eliminated possibility is in one respect richer than actuality, in another respect poorer? Suppose the eliminated possibility has X, which is alien from actuality, but also it lacks Y. Then phenomenal information might eliminate it by revealing the actual presence of Y, without having to reveal the actual absence of X—but then I say there ought to be a third possibility, one with neither X nor Y, poorer and in no respect richer than actuality, and again without any physical difference from actuality. For why should taking away X automatically restore Y? Why can't they vary independently?[9] But this third possibility differs *simpliciter* from actuality without differing physically. Further, it has nothing alien from actuality. So we regain a counterexample to the restricted supervenience thesis.)

The Knowledge Argument works. There is no way to grant the Hypothesis of Phenomenal Information and still uphold Materialism. Therefore I deny the Hypothesis. I cannot refute it outright. But later I shall argue, first, that it is more peculiar, and therefore less tempting, that it may at first seem; and, second, that we are not forced to accept it, since an alternative hypothesis does justice to the way experience best teaches us what it's like.

Three More Ways to Miss the Point

The Hypothesis of Phenomenal Information characterizes information in terms of eliminated possibilities. But there are other conceptions of "information." Therefore the Hypothesis has look-alikes: hypotheses which say that experience produces "information" which could not be gained otherwise, but do not characterize this "information" in terms of eliminated possibilities. These look-alikes do not work as premises for the Knowledge Argument. They do not say that phenomenal information eliminates possibilities that differ, but do not differ physically, from uneliminated possibilities. The look-alike hypotheses of phenomenal "information" are consistent with Materialism, and may very well be true. But they don't make the Knowledge Argument go away. Whatever harmless look-alikes may or may not be true, and whatever conception may or may not deserve the name "information," the only way to save Materialism is fix our attention squarely on the genuine Hypothesis of Phenomenal Information, and deny it. To avert our eyes, and attend to something else, is no substitute for that denial.

Might a look-alike help at least to this extent: by giving us something true that well might have been confused with the genuine Hypothesis, thereby explaining how we might have believed the Hypothesis although it was false? I think not. Each of the look-alikes turns out to imply not only that experience can give us "information" that no amount of lessons can give, but also that lessons in Russian can give us "information" that no amount of lessons in English can give (and vice versa). I doubt that any friend of phenomenal information ever thought that the special role of experience in teaching what it's like was on a par

with the special role of Russian! I will have to say before I'm done that phenomenal information is an illusion, but I think I must look elsewhere for a credible hypothesis about what sort of illusion it might be.

The Fourth Way If a hidden camera takes photographs of a room, the film ends up bearing traces of what went on in the room. The traces are distinctive: that is, the details of the traces depend on the details of what went on, and if what went on had been different in any of many ways, the traces would have been correspondingly different. So we can say that the traces bear information, and that he who has the film has the information. That might be said because the traces, plus the way they depend on what went on, suffice to eliminate possibilities; but instead we might say "information" and just mean "distinctive traces." If so, it's certainly true that new experience imparts "information" unlike any that can be gained from lessons. Experience and lessons leave different kinds of traces. That is so whether or not the experience eliminates possibilities that the lessons leave open. It is equally true, of course, that lessons in Russian leave traces unlike any that are left by lessons in English, regardless of whether the lessons cover the same ground and eliminate the same possibilities.

The Fifth Way When we speak of transmission of "information," we often mean transmission of text. Repositories of "information," such as libraries, are storehouses of text. Whether the text is empty verbiage or highly informative is beside the point. Maybe we too contain information by being storehouses of text. Maybe there is a language of thought, and maybe the way we believe things is to store sentences of this language in some special way, or in some special part of our brains. In that case, we could say that storing away a new sentence was storing away a new piece of "information," whether or not that new piece eliminated any possibilities not already eliminated by the sentences stored previously.

Maybe, also, the language of thought is not fixed once and for all, but can gain new words. Maybe, for instance, it borrows words from public language. And maybe, when one has a new experience, that causes one's language of thought to gain a new word which denotes that experience— a word which could not have been added to the language by any other means. If all this is so, then when Mary sees colors, her language of thought gains new words, allowing her to store away new sentences and thereby gain "information." All this about the language of thought, the storing of sentences, and the gaining of words is speculation. But it is plausible speculation, even if no longer the only game in town. If it is all true, then we have another look-alike hypothesis of phenomenal "information." When Mary gains new words and stores new sentences, that is "information" that she never had before, regardless of whether it eliminates any possibilities that she had not eliminated already.

But again, the special role of experience turns out to be on a par with the special role of Russian. If the language of thought picks up new words by borrowing from public language, then lessons in Russian add new words, and result in the storing of new sentences, and thereby impart "information" that never could have been had from lessons in English. (You might say that the new Russian words are mere synonyms of old words, or at least old phrases, that were there already; and synonyms don't count. But no reason has been given why the new inner words created by experience may not also be synonyms of old phrases, perhaps of long descriptions in the language of neurophysiology.)

The Sixth Way   A philosopher who is skeptical about possibility, as so many are, may wish to replace possibilities themselves with linguistic ersatz possibilities: maximal consistent sets of sentences. And he may be content to take "consistent" in a narrowly logical sense, so that a set with "Fred is married" and "Fred is a bachelor" may count as consistent, and only an overt con-

tradiction like "Fred is married" and "Fred is not married" will be ruled out.[10] The ersatz possibilities might also be taken as sets of sentences of the language of thought, if the philosopher believes in it. Then if someone's language of thought gains new words, whether as a result of new experience or as a result of being taught in Russian, the ersatz possibilities become richer and more numerous. The sets of sentences that were maximal before are no longer maximal after new words are added. So when Mary sees colors and her language of thought gains new words, there are new ersatz possibilities; and she can straightway eliminate some of them. Suppose she knows beforehand that she is about to see green, and that the experience of seeing green is associated with neural firing pattern F. So when she sees green and gains the new word G for her experience, then straightway there are new, enriched ersatz possibilities with sentences saying that she has G without F, and straightway she knows enough to eliminate these ersatz possibilities. (Even if she does not know beforehand what she is about to see, straightway she can eliminate at least those of her new-found ersatz possibilities with sentences denying that she then has G.) Just as we can characterize information in terms of elimination of possibilities, so we can characterize ersatz "information" in terms of elimination of ersatz "possibilities." So here we have the closest look-alike hypothesis of all, provided that language-of-thoughtism is true. But we still do not have the genuine Hypothesis of Phenomenal Information, since the eliminated ersatz possibility of G without F may not have been a genuine possibility at all. It may have been like the ersatz possibility of married bachelors.

Curiouser and Curiouser

The Hypothesis of Phenomenal Information is more peculiar than it may at first seem. For one thing, because it is opposed to more than just Materialism. Some of you may have welcomed the Knowledge Argument because you thought all along that physical information was inadequate to explain the phenomena of mind. You may have been convinced all along that the mind could do things that no physical system could do: bend spoons, invent new jokes, demonstrate the consistency of arithmetic, reduce the wave packet, or what have you. You may have been convinced that the full causal story of how the deeds of mind are accomplished involves the causal interactions not only of material bodies but also of astral bodies; not only the vibrations of the electromagnetic field but also the good or bad vibes of the psionic field; not only protoplasm but ectoplasm. I doubt it, but never mind. It's irrelevant to our topic. The Knowledge Argument is targeted against you no less than it is against Materialism itself.

Let *parapsychology* be the science of all the non-physical things, properties, causal processes, laws of nature, and so forth that may be required to explain the things we do. Let us suppose that we learn ever so much parapsychology. It will make no difference. Black-and-white Mary may study all the parapsychology as well as all the psychophysics of color vision, but she still won't know what it's like. Lessons on the aura of Vegemite will do no more for us than lessons on its chemical composition. And so it goes. Our intuitive starting point wasn't just that *physics* lessons couldn't help the inexperienced to know what it's like. It was that *lessons* couldn't help. If there is such a thing as phenomenal information, it isn't just independent of physical information. It's independent of every sort of information that could be served up in lessons for the inexperienced. For it is supposed to eliminate possibilities that any amount of lessons leave open. Therefore phenomenal information is not just parapsychological information, if such there be. It's something very much stranger.

The genuine Hypothesis of Phenomenal Information, as distinguished from its look-alikes, treats information in terms of the elimination of possibilities. When we lack information, several alternative possibilities are open, when we get the information some of the alternatives are excluded. But a second peculiar thing about phenomenal information is that it resists this treatment. (So does logical or mathematical "information." However, phenomenal information cannot be logical or mathematical, because lessons in logic and mathematics no more teach us what a new experience is like than lessons in physics or parapsychology do.) When someone doesn't know what it's like to have an experience, where are the alternative open possibilities? I cannot present to myself in thought a range of alternative possibilities about what it might be like to taste Vegemite. That is because I cannot imagine either what it *is* like to taste Vegemite, or any alternative way that it *might* be like but in fact isn't. (I could perfectly well imagine that Vegemite tastes just like peanut butter, or something else familiar to me, but let's suppose I've been told authoritatively that this isn't so.) I can't even pose the question that phenomenal information is supposed to answer: is it this way or that? It seems that the alternative possibilities must be unthinkable beforehand; and afterward too, except for the one that turns out to be actualized. I don't say there's anything altogether impossible about a range of unthinkable alternatives; only something peculiar. But it's peculiar enough to suggest that we may somehow have gone astray.

From Phenomenal to Epiphenomenal

A third peculiar thing about phenomenal information is that it is strangely isolated from all other sorts of information; and this is so regardless of whether the mind works on physical or parapsychological principles. The phenomenal aspect of the world has nothing to do with explaining why people seemingly talk about the phenomenal aspect of the world. For instance, it plays no part in explaining the movements of the pens of philosophers writing treatises about phenomenal information and the way experience has provided them with it.

When Mary gets out of her black-and-white cell, her jaw drops. She says "At last! So this is what it's like to see colors!" Afterward she does things she couldn't do before, such as recognizing a new sample of the first color she ever saw. She may also do other things she didn't do before: unfortunate things, like writing about phenomenal information and the poverty of Materialism. One might think she said what she said and did what she did because she came to know what it's like to see colors. Not so, if the Hypothesis of Phenomenal Information is right. For suppose the phenomenal aspect of the world had been otherwise, so that she gained different phenomenal information. Or suppose the phenomenal aspect of the world had been absent altogether, as we materialists think it is. Would that have made the slightest difference to what she did or said then or later? I think not. Making a difference to what she does or says means, at least in part, making a difference to the motions of the particles of which she is composed. (Or better: making a difference to the spatiotemporal shape of the wave-function of those particles. But let that pass.) For how could she do or say anything different, if none of her particles moved any differently? But if something non-physical sometimes makes a difference to the motions of physical particles, then physics as we know it is wrong. Not just silent, not just incomplete—wrong. Either the particles are caused to change their motion without benefit of any force, or else there is some extra force that works very differently from the usual four. To believe in the phenomenal aspect of the world, but deny that it is epiphenomenal, is to bet against the truth of physics. Given the success of physics hitherto, and even with due allowance for the foundational ailments of quantum mechanics, such betting is rash! A friend of the phenomenal aspect would be safer to join Jackson in defense of *epiphenomenal* qualia.

But there is more to the case than just an empirical bet in favor of physics. Suppose there is a phenomenal aspect of the world, and suppose it does make some difference to the motions of Mary's jaw or the noises out of her mouth. Then we can describe the phenomenal aspect, if we know enough, in terms of its physical effects. It is that on which physical phenomena depend in such-and-such way. This descriptive handle will enable us to give lessons on it to the inexperienced. But insofar as we can give lessons on it, what we have is just parapsychology. That whereof we cannot learn except by having the experience still eludes us. I do not argue that *everything* about the alleged distinctive subject matter of phenomenal information must be epiphenomenal. Part of it may be parapsychological instead. But I insist that *some* aspect of it must be epiphenomenal.

Suppose that the Hypothesis of Phenomenal Information is true and suppose that V_1 and V_2 are all of the maximally specific phenomenal possibilities concerning what it's like to taste Vegemite; anyone who tastes Vegemite will find out which one obtains, and no one else can. And suppose that P_1 and P_2 are all the maximally specific physical possibilities. (Of course we really need far more than two Ps, and maybe a friend of phenomenal information would want more than two Vs, but absurdly small numbers will do for an example.) Then we have four alternative hypotheses about the causal independence or dependence of the Ps on the Vs. Each one can be expressed as a pair of counterfactual conditionals. Two hypotheses are patterns of dependence.

K_1: if V_1 then P_1, if V_2 then P_2

K_2: if V_1 then P_2, if V_2 then P_1

The other two are patterns of independence.

K_3: if V_1 then P_1, if V_2 then P_1

K_4: if V_1 then P_2, if V_2 then P_2

These dependency hypotheses are, I take it, contingent propositions. They are made true, if they are, by some contingent feature of the world, though it's indeed a vexed question what sort of feature it is.[11] Now we have eight joint possibilities.

$$K_1V_1P_1 \qquad K_3V_1P_1 \qquad K_3V_2P_1 \qquad K_2V_2P_1$$

$$K_2V_1P_2 \qquad K_4V_1P_2 \qquad K_4V_2P_2 \qquad K_1V_2P_2$$

Between the four on the top row and the four on the bottom row, there is the physical difference between P_1 and P_2. Between the four on the left and the four on the right, there is the phenomenal difference between V_1 and V_2. And between the four on the edges and the four in the middle there is a parapsychological difference. It is the difference between dependence and independence of the physical on the phenomenal; between efficacy and epiphenomenalism, so far as this one example is concerned. There's nothing ineffable about that. Whether or not you've tasted Vegemite, and whether or not you can conceive of the alleged difference between V_1 and V_2, you can still be told whether the physical difference between P_1 and P_2 does or doesn't depend on some part of the phenomenal aspect of the world.

Lessons can teach the inexperienced which parapsychological possibility obtains, dependence or independence. Let it be dependence: we have either K_1 or K_2. For if we had independence, then already we would have found our epiphenomenal difference: namely, the difference between V_1 and V_2. And lessons can teach the inexperienced which of the two physical possibilities obtains. Without loss of generality let it be P_1. Now two of our original eight joint possibilities remain open: $K_1V_1P_1$ and $K_2V_2P_1$. The difference between those is not at all physical, and not at all parapsychological: it's P_1, and it's dependence, in both cases. The difference is entirely phenomenal. And also it is entirely epiphenomenal. Nothing physical, and nothing parapsychological, depends on the difference between $K_1V_1P_1$ and $K_2V_2P_1$. We have the same sort of pattern of dependence either way; it's just that the phenomenal pos-

sibilities have been swapped. Whether it's independence or whether it's dependence, therefore, we have found an epiphenomenal part of the phenomenal aspect of the world. It is the residue left behind when we remove the parapsychological part.

Suppose that someday I taste Vegemite, and hold forth about how I know at last what it's like. The sound of my holding forth is a physical effect, part of the realized physical possibility P_1. This physical effect is exactly the same whether it's part of the joint possibility $K_1V_1P_1$ or part of its alternative $K_2V_2P_1$. It may be caused by V_1 in accordance with K_1, or it may instead be caused by V_2 in accordance with K_2, but it's the same either way. So it does not occur because we have K_1V_1 rather than K_2V_2, or vice versa. The alleged difference between these two possibilities does nothing to explain the alleged physical manifestation of my finding out which one of them is realized. It is in that way that the difference is epiphenomenal. That makes it very queer, and repugnant to good sense.

The Ability Hypothesis

So the Hypothesis of Phenomenal Information turns out to be very peculiar indeed. It would be nice, and not only for materialists, if we could reject it. For materialists, it is essential to reject it. And we can. There is an alternative hypothesis about what it is to learn what an experience is like: the *Ability Hypothesis*. Laurence Nemirow summarizes it thus:

some modes of understanding consist, not in the grasping of facts, but in the acquisition of abilities.... As for understanding an experience, we may construe that as an ability to place oneself, at will, in a state representative of the experience. I understand the experience of seeing red if I can at will visualize red. Now it is perfectly clear why there must be a special connection between the ability to place oneself in a state representative of a given experience and the point of view of experiencer: exercising the ability just *is* what we call "adopting the point of view of experiencer." . . . We can, then, come to terms with the subjectivity of our understanding of experience without positing subjective facts as the objects of our understanding. This account explains, incidentally, the linguistic incommunicability of our subjective understanding of experience (a phenomenon which might seem to support the hypothesis of subjective facts). The latter is explained as a special case of the linguistic incommunicability of abilities to place oneself at will in a given state, such as the state of having lowered blood pressure, and the state of having wiggling ears.[12]

If you have a new experience, you gain abilities to remember and to imagine. After you taste Vegemite, and you learn what it's like, you can afterward remember the experience you had. By remembering how it once was, you can afterward imagine such an experience. Indeed, even if you eventually forget the occasion itself, you will very likely retain your ability to imagine such an experience.

Further, you gain an ability to recognize the same experience if it comes again. If you taste Vegemite on another day, you will probably know that you have met the taste once before. And if, while tasting Vegemite, you know that it is Vegemite you are tasting, then you will be able to put the name to the experience if you have it again. Or if you are told nothing at the time, but later you somehow know that it is Vegemite that you are then remembering or imagining tasting, again you can put the name to the experience, or to the memory, or to the experience of imagining, if it comes again. Here, the ability you gain is an ability to gain information if given other information. Nevertheless, the information gained is not phenomenal, and the ability to gain information is not the same thing as information itself.

Earlier, I mentioned "knowing what an experience is like under a description." Now I can say that what I meant by this was having the ability to remember or imagine an experience while also knowing the egocentric proposition that what one is then imagining is the experience of such-and-such description. One might well know what an experience is like under one description, but not under another. One might even know what some experience is like, but not under any description whatever—unless it be some rather trivial description like "that queer taste that I'm imagining right now." That is what would happen if you slipped a dab of Vegemite into my food without telling me what it was: afterward, I would know what it was like to taste Vegemite, but not under that description, and not under any other nontrivial description. It might be suggested that "knowing what it's like to taste Vegemite" really means what I'd call " knowing what it's like to taste Vegemite under the description 'tasting Vegemite'"; and if so, knowing what it's like would involve both ability and information. I disagree. For surely it would make sense to say: "I know this experience well, I've long known what it's like, but only today have I found out that it's the experience of tasting Vegemite." But this verbal question is unimportant. For the information involved in knowing what it's like under a description, and allegedly involved in knowing what it's like, is anyhow not the queer phenomenal information that needs rejecting.

(Is there a problem here for the friend of phenomenal information? Suppose he says that knowing what it's like to taste Vegemite means knowing that the taste of Vegemite has a certain "phenomenal character." This requires putting the name to the taste, so clearly it corresponds to our notion of knowing what it's like to taste Vegemite under the description "tasting Vegemite." But we also have our notion of knowing what it's like *simpliciter*, and what can he offer that corresponds to that? Perhaps he should answer by appeal to a trivial description, as follows: knowing what it's like *simpliciter* means knowing what it's like under the trivial description "taste I'm imagining now," and that means knowing that the taste one is imagining now has a certain phenomenal character.)

As well as gaining the ability to remember and imagine the experience you had, you also gain the ability to imagine related experiences that you never had. After tasting Vegemite, you might for instance become able to imagine tasting Vegemite ice cream. By performing imaginative experiments, you can predict with some confidence what you would do in circumstances that have never arisen—whether you'd ask for a second helping of Vegemite ice cream, for example.

These abilities to remember and imagine and recognize are abilities you cannot gain (unless by super-neurosurgery, or by magic) except by tasting Vegemite and learning what it's like. You can't get them by taking lessons on the physics or the parapsychology of the experience, or even by taking comprehensive lessons that cover the whole of physics and parapsychology. The Ability Hypothesis says that knowing what an experience is like just *is* the possession of these abilities to remember, imagine, and recognize. It isn't the possession of any kind of information, ordinary or peculiar. It isn't knowing that certain possibilities aren't actualized. It isn't knowing-that. It's knowing-how. Therefore it should be no surprise that lessons won't teach you what an experience is like. Lessons impart information; ability is something else. Knowledge-that does not automatically provide know-how.

There are parallel cases. Some know how to wiggle their ears; others don't. If you can't do it, no amount of information will help. Some know how to eat with chopsticks, others don't. Information will help up to a point—for instance, if your trouble is that you hold one chopstick in each hand—but no amount of information, by itself, will bring you to a very high level of know-how. Some know how to recognize a C-38 locomotive by sight, others don't. If you don't, it won't much help if you memorize a detailed geometrical description of its shape, even though that does all the eliminating of possibilities that there is to be done. (Conversely, knowing the shape by sight doesn't enable you to write down the geometrical description.) Information very often

contributes to know-how, but often it doesn't contribute enough. That's why music students have to practice.

Know-how is ability. But of course some aspects of ability are in no sense knowledge: strength, sufficient funds. Other aspects of ability are, purely and simply, a matter of information. If you want to know how to open the combination lock on the bank vault, information is all you need. It remains that there are aspects of ability that do *not* consist simply of possession of information, and that we *do* call knowledge. The Ability Hypothesis holds that knowing what an experience is like is that sort of knowledge.

If the Ability Hypothesis is the correct analysis of knowing what an experience is like, then phenomenal information is an illusion. We ought to explain that illusion. It would be feeble, I think, just to say that we're fooled by the ambiguity of the word "know": we confuse ability with information because we confuse knowledge in the sense of knowing-how with knowledge in the sense of knowing-that. There may be two senses of the word "know," but they are well and truly entangled. They mark the two pure endpoints of a range of mixed cases. The usual thing is that we gain information and ability together. If so, it should be no surprise if we apply to pure cases of gaining ability, or to pure cases of gaining information, the same word "know" that we apply to all the mixed cases.

Along with information and ability, acquaintance is a third element of the mixture. If Lloyd George died too soon, there's a sense in which Father never can know him. Information won't do it, even if Father is a most thorough biographer and the archives are very complete. (And the trouble isn't that there's some very special information about someone that you can only get by being in his presence.) Know-how won't do it either, no matter how good Father may be at imagining Lloyd George, seemingly remembering him, and recognizing him. (Father may be able to recognize Lloyd George even if there's no longer any Lloyd George to recognize—if *per impossibile* he did turn up, Father could tell it was him.) Again, what we have is not just a third separate sense of "know." Meeting someone, gaining a lot of information about him that would be hard to gain otherwise, and gaining abilities regarding him usually go together. The pure cases are exceptions.

A friend of phenomenal information will agree, of course, that when we learn what an experience is like, we gain abilities to remember, imagine, and recognize. But he will say that it is because we gain phenomenal information that we gain the abilities. He might even say the same about other cases of gaining know-how: you can recognize the C-38 when you have phenomenal information about what it's like to see that shape, you can eat with chopsticks or wiggle your ears when you gain phenomenal information about the experience of doing so, and so on. What should friends of the Ability Hypothesis make of this? Is he offering a conjecture, which we must reject, about the causal origin of abilities? I think not. He thinks, as we do, that experiences leave distinctive traces in people, and that these traces enable us to do things. Likewise being taught to recognize a C-38 or to eat with chopsticks, or whatever happens on first wiggling the ears, leave traces that enable us to do things afterward. That much is common ground. He also interprets these enabling traces as representations that bear information about their causes. (If the same traces had been caused in some deviant way they might perhaps have carried misinformation.) We might even be able to accept that too. The time for us to quarrel comes only when he says that these traces represent special phenomenal facts, facts which cannot be represented in any other way, and therefore which cannot be taught in physics lessons or even in parapsychology lessons. That is the part, and the *only* part, which we must reject. But that is no part of his psychological story about how we gain abilities. It is just a gratuitous metaphysical gloss on that story.

We say that learning what an experience is like means gaining certain abilities. If the causal basis for those abilities turns out also to be a special kind of representation of some sort of information, so be it. We need only deny that it represents a special kind of information about a special subject matter. Apart from that it's up for grabs what, if anything, it may represent. The details of stimuli: the chemical composition of Vegemite, reflectances of surfaces, the motions of well-handled chopsticks or of ears? The details of inner states produced by those stimuli: patterns of firings of nerves? We could agree to either, so long as we did not confuse 'having information' represented in this special way with having the same information in the form of knowledge or belief. Or we could disagree. Treating the ability-conferring trace as a representation is optional. What's essential is that when we learn what an experience is like by having it, we gain abilities to remember, imagine, and recognize.

Acknowledgment

Part of this paper derives from a lecture at La-Trobe University in 1981. I thank LaTrobe for support in 1981, Harvard University for support under a Santayana Fellowship in 1988, and Frank Jackson for very helpful discussion.

Notes

This chapter was collected in *Proceedings of the Russellian Society*, University of Sydney, 1988.

1. See Frank Jackson, "Epiphenomenal qualia," *Philosophical Quarterly* 32 (1982), pp. 127–36; "What Mary didn't know," chapter 36.

2. See B. A. Farrell, "Experience," *Mind* 59 (1950), pp. 170–98; and Thomas Nagel, "What is it like to be a bat?" chapter 32.

3. See Peter Unger, "On experience and the development of the understanding," *American Philosophical Quarterly* 3 (1966), pp. 1–9.

4. For such speculation, see Paul M. Churchland, "Reduction, qualia, and the direct introspection of brain states," *Journal of Philosophy* 82 (1985), pp. 8–28.

5. See my "Attitudes *de dido* and *de se*," *Philosophical Review* 88 (1979), pp. 513–43, also in my *Philosophical Papers*, vol. I (New York: Oxford University Press, 1983); and Roderick Chisholm, *The First Person: An Essay on Reference and Intentionality* (Minneapolis: University of Minnesota Press, 1981).

6. See Gilbert Harman, "The intrinsic quality of experience," chapter 43.

7. See Ned Block and Jerry A. Fodor, "What psychological states are not," *Philosophical Review* 81 (1972), pp. 159–81, also in Ned Block (ed.), *Readings in Philosophy of Psychology*, vol. I (Cambridge, MA: Harvard University Press, 1980); and my "Mad Pain and Martian Pain", in *Readings in Philosophy of Psychology*, vol. I, and in my *Philosophical Papers*, vol. I.

8. See my "New work for a theory of universals," *Australasian Journal of Philosophy* 61 (1983), pp. 343–77, especially pp. 361–4. For a different view about how to state minimal Materialism, see Terence Horgan, "Supervenience and microphysics," *Pacific Philosophical Quarterly* 63 (1982), pp. 29–43.

9. On recombination of possibilities, see my *On the Plurality of Worlds* (Oxford: Blackwell, 1986), pp. 87–92. The present argument may call for a principle that also allows recombination of properties; I now think that would not necessarily require treating properties as non-spatiotemporal parts of their instances. On recombination of properties, see also D. M. Armstrong, *A Combinatorial Theory of Possibility* (Cambridge: Cambridge University Press 1989).

10. See *On the Plurality of Worlds*, pp. 142–65, on linguistic ersatz possibilities.

11. On dependency hypotheses, see my "Causal decision theory," *Australasian Journal of Philosophy* 59 (1981), pp. 5–30, reprinted in my *Philosophical Papers*, vol. II (New York: Oxford University Press, 1986).

12. Laurence Nemirow, review of Nagel's *Mortal Questions*, *Philosophical Review* 89 (1980), pp. 475–6. For a fuller statement, see Nemirow, "Physicalism and the cognitive role of acquaintance," in W. G. Lycan (ed.), *Mind and Cognition: A Reader* (Oxford: Basil Blackwell, 1989) and *Functionalism and the Subjective Quality of Experience* (doctoral dissertation, Stanford, 1979). See also Michael Tye, "The subjective qualities of experience," *Mind* 95 (1986), pp. 1–17.

I should record a disagreement with Nemirow on one very small point. We agree that the phrase "what experience E is like" does not denote some "subjective quality" of E, something which supposedly would be part of the subject matter of the phenomenal information gained by having E. But whereas I have taken the phrase to denote E itself, Nemirow takes it to be a syncategorematic part of the expression "know what experience E is like." See "Physicalism and the cognitive role of acquaintance", section III.

39 Phenomenal States

Brian Loar

On a natural view of ourselves, we introspectively discriminate our own experiences and thereby form conceptions of their qualities, both salient and subtle. These discriminations are of various degrees of generality, from small differences in tactual and color experience to broad differences of sensory modality, for example, those among smell, hearing, and pain. What we apparently discern are ways experiences differ and resemble each other with respect to *what it is like to have them*. Following common usage, I will call these experiential resemblances *phenomenal qualities*, and the conceptions we have of them, *phenomenal concepts*. Phenomenal concepts are formed "from one's own case." They are *type-demonstratives* that derive their reference from a first-person perspective: 'that type of sensation', 'that feature of visual experience'. And so third-person ascriptions of phenomenal qualities are projective ascriptions of what one has grasped in one's own case: 'she has an experience of that type.'

'Phenomenal quality' can have a different sense, namely, how the *object* of a perceptual experience appears. In this sense, a phenomenal quality is ascribed to an object and not directly to an experience. Some have argued that all we discern phenomenologically are phenomenal qualities in this sense; they deny that experiences themselves have introspectible qualities that are not ascribed primarily to their objects (Harman 1990; Block 1990). I will not pursue the issue here, but will assume a certain view of it. For the present objective is to engage antiphysicalist arguments and entrenched intuitions to the effect that conscious mental qualities cannot be identical with ordinary physical properties, or at least that it is problematic to suppose that they are so. Antiphysicalists typically suppose that such mental properties are not relational—that is, that they present themselves as not intrinsically involving relations to things outside the mind. They may allow that, say, visual experiences are in some sense intrinsically representational. That is hard to deny because, as regards ordinary visual experiences, we cannot apparently conceive them phenomenally in a way that abstracts from their *purporting* to represent things in a certain way. The antiphysicalist intuition is compatible with visual experiences' having (some sort of) internally determined intentional structure, so that it is an introspectable and nonrelational feature of a visual experience that it represents things visually as being thus and so. Antiphysicalists suppose that we have conceptions of how visual experiences differ and resemble each other with respect to what it is like to have those experiences. These conceptions then are of qualities of experiences, whatever allowances one may also make for the apparent qualities of the intrinsic objects of those experiences. I will assume that the antiphysicalists' phenomenological and internalist intuitions are correct. The idea is to engage them over the central point, that is, whether those aspects of the mental that we both count as phenomenologically compelling raise substantive difficulties for the thesis that phenomenal qualities (thus understood) are physical properties of the brain that lie within the scope of current science.

We have to distinguish between *concepts* and *properties*, and this chapter turns on that distinction. Antiphysicalist arguments and intuitions take off from a sound intuition about concepts. Phenomenal concepts are conceptually irreducible in this sense: they neither a priori imply, nor are implied by, physical-functional concepts. Although that is denied by analytical functionalists (Levin 1983, 1986), many other physicalists, including me, find it intuitively appealing. The antiphysicalist takes this conceptual intuition a good deal further, to the conclusion that phenomenal qualities are themselves irreducible, are not physical-functional properties, at least not of the ordinary sort. The upshot is a range of anti-reductionist views: that consciousness and phenomenal qualities are unreal because irreducible;[1] that they are irreducibly non–physical-functional facts;[2] that they are forever mysterious, or pose an intellectual problem different from other empirical problems, or require new conceptions of the physical.[3]

It is my view that we can have it both ways. We may take the phenomenological intuition at face value, accepting introspective concepts and their conceptual irreducibility, and at the same time take phenomenal qualities to be identical with physical-functional properties of the sort envisaged by contemporary brain science. As I see it, there is no persuasive philosophically articulated argument to the contrary.

This is not to deny the power of raw metaphysical intuition. Thoughtful people compare phenomenal qualities and kinds of physical-functional property, say the activation of neural assemblies. It appears to them to be an evident and unmediated truth, independent of further premises, that phenomenal qualities cannot be identical with properties of those types or perhaps of any physical-functional type. This intuition is so compelling that it is tempting to regard antiphysicalist arguments as rationalizations of an intuition whose independent force masks their tendentiousness. It is the point of this chapter to consider the arguments. But I will also present a positive account of the relation between phenomenal concepts and physical properties that may provide some relief, or at least some distance, from the illusory metaphysical intuition.

In recent years the central problem with physicalism has been thought by many to be "the explanatory gap." This is the idea that we cannot *explain*, in terms of physical-functional properties, what makes a certain experience 'feel like this', in the way we can explain what makes a certain substance a liquid, say. It is concluded that physicalism is defective in some respect, that there cannot be a (proper) reduction of the mental to the physical. Before we consider this explanatory gap, we must first examine, in some detail, a more basic antiphysicalist line of reasoning that goes back to Leibniz and beyond, a leading version of which is now called the knowledge argument. Answering this argument will generate a framework in which to address antiphysicalist concerns in general.

1 The Knowledge Argument and Its Semantic Premise

The knowledge argument is straightforward on the face of it. Consider any phenomenal quality and any physical property however complex. We can know that a person has the physical property without knowing that she experiences the phenomenal quality. And no amount of a priori reasoning or construction can bridge this conceptual gap. That is the intuitive premise. The conclusion is drawn that the phenomenal quality cannot be identical with the physical property. The argument is equivalent to this: since physical and phenomenal conceptions can be connected only a posteriori, physical properties must be distinct from phenomenal properties.

The best known and liveliest version of the knowledge argument is Frank Jackson's, which features the physiologically omniscient Mary, who has never seen color and so does not know what it is like for us to see red, despite her knowing all the physical-functional facts about us.[4] She later sees colors, and thus learns what it has been like all along for us to see red. She learns a new fact about us. Jackson concludes that this fact is not among the physical facts, since Mary already knew them. It is not difficult to see that this argument depends on a more or less technical premise.

In my view, the physicalist should accept Jackson's intuitive description of Mary: she fails to know that we have certain color experiences even though she knows all relevant physical facts about us. And when she acquires color experience, she does learn something new about us—if you like, learns a new fact or truth. But this is to be granted, of course, only on an *opaque* reading of 'Mary learns that we have such and such color experiences', and on corresponding readings of 'learns a new fact or truth about us'. For as regards the transparent versions of those ascriptions of what Mary did not know and then learned, they would beg the question, amounting to this: 'as for the property of having such and such color experiences, Mary did not know, but then learned, *of* that property that we have it'. Physicalists reject this, for according to us those experiential properties are physical properties, and Mary already knew of all our physical properties that we have them—under their physical descriptions. What she lacked and then acquired, rather, was knowledge of certain such properties couched in experiential terms.

Drawing metaphysical conclusions from opaque contexts is risky. And in fact inferences of Jackson's form, without additional premises, are open to straightforward counterexamples of a familiar sort. Let me describe two cases.

(1) Max learns that the bottle before him contains CH_3CH_2OH. But he does not know that the bottle contains alcohol. This holds on an opaque reading: he would not assert that there's stuff called alcohol in the bottle, or that the bottle contains the intoxicating component of beer and wine. Let sheltered Max even lack the ordinary concept 'alcohol'. After he acquires that ordinary concept, he learns something new—that the bottle contained alcohol. If the knowledge argument has a generally valid form, we could then infer from Max's epistemic situation that alcohol is not identical with CH_3CH_2OH. Evidently this does not follow.

(2) Margot learns about the element Au and reads that people decorate themselves with alloys of Au. But she has never seen gold and cannot visually identify it: she lacks an adequate visual conception. She later is shown some gold and forms a visual conception of it, "that stuff," and she acquires a new piece of information—individuated opaquely—to the effect that those previously read about embellishments are made of that stuff. Again, if the knowledge argument were unrestrictedly valid, it would follow that that stuff is not identical with Au. This case differs from the case of Max by involving not a descriptive mode of presentation but (as we might say) a perceptual mode of presentation.

It is not difficult to find a difference between both these cases and the case of Mary. Max lacks knowledge of the bottle's contents under a contingent description of it—"ingredient of wine and beer that makes you intoxicated." What Margot lacks is a certain visual conception of Au, which is to say gold. This typically would not be a descriptive conception; it would not self-consciously take the form "the stuff that occasions this type of visual experience." Still on the face of it such a concept implicates a visual-experience type. For it picks out the kind it picks out by virtue of that kind's occasioning experiences of that type. And that is a crucial *contingency* in how the concept that Margot lacks is related to its reference. I hope I will be understood, then, if I say that the visual take on Au that Margot lacks would have conceived Au 'under a contingent mode of presentation'.

This brings us back to Mary, whose acquired conception of what it is like to see red does not conceive it under a contingent mode of presentation. She is not conceiving of a property that presents itself *contingently* thus: it is like such and such to experience P. Being experienced like that is essential to the property Mary conceives. She conceives it directly. When Mary later acquires new information about us (construed opaquely), the novelty of this information cannot be explained—as in the case of Margot—as her acquiring a new contingent mode of presentation of something she has otherwise known of all along. She has a *direct* grasp of the property involved in the new information; she conceives of it somehow, but not under a contingent mode of presentation. Proponents of the knowledge argument will say that is why it is valid on an opaque reading: there is no contingency in Mary's conception of the new phenomenal information that explains it as a novel take on old facts. She learns new facts simpliciter and not new conceptions of old facts.

Notice how close this comes to Saul Kripke's well-known antiphysicalist argument (1980).

Kripke assumes that a phenomenal concept such as 'pain' cannot be a priori linked with a physical concept such as that of the stimulation of C-fibers. The case of Mary is a vivid way of making the same point. Kripke points out that property identities can be true even if not a priori, for example, 'heat = such and such molecular property'. It seems fair to represent the next step in his argument as follows. 'Heat' has a contingent higher-order mode of presentation that connotes the property 'feeling like this'. That is what accounts for the a posteriori status of the identity. But, as Kripke points out, this cannot be how 'pain' works: the phenomenal concept 'pain' does not pick out its referent via a contingent mode of presentation; it conceives pain directly and essentially. Kripke concludes that pain is not identical with a physical property.

The two arguments then turn on the same implicit assumption. The only way to account for the a posteriori status of a true property identity is this: one of the terms expresses a contingent mode of presentation. This ought to be given a place of prominence.

(Semantic premise) A statement of property identity that links conceptually independent concepts is true only if at least one concept picks out the property it refers to by connoting a contingent property of that property.

The knowledge argument and Kripke's argument then depend on two assumptions: the conceptual independence of phenomenal concepts and physical-functional concepts, which I accept, and the semantic premise, which I deny.

The antiphysicalist intuition that links concept-individuation and property-individuation (more closely than is in my view correct) is perhaps this. Phenomenal concepts and theoretical expressions of physical properties both conceive their references essentially. But if two concepts conceive a given property essentially, neither mediated by contingent modes of presentation, one ought to be able to see a priori—at least after optimal re-flection—that they pick out the same property. Such concepts' connections cannot be a posteriori; that they pick out the same property would have to be transparent.

But as against this, if a phenomenal concept can pick out a physical property directly or essentially, not via a contingent mode of presentation, and yet be *conceptually independent* of all physical-functional concepts, so that Mary's history is coherent, then Jackson's and Kripke's arguments are ineffectual. We could have two conceptually independent conceptions of a property, neither of which connote contingent modes of presentation, such that substituting one for the other in an opaquely interpreted epistemic context does not preserve truth. Even granting that our conception of phenomenal qualities is direct, physicalism would not entail that knowing the physical-functional facts implies knowing, on an opaque construal, the phenomenal facts; and so the failure of this implication would be quite compatible with physicalism. The next few sections give an account of phenomenal concepts and properties that would justify this claim.

2 Recognitional Concepts

Phenomenal concepts belong to a wide class of concepts that I will call recognitional concepts. They have the form 'x is one of *that* kind'; they are type-demonstratives. These type-demonstratives are grounded in dispositions to classify, by way of perceptual discriminations, certain objects, events, situations. Suppose you go into the California desert and spot a succulent never seen before. You become adept at recognizing instances, and gain a recognitional command of their kind, without a name for it; you are disposed to identify positive and negative instances and thereby pick out a kind. These dispositions are typically linked with capacities to form images, whose conceptual role seems to be to focus thoughts about an identifiable kind in the absence of currently perceived instances. An image is presumably 'of' a given kind by virtue of both past recognitions and current dispositions.

Recognitional concepts are generally formed against a further conceptual background. In identifying a thing as of a recognized kind, we almost always presuppose a more general type to which the kind belongs: four-legged animal, plant, physical thing, perceptible event. A recognitional concept will then have the form 'physical thing of that (perceived) kind' or 'internal state of that kind', and so forth.[5]

Here are some basic features of recognitional concepts that it will help to have in mind in connection with the account of phenomenal concepts that follows.

1. You can understand 'porcelain' from a technical description and only later learn visually, tactually, and aurally to recognize instances. By contrast, in the phenomenon I mean the concept is recognitional at its core; the original concept is recognitional.

2. A recognitional concept need involve no reference to a past instance, or have the form 'is of the same type as that (remembered) one'. You can forget particular instances and still judge 'another one of those'.

3. Recognitional abilities depend on no consciously accessible analysis into component features; they can be irreducibly gestalt.

4. Recognitional concepts are perspectival. Suppose you see certain creatures up close and form a recognitional concept—'those creatures$_1$'; and suppose you see others at a distance, not being able to tell that they are of the same kind (even when they are), and form another recognitional concept—'those creatures$_2$'. These concepts will be a priori independent. Now the respect in which they differ is *perspectival*, in some intuitive sense. A recognitional concept is in part individuated by its constitutive perspective. Here is the important point: a recognitional concept can be ascribed outside its constitutive perspective; 'that thing (seen at distance) is one of those creatures$_1$ (seen up close)' makes perfectly good sense. This plays a key role below in the account of third-person ascriptions of phenomenal concepts.

(This casual invoking of reference-determining dispositions will be a red flag for many who are aware of the vexing foundations of the theory of reference. Problems about referential scrutability, rule-following, naturalizing intentionality—however one wishes to put it—are as frustrating as any in contemporary philosophy. I do not propose to address them here. The idea rather is to appeal to unanalyzed common sense concerning a natural group of concepts and apparent conceptual abilities. The apparent irreducibility of phenomenal qualities itself arises from appeal to intuitions independent of the theory of reference; and it seems reasonable that we should, in resolving that issue, appeal to notions that arise at the same intuitive level. That we *appear* to have recognitional concepts and identifying dispositions that are more or less determinate in their reference is hard to deny. My conception of 'those hedges' (seen around the neighborhood) may unambiguously pick out a variety of eugenia. An example closer to the present topic is this. We can imagine an experiment in which the experimenter tries to determine which internal property is the focus of her subject's identifications: 'again',... 'there it is again'. There seems no commonsensical implausibility—putting aside foundational worries about the inscrutability of reference—in the idea that there is a best possible answer to the experimenter's question, in the scientific long run.[6]

3   Phenomenal Concepts as Recognitional Concepts

Here is the view to be defended. Phenomenal concepts are recognitional concepts that pick out certain internal properties; these are physical-functional properties of the brain. They are the concepts we deploy in our phenomenological reflections; and there is no good philosophical reason to deny that, odd though it may sound, the properties these conceptions *phenomenologically reveal* are physical-functional properties—but not of course under physical-functional descriptions. Granted that brain research might discover that (what we take to be) our phenomenal concepts do not in fact discriminate unified physical-functional properties. Failing that, it is quite coherent for a physicalist to take the phenomenology at face value: the property of *its being like this* to have a certain experience is nothing over and above a certain physical-functional property of the brain.

Phenomenal concepts are conceptually independent of physical-functional descriptions, and yet pairs of such concepts may converge on, pick out, the same properties. Rebutting the semantic premise of the knowledge argument requires making sense of the idea that phenomenal concepts conceive physical-functional properties 'directly', that is, not by way of contingent modes of presentation. The objective is to show that the knowledge argument fails for the same reason in the case of Mary as in the case of Max: both arguments require substitution in opaque contexts of terms that are conceptually independent. In the case of Max, the conceptual independence appears to derive from 'alcohol''s connoting a contingent mode of presentation that is metaphysically independent of the property referred to by the chemical concept. In the case of Mary it has a different source.

What then accounts for the conceptual independence of phenomenal and physical-functional concepts? The simple answer is that recognitional concepts and theoretical concepts are in general conceptually independent. It is true that recognitional concepts other than phenomenal concepts connote contingent modes of presentation that are metaphysically independent of the natural kinds they pick out, and hence independent of the kind referred to by the theoretical term of the pair. But we need not count this metaphysical independence as essential to the conceptual independence of coreferring recognitional and theoretical concepts. Concepts of the two sorts have quite different conceptual roles. It is hardly surprising that a recognitional conception of a physical property should discriminate it without analyzing it in scientific terms. Nor should it be surprising that, if there are recognitional concepts that pick out physical properties *not* via contingent modes of presentation, they do not discriminate their references by analyzing them (even implicitly) in scientific terms. Basic recognitional abilities do not depend on or get triggered by conscious scientific analysis. If phenomenal concepts reflect basic recognitions of internal physical-functional states, they *should* be conceptually independent of theoretical physical-functional descriptions. That is what you expect quite apart from issues concerning physicalism.

An antireductionist may reply that the physicalist view depends on an ad hoc assumption and that it is tendentious to suppose that phenomenal concepts differ from all other recognitional concepts in not having contingent modes of presentation.

But this is not fair. Even on the antiphysicalist view, phenomenal concepts are recognitional concepts, and we have 'direct' recognitional conceptions of phenomenal qualities, that is, conceptions unmediated by contingent modes of presentation. Evidently it would be absurd to insist that the antiphysicalist hold that we conceive of a phenomenal quality of one kind via a phenomenal mode of presentation of a distinct kind. And why should the physicalist not agree that phenomenal recognitional concepts are structured in whatever simple way the antiphysicalist requires? That is after all the intuitive situation, and the physicalist simply claims that the intuitive facts about phenomenal qualities are compatible with physicalism. The physicalist makes the additional claim that the phenomenal quality thus directly conceived is a physical-functional property. On both metaphysical views, phenomenal concepts differ from other recognitional concepts; phenomenal concepts are a peculiar sort of recognitional concept on any account, and that can hardly count against physicalism. The two views agree about conceptual structure and disagree about the nature of phenomenal qualities. To insist that physicalism implies, absurdly, that phenomenal concepts could pick out physical properties only via metaphysically distinct phenomenal modes of presentation is unmotivated. There is, though, still more to be said about whether phenomenal concepts should be regarded as having modes of presentation of some sort, and we continue the account in section 5.

Suppose this account of how phenomenal concepts refer is true. Here is a semantic consequence. The physicalist thesis implies that the judgments "the state a feels like that" and "the state a has physical-functional property P" can have the same truth condition even though their joint truth or falsity can be known only a posteriori. I mean, same condition of truth in a possible world. For truth conditions are determined in part by the possible world satisfaction conditions of predicates; and if a phenomenal predicate directly refers to a physical property, that property constitutes its satisfaction condition.

On this account, a phenomenal concept rigidly designates the property it picks out. But then it rigidly designates the same property that some theoretical physical concept rigidly designates. This could seem problematic, for if a concept rigidly designates a property not via a contingent mode of presentation, must that concept not capture the *essence* of the designated property? And if two concepts capture the essence of the same property, must we not be able to know this a priori? These are equivocating uses of 'capture the essence of'. On one use, it expresses a referential notion that comes to no more than 'directly rigidly designate'. On the other, it means something like 'be conceptually interderivable with some theoretical predicate that reveals the internal structure of' the designated property. But the first does not imply the second. What is correct in the observation about rigid designation has no tendency to imply that the two concepts must be a priori interderivable.

4 The Concept 'Phenomenal Concept'

Not all self-directed recognitional concepts are phenomenal concepts, as may be seen in these two cases.

(1) Cramps have a characteristic feel, but they are not feelings. Cramps are certain muscle contractions, while feelings of cramp are, if physical, brain states. (Witness phantom-limb sufferers.) One has a recognitional concept that picks out certain muscle contractions in the having of them. This is not a phenomenal concept, for it does not purport to pick out a phenomenal quality. But of course, in exercising this concept, one often conceives its reference by way of a phenomenal mode of presentation, a cramp feeling or a cramp-feeling image.

(2) A more fanciful self-directed nonphenomenal concept can be conceived. To begin with, consider blindsight. Some cortically damaged people are phenomenally blind in restricted retinal regions; and yet when a vertical or horizontal line (say) is presented to those regions, they can, when prompted, guess what is there with a somewhat high degree of correctness. We can extend the example by imagining a blindsight that is exercised spontaneously and accurately. At this point we shift the focus to internal properties and conceive of a self-directed recognitional ability, which is like the previous ability in being phenomenally blank and spontaneous but which discriminates an internal property of one's own. If this recognitional ability were suitably governed by the concept 'that state', the resulting concept would be a self-directed recognitional concept that is phenomenally blank.

The two examples show that 'phenomenal concept' cannot mean 'self-directed recognitional concept'. This is compatible with my proposal. For it implies neither (a) that we can reductively explicate the concept 'phenomenal quality' as 'property picked out by a self-directed discriminative ability', or (b) that we can reductively explicate the concept 'phenomenal concept' as 'self-directed recognitional concept'. Phenomenal concepts are certain self-directed recognitional concepts. Our higher-order concept 'phenomenal concept' cannot be reductively explicated, any more than can our concept 'phenomenal quality'. The higher-order concept 'phenomenal concept' is as irreducibly demonstrative as phenomenal concepts themselves.

5 Phenomenal Modes of Presentation

Self-directed recognitional concepts of the blind-sight type might appear to raise a problem for the claim that phenomenal concepts pick out physical-functional properties directly. Here is a way to put the point.

The difference between a self-directed blindsight recognitional concept and a phenomenal concept appears to be that the latter involves a phenomenal mode of presentation while the former conceives its referent in some other, odd, way. So, if the phenomenal concept is taken to discriminate some physical property, it then does so via a phenomenal mode of presentation. But that conflicts with your assertion that phenomenal concepts refer directly, with no contingent mode of presentation. A similar point arises concerning recognitional concepts of cramps and of cramp feelings. Both concepts must presumably have modes of presentation. It is far-fetched to suppose that one of them has and the other lacks a mode of presentation; the phenomenal concept does not pick out a physical state *nakedly*. The 'cramp' concept connotes a mode of presentation of the form 'the physical state that causes such and such phenomenal state'. If we attempt to capture the phenomenal concept analogously, its mode of presentation would have the form 'the state that has such and such phenomenal aspect'. But then, contrary to what the physicalist must say, phenomenal concepts point to physical states only by way of phenomenal modes of presentation.

What might an antiphysicalist say about these various self-directed recognitional concepts? Let me make a good-faith attempt to present a reasonable version.

(1) A cramp concept picks out a muscular property indirectly, by way of a causal chain that is mediated by the phenomenal quality associated with the concept. In addition to this mode of presentation type—the phenomenal quality, we can also note the role of, as we might say, "token modes of presentation." One and the same cramp concept (type) can on different occasions be focussed differently: by an actual cramp feeling, by a cramp-feeling image, or by an imageless inclination to identify cramp feelings when they occur (with a cramp-feeling image on the tip of one's imagination.)

(2) We turn from cramp concepts to cramp-feeling-concepts. These do not refer (i.e., to cramp feelings) by way of contingent modes of presentation. But they can mimic the working of cramp concepts as regards "token modes of presentation." If one can focus attention on the bodily property of cramp by way of a token cramp feeling, surely one can focus attention on the phenomenal quality cramp feeling by way of a token cramp feeling. The same goes for cramp-feeling images and those gossamer identifying inclinations. Should antiphysicalists say that cramp-feeling concepts have 'noncontingent' modes of presentation? We might say that a phenomenal concept has as its mode of presentation the very phenomenal quality that it picks out. We might also say that phenomenal concepts have "token modes of presentation" that are noncontingently tied to the phenomenal qualities to which those concepts point: particular cramp feelings and images can focus one's conception of the phenomenal quality of cramp feeling.

(3) As for self-directed blindsight concepts, the antiphysicalist then ought to say, they differ from phenomenal concepts in the obvious way, whether one puts it by saying that they lack the noncontingent phenomenal modes of presentation (types) that phenomenal qualities have, or that they lack their phenomenal "token modes of presentation."

The main point is by now more than obvious. Whatever the antiphysicalist has said about these cases the physicalist may say as well. The idea that one picks out the phenomenal quality of cramp feeling by way of a particular feeling of cramp (or image, etc.) is hardly incompatible with holding that that phenomenal quality is a physical property. The contrast between phenomenal concepts and self-directed blindsight concepts and cramp concepts finds physicalist and antiphysicalist equally able to say something sensible.

A phenomenal concept exercised in the absence of the phenomenal quality it stands for often involves not merely a recognitional disposition but also an image. And so, as a psychological state in its own right, a phenomenal concept—given its intimate connection with imaging—bears a phenomenological affinity to a phenomenal state that neither state bears to the entertaining of a physical-theoretical concept. When we then bring phenomenal and physical-theoretical concepts together in our philosophical ruminations, those cognitive states are phenomenologically so different that the illusion may be created that their references must be different. It is as though antiphysicalist intuitions rest on a resemblance theory of mental representation, as though we conclude from the lack of resemblance in our phenomenal and physical-functional conceptions a lack of sameness in the properties to which they refer.

6   Third-person Ascriptions

Ascriptions of phenomenal qualities to others ostensibly refer to properties that others may have independently of our ascribing them:[7] we have realist conceptions of the phenomenal states of others. But at the same time they are projections from one's own case; they have the form 'x has a state of this sort', where the demonstrative gets its reference from an actual or possible state of one's own.

Can phenomenal concepts as we predicate them of others be identified with the recognitional concepts we have characterized? A question naturally arises how essentially self-directed recognitional concepts can be applied in cases where it makes no sense to say that one can directly apply

these concepts. This is a question that exercised Wittgensteinians.

As we have already pointed out, recognitional concepts are perspectival, in the sense that their reference is determined from a certain constitutive perspective (depending on the concept). The above concept 'those creatures$_1$' (seen up close) picks out a creature-kind that one discriminates on close sightings. But nothing prevents ascribing the recognitional concept 'one of those creatures$_1$' to something observed from a different perspective, seen in the distance or heard in the dark. We have to distinguish the perspective from which reference is determined and the far broader range of contexts in which the referentially fixed concept can be ascribed. The former perspective hardly restricts the latter contexts. This holds also for phenomenal concepts. We acquire them from a first-person perspective, by discriminating a property in the having of it. Assuming that we successfully pick out a more or less determinate physical property, the extraperspectival ascription 'she is in a state of *this* kind' makes complete sense. And so it is not easy to see that Wittgensteinians succeeded in raising a philosophical problem that survives the observation that we can discriminate physical properties and so fix the reference of phenomenal concepts from a first-person perspective, and then go on to ascribe those concepts third-personally.

There is though a more up-to-date worry about the interpersonal ascribability of first-person concepts, however physical we suppose their references to be. Evidently there will be vagueness, and indeterminacy, concerning whether another person—whose neural assemblies will presumably always differ from mine in various respects— has a certain physical property that I discriminate phenomenally. And this on the face of it poses a problem, which may be framed as follows:

The question whether another person's phenomenal states resemble yours can hardly consist in their neural assemblies' resembling yours. Any physical similarity you choose will be arbitrarily related to a given phenomenal similarity. Suppose there is a small physical difference between a neural state of yours and another person's state. What makes it the case that this small neural difference constitutes a small phenomenal difference or a large one or no phenomenal difference at all? It appears that there cannot be a fact of the matter.

But this objection appears to me to overlook a crucial element of the physicalist view we have presented—that phenomenal concepts are (type-) demonstrative concepts that pick out physical properties and relations. A first step in answering it is to consider the connection between interpersonal and intrapersonal phenomenal similarity. It appears that one's phenomenological conception of how others' phenomenal states resemble one's own has to be drawn from one's idea of how one's own phenomenal states resemble each other. A person's quality space of interpersonal similarity must derive from her quality space of intrapersonal similarity. How else is one to get a conceptual grip on interpersonal phenomenal similarity? This seems inevitable on any account—physicalist or antiphysicalist—on which phenomenal concepts are formed from one's own case.

But conceptions of phenomenal similarity relations are as much type-demonstrative concepts as those of phenomenal qualities. All one can apparently mean by "that spectrum of phenomenal similarity" is "*that ordering* among my phenomenal states." Physicalism implies that if such a type-demonstrative refers, it picks out a physical ordering. And there is no obvious philosophical difficulty (if we put aside scepticism in the theory of reference) in the idea that discriminations of resemblances and differences among one's own phenomenal properties pick out reasonably well defined physical relations.

Now I have to confess some uneasiness about extending this to interpersonal similarity without qualification; but the implications of the foregoing remarks are clear enough. If they are correct, whatever physical ordering relations are picked out by one's personal notions of phenomenal similarity must also constitute (what one

thinks of as) interpersonal phenomenal similarity. It is easy to see that there still is room here for further trouble. But the difficulty the objection raises seems considerably diminished if one insists on the demonstrative nature of all phenomenal concepts, however relational and of whatever order. For the objection then becomes, "Suppose there is a small physical difference between a neural state of yours and another person's state. What makes it the case that this small neural difference constitutes a small difference of *that* type, or a large one, or no difference of *that* type at all?" If "that type" picks out a physical relation, then the question answers itself, and there seems no gloomy philosophical threat of phenomenal incommensurability.

Naturally there is the risk that physical investigation will not deliver the right physical properties and relations. Even if the risk is increased by bringing in interpersonal similarities, the nature of the risk is the same as in one's own case: the phenomenal might turn out to be not adequately embodied.

It goes without saying that one can coherently conceive that another person has P, conceived in physical-functional terms, and doubt that she has any given phenomenal quality; that has been central to this chapter. But one cannot coherently wonder whether another person in a P state has a state with *this* phenomenal quality if one acknowledges that one's concept 'this quality' refers to the property the concept discriminates in oneself (what else?) and that moreover it discriminates P.

Why then is there an apparent problem of other minds? It is as if one wishes to do to others as one does to oneself—namely, apply phenomenal concepts directly, apply phenomenal recognitional capacities to others from a first-person perspective. The impossibility of this can present itself as an epistemological barrier, as something that makes it impossible to know certain facts. Doubtless more can be said in explanation of the naturalness of the conflation of the innocuous conceptual fact with a severe epistemological disability. It is not easy to shake the grip of that conflation or therefore easy to dispel the problem of other minds. The cognitive remedy, the fortification against the illusion, is the idea of recognitional concepts that can be ascribed beyond their constitutive perspective, coupled with the reflection that there is no reason to doubt that it is physical-functional properties that those recognitional concepts discriminate.

7 Knowing How versus Knowing That

Consider a different physicalist reply, to an antiphysicalist argument posed in this form: "knowledge of physical-functional facts does not yield knowledge of the phenomenal facts; therefore phenomenal facts are not physical-functional." Lawrence Nemirow and David Lewis have replied in effect that the premise is true only if you equivocate on "knowledge."[8] The first occurrence means theoretical knowledge, the second the ability to discriminate introspectively or to imagine certain properties. But theoretical knowledge of physical-functional properties that are identical with phenomenal qualities does not yield the other sort of knowledge of the same properties, that is, the ability to discriminate them in introspection or to imagine them. There are two epistemic relations to one class of properties.

Now this suggests something significantly different from my account. On the Nemirow-Lewis proposal, the only knowledge "that such and such" is knowledge couched in physical-functional terms, while what corresponds to (what we have been calling) phenomenal concepts is knowing how to identify or to imagine certain states. What I have proposed is evidently different. Knowing that a state feels a certain way is having distinctive information about it, couched in phenomenal conceptions. There is of course a central role for recognitional abilities, but that is in the constitution of phenomenal concepts. Antiphysicalists are right to count phenomenal knowledge as the possession of distinctive in-

formation, for it involves genuinely predicative components of judgment, whose association with physical-functional concepts is straightforwardly a posteriori.

Physicalists are forced into the Nemirow-Lewis reply if they individuate pieces of knowledge or cognitive information in terms of possible-world truth-conditions, that is, hold that 'knowing that p' and 'knowing that q' ascribe distinct pieces of knowledge just in case 'that-p' and 'that-q' denote distinct sets of possible worlds. Then knowing that x's phenomenal qualities are such and such will be distinct from knowing that x's physical properties are so and so only if the former qualities are distinct from the latter properties. So then a physicalist who counts the basic antiphysicalist premise as true on some interpretation must deny either that knowledge, cognitive information, is individuated in terms of possible-world truth-conditions or deny that knowing the phenomenal facts (in the sense that makes the basic antiphysicalist premise true) is knowing that such and such or having distinctive information about it. Nemirow and Lewis deny the latter. Of course I deny the former; there are ample independent reasons to deny it, and it seems otherwise unmotivated to deny the latter.

There are straightforward reasons to prefer the phenomenal concept view.

1. A person can have thoughts not only of the form "coconuts have *this* taste" but also of the form "if coconuts did not have *this* taste, then Q." You may get away with saying that the former expresses (not a genuine judgment but) the mere possession of recognitional know-how. But there is no comparable way to account for the embedded occurrence of "coconuts have this taste"; it occurs as a predicate with a distinctive content.

2. We entertain thoughts about the phenomenal states of other people—"she has a state of that type"; this clearly calls for a predicative concept. It does of course involve a recognitional ability, but one that contributes to the formation of a distinctive concept.

3. For many conceptions of phenomenal qualities, there is no candidate for an independently mastered term that one then learns how to apply: thinking of a peculiar way my left knee feels when I run (a conception that occurs predicatively in various judgments) is not knowing how to apply an independently understood term. I suppose a functionalist might say that, in such cases, one implicitly individuates the state in terms of some functional description that is fashioned on the spot, but this appears psychologically implausible.

8 The Explanatory Gap

Can we *explain* how a certain phenomenal property might be identical with a certain physical-functional property? The answer is no, and then again, yes.

First, the no. When we explain, say, liquidity in physical-functional terms, the explanation is in crucial part a priori. You may find this surprising; but what we in effect do is analyze liquidity (or more precisely those aspects of liquidity that we count as explained[9]) in terms of a functional description, and then show that the physical theory of water implies, a priori, that the functional description is realized. But given the conceptual independence of phenomenal concepts and physical-functional concepts, we cannot have such an a priori explanation of phenomenal qualities in physical-functional terms.

Does this matter? The explanatory gap, as it appears to me, is an epistemic or conceptual phenomenon, without metaphysical consequences,[10] and it is predictable from the physicalist account we have proposed. But this may seem somewhat glib. As Georges Rey points out (Rey forthcoming), the mere fact of conceptual inequivalence for recognitional type-demonstratives and descriptive terms does not generate an explanatory gap. Many examples would make the point. We do not find a troubling explanatory gap in judgments of the form "that stuff is CH_3CH_2OH," even though this does not hold a priori.

Now what is it that needs accounting for? This seems to me to be it: how identity statements that connect phenomenal concepts and physical-functional concepts can be true despite our sense that, if true, they *ought to be* explanatory and yet are not. We can explain how such identity statements fail to be both explanatory (conceptual independence) and true; but this does not account for the thought that something that ought to be there is missing. We have to explain away the intuition that such identity statements ought to be explanatory.

There must be something special about phenomenal concepts that creates the expectation and the consequent puzzle. We have already seen a significant difference between phenomenal concepts and all other phenomenally mediated recognitional concepts. Might this make the difference here as well? That is what I will try to show.

Perhaps this is why we think that true phenomenal-physical identity judgments ought to be explanatory. It is natural to regard our conceptions of phenomenal qualities as conceiving them as they are in themselves, that is, to suppose we have a direct grasp of their essence. So in this respect there is a parallel with liquidity: the phenomenal concept and the concept 'liquid' both pick out properties directly, that is, not via contingent modes of presentation. And of course the physical-functional theoretical term of the identity, couched in fundamental theoretical terms, also reveals the essence of the property it picks out. Since both conceptions reveal this essence, then, if the psychophysical identity judgment is true, the sameness of that property, it might seem, ought to be evident from those conceptions, as in the liquidity case. The physical-functional concept structurally analyzes the property, and so we expect *it* to explain, asymmetrically, the phenomenal quality, much as physics explains liquidity, on the basis of an a priori analysis. The fact that this is not so makes it then difficult to understand how there can be just one property here.

If this is what makes the explanatory gap troubling, then the idea that phenomenal concepts are recognitional concepts of a certain sort does account for the explanatory gap in a way compatible with physicalism. Phenomenal concepts, as we have seen, do not conceive their reference via contingent modes of presentation. And so they can be counted as conceiving phenomenal qualities directly. Calling this a grasp of essence seems to me all right, for phenomenal concepts do not conceive their references by way of their accidental properties. But this is quite a different grasp of essence than we have in the term "liquid": for that term (or what there is in it that we count as functionally explained) is conceptually equivalent to some functional description that is entailed by the theoretical term of the identity.

The problem of the explanatory gap stems then from an illusion. What generates the problem is not appreciating that there can be two conceptually independent "direct grasps" of a single essence, that is, grasping it demonstratively by experiencing it, and grasping it in theoretical terms. The illusion is of *expected transparency*: a direct grasp of a property ought to reveal how it is internally constituted, and if it is not revealed as physically constituted, then it is not so. The mistake is the thought that a direct grasp of essence ought to be a transparent grasp, and it is a natural enough expectation.

The explanatory gap has led many philosophers of mind seriously astray into mistaken arguments for epiphenomenalism, for mystery, for eliminativism. At the root of almost all weird positions in the philosophy of mind lies this rather elementary and unremarkable conceptual fact, blown up into a metaphysical problem that appears to require an extreme solution. But it is a mistake to think that, if physicalism is true, consciousness as we conceive it at first hand needs explaining in the way that liquidity as we ordinarily conceive it gets explained.

There is another interpretation of "can we understand how physicalism might be true?", for which the answer is clearly yes. For we can explain, and indeed we have explained, how a given phenomenal concept can manage to pick out a particular physical-functional property without remainder: the concept discriminates the property but not via a contingent mode of presentation. This in its way closes the explanatory gap between the phenomenal and the physical. We understand how "such and such phenomenal quality" could pick out physical property P, even though "such and such phenomenal quality $= P$" does not provide an (a priori) explanation in physical terms of why a given phenomenal quality feels as it does. Since the former, when generalized, would entail that physicalism about phenomenal qualities is true, and since we understand both of these things, we thereby understand how physicalism can be true.

9   Subjective Concepts and Subjective Properties

You can ascribe an objective property—one completely expressable in the objective terms of natural science—under a subjective conception: 'x's state has *this* quality'. Thomas Nagel writes that mental facts are "accessible only from one point of view".[11] This does reflect something about phenomenal concepts; they are in some intuitive sense "from a point of view" and moreover subjective. Phenomenal concepts are subjective because they are essentially self-directed, involving capacities to discriminate certain states in the having of them and also involve imaginative capacities anchored in such recognitional capacities. If that is it, then Nagel takes a correct observation about concepts and draws a wrong conclusion about facts and properties. For concepts can in that sense be "from a point of view" and subjective, and still introduce properties that are exhaustively captured in objective science.

But we can go further. Let us grant even that the *property* of experiencing such and such is aptly counted as subjective, as intrinsically involving a point of view. Why should this subjectivity not itself be identical with a physical-functional property, and therefore completely objectively conceivable under its physical-functional description? There is no contradiction in supposing that a property that is subjective—in the sense of being individuated in a way that invokes a relation to a mind—is also conceivable under an objective mode of presentation. There is no incoherence in the thought that the "subjectivity" of a phenomenal quality is identical with an objective physical-functional aspect of that property.

Does a fully objective description of reality not still leave something out, viz. the subjective conceptions? This is a play on 'leave something out'. A complete objective description leaves out subjective conceptions, not because it cannot fully characterize the properties they discriminate or fully account for the concepts themselves as psychological states but simply because it does not employ them.

10 Phenomenal Structure, and Exotic Others

Some functionalists might think this account ignores a major feature of our conceptions of the mental, namely, their systematic structure. We have conceptions of different sensory modalities, and of intramodality comparisons along various spectra, of pitch, timbre, hue, brightness, shape, size, texture, acidity, acridity, and so on. These could be seen as subsidiary functional organizations within a theory of the mental. Antiphysicalists may share something of the point, wanting to speak of phenomenological structures. My account could seem to imply that phenomenal concepts are atomistic, unstructured, unsystematic, for are these recognitional dispositions not in principle independent of each other?

We have phenomenal recognitional concepts of various degrees of generality. Some are of highly determinate qualities, and others are of phenomenal determinables: crimson, dark red, red, warm colored, colored, visual. The last is the recognitional conception of a whole sensory modality. And there is the most general of all, the recognitional concept *phenomenal* (state, quality), the highest ranking phenomenal determinable. (This is a recognitional concept. One discriminates phenomenal states from nonphenomenal states, feeling a twinge from having a bruise, hearing a chirp from jerking a knee, and that highly general discriminative capacity is the basis of the concept of a phenomenal quality.)

There are also relational concepts: quality x is a determinate of quality y; quality x is more like quality y than like quality z; quality x is of a different modality from quality y. These are also recognitional concepts: dispositions to classify together, on phenomenal grounds, certain pairs and triples of phenomenal qualities. Combining them yields complex conceptions of abstract phenomenal structures, for example, of a structured sensory modality. One's general conception of such a structure is in effect one's ability to exercise in concert a group of such general phenomenal concepts

Now it is important that our conceptions of such phenomenal structures, while abstract, are yet phenomenal conceptions. No purely functional conception of a complex structure, however isomorphic to a phenomenal-structure conception it may be, will be cognitively equivalent to it; purely functional conceptions ignore that the structures are of phenomenal similarity relations, of phenomenal determinateness, and so on.

But given the falsity of the semantic minor premise, that is no impediment to holding that those abstract phenomenal conceptions can have purely functional or physical-functional structures as their references. For such structures may well be what these abstract phenomenal recognitional capacities in fact discriminate. Indeed we may go on to say that, if our phenomenal conceptions are to be fully vindicated by brain science, then the brain must have a certain functional structure; any possible totality of (as it were) semantic values for our phenomenal conceptions must have certain functional structures. This perhaps explains the strong intuition of some commonsense functionalists that phenomenal concepts are functional concepts, without our having to accept that counterintuitive view.

"Can your projection analysis accommodate the thought that a bat has highly specific, determinate, phenomenal states that are not like anything I can experience or imagine? It seems to me that your program will require you to bring in the bat's own recognitional-imaginative capacities, such as they are."[12]

When one thinks about a bat's sonar phenomenal states, one thinks about them as phenomenal, that is, as having in common with my phenomenal states what I discriminate them all as having in common, and that may be something physical-functional. One also thinks of them as of a distinctive phenomenal kind or modality, different from one's own states, of roughly that order of determinateness at which one's visual states are marked off from one's auditory states. One has such a general concept from one's own case, and one can project it. Again, that concept—'distinctive phenomenal modality'—may denote a physical-functional property, of sets of phenomenal states. And one thinks of the bat's sonar states as exhibiting phenomenal variation of different degrees of specificity. These conceptions of general phenomenal structure, determinable-determinate relations, resemblance relations, and so on, we have, as I have said, from our own case.

Now nothing in the foregoing requires that a necessary condition of having certain phenomenal qualities is having the capacity to discriminate them. (See, however, the discussion below of transparency.) We ascribe to bats not phenomenal concepts but phenomenal states; and we do that by projection, in the manner characterized above. Other-directed phenomenal conceptions are of others' states, and not as such of their conceptions.

Nagel proposes that we can achieve objectivity about the mental by abstracting from subjective conceptions of our own psychology, fashioning objective mental conceptions that are neither physical nor functional.[13] This would enable us to conceive abstractly of mental lives of which we have no subjective, projective, understanding whatever. Now that is evidentially at odds with my proposal. It appears to me that all mental concepts that are not functional concepts (where the latter include concepts of theoretical psychology) are subjective-projective concepts, however general and abstract they may be. The reason is simple: as far as I can determine, I have no objective nonfunctional mental concepts. If I try to conceive an alien mind in nonfunctional mental terms, I rely on concepts like 'sensory modality' and other general conceptions of phenomenological structure of the sort mentioned above, and I understand them from my own case. They are abstract conceptions; but, it appears to me, they are still recognitional concepts and hence as subjective as the highly specific phenomenal concept of having an itch in the left ankle.

11   Transparency

The following could appear possible on my account: another person is in the state that in me amounts to feeling such and such but sincerely denies feeling anything relevant. It apparently has been left open that others have phenomenal states that are not introspectable at will, for no requirement of transparency has been mentioned. Then the property that is the referent of my concept of feeling like *that* could, even if it occurs transparently in me, occur nontransparently in you. But (the objection continues) denying transparency is tantamount to allowing unconscious experiences; and it would not be unreasonable to say that the topic of phenomenal states is the topic of certain conscious states.

There really is no issue here. Suppose that any phenomenal quality must be essentially transparent, and that no property I correctly identify as phenomenal can be realized in another nontransparently. If cognitive integration is essential to the intuitive property of transparency, so be it; there is no reason to think that such integration itself is not a physical-functional property, as it were implicated by each phenomenal property.

But it is not obvious that phenomenal properties must be transparent in such a reflexive cognitive sense. What about infants and bats? There has always been a philosophical puzzle about how subtracting reflexive cognitive awareness from phenomenal or conscious states leaves something that is still phenomenal or conscious. But that puzzle is independent of the present account. All that is implied here is that if I have a conception of a phenomenal quality that is shared by me and an infant, my conception of it involves a recognitional concept, and there is no reason why that phenomenal quality itself should not be a physical-functional property. Whatever indefinable, elusive aspect of phenomenal qualities might constitute their being conscious—transparent in some appropriately minimal sense— without requiring reflexive conceptualizability, there would be no reason to doubt it is a physical-functional property.

12 Incorrigibility

Physicalism, it may be said, cannot acknowledge the incorrigibility of phenomenal judgments of the form 'it feels like that'. For surely there is no guarantee that a capacity for recognizing a given physical property does not at times misfire; and perhaps even more to the point, there can be no guarantee that to a given recognitional disposition there corresponds a repeatable physical property. Perhaps an antiphysicalist will grant that certain kinds of mistake about phenomenal qualities are possible;[14] but the antiphysicalist will insist that we cannot be wrong in thinking that *there are* phenomenal qualities.

Now suppose it turns out that no system of physical-functional properties corresponds to the system of our phenomenal concepts. Would a physicalist not then have to say there are no phenomenal qualities? And is the fact that physicalism leaves this open not a serious problem?

But that very possibility ought to make us dubious about the incorrigibility of the judgment that there are real phenomenal repeatables. What reason have we to think that our phenomenal judgments discriminate real properties? Memory, one might say, cannot be that mistaken: we can hardly deny that present inner states resemble past states in ways we would recognize again. Despite this conviction, however, if no system of physical-functional properties corresponded to one's putative phenomenal discriminations, an alternative to nonphysical qualities would be this: memory radically deceives us into thinking we discriminate internal features and nonrandomly classify our own states. Strong evidence that no suitable physical-functional properties exist might amaze and stagger one. It would then have emerged that we are subject to a powerful illusion, a cognitive rather than a phenomenal illusion; we would be judging falsely that we thereby discriminate real properties.

It does seem likely that we genuinely discriminate internal physical-functional states in introspection.[15] But with that said, positing nonphysical properties to forestall the *possibility* of radical error, however theoretically adventurous (even reckless) this may be, would in something like a moral sense still be rather faint-hearted. The whole point about the phenomenal is how it appears. And that means there is no introspective guarantee of *anything* beyond mere appearance, even of discriminations of genuine repeatables. The dualist balks at the implications and invents a realm of properties to ensure that the appearances are facts, but this does not respect the truly phenomenal nature of what is revealed by introspection at its least theoretical.

I have to grant that, if it were to turn out that no brain properties are suitably correlated with our ascriptions of phenomenal qualities, one might well feel some justification in questioning physicalism. But that does not imply that one now has such a justification. There is no good reason for prophylactic dualism.

---

13 Functionalism

There are two functionalist theses: that all concepts of mental states are functional concepts, and that all mental properties are functional properties. The first I rejected in accepting the antiphysicalist intuition. I agree with the antiphysicalist that phenomenal concepts cannot be captured in purely functional terms. But nothing in philosophy prevents phenomenal properties from being functional properties. There are two possibilities: they are commonsense-functional properties or they are psychofunctional, and I take the latter to be the interesting one.[16] Might the phenomenal quality of seeing red be identical with a property captured by a detailed psychological theory? This would be so if the repeatable that triggers one's phenomenal concept 'seeing red' has psychofunctional rather than say biochemical identity conditions. That this is possible has been denied by antifunctionalist physicalists on the grounds of inverted qualia and absent qualia possibilities, but I do nor find these arguments persuasive.

The inverted qualia argument is commonly advanced against identifying phenomenal qualities with commonsense functional properties and also against the psychofunctional identification. The position I espouse is agnostic: for all philosophers know, phenomenal qualities are psychofunctional, neurofunctional, or some other fine-grained functional properties. The opposing argument is that it is possible that the functional role that seeing red has in me is had in you by, as I would think of it, seeing green. If this is, as they say, metaphysically possible, then of course phenomenal qualities are not functional properties.

But it seems the only argument for the possibility is the coherent conceivability of inverted qualia. One cannot presuppose that inverted qualia are *nomologically* possible. There seems to be no philosophical reason to assert that, apart from the coherent conceivability of inverted qualia. If there is empirical reason to assert that nomological possibility, then of course we should retreat from agnosticism. The present point is that nothing about the idea of inverted qualia provides philosophical reason to reject functionalism about qualia. For that would require another version of the antiphysicalist argument: it is conceivable that any given functional state can occur without the seeing of green and with the seeing of red, say; therefore the psychofunctional role and the phenomenal quality involve distinct properties. Clearly one cannot accept this argument against functionalism without also accepting the analogous argument against physicalism itself; the philosophical antifunctionalist argument requires a premise that implies antiphysicalism.

There is a well-known absent qualia argument against functionalism by Ned Block (1978). Suppose the Chinese nation were organized so as to realize the psychofunctional organization of a person seeing green. Evidently the Chinese nation would not collectively be seeing green or having any other sensation. Any psychofunctional property could in this way be realized without a given phenomenal quality and hence cannot be identical with one. Now this argument might appear dialectically more telling than the inverted qualia argument, for it apparently rests on more than a conceptual possibility. It seems a plain truth that the Chinese people would not thereby be having a collective sensation. Surely it is barmy to be agnostic about that. Block suggests a principle. "If a doctrine has an absurd conclusion which there is no independent reason to believe, and if there is no way of explaining away the absurdity or showing it to be misleading or irrelevant, and if there is no good reason to believe the doctrine that leads to the absurdity in the first place, then don't accept the doctrine."[17]

While we doubtless find an absurdity in ascribing phenomenal qualities to the Chinese nation as a whole, the matter is not so simple. It is hard to see how such a judgment of absurdity can be *justified* except by our having some intuitive knowledge of the nature of phenomenal qualities whereby we can say that the Chinese nation cannot have them collectively. Have I a special insight into my physical states whereby I can say: the repeatable that I reidentify whenever I attend to my seeing green is not a functional property? One feels sceptical that introspection can yield such knowledge. If the argument is not 'they do not collectively have, by virtue of their functional organization, however fine-grained, what I have when *this* occurs', then what is it? Is a further philosophical argument in the offing? It is difficult to see whence chest-beating to the contrary derives its credibility. Perhaps a dualist conception of Platonic insight into mental essences might help. But, on a naturalist view of human nature, one ought to find it puzzling that we have such a first-person insight into the nature of our mental properties. Perhaps there is reason to suppose that what one introspects and reidentifies is a categorical and not a dispositional property. That has an intuitive ring to it, but it is not that easy to produce a decent argument for it. We are left with this question: how might we know short of detailed brain research that what we reidentify in ourselves when we see green is not a fine-grained functional property? But if we cannot know this by sheer insight into the essence of our own properties, or by philosophical argument, then we cannot know that the Chinese nation lacks what we have. Our ignorance concerns the nature of our own properties, and that ignorance would appear to prevent drawing substantive conclusions from thought experiments of this type.

There is no question that ordinary intuition counts strongly against applying phenomenal concepts to things that are not single organisms, and one cannot deny that the reply just given makes one uncomfortable, at the very least. And yet the alternative appears to be Platonism about mental essences, and that sits awkwardly with naturalism. It is possible that phenomenal qualities are biochemical properties: and yet again it is

difficult to see that philosophers know anything that implies that they are not fine-grained functional, or neurofunctional, properties.[18]

Notes

1. Cf. Rey (forthcoming) and Dennett (1991).

2. Jackson (1982, 1986).

3. Nagel (1974, 1986); McGinn (1993).

4. Jackson (1982, 1986).

5. How such background concepts themselves arise is not my topic; but we might think of them variously as deriving from more general recognitional capacities, or as functions of complex inferential roles, or as socially deferential; or they may be components of innate structures. Background concepts are not always presupposed. Someone may be extremely good at telling stars from other objects (e.g., lightning bugs, airplanes, comets, planets) without having any real idea of what they are.

6. For more on recognitional concepts and on the determinacy of reference, see Loar (1990; 1991; forthcoming).

7. The earlier version of this chapter made heavy weather of third-person ascription of phenomenal concepts. General considerations about the perspectival nature of recognitional concepts permit a far neater account, which I here present.

8. Nemirow (1980); Lewis (1983).

9. This leaves open the possibility of twin-Earth cases in which the apparently defining properties of liquidity—those that are functionally explained—are kept constant across worlds even though the underlying kind changes. The defining properties then turn out to be merely reference fixing.

10. For illuminating accounts of the explanatory gap and its significance see Levine (1983, 1993). Levine's diagnosis of the significance of the explanatory gap is different from mine.

11. Nagel (1974).

12. Thomas Nagel, in a note commenting on an earlier draft.

13. Nagel (1974).

14. See Warner (1986).

15. When I see a ripe lemon in daylight and attend to my visual experience, I form the memory belief that

what I introspect is what I introspected (phenomenologically inclined as I am) the last time I saw a ripe lemon in daylight. It seems a reasonable empirical inference that probably ripe lemons in such circumstances cause in me states that my memory accurately records as the same. But this inference is, I take it, not reasonable on introspective grounds alone; it presupposes much about how the world works.

16. It is empirically unlikely that phenomenal qualities are identical with commonsense functional properties. Here is one way to see this. We know sensations can be produced by nonstandard means, that is, by poking around in the brain; but this of course is no part of the commonsense functional role of the property of seeing red. Now suppose this property is produced in me by a brain probe. What constitutes its being a sensation of red? If it is its commonsense functional role, then that property would be the sensation of red by virtue of (something like) its *normally* having such and such causes and effects (it doesn't have them here). But this makes sense only if the property in question is itself a *distinct* lower-order property about which it is contingently true that normally it has such and such causes and effects although it lacks them here. That lower-order property would then be a far better candidate (than the commonsense functional property) for being the property one's phenomenal conception discriminates. For this reason, such brain probes turn out to be strong and perhaps even conclusive evidence that phenomenal qualities, the ones we discriminate in applying phenomenal concepts, are not identical with commonsense functional properties. There are other ways of reaching the same conclusion.

17. Block 1978.

18. (Original version) For pointing out a substantial error in an ancestor of the paper, I am indebted to George Myro, whose correction put me on the right track as I now see it. I have learned much from conversations on phenomenal qualities with Janet Levin and Richard Warner. Stephen Schiffer made several valuable suggestions about the structure of the paper and got me to clarify certain arguments. I am also grateful for comments on the mentioned ancestor to Kent Bach, Hartry Field, Andreas Kemmerling, Dugald Owen, Thomas Ricketts, Hans Sluga, Stephen Stich, and Bruce Vermazen.

(Revised version) Many thanks to Ned Block for raising questions about modes of presentation and the blindsight case, to Georges Rey for making me see that more needed to be said about the explanatory gap, and to Kent Bach for helpful remarks on a number of points.

References

Block, N. (1978). "Troubles with Functionalism," in C. Wade Savage, ed., *Perception and Cognition: Issues in the Foundations of Psychology*. Vol. 9, *Minnesota Studies in the Philosophy of Science*. Minneapolis: University of Minnesota Press.

———. (1990). "Inverted Earth." *Philosophical Perspectives* **4**, 53–79.

Dennett, Daniel (1991). *Consciousness Explained*. Boston: Little Brown.

Harman, Gilbert (1990). "The Intrinsic Quality of Experience," *Philosophical Perspectives* **4**, 31–52.

Jackson, Frank (1982). "Epiphenomenal Qualia," *Philosophical Quarterly* 1982, 127–136.

———. (1986). "What Mary Didn't Know," *Journal of Philosophy* 83: 291–295.

———. (1994). "Armchair Metaphysics," in M. Michael ed., *Philosophy in Mind*. Norwell, MA: Kluwer.

Kripke, Saul (1980). *Naming and Necessity*. Cambridge, MA: Harvard University Press.

Levin, Janet (1983). "Functionalism and the Argument from Conceivability," *Canadian Journal of Philosophy*, Supplementary Volume 11.

———. (1986). "Could Love Be Like a Heatwave?," *Philosophical Studies*, 49: 245–261.

Levine, Joseph (1983). "Materialism and Qualia: the Explanatory Gap," *Pacific Philosophical Quarterly*, 64: 354–61.

———. (1993). "On Leaving Out What It Is Like," in M. Davies and G. Humphreys, eds., *Consciousness*. Oxford: Blackwell.

Lewis, David (1983a). "Mad Pain and Martian Pain," in *Philosophical Papers*, Vol. 1. Oxford: Oxford University Press.

———. (1983b). "Postscript" to the foregoing.

Loar, Brian (1990). "Personal References," in E. Villanueva, ed., *Information, Semantics and Epistemology*. Oxford: Blackwell.

———. (1991). "Can We Explain Intentionality?," in G. Rey and B. Loewer, eds., *Meaning in Mind*. Oxford: Blackwell.

————. (Forthcoming). "Reference from a First-Person Perspective," in *Philosophical Issues*.

McGinn, Colin (1930). "Consciousness and Cosmology: Hyperdualism Ventilated," in M. Davies and G. Humphreys, eds., *Consciousness*. Oxford: Blackwell.

Nagel, Thomas (1974). "What Is It Like To Be a Bat?", *Philosophical Review*, 1974: 435–450.

————. (1986). *The View From Nowhere*. Oxford: Oxford University Press.

Nemirow, Lawrence (1980). Review of Nagel's *Mortal Questions*, *Philosophical Review*, July 1980.

Rey, Georges (Forthcoming). "Towards a Projectivist Account of Conscious Experience," in T. Metzinger, ed., *Essays on Consciousness*.

Warner, Richard (1986). "A Challenge to Physicalism," *Australasian Journal of Philosophy*, 64; 249–265.

————. (1993). "Incorrigibility," in H. Robinson, ed., *Objections to Physicalism*, Oxford: Oxford University Press.

IX QUALIA

40 Quining Qualia

Daniel C. Dennett

Corralling the Quicksilver

"Qualia" is an unfamiliar term for something that could not be more familiar to each of us: the *ways things seem to us*. As is so often the case with philosophical jargon, it is easier to give examples than to give a definition of the term. Look at a glass of milk at sunset; *the way it looks to you*—the particular, personal, subjective visual quality of the glass of milk is the *quale* of your visual experience at the moment. The *way the milk tastes to you then* is another, gustatory *quale*, and *how it sounds to you* as you swallow is an auditory *quale*. These various "properties of conscious experience" are prime examples of *qualia*. Nothing, it seems, could you know more intimately than your own qualia; let the entire universe be some vast illusion, some mere figment of Descartes' evil demon, and yet what the figment is *made of* (for you) will be the *qualia* of your hallucinatory experiences. Descartes claimed to doubt everything that could be doubted, but he never doubted that his conscious experiences had qualia, the properties by which he knew or apprehended them.

The verb "to quine" is even more esoteric. It comes from *The Philosophical Lexicon* (Dennett 1987a), a satirical dictionary of eponyms: "quine, v. To deny resolutely the existence or importance of something real or significant." At first blush it would be hard to imagine a more quixotic quest than trying to convince people that there are no such properties as qualia; hence the ironic title of this chapter. But I am not kidding.

My goal is subversive. I am out to overthrow an idea that, in one form or another, is "obvious" to most people—to scientists, philosophers, lay people. My quarry is frustratingly elusive; no sooner does it retreat in the face of one argument than "it" reappears, apparently innocent of all charges, in a new guise.

Which idea of qualia am I trying to extirpate? Everything real has properties, and since I do not deny the reality of conscious experience, I grant that conscious experience has properties. I grant moreover that each person's states of consciousness have properties in virtue of which those states have the experiential content that they do. That is to say, whenever someone experiences something as being one way rather than another, this is true in virtue of some property of something happening in them at the time, but these properties are so unlike the properties traditionally imputed to consciousness that it would be grossly misleading to call any of them the long-sought qualia. Qualia are supposed to be *special* properties, in some hard-to-define way. My claim—which can only come into focus as we proceed—is that conscious experience has *no* properties that are special in *any* of the ways qualia have been supposed to be special.

The standard reaction to this claim is the complacent acknowledgment that while some people may indeed have succumbed to one confusion or fanaticism or another, one's own appeal to a modest, innocent notion of properties of subjective experience is surely safe. It is just that presumption of innocence I want to overthrow. I want to shift the burden of proof, so that anyone who wants to appeal to private, subjective properties has to prove first that in so doing they are *not* making a mistake. This status of *guilty until proven innocent* is neither unprecedented nor indefensible (so long as we restrict ourselves to concepts). Today, no biologist would dream of supposing that it was quite all right to appeal to some innocent concept of *élan vital*. Of course one *could* use the term to mean something in good standing; one could use *élan vital* as one's name for DNA, for instance, but this would be foolish nomenclature, considering the deserved suspicion with which the term is nowadays burdened. I want to make it just as uncomfortable for anyone to talk of qualia—or "raw feels" or "phenomenal properties" or "subjective and intrinsic properties" or "the qualitative character" of experience—with the standard presumption that they, and everyone else, knows what on earth they are talking about.[1]

What are qualia, *exactly*? This obstreperous query is dismissed by one author ("only half in jest") by invoking Louis Armstrong's legendary reply when asked what jazz was: "If you got to ask, you ain't never gonna get to know" (Block 1978, p. 281). This amusing tactic perfectly illustrates the presumption that is my target. If I succeed in my task, this move, which passes muster in most circles today, will look as quaint and insupportable as a jocular appeal to the ludicrousness of a living thing—a living thing, mind you!—doubting the existence of *élan vital*.

My claim, then, is not just that the various technical or theoretical concepts of qualia are vague or equivocal, but that the source concept, the "pre-theoretical" notion of which the former are presumed to be refinements, is so thoroughly confused that, even if we undertook to salvage some "lowest common denominator" from the theoreticians' proposals, any acceptable version would have to be so radically unlike the ill-formed notions that are commonly appealed to that it would be tactically obtuse—not to say Pickwickian—to cling to the term. Far better, tactically, to declare that there simply are no qualia at all.[2]

Rigorous arguments only work on well-defined materials, and, since my goal is to destroy our faith in the pre-theoretical or "intuitive" concept, the right tools for my task are intuition pumps, not formal arguments. What follows is a series of fifteen intuition pumps, posed in a sequence designed to flush out—and then flush away—the offending intuitions. In the next section, I will use the first two intuition pumps to focus attention on the traditional notion. It will be the burden of the rest of the chapter to convince you that these two pumps, for all their effectiveness, mislead us and should be discarded. In the following section, the next four intuition pumps create and refine a "paradox" lurking in the tradition. This is not a formal paradox, but only a very powerful argument pitted against some almost irresistibly attractive ideas. In the next section, six more intuition pumps are arrayed in order to dissipate the attractiveness of those ideas, and the following section drives this point home by showing how hapless those ideas prove to be when confronted with some real cases of anomalous experience. This will leave something of a vacuum, and in the final section three more intuition pumps are used to introduce and motivate some suitable replacements for the banished notions.

The Special Properties of Qualia

Intuition pump 1: watching you eat cauliflower. I see you tucking eagerly into a helping of steaming cauliflower, the merest whiff of which makes me feel faintly nauseated, and I find myself wondering how you could possibly relish *that taste*, and then it occurs to me that, to you, cauliflower probably tastes (must taste?) different. A plausible hypothesis, it seems, especially since I know that the very same food often tastes different to me at different times. For instance, my first sip of breakfast orange juice tastes much sweeter than my second sip if I interpose a bit of pancakes and maple syrup, but after a swallow or two of coffee, the orange juice goes back to tasting (roughly? exactly?) the way it did with the first sip. Surely we want to say (or think about) such things, and surely we are not wildly wrong when we do, so ... surely it is quite OK to talk of *the way the juice tastes to Dennett at time t*, and ask whether it is just the same as or different from *the way the juice tastes to Dennett at time t'* or *the way the juice tastes to Jones at time t*.

This "conclusion" seems innocent, but right here we have already made the big mistake. The final step presumes that we can isolate the qualia from everything else that is going on—at least in principle or for the sake of argument. What counts as *the way the juice tastes to x* can be distinguished, one supposes, from what is a mere accompaniment, contributory cause, or byproduct of this "central" way. One dimly imagines taking such cases and stripping them down gradually to the essentials, leaving their common residuum, the way things look, sound, feel, taste, smell to various individuals at various times, independently of how they are subsequently disposed to behave or believe. The mistake is not in supposing that we can in practice ever or always perform this act of purification with certainty, but the more fundamental mistake of supposing that there is such a residual property to take seriously, however uncertain our actual attempts at isolation of instances might be.

The examples that seduce us are abundant in every modality. I cannot imagine, will never know, could never know, it seems, how Bach sounded to Glenn Gould. (I can barely recover in my memory the way Bach sounded to me when I was a child.) And I cannot know, it seems, what it is like to be a bat (Nagel 1974), or whether you see what I see, colorwise, when we look up at a clear "blue" sky. The homely cases convince us of the reality of these special properties—those subjective tastes, looks, aromas, sounds—that we then apparently isolate for definition by this philosophical distillation.

The specialness of these properties is hard to pin down, but can be seen at work in *intuition pump 2: the wine-tasting machine.* Could Gallo Brothers replace their human wine-tasters with a machine? A computer-based "expert system" for quality control and classification is probably within the bounds of existing technology. We now know enough about the relevant chemistry to make the transducers that would replace taste buds and olfactory organs (delicate color vision would perhaps be more problematic), and we can imagine using the output of such transducers as the raw material—the "sense data" in effect—for elaborate evaluations, descriptions, classifications. Pour the sample in the funnel and, in a few minutes or hours, the system would type out a chemical assay, along with commentary: "a flamboyant and velvety Pinot, though lacking in stamina"—or words to such effect. Such a machine might well perform better than human wine-tasters on all reasonable tests of accuracy and consistency the wine-makers could devise,[3] but *surely* no matter how "sensitive" and "discriminating" such a system becomes, it will never have, and enjoy, what *we* do when we taste a wine: the qualia of conscious experience. Whatever informational, dispositional, functional properties its internal states have, none of them will be special in the way qualia are. If you share that intuition, you believe that there are qualia in the sense I am targeting for demolition.

What is special about qualia? Traditional analyses suggest some fascinating second-order properties of these properties. First, since one *cannot say* to another, no matter how eloquent one is and no matter how co-operative and imaginative one's audience is, exactly what way one is currently seeing, tasting, smelling, and so forth, qualia are *ineffable*—in fact the paradigm cases of ineffable items. According to tradition, at least part of the reason why qualia are ineffable is that they are *intrinsic* properties—which seems to imply *inter alia* that they are somehow atomic and unanalyzable. Since they are "simple" or "homogeneous" there is nothing to get hold of when trying to describe such a property to one unacquainted with the particular instance in question.

Moreover, verbal comparisons are not the only cross-checks ruled out. *Any* objective, physiological, or "merely behavioral" test—such as those passed by the imaginary wine-tasting system—would of necessity miss the target (one can plausibly argue), so all interpersonal comparisons of these ways of appearing are (apparently) systematically impossible. In other words, qualia are essentially *private* properties. And, finally, since they *are* properties of *my experiences* (they are not chopped liver, and they are not properties of, say, my cerebral blood flow—or haven't you been paying attention?), qualia are essentially directly accessible to the consciousness of their experiencer (whatever that means), or qualia are properties of one's experience with which one is intimately or directly acquainted (whatever that means), or "immediate phenomenological qualities" (Block 1978) (whatever that means). They are, after all, the very properties the appreciation of which permits us to identify our conscious states. So, to summarize the tradition, qualia are supposed to be properties of a subject's mental states that are

(1) ineffable

(2) intrinsic

(3) private

(4) directly or immediately apprehensible in consciousness.

Thus are qualia introduced onto the philosophical stage. They have seemed to be very significant properties to some theorists because they have seemed to provide an insurmountable and unavoidable stumbling block to functionalism or, more broadly, to materialism or, more broadly still, to any purely "third-person" objective viewpoint or approach to the world (Nagel 1986). Theorists of the contrary persuasion have patiently and ingeniously knocked down all the arguments, and said most of the right things, but they have made a tactical error, I am claiming, of saying in one way or another: "We theorists can handle *those qualia* you talk about just fine; we will show that you are just slightly in error about the nature of qualia." What they ought to have said is: "What qualia?"

My challenge strikes some theorists as outrageous or misguided because they think they have a much blander and hence less vulnerable notion of qualia to begin with. They think I am setting up and knocking down a straw man, and ask, in effect: "Who said qualia are ineffable, intrinsic, private, directly apprehensible ways things seem to one?" Since my suggested fourfold essence of qualia may strike many readers as tendentious, it may be instructive to consider, briefly, an apparently milder alternative: qualia are simply "the qualitative or phenomenal features of sense experience[s], in virtue of having which they re-

semble and differ from each other, qualitatively, in the ways they do" (Shoemaker 1982, p. 367). Surely I do not mean to deny *those* features.

I reply: it all depends on what "qualitative or phenomenal" comes to. Shoemaker contrasts *qualitative* similarity and difference with "intentional" similarity and difference—similarity and difference of the properties an experience represents or is "of." That is clear enough, but what then of "phenomenal"? Among the non-intentional (and hence qualitative?) properties of my visual states are their physiological properties. Might these very properties be the qualia Shoemaker speaks of? It is supposed to be obvious, I take it, that these sorts of features are ruled out, because they are not "accessible to introspection" (S. Shoemaker, personal communication). These are features of my visual *state*, perhaps, but not of my visual *experience*. They are not *phenomenal* properties.

But then another non-intentional similarity some of my visual states share is that they tend to make me think about going to bed. I think this feature of them *is* accessible to introspection—on any ordinary, pre-theoretical construal. Is that a phenomenal property or not? The term "phenomenal" means nothing obvious and untendentious to me, and looks suspiciously like a gesture in the direction leading back to ineffable, private, directly apprehensible ways things seem to one.[4]

I suspect, in fact, that many are unwilling to take my radical challenge seriously, largely because they want so much for qualia to be acknowledged. Qualia seem to many people to be the last ditch defense of the inwardness and elusiveness of our minds, a bulwark against creeping mechanism. They are sure there must be *some* sound path from the homely cases to the redoubtable category of the philosophers, since otherwise their last bastion of specialness will be stormed by science.

This special status for these presumed properties has a long and eminent tradition. I believe it was Einstein who once advised us that science could not give us the *taste* of the soup. Could such

The question is how do we know if they're spectrum really is inverted or if the plug was just upside-down?

a wise man have been wrong? Yes, if he is taken to have been trying to remind us of the qualia that hide forever from objective science in the subjective inner sancta of our minds. There are no such things. Another wise man said so—Wittgenstein (1958, especially pp. 91–100). Actually, what he said was:

The thing in the box has no place in the language-game at all; not even as a *something*; for the box might even be empty.—No, one can "divide through" by the thing in the box; it cancels out, whatever it is (p.100);

and then he went on to hedge his bets by saying "It is not a *something*, but not a *nothing* either! The conclusion was only that a nothing would serve just as well as a something about which nothing could be said" (p. 102). Both Einstein's and Wittgenstein's remarks are endlessly amenable to exegesis, but, rather than undertaking to referee this War of the Titans, I choose to take what may well be a more radical stand than Wittgenstein's.[5] Qualia are not even "something about which nothing can be said"; "qualia" is a philosophers' term which fosters[6] nothing but confusion, and refers in the end to no properties or features at all.

The Traditional Paradox Regained

Qualia have not always been in good odor among philosophers. Although many have thought, along with Descartes and Locke, that it made sense to talk about private, ineffable properties of minds, others have argued that this is strictly nonsense—however naturally it trips off the tongue. It is worth recalling how qualia were presumably rehabilitated as properties to be taken seriously in the wake of Wittgensteinian and verificationist attacks on them as pseudo-hypotheses. The original version of *intuition pump 3: the inverted spectrum* (Locke 1690; see 1959 edn.) is a speculation about two people: how do I know that you and I see the same subjective color when we look at something? Since we both learned

color words by being shown public colored objects, our verbal behavior will match *even if we experience entirely different subjective colors*. The intuition that this hypothesis is systematically unconfirmable (and undisconfirmable, of course) has always been quite robust, but some people have always been tempted to think technology could (in principle) bridge the gap.

Suppose, in *intuition pump 4: the Brainstorm machine*, there were some neuroscientific apparatus that fits on your head and feeds your visual experience into my brain (as in the movie, *Brainstorm*, which is not to be confused with the book, *Brainstorms*). With eyes closed I accurately report everything you are looking at, except that I marvel at how the sky is yellow, the grass red, and so forth. Would this not confirm, empirically, that our qualia were different? But suppose the technician then pulls the plug on the connecting cable, inverts it 180 degrees, and reinserts it in the socket. Now I report the sky is blue, the grass green, and so forth. Which is the "right" orientation of the plug? Designing and building such a device would require that its "fidelity" be tuned or calibrated by the normalization of the two subjects' reports—so we would be right back at our evidential starting point. The moral of this intuition pump is that no intersubjective comparison of qualia is possible, even with perfect technology.

So matters stood until someone dreamed up the presumably improved version of the thought experiment: the *intrapersonal* inverted spectrum. The idea seems to have occurred to several people independently (Gert 1965; Putnam 1965; Taylor 1966; Shoemaker 1969, 1975; Lycan 1973). Probably Block and Fodor (1972) have it in mind when they say, "It seems to us that the standard verificationist counterarguments against the view that the 'inverted spectrum' hypothesis is conceptually incoherent are not persuasive" (p. 172). In this version, *intuition pump 5: the neurosurgical prank*, the experiences to be compared are all in one mind. You wake up one morning to find that the grass has turned red, the sky yellow, and so

(above) ie, which one was what they experienced. How do we find out?

ie, since our own, we could tell.

forth. No one else notices any color anomalies in the world, so the problem must be in you. You are entitled, it seems, to conclude that you have undergone visual color qualia inversion (and we later discover, if you like, just how the evil neurophysiologists tampered with your neurons to accomplish this).

Here it seems at first—and indeed for quite a while—that qualia are acceptable properties after all, because propositions about them can be justifiably asserted, empirically verified, and even explained. After all, in the imagined case, we can tell a tale in which we confirm a detailed neurophysiological account of the precise etiology of the dramatic change you undergo. It is tempting to suppose, then, that neurophysiological evidence, incorporated into a robust and ramifying theory, would have all the resolving power we could ever need for determining whether or not someone's qualia have actually shifted.

But this is a mistake. It will take some patient exploration to reveal the mistake in depth, but the conclusion can be reached—if not secured—quickly with the help of *intuition pump 6: alternative neurosurgery*. There are (at least) two different ways the evil neurosurgeon might create the inversion effect described in intuition pump 5:

1. Invert one of the "early" qualia-producing channels, for example, in the optic nerve, so that all relevant neural events "downstream" are the "opposite" of their original and normal values. *Ex hypothesi* this inverts your qualia.

2. Leave all those early pathways intact and simply invert certain memory-access links—whatever it is that accomplishes your tacit (and even unconscious) comparison of today's hues with those of yore. *Ex hypothesi* this does *not* invert your qualia at all, but just your memory-anchored dispositions to react to them.

On waking up and finding your visual world highly anomalous, you should exclaim, "Egad! *Something* has happened! Either my qualia have been inverted or my memory-linked qualia reactions have been inverted. I wonder which!"

The intrapersonal, inverted spectrum thought experiment was widely supposed to be an improvement, since it moved the needed comparison into one subject's head. But now we can see that this is an illusion, since the link to earlier experiences, the link via memory, is analogous to the imaginary cable that might link two subjects in the original version.

This point is routinely—one might say traditionally—missed by the constructors of "intrasubjective, inverted spectrum" thought experiments, who suppose that the subject's *noticing the difference*—surely a vivid experience of discovery by the subject—would have to be an instance of (directly? incorrigibly?) recognizing the difference *as a shift in qualia*. But as my example shows, we could achieve the same startling effect in a subject without tampering with his presumed qualia at all. Since *ex hypothesi* the two different surgical invasions can produce exactly the same introspective effects, while only one operation inverts the qualia, nothing in the subject's experience can favor one of the hypotheses over the other. So unless he seeks outside help, the state of his own qualia must be as unknowable to him as the state of anyone else's qualia: hardly the privileged access or immediate acquaintance or direct apprehension the friends of qualia had supposed "phenomenal features" to enjoy!

The outcome of this series of thought experiments is an intensification of the "verificationist" argument against qualia. *If* there are qualia, they are even less accessible to our ken than we had thought. Not only are the classical intersubjective comparisons impossible (as the *Brainstorm* machine shows), but we cannot tell in our own cases whether our qualia have been inverted—at least not by introspection. It is surely tempting at this point—especially to non-philosophers—to decide that this paradoxical result must be an artifact of some philosophical misanalysis or other, the sort of thing that might well happen if you took a perfectly good pre-theoretical notion—our everyday notion of qualia—and illicitly stretched it beyond the breaking point. The philosophers

~ (4)
(see p.62

have made a mess; let them clean it up; meanwhile we others can get back to work, relying as always on our sober and unmetaphysical acquaintance with qualia.

Overcoming this ubiquitous temptation is the task of the next section, which will seek to establish the unsalvageable incoherence of the hunches that lead to the paradox by looking more closely at their sources and their motivation.

Making Mistakes About Qualia

The idea that people might be mistaken about their own qualia is at the heart of the ongoing confusion and must be explored in more detail, and with somewhat more realistic examples if we are to see the delicate role it plays.

Intuition pump 7: Chase and Sanborn. Once upon a time there were two coffee-tasters, Mr. Chase and Mr. Sanborn, who worked for Maxwell House.[7] Along with half a dozen other coffee-tasters, their job was to ensure that the taste of Maxwell House coffee stayed constant, year after year. One day, about six years after Chase had come to work for Maxwell House, he confessed to Sanborn:

I hate to admit it, but I'm not enjoying this work anymore. When I came to Maxwell House six yeas ago, I thought Maxwell House coffee was the best-tasting coffee in the world. I was proud to have a share in the responsibility for preserving that flavor over the years. And we've done our job well; the coffee tastes just the same today as it tasted when I arrived. But, you know, I no longer like it! My tastes have changed. I've become a more sophisticated coffee drinker. I no longer like *that taste* at all.

Sanborn greeted this revelation with considerable interest. "It's funny you should mention it," he replied, "for something rather similar has happened to me." He went on:

When I arrived here, shortly before you did, I, like you, thought Maxwell House coffee was tops in flavor. And now I, like you, really don't care for the coffee we're

making. But *my* tastes haven't changed; my . . . *tasters* have changed. That is, I think something has gone wrong with my taste buds or some other part of my taste-analyzing perceptual machinery. Maxwell House coffee doesn't taste to me the way it used to taste; if only it did, I'd still love it, for I still think *that taste* is the best taste in coffee. Now I'm not saying we haven't done our job well. You other tasters all agree that the taste is the same, and I must admit that on a day-to-day basis I can detect no change either. So it must be my problem alone. I guess I'm no longer cut out for this work.

Chase and Sanborn are alike in one way at least: they both used to like Maxwell House coffee, and now neither likes it. But they claim to be different in another way. Maxwell House tastes to Chase just the way it always did, but not so for Sanborn. But can we take their protestations at face value? Must we? Might one or both of them simply be wrong? Might their predicaments be importantly the same and their apparent disagreement more a difference in manner of expression than in experiential or psychological state? Since both of them make claims that depend on the reliability of their memories, is there any way to check on this reliability?

My reason for introducing two characters in the example is not to set up an interpersonal comparison between how the coffee tastes to Chase and how it tastes to Sanborn, but just to exhibit, side by side, two poles between which cases of intrapersonal experiential shift can wander. Such cases of intrapersonal experiential shift, and the possibility of adaptation to them, or interference with memory in them, have often been discussed in the literature on qualia, but without sufficient attention to the details, in my opinion. Let us look at Chase first. If we fall in for the nonce with the received manner of speaking, it appears at first that there are the following possibilities:

(a) Chase's coffee-taste qualia have stayed constant, while his reactive attitudes to those qualia, devolving on his canons of aesthetic judgment, etc., have shifted—which is what he seems, in his informal, casual way, to be asserting.

(b) Chase is simply wrong about the constancy of his qualia; they have shifted gradually and imperceptibly over the years, while his standards of taste have not budged—in spite of his delusions about having become more sophisticated. He is in the state Sanborn claims to be in, but just lacks Sanborn's self-knowledge.

(c) Chase is in some predicament intermediate between (a) and (b); his qualia have shifted some *and* his standards of judgment have also slipped.

Sanborn's case seems amenable to three counterpart versions:

(a) Sanborn is right; his qualia have shifted, due to some sort of derangement in his perceptual machinery, but his standards have indeed remained constant.

(b) Sanborn's standards have shifted unbeknownst to him. He is thus misremembering his past experiences, in what we might call a nostalgia effect. Think of the familiar experience of returning to some object from your childhood (a classroom desk, a tree-house) and finding it much smaller than you remember it to have been. Presumably as you grew larger your internal standard for what was large grew with you somehow, but your memories (which are stored as fractions or multiples of that standard) did not compensate, and hence, when you consult your memory, it returns a distorted judgment. Sanborn's nostalgia-tinged memory of good old Maxwell House is similarly distorted. (There are obviously many different ways this impressionistic sketch of a memory mechanism could be implemented, and there is considerable experimental work in cognitive psychology that suggests how different hypotheses about such mechanisms could be tested.)

(c) As before, Sanborn's state is some combination of (a) and (b).

I think that everyone writing about qualia today would agree that there are all these possibilities for Chase and Sanborn. I know of no one these days who is tempted to defend the high line

on infallibility or incorrigibility that would declare that alternative (a) is—and must be—the truth in each case, since people just cannot be wrong about such private, subjective matters.[8]

Since quandaries are about to arise, however, it might be wise to review in outline why the attractiveness of the infallibilist position is only superficial, so it will not recover its erstwhile allure when the going gets tough. First, in the wake of Wittgenstein (1958) and Malcolm (1956, 1959), we have seen that one way to buy such infallibility is to acquiesce in the complete evaporation of content (Dennett 1976). "Imagine someone saying: 'But I know how tall I am!' and laying his hand on top of his head to prove it" (Wittgenstein 1958, p. 96). By diminishing one's claim until there is nothing left to be right or wrong about, one can achieve a certain empty invincibility, but that will not do in this case. One of the things we want Chase to be right about (if he is right) is that he is not in Sanborn's predicament, so if the claim is to be viewed as infallible it can hardly be because it declines to assert anything.

There is a strong temptation, I have found, to respond to my claims in this chapter more or less as follows: "But after all is said and done, there is still something I know in a special way: I know *how it is with me right now.*" But if absolutely nothing follows from this presumed knowledge—nothing, for instance, that would shed any light on the different psychological claims that might be true of Chase or Sanborn—what is the point of asserting that one has it? Perhaps people just want to reaffirm their sense of proprietorship over their own conscious states.

The infallibilist line on qualia treats them as properties of one's experience one cannot in principle misdiscover, and this is a mysterious doctrine (at least as mysterious as papal infallibility) unless we shift the emphasis a little and treat qualia as *logical constructs* out of subjects' qualia judgments: a subject's experience has the quale F if and only if the subject judges his experience to have quale F. We can then treat such judgings as constitutive acts, in effect, bringing the quale into existence by the same sort of license as novelists have to determine the hair color of their characters by fiat. We do not ask how Dostoevski knows that Raskolnikov's hair is light brown.

There is a limited use for such interpretations of subjects' protocols, I have argued (Dennett 1978a, 1979, especially pp. 109–10, 1982), but they will not help the defenders of qualia here. Logical constructs out of judgments must be viewed as akin to theorists' fictions, and the friends of qualia want the existence of a particular quale in any particular case to be an empirical fact in good standing, not a theorist's useful interpretive fiction, else it will not loom as a challenge to functionalism or materialism or third-person objective science.

It seems easy enough, then, to dream up empirical tests that would tend to confirm Chase and Sanborn's different tales, but if passing such tests could support their authority (that is to say, their reliability), failing the tests would have to undermine it. The price you pay for the possibility of empirically confirming your assertions is the outside chance of being discredited. The friends of qualia are prepared, today, to pay that price, but perhaps only because they have not reckoned how the bargain they have struck will subvert the concept they want to defend.

Consider how we could shed light on the question of where the truth lies in the particular cases of Chase and Sanborn, even if we might not be able to settle the matter definitively. It is obvious that there might be telling objective support for one extreme version or another of their stories. Thus if Chase is unable to re-identify coffees, teas, and wines in blind tastings in which only minutes intervene between first and second sips, his claim to *know* that Maxwell House tastes just the same to him now as it did six years ago will be seriously undercut. Alternatively, if he does excellently in blind tastings, and exhibits considerable knowledge about the canons of coffee style (if such there be), his claim to have become a more sophisticated taster will be supported. Exploitation of the

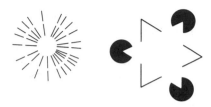

Figure 40.1

standard principles of inductive testing—basically Mill's method of differences—can go a long way toward indicating what sort of change has occurred in Chase or Sanborn—a change near the brute perceptual processing end of the spectrum or a change near the ultimate reactive judgment end of the spectrum. And as Shoemaker (1982) and others have noted, physiological measures, suitably interpreted in some larger theoretical framework, could also weight the scales in favor of one extreme or the other. For instance, the well-studied phenomenon of induced illusory boundaries (see figure 40.1) has often been claimed to be a particularly "cognitive" illusion, dependent on "top-down" processes and hence, presumably, near the reactive judgment end of the spectrum, but recent experimental work (Von der Heydt et al. 1984) has revealed that "edge detector" neurons *relatively* low in the visual pathways—in area 18 of the visual cortex—are as responsive to illusory edges as to real light-dark boundaries on the retina, suggesting (but not quite proving, since these might somehow still be "descending effects") that illusory contours are not imposed from on high, but generated quite early in visual processing. One can imagine discovering a similarly "early" anomaly in the pathways leading from taste buds to judgment in Sanborn, for instance, tending to confirm his claim that he has suffered some change in his basic perceptual—as opposed to judgmental—machinery.

But let us not overestimate the resolving power of such empirical testing. The space in each case between the two poles represented by possibility (a) and possibility (b) would be occupied by phenomena that were the product, somehow, of two factors in varying proportion: roughly, dispositions to generate or produce qualia and dispositions to react to the qualia once they are produced. (That is how our intuitive picture of qualia would envisage it.) Qualia are supposed to affect our action or behavior only via the intermediary of our judgments about them, so any behavioral test, such as a discrimination or memory test, since it takes acts based on judgments as its primary data, can give us direct evidence only about the *resultant* of our two factors. In extreme cases we can have indirect evidence to suggest that one factor has varied a great deal, the other factor hardly at all, and we can test the hypothesis further by checking the relative sensitivity of the subject to variations in the conditions that presumably alter the two component factors. But such indirect testing cannot be expected to resolve the issue when the effects are relatively small— when, for instance, our rival hypotheses are Chase's preferred hypothesis (a) and the minor variant to the effect that his qualia have shifted *a little* and his standards *less than he thinks*. This will be true even when we include in our data any unintended or unconscious behavioral effects, for their import will be ambiguous. (Would a longer response latency in Chase today be indicative of a process of "attempted qualia renormalization" or "extended aesthetic evaluation?")

The limited evidential power of neurophysiology comes out particularly clearly if we imagine a case of adaptation. Suppose, in *intuition pump 8: the gradual post-operative recovery*, that we have somehow "surgically inverted" Chase's taste bud connections in the standard imaginary way: post-operatively, sugar tastes salty, salt tastes sour, etc. But suppose further—and this is as realistic a supposition as its denial—that Chase has subsequently compensated—as revealed by his behavior. He now *says* that the sugary substance we place on his tongue is sweet, and no longer favors gravy on his ice-cream. Let us suppose the compensation is so thorough that on all behavioral and verbal tests his performance is in-distinguishable from that of normal subjects—and from his own pre-surgical performance.

If all the internal compensatory adjustment has been accomplished early in the process—intuitively, pre-qualia—then his qualia today are restored to just as they were (relative to external sources of stimulation) before the surgery. If on the other hand some or all of the internal compensatory adjustment is post-qualia, then his qualia have not been renormalized *even if he thinks they have*. But the physiological facts will not in themselves shed any light on where in the stream of physiological process twixt tasting and telling to draw the line at which the putative qualia appear as properties of that phase of the process. The qualia are the "immediate or phenomenal" properties, of course, but this description will not serve to locate the right phase in the physiological stream, for, echoing intuition pump 6, there will always be at least two possible ways of interpreting the neurophysiological theory, however it comes out. Suppose our physiological theory tells us (in as much detail as you like) that the compensatory effect in him has been achieved by an *adjustment in the memory-accessing process* that is required for our victim to compare today's hues to those of yore. There are *still* two stories that might be told:

(I) Chase's current qualia are still abnormal, but thanks to the revision in his memory-accessing process, he has in effect adjusted his memories of how things used to taste, so he no longer notices any anomaly.

(II) The memory-comparison step occurs just prior to the qualia phase in taste perception; thanks to the revision, it now *yields* the same old qualia for the same stimulation.

In (I) the qualia contribute to the input, in effect, to the memory comparator. In (II) they are part of the output of the memory comparator. These seem to be two substantially different hypotheses, but the physiological evidence, no matter how well developed, will not tell us on which side of memory to put the qualia. Chase's introspective evidence will not settle the issue between (I) and (II) either, since *ex hypothesi* those stories are not reliably distinguishable by him. Remember that it was to confirm or disconfirm Chase's opinion that we turned to the neurophysiological evidence in the first place. We can hardly use his opinion in the end to settle the matter between our rival neurophysiological theories. Chase may think that he thinks his experiences are the same as before *because* they really are (and he remembers accurately how it used to be), but he must admit that he has no introspective resources for distinguishing that possibility from alternative (I), in which he thinks things are as they used to be *because* his memory of how they used to be has been distorted by his new compensatory habits.

Faced with their subject's systematic neutrality, the physiologists may have their own reasons for preferring (I) to (II), or vice versa, for they may have *appropriated* the term "qualia" to their own theoretical ends, to denote some family of detectable properties that strike them as playing an important role in their neurophysiological theory of perceptual recognition and memory. Chase or Sanborn might complain—in the company of more than a few philosophical spokesmen—that these properties the neurophysiologists choose to call "qualia" are not the qualia they are speaking of. The scientists' retort is: "If we cannot distinguish (I) from (II), we certainly cannot support either of your claims. If you want our support, you must relinquish your concept of qualia."

What is striking about this is not just that the empirical methods would fall short of distinguishing what seem to be such different claims about qualia, but that they would fall short *in spite of being better evidence than the subject's own introspective convictions.* For the subject's own judgments, like the behaviors or actions that express them, are the resultant of our two postulated factors, and cannot discern the component proportions any better than external behavioral

tests can. Indeed, a subject's "introspective" convictions will generally be *worse* evidence than what outside observers can gather. For if our subject is—as most are—a "naive subject," unacquainted with statistical data about his own case or similar cases, his immediate, frank judgments are, evidentially, like any naive observer's perceptual judgments about factors in the outside world. Chase's intuitive judgments about his qualia constancy are no better off, epistemically, than his intuitive judgments about, say, lighting intensity constancy or room temperature constancy—or his own body temperature constancy. Moving to a condition inside his body does not change the intimacy of the epistemic relation in any special way. Is Chase running a fever or just feeling feverish? Unless he has taken steps to calibrate and cross-check his own performance, his opinion that his fever-perception apparatus is undisturbed is no better than a hunch. Similarly, Chase may have a strongly held opinion about the degree to which his taste-perceiving apparatus has maintained its integrity, and the degree to which his judgment has evolved through sophistication, but, pending the results of the sort of laborious third-person testing just imagined, he would be a fool to claim to know—especially to know directly or immediately—that his was a pure case (a), closer to (a) than to (b), or a case near (b).

Chase is on quite firm ground, epistemically, when he reports that *the relation* between his coffee-sipping activity and his judging activity has changed. Recall that this is the factor that Chase and Sanborn have in common: they used to like Maxwell House; now they do not. But unless he carries out on himself the sorts of tests others might carry out on him, his convictions about what has stayed constant (or nearly so) and what has shifted *must be sheer guessing.*

But then qualia—supposing for the time being that we know what we are talking about—must lose one of their "essential" second-order properties: far from being directly or immediately apprehensible properties of our experience, they are properties whose changes or constancies are either entirely beyond our ken, or inferrable (at best) from "third-person" examinations of our behavioral and physiological reaction patterns (if Chase and Sanborn acquiesce in the neurophysiologists' sense of the term). On this view, Chase and Sanborn should be viewed not as introspectors capable of a privileged view of these properties, but as autopsychologists, theorists whose convictions about the properties of their own nervous systems are based not only on their "immediate" or current experiential convictions, but also on their appreciation of the import of events they remember from the recent past.

There are, as we shall see, good reasons for neurophysiologists and other "objective, third-person" theorists to single out such a class of properties to study. But they are not qualia, for the simple reason that one's epistemic relation to them is *exactly* the same as one's epistemic relation to such external, but readily—if fallibly—detectable, properties as room temperature or weight. The idea that one should consult an outside expert, and perform elaborate behavioral tests on oneself to confirm what qualia one had, surely takes us too far away from our original idea of qualia as properties with which we have a particularly intimate acquaintance.

So perhaps we have taken a wrong turning. The doctrine that led to this embarrassing result was the doctrine that sharply distinguished qualia from their (normal) effects on reactions. Consider Chase again. He claims that coffee tastes "just the same" as it always did, but he admits—nay insists—that his reaction to "that taste" is not what it used to be. That is, he pretends to be able to divorce his apprehension (or recollection) of the quale—the taste, in ordinary parlance—from his different reactions to the taste. But this apprehension or recollection is itself a reaction to the presumed quale, so some sleight of hand is being perpetrated—innocently no doubt—by Chase. So suppose instead that Chase had insisted that precisely *because* his reaction was now different, the taste had changed for him. (When he told his

wife his original tale, she said "Don't be silly! Once you add the dislike you change the experience!" —and the more he thought about it, the more he decided she was right.)

Intuition pump 9: the experienced beer drinker. It is familiarly said that beer, for example, is an acquired taste; one gradually trains oneself—or just comes—to enjoy that flavor. What flavor? The flavor of the first sip? No one could like *that* flavor, an experienced beer drinker might retort:

Beer tastes different to the experienced beer drinker. If beer went on tasting to me the way the first sip tasted, I would never have gone on drinking beer! Or to put the same point the other way around, if my first sip of beer had tasted to me the way my most recent sip just tasted, I would never have had to acquire the taste in the first place! I would have loved the first sip as much as the one I just enjoyed.

If we let this speech pass, we must admit that beer is *not* an acquired taste. No one comes to enjoy *the way the first sip tasted.* Instead, prolonged beer drinking leads people to experience a taste they enjoy, but precisely their enjoying the taste guarantees that it is not the taste they first experience.[9]

But this conclusion, if it is accepted, wreaks havoc of a different sort with the traditional philosophical view of qualia. For if it is admitted that one's attitudes towards, or reactions to, experiences are in any way and in any degree constitutive of their experiential qualities, so that a change in reactivity *amounts to* or *guarantees* a change in the property, then those properties, those "qualitative or phenomenal features," cease to be "intrinsic" properties and in fact become paradigmatically extrinsic, relational properties.

Properties that "seem intrinsic" at first often turn out on more careful analysis to be relational. Bennett (1965) is the author of *intuition pump 10: the world-wide eugenics experiment.* He draws our attention to phenol-thio-urea, a substance which tastes very bitter to three-fourths of humanity, and as tasteless as water to the rest. Is it bitter? Since the reactivity to phenol-thio-urea is genetically transmitted, we could make it paradigmatically bitter by performing a large-scale breeding experiment: prevent the people to whom it is tasteless from breeding, and in a few generations phenol would be as bitter as anything to be found in the world. But we could also (in principle) perform the contrary feat of mass "eugenics" and thereby make phenol paradigmatically tasteless—as tasteless as water—without ever touching phenol. Clearly, public bitterness or tastelessness is not an intrinsic property of phenol-thio-urea but a relational property, since the property is changed by a change in the reference class of normal detectors.

The public versions of perceptual "qualia" all *seem* intrinsic, in spite of their relationality. They are not alone. Think of the "felt value" of a dollar (or whatever your native currency is). "How much is that in *real* money?" the American tourist is reputed to have asked, hoping to translate a foreign price onto the scale of "intrinsic value" he keeps in his head. As Elster (1985) claims, "there is a tendency to overlook the implicitly relational character of certain monadic predicates." Walzer (1985) points out that "a ten-dollar bill might seem to have a life of its own as a thing of value, but, as Elster suggests, its value implicitly depends on 'other people who are prepared to accept money as payment for goods.'" But even as one concedes this, there is still a tendency to reserve something subjective, felt value, as an "intrinsic" property of that ten-dollar bill. But as we now see, such intrinsic properties cannot be properties to which a subject's access is in any way privileged.

Which way should Chase go? Should he take his wife's advice and declare that since he cannot stand the coffee anymore, it no longer tastes the same to him (it used to taste good and now it tastes bad)? Or should he say that really, in a certain sense, it does taste the way it always did, or at least it sort of does—when you subtract the fact that it tastes so bad now, of course?

We have now reached the heart of my case. The fact is that we have to ask Chase which way he wants to go, and there really are two drastically

different alternatives available to him *if we force the issue*. Which way would *you* go? Which concept of qualia did you "always have in the back of your mind," guiding your imagination as you thought about theories? If you acknowledge that the answer is not obvious, and especially if you complain that this forced choice drives apart two aspects that you had supposed united in your pre-theoretic concept, you support my contention that there is no secure foundation in ordinary "folk psychology" for a concept of qualia. We *normally* think in a confused and potentially incoherent way when we think about the ways things seem to us.

When Chase thinks of "that taste" he thinks equivocally or vaguely. He harkens back in memory to earlier experiences, but need not try—or be able—to settle whether he is including any or all of his reactions or excluding them from what he intends by "that taste." His state then and his state now are different—*that* he can avow with confidence—but he has no "immediate" resources for making a finer distinction, nor any need to do so.[10]

This suggests that qualia are no more essential to the professional vocabulary of the phenomenologist (or professional coffee-taster) than to the vocabulary of the physiologist (Dennett 1978b). To see this, consider again the example of my dislike of cauliflower. Imagine now, in *intuition pump 11: the cauliflower cure*, that someone offers me a pill to cure my loathing for cauliflower. He promises that after I swallow this pill cauliflower will taste exactly the same to me as it always has, but I will like that taste. "Hang on," I might reply, "I think you may have just contradicted yourself." But in any event I take the pill and it works. I become an instant cauliflower-appreciator, but if I am asked which of the two possible effect (Chase-type or Sanborn-type) the pill has had on me, I will be puzzled, and will find nothing *in my experience* to shed light on the question. Of course I recognize that the taste is (sort of) the same—the pill has not made cauliflower taste like chocolate cake, after all—but at the same time my experience is so different now that I resist saying that cauliflower tastes the way it used to taste. There is in any event no reason to be cowed into supposing that my cauliflower experiences have some intrinsic properties behind, or in addition to, their various dispositional, reaction-provoking properties.

"But in principle there has to be a right answer to the question of how it is, intrinsically, with you now, even if you are unable to say with any confidence," Why? Would one say the same about all other properties of experience? Consider *intuition pump 12: visual field inversion created by wearing inverting spectacles*, a phenomenon which has been empirically studied for years. (G. M. Stratton published the pioneering work in 1896, and J. J. Gibson and I. Kohler were among the principal investigators; for an introductory account, see Gregory 1977.) After wearing inverting spectacles for several days subjects make an astonishingly successful adaptation. Suppose we pressed on them this question: "Does your adaptation consist in your re-inverting your visual field or in your turning the rest of your mind upside-down in a host of compensations?" If they demur, may we insist that there has to be a right answer, even if they cannot say with any confidence which it is? Such an insistence would lead directly to a new version of the old inverted spectrum thought experiment: "How do I know whether some people see things upside-down (but are perfectly used to it), while others see things right-side-up?"

Only a very naive view of visual perception could sustain the idea that one's visual field has a property of right-side-upness or upside-downness *independent of one's dispositions to react to it*— "intrinsic right-side-upness" we could call it (see my discussion of the properties of the "images" processed by the robot, SHAKEY, in Dennett 1982). So not all properties of conscious experience invite or require treatment as "intrinsic" properties. Is there something distinguishing about a certain subclass of properties (the "qualitative or phenomenal" subclass, presumably) that forces us to treat them—unlike subjective right-side-upness—as intrinsic properties? If not, such properties have no role to play, in either

physiological theories of experience, or in introspective theories.

Some may be inclined to argue this way: I can definitely imagine the experience of "spectrum inversion" from the inside; after all, I have actually experienced temporary effects of the same type, such as the "taste-displacement" effect of the maple syrup on the orange juice. What is imaginable, or actual, is possible. Therefore spectrum inversion or displacement (in all sensory modalities) is possible. But such phenomena just *are* the inversion or displacement of qualia, or intrinsic subjective properties. Therefore there must be qualia: intrinsic subjective properties.

This is fallacious. What one imagines and what one says one imagines may be two different things. To imagine visual field inversion, of the sort Stratton and Kohler's subjects experienced, is not necessarily to imagine the absolute inversion of a visual field (even if that is what it "feels like" to the subjects). Less obviously, your imagining—as vividly as you like—a case of subjective color-perception displacement is not necessarily your imagining what that phenomenon is typically called by philosophers: an inverted or displaced spectrum *of qualia*. Insofar as that term carries the problematic implications scouted here, there is no support for its use arising simply from the vividness or naturalness of the imagined possibility.

If there are no such properties as qualia, does that mean that "spectrum inversion" is impossible? Yes and no. Spectrum inversion as classically debated is impossible, but something like it is perfectly possible—something that is as like "qualia inversion" as visual field inversion is like the impossible *absolute* visual image inversion we just dismissed.

Some Puzzling Real Cases

It is not enough to withhold our theoretical allegiances until the sunny day when the philosophers complete the tricky task of purifying the everyday concept of qualia. Unless we take active steps to shed this source concept, and replace it with better ideas, it will continue to cripple our imaginations and systematically distort our attempts to understand the phenomena already encountered.

What we find, if we look at the actual phenomena of anomalies of color perception, for instance, amply bears out our suspicions about the inadequacy of the traditional notion of qualia. Several varieties of *cerebral achromatopsia* (brain-based impairment of color vision) have been reported, and while there remains much that is unsettled about their analysis, there is little doubt that the philosophical thought experiments have underestimated or overlooked the possibilities for counterintuitive collections of symptoms, as a few very brief excerpts from case histories will reveal.

Objects to the right of the vertical meridian appeared to be of normal hue, while to the left they were perceived only in shades of gray, though without distortions of form.... He was unable to recognize or name any color in any portion of the left field of either eye, including bright reds, blues, greens and yellows. As soon as any portion of the colored object crossed the vertical meridian, he was able to instantly recognize and accurately name its color. (Damasio et al. 1980)

This patient would seem at first to be unproblematically describable as suffering a shift or loss of color qualia in the left hemifield, but there is a problem of interpretation here, brought about by another case:

The patient failed in all tasks in which he was required to match the seen color with its spoken name. Thus, the patient failed to give the names of colors and failed to choose a color in response to its name. By contrast, he succeeded on all tasks where the matching was either purely verbal or purely nonverbal. Thus, he could give verbally the names of colors corresponding to named objects and vice versa. He could match seen colors to each other and to pictures of objects and could sort colors without error. (Geschwind and Fusillo 1966)

This second patient was quite unaware of any deficit. He "never replied with a simple 'I don't know' to the demand for naming a color" (Geschwind and Fusillo 1966, p. 140). There is a striking contrast between these two patients: both

have impaired ability to name the colors of things in at least part their visual field, but, whereas the former is acutely aware of his deficit, the latter is not. Does this difference make all the difference about qualia? If so, what on earth should we say about this third patient?

His other main complaint was that "everything looked black or grey" and this caused him some difficulty in everyday life.... He had considerable difficulty recognizing and naming colours. He would, for example, usually describe bright red objects as either red or black, bright green objects as either green, blue or black, and bright blue objects as black. The difficulty appeared to be perceptual and he would make remarks suggesting this; for example when shown a bright red object he said "a dirty smudgy red, not as red as you would normally see red." Colours of lesser saturation or brightness were described in such terms as "grey" "off-white" or "black," but if told to guess at the colour, he would be correct on about 50 per cent of occasions, being notably less successful with blues and greens than reds. (Meadows 1974)

This man's awareness of his deficit is problematic to say the least. It contrasts rather sharply with yet another case:

One morning in November 1977, upon awakening, she noted that although she was able to see details of objects and people, colors appeared "drained out" and "not true." She had no other complaint ... her vision was good, 20/20 in each eye.... The difficulty in color perception persisted, and she had to seek the advice of her husband to choose what to wear. Eight weeks later she noted that she could no longer recognize the faces of her husband and daughter.... [So in] addition to achromatopsia, the patient had prosopagnosia, but her linguistic and cognitive performances were otherwise unaffected. The patient was able to tell her story cogently and to have remarkable insight about her defects. (Damasio et al. 1980)

As Meadows notes, "Some patients thus complain that their vision for colors is defective while others have no spontaneous complaint but show striking abnormalities on testing."

What should one say in these cases? When no complaint is volunteered but the patient shows an impairment in color vision, is this a sign that his qualia are unaffected? ("His capacities to discriminate are terribly impaired, but, luckily for him, his inner life is untouched by this merely public loss.") We could line up the qualia this way, but equally we could claim that the patient has simply not noticed the perhaps gradual draining away or inversion or merging of his qualia revealed by his poor performance. ("So slowly did his inner life lose its complexity and variety that he never noticed how impoverished it had become.") What if our last patient described her complaint just as she did above, but performed normally on testing? One hypothesis would be that her qualia had indeed, as she suggested, become washed out. Another would be that in the light of her sterling performance on the color discrimination tests, her qualia were fine; she was suffering from some hysterical or depressive anomaly, a sort of color-vision hypochondria that makes her complain about a loss of color perception. Or perhaps one could claim that her qualia were untouched; her disorder was purely verbal: an anomalous understanding of the words she uses to describe her experience. (Other startlingly specific, color-word disorders have been reported in the literature.)

The traditional concept leads us to overlook genuine possibilities. Once we have learned of the curious deficit reported by Geschwind and Fusillo (1966), for instance, we realize that our first patient was never tested to see if he could still sort colors seen on the left or pass other non-naming, non-verbal, color-blindness tests. Those tests are by no means superfluous. Perhaps he would have passed them; perhaps, *in spite of what he says*, his qualia are as intact for the left field as for the right—if we take the capacity to pass such tests as "criterial." Perhaps his problem is "purely verbal." If your reaction to this hypothesis is that this is impossible, that must mean you are making his verbal, reporting behavior sovereign in settling the issue—but then you must rule out a priori the possibility of the condition I described as color-vision hypochondria.

There is no prospect of *finding* the answers to these brain-teasers in our everyday usage or the intuitions it arouses, but it is of course open to the philosopher to *create* an edifice of theory defending a particular set of interlocking proposals. The problem is that although normally a certain family of stimulus and bodily conditions yields a certain family of effects, any particular effect can be disconnected, and our intuitions do not tell us which effects are "essential" to quale identity or qualia constancy (cf. Dennett 1978a, chapter 11). It seems fairly obvious to me that none of the real problems of interpretation that face us in these curious cases are advanced by any analysis of how the concept of *qualia* is to be applied—unless we wish to propose a novel, technical sense for which the traditional term might be appropriated. But that would be at least a tactical error: the intuitions that surround and *purport* to anchor the current understanding of the term are revealed to be in utter disarray when confronted with these cases.

My informal sampling shows that some philosophers have strong opinions about each case and how it should be described in terms of qualia, but they find they are in strident (and ultimately comic) disagreement with other philosophers about how these "obvious" descriptions should go. Other philosophers discover that they really do not know what to say—not because there are not enough facts presented in the descriptions of the cases, but because it begins to dawn on them that they have not really known what they were talking about over the years.

Filling the Vacuum

If qualia are such a bad idea, why have they seemed to be such a good idea? Why does it seem as if there are these intrinsic, ineffable, private, "qualitative" properties in our experience? A review of the presumptive second-order properties of the properties of our conscious experiences will permit us to diagnose their attractiveness and find suitable substitutes (for a similar exercise, see Kitcher 1979).

Consider "intrinsic" first. It is far from clear what an intrinsic property would be. Although the term has had a certain vogue in philosophy, and often seems to secure an important contrast, there has never been an accepted definition of the second-order property of intrinsicality. If even such a brilliant theory-monger as David Lewis can try and fail, by his own admission, to define the extrinsic/intrinsic distinction coherently, we can begin to wonder if the concept deserves our further attention after all. In fact Lewis (1983) begins his survey of versions of the distinction by listing as one option: "We could Quine the lot, give over the entire family as unintelligible and dispensable," but he dismisses the suggestion immediately: "That would be absurd" (p. 197). In the end, however, his effort to salvage the accounts of Chisholm (1976) and Kim (1982) are stymied, and he conjectures that "if we still want to break in we had best try another window" (p. 200).

Even if we are as loath as Lewis is to abandon the distinction, should we not be suspicious of the following curious fact? If challenged to explain the idea of an intrinsic property to a neophyte, many people would hit on the following sort of example: consider Tom's ball; it has many properties, such as its being made of rubber from India, its belonging to Tom, its having spent the last week in the closet, and its redness. All but the last of these are clearly *relational* or *extrinsic* properties of the ball. Its redness, however, is an intrinsic property. Except that this is not so. Ever since Boyle and Locke we have known better. Redness—public redness—is a quintessentially relational property, as many thought experiments about "secondary qualities" show. (One of the first was Berkeley's [1737] pail of lukewarm water, and one of the best is Bennett's [1965] phenol-thio-urea.) The seductive step, on learning that public redness (like public bitterness, etc.) is a relational property after all, is to cling to intrinsicality ("*something* has to be intrinsic") and move it into the subject's head. It is often thought, in fact, that if we take a Lockean, relational

position on objective bitterness, redness, etc., we *must* complete our account of the relations in question by appeal to non-relational, intrinsic properties. If what it is to be objectively bitter is to produce a certain effect in the members of the class of normal observers, we must be able to specify that effect and distinguish it from the effect produced by objective sourness and so forth.

What else could distinguish this effect but some intrinsic property? Why not another relational or extrinsic property? The relational treatment of monetary value does not require, for its completion, the supposition of items of intrinsic value (value independent of the valuers' dispositions to react behaviorally). The claim that certain perceptual properties are different is, in the absence of any supporting argument, just question-begging. It will not do to say that it is just obvious that they are intrinsic. It may have seemed obvious to some, but the considerations raised by Chase's quandary show that it is far from obvious that any intrinsic property (whatever that comes to) could play the role of anchor for the Lockean, relational treatment of the public perceptual properties.

Why not give up intrinsicality as a second-order property altogether, at least pending resolution of the disarray of philosophical opinion about what intrinsicality might be? Until such time the insistence that qualia are the intrinsic properties of experience is an empty gesture at best; no one could claim that it provides a clear, coherent, understood prerequisite for theory.[11]

What, then, of ineffability? Why does it seem that our conscious experiences have ineffable properties? Because they do have *practically* ineffable properties. Suppose, in *intuition pump 13: the osprey cry*, that I have never heard the cry of an osprey, even in a recording, but know roughly, from reading my bird books, what to listen for: "a series of short, sharp, cheeping whistles, *cheep, cheep* or *chewk chewk*, etc; sounds annoyed" (Peterson 1947) (or words to that effect or better). The verbal description gives me a partial confinement of the logical space of possible bird cries. On its basis I can rule out many bird calls I have heard or might hear, but there is still a broad range of discriminable-by-me possibilities within which the actuality lies hidden from me like a needle in a haystack.

Then one day, armed with both my verbal description and my binoculars, I identify an osprey visually, and then hear its cry. "So *that's* what it sounds like," I say to myself, ostending—it seems—a particular mental complex of intrinsic, ineffable qualia. I dub the complex "*S*" (*pace* Wittgenstein), rehearse it in short-term memory, check it against the bird book descriptions, and see that, while the verbal descriptions are true, accurate, and even poetically evocative—I decide I could not do better with a thousand words— they still fall short of *capturing* the qualia complex I have called *S*. In fact, that is why I need the neologism, "*S*," to refer directly to the ineffable property I cannot pick out by description. My perceptual experience has pin-pointed for me the location of the osprey cry in the logical space of possibilities in a way verbal description could not.

But tempting as this view of matters is, it is overstated. First of all, it is obvious that from a single experience of this sort I do not—cannot— know how to generalize to other osprey calls. Would a cry that differed only in being half an octave higher also be an osprey call? That is an empirical, ornithological question for which my experience provides scant evidence. But more-over—and this is a psychological, not ornitho-logical, matter—I do not and cannot know, from a single such experience, which physical varia-tions and constancies in stimuli would produce an indistinguishable experience in me. Nor can I know whether I would react the same (have the same experience) if I were presented with what was, by all physical measures, a re-stimulation identical to the first. I cannot know the modulat-ing effect, if any, of variations in my body (or psyche).

This inscrutability of projection is surely one of the sources of plausibility of Wittgenstein's skepticism regarding the possibility of a private language:

> Wittgenstein emphasizes that ostensive definitions are always in principle capable of being misunderstood, even the ostensive definition of a color word such as "sepia." How someone understands the word is ex-hibited in the way someone goes on, "the use that he makes of the word defined." One may go on in the right way given a purely minimal explanation, while on the other hand one may go on in another way no matter how many clarifications are added, since these too can be misunderstood. (Kripke 1982, p. 83; see also pp. 40– 6)

But what is inscrutable in a single glance, and somewhat ambiguous after limited testing, can come to be justifiably seen as the deliverance of a highly specific, reliable, and projectible property detector, once it has been field-tested under a suitably wide variety of circumstances.

In other words, when first I hear the osprey cry, I may have identified a property detector in my-self, but I have no idea (yet) what property my newfound property detector detects. It might seem then that I know nothing new at all—that my novel experience has not improved my epis-temic predicament in the slightest. But of course this is not so. I may not be able to describe the property or identify it relative to any readily usable public landmarks (yet), but I am ac-quainted with it in a modest way: I can refer to the property I detected: it is the property I de-tected in *that* event. My experience of the osprey cry has given me a new way of thinking about osprey cries (an unavoidably inflated way of say-ing something very simple) which is practically ineffable both because it has (as yet for me) an untested profile in response to perceptual cir-cumstances, and because it is—as the poverty of the bird book description attests—such a highly informative way of thinking: a deliverance of an informationally very sensitive portion of my nervous system.

In this instance I mean information in the for-mal information theory sense of the term. Consider (*intuition pump 14: the Jello box*) the old spy trick, most famously encountered in the case of Julius and Ethel Rosenberg, of improving on a password system by tearing something in two (a Jello box, in the Rosenberg's case), and giving half to each of the two parties who must be careful about identifying each other. Why does it work? Because tearing the paper in two produces an edge of such informational complexity that it would be virtually impossible to reproduce by deliberate construction. (Cutting the Jello box along a straight edge with a razor would entirely defeat the purpose.) The particular jagged edge of one piece becomes a *practically* unique pattern-recognition device for its mate; it is an apparatus for detecting the shape property M, where M is uniquely instantiated by its mate. It is of the essence of the trick that we cannot replace our dummy predicate "M" with a longer, more complex, but accurate and exhaustive description of the property, for, if we could, we could use the description as a recipe or feasible algorithm for producing another instance of M or another M detector. The only *readily available* way of saying what property M is is just to point to our M detector and say that M is the shape property detected by this thing here.

And that is just what we do when we seem to ostend, with the mental finger of inner intention, a quale or qualia complex in our experience. We refer to a property—a public property of uncharted boundaries—via reference to our personal and idiosyncratic capacity to respond to it. That idiosyncrasy is the extent of our privacy. If I wonder whether your blue is my blue, your middle C is my middle C, I can coherently be wondering whether our discrimination profiles over a wide variation in conditions will be approximately the same. And they may not be; people experience the world quite differently. But that is empiricially discoverable by all the usual objective testing procedures.[12]

Peter Bieri has pointed out to me that there is a natural way of exploiting Dretske's (1981) sense of information in a reformulation of my first three second-order properties of qualia:, intrinsicality, ineffability, and privacy. (There are problems with Dretske's attempt to harness information theory in this way—see my discussion in Dennett 1987b, chapter 8—but they are not relevant to this point.) We could speak of what Bieri would call "phenomenal information properties" of psychological events. Consider the information—what Dretske would call the *natural meaning*—that a type of internal perceptual event might carry. That it carries that information is an objective (and hence, in a loose sense, intrinsic) matter since it is independent of what information (if any) the subject *takes* the event type to carry. Exactly what information is carried is (practically) ineffable, for the reasons just given. And it is private in the sense just given: proprietary and potentially idiosyncratic.

Consider how Bieri's proposed "phenomenal information properties" (let us call them *pips*) would apply in the case of Chase and Sanborn. Both Chase and Sanborn ought to wonder whether their pips have changed. Chase's speech shows that he is under the impression that his pips are unchanged (under normal circumstances—all bets are off if he has just eaten horseradish). He believes that the same objective things in the world—in particular, chemically identical caffeine-rich fluids—give rise to his particular types of taste experiences now as six years ago.

Sanborn is under the impression that his pips are different. He thinks his objective property detectors are deranged. He no longer has confidence that their deliverances today inform him of what they did six years ago. And what, exactly, did they inform him of then? If Sanborn were an ordinary person, we would not expect him to have an explicit answer, since most of us treat our taste detectors as mere M detectors, detecting whatever it is that they detect. (There are good reasons for this, analyzed by Akins, unpublished thesis, 1987.) But professional coffee-tasters are probably different. They probably have some pretty good idea of what kind of chemical-analysis transduction machinery they have in their mouths and nervous systems.

So far, so good. We could reinterpret Chase's and Sanborn's speeches as hypotheses about the constancies or changes in the outputs of their perceptual information-processing apparatus, and just the sort of empirical testing we imagined before would tend to confirm or disconfirm their opinions thus interpreted. But what would justify calling such an information-bearing property "phenomenal"?

Such a pip has, as the testimony of Chase and Sanborn reveals, the power to provoke in Chase and Sanborn acts of (apparent) reidentification or recognition. This power is of course a Lockean, dispositional property on a par with the power of bitter things to provoke a certain reaction in people. It is this power alone, however it might be realized in the brain, that gives Chase and Sanborn "access" to the deliverances of their individual property detectors.

We may "point inwardly" to one of the deliverances of our idiosyncratic, proprietary property detectors, but when we do, what are we pointing at? What does that deliverance itself consist of? Or what are its consciously apprehensible properties, if not just our banished friends the qualia? We must be careful here, for if we invoke an inner perceptual process in which we observe the deliverance with some inner eye and thereby discern its properties, we will be stepping back into the frying pan of the view according to which qualia are just ordinary properties of our inner states.

But nothing requires us to make such an invocation. We do not have to know how we identify or re-identify or gain access to such internal response types in order to be able so to identify them. This is a point that was forcefully made by the pioneer functionalists and materialists, and has never been rebutted (Farrell 1950; Smart 1959). The properties of the "thing experienced" are not to be confused with the properties of the event that realizes the experiencing. To put the matter vividly, the physical difference between someone's imagining a purple cow and imagining a green cow *might* be nothing more than the presence or absence of a particular zero or one in one of the brain's "registers." Such a brute physical presence is all that it would take to anchor the sorts of dispositional differences between imagining a purple cow and imagining a green cow that could then flow, causally, from that "intrinsic" fact. (I doubt that this is what the friends of qualia have had in mind when they have insisted that qualia are intrinsic properties.)

Moreover, it is our very inability to expand on, or modify, these brute dispositions so to identify or recognize such states that creates the doctrinal illusion of "homogeneity" or "atomicity to analysis" or "grainlessness" that characterizes the qualia of philosophical tradition.

This putative grainlessness, I hypothesize, is nothing but a sort of functional invariability: it is close kin to what Pylyshyn (1980, 1984) calls *cognitive impenetrability*. Moreover, this functional invariability or impenetrability is not absolute but itself plastic over time. Just as on the efferent side of the nervous system, *basic actions*—in the sense of Danto (1963, 1965) and others (see Goldman 1970)—have been discovered to be variable, and subject under training to decomposition (one can learn with the help of "biofeedback" to will the firing of a particular motor neuron "directly"), so what counts for an individual as the simple or atomic properties of experienced items is subject to variation with training.[13]

Consider the results of "educating" the palate of a wine-taster, or "ear training" for musicians. What had been "atomic" or "unanalyzable" becomes noticeably compound and describable; pairs that had been indistinguishable become distinguishable, and when this happens we say *the experience changes*. A swift and striking example of this is illustrated in *intuition pump 15: the guitar string*. Pluck the bass or low E string open and listen carefully to the sound. Does it have describable parts or is it one and whole and ineffably guitarish? Many will opt for the latter way of talking. Now pluck the open string again and carefully bring a finger down lightly over the octave fret to create a high "harmonic." Suddenly a *new* sound is heard: "purer" somehow and of course an octave higher. Some people insist that this is an entirely novel sound, while others will describe the experience by saying "the bottom fell out of the note"—leaving just the top. But then on a third open plucking one can hear, with surprising distinctness, the harmonic overtone that was isolated in the second plucking. The homogeneity and ineffability of the first experience is gone, replaced by a duality as "directly apprehensible" and clearly describable as that of any chord.

The difference in experience is striking, but the complexity apprehended on the third plucking was *there* all along (being responded to or discriminated). After all, it was by the complex pattern of overtones that you were able to recognize the sound as that of a guitar rather than of a lute or harpsichord. In other words, although the subjective experience has changed dramatically, the *pip* has not changed; you are still responding, as before, to a complex property so highly informative that it practically defies verbal description.

There is nothing to stop further refinement of one's capacity to describe this heretofore ineffable complexity. At any time, of course, there is one's current horizon of distinguishability—and that horizon is what sets, if anything does, what we should call the primary or atomic properties of what one consciously experiences (Farrell 1950). But it would be a mistake to transform the fact that inevitably there is a limit to our capacity to describe things we experience into the supposition that there are absolutely indescribable properties in our experience.

So when we look one last time at our original characterization of qualia, as ineffable, intrinsic, private, directly apprehensible properties of experience, we find that there is nothing to fill the bill. In their place are relatively or practically ineffable public properties we can refer to indirectly via reference to our private property detectors—

private only in the sense of idiosyncratic. And insofar as we wish to cling to our subjective authority about the occurrence within us of states of certain types or with certain properties, we can have some authority—not infallibility or incorrigibility, but something better than sheer guessing—but only if we restrict ourselves to relational, extrinsic properties like the power of certain internal states of ours to provoke acts of apparent re-identification. So contrary to what seems obvious at first blush, there simply are no qualia at all.

Acknowledgments

The first version of this chapter was presented at University College, London, in November 1978, and in various revisions at a dozen other universities in 1979 and 1980. It was never published, but was circulated widely as Tufts University Cognitive Science Working Paper 7, December 1979. A second version was presented at the Universities of Adelaide and Sydney in 1984, and in 1985 to psychology department colloquia at Harvard and Brown under the title "Properties of conscious experience." The second version was circulated in pre-print in 1985, again under the title "Quining qualia." The present version, the fourth, is a substantial revision, thanks to the helpful comments of many people, including Kathleen Akins, Ned Block, Alan Cowey, Sydney Shoemaker, Peter Bieri, William Lycan, Paul Churchland, Gilbert Harman, and the participants at Villa Olmo.

Notes

1. A representative sample of the most recent literature on qualia would include Block 1980; Shoemaker 1981, 1982; Davis 1982; White 1985; Armstrong and Malcolm 1984; Churchland 1985; and Conee 1985.

2. The difference between "eliminative materialism"— of which my position on qualia is an instance—and a "reductive" materialism that takes on the burden of

identifying the problematic item in terms of the foundational materialistic theory is thus often best seen not so much as a doctrinal issue but as a tactical issue: how might we most gracefully or effectively enlighten the confused in this instance? See my discussion of "fatigues" in the Introduction to *Brainstorms* (Dennett 1978a) and, earlier, my discussion of what the enlightened ought to say about the metaphysical status of *sakes* and *voices* in *Content and consciousness* (Dennett 1969, chapter 1).

3. The plausibility of this concession depends less on a high regard for the technology than on a proper skepticism about human powers, now documented in a fascinating study by Lehrer (1983).

4. Shoemaker (1984, p. 356) seems to be moving reluctantly towards agreement with this conclusion: "So unless we can find some grounds on which we can deny the possibility of the sort of situation envisaged ... we must apparently choose between rejecting the functionalist account of qualitative similarity and rejecting the standard conception of qualia. I would prefer not to have to make this choice; but if I am forced to make it, I reject the standard conception of qualia."

5. Shoemaker (1982) attributes a view to Wittgenstein (acknowledging that "it is none too clear" that this is actually what Wittgenstein held) which is very close to the view I defend here. But to Shoemaker, "it would seem offhand that Wittgenstein was mistaken" (p. 360), a claim Shoemaker supports with a far from offhand thought experiment—which Shoemaker misanalyzes if the present chapter is correct. (There is no good reason, contrary to Shoemaker's declaration, to believe that his subject's *experience* is systematically different from what it was before the inversion.) Smart (1959) expresses guarded and partial approval of Wittgenstein's hard line, but cannot see his way clear to as uncompromising an eliminativism as I maintain here.

6. In 1979, I read an earlier version of this chapter in Oxford, with a commentary by John Foster, who defended qualia to the last breath, which was: "qualia should not be quined but fostered!" Symmetry demands, of course, the following definition for the most recent edition of *The philosophical lexicon* (Dennett 1987a): "foster, v. To acclaim resolutely the existence or importance of something chimerical or insignificant."

7. This example first appeared in print in my reflections on Smullyan in *The Mind's I* (Hofstadter and Dennett 1981, pp. 427–8).

8. Kripke (1982, p. 40) comes close when he asks rhetorically: "Do I not know, directly, and *with a fair degree of certainty*, that I mean plus [by the function I call 'plus']?" [my emphasis]. Kripke does not tell us what is implied by "a fair degree of certainty," but presumably he means by this remark to declare his allegiance to what Millikan (1984) attacks under the name of "meaning rationalism."

9. We can save the traditional claim by ignoring presumably private or subjective qualia and talking always of public tastes—such as the public taste of Maxwell House coffee that both Chase and Sanborn agree has remained constant. Individuals can be said to acquire a taste for such a public taste.

10. "I am not so wild as to deny that my sensation of red today is like my sensation of red yesterday. I only say that the similarity can *consist* only in the physiological force behind consciousness—which leads me to say, I recognize this feeling the same as the former one, and so does not consist in a community of sensation." (Peirce, *Collected Works*, Vol. V, p. 172 fn. 2).

11. A heroic (and, to me, baffling) refusal to abandon intrinsicality is Sellars' (1981) contemplation over the years of his famous pink ice cube, which leads him to postulate a revolution in microphysics, restoring objective "absolute sensory processes" in the face of Boyle and Locke and almost everybody since them (also see my commentary in Dennett 1981).

12. Stich (1983) discusses the implications for psychological theory of incommensurability problems that can arise from such differences in discrimination profiles (see, especially, chapters 4 and 5).

13. See Churchland (1979, especially chapter 2) for supporting observations on the variability of perceptual properties, and for novel arguments against the use of "intrinsic properties" as determiners of the meaning of perceptual predicates. See also Churchland (1985) for further arguments and observations in support of the position sketched here.

References

Akins, K. (1987). Information and organisms: or why nature doesn't build epistemioc engines. Unpublished Ph.D. thesis. University of Michigan.

Armstrong, D., and Malcolm, N. (ed.) (1984). *Consciousness and causality*. Blackwell Scientific Publications, Oxford.

Bennett, J. (1965). Substance, reality and primary qualities. *American Philosophical Quarterly* 2, 1–17.

Berkeley, G. (1713). *Three dialogues between Hylas and Philonous*. London.

Block, N. (1978). Troubles with functionalism. In *Perception and cognition: Issues in the foundations of psychology* (ed. C. W. Savage), pp. 261–326. University of Minnesota Press.

———. (1980). Are absent qualia impossible? *Philosophical Review* 89, 257.

Block, N., and Fodor, J. (1972). What psychological states are not. *Philosophical Review* 81, 159–81.

Chisholm, R. (1976). *Person and object*. Open Court Press, La Salle, IL.

Churchland, P. M. (1979). *Scientific realism and the plasticity of mind*. Cambridge University Press.

———. (1985). Reduction, qualia and the direct inspection of brain states. *Journal of Philosophy* 82, 8–28.

Conee, E. (1985). The possibility of absent qualia. *Philosophical Review* 94, (3), 345–66.

Damasio, A., Yamada, T., Damasio, H., Corbett, J., and McKee, J. (1980). Central achromatopsia: Behavioral, anatomic, and physiological aspects. *Neurology* 30, 1064–71.

Danto, A. (1963). What we can do. *Journal of Philosophy* 60, 435–45.

———. (1965). Basic actions. *American Philosophical Quarterly* 60, 141–48.

Davis, L. (1982). Functionalism and absent qualia. *Philosophical Studies* 41 (2), 231–51.

Dennett, D. C. (1969). *Content and consciousness*. Routledge and Kegan Paul, Andover, Hants.

———. (1976). Are dreams experiences? *Philosophical Review* 73, 151–71.

———. (1978a). *Brainstorms*. MIT Press, Cambridge, MA.

——— (1978b). Two approaches to mental images. In *Brainstorms* (ed. D. C. Dennett), pp. 174–89. MIT Press, Cambridge, MA.

———. (1979). On the absence of phenomenology. In *Body, mind, and method*, (ed. D. F. Gustafson and B. L. Tapscott), pp. 93–114. D. Reidel, Dordrecht.

———. (1981). Wondering where the yellow went. *Monist* 64, 102–8.

———. (1982). How to study human consciousness empirically: or nothing comes to mind. *Synthese* 53, 159–80.

———. (1987a). *The philosophical lexicon*, (8th ed.). Copy available from the American Philosophical Association, University of Delaware, Newark, DE.

———. (1987b). *The intentional stance*. MIT Press, Cambridge, MA.

Dretske, F. (1981). *Knowledge and the flow of information*. MIT Press, Cambridge, MA.

Elster, J. (1985). *Making sense of Marx*. Cambridge University Press.

Farrell, B. (1950). Experience. *Mind* 59, 170–98.

Gert, B. (1965). Imagination and verifiability. *Philosophical Studies* 16, 44–7.

Geschwind, N., and Fusillo, M. (1966). Color-naming defects in association with alexia. *Archives of Neurology* 15, 137–46.

Goldman, A. (1970). *A theory of human action*. Prentice-Hall, Englewood Cliffs, NJ.

Gregory, R. (1977). *Eye and brain* (3d ed.). Weidenfeld and Nicolson, London.

Hofstadter, D., and Dennett, D. C. (1981). *The mind's I: Fantasies and reflections on self and soul*. Basic Books, New York.

Kim, J. (1982). Psychophysical supervenience. *Philosophical Studies* 41, 51–70.

Kitcher, P. (1979). Phenomenal qualities. *American Philosophical Quarterly* 16, 123–9.

Kripke, S. (1982). *Wittgenstein on rules and private language*. Harvard University Press, Cambridge, MA.

Lehrer, A. (1983). *Wine and conversation*. University of Indiana Press.

Lewis, D. (1983). Extrinsic properties. *Philosophical Studies* 44, 197–200.

Locke, J. (1959). *An essay concerning human understanding* (ed. A. C. Fraser). Dover, New York.

Lycan, W. (1973). Inverted spectrum. *Ratio* 15, 315–19.

Malcolm, N. (1956). Dreaming and skepticism. *Philosophical Review* 65, 14–37.

———. (1959). *Dreaming*. Routledge and Kegan Paul, Andover, Hants.

Meadows, J. C. (1974). Disturbed perception of colours associated with localized cerebral lesions. *Brain* 97, 615–32.

Millikan, R. (1984). *Language, thought and other biological categories*. MIT Press, Cambridge, MA.

Nagel, T. (1974). What is it like to be a bat? *Philosophical Review* 83, 435–51.

————. (1986). *The view from nowhere*. Oxford University Press.

Peirce, C. (1931–58). *Collected Works*. Vol. V (ed. C. Hartshorne and P. Weiss). Harvard University Press, Cambridge MA.

Peterson, R. T. (1947). *A field guide to the birds*. Houghton Mifflin, Boston.

Putnam, H. (1965). Brains and behavior. In *Analytical philosophy*, second series, (ed. J. Butler), pp. 1–19. Blackwell Scientific Publications, Oxford.

Pylyshyn, Z. (1980). Computation and cognition: Issues in the foundations of cognitive science. *Behavioral and Brain Sciences* 3, 111–32.

————. (1984). *Computation and cognition: Toward a foundation for cognitive science*. MIT Press, Cambridge, MA.

Sellars, W. (1981). Foundations for a metaphysics of pure process (the Carus Lectures). *Monist* 64, 3–90.

Shoemaker, S. (1969). Time without change. *Journal of Philosophy* 66, 363–81.

————. (1975). Functionalism and qualia. *Philosophical Studies* 27, 291–315.

————. (1981). Absent qualia are impossible—a reply to Block. *Philosophical Review* 90, 581–99.

————. (1982). The inverted spectrum. *Journal of Philosophy* 79, 357–81.

————. (1984). *Identity, cause, and mind*, pp. 351–7. Cambridge University Press.

Smart, J. C. (1959). Sensations and brain processes. *Philosophical Review* 68, 141–56.

Stich, S. (1983). *From folk psychology to cognitive science: The case against belief*. MIT Press, Cambridge, MA.

Taylor, D. M. (1966). The incommunicability of content. *Mind* 75, 527–41.

Von Der Heydt, R., Peterhans, E., and Baumgartner, G. (1984). Illusory contours and cortical neuron response. *Science* 224, 1260–2.

Walzer, M. (1985). What's left of Marx. *New York Review of Books*, 21 November, 43–6.

White, S. (1985). Professor Shoemaker and so-called "qualia" of experience. *Philosophical Studies* 47, 369–83.

Wittgenstein, L. (1958). *Philosophical investigations*. Blackwell Scientific Publications, Oxford.

41 The Inverted Spectrum

Sydney Shoemaker

As best I can determine, the idea of spectrum inversion made its first appearance in the philosophical literature when John Locke, in the *Essay*, entertained the possibility that *"the same Object should produce in several Men's Minds different Ideas at the same time; for example, the Idea, that a Violet produces in one Man's Mind by his Eyes, were the same that a Marigold produced in another Man's, and vice versa."*[1] It was obviously part of Locke's supposition that the color experiences of the two people differ in such a way that the difference could not manifest itself in their behavior and their use of color words, and we will take this as an essential feature of full-fledged intersubjective spectrum inversion. This "inverted spectrum hypothesis" was revived in the early years of this century, and in the heyday of logical positivism it was a favorite target for application of the verificationist theory of meaning; there are classic formulations and discussions of it in the writings of C. I. Lewis, Moritz Schlick, Hans Reichenbach, John Wisdom, Max Black, and J. J. C. Smart,[2] and it lurks beneath the surface, and sometimes at it, in many of Wittgenstein's discussions of "private experience."

I

Wittgenstein seems to have been the first to give this idea a new twist by envisioning the possibility of *intra*subjective spectrum inversion:

Consider this case: someone says "I can't understand it, I see everything red blue today and vice versa." We answer "it must look queer!" He says it does and, e.g., goes on to say how cold the glowing coal looks and how warm the clear (blue) sky. I think we should under these or similar circumstances be inclined to say that he saw red what we saw blue. And again we should say that we know that he means by the words 'blue' and 'red' what we do as he has always used them as we do.[3]

What is imagined here is that there should be a systematic difference between the character of someone's color experience at a certain time and the character of that *same* person's color experience at another time. If Wittgenstein was indeed the first to describe such a case, there is a mild irony in this. For there is a natural line of argument, which we will come to shortly, from the possibility of *intra*subjective inversion to the conclusion that it makes sense to suppose, and may for all we know be true, that *inter*subjective spectrum inversion actually exists—that among normally sighted people, that is, those who are not color blind, there are radical differences in the way things look with respect to color. And Wittgenstein is associated, probably more than any other philosopher, with the view that this supposition makes no sense. In the midst of the attack on the notions of "private language" and "private objects" in the *Philosophical Investigations*[4] there occurs the following passage:

The essential thing about private experience is really not that each person possesses his own exemplar, but that nobody knows whether other people also have *this* or something else. The assumption would thus be possible—though unverifiable—that one section of mankind has one sensation of red and another section another. (p. 95)

I think it is pretty clear from the tenor of the surrounding passages that Wittgenstein thinks that this "assumption" is in fact senseless or conceptually incoherent and takes it to be a *reductio ad absurdum* of the notion of "private experience" he is attacking that it implies that this "assumption" might be true.

I said that there is a natural line of argument from what Wittgenstein seems to admit—the logical possibility of intrasubjective spectrum inversion—to what he apparently denies the meaningfulness of asserting—namely, the possibility that intersubjective spectrum inversion actually exists. One reason why the claim that intrasubjective inversion is logically possible makes a natural starting point for such an argument is that it seems immune from verificationist objections; as Wittgenstein's example shows, it is easy to imagine phenomena we would take as verifying that such a change in color experience had occurred. One can imagine this happening in oneself, one can imagine another person reporting that it had happened to him, and one can imagine nonverbal behavior that would be evidence of such a change. But—and here comes the promised argument—it seems, offhand, that if intrasubjective spectrum inversion is possible, intersubjective inversion must also be possible. For suppose that someone, call him Fred, undergoes intrasubjective inversion at time *t*.[5] Assuming that others did not also undergo inversion at *t*, it would seem that either before *t* or afterward (or both) Fred's color experience must have been radically different from that of others. But if we allow that there can be intersubjective inversion in cases in which there is intrasubjective inversion, it seems that we must allow that there could be intersubjective inversion without intrasubjective inversion; if the color experience of a person can differ from that of others at some point during his career, it should be possible for such a difference to exist throughout a person's career. But if this is a possibility, then it does seem perfectly coherent to suppose, and perfectly compatible with all the behavioral evidence we have about the experiences of others, that, in Wittgenstein's words, "one section of mankind has one sensation of red and another section another."[6]

Suppose one allows the premise of this argument: that intrasubjective inversion is possible; how, if at all, can one resist its conclusion? How is one to reject the inference from the possibility of intrasubjective spectrum inversion to the possibility of intersubjective spectrum inversion? One way is to maintain that the relevant notion of similarity and difference, what I shall call *qualitative* similarity and difference, is well defined only for the intrasubjective case. This allows one to deny the possibility of intersubjective inversion, but does so at the cost of forbidding one from saying that one's color experiences are qualitatively similar to those of others. On this

view (see section IV), experiences belonging to different persons can be neither qualitatively similar nor qualitatively different.

It does not appear, however, that Wittgenstein could have taken this way out. In the passage in which he seems to allow the possibility of intrasubjective inversion he seems to allow that the case he describes would also be a case of intersubjective inversion; he says that "we should under these or similar circumstances be inclined to say that we saw red what he saw blue." Why then is Wittgenstein not committed to the very thing he seems to deny? He was not unaware of the problem, for in a later passage he wrote:

We said that there were cases in which we should say that the person sees green what I see red. Now the question suggests itself: if this can be so at all, why should it not always be the case? It seems, if once we have admitted that it can happen under peculiar circumstances, that it may always happen.... This is a very serious situation. ("Notes for Lectures," p. 316)

A full discussion of how Wittgenstein thought he could solve or avoid this problem would take me too far afield—and the answer is none too clear. Briefly, however, I think that it is only in a qualified sense that he allowed that intrasubjective inversion is possible, and only in a similarly qualified sense that he allowed that in a case of intrasubjective inversion we would also have intersubjective inversion. I think he thought that such a case would have to be one in which the person who has undergone inversion describes things as looking "queer," and says, for example, that the clear sky looks warm and that the glowing coal looks cold. Now, if the difference between someone's color experience and ours went with a tendency on his part to describe his experience in such ways, then of course it would not be a difference that could not manifest itself in behavior (since verbal behavior is behavior), and so would fail to amount to a case of "full-blown" intersubjective spectrum inversion.

But it would seem offhand that Wittgenstein was mistaken if he thought that any case in which we could know that someone's experiences of colors at one time were radically different from his experiences of the same colors at another time would have to be one in which at one or the other of the times the person describes his experiences as "queer." Suppose that it was thirty years ago that Fred underwent his spectrum inversion. We have monitored him closely since then, and at no time has he reported a "reinversion," or given any behavioral indication of one. He has, however, gradually become accustomed to the new look of things and to describing the colors of things in the same words others use; for some time now it has come natural to him to say that the sky is blue and daffodils yellow, and, moreover, that the sky *looks* blue and daffodils *look* yellow. Each day during the last thirty years we have asked him how things looked compared with how he remembered their looking the day before, and each day (after the first) he has confidently reported that things look the same with respect to color as they did the day before—although in the early years of this period he also reported that their looking this way was seeming less strange with the passage of time, that he was again finding it natural to describe glowing coals as looking warm rather than cold, and so on. In such a case I think we could have good reason to think that Fred's color experience now is systematically different from what it was before the inversion, even though he does not now, and did not then, describe his experience as "queer."[7] But if this case is possible, then it seems that full-fledged intersubjective spectrum inversion should also be possible.

II

I have so far talked as if we would have a case of spectrum inversion if blue things looked to you the way yellow things look to me, and vice versa. But a little reflection shows that this is not enough. If you and I differed *only* in this way and if all other colors looked the same to us, it is obvious that the difference would manifest itself in behavior, both verbal and nonverbal. One of us would find yellow things more similar to orange things, and less similar to violet things, than blue things are, while the other would find just the opposite. What is required for full-fledged intersubjective inversion is that the color "quality spaces" of the two people should have the same structure, which requires (among other things) that under the same lighting conditions they make the same judgments of relative color similarity ("A is more similar to B than to C") about the same visually presented objects. If this condition is satisfied, then any difference in how the two people see colors will ramify through all the colors; all, or virtually all, will have to look different to the one person than they do to the other. Pretending, for the moment, that we have only the pure, "saturated," colors to deal with, we might have such a systematic difference if to each of our two persons each color looked the way its complementary color looked to the other.

The same applies, *mutatis mutandis*, to the case of intrasubjective inversion. And this puts us in a position to answer an objection that is sometimes raised against putative cases of intrasubjective spectrum inversion. Suppose Fred claims to have just undergone spectrum inversion. How do we know, it is asked, that what has changed in Fred is his color experience, and not his understanding of color words or his memory of how things looked to him in the past—that he is not the victim of some peculiar sort of aphasia or memory illusion? The suggestion behind such questions is often that the questions are unanswerable and that this undermines the claim that we could know that intrasubjective inversion had occurred. To parry such objections, let me complicate our case slightly. Let us suppose that the relationships between the different colors can be represented by associating each determinate shade of color with a point on the circumference of a circle, the distances between the points along the circumference corresponding to the perceived differences between the shades, and the point corresponding to any shade being opposite the point corresponding to its complementary. Let us label the points on the circle as they are on the face of a clock, with the numerals 1 through 12. I will suppose, indeed, that we have a circle, call it a "color circle," on which the points on the circumference actually have the colors they represent. And now let us imagine our case as follows. At time t_1 Fred was perfectly normal in his use of color words, his discriminatory abilities, and the like. But at time t_2 he tells us that a remarkable change has occurred. Although most things look to him the way they used to, a sizable minority look different. He describes the change by saying that, if he looks at a color circle, it looks the way it would have looked at t_1 if the shades between 12 and 2 had been interchanged with their complementaries (those between 6 and 8), the rest of the circle remaining unchanged. According to this, the structure of Fred's visual color space at t_2 is different from its structure at t_1. And, because of this, we can suppose that Fred's testimony is supported by his nonverbal discriminatory and recognitional behavior—the ease with which he discriminates certain shades that formerly were difficult for him to discriminate (and are so for the rest of us) and the difficulty with which he discriminates other shades that seem to us (and previously seemed to him) very different. At t_3 Fred tells us that another such change has occurred, adding itself to the first one; this time it is the shades between 2 and 4 that have changed places with their complementaries (those between 8 and 10). Again we can suppose there is behavioral evidence to substantiate his claim. Finally, at t_4 he tells us that still another such change has occurred; this time it is the shades between 4 and 6 which have changed places with their complementaries (those between 10 and 12). Again there is behavioral evidence to substantiate his claim. But at t_4, unlike t_2 and t_3, Fred's judgments of color similarity and difference will coincide with ours and those he made at t_1; at t_4 the structure of Fred's color space is the same as it was at t_1. Yet Fred reports that his color experience is systematically different from what it was at t_1; each color looks the way

its complementary looked then. And this claim seems to be supported by the behavioral evidence that supported his claims that there were changes in his color experience between t_1 and t_2, between t_2 and t_3, and between t_3 and t_4; for these partial inversions add up to a total spectrum inversion. It does not appear that any sort of aphasia or memory failure could account for the phenomena imagined here.[8]

Returning to the case of intersubjective spectrum inversion, I suspect that the main reason why many philosophers are hostile to the claim that such spectrum inversion is possible is that they suspect that admitting that claim will put one on a slippery slope which will eventually land one in skepticism about other minds. If I cannot know from the behavior of others that their color experiences are like my own, neither can I know that when they are cut or burned they have experiences phenomenally or qualitatively like my pains; and if I cannot know even that much, it is natural to suppose, then I cannot know anything about their minds. A common counterargument, which argues from the falsity of skepticism to the impossibility of spectrum inversion, goes as follows. According to our ordinary standards of evidence, if two individuals, Jones and Smith, make the same color discriminations, agree in their judgments of color similarity and difference, and apply color words in the same way, this is sufficient evidence that they mean the same by their color words. And if in addition they have learned to use 'looks', 'appears', and so forth in the same ways in the same objective circumstances—for example, both say of what they know to be a white wall illuminated by red light that it "looks" red—this is sufficient evidence that they mean the same by expressions like 'looks red'. But if Jones says, truthfully, that an object looks red to him, and Smith says the same of the object, and if they mean the same by the expression 'looks red', this surely shows that with respect to color the object looks pretty much the same to them and that their experiences of it are similar. Yet, according to the view that intrasubjective spectrum inversion is possible, this information about Jones's and Smith's use of color words, discriminatory abilities, and so forth would leave it an entirely open question whether red things look alike to them. So we must choose between rejecting our ordinary standards of evidence concerning such matters and rejecting the view that intersubjective spectrum inversion is possible. But we cannot abandon our ordinary standards of evidence here without accepting an absurd general skepticism about other minds. So, the argument concludes, we must reject the claim that spectrum inversion is possible.

I will not deny that if it is possible to have some knowledge of other minds, it must be possible to know whether others mean the same as we do by their color words. Nor will I deny that if we can know what someone means by expressions like 'red' and 'looks red', we can also know that something looks to him the way it looks to us. What I dispute in the argument just given is the claim that this conclusion, *in the sense in which it is true*, contradicts the claim that spectrum inversion is possible. What emerges here is that expressions like 'looks the same' are potentially ambiguous. And this can be seen from further reflection on Fred and his introsubjective spectrum inversion.

We have supposed that Fred eventually accommodates to the change in his color experience, and says that an object looks yellow in just those objective circumstances in which others would say this—even though the way something looks to him when he says it looks yellow is the way things formerly looked to him when he said they looked blue. But this accommodation will cause him some difficulty in the use of such expressions as 'looks the same' and 'looked similar in color to'. Others will assume that from the premises "X looked yellow to Fred at time t_1" and "Y looked yellow to Fred at time t_2" we can infer the conclusion "The way X looked to Fred at t_1, with respect to color, is the way Y looked to Fred at t_2, with respect to color." But if t_1 is a time before Fred's spectrum inversion and t_2 is a time

after he has accommodated to it, then that conclusion will be false on one interpretation of it, although true on another, if the premises are true. Fred needs, and we need, a distinction between different senses of the expression 'looks the same', and of related expressions. If Fred's house looked yellow to him at both t_1 and t_2, then with respect to color his house "looked the same" to him at those two times in the sense that his experiences of it on those two occasions were *of* the same objective color, or had the same color as their "intentional object." Call this the *intentional* sense of 'look the same'. But in another sense his house did not "look the same" to him at the two times; call this the *qualitative* sense of that expression. That Fred has undergone spectrum inversion requires that things look different to him than they did before in the qualitative sense, but not (once he has accommodated to the change) that they look different to him in the intentional sense.

Applying this distinction to the case of Jones and Smith in the anti-inversion argument, we can say that it is only in the intentional sense of 'looks the same' that the information about Jones and Smith—their use of color words, their abilities to distinguish and recognize colors, and so forth—establishes that red things look the same to them. What this information does not establish, by itself, is that red things look the same to them in the qualitative sense—that their visual experiences of redness are qualitatively as well as intentionally similar. So long as our ordinary standards of evidence are taken as standards for establishing intentional similarity of experiences, the adherence to these standards is perfectly compatible with allowing the possibility of spectrum inversion. And, I think, it is only if the standards are taken in this way that it is plausible to maintain that abandoning them would lead to general skepticism about other minds.

It may appear that I have conceded part of the claim that allowing the possibility of spectrum inversion leads to skepticism, namely, that it leads to skepticism about our ability to have knowledge of the qualitative character of the experiences of other persons. But I have not conceded that; on the contrary, whether this is so will be one of the main issues under consideration in the rest of this essay. What I have conceded is that it follows from the possibility of spectrum inversion, and is indeed true, that the *behavioral* evidence that establishes intentional similarities and differences between experiences of different persons is not by itself sufficient to establish qualitative similarities and differences between such experiences. And it was such behavioral evidence I had in mind in speaking of our "ordinary standards of evidence." It remains to be considered whether other sorts of evidence, for example, evidence of physiological similarities or differences of some kind, might enable us to make intersubjective comparisons of the qualitative character of experiences.

III

The last objection to the possibility of spectrum inversion which I shall discuss (and there are many I shall have to ignore) is empirical. A brief consideration of it will help me bring into focus some of the problems raised by the possibility of spectrum inversion.

If spectrum inversion is to be possible, there must be a mapping which maps every determinate shade onto some determinate shade and at least some onto shades other than themselves, which preserves, for any normally sighted person, all the "distance" and "between-ness" relationships between the shades, and which maps primary colors onto primary colors. Now as long as we restrict ourselves to the pure saturated colors, various such mappings seem to be possible; one is the mapping of shades onto their complementaries, and others can be got by rotating the "color circle" in different ways. It has been questioned whether even these mappings satisfy the condition that primaries be mapped onto primaries.[9] But it seems even more questionable that we can get a mapping that satisfies these conditions once all the unsaturated colors (beige,

olive, rust, etc.) and non-chromatic colors (black, white, and the various shades of gray) are taken into account. Obviously the simple color circle is inadequate for the representation of the relationships of these to one another and to the "pure" colors.

The question of whether our color experience does have a structure that allows for such a mapping—whether it is "invertible"—is an empirical question about our psychological makeup. And it is one I intend to by-pass. Even if our color experience is not invertible, it seems obviously possible that there should be creatures, otherwise very much like ourselves, whose color experience does have a structure that allows for such a mapping— creatures whose color experience *is* invertible. And the mere possibility of such creatures is sufficient to raise the philosophical problems the possibility of spectrum inversion has been seen as posing.

Let me be more explicit about what these problems are. One problem, call it the *metaphysical* problem, is about the nature of "qualia"— the qualitative or phenomenal features of sense-experience, in virtue of having which they resemble and differ from each other, qualitatively, in the ways they do. If spectrum inversion is so much as a logical possibility—whether or not it is a possibility *for us*, as we are currently constituted—then it is clear that no behavioristic account of qualia will do. For what the possibility of interpersonal spectrum inversion comes to is that two people might be behaviorally indistinguishable, might share all the same behavioral dispositions, even though their color experiences were radically different in qualitative character— and this means that there might be a psychological difference between people who would have to be psychologically identical if behaviorism were true. This is perhaps not such a great problem, since there are plenty of independent reasons for regarding behaviorism as false. But it also appears that the possibility of intersubjective spectrum inversion is incompatible with what many regard as the most respectable descendant of behaviorism, namely functionalism, where this is understood as the view that mental states are definable in terms of their causal relations to sensory inputs, behavioral outputs, and other mental states. Now if spectrum inversion is a logical possibility, then the quale currently involved in my perception of blue things cannot be defined by the functional role it plays in the likes of me, since in someone whose spectrum was inverted related to mine a different quale (perhaps the quale involved in my perception of yellow things) would play that functional role, and this quale would play a different role. This is a version of what has been called the "inverted-qualia objection" to functionalism—spectrum inversion being a special case of "qualia inversion."[10]

The other main problem posed by the possibility of spectrum inversion is what I shall call the *epistemological* problem—the problem of how we can know about the qualitative states of other persons. Now if it turns out that our color experience is not invertible, there is one epistemological problem we do not face: we do not have to worry about the possibility that the color experience of others is inverted relative to our own. But once it is clear that qualia are not behavioristically or functionally definable, other possibilities have to be contemplated. For example, it seems compatible with two creatures having color quality spaces with the same structure that none of the color experiences of either creature should bear any qualitative similarity to any of the color experiences of the other—for example, the sensations of red of the one are not only not like the sensations of red of the other, but also are not like the other's sensations of green or his sensations of any other color. So we must consider what grounds, if any, we have for thinking that we do not differ from our friends and neighbors in this radical way. And the fact, if it is a fact, that our color experience is not invertible, that is, that its structure does not yield mappings of the sort described above, is no reason whatever for thinking this.

I conclude that there is no fundamental epistemological or metaphysical problem here which is solvable on the assumption that our experience is not invertible but not solvable on the assumption that it is. So it will do no harm—and will make exposition easier—to assume from now on that it is.

IV

I now want to take up the view, mentioned earlier, that the relationships of qualitative similarity and difference are well defined only for the intrasubjective case. This view solves the epistemological problem about the qualia of others, not by offering an account of how we know which color experiences of others are qualitatively similar to our own, but by denying that there is anything of this sort for us to know.

A view something like this is suggested by remarks of Frege in his essay "The Thought." Frege discusses the case in which he and a colorblind companion are looking at a strawberry field, and he declares to be "unanswerable, indeed really nonsensical," the question "does my companion see the green leaf as red, or does he see the red berry as green, or does he see both as one colour with which I am not acquainted at all?"[11] He goes on to say that "when the word 'red' does not state a property of things but is supposed to characterize sense-impressions belonging to my consciousness, it is only applicable within the sphere of my consciousness." Putting this in my terminology, Frege is saying that insofar as he uses 'red' as applying to experiences qualitatively similar to certain experiences of his, it will be applicable only to experiences of his. This is not a solipsist claim that assigns a special status to his sense-experiences; it merely asserts that the relationship of qualitative similarity can hold only intrasubjectively. A similar view was held by Moritz Schlick in "Positivism and Realism," on explicitly verificationist grounds: "The proposition that two experiences of different subjects not only occupy the same place in the order of a system but are, in addition, qualitatively similar has no meaning for us. Note well, it is not false, but meaningless: we have no idea what it means" (p. 93).[12]

This view, call it the *Frege-Schlick view*, does not fly as violently in the face of common sense as it may initially seem to do. It does not imply that we are talking nonsense, or that our remarks are without truth-value, when in ordinary circumstances we speak of different persons having similar or dissimilar experiences, or when we say that something looks the same, or different, to two different people. For it is open to us to construe such remarks as about the *intentional* similarity or difference of experiences, rather than as about the *qualitative* similarities and differences; and the view in question does not of course deny that the relationships of intentional similarity and difference are well defined for the intersubjective case.

One attraction of the Frege-Schlick view is that it solves, or dissolves, the epistemological problem about our knowledge of the qualitative states of others. But this view also suggests an answer to the "inverted-qualia objection" to behaviorism and functionalism, and thus a solution to the metaphysical problem. Part of the motivation for holding that qualitative similarity is well defined only for the intrasubjective case is that it is only in the intrasubjective case that we can have direct behavioral evidence of the holding of this relationship. It is this, after all, which makes *intra*subjective spectrum inversion, but not *inter*subjective inversion, behaviorally detectable. Now if intrasubjective qualitative similarity is the only sort of qualitative similarity there is (as the Frege-Schilck view holds), and if it is behaviorally detectable, then for all that has been shown it is behaviorally *definable* as well. But a much more promising view that is suggested by the same considerations is that this relationship is *functionally* definable, that is, definable in terms of how the holding of the relationship between experiences is causally related to sensory inputs,

behavioral outputs, and other mental states. It would be central to the functional account that when this relationship holds between different visual experiences of a person it tends to produce in that person the belief that there are objective similarities in the things he is seeing—to put it roughly, similarity of color qualia tends to produce belief in similarity of seen colors. And, via their effects on the person's beliefs, the qualitative similarities between his experiences would affect his behavior, in particular his recognitional and discriminatory behavior. But in addition, the holding of this relationship between different experiences of a person will produce in that person the belief that the experiences themselves are similar and, via this belief, will affect his verbal behavior—thus it is that Fred's saying that marigolds look today the way violets looked yesterday is taken as evidence that he has undergone inversion. Similar remarks apply to the relationships of qualitative identity (a special case of qualitative similarity) and qualitative difference. It is obvious that it is only when these relationships hold intrasubjectively that the holding of them can play such causal roles. But if, as the Frege-Schlick view holds, the relationships *can* hold only intrasubjectively, then there seems to be no reason why they should not be functionally definable in terms of such causal roles. Given this, there seems no reason why we should not be able to define in functional terms what it is for a state to have a qualitative character—a state will have a qualitative character if it is qualitatively similar to or different from some other state or states, and we are supposing that we already have a functional account of qualitative similarity and difference. And this clears the way for making states like pain functionally definable; at any rate, the fact that pain necessarily has a qualitative character, one that is unpleasant and distracting, is no bar to its being functionally defined. If individual qualia are not functionally definable, then of course no individual quale can be mentioned in the functional definition of pain; but if the similarity and identity conditions of qualia are functionally definable, it will still be possible to quantify over qualia in such a definition, and that is all that seems to be required. If such an account can be made to work, functionalism has nothing to fear from qualia.[13]

It is natural to suppose that a functional account of qualia of the sort just sketched requires the Frege-Schlick view. And it may seem unpromising for just this reason. For the Frege-Schlick view clashes with strongly felt intuitions. Most of us, I suspect, cannot help feeling that a visual experience of mine can be like a visual experience of yours in exactly the way it can be like another visual experience of mine, even though this intersubjective similarity differs from intrasubjective similarity in not being directly experienceable or rememberable by anyone. Call this the *commonsense view*.[14] I shall now try to show that, although the commonsense view is of course incompatible with the Frege-Schlick view, nevertheless, the functional account of qualia, which is suggested by the Frege-Schlick view and may seem to imply it, is in fact not only perfectly compatible with the commonsense view but can be used to defend it.

V

Let us begin by seeing why the functional account of qualitative similarity does not imply the Frege-Schlick view. The word 'qualia', it will be remembered, is intended to refer to those features of sensory states in virtue of which they stand to one another in relationships of qualitative similarity and difference. States will be qualitatively similar in virtue of having identical or similar qualia—so our functional account of qualitative similarity must say what it is for qualia to be qualitatively similar. The first point to be emphasized is that qualia are properties and, therefore, universals. Suppose, then, that Q_1 and Q_2 are two different qualia. What the functional analysis of qualitative similarity tells us is that Q_1 and Q_2 are similar to a certain degree if it is the case that

when Q_1 and Q_2 characterize two different experiences belonging to one and the same person, this tends to have certain effects on that person's beliefs and behavior. There is nothing in this to say that Q_1 and Q_2 can characterize only experiences belonging to one and the same person. And, if they characterize experiences belonging to different persons, those experiences will be similar to the appropriate degree, even though this pair of instantiations of Q_1 and Q_2 will not have, or tend to have, the effects definitive of qualitative similarity; the similarity will hold in virtue of the fact that Q_1 and Q_2 are such that, if they *were* to be instantiated in experiences of the same person, this *would* tend to have these effects.

But these remarks presuppose that one and the same quale can be instantiated in the experiences of different persons, and it may be objected that no sense can be made of this, given the sort of functional account of qualitative similarity and identity I have suggested. The answer to this is, in brief, that qualia can be shared by experiences of different persons in virtue of their being "realized" in other properties, presumably physical properties, that can be shared by experiences of different persons. Here we must remember that although there is a sense in which qualia are not functionally definable (if qualia inversion is a possibility), there is also a sense in which they are—their similarity and identity conditions, I have claimed, are functionally definable. Now functional states and properties can be said to have physical "realizations." A physical state or property *realizes* a functional state or property in a particular creature if in the workings of that creature it plays the "causal role" definitive of that functional state or property, that is, if it interacts causally in the required ways with inputs, outputs, and other internal states of the creature. Given the sense in which they are functionally definable, qualia too can be said to have physical realizations, which in principle we could discover by physiological investigations. The physical properties that realize qualia will be properties that can be instantiated in different people. This makes it possible for the same qualia to be instantiated in different people and, thus, for experiences of different people to be qualitatively similar and different in all the varying degrees. Moreover, it makes it possible that such similarities and differences should be discovered.

I am not saying that it is automatically true that, for any two creatures who have experiences having qualitative character, the color experiences of each will stand to those of the other in determinate relationships of qualitative similarity and difference—or, to abbreviate this, that the color experiences of the two creatures will be "qualitatively comparable." The color experiences of two different creatures will be qualitatively comparable only if those creatures are capable of having states having the same qualia, and on my account this in turn will be true only if, for at least one color quale, both creatures are capable of having states that share at least some of the physical properties that are realizations of that quale. Suppose, to invoke a favorite functionalist fantasy, that we come across a race of Martians who are behaviorally indistinguishable from us and have a "psychology" isomorphic with ours, but whose internal physical makeup—their neurophysiology and biochemistry—is utterly different from ours. These Martians are to be creatures who share our mental states, at least on a functionalist view, but in whom the physical realizations of these states are as different as they could possibly be from their realizations in us. On my functional account of qualia, these Martians would have states having qualia—there would be something it would be like for them to have these states. But their experiences would not share any of the qualia our experiences have; for I am assuming that none of the properties that realize qualia in us could be instantiated in them. When it comes to comparing Martian experiences and ours, something like the Frege-Schlick view holds: their experiences and ours are not qualitatively comparable. But I do not say, with Schlick, that it is meaningless to assert that our experiences are qualitatively similar to those of the Martians;

on my view, that our experiences are not qualitatively comparable with theirs would be something to be discovered empirically, by discovering the physiological differences between them and us.

Now let me fill this account out a bit. Let $Q\text{-}BY$ be the quale currently involved in my perception of the color blue, and let $Q\text{-}YB$ be the quale currently involved in my perception of the color yellow. And let us make the simplifying assumption that only one sort of spectrum inversion is possible for humans and that this involves $Q\text{-}BY$ playing the causal role in the visual perception of one person, or at one time, which $Q\text{-}YB$ plays in another person, or at another time, and vice versa. As I have already said, it is not possible (if spectrum inversion is possible) to give a purely functional characterization of either $Q\text{-}BY$ or $Q\text{-}YB$. But if the notion of a quale can be functionally defined (i.e., if its similarity and identity conditions can be), then the following will be a functional description: 'pair of qualia such that, at any given time, one member of that pair characterizes perceptions of blue while the other characterizes perceptions of yellow'. And, given our simplifying assumption, this description will pick out a unique pair of qualia for each creature having a color quality space with the same structure as our own, although the unique pair may be different in different creatures (e.g., it will be different in a Martian than in one of us). And we can ask how the satisfaction of this description is physically realized in the case of a particular creature at a particular time. In principle we can go hunting in the physiology of a creature for a pair of physical properties which play the functional role of qualia, which are involved only in the perception of blue and yellow, and which are such that, as long as one of them characterizes perceptions of blue the other can characterize only perceptions of yellow, and vice versa (given that the structure of the total color experience is normal). If the creature is me, one member of any such pair will be a realization of $Q\text{-}BY$ and the other will be a realization of $Q\text{-}YB$. There may in fact be a number of different realizations of each of these qualia. To be realizations of the same quale, different properties must be qualitatively identical in the following sense: the experience someone has in virtue of being in a state having the one has the same color quale as the experience he has in virtue of being in a state having the other. These qualia can, in fact, be identified with the disjunctions of the properties in their respective realization classes. What realizes in me the above functional description of a "blue-yellow invertible pair" is the pair of disjunctive properties consisting of the disjunction of the realizations of Q-BY and the disjunction of the realizations of Q-YB.

Having discovered that in a certain creature a certain pair of disjunctive properties realize this description, we could of course discover which of the properties is, at a given time, involved in a creature's perception of blue and which is involved in the creature's perception of yellow. If in another creature we find that the same members of this pair of properties are involved in the perception of the same colors, we know that blue and yellow look qualitatively the same to these two creatures. If we find the reverse, we know that we have a case of spectrum inversion. But for blue to look to me as it does to you, it is not essential that we be in physically similar states. Q-BY, I have said, can be identified with a disjunction of different properties, and it may be that my experience has Q-BY in virtue of having one of these properties while yours has Q-BY in virtue of having a different one. But unless you and I are enough alike physically that there is some physical realization of Q-BY that can be instantiated in both of us, it is impossible for us both to have experiences having Q-BY. What I am supposing about my Martians is that the sets of possible physical realizations in them of their qualia do not overlap at all with the sets of possible realizations in us of our qualia—and from this it follows that none of our qualitative states are qualitatively similar, to any degree at all, to any of theirs.

But now let us confront a problem. Let us suppose that in me having visual experiences is realized in X-fiber firings, and that my visual experiences having a certain color quale, say Q-BY, is realized in the X-fiber firings occurring in a certain pattern. And so it is with you too. In the Martians, let us suppose, the having of visual experiences is realized in having Z-fibers firing, and particular qualia are realized in certain properties of the patterns of Z-fiber firings. Let X_1 be a realization in me of the quale Q-BY, and let Z_1 and Z_2 be realizations in the Martians of a pair of qualia that constitute a blue-yellow invertible pair. Now there are various physical properties that can be instantiated in both us and the Martians, and among these are the disjunctive properties X_1-or-Z_1 and X_1-or-Z_2. Why shouldn't one of these be a physical realization of the quale Q-BY? Of course, it is not possible that *both* should be, since in the Martians Z_1 and Z_2 realize different and incompatible qualia. And I am supposing that the physical differences between the Martians and us are such that there would be no reason for picking one of these rather than the other as a realization of Q-BY? But what is it that disqualifies these disjunctive properties as realizations of qualia? The answer cannot be just that they are disjunctive. For any property that can be shared by things that are different in any way can be construed as disjunctive. You and I will be physically different in a variety of ways; at the very least, our DNA will be different. So the property X_1, which we share, can be construed as the following disjunctive property: (having X_1 and being the experience of someone having my DNA) or (having X_1 and being the experience of someone having a DNA different from mine). But this suggests yet another problem. How could we know, and what could make it true, that what realizes Q-BY in me is X_1 and not a more specific property (a disjunct of X_1) which cannot be instantiated in you—perhaps one that can be instantiated only in creatures having my DNA?

The problem raised is one about the individuation of qualia realizations.[15] What is it that makes it appropriate to say that X_1, but not the disjunctive property X_1-or-Z_1 and also not the more determinate property of having X_1 and being an experience of someone having my DNA, is a particular physical realization of a quale? I think the answer is given by the following rule. Property P realizes a quale if (1) it is a consequence of functional definitions and causal laws that, whenever different states of the same person share P, they are qualitatively identical in some respect (e.g., with respect to color qualia); (2) P is not equivalent to conjunctive property P_1-and-P_2 such that (i) P_1 satisfies condition (1) and P_2 doesn't, and (ii) P satisfies condition (1) because, and only because, P_1 does; and (3) if P is equivalent to a disjunctive property Pa-or-Pb such that Pa and Pb both satisfy conditions (1) and (2), then it must be that Pa and Pb satisfy (1) and (2) because P satisfies them, and not that P satisfies them because Pa and Pb satisfy them.[16] Let me illustrate this with an example.

Suppose the property X_1, which can be instantiated in both you and me, satisfies condition (1); more specifically, it is a consequence of functional definitions, including the functional definition of qualitative identity, that whenever different states of the same person share X_1 they realize experiences identical with respect to color qualia. Suppose, further, that X_1 satisfies condition (2) as well. This means, among other things, that my having the particular DNA I do have plays no essential role in the physiological explanation of the behavior that manifests the existence of my qualitative states and the qualitative similarities and differences between them. This might be because what matters, for purposes of such explanation, is the organization of the brain at the neuronal level, so that, so long as the neurons are such as to interrelate causally in certain ways, differences in their microstructure are irrelevant. On this supposition, of course, the conjunctive property of having X_1 and being an experience of someone with my DNA is ruled out, as a realization of a quale, by condition (2).[17] Both X_1 and the Martian property Z_1, we can suppose, satisfy conditions (1) and (2). But the disjunction of X_1 and Z_1, although it satisfies

conditions (1) and (2), is ruled out by condition (3)—clearly this disjunction satisfies (1) because its disjuncts do, and not vice versa. We can coherently suppose, however, that X_1 itself satisfies (3) (and, if we like, that Z_1 does also). Though it is not coherent to suppose that X_1 is not equivalent to a disjunctive property, it is coherent to suppose that it is not equivalent to any disjunctive property that does not violate condition (3). And if this supposition is true, then X_1 will be a qualia realization of the sort we are looking for.

Conditions (2) and (3) both make use of the notion of something's being the case *because* something else is the case, where this is not simply a matter of the latter thing's being a logically or nomologically sufficient condition of the former. I have no analysis of this notion to offer; but it seems to me that it is clearly a notion we do have, and one that has application. The word 'because' of course signals that something is being said to be explanatory of something. And, on my account, what singles out certain properties as realizations of qualia is the fact that they are suited, and have the right degree of specificity, to play a certain explanatory role. Some properties will be ruled out as too specific because they are analyzable into conjunctions having conjuncts irrelevant to the explanatory role. Others will be ruled out as not specific enough, in that they are analyzable into disjunctions of properties, each of which plays the relevant causal role by itself. But if I am not mistaken, those which satisfy conditions (1)–(3) are just those which are capable of playing the causal role and have just the right degree of specificity.

VI

What I have just been saying was addressed to what I earlier called the "metaphysical problem." Where does all of this leave us with respect to the epistemological problem? On the account I have suggested, there is no reason in principle why we should not be able to discover whether the color experiences of different human beings are qualitatively comparable and, if they are, whether they are qualitatively similar in similar circumstances or, on the other hand, are spectrum-inverted relative to each other. We could discover this by finding how qualia are realized in the brain and by determining whether the relevant physiological similarities hold between the brains of different human beings.[18] But, given that such physiological investigations are still far in the future, what are we to say about our present epistemological situation? Do I have good reason right now to think that my experiences of violets and marigolds are similar to those of others, or even that my color experiences and those of others are qualitatively comparable?

If we do have good grounds for such beliefs, I think it will be an essential part of these grounds that the creatures whose experiences are being compared are members of a single species and, therefore, can be presumed to share a genetic endowment. By and large, different members of our own species have color-quality spaces having the same structure—that is, they make the same color discriminations, see the same similarity relationships between objects, and so forth. Even in the exceptional case of color-blind people, the breakdown of this structural uniformity is very limited. The existence of this uniformity can scarcely be a coincidence, and it calls out for an explanation in terms of our shared genetic endowment. The situation would be altogether different if the structural similarity in question were that between human color-quality spaces and those of my hypothetical Martians, supposing them to exist. The existence of such an interspecies similarity could very well be a coincidence; and in any case, it could not be explained by a shared genetic endowment, since, *ex hypothesi*, the Martian evolutionary history would be entirely independent of our own. The similarity between different Martians could be explained in terms of their genetic endowment, and the similarity between different humans could be explained in terms of ours; but the similarity between humans and Martians

would have to be explained in some quite different way, if at all.

What would seem the simplest explanation of the uniform structure of human color-quality spaces is that, as part of our shared genetic endowment, we are all "wired" in such a way that the same environmental stimuli give rise to the same color qualia in our visual experiences. This, of course, would guarantee both that color experiences of different human beings are qualitatively comparable and that, under similar conditions, they have qualitatively similar color experiences —that is, that there is no intersubjective spectrum inversion among human beings. But if we suppose that our experiences are not qualitatively comparable or that some of us are spectrum-inverted relative to others, then, in order to explain this uniformity of structure, we must suppose there is something in our genetic endowment that compensates for the differences there are in our qualia, so as to make the differences cancel out so far as their effects on behavior are concerned. This is not impossible, but presumably it would call for more complex neural mechanisms than the first arrangement; and from an evolutionary standpoint it seems unlikely that we would have the more complex rather than the less complex arrangement. Obviously no such considerations could be used to support the claim that our experiences are qualitatively comparable with, or similar to, those of my Martians. And this is as it should be; if we know that Martian evolutionary history is completely independent of our own, then even before we discover the physiological differences between them and us, it will not be reasonable to think that our color experiences and theirs are qualitatively similar, or even qualitatively comparable.

It seems to me that if we are indeed entitled to think that, as John Locke put it, "the sensible *Ideas*, produced by any object in different Men's Minds, are most commonly very near and undiscernibly alike,"[19] our entitlement will rest on an empirical argument along the lines of that just sketched. I shall not attempt to elaborate the argument or to rebut the various objections that might be made to it; for part of the point I want to make is that the argument is at best fairly weak. It gives its conclusion—that our experiences are qualitatively comparable with those of others and that spectrum inversion does not occur—the status of a hypothesis which, although perhaps reasonable on the basis of current evidence, could easily be overthrown by future discoveries about how mental states are realized in the brain. We do not, if this is so, know with certainty at the present time that this conclusion is true. If one finds this counterintuitive, one should remember a point I made earlier: given the distinction between qualitative similarity and intentional similarity, our everyday claims about the experiences of others need not be taken as implying anything specific about the qualitative character of those experiences, and thus the certainty we would like to ascribe to some of our everyday claims need not be undermined by the admission that we lack certain knowledge of the qualitative character of the experiences of others.

A more expeditious, if not wholly satisfying, treatment of the epistemological problem is that of John Locke:

I am nevertheless very apt to think, that the sensible *Ideas*, produced by an Object in different Men's Minds, are most commonly very near and undiscernibly alike. For which Opinion, I think, there might be many Reasons offered; but that being besides my present Business, I shall not trouble my reader with them, but only mind him, that the contrary Supposition, if it could be proved, is of little use, either for the Improvement of our Knowledge, or Conveniency of Life: and so we need not trouble ourselves to examine it.[20]

Locke was not always so anxious not to "trouble his reader," and one could wish that he had not been so here.

Postscript (1983)

In the original publication of this essay the following "Note Added in Proof" was appended to it:

Saul Kripke has called my attention to a mistake in what I say in section v about the realization of qualia. Suppose that in person A quale Q_1 has the properties P_1 and P_2 as its only possible realizations, that in person B the quale Q_2 has properties P_2 and P_3 as its only possible realizations, and that in person C the quale Q_3 has properties P_3 and P_4 as its only possible realizations. Suppose further that there is no possible creature in which P_1 and P_4 can both be instantiated. According to what I say in section v, the last supposition implies that P_1 and P_4 are not "qualitatively identical," and thus that Q_1 and Q_3 are not the same quale. Yet plainly Q_1 and Q_3 would have to be the same quale, by the transitivity of identity. Let R be the relationship that holds between two qualia realizations when (a) they can be instantiated in the same creature (i.e., it is possible for there to be a creature in which both are instantiated), and (b) they are such that when they are so instantiated the experiences that have them are qualitatively identical in some respect. Then the relation "being realizations of the same quale" should be equated not with R but with its ancestral R^*; and what I must stipulate about my imaginary Martians is not only that they do not share any qualia realizations with us, or have any that stand in R to any of ours, but also that they do not have any qualia realizations that stand in R^* to any of ours. I believe, however, that an elaboration of the considerations adduced in endnote 16 will show that it is to a very limited extent, if at all, that qualia realizations can be related by R^* without being related by R.

It turns out, I think, that the specific difficulty raised here is fairly easily met (and without the problematic rejection of R in favor of R^* as the qualitative identity relation). But the reflection on the considerations adduced in note 16, which the note encouraged, had the unexpected result of bringing to light a much more serious difficulty with the view presented in section v, one that suggests that the Frege-Schlick view may be right after all.

First let me address the difficulty raised in the note. It is implicit in the account of qualitative similarity given in the essay that the relation of qualitative similarity between qualia, and also the relation of qualitative identity between different quale realizations (the relation that holds between two quale realizations just in case they are realizations of one and the same quale) can hold only between qualia, or quale realizations, that can be instantiated together in experiences of one and the same person—for short, qualia or quale realizations that are capable of cosubjective instantiation. For the basic idea of the account is that these relations are defined in the first instance in terms of what the consequences are when they hold intrasubjectively. The account says that two qualia stand in a certain relation of qualitative similarity if they are such that if they were to be instantiated in the experiences of a single subject, this would have certain effects on the beliefs and behavior of that subject; and it is surely implicit in this that the similarity relationships are well defined only for cases in which the antecedent of that subjective conditional is satisfiable. Similarly, qualitative identity between qualia realizations can be thought of, as a first approximation, as a kind of indistinguishability or functional interchangeability; and only quale realizations that are capable of cosubjective instantiation can be indistinguishable in the sense that the behavioral and introspective effects of their cosubjective instantiation is the same as that of an otherwise identical pattern of property instantiations in which all instantiations of one of the realizations are replaced by instantiations of the other. Of course, indistinguishability is not transitive, so in order to make the relation of qualitative identity an equivalence relation we must complicate the account slightly. We can say that two quale realizations are qualitatively identical if and only if (1) they are indistinguishable in the sense indicated, and (2) any realization indistinguishable from either of them is indistinguishable from the other. This makes the example in the note impossible. If P_1 and P_4 (likewise, P_1 and P_3, and P_2 and P_4) are not capable of cosubjective instantiation, then P_2 and P_3 (likewise P_1 and P_2, and P_3 and P_4) are not qualitatively identical, even if they are indistinguishable. (Kripke's objection was, however, cogent against the somewhat confused version of

section V I had presented to him in conversation; he had not seen the essay.)

But now let us consider a variation on the example described in note 16. Suppose that S_1 is a brainlike system in which quale realization Pa can be instantiated, and S_2 is a brainlike system in which quale realization Pb can be instantiated. If S_1 and S_2 are joined in a certain way—call it "way C"—into a larger system S_3, then each of these systems serves as a "backup system" to the other in the sense indicated in endnote 16, and Pa and Pb are qualitatively identical, or at least indistinguishable, and so realize a common quale, or at least realize very similar qualia. For the moment assume that they realize a single quale. As I explain in endnote 16, strictly speaking it is not Pa and Pb *simpliciter* that realize this single quale, but rather the properties Pa-and-C and Pb-and-C, where C is the relational property a quale has just in case it occurs in a system in which subsystems like S_1 and S_2 are joined in way C. In the terminology of Essay 12,[21] Pa and Pb will be "core realizations" of the single quale, and Pa-and-C and Pb-and-C will be "total realizations" of it.

Now if it is because of the particular way S_1 and S_2 are joined in S_3, that is, the fact that they are joined in way C, that Pa and Pb are core realizations of a single quale (or of very similar qualia), then it would seem that it should be possible for S_1 and S_2 to be joined in a different way, call it C^*, such that when they are so joined Pa and Pb (or the total quale realizations of which they are the "cores") are not qualitatively identical, and instead are qualitatively different to a considerable degree—let it be that they (or the qualia they realize) differ as the character of seeing red differs from the character of seeing green. Of course, the total realizations here are Pa-and-C^* and Pb-and-C^*, so the total realizations that differ in this case are not the ones that are qualitatively identical in the other. There is no difficulty about Pa and Pb being core realizations of the same quale in one sort of system and core realizations of different qualia in another sort of system. So far, then, there is no problem.

The problem begins to emerge when we notice that Pa and Pb can themselves be total quale realizations, namely when they are instantiated in the unjoined systems S_1 and S_2, respectively. Suppose that at t_1, when the systems have not yet been joined, a Pa experience (i.e., an experience having Pa) occurs in S_1. At t_2, after the systems have been joined in way C, another Pa experience occurs in S_1. The latter experience also has the property Pa-and-C (since all experiences in the larger system have C). It will hardly do to say that the experience at t_2 instantiates two different qualia, one realized in Pa and the other realized in Pa-and-C. And we can plausibly suppose (and stipulate as part of the example) that the effects of these successive qualia instantiations are precisely what, on our functional account, the effects of successive instantiations of one and the same qualia should be. It would seem that we must say that just one quale was realized by Pa and Pa-and-C at t_2, and that this is the same quale that was realized by Pa at t_1.

Similar considerations will apparently show that Pb is qualitatively identical to Pb-and-C. But our example is supposed to be one in which Pa-and-C and Pb-and-C are qualitatively identical. Since qualitative identity is a transitive relation, it follows that Pa and Pb are qualitatively identical. But surely something has gone wrong. For the considerations that show that Pa is qualitatively identical to Pa-and-C will also show that Pa is qualitatively identical to Pa-and-C^*, and that Pb is qualitatively identical to Pb-and-C^*. But since Pa-and-C^* and Pb-and-C^* differ significantly in their qualitative character, we can infer from this that Pa and Pb differ qualitatively in exactly the same way. And now we have a contradiction on our hands; for our earlier conclusion was that Pa and Pb were qualitatively identical.

We might attempt to avoid the contradiction by trying to avoid the conclusion that Pa is qualitatively identical to Pa-and-C (likewise with Pb and Pb-and-C, and so on). First, we might insist

that when system S_1 exists by itself (unjoined with S_2), what serves as a total realization is not Pa by itself, but something of the form Pa-and-X, where X is some property which is incompatible with C and C^* (it could be just the property of not occurring in a composite system of the sort S_3 is). Now Pa will be only a core realization, and not a proper term for our qualitative identity relationship. But we still need to block the argument that would seem to show that Pa-and-X is qualitatively identical to Pb-and-X (in virtue of their being qualitatively identical to, respectively, Pa-and-C and Pb-and-C, which in turn are qualitatively identical), since a parallel argument would show that these are qualitatively very different (in virtue of their being qualitatively identical to, respectively, Pa-and-C^* and Pb-and-C^*, which are qualitatively very different). We could block this by strengthening the requirement that qualitatively identical quale realizations must be capable of cosubjective instantiation into the requirement that such realizations must be capable of *simultaneous* cosubjective instantiation. For Pa-and-X and Pa-and-C (and other such pairs) are not capable of simultaneous instantiation in experiences of a single subject. But notice that this will achieve the desired result only if we also strengthen the conditions for qualitative similarity, so that qualia can count as qualitatively similar only if they are capable of simultaneous cosubjective instantiation. For if we allow that Pa-and-X is qualitatively very similar to (even though not qualitatively identical to) both Pa-and-C and Pa-and-C^*, that Pb-and-X is qualitatively identical to both Pb-and-C and Pb-and-C^*, and that Pa-and-C and Pb-and-C are qualitatively identical while Pa-and-C^* and Pb-and-C^* are qualitatively very different, then we still have a contradiction on our hands.

Alternatively, we might try to avoid the contradiction by denying that Pa-and-C and Pb-and-C could be qualitatively identical in the case envisaged. But this will be ineffective unless we also deny that these properties, or the qualia they realize, would be even qualitatively very similar.

For if we allow that they would be qualitatively very similar, and allow that *Pa*-and-*C** and *Pb*-and-*C** would be qualitatively very different, and allow the other qualitative relationships that generated our original contradiction, then we still have a contradiction. We will be able to infer both that *Pa*-and-*X* and *Pb*-and-*X* are qualitatively very similar (being qualitatively identical to, respectively, *Pa*-and-*C* and *Pb*-and-*C*, which are very similar) and that they are qualitatively very different (being qualitatively identical to, respectively, *Pa*-and-*C** and *Pb*-and-*C**, which are qualitatively very different); and both conclusions cannot be true, given that there is here only one relevant dimension of similarity-and-difference.

But is either of these ways of avoiding the contradiction compatible with the view of qualia sketched in section v? It will be useful to resolve that view into two components. First, there is the functional account of qualitative similarity (and difference, etc.) sketched in section IV (and in Essays 8 and 9)—that according to which qualitative similarity is defined in the first instance for the intrasubjective case, and is defined in terms of its effects on the subject's beliefs and behavior. Second, there is what I shall call the standard conception of qualia. This says that qualia are intrinsic properties of experiences (they are not "mere-Cambridge" properties in the sense of Essay 11),[22] that they are the primary relata of the relationships of qualitative similarity and difference, and that the similarity and difference relations of a quale to other qualia are internal to it. On this conception, experiences are qualitatively similar or different in virtue of what qualia they have, that is, in virtue of similarities and differences between their qualia, and each quale essentially and eternally stands to other qualia in whatever relations of qualitative similarity or difference it has to them—so it makes no sense to speak of the same pair of qualia being qualitatively similar under one set of circumstances and qualitatively different under another.

Now consider the consequences of adopting one or the other of the suggested ways of avoiding our contradiction. If we adopt the first, and say that *Pa*-and-*X* and *Pa*-and-*C* cannot be qualitatively identical or even qualitatively very similar (because they are not qualitatively comparable, being incapable of simultaneous cosubjective instantiation), then we must either give up the view that qualia (or quale realizations) are the primary relata of the relations of qualitative identity, similarity, and difference, or else we must deny that the experience at t_1 and the experience at t_2 are qualitatively similar in virtue of their successive instantiation of *Pa*-and-*X* and *Pa*-and-*C*, respectively. But the former denial involves abandoning the standard conception of qualia, and the latter denial is sharply at odds with the functionalist account of qualitative similarity, given that the case is one in which the experiences would count as qualitatively very similar on the functionalist account. And the same is true if we attempt to avoid the contradiction by denying that *Pa*-and-*C* and *Pb*-and-*C* are qualitatively identical or (at least) qualitatively very similar—for the case is one in which experiences having these quale realizations would count as at least qualitatively very similar on the functionalist account. So unless we can find some grounds on which we can deny the possibility of the sort of situation envisaged (one in which there are two different ways of combining brainlike systems into larger brainlike systems, such that on a functionalist account the similarity and difference relations between experiences realized in the different subsystems depend on which mode of connection is in effect) we must apparently choose between rejecting the functionalist account of qualitative similarity and rejecting the standard conception of qualia.

I would prefer not to have to make this choice; but if I am forced to make it, I reject the standard conception of qualia. And to hold the functionalist view of qualitative similarity without the standard conception of qualia is tantamount to holding the Frege-Schlick view. If one adopts this view one must say either that there are no such things as qualia or that the similarity and difference relations between qualia are not internal to them, and that qualia are not the primary relata of the relations of qualitative similarity and difference. And if one says either of these things one will deprive oneself of the way, sketched at the beginning of section v, of giving the functionally defined relations of qualitative similarity and difference an intersubjective application. It will be impossible to say that my experience can resemble yours in virtue of having qualia that resemble those yours have (where the resemblance between qualia consists in their being such that their cosubjective instantiation would have certain effects on beliefs and behavior). Obviously this cannot be said if there are no such things as qualia; and it also cannot be said if the same qualia can stand in different relations of qualitative similarity and difference in different circumstances. On such a view there seems to be no alternative to holding that qualitative identity (and similarity, etc.) is well defined only for the intrasubjective case, just as the Frege-Schlick view holds.

Notes

1. *Essay Concerning Human Understanding*, ed. by Peter H. Nidditch (Oxford, 1975), p. 389 (bk. 11, ch. 32, sect. xv).

2. See Lewis, *Mind and the World Order* (New York, 1929), p. 75; Schlick, "Positivism and Realism," in A. J. Ayer (ed.), *Logical Positivism* (New York, 1959), pp. 92–95; Reichenbach, *Experience and Prediction* (Chicago 1938), pp. 248–258; Wisdom, *Other Minds* (New York, 1952), pp. 10–11; Black, *Language and Philosophy* (Ithaca, N.Y., 1949), pp. 3ff; Smart, *Philosophy and Scientific Realism* (New York, 1963), pp. 66–69.

3. "Notes for Lectures on 'Private Experience' and 'Sense Data,'" ed. by Rush Rhees, *The Philosophical Review*, 77 (1968), p. 284.

4. Trans. by G. E. M. Anscombe, 3rd edn (New York, 1958).

5. For Fred's first appearance in the discussion of this problem see D. M. Taylor, "The Incommunicability of Content," *Mind*, 75 (1966), 527–541.

6. See Taylor, *ibid.*, where this point is made.

7. Though I think we could have good reason to believe this, I do not claim that the behavioral evidence I have described entails it. As Gilbert Harman and David Lewis have pointed out to me, what I have described of Fred's behavior is compatible with there having been over the thirty years a change in Fred's color experience so gradual that the change from one day to the next would not be noticeable (as Lewis put it, a rotation of the color circle so slow that it took it thirty years to go 180 degrees), the net effect of which was to undo the initial inversion. But we could have reason to discount this possibility if we had evidence that over the thirty years there had not occurred in Fred any physiological change such that, if it occurred suddenly rather than gradually, it would produce noticeable behavioral manifestations of intrasubjective inversion. Further possible behavioral evidence of inversion is described in section 11, and the relevance of physiological considerations to questions about inversion is discussed in section v.

8. It might be objected that it is compatible with the behavior I have imagined on the part of Fred that between t_1 and t_2 he underwent a series of experience *cum* memory changes that resulted in his color experience at t_4 being the same as his color experience at t_1, despite his seeming to remember it as being different. I do not deny this, but do not think it follows that in the case as described we would not be justified in thinking that Fred at t_4 was spectrum-inverted relative to Fred at t_1. In general, a memory change having a certain behavioral effect seems far less likely than an experience change having the same effect (where either could produce the effect); on any plausible assumption about how perception and memory are realized physically, a change that alters the way specific kinds of stimuli are linked with specific color qualia (as happens when someone puts on tinted spectacles) seems far more likely than one that systematically modifies all a person's memories of how things looked with respect to color prior to a certain time, leaving these memories otherwise unchanged. And, quite apart from this, in the absence of overriding physiological evidence (and I do not deny that there could be such), the hypothesis that someone has undergone an experience change that would produce a certain behavioral effect is obviously to be preferred, on grounds of simplicity, to the hypothesis that the person has undergone an experience change *and* a memory change which jointly would have the same effect.

9. See Bernard Harrison, "On Describing Colors," *Inquiry*, 10 (1967), 38–52.

10. See Ned Block and Jerry Fodor, "What Psychological States Are Not," *The Philosophical Review*, 81 (1972), 159–181, pp. 172–174.

11. Gottlob Frege, "The Thought: A Logical Inquiry," *Mind*, 65 (1956), 289–311, p. 299.

12. A more recent expression of this view (minus the verificationism) is that of Thomas Nagel: "A type of relation can hold between elements in the experience of a single person that cannot hold between elements in the experience of distinct persons: looking similar in color, for example. Insofar as our concept of similarity of experience in the case of a single person is dependent on his experience of similarity, the concept is not applicable between persons" ("Brain Bisection and the Unity of Consciousness," in *Mortal Questions* (Cambridge, 1979), footnote 10, pp. 160–161). Nagel informs me that he is now doubtful about this view. I suggested such a view myself in my "Critical Notice: *Myself and Others* by Don Locke," *Philosophical Quarterly*, 19 (1969), 272–279, pp. 276–278.

As I am interpreting this view, it regards qualitative similarity as well defined for diachronic intrasubjective comparisons as well as for synchronic ones. But another version of the view is possible. Reichenbach held that "if we call the impression of two persons incomparable, we are obliged to call the impressions of one person at different times incomparable as well" (*Experience and Prediction* p. 252), and this could lead (although I do not find that it did in Reichenbach—he uses his claim to attack the very notion of a quale) to the view that qualitative similarity and difference are well defined only for synchronic intrasubjective comparisons. On such a view intrasubjective inversion is no more possible than intersubjective inversion. I shall not consider this view, partly because it seems to me to have little intrinsic plausibility (especially the sharp epistemological distinction it has to make between synchronic and diachronic intrasubjective comparisons), and partly because I am investigating what options are open to someone who allows the possibility of intrasubjective inversion.

13. See my "Functionalism and Qualia" (Essay 9).

14. It is worth observing that if, as has often been supposed in recent discussions of personal identity (e.g., Derek Parfit's "Personal Identity," *The Philosophical Review*, 80 (1971), 3–27), "fusion" of persons is a logical possibility, then the Frege-Schlick view must be false.

For if persons *A* and *B* fuse to form *C*, and *C's* subsequent mental life is psychologically continuous with the past lives of *A* and *B* (and so, among other things, contains memories of them), then, since the pre-fusion experiences of *A* and *B* must be qualitatively comparable with the post-fusion experiences of *C* (must stand to them in determinate relationships of qualitative similarity and difference), they must be qualitatively comparable to each other. But suppose that *A* and *B* *could* fuse at time *t*, but do not in fact do so. It would seem that, since *A*'s and *B*'s experiences prior to *t* will be qualitatively comparable in the case in which fusion subsequently occurs, they must also be qualitatively comparable in the case in which it doesn't occur; it can scarcely be the case that whether experiences occurring before *t* are qualitatively comparable depends on what happened at *t* or afterward. It thus appears that, if creatures are "fusible," their experiences are qualitatively comparable. But this supports the commonsense view only if human beings are fusible—and that seems rather questionable.

15. I am grateful to John Bennett and Richard Boyd for making me aware of this problem and of the inadequacy of earlier attempts of mine to solve it.

16. In an earlier version of this essay clause (ii) of condition (2) did not contain the word 'only', and condition (3) did not refer to condition (2). That version of the rule was open to the following counterexample (due to Mr. Mark Johnston). Suppose that the brain contains a "backup system" in which qualia are realized quite differently than in the primary system. In the primary system a particular quale is realized by property *Pa*, and in the backup system it is realized by *Pb*. If at a particular point *t* in a person's life the backup system takes over from the primary system, then the person's pre-*t* experiences characterized by *Pa* will be color-qualia-identical to the person's post-*t* experiences characterized by *Pb*. It would seem offhand that the disjunctive property *Pa-or-Pb* should count as a realization of this quale. But though this disjunctive property can be presumed to satisfy conditions (1) and (2), it will fail condition (3) (as originally formulated); for it will satisfy (1) because *Pa* and *Pb* do, whereas, if it is to satisfy (3), it would have to be because it satisfies (1) and (2) that *Pa* and *Pb* do.

Actually, the objection as just stated does not work even against the original formulation, for the disjunctive property *Pa-or-Pb* will not in fact be a realization of the quale (although a closely related property will be). If before *t* an experience realized in the primary system has property Pa and after t an experience realized in the backup system has property Pb, this will not amount to those experiences being color-qualia-identical unless the backup system and the primary system are connected in an appropriate way (e.g., so that they will contribute jointly to the person's recognizing after t things he had seen before t). Let C be a property an experience has in virtue of belonging to a brain in which such a primary system and such a backup system are appropriately connected. What will satisfy (1) in such a case is not Pa-or-Pb but rather $(Pa$-or-$Pb)$-and-C. But the original formulation of the rule is nevertheless in trouble. On a natural interpretation of (2), $(Pa$-or-$Pb)$-and-C fails to satisfy condition (2); for its first conjunct satisfies (1) but its second conjunct doesn't, and it is at least plausible to say that the property as a whole satisfies (1) because the first conjunct does. Moreover, $(Pa$-or-$Pb)$-and-C is equivalent to the disjunctive property $(Pa$-and-$C)$-or-$(Pb$-and-$C)$, and this might be said to fail condition (3) on the grounds that it satisfies condition (1) because its disjuncts do.

The amended version of the rule in the text avoids these difficulties. The inclusion of 'and only because' in (2) enables $(Pa$-or-$Pb)$-and-C to satisfy (2). For it is not the case that the latter satisfies (1) only because its first conjunct does; sometimes (when the similarity is between experiences realized in different subsystems) the second conjunct, i.e., C, plays an essential role. And $(Pa$-or-$Pb)$-and-C (or, equivalently, $(Pa$-and-$C)$-or-$(Pb$-and-$C)$) does not fail the amended version of (3), since it is not the case that it satisfies condition (2) because its disjuncts do, rather than vice versa. For Pa-and-C and Pb-and-C satisfy condition (2) because of the essential role played by C, a common conjunct of both of them, in making Pa experiences realized in the primary system color-qualia-identical to Pb experiences realized in the backup system. And this seems to me tantamount to saying that they satisfy (2) because $(Pa$-or-$Pb)$-and-C satisfies it, and not vice versa.

17. It is worth noting that, if condition (2) did not include clause (ii), X_1 would be ruled out as a quale realization as well, contrary to what we want. For let Z_1 be (as before) a property of Martian states which satisfies condition (1), and let Q be any property of states which is independent of X_1 and Z_1 and is such that possession of Q in the absence of X_1 or Z_1 is not enough to satisfy (1). Then X_1 is equivalent to the complex conjunctive property $(X_1$-or-$Z_1)$-and-$[X_1$-or-$(Q$-and-not-$Z_1)]$. (Here I am indebted to John Bennett.) But whereas the first conjunct of this, X_1-or-Z_1, satisfies condition (1), it surely cannot be said that it is *because* this conjunct of X_1 satisfies (1) that X_1 satisfies it; on the contrary this conjunct satisfies (1) because both X_1 and Z_1 satisfy it. Whereas it plainly is true that the conjunctive property expressed by 'has X_1 and is an experience of someone with my DNA' satisfies (1) because X_1 satisfies it, given what we are assuming about the case. Thus the latter property, but not X_1, is ruled out by condition (2).

18. It may be thought that, if Martian color experiences are not qualitatively comparable with our own, there is one thing that is in principle unknowable—we cannot know "what it is like" to have experiences possessing the Martian color qualia (cf. Thomas Nagel, "What is it Like to be a Bat?," chapter 32). There is a sense in which this is true, but it does not imply that there would be facts about Martian experiences which would be unknowable by us. If, as I have suggested, qualia can be identified with disjunctive physical properties (the disjunctions of their possible realizations), there is no reason in principle why we should not be able to pick out the Martian qualia, assign names to them, and know which of them characterize the experiences of a Martian on a given occasion. Granted, this would not be to know what it is like to have experiences characterized by these various qualia. But what would it be to know this? I suggest that to know what it is like to have an experience having a certain quale is (a) to have such experiences in one's own repertoire of possible experiences, and (b) to be able to recognize such experiences as such "introspectively," i.e., simply by having them. Where we fail to satisfy condition (b) but not condition (a), there is no reason to suppose that our failure to "know what it is like" is irremediable. And our failure to satisfy (a) in the case of Martian color experience, which presumably would be irremediable, would not as such preclude us from knowing any facts; it would merely preclude us from knowing certain facts in a certain way [namely that way which involves the satisfaction of (b)].

19. *Essay*, bk. 11, ch. 32, sect. xv.

20. *Ibid.*

21. See my "Some Varieties of Functionalism" in my *Identity, Cause, and Mind* (Cambridge, 1984).

22. See my "Identity, Properties, and Causality," *ibid.*

42 The Intrinsic Quality of Experience

Gilbert Harman

The Problem

Many philosophers, psychologists, and artificial intelligence researchers accept a broadly functionalist view of the relation between mind and body, for example, viewing the mind in the body as something like a computer in a robot, perhaps with massively parallel processing (as in Rumelhart and McClelland 1986). But this view of the mind has not gone unchallenged. Some philosophers and others object strenuously that functionalism must inevitably fail to account for the most important part of mental life, namely, the subjective feel of conscious experience.

The computer model of mind represents one version of functionalism, although it is not the only version. In its most general form, functionalism defines mental states and processes by their causal or functional relations to each other and to perceptual inputs from the world outside and behavioral outputs expressed in action. According to functionalism, it is the functional relations that are important, not the intrinsic qualities of the stuff in which these relations are instanced. Just as the same computer programs can be run on different computers made out of different materials, so functionalism allows for the same mental states and events in beings with very different physical constitutions, since the very same functional relations might be instantiated in beings with very different physical makeups. According to functionalism, beliefs, desires, thoughts, and feelings are not limited to beings that are materially like ourselves. Such psychological states and events might also occur, for example, in silicon-based beings, as long as the right functional relations obtained.

Functionalism can allow for the possibility that something about silicon makes it impossible for the relevant relations to obtain in silicon-based beings, perhaps because the relevant events could not occur fast enough in silicon. It is even conceivable that the relevant functional relations might obtain only in the sort of material that makes up human brains (Thagard 1986; Dennett 1987, chapter 9). Functionalism implies that in such a case the material is important only because it is needed for the relevant functional relations and not because of some other more mysterious or magical connection between that sort of matter and a certain sort of consciousness.

Various issues arise within the general functionalist approach. For one thing, there is a dispute about how to identify the inputs to a functional system. Should inputs be identified with events in the external environment (Harman 1988) or should they instead be identified with events that are more internal such as the stimulation of an organism's sensory organs (Block 1986)? There is also the possibility of disagreement as to how deterministic the relevant functional relations have to be. Do they have to be completely deterministic, or can they be merely probabilistic? Or might they even be simply nondeterministic, not even associated with definite probabilities (Harman 1973, pp. 51–53)?

I will not be concerned with these issues here. Instead, I will concentrate on the different and more basic issue that I have already mentioned, namely, whether this sort of functionalism, no matter how elaborated, can account for the subjective feel of experience, for "what it is like" (Nagel 1974; see chapter 32) to undergo this or that experience. Furthermore, I will not consider the general challenge, "How does functionalism account for X?" for this or that X. Nor will I consider negative arguments against particular functionalist analyses. I will instead consider three related arguments that purport to demonstrate that functionalism cannot account for this aspect of experience. I will argue that all three arguments are fallacious. I will say little that is original and will for the most part merely elaborate points made many years ago (Quine 1960, p. 235; Anscombe 1965; Armstrong 1961, 1962, and especially 1968; Pitcher 1971), points that I do not think have been properly appreciated. The three arguments are these:

First, when you attend to a pain in your leg or to your experience of the redness of an apple, you are aware of an intrinsic quality of your experience, where an intrinsic quality is a quality something has in itself, apart from its relations to other things. This quality of experience cannot be captured in a functional definition, since such a definition is concerned entirely with relations, relations between mental states and perceptual input, relations among mental states, and relations between mental states and behavioral output. For example, "An essential feature of [Armstrong's functionalist] analysis is that it tells us nothing about the intrinsic nature of mental states ... He never takes seriously the natural objection that we must know the intrinsic nature of our own mental states since we experience them directly" (Nagel 1970).

Second, a person blind from birth could know all about the physical and functional facts of color perception without knowing what it is like to see something red. So, what it is like to see something red cannot be explicated in purely functional terms (Nagel 1974; Jackson 1982, 1986).

Third, it is conceivable that two people should have similarly functioning visual systems despite the fact that things that look red to one person look green to the other, things that look orange to the first person look blue to the second, and so forth (Lycan 1973; Shoemaker 1982). This sort of spectrum inversion in the way things look is possible but cannot be given a purely functional description, since by hypothesis there are no functional differences between the people in question. Since the way things look to a person is an aspect of that person's mental life, this means that an important aspect of a person's mental life cannot be explicated in purely functional terms.

Intentionality

In order to assess these arguments, I begin by remarking on what is sometimes called the intentionality of experience. Our experience of the world has content—that is, it represents things as being in a certain way. In particular, perceptual experience represents a perceiver as in particular environment, for example, as facing a tree with brown bark and green leaves fluttering in a slight breeze.

One thing that philosophers mean when they refer to this as the intentional content of experience is that the content of the experience may not reflect what is really there. Although it looks to me as if I am seeing a tree, that may be a clever illusion produced with tilted mirrors and painted backdrops. Or it may be a hallucination produced by a drug in my coffee.

There are many other examples of intentionality. Ponce de Leon searched Florida for the Fountain of Youth. What he was looking for was a fountain whose waters would give eternal youth to whoever would drink them. In fact, there is no such thing as a Fountain of Youth, but that does not mean Ponce de Leon wasn't looking for anything. He was looking for something. We can therefore say that his search had an intentional object. But the thing that he was looking for, the intentional object of his search, did not (and does not) exist.

A painting of a unicorn is a painting of something; it has a certain content. But the content does not correspond to anything actual; the thing that the painting represents does not exist. The painting has an intentional content in the relevant sense of "intentional."

Imagining or mentally picturing a unicorn is usefully compared with a painting of a unicorn. In both cases the content is not actual; the object pictured, the intentional object of the picturing, does not exist. It is only an intentional object.

This is not to suppose that mentally picturing a unicorn involves an awareness of a mental picture of a unicorn. I am comparing mentally picturing something with a picture of something, not with a perception of a picture. An awareness of a picture has as its intentional object a picture. The picture has as its intentional object a unicorn. Imagining a unicorn is different from imagining a picture of a unicorn. The intentional object of the imagining is a unicorn, not a picture of unicorn.

It is very important to distinguish between the properties of a represented object and the properties of a representation of that object. Clearly, these properties can be very different. The unicorn is pictured as having four legs and a single horn. The painting of the unicorn does not have four legs and a single horn. The painting is flat and covered with paint. The unicorn is not pictured as flat or covered with paint. Similarly, an imagined unicorn is imagined as having legs and a horn. The imagining of the unicorn has no legs or horn. The imagining of the unicorn is a mental activity. The unicorn is not imagined as either an activity or anything mental.

The notorious sense datum theory of perception arises through failing to keep these elementary points straight. According to that ancient theory, perception of external objects in the environment is always indirect and mediated by a more direct awareness of a mental sense datum. Defenders of the sense datum theory argue for it by appealing to the so-called argument from illusion. This argument begins with the uncontroversial premise that the way things are presented in perception is not always the way they are. Eloise sees some brown and green. But there is nothing brown and green before her; it is all an illusion or hallucination. From this the argument fallaciously infers that the brown and green Eloise sees is not external to her and so must be internal or mental. Since veridical, nonillusory, nonhallucinatory perception can be qualitatively indistinguishable from illusory or hallucinatory perception, the argument concludes that in all cases of perception Eloise is directly aware of something inner and mental and only indirectly aware of external objects like trees and leaves.

An analogous argument about paintings would start from the premise that a painting can be a painting of a unicorn even though there are no unicorns. Form this it might be concluded that the painting is "in the first instance" a painting of something else that is actual, for example, the painter's idea of a unicorn.

In order to see that such arguments are fallacious, consider the corresponding argument applied to searches: "Ponce de Leon was searching for the Fountain of Youth. But there is no such thing. So he must have been searching for something mental." This is just a mistake. From the fact that there is no Fountain of Youth, it does not follow that Ponce de Leon was searching for something mental. In particular, he was not looking for an idea of the Fountain of Youth. He already had the idea. What he wanted was a real Fountain of Youth, not just the idea of such a thing.

The painter has painted a picture of a unicorn. The picture painted is not a picture of an idea of a unicorn. The painter might be at a loss to paint a picture of an idea, especially if he is not familiar with conceptual art. It may be that the painter has an idea of a unicorn and tries to capture that idea in his painting. But that is to say his painting is a painting of the same thing that his idea is an idea of. The painting is not a painting of the idea, but a painting of what the idea is about.

In the same way, what Eloise sees before her is a tree, whether or not it is a hallucination. That is to say, the content of her visual experience is that she is presented with a tree, not with an idea of a tree. Perhaps, Eloise's visual experience involves some sort of mental picture of the environment. It does not follow that she is aware of a mental picture. If there is a mental picture, it may be that what she is aware of is whatever is represented by that mental picture; but then that mental picture represents something in the world, not something in the mind.

Now, we sometimes count someone as perceiving something only if that thing exists. So, if there is no tree before her and Eloise is suffering from a hallucination, we might describe this either by saying that Eloise sees something that is not really there or by saying that she does not really see anything at all but only seems to see something. There is not a use of "search or" corresponding to this second use of "see" that would allow us to say that, because there was and is no such thing as the Fountain of Youth, Ponce de Leon was not really searching for anything at all.

But this ambiguity in perceptual verbs does not affect the point I am trying to make. To see that it does not, let us use "see†" ("see-dagger") for the sense of "see" in which the object seen might not exist, as when Macbeth saw a dagger before him.[1] And let us use "see*" ("see-star") for the sense of "see" in which only things that exist can be seen. Macbeth saw† a dagger but he did not see* a dagger.

The argument from illusion starts from a case in which Eloise "sees" something brown and green before her, although there is nothing brown and green before her in the external physical world. From this, the argument infers that the brown and green she sees must be internal and mental. Now if "see" is "see†" here, this is the fallacy already noted, like that of concluding that Ponce de Leon was searching for something mental from the fact that there is no Fountain of Youth in the external world. On the other hand, if "see" is "see*" here, then the premise of the argument simply begs the question. No reason at all has so far been given for the claim that Eloise sees* something brown and green in this case. It is true that her perceptual experience represents her as visually presented with something brown and green; but that is to say merely that she sees† something brown and green, not that she sees* anything at all. (From now on I will suppress the † and * modification of perceptual verbs unless

indication of which sense is meant is crucial to the discussion.)

Here, some philosophers (e.g., Jackson 1977) would object as follows:

You agree that there is a sense in which Eloise sees something green and brown when there is nothing green and brown before her in the external world. You are able to deny that this brown and green thing is mental by taking it to be a nonexistent and merely intentional object. But it is surely more reasonable to suppose that one is in this case aware of something mental than to suppose that one is aware of something that does not exist. How can there be anything that does not exist? The very suggestion is a contradiction in terms, since "be" simply means "exist," so that you are really saying that there exists something that does not exist (Quine 1948). There are no such things as nonexistent objects!

In reply, let me concede immediately that I do not have a well-worded-out theory of intentional objects. Parsons (1980) offers one such theory, although I do not mean to express an opinion as to the success of Parson's approach. Indeed, I am quite willing to believe that there are not really any nonexistent objects and that apparent talk of such objects should be analyzed away somehow. I do not see that it is my job to resolve this issue. However this issue is resolved, the theory that results had better end up agreeing that Ponce de Leon was looking for something when he was looking for the Fountain of Youth, even though there is no Fountain of Youth, and the theory had better *not* have the consequence that Ponce de Leon was looking for something mental. If a logical theory can account for searches for things that do not, as it happens, exist, it can presumably also allow for a sense of "see" in which Macbeth can see something that does not really exist.

Another point is that Eloise's visual experience does not just present a tree. It presents a tree as viewed from a certain place. Various features that the tree is presented as having are presented as relations between the viewer and the tree, for example, features the tree has from here. The tree is presented as "in front of" and "hiding" certain other trees. It is presented as fuller on "the right." It is presented as the same size "from here" as a closer smaller tree, which is not to say that it really looks the same in size, only that it is presented as subtending roughly the same angle from here as the smaller tree. To be presented as the same in size from here is not to be presented as the same in size, period.

I do not mean to suggest that the way the tree is visually presented as being from here is something that is easily expressed in words. In particular, I do not mean to suggest that the tree can thus be presented as subtending a certain visual angle only to someone who understands words like "subtend" and "angle" (as is assumed in Peacoke 1983, chapter 1). I mean only that this feature of a tree from here is an objective feature of the tree in relation to here, a feature to which perceivers are sensitive and which their visual experience can somehow represent things as having from here.

Now, perhaps, Eloise's visual experience even presents a tree as seen by her, that is, as an object of her visual experience. If so, there is a sense after all in which Eloise's visual experience represents something mental: it represents objects in the world as objects of visual experience. But this does not mean that Eloise's visual experience in any way reveals to her the intrinsic properties of that experience by virtue of which it has the content it has.

I want to stress this point, because it is very important. Eloise is aware of the tree as a tree that she is now seeing. So, we can suppose she is aware of some features of her current visual experience. In particular, she is aware that her visual experience has the feature of being an experience of seeing a tree. That is to be aware of an intentional feature of her experience; she is aware that her experience has a certain content. On the other hand, I want to argue that she is not aware of those intrinsic features of her experience by virtue

of which it has that content. Indeed, I believe that she has no access at all to the intrinsic features of her mental representation that make it a mental representation of seeing a tree.

Things are different with paintings. In the case of a painting Eloise can be aware of those features of the painting that are responsible for its being a painting of a unicorn. That is, she can turn her attention to the pattern of the paint on the canvas by virtue of which the painting represents a unicorn. But in the case of her visual experience of a tree, I want to say that she is not aware of, as it were, the mental paint by virtue of which her experience is an experience of seeing a tree. She is aware only of the intentional or relational features of her experience, not of its intrinsic nonintentional features.

Some sense datum theorists will object that Eloise is indeed aware of the relevant mental paint when she is aware of an arrangement of color, because these sense datum theorists assert that the color she is aware of is inner and mental and not a property of external objects. But, this sense datum claim is counter to ordinary visual experience. When Eloise sees a tree before her, the colors she experiences are all experienced as features of the tree and its surroundings. None of them are experienced as intrinsic features of her experience. Nor does she experience any features of anything as intrinsic features of her experience. And that is true of you too. There is nothing special about Eloise's visual experience. When you see a tree, you do not experience any features as intrinsic features of your experience. Look at a tree and try to turn your attention to intrinsic features of your visual experience. I predict you will find that the only features there to turn your attention to will be features of the presented tree, including relational features of the tree "from here."

The sense datum theorists' view about our immediate experience of color is definitely not the naive view; it does not represent the viewpoint of ordinary perception. The sense datum theory is not the result of phenomenological study; it is rather the result of an argument, namely, the argument from illusion. But that argument is either invalid or question-begging, as we have seen.

It is very important to distinguish what are experienced as intrinsic features of the intentional object of experience from intrinsic features of the experience itself. It is not always easy to distinguish these things, but they can be distinguished. Consider the experience of having a pain in your right leg. It is very tempting to confuse features of what you experience as happening in your leg with intrinsic features of your experience. But the happening in your leg that you are presented with is the intentional object of your experience; it is not the experience itself. The content of your experience is that there is a disturbance of a certain specific sort in your right leg. The intentional object of the experience is an event located in your right leg. The experience itself is not located in your right leg. If the experience is anywhere specific, it is somewhere in your brain.

Notice that the content of your experience may not be true to what is actually happening. A slipped disc in your back may press against your sciatic nerve making it appear that there is a disturbance in your right leg when there really is not. The intentional object of your painful experience may not exist. Of course, that is not to say there is no pain in your leg. You do feel something there. But there is a sense in which what you feel in your leg is an illusion or hallucination.

It is true that, if Melvin hallucinates a pink elephant, the elephant that Melvin sees does not exist. But the pain in your leg resulting from a slipped disc in your back certainly does exist.[2] The pain is not an intentional object in quite the way the elephant is. The pain in your leg caused by the slipped disc in your back is more like the afterimage of a bright light. If you look at a blank wall, you see the image on the wall. The image is on the wall, the pain is in your leg. There is no physical spot on the wall, there is no physical disturbance in your leg. The afterimage exists, the pain exists. When we talk about afterimages or referred pains, some of what we say is about our experience and some of what we say is about the intentional object of that experience. When we say the pain or afterimage exists, we mean that the experience. When we say the pain or afterimage exists, we mean that the experience exists. When we say that the afterimage is on the wall or that the pain is in your leg, we are talking about the location of the intentional object of that experience.

Assessment of the First Objection

We are now in a position to reject the first of the three arguments against functionalism which I now repeat:

When you attend to a pain in your leg or to your experience of the redness of an apple, you are aware of an intrinsic quality of your experience, where an intrinsic quality is a quality something has in itself, apart from its relations to other things. This quality of experience cannot be captured in a functional definition, since such a definition is concerned entirely with relations, relations between mental states and perceptual input, relations among mental states, and relations between mental states and behavioral output.

We can now see that this argument fails through confounding a quality of the intentional object of an experience with a quality of the experience itself. When you attend to a pain in your leg or to your experience of the redness of an apple, you are attending to a quality of an occurrence in your leg or a quality of the apple. Perhaps this quality is presented to you as an intrinsic quality of the occurrence in your leg or as an intrinsic quality of the surface of the apple. But it is not at all presented as an intrinsic quality of your experience. And, since you are not aware of the intrinsic character of your experience, the fact that functionalism abstracts from the intrinsic character of experience does not show it leaves out anything you are aware of.

To be sure, there are possible complications. Suppose David undergoes brain surgery which he watches in a mirror. Suppose that he sees certain intrinsic features of the firing of certain neurons in his brain and suppose that the firing of these neurons is the realization of part of the experience he is having at that moment. In that case, David is aware of intrinsic features of his experience. But that way of being aware of intrinsic features of experience is not incompatible with functionalism. Given a functionalist account of David's perception of trees, tables, and the brain processes of other people, the same account applies when the object perceived happens to be David's own brain processes. The awareness David has of his own brain processes is psychologically similar to the awareness any other sighted perceiver might have of those same brain processes, including perceivers constructed in a very different way from the way in which David is constructed.

According to functionalism, the psychologically relevant properties of an internal process are all functional properties. The intrinsic nature of the process is relevant only inasmuch as it is responsible for the process's having the functional properties it has. I have been considering the objection that certain intrinsic features of experience must be psychologically relevant properties apart from their contribution of function, since these are properties we are or can be aware of. The objection is not just that we can become aware of intrinsic features of certain mental processes in the way just mentioned, that is, by perceiving in a mirror the underlying physical processes that realize those mental processes. That would not be an objection to functionalism. The objection is rather that all or most conscious experience has intrinsic aspects of which we are or can be aware in such a way that these aspects of the experience are psychologically significant over and above the contribution they make to function.

Of course, to say that these aspects are psychologically significant is not to claim that they are or ought to be significant for the science of psychology. Rather, they are supposed to be psychologically significant in the sense of mentally significant, whether or not this aspect of experience is susceptible of scientific understanding. The objection is that any account of our mental life that does not count these intrinsic properties as mental or psychological properties leaves out a crucial aspect of our experience.

My reply to this objection is that it cannot be defended without confusing intrinsic features of the intentional object of experience with intrinsic features of the experiences. Apart from that confusion, there is no reason to think that we are ever aware of the relevant intrinsic features of our experiences.

There are other ways in which one might be aware of intrinsic features of our experience without that casting any doubt on functionalism. For example, one might be aware of intrinsic features of experience without being aware of them as intrinsic features of experience, just as Ortcutt can be aware of a man who, as it happens, is a spy without being aware of the man as a spy. When Eloise sees a tree, she is aware of her perceptual experience as an experience with a certain intentional content. Suppose that her experience is realized by a particular physical event and that certain intrinsic features of the event are in this case responsible for certain intentional features of Eloise's experience. Perhaps there is then a sense in which Eloise is aware of this physical process and aware of those intrinsic features, although she is not aware of them as the intrinsic features that they are.

Even if that is so, it is no objection to functionalism. The intrinsic features that Eloise is aware of in that case are no more psychologically significant than is the property of being a spy to Ortcutt's perception of a man who happens to be a spy. The case gives no reason to think that there is a psychologically significant difference between Eloise's experience and the experience of any functional duplicate of Eloise that is made of different stuff from what Eloise is made of.

Similarly, if Eloise undertakes the sort of education recommended by Paul Churchland (1985) so that she automatically thinks of the intentional aspects of her experience in terms of their neurophysiological causes, then she may be aware of intrinsic features of her experience as the very features that they are. But again that would be no objection to functionalism, since it gives no reason to think that there is a psychological difference between Eloise after such training and a robot who is Eloise's functional duplicate and who has been given similar training (Shoemaker 1985). The duplicate now wrongly thinks of certain aspects of its experience as certain features of certain neurological processes—wrongly, because the relevant processes in the duplicate are not neurological processes at all.

Observe, by the way, that I am not offering any sort of positive argument that Eloise and her duplicate must have experiences that are psychologically similar in all respects. I am only observing that the cases just considered are compatible with the functionalist claim that their experiences are similar.

The objections to functionalism that I am considering in this chapter claim that certain intrinsic properties of experience so inform the experience that any experience with different intrinsic properties would have a different psychological character. What I have argued so far is that this objection is not established by simple inspection of our experience.

Perception and Understanding

Now, let me turn to the second objection, which I repeat:

A person blind from birth could know all about the physical and functional facts of color perception without knowing what it is like to see something red. So, what it is like to see something red cannot be explicated in purely functional terms.

In order to address this objection, I have to say something about the functionalist theory of

the content of mental representations and, more particularly, something about the functionalist theory of concepts. I have to do this because to know what it is like to see something red is to be capable of representing to yourself something's being red. You can represent that to yourself only if you have the relevant concept of what it is for something to be red. The blind person lacks the full concept of redness that a sighted person has; so the blind person cannot fully represent what it is for a sighted person to see something red. Therefore, the blind person cannot be said to know what it is like to see something red.

One kind of functionalist account of mental representation supposes that mental representations are constructed from concepts, where the content of a representation is determined by the concepts it contains and the way these concepts are put together to form that representation (Harman 1987). In this view, what it is to have a given concept is functionally determined. Someone has the appropriate concept of something's being red if and only if the person has available a concept that functions in the appropriate way. The relevant functioning may involve connections with the use of other concepts, connections to perceptual input, and/or connections to behavioral output. In this case, connections to perceptual input are crucial. If the concept is to function in such a way that the person has the full concept of something's being red, the person must be disposed to form representations involving that concept as the natural and immediate consequence of seeing something red. Since the blind person lacks any concept of this sort, the blind person lacks the full concept of something's being red. Therefore, the blind person does not know what it is like to see something red.

It is not easy to specify the relevant functional relation precisely. Someone who goes blind later in life will normally retain the relevant concept of something's being red. Such a person has a concept that he or she would be able to use in forming such immediate visual representations except for the condition that interferes in his or her case with normal visual perception. So, the right functional relation holds for such a person. I am supposing that the person blind from birth has no such concept; that is, the person has no concept of something's being red that could be immediately brought into service in visual representations of the environment if the person were suddenly to acquire sight.

We are now in a position to assess the claim that the person blind from birth could know all the physical and functional facts about color perception without knowing what it is like to see something red. I claim that there is one important functional fact about color perception that the blind person cannot know, namely, that there is a concept R such that when a normal perceiver sees something red in good lighting conditions, the perceiver has visual experience with a representational structure containing this concept R. The person blind from birth does not know that fact, because in order to know it the person needs to be able to represent that fact to himself or herself, which requires having the relevant concepts. A key concept needed to represent that fact is the concept of something's being red, because the fact in question is a fact about what happens when a normal perceiver sees something red. Since the person blind from birth does not have the full concept of something's being red, the person cannot fully understand that fact and so cannot know that fact.

The blind person might know something resembling this, for example, that there is a concept R such that, when a normal perceiver sees something that reflects light of such and such a frequency, the perceiver has visual experience with a representational structure containing this concept R. But that is to know something different.

The person blind from birth fails to know what it is like to see something red because he or she does not fully understand what it is for something to be red, that is, because he or she does not have the full concept of something's being red. So, contrary to what is assumed in the second objection, the person blind from birth does not

know all the functional facts, since he or she does not know how the concept R functions with respect to the perception of things that are red.

This response to the second objection appeals to a functionalism that refers to the functions of concepts, not just to the functions of overall mental states. There are other versions of functionalism that try to make do with references to the function of overall mental states, without appeal to concepts. Some of these versions identify the contents of such states with sets of possible worlds (or centered possible worlds). These versions of functionalism cannot respond to the objection in the way that I have responded. It is unclear to me whether any satisfactory response is possible on behalf of such theories. For example, Lewis (1983) is forced to say that although the person blind from birth lacks certain skills, for example, the ability to recognize red objects just by looking at them in the way that sighted people can, this person lacks no information about visual perception. I am not happy with that response, since it is clearly false to say that the person blind from birth does not lack any information.

Inverted Spectrum

I now turn to the third objection to functionalism, which I repeat:

It is conceivable that two people should have similarly functioning visual systems despite the fact that things that look red to one person look green to the other, things that look orange to the first person look blue to the second, and so forth. This sort of spectrum inversion in the way things look is possible but cannot be given a purely functional description, since by hypothesis there are no functional differences between the people in question. Since the way things look to a person is an aspect of that person's mental life, this means that there is an important aspect of a person's mental life that cannot be explicated in purely functional terms.

In order to discuss this objection, I need to say something more about how perceptual states function. In particular, I have to say something about how perceptual states function in relation to belief.

Perceptual experience represents a particular environment of the perceiver. Normally, a perceiver uses this representation as his or her representation of the environment. That is to say, the perceiver uses it in order to negotiate the furniture. In still other words, this representation is used as the perceiver's belief about the environment. This sort of use of perceptual representations is the normal case, although there are exceptions when a perceiver inhibits his or her natural tendency and refrains from using a perceptual representation (or certain aspects of that representation) as a guide to the environment, as a belief about the surroundings. The content of perceptual representation is functionally defined in part by the ways in which this representation normally arises in perception and in part by the ways in which the representation is normally used to guide actions (Armstrong 1961, 1986; Dennett 1969; Harman 1973).

The objection has us consider two people, call them Alice and Fred, with similarly functioning visual systems but with inverted spectra with respect to each other. Things that look red to Alice look green to Fred, things that look blue to Alice look orange to Fred, and so on. We are to imagine that this difference between Alice and Fred is not reflected in their behavior in any way. They both call ripe strawberries "red" and call grass "green" and they do this in the effortless ways in which normal perceivers do who have learned English in the usual ways.

Consider what this means for Alice in a normal case of perception. She looks at ripe strawberry. Perceptual processing results in a perceptual representation of that strawberry, including a representation of its color. She uses this representation as her guide to the environment, that is, as her belief about the strawberry, in particular, her belief about its color. She expresses her belief about the

color of the strawberry by using the words, "it is red." Similarly, for Fred. His perception of the strawberry results in a perceptual representation of the color of the strawberry that he uses as his belief about the color and expresses with the same words, "it is red."

Now, in the normal case of perception, there can be no distinction between how things look and how they are believed to be, since how things look is given by the content of one's perceptual representation and in the normal case one's perceptual representation is used as one's belief about the environment. The hypothesis of the inverted spectrum objection is that the strawberry looks different in color to Alice and to Fred. Since everything is supposed to be functioning in them in the normal way, it follows that they must have different beliefs about the color of the strawberry. If they had the same beliefs while having perceptual representations that differed in content, then at least one of them would have a perceptual representation that was not functioning as his or her belief about the color of the strawberry, which is to say that it would not be functioning in what we are assuming is the normal way.

A further consequence of the inverted spectrum hypothesis is that, since in the normal case Alice and Fred express their beliefs about the color of strawberries and grass by saying "it is red" and "it is green," they must mean something different by their color words. By "red" Fred means the way ripe strawberries look to him. Since that is the way grass looks to Alice, what Fred means by "red" is what she means by "green."

It is important to see that these really are consequences of the inverted spectrum hypothesis. If Alice and Fred meant the same thing by their color terms, then either (a) one of them would not be using these words to express his or her beliefs about color or (b) one of them would not be using his or her perceptual representations of color as his or her beliefs about color. In either case, there would be a failure of normal functioning, contrary to the hypothesis of the inverted spectrum objection.

According to functionalism, if Alice and Fred use words in the same way with respect to the same things, then they mean the same things by those words (assuming also that they are members of the same linguistic community and their words are taken from the common language). But this is just common sense. Suppose Alice and Humphrey are both members of the same linguistic community, using words in the same way, and so on. Alice is an ordinary human being and Humphrey is a humanoid robot made of quite a different material from Alice. Common sense would attribute the same meanings to Humphrey's words as to Alice's, given that they use words in the same way. Some sort of philosophical argument is needed to argue otherwise. No such argument has been provided by defenders of the inverted spectrum objection.

Shoemaker (1982; see chapter 41) offers a different version of the inverted spectrum objection. He has us consider a single person, call him Harry, at two different times, at an initial time of normal color perception and at a later time after Harry has suffered through a highly noticeable spectrum inversion (perhaps as the result of the sort of brain operation described in Lycan 1973, in which nerves are switched around so that red things now have the perceptual consequences that green things used to have, etc.) and has finally completely adapted his responses so as to restore normal functioning. Shoemaker agrees that Harry now has the same beliefs about color as before and means the same things by his color words, and he agrees that there is a sense in which strawberries now look to Harry the same as they looked before Harry's spectrum inversion. But Shoemaker takes it to be evident that there is another sense of "looks" in which it may very well be true that things do not look the same as they looked before, so that in this second sense of "looks" red things look the way green things used to look.

In other words, Shoemaker thinks it is evident that there may be a psychologically relevant difference between the sort of experience Harry had on looking at a ripe strawberry at the initial stage and the experience he has on looking at a ripe strawberry at the final stage (after he has completely adapted to his operation.) That is, he thinks it is evident that there may be a psychologically relevant difference between these experiences even though there is no functional difference and no difference in the content of the experiences.

Now, this may seem evident to anyone who has fallen victim to the sense datum fallacy, which holds that one's awareness of the color of a strawberry is mediated by one's awareness of an intrinsic feature of a perceptual representation. But why should anyone else agree? Two perceptual experiences with the same intentional content must be psychologically the same. In particular, there can be nothing one is aware of in having the one experience that one is not aware of in having the other, since the intentional content of an experience comprises everything one is aware of in having that experience.

I suggest that Shoemaker's inverted spectrum hypothesis will seem evident only to someone who *begins* with the prior assumption that people have an immediate and direct awareness of intrinsic features of their experience, including those intrinsic features that function to represent color. Such a person can then go on to suppose that the intrinsic feature of experience that represents red for Alice is the intrinsic feature of experience that represents green for Fred, and so forth. This prior assumption is exactly the view behind the first objection, which I have argued is contrary to ordinary experience and can be defended only by confusing qualities of the intentional objects of experience with qualities of the experience itself. Shoemaker's inverted spectrum hypothesis therefore offers no independent argument against functionalism.[3]

Conclusion

To summarize briefly, I have described and replied to three related objections to functionalism. The first claims that we are directly aware of intrinsic features of our experience and argues that there is no way to account for this awareness in a functional view. To this, I reply that when we clearly distinguish properties of the object of experience from properties of the experience, we see that we are not aware of the relevant intrinsic features of the experience. The second objection claims that a person blind from birth can know all about the functional role of visual experience without knowing what it is like to see something red. To this I reply that the blind person does not know all about the functional role of visual experience; in particular, the blind person does not know how such experience functions in relation to the perception of red objects. The third objection claims that functionalism cannot account for the possibility of an inverted spectrum. To this I reply that someone with the relevant sort of inverted spectrum would have to have beliefs about the colors of things that are different from the beliefs other have and would have to mean something different by his or her color terms, despite being a functionally normal color perceiver who sorts things by color in exactly the way others do and who uses color terminology in the same way that others do. Functionalism's rejection of this possibility is commonsensical and is certainly not so utterly implausible or counterintuitive that these cases present an objection to functionalism. On the other hand, to imagine that there could be relevant cases of inverted spectrum without inversion of belief and meaning is to fall back onto the first objection and not to offer any additional consideration against functionalism.

Notes

The preparation of this paper was supported in part by research grants to Princeton University from the James S. McDonnell Foundation and the National Science Foundation.

1. W. Shakespeare, *Macbeth*, act 2, scene 1:

Is this a dagger which I see before me,
The handle toward my hand?
Come let me clutch thee.

I have thee not, and yet I see thee still.
Art thou not, fatal vision, sensible
To feeling as to sight? or art thou but
A dagger of the mind, a false creating,
Proceeding from the heat oppressed brain?......
I see thee still;
And on thy blade and dudgeon gouts of blood,
Which was not so before.
There's no such thing; it is the bloody business which informs
Thus to mine eyes.

2. I am indebted to Sydney Shoemaker for emphasizing this to me.

3. I should say that Shoemaker himself does not offer his case as an objection to what he calls functionalism. He claims that his version of functionalism is compatible with his case. But I am considering a version of functionalism that is defined in a way that makes it incompatible with such a case.

References

Anscombe, G. E. M. (1965) "The intentionality of sensation: a grammatical feature," *Analytical Philosophy*, second series, edited by R. J. Butler (Oxford, Blackwell); reprinted in Anscombe, G. E. M., *Metaphysics and 'the Philosophy of Mind: Collected Philosophical Papers*, Volume 2 (Minneapolis, Minnesota; University of Minnesota Press: 1981) pp. 3–20.

Armstrong, David M. (1961) *Perception and the Physical World* (London: Routledge and Kegan Paul).

Armstrong, David M. (1962) *Bodily Sensations* (London: Routledge and Kegan Paul).

Armstrong, David M. (1968) *The Materialist Theory of Mind* (London: Routledge and Kegan Paul).

Block, Ned (1986) "Advertisement for a semantics for psychology," *Midwest Studies in Philosophy* 10:615–678.

Churchland, Paul (1985) "Reduction, qualia, and the direct introspection of mental states," *Journal of Philosophy* 82:8–28.

Dennett, Daniel C. (1969) *Content and Consciousness* (London: Routledge and Kegan Paul).

Dennett, Daniel C. (1987) *The Intentional Stance* (Cambridge, Massachusetts: MIT Press).

Harman, Gilbert (1973) *Thought* (Princeton, New Jersey: Princeton University Press).

Harman, Gilbert (1987) "(Nonsolipsistic) conceptual role semantics," *New Directions in Semantics*, edited by Ernest LePore, London, Academic Press (1987) 55–81.

Harman, Gilbert (1988) "Wide functionalism," *Cognition and Representation*, edited by Stephen Schiffer and Susan Steele (Boulder, Colorado: Westview Press) 11–20.

Jackson, Frank (1977) *Perception: A Representative Theory* (Cambridge, England: Cambridge University Press).

Jackson, Frank (1982) "Epiphenomenal qualia," *Philosophical Quarterly* 32:127–32.

Jackson, Frank (1986) "What Mary didn't know," *Journal of Philosophy* 83:291–295.

Lewis, David K. (1983) "Postscript to 'Mad pain and Martian pain'," *Philosophical Papers*, Volume 1, (New York: Oxford University Press) pp. 130–132.

Lycan, William G. (1973) "Inverted spectrum," *Ratio* 15.

Nagel, Thomas (1970) "Armstrong on the mind," *Philosophical Review* 79, reprinted in *Reading in the Philosophy of Psychology*, Volume 1, edited by Ned Block (Cambridge, Massachusetts: Harvard University Press).

Nagel, Thomas (1974) "What is it like to be a bat?" *Philosophical Review* 83:435–450.

Parsons, Terence (1980) *Nonexistent Objects* (New Haven: Yale University Press).

Peacocke, Christopher (1983) *Sense and Content* (Oxford: Oxford University Press).

Pitcher, George (1971) *A Theory of Perception* (Princeton, New Jersey: Princeton University Press).

Quine, W. V. (1948) "On what there is," *Review of Metaphysics*, reprinted in *From a Logical Point of View* (Cambridge, Masschusetts; Harvard University Press: 1953).

Quine, W. V. (1960) *Word and Object* (Cambridge, Massachusetts: MIT Press).

Rumelhart, David E., and McClelland, James L. (1986) *Parallel Distributed Processing*, 2 volumes (Cambridge, Massachusetts: MIT Press).

Shoemaker, Sydney (1982) "The inverted spectrum," *Journal of Philosophy* 79:357–381.

Shoemaker, Sydney (1985) "Churchland on reduction, qualia, and introspection," *PSA 1984*, Volume 2 (Philosophy of Science Association) pp. 799–809.

Thagard, Paul T. (1986) "Parallel computation and the mind-body problem," *Cognitive Science* 10:301–318.

43 Inverted Earth

Ned Block

This chapter started life as a response to Gilbert Harman's "The Intrinsic Quality of Experience" (see chapter 42), and it retains that format even though the aim of the chapter is to argue that there is an "inversion" argument for qualia realism and against functionalism that is better than the traditional inverted spectrum argument.[1] (Qualia realism in the sense that I will be using the term is the view that there are intrinsic mental features of our experience.) Those who have not read Harman's chapter may want to skip the last section of this chapter.

The Fallacy of Intentionalizing Qualia

To a first approximation, the inverted spectrum hypothesis is that things we agree are red look to you the way things we agree are green look to me (and we are functionally identical). There is a simple argument from the possibility of an inverted spectrum to the falsity of functionalism: if two different mental states can play exactly the same functional role, then there is an aspect of mentality (the "qualitative" aspect) that eludes characterization in terms of functional role. In terms of the machine version of functionalism: even if we are computers, if nonetheless you and I could be computationally exactly alike though mentally different (in what it is like to see something red), then the mental outruns the computational.

The "containment response"[2] to the inverted spectrum would be to give up on functionalism as a theory of experience (or at least of its qualitative aspect), retaining functionalism as a theory of the cognitive aspect of the mind. I favor this approach, but I will not pursue it here. This chapter is directed against the thoroughgoing functionalist who insists on functionalism as a theory of the whole of the mind.[3] The drawback of the containment response is that it arguably commits its proponents to the possibility of a "zombie," a being that is like us in cognitive states but totally lacking in qualia.[4]

I gave a first approximation to the inverted spectrum hypothesis above. But a proper statement of it must make use of a distinction between two kinds of content of experience, one of which is a matter of the way the experience represents the world, the other of which is a matter of "what it is like" (in Tom Nagel's phrase) to have it. The former has been called intentional or representational content; the latter, qualitative or sensational content.[5] In terms of this distinction, the inverted spectrum hypothesis is this: when you and I have experiences that have the intentional content *looking red*, your qualitative content is the same as the qualitative content that I have when my experience has the intentional content *looking green* (and we are functionally identical). This chapter will be concerned with this rather dramatic version of the claim that there is a gap between intentional and qualitative contents of experience. But the emphasis here and in the literature on this dramatic case should not make us forget that if the functionalist theory of qualia were correct, it would also preclude less systematic qualitative differences among functionally identical people, differences the hypothesizing of which though hard to work out in detail is also less vulnerable to the abuse that has been heaped on the inverted spectrum hypothesis.

If blood looks red to both of us, then in the *intentional* sense of 'looks the same', blood looks the same to us. (In respect of color, that is. I will leave out this qualification from now on, and I will also ignore the fact of different shades of red for simplicity.) The *qualitative* sense of 'looks the same' can be defined via appeal to such notions as "what it's like," or alternatively, by direct appeal to the inverted spectrum hypothesis itself. If your spectrum is inverted with respect to mine, then red things look the same to you—in the qualitative sense—as green things look to me.

As Shoemaker points out, it is easy to go from these senses of 'looks' to kinds of content. If blood looks the same to us in the intentional sense, then the intentional contents of our experiences of it are the same. If blood looks the same to you in the qualitative sense as grass looks to me, then the qualitative contents of our experiences are the same.[6]

Now that the intentional/qualitative distinction has been introduced I can correct a vital error made by both sides of the inverted spectrum debate. My point is that if an inverted spectrum is possible, then experiential contents *that can be expressed in public language* (for example, *looking red*) are not qualitative contents, but rather intentional contents. *For suppose that spectrum inversion is rife:* there is no spectrum of the vast majority, despite widespread functional similarity in relevant respects. How could I justify the claim that red things look red to me but not to you? How could I claim that the qualitative content of my experience as of red things is *looking red*, whereas yours is, say, *looking blue*? Any argument I could use against you could equally well be used by you against me. And it will not do to say we are both right, each with our own sense of 'red'. 'Red' is a public language word, not a word that means one thing in your mouth and another thing in mine.

Since I will be appealing to this point later it will be useful to have a name for it. I will tendentiously describe the supposition that experiential contents that can be expressed in public language such as *looking red* are qualitative contents as the fallacy of intentionalizing qualia.[7]

Note that the intentional contents of color experience must be referentially based—these contents are "Californian," not neo-Fregean. The reason is that "modes of presentation" of color experiences are qualitative contents, and qualitative contents are precisely that in which our experiences as of red things—our contents of *looking red*—can differ. What gives an experience the content of *looking red* is its relation to red things, not its qualitative content. One way to put

the point would be that each of us may have our own "concept" of the look of red, where a concept is a qualitative content, but such differences in "concept" of red make no difference to whether something looks red to us. Whether something looks red to us depends on whether we are having an experience as of something red, not on our different "concepts" of red. (Recall that I am ignoring the fact of different shades of a single color.)[8]

I want to note two points about the argument against intentionalizing qualia. First, the argument is not really directed against qualia skeptics like Harman and Dennett, since they don't accept the inverted spectrum premise. Also, they already believe the conclusion on one formulation of it, namely that *looking red* is an intentional content.[9] The second point is that although I hope qualia realists are convinced. I do not intend to go into the matter in much detail here. I mentioned above that the point could be avoided by supposing that 'red' and hence 'looking red' is ambiguous, being privately defined by each of us in terms of his own qualitative content. I scoffed, saying that 'red' is a univocal public language word. But of course the matter need not end here. And there are other more sophisticated ploys the determined defender of a qualitative definition of 'red' might make. I will not pursue the matter because since this paper is directed against the qualia skeptics, a rear-guard action against other members of my team would not be good strategy. Qualia realists who are tempted to intentionalize qualia should note the power of the view that *looking red* is an intentional content in defending qualia realism in the face of the functionalist challenge.

One route to the fallacy of intentionalizing qualia among qualia realists is to define secondary quality terms in terms of the qualitative contents of the experiences they normally produce, a view shared (despite many differences of opinion) by McGinn (op. cit.) and Peacocke (op. cit.). Peacocke defines 'red' in terms of red', 'red'' being the name he gives to "the" quale produced by red things. Since the semantic content of 'looks red' is given by that of 'looks' and 'red', the meaning of 'looks red' is given in terms of red'. Such a view would not be very attractive if there is no "the" quale produced by red things.

McGinn considers the possibility that things to which we and Martians both apply 'red' look to us the way things we and the Martians agree are 'green' look to them. Though he remains agnostic on whether such Martians could be totally functionally identical to us (and thus agnostic on the possibility of an inverted spectrum), he concludes that in such a case, things that are red relative to us (e.g., ripe tomatoes) are green relative to them, even though both groups apply 'red' to things that are the color of ripe tomatoes. Thus, according to McGinn, the Martians might have always spoken a language in which 'red' is applied to things just as we apply it, but nonetheless they mean green by it. But if we are willing to consider such a possibility, why not consider the possibility that those of us with short ear lobes bear a relation to those of us with long ear lobes that McGinn's Earthians bear to McGinn's Martians? This is not as absurd as might appear, given that there are enormous differences among normal people in the physiological machinery of color vision (see Hardin, op. cit.). Why should we try to define 'red' in terms of a quale that red things are supposed to produce in all of us when we don't have any good reason to believe that there is any such thing?

My argument is not based on the idea that spectrum inversion is merely possible (though not actual). I claim that we simply do not know if spectrum inversion obtains or not. Further, even if we were to find good evidence against spectrum inversion actually obtaining, there could be a race of people otherwise very like us who have color vision, color sensations, and color terms for whom spectrum inversion does obtain. Presumably, any good theory of the semantics of color terms will apply to them as well as us.[10]

A defender of a McGinn-Peacocke analysis of color in terms of qualia might wish to allow the possibility of spectrum inversion, but insist that nonetheless our color concepts preclude spectrum inversion. The reasoning might go like this: prior to general relativity, the concept of a straight line presupposed the axioms of Euclidean Geometry, along with the idea that a straight line is the shortest distance between two points, the path of a stretched string or a light ray, the path along which travel uses up the least fuel, and the like. But general relativity plus observations revealed that Euclidean straight lines were not the paths that had the other properties just listed—those properties accompanied Riemmanian straight lines—hence the generally accepted view that space is Riemmanian. The point of the story is that before the development of general relativity and alternative geometries, the unsticking of the notion of a Euclidean straight line from the cluster of other properties was precluded by our concepts—literally inconceivable, though not actually impossible. To conceive of it required a conceptual revolution.

The application of this model to spectrum inversion is this: the application of 'red' to red things, and the production by red things of the same quale in all of us, are joined by our concepts, conceptual revision being required for their unsticking. The analogy is not persuasive. In wondering whether the sunset looks to you as it does to me, I may be imagining you with an experience qualitatively like mine. In daily life, we do not usually take the possibility of spectrum inversion into account. But it would be a mistake to jump from this fact about practice to the idea that spectrum inversion is precluded by our concepts. Spectrum inversion can be understood easily by children (assuming it can be understood at all). Try it out on the next eight-year-old you encounter. Indeed, they sometimes come up with the idea themselves. (My eleven-year-old daughter offered spectrum inversion as an explanation of why people seem to have different favorite colors. Everyone has the same favorite colorquale.)

My brand of qualia realism is quasi-functional. According to me, the *intentional* content of experience is functional. An experience has the intentional content of looking red if it functions in the right way—if it is caused by red things in the right circumstances, and used in thought about red things and action with respect to red things rightly.[11] The functional roles I am talking about are what I call "long-arm" roles, roles that include real things in the world as the inputs and outputs. They are to be distinguished from the "short-arm" roles that functionalists sometimes prefer, roles that stop at the skin. It is essential to the functional role that characterizes the intentional content of *looking red* that it be caused (appropriately) by red things and cause appropriate thought about and action on red things.

So this is why my brand of qualia realism is quasi-*functional*; here is why it is *quasi*-functional: the *qualitative* content of experience is *not* functionally characterizable. Two experiences can differ functionally, hence have different intentional contents, but have the same qualitative content, that is, be alike in "what it is like" to have them. Further, two experiences can be alike in function (and hence have the same intentional content), but have different qualitative contents.

So quasi-functional qualia realism is functionalist about the intentional content of experience. And it is also functionalist about the belief that blood is red, the concept of red, and the meaning of 'red'.[12]

But didn't I identify color "concepts" with qualitative contents earlier? Yes, and this is certainly one reasonable way to use the concept of a concept, but one can equally well individuate concepts in line with public language meanings, as Harman does. Harman says that what makes a concept the concept of red is its production in a natural and immediate way be red things, its role in thinking about and manipulating red things, in causing the subject to judge that two things are the same color, and the like. This is something about which the quasi-functional qualia realist may as well agree with Harman. So let it be common ground that possession of the concept of red is a matter of how our experiences function, not their intrinsic qualitative properties.[13]

Harman's refutation of the inverted spectrum depends on rejecting the distinction I've been talking about between qualitative and intentional content. He claims that experience has only one kind of content: intentional content. According to Harman, two experiences with the same intentional content must be the same in all mental respects. His rejection of the distinction leads him to state and refute a version of the inverted spectrum hypothesis that involves only intentional content. His version of the inverted spectrum hypothesis is: "... things that look red to one person look green to the other, things that look orange to the first person look blue to the second, and so forth," where the people referred to are functionally the same.[14] But this inverted spectrum hypothesis is made of straw. According to this straw inverted spectrum hypothesis, the experience you get on looking at red things, your experience as of red, the one that produces sincere utterances like 'This is red', in the normal way—this experience might be one whose intentional content is *looking green*. But no proponent of the inverted spectrum should accept *this* inverted spectrum hypothesis. The proponent of the inverted spectrum hypothesizes inverted qualitative contents, not inverted *intentional* contents.

Perhaps misunderstanding on this matter is partly responsible for the fact that both sides of the inverted spectrum argument tend to see nothing at all in the other side. To quote Harman on the inverted spectrum from an earlier paper, "I speak of an 'argument' here, although (as D. Lewis has observed in a similar context), the 'argument' really comes down simply to denying the functionalist account of the content of concepts and thoughts without actually offering any reason for that denial."[15] The straw inverted spectrum hypothesis does indeed have this question-begging flavor, supposing as it does that there could be inverted intentional contents. The supposition that there could be inverted intentional contents amounts to the supposition that someone's concept of red might function as a concept of green without thereby being a concept of green. And that does just deny the functionalist account of concepts.

The Inverted Spectrum and Inverted Earth

Let us consider positive arguments for the possibility of an inverted spectrum. If the proponent of the inverted spectrum could establish that the burden of proof is on those who deny the possibility, then positive arguments would be unnecessary. But since no one has succeeded in establishing the burden of proof, the emphasis in the literature has been *epistemic*: science fiction cases which (allegedly) would be *evidence* for an inverted spectrum are produced and discussed.[16] The idea is that if there could be evidence for an inverted spectrum, then it is possible. For example, imagine genetically identical twins one of whom has had color-inverting lenses placed in its eyes at birth.[17]

Both twins are raised normally, and as adults, they both apply 'red' to red things in the normal way. But though the twins are functionally identical in the relevant respects, we may suppose that the internal physiological state that mediates between red things and 'red' utterances in one is the same as the internal physiological state that mediates between green things and 'green' utterances in the other. And one can argue from this to the claim that things that they both call red look to one the way things they both call green look to the other. There is much to be said on both sides of this debate. I do not wish to enter into the argument here.

Interpersonal inverted spectrum cases such as the one just mentioned have not been taken very seriously by the opposition. They suppose (as does Harman) that there is no reason to think that the different physiological realizations of the experience of red things involves any *experiential* difference. Like any mental state, the experience of red has alternative physiological realizations,

and this is held to be just a case of alternative realizations of the very same experience.

The qualia realist reply to Harman is that when we put on the inverting lenses, grass looks red, ripe strawberries green, the sky yellow, and the like. So shouldn't we suppose that the same is true of the twin who wears the inverting lenses? Here, as elsewhere in the disputes about qualia we would do well to follow Searle's (op. cit.) advice of looking to the first-person point of view. This appeal to what happens when we ourselves put on the inverting lenses suggests a version of the inverted spectrum example that involves just such a case—the *intra*personal inverted spectrum.[18]

I think it is best to treat the intrapersonal inverted spectrum as having four stages. First, we have a functionally normal person. Second, inverting lenses are placed in his eyes and he says grass looks red and blood looks green.[19] Third, after a period of confused use of color terms, he finally adapts to the point where he uses color language normally. That is, he naturally and immediately describes blood as 'red' and grass as 'green'. At the third stage, he is functionally normal except in one important respect: he recalls the period before the insertion of the lenses as a period in which "grass looked to me the way blood now looks." Fourth, he has amnesia about the period before the lenses were inserted and is functionally totally normal—just as in the first period. The crucial stage is the third. Here we have the evidence of the victim's testimony that grass used to look to him the way blood now looks. Note that as I have described it there is no use of 'quale' or other technical terms in what he says—he's just talking about the way red things look and used to look as compared with green things. At this point, he is functionally abnormal precisely because he is saying such odd things. But if we are prepared to believe him, then when he gets amnesia and is functionally normal, why should we think that his qualia have re-inverted?

The main advantage of the intrapersonal case over the interpersonal case is the availability of the subject's introspective report at stage 3. Suppose the subject is *you*. By hypothesis, you recall what grass used to look like, and you realize that it used to look to you the way ripe tomatoes now look. Is there anything incoherent about this? Dennett and Rey say yes. Dennett insists that your inclinations to say such things reflect a memory malfunction, and Rey says that we don't know what do make of what you say.[20] I concede that there is some justice in these complaints (though I disagree with them). After all, the adapted subject is not a normal person. Perhaps it can be shown that the hypothesis of confusion will always be more plausible than the hypothesis of spectrum inversion. Certainly if you think the distinction between intentional and qualitative content is a confusion, it will be natural to look for some way of avoiding taking the subject's memory reports at stage 3 at face value.

I believe that these criticisms can be defeated on their own terms, but instead of trying to do that here, I propose to take a different tack. I will describe a case that is the "converse" of the usual inverted spectrum case, a case of inverted *intentional* content and functional inversion combined with identical qualitative content. In the usual inverted spectrum case, we have two persons (or stages of the same person) whose experiences are functionally and intentionally the same but qualitatively inverted. I will describe a case of two persons/stages whose experiences are qualitatively the same but intentionally and functionally inverted. If I am right about this case, the distinction between the intentional and qualitative content of experience is vindicated, and the functionalist theory of qualitative content is refuted.

As with the usual inverted spectrum argument, mine hinges on a science fiction example. (The fancifulness of my example could be much reduced. For example, imagine rooms to which our subjects are confined for their whole lives instead of whole planets.) I will make use of an example of Harman's: Inverted Earth.[21] Inverted Earth differs from Earth in two respects. Firstly, everything has the complementary color of the color on Earth. The sky is yellow, grass is red, fire hydrants are green, and so forth. I mean everything *really* has these oddball colors. If you visited Inverted Earth along with a team of scientists from your university, you would all agree that on this planet, the sky is yellow, grass is red, and so forth. Secondly, the vocabulary of the residents of Inverted Earth is also inverted: If you ask what color the (yellow) sky is, they (truthfully) say "Blue!" If you ask what color the (red) grass is, they say "Green". If you brought a speaker of the Inverted Earth dialect to a neutral place (with unknown sky color, unfamiliar vegetation, and the like) and employed a team of linguists using any reasonable methods to plumb his language, you would have to come to the conclusion that he uses 'red' to mean what we mean by 'green', 'blue' to mean what we mean by 'yellow', and so on. You would have to come to the conclusion that the Inverted Earth dialect differs from ours in "inverted meanings" of color words. If commerce develops between the two planets and painters on Inverted Earth order paint from one of our paint stores, we shall have to translate their order for "green paint" into an order to our stockboy to get red paint. Inverted Earth differs from earth in switched words and switched stimuli.

Further, the intentional contents of attitudes and experiences of Inverted Earthlings are also inverted. If a foreigner misreads a phrase book and comes to the conclusion that 'trash can' means a type of sandwich, despite what he says, he does not actually want a trash can for lunch—he wants a sandwich. Similarly, when a resident of Inverted Earth wonders, as he would put it, "why the sky is blue," he is wondering not why the sky is blue, but why it is yellow. And when he looks at the sky (in normal circumstances for Inverted Earth), the experience he has that he would describe as the sky looking "blue" is actually the experience of the sky looking yellow. There is no mystery or asymmetry here. I am using our language to describe his intentional contents; if he used his language to describe ours, he would correctly describe us as inverted in just the same way.

These two differences that I have mentioned "cancel out" in the sense that the talk on Inverted Earth will *sound* just like talk on Earth. Radio programs from Inverted Earth sound to us like radio programs from faraway places where English is spoken, like New Zealand. Children on both planets ask their parents, "Why is the sky blue?" "Why is grass green?"

Now let's have the analog of the intrasubjective inverted spectrum example. A team of mad scientists knock you out. While you are out cold, they insert color-inverting lenses in your eyes, and change your body pigments so you don't have a nasty shock when you wake up and look at your feet. They transport you to Inverted Earth, where you are substituted for a counterpart who has occupied a niche on Inverted Earth that corresponds exactly (except for colors of things) with your niche at home. You wake up, and since the inverting lenses cancel out the inverted colors, you notice no difference at all. "What it's like" for you to interact with the world and with other people does not change at all. For example, the yellow sky looks blue to you, and all the people around you describe yellow objects such as the sky as "blue." As far as the qualitative aspect of your mental life is concerned, nothing is any different from the way it would have been had you stayed home. Further, we may suppose that your brain is exactly the same in its physiological properties as it would have been had you stayed at home. (Of course, the statements in the science of color would have to be different on both planets. Pure light of 577 nm is described by us as 'yellow' and by them as 'blue'. So let us suppose that you and the twins in the examples to follow know nothing of the science of color, and hence these scientific differences make no difference to you.)[22]

There you are on Inverted Earth. The qualitative content of your experience of the (local) sky is just the same as the day before, when you looked at the sky at home. What about the intentional content of this experience? Here there may be some disagreement. The causal rooting of your color words is virtually entirely at home; your use of 'blue' is grounded in references to blue things and to the uses of 'blue' by other people to refer to blue things. For this reason, I would say that on your first day on Inverted Earth, your intentional contents remain the same as they were—that is, different from the natives. At first, when you look at the sky, thinking the thought that you would express as "It is as blue as ever," you are expressing the same thought that you would have been expressing yesterday at home, only today you are *wrong*. Also, your thought is not the same as the one a native of Inverted Earth would express with the same words. Nonetheless, according to me, after enough time has passed on Inverted Earth, your embedding in the physical and linguistic environment of Inverted Earth would dominate, and so your intentional contents would shift so as to be the same as those of the natives. Consider an analogy (supplied by Martin Davies): if you had a Margaret Thatcher recognitional capacity before your journey to Inverted Earth, and on arriving misidentify twin MT as MT, you are mistaken. But eventually your 'That's MT' judgments get to be about twin MT, and so become right having started out wrong. If you were kidnapped at age 15, by the time 50 years have passed, you use 'red' to mean green, just as the natives do. Once your intentional contents have inverted, so do your functional states. The state that is now *normally* caused by blue things is the same state that earlier was normally caused by yellow things. So once 50 years have passed, you and your earlier stage at home would exemplify what I want, namely a case of functional and intentional inversion together with the same qualitative contents—the converse of the inverted spectrum case. This is enough to refute the functionalist theory of qualitative content and at the same time to establish the intentional/qualitative distinction.

But what if the facts of human physiology get in the way of the case as I described it? My response is the same as the one mentioned earlier (based on Shoemaker's rebuttal of Harrison), namely that it is possible for there to be a race of people very much like us, with color vision, and color sensations, but whose physiology does not rule out the case described (or spectrum inversion). The functionalist can hardly be satisfied with the claim that our experiences are functional states but the other race's experiences are not.

The functionalist theory that I have in mind is a functional state identity theory, a theory that says that each and every mental state *is* some functional state. If mental state M = functional state F, then any instance of M must also be an instance of F. But in the Inverted Earth case just described, two instances of the same qualitative state—yours and Twin's—have different functional roles. And the qualitative state that you share with Twin cannot be identical to *both* your functional state and Twin's functional state, since that would be a case of $Q = F_1$, $Q = F_2$ and $\sim(F_1 = F_2)$, which contravenes transitivity of identity. There is still one loose end to the argument: the existence of one sort of functional description on which the two qualitatively identical states are functionally different does not rule out the possibility of another sort of functional description on which they are the same. I will return to this matter when I consider objections to the Inverted Earth argument later.

Note that this intrapersonal Inverted Earth case does not have the weakness that we saw in the intrapersonal inverted spectrum case. In the latter case, the subject's internal disturbance renders his first-person reports vulnerable to doubt. But you, the subject of the Inverted Earth case, have had no internal disturbance. Your move to Inverted Earth was accomplished without your noticing it—there was no period of confusion or adaptation. All the inversion went on outside your brain—in your inverting lenses, and in your physical and linguistic environment. The intrapersonal case has the considerable advantage of testimony for Inverted Earth as for the inverted spectrum case. But some readers may feel some doubt about the claim that after 50 years your intentional contents and language are the same as that of the Inverted Earth natives. For this rea-

son, it may be helpful to move briefly to the interpersonal Inverted Earth case. I will be talking in terms of the interpersonal case later, but I hope the reader will refer back from time to time to the first-person point of view that is better captured in the intrapersonal case.

Imagine a pair of genetically identical twins, one of whom is adopted on Inverted Earth after having had inverting lenses inserted into his eyes and body pigment changes, the other of whom grows up normally on Earth (without special lenses). To try to bring in the first-person point of view, let the home twin be you. When you two look at your respective skies, you both hear 'blue', and the same retinal stimulation occurs. We may suppose that you and Twin are in relevant respects neurologically the same. (We could even suppose that your brains are molecular duplicates.) But then you two are the same in the qualitative contents of your experiences; just as in the intrasubjective example, your qualitative contents were the same before and after your trip to Inverted Earth. For qualitative contents supervene on physical constitution, and your physical constitutions are relevantly the same.

Though you and Twin have the same qualitative contents at every moment, you are inverted functionally and with respect to intentional contents of experience. For in his intentional contents, Twin is the same as his friends on Inverted Earth. When Twin or any other resident of Inverted Earth thinks the thought that he would express as "The blue of the sky is very saturated," his thought is about *yellow*. Thus your intentional contents of experience are inverted with respect to Twin's. What about functional inversion?

One's mental representation of blue—one's concept of blue, in the psychologists' sense of the term 'concept'—plays a familiar role in being produced in a natural and immediate way by blue things, and in controlling one's behavior toward blue things. (Harman assumes that one's experience of blue *is* one's concept of blue; I am happy to go along; the issue is not relevant to the controversy discussed here.) I speak of the familiar role of one's concept of blue. Perhaps it would help here to think of you and Twin of both being engaged in a game. You are shown something of a certain color, and your task is to find something of the same color. I show you a ripe strawberry, and you look around, finding a matching English double-decker bus. Twin, in his corresponding situation, matches his green strawberries with a green bus.

There you and Twin are, looking at your respective skies, having experiences with just the same qualitative contents. At this very moment, you are in a state produced in a natural and immediate way by blue things, one that plays the aforementioned familiar functional role in controlling your responses to blue things. At the same time, Twin is in a state produced by yellow things, one that plays the same familiar functional role in controlling his responses to yellow things, so you are functionally inverted with respect to Twin. Think of the color-matching game. The qualitative state that functions so as to guide you in matching blue target with blue sample also functions so as to guide Twin in matching yellow target with yellow sample. Of course there is considerable functional similarity between you and Twin; indeed you are functionally exactly alike if we take the border between the inside and the outside so as to exclude the inverter, including your production of the same noise, "Blue again!," when you see the sky. Later I will take up the matter of whether this internal functional description can be used to avoid the criticism of functionalism that I am making.

Further, your perceptual state is about blue things whereas Twin's is about yellow things, so you are intentionally inverted. (The "inversion" has to do with the fact that yellow and blue are simply examples of complementary colors.)

Notice that the argument against functionalism depends on an intentional way of individuating responses. If you and Twin were brought together into my study and asked the color of a red thing, you and Twin would make different noises. You would say "red," Twin would say "green." But

Twin would *mean* red by "green," as would any member of the Inverted Earth Inverted English speech community. In this respect, the Inverted Earth case gets a bit less of a grip on the imagination than the inverted spectrum case, for which no such distinction between ways of individuating responses need be made. And it also points up the fact that the argument is more powerful as a refutation of intentionalism about qualia than of functionalism about qualia. (The issue will be discussed below of whether there is a functionalist theory of qualia that is left untouched by the argument.)

The upshot is that if you and Twin are looking at your respective skies, saying 'Still blue', you have experiences that have the same qualitative content, but inverted intentional content, and they are functionally inverted. Conclusion: the distinction between intentional and qualitative content is vindicated, and the functional and intentional theory of qualia is refuted.

The Inverted Earth argument just given can be attacked in a variety of ways. I will examine a few of them shortly, but first I want to make some comparisons with the more traditional inverted spectrum argument.

The Inverted Earth case is meant to exemplify qualitative identity plus functional and intentional inversion, whereas the inverted spectrum case is meant to exemplify the converse, qualitative inversion plus functional and intentional identity. As I mentioned earlier, the qualitative difference in the best version of the inverted spectrum case (the intrasubjective inversion) is meant to be established by the testimony of the inverted subject. As I also mentioned, the weakness of the case is that unusual things have happened inside this subject (the "adaptation" period), and so there is some doubt (taken more seriously by some philosophers than others) that the subject's words can simply be taken at face value. The contrast with the Inverted Earth case is strong. When you are kidnapped and wake up on Inverted Earth, there is no difference at all in what it is like for you. In this case unlike the intrasubjective inverted spectrum, there is no internal disturbance to throw doubt on the subject's testimony. (Of course, any subject may miss a series of small changes, but there is no reason to suspect these in the Inverted Earth case.) Further, in the intersubjective Inverted Earth case, we have supervenience on our side. Your brain is a molecular doppelganger of Twin's, and since intrinsic properties such as qualitative content are presumably supervenient on physical properties, we can conclude that you are qualitatively identical to Twin. Note that supervenience is asymmetrical with respect to sameness and difference. That is, the molecule-for-molecule identity of your brain with Twin's establishes that intrinsic properties like qualia are the same. But the physical difference between the brains of the inverted spectrum twins does not establish any qualitative difference between them, because the critic can always allege (as Harman does) that the physical difference is just a matter of alternative realizations of the same mental state.

The advantage of the Inverted Earth case is that there is no *internal* switch as in the inverted spectrum case. The switching goes on outside the brain. So far, the Inverted Earth argument is a better argument against functionalism than the inverted spectrum argument. But does it fare as well with respect to objections?

The first objection I want to consider is that Twin does not have the same intentional contents as his friends on Inverted Earth because when he looks at the sky he has a qualitatively different experience from the one his friends have (because he has inverting lenses and they don't). And his color judgments are answerable to the qualitative contents of his experiences. So when he says and his friends echo "The sky looks blue," what they say is true whereas what he says is false because the sky does not look yellow to *him*.[23]

The first thing to note about this objection is that it assumes an inverted spectrum; it claims that Twin's spectrum is inverted with respect to that of his friends, and it uses that claim to argue that Twin's intentional contents are not the same

as those of his friends. For this reason, no functionalist can accept this objection, least of all Harman. Harman insists (as I have) that the intentional content of the experience as of yellow consists in its natural and immediate production by yellow things, its role in manipulating yellow things, and the like. And since Twin is the same as his friends in this respect, Harman cannot suppose he differs from them in intentional content.

Further, those of us who accept the possibility of an inverted spectrum cannot accept the objection either, since it commits the fallacy of intentionalizing qualia. If inverted spectra are possible, then the natives of Inverted Earth may differ from one another in the qualitative content produced by the sky. No one of them can be singled out as the one whose qualitative content on looking at the sky is *really* that of *looking yellow*. Intentional content cannot be reduced to qualitative content.

Note that I have not used the possibility of an inverted spectrum to defend Inverted Earth. The objection assumes an inverted spectrum, and I simply pointed out the consequences of that assumption.

Now onto a more serious objection. I have said that you are qualitatively identical to but functionally inverted with respect to Twin. At the moment when each of you are looking at your respective skies, you are in a state produced by blue things that controls manipulation of blue things, whereas Twin is in a state produced by yellow things that controls manipulation of yellow things. (Recall the example of the color-matching game.) My reasoning involves thinking of inputs and outputs as involving objects in the world. But this is just one way of thinking of inputs and outputs according to one type of functional description. The existence of one functional description according to which your are an invert of Twin does not preclude other functional descriptions according to which you and Twin are functionally the same. If there are other functional descriptions according to which you and

Twin are functionally the same, how can I claim to have refuted functionalism?

Indeed, there are a variety of functional descriptions according to which you are functionally the same as Twin. For example, your brain is physically identical to Twin's, so any functional description that draws the line between the inside and the outside at the surface of the brain will be a functional description according to which you and Twin are functionally the same. For internal functional organization is just as supervenient on internal physical state as is qualitative state.

But brain-internal functional states cannot capture the intentional content of experience. For that content depends on the colors in the outside world. Here is a way of dramatizing the point. The inverting lenses (and the post-retinal inverter as well) invert the color solid 180 degrees.[24] But one can just as well imagine inverters that invert the color solid by smaller amounts, for example, 90 degrees. Imagine a series of clones of yours (and Twin's) whose lenses contain a series of different inverters. Imagine each of these clones confronted with a color patch so chosen as to produce exactly the same neural signal in each of the identical brains. If your brain is confronted with a red patch, another will be confronted with a yellow patch, another with a blue patch, and so forth. But you will all be having exactly the same qualitative content. If * is the neural signal that we are counting as input to your brain, * would be produced by red in your brain, by yellow in one of your clones, and by blue in another clone. So neither * nor any brain-internal functional state triggered by it can correspond to any single color in the world. The intentional content of your experience is *looking red*, whereas that of your clones are *looking yellow*, *looking blue*, and so forth.[25] Your intentional contents are all different, but since your brains are exactly the same (by hypothesis), and since internal functional organization is supervenient on the brain, *all* internal functional descriptions will be shared by all of you. So no purely brain-internal functional description can capture the intentional content of experience.[26]

What I have just argued is that no brain-internal functional state could be suitable for identification with an intentional content of experience. If intentional contents of experience are functional states, they are "long-arm" functional states that reach out into the world of things and their colors. But though Harman commits himself to recognizing *only* long-arm functional states, there is no good reason why the functionalist cannot recognize *both* these long-arm functional roles *and* short-arm functional roles that are purely internal. Why can't the functionalist identify intentional contents with long-arm functional states and qualitative content with short-arm functional states? The result would be a kind of "dualist" or "two-factor" version of functionalism.[27]

My response: perhaps such a two-factor theory is workable, but the burden of proof is on the functionalist to tell us what the short-arm functional states might be. Without some indication of what these functional states would be like we have no reason to believe in such a functional theory of qualia.[28] In terms of machine versions of functionalism, the responsibility of the functionalist is to find a characterization of qualia in terms of the "program" of the mind. Good luck to him![29]

I have conceded that *if* there is some functional characterization of qualia, that will sink the Inverted Earth Argument. But this concession does not yield any superiority of the inverted spectrum over Inverted Earth. For the same possibility would sink the inverted spectrum argument as well. The inverted spectrum twins are supposed to be qualitatively different but functionally identical. And that is supposed to show that qualitative states are not functional states. But if there is a functional theory of qualia, it will be one on which the inverted spectrum twins are functionally different after all.

Perhaps a physiological theory of qualia is possible. If there is a physiological theory of qualia, it can be functionalized.[30] Such a move is changing the subject in the context of the iverted spectrum argument, however. Functionalism in that context is linked to the computer model of the mind. The idea is rather as if two machines with different hardware might have different qualia despite computational identity: having the same computational structure and running all the same programs. Since the issue is whether qualia are computational states, you can't legitimately defend a computationalist theory by appealing to the hardware difference itself.

Let us now turn to what is the most plausible candidate for an alternative functional description designed to make you functionally identical to Twin, namely one that exploits the fact of the inverting lenses. Let's focus on the version in which the inverting lens is installed inside the lens of the eye. Then it may be objected that when you and Twin are looking at your respective skies, you have the *same* inputs. There is blue light in *both* of your eyes, despite the fact that Twin is looking at a yellow sky. So there is no functional inversion.

I've been using a functional description (as does Harman) in which the inputs relevant to experiences as of red are red objects in the world. The objection I am considering is that the boundary between the inside and the outside should be moved inward, and inputs should be thought of in terms of the color of the light hitting the retina, not in terms of colored objects. Here is a first approximation to my reply: you give me an independently motivated conception of the boundary between the inside and the outside of the system, and I will tailor an inverted earth example to suit. In this case the tailoring is done. You will recall that I mentioned an alternative to the inverting lenses, one that seems to me more physically plausible than the lenses, namely a neural inverter behind the retina. The retina reacts in a well-understood way to triples of light wavelengths, transforming them into impulses in the optic nerve. I don't know any reason why it shouldn't be in principle possible for a mini-

aturized silicon chip to register those impulses and substitute transformed impulses for them.

Sensation is generally the product of the action of the world on a transducer that registers some feature of the world and outputs some corresponding signal that conveys information to the brain. The visual apparatus registers light, the auditory apparatus sound, and so forth. The natural way of thinking of inputs and outputs is in terms of impingements on such transducers. With any real transducer, there is often indeterminacy as to exactly where transduction starts or finishes. The lens of the eye could be thought of as the visual transducer, or alternatively the visual transducer could be thought of as ending at the rods and cones or one of the other layers of the retina, or in the optic nerve, or in the lateral geniculate nucleus. I could locate my inverter at any of those places. However, I suppose it could be discovered that there is a "visual sensorium" in the brain with a sharp natural boundary such that any change within it changes qualia and any change outside it does not (except by affecting its inputs). In that case, the choice of the boundary of the sensorium as the border between inside and outside would require placement of the inverter in a place that would change qualia. My response to this possibility is to note as I did in the section on the fallacy of intentionalizing qualia that there could be a type of person otherwise very like us who has color vision and color sensations but no sharp sensorium boundary. Thus I can run my thought experiments on a sort of being (perhaps hypothetical, perhaps us) that has color experience but no sharply bounded sensorium.

Awareness of Intrinsic Properties

Thus far, I have been arguing against Harman's objections to the inverted spectrum, and giving my own argument in terms of Inverted Earth for accepting the qualitative/intentional distinction, and the falsity of a functionalist theory of qualia. But there is one consideration raised by Harman that I have not yet mentioned. He says that the qualitative/intentional distinction depends on the view that we are aware of intrinsic properties of our experience. This latter view is one that he spends more than half the paper arguing against. So in order fully to examine his objection to the inverted spetctrum hypothesis, we shall have to turn to his objection to the view that we are aware of intrinsic features of our experience.

Harman's primary argument is, as far as I can see, an appeal to—of all things—introspection. He says that the idea that we are aware of the "mental paint" is "counter to ordinary visual experience." Here is the main passage where the argument is given.

When Eloise sees a tree before her, the colors she experiences are all experienced as features of the tree and its surroundings. None of them are experienced as intrinsic features of her experience. Nor does she experience any features of anything as intrinsic features of her experience. And that is true of you too ... Look at a tree and try to turn your attention to intrinsic features of your visual experience. I predict you will find that the only features there to turn your attention to will be features of the presented tree ...

In my view, Harman's appeal to introspection here is an error in philosophical method. When I look at my blue wall, I *think* that in addition to being aware of the color I can also make myself aware of what it is like for me to be aware of the color. I'm sure others will disagree. The one thing we should all agree on is that this is no way to do philosophy. Our intuitions can tell us something about our concepts and our experiences so long as we use them rightly. One principle is: *Elicit simple intuitions about complex cases rather than complex intuitions about simple cases.* Looking at a blue wall is easy to do, but it is not easy (perhaps not possible) to answer on the basis of introspection alone the highly theoretical question of whether in so doing I am aware of intrinsic properties of my experience. The point of the complicated science fiction stories described above is to produce complex cases about which one can consult simple intuitions. Harman hopes to argue against the inverted spectrum by appealing to the introspective judgment that we are not aware of intrinsic features of our experience. I think he proceeds the wrong way around. If arguments such as the one I gave convince us that it is possible for qualitative content to remain the same while intentional content is inverted (or conversely), then that will settle the issue of whether we are aware of intrinsic features of our experience. Or at any rate, it will settle the matter that is really at stake: whether *there are* intrinsic mental features of our experience.

Finally, let me turn to Harman's critique of Jackson. Let us put the issue in terms of Jackson's Mary, the scientist who knows all the physical and functional facts about color perception that can be learned in a black-and-white environment. The issue Jackson poses is this: does Mary acquire new knowledge on seeing red? The qualia realist says she acquires genuine knowledge *that*, genuine new information, namely, knowledge that this is what it is like to see red. Lewis, Nemirow, Shoemaker, and other critics have said that what Mary acquires is something more like knowledge *how*: new skills, not new information. Harman's line is that Mary *does* genuinely acquire new information, genuine knowledge *that*— and here he appears (misleadingly) to accommodate the qualia realist intuition—but he goes on to say that functionalism is not refuted because Mary did not know all the functional facts before seeing red. Harman says that knowledge of all the functional facts requires possession of the full concept of red, and that is a matter of being in a certain functional state. More specifically, the full concept of red must be produced in a natural and immediate way by red things and must play a certain role in thought and action with respect to red things. While she is still locked in the black-and-white room, Mary has no state that is produced in a natural and immediate way by red things, and plays the appropriate role in thought and action. So Mary had no such functional state before seeing red; hence she did not know all the functional facts. When she sees a red thing for the first time she acquires the concept of red, and with it the functional facts that she lacked for lack of that concept. Further, she now can be said to know that blood is red, apples are red, and the like, whereas earlier she could mouth those words, but lacking the concept of red, she did not really possess the knowledge.

In sum: Jackson says that Mary knows all the functional facts before she sees anything red, yet she learns a new fact, so the functional facts do not include all the facts. Some of Jackson's critics deny that Mary learns a new fact. Harman, by contrast, allows that Mary learns new facts on seeing red, but he denies that Mary knew all the functional facts before she saw anything red. He says she acquires a new functional fact as well, in acquiring the concept of red itself.

If Harman is right about all this—and for the sake of argument, let's suppose that he is—he has provided no argument against qualia realism; rather, he has shown that the Jackson argument does not serve very well as a locus of controversy between the qualia realist and the qualia skeptic. The knowledge that Harman shows Mary lacks in the black-and-white room has little to do with the real issues about qualia. Until Mary sees green for the first time, she cannot have the full concept of green, and so she cannot have the knowledge that some olives are green. Indeed, she can't even have the false belief that all olives are green. This fact has little to do with the disagreement between the qualia skeptic and the qualia realist.

If one accepts Harman's claim that Mary can't have any beliefs about the colors of things until she leaves the black-and-white room, then the real issue between the qualia realist and the qualia skeptic about Mary is that the qualia realist says Mary acquires *two* types of knowledge *that* when she sees colors for the first time, whereas the qualia skeptic says she acquires only one. All can agree (assuming Harman is right about concepts) that she acquires knowledge involving *intentional* contents. For example, she acquires the concept of green and having already read the *Encyclopaedia Brittanica*, she acquires the knowledge that olives are green. However, the qualia realist says she acquires knowledge involving qualitative contents in addition to the intentional contents. This is the crux of the matter, and on this, Harman's reply to Jackson is silent.

Notes

1. The reply was delivered at the Chapel Hill Colloquium, October 17, 1987. A later version of this paper was delivered at the Universities of Oxford, Cambridge, and Edinburgh; at Birkbeck College and Kings College London; and at a meeting of the Anglo-French Philosophy Group. I am grateful for support to the American Council of Learned Societies and to the National Science Foundation (DIR88 12559). I am also grateful to Martin Davies and Christopher Peacocke for comments on an earlier version, and I am grateful for useful discussions on these matters with Davies and with Sam Guttenplan.

2. John Haugeland, "The Nature and Plausibility of Cognitivism," *The Behavioral and Brain Sciences* 1/215–226, 1978.

3. In "Functionalism and Qualia," *Philosophical Studies* 27/291–315, 1975 (reprinted in my *Readings in Philosophy of Psychology*, Vol 1, Harvard University Press, 1980). Sydney Shoemaker shows how functionalism can provide identity conditions for qualia even if it abandons an attempt to characterize particular qualiatative states. Shoemaker's technique does, however, assume that "absent" qualia are impossible, an assumption that I dispute.

4. For arguments against the possibility of such a zombie, see Shoemaker, op. cit.; see also Colin McGinnn, *The Subjective View*, Oxford University Press: Oxford, 1983; and John Searle, *What's Wrong with the Philosophy of Mind*, MIT Press: Cambridge, forthcoming. I reply to Shoemaker in "Are Absent Qualia Impossible?," *The Philosophical Review* 89/257–274, 1980. Shoemaker responds in "Absent Qualia are Impossible—a Reply to Block," *The Philosophical Review* 90, 4/581–599, 1981.

5. The intentional/qualitative terminology is from Shoemaker's, "The Inverted Spectrum," *The Journal of Philosophy* 74, 7, 1981, 357–81 and chapter 41, this book. This essay is reprinted with a new postscript to-

gether with other papers of Shoemaker's on the same topic (including "Functionalism and Qualia") in *Identity, Cause and Mind: Philosophical Essays*, Cambridge University Press: Cambridge, 1984. The representational/sensational terminology is from Christopher Peacocke, *Sense and Content*, Oxford University Press: Oxford, 1983, chapters 1 and 2. Peacocke uses 'what it is like' in a way that includes both representational and sensational content. Frank Jackson's distinction between comparative and phenomenal senses of 'looks' comes to much the same thing. See chapter 2 *of Perception*, Cambridge University Press: Cambridge, 1977.

6. Peacocke, op. cit., uses a number of intriguing examples to argue for the representational/sensational distinction without any commitment to an inverted spectrum. For example, he argues that in looking at a room through one eye, one has an experience with a representational content that is the same as that of the experience one gets on looking with two eyes (the same objects are represented to be the same distances away), but the sensational contents differ. If he is right, then there is a much greater distance between the representation/sensational distinction and the inverted spectrum than I suppose. I will sidestep the issue by individuating intentional contents *functionally*. So the monocular and binocular intentional contents will be different because they function differently. For example, since we are fully aware of the difference, and can make use of it in our verbal reports of our experiences, the binocular experience can produce different reports from those produced by the monocular experience. See Michael Tye's review of Peacocke's book in *Canadian Philosophical Reviews* V/173–175, 1985, for a discussion of another of Peacocke's examples from the same point of view.

7. One qualification: It is useful to have some terms to refer to that content of experience that is mental without being intentional. I have used 'what it is like' and 'qualitative content' in this way, and so I do not wish to regard these terms as referring to intentional contents.

8. The point I have been making does assume that it is often the case that objects have colors, for example, the book I am now looking at is blue. It does not assume that questions of what color something is always have a determinate answer, nor does it deny that what color an object is is relative to all sorts of things, for example, the position of the perceiver. An expanse of color in a comic strip may be orange from a distance yet also be red and

yellow from close up. If this is objectivism, I am happy to be an objectivist. See C. L. Hardin, *Color for Philosophers: Unweaving the Rainbow*, Indianapolis: Hackett Publishing Co, 1988, for a forceful argument against objectivism (and subjectivism).

9. Some qualia skeptics hold that there is no such thing as qualitative content whereas others believe that there is such a thing but that it is identical to intentional content. Dan Dennett seems to me to have vacillated on this issue. In "Quining Qualia," 1988 in A. Marcel and E. Bisiach, eds., *Consciousness in Contemporary Society*. Oxford: Oxford University Press, 1988 (chapter 40, this book). He takes a functionalist view of qualia, as he does in "Toward a Cognitive Theory of Consciousness," in *Brainstorms: Philosophical Essays on Mind and Psychology*, MIT Press: Cambridge, 1978, 149–173. But in other papers he has been more of an eliminativist about qualia. See especially "On the Absence of Phenomenology," in *Body, Mind and Method: Essays in Honor of Virgil Aldrich*, D. Gustafson and B. Tapscott, eds., D. Reidel: Dordrecht, 93–113, 1979; and "Why You Can't Make a Computer that Feels Pain," *Synthese* 38.3, 1978, reprinted in *Brainstorms*, 190–229. The answer to the title question (why you can't make a computer that feels pain) is that there isn't any such thing as pain.

10. This point is stimulated by Shoemaker's (op. cit.) argument against Harrison.

11. Note that I've said that the function of *an experience* is what gives it the intentional content of *looking red*; I did not say that anything at all (even something that isn't an experience) that has that function has that content. This issue—the issue of "absent qualia"—is not taken up in this chapter.

12. But it is not functionalist, for reasons mentioned earlier, about the meaning of 'what it is like' and 'qualitative content'. The view I'm defending of the semantics of color terms is similar to Paul Churchland's in *Scientific Realism and the Plasticity of Mind*, Cambridge: Cambridge University Press, 1979, chapter 2.

13. So long as the experience has *some* qualitative content or other—which it must have, being an experience. As I said in the last note, whether a non-experience could have the functional role of an experience is a matter I do not intend to discuss here.

14. W. Lycan, *Consciousness*, MIT Press: Cambridge, 1987 also puts the inverted spectrum hypothesis in this way.

15. "Conceptual Role Semantics," *The Notre Dame Journal of Formal Logic* 23, 2, 1982, p. 250. Lycan, op. cit., p. 60, says that proponents of the inverted spectrum hypothesis "simply . . . deny the truth of Functionalism . . . without argument."

16. See, for example, Sydney Shoemaker, "The Inverted Spectrum", op. cit., and William Lycan, "Inverted Spectrum", *Ratio* 15, 1973.

17. A perhaps more realistic possibility would be that of a miniature computer placed in a sinus cavity hooked into the optic nerve behind the retina that registers the output of the retina and changes the signals that represent red to signals that represent green, and so forth, feeding the transformed signals to the lateral geniculate nucleus. Many of the objections to the empirical possibility of an inverted spectrum by Harrison and Hardin are also objections to the possibility of a color inverter. See Bernard Harrison, *Form and Content*, Oxford University Press: Oxford, and C. L. Hardin, op. cit. See also Shoemaker's comment on Harrison in the paper referred to earlier (p. 336 of *Identity, Cause and Mind*). Harrison and Hardin both argue in different ways that the color solid has asymmetries that prevent indetectable color inversion. As will become clear later, the main claim of this paper is one that would not be damaged if they are right, for I am claiming only that the "Inverted Earth" argument to be presented is a better argument against functionalism than the inverted spectrum argument. (Further, both arguments can avoid inverting spectacles.) However, I cannot resist mentioning that neither Harrison's nor Hardin's objections work. Hardin points out the main problems with Harrison. For example, Harrison argues that there may be more shades between some unique (primary) colors than others, rendering an inversion detectable. Hardin points out that the number of shades seen between any two colors is a highly variable matter among people with perfectly normal color vision. Hardin's own objection is that some colors (red and yellow) are warm whereas others (blue and green) are cool. But he gives no argument against the possibility of warm/cool inversion. That is, he gives no argument against the possibility that things we agree have a warm color produce the same qualitative character in you that things we agree have a cool color produce in me.

Hardin also argues that if the color-inverted person sees blood as green plus cool, epiphenomenalism would have to be true, whereas supposing he sees blood as green plus warm verges on incoherence. These claims—

at least the first—draw their plausibility from the fallacy of intentionalizing qualia. The reason that the possibility of seeing blood as green plus cool is supposed to involve epiphenomenalism is that it is supposed that seeing blood as cool-colored would lead to saying and acting as if it were cool-colored, which is incompatible with the functional (and therefore behavioral) identity presupposed in the inverted spectrum hypothesis. But this claim depends on thinking of the inverted spectrum as intentional inversion. Suppose that the qualitative property that leads you to say something is red and leads me to say something is green is Q_a, whereas Q_b has the opposite effect. And suppose that the qualitative property that leads you to say something is warm-colored and leads me to say something is cool-colored is Q_x, whereas Q_y has the opposite effect. There is no threat of epiphenomenalism in my experiencing red things via the qualitative content $Q_b + Q_y$. The appearance of an epiphenomenalism problem comes only from the fallacy of intentionalizing qualia via thinking of $Q_b + Q_y$ as having an intentional content involving coolness.

18. I said that when we put on the inverting lenses, grass looks red, so am I not committed to the claim that for the inverted twin as well grass looks red? No. Grass looks to the *temporary* wearer of the lenses the way red things normally look. But the inverted twin is not a temporary wearer: grass looks to him the way green things normally look.

19. This stage is broken into parts in a way that adds to its power to convince in Shoemaker, op. cit.

20. See Dennett's "Quining Qualia," op. cit., and Rey's *Mind Without Consciousness: A Discrepancy Between Explanatory and Moral Psychology*, forthcoming from MIT Press.

21. "Conceptual Role Semantics," op. cit., p. 251. I have an earlier but clumsier example to the same effect, in "Troubles with Functionalism," pp. 302–303 (fn. 21), in my *Readings in Philosophy of Psychology*, Vol 1, Harvard University Press: Cambridge, 1980. See also Ron McClamrock's use of Harman's example for a different purpose in his 1984 Ph.D. thesis, MIT.

22. In my clumsier example (mentioned in the last footnote) I had the inverting lenses and the switched color words, but instead of the yellow sky and the like on Inverted Earth, I had my events take place in a remote Arctic village where (I supposed) the people had no standing beliefs about the colors of things.

23. This objection is suggested by the McGinn-Peacocke view mentioned earlier according to which the intentional content ('representational content' in Peacocke's terminology) of an experience as of red is defined in terms of its qualitative content (sensational content).

24. I am thinking of an inversion of the constant brightness hue-saturation wheel.

25. Since your qualitative contents are the same but your intentional contents are all different, *looking red* is not a qualitative content. Thus we see that the Inverted Earth case can be used to unmask the fallacy of intentionalizing qualia, just as the inverted spectrum case can.

26. What makes the difference between the intentional content of the experience of *looking red* and *looking blue* is the connection between these experiences and the colored objects in the world. Therefore any conception of content that leaves out the connection between experience and the world will have no way of distinguishing between these different intentional contents. "Narrow content," the aspect of content that is "inside the head" is just such a conception of content, and so it is not hard to see that the "narrow content" of *looking red* and *looking green* must be the same. In my "Functional Role and Truth Conditions," *Proceedings of the Aristotelian Society*: Supplementary Volume LXI/157–181 I argue that a theory that uses Harman's "long-arm" functional roles (the ones that I have adopted here) is equivalent to a "two-factor" theory utilizing "short-arm" functional roles plus a referential component.

27. See the paper referred to in the last note for a discussion of such a two-factor theory in the context of propositional attitudes.

28. I also think an "absent qualia" argument would doom any such proposal; but I cannot go into that here.

29. I take the view that thought is functional, but that the best bet for a theory of qualia lies in neurophysiology. See my "Troubles with Functionalism," op. cit.

30. As advocated by Lycan, op. cit., 1987. I described this idea as "physiofunctionalism" in my "Troubles with Functionalism," op. cit.

44 Curse of the Qualia

Stephen L. White

1 Introduction

The functionalist project of characterizing mental states in terms of their causal and relational properties has seemed to many a promising alternative to such competing theories of mind as dualism, physicalism and behaviorism. Though functionalism continues to attract a significant following, resistance to this approach, at least where qualitative states such as pain are concerned, almost completely overshadows the original theory. In spite of the plausibility of characterizing beliefs and desires in terms of their causal roles in mediating between perceptual input and behavioral output, states such as pain seem to demand an analysis which accounts for the *feelings* involved in experiencing them. Such feelings, however, appear to be left untouched by any conceivable form of functional analysis.

A recent alternative to functionalism, which is rapidly becoming (if only by default) the accepted view of qualitative states, involves a compromise between functionalist and physicalist intuitions. On this view, which I shall call *physicalist-functionalism*, even those aspects of a subject's physiological makeup which can be varied without varying any functional properties would be relevant to the exact nature of the subject's qualitative states. Versions of this view have recently been defended by Sydney Shoemaker and Ned Block.[1] The list of its proponents, however, is far longer, including the majority of those whose work in the philosophy of mind touches on questions of qualia.[2]

I shall argue that the reaction against functionalism and the attempt to compromise between functionalism and physicalism are mistaken. I shall claim, in fact, that physicalist-functionalism is untenable in any form. Given the alternatives available, this amounts to a defense of functionalism in its orthodox form. I shall begin by sketching the conceptions of qualia which underlie orthodox functionalism, Shoemaker's version of physicalist-functionalism, Block's alternative version of the theory and a view I shall call *transcendentalism*. This list does not exhaust the logically possible alternatives to functionalism, which include behaviorism and eliminativism among others. But since this chapter concerns the challenge that physicalist-functionalism poses to functionalism regarding *qualia*, the list exhausts the relevant alternatives. Those who are unsympathetic to the functionalist attempt to deal with qualia are unlikely to be more impressed with the behaviorist or eliminativist options.

Orthodox Functionalism (Harman)

In its most general form, orthodox functionalism is the theory that a subject's psychological states can be explained solely in terms of their causal and dispositional relations to the subject's perceptual inputs, behavioral outputs and other internal states.[3] Any causal system whose input states, output states and internal states bear the right relation to one another has the psychological states in question, regardless of whether its physical makeup consists in neural networks, computer chips or beer cans and bits of string.

Construed as an account of propositional attitudes, this theory has a genuine intuitive appeal. It is not implausible to suppose that the essence of belief lies in its evolutionary role in mediating between our stimulus inputs and behavioral outputs in such a way as to permit flexible responses to new environmental conditions. For the orthodox functionalist, this theory applies equally well to qualitative states. Pain, for example, plays its evolutionary role in shifting our desires away from our current projects when these projects lead to bodily damage. According to orthodox functionalism, the essential property of pain, like the essential property of belief, is its causal role fixed by evolution. Pain can be functionally defined in terms of its typical causes—bodily damage; and its typical effects—behavioral changes brought about by an intense desire to change one's current state and a belief that one can do so by changing one's behavior.[4] This is not to say that for the orthodox functionalist pain need not be painful. What it *is* for something to hurt, on this view, is for it to cause a state with the functional properties of pain, particularly the overriding desire that that state cease.

Physicalist-Functionalism$_1$ (Block)

This theory, which may be viewed as a compromise between functionalism and physicalism, stems from the same conception of belief and desire as orthodox functionalism, but a different conception of qualitative states. For the physicalist-functionalist$_1$, the dispositional tendency of an internal state to shift our immediate desires away from our current projects toward behavior which would prevent further bodily damage is insufficient to ensure that it feels like pain. Indeed, for the physicalist-functionalist$_1$, such a dispositional property is insufficient to ensure that the state is associated with any feeling at all. According to this theory, the orthodox functionalist has no way of ruling out the possibility that some internal state might play the evolutionary role of pain without its feeling like *anything*, much less like pain, to be in that state. And while a physicalist-functionalist$_1$ might allow the possibility that pain in another subject could involve a different feeling from the one it has for us, such theorists find the possibility that pain could be unaccompanied by any feeling whatsoever an unacceptable consequence of orthodox functionalism. Thus according to physicalist-functionalism$_1$, functional states underdetermine qualitative states, and only further specification of the physical details of the way in which the functional states are realized would determine which, if any, qualitative states the subject occupies. Being a condition of neurons, as opposed to being a con-

dition of silicon chips, is, on this theory, very possibly part of the essence of pain.

Physicalist-Functionalism$_2$ (Shoemaker)

If physicalist-functionalist$_1$ is a compromise between functionalism and physicalism, physicalist-functionalism$_2$ is a compromise between functionalism and physicalist-functionalism$_1$. Although this view of Shoemaker's grows out of the same dissatisfaction over the orthodox functionalist treatment of qualia as does physicalist-functionalism$_1$, it is also motivated by an objection to physicalist-functionalism$_1$ and an alternative conception of what is essential to qualitative states. The objection is that for the physicalist-functionalist$_1$, a functional duplicate of a normal human subject might lack the qualitative experience of pain for purely physiological reasons. Such a subject, however, would mistakenly believe that he or she experienced all of the usual pain sensations. If this were genuinely possible, then the question would arise how we, in our own cases, could rule out the possibility that we lacked pain experience. But, at least in our own cases, Shoemaker claims, skepticism about qualia seems absurd. That it entails this form of skepticism points up, for Shoemaker, the inadequacy of physicalist-functionalism$_1$.

On the positive side, Shoemaker's view is that while part of the essence of pain is that there is *something* it feels like to experience it, it is not essential that this should be exactly what it feels like when *we* experience it. On Shoemaker's account, we can give a functionalist characterization of what it is like to have states with qualitative content, though not of what it is like to have states with any *particular* qualitative content. Since having states with some qualitative content or other is sufficient for mentality, functionalism as a theory of mind is vindicated, and skepticism about the existence of our own qualitative states is forestalled. Physicalist-functionalism$_2$ represents the hope that we can compromise with physicalism over the *particular* qualitative content of qualitative states but that we can save sentience for functionalism.

Transcendentalism (Nagel)

For transcendental theories of mind, as for orthodox functionalism,[5] it is essential to being in pain that it *feel* like pain. But for the transcendentalist, this feeling is not captured by either functional or physical conditions. That one is in pain is a first person fact, irreducible to any third person facts, whether these include the details of one's neurophysiology or not. For the transcendentalist, mention of the subject's physical states brings us no closer to what the subject feels than does mention of the subject's functional states. On this score even Cartesian dualism is no improvement. Mental substance is simply one more entity bound up in the causal nexus of objective, third person relations. If facts about physical substance tell us nothing about what pain feels like, neither do facts about mental substance. As Nagel puts the point,

> [t]he question of how one can include in the objective world a mental substance having subjective properties is as acute as the question how a physical substance can have subjective properties.[6]

Contrary to Descartes's assumption, facts about the mind are not determined by objective facts of any kind whatsoever. Transcendental theories include transcendental dualism, transcendental idealism, and any of the transcendental pluralisms that might, in principle, be formulated.

Regardless of the form it takes, any version of physicalist-functionalism is committed to at least one of the following two theses:

(1) Absent qualia are possible; that is, there could be a subject who was functionally equivalent to a normal subject and who lacked qualitative states.

(2) Qualia differences are possible; that is, there could be a subject who was functionally equivalent to a normal subject and whose mental states differed in qualitative character from those of the normal subject.

Block's physicalist-functionalism$_1$ entails both (1) and (2), as does transcendentalism. The transcendentalist, in fact, holds the even stronger thesis that two subjects who are alike in respect to all objective, third person facts may nonetheless differ in the presence or character of their qualitative experiences. Shoemaker is committed to the truth of (2), while the orthodox functionalist is committed to the falsity of both.

Shoemaker's claim that absent qualia are impossible might seem to commit him to the negation of (1) as well as the truth of (2), but this is not the case. Shoemaker's claim—the only claim for which he argues—is couched in terms of a different concept of absent qualia, and it is significantly weaker than the negation of the claim made by thesis (1). Shoemaker's claim is that no subject who is functionally equivalent to a normal subject *and whose nonqualitative states are all genuine* could lack qualitative states. And this weaker claim is obviously compatible with the truth of thesis (1). Thesis (1) would be true if there could be a subject who was a functional duplicate of a normal subject and who had no mental states whatsoever—nonqualitative or qualitative. Such a case would be compatible with Shoemaker's claim because the subject would lack genuine nonqualitative states. Hence if Shoemaker wanted to defend the negation of thesis (1) as well as his weaker claim, he would have to argue for the impossibility of such a case, and he provides no such argument.

In section 2 I shall show that in spite of the weakness of the claim Shoemaker actually defends, his arguments for the claim raise serious difficulties. Shoemaker's definition of "absent qualia" requires that an absent qualia subject have genuine nonqualitative states. However, Shoemaker's understanding of the notion of a genuine nonqualitative state rules out by fiat the most plausible case for the physicalist-functionalist$_1$'s thesis that absent qualia are possible. Shoemaker's definition, in other words, eliminates a case which the physicalist-functionalist$_1$ would rightly regard as a case of an absent qualia subject not because the case has been shown to be incoherent, but because it fails to meet Shoemaker's restrictive definition of "absent qualia." Furthermore, the restrictive definition is not justified by Shoemaker's claim for the scope of his undertaking; nor does the definition find any independent support in Shoemaker's arguments against absent qualia.

My own arguments against absent qualia in sections 3 and 4, which are also general arguments against physicalist-functionalism, share some of the same intuitive motivation as Shoemaker's argument.[7] Shoemaker's argument against absent qualia (in his sense) appears to be motivated, at least in part, by the intuition that physical facts per se are irrelevant to the question of a subject's mental experiences. Shoemaker says, for example, that

if we are given that a man's state is functionally identical with a state that in us is pain, it is hard to see how a neurophysiological difference between him and us could be any evidence at all that his states lack qualitative character. (Shoemaker 1975, p. 296)

This intuition that mental differences could not consist in neurophysiological differences alone is one that I share with Shoemaker. The basic idea is that unless there is some non–a posteriori connection between the neurophysiological difference and the alleged mental difference, we have no explanation of the relevance to the mental of the difference in neurophysiology. Even if we discovered that every subject to whom we were tempted to ascribe pain had the same neurophysiological makeup, the possibility of there being a subject who satisfied every other condition for pain ascription except the possession of the neurophysiology in question would make the empirical correlation irrelevant. If there is no connection between the neurophysiological facts and the grounds for the ascription of pain which is *prior* to the empirical correlation, the correlation itself could have no relevance to the question of whether the neurophysiological deviant felt pain.

As a result of my agreement with Shoemaker over this intuition, my arguments in sections 3

and 4 will overlap with his in their intuitive motivation as well as in the consequence that absent qualia (in Shoemaker's sense) are impossible. I argue in section 3 that physicalist-functionalists inherit the problem of property dualism that originally plagued central state materialists and helped to motivate orthodox functionalism. It was the claim of central state materialism that particular mental events such as one's pain at t would turn out to be identical with particular physical events such as one's brain state X at t. This identity, it was held, would be an empirical discovery and, hence, known a posteriori. The following principle suggested that there had to be two modes of presentation of any such mental event, one of which was a mental property or feature: if two expressions refer to the same object, and this fact cannot be established a priori, then the modes of presentation in virtue of which they pick out their common referent must be distinct. And this suggested that central state materialism would be committed to the existence of irreducible mental properties or features. The solution that emerged consisted in the claim that mental terms *were* coreferential a priori with their translations in a topic neutral vocabulary—expressions which were neither mentalistic nor physicalistic. Thus it was claimed that central state materialism was committed only to the existence of physical and topic neutral properties. Since functional definitions are instances of topic neutral translation, orthodox functionalism allows essentially the same response. The insistence of the physicalist-functionalist that no topic neutral expression is coreferential a priori with a mentalistic term for a qualitative mental state, however, leaves the problem of property dualism with no plausible solution.

In section 4 I argue that physicalist-functionalism precludes our making a principled distinction between those physiological differences between subjects which provide grounds for ascribing differences in their qualitative experiences and those which do not. The reason is that there is no evidence for a difference in the qualitative experiences of functionally equivalent subjects which is *independent* of their physiological differences. This contradicts Shoemaker's claim that intra-subjective qualia inversions provide evidence which allows us to correlate qualitative with neurophysiological changes. I argue, however, that if we keep a subject's functional states constant, no change in the neurophysiology, however drastic, will produce evidence of an intrasubjective inversion.

The thought that physicalist-functionalism justifies intuitions that functionalism could not accommodate helps to explain its popularity, but it represents a confusion between physicalist-functionalism and transcendentalism. It is transcendentalism, not physicalist-functionalism, that can accommodate more radical pretheoretical intuitions than orthodox functionalism. To the extent that physicalist-functionalism makes room for qualia differences functionalism does not, it severs the link between physical facts and the qualia distinctions they are supposed to explain. In so doing, it makes every physical fact equally relevant to the facts of qualitative experience. Nonetheless, the picture of qualitative character offered by the physicalist-functionalist has an appeal which is likely to survive any single argument. Shoemaker's version in particular represents the most detailed and sophisticated treatment available of the constellation of problems surrounding qualitative states. Only by investigating the source of the picture's appeal, as well as the picture's consequences and alternatives, are we likely to have any hope of dispelling it.

2 The Absent Qualia Arguments

Shoemaker's longest and most explicit argument for the thesis that absent qualia are impossible is based on the premise that if absent qualia were possible, qualia would be unknowable (Shoemaker 1981, pp. 587–596). As Shoemaker himself points out, however, there is a serious objection to this argument (Shoemaker 1981, p. 596, fn. 20).

One might hold the view, defended by Goldman[8] among others, that if one's belief in a proposition is acquired in virtue of a reliable mechanism, then the merely logical possibility of its falsehood does not rule out our knowing the proposition to be true. On this view, the logical possibility of absent qualia would be compatible with one's knowing one experienced genuine qualitative states. Since for Shoemaker it was the absurdity of skepticism about the existence of one's own qualitative states that made the possibility of absent qualia seem unacceptable, Goldman's epistemological position appears to undermine Shoemaker's argument.

Because of this objection, Shoemaker relies on a pair of alternative arguments against the possibility of absent qualia, and it is these arguments which I shall discuss. Before presenting the arguments, however, it will be necessary to set out Shoemaker's definitions of "functional definability" and "absent qualia."

A mental state is *functionally definable in the strong sense* if and only if it is definable in terms of its causal relations to inputs, outputs and other mental states, all of which must themselves be functionally definable. (Shoemaker 1981, p. 583)

A mental state is *functionally definable in the weak sense* if and only if it is definable in terms of its causal relations to inputs, outputs and nonqualitative mental states, where it is not required that these nonqualitative mental states must themselves be functionally definable. (Shoemaker 1981, p. 584, fn. 8)[9]

Among qualitative mental states Shoemaker means to include, besides qualitative states proper such as pain, qualitative beliefs to the effect that one is in a state with a *particular* qualitative character, such as the feeling of one's headache on a particular occasion (Shoemaker 1975, p. 309).

In terms of these two senses of functional definability we have two corresponding senses of "absent qualia."

Absent Qualia Thesis One (AQT-1) holds that qualitative states are not functionally definable even in the weak sense. (Shoemaker 1981, p. 584, fn. 8)

Absent Qualia Thesis Two (AQT-2) holds that qualitative states are not functionally definable in the strong sense. (Shoemaker 1981, p. 585)

The thesis to which Shoemake's actual arguments commit him is not the negation of AQT-2, which would commit him to the negation of thesis (1) of section 1, but the negation of AQT-1 (Shoemaker 1981, p. 587).[10] Shoemaker, then, is committed to the thesis that qualitative states are definable in terms of their causal relations to inputs, outputs and nonqualitative mental states which need not themselves be functionally definable.[11] Let us call, as Shoemaker does, a mental state which satisfies the best functional definition for states of type M, but is not in fact a genuine (token of) M an *ersatz* M (e.g., an "ersatz pain").[12] Suppose that Shoemaker is wrong, that AQT-1 is *true*, and that qualitative states are *not* functionally definable even by reference to nonqualitative mental states which are not themselves functionally definable. Then there is a possible creature, all of whose nonqualitative mental states are genuine and whose qualitative mental states are ersatz. Call such a creature an *imitation man*.[13] Shoemaker's claim is that such an imitation man is impossible (Shoemaker 1981, p. 584). Table 44.1 should make the relations between these theses clear. Logically equivalent propositions are grouped together under bold-faced headings, each of which names the thesis of which the members of the group are alternative formulations.

There is one ambiguity in these definitions which has yet to be clarified. To say that a nonqualitative state which is functionally equivalent to one of our mental states is genuine could mean either of two things. Suppose the state which it is claimed is genuine is functionally equivalent to our belief that water is wet. The claim that it is genuine might mean that it is a genuine *belief*, or it might mean that it is a genuine *belief that water is wet*. The difference lies in the fact that on the causal theory of reference, the content of a belief that water is wet is determined in part by environmental circumstances which are independent of the subject's functional makeup. Among those

subjects who share our functional states, only those who have beliefs caused in the right way by *water* have the belief that water is wet. Consider a possible subject who is functionally equivalent to a normal human subject and who has a belief that would be expressed by saying, "Water is wet." If that belief was not caused by water, but by a substance like water in all respects except its microstructure, the subject would not have a genuine belief that *water* is wet.[14] Hence on the second, stronger interpretation of "genuine nonqualitative state" such a subject's nonqualitative states would not all be genuine. Shoemaker has made it clear that it is this second interpretation he has in mind.[15]

Finally, let us define *the parochial theory of the meaning of mental terms* as the theory according to which mental terms have their references fixed, à la Kripke, to what are in fact (although the users of the terms need not know this) certain physiological states. These states are the physical realizations *in us* of the best functional definitions of the mental states (Shoemaker 1981, p. 592). If an absent qualia subject (in Shoemaker's sense) were possible, it would be a subject who was functionally equivalent to us and who shared our nonqualitative states, but who lacked our qualitative states. Since the only objective difference between such a subject and us would lie in the realization of the functional states, consider a case in which the members of some group of creatures (say Martians) are functionally equivalent to us but differ radically in their neurophysiology. Given the definition of the parochial theory, there are three possible ways in which the Martians' pains and pain beliefs might be related to ours.

Case 1

Assume the parochial theory is true. Our term "pain" refers to any mental state whose neurophysiological realization belongs to the same natural kind as the state which realizes *in us* the best functional definition of "pain." Since the Martians have a neurophysiology which differs radically from ours, our term "pain" cannot refer

Table 44.1

STRONG ABSENT QUALIA THESIS	WEAK DEFINABILITY THESIS
(= The negation of the Weak Definability Thesis)	(Shoemaker's Claim)
Possibility of an Imitation Man:	Impossibility of an Imitation Man:
There could be a subject who was functionally equivalent to a normal subject and whose nonqualitative states were all genuine, *but who lacked qualitative states.*	*No subject who was functionally equivalent to a normal subject* and whose nonqualitative states were all genuine *could lack qualitative states.*
$\updownarrow$	$\updownarrow$
AQT-1:	~AQT-1:
Qualitative states are not *definable in terms of their causal relations to inputs, outputs and nonqualitative mental states, where it is not required that these non-qualitative mental states must themselves be functionally definable.*	*Qualitative states are definable in terms of their causal relations to inputs, outputs and nonqualitative mental states, where it is not required that these nonqualitative mental states must themselves be functionally definable.*
$\downarrow$	$\uparrow$
WEAK ABSENT QUALIA THESIS	STRONG DEFINABILITY THESIS
(Block's claim)	(= The negation of the Weak Absent Qualia Thesis)
Thesis (1):	Negation of Thesis (1):
There could be a subject who was functionally equivalent to a normal subject and who lacked qualitative states.	*No subject who was functionally equivalent to a normal subject could lack qualitative states.*
$\updownarrow$	$\updownarrow$
AQT-2:	~AQT-2:
Qualitative states are not definable in terms of their causal relations to inputs, outputs and other mental states, all of which must themselves be functionally definable.	*Qualitative states are definable in terms of their causal relations to inputs, outputs and other mental states, all of which must themselves be functionally definable.*

to the physiological states which realize *in them* the best functional definition of "pain." Since, however, the Martians are functionally equivalent to us, their term "pain" bears the same causal relation to their physical states that our term bears to ours. Hence, since our term refers to our neurophysiological realization of the best functional definition of "pain," their term refers to theirs. Thus the Martian term "pain" does not refer to pain, the Martians' pain beliefs are nongenuine and the Martians, since their non-qualitative states are not all genuine, are not ex-amples of imitation men.

Suppose the parochial theory is false. Then there are two possibilities as to how our term "pain" refers. It might refer to anything which *feels like* what we have when we are in pain, or it might refer to anything which is functionally equivalent to the state we are in when we are in pain.

Case 2a

Assume that "pain" refers to any state that *feels like* the state we are in when we are in pain. In contrast to case (1), whether the Martians experience pain in this case is not an immediate con-sequence of the definition of "pain" alone. It is not *stipulated in advance* that any subject whose functional counterparts of our mental states are realized by states of a different physical natural kind lacks genuine pain. For the physicalist-functionalist$_1$ who does not hold the parochial theory, the usual assumption is that *as a matter of fact* such subjects do lack genuine pain and, in-deed, may lack states with any qualitative char-acter whatsoever. This assumption, if it is true, will be true in virtue of a connection between the physical realization of those states and the way those states feel which is *preconventional*. The nature of this connection for the physicalist-func-tionalist$_1$ who is not a parochial theorist is, admittedly, unclear, and I shall go on to examine this problem in the context of my own arguments against physicalist-functionalism$_1$. Nevertheless, the difference between case (1) and case (2a) is genuine. A convention of the kind postulated by the parochial theory would be justified for one who rejected that theory (if it were justified at all) by the following claim: all and only those subjects whose functional counterparts of pain are realized in states of the same physical natural kind as ours actually feel pain. Unless one accepts the parochial theory, it is this claim that would justify the convention and not the convention the claim.

For the same reasons as those cited in case (1), the Martians' term "pain" will refer to their own states and to any states which feel like theirs—which, by hypothesis, ours do not. Hence, in this case too, our term "pain" and theirs have different meanings, and the Martians lack genuine pain beliefs. Thus, again, they are not examples of imitation men.

Case 2b

Assume that our term "pain" refers to any state which is functionally equivalent to pain. In this case the Martian pains will be genuine, their pain beliefs will be genuine, and again they will not qualify as imitation men.

These three cases should make at least one difficulty with Shoemaker's position apparent. The fact that none of the possible cases provides a case of an imitation man, and hence that an imitation man is impossible (and thus that absent qualia in Shoemaker's sense are impossible), is a direct consequence of his definitions alone, given his construal of "genuine nonqualitative state." Shoemaker does have, it is true, an argument (which is independent of the immediate consequences of his definitions) that the possibility described in case (1) is not a real case of absent qualia. Shoemaker claims that if the parochial theory were true, the question of whether a creature in a state functionally equivalent to pain had genuine or ersatz pain would be irrelevant to the question of whether there was anything it felt like

to occupy that state. In case (2a), however, Shoemaker has ruled out by fiat a possibility against which he has no independent argument.

Although Shoemaker might want to object to the distinction between case (1) and case (2a), this is not an objection open to him; it is not open to Shoemaker, that is, to claim that case (2a) should be counted as a case in which the parochial theory is true. Such a claim would undermine Shoemaker's argument against the relevance of the parochial theory. Case (2a) is obviously one in which the question of whether the Martians have real or ersatz pain is *identical* to the question of what it feels like to be a Martian in a state functionally equivalent to pain. Hence if case (2a) is an instance of the parochial theory, then the parochial theory does not *always* render the question of whether Martians have genuine pains philosophically uninteresting.

Shoemaker does attempt to justify ruling out cases in which a creature's *non*qualitative (as well as qualitative) states are ersatz as cases of absent qualia (as he does in his definition of AQT-1), but the justification fails to apply to case (2a). Shoemaker claims that since he is concerned only with the objections to functionalism specifically concerning qualia, cases in which a subject's *non*qualitative states are ersatz can be legitimately ignored (Shoemaker 1981, p. 586). This claim does not take account of the distinction made above between states which are not genuine pain beliefs because they are not genuine beliefs and those which are not genuine pain beliefs because they are not about pain. If we take a state functionally equivalent to one of our pain beliefs (a "pain" belief for short), then if functionalism is inadequate as a theory of belief, such a state may not even be a belief at all. If functionalism *is* an adequate theory of belief, however, such a state may still fail to be a belief about pain because the subject never experiences pain. Given Shoemaker's concern with qualia, the possibility of states of the first sort is one which he is justified in ignoring. There is nothing about the possibility of states of the second sort, however, which would undermine functionalism as a theory of *belief*. The "pain" beliefs in question *would have been* genuine pain beliefs had the subject had genuine pains. Because these nongenuine pain beliefs cast no doubt on functionalism as a theory of *belief*,[16] Shoemaker is not entitled to disregard the cases in which they occur. Since (2a) is such a case and since it is the central case for the physicalist-functionalist$_1$, Shoemaker needs an independent argument against such a possibility, or his claim that absent qualia are impossible will not have the philosophical significance he intended.

I should make it clear at this stage that I am not defending the possibility or the ultimate coherence of case (2a). In sections 3 and 4, I shall argue that such a case does *not* represent a genuine possibility. My objection is to Shoemaker's excluding the case by fiat without challenging its intelligibility or coherence. Shoemaker, however, does not seem to regard his conclusion that absent qualia are impossible as a direct consequence of his definition of "absent qualia," because he provides a number of arguments in support of the thesis. Therefore, in the remainder of this section, I shall review these arguments and show that they fail to provide the independent argument against (2a) that Shoemaker needs.

In addition to the arguments against absent qualia which stem directly from Shoemaker's statement of AQT-1 and the definitions which support it, I can find two distinct arguments of Shoemaker's for the thesis that absent qualia are impossible. The simplest of these I shall call the *Symmetry Argument*. Shoemaker argues that in virtue of the symmetry between the case of the Martians and our own case, anything that we could say to support our claim to experience qualitative states will have a counterpart in something the Martians could say to bolster their own claim to qualitative experience. Though the Martians lack our neurophysiological makeup, we in turn lack theirs. The relation between the Martians and us seems to be perfectly symmetrical, whereas the relation postulated by the friends of absent qualia is asymmetrical—the

Martians lack something significant that we possess, while we suffer no comparable lack in relation to them.

This argument, though it has an intuitive appeal, does not establish the desired conclusion. It is open to the physicalist-functionalist$_1$ to reply that the asymmetry lies precisely in the facts of the subjects' physical realizations. The normal subject has a neurophysiology in virtue of which he or she has qualitative experience; the absent qualia subject does not. Such an asymmetry may well exist in the absence of any corresponding asymmetry in what can be *said* by a sincere and rational subject.[17]

Compare this with the case of the brain in the vat. The difference between a normal subject and the brain in the vat consists in a physical fact that has no bearing on what a rational and sincere subject could *say* in support of a claim to knowledge of external objects. The fact that either sort of abnormal subject—the absent qualia subject or the brain in the vat—could say anything a normal subject could by way of justifying his or her belief in qualitative experiences or external objects is less significant than it might appear. It does not necessarily follow that the abnormal subject would have the same justification for saying those things the normal subject would. Nor does it follow that the abnormal subject would mean the same things in saying them. What the physicalist-functionalist$_1$ would claim is that the symmetries that exist between the normal and abnormal subjects are no more than can be explained by their functional equivalence; it is their physical differences which explain the asymmetries.

There is, admittedly, an important difference between the absent qualia subject and the brain in the vat. Whereas the brain in the vat would know itself to be such given *all* the physical facts about itself and its environment, this is not the case for the absent qualia subject. Even given the facts of its own neurophysiology, the absent qualia subject would continue to believe in the existence of its own qualitative experience. This fact does suggest that there is at least something a bit odd about the absent qualia hypothesis. This suggestion of oddness, however, is just another instance of the intuition, which I have already touched upon in section 1, that mental differences could not be completely manifest in purely physical facts. This intuition, which Shoemaker himself makes explicit, will provide the basis of the arguments against absent qualia (and against physicalist-functionalism generally) in sections 3 and 4.

Shoemaker's answer to this line of argument poses a dilemma for the physicalist-functionalist$_1$.[18] Either the parochial theory is correct, in which case words such as "pain" as used by the alleged absent qualia subject refer to something other than pain, or the absent qualia subject succeeds in referring to genuine pain. In either case, what is alleged to be an absent qualia subject turns out not to qualify—in the first case because the nonqualitative states are nongenuine and in the second because if the alleged absent qualia subject succeeds in referring to qualia, then given that it is referring to its own states, it must enjoy qualitative experience after all. Unfortunately, this is not the independent argument Shoemaker needs against the possibility of case (2a). First, the argument assumes incorrectly that only on the parochial theory will the absent qualia subject refer to something other than that to which we refer in using "pain." And we have seen that case (2a) provides an example in which the parochial theory is false and yet an absent qualia subject refers to something other than pain in using "pain." Secondly, the argument presupposes the restrictive definition of absent qualia entailed by the statement of AQT-1. Given that case (2a) exists, the restrictive definition is required if Shoemaker is to rule this case out as a case of absent qualia. But, as we have seen above, Shoemaker's motivation for ruling out case (1), namely, that the parochial theory trivializes the question of whether other subjects experience qualia, does not apply to case (2a). Thus this argument presupposes the restrictive definition, and it is the fact that it presupposes this definition that makes

it useless to provide the independent justification which the definition requires.

The second argument against the possibility of absent qualia I shall call the *Common Language Argument*. Let us imagine a possible world in which alleged absent qualia subjects and normal subjects belong to the *same* linguistic community. The argument, then, goes as follows:

(1) Since the alleged absent qualia subjects and the normal subjects are functionally equivalent and since "pain" as used by the normal subjects refers to a state they possess, "pain" as used by the alleged absent qualia subjects must refer to a state they possess as well.

(2) Since the alleged absent qualia subjects and the normal subjects belong to the same linguistic community, they must mean the same thing by "pain" (i.e., they must associate "pain" with the same intension, that is, with the same function from possible worlds to extensions).

(3) Hence the state to which the alleged absent qualia subjects refer must be part of the extension of "pain" at this world as the term is used by the normal subjects.

(4) Hence the alleged absent qualia subjects have genuine pain.

The problem with this is that Shoemaker's assumption that members of our community *must* use the word "pain" with the same intension we do is unwarranted. If we think of "pain" on the model of a natural kind term, as the physicalist-functionalist$_1$ does, there is no problem in imagining different members of the community associating the same term with different intensions. It might turn out, for example, that "*Homo sapiens*" does not pick out a natural kind—that, in fact, there are two distinct natural kinds equally represented in our linguistic community. Call these "*Homo sapiens$_1$*" and "*Homo sapiens$_2$*." When we, members of *Homo sapiens$_1$*, discover the existence of members of *Homo sapiens$_2$*, we might naturally describe the situation as one in which we had used "*Homo sapiens*" to refer to members of *Homo sapiens$_1$* and members of *Homo sapiens$_2$* had used it to refer to members of *Homo sapiens$_2$*. Hence our being members of the same linguistic community does not guarantee that our terms are used with the same intension or extension. But without the second premise that our term "pain" has the same extension that it has when used by the alleged absent qualia subjects, Shoemaker's argument does not go through.

Even if we grant Shoemaker's second premise, however, the argument does not establish the conclusion Shoemaker needs. All that follows is that at a possible world in which alleged absent qualia subjects and normal subjects belonged to the same community, "pain," as used at that world, *would* include the internal states of the alleged absent qualia subjects in its extension. Thus it would be true that as "pain" is used at *that* world, the alleged absent qualia subjects would experience genuine pain. Since Shoemaker is not suggesting that this is *actually* the case, however, nothing follows about whether an alleged absent qualia subject would experience genuine pain as the term is *actually* used. Thus there is no shortcut to the conclusion that absent qualia are impossible, and Shoemaker has failed to supply an argument that supports this conclusion.

3   The Property Dualism Argument

The basic difficulty with Shoemaker's objections to absent qualia and to physicalist-functionalism[1] is that while he explicitly addresses a number of epistemological and metaphysical problems, there is nothing specific to the mental in any of the difficulties he treats. Although the intuition that a mental difference cannot have a purely physical manifestation seems to provide at least part of the motivation for his arguments, it is an intuition that they never successfully capture. If we limit the discussion of qualitative states to those features which they share with ordinary objects, we make things far too easy for the friends of absent qualia.

Could there be any objection, if we ignore the peculiarities of the mental, to the thesis that whereas some of the physical realizations of

the best functional descriptions of normal human subjects yield subjects with qualitative states, others do not? We can assume, to begin with, that there is a necessary connection between the physical states of a subject and that subject's qualitative states. (If not, there would be a possible world in which that subject exists unchanged in every physical detail but lacks qualitative states. This would rule out Shoemaker's position from the start.) Given this necessary connection, we can assume for the sake of simplicity that the connection is one of identity—nothing in the objection to Block that follows depends on this assumption. Now, abstracting from the peculiarities of the mental, there are no objections to the possibility that while all qualitative states are identical with some physical states of normal subjects, not all subjects which are functional duplicates of normal subjects have physical states which are qualitative states. Given such a possibility, it is entirely plausible that the terms "pain" and "qualia," as used by the absent qualia subject, should fail to refer because they are not causally connected with the right kinds of entities (or that they should refer to states different in kind from the ones to which our terms refer). In either event, the answer to the question whether we can refer, in our own case, to something the absent qualia subject lacks is yes.

The problem for Block's theory emerges when we examine what is specific to the epistemology and metaphysics of the mental. And it is a problem that should, at least since the the heyday of central state materialism, be relatively familiar. We are assuming, for simplicity, that a person's qualitative state of pain at t, say Smith's, is identical with a physical state, say Smith's brain state X at t. Even if this is the case, however, not only do the sense of the expression "Smith's pain at t" and the sense of the expression "Smith's brain state X at t" differ, but the fact that they are coreferential cannot be established on a priori grounds.[19] Thus there must be different properties of Smith's pain (i.e., Smith's brain state X) in virtue of which it is the referent of both terms. In the case of the expressions "the morning star" and "the evening star," it is in virtue of the property of being the last heavenly body visible in the morning that Venus is the referent of the first expression. And (since "the evening star" is not coreferential a priori with "the morning star") it is in virtue of the *logically distinct* property of being the first heavenly body visible in the evening that it is the referent of the second. The general principle is that if two expressions refer to the same object, and this fact cannot be established a priori, they do so in virtue of different routes to the referent provided by different modes of presentation of that referent.[20] These modes of presentation of the object fall on the object's side of the language/world dichotomy. In other words they are aspects of the object in virtue of which our conceptual apparatus picks the object out; they are not aspects of that conceptual apparatus itself. Hence the natural candidates for these modes of presentation are properties.

Suppose that this is not the case. Suppose, that is, that two descriptions are coreferential and that this fact cannot be established a priori and has not been established a posteriori. And suppose that there are *not* two different properties in virtue of which the two descriptions pick out the same referent. That the descriptions are not coreferential a priori (and not known to be a posteriori) means there is a possible world in which speakers who are epistemically equivalent to us use these terms to refer to different objects. There is, for example, a possible world in which the inhabitants are epistemically equivalent to those of our ancestors who used "the morning star" and "the evening star" before the discovery that the terms were coreferential and in which the inhabitants use the terms to refer to different planets. As used by the inhabitants of this possible world, these terms must pick out their referents in virtue of distinct properties, because unlike our terms, theirs pick out different objects. Hence the expressions, as used by our ancestors, must, contrary to our assumption, pick out their common referent in vir-

tue of two logically distinct properties of that referent.

To this argument it might be objected that properties are not individuated as finely as the argument requires. It might be suggested, that is, that there are not distinct properties corresponding to every distinction in meaning between linguistic expressions which are not coreferential a priori. On this view, the same property might be required to provide the route from two referring expressions which are not coreferential a priori. Such a view is tenable, but it simply postpones the problem of explaining how two referring expressions which are distinct in meaning and not coreferential a priori come to pick out the same object. If they do so in virtue of the same property of the referent, then that referent must have other *features* which differ in such a way as to provide two distinct routes by which the referring expressions pick it out. It would then be these features that play the role assigned by the argument to properties, and the argument could be rephrased accordingly.

Let us stipulate that a property which is neither physical nor mental is topic neutral. Since there is no physicalistic description that one could plausibly suppose is coreferential a priori with an expression like "Smith's pain at t," no physical property of a pain (i.e., a brain state of type X) could provide the route by which it was picked out by such an expression. Thus we are faced with a choice between topic neutral and mental properties. Postulating a mental property distinct from the property of being a brain state of type X would, needless to say, run counter to Block's commitment to minimal physicalism (Block 1980, p. 266). Suppose, then, that certain causal (though not necessarily physical) features are what constitute the route by which "Smith's pain at t" picks out a pain of Smith's. This is what J. J. C. Smart has claimed regarding the topic neutral properties of pain states. Smart holds that the expression "an event like the event that occurs in one when one is stabbed with a pin (and so forth)" is a topic neutral *translation* of "pain."[21]

That is, the expression contains no irreducibly mentalistic (or physicalistic) vocabulary, and it has the same sense as "pain"—or, at any rate, a description in which the topic neutral expression is substituted for "pain" is coreferential a priori with the original description.

If descriptions containing "pain" have a topic neutral translation (say Smart's) with which they are coreferential a priori, then both the description and its translation share the same route to their referent. Hence both expressions pick out the referent in virtue of the same property. The property of being a pain, therefore, is the same property as the property of being an event like the event that occurs in one when one is stabbed with a pin (and so forth). Since the topic neutral expression corresponding to this property involves no irreducibly mentalistic terms, the property, like the expression, is topic neutral; i.e., it is neither mental nor physical. (It follows that the expression "pain" itself is implicitly topic neutral; since it has a topic neutral translation, it is not *irreducibly* mentalistic.) If there are no topic neutral expressions which are at least coreferential a priori with such mentalistic descriptions as "Smith's pain at *t*," then these mentalistic descriptions refer in virtue of a property distinct from that in virtue of which any physicalistic or topic neutral expression refers. Such a property or feature could only be regarded as an irreducibly mental entity.[22]

This argument, which I shall call the *Property Dualism Argument*, shows that unless there are topic neutral expressions with which mentalistic descriptions of particular pains are coreferential a priori, we are forced to acknowledge the existence of mental properties. The claim that there are such topic neutral expressions—a claim which Smart shares with the orthodox functionalist, who claims that functional definitions are a priori—is not, however, a solution which is open to Block.[23] For Block, a topic neutral property would be unacceptable as the route from a mentalistic description to a pain since Smart's claim that "pain" has a topic neutral translation is just

the claim that "pain" has a definition in terms of its typical causes. And this claim is nothing more than the claim that "pain" has a protofunctionalist definition. Thus it is an instance of precisely the orthodox functionalist view that Block is attacking. It is, in fact, the alleged inadequacy of *any* topic neutral definition of "pain" that motivates Block's physicalist-functionalism. The upshot for Block is that by reverting from functionalism to a theory more akin to prefunctionalist identity theories, he has saddled himself with all the problems those theories entailed. And by insisting on the inadequacy of topic neutral translations of sensation terms, he has deprived himself of the only plausible solution those problems had generated.

One might assume that Block could solve this problem by dropping his commitment to physicalism. In that case a mental property, such as the property of being a pain, would provide the route by which mentalistic descriptions refer. Surprisingly, however, even dualism does not automatically provide one of the possible alternatives to functionalism. If we ask how the mental property of being a pain is to be explained, we are faced with a choice between a causal and a transcendentalist response. For the Cartesian dualist, pain is a modification of mental substance which has certain typical physical causes and results in a propensity toward certain behavioral effects. Spelling out the causal role that pain plays and then specifying that this role must be instantiated in a mental substance results in a theory which is formally analogous to physicalist-functionalism[24]—and a theory which shares all of that theory's defects. In particular the same question arises whether "pain" could be discovered a priori to be coextensive with any description couched in terms of mental substance. The answer is also analogous: either we drop the condition that pain's causal role *must* be instantiated by a mental substance and Cartesian dualism collapses into functionalism, or Cartesian dualism is no solution to the problem raised by the Property Dualism Argument.

For the transcendental dualist, on the other hand, pain cannot be explained in terms of mental substance, causal dispositions, or any combination of the two. Facts about mental states are not determined by *any* objective, third person facts, and mental substance is no less objective than physical substance. This position alone, among the alternatives to functionalism, is not susceptible to the argument I have been developing, but it is a position which seems too radical to tempt any but the most ardent antifunctionalists.

Given the Property Dualism Argument, absent qualia are impossible (unless one adopts some version of transcendentalism). The possibility of absent qualia depends on there being some non—topic neutral condition on the existence of the qualitative state in question. But in adding conditions beyond those which make up a topic neutral analysis of qualitative states, we make it impossible to establish a priori that a qualitative term and its analysans are coextensive. And it is in virtue of the lack of any a priori connection between the qualitative term and its analysans that the expressions refer to the same subject via different routes—and in virtue of these different routes that we are forced to acknowledge transcendental properties. Thus there is a direct connection between the intuitions that absent qualia and that inverted qualia are possible—the intuitions which motivate physicalist-functionalism—and transcendentalism. Hence we have a choice between abandoning the intuitions, and with them physicalist-functionalism, or retaining them and taking their transcendental consequences seriously. Whether these intuitions could plausibly be abandoned will be the subject of the next section.

4 DNA Physicalist-Functionalism

I have argued that Shoemaker's objections to absent qualia fail because they do not capture those features which distinguish the mental. The Property Dualism Argument, which does seem to capture an essential part of the peculiarity of the mental, rules out not only Block's position, but *any* version of physicalist-functionalism.[25] Although physicalist-functionalism is motivated by the intuition that functionalism cannot do justice to qualia, there is a crucial respect in which the functionalist account of qualia is superior: the problem of property dualism does not arise. Shoemaker, however, in his attempt to establish the claims of physicalist-functionalism$_2$, produces an important argument that might be thought to count against functionalism. This is the argument that an adequate theory of qualitative experience should allow for the possibility of qualia inversion. And if there is an argument against orthodox functionalism which does not lead to some version of transcendentalism, then functionalism may lose the advantage that it holds over physicalist-functionalism.

Let us distinguish, as Shoemaker does, between intrasubjective and intersubjective qualia inversion. An example of *intra*subjective inversion is the case in which things that look green to a subject at t_1 look red at t_2 and in which the way the rest of the colors look at t_2 is so related to the way they looked at t_1 that all of the subject's synchronic similarity judgments and discriminatory dispositions are preserved. This means, for example, that the subject will find that traffic light at the top more similar in color to the light in the middle than to the light at the bottom after the inversion as before. Furthermore, all the usual tests for color blindness will yield normal results. Only if the subject is asked how the way the lights at the top and bottom look *now* compares to the way they looked at t_1 will there be a manifest deviation from the norm. Associations such as that between red and danger, including such nonverbal responses to red as a slight increase in pulse rate, might survive the inversion intact, but we can assume for the sake of simplicity that either at the time of the inversion or gradually thereafter these associations will be inverted as well.

In the case of *inter*subjective qualia inversion the qualitative experiences of two subjects are related as the later experiences of the intrasubjective inversion subject are related to the earlier ones. In this case, however, there is no analogue of the anomolous diachronic judgments of the intrasubjective inversion victim. If subject A's qualitative states are inverted relative to B's, nothing in their observable behavior or functional makeup will make this apparent. Whereas an intrasubjective inversion subject will differ functionally from a normal subject, two subjects' qualitative states may be inverted relative to one another's while they remain perfect functional duplicates.

Shoemaker's objection to orthodox functionalism is that while *intra*subjective qualia inversion can be characterized in orthodox functional terms, it could not account for *inter*subjective inversion. This is a drawback, according to Shoemaker, because he claims that

there is a natural line of argument ... from the possibility of *intra*subjective inversion to the conclusion that it makes sense to suppose, and may well for all we know be true, that *inter*subjective spectrum inversion actually exists. (Shoemaker 1982, p. 358)

Shoemaker also claims that

[m]ost, of us, I suspect, cannot help feeling that a visual experience of mine can be like a visual experience of yours in exactly the same way it can be like another visual experience of mine. (Shoemaker 1982, p. 358)

If these claims are correct, functionalism would seem to contain a significant source of internal tension.

This feeling of tension, however, is largely illusory. Shoemaker's argument that the possibility of *intra*subjective inversion leads naturally to the possibility of *inter*subjective inversion is based on the intuition that if Smith undergoes a qualia shift at t, then either before or after t, Smith's experience must be qualitatively distinct from that of Jones who has undergone no such shift. But this is not an intuition that need worry an orthodox functionalist. The basic functionalist intuition is that all mental differences correspond to functional differences. This claim is conceptual rather

than empirical: a psychological state has, as a matter of conceptual necessity, no qualitative properties which cannot be reduced to functional properties. Thus the claim that functional duplicates might experience inverted qualia relative to one another is, for the orthodox functionalist, self-contradictory in a way that the possibility of intrasubjective qualia inversion is not. Consequently the claim that *intra*subjective inversion has a functionalist characterization provides the *functionalist* no reason to take *inter*subjective inversion seriously.

Whether the functionalist *should* admit the possibility of intrasubjective inversion is a question I shall not try to answer in this chapter, but the functionalist, if he does so, takes intrasubjective inversion seriously only when it makes a functional difference. If, as it is plausible to suppose, there is no functional difference between intrasubjective qualia inversion and qualia constancy coupled with nonveridical memories, then intrasubjective inversion is no more intelligible to the functionalist than intersubjective inversion. Hence, whatever the defects of the functionalist position, there are no internal sources of tension.

If Shoemaker is to produce an argument that will force us beyond functionalism, it will have to be an argument not that there are tensions internal to functionalism, but that it fails to explain our *pretheoretical* intuitions. We do, after all, *seem* to understand the possibility that things which we both call "red" look to me the way things which we both call "green" look to you. But if this is the source of Shoemaker's dissatisfaction, we shall have no reason to prefer physicalist-functionalism to orthodox functionalism. This is because nothing in my statement about what we seem to understand when we claim to understand the possibility of intersubjectively inverted qualia involves any reference to functionalism. If our pretheoretical intuitions make it possible to imagine two functional duplicates who differ in their qualitative experiences, they make it equally possible to imagine two *physical* duplicates who differ in the same way. Hence the intuition to which Shoemaker appeals is every bit as effective against physicalist-functionalism as it is against functionalism. Indeed, it should come as no surprise that our pretheoretical intuitions fail to discriminate between physicalist and orthodox functionalism, given that the interest in the possibility of spectrum inversion so conspicuously predates functionalist developments.

It might be maintained, by way of reply, that physicalist-functionalism comes closer, at least, to accommodating those dualistic, pretheoretical intuitions we seem to possess. Even this reply, though, is unavailable to Shoemaker. Imagine a theory which takes the physical difference in DNA structure between two subjects as evidence of qualia difference. We can call such a theory *DNA physicalist-functionalism*. To see physicalist-functionalism as superior to orthodox functionalism on the basis of our *pretheoretical* intuitions would require that we see DNA physicalist-functionalism as an even better alternative. DNA physicalist-functionalism would allow for qualia differences even between functional states whose physical realizations belonged to the same natural kind. Thus by taking physical differences which are independent of any functional manifestation as evidence of possible qualia differences, we deprive ourselves of any natural point at which to draw the line between relevant and irrelevant physical differences. No doubt one would like to associate qualia differences only with "significant" physical differences, but the physicalist-functionalist has no principled way of doing so.

Shoemaker might deny that this last claim raises a problem on the grounds that there is no absurdity in the suggestion that DNA differences might lead to qualia differences if it is possible, in principle, to settle the question. As a result, the physicalist-functionalist could not be embarrassed by the objection that no physical difference would be too trivial to count as evidence of a qualia difference. If a test is possible, the physicalist-functionalist can establish *empirically* the point at which physical differences become irrelevant to qualia.

This possible reply of Shoemaker's goes to the heart of his position because it points to the fundamental gap in any physicalist-functionalist account of qualia difference. Shoemaker's remarks suggest the following test to determine whether two different types of physiological realization of the same functional states in two subjects lead to qualia differences. If we change the neurophysiology of one subject to match that of the other (assuming that the physical replacements are not so extensive as to threaten personal identity), and if the subject undergoes an *intra*subjective qualia change, this is a very strong indication of the existence of *inter*subjective qualia differences. If there is no intrasubjective switch, then there is no intersubjective qualia difference between the two subjects. If neither subject's physiology can be realized in the other, the question of intersubjective qualia difference does not arise (Shoemaker 1982, pp. 372–375).

The problem with this reply is that a change in the *type* of physiology per se has *no* tendency to produce functional evidence of intrasubjective qualia change. If the functional states are fixed, changing the type of realization could only produce a subject who claims sincerely to have undergone *no* change in qualitative experience— exactly what the subject would have claimed had there been no change at all. If the functional states are not fixed, then no change in the *type* of physiology is even necessary to produce evidence of inversion. A functional change alone is sufficient to produce a subject who claims sincerely to have experienced an intrasubjective inversion of his or her qualitative states. In other words, we cannot test the relevance of different kinds of physiological differences to qualitative experiences by testing their tendency to produce evidence of intrasubjective qualia inversion. Physiological changes, by themselves, are *irrelevant* to the evidence of either intrasubjective or intersubjective qualia inversion; only if the physiological changes amount to a change in functional states could any evidence of qualia inversion emerge.[26]

The fact that we can hold a subject's functional states fixed and vary the type of neurophysiology without producing anything an orthodox functionalist would count as evidence of qualia change leads to a dilemma for Shoemaker. Consider the following principle.

Manifestation Principle Differences in the qualitative content of mental states cannot be postulated on the basis of physical differences which have no actual or possible functional manifestation.

This means that the physical difference in the way the functional states of a pair of functional duplicates are realized could not be the basis of an ascription to them of qualitatively different states. It also means that if, as Shoemaker seems to suggest, there are no functional differences between a subject who has undergone intrasubjective qualia inversion and one who has suffered a memory failure producing beliefs to that effect, then the distinction between the two is meaningless. One cannot, as Shoemaker does (Shoemaker 1982, p. 363, fn. 8), appeal to facts about the way perception and memory are realized physically to make the distinction.

These consequences of the Manifestation Principle make it clear that Shoemaker cannot accept it. Unless the principle is rejected, intrasubjective qualia inversion is by Shoemaker's own account impossible, and regardless of whether it is possible or not, intersubjective inversion is ruled out. Adopting the principle amounts, in fact, to abandoning physicalist-functionalism for its orthodox counterpart.

For equally decisive reasons, however, Shoemaker cannot reject the principle. First, Shoemaker is committed to the principle by the fact that he uses it against Block when he says that if a subject shares with us all of the functional aspects of pain,

it is hard to see how a physiological difference between him and us could be any evidence at all that his states lack qualitative character. (Shoemaker 1975, p. 296)

Secondly, there is the problem that we have just seen of DNA physicalist-functionalism. Without the principle, there is no way of ruling out the claim that trivial physical differences correspond to qualia differences. Finally, Shoemaker is committed to the principle by his claim that qualia similarities and differences can be functionally defined. Physicalist-functionalism$_2$ is distinguished from physicalist-functionalism$_1$ by the claim that the class of qualitative states can be functionally defined, even if individual states cannot (Shoemaker 1975, p. 309). Rejecting the principle means rejecting Shoemaker's position for Block's. The dilemma for Shoemaker is that whatever his stance toward the principle, his position collapses—either into orthodox functionalism or into Block's physicalist-functionalism$_1$.

Although Shoemaker's dilemma is not a problem for physicalist-functionalism generally, DNA physicalist-functionalism is. Regardless of its form, any version of physicalist-functionalism entails the denial of the Manifestation Principle. And it is this principle which provides the functionalist with a link between the neurophysiological level and the facts of qualitative experience. Physical facts gain their relevance by making a difference to the functional facts which are conceptually linked to qualia differences. The denial of the Manifestation Principle breaks this link, leaving the physicalist-functionalist vulnerable to the arguments of DNA physicalist-functionalism. As a result, we have a second argument which works against physicalist-functionalism in any form.

The DNA Physicalist-Functionalism Argument and the Property Dualism Argument grow out of the same general problem for physicalist-functionalism: that it has no principled way of establishing the relevance (or the lack of relevance) of the physical differences between subjects—physical differences, that is, which have no functional significance. The Manifestation Principle is the orthodox functionalist version of the pretheoretical intuition that mental differences cannot have a purely physical manifestation.

Unlike the proponents of physicalist-functionalism, the orthodox functionalist can point to an a priori connection between the properties he or she takes to be relevant to qualia—the functional properties—and the qualitative properties themselves. This is a connection in virtue of the meaning of "pain" and the meaning of the expression describing the corresponding functional disposition. In contrast, the advocate of physicalist-functionalism who holds the parochial theory can only point to a connection between physical properties and qualitative properties in virtue of a *dispensable* linguistic convention. Nothing would be lost by couching the question of intersubjective qualitative similarity in terms of a concept—"pain*"—to which it is stipulated that the parochial theory does not apply. It would allow us, in fact, to ask a question which is clearly intelligible given the antifunctionalist intuitions to which physicalist-functionalism purports to do justice: whether qualitative similarity among alleged pains corresponds to identity in natural kind of their physical realizations. In the case of the nonparochial version of physicalist-functionalism, the problem is even more acute: there is *no* connection between a subject's physical and qualitative states. Hence the Manifestation Principle presents a problem for any version of physicalist-functionalism.

The question with which we began this section was whether there were arguments against orthodox functionalism which might counterbalance the Property Dualism Argument against physicalist-functionalism. We have been concerned, in particular, with the claim that physicalist-functionalism more adequately captures our pretheoretical intuitions than functionalism. One class of intuitions which have not yet been mentioned are those concerning the privileged access we may be thought to enjoy regarding our own qualitative states. Though these are not irrelevant to an assessment of orthodox functionalism, since they provide physicalist-functionalism with no claim to any advantage, they can in this context safely be ignored. As regards our pretheoretical

intuitions about qualia inversion, however, we have now seen that they fail to provide physicalist-functionalism any support. Furthermore, physicalist-functionalism violates Shoemaker's intuition that mental differences cannot have a purely physical manifestation. Hence among the intuitions which favor either physicalist-functionalism or functionalism, the advantage goes entirely to functionalism. Functionalism, it is true, fails to capture *all* of our intuitions regarding qualia, but those which it fails to accommodate point beyond physicalist-functionalism to transcendentalism. And though I have left open the possibility of a transcendentalist account of qualia, such a position will have little appeal to most of functionalism's current critics.[27]

Notes

1. Shoemaker (1975, 1981, 1982) and Block (1980). The term "physicalist-functionalism" is unlikely to please either Shoemaker or Block. Shoemaker regards himself as defending functionalism, at least where qualia are concerned, rather than offering an alternative theory. Block, on the other hand, has little sympathy for functionalism, and even the category of physicalist-functionalism that I shall sketch might seem objectionable. Nonetheless, I think this term is appropriate. As in every question of terminology, we can distinguish two components. There is, first of all, the question of where to divide the space of possible positions. Since I shall claim that both Shoemaker's position and Block's are vulnerable to the same set of arguments and that this is a vulnerability that functionalism does not share, the distinction between functionalism and physicalist-functionalism is not only motivated but is dictated by my substantive position. The second question is how the subspaces of the space of possible positions should be labeled. On this point it is open to Shoemaker to argue that his position bears a stronger similarity to the positions historically associated with the term "functionalism" than the position for which I am using the term. If this were the case, it might be more appropriate to call what I shall call "functionalism" and "orthodox functionalism" by another name. Such a claim, however, does not seem to me to be supported by the evidence. Shoemaker's claim that particular qualia are not func-

tionally definable would rule out functionalism as a *complete* theory of mind. And this is sufficiently at odds with the spirit in which functionalism was advanced to justify treating Shoemaker's position as an alternative to functionalism as it is ordinarily understood. Moreover, since I shall argue that what I call "functionalism" is the only viable descendant of the original theory, it seems reasonable to reserve for it the shorter and simpler term.

The case of Block is more complicated, since if we compromise the functionalist principle that the nature of the realization of a functional system is irrelevant to the psychological properties of that system, it is hard to know where to draw the line between physicalist-functionalism and (type-type) physicalism. Fortunately, for the purposes at hand, we can stipulate that (type-type) physicalism is to count as a version of physicalist-functionalism. The difficulties that arise for physicalist-functionalism over qualia are difficulties for physicalism as well. The choice of terminology is further complicated by the fact that if the nature of the realization of functional states is relevant to mentality, then mentality may depend on more than physical facts. Functionalism has always left open the possibility in principle of non-physical realizations of functional systems. If for the physicalist-functionalist it is the nature of the functional realization that matters, then physicalist-functionalism should leave open this possibility as well. Hence at least some versions of Cartesian dualism could count as versions of physicalist-functionalism. I shall ignore this qualification in most of what follows.

2. Besides those mentioned above: Armstrong (1968, pp. 73–125), Lewis (1980), Rey (1980), Searle (1980, 1981), Churchland and Churchland (1981), and Putnam (1981, pp. 75–102).

3. Harman (1982). See also Dennett (1978), Kitcher (1979), and Lycan (1981). Dennett's claim that all instantiations of a flowchart theory of pain might feel pain suggests that where qualia are concerned Dennett's functionalism is orthodox. However, his idea that pain might be identified with a "natural kind" (p. 228) points in the other direction. Lycan's criticisms of Block make it clear that orthodox functionalism is the correct category, but his skepticism about the functional/physical distinction necessarily blurs the line between orthodox and physicalist-functionalism. And Kitcher's more recent article (Kitcher, 1982) makes it clear that she is an agnostic where the merits of orthodox as opposed to physicalist-functionalism are concerned. In what fol-

lows, I shall sometimes use the term "functionalism" for "orthodox functionalism" where there is no chance of confusion.

4. This, of course, is an oversimplification. The correct functional description of the subject's inputs and outputs is a matter of long-standing debate. For an argument that inputs and outputs must themselves be described relationally see White (1982a, chapter one).

5. Nagel (1979). The term "transcendentalism" is intended to suggest the affinities between Nagel's criticism of Cartesian (substance) dualism and those of Kant and Husserl. See Kant (1965, A341–A405, B399–B432), and Husserl (1973, pp. 18–26).

6. Nagel (1979, p. 201).

7. The argument, strictly speaking, is not that absent qualia are impossible, but that absent qualia raise insurmountable obstacles for any *nontranscendental* theory.

8. Goldman (1976).

9. The notion of functional definability that occurs in the *definiens* of Shoemaker's definitions is strong definability. In other words, a state is functionally definable in the strong sense if and only if it has a definition in which no mental terms occur in the definiens. A mental state is functionally definable in the weak sense if it has a functional definition given that we allow in the *definiens* terms which are not themselves strongly functionally definable.

10. To see that the negation of AQT-2 is equivalent to the negation of thesis (1), suppose that qualitative states are only weakly functionally definable. Then whether a subject has qualitative states will depend on whether that subject has nonqualitative states which themselves are not (strongly) functionally definable. Let us suppose that such a subject is functionally equivalent to a normal subject. In spite of the equivalence, such a subject may lack some of the nonqualitative states of the normal subject which are not functionally definable and hence may lack qualitative states. If qualitative states are strongly functionally definable, this possibility is ruled out. Hence the negation of AQT-2 is equivalent to the negation of thesis (1).

11. Shoemaker's claim that qualitative states are weakly definable, however, is compatible with the claim, which he also makes, that two subjects who are functional duplicates may *differ* in the particular character of their qualitative experience. (Shoemaker's thesis that inverted qualia are possible is merely a special instance of this

latter claim.) These two claims are compatible because, as we have seen, Shoemaker does not regard it as essential to ordinary qualitative states such as pain that they feel like what we have when we experience them. All that is essential to pain, besides its functional role, is that it involve some kind of qualitative experience. The same is true for all the qualitative states picked out by our normal vocabulary of mental terms. Thus Shoemaker can hold that as long as absent qualia are impossible, our ordinary terms for qualitative states are weakly functionally definable. We could, however, artificially define qualitative states whose *particular* qualitative character would be essential to their identity. We might, for example, define "pain$_s$" as any state which feels exactly like the last headache of some particular subject *S*. Such artificial qualitative states do not fall within the scope of Shoemaker's claim that qualitative states are weakly functionally definable.

It follows that Shoemaker uses "qualitative states" in two senses. When in the statement of the negation of AQT-2 (see Table 44.1) he says that qualitative states are weakly definable, he means *ordinary* qualitative states such as pain. When in the definition of functional definability in the weak sense he uses the expression "nonqualitative mental states," this contrasts not only with *ordinary* qualitative states, but also with such artificially defined states as pain$_s$. In particular contexts it is usually clear which sense Shoemaker has in mind.

12. The term "ersatz pain" is due to Lawrence Davis. See Block (1980, p. 259).

13. The term "imitation man" is Keith Campbell's. See Campbell (1970, p. 100).

14. See Putnam (1975) and Kripke (1980).

15. In correspondence.

16. This claim is defended in the context of a more detailed discussion of the distinction between beliefs narrowly and widely construed and an argument that functionalism is a theory of narrow belief in White (1982b).

17. Even if some version of the Symmetry Argument did yield the conclusion which is needed, Shoemaker has failed to notice that this argument would prove too much. We could use the same argument to show that the Martians, who are functionally but not neurophysiologically equivalent to us, not only have pains, but have pains that feel exactly like ours. Suppose, for example, the hypothesis is that Martian pains differ from ours in that theirs are never "shooting" pains.

Since they are functionally equivalent to us, they will *claim* to have shooting pains under exactly the same circumstances that we claim to have them. If the difference between the Martians' neurophysiology and ours is irrelevant to their claims to have pain, it is equally irrelevant to their claims to have shooting pains. Hence any argument which supports their claim to have pains will support their claim to have pains with *any* qualitative characteristics we attribute to ours. Of course, it is possible to object that the feelings the Martians experience when they experience pain may be unlike the feelings we experience, though they describe their pains in exactly the same ways. If this were possible, however, there would be no argument from the symmetry between what Martians and humans could sincerely say about what they feel to any symmetry between their actual feelings and ours. Hence either the Symmetry Argument proves that qualia differences between Martians and humans are impossible, and thereby undermines Shoemaker's version of physicalist-functionalism, or it fails to prove that absent qualia are impossible. Thus Shoemaker's argument for the symmetry of the Martian and human claims to experience pain undermines his own version of physicalist-functionalism.

18. Shoemaker has made this argument explicit in correspondence.

19. The distinction between expressions which are synonymous or which have the same sense and expressions which are coreferential a priori is meant to accommodate the kinds of cases which are familiar in mathematics. Two mathematical expressions may be coreferential a priori and this fact may be sufficiently far from obvious, even to a fully competent speaker, that we would not want to call them synonymous.

20. See Smart (1971, p. 59). As the statement of the general principle suggests, the crucial distinction for this argument is not between expressions which are synonymous and expressions which are nonsynonymous, but between expressions which are coreferential a priori and expressions which are coreferential a posteriori. Nonsynonymy is not sufficient to generate a duality of properties, since the nonsynonymy of two expressions which pick out the same referent does not require that the referent have *logically distinct* features in virtue of which the two expressions pick it out.

21. Smart does not provide a topic neutral translation of "the experience of having pain." What I have provided is one natural analogue of his translation of "the

experience of seeing an after-image." "And so forth" should be taken to stand in for a long list of typical causes of pain, since the description is intended as a description of pain and not of the particular kind of pain associated with pin pricks. Needless to say, neither the merits of this nor of any other particular topic neutral translations are at issue here.

22. As the argument suggests, the existence of a physicalist or a topic neutral description which picks out the same event as the mentalistic expression "Smith's pain at t" is irrelevant so long as no such description is coreferential a priori with the mentalistic expression. This is true regardless of whether the physicalistic or topic neutral description is rigid or nonrigid. (Skeptics about the existence of a rigid reading of such a description may take the term derived from the original description by the addition of Kaplan's operator "Dthat." The operator transforms the description into a term which rigidly designates the object *actually* satisfying the description. See Kaplan (1977).) Any such description which is *not* coreferential a priori with the mentalistic expression refers to Smith's pain in virtue of a different property from that in virtue of which the mentalistic expression picks it out. If, for example, the topic neutral and nonrigid description "the state of Smith at t of the type which typically causes him to say 'ow'" picks out Smith's pain at t, it does so in virtue of a topic neutral property that Smith's pain has at the actual world but lacks at those possible worlds where Smith says "damn" when in pain and "ow" when mildly embarrassed (assuming that "Smith's pain at t" is rigid). If we give the topic neutral description a rigid reading, then it picks out Smith's pain at t at every possible world. Unless the mentalistic expression is coreferential with this topic neutral description a priori, however, it will still pick out Smith's pain in virtue of a *different* property from the topic neutral one, and the problem of property dualism will remain.

It might be objected with reference to this last case that the topic neutral property corresponding to the rigid topic neutral description "Dthat the state of Smith at t of the type which typically causes him to say 'ow'" is identical with the mental property corresponding to the mentalistic description "Smith's pain at t" on the grounds that they have the same extension. I am not, however, committed to the thesis that if two descriptions are not coreferential a priori, then the properties expressed by those descriptions can be shown to be distinct by the fact that they have different extensions.

Consider the descriptions "Dthat the first Postmaster General" and "Dthat the inventor of bifocals." These are not coreferential a priori, but they are satisfied by the same individual at each possible world, namely, Franklin. And if there are rigid properties expressed by these two rigid descriptions, then these properties have the same extension at very possible world. What I claim is that *there are* two properties in virtue of which these descriptions pick out Franklin which can be shown to be distinct because they *do* differ in their extension. These are the property of being the first Postmaster General and the property of being the inventor of bifocals. It is these properties which provide the two routes to Franklin in virtue of which he is picked out by descriptions which are not coreferential a priori.

This argument assumes that the mentalistic and topic neutral descriptions would pick out a *token* physical state. It is possible that a topic neutral description might purport to pick out a *type* of physical state instead of a token. For a topic neutral description, however, this will not be the case unless the description is rigid and contains an explicit reference to a particular species. This is because no one seriously disputes the assumption that the topic neutral properties associated with pain might be realized in different physical state types in different actual species or in the same species at different possible worlds. Suppose that it *is* claimed that our actual use of "pain" is such that we can fix the reference of "pain" to a type of physical state by the use of a rigid, topic neutral description which is coextensive with "pain" a priori. Call the topic neutral properties of pain the "causal-role-of-pain." Such a claim might be made for the description "the state (type) which realizes the causal-role-of-pain in humans" on a rigid reading. This would not raise the problem of property dualism, since, by hypothesis, both the topic neutral expression and the expression "pain" share the same route to the referent. This suggestion, however, merely restates the parochial view of the meaning of mental terms whose inadequacy Shoemaker points out (Shoemaker 1981, p. 595). The parochial view *trivializes* physicalist-functionalism by making the claim that there could be subjects who were functionally equivalent to us and who felt no pain true as a matter of linguistic convention. If "pain" did have the meaning suggested, we would be forced to coin a new term (to which it would be stipulated that the parochial theory did not apply and) which would be true of a state just in case it had the same phenomenal quality as one of our pains. The philosophically interesting question would then become whether subjects who were functionally equivalent to us could lack the states thus defined.

23. This argument that we are forced to postulate irreducibly mentalistic properties unless "pain" has a topic neutral translation is similar to Smart's argument for the same conclusion. (How far the similarity goes will depend on a number of issues in the interpretation of Smart's position which cannot be settled here.) I have recast Smart's talk of contingent identity statements in terms of identity statements which are known a posteriori.

Richard Rorty has claimed (Rorty 1970, p. 400) that there are three possible responses to Smart's argument for property dualism: (1) Formulate adequate topic neutral translations. (2) Drop the principle that properties are identical only if the terms referring to them are synonymous. (3) Adopt the principle that two things can be identical in some sense even if they do not share all and only the same properties. Rorty's second proposal is obviously no help to the physicalist-functionalist, since the criteria of property identity have already been fixed by the theoretical role that properties have to play in explaining the fact that "pain" and the relevant neurophysiological description are coreferential despite the fact that they are not coreferential a priori. I discuss the first proposal below in the context of the orthodox functionalist approach to qualia; the third proposal does not provide a genuine alternative to the transcendental property dualist position, which I claim is a consequence of Shoemaker's and Block's antifunctionalist intuitions.

24. It was because of this formal analogy that I claimed in footnote 1 that some versions of Cartesian dualism—those which emphasize the causal role of mental substance—could be counted as instances of physicalist-functionalism.

25. On Shoemaker's view, ordinary qualitative states such as pain present no problem, because he is committed to the possibility of giving *them* a topic neutral analysis. As we saw in footnote 11, however, if we define "pain$_s$" as any state which feels like some particular individual's last headache, such an expression will *not*, according to Shoemaker, have even a weak functional definition. Thus it will not have a topic neutral translation. Hence it will raise the same problems for Shoemaker that "pain" raises for Block. Notice that the issue is not whether functionalism must provide an analysis of

such artificial terms as "pain$_s$" as well as our ordinary mentalistic vocabulary. The problem for Shoemaker is not that he fails to provide a *functionalist* account of terms such as "pain$_s$." The problem is that since such terms are definable, Shoemaker must provide *some* account of their meaning, and the account he does provide has, as does every physicalist-functionalist account, two unacceptable consequences. The first, as we have seen, is the existence of transcendental properties; the second, as we shall see, is the lack of a principled distinction between those physical facts which are relevant to a subject's qualitative experiences and those which are not.

26. After completing this chapter, I discovered that this last point against Shoemaker is also made in Seager (1983). Seager's point occurs in the context of a different assessment of functionalism, which, unfortunately, I cannot discuss here.

27. I am grateful to Akeel Bilgrami, Jaegwon Kim, William Lycan, Joseph Mendola, Stephen Schiffer, and Sydney Shoemaker for their comments and advice on earlier drafts of this chapter.

References

Armstrong, D. M. 1968, *A Materialist Theory of the Mind*, Humanities Press, New York.

Block, Ned. 1980, "Are Absent Qualia Impossible?" *Philosophical Review* 89, 257–274.

Campbell, Keith. 1970, *Body and Mind*, Doubleday, Garden City, New York.

Churchland, Paul M., and Patricia Smith Churchland, 1981, "Functionalism, Psychology and the Philosophy of Mind," *Philosophical Topics* 12, 121–146.

Dennett, Daniel. 1978, "Why You Can't Make a Computer that Feels Pain," in *Brainstorms*, Bradford Books, Montgomery, VT, pp. 190–229.

Goldman, Alvin. 1976, "Discrimination and Perceptual Knowledge," *Journal of Philosophy* 73, 771–791.

Harman, Gilbert. 1982, "Conceptual Role Semantics," *Notre Dame Journal of Formal Logic* 23, 242–256.

Husserl, Edmund. 1973, *Cartesian Meditations*, Martinus Nijhoff, The Hague.

Kant, Immanuel. 1965, *Critque of Pure Reason*, St. Martin's Press, New York.

Kaplan, David. 1977, *Demonstratives*, mimeographed, Department of Philosophy, UCLA.

Kitcher, Patricia. 1979, "Phenomenal Qualities," *American Philosophical Quarterly* 16, 123–129.

———. 1982, "Two Versions of the Identity Theory," *Erkenntnis* 17, 213–228.

Kripke, Saul. 1980, *Naming and Necessity*, Harvard University Press, Cambridge, Mass.

Lewis, David. 1980, "Mad Pain and Martian Pain," in N. J. Block (ed.), *Readings in the Philosophy of Psychology*, Vol. I, Harvard University Press, Cambridge, Mass., pp. 216–222.

Lycan, William. 1981, "Form, Function and Feel," *Journal of Philosophy* 78, 24–50.

Nagel, Thomas. 1979, "Subjective and Objective," in *Mortal Questions*, Cambridge University Press, New York, pp. 196–213.

Putnam, Hilary. 1975, "The Meaning of 'Meaning,'" in *Mind, Language and Reality*, Cambridge University Press, New York, pp. 215–271.

———. 1981, *Reason, Truth and History*, Cambridge University Press, New York.

Rey, Georges. 1980, "Functionalism and the Emotions," in Amélie Rorty (ed.), *Explaining the Emotions*, University of California Press, Berkeley, pp. 163–195.

Rorty, Richard. 1970, "Incorrigibility as the Mark of the Mental," *Journal of Philosophy* 68, 399–424.

Seager, W. 1983, "Functionalism, Qualia and Causation," *Mind* 92, 174–188.

Searle, John. 1980, "Minds, Brains, and Programs," *Behavioral and Brain Sciences* 3, 417–457.

———. 1981, "Analytic Philosophy and Mental Phenomena," *Midwest Studies in Philosophy* 6, 405–423.

Shoemaker, Sydney. 1975, "Functionalism and Qualia," *Philosophical Studies* 27, 291–315.

———. 1981, "Absent Qualia Are Impossible—A Reply to Block," *Philosophical Review* 90, 581–599.

———. 1982, "The Inverted Spectrum," *Journal of Philosophy* 79, 357–381.

Smart, J. J. C. 1971, "Sensations and Brain Processes," in David Rosenthal (ed.), *Materialism and the Mind-Body Problem*, Prentice-Hall, Englewood Cliffs, pp. 53–66, 59.

White, Stephen. 1982a, *Functionalism and Propositional Content*, dissertation, University of California, Berkeley.

———. 1982b, "Partial Character and the Language of Thought," *Pacific Philosophical Quarterly* 63, 347–365.

X HIGHER-ORDER MONITORING CONCEPTIONS OF CONSCIOUSNESS

45 What Is Consciousness?

David Armstrong

The notion of consciousness is notoriously obscure. It is difficult to analyze, and some philosophers and others have thought it unanalyzable. It is not even clear that the word "consciousness" stands for just one sort of entity, quality, process, or whatever. There is, however, one thesis about consciousness that I believe can be confidently rejected: Descartes's doctrine that consciousness is the essence of mentality. That view assumes that we can explain mentality in terms of consciousness. I think that the truth is in fact the other way round. Indeed, in the most interesting sense of the word "consciousness," consciousness is the cream on the cake of mentality, a special and sophisticated development of mentality. It is not the cake itself. In what follows, I develop an anti-Cartesian account of consciousness.

Minimal Consciousness

In thinking about consciousness, it is helpful to begin at the other end and consider a totally unconscious person. Somebody in a sound, dreamless sleep may be taken as an example. It has been disputed whether unconsciousness is really ever total. There is some empirical evidence that a person in dreamless sleep, or even under a total anesthetic, still has some minimal awareness. Minimal behavioral reactions to sensory stimuli have been observed under these conditions. But let us take it, if only as a simplifying and perhaps unrealistic assumption, that we are dealing with *total* unconsciousness.

Notice first that we are perfectly happy to concede that such a person, while in this state of total unconsciousness, has a *mind*. Furthermore, although by hypothesis this mind is in no way active—no mental events take place, no mental processes occur within it—we freely allow that this mind is in various *states*.

The totally unconscious person does not lack knowledge and beliefs. Suppose him to be a his-torian of the medieval period. We will not deny him a great deal of knowledge of and beliefs about the Middle Ages just because he is sound asleep. He cannot give current expression to his knowledge and his beliefs, but he does not lack them. The totally unconscious person also may be credited with memories. He also can be said to have skills, including purely mental skills such as an ability for mental arithmetic. The ability is not lost during sound sleep just because it then cannot be exercised, any more than an athlete loses his athletic abilities during sound sleep, when he cannot exercise them. A totally unconscious person may be credited with likes and dislikes, attitudes and emotions, current desires and current aims and purposes. He may be said to have certain traits of character and termperament. He may be said to be in certain moods: "He has been depressed all this week."

How are we to conceive of these mental states (it seems natural to call them "states") we attribute to the unconscious person? Some decades ago, under the influence of positivistic and phenomenalistic modes of thought, such attributions of mental states to an unconscious person would not have been taken very seriously, ontologically. It would have been thought that to say that the currently unconscious person A believes that p, is simply to refer to various ways in which A's mind works, or would work in suitable circumstances, before and/or after he wakes up. (The same positivist spirit might try further to reduce the way that A's mind works to A's peripheral bodily behavior or to the behavior A would exhibit in suitable circumstances.)

In historical perspective, we can see clearly how unsatisfactory such a view is. Consider two persons, A and B, unconscious at the same time, where it is true of A that he believes that p, but false of B. Must there not be a difference between A and B at that time to constitute this difference in belief-state? What else in the world could act as a truth-maker (the ground in the world) for the different conditional statements that are true of A and B? The mind of the unconscious person cannot be dissolved into statements about what would be true of the person *if* the situation were other than it was; if, in particular, he were not unconscious.

In considering this point, I find very helpful the analogy between an unconscious person and a computer that has been programmed in various ways, that perhaps has partially worked through certain routines and is ready to continue with them, but is not currently operating. (I do not think that anything in the analogy turns on the material, physical nature of the computer. Even if the mind has to be conceived of in some immaterial way, the analogy will still hold.) The computer, perhaps, will have a certain amount of information stored in its memory banks. This stored information may be compared to the knowledge, belief, and memories the unconscious person still has during unconsciousness. If a Materialist account of the mind is correct, then, of course, knowledge, belief, and memory will be physically encoded in the brain in some broadly similar way to the way in which information is stored in the computer. But the Dualist, say, will equally require the conception of immaterial storage of knowledge, belief, and memory.

What we can say both of the knowledge, beliefs, and so forth possessed by the totally unconscious person, and also of the information stored in the switched-off computer, is that they are *causally quiescent*. Of course, nothing is causally quiescent absolutely: while a thing exists, it has effects upon its environment. But the information stored in the switched-off computer is causally quiescent with respect to the computing operations of the computer, and for our purposes this may be called causal quiescence. (The information may remain causally quiescent even after the computer has been switched on, unless that piece of information is required for current calculations.) In the same way, knowledge and beliefs may be said to be causally quiescent while they are not producing any *mental* effect in the person. The mental states of a totally unconscious person are thus causally quiescent (if they are not, we may stipulate that the person is not totally unconscious). Knowledge, beliefs, and so on may remain causally quiescent in this sense even when the mind is operational, for instance, where there is no call to use a particular piece of knowledge.

It seems, then, that we attribute mental states of various sorts to a totally unconscious person. But there are certain mental attributions we do not make. The totally unconscious person does not perceive, has no sensations, feelings, or pangs of desire. He cannot think, contemplate, or engage in any sort of deliberation. (He can have purposes, because purposes are capable of causal quiescence, but he cannot be engaged in carrying them out.) This is because perception, sensation, and thinking are mental *activities* in a way that knowledge and beliefs are not. The distinction appears, roughly at any rate, to be the distinction between events and occurrences on the one hand, and states on the other. When a mental state is producing mental effects, the comings-to-be of such effects are mental events: and so mental activity is involved.

We now have a first sense for the word "consciousness." If there is mental activity occurring in the mind, if something mental is actually happening, then that mind is not totally unconscious. It is therefore conscious. A single faint sensation is not much, but if it occurs, to that extent there is consciousness. Unconsciousness is not total. I call consciousness in this sense "minimal" consciousness.

It is alleged that it sometimes occurs that someone wakes up knowing the solution to, say, a mathematical problem, which they did not know when they went to sleep. If we rule out magical explanations, then there must have been mental activity during sleep. To that extent, there was minimal consciousness. This is compatible with the completest "unconsciousness" in a sense still to be identified.

Perceptual Consciousness

Among the mental activities, however, it appears that we make a special link between consciousness and *perception*. In perception, there is consciousness of what is currently going on in one's environment and in one's body. (Of course, the consciousness may involve illusion.) There is an important sense in which, if a person is not perceiving, then he is not conscious, but if he is perceiving, then he is conscious. Suppose somebody to be dreaming. Since there is mental activity going on, the person is not totally unconscious. He is minimally conscious. Yet is there not some obvious sense in which he is unconscious? Now suppose that this person starts to perceive his environment and bodily state. (I do not want to say "suppose he wakes up", because perhaps there is more to waking up than just starting to perceive again.) I think that we would be inclined to say that the person was now conscious in a way that he had not been before, while merely dreaming. Let us say, therefore, that he has regained "perceptual" consciousness. This is a second sense of the word "consciousness." Perceptual consciousness entails minimal consciousness, but minimal consciousness does not entail perceptual consciousness.

Introspective Consciousness

Let us suppose, now, that there is mental activity going on in a person, and that this activity includes perception. If what has been said so far is accepted, then there are two senses in which such a person can be said to be conscious. He or she has *minimal* consciousness and has *perceptual* consciousness. There is, nevertheless, a third sense, in which such a person may *still* "lack consciousness." Various cases may be mentioned here. My own favorite is the case of the long-distance truck driver. It has the advantage that many people have experienced the phenomenon.

After driving for long periods of time, particularly at night, it is possible to "come to" and realize that for some time past one has been driving without being aware of what one has been doing. The coming-to is an alarming experience. It is natural to describe what went on before one came to by saying that during that time one lacked consciousness. Yet it seems clear that, in the two senses of the word that we have so far isolated, consciousness was present. There was mental activity, and as part of that mental activity, there was perception. That is to say, there was minimal consciousness and perceptual consciousness. If there is an inclination to doubt this, then consider the extraordinary sophistication of the activities successfully undertaken during the period of "unconsciousness."

A purpose was successfully advanced during that time: that of driving a car along a road. This purpose demanded that various complex subroutines be carried out, and carried out at appropriate points (for instance, perhaps the brake or the clutch was used). Were not these acts purposeful? Above all, how is it possible to drive a car for kilometers along a road if one cannot perceive that road? One must be able to see where one is going, in order to adjust appropriately. It would have to be admitted, at the very least, that in such a case, eyes and brain have to be stimulated in just the same way as they are in ordinary cases of perception. Why then deny that perception takes place? So it seems that minimal consciousness and perceptual consciousness are present. But something else is lacking: consciousness in the most interesting sense of the word.

The case of the long-distance truck driver appears to be a very special and spectacular one. In fact, however, I think it presents us with what is a relatively simple, and in evolutionary terms relatively primitive, level of mental functioning. Here we have more or less skilled purposive action, guided by perception, but apparently no other mental activity, and in particular no consciousness in some sense of "consciousness," which differs from minimal and perceptual consciousness.

It is natural to surmise that such relatively simple sorts of mental functioning came early in the course of evolutionary development. I imagine that many animals, particularly those whose central nervous system is less developed than ours, are continually, or at least normally, in the state in which the long-distance truck driver is in temporarily. The third sort of consciousness, I surmise, is a late evolutionary development.

What is it that the long-distance truck driver lacks? I think it is an additional form of perception, or, a little more cautiously, it is something that resembles perception. But unlike *sense*-perception, it is not directed toward our current environment and/or our current bodily state. It is perception of the mental. Such "inner" perception is traditionally called introspection, or introspective awareness. We may therefore call this third sort of consciousness "introspective" consciousness. It entails minimal consciousness. If perceptual consciousness is restricted to sense-perception, then introspective consciousness does not entail perceptual consciousness.

Introspective consciousness, then, is a perception-like awareness of current states and activities in our own mind. The current activities will include sense-perception: which latter is the awareness of current states and activities of our environment and our body. And (an important and interesting complication) since introspection is itself a mental activity, it too may become the object of introspective awareness.

Sense-perception is not a *total* awareness of the current states and activities of our environment and body. In the same way, introspective consciousness is not a total awareness of the current states and activities of our mind. At any time there will be states and activities of our mind of which we are not introspectively aware. These states and activities may be said to be unconscious mental states and activities in one good sense of the word "unconscious." (It is close to the Freudian sense, but there is no need to maintain that it always involves the mechanism of repression.) Such unconscious mental states and

activities of course may involve minimal and/or perceptual consciousness, indeed the *activities* involve minimal consciousness by definition.

Just as perception is selective—not all-embracing—so it also may be mistaken. Perceptions may fail to correspond, more or less radically, to reality. In the same way, introspective consciousness may fail to correspond, more or less radically, to the mental reality of which it is a consciousness. (The indubitability of consciousness is a Cartesian myth, which has been an enemy of progress in philosophy and psychology.)

Following Locke, Kant spoke of introspection as "inner sense," and it is essentially Kant's view I am defending here. By "outer sense," Kant understood sense-perception. There is, however, one particular form of "outer sense" that bears a particularly close formal resemblance to introspection. This is bodily perception or *proprioception*, the perception of our own current bodily states and activities. If we consider the objects of sight, sound, touch, taste, and smell, then we notice that such objects are intersubjectively available. Each of us is capable of seeing or touching numerically the very same physical surface, hearing numerically the very same sound, tasting numerically the same tastes, or smelling numerically the same smell. But the objects of proprioception are not intersubjectively available in this way.

Consider, for instance, kinesthetic perception, which is one mode of proprioception. Each person kinesthetically perceives (or, in some unusual cases, misperceives) the motion of his own limbs and those of nobody else. There is no overlap of kinesthetic objects. This serves as a good model for, and at the same time it seems to demystify, the privacy of the objects of introspection. Each of us perceives current states and activities in our own mind and that of nobody else. The privacy is simply a little more complete than in the kinesthetic case. There are other ways to perceive the motion of my limbs besides kinesthetic perception—for instance, by seeing and touching. These other ways are intersubjective. But, by contrast, nobody else can have the direct awareness of my mental states and activities that I have. This privacy, however, is contingent only. We can imagine that somebody else should have the same direct consciousness of my mental states and activities that I enjoy. (They would not *have* those states, but they would be directly aware of them.)

Perception is a causal affair. If somebody perceives something, then it is involved in the perception; it is even involved in the concept of perception: that the thing perceived acts upon the perceiver, causing the perception of the object. If introspective consciousness is to be compared to perception, then it will be natural to say that the mental objects of introspection act within our mind so as to produce our introspective awareness of these states. Indeed, it is not easy to see what other naturalistic account of the coming-to-be of introspections could be given. If introspection is a causal process, then it will follow, incidentally, from our earlier definition of causal quiescence that whenever we are introspectively aware of one of our mental states, then that state is not at that time causally quiescent.

Types of Introspective Consciousness

Perhaps we still have not drawn enough distinctions. Sometimes the distinction is drawn between mere "reflex" consciousness, which is normally always present while we are awake (but which is lost by the long-distance truck driver), and consciousness of a more explicit, self-conscious sort.

This difference appears to be parallel to the difference between mere "reflex" seeing, which is always going on while we are awake and our eyes are open, and the careful *scrutinizing* of the visual environment that may be undertaken in the interest of some purpose we have. The eyes have a watching brief at all times that we are awake and have our eyes open; in special circumstances, they are used in a more attentive manner. (In close scrutiny by human beings, introspective consciousness is often, although not invariably, also called into play. We not only give the object more

attention but have a heightened awareness of so doing. But, presumably, in lower animals such attentive scrutiny does not have this accompaniment.) Similarly, introspective consciousness normally has only a watching brief with respect to our mental states. Only sometimes do we carefully scrutinize our own current state of mind. We can mark the distinction by speaking of "reflex" introspective awareness and opposing it to "introspection proper." It is a plausible hypothesis that the latter will normally involve not only introspective awareness of mental states and activities but also introspective awareness of that introspective awareness. It is in any case a peculiarly sophisticated sort of mental process.

What Is So Special about Introspective Consciousness?

There remains the feeling that there is something quite special about introspective consciousness. The long-distance truck driver has minimal and perceptual consciousness. But there is an important sense, we are inclined to think, in which he has no experiences, indeed is not really a person, during his period of introspective unconsciousness. Introspective consciousness seems like a light switched on, which illuminates utter darkness. It has seemed to many that with consciousness in this sense, a wholly new thing enters the universe.

I now will attempt to explain why introspective consciousness *seems to have*, but does not necessarily *actually* have, a quite special status in the world. I proceed by calling attention to two points, which will then be brought together at the end of the section.

First, it appears that introspective consciousness is bound up in a quite special way with consciousness of self. I do not mean that the self is one of the particular objects of introspective awareness alongside our mental states and activities. This view was somewhat tentatively put forward by Russell in *The Problems of Philosophy*

(1912, chapter 5), but had already been rejected by Hume and by Kant. It involves accepting the extraordinary view that what seems most inward to us, our mental states and activities, are not really us. What I mean rather is that we take the states and activities of which we are introspectively aware to be states and activities of a single continuing thing.

In recent years, we have often been reminded, indeed admonished, that there is a great deal of theory involved even in quite unsophisticated perceptual judgments. To see that there is a tomato before our body is already to go well beyond anything that can be said to be "given," even where we do not make excessive demands (such as indubitability) upon the notion of the given. Consider knowingly perceiving a tomato. A tomato, to be a tomato, must have sides and back, top and bottom, a certain history, certain causal powers; and these things certainly do not seem to be given in perception. If we consider the causal situation, it is only the shape, size, and color of some portions of the surface of the tomato (the facing portions) that actually determine the nature of the stimulation that reaches our eyes. This suggests that, at best, it is only these properties that are in any way "given" to us. The rest is, in some sense, a matter of theory, although I do not think that we should take this to mean that the perceptual judgment that there is a tomato before us is a piece of risky speculation.

It is therefore natural to assume that the perceptions of "inner sense" involve theory, involve going beyond the "given," in the same general way that the perceptions of "outer sense" do . In particular, whatever may be the case with other animals, or with small children, or with those who, like the Wild Boy of Aveyron, have not been socialized, for ordinary persons, their mental states and activities are introspected as the states and activities of a single thing.

Once again, the comparison with proprioception seems to be instructive. We learn to organize our proprioceptions so that they yield us perceptions of a single, unitary, physical object, our body, concerning which our proprioceptions give us certain information: its current posture, temperature, the movement of its limbs, and so on. This is clearly a theoretical achievement of some sophistication.

In the same way, we learn to organize what we introspect as being states of, and activities in, a single continuing entity: our self. Mere introspective consciousness, of course, is not at all clear just what this self is. At a primitive level perhaps, no distinction is made between the self and the body. Identification of the thing that is introspected as, say, a spiritual substance, or as the central nervous system, goes far beyond the level of theorizing involved in ordinary introspection. But the idea that the states and activities observed are states and activities of a unitary thing *is* involved. Introspective consciousness is consciousness of self.

If it is asked why introspection is theory-laden in this particular way, then an answer can be suggested. It is always worth asking the question about any human or animal organ or capacity: "What is its biological function?" It is therefore worth asking what is the biological function of introspective consciousness. Once the question is asked, then the answer is fairly obvious: it is to sophisticate our mental process in the interests of more sophisticated action.

Inner perception makes the sophistication of our mental processes possible in the following way. If we have a faculty that can make us aware of current mental states and activities, then it will be much easier to achieve *integration* of the states and activities, to get them working together in the complex and sophisticated ways necessary to achieve complex and sophisticated ends.

Current computer technology provides an analogy, though I would stress that it is no more that an analogy. In any complex computing operation, many different processes must go forward simultaneously: in parallel. There is need, therefore, for an overall plan for these activities, so that they are properly coordinated. This cannot be done simply in the manner in which a "command economy" is supposed to be run: by a series of instructions from above. The coordination can only be achieved if the portion of the computing space made available for administering the overall plan is continuously made "aware" of the current mental state of play with respect to the lower-level operations that are running in parallel. Only with this feedback is control possible. Equally, introspective consciousness provides the feedback (of a far more sophisticated sort than anything available in current computer technology) in the mind that enables "parallel processes" in our mind to be integrated in a way that they could not be integrated otherwise. It is no accident that fully alert introspective consciousness characteristically arises in *problem* situations, situations that standard routines cannot carry one through.

We now can understand why introspection so naturally gives rise to the notion of the self. If introspective consciousness is the instrument of mental integration, then it is natural that what is perceived by that consciousness should be assumed to be something unitary.

There is nothing necessary about the assumption. It may even be denied on occasion. Less sophisticated persons than ourselves, on becoming aware of a murderous impulse springing up, may attribute it not to a hitherto unacknowledged and even dissociated part of themselves, but to a devil who has entered them. In Dickens's *Hard Times*, the dying Mrs. Gradgrind says that there seems to be a pain in the room, but she is not prepared to say that it is actually *she* that has got it. In her weakened condition, she has lost her grip upon the idea that whatever she introspects is a state of one unitary thing: herself.

But although the assumption of unity is not necessary, it is one we have good reason to think true. A Physicalist, in particular, will take the states and activities introspected to be all physical states and activities of a continuing physical object: a brain.

That concludes the first step in my argument: to show that, and in what sense, introspective

awareness is introspective awareness of self. The second step is to call attention to the special connection between introspective consciousness and event-memory, that is, memory of individual happenings. When the long-distance truck driver recovers introspective consciousness, he has no memory of what happened while it was lacking. One sort of memory processing cannot have failed him. His successful navigation of his vehicle depended upon him being able to *recognize* various things for what they were and treat them accordingly. He must have been able to recognize a certain degree of curve in the road, a certain degree of pressure on the accelerator, for what they were. But the things that happened to him during introspective unconsciousness were not stored in his event-memory. He lived solely in the present.

It is tempting to suppose, therefore, as a psychological hypothesis, that unless mental activity is monitored by introspective consciousness, then it is not remembered to have occurred, or at least it is unlikely that it will be remembered. It is obvious that introspective consciousness is not sufficient for event-memory. But perhaps it is necessary, or at least generally necessary. It is notoriously difficult, for instance, to remember dreams, and it is clear that, in almost all dreaming, introspective consciousness is either absent or is at a low ebb.

So it may be that introspective consciousness is essential or nearly essential for event-memory, that is, memory of the past as past. *A fortiori*, it will be essential or nearly essential for memory of the past of the self.

The two parts of the argument now may be brought together. If introspective consciousness involves (in reasonably mature human beings) consciousness of self, and if without introspective consciousness there would be little or no memory of the past history of the self, the apparent special illumination and power of introspective consciousness is explained. Without introspective consciousness, we would not be aware that we existed—our self would not be self to itself. Nor would we be aware of what the particular history of that self had been, even its very recent history. Now add just one more premise: the overwhelming interest that human beings have in themselves. We can then understand why introspective consciousness can come to seem a condition of anything mental existing, or even of anything existing at all.

46   A Theory of Consciousness

David M. Rosenthal

A judicious division of labor often advances our understanding of things. This is no less true in the study of mind than in other areas of investigation. For example, because the intentional and sensory features of mental states differ radically, it is widely accepted that we will make progress by studying each kind of property independently of the other. Of course many mental phenomena, such as perceptual states and emotions, have both kinds of property; but other mental states exhibit only one of the two. And the difference between intentional and sensory character is so pronounced that the study of each raises problems unlike those encountered with the other. Pursuing independent investigations allow us to ignore the irrelevant problems.

Is a similar division of labor desirable in the case of consciousness? Can we profitably investigate consciousness independently of intentionality and sensory character? In particular, can we usefully separate the question of what it is for mental states to be conscious from the question of what it is for those states to have intentional or sensory character?

Some have held that when it comes to consciousness such a division of labor is not only undesirable; it is not even possible. On this view consciousness is intrinsic to being an intentional or sensory mental state; so one cannot understand what it is for states to have sensory or intentional character without knowing what it is for those states to be conscious. Nor, then, can we fully grasp what it is for a state to be a conscious state unless we understand why a state's being conscious is intrinsic to its having intentional or sensory character.

I shall argue that this view is mistaken, and that a separation of these questions is necessary to any satisfactory understanding of what it is for a mental state to be a conscious state. More specifically, I argue that if such consciousness were intrinsic to sensory or intentional character, no theoretical understanding of what it is to be a conscious state would be possible at all.

My argument proceeds in several steps. After drawing some preliminary distinctions in section I, I argue in section II that mental states can occur without being conscious. In section III, then, I show that if mental states were all conscious, or if being conscious were intrinsic to those states which are conscious, an informative explanation of such consciousness would be impossible. This provides a powerful reason to deny that being conscious is such an intrinsic property and, thus, to embrace the division of labor just described. I then show that accepting this division of labor paves the way for a natural and independently defensible theory of what such consciousness consists in. Section IV draws a distinction that points to this positive theory, which I develop and defend in sections V through VII.

I   Preliminary Distinctions

Two distinct issues are often run together in discussions of consciousness. One is the question of what it is for a mental state to be conscious. Assuming that not all mental states are conscious, we want to know how the conscious ones differ from those which are not. And, even if all mental states are conscious, we can still ask what their being conscious consists in. We can call this the question of state consciousness. This is my main concern in what follows.

But we not only describe mental states as being conscious or not; we also ascribe consciousness to creatures. So there is a second question, that of what it is for a person or other creature to be conscious, that is, how conscious creatures differ from those which are not conscious. We can call this the question of creature consciousness. No special puzzle exists about what it is for a creature not to be conscious; so in this case the contrast between being conscious and not being conscious is reasonably transparent. Accordingly, the answer to this question is tolerably clear, at least in rough outline: To be conscious, a person or other creature must be awake and sentient. Though this answer is schematic, it does tell us what a full account would have to look like.[1]

The questions about creature consciousness and state consciousness are plainly distinct. The property of a state's being conscious is different from that of a creature's being conscious. Indeed, since mental states are states of creatures, the properties of such states cannot be the same as the properties of creatures.

Issues about the two kinds of consciousness are of course not entirely independent. Perhaps being in conscious states implies that a creature is awake, and therefore conscious. And some might insist that the converse connection holds, perhaps because being sentient implies that at least some of one's sensory states are conscious.

Nonetheless, answers to one question will not help much with the other. Knowing that a creature's being conscious means that it is awake and sentient does not help us understand what it is for a mental state to be conscious, or place useful constraints on what such state consciousness consists in. Nor is there reason to think that a complete account of creature consciousness would help more. And even if creatures must themselves be conscious for their mental states to be conscious states, knowing what it is for mental states to be conscious would tell us little about creature consciousness.

Despite this, state consciousness and creature consciousness not only are seldom explicitly distinguished, but are often run together. Perhaps this is due in part to a natural tendency to speak of consciousness, rather than of something's being conscious. This seemingly innocuous shorthand encourages one to lose sight of the fact that there are two very different sorts of things we describe as being conscious, and hence which of the two is at issue. Intuitions that pertain to one of the two properties thus get invoked in support of claims about the other.

It will be helpful to draw a second preliminary distinction. When we pay deliberate attention to what mental state we are in, we are introspectively conscious of that state. This is different from the way in which mental states are conscious when we are not intentionally focusing on them. Introspection is attentive, deliberately focused consciousness of our mental states. It is relatively rare, and it is more elaborate than the way in which mental states are ordinarily conscious states. When we introspect, we are not only aware of what mental states we are in; we are aware of being thus aware. The difference between introspective and nonintrospective consciousness emerges vividly if we note that, when a state is nonintrospectively conscious, it normally has the potential to be an object of introspection; ordinary conscious states are normally introspectible. These differences form the basis of the argument I advance in section VI in support of my positive theory of state consciousness.

Consciousness is a notoriously puzzling topic. One way in which this is so has to do with how physical systems can be conscious, or how they can be in conscious states. We have a sense of ourselves that seems to make it difficult to understand how, as conscious selves, we could be located among the physical furniture of the universe.

But there is also an independent, and conceptually prior, sense of mystery simply about what consciousness is. This sense of puzzlement has to do mainly with the nonintrospective consciousness of mental states, rather than either creature consciousness or introspective consciousness. We know in general terms what it is for a creature to be conscious; it is conscious if it is awake and sentient. So there is no special mystery about what creature consciousness is.

By contrast, we lack even the sketch of a generally accepted answer to what kind of property the consciousness of mental states is. This lack of a schematic answer makes it difficult to say even what it could be for a mental state to be conscious. And the absence of even a general idea of what such consciousness consists in has led some to see it as a primitive, unanalyzable property of mental states. Moreover, the consciousness of mental states is often held to have a number of special features, such as transparency, immediacy, and epistemic privilege of one sort or another. These considerations strongly reinforce whatever initial sense of mystery we may have about the nature of state consciousness.

As with creature consciousness, there is no particular mystery about introspective consciousness. Introspection is the attentive, deliberately focused consciousness of our mental states. So whatever puzzles we have about its nature are not special to it. There may well be problems about attention, but those are not puzzles about consciousness, per se. If we understood what it is for a mental state to be conscious, we would have at least the outline of an account of introspective consciousness.

The first puzzle, about how a physical system could be in conscious states, is often discussed independently of the problem about what it is for a state to be conscious. But this puts the cart before the horse. Only if we first understand what a conscious state is can we determine whether there is a real problem about how physical objects could be in such states, and if so exactly what that problem is.

The consciousness of states is in a certain way intermediate between the other two phenomena involving consciousness. Since only conscious creatures can be in conscious states, but the mental states of a conscious creature may not all be conscious states, state consciousness presupposes creature consciousness. Similarly, all states of which we are introspectively aware are conscious states, though not conversely.

II Are All Mental States Conscious?

It is sometimes held that all mental states are conscious states, indeed, that part of what it is for a state to be a mental state is that it be conscious. This claim is central to the Cartesian concept of mind, and was forcefully articulated by both Descartes and Locke.[2] And even when it is not explicitly put forth, this idea figures centrally in the writing of many contemporary theorists.[3] Whether or not it is true may well be the most important and pressing question about the nature of mind and consciousness.

This issue is connected to the distinction between creature consciousness and state consciousness. It might be held that only conscious creatures can be in conscious mental states. Moreover, to be conscious a creature must be in at least some mental states; so if all such states were conscious, conscious creatures would perforce be in conscious states. A creature's being conscious would then be coextensive with its being in conscious states, and the distinction between the two would arguably be idle.

It is far from obvious, however, that all mental states are conscious. For one thing, our ordinary picture of mentality plainly allows room for mental states that are not conscious states. We sometimes see that somebody wants something or thinks that something is so before that person is at all aware of that desire or thought. Similarly with emotions; we will occasionally recognize that we ourselves are sad or angry only after somebody else points it out to us. Subliminal perception and peripheral vision remind us that perceptual sensations can occur without our being aware of them. It is arguable that even bodily sensations such as pains can at times go wholly unnoticed, and so can exist without being conscious. When one is intermittently distracted from a relatively minor pain or headache, it is natural to speak of having had a single, persistent pain or ache during the entire period. It would be odd to say that one had had a sequence of brief, distinct, but qualitatively identical pains or aches.

Despite these considerations, there does exist an intuitive temptation to hold that mental states are invariably conscious. This should not, however, lead us to conclude[4] that our commonsense concept of mind is irredeemably Cartesian. In part, this temptation is due to the tendency noted earlier to run together the consciousness of states with that of creatures. If a creature's being conscious coincided with its mental states' being conscious, all its waking mental states would be conscious states. And it is possible to deny that apart from dreams, whose nature is notoriously far from clear, we have any mental states while asleep.[5]

Whatever commonsense pull there is toward thinking that all mental states are conscious states may also result in part from our relative lack of interest in nonconscious mental states. Some kinds of nonconscious mental states do interest us, because they help us understand other people's behavior even when they are unaware of being in those states. Still, our concern with the mental states of others is set in a social context that largely precludes our remarking on mental states of which they are unaware. So we tend not to pay explicit or conscious attention to such states. And of course we normally disregard whatever nonconscious mental states we ourselves may be in.

Even more telling, the tie between mental states and their consciousness is stronger with some types of state than with others. And the more plausible it is to hold that a particular kind of mental state must be conscious, the less interest we would have in cases that are not conscious. This temptation is perhaps strongest with bodily sensations such as pains and tickles, less compelling with emotions, and very likely weakest with intentional states such as thoughts and desires. Correspondingly, we have the least interest in nonconscious bodily sensations, whether our own or anybody else's, and far the most in nonconscious beliefs and desires, because of their role in explaining behavior. This variable lack of interest in the nonconscious cases is very likely a major source of the intuition that at least some kinds of mental state are invariably conscious.

One might try to sustain the idea that all mental states are conscious by insisting that nonconscious states would be mere dispositions. Only occurrent states could qualify as genuine mental states and these, one might claim, would all be conscious.[6]

This suggestion conflates two ways of being dispositional. By 'dispositional mental state' one might mean a state that is simply a disposition to be in some occurrent mental state. But one might also mean a mental state whose nature we can usefully describe at least partly in dispositional terms. Being dispositional in the first way is incompatible with being occurrent, but being dispositional in the second way is not. Most states we describe dispositionally are dispositional in just this second way. Being flammable, for example, is both a disposition to burn and an occurrent, albeit possibly disjunctive, chemical property. Most mental states are like this. Since we detect nonconscious mental states by way of their dispositional connections to other things, we can assume that nonconscious mental states are dispositional in this second way. But that in no way implies that they are not also occurrent states.

Still, our intuitive reluctance to countenance nonconscious bodily sensations may persist. For one thing, we speak roughly interchangeably of feeling a pain or tickle or itch and of having the relevant sensation. And when we feel a pain or tickle or itch, is not that sensation automatically conscious?

Such terms as 'feeling' do carry this implication of consciousness; a felt pain is perforce a conscious pain. This is also true of something's hurting, and perhaps even of one's simply being in pain. But these things are not the same as having a pain, or a pain's existing. If we are intermittently unaware of a pain by being distracted from it, we feel the pain only intermittently; similarly with its hurting and our being in pain. Still, it is natural to speak of having had a pain that lasted throughout the day, and even to say that one was not always aware of that pain. This provides evidence that commonsense countenances the existence of nonconscious pains.[7] Feeling pains and having them seem equivalent only because of our lack of interest in the nonconscious cases.

We cannot of course know what it is like to have a nonconscious pain or tickle or itch.[8] But that is not relevant here. The reason we cannot know what it is like to have a nonconscious pain is simply that unless the pain is conscious there is no such thing as what it is like to have it. What it is like to be in pain, in the relevant sense of that idiom, is simply what it is like to be conscious of being in pain. None of this shows that nonconscious pains do not occur.

Reflection on what it is like to feel sensations does, however, suggest an important source for doubt about whether nonconscious sensations can occur. We classify sensory states and discriminate among their various tokens on the basis of what it is like for us to be in those states. This is true equally for bodily and perceptual sensations; we appeal to what it is like to be in pain and to what it is like to see red or hear a trumpet. And there is no such thing as what it is like to have these sensations unless the sensation is conscious.

One might conclude from this that there is no such thing as a sensation's having some distinctive sensory quality unless that sensation is conscious. If that were so, the very properties by reference to which we classify and discriminate among sensory states could occur only when those states are conscious. And if these qualities cannot occur except consciously, then plainly sensory states cannot either.

The premise of this argument is correct; we do classify and discriminate among sensory states by appeal to the conscious cases. But this hardly shows that the properties by reference to which we classify sensory states cannot occur nonconsciously. The distinctive qualities by means of which we type sensations form families of properties that pertain to color, visual shape, sound, and so forth. The members of these families resemble and differ from one another in ways that parallel the similarities and differences among the corresponding perceptible properties of physical objects. For example, the red sensory quality of visual sensations resembles the orange sensory quality of such sensations more than either re-

sembles the sensory green or blue of such sensations. The same holds for the distinctive qualities of pains. The qualities of being dull, stabbing, burning, or sharp resemble and differ in ways that reflect the similarities and differences among the corresponding physical objects and processes. Moreover, piercing and stabbing pains are both species of sharp pains, and typically result from piercing and stabbing objects or processes. Similarly, throbbing and pounding pains are species of dull pains.[9]

Sensory qualities are sometimes held to be problematic in some way that precludes this kind of account. Common sense does not support this. Sensory qualities are simply those properties in virtue of which we distinguish among our sensations. They are the properties in virtue of which sensory states differ from one another in respect of sensory content. We have access to these properties in the first instance by way of the conscious cases, but that by itself does not show that there is anything problematic about the properties themselves.

Nor is there reason to hold that these similarities and differences cannot obtain except when the sensation in question is conscious. So we have no basis to deny that sensory qualities can occur nonconsciously. The distinctive sensory properties of nonconscious sensations resemble and differ in just the ways that those of conscious sensations resemble and differ. They diverge only in that one group is conscious and the other not. We do rely on conscious sensations in typing sensory states. Indeed, we fix the extensions of our terms for the various kinds of sensation by way of the conscious cases, both our own and those of others. But this in no way shows that all sensory states are conscious states.[10]

Our goal is to understand and thereby disarm whatever intuitive doubts we have about whether mental states can occur nonconsciously. In addition to the concern we may have about sensory states specifically, doubts may also linger about mental states in general, whether sensory or intentional. And the foregoing considerations will not help with intentional states. Can we explain whatever temptation exists to hold that mental states generally cannot occur nonconsciously?

Perhaps the most important source of such temptation stems from our intuitive sense that mental phenomena are in some special way different from everything else. And being conscious may well seem to be the only way to demarcate the distinctively mental. The problem is pressing because no other single mark will do for all mental phenomena. Intentional and sensory properties constitute the most likely candidate; all mental states have one or the other. But mark neither covers all mental states, and the two kinds of property have so little in common that using them disjunctively may well seem artificial.[11]

Here again it will help to distinguish what fixes the extension of a term from those properties which hold of all the items in that extension. We can satisfy our need for a uniform mark of the mental by having a single property in terms of which we fix the extension of 'mental'. We need not also have a single property that all mental states exhibit. As a way of fixing this extension, consciousness very likely does provide a single mark of the mental. We fix the extension of 'mental' by way of conscious mental states, even though not all mental states are conscious.

Nonconscious mental states apart, there are commonsense reasons to prefer a mark of the mental based on intentional and sensory properties rather than consciousness. For one thing, the way we are aware of conscious mental states resembles the way we are aware of such bodily states and events as the positions of our limbs and perturbations of our viscera. In both cases our awareness is intuitively unmediated and strikingly unlike the way we may know about such states and events in others. So using consciousness as a mark of mental states may leave unexplained why those bodily states and events are not mental. Using intentional and sensory properties to demarcate the mental excludes such cases.[12]

Is a first-person perspective somehow essential to mental states? Is it impossible to grasp the na-

ture of those states from a third-person point of view? This seductive idea is sometimes invoked in support of the suggestion that being conscious is an inseparable aspect of what it is to be a mental state, or perhaps a mental state of a particular kind. Since the very existence of a first-person viewpoint depends on a state's being a conscious state, consciousness would then be intrinsic to its nature.[13]

But any serious theory of mental states must capture both their first-person and third-person dimensions, and do so without shortchanging either. If you feel pain or think that it's raining, your first-person viewpoint provides access to the very same states which I may know about from my third-person perspective. Since this third-person knowledge can be independent of those states' being conscious, consciousness cannot be essential to the state you may be able to grasp from your first-person point of view.

This conclusion does not diminish the importance of consciousness. We fix the extension of our terms not only for sensations but for mental states generally by reference to the conscious cases; so our first-person access to mental states figures in fixing those extensions. It does not follow that the first-person perspective is essential to the states thus determined.

Still, one might urge that without some essential tie to consciousness, the genuine intentionality of mental states would be indistinguishable from the merely derivative intentionality of speech.[14] It is far from clear that any such difference of status does distinguish the intentionality of thought from that of speech.[15] But we can in any case describe the distinction without reference to consciousness. The intentionality of speech is derivative, if at all, because speech acts are caused by mental states with the same content and a mental attitude parallel to the illocutionary force of the speech acts. Since mental states are not caused by anything that has the same content and mental attitude, their intentionality is in this way not derived.[16]

III   Can Consciousness Be Explained?

On balance, then, common sense rejects the claim that all mental states are conscious states. But there are also serious theoretical reasons to reject that claim. It turns out that if all mental states were conscious states, it would be impossible to give any nontrivial, informative explanation of the nature of state consciousness.

An explanation of what it is for mental states to be conscious either will itself appeal to mental states or it will not. Suppose now that all mental states are conscious, and that our explanation of what it is for mental states to be conscious does invoke mental states. Such an explanation will be circular, since the appeal to mental states is then automatically an appeal to conscious states. Invoking the very phenomenon we want to explain trivializes the explanation and prevents it from being informative.[17]

Alternatively, our explanation might appeal only to what is nonmental. Some mental phenomena can, perhaps, be fully explained in that way. To give such an explanation is, in effect, the project of naturalizing the mental.[18] Many would accept the possibility of an essentially nonmental explanation of what it is for states to have intentional properties, at least in the case of nonconscious intentional states. And given some such account as that sketched in the previous section, perhaps the same is true of sensory states as well.

But it is far less likely that we can successfully do this in any direct way with consciousness. Nothing in nonmental reality seems suited to explain what it is for a mental state to be conscious; as Thomas Nagel insists, the gulf between mental and physical seems unbridgeable primarily in respect of consciousness.[19] Moreover, the consciousness of mental states is the most sophisticated and difficult to understand of any mental phenomenon; so such consciousness is unlikely to yield directly to explanation in nonmental terms. Both intuitively and theoretically, the opposition between consciousness and matter seems to defy the possibility of directly explaining one in terms of the other.[20]

To those with Cartesian leanings, this picture will seem exactly right. We cannot explain consciousness in terms of what is not mental, and explaining consciousness in terms of conscious states will be trivial and uninformative. We must therefore acquiesce in our inability to give any genuine explanation of consciousness at all; at best we can render the phenomenon more intelligible by tracing the merely conceptual connections that hold among such cognate notions as mind, consciousness, subjectivity, viewpoint, first-person perspective, and self.[21]

But the dichotomy is false. Since mental states are not all conscious, there is a third strategy. We can explain what it is for mental states to be conscious by appeal to mental states that are not, themselves, conscious states. We bridge the intuitive gulf between consciousness and matter by explaining consciousness in terms of states that are mental, but not conscious.[22]

This strategy not only preserves the possibility of an informative explanation of consciousness; it also holds out hope for a naturalist account of mind. If we can explain consciousness by appeal to states that are mental but not conscious, perhaps we can in turn explain those nonconscious mental states in nonmental terms. This tiered picture would sustain naturalism. We still would not explain consciousness directly in nonmental terms, but the explanatory chain would reach nonmental reality by way of some nonconscious but mental intermediate. The intermediate step would dispel the apparent unintelligibility of explaining consciousness straightaway in nonmental terms.[23] Since it explains conscious states in terms of nonconscious mental states, moreover, this approach would vindicate the division of labor described at the outset. But naturalism is not the main issue here. Whatever the case about that, no nontrivial, informative explanation of state consciousness will be possible unless we reject the idea that all mental states are conscious.

As we have seen, the idea that all mental states are conscious is considerably more compelling with sensory states than with intentional states. So one might concede that nonconscious intentional states exist, but insist that nonetheless sensory states are all conscious. Nothing so far shows that this modified position would preclude an informative explanation of consciousness. So we might try to salvage this much of the Cartesian position.

Once we drop the idea that mental states are all conscious, what reason could we have to insist that all sensory states are? The considerations of section II suggest an answer: The distinctive sensory quality of sensory states can exist only if those states are conscious. If so, being conscious would be part of what it is to be a sensory state. It would be intrinsic to having sensory character, and thus intrinsic to being a sensation in the first place. Some such line of thought very likely underlies the idea that sensory states cannot occur nonconsciously.

A property is intrinsic if something's having it does not consist, even in part, in that thing's bearing some relation to something else. If being conscious is at least partly relational, a mental state could be conscious only if the relevant relation held between the state and some other thing. Because the other thing would be a distinct existence, it would be natural to conclude that being conscious is a contingent property of mental states; any particular conscious state could be the very same state and yet not be conscious. Some special reason would be needed to avoid that conclusion. So, if all sensory states were conscious, the best explanation of that generalization would be that being conscious is an intrinsic property of sensory states. Similarly with the more general claim that all mental states, of whatever sort, are conscious.

If mental states are all conscious states, we cannot explain what it is for mental states to be conscious. This difficulty also arises if being conscious is an intrinsic property of mental states, even if not all mental states are conscious.

No informative explanation of state consciousness is possible unless we can represent it as having some articulated structure. But it will be hard to justify the idea that being conscious is an intrinsic property of mental states if that property does have some informative structure. Once an explanation assigns such structure, it will be equally plausible to regard being conscious as an extrinsic property of mental states.[24] So the only reason to see consciousness as an intrinsic property of mental states will be that it lacks such structure, and is therefore simple and unanalyzable. And its being simple would effectively preclude our explaining it by appeal to anything else. Simple properties are those we take to be primitive in our hierarchies of explanation.[25]

The reason for insisting that being conscious is intrinsic to sensations is its supposed inseparability from sensory quality. On this view, the property of being conscious is not only intrinsic to sensations, but it is actually an intrinsic aspect of the qualitative properties that distinguish types of sensations.[26] This would mean the failure of the division of labor envisaged at the outset between sensory character and consciousness.

The inseparability of sensory quality and consciousness would also exacerbate the difficulty about simplicity. Not only would the property of being conscious be simple and unanalyzable; it would also include the relevant sensory quality. There seems no hope on this model for any useful, informative explanation of what it is for a sensory state to be conscious.

These considerations reinforce the earlier argument that no satisfactory explanation of state consciousness is possible if mental states are all conscious. Even if all mental states are indeed conscious, perhaps we cannot preclude the possibility of a noncircular explanation that appeals to conscious mental states, but not to the property of their being conscious (see note 17). Only if being conscious were an intrinsic property of mental states would we have reason to hold that mental states are invariably conscious. And it will be arbitrary to hold that being conscious is an intrinsic property unless that property lacks the articulated structure necessary for an informative explanation.

The idea that being conscious is an intrinsic property has strong intuitive appeal. A parallel may be useful. On the pre-Galilean idea, bodies move toward a natural resting place, and having a particular natural resting place is an intrinsic property of every kind of body. This conception is intuitively natural; it is inviting to see bodies as intrinsically tending toward upward or downward movement.[27] Still, we get vastly more accurate and powerful explanations of bodily motions if we see a body's tendency to move in terms of its relations to other bodies. Similarly, it is pretheoretically tempting to see the property of being conscious as intrinsic to sensations, or perhaps to all mental states. Nonetheless, it is only if we regard being conscious as a relational property that we can explain what such consciousness consists in.

IV Transitive and Intransitive Consciousness

To be able to explain what it is for a mental state to be conscious, we must reject the claim that all mental states are conscious as well as the related idea that being conscious is an intrinsic property. We must see consciousness as a property of only some mental states, and as a relational property of whatever states have it. Does any reasonable account of consciousness meet these conditions?

Putting creature consciousness to one side, we can distinguish two ways in which we use the word 'conscious'. One is when we speak of our being conscious of something. Because of the direct object, I shall call this the transitive use.

But we also apply the term 'conscious' to mental states, to say of them that they are conscious states. This is what I have labeled state consciousness. The lack of a direct object suggests calling this the intransitive use. This intransitive use figures only when talking about mental states, whereas we speak of being conscious, transitively, of mental and physical things alike. We may be transitively conscious of a stone or a symphony, or of a mental state.[28]

We want an account of what it is for mental states to be intransitively conscious on which that property is relational and not all mental states are conscious. The natural suggestion is to explain intransitive consciousness in terms of transitive consciousness. As a first try, we can say that a mental state is intransitively conscious just in case we are transitively conscious of it.[29]

Explaining intransitive by way of transitive consciousness would be circular if transitive consciousness were a type of state consciousness. But transitive consciousness can occur without intransitive state consciousness. One is transitively conscious of something if one is in a mental state whose content pertains to that thing—a thought about the thing, or a sensation of it. That mental state need not be a conscious state. And if, as is likely, mental states are possible during sleep, transitive consciousness will not even presuppose creature consciousness.

Explaining intransitive in terms of transitive consciousness squares reasonably well with our pretheoretic intuitions about what it is for a mental state to be conscious. Plainly, if a state is a conscious state, we are transitively conscious of it. But the converse claim requires a bit of qualification. One can be conscious of being in a mental state even when we would not count that state as being a conscious state. We regard mental states as conscious states only if we are transitively conscious of them in some suitably unmediated way.

Suppose I am angry, but unaware of it, and suppose that you see this from my behavior, and tell me. I trust your judgment, but still consciously experience no anger. In this case I am conscious that I am angry even though my anger is not a conscious state. Or suppose that I myself notice my angry behavior and infer that I am angry, but again experience no conscious feeling of anger.

These kinds of case require only a minor adjustment. We must specify that our transitive consciousness of our mental state relies on neither inference nor observation.[30] Mental states are intransitively conscious just in case we are non-inferentially and nonobservationally conscious of them.

Conscious states are states we are conscious of, without benefit of inference or observation. But suppose that inference can be nonconscious,[31] and that such inference sometimes figures in our becoming conscious of our mental states. Common sense would say these are cases of conscious states, but our excluding all reliance on inference rules them out.

The natural rejoinder is to require that conscious states be those we are intransitively conscious of without benefit of inference or observation in the ordinary sense. The trouble is that the natural way to understand that ordinary sense is circular; ordinary inference is conscious inference. The proposal about transitive and intransitive consciousness disarms this difficulty. Ordinary inference is inference of which we are transitively conscious. So conscious mental states are mental states we are transitively conscious of, but without relying on any inference or observation of which we are transitively conscious.

This proposal captures our commonsense intuitions. It also has the advantage, at least on the most natural construal, of providing a relational account of the property of being a conscious state. Bracketing the qualifications about inference and observation, a state is intransitively conscious if one is transitively conscious of it. And being transitively conscious so something is a relation that a person or other creature bears to that thing. Accordingly, a conscious mental state is a compound of two things: the mental state, which by itself is not conscious, and one's being transitively conscious of it. So being in the state and being transitively conscious of it are distinct, and the property of being conscious is not intrinsic to the state itself. The proposal thus avoids the problems raised earlier about explaining consciousness.

Care is necessary on this point. If by 'conscious state' one means the state, which as it happens is conscious, then the property of being conscious is not intrinsic to conscious states. But one might instead mean by 'conscious state' to refer to a state together with the property of its being conscious. Then being conscious is of course intrinsic to the state. Being intrinsic in this way is trivial, since one can in this way make any property intrinsic. It is also question begging, since only if one assumed that being conscious was intrinsic to conscious states would one use 'conscious state' in that way.

The distinction between transitive and intransitive consciousness also dispels one widespread reason for insisting that intransitive consciousness is an intrinsic property. Being conscious is often thought of as a reflexive property of conscious states, as though such states were somehow conscious of themselves. Ryle vividly captures this idea with his disparaging metaphors of conscious states as "self-intimating" or "self-luminous."[32]

It is doubtful that any states have the epistemic privilege that self-intimating states would presumably exhibit. But whatever the case about that, explaining what it is for a mental state to be conscious in terms of our being conscious of those states undercuts the metaphor of a state's being conscious of itself. Being transitively conscious of something is a relation that a person or other creature bears to that thing. So only creatures can be transitively conscious of things. A mental state may well be that state in virtue of which somebody is conscious of a thing, but the state cannot itself literally be conscious of anything.

One might object that being transitively conscious of things does not in general make them intransitively conscious. My being conscious of a stone does not make it conscious. What is relevantly different in the case of mental states? Why should being transitively conscious of such states make them conscious states?[33]

We must distinguish two ways of understanding the present proposal. Being transitively conscious of a mental state does in a sense make it intransitively conscious. But that is not because being conscious of a mental state causes that state to have the property of being intransitively conscious; rather, it is because a mental state's being intransitively conscious simply consists in one's being transitively conscious of it. The mistake here is to suppose that a state's being intransitively conscious is an intrinsic property of that state. If it were, then being intransitively conscious could not consist in one's being transitively conscious of being in that state unless being thus conscious induced a change in that state's intrinsic properties. This objection is at bottom just a disguised version of the doctrine that being intransitively conscious is an intrinsic property.

The foregoing considerations help explain the intuitive appeal of the idea that being conscious is an intrinsic property. For one thing, one-place predicates typically suggest nonrelational properties; so speaking of mental states as intransitively conscious doubtless encourages this picture. An even more telling point derives from the need for our transitive consciousness of conscious states to be independent of inference and observation. Because of this independence, we normally have no idea how we come to be conscious of those states and thus, on this proposal, no idea of why those states are intransitively conscious. Since we cannot trace this consciousness to anything, it can seem tempting to suppose that a state's being intransitively conscious is something intrinsic to the state itself.

It is tempting to suppose that consciousness reveals its own nature. How better, one might think, to learn about what being conscious consists in than from the very dictates of consciousness? And, since consciousness does not reveal itself as an extrinsic property of conscious states, can we not conclude that it is an intrinsic property? But the deliverances of consciousness are compatible both with its being an intrinsic property and with its being an extrinsic property. And there is no reason to think that if it were in fact intrinsic, that would help explain the intuitive appeal of the idea that it is intrinsic; the best ex-

planation of that intuition is that consciousness itself is mute about its own nature. Our intuition that it is intrinsic, therefore, is arguably idle. Indeed, if consciousness gave us privileged knowledge about what mental states we are in, it might still provide no special insight into its own nature.

V   A Theory of Consciousness

On the foregoing proposal, a mental state's being intransitively conscious is simply one's being transitively conscious of that state in a certain way. What kind of positive account might be given of how we are transitively conscious of our conscious mental states?

Cases of being conscious of things fall into two broad categories. One is perceptual; we are conscious of things when we see or hear them, or perceive them in some other way. The other way we are conscious of things has to do with thinking; when we think about something, we are conscious of that thing. Which of the two ways is needed here?

There are analogies between sense perception and the way mental states are conscious that may encourage the adoption of a perceptual model. For one thing, the various sense modalities each enable us to respond differentially to a distinctive range of stimuli. Because being conscious of our mental states is an ability to respond differentially to the mental states we are in, it may seem somewhat like a sense modality dedicated to mental states. For another thing, some sensory modalities exhibit a characteristic directness. The sensory mechanisms subserving taste, touch, proprioception, and enteroceptive perception enable each of these senses to operate without any intervening medium. Given the apparent immediacy of our consciousness of our mental states, these sense modalities may seem to be apt models for such consciousness.

These two analogies are important in the way we discriminate the several sensory modalities.

Each modality has a characteristic range of properties or stimuli to which it responds, and a characteristic sense organ or sensory mechanism by means of which it operates. But other commonsense intuitions suggest a perceptual model as well. Sensory quality and the consciousness of mental states both seem intuitively inexplicable, as though the two must somehow be emergent phenomena. That the two seem mysterious in similar ways may make it inviting to adopt a single model for both. Another apparent similarity is that the consciousness of our mental states seems to occur organized into a kind of field, somewhat like the fields that characterize the various sensory modalities.[34]

However, the perceptual model does not withstand scrutiny. Whereas a range of stimuli is characteristic of each sensory modality, mental states do not exemplify a single range of properties. Rather, as noted in section II, mental states exhibit intentional or sensory character, and these two have little in common; nor do the sensory qualities special to the various modalities resemble each other.[35] The other analogy fares no better. Doubtless some central neural process subserves our being conscious of our mental states, and presumably that process is responsible for the apparent immediacy in the way we are conscious of those states. But there is no reason to suppose that the operation of that process explains that apparent immediacy in anything like the way that the mechanisms of sensory modalities like touch and proprioception do explain the apparent immediacy of such perception.

The perceptual model fails even apart from these points. Perceiving something involves the occurrence of some sensory quality, which in standard circumstances signals the presence of that thing. If our being conscious of a mental state is like perceiving something, our being conscious of it will involve the occurrence of some mental quality; otherwise the analogy with perception will be idle.

What might that mental quality be? In the case of our being conscious of a sensory state, it is tempting to hold that the mental quality in virtue of which we perceive that state is the sensory quality of the sensation in question. But this answer is theoretically unmotivated. When we see a tomato, the redness of our sensation is not literally the same property as the redness of the tomato. If being conscious of a sensory state is like perceiving that state, why should the quality involved in our being conscious of that state be the same quality as that of the state itself? Moreover, this answer, by reducing the quality involved in our being conscious of a state to the quality of that state, in effect reduces our being conscious of the state to our simply having that state. But that results in consciousness being intrinsic to such states,[36] and the point of the perceptual model was to avoid that conclusion.

But, if being conscious of a mental state is like perceiving, there is no other remotely plausible candidate for the mental quality involved in being conscious of a sensory state.[37] The difficulty is even more acute with intentional states; being conscious of them seems plainly to involve no mental quality whatever. Moreover, even when the conscious state is sensory, it is the quality of that state we are conscious of; so how could the sensory quality of a higher-order state explain our being conscious of the lower-order quality? We must therefore reject the perceptual model of how we are transitively conscious of our conscious mental states.

Nor do the two intuitive factors help. As already argued, the mystery that seems to attend our mental states being conscious is due largely to our conceiving of such consciousness as an intrinsic property. And only when the states that are conscious occur in a sensory field does the consciousness seem to come organized in a field. In such cases as emotions and thoughts, the property of their being conscious resists being so located.

The other model for transitive consciousness, which relies on thinking, encounters no such difficulties. Thinking is not specific to a particular range of objects, and it involves no dedicated organ in the way sense modalities do. Moreover, the relation between thinking and its object is intuitively at least as unmediated as that between perceiving and the object of perception. Nor does having thoughts about things involve any characteristic qualities. It seems, therefore, that such a model provides the best hope for explaining what it is for mental states to be conscious in terms of our being conscious of those states.

We are conscious of something, on this model, when we have a thought about it. So a mental state will be conscious if it is accompanied by a thought about that states. The occurrence of such a higher-order thought (HOT) makes us conscious of the mental state; so the state we are conscious of is a conscious state. Similarly, when no such HOT occurs, we are unaware of being in the mental state in question, and the state is then not a conscious state. The core of the theory, then, is that a mental state is a conscious state when, and only when, it is accompanied by a suitable HOT.

Because being conscious of something is factive, using HOTs to explain the relevant transitive consciousness may seem less plausible than a perceptual model. After all, perceiving something is also arguably factive, whereas having thought is not. This should not lead one to adopt the perceptual model, however; if the relevant consciousness really is factive, we can stipulate that for our HOTs. In any case, there is good reason to doubt that the way we are conscious of our conscious mental states guarantees truth; special views about privileged access notwithstanding, we can and do make mistakes about what conscious states we are in.[38]

When a mental state is conscious, it is not simply that we are conscious of the state; we are conscious of being in that state. This places constraints on what the content of these HOTs must be; their content must be that one is, oneself, in that very mental state. Independent considerations point to the same conclusion. One cannot think about a particular mental-state token, as opposed to thinking simply about a type of mental state, unless what one thinks is that some in-

dividual creature is in that mental state. So HOTs will not be about mental-state tokens unless their content is that one is, oneself, in the mental state.[39]

How demanding are these requirements? One way to answer this is to see whether creatures without language can have such thoughts. Language is not required in order for a creature to be able to have any thoughts at all.[40] To have thoughts a command of some concepts is of course necessary. But those conceptual abilities need not be anything like as powerful as ours, nor need the concepts be nearly so fine grained. More important, a creature's thoughts need not be articulated into syntactic components. Just as people can deploy one-word sentences, so thoughts can occur without syntactic structure.

We would not, however, be warranted in interpreting a creature's behavior as the using of sentences or the expressing of thoughts unless we had reason to see that behavior as involving affirmation or denial. To do that we must be able to distinguish affirmations and denial in the creature's behavior, and perhaps other illocutionary acts as well. This suggests that the ability to have thoughts may depend more on a creature's being able to have some minimal variety of mental attitudes, such as believing and desiring, than on its having resources for fine-grained content with some compositionally articulated structure.

But is language necessary for a creature to have HOTs with the content required by the present theory? HOTs refer both to oneself and to one's mental states; can a nonlinguistic creature have thoughts with sufficiently sophisticated content? A minimal concept of self will suffice for reference to oneself; no more is needed than a concept that allows distinguishing between oneself and other things. Such a minimal concept need not specify what sort of thing the self is. Thus it need not imply that the self has some special sort of unity, or is a center of consciousness, or is transparent to itself, or even that it has mental properties.[41]

Nor is there reason to suppose that rich conceptual resources are necessary for a thought to refer to one's own mental states. We refer in thought to physical objects by way of their position in our visual field. It is natural to suppose that a thought can similarly refer to sensory states by way of their position in the relevant sensory field. In any case, conscious differentiation of sensory detail quickly outstrips one's conceptual resources; so some such means of referring to sensory states is necessary.

Doubtless one cannot thus refer in thought to all the sensory states to which richer conceptual resources would enable us to refer. Nor can one's HOTs refer in that way to intentional states that lack suitable perceptual content. Richer conceptual resources would thus expand the range of one's conscious states. Though this may initially seem surprising, on reflection it is plain that this happens in our own experience. Having more fine-grained conceptual distinctions often makes us aware of more fine-grained differences among sensory qualities. Vivid examples come from wine tasting and musical experience, where conceptual sophistication seems to generate experiences with more finely differentiated sensory qualities.

The term 'thought' sometimes has a generic sense, in which it applies to any propositional mental state, regardless of its mental attitude. On this construal, such diverse states as believing, hoping, expecting, desiring, wondering, and suspecting all count as thoughts. Will any propositional state make a mental state conscious, as long as it has the right content?

The requisite content is that one is, oneself, in a particular mental state. If one doubts or wonders whether one is in a particular mental state, or desires, hopes, or suspects that one is, that plainly will not make the state a conscious state.

Still, we often are conscious of things by virtue of such states as doubting and wondering. For example, if I doubt or wonder whether some physical object is red, I am conscious of the object; similarly if I expect, hope, or desire that it is. So perhaps if one doubts or wonders whether a mental state has some particular property, or hopes, desires, or expects that it does, one will thereby be conscious of the mental state.[42]

But it is not the doubt, wonder, hope, or desire that makes us conscious of the object. If I doubt whether that object is red, or desire or suspect that it is, I must at least think assertorically that the object is there. Similarly with doubting, hoping, or expecting that my mental state has some property; I must at least have the assertoric thought that I am in that state. Similarly, we must not suppose that these nonassertoric attitudes will make one conscious of one's being in that state unless having the attitude also leads one to have an affirmative thought that one is in that state.[43] The same holds of such states as anger and pleasure, when these are construed propositionally.

Nor will one's mental states be conscious if accompanied merely by a dispositional higher-order mental state. Being disposed to have a thought about something does not by itself make one conscious of it.[44] To be transitively conscious of something, therefore, we must have a thought about it in a relatively narrow sense: It must be an assertoric, occurrent propositional state.[45]

The HOT theory sustains in one direction the division of labor proposed at the outset. Being conscious and having sensory character are totally independent on this theory. Moreover, since being conscious is not intrinsic to intentional states, we can study intentionality independently of consciousness. And, although the HOT theory does presuppose that we understand intentionality, it remains neutral about the main issues that divide theorists about intentional states.

On the HOT theory, every conscious mental state is accompanied by a HOT about that state. This may seem hard to accept; after all, we are seldom aware of such HOTs. But the theory actually predicts that we would not be. A mental state is conscious only if it is accompanied by a HOT. So that HOT will not itself be a conscious thought unless one also has a third-order thought about the second-order thought. And if our second-order thought is not a conscious thought, we will be unaware of it. Only if one assumed that all mental states are conscious would one urge that being unaware of a state shows it is not there.

Given the multitude of conscious states we are in during most of our waking life, is it plausible to suppose we have such a great number of HOTs? We do, in any case, have very many thoughts that are not conscious. There are vast numbers of nonconscious first-order thoughts by means of which we negotiate our way trough the world and adjust both our plans and our conscious trains of thought. Why should there not also be a multitude of nonconscious HOTs? Moreover, we may need fewer than might at first appear. The content of HOTs may typically be reasonably specific for mental states that are near our focus of attention. But it is unlikely that this is so for our more peripheral states. For example, the degree of detail we are conscious of in our visual sensations decreases surprisingly rapidly as sensations get farther from the center of our visual field. It is natural to suppose that the content of one's HOTs becomes correspondingly less specific, and that a progressively smaller number of HOTs will refer to successively larger portions of the visual field.[46]

The nonconscious character of most HOTs leads, however, to another objection. HOTs are supposed to make the mental states they are about conscious. How can nonconscious HOTs do this? How can HOTs be a source of consciousness if they are not themselves conscious?[47]

This objection disregards the distinction between transitive and intransitive consciousness. HOTs confer intransitive consciousness on the mental states they are about because it is in virtue of those thoughts that we are transitively conscious of those mental states.

The situation emerges vividly when we consider a ceratin ambiguity of the phrase, 'state of consciousness'. A state of consciousnes can be a conscious state, that is, a state one is conscious of being in. Or it can be a mental state in virtue of which one is conscious of something. Adapting our terminology, we can call these intransitive and transitive states of consciousness, respectively. For a mental state to be conscious is for it to be a state one is conscious of being in. So a

HOT can be a source of consciousness for the mental state it is about because the HOT is a transitive state of consciousness; it does not also need to be an intransitive state of consciousness.

One might insist that this misunderstands the objection about a source of consciousness; such a source must be conscious in just the way conscious states are conscious. But without some independent substantiation, this claim begs the question at hand, since on the HOT theory a state's being intransitively conscious just is one's being transitively conscious of it in a suitable way. More important, the objection so understood is simply a version of the claim that we can have no noncircular explanation of state consciousness, since a satisfactory explanation would itself have to appeal to state consciousness.

But are transitive and intransitive states of consciousness really distinct in this way? Or must every transitive state of consciousness be an intransitive state of consciousness as well? Suppose I see or think about some physical object, and am thereby conscious of it. Must not my visual experience or thought be a conscious experience or thought?

The cases that come immediately to mind do indeed work that way, but often this connection does not hold. To make one's way when driving or walking somewhere, one must be visually conscious of many obstacles. But one may well be wholly unaware that one is conscious of those obstacles if, for example, one is immersed in conversation. Other cases abound. The so-called cocktail-party effect occurs when one screens out the sounds of conversations other than one's own. Still, if one's name is mentioned in a conversation one had screened out, one's attention immediately shifts to that conversation, showing that one must have had auditory consciousness of what was being said. Such cases do not immediatiely occur to us precisely because in these cases we are not aware of being conscious of these things.[48]

Perhaps one reason why the two notions often fail to be distinguished may be that all intransitive states of consciousness are also transitive states of consciousness. To be a conscious state implies being a mental state, and mental states are all states of being conscious of something or other. But the two notions still apply differently; although all intransitive states of consciousness are transitive states of consciousness, the converse does not hold.

Must the relationship between mental state and HOT be closer than mere accompaniment? In particular, must we postulate a causal connection between the two? It is natural to suppose that the mental state must in some way be implicated in causing the HOT. But requiring that the mental state be the principal factor in causing the HOT is very likely too strong.[49] For one thing, mere accompaniment is all one needs to spell out the proposal to explicate intransitive in terms of transitive consciousness. Moreover, it is not uncommon that a particular mental state is sometimes conscious and sometimes not. In these cases some causal factor other than the mental state must figure in explaining why the HOT does or does not occur. It is possible that the mental state does by itself cause the HOT while other factors, such as mental distractions, intermittently block that causal link. But we have no reason to prefer that model to one in which other factors, such as the mental state's immediate mental environment, contribute to causing the HOT.[50] In any case, since mere accompaniment suffices to explain our being conscious of our conscious states, we can remain noncommittal about the causal history of HOTs.

One motive for supposing that mental states will be implicated in causing HOTs is a desire for a mechanism to inhibit the occurrence of HOTs in the absence of the mental states they are about. But the occurrence of such HOTs in not a difficulty so long as they do not occur too often. Indeed, there is good reason to think that we sometimes in effect invent the mental states that we take ourselves to be in.[51] It is natural to interpret such confabulation as the occurrence of suitable HOTs in the absence of the mental states they purport to be about.

Strictly speaking, having a HOT cannot of course result in a mental state's being conscious if that mental state does not even exist. Our ordinary notion of transitive consciousness reflects this fact; since being conscious of something is factive, we cannot be conscious of something that is not there. Still, a case in which one has a HOT along with the mental state it is about might well be subjectively indistinguishable from a case in which the HOT occurs but not the mental state. If so, folk psychology would count both as cases of conscious states.

It is sometimes argued that one can do justice to our pretheoretic intuitions about consciousness only on the assumption that being conscious is intrinsic to mental states. This is not so. The HOT theory can save the phenomenological appearances at least as well as one can by assuming that consciousness is an intrinsic property, and very likely more successfully. Several examples will illustrate this.[52]

When we focus on a particular conscious state, what we focus on is the state we are conscious of; it is notoriously difficult to isolate that aspect of the situation in which its being conscious consists. The consciousness of mental states is somehow transparent, or diaphanous.[53] The idea that consciousness is intrinsic seems superficially to help; perhaps it would be hard to isolate the property of being conscious if that property were intrinsic to the state itself. We get a more satisfactory explanation from the HOT theory. A conscious state's being conscious consists in there being an accompanying HOT. Since that HOT is not usually a conscious thought, we normally are unaware of anything that could count as the property of the mental state's being conscious.

A strong intuitive connection obtains between being in a conscious state and being conscious of oneself. Again, the idea that consciousness is intrinsic may seem to help, by implying some sort of self-reference. This is a confusion. If being conscious were intrinsic to mental states, perhaps those states would refer to themselves, but what is needed is reference to the self, which is different.

Again, the HOT theory explains the phenomenon more successfully, since one's HOTs must refer to oneself.

Sometimes the idea that being conscious is intrinsic to mental states makes it actually harder to save the appearances. Some mental states seem to be conscious only some of the time, largely through shifts in attention; examples considered earlier are pains or auditory sensations from which we are temporarily distracted. It is doubtful that we can explain such shifts between a state's being conscious and not being conscious if the property of being conscious is intrinsic to those mental states which are.[54]

There are, finally, phenomena that seem to point directly to the HOT theory, with which no other theory could deal at all. One has to do with sensory qualities, which supposedly lend intuitive support to the idea that consciousness is intrinsic. As noted earlier in this section, we are often aware of more fine-grained differences among sensory qualities when we have more fine-grained conceptual distinctions. The HOT theory predicts this. The degree to which we are conscious of differences among sensory qualities is a function of how fine-grained the concepts are that figure in our HOTs. It is difficult to see how a theory that does not rely on HOTs could explain this role that concepts have.[55]

As noted at the end of section IV, we can explain the apparent force of the idea that being conscious is intrinsic to conscious states as due to our normally having no idea how we come to be conscious of them. The HOT theory enables us to expand on that explanation. Because the HOTs are typically not conscious thoughts, we are unaware of what the consciousness of our mental states consists in. This not only makes the property of being conscious seem diaphanous; it also makes it tempting to hold that such consciousness is intrinsic to those states. The sense that a state is inseparable from our consciousness of it may be further strengthened by the reference the HOT makes to that state. But this inseparability is of course merely notional; it is the inseparability

of a thought from its object. So it cannot help show that being conscious is intrinsic to mental states.

VI   The Argument from Introspection

In closing I turn briefly to two arguments that provide independent support for the HOT theory. As noted in section I, introspection involves more than a mental state's being a conscious state. Introspecting a mental state is deliberately and attentively focusing on that state. Nonintrospective consciousness, by contrast, requires no special act of attention. Every introspected state is therefore a conscious state, but not conversely.

Mental states are conscious just in case they are introspectible.[56] All and only conscious states can become subjects of introspective consciousness by a more or less deliberate shift of attention. This equivalence of being conscious with being introspectible may lead to eliding the difference between introspective and nonintrospective consciousness.

If a mental state's being conscious consists in our being conscious of being in that state, what more occurs when we introspect that state? Focusing on a mental-state token means focusing on somebody's being in that state; so introspecting one's own mental state implies deliberately focusing on one's being in that state. And that involves not merely being conscious of being in that state, but being actually aware that one is thus aware. Introspection is a kind of higher-order consciousness; it is the transitive consciousness of being conscious of one's mental states.[57]

The HOT theory readily accounts for the difference between introspective and nonintrospective consciousness. A mental state is non-introspectively conscious when accompanied by a relevant HOT; introspection occurs when there is a third-order thought that makes the second-order thought conscious. Introspective consciousness is the special case of conscious states in which the accompanying HOT is itself a conscious thought.[58]

HOTs are sometimes invoked to explain introspective consciousness; introspecting a mental state is, on such an account, one's having an accompanying thought about that state.[59] But when we introspect a mental state, the HOT that accompanies the state is always conscious; we are conscious of thinking about that state. The idea that introspection consists simply in having HOT about the introspected state must thus rely on the tacit assumption that HOTs are all conscious. So that view would seem plausible only if one already held that mental states are automatically conscious.

In any case, the idea that HOTs can explain introspection seems to many to be more intuitively compelling than the proposal that HOTs can explain nonintrospective consciousness. Conscious HOTs may seem to provide a more intuitively satisfactory explanation of introspection that HOTs, of whatever sort, can provide of nonintrospective consciousness.

Nonetheless, the idea that we should explain introspection by appeal to conscious HOTs actually provides the basis of an argument for the HOT explanation of nonintrospective consciousness. There is more to being a mental state's being introspectively conscious than to its just being nonintrospectively conscious. Similarly, there is more to being nonintrospectively conscious than to not be conscious at all. So nonintrospectively conscious states are intermediate between introspected mental states and those which are simply not conscious.

Introspected states are accompanied by conscious HOTs. And nonconscious mental states are presumably unaccompanied by HOTs, whether conscious or not. What can we say of nonintrospectively conscious states that preserves their intermediate status between introspected states and nonconscious states? The natural answer is that they are accompanied by HOTs, but unlike the introspective case those HOTs are not conscious thoughts.

The only alternative is that nonintrospective consciousness consists instead in a disposition for a conscious HOT. A dispositional account would represent such consciousness as intermediate between introspected and nonconscious mental states, and might at the same time capture the equivalence of being nonintrospectively conscious and being introspectible.

This is hardly satisfactory. For one thing, there is no reason to adopt this view save the unfounded insistence that all mental states are conscious states. And as noted earlier, it is unclear how being disposed to have a HOT could make one conscious of one's mental states. In any event, because being disposed to have a conscious thought is the same as having that thought without its being conscious, the putative alternative very likely reduces to the HOT theory itself.

VII The Argument from Reporting and Expressing

Brentano held that all mental states are, in part, about themselves: All mental acts, he wrote, "apprehend [themselves,] albeit indirectly" (p. 128). His reason was that that there is no difference between the mental act of, say, perceiving or thinking something, and the mental act of thinking that one so perceives or thinks. Since mental states are individuated by way of the mental act involoved, HOTs are indistinguishable from the mental states they are about (pp. 127–128). The property of being conscious is thus intrinsic to mental states.

It is not easy to know what to make of Brentano's notion of a mental act. But in any case the two nemtal acts are not indistinguishable. The thought that it's raining does have the same mental analogue of performance conditions as the thought that I think it's raining. There is no difference between the circumstances in which it would be appropriate to think the two things. Still, the two have distinct truth conditions.[60] And, if the lower-level state is anything other than an assertoric propositional state, the mental attitudes of the two will differ as well. Identity of performance conditions does not imply identity of intentional acts.

These considerations suggest another argument for the HOT theory. Reporting one's mental states is distinct from verbally expressing those states. Suppose I have the thought that it's raining. I can report that thought by saying that I think that it's raining, thereby explicitly telling you about my thought. Or I can instead verbally express the thought, without referring to it, by saying simply that it's raining.

As with Brentano's argument, it is crucial to distinguish performance conditions from truth conditions. The speech acts of saying that it's raining and saying that I think it's raining are indistinguishable with respect to performance conditions. But they are different in truth conditions. And though the speech act of asking whether it's raining would have the same performance conditions as the speech act of saying that I ask, the two are distinct not only in truth conditions, but in illlocutionary force as well.

Reporting, moreover, has a special connection to consciousness. If we restrict attention to creatures with the relevant linguistic ability, a mental state is conscious if, and only if, one can report being in that state. I cannot tell you about my mental states if I am not conscious of them, and given the requisite linguistic capacity, I can tell you about those I am conscious of.[61] Every sincere, meaningful speech act, finally, expresses a propositional state with the same content and a mental attitude analogous to the illocutionary force of the speech act. I cannot meaningfully and sincerely say it's raining unless I have the assertoric thought that it's raining.[62]

When I report being in a mental state, therefore, my speech act expresses my HOT that I am, myself, in that very mental state. The ability to report a mental state is thus the same as the ability to express the very thought posited by the HOT theory. So a mental state is conscious if, and only

if, one can express a suitable HOT about that state.

The best explanation of our ability to express these HOTs about all our conscious states is that our conscious states are actually accompanied by such HOTs. Similarly, we can best explain our inability to report mental states when they are not conscious by assuming that we lack the relevant HOTs. The HOT theory therefore provides the best explanation of our ability to report mental states if, and only if, they are conscious states.[63]

Any theory of conscious mental states must do justice to our pretheoretic intuitions. The Cartesian doctrines that all mental states are conscious and that being conscious is an intrinsic property of mental states make explaining such consciousness impossible. So it is a reasonable goal to reject those claims if we can still do justice to our intuitions. That the HOT theory provides our best hope of doing this, and also receives support from independent arguments, gives us good reason to adopt it as a working hypothesis.[64]

Notes

1. Thus creatures are conscious only for various periods of time. Describing creatures as conscious may also mean just that unlike stones, for example, they have the capacity to be awake and sentient. I reserve 'creature consciousness' for occurrent consciousness, rather than this extended notion.

2. Perhaps Descartes's clearest remarks are that "no thought can exist in us of which we are not conscious at the very moment it exists in us" (*Fourth Replies, Oeuvres de Descartes*, ed. Charles Adam and Paul Tannery, Paris: J. Vrin, 1964–75 [henceforth *AT*] VII, 246); and "the word 'thought' applies to all that exists in us in such a way that we are immediately conscious of it" (Geometrical Exposition of the *Second Replies, AT* VII, 160). See also *First Replies, AT* VII, 107, letter to Mersenne, December 31, 1640, *AT* III, 273, *Fourth Replies, AT* VII, 232, and *Principles* I, ix, *AT* VIII–1, 7. (Translations of Descartes are mine; *AT* volume and page numbers can be found in *The Philosophical Writings of Descartes*, translated by John Cottingham,

Robert Stoothoff, and Dugald Murdoch, 3 volumes, Cambridge: Cambridge University Press, 1984–91.) Cf. Locke's rather compressed remark that "thinking consists in being conscious that one thinks" (*Essay* II, i, 19); see also *Essay* II, i, 10–12 and IV, vii, 4 for somewhat clearer versions.

3. Even writers with explicitly anti-Cartesian views. Thus J. C. C. Smart, for example, holds that "[t]o say that a process is an ache is simply to classify it with other processes that are felt to be similar" ("Materialism," *The Journal of Philosophy* 60, 22 [October 24, 1963]: 651–62, p. 655).

On the Cartesian assumptions of contemporary mind-body materialists, see my "Mentality and Neutrality," *The Journal of Philosophy* 73, 13 (July 15, 1976):386–415.

4. With Stuart Hampshire, "Critical Notice of *The Concept of Mind*, by Gilbert Ryle," *Mind* 59, 234 (April 1950):237–225; and Richard Rorty, "Incorrigibility as the Mark of the Mental," *The Journal of Philosophy* 67, 12 (June 25, 1970):399–424, p. 406, fn. 11.

5. For a useful study, see Daniel C. Dennett, "Are Dreams Experiences?," *The Philosophical Review* 73, 2 (April 1976):151–171.

6. I am grateful to Ernest Sosa for having put this idea especially forcefully.

7. One could insist here that only a single, temporally discontinuous state of pain occurs, on the model of the temporally discontinuous bursts of sound as a single siren sound. (I owe this idea to Jaegwon Kim.) But all the argument here needs is that common sense be open to nonconscious pains, and it is doubtful that common sense countenances single, temporally discontinuous pains.

8. See Thomas Nagel's important article, "What Is It Like To Be a Bat?", *The Philosophical Review* 83, 4 (October 1974):435–450; and chapter 32 of this book. See also Nagel's "Panpsychism," in *Mortal Questions*, Cambridge: Cambridge University Press, 1979, pp. 181–195, and *The View From Nowhere*, chapters 1–4, New York: Oxford University Press, 1986.

9. I develop and defend this claim in "Armstrong's Causal Theory of Mind," in *Profiles: David Armstrong*, ed. Radu J. Bogdan, Dordrecht: D. Reidel Publishing Co., 1984, pp. 79–120, section V: pp. 100–108; in my review of *Perception: A Representative Theory*, by Frank Jackson, *The Journal of Philosophy* 82, 1 (January 1985):28–41; and in "The Colors and Shapes of Visual Experiences," Report No. 28/1990, Center for Interdisciplinary Research (ZiF), Research Group on Mind and Brain, University of Bielefeld.

10. For the notion of fixing extensions, see Saul A. Kripke, *Naming and Necessity*, Cambridge, Mass.: Harvard University Press, 1980, pp. 54–159; "Identity and Necessity," in *Identity and Individuation*, ed. Milton K. Munitz, New York: New York University Press, 1971: pp. 135–164, pp. 156–161; and Hilary Putnam "The Meaning of 'Meaning'," in Putnam's *Philosophical Papers*, vol. 2 (Cambridge: Cambridge University Press, 1975): pp. 215–271, pp. 223–35. Both Kripke and Putnam maintain that, in general, what fixes the extension of a term need not coincide with what is essential or necessary to the things in that extension. See, however, note 26.

11. For this kind of argument, see Rorty, "Incorrigibility as the Mark of the Mental," pp. 409, 412.

12. We could also exclude them by insisting that, unlike the mental case, our intuitively immediate access to them relies on observation. But such a stipulation would in this context be ad hoc.

13. For such claims about the first-person perspective and viewpoint, see Nagel, *op. cit.*; John R. Searle ("Indeterminacy, Empiricism, and The First Person," *The Journal of Philosophy* 84, 3 [March 1987]:123–146; "Consciousness, Explanatory Inversion, and Cognitive Science," *The Behavioral and Brain Sciences* 13, 4 (1990):585–696; and *The Rediscovery of the Mind*, Cambridge, Mass.: MIT Press, 1992, esp. chapter 7; and Colin McGinn, *The Problem of Consciousness*, Oxford: Basil Blackwell, 1991.

14. Searle defends a version of this claim in "Consciousness, Explanatory Inversion and Cognitive Science" and in "Consciousness, Unconsciousness and Intentionality." On the idea that the intentionality of speech is merely derived, see Searle, *Intentionality: An Essay in the Philosophy of Mind* (Cambridge: Cambridge University Press, 1983). See also Zeno Vendler, *Res Cogitans* (Ithaca: Cornell University Press, 1972).

15. See Dennett, "Evolution, Error, and Intentionality," chapter 8 of his *The Intentional Stance*, Cambridge, Mass.: MIT Press/Bradford Books, 1987.

16. See my "Intentionality," *Midwest Studies in Philosophy* 10 (1986):151–184.

17. Things are actually a bit more complicated. Such an explanation can refer to conscious states without being circular if it does not rely on the property of their being

conscious; perhaps only other properties of conscious states are relevant to explaining what it is for states to be conscious. (I am grateful to Frances Egan for insisting on this.) But it will be difficult, if possible at all, to disarm a skeptic's charge that relying on conscious states harbors a tacit appeal to the property of being conscious.

18. See, for example, Dennett, *The Intentional Stance*, especially "Evolution, Error, and Intentionality"; and Jerry A. Fodor, *Psychosemantics*, Cambridge, Mass.: MIT Press/Bradford Books, 1987, esp. chapter 4.

19. "What Is It Like To Be a Bat?", *op. cit.* p. 435; also chapter 32, this book.

20. The difficulty here, and in what follows, affects only the nonintrospective consciousness of mental states; there is no difficulty about explaining introspection in terms of nonintrospective consciousness. See section VI.

21. Such acquiescence is not uncommon; see, for example, Nagel and McGinn. Nagel explicitly insists that any satisfactory account must be based on a full conceptual analysis ("What Is It Like To Be a Bat?," *op. cit.*, pp. 436–437; also chapter 32, this book.

Such acquiescence also occurs in those who take Cartesian ideas about consciousness to support an eliminativist position. See Georges Rey, "A Question about Consciousness," in *Perspectives on Mind*, ed. H. R. Otto and J. A. Tuedio, Dordrecht: D. Reidel Publishing Company, 1986, pp. 5–24; and to some extent Kathleen V. Wilkes, *Real People: Personal Identity Without Thought Experiments*, Oxford: Oxford University Press, 1988, chapter 6.

22. One version of this gulf has to to do with how creatures with the capacity to be in conscious states could have evolved from nonmental organisms. One might speculate that this capacity relied on the intermediate capacity to be in nonconscious mental states.

23. Compare trying to explain cell mitosis by appealing directly to the laws of particle physics.

24. Franz Brentano's idea that a mental state's being conscious is due to its being in part about itself is a rare attempt to assign informative structure to state consciousness, conceived of as an intrinsic property. (*Psychology from an Empirical Standpoint*, tr. Antos C. Rancurello, D. B. Terrell, and Linda L. McAlister [London: Routledge & Kegan Paul, 1973], pp. 129–130.) But he gives no reason to sustain his insistence that this awareness of conscious mental states is intrinsic to those states. Other difficulties for Brentano's view are noted in section VII.

25. Thus, mental properties aside, we generally regard properties as truly simple only in sciences such as particle physics, whose properties we think cannot be explained, but must be taken for granted.

It is striking that even Freud saw consciousness as in this way simple. Moreover, he explicitly accepted the consequence that we could give no explanation of it. Freud did maintain that "[l]ike the physical, the psychical is not necessarily in reality what it appears to us to be." ("The Unconscious," in *The Complete Psychological Works of Sigmund Freud*, tr. and ed. James Strachey, London: The Hogarth Press, 1966–74, vol. 14: pp. 166–215, p. 171.) But while he countenanced unconscious intentional states, he denied that feelings can strictly speaking be unconscious (*The Ego and the Id*, *Works*, vol. 19: pp. 3–68, pp. 22–23). Perhaps for this reason, he insisted that consciousness is a "unique, indescribable" quality of mental states ("Some Elementary Lessons," *Works*, vol. 23: pp. 279–286, p. 282), and that "the fact of consciousness" "defies all explanation or description" (*An Outline of Psycho-Analysis*, *Works*, vol. 23: pp. 141–208, p. 157).

26. Thus Kripke urges that the way pains appear to us cannot diverge from how they really are: "For a sensation to be *felt* as pain is for it to *be* pain" ("Identity and Necessity," p. 163, n. 18; author's emphasis throughout) and, conversely, that "for [something] to exist without being *felt as pain* is for it to exist without there *being any* pain" (*Naming and Necessity*, p. 151). Thus "[i]f any phenomenon is picked out in exactly the same way that we pick out pain, then that phenomenon *is* pain" (*Naming and Necessity*, p. 153).

These claims lead Kripke to his famous insistence that what fixes the extension of the term 'pain' must coincide with what is essential to the items thereby picked out ("Identity and Necessity," pp. 157–161; *Naming and Necessity*, pp. 149–154). But this is so only if it is necessary that pains affect us in the way they do, that is, only if being conscious is intrinsic to pains. Kripke gives no independent reason to accept these claims.

27. Similarly, Michael McCloskey has elegantly and convincingly argued that commonsense predictions about bodily motions systematically err in ways that reveal the tacit assumption that those motions are due to an internal force imparted by the source of motion. ("Intuitive Physics," *Scientific American* 248, 4 [April 1983]:114–122.)

28. I use interchangeably the notions of being conscious of something and being aware of it.

We of course speak also of creature consciousness intransitively, but in that case there is no distinction to mark between transitive and intransitive.

29. This proposal is a substantive hypothesis about what intransitive consciousness is, not a recommendation about how to conceive of it. The goal is to explain our ordinary folk-psychological notion of a mental state's being a conscious state in terms of our being conscious of that state.

30. Including proprioception and enteroceptive perception as well as ordinary exteroceptive perception. Perhaps whenever our transitive consciousness relies on observation it also relies on inference; I rule out both so as to remain neutral on that question.

31. See, for example, Gilbert Harman, *Thought*, Princeton: Princeton University Press, 1973, especially chapters 1 and 2; and Irvin Rock, *The Logic of Perception*, Cambridge, Mass.: MIT Press/Bradford Books, 1983, esp. chapter 9.

32. Gilbert Ryle, *The Concept of Mind* (London: Hutchinson and Company, 1949), pp. 158, 159.

33. I am grateful to Peter Bieri and Fred Dretske for forcefully advancing this objection.

34. For more on the analogy between sense perception and consciousness, see D. M. Armstrong, "What is Consciousness?," *Proceedings of the Russellian Society* (1978), reprinted in his *The Nature of Mind*, St. Lucia, Queensland: University of Queensland Press, 1980, pp. 55–67, especially pp. 60–62; and *A Materialist Theory of the Mind*, New York: Humanities Press, 1968, pp. 94–107, 323–338. See also D. H. Mellor, "Conscious Belief," *Proceedings of the Aristotelian Society*, New Series, 88 (1977–78):87–101, pp. 98–100; and "Consciousness and Degrees of Belief," *Prospects for Pragmatism*, ed. D. H. Mellor (Cambridge: Cambridge University Press, 1980): pp. 139–173.

35. According to Armstrong, all mental properties are intentional, so on his account the perceptual analogy may not face this particular difficulty. But it is doubtful whether perceptual states can be satisfactorily explained by way of intentional properties. See my "Armstrong's Causal Theory of Mind," section V.

36. There is another way in which the perceptual model seems to suggest that being conscious is intrinsic. Since perceiving depends on a dedicated organ or mechanism, the perceptual model raises the question of what special organ or mechanism subserves being conscious of one's mental states. The absence of any such organ or mechanism may tempt one to conclude that being conscious must be something internal to conscious states.

37. The difficulty is reminiscent of Aristotle's concern about whether or not the sense we use to see that we see is the same as the sense of sight (*de Anima* III 2, 425b13–4). Aristotle concludes that it is, since otherwise the sense of sight and the other sense would both have color as their proper object, and no two distinct senses can share the same proper object.

38. See below, especially note 51.

39. Only if one's thought is about oneself as such, and not just about someone that happens to be oneself, will the mental state be a conscious state. Otherwise it might turn out in any particular case that the state was a state of somebody else instead. For this special sort of reference to oneself, see, for example, G. E. M. Anscombe, "The First Person," in *Mind and Language*, ed. Samuel Guttenplan (Oxford: Oxford University Press, 1975), pp. 45–65; Hector-Neri Castañeda, "On the Logic of Attributions of Self-Knowledge to Others," *The Journal of Philosophy* 65, 15 (August 8, 1968), 439–456; Roderick M. Chisholm, *The First Person* (Minneapolis: University of Minnesota Press, 1981), chapters 3 and 4; David Lewis, "Attitudes *De Dicto* and *De Se*," *The Philosophical Review* 88, 4 (October 1979):513–543; and John Perry, "The Problem of the Essential Indexical," *Nous* 13, 1 (March 1979), 3–21.

40. *Pace* Donald Davidson ("Thought and Talk," in *Mind and Language*, ed. Samuel Guttenplan, Oxford: Oxford University Press, 1975, pp. 7–23). Davidson argues that believing something presupposes understanding the difference between believing truly and believing erroneously, and that only language provides a context in which that distinction can take hold. His arguments seem better adapted, however, to showing that what the distinction between truth and error is necessary for is our having the concept of belief, and it is far from obvious that having beliefs presupposes having the concept of a belief. Moreover, though language and its interpretation may well presuppose the distinction between believing truly and erroneously, the converse is far less clear.

41. Moreover, it is probable that being nonobservational will ensure that HOTs refer to oneself in the way suggested in note 20.

To illustrate such a minimal idea of oneself, I once proposed that each HOT could refer to the self as whatever individual has that very HOT. The content of HOTs would then be that whatever individual has this very thought is in that very mental state ("Two Concepts of Consciousness," *Philosophical Studies* 49, 3 [May 1986]: 329–359, p. 344). Thomas Natsoulas assumes that a self-referential thought is automatically self-intimating, and infers that since HOTs thus construed are about themselves, they would make themselves conscious. He also supposes that I would accept this inference ("An Examination of Four Objections to Self-Intimating States of Consciousness," *The Journal of Mind and Behavior* 10, 1 [Winter 1989]:63–116, pp. 70–72).

It is worth stressing that I disavow the idea that HOTs are ever self-intimating, and also reject the inference from mere self-reference to a thought's being self-intimating. Plainly an intentional state could refer to itself and yet not be conscious. To be conscious, an intentional state one is in would, in any case, have to affirm that one is, oneself, in that very state (see section V). On my earlier proposal, the HOT does not say of an independently identified self that it has that HOT, but rather identifies the self as being whatever has the HOT. Natsoulas might argue that this difference is too esoteric to matter to whether a state is self-intimating, especially given my acceptance of a minimal concept of the self. But in any case the earlier proposal about how we can understand the content of HOTs is at best peripheral to the overall theory.

42. Such nonassertoric propositional attitudes would of course be relatively rare. Our knowledge of our own mental states is neither exhaustive nor infallible, though we typically act as though it is.

43. Terms for propositional mental states, such as 'belief', 'doubt', and 'expectation', can refer to tokens or types. And as just noted, the term 'thought' can refer generically to such states. So 'thought' can refer to a type, independently of what mental attitude is involved. In this case, the term in effect refers to some propositional content, rather than those states themselves.

All propositional states about one's mental states will involve the thought, so construed, that I am in those states. But to make that state conscious, that content must occur with an assertoric mental attitude.

44. As noted in section II, a particular property may be described in both dispositional and nondispositional terms. Relative to the categories of folk psychology, we need nondispositional states to make mental states conscious; but at a subpersonal level of description we might end up describing those states in dispositional terms. I am grateful to Daniel Dennett for arguing the virtues of a dispositional treatment, and for much useful conversation on these topics in general.

45. In discussing my "Two Concepts of Consciousness," Rey urges that it is arbitrary for consciousness to result from any particular level of nested intentionality, rather than from some other (section II). This misunderstands the motivation of the theory. It is because a HOT of the requisite sort constitutes one's being conscious of one's mental state that HOTs make one's mental states conscious.

Without the foregoing restrictions on the type of HOT, the connection between higher-order cognition and a state's being intransitively conscious will seem implausible. Both Rey and Robert Van Gulick, ("A Functionalist Plea for Self-Consciousness," *The Philosophical Review* 97, 2 [April 1988]:149–181) disregard those restrictions.

46. Moreover, HOTs presumably often refer to perceptual states demonstratively, aided by location in the relevant sensory field.

47. See, for example, David Woodruff Smith, "The Structure of (Self-) Consciousness," *Topoi* 5, 2 (September 1986): 149–156, p. 50.

48. As Brentano put it, with an unnecessary air of paradox, "[a]n unconscious consciousness is no more a contradiction in terms than an unseen case of seeing" (p. 102).

49. Natsoulas assumes I would appeal to some causal connection to explain how HOTs refer to the mental states they are about (p. 65). But whatever puzzles arise about how HOTs refer to mental states are due to general problems about reference, and require nothing special in this case. If something like causal ties is needed to explain reference generally, it will figure here as well.

50. Nor can we conceive the connection as one of inferring from a mental state to the relevant HOT (though some other inference may well be involved). Suppose I think it's raining; the relevant HOT is then that I have the thought that it's raining. But the inference from it's raining to my having the thought that it is would at best be irrational. A similar point is attributed to Michael Rohr by D. M. Armstrong in *A Materialist Theory of the Mind*, New York: Humanities Press, 1968, p. 200.

51. This supports our choice of HOTs over a perceptual model to capture the way we are transitively conscious

of our conscious states, since perceiving is factive and thinking is not.

On the confabulation of intentional states, see Richard E. Nisbett and Timothy DeCamp Wilson, "Telling More Than We Can Know: Verbal Reports on Mental Processes," *Psychological Review* 84, 3 (May 1977):231–259.

Our visual field seems to be replete with visual detail throughout. This is because eye movements provide foveal vision over a wide area, and we retain the visual information thus gained. Nonetheless, as noted in section V, we are at any given moment aware of little visual detail outside the center of our visual field. It is natural to speculate that our seeming to see much of this detail may in effect be due to our confabulating detailed visual sensations.

52. For a more extended discussion of these intuitions, see my "Two Concepts of Consciousness."

53. The terms are G. E. Moore's: "The Refutation of Idealism," in his *Philosophical Studies*, (London: Routledge & Kegan Paul, 1922):1–30, pp. 20, 25.

54. It is a familiar Cartesian tactic to define these phenomena away. Descartes, for example, having insisted that, "we do not have any thoughts in sleep without being conscious of them at the very moment they occur," goes on to concede that "commonly we forget them immediately" (letter to Arnauld, July 29, 1648, *AT* V, 221).

55. Another striking phenomenon that it is likely only a HOT theory can explain is that thoughts are generally conscious whenever we express them verbally, though not necessarily when we express them nonverbally. For this explanation, see my "Why Are Verbally Expressed Thoughts Conscious?", Report No. 32/1990, Center for Interdisciplinary Research (ZiF), Research Group on Mind and Brain, University of Bielefeld; and "Consciousness and Speech."

56. Van Gulick proposes detaching our concept of introspection from that of self-consciousness and, presumably, of a state's being conscious (p. 162). But he understands self-consciousness and state consciousness in terms of the subpersonal possession of "reflexive meta-psychological information" (pp. 160ff.), and it is unclear that this has much to do with the relevant folk-psychological concepts.

57. Any alternative account of introspection—say, in terms of attention or phenomenological *epoché*—would at the very least face the challenge of showing that these concepts themselves need not be explicated in turn by reference to higher-order transitive consciousness.

58. We intuitively regard introspective consciousness as somehow active, in contrast to the nonintrospective consciousness of mental states. (I am grateful to Jay Rosenberg for insisting on this.) The HOT theory readily explains this. Introspection is having a conscious HOT, whereas in nonintrospective consciousness the HOT is not conscious; and, although the having of conscious thoughts is intuitively an active matter, the having of nonconscious thoughts plainly is not.

59. See, for example, Armstrong, *A Materialist Theory of the Mind*, pp. 94–107 and 323–338, and "What is Consciousness?", especially pp. 59–63; Dennett, "Toward a Cognitive Theory of Consciousness," in *Minnesota Studies in the Philosophy of Science*, ed. C. Wade Savage (Minneapolis: University of Minnesota Press, 1978): pp. 201–228, esp. pp. 216–222; Lewis, "An Argument for the Identity Theory," *The Journal of Philosophy* 63, 1 (January 6, 1966):17–25, p. 21, and "Psychophysical and Theoretical Identifications," *Australasian Journal of Philosophy* 50, 3 (December 1972):249–258, p. 258; and Wilfrid Sellars, "Empiricism and the Philosophy of Mind," in *Science, Perception and Reality* (London: Routledge & Kegan Paul, 1963): pp. 127–196, 188–189, and 194–195. Except for Armstrong's reliance on the perceptual model (see note 34), these views about introspective consciousness are similar in spirit to the theory of nonintrospective consciousness developed here.

Mellor, like Armstrong, relies on a perceptual metaphor; but unlike Armstrong he seeks to explain nonintrospective consciousness. And unlike both Armstrong and the present theory, Mellor insists that his account cannot explain the consciousness of mental states generally, but only beliefs.

60. And insofar as truth conditions are relevant to content, distinct content.

Brian Loar argues that the concepts in a lower-order thought will occur in a HOT, and concludes that the conceptual role of the lower-order thought is included in that of the HOT. ("Subjective Intentionality," *Philosophical Topics* 15, 1 [Spring 1987]:89–124, p. 103.) This claim about conceptual role seems to capture the spirit if not the letter of Brentano's view about HOTs (though as Loar notes [p. 89], it is of course independent of Brentano's antinaturalism).

61. This does not mean that the mental states of nonlinguistic creatures are never conscious states. The

ability to report our mental states in effect fixes the extension of the term 'conscious state'. And as with other mental categories, what fixes the extension of a term need not be a property common to everything in that extension. So, *pace* Van Gulick, the fact that many mental states of nonlinguistic creatures are conscious provides no reason to deny the connection between a state's being conscious and our being able to report about it (p. 162).

62. On the connection between thought and sincere speech, see my "Intentionality."

63. This argument is developed in detail in my "Thinking That One Thinks," in *Consciousness*, ed. Glyn W. Humphreys and Martin Davies (Oxford: Basil Blackwell, 1993), pp. 197–223; originally issued as Report No. 11/1989, Center for Interdisciplinary Research (ZiF), Research Group on Mind and Brain, University of Bielefeld.

64. This chapter was written during a research year spent at the Center for Interdisciplinary Research (ZiF), University of Bielefeld, Germany, and was originally issued there as Report 40, 1990, Research Group on Mind and Brain, Center for Interdisciplinary Research (ZiF). I am indebted to the Center for their generous support, and for the exceptionally congenial and stimulating environment provided there. I am also grateful to many friends and colleagues there and elsewhere for helpful discussion, especially Peter Bieri, Daniel Dennett, Jerry Fodor, Jaegwon Kim, Jay Rosenberg, and Robert Schwartz.

47 Consciousness as Internal Monitoring

William G. Lycan

Locke put forward the theory of consciousness as "internal Sense" or "reflection"; Kant made it "inner sense, by means of which the mind intuits itself or its inner state."[1] On that theory, consciousness is a perception-like second-order representing of our own psychological states events.

The term "consciousness," of course, has many distinct uses.[2] My concern here is with that use according to which much of one's mental or psychological activity is unconscious or subconscious even when one is wide awake and well aware of other goings-on, both external and internal. I shall argue that what distinguishes conscious mental activity from un- and subconscious mental activity is indeed second-order representing.

Locke's idea has been urged in our own time by philosophers such as D. M. Armstrong and by psychologists such as Bernard Baars; I have previously defended it too.[3] But some interesting criticisms have been raised against the view by a number of theorists. In this chapter I shall rebut a few; I am particularly concerned to overcome an objection due to Georges Rey.[4]

1

Armstrong states the Inner Sense doctrine as follows: "Introspective consciousness ... is a perception-like awareness of current states and activities in our own mind. The current activities will include sense-perception: which latter is the awareness of current states and activities of our environment and our body."[5] As I would put it, consciousness is the functioning of internal attention mechanisms directed upon lower-order psychological states and events. I would also add (or make more explicit) a soupçon of teleology: Attention mechanisms are devices that have the job of relaying and/or coordinating information about ongoing psychological events and processes.[6]

Armstrong offers a plausible Just-So Story to explain the prevalence of introspective consciousness:

The biological function of introspective consciousness ... is to sophisticate our mental processes in the interests of more sophisticated action.

Inner perception makes the sophistication of our mental processes possible in the following way. If we have a faculty that can make us aware of current mental states and activities, then it will be much easier to achieve *integration* of the states and activities, to get them working together in the complex and sophisticated ways necessary to achieve complex and sophisticated ends.

... [C]o-ordination [of many parallel processes] can only be achieved if the portion of the computing space made available for administering the overall plan is continuously made "aware" of the current mental state of play with respect to the lower-level operations that are running in parallel. Only with this feedback is control possible.... It is no accident that fully alert introspective consciousness characteristically arises in *problem* situations, situations that standard routines cannot carry one through.[7]

A slightly deflated version of this idea will figure in my own defense of the Inner Sense theory.

The Lockean thesis is a component of a wider project of mine: that of establishing the *hegemony of representation*. I am concerned to maintain a weak version of Brentano's doctrine that the mental and the intentional are one and the same— weak, because I am not sure that intentionality suffices for representation; but my claim is strong enough: that the mind has no special properties that are not exhausted by its representational properties. It would follow that once representation is (eventually) understood, then not only consciousness in our present sense but subjectivity, qualia, "what it's like," and every other aspect of the mental will be explicable in terms of representation, without the positing of any other ingredient not already well understood from the naturalistic point of view.[8]

I should repeat and emphasize that my concern in this chapter is solely with the notion of conscious awareness, with the distinction between conscious mental states and un-, sub-, pre- or otherwise nonconscious mental states. In particular, I am not here addressing issues of qualia or phenomenal character, which I have resolved almost entirely satisfactorily elsewhere.[9] There may be Inner Sense theorists who believe that their views solve problems of qualia; I make no such claim, for I think qualia problems and the nature of conscious awareness are mutually independent and indeed have little to do with each other.[10]

2

The Inner Sense view of consciousness has a number of advantages, the first of which is that it does distinguish awareness from mere psychology and conscious states/events (in the sense indicated above) from mere mentation. We may plausibly suppose that many lower animals have psychologies and mentation, or at least internal representation, without awareness. Second, the view affords some grades of un- or subconsciousness; for example, a state/event may be unconscious just because it is unattended, but a Freudian wish to kill one's father may have been rendered unattend*able* by some masterful Censor. Further distinctions are available, for both animals and human beings.

Third, the Inner Sense account affords the best solution I know to the problem of subjectivity and "knowing what it's like," raised by B. A. Farrell, Thomas Nagel, and Frank Jackson. Georges Rey and I hit upon that solution independently a few years ago.[11] It involves the behavior of indexical terms in the proprietary vocabulary mobilized by the relevant attention mechanisms. But there is no time to rehearse it here.

Fourth, the Inner Sense view sorts out a longstanding issue about sensations and feeling. Consider pain. A minor pain may go unfelt, or so we sometimes say.[12] Even quite a bad pain may not be felt if attention is distracted by sufficiently pressing concerns. Yet such assertions as my last two can sound anomalous. As David Lewis once said, meaning to tautologize, "Pain is a feeling." When one person's commonplace sounds to another contradictory on its face, we should suspect equivocation, and the Inner Sense model delivers. Sometimes the word "pain" is used to mean just the first-order representation of damage or disorder, a representation that can go unnoticed. But sometimes "pain" means a conscious feeling or mode of awareness, and on that usage the phrase "unfelt pain" is simply self-contradictory; it comprehends both the first-order representation and the second-order scanning together. Thus the equivocation, which gave rise to the issue; the issue is dissolved.

3

The preceding point reveals a consequence of the Inner Sense theory that may disturb: Since an internal monitor is a physical device and so subject to malfunction, it might report falsely; the very fallibility of monitoring guarantees that a subject might register a first-order event incorrectly. Thus, the Inner Sense theory implies an appearance/reality distinction for subjectivity.

A Cartesian incorrigibilist would be appalled, of course. So would the Cartesian's unlikely bedfellow, the Wittgensteinian incorrigibilist. Neither such animal abounds nowadays, thanks to the decline of Cartesian doctrine generally, the weakening of Wittgensteinian "conceptual truths," and Armstrong's specific arguments against incorrigibility of both sorts.[13] It is generally conceded, at least, that one can or in theory might mistake and misdescribe the contents of one's own experience. Yet the Inner Sense view has two further implications that may be more troubling to the contemporary reader.

First, in addition to misreporting the character of a first-order state, an internal monitor could in principle fire without anything like a proper cause, giving a false positive. Thus, the Inner Sense view predicts that it is possible for a person to be unveridically conscious or aware of a sensation that simply does not exist. You might introspect a sharp, severe pain, when there was in fact no pain at all.

I am happy to live with that theoretical possibility. Notice, first, that it is not as conceptually anomalous as it sounds. My description misleadingly suggests that you might feel a severe pain, with everything that is involved in feeling a severe pain, which would include all the first-order functional effects of the pain—withdrawal, wincing, involuntary crying out, favoring, and the like—while having no actual pain whatever. That suggestion is, I agree, truly weird. But it is not in fact a consequence of the Inner Sense theory. If (as the present hypothesis has it) there is no first-order pain sensation at all but merely a mendacious representation of one, there is no reason to think that every or any of those usual functional effects would indeed ensue. You would be introspecting something that had some of the qualitative aspect of a pain, but important elements would be missing. You might be in the position of the morphine patients who manifest "reactive dissociation," saying that they still feel the pain as intensely as ever but no longer mind it. (Remember that on my view, introspective awareness itself is just one of several normal effects of a first-order pain sensation, and largely independent of the sensation's other normal effects.)

Second, the mere theoretical possibility of the false positive does little to encourage the idea that such things can happen easily. Perhaps they do happen, as when an apprehensive child or medical patient mistakes a light touch or a sensation of cold for a pain, but those examples are usually mistaken perceptions of actual sensations. It is at best rare for a person to be aware of a pain but give no behavioral or other functional sign of pain. I suspect that our introspectors are well wired and virtually never fire for no reason at all. It is not as though they were external sense organs, prey to predictable perceptual illusions and

at the mercy of unusual environmental setups; the first-order sectors they scan are immured right there in the brain with them, and there is little to threaten the informational connection. (Though one must never underestimate the power of drugs or lesions to sever what are normally very tight psychological connections; Wittgensteinian "conceptual truths" about mental states are often counterexampled by unusual clinical conditions.)

In making these two replies to the objection from false positives, I have used the vernacular of felt and unfelt pains, that is, the terminology that applies "pain" to the first-order representation of damage or disorder without requiring introspective awareness of that representation. If instead one prefers the more comprehensive use of "pain," then one will be frustrated in trying to use the term, for a false positive will not count as pain in that sense but will merely feel like pain, or have the introspective component of pain without the first-order sensory component. Perhaps we should now recognize a third sense of "pain," meaning just the introspective awareness (as) of pain, whether or not that awareness is veridical. In that third sense, trivially, you cannot feel pain when there is no pain, even if there is no first-order representation of disorder. (On the other hand, as against acknowledging the third sense, remember that an unveridical awareness of pain would not be accompanied by the other usual effects of the first-order sensation and would probably not be phenomenally very like veridical awareness of pain. Knowing oneself to be the victim of a false positive, one might or might not be moved to call one's state of awareness "pain"; this is something we cannot tell until we have documented and investigated an actual false-positive case.)

The Inner Sense theory's second potentially disturbing implication was recently noted by D. C. Dennett in *Consciousness Explained.*[14] He raises the question of second-order seeming: "the bizarre category of the objectively subjective— the way things actually, objectively seem to you even if they don't seem to seem that way to you!"

He thereupon "brusquely denies the possibility in principle of consciousness of a stimulus in the absence of the subject's belief in that consciousness." But the Inner Sense view affords a perfect model of just such a state of affairs: a first-order state is conscious in virtue of being scanned, and seems a certain way to its subject, but the scanning is not itself scanned. This would be precisely a case of consciousness of a stimulus in the absence of the subject's belief in that consciousness. Moreover, a second-order monitor could break down and make a first-order state seem to seem to me in a way that the state does not in fact seem to me.

Dennett calls this idea "metaphysically dubious" as well as impossible in principle. But his only argument is as follows, based on "first-person operationalism":

Opposition to this operationalism appeals, as usual to possible facts beyond the ken of the operationalist's test, but now the operationalist is the subject himself, so the objection backfires: "Just because you can't tell, by your preferred ways, whether or not you were conscious of x, that doesn't mean you weren't. Maybe you were conscious of x but just can't find any evidence for it!" Does anyone, on reflection, really want to say that? Putative facts about consciousness that swim out of reach of both "outside" and "inside" observers are strange facts indeed.

Well. Just to gratify Dennett's rhetorical curiosity: Yes, *I*, on reflection, really want to say that, or rather to insist on its perfect coherence as a factual possibility. Since the Inner Sense theory provides an excellent model for the second-order situation that appalls Dennett and since the theory may well be true, the second-order situation is without question a genuine possibility. (Remember, if the Inner Sense theory is false, that is a brutely empirical fact; certainly Mother Nature could have equipped us with banks of first- and second-order internal monitors, whether or not She did in fact choose to do so.) As for the strange aquatic facts, I see no reason to grant that they do "swim out of reach of" the outside observers, at least, since in principle a neuroscientist

could observe a first-order state being scanned by an unscanned monitor and know just what was going on.

As before, I agree that the notion of an appearance/reality distinction for conscious awareness is odd on its face, and I am inclined to think that dramatic cases of appearance/reality gap are rare and pathological, but I see here no powerful objection to the Inner Sense view.

4

In correspondence,[15] Fred Dretske has asked a good pair of questions about the Inner Sense theory: Why is consciousness (or just representation) *of* certain physical states enough to make those states *themselves* "conscious"? And more specifically, what is it that is so special about physical states of that certain sort, that consciousness of them makes them—but not just any old physical state—conscious? After all, we are conscious *of* (what are in fact) physical states of our stomachs; for that matter, through ordinary perception we are conscious of physical states of our skins, such as their being freckled, but no one would distinguish between "conscious" *stomachs* and "unconscious" stomachs, or between "conscious" and "unconscious" frecklednesses.

Indeed, why does the concept work that way (assuming it does work that way)? It may have something historically to do with the fact that until the twentieth century, the mental/psychological was simply identified with the conscious, and so only recently have we had to adopt a taxonomic distinction between states we are aware of holding and states we are not. (I am assuming that there is such a distinction in reality, and I believe—what is not uncontroversial—that the distinction in theory applies to any ordinary mental state, not counting states already described as "being consciously aware of [such-and-such].")

What is it that is so special about physical states of that certain sort, that consciousness *of* them makes them "conscious"? That they are themselves mental. Stomachs and freckled patches of skin are not mental. It seems psychological states are called "conscious" states when we are conscious of them, but nonpsychological things are not.

Given the reality of the distinction between states we are aware of being in and states we are not aware of being in, the only remaining question is that of why the *word* "conscious" is thus dragged in as an adjective to mark it. My bet is that there is a grammatical answer. Maybe it is a transferred epithet: We begin with the adverbial form, as in "consciously thought" or "consciously felt," and when we make the verb into a noun, the adverb automatically becomes an adjective—as in the move from "meditatively sipped" to "took a meditative sip." That is fairly plausible; at any rate it is the best I can do for now.

In any case, it is important to see that the question pertains to the notion of conscious awareness itself; it is not a problem for or objection to the Inner Sense theory of awareness in particular.

5

Dretske makes a related, ostensibly more substantive criticism of the theory as I have stated it. He argues at some length that there is a sense of "conscious" in which, as he oxymoronically puts it, "an experience can be conscious without anyone—including the person having it—being conscious of having it" (p. 263). As he says, this usage sounds "odd, perhaps even contradictory, to those philosophers who ... embrace an inner spotlight view of consciousness" (as targets he cites Armstrong, David Rosenthal, and me in particular). In brief, his argument is that to perceive anything, whether or not one is conscious of doing that perceiving, is to be conscious of the thing perceived, and so to be "in a conscious state of some sort." (He notes that Armstrong actually agrees in principle, for Armstrong grants a sense

in which any perceiver *eo ipso* enjoys "perceptual consciousness," whether or not she or he is conscious or aware of the perceiving itself.)[16] Thus, the Inner Sense or "inner spotlight" view has gone wrong, at least by its implication that for a state to be a conscious state, its subject must be aware of being in it.

Here I believe the issue is purely verbal. Although I cannot myself hear a natural sense of the phrase "conscious state" other than as meaning "state one is conscious of being in," the philosophical use of "conscious" is by now well and truly up for grabs, and the best one can do is to be as clear as possible in one's technical specification.[17] Let us then grant a sense, whether natural or merely technical, in which a state of perceiving is a conscious state, whether or not its subject is conscious of being in it.[18] But the Inner Sense theory of consciousness is not and has never pretended to be a theory of "perceptual consciousness' in Dretske's and Armstrong's sense. It is a theory of conscious awareness, of "conscious states" in my original sense of: states one is conscious of being in.

Dretske adds a more specific objection to the Inner Sense theory (pp. 279–280). Distinguishing between awareness of things, which is referentially transparent, and awareness of facts, which presupposes mobilization of particular concepts, he argues as follows. Suppose a person has two experiences, E(Alpha) and E(Beta), which differ subtly in their contents, and the person does introspect the two but fails to register the difference.[19] If the person is merely "thing-aware" of a first-order psychological state without being "fact-aware" of the state, and if that thing-awareness is supposed to constitute the state's being a conscious state, then the person's

failure to realize, [her or his] total unawareness of the fact *that* there is a difference between E(Alpha) and E(Beta), is irrelevant to whether there is a conscious difference between these two experiences. This being so, the "inner sense" theory of what makes a mental state conscious does nothing to *improve* one's epistemic access to one's own conscious states.... What good is an inner spotlight, an introspective awareness of mental events, if it doesn't give one epistemic access to the events on which it shines?

(Further, the Inner Sense theory "multiplies the problems by multiplying the facts of which we are not aware.")

This is puzzling on its face, since the topic of epistemic access arises rather suddenly; the Inner Sense account was offered as a theory of the "conscious"/"nonconscious" distinction in our original sense, not as a contribution to epistemology. Besides, introspection conceived as inner perception normally does improve one's epistemic position, for although it is indeed possible for one to be thing-aware of a first-order state without being fact-aware of being in that state, the thing-awareness will often directly *give rise to* fact-awareness, just as in the case of ordinary external perception.

I suspect that what motivated these remarks of Dretske's was as follows: In the section of his paper that surrounds the present objection, Dretske is contrasting the Inner Sense view with a close relative, David Rosenthal's "Higher-Order Thought" theory,[20] which is also a major target of his essay; and it seems Dretske means the objection comparatively. This is, I believe he means to say that if his original criticism is damaging to the Higher-Order Thought account, it refutes the Inner Sense view even more decisively. Thus, he has argued (correctly) that being the object of a higher-order thought is not what makes a state conscious in the sense of "perceptual consciousness." But at least a higher-order thought would make the state's subject aware *that* she or he was in that state, which is something; by contrast, a mere higher-order thing-awareness of the state would not (*eo ipso*) even yield that fact-awareness, and so is *completely* irrelevant to perceptual consciousness.

If this interpretation of Dretske's objection is correct, the objection again simply goes wide of my own position. For (again) I am using Inner Sense to explicate conscious awareness, not "perceptual consciousness."

Dretske's point is of independent interest, however. Whatever the exact function(s) of introspection may be, we may be fairly sure that Mother Nature intended introspection to confer some cognitive benefit, and a theory of introspective awareness that masked this or made it unintelligible would be to that extent a bad theory. Dretske is right to insist that *mere* thing-awareness of a first-order state would be a cognitive idler. So I must reemphasize my presumption that internal monitoring normally or often does give rise to introspective belief; and it should also be noted that, again on the model of external perception, introspection presents its object under an aspect, *as* being a certain way. I have argued elsewhere that such introspective aspects and "ways" are important, though ineffable.[21]

6

Rosenthal makes a direct argument against the Inner Sense account.[22] It begins with the claim that "perceiving always involves some sensory quality." That claim might be taken by a naive Inner Sense theorist to help explain the qualitative dimension of a conscious first-order sensory state: perhaps the first-order state is felt to have a qualitative or phenomenal aspect because it gives rise to an internal perception that itself "involves some sensory quality." But as Rosenthal briskly points out, that way lies regress, for the sensory quality of the second-order state would remain to be explained.

The failure of the naive idea just mentioned is no embarrassment to my own Inner Sense view, since that view bears no responsibility for explaining qualia or phenomenal character. But Rosenthal rides his initial claim further. If perceiving always involves some sensory quality and if internal monitoring is perceiving, then internal monitoring itself must indeed involve some sensory quality. A dilemma ensues: Either the quality is just the same quality as that exhibited by the first-order state being scanned, or it is some second, higher-order sensory quality. But the former is at best unmotivated and presumably false: "When we see a tomato, the redness of our sensation is not literally the same property as the redness of the tomato." And if the latter, "it's a mystery just what mental quality a higher-order perception could have. What mental qualities are available other than those we're conscious of when we're conscious of our first-order sensory states?"

My main reply to this is to reject the extension of Rosenthal's initial claim to internal monitoring itself. The Inner Sense theorist does not contend (at least neither Armstrong nor I contend) that internal monitoring is like external perception in every single respect. And in particular, we should not expect internal monitoring to share the property of involving some sensory quality at its own level of operation. The sensory properties involved in first-order states are, according to me,[23] the represented features of physical objects; for example, the color presented in a visual perception is the represented color of a physical object. First-order states themselves do not have ecologically significant features of that sort, and so we would not expect internal representations of first-order states to have sensory qualities representing or otherwise corresponding to such features.

I did concede that introspection represents a first-order state under an aspect, or as being a certain way, and that "way" doubtless has *something* to do with the first-order state's own quale or sensory quality. So if Rosenthal's term "mental quality" is taken more broadly than "sensory quality" in his original sense, it is possible that the second horn of his dilemma can be grasped, and every scanning of a first-order sensory state does "involve" some distinctive mental quality that is distinctively related to the first-order sensory quality. I agree with Rosenthal that if one wants to maintain this, one must demystify it, but I shall leave that discussion for another time,[24] especially since I have blocked the inference to his disjunctive step in the first place.

A word about the notion of an "experience". Prosecuting Rosenthal's objection against me in correspondence, Fred Dretske has asked whether unscanned perceivings or unfelt pains count as *experiences* and whether there is an introspective "experience" involved in scanning over and above the first-order perceiving itself. To this I reply that the term "experience" is subject to the same sort of ambiguity I ascribed in section 2 to the word "feeling." One can use "experience" merely to mean a first-order perceiving or sensory state, in which case there can be unconscious experiences, or one can reserve the term for monitored sensings or monitorings of sensings, in which case "conscious experience" becomes a redundancy. I do not see any substantive issue that outruns this verbal choice.

7

An initial flaw in the version of the Inner Sense theory as stated so far is that it makes a Cartesian assumption recently highlighted by Dan Dennett:[25] that there is some determinate stage of information processing that constitutes the locus of conscious mental states/events. More specifically, "Cartesian materialism" is the (usually tacit) assumption that there is a *physically realized* spatial or temporal turnstile in the brain, a stage where "it all comes together" and the product of preprocessing is exhibited "to consciousness."

Dennett attacks that assumption. However natural it may be, it is gratuitous and empirically implausible. First, it is a priori unlikely that Mother Nature has furnished the human brain with any central viewing room or single monitor to do the viewing, nor is there any positive neurophysiological of such an organ. Second, Dennett argues at length that the famous "temporal anomalies" of consciousness discovered by psychophysical research, such as color phi, the cutaneous rabbit, and Libet's "backward referral" of sensory experiences,[26] are anomalous only so long as Cartesian materialism is being assumed; jettison the assumption, and the phenomena are readily explained. Dennett's analyses of the experimental data are not completely uncontroversial,[27] but I find them convincing on the whole, and it is hard to think how anyone might defend Cartesian materialism on purely neurophysiological grounds.

The point is not just that there is no *immaterial audience* in the brain or just that there is no undischargeable homunculus but that there is no such locus at all, however physically characterized—no single Boss Unit or even CPU within the brain to serve as chief executive of my utterings and other actions. The central nervous system is as central as it gets. There is, if you like, a "stream of consciousness": "We are more-or-less serial virtual machines implemented— inefficiently—on the parallel hardware that evolution has provided for us, " "Joycean" machines that formulate synthesized reports of our own passing states,[28] though the reports are never entirely accurate.

The Inner Sense theory has it that conscious awareness is the successful operation of an internal scanner or monitor that outputs second-order representations of first-order psychological states.[29] But an "internal scanner" sounds very much as though it presupposes an internal audience seated in a Cartesian Theater, even if it and the theater are made of physical stuff. Is the Inner Sense view not then committed to Cartesian materialism?

It is not hard to come up with a pretty damning collection of direct quotations. Armstrong spoke of "*the* portion of the computing space made available for administering the *overall plan*." And (just to save you looking) I myself wrote of an internal scanner's "delivering information about ... [a first-order] psychological state to one's *executive control unit*."[30] For shame. There may be an "executive control unit" in some functional sense, but very probably not in the sense of being: that agency, arrival at which makes information conscious.

But it should be clear that the Inner Sense view is not per se committed to Cartesian materialism. For even if an internal scanner resembles an internal audience in some ways, the "audience" need not be seated in a Cartesian Theater. There need be no *single*, executive scanner, and no one scanner or monitor need view the entire array of first-order mental states accessible to consciousness. Accordingly, there need be neither a "turnstile of consciousness" nor one central inner stage on which the contents of consciousness are displayed in one fixed temporal order. An internal monitor is an attention mechanism that presumably can be directed upon representational subsystems and stages of same; no doubt internal monitors work selectively and piecemeal, and their operations depend on control windows and other elements of conative context. On this point, the Inner Sense theory has already parted with Cartesian materialism.

A qualification: We should not throw out the integration-and-control baby with the Cartesian bathwater. The operation of an internal monitor does not *eo ipso* constitute consciousness. We can imagine a creature that has a panoply of first-order states and a rich array of monitors scanning those states but in such a way that the monitors' output contributes nothing at all to the creature's surrounding psychology, maintenance, or welfare. The outputs might just go unheard, or they might be received only by devices that do nothing but turn patches of the creature's skin different colors. For consciousness constituting, we must require that monitor output contribute—specifically to the integration of information in a way conducive to making the system's behavior appropriate to its input and circumstances. Though the latter formulation is vague, it will do for present purposes; the requirement rules out the ineffectual monitors without falling back into the idea of a Cartesian Theater or single CPU.

(This is a good juncture at which to underscore and deepen the teleological cast I am imparting to the Inner Sense theory. I said that for an internal monitor to count in the analysis of consciousness, in the present sense of "conscious," the monitor must have monitoring as its function, or one of its functions. But that is not all. To count in the analysis of *my* consciousness, the monitor must do its monitoring *for me*. A monitor might have been implanted in me somewhere that sends its outputs straight to Reuters and to CNN, so that the whole world may learn of my first-order psychological states as soon as humanly possible. Such a device would be teleologically a monitor, but the wire services' monitor rather than mine. More important, a monitor functioning within one of my subordinate homunculi might be doing its distinctive job for that homunculus *rather than* for me; for example, it might be serving the homunculus's event memory rather than my own proprietary event memory.[31] This distinction blocks what would otherwise be obvious counterexamples to the Inner Sense view as stated so far.)

Rejection of Cartesian materialism is not only compatible with the Lockean view. In an important way, it supports the Inner Sense theory. It predicts introspective fallibility of two characteristic sorts. First, as Dennett emphasizes, the result of an introspective probe is a judgment made by the subject, which judgment does not (or not eo ipso) simply report a "presentation" to an inner audience. And the "temporal anomalies" alone should have made us question the reliability of introspective reports. Introspection gets small temporal details wrong. That tends to confirm rather than to impugn the Inner Sense view of consciousness. If conscious awareness is indeed a matter of introspective attention and if introspection is the operation of a monitor or self-scanner, then such anomalies were to be expected, for monitors and scanners are characteristically fallible on details, and Dennett shows admirably how such devices might corporately mix up temporal sequence in particular.

Second, if there is no single Cartesian Theater, then there should be no single optimal time of probing a first-order process. More strongly, Dennett argues that probing "changes the task", it interferes with the very process it purports to be monitoring. That too is good news for the Inner

Sense theory, for if introspection is the operation of a monitor or self-scanner, then revisionary effects of the present sort are again just what we should have expected; monitoring instruments (such as ammeters) typically do affect the values of the magnitudes they measure.[32]

Thus the Inner Sense theory of consciousness survives the collapse of Cartesian materialism, and is even strengthened by it.

8

Christopher Hill offers a putative criticism of the Inner Sense theory (which he calls "the inner eye hypothesis"):[33]

There has been little recognition of the fact that a sensation may be transformed by the act of coming to attend to it, and even less of the fact that a sensation may be brought into existence by attention. Instead of facing these facts and attempting to explain them, philosophers have often waged an imperialist struggle on behalf of inner vision and the inner eye hypothesis. They have maintained, either explicitly or implicitly, that inner vision is the only important form of active introspection, and they have attempted to deny or reinterpret the data that are incompatible with this view. (pp. 123–24)

When a sensation is transformed by being attended to, Hill calls this "volume adjustment"; when a sensation is brought into being by active introspection, Hill speaks of "activation." It becomes clear (p. 126) that these two phenomena are themselves the "data" on which Hill thinks the Inner Sense theory founders.

Now what exactly is the difficulty? In particular, why cannot the Inner Sense theorist grant both that scanning a first-order state can cause a change in the character of that state and that aiming one's internal monitor at a particular sector of one's phenomenal field can bring a sensation into existence? Either of these scenarios seems entirely realistic, and I for one do not doubt that they are sometimes realized.

In making the reply just offered, I am in effect advancing the claim that volume adjustment and activation are matters of internal scanning plus certain causal results, and perhaps Hill would object to that reductive analysis. But he uses almost overtly causal language himself: "The phenomenal field is often profoundly *changed by* the process of coming to attend to a sensation" (p. 125, italics mine); and if he has in mind some noncausal understanding of volume control or of activation, he does not make it explicit.

A clue is provided by the following passage.

Think of a laboratory technician who is trying to determine the composition of a sample by chemical analysis. The technician may find it perfectly natural to say that he or she is "taking a closer look" at the sample. In saying this, however, the technician does not mean to assert that he or she is doing something that is fundamentally akin to what we do when we subject an object to visual scrutiny. When one subjects an object to closer visual scrutiny, one simply changes the relation between the object and one's eyes. But a technician who is analyzing a sample may well be changing many of its intrinsic qualities. (pp. 124–25)

This suggests that Hill is thinking of visual scanning as entirely passive, as unable to affect the intrinsic properties of the object scanned; analogously, he may think of "inner vision" or internal monitoring as passive in just the same way.[34] At any rate, that would explain why he thinks the phenomena of volume adjustment and activation require different sorts of active introspection, additional to the "inner eye" sort. But as I have emphasized, I do not think of internal monitoring in that passive, vicarious way; I not only grant but insist that it often does affect the phenomenal field being scanned. So if I am understanding Hill's critique correctly, my own Inner Sense theory is immune to it.

9

On at last to Rey's objection. The objection is that if all it takes to make a first-order state a conscious state is that the state be monitored by a scanner that makes integrative use of the infor-

mation thus gleaned, then consciousness is a lot more prevalent than we think. Any notebook computer, for example, has devices that keep track of its "psychological" states. (If it be protested that no computer has genuinely psychological states—for example, because it has neither authentic intentional states nor sensory states—that is inessential to the point. Once we had done whatever needs to be done in order to fashion a being that does have first-order intentional and sensory states, the addition of an internal monitor or two would be virtually an afterthought, a trifling wrinkle, surely not the sort of thing that could turn a simply nonconscious being into a conscious being.) For that matter, individual subsystems of our own human psychologies doubtless involve their own internal monitors, and it is implausible to grant that those subsystems are themselves conscious.

Several replies may be made to this. First, for consciousness we should require that our monitor emit a genuine representation, not just physical "information" in the Bell Telephone sense or a simple nomological "indication" in the Wisconsin sense. But that is of little help, since surely our subsystems do contain monitors that output genuine representations.

Second, it should trouble no one that he or she has proper parts that are conscious. The proper part of you that consists of you minus your left arm is conscious, as is the part consisting of you minus your skin and most of your musculature. Other (individually) expendable chunks include your entire gastrointestinal tract, your auditory system, much of your cortex, and possibly much of a hemisphere. Each of your respective complementary proper parts is conscious, even as we speak.

But it may be said that the second reply is of little more help than the first, for each of the large proper parts I have mentioned would qualify, mentally speaking, as being *you*, if taken on its own. Its consciousness is your consciousness; at least, there is nothing present to its consciousness that is not also present to yours. But the sort of case that worries Rey is one in which self-monitoring is performed by a *silent*, subterranean subsystem, perhaps one of "all those unconscious neurotic systems postulated in so many of us by Freud,... [or] all those surprisingly intelligent, but still unconscious, subsystems for perception and language postulated in us by contemporary cognitive psychology" (p. 11). What troubles Rey is that he or you or I should contain subsystems that are conscious on their own though we know nothing of them, and whose conscious contents are not at all like ours.

It does sound eerie. But I am not so sure that the individuation of consciousnesses is so straightforward a business. For one thing, that the contents of one consciousness coextend with those of mine hardly entails that the first consciousness *is* (=) mine; they still may be two. For another, the commissurotomy literature has raised well-known thorny questions about the counting of consciousnesses in the first place,[35] and it is abetted in that by thought experiments such as Dan Dennett's in his classic "Where Am I?" and a more recent one by Stephen White.[36] My own preference is to doubt there to be any fact of the matter, as to how many consciousnesses live in a single human body (or as to how many bodies can be animated by the same consciousness).

A third reply to the argument: In his own essay on Rey's objection,[37] Stephen White enforces a distinction that Rey himself acknowledged but slighted: the difference between consciousness and *self*-consciousness. Rey had argued that if we already had a nonconscious perception-belief-desire machine, the addition of a "self" concept would be trifling (just as would be that of a simple internal monitor); one need only give the machine a first-person representation whose referent was the machine itself—that is, add the functional analogue of the pronoun "I" to the machine's language of thought. But White argues on the basis of an ingenious group-organism example that the matter is hardly so simple and that the difference between consciousness and self-con-

sciousness is far larger and more important than Rey allowed. Surprisingly, having a functional inner "I" does not suffice for being able to think of oneself as oneself; nor does mere consciousness as opposed to self-consciousness confer personhood or any moral status. And it turns out on White's analysis that although subsystems of ours might count as conscious, they would not be self-conscious in the way we are. That difference helps to explain and assuage our reluctance to admit them to our own country club.[38] I find White's defense of these claims quite convincing.[39]

But I do not invest much in these second and third meditations as replies to Rey's objection. I have presented them mainly for the purpose of softening you up.

10

So I turn to my fourth and (*chez* me) most important reply. It is emphatically to deny (what John Searle has recently asserted with unsurprising boldness)[40] that consciousness is an on-off affair—that a creature is either simply conscious or simply not conscious. (If Searle did not exist I would have to invent him, for he actually puts it that way: "Consciousness is an on/off switch; a system is either conscious or not" [p. 83].) I maintain that consciousness comes in degrees, which one might describe as degrees of richness or fullness.[41] We human beings are very richly conscious, but there might be more complex and/or more sophisticated organisms that are more fully conscious than we. "Higher animals" are perhaps less fully so; "lower" animals still less, and so forth.

In saying this, I am shifting my sense of "conscious" slightly, for there is not obviously any great spectrum of degrees of whether something has an internal monitor scanning some of its psychological states. (Actually there probably is a *significant* spectrum, based on the extent to which monitor output contributes to integration of information and to control; as was conceded at the time, I did leave the formulation vague. But I will not rest anything on this.) The paronymy works as follows. A thing is conscious, at all, if it is conscious to any degree at all—that is, if it has at least one internal monitor operating and contributing etc. We might call this "bare" or "mere" consciousness. The thing may be *more richly or more fully* conscious if it has more monitors, monitors more, integrates more, integrates better, integrates more efficiently for control purposes, and so forth.

Actually I have not yet achieved paronymy, for I have located the degrees in the modifers ("richly" and "fully") rather than in the basic term "conscious" itself, which so far retains its original sense. But I do still mean to shift its meaning, for I want to allow at least a very vague sense in which some "barely" conscious devices are not really conscious; I take that one to be the ordinary sense of the word. But I would insist that that sense still affords a largeish spectrum of degrees. (Granted, this needs defense, and I shall provide some shortly.)

My principal answer to Rey is, then, to deny his intuition. So long as it contributes in the way aforementioned, one little monitor does make for a little bit of consciousness. More monitors and better integration and control make for fuller and fuller consciousness.[42]

Rey conjectures (p. 24), as a diagnosis of his own chauvinist intuitions about machines, that *if* consciousness is anything, it is like an "inner light" that is on in us but could be off or missing from other creatures that were otherwise first-order-psychological and functionally very like us; that is why he finds it so obvious that machines are not conscious even when they have been hypothetically given a perception-belief-desire system like ours. (Naturally given his conditional assumption, he asks why we should believe that *we* are not just very complicated perception-belief-desire machines and offers the eliminative suggestion that we are therefore not conscious either; consciousness *is not* anything.)[43] But I see no reason to grant the conditional con-

jecture. I have no problem saying that a device whose internal monitor is contributing integration-and-control-wise is conscious *of* the states reported by the monitor. There is a rhetorical difference between saying that a device is conscious *of* such-and-such and saying that it, itself, is ... conscious! But that is *only* a rhetorical difference, barring my slight paronym above. What is special about us is not our being conscious per se but that we monitor so much at any given time and achieve so high a degree of integration and control.

Thus two remarks made by psychologists and quoted by Rey as "astonishing" him by their naiveté do not astonish me in the slightest:

Perceptions, memories, anticipatory organization, a combination of these factors into learning—all imply rudimentary consciousness. (Peter H. Knapp)[44]

Depending on what Knapp meant by "anticipatory organization," this is not far wrong. If anticipatory organization implies internal monitoring that contributes, or if the "combination of ... [the] factors into learning" involves such monitoring, or both, I endorse the statement.

Consciousness is a process in which information about multiple individual modalities of sensation and perception are combined into a unified, multidimensional representation of the state of the system and its environment and is integrated with information about memories and the needs of the oaganism, generating emotional reactions and programs of behavior to adjust the organism to its environment. (E. Roy John)[45]

No quarrel there either, assuming again that the "combining" is done in part by contributory monitoring.

The main obstacle to agreement with my matter-of-degree thesis is that we ourselves know only one sort of consciousness from the inside, and that one is particularly rich and full. We have elaborate and remarkably non-gappy visual models of our environment; we have our other four main sense modalities, which supplement the blooming, bursting phenomenological garden already furnished by vision; we have proprioception of various sorts that orient us within our surroundings; and (most important) we have almost complete freedom of attention within our private worlds; we can at will attend to virtually any representational aspect of any of our sensations that we choose. (All this creates the Cartesian illusion of a complete private world of sensation and thought, a seamless movie theater. There is no such completeness even phenomenologically, what with failings like the blind spot and the rapid decay of peripheral vision, but the illusion is dramatic.) Now, since this is the only sort of consciousness we have ever known from the inside and since the only way to *imagine* a consciousness is to imagine it from the inside, we cannot imagine a consciousness very different at all from our own, much less a greatly impoverished one. What we succeed in imagining, if we try to get inside the mind of a spider or a notebook computer, is either an implausible cartoon (with anthropomorphic talk balloons) or something that hardly seems to us to deserve the title "consciousness." It is a predicament: We are not well placed to receive the idea that there can be very low degrees of consciousness.[46]

11

Now, finally, for a bit of argument:

1. Consider the total mental states of people who are very ill, or badly injured, or suffering the effects of this or that nefarious drug. Some such people are at some times called "semiconscious." Any number of altered states are possible, many of them severely diminished mental conditions. For some of these, surely, there will be no clear Searlean "yes" or "no" to the question, "Is the patient conscious?" but only a "To a degree" or "Sort of."

2. We could imagine thousands of hypothetical artifacts, falling along a multidimensional spectrum having at its low end ordinary hardware store items like record changers and air-conditioners and at its high end biologic human duplicates (indistinguishable from real living human beings save by their histories).[47] Along the way(s) will be robots of many different sorts, having wildly different combinations of abilities and stupidities, oddly skewed and weighted psychologies of all kinds. Which are "conscious"? How could one possibly draw a single line separating the whole seething profusion of creatures into just two groups?

3. For that matter, the real world provides a similar argument (for those who favor the real world over science fiction). Consider the phylogenetic scale. Nature actually contains a fairly smooth continuum of organisms, ranked roughly by complexity and degree of internal monitoring, integration, and efficient control. Where on this continuum would God tell us that Consciousness begins? (Appropriately enough, Searle himself declares deep ignorance regarding consciousness and the phylogenetic scale.)[48]

4. If argument 3 does not move you (or even if it does), consider human infants as they develop from embryo to fetus to neonate to baby to child. When in that sequence does consciousness begin?

I do not say that any of these arguments is overwhelming. But taken together—and together with recognition of the imaginative predicament I mentioned prior to offering them—I believe they create a presumption. At the very least, they open the door to my matter-of-degree view and make it a contender. Therefore, one cannot simply assume that consciousness (if any) is an on-off switch. And Rey's argument does assume that.

Thus I do not think Rey has refuted the Inner Sense view.

Notes

This chapter is a very much expanded version of "Consciousness as Internal Monitoring, I," in J. E. Tomberlin (ed.), *Philosophical Perspectives, 9: AI, Connectionism, and Philosophy of Psychology* (Atascadero,

CA: Ridgeview Publishing, 1995). I had planned a separate sequel but instead have been allowed by the editors to incorporate all the additional material here.

I am grateful to Joe Levine, Ned Block, Georges Rey, Chris Hill and Fred Dretske for extensive comments and discussion.

1. Locke, *An Essay Concerning Human Understanding*, ed. A. C. Fraser (New York: Dover Publications, 1959), II, ch. I, sec. 3, p. 123; Kant, *Critique of Pure Reason*, trans. Norman Kemp Smith (New York: St. Martin's Press, 1965), A23/B37, p. 67.

2. See my " What Is 'The' Problem of Consciousness?," manuscript.

3. D. M. Armstrong, *A Materialist Theory of the Mind* (London: Routledge and Kegan Paul, 1968), and "What Is Consciousness?" in *The Nature of Mind and Other Essays* (Ithaca, NY: Cornell University Press, 1980). Baars, "Conscious Contents Provide the Nervous System with Coherent, Global Information," in R. Davidson, G. E. Schwartz, and D. Shapiro (eds.), *Consciousness and Self-Regulation, Vol. 3* (New York: Plenum Press, 1983), 3: 41–79; *A Cognitive Theory of Consciousness*. Lycan, *Consciousness* (Cambridge, MA: Bradford Books/MIT Press, 1987), ch. 6.

4. "A Reason for Doubting the Existence of Consciousness," in Davidson, Schwartz, and Shapiro, *Consciousness*, pp. 1–39.

5. Armstrong, "What Is Consciousness?" p. 61.

6. There is a potential ambiguity in Armstrong's term "introspective consciousness": Assuming there are attention mechanisms of the sort I have in mind, they may function automatically, on their own, or they may be deliberately mobilized by their owners. Perhaps only in the latter case should we speak of introspect*ing*. On this usage, "introspective" consciousness may or may not be a result of introspecting. Armstrong himself makes a similar distinction between "reflex" introspective awareness and "introspection proper," adding the suggestion that "the latter will normally involve not only introspective awareness of mental states but also introspective awareness of that introspective awareness" ("What Is Consciousness?" p. 63).

7. Armstrong, "What Is Consciousness?" pp. 65–66. Robert Van Gulick has also written illuminatingly on the uses of consciousness, though he does not focus so specifically on introspection; see particularly "What Difference Does Consciousness Make?" *Philosophical Topics* 17(1989):211–30.

8. I began this project with respect to subjectivity and qualia respectively in chapters 7 and 8 of *Consciousness*. Parts of it have also been pursued by Gilbert Harman ("The Intrinsic Quality of Experience," in J. E. Tomberlin (ed.), *Philosophical Perspectives*, 4: *Action Theory and Philosophy of Mind* (Atascadero, CA: Ridgeview Publishing, 1990), Sydney Shoemaker ("Phenomenal Character," *Noûs* 28[1994]:21–38), and Michael Tye ("Qualia, Content, and the Inverted Spectrum." *Noûs* 28[1994]:159–83).

9. In *Consciousness*. See also my "Functionalism and Recent Spectrum Inversions," unpublished manuscript, and "True Colors," in preparation.

10. When I made this point emphatically after a presentation of this material at the National Endowment for The Humanities (NEH) Summer Institute on "The Nature of Meaning" (Rutgers University July, 1993), Bill Ramsey responded much as follows: "I see; once you've got the explanandum whittled all the way down, as specific and narrow as you want it, the big news you're bringing us is that what *internal monitoring* really is, at bottom, is ... internal monitoring!" That characterization is not far wrong. Though the Inner Sense doctrine is not tautologous and faces some objections, I think it is very plausible, once it has been relieved of the extraneous theoretical burden of resolving issues that are not directly related to the "conscious"/ "nonconscious" distinction per se.

Incidentally, I do not offhand know of any Inner Sense proponent who does claim that the theory resolves qualia problems. Yet there is a tendency among its critics to criticize it from that quarter; I conjecture that such critics are themselves confusing issues of awareness with issues of qualitative character.

11. Rey, "Sensations in a Language of Thought," in E. Villanueva (ed.), *Philosophical Issues, I: Consciousness* (Atascadero, CA: Ridgeview Publishing, 1991), and "Sensational Sentences," in M. Davies and G. Humphreys (eds.), *Consciousness* (Oxford: Basil Blackwell, 1992); Lycan, "What Is the 'Subjectivity' of the Mental?" in Tomberlin, *Philosophical Perspectives*.

12. From a current novel: "Each step was painful, but the pain was not felt. He moved at a controlled jog down the escalators and out of the building." John Grisham, *The Firm* (New York: Island Books, Dell Publishing, 1991), p. 443.

David Rosenthal offers a nice defense of unfelt pain, in "The Independence of Consciousness and Sensory Quality," in Villanueva, *Philosophical Issues*. See also

David Palmer's "Unfelt Pains," *American Philosophical Quarterly* 12(1975):289–98.

13. Armstrong, *A Materialist Theory of the Mind*, pp. 100–15. But see also G. Sheridan, "The Electro-encephalogram Argument Against Incorrigibility," *American Philosophical Quarterly* 6 (1969):62–70.

14. D. C. Dennett, *Consciousness Explained* (Boston: Little, Brown, 1991), pp. 132–33.

15. See also Dretske's "Conscious Experience," *Mind* 102(1993):263–83.

16. Armstrong, "What Is Consciousness?" p. 59.

17. Certainly we should all conscientiously obey Mary Lycan's Maxim: "No *professional philosopher* is qualified to pronounce on the 'folk sense' or 'ordinary use' of any philosophically contentious term (unless the philosopher happens also to be a professional anthropologist and has done the requisite surveys)." None of us gets to kidnap words like "conscious." Perhaps it is time for "conscious" to take its proud place on Neurath's list of forbidden terms, but I will not urge that as yet.

To illustrate the terminological situation (and to vent some annoyance): At least two reviewers of my book have emphatically complained that its title is false advertising and that it is not about *consciousness* at all— despite its offering accounts of conscious awareness (ch. 6), "what it's like" (ch. 7), subjectivity/perspectivalness (ch. 7), and qualia (ch. 8). Though I insist on keeping all those issues and further close relatives sharply separate from each other, I am baffled as to what matter of "consciousness" I have ignored.

18. However, I will not resist remarking that the Dretske-Armstrong usage has the vice of making Armstrong's own term, "perceptual consciousness," redundant; the occurrence of "consciousness" within it is gratuitous. Also, we need no special *theory of* consciousness in the perceptual sense, since a theory of "perceptual consciousness" would just be a theory of perception itself and its intentionality.

I note that Rosenthal's usage agrees with mine: "Whatever we may discover about consciousness, it is presumably uncontroversial that, if one is wholly unaware of some mental state, that state is not a conscious state." "Explaining Consciousness," manuscript, p. 3.

19. Cf. Irvin Rock, *The Logic of Perception* (Cambridge, MA: Bradford Books/MIT Press, 1983).

20. David Rosenthal, "Two Concepts of Consciousness," *Philosophical Studies* 94(1986):329–59; "Think-ing That One Thinks," in Davies and Humphreys, *Consciousness*, Dretske's nomenclature confuses the issues a bit, for he lumps both Rosenthal's theory and mine under the heading of "inner spotlight" theories, while in the present context he also rightly distinguishes Higher-Order Thought from Inner Sense, and acknowledges that the two are mutual competitors at least in a small way. See Rosenthal's own objection to Inner Sense, discussed in section 5 below.

21. Lycan, "What Is the 'Subjectivity' of the Mental?" See also "A Limited Defense of Phenomenal Information," in T. Metzinger (ed.), *Consciousness* (Ferdinand Schöningh-Verlag 1995).

22. "A Theory of Consciousness," Report No. 40, Research Group on Mind and Brain, Zentrum für Interdisziplinäre Forschung, Bielefeld, Germany, 1990; and "Explaining Consciousness," pp. 7–8. Besides his direct argument against Inner Sense, Rosenthal deploys an ingenious line of reasoning designed to show that every conscious state is accompanied by a higher-order thought, which if sound would support the Higher-Order Thought theory. Rosenthal might then argue further that Inner Sense is expendable and should be expended by means of Occam's Razor. His argument is based on the distinction between expressing a thought and reporting a thought and on the claim that all and only conscious states are reportable by their owners; for the record, I reject the latter claim.

23. *Consciousness*, ch. 8.

24. For some predominantly negative discussion of the issues involved here, see my "Functionalism and Recent Spectrum Inversions."

25. Dennett, *Consciousness Explained*, D. C. Dennett and M. Kinsbourne, "Time and the Observer: The Where and When of Consciousness in the Brain," *Behavioral and Brain Sciences* 15(1992):183–201.

26. P. Kolers and M. von Grünau, "Shape and Color in Apparent Motion," *Vision Research* 16(1976):329–35; F. A. Geldard and C. E. Sherrick, "The Cutaneous 'Rabbit': A Perceptual Illusion," *Science* 178(1972): 178–79; B. Libet, "Cortical Activation in Conscious and Unconscious Experience," *Perspectives in Biology and Medicine* 9(1965):77–86.

27. E.g., B. J. Baars and M. Fehling, "Consciousness Is Associated with Central as Well as Distributed Processes," *Behavioral and Brain Sciences* 15(1992):203–4, and B. Libet, "Models of Conscious Timing and the Experimental Evidence," *Behavioral and Brain Sciences*

213–15. Dennett and Kinsbourne reply to their critics in "Authors' Response," *Behavioral and Brain Sciences,* 234–43.

28. Dennett, *Consciousness Explained*, pp. 218, 225.

29. For convenience, I shall continue to speak of the states that get monitored as "first-order" states, but this is inaccurate, for introspective states can themselves be scanned. This will be important later on.

30. *Consciousness*, p. 72.

31. On such distinctions, and for more illuminating examples, see chs. 3 and 4 of ibid.

32. One might be tempted to infer (something highly congenial to Dennett himself) that introspection is *woefully* fallible, unreliable to the point of uselessness. But that inference would be unjustified. Though the "temporal anomalies" alone should have made us question the reliability of introspective reports, notice that the scope of unreliability exhibited by the anomalies is very small, tied to temporal differences within the tiny intervals involved, a small fraction of a second in each case.

33. Christopher Hill, *Sensations* (Cambridge: Cambridge University Press, 1991), ch. 5. That piece and this section of the chapter continue a dialogue begun by a preprint of Hill's paper, "Introspective Awareness of Sensations," *Topoi* 6(1987):9–22, and my response in ch. 6 of *Consciousness*.

34. This likely possibility was called to my attention by Roger Sansom.

35. For a survey and discussion, see C. Marks, *Commissurotomy, Consciousness and the Unity of Mind* (Montgomery, VT: Bradford Books, 1979).

36. Dennett, "Where Am I?" in *Brainstorms* (Montgomery, VT: Bradford Books, 1978), reprinted in D. R. Hofstadter and D. C. Dennett (eds.), *The Mind's I: Fantasies and Reflections on Self and Soul* (New York: Basic Books, 1981); see also D. H. Sanford, "Where Was I?" in Hofstadter and Dennett, *The Mind's I.* White, "What Is It Like to Be a Homunculus?" *Pacific Philosophical Quarterly* 68(1987):148–74.

37. White, "What Is It Like to Be a Homunculus?"

38. Moreover, as he observes (p. 168), we have no access to unproblematic examples of consciousness in the absence of self-consciousness, and that fact contributes to an important predicament that I shall expound below.

39. He maintains that no notebook computer is self-conscious even if some are conscious in a less demanding functional sense. (I believe White would accept my claim that mere consciousness is more prevalent than philosophers think; see p. 169.) But I do not see that his analysis of self-consciousness generates that result, since his main concern was to argue only that self-consciousness is restricted to the highest level of organization in a group organism, a result that does not help deny self-consciousness to whole computers. (White has explained in conversation that his analysis alone was not intended to do that; he has other means.)

40. John Searle, *The Rediscovery of the Mind* (Cambridge, MA: MIT Press, 1992).

41. I have defended this thesis before, in "Abortion and the Civil Rights of Machines," in N. Potter and M. Timmons (eds.), *Morality and Universality* (Dordrecht: D. Reidel, 1985), pp. 144–45.

Searle himself goes on, in *Rediscovery of the Mind*, to qualify his "on-off" claim: "But once conscious, the system is a rheostat: there are different degrees of consciousness"; he speaks of levels of intensity and vividness. Thus, it seems, our real disagreement is over not degrees per se but the question of whether a creature or device could have a much lower degree of consciousness than is ordinarily enjoyed by human beings and still qualify as being conscious at all.

42. I should emphasize again that a monitor makes for consciousness when *what* it monitors is itself a psychological state or event. My suggestion that notebook computers are after all conscious is conditional on the highly controversial assumption that such computers have psychological states such as beliefs and desires in the first place.

43. By way of further diagnosis (p. 25), Rey offers the additional conjecture that our moral concern for our living, breathing conspecifics drives us to posit some solid metaphysical difference between ourselves and mere artifacts, as a ground of that concern. He opines that we need no such ground in order to care more for human beings than for functionally similar machines, but he does not say what he thinks *would* ground that difference in care.

44. Peter H. Knapp, "The Mysterious 'Split': A Clinical Inquiry into Problems of Consciousness and Brain," in G. Globus, G. Maxwell and I Savodnik (eds.), *Consciousness and the Brain* (New York: Plenum Press, 1976), pp. 37–69.

45. E. Roy John, "A Model of Consciousness," in G. E. Schwartz and D. Shapiro (eds.), *Consciousness and Self-Regulation* (New York: Plenum Press, 1976), 1:1–50.

46. Samuel Butler said, "Even the potato, rotting in its dank cellar, has a certain low cunning." But I grant the potato has no internal monitors.

47. This is the one argument I gave in "Abortion and the Civil Rights of Machines."

48. "I have no idea whether fleas, grasshoppers, crabs, or snails are conscious" (p. 74). He suggests that neurophysiologists might find out, by a method of apparent-consciousness-debunking, viz., looking for evidence of "mechanical-like tropism to account for apparently goal-directed behavior in organisms that lacked consciousness" (p. 75); he pooh-poohs "mechanical-like" functional processing as being in no way mental or psychological. On this, see D. C. Dennett's review of *The Rediscovery of the Mind*, *Journal of Philosophy* 90(1993):193–205.

48 Conscious Experience

Fred Dretske

There is a difference between hearing Clyde play the piano and seeing him play the piano. The difference consists in a difference in the kind of experience caused by Clyde's piano playing. Clyde's performance can also cause a belief—the belief that he is playing the piano. A perceptual belief that he is playing the piano must be distinguished from a perceptual experience of this same event. A person (or an animal, for that matter) can hear or see a piano being played without knowing, believing, or judging that a piano is being played. Conversely, a person (I do not know about animals) can come to believe that Clyde is playing the piano without seeing or hearing him do it—without experiencing the performance for themselves.

This distinction between a perceptual experience of x and a perceptual belief about x is, I hope, obvious enough. I will spend some time enlarging upon it, but only for the sake of sorting out relevant interconnections (or lack thereof). My primary interest is not in this distinction, but, rather, in what it reveals about the nature of conscious experience and, thus, consciousness itself. For unless one understands the difference between a consciousness of things (Clyde playing the piano) and a consciousness of facts (that he is playing the piano), and the way this difference depends, in turn, on a difference between a concept-free mental state (e.g., an experience) and a concept-charged mental state (e.g., a belief), one will fail to understand how one can have conscious experiences without being aware that one is having them. One will fail to understand, therefore, how an experience can be conscious without anyone—including the person having it—being conscious of having it. Failure to understand how this is possible constitutes a failure to understand what makes something conscious and, hence, what consciousness is.

The possibility of a person's having a conscious experience she is not conscious of having will certainly sound odd, perhaps even contradictory, to those philosophers who (consciously or not) embrace an inner spotlight view of consciousness according to which a mental state is conscious insofar as the light of consciousness shines *on* it—thus making one conscious *of* it.[1] It will also sound confused to those like Dennett (1991) who, though rejecting theatre metaphors (and the spotlight images they encourage), espouse a kind of first person operationalism about mental phenomena that links conscious mental states to those that can be reported and of which, therefore, the reporter is necessarily aware of having.

There is, however, nothing confused or contradictory about the idea of a conscious experience that one is not conscious of having. The first step in understanding the nature of conscious experience is understanding why this is so.

1 Awareness of Facts and Awareness of Things

For purposes of this discussion I regard "conscious" and "aware" as synonyms.[2] Being conscious of a thing (or fact) is being aware of it. Accordingly, "conscious awareness" and "consciously aware" are redundancies.

A. White (1964) describes interesting differences between the ordinary use of "aware" and "conscious." He also describes the different liaisons they have to noticing, attending, and realizing. Though my treatment of these expressions (for the purposes of this inquiry) as synonymous blurs some of these ordinary distinctions, even (occasionally) violating some of the strictures White records, nothing essential to my project is lost by ignoring the niceties. No useful theory of consciousness can hope (nor, I think, should it even aspire) to capture all the subtle nuances of ordinary usage.

By contrasting our awareness of things (x) with our awareness of facts (that P) I mean to be distinguishing particular (spatial) objects and (temporal) events[3] on the one hand from facts involving these things on the other. Clyde (a physical object), his piano (another object), and Clyde's playing his piano (an event) are all things as I am using the word "thing"; that he is playing his piano is a fact. Things are neither true nor false though, in the case of events, states of affairs, and conditions, we sometimes speak of them as what makes a statement true. Facts are what we express in making true statements about things. We describe our awareness of facts by using a factive complement, a that-clause, after the verb; we describe our awareness of things by using a (concrete) noun or noun phrase as direct object of the verb. We are aware of Clyde, his piano, and of Clyde's playing his piano (things); we are also aware that he is playing the piano (a fact).

Seeing, hearing, and smelling x are ways of being conscious of x.[4] Seeing a tree, smelling a rose, and feeling a wrinkle is to be (perceptually) aware (conscious) of the tree, the rose, and the wrinkle. There may be other ways of being conscious of objects and events. It may be that thinking or dreaming about Clyde is a way of being aware of Clyde without perceiving him.[5] I do not deny it (though I think it stretches usage). I affirm, only, the converse: that to see and feel a thing is to be (perceptually) conscious of it. And the same is true of facts: to see, smell, or feel that P is to be (or become) aware that P. Hence,

(1)   S sees (hears, etc.) x (or that P) $\Rightarrow$ S is conscious of x (that P)[6]

In this chapter I shall be mainly concerned with *perceptual* forms of consciousness. So when I speak of S's being conscious (or aware) of something I will have in mind S's seeing, hearing, smelling, or in some way sensing a thing (or fact).

Consciousness of facts implies a deployment of concepts. If S is aware that x is F, then S has the concept F and uses (applies) it in his awareness of x.[7] If a person smells that the toast is burning, thus becoming aware that the toast is burning,

this person applies the concept *burning* (perhaps also the concept *toast*) to what he smells. One cannot be conscious that the toast is burning unless one understands what toast is and what it means to burn—unless, that is, one has the concepts needed to classify objects and events in this way. I will follow the practice of supposing that our awareness of facts takes the form of a belief. Thus, to smell that the toast is burning is to be aware that the toast is burning is to believe that the toast is burning. It is conventional in epistemology to assume that when perceptual verbs take factive nominals as complements, what is being described is not just belief but knowledge. Seeing or smelling that the toast is burning is a way of coming to *know* (or, at least, verifying the knowledge) that the toast is burning. It will be enough for present purposes if we operate with a weaker claim: that perceptual awareness of facts is a mental state or attitude that involves the possession and use of concepts, the sort of cognitive or intellectual capacity involved in thought and belief. I will, for convenience, take belief (that P) as the normal realization of an awareness that P.

Perceptual awareness of facts has a close tie with behavior—with, in particular (for those who have language), an ability to *say* what one is aware of. This is not so with a consciousness of things. One can smell or see (hence, be conscious of) burning toast while having little or no understanding of what toast is or what it means to burn. "What is that strange smell?" might well be the remark of someone who smells burning toast but is ignorant of what toast is or what it means to burn something. The cat can smell, and thus be aware of, burning toast as well as the cook, but only the cook will be aware that the toast is burning (or that it is the toast that is burning).

The first time I became aware of an armadillo (I saw it on a Texas road), I did not know what it was. I did not even know what armadillos were, much less what they looked like. My ignorance did not impair my eyesight, of course. I saw the animal. I was aware of it ahead of me on the road.

That is why I swerved. Ignorance of what armadillos are or how they look can prevent someone from being conscious of certain facts (that the object crossing the road is an armadillo) without impairing in the slightest one's awareness of the things—the armadillos crossing roads—that (so to speak) constitute these facts. This suggests the following important result. For all things (as specified above) x and properties F,

(2) S is conscious of $x \nRightarrow$ S is conscious that x is F.

Though (2) strikes me as self-evident, I have discovered, over the years, that it does not strike everyone that way. The reason it does not (I have also found) is usually connected with a failure to appreciate or apply one or more of the following distinctions. The first two are, I hope, more or less obvious. I will be brief. The third will take a little longer.

(a) *Not Implying vs. Implying Not.* There is a big difference between denying that A implies B and affirming that A implies not-B. (2) does not affirm, it denies, an implication. It does not say that one can only be aware of a thing by *not* being aware of what it is.

(b) *Implication vs. Implicature.* The implication (2) denies is a logical implication, not a Gricean (1989) implicature. *Saying* you are aware of an F (i.e., a thing, x, which is F) implies (as a conversational implication) that you are aware that x is F. Anyone who said he was conscious of (e.g., saw or smelled) an armadillo would (normally) imply that he thought it was an armadillo. This is true, but irrelevant.

(c) *Concrete Objects vs. Abstract Objects.* When perceptual verbs (including the generic "aware of" and "conscious of") are followed by abstract nouns (the difference, the number, the answer, the problem, the size, the color) and interrogative nominals (where the cat is, who he is talking to, when they left), what is being described is normally an awareness of some (unspecified) fact.

The abstract noun phrase or interrogative nominal stands in for some factive clause. Thus, seeing (being conscious of) the difference between A and B is to see (be conscious) *that* they differ. If the problem is the clogged drain, then to be aware of the problem is to be aware that the drain is clogged. To be aware of the problem it isn't enough to be aware of (e.g., to see) the thing that is the problem (the clogged drain). One has to see (the fact) *that* it is clogged. Until one becomes aware of this fact, one hasn't become aware of the problem. Likewise, to see where the cat is hiding is to see that it is hiding *there*, for some value of "there."

This can get tricky, and is often the source of confusion in discussing what can be observed. This is not the place for gory details, but I must mention one instance of this problem since it will come up again when we discuss which aspects of experience are conscious when we are perceiving a complicated scene. To use a traditional philosophical example, suppose S sees a speckled hen on which there are (on the facing side) 27 speckles. Each speckle is clearly visible. Not troubling to count, S does not realize that (hence, is not aware that) there are 27 speckles. Nonetheless, we assume that S looked long enough, and carefully enough, to see each speckle. In such a case, although S is aware of all 27 speckles (things), he is not aware of the number of speckles because being aware of the number of speckles requires being aware that there is that number of speckles (a fact), and S is not aware of this fact.[8] For epistemological purposes, abstract objects are disguised facts; you cannot be conscious of these objects without being conscious of a fact.

(2) is a thesis about concrete objects. The values of x are *things* as this was defined above. Abstract objects do not count as things for purposes of (2). Hence, even though one cannot see the difference between A and B without seeing that they differ, cannot be aware of the number of speckles on the hen without being aware that there are 27, and cannot be conscious of an

object's irregular shape without being conscious that it has an irregular shape, this is irrelevant to the truth of (2).

As linguists (e.g., Lees 1963, p. 14) observe, however, abstract nouns may appear in copula sentences opposite both factive (that) clauses and concrete nominals. We can say that the problem is *that his tonsils are inflamed* (a fact); but we can also say that the problem is, simply, *his* (inflamed) *tonsils* (a thing). This can give rise to an ambiguity when the abstract noun is the object of a perceptual verb. Though it is, I think, normal to interpret the abstract noun as referring to a fact in perceptual contexts, there exists the possibility of interpreting it as referring to a thing. Thus, suppose that Tom at time t_1 differs (perceptibly) from Tom at t_2 only in having a moustache at t_2. S sees Tom at both times but does not notice the moustache—is not, therefore, aware that he has grown a moustache. Since, however, S spends twenty minutes talking to Tom in broad daylight, it is reasonable to say that although S did not notice the moustache, he (must) nonetheless have seen it.[9] If S did see Tom's moustache without (as we say) registering it at the time, can we describe S as seeing, and thus (in this sense) being aware of, a difference in Tom's appearance between t_1 and t_2? In the factive sense of awareness (the normal interpretation, I think), no; S was not aware that there was a difference. S was not aware at t_2 that Tom had a moustache. In the thing sense of awareness, however, the answer is: yes. S was aware of the moustache at t_2, something he was not aware of at t_1, and the moustache is a difference in Tom's appearance.

If, as in this example, "the difference between A and B" is taken to refer, not to the fact that A and B differ, but to a particular element or condition of A and B that constitutes their difference, then seeing the difference between A and B would be seeing this element or condition—a thing, not a fact. In this thing sense of "the difference" a person or animal who had not yet learned to discriminate (in any behaviorally relevant way) between (say) two forms might nonetheless be said

to see (and in this sense be aware of) the difference between them if it saw the parts of one that distinguished it from the other. When two objects differ in this perceptible way, one can be conscious of the thing (speckle, line, star, stripe) that is the difference without being conscious of the difference (= conscious *that* they differ). In order to avoid confusion about this critical (for my purposes) point, I will, when speaking of our awareness or consciousness of something designated by an abstract noun or phrase (the color, the size, the difference, the number, etc.), always specify whether I mean thing-awareness or fact-awareness. To be thing-aware of a difference is to be aware of the thing (some object, event, or condition, x) that makes the difference. To be fact-aware of the difference is to be aware of the fact that there is a difference (not necessarily the fact that x is the difference). In the above example, S was thing-aware, but not fact-aware, of the difference between Tom at t_1 and t_2. He was (at t_2) aware of the thing that made the difference, but not fact-aware (at t_2 or later) of this difference.

So much by way of clarifying (2). What can be said in its support? I have already given several examples of properties or kinds, F, which are such that one can be aware of a thing which is F without being aware that it is F (an armadillo, burning toast, a moustache). But (2) says something stronger. It says that there is no property F which is such that an awareness of a thing which is F requires an awareness of the fact that it is F. It may be felt that this is much too strong. One can, to be sure, see armadillos without seeing that they are armadillos, but perhaps one must, in order to see them, see that they are (say) animals of some sort. To see x (which is an animal) is to see that it is an animal. If this sounds implausible (one can surely mistake an animal for a rock or a bush) maybe one must, in seeing an object, at least see that it is an object of some sort. To be aware of a thing is at least be aware that it is ... how shall we say it? ... a thing. *Something or other*. Whether or not this is true depends, of course, on what is involved in being aware that a thing is a thing. Since we can certainly see a physical object without being aware that it is a physical object (we can think we are hallucinating), the required concept F (required to be aware that x is F) cannot be much of a concept. It seems most implausible to suppose infants and animals (presumably, conscious of things) have concepts of this sort. If the concept one must have to be aware of something is a concept that applies to *everything* one can be aware of, what is the point of insisting that one must have it to be aware?

I therefore conclude that awareness of things (x) requires no fact-awareness (that x is F, for any F) of those things.[10] Those who feel that this conclusion has too little support are welcome to substitute a weaker version of (2): namely, there, is no *reasonably specific property F* which is such that a awareness of a thing which is F requires fact-awareness that it is F. This will not affect my use of (2).

---

2 Conscious Beings and Conscious States

Agents are said to be conscious in an intransitive sense of this word (he regained consciousness) and in a transitive sense (he was conscious of her). I will follow Rosenthal (1990) and refer to both as *creature* consciousness. Creature consciousness (whether transitive or intransitive) is to be contrasted with what Rosenthal calls *state* consciousness—the (always intransitive) sense in which certain internal states, processes, events and attitudes (typically in or of conscious beings) are said to be conscious.

For purposes of being explicit about my own (standard, I hope) way of using these words, I assume that for any x and P,

(3)　S is conscious of x or that $P \Rightarrow$ S is conscious (a conscious being).

That is, transitive (creature) consciousness implies intransitive (creature) consciousness. You cannot see or hear, taste or smell, a thing without

(thereby) being conscious.[11] You cannot be aware that your check-book doesn't balance or conscious that you are late for an appointment (a fact) without being a conscious being.[12]

The converse of (3) is more problematic. Perhaps one can be conscious without being conscious of anything. Some philosophers think that during hallucination, for example, one might be fully conscious but (*qua* hallucinator) not conscious of anything. To suppose that hallucination (involving intransitive consciousness) is a consciousness of something would (or so it is feared) commit one to objectionable mental particulars—the sense data that one hallucinates. Whether or not this is so I will not try to say. I leave the issue open. (3) only endorses the innocent idea that beings who are conscious of something are conscious; it does not say that conscious beings must be conscious of something.

By way of interconnecting creature and state consciousness I also posit:

(4)　S is conscious of x or that $P \Rightarrow$ S is in a conscious state of some sort.

Transitive creature consciousness requires state (of the creature) consciousness. S's consciousness of x or that P is a relational state of affairs; it involves both the agent, S, and the object (or fact) S is conscious of. The conscious state which (according to (4)) S must be in when he is conscious of x or that P, however, is not the sort of state the existence of which logically requires x or the condition described by P. Tokens of this state type may be caused by x or the condition described by "P" (and when they are, they may qualify as experiences of x or knowledge that P), but to qualify as a token of this type, x and the condition described by "P" are not necessary.

Thus, according to (4), when I see or hear Clyde playing the piano (or that he is playing the piano) and (thus) am conscious of him playing the piano (or that he is playing the piano), I am in a conscious state of some kind. When hallucinating (or simply when listening to a recording) I can be in the same kind of conscious state even if Clyde is not playing the piano (or I do not perceive him playing the piano). When Clyde is not playing the piano (or I am not perceiving him play the piano), we speak of the conscious state in question not as knowledge (that he is playing the piano) but as belief, not as perception (of Clyde playing the piano) but as hallucination (or perception of something *else*).[13]

I do not know how to argue for (4). I would like to say that it states the obvious and leave it at that. I know, however, that nothing is obvious in this area. Not even the obvious. (4) says that our perceptual awareness of both things (smelling the burning toast) and facts (becoming aware that it is burning) involves, in some essential way, conscious subjective (i.e., non-relational and, in this sense, internal or subjective) states of the perceive—beliefs (in the case of awareness of facts) and experiences (in the awareness of things). Not everything that happens in or to us when we become conscious of some external object or fact is conscious, of course. Certain events, processes, and states involved in the processing of sensory information are presumably not conscious. But *something*, some state or other of S, either an experience or a belief, has to be conscious in order for S to be made conscious of the things and facts around him. If the state of S caused by x is not a conscious state, then the causation will not make S conscious of x. This is why one can *contract* poison ivy without ever becoming aware of the plant that poisons one. The plant causes one to occupy an internal state of some sort, yes, but this internal state is not a conscious state. Hence, one is not (at least not in contracting poison ivy) conscious of the plant.

David Armstrong (1980, p. 59) has a favorite example that he uses to illustrate differences in consciousness. Some may think it tells against (4). I think it does not. Armstrong asks one to imagine a long-distance truck driver:

After driving for long periods of time, particularly at night, it is possible to "come to" and realize that for some time past one has been driving without being aware of what one has been doing. The coming-to is an alarming experience. It is natural to describe what went on before one came to by saying that during that time one lacked consciousness. Yet it seems clear that, in the two senses of the word that we have so far isolated, consciousness was present. There was mental activity, and as part of that mental activity, there was perception. That is to say, there was minimal consciousness and perceptual consciousness. If there is an inclination to doubt this, then consider the extraordinary sophistication of the activities successfully undertaken during the period of "unconsciousness." (p. 59)

Armstrong thinks it plausible to say that the driver is conscious (perceptually) of the road, the curves, the stop signs, etc. He *sees* the road. I agree. There is transitive creature consciousness of both things (the roads, the stop signs) and facts (that the road curves left, that the stop sign is red, etc.). How else explain the extraordinary performance?

But does the driver thereby have, in accordance with (4), conscious experiences of the road? Armstrong thinks there is a form of consciousness that the driver lacks. I agree. He thinks what the driver lacks is an introspective awareness, a perception-like awareness, of the current states and activities of his own mind. Once again, I agree. The driver is neither thing-aware nor fact-aware of his own mental states (including whatever experiences he is having of the road). I am not sure that normal people have this in normal circumstances, but I'm certainly willing to agree that the truck driver lacks it. But where does this leave us? Armstrong says (p. 61) that if one is not introspectively aware of a mental state (e.g., an experience), then it (the experience) is "in one good sense of the word" unconscious. I disagree. The only sense in which it is unconscious is that the person whose state it is is not conscious of having it. But from this it does not follow that the state itself is unconscious. Not unless one accepts a higher-order theory according to which state-consciousness is analyzed in terms of creature-consciousness of the state. Such a theory may be true, but it is by no means obvious. I shall, in fact, argue that it is false. At any rate, such a theory cannot be invoked at this stage of the proceedings as an objection to (4). (4) is, as it should be, neutral about what makes the state of a person (who is transitively conscious of x or that P) a conscious state.

I therefore accept Armstrong's example, his description of what forms of consciousness the driver has, and the fact that the driver lacks an important type of higher level (introspective) consciousness of his own mental states. What we disagree about is whether any of this implies that the driver's experiences of the road (whatever it is in the driver that is required to make him conscious *of* the road) are themselves unconscious. We will return to that question in the final section.

Many investigators take perceptual experience and belief to be paradigmatic conscious phenomena.[14] *If* one chooses to talk about state consciousness (in addition to creature consciousness) at all, the clearest and most compelling instance of it is in the domain of sensory experience and belief. My present visual experience of the screen in front of me and my present perceptual beliefs about what is on that screen are internal states that deserve classification as conscious if anything does. (4) merely records a decision to regard such perceptual phenomena as central (but by no means the only) instances of conscious mental states.

Such is my justification for accepting (4). I will continue to refer to the conscious states associated with our consciousness of things (hearing Clyde playing the piano) as experiences and our consciousness of facts (that he is playing the piano) as beliefs. This is, I think, fairly standard usage. I have not, of course, said what an experience or a belief is. I won't try. That is not my project. I am trying to say what makes (or doesn't make) an experience conscious, not what makes it an experience.

Consciousness of things—e.g., seeing a stoplight turn green—requires a conscious experience of that thing. Consciousness of a fact —that the stop light is turning green—requires a conscious belief that this is a fact. And we can have the first without the second—an awareness of the stoplight's turning green without an awareness that it is turning green—hence a conscious experience (of the light's turning green) without a conscious belief (that it is turning green). Likewise, we can have the second without the first—a conscious belief about the stoplight, that it is turning green, without an experience of it. Someone I trust tells me (and I believe her) that the stoplight is turning green. So much by way of summary of the relationships between the forms of consciousness codified in (1) through (4).

We are, I think, now in a position to answer some preliminary questions. First: can one have conscious experiences without being conscious that one is having them? Can there, in other words, be conscious states without the person in whom they occur being fact-aware of their occurrence? Second: can there be conscious states in a person who is not thing-aware of them? These are important preliminary questions because important theories of what makes a mental state conscious, including what passes as orthodox theory today, depend on negative answers to one (or, in some cases both) of these questions. If, as I believe, the answers to both questions are affirmative, then these theories are simply wrong.

3 Experienced Differences Require Different Experiences

Glance at figure 48.1 long enough to assure yourself that you have seen all the elements composing constellation Alpha (on the left) and constellation Beta (on the right). It may be necessary to change fixation points in order to foveate (focus on the sensitive part of the retina) all parts of Alpha and Beta. If the figure is being held at arm's length, though, this should not be necessary though it may occur anyway via the frequent involuntary saccades the eyes make. A second or two should suffice.

During this brief interval some readers may have noticed the difference between Alpha and

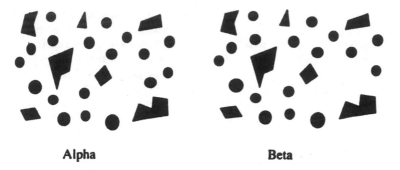

Alpha   **Beta**

Figure 48.1

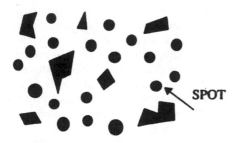

SPOT

Figure 48.2

Beta. For expository purposes, I will assume no one did. The difference is indicated in figure 48.2. Call the spot, the one that occurs in Alpha but not Beta, Spot.

According to my assumptions, then, everyone (when looking at figure 48.1) saw Spot. Hence, according to (1), everyone was aware of the thing that constitutes the difference between Alpha and Beta. According to (4), then, everyone consciously experienced (i.e., had a conscious experience of) the thing that distinguishes Alpha from Beta. Everyone, therefore, was thing-aware, but not fact-aware, of the difference between Alpha and Beta. Spot, if you like, is Alpha's moustache.

Let E(Alpha) and E(Beta) stand for one's experience of Alpha and one's experience of Beta respectively. Alpha and Beta differ, Alpha has Spot as a part, Beta does not. E(Alpha) and E(Beta) must also differ. E(Alpha) has an element corresponding to (caused by) Spot. E(Beta) does not. E(Alpha) contains or embodies, as a part, an E(Spot), an experience of Spot, while E(Beta) does not. If it did not, then one's experience of Alpha would have been the same as one's experience of Beta and, hence, contrary to (4), one would not have seen Spot when looking at Alpha.[15]

One can, of course, be conscious of things that differ without one's experience of them differing in any intrinsic way. Think of seeing visually indistinguishable objects—similar looking thumb tacks, say. One sees (experiences) numerically different things, but one's experience of them is the same. Both experiences are conscious, and they are experiences of different things, but the differences in the experiences are not conscious differences. The differences are extrinsic to the experience itself. It is like having an experience in Chicago and another one in New York. The numerically different experiences may be qualitatively identical even though they have different (relational) properties—one occurs in Chicago, the other in New York. The perception of (visually) indistinguishable thumb tacks is like that.

The experiences of Alpha and Beta, however, are not like that. They are qualitatively different. They differ in their relational properties, yes, as all numerically different objects do, but they also differ in their intrinsic properties. These two experiences are not only experiences of qualitatively different objects (Alpha and Beta), they are experiences of the qualitative differences. The respects in which Alpha and Beta differ are not only visible, they are (by hypothesis) seen. One is, after all, thing-aware of Spot, the difference between Alpha and Beta. The experiences are not distinguished in terms of their intrinsic qualities by the person who has the experiences, of course, but that is merely to say that there is, on the part of this person, no fact-awareness of any differences in his experience of Alpha and his experience of Beta. That, though, is not the issue. The question is one about differences in a person's conscious experiences, not a question about a person's awareness of differences in his experiences. It is a question about *state* consciousness, not a question about *creature* consciousness.

Once one makes the distinction between state and creature consciousness and embraces the distinction between fact- and thing-awareness, there is no reason to suppose that a person must be able to distinguish (i.e., tell the difference between) his conscious experiences. Qualitative differences in conscious experiences are *state* differences; distinguishing these differences, on the other hand, is a fact about the *creature* consciousness of the person in whom these experiences occur.

The argument assumes, of course, that if one is thing-aware of the difference between Alpha and Beta (i.e., thing-aware of Spot), then E(Alpha) and E(Beta) must differ. It assumes, that is, that *experienced* differences require different experiences. What else could experienced differences be? The difference between E(Alpha) and E(Beta), then, is being taken to be the same as the difference between seeing, in broad daylight, directly in front of your eyes, one finger raised and two fingers raised. Seeing the two fingers is not like seeing a flock of geese (from a distance) where individual geese are "fused" into a whole and not seen. In the case of the fingers, one sees both the finger on the left and the finger on the right. Quite a different experience from seeing only the finger on the left. When the numbers get larger, as they

do with Alpha and Beta, the experiences are no longer discernibly different to the person having them. Given that each spot is seen, however, the experiences *are*, nonetheless, different. Large numbers merely make it harder to achieve fact-awareness of the differences on the part of the person experiencing the differences. E(Spot) is really no different than the difference between experiencing one finger and two fingers in broad daylight. The only difference is that in the case of Alpha and Beta there is no fact-awareness of the thing that makes the difference.[16]

Since the point is critical to my argument, let me emphasize the last point. In speaking of conscious differences in experience it is important to remember that one need not be conscious of the difference (= conscious that such a difference exists) in order for such differences to exist. Readers who noticed a difference between Alpha and Beta were, thereby, fact-aware of the difference between Alpha and Beta. Such readers may also have become fact-aware (by inference?) of the difference between their experience of Alpha and their experience of Beta—i.e., the difference between E(Alpha) and E(Beta). But readers who were only thing-aware of the difference between Alpha and Beta were not fact-conscious of the difference between Alpha and Beta. They were not, therefore, fact-conscious of any difference between E(Alpha) and E(Beta)—their conscious experience of Alpha and Beta. These are conscious differences of which no one is conscious.

In saying that the reader was conscious of Spot—and, hence, in this sense, the difference between Alpha and Beta—without being conscious of the fact that they differed, we commit ourselves to the possibility of differences in conscious experience that are not reflected in conscious belief. Consciousness of Spot requires a conscious experience of Spot, a conscious E(Spot); yet, there is nothing in one's conscious beliefs—either about Spot, about the difference between Alpha and Beta, or about the difference between E(Alpha) and E(Beta)—that registers this difference. What we have in such cases is

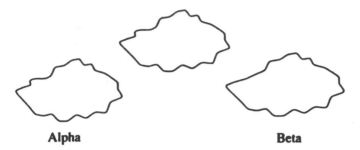

Alpha   **Beta**

Figure 48.3

internal *state* consciousness with no corresponding (transitive) *creature* consciousness of the conscious state.[17] With no creature consciousness we lack any way of discovering, *even in our own case*, that there exists this difference in conscious state. To regard this as a contradiction is merely to confuse the way an internal state like an experience can be conscious with the way the person who is in that state can be, or fail to be, conscious of it.

It may be supposed that my conclusion rests on the special character of my example. Alpha contains a numerically distinct element, Spot, and our intuitions about what is required to see a (distinct) thing are, perhaps, shaping our intuitions about the character of the experience needed to see it. Let me, therefore, borrow an example from Irvin Rock (1983). Once again, the reader is asked to view Figure 48.3 (after Rock 1983. p. 54) for a second and then say which, Alpha or Beta at the bottom, is the same as the figure shown at the top.

As closer inspection reveals, the upper left part of Alpha contains a few wiggles found in the original but not in Beta. Experimental subjects asked to identify which form it was they had seen did no better than chance. Many of them did not notice that there were wiggles on the figure they were shown. At least they could not remember having seen them. As Rock (1983, p. 55) observes:

Taken together, these results imply that when a given region of a figure is a nonconsequential part of the whole, something is lacking in the perception of it, with the result that no adequate memory of it seems to be established.

No adequate *memory* of it is established because, I submit, at the time the figure is seen there is no fact-awareness of the wiggles. You cannot remember *that* there are wiggles on the left if you were never aware that there were wiggles on the left.[18] Subjects were (or may well have been) aware (thing-aware) of the wiggles (they saw them), but never became aware that they were there. The wiggles are what Spot (or Tom's moustache) is: a thing one is thing-aware of but never notices. What is lacking in the subject's perception of the figure, then, is an awareness of certain facts (that there are wiggles on the upper left), not (at least not necessarily) an awareness of the things (the wiggles) on the left.

In some minds the second example may suffer from the same defects as the first: it exploits subtle (at least not easily noticeable) differences in detail of the object being perceived. The differences are out there in the objects, yes, but who can say whether these differences are registered in here, in our experience of the objects? Perhaps our conviction (or *my* conviction) that we do see (and, hence, consciously experience) these points of detail, *despite* not noticing them, is simply a result of the fact that we see figures (Alpha and Beta, for instance) between which there are visible differences, differences that *could* be identified (noticed) by an appropriate shift of attention. But just because the details are visible does not mean that we see them or, if we do, that there must be some intrinsic (conscious) difference in the experience of the figures that differ in these points of detail.

This is a way of saying that conscious experiences, the sort of experiences you have when looking around the room, cannot differ unless one is consciously aware that they differ. Nothing mental is to count as conscious (no state consciousness) unless one is conscious of it (without creature consciousness). This objection smacks of verificationism, but calling it names does nothing to blunt its appeal. So I offer one final example. It will, of necessity, come at the same point in a more indirect way. I turn to perceptually salient conditions, conditions it is hard to believe are not consciously experienced. In order to break the connection between experience and belief, between thing-awareness and fact-awareness, then, I turn to creatures with a diminished capacity for fact-awareness.[19]

Eleanor Gibson (1969, p. 284), in reporting Kluver's studies with monkeys, describes a case in which the animals are trained to the larger of two rectangles. When the rectangles are altered in size, the monkeys continue to respond to the larger of the two—whatever their absolute size happens to be. In Kluver's words, they "abstract" the LARGER THAN relation. After they succeed in abstracting this relation, and when responding appropriately to the larger (A) of two presented rectangles (A and B), we can say that they are aware of A, aware of B (thing-awareness), and aware that A is larger than B (fact awareness). Some philosophers may be a little uncomfortable about assigning beliefs to monkeys in these situations, uncomfortable about saying that the monkey is aware *that* A is larger than B, but let that pass. The monkeys at least exhibit a differential response, and that is enough. How shall we describe the monkeys' perceptual situation *before* they learned to abstract this relation? Did the rectangles *look* different to the monkeys? Was there any difference in their experience of A and B *before* they became aware that

A was larger than B? We can imagine the difference in size to be as great as we please. They were not fact-aware of the difference, not aware that A is larger than B, to be sure. But that isn't the question. The question is: were they conscious of the condition of A and B that, so to speak makes it true that A is larger than B?[20] Does their experience of objects change when, presented with two objects the same size, one of these objects expands making it much larger than the other? If not, how could these animals ever learn to do what they are being trained to do—distinguish between A's being larger than B and A's not being larger than B?

It seems reasonable to suppose that, prior to learning, the monkeys were thing-aware of a difference which they only became fact-aware of after learning was complete. Their experience of A and B was different, consciously so, before they were capable of exhibiting this difference in behavior. Learning of this sort is simply the development of fact-awareness from thing-awareness.

The situation becomes even more compelling if we present the monkeys with three rectangles and try to get them to abstract the INTERMEDIATE IN SIZE relation. This more difficult problem proves capable of solution by chimpanzees, but monkeys find it extremely difficult. Suppose monkey M cannot solve it. What shall we say about M's perceptual condition when he sees three rectangles, A, B and C of descending size. If we use behavioral criteria for what kind of facts M is conscious of and assume that M has already mastered the first abstraction (the LARGER THAN relation), M is aware of the three rectangles, A, B and C. M is also aware that A is larger than B, that B is larger than C, and that A is larger than C. M is not, however, aware that B is INTERMEDIATE IN SIZE even though this is logically implied by the facts he is aware of. Clearly, although M is not (and, apparently, cannot be made) aware of the fact that B is intermediate in size, he is nonetheless aware of the differences (A's being larger than B, B's being larger than C) that logically constitute the fact that he is not aware of. B's being intermediate in size is a condition the monkey is thing-aware of but cannot be made fact-aware of. There are conscious features of the animal's experiences that are not registered in the animal's fact-awareness and, hence, not evinced in the animal's deliberate behavior.

4   What, Then, Makes Experiences Conscious?

We have just concluded that there can be conscious differences in a person's experience of the world—and, in this sense, conscious features of his experience—of which that person is not conscious. If this is true, then it cannot be a person's awareness of a mental state that makes that state conscious. E(Spot) is conscious, and it constitutes a conscious difference between E(Alpha) and E(Beta) even though no one, including the person in whom it occurs, is being conscious of it. It follows, therefore, that what *makes* a mental state conscious cannot be our consciousness of it. If we have conscious experiences, beliefs, desires, and fears, it cannot be our introspective awareness of them that makes them conscious.

This conclusion is a bit premature. The argument mounted in §3 was primarily directed at higher-order-thought (HOT) theories that take an experience or a belief (mental states) to be conscious in virtue of their being the object of some higher-order-thought-like entity, a higher-order mental state that (like a thought) involves the deployment of concepts. My concern in §3, therefore, was to show that conscious experience required no fact-awareness—either of facts related to what one experiences (e.g., Spot) or of facts related to the experience itself (e.g., E(Spot)). One does not have to be fact-aware of E(Spot) in order for E(Spot) to be conscious.

This leaves the possibility, however, that in order for one's experience of Spot to be conscious, one must be thing-aware of it. Perhaps, that is, E(Spot) is conscious, not because there is some higher order *thought* (involving concepts) about E(Spot), but rather because there is a higher-order *experience* (a non-conceptual mental state) of E(Spot), something that makes one thing-aware of E(Spot) in the same way one is thing-aware (perceptually) of Spot. This is a form of the HOT theory that Lycan (1992, p. 216) describes as Locke's "inner sense" account of state-consciousness. What makes an experience conscious is not one's (fact) awareness that one is having it, but one's (thing) awareness of it.

To my mind, Rosenthal (1990, pp. 34ff.) makes a convincing case against this "inner sense" version of state consciousness. He points out, for example, that one of the respects in which experiences are unlike thoughts is in having a sensory quality to them. E(Alpha), for instance, has visual, not auditory or tactile qualities. If what made E(Alpha) into a conscious experience was some higher order experience of E(Alpha), one would expect some distinctive qualia of this higher-order experience to intrude. But all one finds are the qualia associated with E(Alpha), the lower-order experience. For this reason (among others) Rosenthal himself prefers a version of the inner spotlight theory of consciousness in which the spotlight is something in the nature of a fact-awareness, not thing-awareness, of the lower order mental state or activity.

Aside, though, from the merits of such specific objections, I think the "inner sense" approach loses all its attraction once the distinction between thing-awareness and fact-awareness is firmly in place. Notice, first, that if it is thing-awareness of a mental state that is supposed to make that mental state conscious, then the "inner sense" theory has no grounds for saying that E(Spot) is not conscious. For a person might well be thing-aware of E(Spot)—thus making E(Spot) conscious—just as he is thing-aware of Spot, without ever being fact-aware of it. So on this version of the spotlight theory, a failure to realize, a total unawareness of the fact *that* there is a difference between E(Alpha) and E(Beta), is irrelevant to whether there is a conscious difference between these two experiences. This being so, the "inner sense" theory of what makes a mental state conscious does nothing to *improve* one's epistemic access to one's own conscious states. *As far as one can tell*, E(Spot) (just like Spot) may as well not exist. What good is an inner spotlight, an introspective awareness of mental events, if it doesn't give one epistemic access to the events on which it shines? The "inner sense" theory does nothing to solve the problem of what makes E(Spot) conscious. On the contrary, it multiplies the problems by multiplying the facts of which we are not aware. We started with E(Spot) and gave arguments in support of the view that E(Spot) was conscious even though the person in whom it occurred was not fact-aware of it. We are now being asked to explain this fact by another fact of which we are not fact-aware: namely, the fact that we are thing-aware of E(Spot). Neither E(Spot) nor the thing-awareness of E(Spot) makes any *discernible* difference to the person in whom they occur. This, surely, is a job for Occam's Razor.

If we do not have to be conscious of a mental state (like an experience) for the mental state to be conscious, then, it seems, consciousness of something cannot be what it is that makes a thing conscious. Creature consciousness (of either the factive or thing form) is not necessary for state consciousness.[21] What, then, makes a mental state conscious? When S smells, and thereby becomes aware of, the burning toast, what makes his experience of the burning toast a conscious experience? When S becomes aware that the light has turned green, what makes his belief that the light has turned green a conscious belief?

This is the big question, of course, and I am not confronting it in this chapter. I am concerned only with a preliminary issue—a question about the relationship (or lack thereof) between creature consciousness and state consciousness. For it is the absence of this relation (in the right form) that undermines the orthodox view that what makes certain mental states conscious is one's awareness of them. Nonetheless, though I lack the space (and, at this stage, the theory) to answer the big question, I would like to indicate, if only

briefly, the direction in which these considerations lead.

What makes an internal state or process conscious is the role it plays in making one (intransitively) conscious—normally, the role it plays in making one (transitively) conscious of some thing or fact. An experience of x is conscious, not because one is aware of the experience, or aware that one is having it, but because, being a certain sort of representation, it makes one aware of the properties (of x) and objects (x itself) of which it is a (sensory) representation. My visual experience of a barn is conscious, not because I am introspectively aware of it (or introspectively aware that I am having it), but because it (when brought about in the right way) makes me aware of the barn. It enables me to perceive the barn. For the same reason, a certain belief is conscious, not because the believer is conscious of *it* (or conscious of having it[22]), but because it is a representation that makes one conscious of the fact (that *P*) that it is a belief about. Experiences and beliefs are conscious, not because you are conscious of them, but because, so to speak, you are conscious *with* them.

This is not to deny that one may, in fact, be conscious of one's own experiences in the way one is, in ordinary perception, conscious of barns and other people. Perhaps we are equipped with an introspective faculty, some special internal scanner, that takes as its objects (the xs it is an awareness of), one's experiences of barns and people. Perhaps this is so. Perhaps introspection is a form of meta-spectation—a sensing of one's own sensing of the world. I doubt this. I think introspection is best understood, not as thing-awareness, but as fact-awareness—an awareness that one has certain beliefs, thoughts, desires and experiences *without* a corresponding awareness of the things (the beliefs, thoughts, experiences and desires) themselves. Introspection is more like coming to know (be aware) that one has a virus than it is like coming to see, hear, or feel (i.e., be aware of) the virus (the thing) itself.

Whether these speculations on the nature of introspection are true or not, however, is independent of the present thesis about consciousness. The claim is not that we are unaware of our own conscious beliefs and experiences (or unaware that we have them). It is, instead, that our being aware of them, or that we have them, is not what makes them conscious. What make them conscious is the way they make us conscious of something else—the world we live in and (in proprioception) the condition of our own bodies.

Saying just what the special status is that makes certain internal representations conscious while other internal states (lacking this status) remain unconscious is, of course, the job for a fully developed theory of consciousness. I haven't supplied that. All I have tried to do is to indicate where not to look for it.

Acknowledgments

I am grateful to Berent Enç, Güven Güzeldere, Lydia Sanchez, Ken Norman, David Robb and Bill Lycan for critical feedback. I would also like to thank the Editor and anonymous referees of *Mind* for a number of very helpful suggestions.

Notes

1. I am thinking here of those who subscribe to what are called higher order thought (HOT) theories of consciousness, theories that hold that what makes an experience conscious is its being an object of some higher-order thought or experience. See Rosenthal (1986, 1990, 1991), Armstrong (1968, 1980, especially Ch. 4, "What is Consciousness?") and Lycan (1987, 1992). I return to these theories in §4.

2. This section is a summary and minor extension of points I have made elsewhere; see especially Dretske 1969, 1978, 1979.

3. When I speak of events I should be understood to be including any of a large assortment of entities that occupy temporal positions (or duration): happenings, occurrences, states, states-of-affairs, processes, conditions, situations, and so on. In speaking of these as temporal entities, I do not mean to deny that they have spatial attributes—only that they do so in a way that is derived from the objects to which they happen. Games occur in stadiums because that is where the players are when they play the game. Movements (of a passenger, say) occur in a vehicle because that is where the person is when she moves.

4. White (1964, p. 42) calls "aware" a polymorphous concept (p. 6); it takes many forms. What it is to become or be aware of something depends on what one is aware of. To become aware of a perceptual object takes the form of seeing or hearing or smelling or tasting or feeling it.

5. One must distinguish Clyde from such things as Clyde's location, virtues, etc. One can be aware of Clyde's location and virtues without, at the time, perceiving them. But unlike Clyde, his virtues and location are not what I am calling things. See the discussion of abstract objects below.

6. I will not try to distinguish direct from indirect forms of perception (and, thus, awareness). We speak of seeing Michael Jordan on TV. If this counts as seeing Michael Jordan, then (for purposes of this essay), it also counts as being aware or conscious of Michael Jordan (on TV). Likewise, if one has philosophical scruples about saying one smells a rose or hears a bell—thinking, perhaps, that it is really only scents and sounds (not the objects that give off those scents or make those sounds) that one smells and hears—then, when I speak of being conscious of a flower (by smelling) or bell (by hearing), one can translate this as being indirectly conscious of the flower via its scent and the bell via the sound it makes.

7. Generally speaking, the concepts necessary for awareness of facts are those corresponding to terms occurring obliquely in the clause (the that-clause) describing the fact one is aware of.

8. I am here indebted to Perkins' (1983, pp. 295–305) insightful discussion.

9. If it helps, the reader may suppose that later, at t_3, S remembers having seen Tom's moustache at t_2 while being completely unaware at the time (i.e., at t_2) that Tom had a moustache. Such later memories are not essential (S may see the moustache and *never* realize he saw it), but they may, at this point in the discussion, help calm verificationists' anxieties about the example.

10. For further arguments see Dretske (1969, Ch. 2; 1979; 1981, Ch. 6; and my reply to Heil in McLaughlin, 1991, pp. 180–185).

11. White (1964, p. 59): "Being conscious or unconscious *of* so and so is not the same as simply being conscious or unconscious. If there is anything of which a man is conscious, if follows that he is conscious; to lose consciousness is to cease to be conscious of anything."

12. One might mention dreams as a possible exception to (3): one is (in a dream) aware of certain things (images?) while being asleep and, therefore, unconscious in the intransitive sense. I think this is not a genuine exception to (3), but since I do not want to get sidetracked arguing about it, I let the possibility stand as a "possible" exception. Nothing will depend on how the matter is decided.

13. For purposes of illustrating distinctions I use a simple causal theory of knowledge (to know that *P* is to be caused to believe that *P* by the fact that *P*) and perception (to perceive *x* is to be caused to have an experience by *x*). Though sympathetic to certain versions of these theories, I wish to remain neutral here.

14. E.g., Baars (1988), Velmans (1991), Humphrey (1992).

15. I do not think it necessary to speculate about how E (Spot) is realized or about its exact relation to E(Alpha). I certainly do not think E(Spot) must literally be a *spatial* part of E(Alpha) in the way Spot is a spatial part of Alpha. The argument is that there is an intrinsic *difference* between E(Alpha) and E(Beta). E(Spot) is just a convenient way of referring to this difference.

16. Speaking of large numbers, Elizabeth, a remarkable eidetiker (a person who can maintain visual images for a long time) studied by Stromeyer and Psotka (1970), was tested with computer-generated random-dot stereograms. She looked at a 10,000 dot pattern for one minute with one eye. Then she looked at another 10,000 dot pattern with the other eye. Some of the individual dots in the second pattern were systematically offset so that a figure in depth would emerge (as in using a stereoscope) if the patterns from the two eyes were fused. Elizabeth succeeded in superimposing the eidetic image that she retained from the first pattern over the second pattern. She saw the figure that normal subjects can only see by viewing the two patterns (one with each eye) simultaneously.

I note here that to fuse the two patterns the *individual dots* seen with one eye must somehow be paired with those retained by the brain (*not* the eye; this is not an after-image) from the other eye.

17. I return, in the next section, to the question of whether we might not have thing-awareness of

E(Spot)—that is, the same kind of awareness of the difference between E(Alpha) and E(Beta) as we have of the difference between Alpha and Beta.

18. Though there may be other ways of remembering the wiggles. To use an earlier example, one might remember seeing Tom's moustache without (at the time) noticing it (being fact-aware of it). Even if one cannot remember *that* Tom had a moustache (since one never knew this), one can, I think, remember *seeing* Tom's moustache. This is the kind of memory (episodic vs. declarative) involved in a well-known example: remembering how many windows there are in a familiar house (e.g., the house one grew up in) by imagining oneself walking through the house and counting the windows. One does not, in this case, remember that there were 23 windows although one comes to know that there were 23 windows by using one's memory.

19. The following is an adaptation of the discussion in Dretske (1981, pp. 151–2).

20. *Conditions*, recall, are things in my sense of this word. One can be aware of an object's condition (its movement, for instance) without being aware that it is moving. This is what happens when one sees an adjacent vehicle's movement *as* one's own movement or an object's movement as an expansion or contraction. It is also what occurs in infants and, perhaps, animals who do not have the concept of movement: they are aware of O's movement, but not aware that O is moving.

21. Neither is it sufficient. We are conscious of a great many internal states and activities that are not themselves conscious (heart beats, a loose tooth, hiccoughs of a fetus, a cinder in the eye).

22. If fact-awareness was what made a belief conscious, it would be very hard for young children (those under the age of three or four years, say) to have conscious beliefs. They don't yet have a firm grasp of the concept of a belief and are, therefore, unaware of the fact that they have beliefs. See Flavell (1988), Wellman (1990).

References

Armstrong, D. M. (1986). A *Materialist Theory of the Mind*. London: Routledge and Kegan Paul.

———. (1980). *The Nature of Mind and Other Essays*. Ithaca, New York: Cornell University Press.

Astington, J., P. Harris, and D. Olson, eds. (1988). *Developing Theories of the Mind*. New York: Cambridge University Press.

Baars, B. (1988). *A Cognitive Theory of Consciousness*. Cambridge: Cambridge University Press.

Dennett, D. C. (1991). *Consciousness Explained*. Boston: Little, Brown.

Dretske, F. (1969). *Seeing and Knowing*. Chicago: University of Chicago Press.

——. (1978). "The role of the percept in visual cognition," in Savage 1978, pp. 107–127.

——. (1979). "Simple seeing," in Gustafson and Tapscott 1979, pp. 1–15.

——. (1981). *Knowledge and the Flow of Information*. Cambridge, Massachusetts: MIT Press/A Bradford Book.

——. (1990). "Seeing, believing and knowing," in Osherson, Kosslyn and Hollerbach 1990.

Flavell, J. H. (1988). "The development of children's knowledge about the mind: From cognitive connections to mental representations," in Astington, Harris, and Olson 1988.

Gibson, E. (1969). *Principles of Perceptual Learning and Development*. New York: Appleton Century & Crofts.

Grice, P. (1989). *Studies in the Way of Words*. Cambridge, Massachusetts: Harvard University Press.

Gustafson, D. F., and B. L. Tapscott, eds. (1979). *Body, Mind and Method: Essays in Honor of Virgil Aldrich*. Dordrecht, Holland: Reidel.

Humphrey, N. (1992). *A History of the Mind: Evolution and the Birth of Consciousness*. New York: Simon and Schuster.

Lees, R. B. (1963). *The Grammar of English Nominalizations*. Bloomington, Indiana: Indiana University Press.

Lycan, W. (1987). *Consciousness*. Cambridge, Massachusetts: MIT Press.

——. (1992). "Uncertain Materialism and Lockean introspection." *Behavioral and Brain Sciences* 15.2, pp. 216–17.

McLaughlin, B., ed. (1991). *Critical Essays on the Philosophy of Fred Dretske*. Oxford: Basil Blackwell.

Milner, A. D., and M. D. Rugg, eds. (1992). *The Neuropsychology of Consciousness*. London: Academic Press.

Osherson, D., S. Kosslyn, and J. Hollerback, eds. (1990). *An Invitation to Cognitive Science, Volume 2, Visual Cognition and Action*. Cambridge, Massachusetts: MIT Press.

Perkins, M. (1983). *Sensing the World*. Indianapolis, Indiana: Hackett Publishing Company.

Rock, I. (1983). *The Logic of Perception*. Cambridge, Massachusetts: MIT Press/A Bradford Book.

Rosenthal, D. (1986). "Two concepts of consciousness." *Philosophical Studies* 94.3, pp. 329–59.

——. (1990). "A theory of consciousness." Report No. 40, Research Group on Mind and Brain, ZiF, University of Bielefeld.

——. (1991). "The independence of consciousness and sensory quality," in Villanueva (1991), pp. 15–36.

Savage, W., ed. (1978). *Minnesota Studies in the Philosophy of Science: Perception and Cognition*, Vol IX. Minneapolis, Minnesota: University of Minnesota Press.

Stromeyer, C. F., and J. Psotka (1970). "The detailed texture of eidetic images." *Nature*, 225, pp. 346–349.

Velmans, M. (1991). "Is human information processing conscious?" *Behavioral and Brain Sciences* 14.4, pp. 651–668.

Villanueva, E., ed. (1991). *Consciousness*. Atascadero, CA: Ridgeview Publishing Company.

Wellman, H. M. (1990). *The Child's Theory of the Mind*. Cambridge, Massachusetts; MIT Press/A Bradford Book.

White, A. R. (1964). *Attention*. Oxford: Basil Blackwell.

Is Consciousness the Perception of What Passes in One's Own Mind?

Güven Güzeldere

There is a strong intuition, which dates back several centuries, that consciousness is not, or does not consist in, an ordinary mental state or process itself, but it is, or it consists in, the *awareness* of such states and processes. Locke (1959) epitomized this intuition in his celebrated statement: "Consciousness is the perception of what passes in a man's own mind" (p. 138). Various versions of this maxim have appeared in the writings of philosophers and psychologists from William James (1950) to Franz Brentano (1973)[1] and more recently have received endorsement by David Armstrong (1980), Paul Churchland (1988), David Rosenthal (1986, chap. 46, this book), Peter Carruthers (1989), and William Lycan (1987, chap. 47, this book), as well as (though rather indirectly) by Daniel Dennett (1991). Armstrong (1980) calls this form of consciousness the "perception of the mental," or "introspective consciousness," and promotes it as "consciousness in the most interesting sense of the word":

Introspective consciousness ... is a perception-like awareness of current states and activities in our own mind. The current activities will include sense-perception: which latter is the awareness of current states and activities of our environment and our body. (p. 61)

Churchland (1988) echoes Armstrong's conviction in calling introspective consciousness "just a species of perception: *self-perception*" (p. 74). According to Rosenthal (chap. 46, this book), the awareness of mental states and activities comes in the form of a cognitive, rather than a perceptual, state: "[A] mental state is a conscious state when, and only when, it is accompanied by a suitable higher-order thought" (p. 741). And Lycan (chap. 47, this book) characterizes consciousness as a "perception-like second-order representing of our own psychological states and events" (p. 755).[2]

These assertions constitute the core of a substantial body of work among the philosophical theories of consciousness today. What is common to all these theories is the claim that consciousness is, or consists in, some kind of higher-order representing of lower-level mental states and processes. This representing may be perception-like (as Armstrong, Churchland, and Lycan claim, after Locke), or thought-like (as Rosenthal, and to some extent, Carruthers and Dennett, claim).[3]

The psychological plausibility and philosophical merit of such accounts depend on how well the specifics of such representings are spelled out—whether it is the perception or the thinking about of "what passes in one's own mind." Paying attention to the mechanics of higher-order representation is important especially for two reasons. First, it is these mechanics that determine the degree to which consciousness is literally, and not just metaphorically, taken to be the "perception (or, thinking) of what passes in one's own mind." Second, assuming a literal reading of this conception of consciousness, it is the specifics of just how certain mental states can be represented by certain others that reveal the substantive differences, if any, between the perception-like and the thought-like higher-order representings of first-order mental states.

I will lay out these details in this chapter. In doing so, I hope to show that the two varieties of higher-order representation accounts of consciousness, if taken literally, do not survive as two distinct competing models. In particular, I try to demonstrate that the "higher-order perception" accounts of consciousness, upon close examination, face a serious trilemma: they get forced to abandon their characteristic two-tiered structure, or commit themselves to what I call the "fallacy of the representational divide," or turn into a species of their competitor.

Taking the first horn of the trilemma means simply giving up the essential introspective element of the theory. The fallacy inherent in the second horn stems from a confusion between properties of what is represented and properties of that which represents what is represented, in these accounts of second-order, introspective awareness. Avoiding this fallacy is possible only under a particular interpretation of the phrase "perception of what passes in one's mind," which forces the "higher-order perception theories" to transform into a species of "higher-order thought" theories. That is the third horn of the trilemma.

This construal can constitute only half of a full analysis of the higher-order representation accounts of consciousness. The other half would consist in an examination of how plausible the remaining accounts of the higher-order thought variety are and to what extent they do justice to explaining the nature and mechanism of consciousness. That half I do not attempt to give here. My goal is only to point out that the presumed distinction between the two kinds of higher-order accounts of consciousness, based on which there is a growing literature, is unfounded as it stands. In particular, the higher-order perception accounts, taken literally, can only be a species of higher-order thought accounts.[4]

1 The Higher-Order Representation (HOR) Theories of Consciousness

Two Senses of Consciousness

Let me start with a simple set of distinctions with respect to consciousness. Among the things that the term *conscious* can be used to predicate upon, the two most important kinds are individual beings and mental states that belong to, or occur in, these individuals. For example, there is a difference in my being conscious (as opposed to, say, in a coma) and my having a mental state that is conscious (as opposed to, say, subconscious).[5] The former involves one's being conscious in the sense of being awake and alert. Furthermore one's consciousness can be directed upon something, such as a tune coming from the radio or a

lingering thought about a past conversation. This is the *individual* sense of consciousness.

On the other hand, it makes sense to talk about whether a particular mental state is conscious. This is not quite the same as someone's being conscious. The individual sense of consciousness denotes an overall state one is in; the other one classifies one's (mental) states as of one type or another. Following Rosenthal (chap. 46, this book), I will call this sense of consciousness, which functions as a type identifier for mental states, *state consciousness*. (Rosenthal's term for what I call "individual consciousness" is "creature consciousness.")[6]

Given this distinction, the natural next step is to investigate the relation between these two senses of consciousness. One way of doing this is to formulate a tighter relation between the (state-)consciousness of some particular mental state and one's (individual-)consciousness of *that* state.[7]

So far, I have not specified the domain of objects toward which individual consciousness can be directed. For the purposes of this chapter, I will adopt a fairly nondetailed position: One can be individual conscious of physical things (cups, telephones, etc.), abstract objects (relations, theorems, etc.), facts, states of affairs, and events.[8] These are all "external," in the sense that they can be objects of other peoples's consciousnesses as well. Alternatively, one can be conscious of the proprioceptive states of one's own body (the muscular strain in one's leg) or, as it is generally accepted, of one's own mental states (a desire for a chocolate bar). Broadly speaking, both of these are "internal" to the subject; only I have access to my proprioceptive states or desires, at least in the way that I do (cf. Lyons 1986, esp. chapters 1 and 7).

This classification roughly corresponds to a commonsense understanding of perception (seeing a cup on the counter, seeing that the cup is on the counter), proprioception (feeling one's foot getting numb), and introspection (dwelling on one's thoughts, desires, motives, etc.). That is, I want to spell out individual consciousness in terms of familiar mental phenomena and remain neutral about further details at this stage. This is not to say, however, that this usage is entirely unproblematic. In particular, the claim that mental states can be the object of one's individual consciousness, which makes it a "second-order" mental state, is multiply ambiguous, and, as such, requires further analysis.

What does "being conscious of one's belief" mean? Being conscious of the *content* of that belief, being conscious of *the fact that one has a belief* with the content that it has, or being conscious of *the belief state qua the vehicle* that it is (i.e., the mental state that does the representing, not what it represents)? The discussion of these issues will constitute the core of my assessment of the "higher-order perception theories" of consciousness in section 2.

Linking Individual Consciousness with State Consciousness

Let me now state a canonical formulation of the relation between the state and the individual senses of consciousness. This formulation is meant to capture the thesis that underlies both the perception-like and the thought-like higher order theories of consciousness.

The Introspective Link Principle A mental state M in a subject S is *state-conscious* if and only if S is *individual-conscious* of M.

I would like to give the consciousness accounts that are built around this general linking principle a common name: the theories of higher-order (mental) representation (HOR). Implicit in the *Introspective Link Principle*, and hence in all the HOR theories, is the employment of a metalevel mental state, which is responsible for the consciousness of the lower-level states. S's (individual-)consciousness of M is itself a (second-order) mental state, M' in S, presumably directed upon M. M', then, *endows* M with state-consciousness,

in virtue of being a mental state in S itself, directed upon M. In other words, M' is second-order state that *represents* M, an ordinary first-order mental state. M may, for instance, just be a visual perceptual state whose content is a scene S is looking at or a thought S is entertaining about her dinner plans.

Representation as Perception or Thought? HOP versus HOT

HOR comes in two main flavors, depending on the nature of the postulated higher-order mental representation. This is only natural since mental representation is possible via both perceptual and (nonperceptual) cognitive states. Indeed, there is a significant number of philosophers taking each route in spelling out the "R" of HOR.

If M' is regarded as a perception-like state, where M' relation to its object M is somehow like the relation between perceptual state and its object, I call this version of HOR the thesis of higher-order perception, or HOP. As indicated earlier, David Armstrong, Paul Churchland, and William Lycan, following Locke, all defend this view.

Alternatively, M' can be taken to be a type of cognitive mental representation, a higher-level thought-like state, the content of which is either the content of M or (roughly speaking) a fact involving M (e.g., that S is having M). This is the thesis of higher-order thought, or HOT. David Rosenthal and Peter Carruthers subscribe to the HOT thesis, and Dan Dennett comes close, though they all defend different variations of it.[9]

In either case, some form of hierarchical mental structure and of higher-order representing is the key idea for explaining consciousness in these accounts. For that reason, I call them "double-tiered" theories. The HOR accounts constitute the orthodox line with regard to theories of "introspective consciousness" in analytic philosophy today.[10] Dretske (1993, 1995) and Shoemaker (1994) provide forceful contemporary critiques of these accounts.[11]

2 Spelling out the "P" in "HOP": What Is Wrong with Higher-Order Perception?

Locke, Armstrong, Churchland, and Lycan all talk about consciousness as the awareness, or perception, or monitoring, or scanning of one's mental states. There is an ambiguity inherent in all these statements concerning the nature of the proper object of such internal, perception-like awareness. What exactly is being perceived in the "perception of what passes in one's own mind": the content of the mental state that happens to be "passing through" one's mind at the time or the mental state itself? Or the content of another thought to the effect that one is having such a mental state?

There is surprisingly little attention paid to spelling out the answer to this question in any detail. Perhaps it is because the answer seems obvious or self-evident to everyone. Or perhaps not much is thought to depend on it. I will argue that, taken literally, there is actually nothing quite obvious or self-evident about such an answer, especially when the implicit ontological assumptions underlying it are made explicit. Nor is it true that not much turns on providing such details. What is at stake is simply the plausibility of the whole class of HOP-style theories.

Three Options for the HOP Theorist

So far, one of the predominant distinctions on which the discussion has been resting has been perceptual versus cognitive mental states—for example, one's seeing a cup on the desk versus one's believing that the cup is on the desk (seeing *that* the cup is on the desk). Since vision is paradigmatic of perception, and beliefs are paradigmatic of cognitive states, let me proceed as such, assuming no loss of generality.[12]

Assume that our subject S is sitting on her desk and looking at her cup right in front of her, under all the "normal circumstances": perfect light, veridical experience, no demons or "evil neuro-

surgeons" playing tricks on S, and so forth. And despite the immense complexity and dynamical nature of perception, let us, in all simplicity, assume that we can capture a single instant of S's perceptual processing as she continues to eye the cup, freezing time, and thus securing a momentary state of her bodily-mental conditions—"a Polaroid snapshot of S's mind," if you will. Call the visual state S is in at this moment, the state which is in her (as well as for her), a representation of the cup, V. In other words, V is the state in virtue of which S sees the cup in the way she does. Let me denote the content of S's visual state concisely as: [cup in front].

According to the HOP theorists, S's consciousness consists in her "perception of V." Call this S's second-order "perception-like awareness" of V, her "monitoring" or "scanning" of her first-order mental state. Whatever we may call it (and henceforth I use the term *awareness* to cover all these), this is a junction in the conceptual landscape where some unpacking is necessary.

I can come up with at least three different readings of "S is aware of of her visual state V, which has the content: [cup in front]":

1. S is aware of *the cup* in front of her, simpliciter.

2. S is aware of *her visual state V* (i.e., she is aware of V-*qua*-vehicle, the cup-representing internal state.)

3. S is aware of *the fact that she has a visual state V*, which has the content: [cup in front].

Which one of these three readings truly reflects what the HOP theorists have in mind?

3 Option 1: Higher-Order Perception as Perception Simpliciter

Option 1 will not do. An (introspective) awareness of one's mental state is not, by the HOP theorists' definition, nothing but just having that mental state. This option would no longer leave room for higher-order representing, and hence not allow for a double-tiered account, collapsing the (first) level of an ordinary mental state and the (second) level of an introspective mental state into one.

Such an option may be available to those (single-tiered theorists of consciousness) who would like to claim that introspection is but an illusion, and that every time one tries to become introspectively aware of one's mental state, one finds oneself simply in that very mental state. But this would mean doing away with second-order representing altogether, something central to HOP accounts. Option 1 is therefore really a nonoption for the HOP theorist.[13]

4   Option 2: Higher-Order Perception as Perception of the Representational Vehicle

What about Option 2? The idea that introspective consciousness may be the direct awareness of mental states (*qua* the representational vehicles, the carriers of content) rather than of what those states represent (their content) is an interesting one. Furthermore, it can also be defended in one of two different ways, depending on the accompanying theory of mental representations. I will look at them both in some detail, but my conclusion will not be any different from what I reached for the first option: There is no reading under which "higher-order perception" can be taken literally as an account of introspective consciousness.

Two Interpretations for Option 2

Most contemporary materialist theories of mental representations, details aside, have this much in common: Mental representations are states of the nervous system, which represent to the subject in whom they occur various objects in, and facts about, the subject's environment, as well as the subject's bodily states. These representations, being neuronal structures interacting in various electrochemical ways, themselves possess such properties as spiking frequencies and synaptic densities. In turn, they represent the world to the subject as being a certain way, via (at least, seemingly) different properties—those properties we are all familiar with in our phenomenology: colors, textures, temperature, and so on. So at least on the face of it, it seems that the properties of the representers and those of the represented do not always coincide; in fact, they often seem radically different.

On the other hand, there used to be a time when the relation between (what can roughly be called today) "mental images" in the mind and objects in the world external to the mind was taken to be one of resemblance.[14] Under this conception of mental representation, perception was thought to involve literally "seeing with the mind's eye." Although it is not easy to come by anyone today who would explicitly defend the "resemblance theory of mental representations," I think that it is still an operant intuition, albeit in disguise, in many discussions in the philosophy of perception. In fact, I will argue that one way to take the "perception of the mental" claim literally commits the HOP theorists to such a resemblance account of mental representations.

In sum, it is possible to give two distinct interpretations of introspective consciousness construed as "internally directed perception," depending on what the "internal objects" of this perceptual activity are taken to be. Under the former materialist framework, this would amount to, I will argue, an account of introspection as some form of "direct access" to one's brain states, in terms of the intrinsic, physical properties of those states. In the latter version, where the introspected "internal objects" are assumed to share the properties of the external objects they resemble, I will show that introspective consciousness in essence becomes a literal account of "seeing with the mind's eye." Neither account has desirable consequences, but both deserve a more detailed treatment.

First Interpretation of Option 2: Higher-Order Perception as "Direct Introspection of Brain States"

Let me start with the former version. Even though the phrase "direct introspection of brain states" exclusively belongs to Churchland (1985), I will argue that the same basic idea can be used in filling in the details of what both Armstrong (1968, 1980) and Lycan (1987, chap. 47, this book) leave unspecified in their accounts. I will come back to Churchland following an analysis of Armstrong and Lycan.

Armstrong and Lycan

Armstrong (1980) contrasts introspective consciousness with ordinary perception and talks about the consciousness of one's mental states as "simply the scanning of one part of our central nervous system by another." He states (Armstrong 1968):

[I] suggest that consciousness is no more than *awareness* (perception) of inner mental states by the person whose states they are.... In perception the brain scans the environment. In awareness of the perception another process in the brain scans that scanning. (p. 94)

In Armstrong's view, this "second-order scanning" is just what is missing in a long-distance truck driver, who has been driving on "autopilot," perceiving the road and steering accordingly but lacking any "inner perception" of his mental states, any introspective awareness of what he has been doing (seeing other vehicles, stopping at red light, swerving to avoid collisions, etc.). The truck driver, Armstrong maintains, although "perceptually conscious" of his environment, is nonetheless *unconscious* in a very important sense: he lacks "introspective consciousness." As a result, he will have been surprised that he has been driving for hours at the moment he (re)gains introspective consciousness and will have no recollection of his experiences that belong to this period of introspective unconsciousness.[15]

Lycan (chap. 47, this book) follows suit in characterizing consciousness as "the successful operation of an internal scanner or monitor" in the brain and asserts that "consciousness is the functioning of internal *attention mechanisms* directed upon lower-order psychological states and events" (p. 755).

Unfortunately these claims, once asserted, are left at that: mere just-so stories. Neither the neurophysiological nor the psychological details of such a monitoring process are anywhere to be found in either author's account. It can perhaps be argued that Armstrong and Lycan cannot be expected to make a neurophysiological case; it is the job of neuroscientists to determine the validity of the higher-order scanning claim with further research. It should be noted, however, that the claim that there are self-scanners in the nervous system that are responsible for introspective consciousness, in accordance with Armstrong's and Lycan's characterization, has no solid physiological or anatomical basis in the neuroscientific literature at present either.[16] Moreover, even if that was not the case, there would still be a missing philosophical component in these accounts: the construal of the nature of those properties that figure in the internal monitoring process such that their scanning gives rise to introspective consciousness.

For instance, Lycan (1987) asserts that "to be actively-introspectively aware that P is for one to have an internal scanner in working order that is operating on some state that is itself psychological and delivering information about that state to one's executive control unit" (p. 72). He leaves it unspecified, however, just what kind of information about the first-order states needs to be delivered to the "executive control unit." Surely such information is to bear *some* relation to the state in question. It could be constitutive of the relevant state's *content*, for example, or it could just indicate the *presence* (or absence) of that state. Lycan does not say which.

In fact, neither of these construals can account for the "higher-order perception" hypothesis. If the output of the second-order scanner simply provides the system with the *content* of the first-order state, this collapses the double-tiered structure of the HOP accounts into a unilevel account (transforming Option 2 to Option 1). If, on the other hand, the output of the scanning process is taken merely to deliver information about whether the system is currently in possession of a certain first-order state (*that* a particular first-order state is tokened), then the HOP account transforms into a species of a HOT account (transforming Option 2 to Option 3). As such, neither Armstrong's nor Lycan's account provides sufficient detail to uphold the first interpretation of Option 2 of the HOP thesis on its own.

Churchland

Churchland (1988) tries out a somewhat different tack, and his account is more explicit in its details. Furthermore, if valid, it could also provide a new way out for both Armstrong's and Lycan's accounts. Churchland too takes introspective consciousness as a species of perception:

[O]ne's introspective consciousness of oneself appears very similar to one's perceptual consciousness of the external world. The difference is that, in the former case, whatever mechanisms of discrimination are at work are keyed to internal circumstances instead of to external ones.... Self-consciousness is no more (and no less) mysterious than perception generally. It is just directed internally rather than externally. (p. 74)

So what are the internal circumstances to which one's discriminatory introspective powers are keyed? Or, to put the question in another way, in virtue of what kinds of properties of internal goings on does one gain introspective consciousness of one's mental states? What sort of "self-perception," in other words, would make the truck driver who is driving on "auto-pilot" to become introspectively aware that he has just stopped because the traffic light turned red?

A possible answer could be found in Churchland's (1985) discussion of the direct introspec-

tion of brain states. Although Churchland's intention there seems to be promoting a general ontological position about the mind (a blend of reductionism and eliminativism), the framework he lays out is sufficiently detailed, and it subsumes several pointers to pursue questions about the nature of introspective consciousness, especially when combined with his more specific remarks.

Churchland claims that a finer grained account of "human subjective consciousness" can be given in the language of a highly advanced neuroscience. Provided that we acquaint ourselves with such a new, sophisticated conceptual framework, he maintains, the direct introspection of brain states, which amounts to a form of "internally directed perception," will give us greater powers of discrimination.

Dopamine levels in the limbic system, the spiking frequencies in specific neural pathways, resonances in the *n*th layer of the occipital cortex, inhibitory feedback to the lateral geniculate nucleus, and countless other neurophysiological niceities could be moved into the objective focus of our introspective discrimination, just as *Gm7* chords and *Adim* chords are moved into the objective focus of a trained musician's auditory discrimination. We will of course have to *learn* the conceptual framework of a matured neuroscience in order to pull this off. And we will have to *practice* its noninferential application. But that seems a small price to pay for the quantum leap in self-apprehension. (p. 55)

Perhaps so. Perhaps we can learn to discriminate among our brain states in terms of their intrinsic properties and become very good at it. Note that underlying Churchland's claim is the conviction that not only are mental states identical to brain states, but also the properties of the former will turn out to be identical to, or will replace the properties of, the latter (or a combination of both). And perhaps that too is true. But would any amount of such "direct access" to the neurophysiological properties of our brain states help us in gaining *introspective consciousness* of our first-order perceptual states?

The answer is no. Consider Armstrong's truck driver who, after having been driving for the last half-hour with no introspective awareness, "comes to realize" that he has just stopped because he is at a red traffic light. What does his realization, his gaining introspective consciousness, amount to? Note that the question is not whether spiking frequencies or dopamine levels in his brain underlay or played a causal role in his becoming introspectively conscious of his circumstances. (Of course, they did.) We are, rather, interested in how far we can go by taking the idea of "direct introspection of brain states" literally. Certainly the driver is now aware of something he was not before. But is it the dopamine levels or spiking frequencies in his brain that he "perceived" and became aware of?

The Fallacy of the Representational Divide

Looking inside someone's head to find out about the content of his or her introspective awareness is a mistake. Not only does the truck driver not need to be aware of the intrinsic properties of his brain states in order to come to realize that he is at a red traffic light, his awareness of such properties would not necessarily suffice to wake him up to his circumstances either. According to Armstrong, he has always been aware of the road and the traffic lights in some sense of the word *consciousness*. (Armstrong calls this "perceptual consciousness.") Perhaps what changes in his situation is the way he becomes aware of the red light or the amount of attention he pays to what he is up to. All of this has a lot to do with the intrinsic properties of one's brain, but none of it has to involve one's awareness or knowledge of those properties per se.

Conversely, the driver could, in some bizzarely concocted way, "perceive" his brain states and processes (say, through real-time functional magnetic resonance imaging [FMRI] viewing), in the same nonintrospective way he has been perceiving the road. Or (if we were to insist) matters could be arranged such that he could get to take a peek at the soggy, gray surface of his own brain with the help of a set of mirrors through his

open skull. But why should any of that provide him with the sort of extra awareness Armstrong describes?

True, both an FMRI plate and a reflected image on a mirror of a brain are, in some sense, representations of that brain or of its states. But perceiving (the states of) one's own brain this way does not bring about the desired effect; it neither makes those states conscious, nor does it make one introspectively conscious of what those states represent. There can be various ways to encode states of a brain in different media—whether in terms of magnetic resonance distribution, positron emission levels, electroencephalographic patterns, or simply light waves bouncing off its surface. But these are representations *of* the states of a brain (in the intentional sense), not representation *in* a brain. As such, they do not play the right causal role in the cognitive economy of the brain's owner. So the truck driver can actually get to perceive (the states of) his own brain literally, thanks to recent technology or an ingenious setup, but this does not help contribute to his introspective consciousness in any way. I am afraid this is nothing but just belaboring the obvious.[17]

Now, notice that what Armstrong is trying to give an account of is some form of (heightened, attentive, observant, but, after all) *externally directed*, awareness. Why, then, try to explain that in terms of another form of, *internally directed*, awareness? I think that the reasoning that tries to account for the changes in the attentiveness, vividness, and so forth of the externally directed ordinary perception (from the truck driver's autopilot mode to his attentive condition) in terms of an internally directed, higher-order perception of lower-order perceptual states, is based on a fundamental mistake worthy of a name. I will call it the "fallacy of the representational divide."[18]

Mental states qua brain states (in a materialist ontology) are the vehicles that represent for us the world around, as well as in, us. What we thus become aware of is what those states represent as being a certain way, that is, their *content*, in terms of the properties of what is represented. The mistake in the reasoning I am targeting here seems to result from a tacit attempt to replace what is being represent-*ed* with that which is the represent-*er*. Armstrong talks as though we should expect the truck driver to become (attentively) aware of the red light in virtue of his "internally perceiving" (scanning, monitoring) his ordinary perception of the light. Notice that there seems to be some causal role for the second-order perception involved in what the first-order state is about here. The force of the example comes from the conviction that when the truck driver "comes to," he does not merely gain access to an inventory of what kind of internal states he is currently having but that the content of one of his first-order states starts to figure in his behavior. Perhaps this is only to be expected—that gaining access to an inventory of one's ongoing mental states automatically (by nomological necessity) makes the contents of some of those states causally relevant to one's behavior. But this intuition, which seems crucial for rationalization of the HOP theorist's most celebrated example, has to be spelled out.

The explication of the relation of higher-order perceptions to the contents of first-order states that become the objects of such perceptions is of utmost importance, especially in the presence of close-kin, competing theories, such as HOT accounts. (Although HOT accounts are to be held equally liable for having to provide such details as well.) The underlying operative presumption in Armstrong's truck driver example seems to be that the (second-order) perception of the (first-order) perception of an object should furnish one's (first-order) perception of that object with more attentiveness. More generally, it seems to be assumed that by gaining higher-order access to the intrinsic, nonrepresentational properties of a first-order state (a visual perception), which happens to represent something (the red light), one gains access, perhaps more attentively, to the extrinsic, representational properties of that state itself (its content, the red light). But why should that be the case? In Armstrong and Lycan, this issue is left unexpounded, though some form of

the intuition I sketched above seems implicitly to be in operation on a fundamental level.

When it comes to utilizing representational states in behavior, finding out all the facts inside the head (facts about the representations) may not suffice by itself in providing all the facts outside the head (facts about what are being represented by those representations). In other words, no matter how much we find out about the intrinsic properties of representational states, we may simply not be able to reach the other side of the "representational divide," in virtue of this alone, and get to the extrinsic, relational properties of those states.[19]

But if it is impossible to understand one's first-order states as intentional states of sorts, and find out about their content simply by examining the nonrelational features of those states, insisting on an Armstrongian account of introspective consciousness is a moot endeavor. Such insistence, I suspect, has its roots in a commitment to an implicit but misguided assumption: that a case can be made by using the properties of the representers when what is called for is how the representers represent what they represent, that is, the properties of the represented. Operating on the basis of this unacknowledged assumption is somewhat like trying to figure out what a stop sign is by studying only the color, shape, material, and mass of the actual sign. Surely one would learn a lot of facts, but expecting to find out in this way what the stop sign *qua* a traffic symbol really is would be a mistake. Making this mistake is what I have in mind by the term "fallacy of the representational divide."

In a similar vein, the neurophysiological properties Churchland thinks will be revealed to our discriminatory powers in the future involve only the intrinsic properties of the brain states themselves, whereas figuring out what they are about needs to bring into the picture their extrinsic, intentional properties as well. One cannot become introspectively conscious of what an ongoing perceptual state is about in terms of identifying only the neural properties of that state. Insisting that such is the case, that the direct introspection of brain states as a method will reveal not only which type of states they are but also what they are about (e.g., a visual state, about a cup in front of the subject), is, once again, conflating the properties of the representer and those of the represented. It is almost never the case, except in iconic representation (and then only if one knows it is iconic), that one can find out about the nature of what is being represented via the properties of whatever it is that does the representing. Why should we expect, then, to find out all about the cup a subject sees by examining the neural properties of the visual state that subject happens to have in looking at that cup?[20]

In conclusion, the "perception of what passes in one's mind," taken literally, is neither a necessary nor a sufficient condition for the sort of introspective awareness that furnishes one with "consciousness in the most interesting sense of the word." But Option 2 has yet another possible interpretation, based on the mind's-eye model of introspective consciousness, which involves a variation of the fallacy of the representational divide. The mind's-eye model is based on a defunct account of mental representation of the long gone past, but it is nonetheless worthy of examination, especially to provide contrast with the former interpretation.

Second Interpretation of Option 2: Higher-Order Perception as "Seeing with the Mind's Eye"

Is there absolutely no way to make sense out of the idea of "internally perceiving" (the properties of) one's mental states, and thereby becoming introspectively conscious of what those states are states of? That is, can't there be a plausible interpretation within which to accommodate the idea of "perceiving one's perception" of a cup, for instance, and in virtue of this introspective awareness, becoming (attentively) aware of the cup itself?

This scheme could actually work if the properties of one's representational states resembled (or were identical to) the properties that those states represented. This would mean taking the idea of "seeing with the mind's eye" literally. Here is how it would go: By a first-order visual perception, the subject S forms, in her mind, a representation of the cup in front of her. This representation is her visual state, V. By second-order introspective consciousness, she goes on to "internally perceive" this representation. The representation of the cup has cuplike properties that resemble properties of the cup itself. Thus, by her second-order perception, S gets to "see the cup in her mind's eye."

Such a story doesn't make sense unless we commit ourselves literally to a mind's eye and to mental representations that bear a resemblance relation to what they represent. If S had in her mind, as Scholastic Aristotelians thought, something like a little replica of what she saw in front of her, and with the aid of an "internal third eye" she were able to view this replica and had, as a result, a conscious visual experience of the real cup, only then would her case have constituted a true example of this reading of the HOP account. To my mind, all this is more like fairy tales, which makes this interpretation of Option 2, not unlike the previous alternatives, a nonoption for the HOP theorist.[21]

Notice how both cases—the "direct introspection of brain states" as well as the "resemblance theory of mental representations"—involve a confusion about the nature of the representational divide—a conflation of the properties of that which represents and of what is represented—though in a mirror-imaged way. In the former case, the properties of the representer are taken to be the properties of the represented, identifying what is in the head with the properties of what is perceived (something outside the head). In the latter, the properties of the represented are taken to be the properties of the representer, importing the properties of what are outside the head as the properties of the representers inside the head. Under either interpretation, Option 2 is committed to the fallacy of the representational divide.

5   Option 3: Higher-Order Perception as Higher-Order Thought

It can perhaps be argued now that all the circumlocution in the previous section was really not necessary, for isn't there just a simple, straightforward way to account for the truck driver's psychology? More specifically, I have in mind the following proposition: The driver's gaining of introspective consciousness while he was driving on auto-pilot comes down simply to the occurrence of a thought about his circumstances. "Oh, there is the railroad crossing; I must have been driving for the past hour!" he thinks, and this, in Armstrong's story, is precisely what marks his transition from a state of mere perceptual consciousness to one of introspective consciousness.

This proposal is simple and straightforward, indeed. Moreover, it seems to have folk psychological plausibility. In ordinary circumstances, we are generally aware of having a variety of mental states and can easily report the presence of "what is passing in our minds."[22] At least, it seems commonplace to be able to make judgments of the sort: "I am now looking at a coffee cup with bird motifs on it that sits right in front of me, on my desk."[23]

But notice: this way of construing "introspective awareness" as an ability to think a thought or entertain a belief about the mental state one is currently having can no longer be regarded as a case of higher-order perception. As it happens, this is precisely the thesis of a competing theory—that of higher-order thought (HOT). The HOP theorist cannot opt for this route while defending an account separate from and independent of the HOT account. Thus, Option 3 is really not an option for HOP accounts either.

6   The Trilemma for the HOP Theorist

The HOP theorists are at a crossroads where neither of the directions looks promising. In fact, a serious trilemma looms: They have to abandon the two-tiered structure of their account of introspective consciousness, or commit themselves to the "fallacy of the representational divide," or allow the central HOP thesis to transform into the thesis of the competing HOT theory.

Options 1, 2, and 3 present the first, second, and third horns of this trilemma, respectively. Embracing either one of Option 1 or Option 3 simply means trading in the HOP thesis in favor of a different type of account. Accepting Option 2 avoids this sort of a theoretical surrender, but it burdens the HOP account with a fundamental fallacy regarding the nature of representational states. Neither alternative is desirable.

In sum, there is no single construal of an HOP theory of consciousness that does not look substantially problematic. Furthermore, it is not clear that the four major proponents of HOP theories I talked about—Locke, Armstrong, Lycan, and Churchland—would all opt for the same interpretation. In fact, everyone may be forced to take a different path, given their prior theoretical commitments.[24] If the Locke-Armstrong-Churchland-Lycan pact could thereby disintegrate under this sort of argumentative pressure, it would be hard to say whether there was any genuine theoretical backbone in the HOP paradigm to begin with.

In closing, let me note that I *do* intend this analysis to be exhaustive of all possible readings, but of course there can be no saying on my part that such is the case. Nonetheless, I hope to have hereby posed a challenge to the HOP theorists—the challenge of spelling out the specifics of the "perception of what passes in one's own mind," taken literally. Given that the HOP accounts lack any such analysis, it is up to the defenders of this view to fill in the gaps in order to show that they can deliver what they promise: a separate higher-order account of consciousness that does not collapse into the HOT characterization.

Acknowledgments

This chapter first appeared in *Conscious Experience*, Thomas Metzinger (ed.), Paderborn: Schöningh-Verlag, 1995. I would like to thank Fred Dretske, John Perry, Owen Flanagan, William Lycan, David Armstrong, Murat Aydede, Stefano Franchi, and Lisa Taliano for helpful discussion and correspondence, as well as valuable comments on earlier drafts of this chapter.

Notes

1. The first instance of giving philosophical expression to this kind of an intuition could be said to go back to Aristotle's discussion of the "sense that perceives other (ordinary) senses," which starts out with the reasoning that "since we perceive that we see and hear, we must see that we see either by sight or by another sense" (Aristotle 1951, BK. III, Chap. II, §584–586). James had talked about the awareness of mental states, under the name "introspective observation," as the most fundamental method of all psychology, and characterized it as "the looking into (of) our own minds and reporting what we there discover—states of consciousness" (James 1950, p. 185). But it was really Franz Brentano, more than perhaps any other philosopher or psychologist, who was preoccupied with the role of higher-order, "meta-awareness" in human psychology. In the case of auditory perception, for instance, he wrote: "The presentation of the sound and the presentation of the presentation of the sound form a single mental phenomenon.... In the same mental phenomenon in which the sound is present to our minds we simultaneously apprehend the mental phenomenon itself." (Brentano 1973, pp. 121–127).

These "double-tiered" accounts of consciousness come with the threat of infinite regress (having a commitment to a third-level awareness to account for the second, a fourth for the third, and so on). Aristotle was very much aware of this problem, and Brentano devoted a good deal of his philosophical career trying to come up with a satisfactory account that was free of such regress. The details are fascinating, but that kind of historical scholarship lies beyond the scope of this chapter.

2. While drawing a distinction between "knowledge by acquaintance" and "knowledge by description," Bertrand Russell (1912) makes the following observation regarding introspection: "We are not only aware of things, but we are often aware of being aware of them. When I see the sun, I am often aware of my seeing the sun; thus 'my seeing the sun' is an object with which I have acquaintance" (p. 76–77). As such, Russell's remarks can also be taken to endorse the Lockean characterization of (introspective) consciousness as the "perception of what passes in one's own mind," even though his overarching aim of defending a sense-data theory of perception is espoused by neither Armstrong, nor Churchland, nor Lycan.

3. There is a certain amount of terminological calibration required here. What Lycan (and most others) describes under the title "consciousness" or "conscious awareness," Armstrong refers to as "introspective consciousness." This is in contrast with, for example, Armstrong's notion of "perceptual consciousness." In the rest of the chapter, I will use *consciousness* and *introspective consciousness* interchangeably and point out other uses involving the term *consciousness* wherever necessary.

4. The further question of whether higher-order thought accounts provide a fully satisfactory account of consciousness is one I leave unaddressed in the chapter. Although I cannot pursue this question here. I believe that the higher-order thought models account well for certain aspects of consciousness, especially "introspective consciousness" (which typically consists in the awareness of one's own mental states). But I take that to be only part of the whole picture. I believe that not all consciousness is of the introspective sort. More specifically, those aspects of consciousness that humans share with other animals of lesser cognitive capabilities have to be accounted for by a nonintrospective, unilevel model. Although I cannot substantiate my claim here, I would like to point out that rudimentary elements of such a model are already present in the notion of "attention," characterized as a limited resource in various information processing models developed in cognitive psychology.

5. Of course, none of this is really new. Variations on such distinctions can be found in James (1950) and Brentano (1973). The contemporary formulation is due to Rosenthal.

6. There are further distinctions that I talk about elsewhere (Güzeldere 1995a, 1995b). For instance, individual consciousness can be used to classify organisms (or systems) into two kinds: those that are, or are potentially, conscious (e.g., a person, even if knocked out or asleep) and those that are not (e.g., a calculator), much in the same sense as theoretical biology tries to accomplish with the predicate "living" in drawing a line between animate and nonanimate things. (See also the preface of Lycan (1987) for a brief but useful classification.) For the purposes of this chapter, I am mainly interested in the "intentional" sense of individual consciousness, which always involves directedness toward something, and will use it as such.

See also Block (1995) for another important and inherently related distinction: access consciousness versus phenomenal consciousness. Block is responsible for coining these terms (in the contemporary discussion), and he treats them at length in his 1995 article. Martin Davies has a carefully crafted discussion based on Block's distinction (Introduction, Davies and Humphreys 1993). A somewhat related distinction, between sensational and representational properties of perceptual experience, can be found in Peacocke (1983).

7. Here, I take the sense in which a mental state is said to be conscious at least conceptually distinct from the subject's consciousness *of* it. Not everyone thinks so. Lycan, for instance, states in chapter 47 of this book, "I cannot myself hear a natural sense of the phrase 'conscious state' other than as meaning 'state one is conscious of being in.'" He quotes a statement from Dretske (1993) that "an experience can be conscious without anyone—including the person having it—being conscious of having it" and labels it "oxymoronic." However, he also adds that "the philosophical use of 'conscious' is by now well and truly up for grabs, and the best one can do is to be as clear as possible in one's technical specification."

Although generally in agreement with Lycan's latter observation (but not the former claim), let me nonetheless note that there are various established uses of the term that one ought to pay attention to—if not the folk psychological use, then, for instance, the use grounded in the Freudian tradition. In any case, "giving a clear technical specification" (albeit alternative to Lycan's) is precisely what I aim at doing here. Furthermore, as evidenced from contemporary psychology literature, research on type-identifying mental states as conscious versus nonconscious, and research on the nature of

consciousness of the subjects who have such states, is being pursued on independent conceptual grounds.

8. Dretske (1993) makes a distinction between "consciousness of" something versus "consciousness that" something is the case. This distinction is along the same lines with Dretske's earlier work in epistemology (1969), in particular his distinction between "nonepistemic seeing" versus "epistemic seeing," or "seeing" versus "seeing that," and it is fundamentally based on the lack or presence of conceptual involvement in perception. Dretske's position is not a unanimously received view; for some, perception is an affair fundamentally mingled with concepts, and hence it is always "epistemic." Armstrong (1968), for instance, talks about perception as the "acquiring of beliefs." I would like to remain neutral on this issue for the time being. I therefore intend my use of "consciousness of" in a generic way and mean it also to include the "consciousness that" sense, at least when the content in question is an abstract entity, such as a postulate of arithmetic or a proposition about one's beliefs.

9. In a letter to Mersenne, dated June 11, 1640, Descartes makes the following point about why he thinks animals cannot be said, strictly speaking, to feel pain: "[I]n my view, pain exists only in the understanding. What I do explain is all the external movements which accompany this feeling in us; in animals it is these movements alone which occur, and not pain in the strict sense" (Descartes 1993b, AT III: 85, p. 148). Descartes seems to have an intuition here that comes very close to that which underlies the HOT thesis. Pain, or an essential aspect of it anyway, consists not in the first-order state itself, he thinks, but in a cognitive, second-level state involving (or about) it. This is basically the position Carruthers (1989) adopts in arguing for his rather baroque conclusion that animal pain cannot really count as pain due to the lack of higher cognitive faculties in animals, and hence it should not be of any moral concern to humans. See Jamieson and Bekoff (1992) for a critique of Carruthers' argument.

10. There are, of course, other accounts that say interesting things about consciousness (e.g., Dennett 1991; Flanagan 1992; Searle 1992; Block 1995; Tye 1995), but they do not always explicitly address the HOR thesis. It is instructive, however, to examine these accounts in the light of HOR, for in some cases, they turn out to be not orthogonal to it but rather tacitly in agreement (e.g., Dennett). Hence, the discrediting of the HOR thesis

may very well undermine the plausibility of some of the seemingly unrelated accounts.

11. It is possible to find earlier criticisms against the "self-perception" model of consciousness in the context of the debate on self-knowledge and self-reference. Shoemaker (1984) finds it problematic, for instance, "to think of awareness as a kind of perception, i.e., to think of it on the model of sense perception," and denies that "self-awareness involves any sort of perception of oneself" (pp. 14–15). In a somewhat similar vein, Evans (1992), in discussing the question of self-identification, observes that in forming a (higher-order) cognitive state about a (lower-order) informational state, the latter cannot be regarded as an object of the former, in analogy with perceptual states and perceived objects, for "there is nothing that constitutes 'perceiving that state.'" That is, he goes on to say, "there is no *informational* state which stands to the internal state as that internal state stands to the state of the world." (p. 228)

12. That is, nothing specific turns on my choice of using a visual state for my analysis. The same analysis could straightforwardly be given using a different perceptual state or another (first-order) belief.

13. Rosenthal (chap. 46, this book) raises an objection to HOP theories that aims at forcing them into something like Option 1. All perception involves some sensory quality, he maintains, and if introspective consciousness is higher-order perception, so should it. It is not obvious, however, what sort of sensory quality, if any, is involved in higher-order perceiving.

I think this is a powerful objection. One possible move for the HOP theorist could be to claim that the sensory quality involved in second-order perception is the same as the one involved in the first-order mental state being introspected. But this is entirely ad hoc as an answer to the objection. Furthermore, if all we can report are sensory qualities associated with our first-order perceptions while we are trying to introspect, this constitutes fair reason to think that something like what is outlined in Option 1 is actually the case: that the proposed double-tiered structure of introspective awareness is nothing but an illusion.

Lycan in chapter 47 of this book tries to counter Rosenthal's objection by stating that higher-order perception is not like ordinary perception in every aspect. He also concedes that one can perhaps talk about a broadly construed "mental quality" (though not necessarily a "sensory quality," but rather some kind of

"psychological mode of presentation") associated with every higher-order perceiving, and that the HOP theorist owes to give an account of this. Unfortunately, Lycan then chooses to "leave that discussion for another time" (p. 761).

14. The idea that in sensation, objects produce "resemblances" of themselves in the sensing subject is quite common among the medieval Aristotelian scholars. Descartes (1993a) describes this view as "the intervention of 'intentional forms'" in "Fourth Set of Replies" (pp. 173–174), and Cottingham et al. add, in an editorial footnote, that "according to the scholastic theory referred to here, what is directly perceived via the senses is not the object itself but a 'form' or 'semblance' transmitted from object to observer" (ibid., n. 1, p. 174). Descartes later rejects this view in "Sixth Set of Replies," objection 9, p. 295: "For example, when I see a stick, it should not be supposed that certain 'intentional forms' fly off the stick towards the eye."

Sellars (1991) characterizes the Thomist-Aristotelian view of the relation between sense impressions and their objects as being identical with respect to their properties while differing in "mode of exemplification." Chisholm (1982) dubs this view (which he takes as maintaining that "a state of mind refers to a thing if and only if it takes on the properties of that thing") the "copy theory of reference" (p. 190) and discusses its impact on the work of Arthur Lovejoy and the American school of "Critical Realism" in general. A somewhat related view was also upheld in gestalt psychology as a fundamental postulate, based on a hypothesized isomorphic relation between "the structural characteristics of brain processes and of related phenomenal events." (Köhler 1971, p. 81; see also Köhler 1980). An exposition of the issue of resemblance in the context of contemporary theories of mental representation can be found in Cummins (1991).

15. The relation between introspective consciousness and memory is a very interesting one in its own right. Armstrong seems to think that the lack of the former would be somehow responsible for the lack of the latter, or at least the lack of long-term memory, but he does not pursue this point any further.

Tracing this issue back in history, one encounters a passage in *New Essays* where Leibniz uses an example much like Armstrong's truck driver. Leibniz (1981) suggests that attention (the lack of which seems closely related to the lack of introspective consciousness in Armstrong's example) and memory must be closely related: "[T]here are hundreds of indications leading us to conclude that at every moment there is in us an infinity of perceptions, unaccompanied by awareness or reflection.... This is how we become so accustomed to the motion of a mill or a waterfall, after living beside it for a while, that we pay no heed to it. Not that this motion ceases to strike on our sense-organs, ... but these impressions, ... lacking the appeal of novelty, are not forceful enough to attract our attention and our memory, which are applied only to more compelling objects. Memory is needed for attention; when we are not alerted, so to speak, to pay heed to certain of our own present perceptions, we allow them to slip by unconsidered and even unnoticed" (p. 54).

It would probably not be too far-fetched to say that Leibniz can be characterized as an early HOR theorist of sorts, given his remarks on perceptions gone unnoticed in the absence of a second-order awareness or reflection.

16. Among the few articles that can be taken somewhat as support for such a hypothesis are Crick (1984) and Barker (1988), where the thalamic reticular complex and the basal ganglia are proposed as candidate structures in charge of processes that accomplish some form of "selective attention" and control in the central nervous system. It is not clear whether the existence of such structures really provides evidence for the "consciousness as self-scanning" claim, however. At best, Crick's and Barker's accounts remain sketchy and speculative to date with respect to the HOP thesis.

17. What is not so obvious is the specification of conditions under which a given representational state in a subject plays the right causal role in making the subject conscious of various things or facts. Van Gulick (1993) presents an insightful proposal in this direction in his attempt to secure a functional role for phenomenal states. His account is based on the notion of *semantic transparency*, which "concerns the extent to which a system can be said to understand the content of the internal symbols or representations on which it operates" (p. 149).

In terms of higher-order representations, Dretske (1995) talks about what makes something truly a "representation of a representation"—a *metarepresentation*—such that it plays the right causal role, in virtue of being a metarepresentation, in one's cognitive functioning.

Both accounts are very promising and deserve a more detailed treatment.

18. Harman (1990) presents a strong case against sense-data theories of perception on the basis of similar observations about the nature of representation, and remarks that the sense-data theorists confuse "intrinsic features of the intentional object of experience with intrinsic features of the experiences" (p. 42). Dretske (1995) also adopts this line of criticism while defending externalist theories of experience (pp. 127–130). Much of my discussion of what I call the "fallacy of the representational divide" involves extending the kind of reasoning found in Harman and Dretske from a critique of theories of experience and perception to a critique of higher-order perceptual theories of introspective consciousness.

19. The point I am making does not depend on Twin Earth-like scenarios. That is, I take the "representational divide" to pose a problem for the project of giving a full account of mental states only in terms of their intrinsic properties even in the most ordinary cases of human psychology. Problems about widely individuated content do, *a fortiori*, pose a further challenge to HOP accounts.

A fully externalist representational account of not only propositional attitudes but also sensory experience, which deals with various issues involving wide content and Twin Earth cases, can be found in Dretske (1995). Tye (1995) also presents a representational theory of phenomenal consciousness, extending his analysis from sensations to emotions and moods.

20. Churchland's case may have more plausibility regarding brain states that do not have any obvious representational content (e.g., emotions and moods). Perhaps we can indeed learn to individualize such states, which do not (if such is the case) represent anything "outside the head" via their intrinsic qualities. I think that view has some truth in it, but for the purposes of this chapter, I will choose to leave this issue open and make my point in terms of straightforwardly representational states, such as visual states and beliefs.

Also in this chapter, I eschew the traditional debates regarding the status of identity theory that heavily dominated philosophy of the mind in the late 1950s and the 1960s—not because they are irrelevant; on the contrary, the question of identity between "mental" and "physical" properties (properties of the mind versus those of the brain, or the body in general) lies at the heart of the matter being discussed here. However, given the voluminous literature of this era, it is virtually impossible to consider the debate in its entirety. My discussion is just one of several possible approaches to the larger "mental-physical" question, but it proceeds along the relatively recent "intrinsic-extrinsic" axis in the context of the representational content of mental states. For classics of this debate, see Smart (1959), Sellars (1964), and Feigl (1967), among others.

21. William Lycan pointed out to me (in personal communication) that the interpretation of higher-order perception as "seeing with the mind's eye" may not be "all fairy tales" after all. "Not all resemblance is first-order resemblance" Lycan says. "Isomorphism is resemblance too." He then continues, "It is not only possible but a known fact that, especially in perceptual processing, the brain constructs certain isomorphs of external scenes."

As I have been arguing, I find the idea of the necessity of a resemblance relation (or, some form of isomorphism in general) between representational vehicles in the mind and represented entities, although philosophically interesting, ultimately ungrounded and misleading. (However, I acknowledge the pervasiveness of this idea in the history of philosophy and psychology; see note 13.) But what about the empirical plausibility of the isomorphism thesis in the present neuroscientific framework? It is indeed an interesting point to note that there actually exist certain topographical relations between objects perceived and the representational brain structures involved in the perception of them, which go deeper than the receptor surfaces. That is, in the case of vision, for example, there exist order-preserving systematic relations not only between visual stimuli and the retinal image caused by them but also between the retinal image and the cortical areas that are responsible for processing the retinal input. Rosenzweig and Leiman (1989) report the following: "Recent examination of the cortex of the owl monkey (a New World monkey) reveals at least six visual areas, each of which is a topographic representation of the retina. No other species has yet been mapped as completely, but in the macaque (an Old World monkey) it also appears that most of the cortical visual regions consist of orderly maps of the retina" (p. 323; a detailed account of cortical processing topography in visual perception can be found in Woolsey 1981).

But does this provide any support for the "mind's-eye" model? I think not. First, the relation between objects perceived and cortical areas involved in perception is, strictly speaking, not an isomorphism of any order. It is simply a topographical relation of a very crude sort,

preserving only order, but not size and not really shape. (Secondary properties are never preserved; for example, no part of the occipital cortex ever turns red upon perceiving a red object! Also note that although a similar topographical relation exists in auditory perception, it is even more difficult to talk about *any* kind of resemblance there.) Second, even if the "representations as replicas" part of the "mind's-eye" story was correct, one would still need to account for how it was that those replicas got perceived by an "internal eye" in the absence of any neuroanatomical evidence and also without falling into the infinite regress of requiring yet a second "internal eye" to account for the perception of the replicas themselves, and so forth. In short, although the topography of the cortex in relation to the perceived objects is a very interesting research area to pursue, it does not provide any credibility, or even plausibility, to the "mind's-eye" model of perception.

22. Easily, but not necessarily accurately. Above and beyond some rudimentary ability to report what we are experiencing, human subjects are notoriously bad in making correct and accurate judgments about the causes of their reasoning and behavior. For many "surprising" results along these lines, see Nisbett and Wilson (1977), Wilson and Dunn (1986), and Lyons (1986).

23. There are further issues here that are worthy of pursuing, especially regarding the nature of the relation between the ability to make judgments about the mental state one is in and the ability to verbalize or report the presence and/or the content of that state. For a detailed account, which deals with such issues, see Rosenthal (chap. 46, this volume).

24. For example, although David Armstrong explicitly talks about (introspective) consciousness as a "perception-like awareness of current states and activities of one's own mind," and Lycan locates Armstrong in the same lineage with Locke and himself, Armstrong's position may ultimately be closer to those of the HOT theorists, such as David Rosenthal. Armstrong thinks that "perception is the acquiring of beliefs" (cf. Armstrong 1968, chap. 10, pp. 208–244). From the writings of these authors, it is hard to judge comparatively just how conceptually loaded Armstrong wants to view perception vis-à-vis Lycan. But it is at least a possibility that Armstrong may turn out to be on the same side of the fence with Rosenthal, not with Lycan, despite the prima facie dissimilarity of their respective vocabulary.

In fact, Armstrong kindly acknowledged (in subsequent personal communication) that he thought his position "fell in between" the HOP and and HOT characterizations. He writes: "For me, perception, taken as a mental act, is always *propositional*, by which I do not of course mean it is in any way linguistic, but that the content of the perception will have a form **Fa** or **Rab** or ... some state-of-affairs structure.... When the truck driver "comes to" and introspective consciousness resumes, to [the current content of his perception] will be added the further content that 'I am perceiving these things.' ... This is HOT-like. But, following Locke and Kant, I think the introspective awareness is perception-like. For instance, it is very like proprioception, and seems not to involve any linguistic capacity. Perhaps chimpanzees and even dogs have such consciousness."

It is not immediately obvious to what extent Armstrong's HOP account, under his particular characterization of perception, succeeds in avoiding the difficulties of HOP accounts in general while actually remaining distinct from HOT accounts. Further pursuit of this issue elsewhere (on the basis of Armstrong 1968, 1980) would certainly be useful.

References

Aristotle (1951). *De Anima*. London: Routledge and Kegan Paul.

Armstrong, D. (1968). *A Materialist Theory of the Mind*. New York: Humanities Press.

———. (1980). *The Nature of Mind and Other Essays*. Ithaca: Cornell University Press.

Barker, R. (1988). How Does the Brain Control Its Own Activity? A New Function for the Basal Ganglia? *Journal of Theoretical Biology* 131, 497–507.

Block, N. (1995). On a Confusion About a Function of Consciousness. *Behavioral and Brain Sciences* 18:12, 227–287.

Brentano, F. (1973). *Psychology from an Empirical Standpoint*. Rancurello, A., Terrell, D. B., and McAlister, L. (trans.). New York: Humanities Press.

Carruthers, P. (1989). Brute Experience. *Journal of Philosophy* 86, 5, 258–269.

Chisholm, R. (1982). *The Foundations of Knowing*. Minneapolis: University of Minnesota Press.

Churchland, P. (1985). Reduction, Qualia, and the Direct Introspection of Brain States. *Journal of Philosophy* 82:1, 8–28.

———. (1988). *Matter and Consciousness*. Cambridge: MIT Press.

Crick, F. (1984). Function of the Thalamic Reticular Complex: The Search-light Hypothesis. *Proceedings of the National Academy of Sciences* 81, 4586–4590.

Cummins, R. (1991). *Meaning and Mental Representation*. Cambridge: MIT Press.

Davies, M., and Humphreys, G., eds. (1993). Introduction to *Consciousness: Psychological and Philosophical Essays*. Oxford: Basil Blackwell.

Dennett, D. (1991). *Consciousness Explained*. Boston: Little, Brown.

Descartes, R. (1993a). Objections and Replies. In *The Philosophical Writings of Descartes*, vol. 2. Cottingham, J., Stoothoff R., and Murdoch, D. (eds.). Cambridge: Cambridge University Press.

———. (1993b). The Correspondence. In *The Philosophical Writings of Descartes*, vol. 3. Cottingham, J., Kenny, A., Stoothoff R., and Murdoch, D. (eds.). Cambridge: Cambridge University Press.

Dretske, F. (1969). *Seeing and Knowing*. Bloomington: University of Chicago Press.

———. (1993). Conscious Experience. *Mind* 102:406, 262–283.

———. (1995). *Naturalizing the Mind*. Cambridge: MIT Press.

Evans, G. (1992). Self-Identification. In *The Varieties of Reference*. McDowell, J. (ed.). Oxford: Clarendon Press.

Feigl, H. (1967). *The "Mental" and the "Physical."* Minneapolis: University of Minnesota Press.

Flanagan, O. (1992). *Consciousness Reconsidered*. Cambridge: MIT Press.

Güzeldere, G. (1995a). Consciousness: What it is, how to study it, what to learn from its history. *Journal of Consciousness Studies*, 2:1, 30–51.

———. (1995b). Problems of Consciousness: A Perspective on Contemporary Issues, Current Debates. *Journal of Consciousness Studies*, 2:2, 112–143.

Harman, G. (1990). The Intrinsic Quality of Experience. *Philosophical Perspectives* 4, 31–52.

James, W. (1950). *The Principles of Psychology*, vol. 1. New York: Dover Publications.

Jamieson, D. and Bekoff, M. (1992). Carruthers on Nonconscious Experience. *Analysis* 52, 23–28.

Köhler, W. (1971). The Mind-Body Problem. In *The Selected Papers of Wolfgang Köhler*, New York: Liveright Publishing Corporation, 62–82.

———. (1980). *Gestalt Psychology*. New York: New American Library.

Leibniz, G. (1981). *New Essays on Human Understanding*. Remnant, P., and Bennett, J. (eds.). Cambridge: Cambridge University Press.

Locke, J. (1959). *An Essay Concerning Human Understanding*, vol. 1. New York: Dover Publications.

Lycan, W. (1987). *Consciousness*. Cambridge: MIT Press.

Lyons, W. (1986). *The Disappearance of Introspection*. Cambridge: MIT Press.

Nisbett, R., and Wilson, T. (1977). Telling More Than We Can Know: Verbal Reports on Mental Processes. *Psychological Review* 84:3, 231–258.

Peacocke, C. (1983). *Sense and Content*. Oxford: Clarendon Press.

Rosenthal, D. (1986). Two Concepts of Consciousness. *Philosophical Studies* 94:3, 329–359.

Rosenzweig, M., and Leiman, A. (1989). *Physiological Psychology*. New York: Random House.

Russell, B. (1912). *The Problems of Philosophy*. New York: Henry Holt and Co.

Searle, J. (1992). *The Rediscovery of the Mind*. Cambridge: MIT Press.

Sellars, W. (1964). The Identity Approach to the Mind-Body Problem. *Review of Metaphysics* 18:2, 430–51.

———. (1991). Being and Being Known. In *Science, Perception, and Reality*. Atascadero: Ridgeview Publishing Co., 41–59.

Shoemaker, S. (1984). Self-Reference and Self-Awareness. In *Identity, Cause, and Mind*. Cambridge: Cambridge University Press, 6–18.

———. (1994). Self-Knowledge and "Inner Sense." *Philosophy and Phenomenological Research*. LIV:2, 249–314.

Smart, J. J. C. (1959). Sensations and Brain Processes. *Philosophical Review* 68, 141–156.

Tye, M. (1995). *Ten Problems of Consciousness*. Cambridge: MIT Press.

van Gulick, R. (1993). Understanding the Phenomenal Mind: Are We All just Armadillos? In Davies and Humphreys (1993), 137–154.

Wilson, T., and Dunn, D. (1986). Effects of Introspection on Attitude-Behavior Consistency: Analyzing Reasons versus Focusing on Feelings. *Journal of Experimental and Social Psychology* 22, 249–263.

Woolsey, C., ed. (1981). *Cortical Sensory Organization*. Vol. 2: *Multiple Visual Areas*. Clifton: Humana Press.

References to Introduction

Abramson, H. S., ed. (1951–55). *Problems of Consciousness*. New York: Josiah Macy Jr. Foundation.

Ackerknecht, E. H. and Vallois, H. V. (1956). *Franz Joseph Gall, Inventor of Phrenology and his Collection*. Translated by Claire St. Leon. Madison: Department of History of Medicine, University of Wisconsin.

Adams, R. (1987). Flavors, Colors, and God. In *The Virtue of Faith and Other Essays in Philosophical Theology*. Oxford: Oxford University Press, 243–262.

Akins, K. (1993). What is it like to be boring and myopic? In *Dennett and his Critics*. Edited by B. Dahlbom. Cambridge: Blackwell Publishers, 124–160.

Anscombe, G. E. M. (1965). The Intentionality of Sensation: A Grammatical Feature. In *Analytical Philosophy*. Second series. Edited by R. J. Butler. Oxford: Basil Blackwell, 158–80.

Armstrong, D. (1980a). What is consciousness? In Armstrong (1980b), 55–67.

Armstrong, D. (1980b). *The Nature of Mind and Other Essays*. Ithaca: Cornell University Press.

Armstrong, D. (1993). *A Materialist Theory of the Mind*. Revised edition (first published in 1968). London: Routledge.

Atkinson, R. and Shiffrin, R. (1968). Human memory: A proposed system and its control processes. In *The Psychology of Learning and Motivation*, Vol 2. Edited by K. Spence and J. Spence. New York: Academic Press, 89–195.

Augustine of Hippo, St. (1961). *The Confessions of Saint Augustine*. Translated by E. B. Pusey. New York: Collier Books.

Baars, B. (1985). *The Cognitive Revolution in Psychology*. New York: Guilford Press.

Baars, B. (1988). *A Cognitive Theory of Consciousness*. Cambridge: Cambridge University Press.

Baddeley, A. (1990). *Human Memory: Theory and Practice*. Boston: Allyn and Bacon.

Baddeley, A. (1993). Working Memory and Conscious Awareness. In *Theories of Memory*. Edited by A. Collins, S. Gathercole, M. Conway, and P. Morris. Hove: L. Erlbaum Associates.

Baldwin, J. M. (1901). Consciousness. In *Dictionary of Philosophy and Psychology*, Vol. I. Edited by J. M. Baldwin. New York: The MacMillan Co., 197–237.

Beckermann, A., Flohr, H., and Kim, J., eds. (1992). *Emergence or Reduction?* Berlin: Walter de Gruyter.

Berkeley, G. (1977). *A Treatise Concerning the Principles of Human Knowledge*. Edited by C. Turbayne. Originally published in 1710. Indianapolis: Bobbs-Merrill Publishing.

Biro, J. (1991). Consciousness and subjectivity. In *Philosophical Issues*, Vol. 1. Edited by E. Villanueva. Atascadero: Ridgeview Publishing Co., 113–33.

Block, N. (1978). Troubles with Functionalism. Reprinted in Block (1980a), 268–305.

Block, N., ed. (1980a). *Readings in Philosophy of Psychology*, Vol. I. Cambridge: Harvard University Press.

Block, N. (1980b). Are Absent Qualia Impossible? *The Philosophical Review*, 89, 257–274.

Block, N. (1993a). Inverted Earth. In Tomberlin (1990), 53–79.

Block, N. (1993b). Other Things Explained (Review of Dennett, 1991). *Journal of Philosophy*, 90, 181–93.

Block, N. (1994). Consciousness. In *A Companion to the Philosophy of Mind*. Edited by S. Guttenplan. Oxford: Blackwell Publishers, 210–219.

Block, N. (1995). On a Confusion about a Function of Consciousness. *Behavioral and Brain Sciences*, 18:2, 227–287.

Block, N. and Fodor, J. (1980). What Psychological States Are Not. Reprinted in Block (1980a), 237–250.

Block, N., Flanagan, O., and Güzeldere, G. eds. (1997). *The Nature of Consciousness: Philosophical Debates*. Cambridge: MIT Press.

Boring, E. (1929). *A History of Experimental Psychology*. New York: The Century Co.

Boring, E. (1942). *Sensation and Perception in the History of Experimental Psychology*. New York: Appleton-Century Co.

Boring, E. (1953). A History of Introspection. *Psychological Bulletin*, 50:3, 169–189.

Boring, E. (1963). The Physiology of Consciousness. In *History, Psychology, and Science: Selected Papers*. Originally published in 1932. New York: Wiley and Sons, 274–286.

Bowers, K. and Meichenbaum, D., eds. (1984) *The Unconscious Reconsidered*. New York: John Wiley and Sons.

Brandon, R. (1996). Reductionism versus Holism versus Mechanism. In *Concepts and Methods in Evolutionary Biology*. Cambridge: Cambridge University Press, 179–204.

Brentano, F. (1973). *Psychology from an Empirical Standpoint*. Translated by A. Rancurello, D. B. Terrell, and L. McAlister. Original edition in 1874. New York: Humanities Press.

Broad, C. D. (1962). *The Mind and its Place in Nature*. First published in 1925. London: Routledge and Kegan Paul.

Broadbent, D. (1958). *Perception and Communication*. Oxford: Pergamon Press.

Capek, M. (1954). James's Early Criticism of the Automaton Theory. *Journal of the History of Ideas*, XV:2, 260–279.

Capron, A. M. (1988). The report of the President's Commission on the uniform determination of death act. In Zaner (1988), 147–170.

Carruthers, P. (1989). Brute Experience. *Journal of Philosophy*, 86, 258–269.

Carruthers, P. (1996). *Language, Thought, and Consciousness: An Essay in Philosophical Psychology*. Cambridge: Cambridge University Press.

Chalmers, D. (1993). Self-Ascription without Qualia: A Case-Study. *Behavioral and Brain Sciences*, 16:1, 35–36.

Chalmers, D. (1995). Facing Up to the Problem of Consciousness. *Journal of Consciousness Studies*, 2:3, 200–219.

Chalmers, D. (1996). *The Conscious Mind*. Oxford: Oxford University Press.

Chappel, V. C., ed. (1981). *The Philosophy of Mind*. First printed by Prentice-Hall in 1962. New York: Dover Publications.

Chisholm, R. (1981). *The First Person: An Essay on Reference and Intentionality*. Minneapolis: University of Minnesota Press.

Chomsky, N. (1959). A Review of B. F. Skinner's *Verbal Behavior*. *Language*, 35:1, 26–58.

Churchland, P. (1988). *Matter and Consciousness*. First printed in 1984. Cambridge: MIT Press.

Churchland, P. (1989). Knowing Qualia: A Reply to Jackson. *A Neurocomputational Perspective*. Cambridge: MIT Press, 67–76.

Churchland, P. S. (1983). Consciousness: The Transmutation of a Concept. *Pacific Philosophical Quarterly*, 64, 80–95.

Churchland, P. and Churchland, P. S. (1982). Functionalism, Qualia, and Intentionality. In *Mind, Brain, and Function*. Edited by J. Biro and R. Shahan. Norman: University of Oklahoma Press, 121–145.

Clarke, S. (1707). A Defense of an Argument Made Use of in a Letter to Mr. Dodwell, to Prove the Immateriality and Natural Immortality of the Soul. Quoted in Mijuskovic (1974), p. 82.

Corsini, R., ed. (1984). *Encyclopedia of Psychology*. New York: Wiley and Sons.

Crick, F. and Koch, C. (1990). Towards a Neurobiological Theory of Consciousness. *Seminars in the Neurosciences*, 2, 263–275.

Crook, J. (1980). *The Evolution of Human Consciousness*. Oxford: Clarendon Press.

Davidson, D. (1970). Mental Events. Reprinted in *Essays on Actions and Events*. Oxford: Clarendon Press, 1980, 207–225.

Davidson, D. (1987). Knowing One's Own Mind. *Proceedings and Addresses of the American Philosophical Association*, 60, 441–458.

Davies, M. and Humphreys, G., eds. (1993). *Consciousness: Psychological and Philosophical Essays*. Oxford: Blackwell.

Dennett, D. (1979). On the absence of phenomenology. In *Body, Mind, and Method*. Edited by D. Gustafson and B. Tapscott. Dordrecht: D. Reidel, 93–113.

Dennett, D. (1981). Toward a Cognitive Theory of Consciousness. In Dennett (1986), 149–173.

Dennett, D. (1982). How to Study Human Consciousness Empirically or Nothing Comes to Mind. *Synthese*, 53:2, 159–79.

Dennett, D. (1986). *Brainstorms*. First published in 1981. Cambridge: MIT Press.

Dennett, D. (1987). Consciousness. In *The Oxford Companion to the Mind*. Edited by R. L. Gregory. Oxford: Oxford University Press, 160–164.

Dennett, D. (1988). Quining Qualia. In Marcel and Bisiach (1992), 42–77.

Dennett, D. (1991). *Consciousness Explained*. Boston: Little, Brown, and Co.

Dennett, D. (1995). The path not taken. *Behavioral and Brain Sciences*, 18:2, 252–253.

Dennett, D. (1995). The Unimagined Preposterousness of Zombies. *Journal of Consciousness Studies*, 2:4, 322–326.

Dennett, D. and Kinsbourne, M. (1992). Time and the Observer. *Behavioral and Brain Sciences*, 15, 183–247.

Descartes, R. (1991). *The Philosophical Writings of Descartes*, Vol. III. Translated by J. Cottingham, R. Stoothoff, D. Murdoch, and A. Kenny. Cambridge: Cambridge University Press.

Descartes, R. (1992). *The Philosophical Writings of Descartes*, Vol. I. Translated by J. Cottingham, R. Stoothoff, and D. Murdoch. First published in 1985. Cambridge: Cambridge University Press.

Descartes, R. (1993a). *The Philosophical Writings of Descartes*, Vol. II. Translated by J. Cottingham, R. Stoothoff, and D. Murdoch. First published in 1984. Cambridge: Cambridge University Press.

Descartes, R. (1993b). Objections and Replies. In Descartes (1993a).

Descartes, R. (1993c). The Correspondence. In Descartes (1991).

Dewey, J. (1940). The Vanishing Subject in the Psychology of James. *Journal of Philosophy*, 37, 589–598.

Dilman, I. (1972). Is the Unconscious a Theoretical Construct? *The Monist*, 56:3, 313–342.

Dixon, N. F. (1971). *Subliminal Perception: The Nature of a Controversy.* New York: McGraw Hill.

Dixon, N. F. (1981). *Preconscious Processing.* New York: Wiley and Sons.

Dretske, F. (1988). *Explaining Behavior.* Cambridge: MIT Press.

Dretske, F. (1993). Conscious Experience. *Mind*, 102: 406, 263–283.

Dretske, F. (1995). *Naturalizing the Mind.* Cambridge: MIT Press.

Dretske, F. (1996). Differences that make no difference. *Philosophical Topics*, 22:1–2, 41–57.

Dretske, F. (forthcoming). What good is consciousness? Forthcoming in *Canadian Journal of Philosophy*.

Dreyfus, H. (1979). *What Computers Can't Do: The Limits of Artificial Intelligence*. First published in 1972. New York: Harper and Row, Publishers.

Dreyfus, H. (1992). *What Computers Still Can't Do: A Critique of Artificial Reason*. Revised edition of Dreyfus 1979. Cambridge: MIT Press.

Eccles, J. (1991). *Evolution of the Brain: Creation of the Self.* First printed in 1989. London: Routledge Publishers.

Ellenberger, H. (1970). *The discovery of the unconscious: The history and evolution of dynamic psychiatry.* New York: Basic Books.

Enç, B. (1983). In defense of the identity theory. *Journal of Philosophy*, 80, 279–98.

English, H. B. and English, A. C. (1958). *A comprehensive dictionary of psychological and psychoanalytical terms: A guide to usage.* New York: McKay Publishing.

Erdelyi, M. H. (1985). *Psychoanalysis: Freud's Cognitive Psychology.* New York: W. H. Freeman and Co.

Eriksen, C. W. (1960). Discrimination and learning without awareness: A methodological survey and evaluation. *The Psychological Review*, 67, 279–300.

Farah, M. (1995). Visual perception and visual awareness after brain damage: A tutorial overview. In *Attention and Performance*: XV. Edited by C. Umilta and M. Moscovitch. Cambridge: MIT Press, 37–75.

Farrell, B. A. (1950). Experience. In Chappel (1981), 23–48.

Fechner, G. T. (1966). *Elements of Psychophysics*. Translated by H. Adler. Edited by D. Howes and E. Boring. Originally published in 1860. New York: Holt, Rinehart and Winston.

Feigl, H. (1967). *The "Mental" and the "Physical"*. First published in 1958. Minneapolis: University of Minnesota Press.

Flanagan, O. (1991). *The Science of the Mind*. First published in 1984. Cambridge: MIT Press.

Flanagan, O. (1992). *Consciousness Reconsidered*. Cambridge: MIT Press.

Flanagan, O. (1995). Deconstructing Dreams: The Spandrels of Sleep. *Journal of Philosophy*, 92:1, 5–27.

Flanagan, O. and Polger, T. (1995). Zombies and the Function of Consciousness. *Journal of Consciousness Studies*, 2:4, 313–321.

Flohr, H. (1995). An Information Processing Theory of Anaesthesia. *Neuropsychologia*, 9, 1169–1180.

Fodor, J. (1987). *Psychosemantics*. Cambridge: MIT Press.

Fodor, J. (1991a). Meaning in Mind. In *Fodor and his Critics*. Edited by B. Loewer and G. Rey. Oxford: Blackwell.

Fodor, J. (1991b). Too hard for our kind of mind? *London Review of Books*, 13:12 (June 27, 1991), 12.

Fodor, J. (1992). The big idea. *Times Literary Supplement* 4657 (July 3, 1992), 5–7.

Fox, I. (1989). On the Nature and Cognitive Function of Phenomenal Content—Part One. *Philosophical Topics*, 17, 81–103.

Frege, G. (1892). On Sense and Reference. Translated by Max Black. In *Translations from the Philosophical Writings of Gottlob Frege*. Edited by P. Geach and M. Black. Second edition. Oxford: Basil Blackwell, 25–50.

Freud, S. (1949). *An Outline of Psychoanalysis*. Originally published in 1940. New York: Norton Publishers.

Freud, S. (1950). *The Interpretation of Dreams*. Originally published in 1900. Translated by A. A. Brill. New York: The Modern Library.

Freud, S. (1962). *The Ego and the Id*. Originally published in 1923. New York: Norton Publishers.

Freud, S. (1964). *New Introductory Lectures on Psychoanalysis*. Originally published in 1933. In *Complete Psychological Works of Sigmund Freud*, Vol. 20. Translated by J. Strachey. London: Hogarth Press.

Galin, D. (1974). Implications for psychiatry of left and right cerebral specialization. *Archives of General Psychiatry*, 31, 572–583.

Garver, M. M. (1880). The Periodic Character of Voluntary Nervous Action. *American Journal of Science*. Third Series, XX:117, 189–193.

Gazzaniga. M. (1970). *The Bisected Brain*. New York: Appleton Century Crofts.

Gazzaniga. M. (1993). Brain Mechanisms and Conscious Experience. In *Experimental and Theoretical Studies of Consciousness*. Edited by G. Bock and J. Marsh. Chichester: John Wiley and Sons, 247–257.

Gazzaniga. M., ed. (1994). *The Cognitive Neurosciences*. Cambridge: MIT Press.

Ginet, C. and Shoemaker, S., eds. (1983). *Knowledge and Mind*. New York: Oxford University Press.

Goldman, A. (1993). Consciousness, Folk Psychology, and Cognitive Science. *Consciousness and Cognition*, 2, 364–382.

Goodman, N. (1978). *Ways of Worldmaking*. Indianapolis: Hackett Publishing Co.

Graham, G. and Stephens, L. (1985). Are qualia a pain in the neck for functionalists? *American Philosophical Quarterly*, 22, 73–80.

Gunderson, K. (1970). Asymmetries and Mind-Body Perplexities. In Rosenthal (1971), 112–127.

Güzeldere, G. (1993). Stanford Consciousness Survey. Unpublished study. Stanford University.

Güzeldere, G. (1995a). Is consciousness the perception of what passes in one's own mind? In Metzinger (1995b), 335–357.

Güzeldere, G. (1995b). Varieties of Zombiehood. *Journal of Consciousness Studies*, 2:4, 326–333.

Güzeldere, G. (1995c). Cartesian Modularism, Blindsight, and the Function of Consciousness. Manuscript, presented at the *Cognitive Neuroscience Society*, Second Annual Meeting, March 26–28, 1995, San Francisco.

Güzeldere, G. (1996). Consciousness and the introspective link hypothesis. In *Towards a Scientific Basis for Consciousness*. Edited by S. Hameroff, A. Kaszniak, and A. C. Scott. Cambridge: MIT Press, 29–39.

Güzeldere, G. and Aydede, M. (forthcoming). On the Relation between Phenomenal and Representational Properties. Forthcoming in *Behavioral and Brain Sciences*.

Hamlyn, D. W. (1968a). *De Anima*. Selections. Oxford: Clarendon Press.

Hamlyn, D. W. (1968b). Koine Aisthesis. *The Monist*, 52:2, 195–209.

Hannay, A. (1990). *Human Consciousness*. London: Routledge Publishers.

Hardcastle, V. (1996). Functionalism's Response to the Problem of Absent Qualia. *Journal of Consciousness Studies*, 3:4, 357–373.

Hardie, W. F. R. (1976). Concepts of Consciousness in Aristotle. *Mind*, 85, 388–411.

Hardin, C. (1987). Qualia and Materialism: Closing the Explanatory Gap. *Philosophy and Phenomenological Research*, XLVIII:2, 281–298.

Hardin, C. (1988). *Color for Philosophers*. Indianapolis: Hackett Publishing Co.

Hare, R. (1952). *The Language of Morals*. Oxford: Clarendon Press.

Harman, G. (1990). The Intrinsic Quality of Experience. In Tomberlin (1990), 31–52.

Harman, G. (1993a). *Conceptions of the Mind: Essays in Honor of George A. Miller*. Edited by G. Harman. Hillside: Lawrence Erlbaum.

Harman, G. (1993b). Can science understand the mind? In Harman (1993a), 111–121.

Harnad, S. (1982). Consciousness: An Afterthought. *Cognition and Brain Theory*, 5, 29–47.

Harris, E. (1993). *The Foundations of Metaphysics in Science*. First printed in 1965. Atlantic Highlands: Humanities Press.

Hebb, D. (1949). *The Organization of Behavior*. New York: John Wiley and Sons.

Hempel, C. (1949). The Logical Analysis of Psychology. In *Readings in Philosophical Analysis*. Edited by H. Feigl and W. Sellars. New York: Appleton-Century-Crofts, 373–384.

Herbert, N. (1993). *Elemental Mind: Human consciousness and the new physics*. New York: Dutton Publishing.

Hilgard, E. (1956). *Theories of Learning*. New York: Appleton-Century Press.

Hilgard, E. (1980). Consciousness in Contemporary Psychology. *Annual Review of Psychology*, 31, 1–26.

Hilgard, E. (1987). *Psychology in America: A Historical Survey*. San Diego: H. B. Jovanovich Publishers.

Hill, C. (1991). *Sensations: A Defense of Type Materialism*. Cambridge: Cambridge University Press.

Hofstadter, D. (1979). *Gödel, Escher, Bach: An Eternal Golden Braid*. New York: Basic Books.

Holender, D. (1986). Semantic activation without conscious identification in dichotic listening, parafoveal vision, and visual masking: A survey and appraisal. *Behavioral and Brain Sciences*, 9, 1–23.

Holt, E. (1914). *The Concept of Consciousness*. New York: The MacMillan Co.

Holt, F. (1915). *The Freudian Wish and Its Place in Ethics*. New York: Henry Holt.

Holyoak, K. and Spellman, B. (1993). Thinking. *Annual Review of Psychology*, 44:51, 265–315.

Horgan, T. (1987). Supervenient qualia. *Philosophical Review*, 96, 491–520.

Hume, D. (1955). *The Treatise of Human Nature*. (Originally published in 1739.) In *Hume: Selections*. Edited by Charles Hendel. New York: C. Scribner's Sons.

Humphrey, N. (1992). *A History of the Mind*. New York: Simon and Schuster.

Husserl, E. (1913). *Ideas*. English edition, fourth printing, 1972. Translated by B. Gibson. New York: Collier Books.

Husserl, E. (1928). *The Phenomenology of Internal Time Consciousness*. English edition, third printing, 1969. Translated by C. Schrag. Bloomington: Indiana University Press.

Hut, P. and Shepard, R. (1996). Turning the Hard Problem Upside Down and Sideways. *Journal of Consciousness Studies*, 3:4, 313–329.

Huxley, T. H. (1866). *Lessons in Elementary Physiology*. London: The MacMillan Co.

Huxley, T. H. (1876). *Lessons in Elementary Physiology*. 10th edition. London: The MacMillan Co.

Huxley, T. H. (1901). *Methods and Results*. New York: Appleton Co.

Jackendoff, R. (1987). *Consciousness and the Computational Mind*. Cambridge: MIT Press.

Jackson, F. (1982). Epiphenomenal Qualia. *Philosophical Quarterly*, XXXII:127, 127–136.

Jackson, F. (1986). What Mary Didn't Know. *Journal of Philosophy*, LXXXIII:5, 291–295.

James, W. (1879). Are We Automata? *Mind*, 4:13, 1–22.

James, W. (1950a). *The Principles of Psychology*, Vol. I. New York: Dover Publications.

James, W. (1950b). *The Principles of Psychology*, Vol. II. New York: Dover Publications.

James, W. (1956). *Human Immortality*. New York: Dover Publications.

James, W. (1971). Does 'Consciousness' Exist? Reprinted in *Essays in Radical Empiricism*. Edited by R. B. Perry. New York: Dutton and Co., 3–22.

Jaynes, J. (1976). *The Origin of Consciousness in the Breakdown of the Bicameral Mind*. Boston: Houghton Mifflin Co.

Johnson-Laird, P. (1983a). *Mental Models*. Cambridge: Harvard University Press.

Johnson-Laird, P. (1983b). A computational analysis of consciousness. *Cognition and Brain Theory*, 6:4, 499–508.

Joynt, R. J. (1981). Are Two Heads Better than One? *Behavioral and Brain Sciences*, 4, 108–109.

Kahn, C. (1966). Sensation and Consciousness in Aristotle's Psychology. *Archiv für Geschichte der Philosophie*, 48, 43–81.

Kanellakos, D. and Lukas, J. (1974). *The Psychobiology of transcendental meditation: A literature review*. Menlo Park: W. A. Benjamin Press.

Kihlstrom, J. (1984). Conscious, Subconscious, Unconscious: A Cognitive Perspective. In Bowers and Meichenbaum (1984), 149–211.

Kihlstrom, J. (1987). The Cognitive Unconscious. *Science*, 237:4821, 1445–1452.

Kim, J. (1972). Materialism and the Criteria of the Mental. *Synthese*, 22, 323–345.

Kim, J. (1993). *Supervenience and Mind*. Cambridge: Cambridge University Press.

Kim, J. (1996). *Philosophy of Mind*. Boulder: Westview Press.

Kirk, R. (1974). Zombies v. Materialists. *Proceedings of the Aristotelian Society*, 48, 135–152.

Kirk, R. (1994). *Raw Feeling*. Oxford: Clarendon Press.

Kitcher, P. S. (1979). Phenomenal Qualities. *American Philosophical Quarterly*, 16:2, 123–129.

Kitcher, P. (1992). The Naturalists Return. *The Philosophical Review*, 101:1, 53–114.

Kolb, B. and Whishaw, I. (1990). *Fundamentals of Human Neuropsychology*. New York: Freeman and Co.

Köhler, W. (1971). The Mind-Body Problem. In *The Selected Papers of Wolfgang Köhler*. New York: Liveright Publishing Co., 62–82.

Köhler, W. (1980). *Gestalt Psychology*. New York: New American Library.

Kripke, Saul (1980). *Naming and Necessity*. First published in 1972. Cambridge: Harvard University Press.

Külpe, O. (1901). *Outlines of Psychology*. New York: The MacMillan Co.

Ladd, G. (1909). *Psychology: Descriptive and Explanatory*. New York: C. Scribner's Sons.

Lashley, K. S. (1923). The Behavioristic Interpretation of Consciousness: I. *The Psychological Review*, 30:4, 237–272.

Leibniz, G. W. (1951). *Selections*. New York: Charles Scribner's Sons.

Lerner, G. (1993). *The Creation of Feminist Consciousness*. New York: Oxford University Press.

Levin, J. (1985). Functionalism and the argument from conceivability. *Canadian Journal of Philosophy Supplement*, 11, 85–104.

Levine, J. (1983). Materialism and Qualia: The Explanatory Gap. *Pacific Philosophical Quarterly*, 64, 354–361.

Levine, J. (1988). Absent and Inverted Qualia Revisited. *Mind and Language*, 3:4, 271–287.

Levine, J. (1993). On Leaving Out What It's Like. In Davies and Humphreys (1993), 121–136.

Lewis, D. (1966). An Argument for the Identity Thesis. *Journal of Philosophy*, LXIII:1, 17–25.

Lewis, D. (1972). Psychological and Theoretical Identifications. *Australasian Journal of Philosophy*, L:3, 248–259.

Lewis, D. (1980). Mad Pain and Martian Pain. In Block (1980a), 216–222.

Lewis, D. (1990). What experience teaches. In *Mind and Cognition*. Edited by W. Lycan. Oxford: Blackwell Publishers, 499–519.

Lewis, D. (1995). Should a Materialist Believe in Qualia? *Australasian Journal of Philosophy*, 73:1, 140–144.

Llinás, R. and Ribary, U. (1994). Coherent 40 Hz oscillation characterizes dream state in humans. *Proceedings of the National Academy of Science USA*, 90, 2078–2081.

Loar, B. (1990). Phenomenal States. In Tomberlin (1990), 81–108.

Locke, J. (1959). *An Essay Concerning Human Understanding*. Originally published in 1690, annotated by A. C. Fraser. New York: Dover Publications.

Lovejoy, A. (1963). James's *Does Consciousness Exist?* In *The Thirteen Pragmatisms and Other Essays*. Baltimore: The Johns Hopkins Press, 113–132.

Lycan, W. (1981). Form, function and feel. *Journal of Philosophy*, 78, 24–50.

Lycan, W. (1987). *Consciousness*. Cambridge: MIT Press.

Lycan, W. (1990). What is the subjectivity of the mental? *Philosophical Perspectives*, 4, 109–130.

Lycan, W. (1997a). *Consciousness and Experience*. Cambridge: MIT Press.

Lycan, W. (1997b). Consciousness as Internal Monitoring. In Block, Flanagan, and Güzeldere (1997), 755–771.

Lyons, W. (1986). *The Disappearance of Introspection*. Cambridge: MIT Press.

MacIntyre, A. (1958). *The Unconscious*. London: Routledge and Kegan Paul.

Malebranche, N. (1923). *Dialogues on Metaphysics and on Religion*. London: G. Allen and Unwin Ltd.

Mandler, G. (1975). Consciousness: Respectable, Useful, and Probably Necessary. In *Information Processing and Cognition: The Loyola Symposium*. Edited by R. Solso. Hillsdale: Erlbaum Press, 229–254.

Mangan, B. (1993). Taking Phenomenology Seriously: The Fringe and Its Implications for Cognitive Research. *Consciousness and Cognition*, 2:2, 89–108.

Marcel, A. J. (1983a). Conscious and Unconscious Perception: Experiments on Visual Masking and Word Recognition. *Cognitive Psychology*, 15, 197–237.

Marcel, A. J. (1983b). Conscious and Unconscious Perception: An Approach to the Relations between Phenomenal Experience and Perceptual Processes. *Cognitive Psychology*, 15, 238–300.

Marcel, A. J. and Bisiach, E., eds. (1992). *Consciousness in Contemporary Science*. First published in 1988. Oxford: Oxford University Press.

Marr, D. (1982). *Vision*. San Francisco: W.H. Freeman and Co.

Matson, W. I. (1966). Why Isn't the Mind-Body Problem Ancient? In *Mind, Matter, and Method*. Edited by P. Feyerabend and G. Maxwell. Minneapolis: University of Minnesota Press, 92–102.

McGinn, C. (1989). Can we solve the mind-body problem? *Mind*, XCVIII:891, 349–366.

McGinn, C. (1991). *The Problem of Consciousness*. Oxford: Blackwell Publishers.

McLaughlin, B. (1989). Type Epiphenomenalism, Type Dualism, and the Causal Priority of the Physical. *Philosophical Perspectives*, 3, 109–135.

McLaughlin, B. (1992). The Rise and Fall of British Emergentism. In Beckermann, Flohr, and Kim (1992), 49–93.

Mercier, Charles (1888). *The nervous system and the mind: A treatise on the dynamics of the human organism*. London: TheMacMillan Co.

Metzinger, T. (1995a). Faster than Thought: Holism, Homogeneity and Temporal Coding. In Metzinger (1995b), 425–461.

Metzinger, T., ed. (1995b). *Conscious Experience*. Paderborn: Schöningh-Verlag.

Michenfelder, J. D. (1988). The Anesthesized Brain. In *Anesthesia and the Brain: Clinical, Functional, Metabolic, and Vascular Correlates*. New York: Churchill Livingstone Publishers, 35–48.

Mijuskovic, B. (1974). *The Achilles of Rationalist Arguments*. The Hague: Martinus Nijhoff.

Miller, G. (1962). *Psychology: The science of mental life*. New York: Harper and Row Publishers.

Moody, T. (1994). Conversations with Zombies. *Journal of Consciousness Studies*, 1:2, 196–200.

Morgan, M. (1977). *Molyneux's Question*. Cambridge: Cambridge University Press.

Myers, G. (1986). *William James: His life and thought*. New Haven: Yale University Press.

Nagel, T. (1965). Physicalism. In Rosenthal (1971), 96–111.

Nagel, T. (1974). What is it like to be a bat? Reprinted in Nagel (1988b), 165–180.

Nagel, T. (1979). Subjective and Objective. Reprinted in Nagel (1988b), 196–213.

Nagel, T. (1983). The Objective Self. In Ginet and Shoemaker (1983), 211–232.

Nagel, T. (1986). *The View from Nowhere*. Oxford: Oxford University Press.

Nagel, T. (1988a). Panpsychism. In Nagel (1988b), 181–195.

Nagel, T. (1988b). *Mortal Questions*. First printed in 1979. Cambridge: Cambridge University Press.

Natsoulas, T. (1983). Concepts of Consciousness. *Journal of Mind and Behavior*, 4:1, 13–59.

Natsoulas, T. (1986). The Six Basic Concepts of Consciousness and William James' Stream of Thought. *Imagination, Cognition, and Personality*, 6:4, 289–317.

Natsoulas, T. (1992). Is consciousness what psychologists actually examine? *The American Journal of Psychology*, 105:3, 363–384.

Neisser, U. (1967). *Cognitive Psychology*. Englewood Cliffs: Prentice-Hall.

Neisser, U. (1976). *Cognition and Reality*. San Francisco: Freeman and Co.

Nemirow, L. (1980). Review of Nagel's *Mortal Questions*. *Philosophical Review*, 89, 473–477.

Newell, A. and Simon, H. (1972). *Human Problem Solving*. Englewood Cliffs: Prentice Hall.

Nikolinakos, D. (1994). General Anesthesia, Consciousness, and the Skeptical Challenge. *The Journal of Philosophy*, XCI:2, 88–104.

Nisbett, R. and Wilson, T. (1977). Telling More Than We Can Know: Verbal Reports on Mental Processes. *The Psychological Review*, 84:3, 231–258.

Norman, D. (1968). Toward a Theory of Memory and Attention. *The Psychological Review*, 75, 522–536.

Ostenfeld, E. (1987). *Ancient Greek Psychology and the Modern Mind-Body Debate*. Aarhus: Aarhus University Press.

Papineau, D. (1993). Physicalism, Consciousness and the Antipathetic Fallacy. *Australasian Journal of Philosophy*, 71:2, 169–182.

Perry, R. B. (1904). Conceptions and Misconceptions of Consciousness. *The Psychological Review*, XI, 282–296.

Perry, C. and Laurence, J-R. (1984). Mental Processing Outside Awareness: The Contributions of Freud and Janet. In Bowers and Meichenbaum (1984), 9–48.

Perry, J. (1979). The Problem of the Essential Indexical. *Noûs*, 13, 3–21.

Perry, J. (1993). *The Problem of the Essential Indexical*. New York: Oxford University Press.

Perry, J. (1995). Knowledge, Objectivity, and Consciousness. Manuscript, presented at the American Philosophical Association Pacific Division Meeting, April 1, 1995.

Perry, J. (forthcoming). Self-Knowledge and Self-Consciousness. Manuscript. Stanford University.

Place, U. T. (1956). Is Consciousness a Brain Process? In Chappel (1981), 101–109.

Poland, J. (1994). *Physicalism: The Philosophical Foundations*. Oxford: Clarendon Press.

Popper, K. and Eccles, J. (1993). *The Self and Its Brain: An Argument for Interactionism*. First printed in 1977. London: Routledge Publishers.

Posner, M. and Boies, S. J. (1971). Components of Attention. *The Psychological Review*, 78, 391–408.

Post, J. (1987). *The Faces of Existence*. Ithaca: Cornell University Press.

President's Commission. (1981). *President's Commission for the Study of Ethical Problems in Medicine and Biomedical and Behavioral Research: Defining Death*. Washington D.C.: Government Printing Office. (Quoted in Capron 1988.)

Putnam, H. (1963). Brains and Behavior. Reprinted in Block (1980a), 24–36.

Putnam, H. (1981). *Reason, Truth and History*. Cambridge: Cambridge University Press.

Reck, A. (1972). Dualisms in William James's *Principles of Psychology*. *Tulane Studies in Philosophy*, 21:23–38.

Reeves, A. (1981). *Disorders of the Nervous System: A Primer*. Chicago: Year Book Medical Publishers.

Reingold, E. and Merikle, P. (1990). On the Interrelatedness of Theory and Measurement in the Study of Unconscious Processes. *Mind and Language*, 5:1, 9–28.

Revonsuo, A. (1994). The fragile smell of rose, the peculiar aboutness of thought, and the elusive subject of conscious experience. In *Consciousness in Philosophy and Cognitive Neuroscience*. Edited by A. Revonsuo and M. Kamppinen. Hillsdale: L. Erlbaum, 105–114.

Rey, G. (1988). A question about consciousness. In *Perspectives on Mind*. Edited by H. Otto and J. Tuedio. Dordrecht: D. Reidel, 5–24.

Robinson, H., ed. (1993). *Objections to Physicalism*. Oxford: Clarendon Press.

Roche (1979). *Roche Handbook of differential diagnosis. Signs and symptoms in the central nervous system: Coma*. Nutley: Roche Laboratories.

Roche (1989). *Roche Handbook of differential diagnosis. Emergency medicine: Transient loss of consciousness*. Nutley: Roche Laboratories.

Rock, I. (1983). *The Logic of Perception*. Cambridge: MIT Press.

Rorty, R. (1970a). Incorrigibility as the Mark of the Mental. *Journal of Philosophy*, 67, 399–424.

Rorty, R. (1970b). Cartesian Epistemology and Changes in Ontology. In *Contemporary American Philosophy*. Second series. Edited by J. Smith. New York: Humanities Press, 273–292.

Rorty, R. (1979). *Philosophy and the Mirror of Nature*. Princeton: Princeton University Press.

Rosen, M. and Lunn, J. N., eds. (1987). *Consciousness, Awareness, and Pain in General Anaesthesia*. London: Butterworths Press.

Rosenthal, D., ed. (1971). *Materialism and the Mind Body Problem*. Englewood Cliffs: Prentice-Hall.

Rosenthal, D. (1986). Two Concepts of Consciousness. *Philosophical Studies*, 94:3, 329–359.

Rosenthal, D. (1997). A Theory of Consciousness. In Block, Flanagan, and Güzeldere (1997), 729–753.

Ryle, G. (1949). *The Concept of Mind*. London: Hutchinson and Co.

Sacks, O. (1974). *Awakenings*. New York: Doubleday and Co., Inc.

Sanford, D. (1983). The Perception of Shape. In Ginet and Shoemaker (1983), 130–158.

Sartre, J. P. (1956). *Being and Nothingness*. Translated by H. Barnes. New York: Philosophical Library.

Savellos, E. and Yalçın, Ü., eds. (1995). *Supervenience: New Essays*. Cambridge: Cambridge University Press.

Schacter, D. (1988). On the relation between memory and consciousness: Dissociable interactions and conscious experience. In *Varieties of Memory and*

Consciousness. Edited by H. Roediger and F. Craik. Hillsdale: Lawrence Erlbaum Associates, 355–389.

Schmaltz, T. (1996). *Malebranche's Theory of the Soul: A Cartesian Interpretation*. New York: Oxford University Press.

Seager, W. (1991). *Metaphysics of Consciousness*. London: Routledge.

Seager, W. (1995). Consciousness, Information and Panpsychism. *Journal of Consciousness Studies*, 2:3, 272–288.

Searle, J. (1980). Minds, Brains, and Programs. *Behavioral and Brain Sciences*, 3, 417–424.

Searle, J. (1984). *Minds, Brains, and Science*. Cambridge: Harvard University Press.

Searle, J. (1992). *The Rediscovery of the Mind*. Cambridge: MIT Press.

Sellars, W. (1964). The Identity Approach to the Mind-Body Problem. *Review of Metaphysics*, 18:2, 430–451.

Sellars, W. (1991). Philosophy and the Scientific Image of Man. In *Science, Perception, and Reality*. Atascadero: Ridgeview Publishing Co., 1–40.

Shallice, T. (1972). Dual Functions of Consciousness. *The Psychological Review*, 79:5, 383–393.

Shallice, T. (1988). *From Neuropsychology to Mental Structure*. Cambridge: Cambridge University Press.

Shepard, R. (1993). On the physical basis, linguistic representation, and conscious experience of colors. In Harman (1993a), 217–245.

Shepard, R. and Cooper, L. (1992). Representation of colors in the blind, color-blind, and normally sighted. *Psychological Science*, 3, 97–104.

Shoemaker, S. (1975). Functionalism and Qualia. *Philosophical Studies*, 27, 292–315.

Shoemaker, S. (1981a). Absent Qualia are Impossible: A Reply to Block. *The Philosophical Review*, 90:4, 581–599.

Shoemaker, S. (1981b). The Inverted Spectrum. *The Journal of Philosophy*, 74:7, 357–381.

Shoemaker, S. (1991). Qualia and Consciousness. *Mind*, 100:4, 507–524.

Shoemaker, S. (1994). Self-Knowledge and "Inner Sense." *Philosophy and Phenomenological Research*, LIV:2, 249–314.

Skinner, B. F. (1957). *Verbal Behavior*. New York: Appleton-Century-Crofts.

Skinner, B. F. (1974). *About Behaviorism*. New York: Alfred A. Knopf.

Smart, J. J. C. (1959). Sensations and Brain Processes. *Philosophical Review*, LXVIII, 141–156.

Smith, B. C. (1996). *On the Origin of Objects*. Cambridge: MIT Press.

Smith, B. C. (forthcoming). Who's on Third? The Physical Bases of Consciousness. Manuscript. Indiana University, Bloomington.

Smith, L. (1986). *Behaviorism and Logical Positivism: A Reassessment of the Alliance*. Stanford: Stanford University Press.

Sommerhoff, G. (1990). *Life, Brain and Consciousness*. Amsterdam: North Holand.

Sommerhoff, G. (1996). Consciousness Explained as an Integral Integrating System. *Journal of Consciousness Studies*, 3:2, 139–157.

Spence, P. (1879). Space and time considered as negations. *Journal of Speculative Philosophy*, XIII:4, 337–346.

Spencer, H. (1891). *The Principles of Biology*. 2 volumes. New York: D. Appleton and Co.

Spencer, H. (1898). *The Principles of Psychology*. 2 volumes. New York: D. Appleton and Co.

Sprigge, T. (1971). Final Causes. *Supplement of the Aristotelian Society*, XLV, 149–170.

Stapp, H. (1996). Chance, Choice, and Consciousness: A Causal Quantum Theory of the Mind/Brain. Technical report, LBL-37944MOD. Berkeley: Lawrence Berkeley Laboratory.

Stillings, N. et al. (1987). *Cognitive Science: An Introduction*. Cambridge: MIT Press.

Stout, G. F. (1899). *A Manual of Psychology*. New York: Hinds, Noble, and Eldredge Publishers.

Strawson, G. (1994). *Mental Reality*. Cambridge: MIT Press.

Stroud, B. (1996). The Charm of Naturalism. *Proceedings and Addresses of the American Philosophical Association*, 70:2, 43–55.

Sutherland, S. (1995). Consciousness. In *MacMillan Dictionary of Psychology*. Second edition. London: The MacMillan Press, 95.

Thatcher, R. and John, R. (1977). *Foundations of Cognitive Processes*. Hillsdale: Lawrence Erlbaum Associates.

Titchener, E. B. (1902). *An Outline of Psychology*. New York: The MacMillan Co.

Titchener, E. B. (1915). *A Beginner's Psychology*. New York: The MacMillan Co.

Tolman, E. (1927). A Behaviorist's Definition of Consciousness. *The Psychological Review*, 34, 433–439.

Tolman, E. (1967). *Purposive Behavior in Animals and Men*. First published in 1932. New York: Irvington Publishers, Inc.

Tomberlin, J., ed. (1990). *Philosophical Perspectives*, Vol. 4: *Action Theory and Philosophy of Mind*. Atascadero: Ridgeview Publishing Co.

Treisman, A. M. (1969). Strategies and models of selective attention. *The Psychological Review*, 76:3, 282–299.

Tye, M. (1992). Visual Qualia and Visual Content. In *The Contents of Experience: Essays on Perception*. Edited by T. Crane. Cambridge: Cambridge University Press, 158–176.

Tye, M. (1995). *Ten Problems of Consciousness*. Cambridge: MIT Press.

Tyndall, J. (1868). Scientific Materialism. In Tyndall (1898), 75–90.

Tyndall, J. (1874). The Belfast Address. In Tyndall (1898), 135–201.

Tyndall, J. (1898). *Fragments of Science*, Vol. II. New York: Appleton and Co.

Van Gulick, R. (1988). A Functionalist Plea for Self-Consciousness. *Philosophical Review*, 97, 149–188.

Van Gulick, R. (1989). What Difference Does Consciousness Make? *Philosophical Topics*, 17, 211–230.

Van Gulick, R. (1993). Understanding the Phenomenal Mind: Are We All just Armadillos? In Davies and Humphreys (1993), 137–154.

Vickers, M. D. (1987). Final Discussion and Conclusions. In Rosen and Lund (1987), 180–183.

Velmans, M. (1990). Consciousness, Brain, and the Physical World. *Philosophical Psychology*, 3:1, 77–99.

Velmans, M. (1991). Is Human Information Processing Conscious? *Behavioral and Brain Sciences*, 14, 651–726.

Watson, J. (1913). Psychology as the Behaviorist Views It. *The Psychological Review*, XX, 158–177.

Watson, J. (1970). *Behaviorism*. First published in 1924. New York: Norton and Co.

White, S. (1986). Curse of the qualia. *Synthese*, 68, 333–368.

Whyte, L. (1960). *The Unconscious Before Freud*. New York: Basic Books, Inc.

Wilkes, K. (1984). Is Consciousness Important? *British Journal of Philosophy of Science*, 35, 223–243.

Wilkes, K. (1988). —, yishi, duh, um and consciousness. In Marcel and Bisiach (1992), 16–41.

Wilkes, K. (1995). *Psyche* versus the Mind. In Nussbaum and Rorty (1995), 109–127.

Wilson, T. and Dunn, D. (1986). Effects of Introspection on Attitude-Behavior Consistency: Analyzing Reasons versus Focusing on Feelings. *Journal of Experimental and Social Psychology*, 22, 249–263.

Wimsatt, W. (1976). Reductionism, Levels of Organization, and the Mind-Body Problem. In *Consciousness and the Brain*. Edited by G. Globus, G. Maxwell, and I. Savodnik. New York: Plenum, 205–267.

Wittgenstein, L. (1958). *Philosophical Investigations*. Third Edition. Translated by G. E. M. Anscombe. New York: Prentice-Hall Publishing Co.

Wittgenstein, L. (1974). *Tractatus Logico-Philosophicus*. Translated by D. F. Pears and B. F. McGuinnes. First German edition in 1921. London: Routledge and Kegan Paul.

Zaner, R., ed. (1988). *Death: Beyond the Whole-Brain Criteria*. Dordrecht: Kluwer Academic Publishers.

Suggested Readings

compiled by Güven Güzeldere

Articles on Consciousness

Stream of Consciousness

Ericsson K. A., and H. A. Simon (1980). "Verbal Reports as Data." *Psychological Review* 87:215–251.

Lyons, W. (1986). "Noticing with the Inner Eye." Chapter 1 of *The Disappearance of Introspection.* Cambridge: MIT Press.

Meyers, G. E. (1986). "Consciousness." Chapter 2 of *William James: His Life and Thought.* New Haven: Yale University Press.

Natsoulas, T. (1992–93). "The Stream of Consciousness: William James's Pulses." *Imagination, Cognition, and Personality* 12:3–21.

Titchener, E. B. (1912). "The Schema of Introspection." *The American Journal Psychology* XXIII:485–508.

Consciousness, Science, and Methodology

Boring, E. G. (1932). "The Physiology of Consciousness." *Science* 75:32–39.

Chalmers, D. J. (1995). "Facing Up to the Problem of Consciousness." *Journal of Consciousness Studies* 2: 200–219.

Churchland, P. M. (1985). "Reduction, Qualia, and the Direct Introspection of Brain States." *Journal of Philosophy* 82:8–28.

Churchland, P. S. (1983). "Consciousness: the Transmutation of a Concept." *Pacific Philosophical Quarterly* 64:80–95.

Churchland, P. S. (1988). "Reduction and the Neurobiological Basis of Consciousness." In *Consciousness in Contemporary Science*, A. Marcel and E. Bisiach (eds.). Oxford: Oxford University Press.

Dennett, D. C. (1978). "Toward a Cognitive Theory of Consciousness." In *Brainstorms*, D. C. Dennett. Cambridge: MIT Press.

Dennett, D. C. (1982). "How to Study Human Consciousness Empirically, or Nothing Comes to Mind." *Synthese* 53:159–80.

Gillett, G. (1988). "Consciousness and Brain Function." *Philosophical Psychology* 1:325–139.

Hannay, A. (1987). "The Claims of Consciousness: A Critical Survey." *Inquiry* 30:395–434.

Harnad, S. (1982). "Consciousness: An Afterthought." *Cognition and Brain Theory* 5:29–47.

Hilgard, E. R. (1977). "Controversies over Consciousness and the Rise of Cognitive Psychology." *Australian Psychologist* 12:7–26.

James, W. (1904). "Does Consciousness Exist?" *Journal of Philosophy, Psychology, and Scientific Methods* 1:477–491.

McGinn, C. (1991). "Consciousness and the Natural Order." In *The Problem of Consciousness*, C. McGinn. Oxford: Blackwell.

Maudlin, T. (1989). "Computation and Consciousness." *Journal of Philosophy* 86:407–432.

Natsoulas, T. (1978). "Consciousness." *American Psychologist* 33:906–914.

O'Shaughnessy, B. (1991). "The Anatomy of Consciousness." *Philosophical Issues*, Vol. 1, E. Villanueva (ed.). Atascadero, CA: Ridgeview Publishing Co.

Wilkes, K. V. (1984). "Is Consciousness Important?" *British Journal for the Philosophy of Science* 35:223–243.

The Psychology and Neuropsychology of Consciousness

Baars, B. J. (1983). "Conscious Contents Provide the Nervous System with Coherent, Global Information." In *Consciousness and Self-Regulation: Advances in Research and Theory*, Vol. 3. R. J. Davidson, G. E. Schwartz, and D. Shapiro (eds.). New York: Plenum Press.

Bisiach, E. (1988). "Language Without Thought." In *Thought Without Language*, Chap. 18, L. Weiskrantz (ed.). Oxford: Clarendon Press.

Bisiach, E. (1988). "The (Haunted) Brain and Consciousness." In *Consciousness in Contemporary Science*, A. Marcel and E. Bisiach (eds.). Oxford: Oxford University Press.

Cowey, A. and P. Stoerig (1991). "The Neurobiology of Blindsight." *Trends in Neurosciences* 14:140–145.

Davis, L. H. (1989). "Self-Consciousness in Chimps and Pigeons." *Philosophical Psychology* 2:249–257.

Dimond, S. (1976). "Brain Circuits for Consciousness." *Brain, Behavior, and Evolution* 13:376–395.

Edelman, G. M. (1993). "Neural Darwinism: Selection and Re-entrant Signaling in Higher Brain Function." *Neuron* 10:115–125.

Farah, M. J. (1988). "Is Visual Imagery Really Visual? Overlooked Evidence from Neuropsychology." *Psychological Review* 95:307–317.

Flohr, H. (1995). "An Information Processing Theory of Anaesthesia." *Neuropsychologia* 9:1169–1180.

Freeman, W. J. (1990). "On the Fallacy of Assigning an Origin to Consciousness." In *Machinery of the Mind: Data, Theory, and Speculations about Higher Brain Function*, Chap. 2, E. Roy John (ed.). Boston: Birkhauser.

Frost, E. P. (1912). "Can Biology and Physiology Dispense with Consciousness?" *Psychological Review* 19:246–252.

Gazzaniga, M. S. (1995). "Consciousness and the Cerebral Hemispheres." In *The Cognitive Neurosciences*, M. S. Gazzaniga (ed.). Cambridge: MIT Press.

Hameroff, S. (1994). "Quantum Coherence in Microtubules." *Journal of Consciousness Studies* 1:91–118.

Hardcastle, V. G. (1994). "Psychology's Binding Problem and Possible Neurobiological Solutions." *Journal of Consciousness Studies* 1:66–90.

Holender, D. (1986). "Semantic Activation Without Conscious Identification in Dichotic Listening, Parafoveal Vision, and Visual Masking: A Survey and Appraisal." *Behavioral and Brain Sciences* 9:1–66.

Jacoby, L. L., V. Woloshyn, and C. Kelley. (1989). "Becoming Famous Without Being Recognized: Unconscious Influences of Memory Produced by Dividing Attention." *Behavioral and Brain Sciences* 118:115–125.

Johnson-Laird, P. (1983). "A Computational Analysis of Consciousness." *Cognition and Brain Theory* 6:499–508.

Kihlstrom, J. F. (1984). "Conscious, Subconscious, Unconscious: A Cognitive Perspective." In *The Unconscious Reconsidered*, K. S. Bowers and D. Meichenbaum (eds.). New York: Wiley.

Kinsbourne, M. (1995). "Awareness of One's Own Body: An Attentional Theory of its Nature, Development, and Brain Basis." In *The Body and the Self*, J. L. Bermúdez, A. Marcel, and N. Eilan (eds.). Cambridge: MIT Press.

LaBerge, S. (1990). "Psychophysiological Studies of Consciousness During Sleep." In *Sleep and Cognition*, R. R. Bootzen, J. F. Kihlstrom, and D. L. Schacter (eds.). Washington D.C.: American Psychological Association.

Lahav, R. (1993). What Neuropsychology Tells Us about Consciousness. *Philosophy of Science* 60:67–85.

Lashley, K. S. (1923). "The Behavioristic Interpretation of Consciousness I." *Psychological Review* 30:237–272.

Lashley, K. S. (1923). "The Behavioristic Interpretation of Consciousness II." *Psychological Review* 30:329–353.

Libet, B. (1985). "Unconscious Cerebral Initiative and the Role of Conscious Will in Voluntary Action." *Behavioral and Brain Sciences* 8:529–566.

Libet, B. (1989). "Conscious Subjective Experience vs. Unconscious Mental Functions: A Theory of the Cerebral Processes Involved." In *Models of Brain Function*, R. M. J. Cotterill (ed.). Cambridge: Cambridge University Press.

Luria, A. R. (1978). "The Human Brain and Conscious Activity." In *Consciousness and Self-Regulation Advances in Research and Theory*, Vol. 2, G. E. Schwartz and David Shapiro (eds.). New York: Plenum Press.

Mandler, G. (1975). "Consciousness: Respectable, Useful, and Probably Necessary." In *Information Processing and Cognition: The Loyola Symposium*, Chap. 8. Hillsdale, NJ: Erlbaum.

Mangan, B. (1993). "Taking Phenomenology Seriously: The 'Fringe' and Its Implications for Cognitive Research." *Consciousness and Cognition* 2:89–108.

Marcel, A. (1983). "Conscious and Unconscious Perception: An Approach to the Relations between Phenomenal Experience and Perceptual Processes." *Cognitive Psychology* 15:238–300.

Marcel, A. J. (1983). "Conscious and Unconscious Perception: Experiments on Visual Masking and Word Recognition." *Cognitive Psychology* 15:197–237.

Nisbett, R., and T. D. Wilson. (1977). "Telling More Than We Can Know: Verbal Reports on Mental Processes." *Psychological Review* 84:231–258.

Premack, D. (1988). "Minds With and Without Language." In *Thought Without Language*, Chap. 3, L. Weiskrantz (ed.). Oxford: Clarendon Press.

Pribram, K. H. (1990). "Brain and Consciousness: A Wealth of Data." In *Machinery of the Mind: Data,*

Theory, and Speculations about Higher Brain Functions, E. R. John (ed.). Boston: Birkhauser.

Schacter, D. (1987). "Implicit Memory: History and Current Status." *Journal of Experimantal Psychology* 13:501–518.

Schacter, D. L., M. P. McAndrews, and M. Moscovitch. (1988). "Access to Consciousness: Dissociations between Implicit and Explicit Knowledge in Neuropsychological Syndromes." In *Thought Without Language*, Chap. 10, L. Weiskrantz (ed.). Oxford: Clarendon Press.

Shallice, T. (1972). "Dual Functions of Consciousness." *Psychological Review* 79:383–393.

Shallice, T. (1988). "Information-Processing Models of Consciousness: Possibilities and Problems." In *Consciousness in Contemporary Science*, A. Marcel and E. Bisiach (eds.). Oxford: Oxford University Press.

Shepard, R. N. (1992). "On the Physical Basis, Linguistic Representation, and Conscious Experience of Colors." In *Conceptions of the Mind: Essays in Honor of George Miller*, G. Harman (ed.). Hillsdale, NJ: Lawrence Erlbaum Associates.

Tulving, E. (1985). "Memory and Consciousness." *Canadian Psychology* 26:1–12.

Wilson, T. D., and D. S. Dunn. (1986). "Effects of Introspection on Attitude-Behavior Consistency: Analyzing Reasons versus Focusing on Feelings." *Journal of Experimental Psychology* 22:249–263.

Young, A. W. (1988). "Functional Organization of Visual Recognition." In *Thought Without Language*, Chap. 4, L. Weiskrantz (ed.). Oxford: Clarendon Press.

Consciousness and Content

Boghossian, P. (1989). "Content and Self-Knowledge." *Philosophical Topics* 17:5–26.

Burge, T. (1988). "Individualism and Self-Knowledge." *Journal of Philosophy* 85:649–663.

Crane, T. (1992). "The nonconceptual content of experience." In *The Contents of Experience*, T. Crane (ed.). Cambridge: Cambridge University Press.

Davidson, D. (1987). "Knowing One's Own Mind." *Proceedings and Addresses of the American Philosophical Association*, 60.

Gunderson, K. (1990). "Consciousness and Intentionality: Robots with and without the Right Stuff." In *Propositional Attitudes: The Role of Content in Language, Logic, and Mind*, C. A. Anderson and J. Owens (eds.). Stanford: CSLI Publications.

Hamlyn, D. W. (1994). "Perception, Sensation, and Non-Conceptual Content." *Philosophical Quarterly* 44:139–153.

McDowell, J. (1994). "The Content of Perceptual Experience." *Philosophical Quarterly* 44:190–205.

Nelkin, N. (1989). "Propositional Attitudes and Consciousness." *Philosophy and Phenomenological Research* 49:413–430.

Pendlebury, M. (1990). "Sense Experiences and Their Contents: A Defense of the Propositional Account." *Inquiry* 33:215–230.

Function of Consciousness

Bechtel, W. and R. C. Richardson (1983). "Consciousness and Complexity: Evolutionary Perspectives on the Mind-Body Problem." *Australasian Journal of Philosophy* 61:378–395.

Dretskes, F. (forthcoming). "What Good is Consciousness?" *Canadian Journal of Philosophy*.

Flanagan, O. and T. Polger (1995). "Zombies and the Function of Consciousness." *Journal of Consciousness Studies* 2:313–321.

McGinn, C. (1981). "A Note on Functionalism and Function." *Philosophical Topics* 12:169–170.

van Gulick, R. (1989). "What Difference Does Consciousness Make?" *Philosophical Topics* 17:211–230.

Velmans, M. (1992). "Is Human Information-Processing Conscious?" *Behavioral and Brain Sciences* 14:651–669.

The Metaphysics of Consciousness

Feigl, H. (1958). "The 'mental' and the 'physical'." *Minnesota Studies in the Philosophy of Science* 2:370–497.

Kirk, R. (1974). "Zombies vs. Materialists." *Proceedings of the Aristotelian Society*, Supplement 48:135–152.

Kirk, R. (1982). "Physicalism, Identity, and Strict Implication." *Ratio* 24:131–141.

Lewis, D. (1965). "An Argument for the Identity Theory." *Journal of Philosophy* 63:17–25.

Nagel, T. (1979). "Panpsychism." In *Mortal Questions*. Cambridge: Cambridge University Press.

Place, U. T. (1956). "Is Consciousness a Brain Process?" *British Journal of Psychology* 47:44–50.

Place, U. T. (1988). "Thirty Years On—Is Consciousness Still a Brain Process?" *Australasian Journal of Philosophy* 66:208–219.

Searle, J. R. (1990). "Consciousness, Explanatory Inversion, and Cognitive Science." *Behavioral and Brain Sciences* 13:585–642.

Sellars, W. (1981). "Is Consciousness Physical?" *Monist* 64:66–90.

Smart, J. J. C. (1959). "Sensations and Brain Processes." *Philosophical Review* 68:141–156.

Subjectivity and Explanatory Gap

Akins, K. (1993). "A bat without qualities?" In *Consciousness: Psychological and Philosophical Essays*, M. Davies and G. Humphreys (eds.). Oxford: Blackwell.

Biro, John I. (1991). "Consciousness and Subjectivity." *Philosophical Issues*, Vol. 1, E. Villanueva (ed.). Atascadero, CA: Ridgeview Publishing Co.

Foss, J. (1989). "On the Logic of What It Is Like to Be a Conscious Subject." *Australasian Journal of Philosophy* 67:305–320.

Hardin, C. L. (1987). "Qualia and Materialism: Closing the Explanatory Gap." *Philosophy and Phenomenological Research* 48:281–298.

Levine, J. (1983). "Materialism and Qualia: The Explanatory Gap." *Pacific Philosophical Quarterly* 64:354–361.

Lycan, W. G. (1990). "What Is the 'Subjectivity' of the Mental?" In *Philosophical Perspectives*, Vol. 4: *Action Theory and Philosophy of Mind*, J. Tomberlin (ed.) Atascadero, CA: Ridgeview.

McGinn, C. (1991). "The Hidden Structure of Consciousness." In *The Problem of Consciousness*, C. McGinn. Oxford: Blackwell.

Malcolm, N. (1988). "Subjectivity." *Philosophy* 63:147–160.

Nagel, T. (1979). "Subjective and Objective." In *Mortal Questions*. Cambridge: Cambridge University Press.

Nemirow, L. (1990). "Physicalism and the Cognitive Role of Acquaintance." In *Mind and Cognition*, W. Lycan (ed.). Oxford: Blackwell.

Russow, L. (1982). "It's Not Like That to Be a Bat." *Behaviorism* 10:55–63.

Teller, P. (1992). "Subjectivity and Knowing What It's Like." In *Emergence or Reduction?: Prospects for Nonreductive Physicalism*, A. Beckermann, H. Flohr, and J. Kim (eds.). Berlin: De Gruyter.

Tilghman, B. R. (1991). "What Is It Like to Be an Aardvark?" *Philosophy* 66:325–338.

van Gulick, R. (1985). "Physicalism and the Subjectivity of the Mental." *Philosophical Topics* 13:51–70.

White, S. (1987). "What Is It Like to Be a Homunculus?" *Pacific Philosophical Quarterly* 68:148–174.

The Knowledge Argument

Churchland, P. M. (1985). "Reduction, Qualia and the Direct Introspection of Brain States." *Journal of Philosophy* 82:8–28.

Horgan, T. (1984). "Jackson on Physical Information and Qualia." *Philosophical Quarterly* 34:147–183.

Jackson, F. (1982). "Epiphenomenal Qualia." *Philosophical Quarterly* 32:127–136.

Levin, J. (1986). "Could Love Be Like a Heatwave?: Physicalism and the Subjective Character of Experience." *Philosophical Studies* 49:245–261.

Papineau, D. (1993). "Physicalism, Consciousness, and the Antipathetic Fallacy." *Australasian Journal of Philosophy* 71:169–183.

Stemmer, N. (1989). "Physicalism and the Argument from Knowledge." *Australasian Journal of Philosophy* 67:84–91.

Qualia

Block, N. (1980). "Troubles with Functionalism." In *Readings in the Philosophy of Psychology*, Vol. 1, N. Block (ed.). Cambridge: Harvard University Press.

Block, N. (1980). "Are Absent Qualia Impossible?" *Philosophical Review* 89:257–274.

Churchland, P. M., and P. S. Churchland. (1981). "Functionalism, Qualia and Intentionality." *Philosophical Topics* 12:121–132.

Cole, D. (1990). "Functionalism and Inverted Spectra." *Synthese* 82:207–222.

Conee, E. (1985). "The Possibility of Absent Qualia." *Philosophical Review* 94:345–366.

Conee, E. (1985). "Physicalism and Phenomenal Properties." *Philosophical Quarterly* 35:296–302.

Davis, L. (1982). "Functionalism and Absent Qualia." *Philosophical Studies* 41:231–249.

Dennett, D. C. (1978). "Why You Can't Make a Computer That Feels Pain." *Synthese* 38:3.

Fox, I. (1989). "On the Nature and Cognitive Function of Phenomenal Content—Part One." *Philosophical Topics* 17:81–103.

Graham, G., and G. Stephens. (1985). "Are Qualia a Pain in the Neck for Functionalists?" *American Philosophical Quarterly* 22:73–80.

Horgan, T. (1984). "Functionalism, Qualia, and the Inverted Spectrum." *Philosophy and Phenomenological Research* 44:453–469.

Horgan, T. (1987). "Supervenient Qualia." *Philosophical Review* 96:491–520.

Kitcher, P. S. (1979). "Phenomenal Qualities." *American Philosophical Quarterly* 16:123–129.

Levin, J. (1985). "Functionalism and the Argument from Conceivability." *Canadian Journal of Philosophy*, Supplement 11:85–104.

Levine, J. (1988). "Absent and Inverted Qualia Revisited." *Mind and Language* 3:271–287.

Levine, J. (1994). "Out of the Closet: A Qualophile Confronts Qualophobia." *Philosophical Topics* 22:107–126.

Lewis, D. (1980). "Mad Pain and Martian Pain." In *Readings in the Philosophy of Psychology*, Vol 1., N. Block (ed.). Cambridge: Harvard University Press.

Lewis, D. (1983). "Postscript to 'Mad Pain and Martian Pain.'" In *Philosophical Papers*, Vol. 1. Cambridge: Cambridge University Press.

Lewis, D. (1995). "Should a Materialist Believe in Qualia?" *Australasian Journal of Philosophy* 73:140–144.

Linsky, B. (1984). "Phenomenal Qualities and the Identity of Indistinguishables." *Synthese* 59:363–380.

Lycan, W. G. (1973). "Inverted Spectrum." *Ratio* 15:315–319.

Lycan, W. G. (1981). "Form, Function and Feel." *Journal of Philosophy* 78:24–50.

Nelkin, N. (1986). "Pains and Pain Sensations." *Journal of Philosophy* 83:129–148.

Nelkin, N. (1989). "Unconscious Sensations." *Philosophical Psychology* 2:129–141.

Newton, N. (1989). "On Viewing Pain as a Secondary Quality." *Nous* 23:569–598.

Pitcher, G. (1970). "The Awfulness of Pain." *Journal of Philosophy* 48.

Rey, G. (1992). "Sensational Sentences Switched." *Philosophical Studies* 67:73–103.

Seager, W. E. (1983). "Functionalism, Qualia and Causation." *Mind* 92:174–188.

Shoemaker, S. (1975). "Functionalism and Qualia." *Philosophical Studies* 27:291–315.

Shoemaker, S. (1981). "Absent Qualia Are Impossible—A Reply to Block." *Philosophical Review* 90:581–599.

Shoemaker, S. (1984). "Churchland on Reduction, Qualia, and Introspection." *Philosophy of Science Association* 2:799–809.

Shoemaker, S. (1991). "Qualia and Consciousness." *Mind* 100:507–524.

Tye, M. (1986). "The Subjective Qualities of Experience." *Mind* 95:1–17.

Wilson, F. (1974). "Why I Am Not Aware of Your Pain." In *The Ontological Turn: Studies in the Philosophy of Gustav Bergmann*, M. S. Gram and E. D. Klemke (eds.). Dobuqve: University of Iowa Press.

Higher-Order Monitoring Conceptions of Consciousness

Aquila, R. (1990). "Consciousness as Higher-Order Thoughts: Two Objections." *American Philosophical Quarterly* 27:81–87.

Byrne, A. (forthcoming). "Some Like It HOT: Consciousness and Higher-Order Thoughts." *Philosophical Studies*.

Carruthers, P. (1989). "Brute Experience." *Journal of Philosophy*, 435–451.

Rosenthal, D. M. (1986). "Two Concepts of Consciousness." *Philosophical Studies* 49:329–359.

Rosenthal, D. M. (1991). "The Independence of Consciousness and Sensory Quality." In *Consciousness*, E. Villanueva (ed.). Atascadero, CA: Ridgeview.

Shoemaker, S. (1968). "Self-Reference and Self-Awareness." *Journal of Philosophy* 65:555–567.

Books on Consciousness

Philosophy

Armstrong, David M., and Norman Malcolm. (1984). *Consciousness and Causality: A Debate on the Nature of Mind.* Oxford: Basil Blackwell.

Carruthers, P. (1996). *Language, Thought, and Consciousness.* Cambridge: Cambridge University Press.

Chalmers, D. J. (1996). *The Conscious Mind.* New York: Oxford University Press.

Churchland, Paul. (1984). *Matter and Consciousness: A Contemporary Introduction to the Philosophy of Mind.* Cambridge: MIT Press/Bradford Book.

Churchland, Paul. (1995). *The Engine of Reason, the Seat of the Soul.* Cambridge: MIT Press.

Dennett, Daniel C. (1969). *Content and Consciousness.* London: Routledge & Kegan Paul.

Dennett, Daniel C. (1991). *Consciousness Explained.* Boston: Little, Brown.

Dretske, F. (1995). *Naturalizing the Mind.* Cambridge: MIT Press.

Evans, C. O. (1970). *The Subject of Consciousness.* London: George Allen & Unwin.

Flanagan, Owen. (1992). *Consciousness Reconsidered.* Cambridge: MIT Press/Bradford Book.

Hannay, Alastair. (1990). *Human Consciousness.* London: Routledge.

Hardcastle, V. G. (1996). *Locating Consciousness.* Amsterdam: John Benjamins.

Hill, Christopher S. (1991). *Sensations: A Defense of Type Materialism.* Cambridge: Cambridge University Press.

Jackendoff, Ray. (1987). *Consciousness and the Computational Mind.* Cambridge: MIT Press/Bradford Book.

Kirk, Robert. (1994). *Raw Feeling: A Philosophical Account of the Essence of Consciousness.* Oxford: Clarendon Press.

Lockwood, M. (1989). *Mind, Brain, and the Quantum.* Oxford: Oxford University Press.

Lycan, William G. (1987). *Consciousness.* Cambridge: MIT Press/Bradford Book.

Lycan, W. G. (1996). *Consciousness and Experience.* Cambridge: MIT Press.

Marks, Charles E. (1980). *Commissurotomy, Consciousness, and the Unity of Mind.* Montgomery: Bradford Books.

Nelkin, N. (1996). *Consciousness and the Origins of Thought.* Oxford: Oxford University Press.

Seager, William. (1991). *Metaphysics of Consciousness.* London: Routledge.

Searle, John. (1992). *The Rediscovery of the Mind.* Cambridge: MIT Press/Bradford Book.

Strawson, G. (1994). *Mental Reality.* Cambridge: MIT Press.

Stubenberg, L. (1996). *Consciousness and Qualia.* Amsterdam: John Benjamins.

Tye, M. (1995). *Ten Problems of Consciousness.* Cambridge: MIT Press.

White, Alan R. (1964). *Attention.* Oxford: Basil Blackwell.

Philosophy Anthologies

Davies, Martin, and Glyn W. Humphreys, eds. (1993). *Consciousness.* Oxford: Blackwell.

Metzinger, T., ed. (1995). *Conscious Experience.* Paderborn: Ferdinand Schöningh.

Revonsuo, Antti, and Matti Kamppinen, eds. (1994). *Consciousness in Philosophy and Cognitive Neuroscience,* Hillsdale, NJ: Lawrence Erlbaum Associates.

Villanueva, Enrique, ed. (1991). *Consciousness.* Atascadero, CA: Ridgeview Publishing Co.

Warner, R. and T. Szubka, eds. (1994). *The Mind-Body Problem: A Guide to the Current Debate.* Oxford: Blackwell.

Psychology and Neuroscience

Baars, Bernard J. (1988). *A Cognitive Theory of Consciousness.* Cambridge: Cambridge University Press.

Boring, Edwin. (1933). *The Physical Dimensions of Consciousness.* New York: Century Co.

Farah, Martha. (1991). *Visual Agnosia: Disorders of Object Recognition and What They Tell Us about Normal Vision.* Cambridge: MIT Press.

Farthing, William G. (1992). *The Psychology of Consciousness.* Englewood Cliffs, NJ: Prentice-Hall.

Hilgard, Ernest R. (1986). *Divided Consciousness: Multiple Controls in Human Thought and Action.* Exp. ed. New York: Wiley.

Klein, David Ballin. (1984). *The Concept of Consciousness: A Survey*. Lincoln: University of Nebraska Press.

Pöppel, E. (1985). *Mindworks: Time and Conscious Experience*. New York: H. B. Jovanovich.

Popper, K. R. and J. C. Eccles (1977). *The Self and Its Brain*. Berlin: Springer Verlag.

Rosenfield, I. (1992). *The Strange, Familiar, and Forgotten: An Anatomy of Consciousness*. New York: Alfred Knopf.

Shallice, Tim (1988). *From Neuropsychology to Mental Structure*. Cambridge: Cambridge University Press.

Weiskrantz, L. (1986). *Blindsight: A Case Study and Implications*. Oxford: Clarendon Press.

Psychology and Neuroscience Anthologies

Bermúdez, J. L., A. Marcel, and N. Eilan, eds. (1995). *The Body and the Self*. Cambridge: MIT Press.

Blakemore, C. and S. Greenfield, eds. (1987). *Mindwaves: Thoughts on Intelligence, Identity, and Consciousness*. Oxford: Basil Blackwell.

Bock, Gregory R., and Joan Marsh, eds. (1993). *Experimental and Theoretical Studies of Consciousness*. Chichester: Wiley.

Bowers, K. S. and D. Meichenbaum, eds. (1984). *The Unconscious Reconsidered*. New York: Wiley.

Cohen, J. and J. Schooler, eds. (in press). *Scientific Approaches to the Study of Consciousness: 25th Carnegie Symposium*. Hillsdale: L. Erlbaum.

Davidson, J. M. and R. J. Davidson, eds. (1980). *Psychology of Consciousness*. New York: Plenum Press.

Gackenbach, J. and S. LaBerge, eds. (1988). *Conscious Mind, Sleeping Brain*. New York: Plenum Press.

Gazzaniga, M., ed. (1995). *The Cognitive Neurosciences*. Cambridge: MIT Press.

Hameroff, Stuart, A. Kazniak, and A. Scott, eds. (1996). *Toward a Science of Consciousness*. Cambridge: MIT Press.

Marcel, Anthony J., and Eduardo Bisiach, eds. (1988). *Consciousness in Contemporary Science*. Oxford: Oxford University Press.

Milner, A. D., and M. D. Rugg, eds. (1992). *The Neuropsychology of Consciousness*. London: Academic Press.

Ornstein, Robert E., ed. (1973). *The Nature of Human Consciousness: A Book of Readings*. New York: Viking Press.

Pickering, John, and Martin Skinner, eds. (1990). *From Sentience to Symbols: Readings on Consciousness*. Toronto: University of Toronto Press.

Robertson, I. H. and J. C. Marshall, eds. (1993). *Unilateral Neglect: Clinical and Experimental Studies*. Hillsdale: L. Erlbaum.

Roediger III, Henry L., and Fergus I. M. Craik, eds. (1989). *Varieties of Memory and Consciousness: Essays in Honour of Endel Tulving*. Hillsdale, NJ: Lawrence Erlbaum Associates.

Schwartz, G. E. and D. Shapiro (1976–83), eds. *Consciousness and Self-Regulation*. Volumes 1–3. (Volume 3 co-edited by R. J. Davidson.) New York: Plenum Press.

Underwood, G. and R. Stevens, eds. (1979–82). *Aspects of Consciousness*. Volumes 1–3. (Volume 3 edited solely by G. Underwood.) London: Academic Press.

Velmans, M., ed. (1996). *The Science of Consciousness*. London: Routledge.

Weiskrantz, L., ed. (1988). *Thought without Language*. Oxford: Clarendon Press.

Other Recent Books on Consciousness

Calvin, William. (1990). *The Cerebral Symphony: Seashore Reflections on the Structure of Consciousness*. New York: Bantam Books.

Crick, Francis. (1994). *The Astonishing Hypothesis: The Scientific Search for the Soul*. New York: Charles Scribner's Sons.

Dennett, Daniel C. (1996). *Kinds of Minds: Toward an Understanding of Consciousness*. New York: Basic Books.

Edelman, Gerald M. (1989). *The Remembered Present: A Biological Theory of Consciousness*. New York: Basic Books.

Edelman, Gerald M. (1992). *Bright Air, Brilliant Fire*. New York: Basic Books.

Humphrey, Nicholas. (1983). *Consciousness Regained*. Oxford: Oxford University Press.

Humphrey, Nicholas. (1992). *A History of the Mind*. New York: Simon & Schuster.

Jaynes, Julian. (1976). *The Origin of Consciousness in the Breakdown of the Bicameral Mind*. Boston: Houghton Mifflin.

Ornstein, Robert. (1972). *The Psychology of Consciousness*. 2d ed. New York: Harcourt Brace Jovanovich.

Penrose, Roger. (1994). *Shadows of the Mind.* Oxford: Oxford University Press.

Scott, Alwyn. (1995). *Stairway to the Mind: The Controversial New Science of Consciousness.* New York: Springer.

Index

A posteriori stipulation, 483, 487–491
A priori stipulation, 486, 490–491
Ability Hypothesis, 591–594
Above-threshold stimulus, 190
Absent qualia. *See also* Qualia
  epiphenomenalism and, 39
  possibility of, 39, 175
  as problem of phenomenal consciousness, 30,
    39
  Property Dualism Argument and, 708
  Shoemaker and, 699–700
Absent Qualia Argument
  functionalism and, 435–441, 559, 613, 699–705
  materialism and, 559
  reconstruction of, 435–436
Absent-minded processing of vision, 248
Access (A) consciousness
  availability for global control and, 421–422
  Block and, 417–419, 421, 425, 427
  conflation of, 392–397
  defined, 425
  Dennett and, 395
  epiphenomenalism and, 369–371
  function of consciousness and, 382–386, 423
  Multiple Drafts model and, 395
  pain and, 405–407
  perceptual state and, 379
  without phenomenal consciousness, 385–386
  phenomenal consciousness vs., 28–30, 113, 421–422,
    426–427
  phenomenal consciousness without, 386–389
  zombies and, 387
Accessibility, 426
Activation inhibition modulation (AIM) theory, 101–
  104
Adams, Robert, 4
Additional characterization problem, 344–345
Adequacy Thesis (AT), 343–350
Afterimages, 329–331
AI, 465
AIM theory, 101–104
Akelaitis, 262
Akins, Kathleen, 387
Alexia
  without agraphia, 117
  implicit reading in pure, 228–231
    awareness of perception, 229–230
    awareness of vision, 203

comparisons with other syndromes, 231–233
described, 228
explanations, 230–231
representative findings, 228–229
  Schacter's model and, 380
Allman, John, 289
Allport, Alan, 115–116, 233, 241, 243, 245
Ambiguity concept, 391
Ames, Adelbert, 191
Amnesia, 117
Analytic method of studying stream of consciousness,
  71
Anderson, John, 189
Andrade, J., 392–393
Anesthesia, consciousness under, 1–2
Anosognosia, 266–269
Anterior cingulate as proposed site of Cartesian
  Theater, 83
Anti-physicalism. *See also* Knowledge Argument
  arguments
    Jackson's, 543, 545–546, 598–599
    Kripke's, 543–545, 548, 599–600
    replies to, 546–547
  intuition, 597, 600
Anton, G., 266
Aphasia, 117, 266
Armstrong, David M., 112, 755, 762, 778–779, 789,
  791, 794–797, 799
Artificial intelligence (AI), 465
As-if intentionality, 499–501
AT, 343–350
Atkinson, R., 17, 196, 269
Attended messages, unattended vs., 194
Attention
  in iconic memory, 288
  as input selection, 193–195
  mechanisms, 277, 794
  in neglect, unilateral, 247–248
  role of, 284–285
  selective, 80, 188
  spatial, 247
  visual
    binding and selective, 282–285
    oscillations and, neuronal, 286–287
  voluntary vs. involuntary control of, 194–195
Automaticity in learning, 195
Automaton theory of consciousness, 41
Availability for global control, 421–423, 425

Awareness. *See also* Visual perception and awareness
  after brain damage
  conscious experience and, 773–777, 789
  experimental approaches to, 289–290
  experimental problems and, 288–289
  fleeting, 288
  higher-order, 12–13
  of intrinsic properties, 688–690
  knowledge with, 364
  knowledge without, 117, 261–262, 364, 370
  of mental states, 792–793
  perceptual, 203, 208, 213, 224–225, 229–230, 774–775
  second-order reflective, 12
  of stimuli in central vision, 247–248, 250
  subjective, 372
  as synonym for "consciousness", 111
  visual, 135–138, 203, 281–282
  working, 288–290

Baars, Bernard J., 18, 111–112, 269, 392, 401–402, 422,
  440, 755
Backwards projection, 163
Backwards referral, 146–147, 162–165, 761–762
Barbur, J. L., 258
Bat's experience, 520–522, 525
Bauer, R. M., 213, 215, 217, 261–262
Behaviorism
  Frege-Schlick view and, 650
  functionalism and, 695
  in historical perspective of consciousness, 15–17, 29,
    255
  introspection and, 16
  mental states and, 119, 473
Behrmann, M., 227
Beliefs, 187, 313–315, 338, 463, 791
Believer System, 466–468
Bennett, 406
Berti, A., 223, 227, 266–268, 270
Bieri, Peter, 637
Binding problem
  in neuroscientific research, 85
  oscillations and, neuronal, 286–288, 381
  stream of consciousness and, 90–91, 93
  visual attention and, binding and
    selective, 282–284, 286–288
Binocular rivalry, 289
Biological naturalism, 6
Bisiach, Edoardo, 113, 115, 118, 224–225, 227, 256,
  266–270

Black-box approach to research, 277
Blind spot region, 86–87
Blindsight
  as general aspect of neurobiological theory, 280–281
  information and, 365–366
  knowledge without awareness and, 117
  literature on, 375
  as model of consciousness, 256–261
  phenomenal consciousness and, 385–386
  phenomenal experience and, 248
  restoring of consciousness and, 418
  Schacter's model and, 376–377
  stimuli in blind field and, 365
  study of consciousness and, 237
  super, 385–386, 426
  visual perception and awareness in, 206–210
    awareness of perception, 208
    awareness of vision, 203
    comparisons with other syndromes, 231–233
    described, 206
    explanations, 208–210
    representative findings, 206–208
  zombies and, 385
Block, Ned J., 28–30, 33, 36, 40–41, 113, 119, 330–332,
  368–371, 417–419, 421, 423, 425–426, 473–474,
  613, 623, 695–696, 705
Block, R., 406
Body-mind problem. *See* Mind-body problem
Bogen, J. E., 262
Boies, S. J., 18
Boring, Edwin, 15–16
Brain
  consciousness and
    cause of, 132–133, 531
    as graded property of neural information, 205–206
    as privileged role of particular systems in, 203–204
    as state of integration among systems in, 204–205
  fallacies about special center in, 83–85
  perception and, understanding, 533–535
  philosophical problem of, 537
  visual perception and awareness and, 203–206
Brain-damaged patients, 117, 240–243. *See also* Visual
  perception and awareness after brain damage
Brentano, Franz, 23, 746–747, 789
Brentano's problem, 298–299
Broadbent, D. E., 194
Broca's aphasia, 117
Brown, G., 466
Brunn, J. L., 227

Brute fact explanation, 437
Bruyer, R., 211
Buffer memories, 149
Burge, Tyler, 315–317, 321, 324

Campion, J., 209, 258–260
Capgras delusion, 388–389
Caramazza, A., 246, 249
Carruthers, Peter, 789, 791
Cartesian bottleneck, 143
Cartesian dualism, 529, 697
Cartesian intuition, 362, 461–462, 471–474
Cartesian Materialism, 83–87
  Cartesian modularism vs., 34–35
  D & K's argument against, 176, 178, 181, 377
  defined, 83
  Filling In model and, 85–87
  identity theory and, 545
  imagery of, 83
  Inner Sense theory and, 761–764
  Jackson's argument and, 545–546
  Kripke's argument and, 544–545
  mental states and, 18–19
  as model of consciousness, 141–145, 377
  Multiple Drafts model and, 83–85, 93
  rejection of, 763
  temporal anomalies and, 145–153
Cartesian modularism, 34–35, 178, 377, 379
Cartesian Theater
  D & K's argument against, 176, 178, 181
  Filling In model and, 85–87
  imagery of, 144
  Inner Sense theory and, 762–763
  Multiple Drafts model and, 83–85, 141, 143–145
  Orwellian revisions and, 153–162
  sites of, proposed, 83–85, 249–250
  Stalinesque revisions and, 153–162
CAS, 117–118, 203, 393
Causal characterization of consciousness, 11, 27
Causal emergence, 451
Causal reduction, 452
Causal role, 529
Causal/creature conception of consciousness, 729–731, 777–779
Causal/state conception of consciousness, 791
Cerebral achromatopsia, 633
C-fiber stimulation, 445–449, 505–506
Chalmers, David J., 29–32, 392
Chisholm, R., 635

Chomsky, Noam, 296
Churchland, Patricia, 5, 32, 40, 105, 114–115
Churchland, Paul M., 32, 40, 164–165, 177, 567–569, 669–670, 789, 791, 794–796
Cluster concept, 391–392
Cognitive closure, 529–531, 536
Cognitive functions of consciousness, as easy problems, 29, 381
Cognitive impenetrability, 638
Cognitivism
  cognitive science, 119–123
  consciousness and
    historical perspective of, 16–18, 27–28
    phenomenal, 381
    study of, 278–279
  neurobiological theory of consciousness and, 278–279
  pain and, 329
  research in, 381–382
  states of mind and, 79–82
Collapse Hypothesis, 402–404
Color phi phenomenon, 145–146, 156, 161
Common Language Argument, 704–705
Conceptual analysis, 483–491
  completeness and, 484–485
  entry by entailment thesis and, 485–487
  location problem and, 483–484
  materialism and, 483–486
  metaphysics and, 483–484
  a posteriori stipulation and, 483, 487–491
  a priori stipulation, 486, 490–491
  supervenience and, 484–485
Conceptual truths, 756
Conflations of access and phenomenal consciousness, 392–397, 419
Connection principle, 22
Connectionist research program, 382
Conscious Awareness System (CAS), 117–118, 203, 393
Conscious creatures, unconscious creatures vs., 729–731, 777–779
Conscious decisions, 147
Conscious experience, 773–786. See also Experience
  awareness and, 773–777, 789
  conscious being and states and, 777–779
  differences in, 779–784
  higher-order thought theory and, 784
  occurrence of, 519, 784–786
  perceptual experience vs., 773, 779
Conscious inessentialism, 357

Conscious representation, levels of processing, 244–247, 250

Conscious robots thought experiment, 495–496

Conscious states, 777–779

Consciousness, 1–46, 721–728. *See also* Access (A) consciousness; Phenomenal (P) consciousness; Stream of consciousness; *specific theories*
 claims about, 97–98
 conceptual foundations, 1–11, 721
  conceptions of, 8, 26–30, 45–46, 375
  explanatory gap, 2–4, 26, 30–32, 40–41, 45, 175
  intuitions, 11
  mystery of, 1–5, 290
  naturalism, 5–6
  nature of, difficulties with, 9–10
  philosophical problems, 1–2
  puzzlement of, 1–6
  semantic confusion, 7–8
  skepticism, 5
  studying, difficulties with, 6–9
 as cultural construction, 394–395
 defined, 6–9, 27, 111–114
 Dennett and, 394
 division of labor in, 729
 future investigation of, 250–251
 historical perspective, 12–21
  behaviorism, 14–16, 27–28, 255
  cognitivism, 16–18, 28
  current status, 21
  functionalism, 17, 28
  introspectionism, 13–15
  James, 13
  philosophy, early modern, 12–13
  unconscious study, 18–21
 problems of, 21–46
  access vs. phenomenal consciousness, 28–32
  characterization of, 27–28, 45
  dispute of phenomenal consciousness, 42–46
  easy vs. hard problems, 29–30, 45
  epiphenomenalism, 40, 41–42, 45
  experience, 30
  first-person vs. third-person accounts, 24–26, 45, 575–577
  four W questions and further-How question, 30–36
  intentionality, 22–23
  perspectivity and epistemic asymmetry, 24–25, 44
  qualia, 36–41, 278
  road map for phenomenal consciousness, 36–38
 Rey's question about, 461–475

Conservative stance of individualist, 315

Constitutive externalism/individualism, 312–313

Containment response, 677

Content problem, 295–305
 conscious perceptual experiences and, 297–299
 eliminativism and, 299
 individuation and, 302
 insulation strategy and, 299–300, 304
 intentionality and, 302–304
 medium conception and, 300–301
 naturalism and, 295–297, 301, 304–305
 pessimism regarding, 297–298
 theory of content and, 299–302

Continuity of stream of consciousness, 89–90

Contrastive phenomenology (CP), 187–198
 attention as input selection and, 193–195
 consciousness as variable and, 187–189
 defined, 187
 imagery and, 192–193
 inner speech and, 192–193
 learning and memory contrasts and, 195–196
 perception as input representation and, 189–192
 problem-solving and, spontaneous, 196–197

Convergence zones, 282

Cooper, L. A., 193, 402

Cornell school, 14

Cortical blindness, 266, 280

Coslett, H. B., 229–231, 380

Couture, L., 406

Covert recognition of faces in prosopagnosia, 210–219
 awareness of perception, 213
 awareness of vision, 203
 comparisons with other syndromes, 231–233
 described, 210
 explanations, 213–219
 representative findings, 210–213

Cowey, A., 206, 210, 383, 386

CP. *See* Contrastive phenomenology (CP)

Creature conception of consciousness, 729–731, 777–779

Crick, Francis, 3, 7, 33, 117, 119, 134, 176–177, 205, 381, 383, 396–397, 406, 422

Crick hypothesis of visual awareness, 135–136

Crick-Koch hypothesis
 oscillations and, neuronal, 117, 119, 422
 phenomenal consciousness and, 33, 177
 What question and, 33

Crowne, D. P., 248

Cummings, 241

Cummins, Robert, 549
Cutaneous rabbit example, 146, 161

D & K's argument, 175–178, 181–182
D'Addami, G., 466
Damasio, A. R., 205, 211, 213, 225, 261–262, 268, 282
Damasio, H., 211, 213
Darwin, Charles, 358–359
Davidson, Donald, 525
De Haan, E. H. F., 211, 213, 215–216, 261
Decisions, 147
Defects of consciousness, 363–368
Definitional reduction, 452–453
Déjà vu experience, 101
Delay loop mechanism, 149
Deliberative will, 80
Denial of deficit, 266–269
Dennett and Kinsbourne's (D & K's) argument, 175–178, 181–182
Dennett, Daniel, 2–3, 18, 34–36, 39, 42–43, 89–92, 101–102, 104, 115–116, 118–119, 175–178, 250, 269, 377, 391, 394–396, 464, 466–467, 678, 682, 757–758, 761–763, 765, 773, 789, 791
Derived intentionality, 499–501
Descartes, Rene, 4, 12–13, 19, 25, 41–42, 83–85, 143–144, 203, 445, 461, 465, 543–544, 619, 623, 721, 731
DICE model, 34, 203, 213, 230, 233
Dimond, S. J., 118
Directional hypokinesia, 241
Disembodiment, 538
Dispositional mental states, 732
Dissociated interactions and conscious experience (DICE) model, 34, 203, 213, 230, 233
Distorted room of Ames, 191
Distribution of consciousness, 189
Disunity of consciousness, 243–244, 250
DNA, 131–132
DNA physicalist-functionalism, 708–712
Dreams, 101–105, 111
Dretske, Fred, 5, 35–36, 40, 637, 758–761, 791
Dualism
  Cartesian, 529, 697
  functionalism and, 695
  mental states and, 614
  Property Dualism Argument and, 705–708
  split-brain and, 262–266
  substance, 573–574
Dupreé, John, 115

Eccles, John C., 4, 147, 264
Ectoplasmic story, 574
Edelman, G., 87, 392
EEG, 1
Efron, R., 151, 162
Electroencephalogram (EEG), 1
Eliminativism
  content problem and, 299
  Dennett and, 39–40
  materialism and, 129
  mental states and, 473
  phenomenal consciousness and, 43, 177
  qualia and, 39–40, 44
Ellenberger, H., 19
Elster, J., 631
Emergentism, 451–453
Empathic explanation, 463
Empiricism, 496. See also Contrastive phenomenology (CP)
Entry by entailment thesis, 486–487
Epilepsy, 376, 399
Epiphenomenalism, 357–373
  absent qualia and, 39
  access consciousness and, 369–371
  arguments from design and, 359–361
  challenges facing, 372
  conscious inessentialism and, 357
  defects of consciousness and, 363–368
  ephiphenomenalist suspicion and, 357–359, 371–373
  experiment in, 361–363, 372
  information and, 589–591
  James and, 358
  phenomenal consciousness and, 369–371, 423
  as problem of consciousness, 39, 41–42, 45
  qualia and, 590
  teleological functionalism and, 363–368, 371–373
  zombies and, 41–42
Epistemic asymmetry, perspectivity and, 24–25
Equivocation fallacy, 425
Erdelyi, M. H., 20
Ethics, 82
Evans, Gareth, 310–312
Executive System, 377–380
Expectations, stimulus, 192
Experience, 579–594. See also Conscious experience; Externalism and experience; Sense experience
  Ability Hypothesis and, 591–594
  Adequacy Thesis and, 343–350
  availability for global control and, 421–423, 425

Experience (cont.)
  of bat, 520–522, 525
  content of, 341–343
  déjà vu, 101
  different, 779–784
  discrimination of, 597
  facts of, 522
  functionalism and, 663–664, 668–673
  Hypothesis of Phenomenal Information and, 583–587, 589–591
  information and, 342
  intentionality and, 664–668, 679–680
  intrinsic quality of, 663–674, 688–690
  Knowlege Argument and, 585–587
  learning from, 579
  missing point of, 580–583, 587–589
  other ways of learning and, 579–580
  pain and, 332–334, 336–337
  perceptual, 297–299, 341, 672, 773, 779
  Percy's, 319–320
    with twist, 320–322
  phenomenal, 239, 248–249
  phenomenal concepts and qualities of, 597–598
  physical information and, 583–585, 589–591
  as problem of consciousness, 30
  putative perceptual, 341
  sensational properties of, 324–325
  sense datum theory and, 667–668
  in sleep, 101–104
  subjective, 248–249, 519–520
  visual perceptual, 341
Experimental approaches to awareness, 289–290
Experimental problems and awareness, 288–289
Explanatory Gap Argument, 563–565
  functionalism and, 559
  materialism and, 435, 559, 563
  reconstruction of, 563–565
  strength of, 563
Explanatory gap
  basis of, conceptual, 550
  in conceptual foundations of consciousness, 2–4, 26, 30, 40–41, 45, 175
  consequence of discussing, 553
  leaving out qualia and, 543, 550, 553
  phenomenal concepts and qualities and, 608–609
  phenomenal consciousness and, 381–382
  physicalism and, 543, 598
  qualia and, 552–553
Explanatory reduction, 550–551, 553

Explicit memory, 117
Externalism and experience
  argument for externalism and, 313–315
  claims of externalism and, 312–313
  dilemma for externalist and, 315–318
  individualist stances and, 315–318
  perceptual content of consciousness and, 309–312, 322–326
  phenomenal character and, 325–326
  views of, 309
  vindication of externalism and, 318–322
    Percy's experience, 319–320
    Percy's experience with twist, 320–322
    schematic example, 318–319
Externalist claim, 312–313

Facile materialism, 462
Farah, Martha J., 217, 222, 226–227, 378–379, 386, 422
Farrell, B. A., 38, 756
Fechner, 19
Fendrich, R., 209
Fichte, 19
Field, H., 463
Filling In model, 85–87
First-person accounts, 503–514
  Kripke's argument and, 503–507
  phenomenal concepts and qualities and, 597
  in philosophical reflection, 503–504
  as problem of consciousness, 26, 45
  Searle's argument and, 504, 507–514
  third-person accounts and, 26, 45, 575–577
  thought experiments and, 503–514
Flanagan, Owen, 3, 36, 40, 116–117, 119, 388, 400–401
Fodor, Jerry A., 22, 270, 463, 469, 552, 623
Folk psychology concept of consciousness, 114–119, 631
Foveal vision, 86
Free will, 187
Frege, Gottlob, 649–651
Freud, Sigmund, 7, 18–20, 102
Fringe, in stream of consciousness, 77–78
Frontal lobe as proposed site of Cartesian Theater, 83
Frost, D., 206, 256
Function of consciousness, 375–407
  access consciousness and, 382–386, 423
  cognitive, 29–30, 381
  conflations and, 392–397
  confusion about, 375–376

distinguishing between models and, 403–407
phenomenal consciousness and, 380–382, 386–389, 423
Schacter's model and, 376–380, 403
self-consciousness and, 390–392, 395
target reasoning and, 377, 379, 397–403, 407
Functionalism, 695–712
Absent Qualia Argument and, 435–441, 559, 613, 699–705
alternative to, 695–697, 708–712
behaviorism and, 695
DNA physicalist, 708–712
dualism and, 695
experience and, 663–664, 668–673
Explanatory Gap Argument and, 559
Frege-Schlick view and, 650
in historical perspective of consciousness, 17, 28
intrinsic quality of experience and, 663–664
Knowledge Argument and, 559
mental states and, 120–121
mind-body problem and, 269, 663
models of consciousness and, 255
objections to, 668–674
orthodox, 695–696, 712
phenomenal access and, 369–371
phenomenal concepts and qualities, 613–614
physicalism and, 695–697, 708–712
Property Dualism Argument and, 705–708, 712
property of, 529
qualia and, 39, 695–696
teleological, 363–369, 371–373
transcendentalism and, 695, 697–699
Fundamentalism, 473
Further-How question, 31–34, 45
Fusillo, M., 634
"Fuzzy-jittery" neuronal assemblies, 239

Gall, 271
Gallup, G., 395
Galvanic skin response (GSR), 261–262
Gazzaniga, M. S., 203–204, 209, 219, 222–226, 262–263, 265–266, 396
Gedankenexperiment, 493–496
Geschwind, N., 634
Gestalt psychologists, 350–351
Ghoneim, M., 406
Ghost in the Machine idea, 143
Gibson, Eleanor, 783

Gibsonian visual field, 350, 352
GIPS model, 182–183
Global Integrative Phenomenal State (GIPS) model, 182–183
Global Workspace (GW) theory, 189
Goethe, Johann Wolfgang, 19
Goldman, Alvin, 699
Goodman, Nelson, 145–146, 159–160, 344
Gopnik, Alison, 119
Grammars, implicit learning of, 195
Gray, C. M., 205
Gregory, 268
Greve, K. W., 213, 217
Grice, H. P., 467
Grossi, D., 228
Grouping phenomena, 350–352
GSR, 261–262
Guillain-Barré syndrome, 494
GW theory, 189

Habituated stimulus, 190–191
Halligan, P. W., 224–225, 241, 246–247
Hardin, Larry, 564
Hare, R. M., 458
Harman, Gilbert, 463, 677–678, 680, 682, 688–690
Harnad, S., 177
Hebb, D. O., 239
Hebbian form of modification, 285–286, 289
Hécaen, H., 243
Heisenbergian uncertainty, 167
Held, R., 206, 256
Hellawell, D., 211, 216
Helmholtz, 20
Hemianopia, 219, 249
Hemiplegia, 249, 266
Hempel, Carl G., 116, 549
Herbert, Nick, 32
Heterogeneity claim of consciousness, 98–100
"Hidden observer" technique, 406
Higher-order perception (HOP) theory, 789–800
higher-order thought theory and, 797, 799
individual consciousness and, 790–791
Introspective Link Principle and, 791
perception and, 789–792
as higher-order thought, 799
as representational vehicle, 793–799
as simpliciter, 792–793

Higher-order perception (HOP) theory (cont.)
  state consciousness and, 790–791
  trilemma for, 799–800
Higher-order representation (HOR) theories, 789–791
Higher-order thought (HOT) theory
  conscious experience and, 784
  higher-order perception theory and, 797, 799
  Inner Sense theory and, 760
  intransitive consciousness and, 743–745
  mental states and, 741–745, 784
  perception and, 797, 799
  transitive consciousness and, 741–745
Hilgard's "hidden observer" technique, 406
Hill, Christopher, 763–764
Hillis, A., 246, 249
Hintikka, J., 344
Hinton, G., 218
Hippocampus, as mechanism of consciousness, 134
Hobson, Allan, 101–104
Holt, Edwin, 15
Holyoak, K., 21
Homogeneity principle, 534
HOP theory. See Higher-order perception (HOP)
  theory
HOR theories, 789–791
Horgan, T., 545–546
Horizon of simultaneity, 141–142
HOT theory. See Higher-order thought (HOT)
  theory
Hume, D., 461–462, 530, 726
Humean mind, 530, 537, 539
Humphrey, N., 386
Huxley, Thomas H., 41–42, 358, 381
Hypnosis, 405
Hypothesis of Phenomenal Information, 583–587, 589–591
Hypothesis-testing, 190–191

Iconic memory, 285–286, 288
Identity theory, 445–449
  afterimages and, 329–331
  Cartesian Materialism and, 545
  identifications and, 445–447
  Kripke's criticism of, 504, 545
  pain and, 329, 445–449
Imagery, 83, 144, 192–193
Immaterial realm, 4
Immediate memory, 195–196
Implicit memory, 117

Implicit reading in pure alexia, 228–231
  awareness of perception, 229–230
  awareness of vision, 203
  comparisons with other syndromes, 231–233
  described, 228
  explanations, 230–231
  representative findings, 228–229
Incorrigibility, 612–613, 756
Individual consciousness, 790–791
Individualism, constitutive, 312–313
Individualist claims/stances, 312–313, 315–318
Individuation, 302, 600
Inessentialism, conscious, 357
Information
  blindsight and, 365–366
  epiphenomenal, 589–591
  experience and, 342
  Hypothesis of Phenomenal Information and, 583–587, 589–591
  methods of gaining, 364–366
  phenomenal, 583–587, 589–591
  physical, 583–585, 589–591
  term of, 342
Information-processing models, 18, 379
Inner eye hypothesis, 763–764
Inner Sense theory, 755–767
  advantages of, 756
  arguments of, 767
  Armstrong and, 755, 762
  Cartesian Materialism and, 761–764
  Cartesian Theater and, 762–763
  conscious states and, 784–785
  Dennett and, 757–758, 761–763
  Dretske and, 758–760
  higher-order thought theory and, 760
  Hill and, 763–764
  Kant and, 755
  Locke and, 755
  pain and, 757
  Rey and, 764–767
  Rosenthal and, 760–761
  Searle and, 765
  second-order monitoring and, 757–758
  subjectivity and, 755–756
Inner speech, 192–193
Insulation strategy, 299–300, 304
Integrated field theory, 204
Integration accounts, 204–205
Intellectualism, 76

Intentionality
  afterimages and, 331
  artificial, 465
  as-if, 499–501
  beliefs and, 463
  content problem and, 302–304
  derived, 499–501
  experience and, 664–668, 679–680
  intrinsic, 499–501
  mental phenomena and, 499–501
  naturalism and, 295–296
  pain and, 332–333
  as problem of consciousness, 22–23
  qualia and, 677–681
  subjective delay of consciousness of, 147–148, 165–168
Internal monitoring, consciousness as. See Inner Sense
    theory
Internalist claim, 312–313
Interruptions in stream of consciousness, 74–75
Intransitive consciousness, 737–739, 743–745
Intrinsicalism
  consciousness and, qualities of, 119–123, 621, 736
  defined, 113
  intentionality and, 499–501
Introspected states, 745–746
Introspection
  arguments from, 745–747
  behaviorism and, 15
  mental states and, 745–747, 761
  by proxy, 238
  term of, 13, 238
Introspectionism, 13–15
Introspective consciousness, 723–728, 789, 793–796
Introspective Link Principle, 791
Inverted Earth argument, 113, 682–686
Inverted spectrum. See Spectrum inversion
Irreducibility of consciousness, 453–457

Jackendoff, R., 169, 244–246, 279
Jackson, Frank, 38, 382, 453, 543, 545–546, 559–560,
    585, 590, 598–599, 689–690, 756
Jacoby, L., 393
James, William, 7, 13, 27, 34, 90, 189, 193–194, 197,
    358, 363, 387, 789
Jasper, H., 146, 166
Jaynes, Julian, 16, 37, 396
Joanette, Y., 241

Johnson-Laird, Philip N., 18, 21, 112, 269, 279, 392, 436
Jones, Ernest, 19
Joynt, R. J., 8
Judgment, content of, 341–342

Kant, Immanuel, 296, 503, 534, 559, 724, 726, 755
Kaplan, David, 464
Kaplan's Logic of Demonstratives, 467
Kay, J., 228–229
Kihlstrom, J., 392, 406
Kim, J., 458, 635
Kinesthetic perception, 724–725
Kinsbourne, Marcel, 34–35, 175–178, 204, 225, 227,
    232, 247, 265, 377
Klein, Karen, 229, 231
Klein, R. M., 269
Kluver's studies, 783
Knapp, Peter H., 766
Knowledge
  with awareness, 364
  without awareness, 117, 261–262, 364, 370
  kinds of, 568–569
  knowing how vs. knowing that, 607–608, 689
  spectrum inversion and, 647–648
Knowledge Argument, 559–563
  assumption of, basic, 559
  clarifications of, 567–568
  equivocal, 571–573
  experience and, 585–587
  functionalism and, 559
  Jackson and, 567–569, 598–599
    reply to, 571–577
  materialism and, 435, 489–491, 559–560, 585–587,
    589
  nonequivocal, 574–575
  objections to
    Churchland's, 568–577
    questions classifying, 560–563
  phenomenal concepts and qualities and, 598–600
  physicalism and, 560, 567–569
  as problem of phenomenal consciousness, 38
  semantic premise of, 598–600
  two-dimensionalism and, 489–491
Koch, Christof, 3, 7, 33, 117, 119, 176–177, 205, 381,
    383, 396, 406, 422. See also Crick-Koch hypothesis
Koenig, O., 392
Kohler, I., 632
Kolers, P. A., 145–146, 159–161

Kosslyn, S., 392, 402
Kripke, Saul, 30, 348–349, 453–454, 483, 504–508,
    543–545, 548, 550, 599–600, 656, 700
Külpe, O., 14–15

Ladd, George Trumbull, 6
Laing, R., 467
Landis, T., 228–229, 380
Language of thought theory, 382, 463–464, 468
Language, philosophy of, 130–131
Lashley, Karl, 16
Latto, R., 209, 258–260
LC, as mechanism of consciousness, 134
Learning
  automaticity in, 195
  from experience, 579
    other ways, 579–580
  implicit, 195, 370
  memory and, contrasts with, 195–196
Leaving out qualia, 543–553
  anti-physical argument and, 543, 546–547
  concepts and, 551–552
  epistemological reading of, 548–550
  explanatory gap of consciousness and, 543, 550, 553
  Jackson's argument and, 543, 545–546
  Kripke's argument and, 543–545, 548
  metaphysical reading of, 543
  physicalism and, 543
  qualia properties and, 552–553
  reductionism and, 550–551
LeDoux, J. E., 219, 222–226, 265, 396
Lee, A., 467
Leeds, S., 474
Leibniz, G. W., 4, 19, 598
Leibnizian pre-established harmony, 529
Leibniz's Law, 489
Levander, M., 240, 242, 250–251
Levine, Joseph, 4, 6, 30, 563–564
Levophobia, 249
Lewis, David, 483, 560, 562, 568, 607, 635, 671, 756
Libet, B., 141, 145–147, 160, 162–169, 361–363, 422,
    761–762
Llinás hypothesis of visual awareness, 135–138
Llinás, Rodolfo, 103, 136
Loar, Brian, 474, 562–563
Locke, John, 9, 12–13, 19, 38, 366, 465, 530, 563–564,
    623, 643, 655–656, 724, 731, 755, 789, 791
Locus cereleus (LC), as mechanism of consciousness,
    134

Locus of subjectivity, mind as, 141
Logical reduction, 452–453
Long-term memory, 197, 279
Long-term potentiation (LTP), 285
Lorenz, Konrad, 439
LTP, 285
Luria, Alexsandr Romanovich, 243, 269, 366–368,
    400
Luzzatti, C., 266
Lycan, William, 112, 474, 784, 789, 791, 794–795, 797
Lying, 357

McAndrews, M. P., 203
McFetridge, I. G., 312–313
McGinn, Colin, 3–4, 25, 32, 318–320, 322–324, 563,
    678–679
McGlinchey-Berroth, R., 223–226
MacKay, D. G., 194
MacKay, D. M., 264, 269
Malcolm, Norman, 101–102
Malebranche, N., 13
Mandler, G., 17–18, 269, 392
Manifestation Principle, 711
Marcel, Anthony J., 112, 115, 118, 188, 190, 226, 238,
    241, 245, 269, 375–376, 385, 401–402, 436
"Mark test" evidence, 389–390, 395
Marr, David, 20
Marshall, J. C., 224–225, 241, 246–247, 256, 269
Marzi, C. A., 206, 208
Materialism. See also Cartesian Materialism
  Absent Qualia Argument and, 559
  conceptual analysis and, 483–486
  eliminativism and, 129
  Explanatory Gap Argument and, 435, 559, 563
  facile, 462
  Knowledge Argument and, 435, 489–491, 559–560,
    585–587, 589
  mental representations and, 793, 796–797
  Minimal, 585–586
  physicalism and, 484
Matthews, Robert, 315–317
MD model. See Multiple Drafts (MD) model
Meadows, J. C., 633
Mechanisms of consciousness, neural, 134–138, 277.
    See also Neurobiological theory of consciousness
Medium conception, 300–301
Mellor, H., 152, 177, 183
Melzack, R., 337
Memes, 394

Memory
 buffer, 149
 explicit, 117
 iconic, 285–286, 288
 immediate, 195–196
 implicit, 117
 learning and, contrasts with, 195–196
 long-term, 197, 279
 procedural, 279
 sensory, 195–196
 short-term, 277, 279, 285–286
 views of, 360–361
 working, 188–189, 196, 285–286
Mental images, 329
Mental phenomena
 empiricism and, 496
 intentionality and, 499–501
 mind problems and, 496–499
 physical phenomena vs., 23
 thought experiments
  conscious robots, 495–496
  first-person accounts and, 503–514
  silicon brains, 493–495
Mental states
 awareness of, 792–793
 behaviorism and, 119, 473
 brain states and, 449, 706–707
 Cartesian Materialism and, 18–19
 dispositional, 732
 dualism and, 614
 eliminativism and, 473
 functionalism and, 120–121
 higher-order thought theory and, 741–745, 784
 intransitive consciousness and, 737–739
 introspection and, 745–747, 761
 nonconscious, 734
 representation and, 796–797
 sense perception and, 739–740
 supervenience and, 457–458
 theory of consciousness and, 729, 731–734
  explanation of, 735–737
 transitive consciousness and, 737–739
Meregalli, S., 266, 268
Messages, attended vs. unattended, 194
Mesulam, M.-M., 118, 240
Meta-cognition, 437
Metacontrast, 118, 182
Metaphysics, 483–484
Methodological issues of studying consciousness, 237–238, 251

Miller, George, 8, 21–22, 24
Mind-body problem, 529–539
 Cartesian (re)formulation of, 12
 cognitive closure and, 529–531, 536
 consciousness and, 519
 Descartes's theory of, 203
 functionalism and, 269, 663
 Humean mind and, 530, 537, 539
 reductionism and, 452–453, 519
 solving, 529–539, 553
Mindful processing of vision, 248
Minimal consciousness, 721–723
Minimal Materialism, 585–586
Minsky, M., 87
Misoplegia, 249
Modal externalist/individualist claims, 312–313, 325
Models of consciousness, 255–273. See also specific types
 Bisiach's argument and, 256, 266–269
 blindsight, 256–261
 Cartesian Materialism, 141–145, 377
 functionalism and, 255
 knowledge without awareness, 261–262
 relevance of, 255–256
 split-brain patient and dual consciousness, 262–266
Monheit, M. A., 222, 226–227
Monitoring consciousness, 390–392, 395. See also Inner Sense theory
Moore, G. E., 458
Morton, J., 269
Moruzzi, G., 473
Moscovitch, M., 203
Motion, apparent, 145–146
Mozer, M. C., 227
Multiple Drafts (MD) model
 access consciousness and, 395
 Cartesian Materialism and, 83–85, 93
 Cartesian Theater and, 83–85, 141, 143–145
 D & K's argument and, 181
 Dennett and, 395
 as model of consciousness, 145–148
 Orwellian revisions and, 153–162
 Stalinesque revisions and, 153–162
 temporal anomalies and, 145–153
 Walter's experiment and, 168–169
Mystery of consciousness, 1–5, 290

Nagel, Thomas, 2, 6, 25, 30, 37–39, 175, 264, 298, 396, 453, 510, 559, 562–563, 611, 697, 735, 756
Natsoulas, Thomas, 8, 188

Natural method and unified theory of consciousness, 97, 100–101
Naturalism, 5–6
  biological, 6
  Cartesian intuition and, 362
  in conceptual foundations of consciousness, 5–6
  content problem and, 295–297, 301, 304–305
  defined, 295
  intentionality and, 295–296
  problem facing, 295
Necker cube drawing, 289
Neglect, 237–251
  attention in unilateral, 247–248
  clues from unilateral breakdown of awareness of stimuli in central vision, 247–248, 250
    levels of processing conscious representations, 244–247, 250
    methodological issues, 237–238, 251
    spatiotemporal structure of consciousness, 238–243, 250
    unilateral distortion of content of subjective experience, 248–249
    unity and disunity of consciousness, 243–244, 250
  and extinction, unconscious perception in, 219–227
    awareness of perception, 224–225
    awareness of vision, 203
    comparisons with other syndromes, 231–233
    described, 219
    explanations, 225–227
    representative findings, 219–224
Neisser, Ulric, 16–18, 21, 196
Nemirow, Laurence, 560, 568, 591–592, 607
Neumann, O., 87
Neural mechanisms of consciousness, 134–138, 277. See also Neurobiological theory of consciousness
Neurobiological theory of consciousness, 277–290
  background information on, 277
  cognitive approach to, 278–279
  experimental approaches to, 289–290
  experimental problems and, 288–289
  general aspects of, 279–281
  oscillations and, neuronal, 286–288
  prolegomenon to studying, 277–278
  research program for, 290
  short-term memory and, 277, 279, 285–286
  sketch of, 286–288
  visual attention and, binding and selective, 282–285
  visual awareness and, 281–282

Neurobiology, 127–138
  neural mechanisms of consciousness and, 134–138
  rationale behind research on, 127–129
  reductionist research strategy, 129–134
Neuronal firing, 281, 286
Neuronal oscillations. See Oscillations, neuronal
Neuropsychological syndromes. See specific types
Neuroscience, 115, 127–129, 134, 533
New Mysterians, 3
Newcombe, F., 211, 213, 215, 261
Newell, Allan, 20, 189
Nietzsche, Friedrich, 19
Non-conceptual content, 310–311, 338
Non-Hebbian form of modification, 285–286
Non-rapid eye movement (NREM) sleep, 103
Norman, D., 18
NREM sleep, 103

Objective conception, 520–526
O'Keefe, J., 269
Ontological reduction, 452
Ontology of consciousness, 24–25, 45
OR, 191
O'Reilly, R. C., 217, 226–227
Orienting Response (OR), 191
Orthodox functionalism, 695–696, 712
Orwell, George, 153
Orwellian revisions
  Cartesian Theater and, 153–162
  D & K's argument and, 182
  Dennett and, 118, 250
  examples of, 118
  Libet's experiment and, 166
  Multiple Drafts model and, 153–162
  phenomenal consciousness and, 176–177
Oscillations, neuronal
  binding problem and, 286–288, 381
  connections of, 136
  Crick-Koch hypothesis and, 117, 119, 422
  firing of, 281, 286
  neurobiological theory of consciousness and, 286–288
  non-rapid eye movement sleep and, 103
  rapid eye movement sleep and, 103–104
"Other minds problem," 496–499

Pain, 329–339
  access consciousness and, 405–407
  Block and, 331–332
  cognitivism and, 329

experience and, 332–334, 336–337
feeling, 432
identity theory and, 329, 445–449
Inner Sense theory and, 757
intentionality and, 332–333
intrinsic features of, 337–338
introspectible features of, 338
Kripke's argument and, 504–507
observational features of, 339
orthodox functionalism and, 695–696
phenomenal consciousness and, 405–407, 433
Property Dualism Argument and, 706–708
qualia and, 337–339, 700–705
rational-access thought and, 432
representational theory of, 333–336
transcendentalism and, 697
unfelt, 432–433
Pani, J. R., 193
Panpsychism, 23
Parafoveal vision, 86
Parallelism of stream of consciousness, 91–93
Paramnesia, reduplicative, 388
Parapsychology, 589
Paré, D., 103
Parsons, Terence, 666
PAs, 334
Patterson, K. E., 228–229
Peabody test, 263
Peacocke, Christopher, 309–310, 324–325, 678–679
Penfield, W., 146, 376, 397–398, 473
Penfield-Van Gulick-Searle reasoning, 397
Perani, D., 266
Perception. *See also* Higher-order perception (HOP)
    theory; Unconscious; Visual perception and
    awareness after brain damage
  awareness of, 203, 208, 213, 224–225, 229–230, 774–
    775
  brain and, understanding, 533–535
  conscious experiences of, 297–299
  consciousness and, 723
  contextual constraints on, 191–192
  Descartes and, 12–13, 19
  errors in, 724
  Helmholtz and, 20
  higher-order thought theory and, 797, 799
  as input representation, 189–192
  kinesthetic, 724–725
  Leibniz and, 19
  Locke and, 12–13, 19

reflection and, 12–13
reorganization and, 197
sense, 724, 739–740
understanding and, 670–671
Perceptual closure, 533–534
Perceptual content of consciousness, 309–312, 322–326
Perceptual experience, 297–299, 341, 672, 773, 779
Perceptual forms of consciousness, 723, 774–777, 796
Perspectivity, 24–25, 45
Phenomenal characterization of consciousness, 11, 30
Phenomenal concepts and qualities, 597–614
  concepts of, 603–604
  defined, 597
  of experience, 597–598
  explanatory gap of consciousness and, 608–609
  first-person accounts and, 597
  functionalism, 613–614
  incorrigibility, 612–613
  knowing how vs. knowing that, 607–608
  Knowledge Argument and, 598–600
  phenomenal structure and, 610–611
  physicalism and, 601–603
  presentation modes, 604–605
  question about, 325–326
  as recognitional concepts, 600–603
  subjective concepts and properties and, 609–610
  third-person accounts and, 597, 605–607
  transparency, 609, 611–612
Phenomenal experience, 239, 248–249
Phenomenal information, 583–587, 589–591
Phenomenal (P) consciousness, 175–178
  without access consciousness, 386–389
  access consciousness vs., 28–29, 113, 421–422, 426–
    427
  access consciousness without, 385–386
  availability for global control and, 421–423
  blindsight and, 385–386
  Block and, 417–419, 421, 425, 427
  Cartesian modularism and, 178
  concept of, 380–382
  conflation of, 392–397
  Crick-Koch hypothesis and, 33, 177
  D & K's argument and, 175–178
  defined, 175, 380, 425
  degrees of, 399
  Dennett and, 394–396
  dispute of, 42–44
  as distinct system, rejection of, 377–378
  eliminativism and, 43, 177

Phenomenal (P) consciousness (cont.)
  epiphenomenalism and, 369–371, 423
  outside events and, 176–178
  explanatory gap of consciousness and, 381–382
  Freudian theory and, 388
  function of consciousness and, 380–382, 386–389, 423
  independence of, 426
  information-process function of, 379
  module, 422–423
  Orwellian vs. Stalinesque revisions and, 176–177
  pain and, 405–407, 433
  phenomenal properties and, 427–428
  problems of
    absent qualia, 30, 38
    Knowledge Argument, 38
    qualia, 38–41, 278
    subjectivity, 39
  rational-access consciousness and, 428–433
  road map for, 36–38
  superficiality and, 104–107
  zombies and, 43–44, 385, 387
Phenomenal structure, 610–611
Phenomenal/creature conception of consciousness,
    729–731, 777–779
Phillipson, H., 467
Philosophy, early modern, 12–13
Physical information, 583–585, 589–591
Physical phenomena, mental phenomena vs., 23
Physicalism
  arguments against
    Jackson, 543, 545–546
    Kripke, 543–545, 548
    replies to, 546–547, 607–608
  explanatory gap of consciousness and, 543, 598
  functionalism and, 695–697, 708–712
  incorrigibility and, 612–613
  Knowledge Argument and, 560, 567–569
  leaving out qualia and, 543
  materialism and, 484
  phenomenal concepts and qualities and, 601–603
  status of, 524–525
  subjective phenomena and, 520
  third-person accounts and, 606
Physicalist-functionalism
  as alternative to functionalism, 695–697, 708–712
  Block and, 696
  DNA, 708–712
  Shoemaker and, 696–697

Piaget, Jean, 469
Pineal gland as proposed site of Cartesian Theater, 83–
    85
Place, U. T., 38
Pollatsek, A., 224
Pöppel, E., 141–142, 206, 256
Popper, Karl, 3–4
Positivism, 14
Posner, M. I., 18, 224, 247–248, 269
Post-tetanic potentiation, 285
Povinelli, D., 395
Preconscious, 20
Pribram, Karl, 473
Privileged role accounts, 203–204
Problem-solving, spontaneous, 196–197
Procedural memory, 279
Productive phenomena, 248–249
Progressive Matrices non-verbal reasoning test, 264
Property Dualism Argument, 543, 705–708, 712
Property ontological reduction, 452
Propositional attitudes (PAs), 334
Prosopagnosia
  covert recognition of faces in, 210–219
    awareness of perception, 213
    awareness of vision, 203
    comparisons with other syndromes, 231–233
    described, 210
    explanations, 213–219
    representative findings, 210–213
  knowledge without awareness and, 117, 261–262
  non-anosognosic, 394
  Schacter's model and, 376–380
Psychological conception of consciousness, 9, 27–30
Psychons (mental units), 4
Puccetti, R., 264
Putative perceptual experience, 341
Putnam, Hilary, 483, 504
Puzzlement of consciousness, 1–6, 730–731
Pylyshyn, Z. W., 269, 638

Qualia, 619–639. See also Absent qualia; Leaving out
    qualia
  Block and, 417, 696–697
  cases of, 632–634
  concept of, 619–620
  eliminativism and, 39–40, 43
  epiphenomenal, 590
  explanatory gap of consciousness and, 552–553

functionalism and, 40, 695–696
identity condition for, 344
intentionality and, 677–681
intersubjective and, 708–709
intrasubjective, 708–709
intrinsic qualities of consciousness and, 122–123, 621
inverted, 613, 648–649
Kripke's argument and, 544, 548–549
mistakes about, 625–632
of orthodox functionalism, 695–696
pain and, 337–339, 700–705
paradox of, 620, 623–625
phenomenal information and, 585
as problem of phenomenal consciousness, 38–41, 278
properties, 439, 552–553, 620–623, 634–639
quining, 118, 619–620, 635
realism, 677, 690
Shoemaker and, 622, 696–697, 699, 702–704, 708–711
spectrum inversion and, 623–625, 656–660
theoretical reduction of, 552–553
of transcendentalism, 697–699
Quality of representation account, 205–206
Question-answering, 197
Quine, W. V., 177, 351

Rafal, R., 206, 208–210
Rapid eye movement (REM) sleep, 101–104, 279–280
Rational Regularities, 463, 466
Rational-access consciousness, 428–433
"Raw feels," 23, 43, 114
Reaction time (RT) study, 211, 214, 216
Recognitional concepts, 600–603
Reductionism, 451–453
  causal, 452
  definitional, 452–453
  discussions of, 451–453
  explanatory, 550–551, 553
  leaving out qualia and, 550–551
  logical, 452–453
  mind-body problem and, 452–453, 519
  ontological, 452
  property ontological, 452
  psychophysical, 519, 523–524
  research strategy using, 127–129
    criticisms of, 129
    goals of, 129–134
  theoretical, 452, 551–553
Reduplicative paramnesia, 388

Referral backwards in time, 146–147, 162–165, 761–762
Reflection, perception and, 12–13
Regard, M., 228–229
REM sleep, 101–104, 279–280
Reorganization, perceptual, 197
Representational theory of pain, 333–336
Res cogitans realm, 4
Response
  Orienting, 191
  System, 377, 379
Reticular formation as proposed site of Cartesian Theater, 83
Revisionary stance of individualist, 315
Rey, Georges, 5, 461–475, 608, 682, 755–756, 764–767
Ribary, U., 103
Rivalry process, 289
Rock, Irvin, 20, 345, 348–349, 782
Roelofs, C. O., 146, 160
Rorty, Richard, 23, 43, 237
Rosenthal, David, 112, 467, 759–761, 777, 784, 789–791
Rousseau, Jean-Jacques, 19
RT study, 211, 214, 216
Ruddock, K. H., 258
Rusconi, L. L., 224
Russell, Bertrand, 725–726
Ryle, G., 143

Sacks, Oliver, 439
Saffran, E., 228–230
Saffran, E. M., 229–231, 380
Sanders, M. D., 256
Scattering hypothesis, 258
Schacter, Daniel, 36, 117–118, 203, 377, 393, 401, 403, 406
Schacter's model, 376–380, 403
Schiffer, 467
Schlick, Moritz, 649–651
Schmidt, C., 466
SCR, 210–211, 216
Searle, John, 6, 22, 36, 42, 113, 132, 376, 380, 397–400, 462, 504, 507–514, 681, 765
Second-order monitoring, 757–758
Selective attention, 80, 188
Self-attribution, 119–123
Self-consciousness, 381, 389–390, 395, 436

Self-perception, 789
Semantic transparency, 437–438
Semantics, 7–8, 192, 598–600
Sensation, 341–343, 351–352
Sensationalism, 76
Sense datum theory, 667–668, 673
Sense experience, 341–352
  additional characterization problem and, 344–345
  Adequacy Thesis and, 343–350
  content of experience and, 341–343
  defined, 341
  duality of representational properties and, 345–347
  grouping phenomena and, 350–352
  independence of, 341–342
  nonrepresentational similarities between experiences and, 347
  sensation and, 341–343, 351–352
  tactile-vision substitution system and, 346
Sensory memory, 195–196
Sensory qualities, 733
Sensory stimulus, 190
Serrat, A., 228–229
Seymour, P. H. K., 262
Shallice, T., 17–18, 36, 228–230, 392, 422
Shepard, R., 193, 402
Shiffrin, R., 18, 196, 269
Shoemaker, Sydney, 622, 673, 678, 689, 695–700, 702–712
Short-term memory, 277, 279, 285–286
Short-term synaptic modification, 285
Sieroff, E., 224
Silicon brains thought experiment, 493–495
Simon, Herbert, 20, 189
Singer, W., 205
Skin conductance response (SCR), 210–211, 216
Skinner, B. F., 189–190
Sleep
  dreams, 101–105, 111
  experience in, 101–104
  non-rapid eye movement, 103
  rapid eye movement, 101–104, 279–280
  somnambulism, 114–115
Smart, J. J. C., 38, 329, 706–707
Smith, Y. M., 209, 258–260
Social conception of consciousness, 9
Sokolov, E. N., 191
Somnambulism, 114–115
Spatiotemporal structure of consciousness, 238–243, 250

Spectrum inversion, 643–660
  arguments for possibility of, 681–688
  consequences of, 671–673
  containment response to, 677
  epistemological problem of, 649, 655–656
  Frege-Schlick view and, 649–651, 656
  intersubjective, 643
  intrasubjective, 643, 645–647, 650
  Inverted Earth argument and, 682–686
  knowledge and, 647–648
  Locke and, 38, 643
  mapping and, 648
  metaphysical problem of, 648–649, 654–655
  origin of, 643
  philosophical problems posed by, 648–649
  possibility of, 38, 175
  qualia and, 623–625, 656–660
  qualitative similarities and differences and, 649–660
  revival of, 38, 643
  Shoemaker and, 673
  Twin Earth argument and, 686–688
  uniformity and, 655–656
  Wittgenstein and, 643–645
Speech, inner, 192–193
Spellman, B., 21
Sperling, G., 405, 421
Sperry, R. W., 263–264
Split brain, 262–266, 280
Spontaneous decisions, 147
Stalinesque revisions
  Cartesian Theater and, 153–162
  D & K's argument and, 182
  Dennett and, 118
  examples of, 118
  Global Integrative Phenomenal State model and, 182
  Libet's experiment and, 163, 165–166
  Multiple Drafts model and, 153–162
  phenomenal consciousness and, 176–177
Stamm, J. S., 167
Stampe, D., 464
Stapp, Henry, 32
State conception of consciousness, 790–791
States of mind
  cognitive function of different, 79–82
  duration of, 72
  fundamental fact of, 71
  substantive, 75–78
  transitive, 75–78
Stich, S. P., 463

Stimulus
  above-threshold, 190
  in blind field, 365
  in central vision, 247–248, 250
  C-fiber, 445–449, 505–506
  expectations, 192
  habituated, 190–191
  sensory, 190
  unawareness of, 281
Stoerig, P., 206, 210, 383, 386
Stout, George, 7
Stratton, G. M., 632
Stream of consciousness, 71–82, 89–93
  binding problem and, 90–91, 93
  characters in process of, 71–75
  continuity of, 89–90
  Fringe in, 77–78
  fundamental fact of, 71
  interruptions in, 74–75
  parallelism of, 91–93
  phenomenology of, 89–93
  problem-solving and, spontaneous, 197
  studying, 71
  substantive and transitive states of mind in, 75–78
  time-gaps in, 74–75
  topic of thought in, 79–82
Strong externalism, 319
Subjective conception, 520–526
Subjective concepts and properties, 609–610
Subjective delay of consciousness of
      intention, 147–148, 163, 165–168
Subjective experience, 248–249
Subjectivity problem of phenomenal consciousness, 37
Substance dualism, 573–574
Substantive states of mind, 75–78
Super-blindsight, 385–386, 426
Superficiality and unified theory of consciousness, 104–107
Supervenience
  causal, 458
  completeness and, 484–485
  conceptual analysis and, 484–485
  constitutive, 458
  kinds of, 323–324
  mental states and, 457–458
  modal individualist claims and, 312–313
  restricted, 586
Supervisory System, 269–271, 422
Sutherland, Stuart, 8

Symmetry Argument, 703
Syntax, 192
Synthetic method of studying stream of consciousness, 71

Tactile-vision substitution system (TVSS), 346
Target reasoning, 377, 379, 397–403, 407
Taylor, A. M., 261
Tegnér, R., 240, 242, 250–251
Teleological functionalism, 363–369, 371–373
Temporal anomalies of consciousness, 145–153
Theoretical reduction, 452, 551–553
Theory of consciousness, 299–300, 729–747. See also
      specific types
  higher-order thought theory and, 741–743, 745–747
  intransitive consciousness, 737–739
  introspected states and, 745–746
  issues in, 729–731
  mental states and, 729, 731–734
    explanations of, 735–737
  proposal of, 739–745
  transitive consciousness, 737–739
Theory of content, 299–302
Third-person accounts
  first-person accounts and, 24–25, 44–45, 575–577
  Kripke's argument and, 505
  phenomenal concepts and qualities and, 597, 605–607
  physicalism and, 606
  as problem of consciousness, 24–25, 45–46
Thought
  experiments
    conscious robots, 495–496
    first-person accounts and, 503–514
    silicon brains, 493–495
  rational-access consciousness and, 428–431
  topic of, 79–82
  unconscious, 188
Time-gaps in stream of consciousness, 74–75
Titchener, E., 7, 14, 19, 27
Tower of Hanoi puzzle, 366
Tranel, D., 211, 213, 261–262, 268
Transcendentalism, 695, 697–699
Transitive consciousness, 737–739, 741–745
Transitive states of mind, 75–78
Transparency, 609, 611–612
Treisman, A. M., 18
Truths, conceptual, 756
TVSS, 346
Twin Earth argument, 313, 551, 686–688

Two-dimensionalism, 489–491
Tye, Michael, 5, 389
Tyndall, John, 3
Type-demonstratives. *See* First-person accounts;
 Third-person accounts

Unattended messages, attended vs., 194
Unconscious, 18–21
 cognitive, 20–21
 Freudian, 18–20, 388
 input representation, 190
 natural contrasts between conscious and, 187
 perception in neglect and extinction, 219–227
  awareness of perception, 224–225
  awareness of vision, 203
  comparisons with other syndromes, 231–233
  described, 219
  explanations, 225–227
  representative findings, 219–224
 total, 721–722
Unconscious creatures, conscious creatures vs., 729–
 731, 777–779
Unified Theories of Cognition, 189
Unified theory of consciousness, 97–107
 claims about consciousness and, 97–98
 dreams and, 101–105
 heterogeneity and, 97–100
 natural method and, 97, 100–101
 prospects for, 97
 superficiality and, 104–107
Unit of consciousness, 243–244, 250

Vallar, G., 270
Van der Waals, H. G., 146, 160
Van Gulick, Robert, 376, 397–398
Vecera, S. P., 217, 226–227
Velmans, Max, 364, 366
Verifiability, 426
Verstehen explanation, 463
Vision. *See also* Visual perception and awareness after
 brain damage
 absent-minded processing of, 248
 attention and
  binding and selective, 282–285
  oscillations and, neuronal, 286–287
 awareness of, 135–138, 203, 281–282
 blind spot region and, 86–87
 experiences of, 83, 341
 foveal, 86

Gibsonian visual field and, 350, 352
 images and, 192–193
 mammalian, 281–282
 mindful processing of, 248
 parafoveal, 86
 stimulus in central, 247–248, 250
Visual perception and awareness after brain damage,
 203–233
 blindsight, 206–210
  awareness of perception, 208
  awareness of vision, 203
  comparisons with other syndromes, 231–233
  described, 206
  explanations, 208–210
  representative findings, 206–208
 brain mechanisms and, 203–206
 comparing, in various syndromes, 231–233
 covert recognition of faces in prosopagnosia, 210–
  219
  awareness of perception, 213
  awareness of vision, 203
  comparisons with other syndromes, 231–233
  described, 210
  explanations, 213–219
  representative findings, 210–213
 implicit reading in pure alexia, 228–231
  awareness of perception, 229–230
  awareness of vision, 203
  comparisons with other syndromes, 231–233
  described, 228
  explanations, 230–231
  representative findings, 228–229
 unconscious perception in neglect and extinction, 219–
  227
  awareness of perception, 224–225
  awareness of vision, 203
  comparisons with other syndromes, 231–233
  described, 219
  explanations, 225–227
  representative findings, 219–224
Visual perceptual experience, 341
Vogel, P. J., 262
Volpe, B. T., 219, 222–226
Von Cramon, D., 241
Von der Malsburg, C., 286
Von Grünau, M., 145–146, 161

W questions, 30–36
Wallace, M. A., 217, 222, 226–227

Walter, Grey, 168–169
Walzer, M., 631
Warrington, E. K., 245, 256, 261
Wasserman, G. S., 166
Watson, J., 16
Watson, R. T., 240
Weber, Max, 463
Weiskrantz, Lawrence, 122–123, 206, 256, 258, 386
Werneicke's aphasia, 117
Wertheimer, M., 145
Wessinger, C. M., 209
What question, 31, 33
Whatitisliketobe wild card, 37
When neurobiological aspect, 279–280
Where neurobiological aspect, 280
Where question, 31, 34–35
White, A., 773
White, Stephen, 765
Who question, 31, 35
Why/Which question, 31, 35–36
Wiener, N., 466
Wilkes, Kathleen, 5, 8, 98–100, 115
Will, 80, 187
Wilson, D. H., 263, 265
Wittgenstein, Ludwig, 458, 473, 503, 563, 623, 636, 643–645
WM, 118–189, 196, 285–286
Word-retrieval, 197
Working awareness, 288–290
Working memory (WM), 188–189, 196, 285–286
World 1 (physical), 4
World 2 (mental), 4
Wundt, W., 343
Würzburg school, 14

Young, A. W., 211, 213, 215–216, 261, 388, 393–394

Zaidel, D. W., 264
Zaidel, E., 263, 264
Zihl, J., 241, 260
Zombies
  access consciousness and, 387
  blindsight and, 385, 387
  Cartesian modularism and, 379
  epiphenomenalism and, 41–42
  higher-order beliefs and, 112
  phenomenal consciousness and, 44–45, 385
  types of, 387